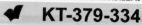

Montmartre

Opera Quarter

Tuileries Quarter

Beaubourg and Les Halles

The Marais

St-Germain-des-Prés

Ile de la Cité

Ile St-Louis

Latin Quarter

Luxembourg Quarter

Jardin des Plantes Quarter

Montparnasse

PAGES 218–27
Street Finder maps 2, 6, 7

PAGES 210–17
Street Finder maps 5–6

PAGES 104–15
Street Finder map 13

PAGES 90–103
Street Finder maps 13–14

PAGES 168–73
Street Finder maps 12, 16

PAGES 148–59
Street Finder maps 12, 13, 17

PAGES 160–67
Street Finder maps 17–18

PAGES 76–89
Street Finder maps 12–13

EYEWITNESS TRAVEL GUIDES

PARIS

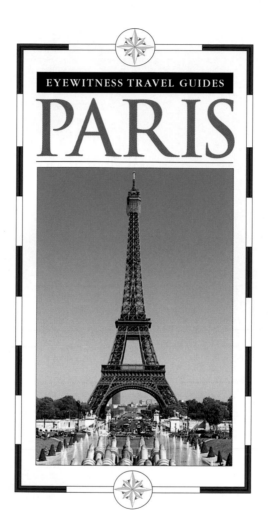

EYEWITNESS TRAVEL GUIDES

PARIS

Main contributor: ALAN TILLIER

LONDON, NEW YORK,
MELBOURNE, MUNICH AND DELHI
www.dk.com

PROJECT EDITOR Heather Jones
ART EDITOR Janis Utton
EDITOR Alex Gray
DESIGNER Vanessa Hamilton
DESIGN ASSISTANT Clare Sullivan

CONTRIBUTORS
Chris Boicos, Michael Gibson, Douglas Johnson

PHOTOGRAPHERS
Max Alexander, Neil Lukas, Robert O'Dea

ILLUSTRATORS
Stephen Conlin, Stephen Gyapay,
Maltings Partnership

This book was produced with the assistance of
Websters International Publishers.

Reproduced by Colourscan, Singapore
Printed and bound by South China Printing Co. Ltd., China

First published in Great Britain in 1993
by Dorling Kindersley Limited
80 Strand, London WC2R 0RL

**Reprinted with revisions 1994, 1995, 1997 (twice),
1999, 2000, 2001, 2002, 2003, 2004, 2005, 2006, 2007**

Copyright © 1993, 2007 Dorling Kindersley Limited, London
A Penguin Company

ALL RIGHTS RESERVED. NO PART OF THIS PUBLICATION MAY BE
REPRODUCED, STORED IN A RETRIEVAL SYSTEM, OR TRANSMITTED IN ANY
FORM OR BY ANY MEANS, ELECTRONIC, MECHANICAL, PHOTOCOPYING,
RECORDING OR OTHERWISE, WITHOUT THE PRIOR WRITTEN PERMISSION
OF THE COPYRIGHT OWNER.

A CIP CATALOGUE RECORD IS AVAILABLE FROM THE BRITISH LIBRARY.

ISBN 978 1 40531 733 7

FLOORS ARE REFERRED TO THROUGHOUT IN ACCORDANCE WITH FRENCH
USAGE; IE THE "FIRST FLOOR" IS THE FLOOR ABOVE GROUND LEVEL.

Front cover main image: Arc de Triomphe with Champs-Elysées

**The information in this
Dorling Kindersley Travel Guide is checked annually.**
Every effort has been made to ensure that this book is as
up-to-date as possible at the time of going to press. Some details,
however, such as telephone numbers, opening hours, prices, gallery
hanging arrangements and travel information are liable to change.
The publishers cannot accept responsibility for any consequences
arising from the use of this book, nor for any material on third-party
websites, and cannot guarantee that any website address in this book
will be a suitable source of travel information.
We value the views and suggestions of our readers very highly.
Please write to: Publisher, DK Eyewitness Travel Guides,
Dorling Kindersley, 80 Strand, London WC2R 0RL, Great Britain.

◁ **Sacré-Coeur and the Butte Montmartre**

CONTENTS

Henri II (1547–59)

INTRODUCING
PARIS

Pont Alexandre III

The Panthéon

HOW TO USE THIS GUIDE

This Eyewitness Travel Guide helps you get the most from your stay in Paris with the minimum of practical difficulty. The opening section, *Introducing Paris*, locates the city geographically, sets modern Paris in its historical context and explains how Parisian life changes through the year. *Paris at a Glance* is an overview of the city's specialities. The main sightseeing section of the book is *Paris Area by*

Area. It describes all the main sights with maps, photographs and detailed illustrations. In addition, eight planned walks take you to parts of Paris you might otherwise miss.

Carefully researched tips for hotels, shops and markets, restaurants and bars, sports and entertainment are found in *Travellers' Needs*, and the *Survival Guide* has advice on everything from posting a letter to catching the metro.

PARIS AREA BY AREA

The city has been divided into 14 sightseeing areas. Each section opens with a portrait of the area, summing up its character and history, with a list of all the sights to be covered. These are clearly located by numbers on an *Area Map*. This is followed by a large-scale *Street-by-Street Map* focusing on the most interesting part of the area. Finding your way about the section is made simple by the numbering system used throughout the book for the sights. This refers to the order in which they are described on the pages that complete the section.

Sights at a Glance
lists the sights in the area by category: Historic Streets and Buildings, Churches, Museums and Galleries, Monuments, Parks and Gardens.

The area covered in greater detail on the *Street-by-Street Map* is shaded red.

Travel tips help you reach the area quickly.

1 **Area Map** *For easy reference, the sights in each area are numbered and located on an area map. To help the visitor, the map also shows metro and mainline RER stations and car parks.*

The Conciergerie 8 is shown on this map as well.

Colour-coding on each page makes the area easy to find in the book.

2 **Street-by-Street Map** *This gives a bird's-eye view of the heart of each sightseeing area. The most important buildings are picked out in stronger colour, to help you spot them as you walk around.*

A locator map shows you where you are in relation to surrounding areas. The area of the *Street-by-Street Map* is shown in red.

Photographs of facades and distinctive details of buildings help you to locate the sights.

Numbered circles pinpoint all the listed sights on the area map. The Conciergerie, for example, is **8**

A suggested route for a walk takes in the most attractive and interesting streets in the area.

Stars indicate the sights that no visitor should miss.

PARIS AT A GLANCE

Each map in this section concentrates on a specific theme: *Museums and Galleries, Churches, Squares, Parks and Gardens, Remarkable Parisians*. The top sights are shown on the map; other sights are described on the following two pages.

Each sightseeing area is colour-coded.

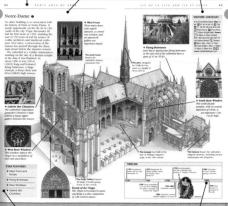

The theme is explored in greater detail on the pages following the map.

3 Detailed information on each sight
All important sights in each area are described in depth in this section. They are listed in order, following the numbering on the Area Map. *Practical information is also provided.*

4 Paris's major sights *These are given two or more full pages in the sightseeing area in which they are found. Historic buildings are dissected to reveal their interiors; and museums and galleries have colour-coded floor plans to help you find important exhibits.*

PRACTICAL INFORMATION

Each entry provides all the information needed to plan a visit to the sight. The key to the symbols used is on the inside back cover.

The Visitors' Checklist provides the practical information you will need to plan your visit.

The facade of each major sight is shown to help you spot it quickly.

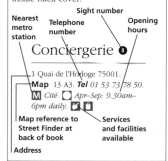

Nearest metro station — Sight number — Telephone number — Opening hours

Conciergerie 8

1 Quai de l'Horloge 75001.
Map 13 A3. **Tel** 01 53 73 78 50.
M Cité. **⏰** Apr–Sep: 9.30am–6pm daily.

Map reference to Street Finder at back of book — **Services and facilities available**

Address

Stars indicate the most interesting architectural details of the building, and the most important works of art or exhibits on view inside.

A timeline charts the key events in the history of the sight.

INTRODUCING PARIS

FOUR GREAT DAYS IN PARIS

Paris is a city packed with wonderful things to see and do. There may be a temptation to spend the trip in a café letting the French way of life wash over you, but it would be a shame to miss its treasures. Here are the best of the city's must-dos. Energetic sightseers should manage everything on these itineraries, but this selection can also be dipped into for ideas. All are reachable by public transport. Price guides are for two adults or for a family of two adults and two children, excluding meals.

Rodin's Thinker

Pyramide du Louvre, from across the fountain pools

ARTISTIC TREASURES

- Fabulous art at the Louvre
- Lunch at chic Café Marly
- A visit to the Rodin sculpture garden or take in the Musée Picasso
- Dine at Tokyo Eat

TWO ADULTS allow at least €60

Morning
Begin with the **Musée du Louvre** *(see pp122–9)*, one of the world's most impressive museums. Beat the crowds by using the little-known entrance at the Carrousel du Louvre (99 Rue de Rivoli). Save time by getting a floorplan and working out where you want to go and sticking to it.

Lunch
There are many cheap eateries nearby, but for a great lunch experience head to smart **Café Marly** *(see p304)*. On warm days sit in the outside gallery or revel in the cozy red velvet and gilt splendour of the interior.

Afternoon
Choose from three museums for the afternoon. The fatigued should head to the sublime **Musée Rodin** *(see p187)* for a soothing stroll in the sculpture garden and a pensive moment next to *The Thinker*. Those seeking modern masterpieces should visit the **Musée Picasso** *(see pp100–1)*, which has works by Pablo Picasso, from early portraits and sketches to an amazing range of later paintings. To go even more modern, explore the crop of galleries that are known as "Scene Est" in the 13th arrondissement (district). "Scene Est" is three roads' full of cutting-edge galleries, with the **Rue Louise Weiss** *(Map 18 E4)* the most important and the Air de Paris gallery the most funky.

Evening
The **Palais de Tokyo** *(see p201)* is currently Paris' most fashionable exhibition space, with its multimedia displays open till midnight. After a quick tour around, stop at restaurant Tokyo Eat.

RETAIL THERAPY

- Buy foody treats at Le Bon Marché
- Lunch at a top department store restaurant
- Drinks and dinner at Kong

TWO ADULTS allow at least €22

Morning
One-stop shops for gourmets and gluttons include **Fauchon, Hediard** and **La Grande Epicerie** at **Le Bon Marché** *(see pp320–1)*. In fact, anything that is edible – as long as it's delicious – can be found here. Specialist shops include **Poilâne** for bread, **Richart** for chocolate, **Legrand** for wine and **Pierre Hermé** for cakes. Or head down the Rue Mouffetard, one of the city's best market streets.

Lunch
Shopaholics can eat in one of the main department stores. The World Bar at **Au Printemps**, designed by Paul Smith, is a super-cool eatery *(see pp320–1)*, for example.

Ultra-hip interior of Kong, which also has stunning rooftop views

◁ *The Market and Fountain of the Innocents, by John James Chalon*

The surrounding area is a busy shopping and eating hub, so you can combine the two with no difficulty.

Afternoon
Either shop on till you drop, or go esoteric and visit the **Musée de la Mode** at the Louvre *(see p121)*; a true temple to fashion, dedicated to beautiful clothes and accessories. Boutique lovers should go to **Claudie Pierlot, Agnes B, Isabelle Marant, Vanessa Bruno** *(see pp324–7)*.

Evening
Head for restorative drinks and dinner at **Kong** on top of Kenzo's flagship store and fashion shrine *(see pp317–8)*.

Reflections in La Géode, giant sphere at the Parc de la Villette

CHILD'S PLAY

- Explore Parc de la Villette
- See animals at the zoo at Jardin des Plantes
- Stop for a café lunch
- Go up the Eiffel Tower

FAMILY OF FOUR allow at least €128

Morning
Take receptive young minds to **Parc de la Villette**, which has an impressive children's programme. **La Cité des Sciences et de l'Industrie** (Science City) is packed with interesting interactive exhibits for budding Einsteins *(see pp234–9)*. Family fun can be found at the **Ménagerie** *(see pp164)* in the Jardin des Plantes area where the zoo

is very popular. Even more exciting than the live animals for some are the skeletons and stuffed beasts in the **Muséum National d'Histoire Naturelle** *(see p167)*.

Lunch
There are lots of cafés in the Jardin des Plantes area or a more formal lunch can be had at **Mavromatis** *(see p307)*.

Afternoon
No child can resist a trip up the **Eiffel Tower**, so take them up in the afternoon for a proper view of the city, or wait until nightfall and time your trip to coincide with the changing of the hour when thousands of lights twinkle for ten minutes *(see pp192–3)*. If there's time, take a tour of the waxworks at the **Grévin** museum *(see p216)*. Most of the models are of French celebrities, but big international names in art and sport can also be spotted.

THE GREAT OUTDOORS

- Boat trip on the Seine
- Lunch on the Rue de Rivoli
- A walk to Luxembourg Garden
- Take a balloon ride

TWO ADULTS allow at least €62

Morning
For today's trip the metro is banned, so instead take the hop-on-hop-off bateaubus up the Seine. The first "stop" is near the **Eiffel Tower** so a quick look around the

Modern water sculpture and glasshouse, Parc André Citroën

Champ-de-Mars underneath Gustave Eiffel's monument is recommended *(see p191)*. Continue on the bateaubus to the Louvre stop, jump off and wander around the **Jardin des Tuileries** *(see p130)*.

Lunch
The tea salon **Angélina** *(see p318)* is a cut above other cafés on Rue de Rivoli. Leave space for the famous Mont Blanc cake of chestnut purée and cream.

Afternoon
Reboard the boat and head up to **Notre-Dame** *(see pp82–5)*, then it's a good walk down the Boulevard St Michel to the **Jardin du Luxembourg** *(see p172)*. There's lots to see – chess tables, beehives and donkey rides – and the **Senat Art Gallery**, which hosts blockbuster shows. For a final blast of fresh air, cross the city to the **Parc André Citroën** and take a tethered balloon ride *(see p247)*.

A floral display in the Jardin des Plantes

Putting Paris on the Map

Paris, the capital of France, is a city of over two million people covering 1,200 sq km (460 sq miles) of northern France. It is on the River Seine at the centre of the Ile-de-France, the region which is home to ten million people, around one-fifth of the French population. An important European business and cultural centre, it is the focus of activity in the north of France.

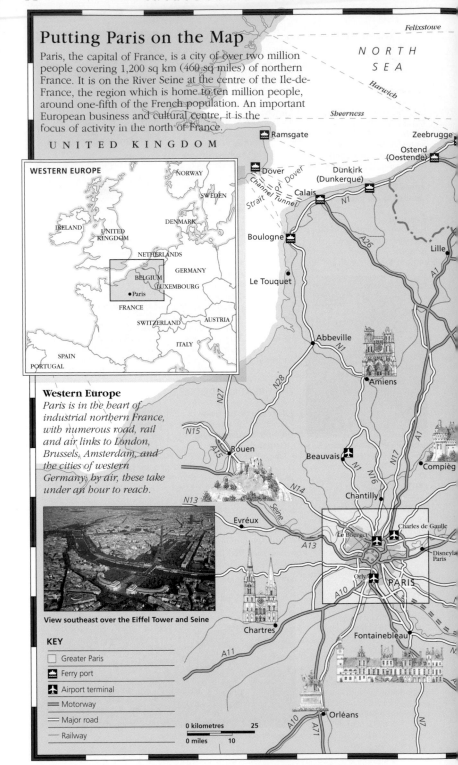

UNITED KINGDOM

WESTERN EUROPE

NORWAY

SWEDEN

DENMARK

IRELAND
UNITED
KINGDOM

NETHERLANDS

GERMANY

BELGIUM
LUXEMBOURG

• Paris

FRANCE

SWITZERLAND
AUSTRIA

ITALY

SPAIN
PORTUGAL

Felixstowe

NORTH
SEA

Harwich

Sheerness

Ramsgate

Zeebrugge

Ostend
(Oostende)

Dover
Channel / Strait of Dover
Strait / Channel Tunnel
Calais
Dunkirk
(Dunkerque)
N1

Boulogne
A26
Lille
A1

Le Touquet

Abbeville
N1
Amiens

N28

N27

Western Europe
Paris is in the heart of industrial northern France, with numerous road, rail and air links to London, Brussels, Amsterdam, and the cities of western Germany: by air, these take under an hour to reach.

N15
A15
Rouen

N14
Seine

N13

Évreux

Seine

Beauvais
N1
N16
N17
Compièg
A1

Chantilly

Le Bourget
A13
Charles de Gaulle
Disneyla
Paris

Orly
A10
PARIS

Chartres

Fontainebleau

View southeast over the Eiffel Tower and Seine

A11

A10
A71
Orléans

KEY

☐ Greater Paris

⛴ Ferry port

✈ Airport terminal

▬ Motorway

▬ Major road

▬ Railway

| 0 kilometres | 25 |
| 0 miles | 10 |

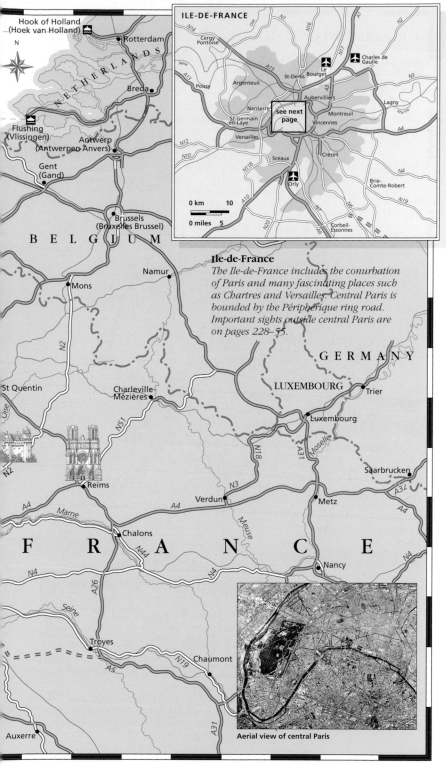

ILE-DE-FRANCE

Cergy-Pontoise
Charles de Gaulle
St-Denis
Le Bourget
Poissy
Argenteuil
Aubervilliers
Lagny
Nanterre
Montreuil
St-Germain-en-Laye
Vincennes
Versailles
Créteil
Sceaux
Orly
Brie-Comte-Robert
Corbeil-Essonnes

see next page

0 km   10
0 miles   5

Ile-de-France

*The Ile-de-France includes the conurbation
of Paris and many fascinating places such
as Chartres and Versailles. Central Paris is
bounded by the Périphérique ring road.
Important sights outside central Paris are
on pages 228–55.*

Hook of Holland
(Hoek van Holland)
Rotterdam
NETHERLANDS
Breda
Flushing
(Vlissingen)
Antwerp
(Antwerpen Anvers)
Gent
(Gand)
Brussels
(Bruxelles Brussel)
BELGIUM
Namur
Mons
St Quentin
Charleville-Mézières
GERMANY
LUXEMBOURG
Trier
Luxembourg
Saarbrucken
Reims
Verdun
Metz
FRANCE
Chalons
Nancy
Seine
Troyes
Chaumont
Auxerre

Aerial view of central Paris

Central Paris

Napoleon's Arc de Triomphe

This book divides Paris into 14 areas, comprising central Paris and the nearby area of Montmartre. Most of the sights covered in the book lie within these areas, each one of which has its own chapter. Each area contains a range of sights that convey some of its history and distinctive character. The sights of Montmartre, for example, reveal its village charm and its colourful history as a thriving artistic enclave. In contrast, Champs-Elysées is renowned for its wide avenues, expensive fashion houses and opulent mansions. Most of the city's famous sights are within reach of the heart of the city and are easy to reach on foot or by public transport.

Dôme Church
The gilded Dôme Church (see pp188–9) lies at the heart of the Invalides.

Eiffel Tower
Named after the engineer who designed and built it in 1889, the Eiffel Tower is the city's best-known landmark (see pp192–3). It towers more than 320 m (1,050 ft) above Champ-de-Mars park.

KEY

▪	Star sights
Ⓜ	Metro station
🚆	SNCF (train) station
RER	RER station
⛴	Boat service boarding point
ℹ	Tourist information office

Musée du Louvre
Right in the heart of Paris, adjacent to the River Seine and the Tuileries garden, lies the city's most impressive museum, with an unrivalled collection of artifacts from around the world (see pp122–9).

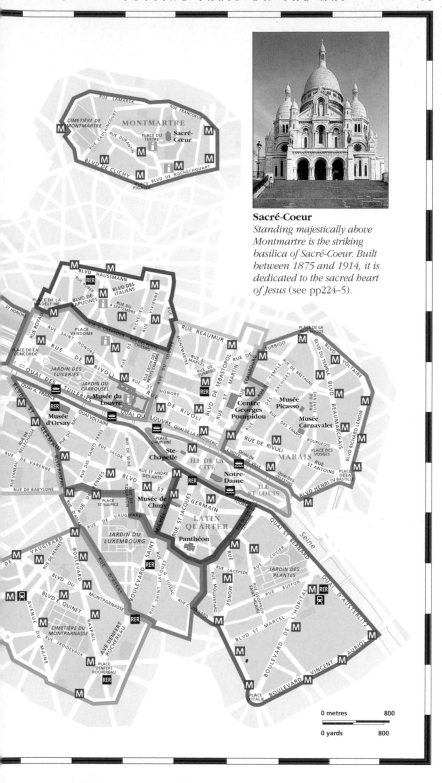

Sacré-Coeur
Standing majestically above Montmartre is the striking basilica of Sacré-Coeur. Built between 1875 and 1914, it is dedicated to the sacred heart of Jesus (see pp224–5).

REPUBLIQUE FRANCAISE

LIBERTE EGALITE · FRATERNITE

THE HISTORY OF PARIS

The Paris conquered by the Romans in 55 BC was a small flood-prone fishing village on the Ile de la Cité, inhabited by the Parisii tribe. A Roman settlement soon flourished and spread on to the Left Bank of the Seine. The Franks succeeded the Romans, named the city Paris and made it the centre of their kingdom.

During the Middle Ages the city flourished as a religious centre and architectural masterpieces such as Sainte-Chapelle were erected. It also thrived as a centre of learning, enticing European scholars to its great university, the Sorbonne.

Paris emerged during the Renaissance and the Enlightenment as a great centre of culture and ideas, and under the rule of Louis XIV it also became a city of immense wealth and power. But rule by the monarch gave way to rule by the people in the bloody Revolution of 1789. By the early years of the new century, revolutionary fervour had faded and the brilliant militarist Napoleon Bonaparte proclaimed himself Emperor of France and pursued his ambition to make Paris the centre of the world.

Soon after the Revolution of 1848 a radical transformation of the city began. Baron Haussmann's grand urban scheme replaced Paris's medieval slums with elegant avenues and boulevards. By the end of the century, the city was the driving force of Western culture. This continued well into the 20th century, interrupted only by the German military occupation of 1940–44. Since the war, the city has revived and expanded dramatically, as it strives to be at the heart of a unified Europe.

The following pages illustrate Paris's history by providing snapshots of the significant periods in the city's evolution.

Fleur-de-lys, the royal emblem

A map of Paris (about 1845)

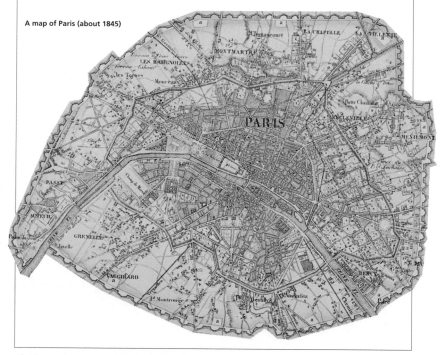

◁ *Allegory of the Republic* (1848) by Dominique Louis Papety

Kings and Emperors in Paris

Paris became the power base for the kings of France at the beginning of the Capetian dynasty, when Hugh Capet ascended the throne. Successive kings and emperors have left their mark and many of the places mentioned in this book have royal associations: Philippe-Auguste's fortress, the Louvre Palace, is now one of the world's great museums; Henri IV's Pont Neuf bridge links the Ile de la Cité with the two banks of the Seine; and Napoleon conceived the Arc de Triomphe to celebrate his military victories. The end of the long line of kings came with the overthrow of the monarchy in 1848, during the reign of Louis-Philippe.

768–814 Charlemagne

743–751 Childéric III
716–721 Chilpéric II
695–711 Childebert II
566–584 Chilpéric I
558–562 Clotaire I
447–458 Merovich
458–482 Childéric I
674–691 Thierri III
655–668 Clotaire III
628–637 Dagobert I

954–986 Lothaire
898–929 Charles III, the Simple
884–888 Charles II, the Fat
879–882 Louis III
840–877 Charles I, the Bald
1137–80 Louis VII
987–996 Hugh Capet
1031–60 Henri I
1060–1108 Philippe I

400	500	600	700	800	900	1000	1100
MEROVINGIAN DYNASTY				CAROLINGIAN DYNASTY		CAPETIAN DYNASTY	
400	500	600	700	800	900	1000	1100

751–768 Pépin the Short
721–737 Thierri IV
711–716 Dagobert III
691–695 Clovis III
668–674 Childéric II
637–655 Clovis II
584–628 Clotaire II
562–566 Caribert
511–558 Childebert I

996–1031 Robert II, the Pious
986–987 Louis V
936–954 Louis IV, the Foreigner
888–898 Odo, Count of Paris
882–884 Carloman
877–879 Louis II, the Stammerer
814–840 Louis I, the Debonair

482–511 Clovis I

1108–37 Louis VI, the Fat

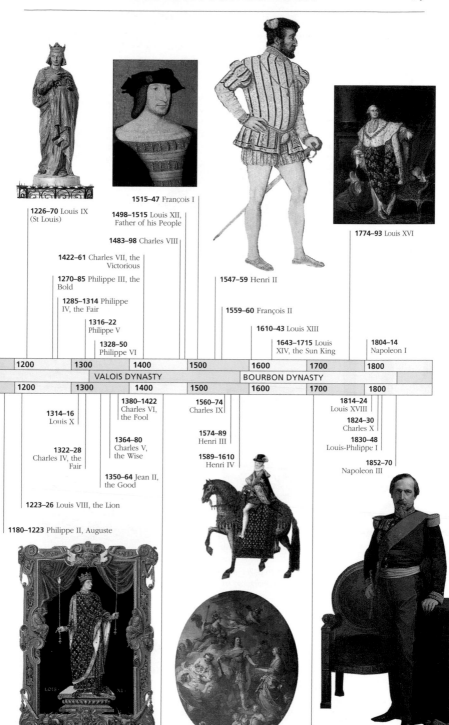

1515–47 François I

1226–70 Louis IX (St Louis)

1498–1515 Louis XII, Father of his People

1483–98 Charles VIII

1422–61 Charles VII, the Victorious

1270–85 Philippe III, the Bold

1285–1314 Philippe IV, the Fair

1316–22 Philippe V

1328–50 Philippe VI

1547–59 Henri II

1559–60 François II

1610–43 Louis XIII

1643–1715 Louis XIV, the Sun King

1774–93 Louis XVI

1804–14 Napoleon I

| 1200 | 1300 | 1400 | 1500 | 1600 | 1700 | 1800 |

VALOIS DYNASTY **BOURBON DYNASTY**

| 1200 | 1300 | 1400 | 1500 | 1600 | 1700 | 1800 |

1314–16 Louis X

1380–1422 Charles VI, the Fool

1560–74 Charles IX

1814–24 Louis XVIII

1824–30 Charles X

1574–89 Henri III

1830–48 Louis-Philippe I

1322–28 Charles IV, the Fair

1364–80 Charles V, the Wise

1589–1610 Henri IV

1852–70 Napoleon III

1350–64 Jean II, the Good

1223–26 Louis VIII, the Lion

1180–1223 Philippe II, Auguste

1461–83 Louis XI, the Spider

1715–74 Louis XV

Gallo-Roman Paris

Paris would not have existed without the Seine. The river provided early peoples with the means to exploit the land, forests, marshes and islands. Recent excavations have unearthed canoes dating back to 4,500 BC, well before a Celtic tribe, known as the Parisii, settled there in the 3rd century BC,

Roman enamel brooch in an area known as Lutetia. From 59 BC, the Romans undertook the conquest of Gaul (France). Seven years later Lutetia was sacked by the Romans. They fortified and rebuilt it, especially the main island (the Ile de la Cité) and the Left Bank of the Seine.

EXTENT OF THE CITY

▦ 200 BC	☐ Today

Bronze-Age Harness
Everyday objects like harnesses continued to be made of bronze well into the Iron Age, which began in Gaul around 900 BC.

Iron Daggers
From the 2nd century BC, short swords of iron replaced long swords and were sometimes decorated with human and animal shapes.

Baths

Theatre

Forum

Present-day
Rue Soufflot

Glass Beads
Iron-Age glass beads and bracelets have been found on the Ile de la Cité.

Fired-Clay Vase
Pale ceramics with coloured decoration were common in Gaul.

Present-day
Rue St-Jacques

TIMELINE

Helmet worn by Gaulish warriors

52 BC Labienus, Caesar's lieutenant, defeats the Gauls under Camulogenes. The Parisii destroy their own city

4500 BC Early boatmen operate from the banks of the Seine

4500	400		200	

Parisii gold coin minted on the Ile de la Cité

300 BC Parisii tribe settle on the Ile de la Cité

100 BC Romans rebuild the Ile de la Cité, and create a new town on the Left Bank

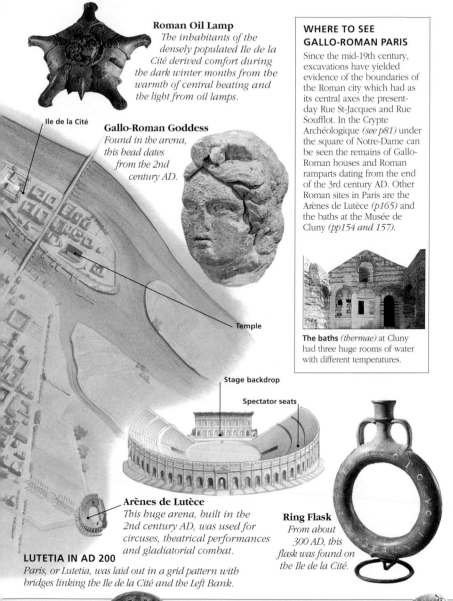

Roman Oil Lamp
The inhabitants of the densely populated Ile de la Cité derived comfort during the dark winter months from the warmth of central heating and the light from oil lamps.

Ile de la Cité

Gallo-Roman Goddess
Found in the arena, this head dates from the 2nd century AD.

Temple

WHERE TO SEE GALLO-ROMAN PARIS

Since the mid-19th century, excavations have yielded evidence of the boundaries of the Roman city which had as its central axes the present-day Rue St-Jacques and Rue Soufflot. In the Crypte Archéologique *(see p81)* under the square of Notre-Dame can be seen the remains of Gallo-Roman houses and Roman ramparts dating from the end of the 3rd century AD. Other Roman sites in Paris are the Arènes de Lutèce *(p165)* and the baths at the Musée de Cluny *(pp154 and 157)*.

The baths *(thermae)* at Cluny had three huge rooms of water with different temperatures.

Stage backdrop

Spectator seats

Arènes de Lutèce
This huge arena, built in the 2nd century AD, was used for circuses, theatrical performances and gladiatorial combat.

Ring Flask
From about 300 AD, this flask was found on the Ile de la Cité.

LUTETIA IN AD 200
Paris, or Lutetia, was laid out in a grid pattern with bridges linking the Ile de la Cité and the Left Bank.

Roman floor mosaic from the Cluny baths

200 Romans add arena, baths and villas

285 Barbarians advance, Lutetia swept by fire

360 Julien, prefect of Gaul, is proclaimed Emperor. Lutetia changes its name to Paris after the Parisii

0	200	400

250 Early Christian martyr, St Denis, beheaded in Montmartre

451 Sainte Geneviève galvanizes the Parisians to repulse Attila the Hun

485–508 Clovis, leader of the Franks, defeats the Romans. Paris becomes Christian

Medieval Paris

Manuscript illumination

Throughout the Middle Ages, strategically placed towns like Paris, positioned at a river crossing, became important centres of political power and learning. The Church played a crucial part in intellectual and spiritual life. It provided the impetus for education and for technological advances such as the drainage of land and the digging of canals. The population was still confined mainly to the Ile de la Cité and the Left Bank. When the marshes *(marais)* were drained in the 12th century, the city was able to expand.

EXTENT OF THE CITY

■ *1300*   □ *Today*

Sainte-Chapelle
The upper chapel of this medieval masterpiece (see pp88–9) *was reserved for the royal family.*

The Ile de la Cité, including the towers of the Conciergerie and Sainte-Chapelle, features in the pages for June.

Octagonal Table
Medieval manor houses had wooden furniture like this trestle table.

Drainage allowed more land to be cultivated.

Weavers' Window
Medieval craftsmen formed guilds and many church windows were dedicated to their crafts.

A rural life was led by most Parisians, who worked on the land. The actual city only occupied a tiny area.

TIMELINE

512 Death of Sainte Geneviève. She is buried next to Clovis

725–732 Muslims attack Gaul

845–862 Normans attack Paris

| 500 | 700 | 800 | 900 |

543–556 Foundation of St-Germain-des-Prés

Golden hand reliquary of Charlemagne

800 Charlemagne crowned Emperor by the Pope

Notre-Dame
The great Gothic cathedrals took many years to build. Work continued on Notre-Dame from 1163 to 1334.

University Seal
The University of Paris was founded in 1215.

The Monasteries
Monks of many different orders lived in monasteries in Paris, especially on the Left Bank of the Seine.

The Louvre of Charles V with its defensive wall is seen here from the Ile de la Cité.

The Nobility
From the mid-14th century, dress was considered to be a mark of class; noble ladies wore high, pointed hats.

THE MONTHS: JUNE AND OCTOBER
This illuminated prayer book and calendar, the Très Riches Heures (left and above), was made for the Duc de Berri in 1416. It shows many Paris buildings.

A MEDIEVAL ROMANCE
It was in the cloisters of Notre-Dame that the romance between the monk Pierre Abélard and the young Héloïse began. Abélard was the most original theologian of the 12th century and was hired as a tutor to the 17-year-old niece of a canon. A love affair soon developed between the teacher and his pupil. In his wrath, Héloïse's uncle had the scholar castrated; Héloïse took refuge in a convent for the rest of her life.

1010–22 Christians burn Jews and heretics

1167 Les Halles food market created on the Right Bank of the Seine

1253 The Sorbonne opens

1380 The Bastille fortress completed

Joan of Arc

| 1000 | 1100 | 1200 | 1300 | 1400 |

1079 Birth of Pierre Abélard

1163 Work starts on Notre-Dame cathedral

1215 Paris University founded

1245 Work starts on Sainte-Chapelle

1226–70 Reign of Louis IX, St Louis

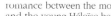

1430 Henry VI of England crowned King of France after Joan of Arc fails to defend Paris

Renaissance Paris

Couple in fine courtly dress

At the end of the Hundred Years' War with England, Paris was in a terrible state. By the time the occupying English army had left in 1453, the city lay in ruins, with many houses burned. Louis XI brought back prosperity and a new interest in art, architecture, decoration and clothes. During the course of the 16th and 17th centuries, French kings came under the spell of the Italian Renaissance. Their architects made the first attempts at town planning, creating elegant, uniform buildings and open urban spaces like the magnificent Place Royale.

EXTENT OF THE CITY

▨ *1590* ☐ *Today*

A Knight Preparing to Joust
The Place Royale was the setting for jousting displays well into the 17th century.

Jewel-Encrusted Pendant
A sign of the new prosperity, jewels became an important part of dress.

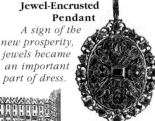

Printing Press (1470)
Religious tracts, mainly in Latin, were printed on the first press at the Sorbonne.

Pont Notre-Dame
This bridge with its row of houses was built at the start of the 15th century. The Pont Neuf (1589) was the first bridge without houses.

PLACE ROYALE
Built by Henri IV in 1609, with grand symmetrical houses round an open, central space, this was Paris's first square. Home to the aristocracy, it was re-named Place des Vosges in 1800 (see p94).

TIMELINE

François I

1453 End of the Hundred Years' War with England

1516 François I invites Leonardo da Vinci to France. He brings the *Mona Lisa* with him

1450	1460	1470	1480	1490	1500	1510	1520

1469 First French printing works starts operating at the Sorbonne

1528 François I takes up residence in the Louvre

16th-Century Knife and Fork Set
Ornate knife and fork sets were used in the dining rooms of the wealthy to carve joints of meat. Diners used hands or spoons for eating.

WHERE TO SEE RENAISSANCE PARIS TODAY

Besides the Place des Vosges, there are many examples of the Renaissance in Paris. Churches include St-Etienne-du-Mont *(p153)* and St-Eustache *(p114)*, as well as the Tour St-Jacques *(p115)*, the tower of a church no longer in existence. Mansions such as the Hôtel Carnavalet *(pp96–7)* have been restored, and the staircases, courtyard and turrets of the Hôtel de Cluny *(pp154–5)* date from 1485–96.

The rood screen of St-Etienne-du-Mont (about 1520) is of outstanding delicacy.

Walnut Dresser (about 1545)
Elegant carved wooden furniture decorated the homes of the wealthy.

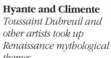

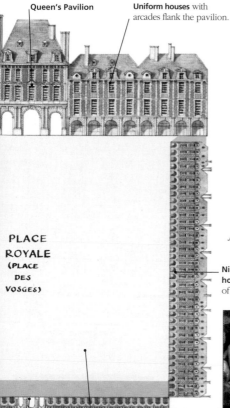

Queen's Pavilion

Uniform houses with arcades flank the pavilion.

PLACE ROYALE (PLACE DES VOSGES)

Nine symmetrical houses line each side of the square.

Hyante and Climente
Toussaint Dubreuil and other artists took up Renaissance mythological themes.

King's Pavilion

Duels were fought in the centre of the square in the 17th century.

1534 Ignatius of Loyola founds the Society of Jesus	**1546** Work starts on new Louvre palace; first stone quay built along Seine	**1559** Primitive street lanterns introduced; Louvre completed		**1572** St Bartholomew's Day massacre of Protestants		**1589** Henri III assassinated at St-Cloud, near Paris	**1609** Henri IV begins building Place des Vosges

1530	1540	1550	1560	1570	1580	1590	1600

1547 François I dies

1534 Founding of the Collège de France

1533 Hôtel de Ville rebuilt

1559 Henri II killed in a Paris tournament

1589 Protestant Henri of Navarre converts to Catholicism, crowned as Henri IV

1589 Henri IV completes Pont-Neuf and improves capital's water supply

1610 Henri IV is assassinated by Ravaillac, a religious fanatic

The assassin Ravaillac

The Sun King's Paris

Emblem of the Sun King

The 17th century in France, which became known as *Le Grand Siècle* (the great century), is epitomized by the glittering extravagance of Louis XIV (the Sun King) and his court at Versailles. In Paris, imposing buildings, squares, theatres and aristocratic *hôtels* (mansions) were built. Beneath this brilliant surface lay the absolute power of the monarch. By the end of Louis' reign the cost of his extravagance and of waging almost continuous war with France's neighbours led to a decline in the monarchy.

EXTENT OF THE CITY

▢ 1657	▢ Today

The mansard roof, with its slopes at both sides and both ends, came to typify French roofs of this period.

An open staircase rose from the internal courtyard.

Cross section of the living quarters

The Gardens of Versailles
Louis XIV devoted a lot of time to the gardens, which were designed by André Le Nôtre.

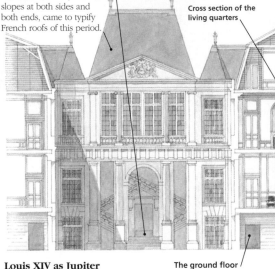

Louis XIV as Jupiter
On ascending the throne in 1661, Louis, depicted here as Jupiter triumphant, ended the civil wars that had been raging since his childhood.

The ground floor contained the servants' quarters.

Chest of Drawers
This gilded piece was made by André-Charles Boulle for the Grand Trianon at Versailles.

TIMELINE

1610 Louis XIII's accession marks the start of *Le Grand Siècle*

Louis XIII

1624 Completion of Tuileries Palace

Cardinal Mazarin

1631 Launch of *La Gazette*, Paris's first newspaper

1643 Death of Louis XIII. Regency under control of Marie de Médicis and Cardinal Mazarin

1661 Louis XIV becomes absolute monarch. Enlargement of Château de Versailles begun

1610	1620	1630	1640	1650	1660

1622 Paris becomes an episcopal see

1629 Richelieu, Louis XIII's first minister, builds Palais Royal

1638 Birth of Louis XIV

1662 Colbert, Louis XIV's finance minister, founds Gobelins tapestry works

1614 Final meeting of the Estates Council (the main legislative assembly) before the Revolution

1627 Development of the Ile St-Louis

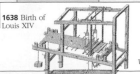

Weaving frame

Ceiling by Charles Le Brun
Court painter to Louis XIV, Le Brun decorated many ceilings like this one at the Hôtel Carnavalet (see p96).

Madame de Maintenon
When the queen died in 1683, Louis married Madame de Maintenon, shown here in a framed painting by Caspar Netscher.

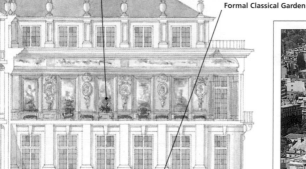

Decorated Fan
For special court fêtes, Louis XIV often stipulated that women carry fans.

The Galerie d'Hercule with Le Brun ceiling

Formal Classical Garden

Dôme Church (1706)

HOTEL LAMBERT (1640)
In the 17th century, the aristocracy built luxurious town houses with grand staircases, courtyards, formal gardens, coach houses and stables.

Neptune Cup
Made from lapis lazuli with a silver Neptune on top, this cup was part of Louis' vast collection of art objects.

WHERE TO SEE THE SUN KING'S PARIS
Many 17th-century mansions such as the Hôtel Lambert still exist in Paris, but not all are open to the public. However, Hôtel des Invalides (p187), the Dôme Church (pp188–9), the Palais du Luxembourg (p172) and Versailles (pp248–53) give a magnificent impression of the period.

1667 Louvre rebuilt and observatory established

1682 Court moves to Versailles where it stays until the Revolution

1686 Le Procope, Paris's first café

1702 Paris first divided into 20 arrondissements (districts)

1715 Louis XIV dies

1670	1680	1690	1700	1710

1692 Great famines due to bad harvests and wars

1670 Hôtel des Invalides built

1689 Pont Royal built

Statue of Louis XIV at Musée Carnavalet

Paris in the Age of Enlightenment

Bust of François Marie Arouet, known as Voltaire

The Enlightenment, with its emphasis on scientific reason and a critical approach to existing ideas and society, was centred on the city of Paris. In contrast, nepotism and corruption were rife at Louis XV's court at Versailles. Meanwhile the economy thrived, the arts flourished as never before and intellectuals, such as Voltaire and Rousseau, were renowned throughout Europe. In Paris, the population rose to about 650,000: town planning was developed, and the first accurate street map of the city appeared in 1787.

EXTENT OF THE CITY

■ *1720*   ☐ *Today*

Nautical Instruments
As the science of navigation advanced, scientists developed telescopes and trigonometric instruments (used for measuring longitude and latitude).

18th-Century Wigs
These were not only a mark of fashion but also a way of indicating the wearer's class and importance.

COMEDIE FRANÇAISE
The Age of Enlightenment saw a burst of dramatic activity, and new theatres opened. Among them was the Comédie Française (see p120), still one of the most prestigious theatres in the world.

The auditorium, with 1,913 seats, was the largest in Paris.

TIMELINE

Fireman

1720	1730	1740	1750

1722 City's first fire brigade founded

1734 Fontaine des Quatre Saisons built

1748 Montesquieu's *L'Esprit des Lois* (an influential work about different forms of government) published

1751 First volume of Diderot's *Encyclopedia* published

Madame de Pompadour
*Although generally
remembered as the
mistress of Louis XV, she
was renowned as a patron
of the arts and had great
political influence.*

Chocolate Pot
*By the 18th century,
bourgeois families
could afford tobacco, tea,
chocolate and coffee from Asia
and the New World.*

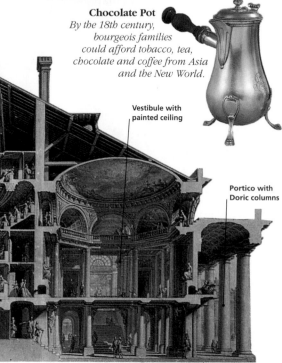

Vestibule with
painted ceiling

Portico with
Doric columns

The Catacombs
*These were set up in
1785 as a more
hygienic alternative
to Paris's cemeteries
(see p179).*

WHERE TO SEE ENLIGHTENMENT PARIS

The district around the Rue
de Lille, the Rue de Varenne
and the Rue de Grenelle
(p187) has many luxurious
town houses, or *hôtels*,
which were built by the
aristocracy during the first
half of the 18th century.
Memorabilia from the lives
of the great intellectuals
Voltaire and Jean-Jacques
Rousseau is in the Musée
Carnavalet *(pp96–7)*, along
with 18th-century interior
designs and paintings.

Churches were built throughout
the Enlightenment. St-Sulpice
(p172) was completed in 1776.

Le Procope *(p140)* is the oldest
café in Paris. It was frequented
by Voltaire and Rousseau.

1757 First oil
street lamps

c.1760 Place de
la Concorde,
Panthéon and
Ecole Militaire
built

1760

1762
Rousseau's
Emile and
the *Social
Contract*

1764 Madame
de Pompadour
dies

*Rousseau, philosopher
and writer, believed
that humans were
naturally good
and had been
corrupted by
society.*

1770

1774 Louis XV,
great grandson of
Louis XIV, dies

1778 France supports
American independence

1780

1782 First
pavements built,
in the Place du
Théâtre Français

1783
Montgolfier
brothers make
the first hot-air
balloon ascent

1785
David paints
the *Oath of
the Horatii*

Paris During the Revolution

In 1789 most Parisians were still living in squalor and poverty, as they had since the Middle Ages. Rising inflation and opposition to Louis XVI culminated in the storming of the Bastille, the king's prison; the Republic was founded three years later. However, the Terror soon followed, when those suspected of betraying the Revolution were executed

A plate made in celebration of the Revolution

without trial: more than 60,000 people lost their lives. The bloody excesses of Robespierre, the zealous revolutionary, led to his overthrow and a new government, the Directory, was set up in 1795.

EXTENT OF THE CITY

■ *1796*   □ *Today*

The prison turrets were set alight.

The French guards, who were on the side of the revolutionaries, arrived late in the afternoon with two cannons.

Declaration of the Rights of Man and the Citizen

The Enlightenment ideals of equality and human dignity were enshrined in the Declaration. This illustration is the preface to the 1791 Constitution.

Drawbridge

REPUBLICAN CALENDAR

The revolutionaries believed that the world was starting again, so they abolished the existing church calendar and took 22 September 1792, the day the Republic was declared, as the first day of the new era. The Republican calendar had 12 equal months, each sub-divided into three ten-day periods, with the remaining five days of each year set aside for public holidays. All the months of the year were given poetic names which linked them to nature and the seasons, such as fog, snow, seed-time, flowers and harvest.

A coloured engraving by Tresca showing *Ventôse*, the windy month (19 Feb–20 Mar) from the new Republican calendar

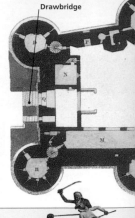

TIMELINE

14 Jul Fall of the Bastille

4 Aug Abolition of feudalism

26 Aug Declaration of the Rights of Man and the Citizen

17 Sep Law of Suspects passed: the Terror begins

10 Aug The storming of the Tuileries

1789	1790	1791	1792

Cartoon on the three Estates: the clergy, the nobility and the awakening populace

Lafayette, Commander of the National Guard, takes his oath to the Constitution

17 Jul Champ de Mars massacre

25 Apr *La Marseillaise* composed

5 May The Estates council meets

14 Jul Fête de la Fédération

Paper Money
Bonds, called assignats, *were used to fund the Revolution from 1790–93.*

La Marseillaise
The revolutionaries' marching song is now the national anthem.

The Sans Culottes
By 1792, the wearing of trousers instead of breeches (culottes) was a political symbol of Paris's artisans and shopkeepers.

"Patriotic" Chair
The back of this wooden chair is topped by red bonnets, symbol of revolutionary politics.

Wallpaper
Commemorative wallpaper was produced to celebrate the Revolution.

The dead and wounded totalled 171 by the end of the day.

Coin tower

Great court

Well court

Guillotine
This was used for the first time in France in April 1792.

STORMING OF THE BASTILLE
The Bastille was overrun on 14 July 1789 and the seven prisoners held there released. The defenders (32 Swiss guards, 82 wounded soldiers and the governor) were massacred.

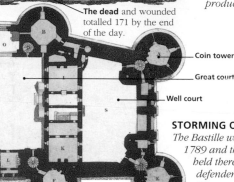

Napoleonic Paris

Napoleon Bonaparte was the most brilliant general in the French army. The instability of the new government after the Revolution gave him the chance to seize power, and in November 1799 he installed himself in the Tuileries Palace as First Consul. He crowned himself Emperor in May 1804. Napoleon established a centralized administration and a code of

Napoleon's imperial crown

laws, reformed France's educational system and set out to make Paris the most beautiful city in the world. The city was endowed with grand monuments and embellished with the spoils of conquest. His power was always fragile and dependent on incessant wars. In March 1814 Prussian, Austrian and Russian armies invaded Paris and Napoleon fled to Elba. He returned to Paris in 1815 but was defeated at Waterloo and died in exile in 1821.

EXTENT OF THE CITY

◼ *1810*   ☐ *Today*

Château de Malmaison
This was the favourite home of Josephine, Napoleon's first wife.

Ladies-in-Waiting hold Josephine's train.

Opaline-Glass Clock
The decoration on this clock echoed the fashion for draperies.

Elephant Project
This monument was planned for the centre of the Place de la Bastille.

Eagle's Flight
Napoleon's flight to Elba in 1814 was satirized in this cartoon.

TIMELINE

1799 Napoleon seizes power	**1800** Banque de France founded			**1815** Waterloo; second abdication of Napoleon. Restoration of the monarchy	
1797 Battle of Rivoli		**1802** Legion of Honour established	**1812** Russian campaign ends in defeat		
1800		**1805**	**1810**	**1815**	**1820**
	1804 Napoleon crowned	**1806** Arc de Triomphe commissioned			**1821** Napoleon dies
			1814 Napoleon abdicates		*Napoleon's death mask*
	1800 Napoleon returns from Egypt on his ship *L'Orient*		**1809** Napoleon divorces Josephine and marries Marrie-Louise		

Bronze Table Top
Inlaid with Napoleon's portrait, this table marks the victory at Austerlitz.

Josephine kneels before Napoleon.

Napoleon holds the crown for his Empress, Josephine.

Russian Cossacks in the Palais Royal
After Napoleon's defeat and flight in 1814, Paris suffered the humiliation of being occupied by foreign troops, including Austrians, Prussians and Russians.

The Pope makes the sign of the cross.

The Arc de Triomphe du Carrousel was erected in 1806 and crowned with the horses looted from St Mark's, Venice.

WHERE TO SEE NAPOLEONIC PARIS

Many of the grand monuments Napoleon planned for Paris were never built, but two triumphal arches, the Arc de Triomphe (*pp208–9*) and Arc de Triomphe du Carrousel (*p122*), were a major part of his legacy. La Madeleine church (*p214*) was also inaugurated in his reign and much of the Louvre was rebuilt (*pp122–3*). Examples of the Empire style can be seen at Malmaison (*p255*) and at the Carnavalet (*pp96–7*).

NAPOLEON'S CORONATION

Napoleon's rather dramatic crowning took place in 1804. In this recreation by J L David, the Pope, summoned to Notre-Dame, looks on as Napoleon crowns his Empress just before crowning himself.

The Empress
Josephine was divorced by Napoleon in 1809.

1842 First railway line between Paris and St-Germain-en-Laye opens

1825	1830	1835	1840	1845

1830 Revolution in Paris and advent of constitutional monarchy

1831 Victor Hugo's *Notre-Dame de Paris* published Cholera epidemic hits Paris

1840 Reburial of Napoleon at Les Invalides

Napoleon's tomb

The Grand Transformation

In 1848 Paris saw a second revolution which brought down the recently restored monarchy. In the uncertainties that followed, Napoleon's nephew assumed power in the same way as his uncle before him – by a *coup d'état*. He proclaimed himself Napoleon III in 1851. Under his rule Paris was transformed into the most magnificent city in Europe. He entrusted the task of modernization to Baron Haussmann. Haussmann demolished the crowded, unsanitary streets of the medieval city and created a well-ordered capital within a geometrical grid of avenues and boulevards. Neighbouring districts such as Auteuil were annexed, creating the suburbs.

EXTENT OF THE CITY

▨ *1859*　　☐ *Today*

Lamppost outside the Opéra

Arc de Triomphe

Boulevard des Italiens
This tree-lined avenue, painted by Edmond Georges Grandjean (1889), was one of the most fashionable of the new boulevards.

Twelve avenues formed a star *(étoile).*

Laying the Sewers
This engraving from 1861 shows the early work for laying the sewer system (see p190) from La Villette to Les Halles. Most was the work of the engineer Belgrand.

Circular Hoarding
Distinctive hoardings advertised opera and theatre performances.

Grand mansions were built around the Arc de Triomphe between 1860 and 1868.

TIMELINE

1850	1852	1854	1856	1858

1851 Napoleon III declares the Second Empire

Viewing the exhibits at the World Exhibition

1852 Haussmann begins massive town-planning schemes

1855 World Exhibition

20 centimes stamp showing Napoleon III

1857 The poet, Baudelaire, prosecuted for obscenity for *The Flowers of Evil*

PLACE DE L'ETOILE

The new scheme for the centre of Paris included redesigning the area at one end of the Champs-Elysées (Elysian Fields). Haussmann created a star of 12 broad avenues around the new Arc de Triomphe.
(The inset map shows the area as it was in 1790.)

Fields

Avenue des Champs-Elysées

Site of Arc de Triomphe

Drinking Fountain

In 1840, fifty fountains were erected in poor areas of Paris through the generosity of the English francophile, Richard Wallace.

AVE DES CHAMPS ELYSEES

AVE MARCEAU

AVE D'IENA

AVE KLEBER

L'ETOILE

DE

AVE DE LA GRANDE ARMEE

AVE VICTOR HUGO

AVE FOCH

Bois de Boulogne

Given to the city in 1852 by Napoleon III, this park became a popular place for walking and riding (see pp254–5).

BARON HAUSSMANN

Lawyer by training and civil servant by profession, Georges-Eugène Haussmann (1809–91) was appointed Prefect of the Seine by Napoleon III. For 17 years he was in charge of urban planning. With the best architects and engineers of the day, he planned a new city, improved the water supply and sewerage, and created beautiful parks.

Some avenues were named after French generals.

1861 Garnier designs new Opera House

1863 The nudity in Manet's *Le Déjeuner sur l'Herbe* causes a scandal and is rejected by the Academy *(see pp144–5)*

1867 World Exhibition

1870 Napoleon's wife, Eugénie, flees Paris at threat of war

| 1860 | 1862 | 1864 | 1866 | 1868 |

1863 Credit Lyonnais bank established

1862 Victor Hugo's epic novel of Paris's poor, *Les Misérables,* published

1868 Press censorship relaxed

1870 Start of Franco-Prussian War

The Belle Epoque

The Franco-Prussian War culminated in the terrible Siege of Paris. When peace came in 1871, it fell to the new government, the Third Republic, to bring about economic recovery. From about 1890 life was transformed: the motor-car, aeroplane, cinema, telephone and gramophone all contributed to the enjoyment of life and the *Belle Epoque* (beautiful age) was born. Paris became a glittering city where the new style, *Art Nouveau*, decorated buildings and objects. The paintings of the Impressionists, such as Renoir, reflected the *joie de vivre* of the times, while later those of Matisse, Braque and Picasso heralded the modern movement in art.

Art Nouveau pendant

EXTENT OF THE CITY
▨ 1895   ▢ Today

The interior was arranged as tiers of galleries around a central grand staircase.

Cabaret Poster
Toulouse-Lautrec's posters immortalized the singers and dancers of the cafés and cabaret clubs of Montmartre, where artists and writers congregated in the 1890s.

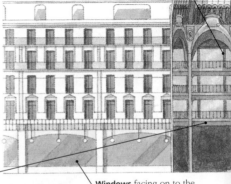

Electricity illuminated the window displays.

Windows facing on to the Boulevard Haussmann displayed the goods on offer.

Central Hall of the Grand Palais
The Grand Palais (p206) was built to house two huge exhibitions of French painting and sculpture at the World Exhibition of 1889.

Art Nouveau Cash Till
Even ordinary objects like this cash till were beautified by the new style.

TIMELINE

1871 Third Republic established

1874 Monet paints first Impressionist picture: *Impression: Soleil levant*

Louis Pasteur

1889 Eiffel Tower built

| 1870 | 1875 | 1880 | 1885 | 1890 |

Zoo animals were shot to feed the hungry (see p224)

1870 Siege of Paris

1885 Louis Pasteur discovers rabies vaccine

Entrance ticket to the exhibition

1891 First metro station opens

1889 Great Exhibition

Citroën 5CV

France led the world in the early development of the motor-car. By 1900 the Citroën began to be seen on the streets of Paris, and long-distance motor racing was popular.

The glass dome could be seen from all parts of the store.

Moulin Rouge (1890)

The old, redundant windmills of Montmartre became nightclubs, like the world-famous Moulin Rouge (red windmill) (see p226).

WHERE TO SEE THE BELLE EPOQUE

Art Nouveau can be seen in monumental buildings like the Grand Palais and Petit Palais *(p206)*, while the Galeries Lafayette *(p321)* and the Pharamond restaurant *(p303)* have beautiful Belle Epoque interiors. The Musée d'Orsay *(pp144–7)* has many objects from this period.

The entrance to the metro at Porte Dauphine was the work of leading Art Nouveau designer Hector Guimard *(p226)*.

The doorway of No. 29 Avenue Rapp *(p191)*, in the Eiffel Tower quarter, is a fine example of Art Nouveau.

GALERIES LAFAYETTE (1906)

This beautiful department store, with its dome a riot of coloured glass and wrought ironwork, was a sign of the new prosperity.

The Naughty Nineties

The Lumière brothers captured the daring negligée fashions of the 1890s in the first moving images of the cinematograph.

1894–1906 Dreyfus affair

Captain Dreyfus was publicly humiliated for selling secrets to the Prussians. He was later found innocent.

1907 Picasso paints *Les Demoiselles d'Avignon*

1913 Proust publishes first volume of *Remembrance of Things Past*

1895	1900	1905	1910

1898 Pierre and Marie Curie discover radium

1909 Blériot flies across the English Channel

1911 Diaghilev brings the Russian ballet to Paris

1895 Lumière brothers introduce cinematography

Avant-Garde Paris

Office chair by Le Corbusier

From the 1920s to the 1940s, Paris became a mecca for artists, musicians, writers and film-makers. The city was alive with new movements such as Cubism and Surrealism represented by Cézanne, Picasso, Braque, Man Ray and Duchamp. Many new trends came from the USA, as writers and musicians including Ernest Hemingway, Gertrude Stein and Sidney Bechet took up residence in Paris. In architecture, the geometric shapes created by Le Corbusier changed the face of the modern building.

EXTENT OF THE CITY

■ 1940	□ Today

Napoleon by Abel Gance
Paris has always been a city for film-makers. In 1927 Abel Gance made an innovative movie about Napoleon, using triple screens and wide-angle lenses.

Occupied Paris
Paris was under occupation for most of World War II. The Eiffel Tower was a favourite spot for German soldiers.

Josephine Baker
Arriving in Paris in 1925, the outlandish dancer catapulted to fame in "La Revue Nègre" wearing nothing but feathers.

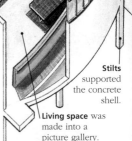

Stilts supported the concrete shell.

Living space was made into a picture gallery.

LA ROCHE VILLA BY LE CORBUSIER
Made from concrete and steel, with straight lines, horizontal windows and a flat roof, this house (1923) epitomized the new style.

Sidney Bechet
In the 1930s and 1940s the jazz clubs of Paris resounded to the swing music of black musicians such as the saxophonist Sidney Bechet.

TIMELINE

1919 Treaty of Versailles signed in the Hall of Mirrors

1924 Olympic Games held in Paris

1924 André Breton publishes Surrealist Manifesto

1925 Art Deco style first seen at the Exposition des Arts Décoratifs

1914	1916	1918	1920	1922	1924	1926	1928

1914–18 World War I. Paris is under threat of German attack, saved by the Battle of the Marne. A shell hits St-Gervais–St-Protais.

World War I soldier in uniform

1920 Interment of the Unknown Soldier

An eternal flame for the Unknown Soldier burns under the Arc de Triomphe

Fashion in the 1940s

After World War II, the classic look for men and women was reminiscent of military uniforms.

The roof was designed as a garden terrace.

The old Trocadéro was changed to the Palais de Chaillot (*see p198*) for the World Exhibition.

WHERE TO SEE AVANT-GARDE PARIS

La Roche Villa is now part of the Fondation Le Corbusier (*p254*) and can be visited in the Paris suburb of Auteuil. Hemingway's haunt, the bar-brasserie La Closerie des Lilas in Montparnasse (*p179*), has retained much of its period decor. For fashion don't miss the Musée Galliera (*p201*).

Airmail Poster
Airmail routes developed during the 1930s, especially to French North Africa.

The bedroom was above the dining room.

The kitchen was built at the back with a sloping glass roof.

The garage was built into the ground floor.

Claudine in Paris by Colette
The Claudine series of novels, written by Colette Willy, known simply as "Colette", were extremely popular in the 1930s.

Windows were arranged in a horizontal strip.

1931 Colonial Exhibition

A visitor to the exhibition in colonial dress

1937 Picasso paints *Guernica* in protest at the Spanish Civil War

1940 World War II: Paris bombed and occupied by Nazis

1930	1932	1934	1936	1938	1940	1942

Symbol of Free French superimposed on the victory sign

1934 Riots and strikes in response to the Depression

1937 Palais de Chaillot built

Aug 1944 Liberation of Paris

The Modern City

In 1962 a programme of renovation was started in Paris, with run-down districts like the Marais being restored. This work was continued by François Mitterrand's *Grand Travaux* (great works) scheme. Access was improved to historical monuments and art collections, such as the Grand Louvre *(see pp122–9)* and the Musée d'Orsay *(pp144–7)*. The scheme was responsible for several monuments to the modern age, including the Opéra National de Paris Bastille *(p98)*, the Cité des Sciences *(pp236–9)* and the Bibliothèque Nationale at Quai de la Gare *(p246)*. With these, and the boldly modern Défense, Grande Arche and Stade de France, Paris prepared herself for the 21st century.

Late President, François Mitterrand

EXTENT OF THE CITY

☐ *1959* ☐ *Today*

La Grande Arche is taller and wider than Notre-Dame and runs in an axis linking the Arc de Triomphe and the Louvre Pyramid.

Christo's Pont Neuf
To create a work of art, the Bulgarian-born artist Christo wrapped Paris's oldest bridge, the Pont Neuf, in fabric in 1985.

Simone de Beauvoir
Influential philosopher and life-long companion of J-P Sartre, de Beauvoir fought for the liberation of women in the 1950s.

Shopping centre

Citroën Goddess (1956)
With its ultra-modern lines, this became Paris's most prestigious car.

TIMELINE

1950 Construction of UNESCO, and the Musée de Radio-France

1962 André Malraux, Minister of Culture, begins renovation programme of run-down districts and monuments

Ducting at the Pompidou Centre

1977 Pompidou Centre opens. Jacques Chirac is installed as first elected Mayor of Paris since 1871

1945	1950	1955	1960	1965	1970	1975

President de Gaulle

1958 Establishment of Fifth Republic with de Gaulle as President

1964 Reorganization of the Ile de France

1968 Student riots and workers strikes in the Latin Quarter

1969 Les Halles market transfers to Rungis

1973 Construction of Montparnasse Tower and the Périphérique (ring road)

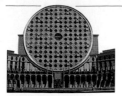

Marne La Vallée
Like a gigantic loud speaker, this residential complex is in one of Paris's dormitory towns near Disneyland Resort Paris.

Chanel Designs
Paris is the centre of the fashion world with important shows each year.

The Pompidou Centre
The nation's collection of modern art is housed here in this popular building (see pp110–13).

The Fiat Tower is one of Europe's tallest buildings.

Opéra National de Paris Bastille (1989)
It marks the bicentenary of the fall of the Bastille.

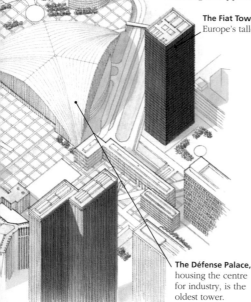

The Défense Palace, housing the centre for industry, is the oldest tower.

LA DEFENSE
This huge business centre was started on the edge of Paris in 1958. Today 30,000 people commute here from Paris's surrounding areas.

STUDENTS AT THE BARRICADES

In May 1968 Paris saw a revolution of a kind. The Latin Quarter was taken over by students and workers. What began as a protest against the war in Vietnam spread to other issues and became an expression of discontent with the Government. President de Gaulle rode out the storm but his prestige was severely damaged.

Rioting students clash with police

1985 Christo wraps Pont Neuf

Participant of the bicentenary wearing the French national colours

Victorious French football team holding aloft the World Cup trophy in Paris

1980	1985	1990	1995	2000	2005	2010

1980 Thousands greet Pope John-Paul on his official visit

1994 Eurostar inaugurated: Paris to London in 3 hrs

1989 Bicentenary celebrations to mark the French Revolution

2002 The Euro replaces the Franc as exclusive legal tender

1999 December hurricanes hit Paris: Versailles loses 10,000 trees

1998 France hosts – and wins – the 1998 football World Cup tournament

PARIS AT A GLANCE

There are nearly 300 places of interest described in the *Area by Area* section of this book. A broad range of sights is covered: from the ancient Conciergerie and its grisly associations with the guillotine *(see p81)*, to the modern opera house, the Opéra de la Bastille *(see p98)*; from No. 51 Rue de Montmorency *(see p114)*, the oldest houses in Paris, to the elegant Musée Picasso *(see pp100–1)*. To help make the most of your stay, the following 20 pages are a time-saving guide to the best Paris has to offer. Museums and galleries, historic churches, spacious parks, gardens and squares all have a section. There are also guides to Paris's famous personalities. Each sight has a cross reference to its own full entry. Below are the top tourist attractions to start you off.

PARIS'S TOP TOURIST ATTRACTIONS

La Défense
See p255.

Sainte-Chapelle
See pp88–9.

Palace of Versailles
See pp248–53.

Pompidou Centre
See pp110–13.

Musée d'Orsay
See pp144–7.

Musée du Louvre
See pp122–9.

Jardin du Luxembourg
See p172.

Eiffel Tower
See pp192–3.

Bois de Boulogne
See pp254–5.

Notre-Dame
See pp82–5.

Arc de Triomphe
See pp208–9.

◁ The Dôme Church, adjoining the Hôtel des Invalides

Remarkable Parisians

By virtue of its strategic position on the Seine, Paris has always been the economic, political and artistic hub of France. Over the centuries, many prominent and influential figures from other parts of the country and abroad have come to the city to absorb her unique spirit. In return they have left their mark: artists have brought new movements, politicians new schools of thought, musicians and film-makers new trends, and architects a new environment.

Actress Catherine Deneuve

ARTISTS

Sacré-Coeur by Utrillo (1934)

In the early 18th-century, Jean-Antoine Watteau (1684– 1721) took the inspiration for his paintings from the Paris theatre. Half a century later, Jean-Honoré Fragonard (1732– 1806), popular painter of the Rococo, lived and died here, financially ruined by the Revolution. Later, Paris became the cradle of Impressionism. Its founders Claude Monet (1840– 1926), Pierre-Auguste Renoir (1841–1919) and Alfred Sisley (1839–99) met in a Paris studio. In 1907, Pablo Picasso

(1881–1973) painted the seminal work *Les Demoiselles d'Avignon* at the Bateau-Lavoir, *(see p226)* where Georges Braque (1882–1963), Amedeo Modigliani (1884–1920) and Marc Chagall (1887–1985) also lived. Henri de Toulouse-Lautrec (1864–1901) drank and painted in Montmartre. So did Salvador Dalí (1904–89) who frequented the Café Cyrano, centre of the Surrealists. The Paris School eventually moved to Montparnasse, home to sculptors Auguste Rodin (1840–1917), Constantin Brancusi (1876–1957) and Ossip Zadkine (1890–1967).

POLITICAL LEADERS

Hugh Capet, Count of Paris, became King of France in 987. His palace was on the Ile de la Cité. Louis XIV, XV and XVI lived at Versailles *(see pp248–53)* but Napoleon *(see pp32–3)* preferred the Tuileries. Cardinal Richelieu (1585–1642), the power behind Louis XIII, created the Académie Française and the Palais-Royal *(see p120)*. Today the President lives in the Palais de l'Elysée *(p207)*.

FILMS AND FILM-MAKERS

Paris has always been at the heart of French cinema. The prewar and immediate post-war classics were usually made on the sets of the Boulogne and Joinville studios, where whole areas of the city were reconstructed, such as the Canal St-Martin for Marcel Carné's *Hôtel du Nord*. Jean-Luc Godard and other New Wave directors preferred to shoot outdoors. Godard's *A Bout de Souffle* (1960) with Jean-Paul Belmondo and Jean Seberg was filmed in and around the Champs-Elysées.

Simone Signoret (1921– 1985) and Yves Montand (1921– 1991), the most celebrated couple of French cinema, were long associated with the Ile de la Cité. Actresses, such as Catherine Deneuve (b.1943) and Isabelle Adjani (b.1955), live in the city to be near their couturiers.

MUSICIANS

Jean-Philippe Rameau (1683– 1764), organist and pioneer of harmony, is associated with St-Eustache *(see p114)*. Hector Berlioz (1803– 69) had his *Te Deum* first performed there in 1855, and Franz Liszt (1811– 86) his *Messe Solemnelle* in 1866. A great dynasty of organists, the Couperins, gave recitals in St-Gervais–St-Protais *(see p99)*.

The stage of the Opéra *(see p215)* has seen many talents, but audiences have not always been appreciative. Richard Wagner (1813–83) had his *Tannhäuser* hooted down. George Bizet's *Carmen*

Portrait of Cardinal Richelieu by Philippe de Champaigne (about 1635)

(1838–75) was booed, as was *Peléas et Mélisande* by Claude Debussy (1862–1918).

Soprano Maria Callas (1923–77) gave triumphal performances here. The composer and conductor Pierre Boulez (b.1925) has devoted his talent to experimental music at IRCAM near the Pompidou Centre *(see p346)*, which he helped to found.

The diminutive *chanteuse* Edith Piaf (1915–63), known for her nostalgic love-songs, began singing in the streets of Paris and then went on to tour the world. There is now a museum devoted to her life and work *(see p232–3)*.

Renée Jeanmaire as Carmen (1948)

ARCHITECTS

Gothic, Classical, Baroque and Modernist – all co-exist in Paris. The most brilliant medieval architect was Pierre de Montreuil, who built Notre-Dame and

The Grand Trianon at Versailles, built by Louis Le Vau in 1668

Sainte-Chapelle. Louis Le Vau (1612–70) and Jules Hardouin-Mansart (1646–1708) designed Versailles *(see pp248–53)*. Jacques-Ange Gabriel (1698–1782) built the Petit Trianon *(see p249)* and Place de la Concorde *(see p131)*. Haussmann (1809–91) gave the city its boulevards *(see pp34–5)*. Gustave Eiffel (1832–1923) built his tower in 1889. A century later, I M Pei added the Louvre's glass pyramid *(see p129)*, Jean Nouvel created the Institut du Monde Arabe *(see p164)* and Dominique Perrault the new Bibliothèque Nationale de France *(see p246)*. The 21st century already has several new landmarks underway.

WRITERS

French has been dubbed "the language of Molière", after playwright Jean-Baptiste Poquelin, alias Molière, (1622–73), who helped create the Comédie-Française, now situated near his home in Rue Richelieu. On the Left Bank, the Odéon Théâtre de l'Europe was home to playwright Jean Racine (1639–99). It is near the statue of Denis Diderot (1713–84), who published his

L'Encyclopédie between 1751 and 1776. Marcel Proust (1871–1922), author of the 13-volume *Remembrance of Things Past*, lived on the Boulevard Haussmann. To the existentialists, the district of St-Germain was the only place to be *(see pp142–3)*. Here Sylvia Beach welcomed James Joyce (1882–1941) to her bookshop on the Rue de l'Odéon. Ernest Hemingway (1899–1961) and F Scott Fitzgerald (1896–1940) wrote novels in Montparnasse.

Proust by J-E Blanche (about 1910)

SCIENTISTS

Paris has a Quartier Pasteur, a Boulevard Pasteur, a Pasteur metro and the world-famous Institut Pasteur *(see p247)*, all in honour of Louis Pasteur (1822–95), the great French chemist and biologist. His apartment and laboratory are faithfully preserved. The Institut Pasteur is today home to Professor Luc Montagnier, who first isolated the AIDS virus in 1983. Discoverers of radium, Pierre (1859–1906) and Marie Curie (1867–1934), also worked in Paris. The Curies have been the subject of a long-running play in Paris, *Les Palmes de M. Schutz*.

EXILED IN PARIS

The Duke and Duchess of Windsor married in France after his abdication in 1936 as King Edward VIII. The city granted them a rent-free mansion in the Bois de Boulogne. Other famous exiles have included Chou En-Lai (1898–1976), Ho Chi Minh (1890–1969), Vladimir Ilyich Lenin (1870–1924), Oscar Wilde (1854–1900) and ballet dancer Rudolf Nureyev (1938–93).

The Duke and Duchess of Windsor

Paris's Best: Churches

The Catholic Church has been the bastion of Parisian society through time. Many of the city's churches are worth visiting. Architectural styles vary and the interiors are often spectacular. Most churches are open during the day and many have services at regular intervals. Paris's tradition of church music is still alive. You can spend an evening enjoying the interiors while listening to an organ recital or classical concert *(see p346).* A more detailed overview of Paris churches is on pages 48–9.

Early crucifix in St-Gervais-St-Protais

La Madeleine
Built in the style of a Greco-Roman temple, this church is known for its fine sculptures.

Chaillot Quarter

Champs-Elysées

Tuileries Quarte

RIVER SEINE

Invalides and Eiffel Tower Quarter

St-Germain des-Prés

Dôme Church
This memorial to the military engineer Vauban lies in the Dôme Church, where Napoleon's remains were buried in 1840.

Montparnasse

Sainte-Chapelle
With its fine stained glass, this chapel is a medieval jewel.

Panthéon
The Neo-Classical Sainte-Geneviève, now the Panthéon, was inspired by Wren's St Paul's Cathedral in London.

| 0 kilometres | | 1 |
| 0 miles | | 0.5 |

Sacré-Coeur
Above the altar in this massive basilica, the chancel vault is decorated with a vast mosaic of Christ by Luc-Olivier Merson.

Montmartre

St-Eustache
With its mixture of Gothic and Renaissance styles, this is one of the finest churches in Paris.

St-Paul–St-Louis
This Christ figure is one of the many rich furnishings in this Jesuit church, built in 1641 for Cardinal Richelieu.

Opéra Quarter

Beaubourg and Les Halles

The Marais

Ile de la Cité

Ile St-Louis

Notre-Dame
The great cathedral was left to rot after the Revolution, until Victor Hugo led a restoration campaign.

Latin Quarter

Luxembourg Quarter

Jardin des Plantes Quarter

St-Séverin
The west door leads to one of the finest medieval churches in the city.

Mosquée de Paris
The minaret of this 1920s mosque is 33 m (100 ft) tall.

Exploring Paris's Churches

Some of Paris's finest architecture is reflected in the churches. The great era of church building was the medieval period but examples survive from all ages. During the Revolution *(see pp30–31)* churches were used as grain or weapons stores but were later restored to their former glory. Many churches have superb interiors with fine paintings and sculptures.

Facade of Eglise de la Sorbonne

MEDIEVAL

Tower of St-Germain-des-Prés

Both the pointed arch and the rose window were born in a suburb north of Paris at the Basilica de St-Denis, where most of the French kings and queens are buried. This was the first Gothic building, and it was from here that the Gothic style spread. The finest Gothic church in Paris is the city cathedral, **Notre-Dame**, tallest and most impressive of the early French cathedrals. Begun in 1163 by Bishop Maurice de Sully, it was completed in the next century by architects Jean de Chelles and Pierre de Montreuil, who added the transepts with their fine translucent rose windows. Montreuil's masterpiece is Louis IX's medieval palace chapel, **Sainte-Chapelle**, with its two-tier structure. It was built to house Christ's Crown of Thorns. Other surviving churches in Paris are **St-Germain-des-Prés**, the oldest surviving abbey church in Paris (1050); the tiny, rustic Romanesque **St-Julien-le-Pauvre**; and the Flamboyant Gothic **St-Séverin, St-Germain l'Auxerrois** and **St-Merry**.

RENAISSANCE

The effect of the Italian Renaissance swept through Paris in the 16th century. It led to a unique architectural style in which fine Classical detail and immense Gothic proportions resulted in an impure, but attractive, cocktail known as "French Renaissance". The best example in Paris is **St-Etienne-du-Mont**, whose interior has the feel of a wide and light basilica. Another is **St-Eustache**, the massive market church in Les Halles, and the nave of **St-Gervais–St-Protais** with its stained glass and carved choir stalls.

BAROQUE AND CLASSICAL

Churches and convents flourished in Paris during the 17th century, as the city expanded under Louis XIII and his son Louis XIV. The Italian Baroque style was first seen on the majestic front of **St-Gervais–St-Protais**, built by Salomon de Brosse in 1616. The style was toned down to suit French tastes and the rational temperament of the Age of Enlightenment *(see pp28–9)*. The result was a harmonious and monumental Classicism in the form of columns and domes. One example is the **Eglise de la Sorbonne**, completed by Jacques Lemercier in 1642 for Cardinal Richelieu. Grander and more richly decorated, with a painted dome, is the church built by François Mansart to honour the birth of the Sun King at the **Val-de-Grâce** convent. The true gem of the period is Jules Hardouin-Mansart's **Dôme Church**, with its enormous gilded

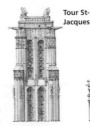

St-Gervais–St-Protais

TOWERS, DOMES AND SPIRES

Paris's many churches have dominated her skyline since early Christian times. The Gothic Tour St-Jacques, the only element still extant from a long-gone church, reflects the medieval love of the defensive tower. St-Etienne-du-Mont, with its pointed gable and rounded pediment, shows the transition from Gothic to Renaissance. The dome, a much-used feature of the French Baroque, was used to perfection in the Val-de-Grâce, while St-Sulpice with its severe arrangement of towers and portico is typically Neo-Classical. With its ornate spires, Ste-Clotilde is a Gothic Revival church. Modern landmarks include the mosque, with its minaret.

Tour St-Jacques

St-Etienne-du-Mont

Gothic

Renaissance

dome. Jesuit extravagance can be seen in **St-Paul–St-Louis** built in the style of Il Gesú in Rome. In contrast are Libéral Bruand's chapels, the **Salpêtrière** and **St-Louis-des-Invalides** with their severe geometry and unadorned simplicity. Other fine Classical churches are **St-Joseph-des-Carmes** and the 18th-century bankers' church, **St-Roch**, with its Baroque Marian chapel.

NEO-CLASSICAL

Interior of the Panthéon

An obsession with all things Greek and Roman swept France in the mid-18th century and well into the 19th century. The excavations at Pompeii (1738) and the influence of the Italian architect Andrea Palladio produced a generation of architects fascinated by the column, geometry and engineering. The best example of such churches is Jacques-Germain Soufflot's Sainte-Geneviève, now the **Panthéon**. Begun in 1773, its colonnaded dome was also inspired by Christopher Wren's St Paul's in London. The dome is supported by four pillars, built by Guillaume Rondelet, linking four great arches. The first colonnaded facade was Giovanni Niccolo Servandoni's **St-Sulpice**. Construction of this church began in 1733 and consisted of a two-storey portico, topped by a triangular pediment. **La Madeleine**, Napoleon's grand temple to his victorious army, was constructed on the ground plan of a Greco-Roman temple.

SECOND EMPIRE AND MODERN

Franz Christian Gau's **Sainte-Clotilde** of the 1840s is the first and best example in Paris of the Gothic Revival or *style religieux*. Showy churches were built in the new districts created by Haussmann in the Second Empire *(pp34–5)*. One of the most lovely is Victor Baltard's St-Augustin, at the intersection of the Boulevard de Malesherbes and the Boulevard de la Madeleine. Here historic detail combines with modern iron columns and girders in a soaring interior space. The great basilica of the late 19th century, **Sacré-Coeur**, was built as a gesture of religious defiance. **St-Jean l'Evangéliste** by Anatole de Baudot is an interesting modern church combining the Art Nouveau style with Islamic arches. The modern gem of Islamic architecture, the **Mosquée de Paris**, is an attractive 1920s building in the Hispanic-Moorish style. It has a grand patio, inspired by the Alhambra, woodwork in cedar and eucalyptus, and a fountain.

The arches of St-Jean L'Evangéliste, reminiscent of Islamic architecture

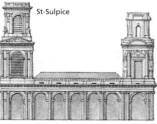

Val-de-Grâce   **St-Sulpice**   **Sainte-Clotilde**   **Mosquée de Paris**

Baroque and Classical   **Neo-Classical**   **Second Empire**   **Modern**

Paris's Best: Gardens, Parks and Squares

Few cities can boast the infinite variety of styles found in Parisian gardens, parks and squares today. They date from many different periods and have been central to Parisian life for the past 300 years. The Bois de Boulogne and the Bois de Vincennes enclose the city with their lush, green open spaces, while elegant squares and landscaped gardens, such as the Jardin du Luxembourg, brighten the inner city and provide a retreat for those craving a few moments peace from the bustling city.

Parc Monceau
This English-style park features many follies, grottoes, magnificent trees and rare plants.

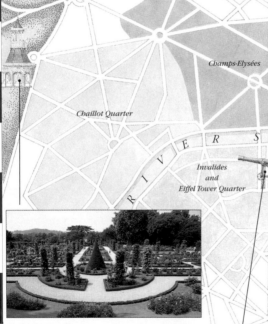

Champs-Elysées

Opéra Quarter

Chaillot Quarter

Tuilerie Quarter

R I V E R S E I N E

Invalides and Eiffel Tower Quarter

St-Germain-des-Prés

Luxembourg Quarter

Bois de Boulogne
The Bagatelle gardens, set in this wooded park, have an amazing array of flowers including the spectacular rose garden.

Montparnasse

Esplanade des Invalides
From this huge square, lined with lime trees, are some brilliant views over the quays.

Jardin des Tuileries
These gardens are renowned for ornamental ponds, terraces and the collection of bronze figures by Aristide Maillol.

Parc des Buttes-Chaumont
Once a scraggy hilltop, this park was transformed to provide open spaces for the growing city. It is now beautifully landscaped with huge cliffs revealing caves.

0 kilometres 1

0 miles 0.5

Square du Vert-Galant
The square, named after Henri IV's nickname, forms the west point of the Ile de la Cité.

Place des Vosges
Considered one of the most beautiful squares in the world, it was finished in 1612 and is the oldest square in Paris.

Beaubourg
and
Les Halles

The Marais

Jardin des Plantes
The botanical garden has a vast collection of plants and flowers from around the world.

Ile de la
Cité

Ile St-Louis

Latin Quarter

Jardin des Plantes
Quarter

Jardin du Luxembourg
This park is a favourite with Parisians wanting to escape the bustle of the Latin Quarter.

Bois de Vincennes
The flower garden in this charming park is the perfect place to relax.

Exploring Gardens, Parks and Squares

Paris is dotted with many areas of parkland, intimate gardens and attractive tree-lined squares. Each is a reminder of the French capital's illustrious past. Many squares were formed during Napoleon III's transformation of the city, creating a pleasant environment for Parisians to live in *(see pp34–5)*. This aim has been preserved right up to the present day. Paris's parks and gardens have their own character: some are ideal for a stroll, others for romance, while some provide space for sporting activities such as a game of *boules*.

Royal built by Cardinal Richelieu in the 17th century. An elegant arcade encloses the garden. The 19th-century **Parc Monceau**, in the English picturesque style, has follies and grottoes. The flat **Jardins des Invalides** and the land-scaped **Champ-de-Mars** were the grounds of the Hôtel des Invalides and the Ecole Militaire. They were the site of the Paris Universal Exhi-bition, whose reminder is the Eiffel Tower *(pp192–3)*.

An attractive public garden is attached to the lovely Hôtel Biron, home of the **Musée Rodin**. The 17th-century bot-anical garden **Jardin des Plantes** is famous for its ancient trees, flowers, alpine garden, hothouses and small zoo.

Engraving of the Jardin du Palais Royal (1645)

HISTORIC GARDENS

The oldest public gardens in Paris were made for queens of France – the **Jardin des Tuileries** for Catherine de Médicis in the 16th century, and the **Jardin du Luxembourg** for Marie de Médicis in the 17th century. The Tuileries form the beginning of the axis running from the Arc du Triomphe du Carrousel through the Arc de Triomphe *(pp208–9)* to La Défense *(p255)*. These gardens retain the formality devised by landscape architect André Le Nôtre, originally for the **Palace of Versailles**. Many of the Jardin des Tuileries's original sculptures survive, as well as modern pieces, notably the bronze nudes by Aristide Maillol (1861–1944).

The Jardin du Luxembourg also has the traditional formal plan – straight paths, clipped lawns, Classical sculpture and a superb 17th-century fountain. It is shadier and more intimate than the Tuileries, with lots of seats, pony rides and puppet shows to amuse the children.

The **Jardins des Champs-Elysées**, also by Le Nôtre, were reshaped in the English style during the 19th century. The gardens have Belle Epoque pavilions, three theatres (L'Espace Pierre Cardin, Théâtre Marigny and the Théâtre du Rond Point), smart restaurants – and the ghost of the novelist Marcel Proust, who once played here as a child.

A haven of peace in a busy district is the **Jardin du Palais**

19TH-CENTURY PARKS AND SQUARES

Aquatic Garden, Bois de Vincennes

The great 19th-century parks and squares owe much to Napoleon III's long exile in London before he came to power. The unregimented planting and rolling lawns of Hyde Park and the leafy squares of Mayfair inspired him to bring trees, fresh air

FOLLIES AND ROTUNDAS

Dramatic features of Paris's parks and gardens are the many follies and rotundas. Every age of garden design has produced these ornaments. The huge Gloriette de Buffon in the Jardin des Plantes was erected as a memorial to the great naturalist *(p166)*. It is the oldest metal structure in Paris. The pyramid in the Parc Monceau, the oriental temple in the Bois de Boulogne, and the recently restored 19th-century temple of love in the Bois de Vincennes reflect a more sentimental age. In contrast are the stark, painted-concrete follies that grace the Parc de la Villette.

Egyptian pyramid

Parc Monceau

Relaxing in Jardin du Luxembourg

and park benches to what was then Europe's most congested and dirty capital. Under his direction, landscape gardener Adolphe Alphand turned two woods at opposite ends of the city, the **Bois de Boulogne** (known as the "Bois") and the **Bois de Vincennes**, into English-style parks with duck ponds, lakes and flower gardens. He also added a race course to the "Bois". Today it is traversed by traffic and by prostitutes at night. Its most attractive feature is the Bagatelle rose garden.

Far more pleasant are the two smaller Alphand parks, **Parc Montsouris** in the south and the **Parc des Buttes-Chaumont** in the northeast. The "Buttes" (hills), a favourite with the Surrealists, was a quarry transformed into two craggy mini-mountains with overhanging vegetation, suspended bridge, temple of love and a lake below.

Part of the town-planning schemes for the old city included squares and avenues with fountains, sculptures, benches and greenery. One of the best is the **Square du Vert-Galant** on the Ile de la Cité. The Avenue de l'Observatoire in the **Jardin du Luxembourg** is rich in sculptures made by Jean-Baptiste Carpeaux.

Parc Montsouris

Fountains and sculpture in the Jardins du Trocadéro

MODERN PARKS AND GARDENS

The shady **Jardins du Trocadéro** sloping down to the river from the Palais de Chaillot were planted after the 1937 Universal Exhibition. Here is the largest fountain in Paris and fine views of the river and the Eiffel Tower.

More recent Paris gardens eschew formality in favour of wilder planting, multiple levels, maze-like paths, children's gardens and modern sculpture. Typical are the **Parc André-Citroën**, the **Parc de la Villette** and the Jardins Atlantique, next to the Gare Montparnasse.

Pleasant strolls may be taken in Paris's waterside gardens: in the modern sculpture park behind Notre-Dame, at the Bassin de l'Arsenal at the Bastille, and along the quays of the Seine between the Louvre and the Place de la Concorde, or on the elegantly residential Ile St-Louis. The planted walkway above the **Viaduc des Arts** is a peaceful way to observe eastern Paris.

FINDING THE GARDENS, PARKS AND SQUARES

Gloriette de Buffon

Jardin des Plantes

Oriental temple

Bois de Boulogne

Temple of love

Bois de Vincennes

Modern folly

Parc de la Villette

Paris's Best: Museums and Galleries

Some of the oldest, the newest, and certainly
some of the finest museums and galleries are to
be found in Paris – many are superb works of
art in their own right. They house some of the
greatest and strangest collections in the world.
Some of the buildings complement their
themes, such as the Roman baths and Gothic
mansion which form the Musée de Cluny, or
the Pompidou Centre, a modern masterpiece.
Elsewhere there is pleasing contrast, such as
the Picassos in their gracious 17th-century
museum, and the Musée d'Orsay
housed in its grand old railway
station. Together they make an
unrivalled feast for visitors.

Musée des Arts Décoratifs
*Decorative and ornamental art like
this Paris bathroom by Jeanne
Lanvin is displayed here.*

Champs-Elysées

Chaillot Quarter

Petit Palais
*A collection of works
by the 19th-century
sculptor Jean-
Baptiste Carpeaux is
housed here, including
The Fisherman and Shell.*

*Invalides
and
Eiffel Tower Quarter*

Musée Guimet
*This 4th-century head of
Buddha from India is part of a
vast collection of Asian art
and artefacts housed here.*

Montparnasse

Musée Rodin
*The museum brings together
works bequeathed to the
nation by sculptor Auguste
Rodin, like the magnificent
Gates of Hell doors.*

Musée d'Orsay
*Carpeaux's Four Quarters of the
World (1867–72) can be found
among this collection of 19th-
century art.*

Musée du Louvre
The museum boasts one of the world's great collections of paintings and sculpture, from the ancient civilizations to the 19th century. This Babylonian monument, the Code of Hammurabi, *is the oldest set of laws in existence.*

Pompidou Centre
Paris's modern art collection from 1905 to the present day is housed here. The centre also has art libraries and an industrial design centre.

Musée Picasso
Sculptor and Model *(1931) is one of many paintings on display in Picasso's private collection, "inherited" in lieu of tax by the French government after his death in 1973.*

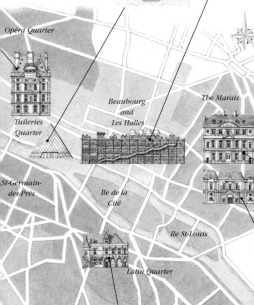

Opéra Quarter

Beaubourg and Les Halles

The Marais

Tuileries Quarter

St-Germain-des-Prés

Ile de la Cité

Ile St-Louis

Latin Quarter

Luxembourg Quarter

Jardin des Plantes Quarter

Musée Carnavalet
The museum is devoted to the history of Paris. Its historic buildings surround attractive garden courtyards.

Musée de Cluny
The remains of the old Gallo-Roman baths are part of this fine museum of ancient and medieval art.

0 kilometres 1

0 miles 0.5

Exploring Paris's Museums and Galleries

Paris holds great treasures in its museums and art galleries. The major national art collection is to be found at the **Musée du Louvre**, which began collecting 400 years ago and is still growing. Other important museums, such as the **Musée d'Orsay,** the **Musée Picasso** and the **Pompidou Centre**, have their own treasures, but there are scores of smaller, specialized museums, each with its own interest.

Dante and Virgil in the Underworld (1822) by Delacroix, Musée du Louvre

GREEK, ROMAN AND MEDIEVAL ART

Golden altar in the Musée de Cluny

Sculpture from Greek and Roman times is well represented in the **Musée du Louvre**, which also has fine medieval sculptures. The major medieval collection is at the **Musée de Cluny**, a superb 15th-century mansion. Among the highlights are the Unicorn Tapestries, the Kings' Heads from Notre-Dame and the golden altar from Basel Cathedral. Adjoining the Cluny are the 3rd-century Roman baths. Remains of houses from Roman and medieval Paris can be seen in the **Crypte Archéologique** near Notre-Dame cathedral.

OLD MASTERS

The Mona Lisa was one of the **Musée du Louvre's** first paintings, acquired 400 years ago. It also has other fine Leonardos. They are to be found along with superb Titians, Raphaels and other Italian masters. Other works include Rembrandt's *Pilgrims at Emmäus*, Watteau's *Gilles* and Fragonard's *The Bathers*. The **Musée Cognacq-Jay** has a small, but exquisite, collection of paintings and drawings by 18th-century French painters. The **Musée Jacquemart-André** has works by such masters as Mantegna, Uccello, Canaletto, Rembrandt and Chardin.

IMPRESSIONIST AND POST-IMPRESSIONIST ART

Installed in a converted 19th-century railway station, the **Musée d'Orsay** boasts the world's largest collection of art from the period 1848–1904. Admired for its fine Impressionist and Post-Impressionist collections, it also devotes a lot of space to the earlier Realists and the formerly reviled 19th-century academic and "Salon" masters. There are superb selections of Degas, Manet, Courbet, Monet, Renoir, Millet, Cézanne, Bonnard and Vuillard, and some fine Gauguins, Van Goghs and Seurats, but these have to contend with poor lighting and an intrusive stone decor.

A great ensemble of late Monets is to be found at the **Musée Marmottan-Claude Monet** and another at the **Musée de l'Orangerie**, including Monet's last great waterlily murals (1920–5). Here also is a good collection of Cézannes and late Renoirs.

Three artists' studios and homes are now museums of their life and work. The **Musée Rodin**, in an attractive 18th-century mansion and garden, offers a complete survey of the master's sculptures, drawings and paintings. The **Musée Delacroix**, set in a garden near St-Germain-des-Prés, has sketches, prints and oils by the Romantic artist. The **Musée Gustave Moreau**, in an oppressive 19th-century town house, has an extraordinary collection of intricately painted canvases of legendary *femmes fatales* and dying youths. The **Petit Palais** has an interesting collection of 19th-century paintings with four major Courbets, including *The Sleep*.

Dead Poet in Musée Gustave Moreau

MODERN AND CONTEMPORARY ART

As the international centre of the avant-garde from 1900 to 1940, Paris has a great concentration of modern painting and sculpture. The Pompidou Centre houses the **Musée National d'Art Moderne**, covering from 1905 to the present. It has a good selection of Fauvist and Cubist works, particularly by Matisse, Rouault, Braque, Delaunay, and Leger, as well as works by the 1960s' *Nouveaux Réalistes*.

The **Musée d'Art Moderne de la Ville de Paris**, in the elegant 1930s Palais de Tokyo also has an excellent collection, including Delaunays, Bonnards and Fauvist paintings. The highlight is Matisse's 1932 mural, *The Dance*.

The **Musée Picasso**, in a lovely 17th-century mansion, has the world's largest Picasso collection. It also has his own personal collection of the work of his contemporaries. Picasso, Matisse, Modigliani, Utrillo and late Derains make up the collection of 1920s art dealer Paul Guillaume on display at the **Musée de l'Orangerie**. For modern sculpture, the small **Musée Zadkine** has Cubist work by a minor school whose leading light was Ossip Zadkine. The **Musée Antoine Bourdelle** and the **Musée Maillol** house work by these two sculptors, who were both influenced by Rodin, in very different ways.

Penelope by Bourdelle

FURNITURE, DECORATIVE ARTS AND OBJETS D'ART

Pride of place after painting must go to furniture and the decorative arts, contained in a plethora of museums. Fine ensembles of French furnishings and decoration are in the **Louvre** (medieval to Napoleonic) and at the Palace of Versailles (17th–18th century). Furniture and *objets d'art* from the Middle Ages to the present century are arranged in period rooms at the **Musée des Arts Décoratifs**. The **Musée d'Orsay** has a large collection of 19th-century furniture, notably Art Nouveau. A superb example of Louis XV (1715–74) and Louis XVI (1774–93) furniture and decoration is in the **Musée Nissim de Camondo**, a mansion from 1910 facing the Parc Monceau. Other notable collections are the **Musée Cognacq-Jay**; the **Musée Carnavalet** (18th-century); the **Musée Jacquemart-André** (French furniture and earthenware); the **Musée Marmottan-Claude Monet** (Empire) and **Musée d'Art Moderne de la Ville de Paris** (Art Deco).

Jeweller's shop in the Carnavalet

SPECIALIST MUSEUMS

Devotees of antique sporting guns, muskets and hounds of the chase should make for the attractive Marais **Hôtel Guénégaud** (Musée de la Chasse et de la Nature). This museum also has some fine 18th-century animal paintings by Jean-Baptiste Oudry and Alexandre-François Desportes, as well as others by Rubens and Brueghel. The **Musée de la Contrefaçon** gives a fascinating insight into the world of counterfeit with examples from every luxury trade, including perfume, wines and spirits, and clothing. Numismatists will find an extensive coin and medallion collection housed in luxurious surroundings at the 18th-century Paris Mint at the **Musée de la Monnaie**. French coins are no longer minted here, but the old Mint still makes medals which are on sale. Stamps are on show at the **Musée de la Poste**. The history of postal services is also covered, as are all aspects of philately old and new, with temporary shows on current philatelic design. Sumptuous silver dinner services and other antique glass- and silverware can be seen at the **Galerie Royale**. The items were made over a period of 150 years by the Paris firm whose founder was Charles Bouilhet-Christofle, silversmith to King Louis-Philippe and Napoleon III. Contemporary glass- and silverware is also for sale in nearby workshops.

Candelabra in the Galerie Royale

FASHION AND COSTUME

The two rival fashion museums in Paris are the **Musée Galliera** at the Palais Galliera and the more recent national museum within the **Musée des Arts Décoratifs**. Neither displays a permanent collection, but both hold regular shows devoted to the great Paris couturiers, such as Saint Laurent and Givenchy. They also display fashion accessories and – more rarely but always fascinatingly – historical costumes.

Poster for the Musée Galliera

ASIAN, AFRICAN AND OCEANIAN ART

The major collection of Asian art in France is housed at the **Musée National des Arts Asiatiques Guimet**, covering China, Tibet, Japan, Korea, Indonesia, India and Central Asia. It includes Chinese bronzes and lacquerware and some of the best Khmer art outside Cambodia. The **Musée Cernuschi** has a smaller but well-chosen Chinese collection, noted for its ancient bronzes and reliefs. France's premier showcase for African, Asian, American tribal and Oceanian arts and cultures is the **Musée du Quai Branly**, which displays more than 300,000 objects in truly breathtaking surroundings. The **Musée Dapper** also houses African art and is part of an important ethnographic research centre, housed in an elegant 1910 *hôtel particulier* with an "African" garden. Its collection of tribal masks is particularly dazzling.

Sri Lankan theatrical mask

HISTORY AND SOCIAL HISTORY

Café in Musée de Montmartre

Covering the entire history of the city of Paris, the **Musée Carnavalet** is housed in two historic Marais *hôtels*. It has period interiors, paintings of

the city and old shop signs, a fascinating section covering events and artefacts from the French Revolution, and even Marcel Proust's bedroom. Also in the Marais, the **Musée d'Art et d'Histoire du Judaisme** explores the culture of French Jewry. The **Musée de l'Armée**, in the Hôtel des Invalides, recounts French military history, and the Musée de l'Histoire de France, in the Rococo **Hôtel de Soubise**, has historical documents from the national archives on display. Famous *tableaux vivants* and characters, both current and historical, await the visitor at the **Grévin** wax museum. The intriguing

Musée de Montmartre, overlooking Paris's last surviving vineyard, holds exhibitions on the history of Montmartre.

ARCHITECTURE AND DESIGN

The Centre de la Création Industrielle holds modern and contemporary design and architecture exhibitions at the **Pompidou Centre**. Superb scale models of fortresses built for Louis XIV and later are on display at the **Musée des Plans-Reliefs**. The work of the celebrated Franco-Swiss architect forms the basis of the **Fondation Le Corbusier**. The showpiece is his 1920s villa for his friend, art collector Raoul La Roche. Some of his furniture is also on display.

THE FRENCH IMPRESSIONISTS

Impression: Sunrise by Monet

Impressionism, the great art revolution of the 19th century, began in Paris in the 1860s, when young painters, influenced in part by the new art of photography, started to break with the academic values of the past. They aimed to capture the "impression" of what the eye sees at a given moment and used brushwork designed to capture the fleeting effects of light falling on a scene. Their favourite subjects were landscapes and scenes from contemporary urban life.

The movement had no founder, though Edouard Manet (1832–83) and the radical Realist painter Gustave Courbet (1819–77) both inspired many of the

Monet's sketchbooks

younger artists. Paintings of scenes of everyday life by Manet and Courbet often offended the academicians who legislated artistic taste. In 1863 Manet's *Le Déjeuner sur l'Herbe (see p144)* was exhibited at the Salon des Refusés, an exhibition set up for paintings rejected by the official Paris Salon of that year. The first time the term "Impressionist" was used to describe this new artistic movement was at another unofficial exhibition, in 1874. The name came from a painting by Claude Monet, *Impression: Sunrise*, a view of Le Havre in the mist from 1872. Monet was almost exclusively a landscape artist, influenced by the works of the English

Harvesting (1876) by Pissarro

The living room of La Roche Villa by Le Corbusier (1923)

SCIENCE AND TECHNOLOGY

In the Jardin des Plantes the **Muséum National d'Histoire Naturelle** has sections on palaeontology, minerology, entomology, anatomy and botany, plus a zoo and a botanical garden. In the Palais de Chaillot, the **Musée de l'Homme** is a museum of anthropology and prehistory with displays on anatomy and the environment. Next door, the **Musée de la Marine** covers French naval history from the 17th century onwards, with fine 18th-century models of ships and sculpted figure-heads. The **Musée des Arts et Métiers** displays the world of science and industry, invention and manufacturing. The **Palais de la Découverte** covers the history of science and has a good planetarium, somewhat overshadowed by the specta-cular one at the **Cité des Sciences** in the Parc de la Villette. This museum is on several levels, with a spherical movie screen, the Géode.

Gabrielle **(1910) by Renoir**

artists, Constable and Turner. He always liked to paint out of doors and encouraged others to follow his example.

At the 1874 exhibition, a critic wrote that one should stand well back to see these "impressions" – the further back the better – and that members of the establishment should retreat altogether. Other exhibitors at the show were Pierre-Auguste Renoir, Edgar Degas, Camille Pissarro, Alfred Sisley and Paul Cézanne.

There were seven more Impressionist shows up to 1886. By then the power of the Salon had waned and the whole direction of art had changed. From then on, new movements were defined in terms of their relation to Impressionism. The leading Neo-Impressionist was Georges Seurat, who used thousands of minute dots of colour to build up his paintings. It took later generations to fully appreciate the work of the Impressionists. Cézanne was rejected all his life, Degas sold only one painting to a museum, and Sisley died unknown. Of the great artists whose genius is now universally recognized, only Renoir and Monet were ever acclaimed in their lifetimes.

Profile of a Model **(1887) by Seurat**

Artists in Paris

The city first attracted artists during the reign of Louis XIV (1643–1715), and Paris became the most sophisticated artistic centre in Europe; the magnetism has persisted. During the 18th century, all major French artists lived and worked in Paris. In the the latter half of the 19th century and early part of the 20th century, Paris was the European centre of modern and progressive art, and movements such as Impressionism and Post-Impressionism were founded and blossomed in the city.

Monet's palette

BAROQUE ARTISTS

Champaigne, Philippe de (1602–74)
Coysevox, Antoine (1640–1720)
Girardon, François (1628–1715)
Le Brun, Charles (1619–90)
Le Sueur, Eustache (1616–55)
Poussin, Nicolas (1594–1665)
Rigaud, Hyacinthe (1659–1743)
Vignon, Claude (1593–1670)
Vouet, Simon (1590–1649)

ROCOCO ARTISTS

Boucher, François (1703–70)
Chardin, Jean-Baptiste-Siméon (1699–1779)
Falconet, Etienne-Maurice (1716–91)
Fragonard, Jean-Honoré (1732–1806)
Greuze, Jean-Baptiste (1725–1805)
Houdon, Jean-Antoine (1741–1828)
Oudry, Jean-Baptiste (1686–1755)
Pigalle, Jean-Baptiste (1714–85)
Watteau, Jean-Antoine (1684–1721)

Boucher's Diana Bathing *(1742), typical of the Rococo style (Louvre)*

1600	1650	1700	1750	
BAROQUE		ROCOCO	NEO-CLASSICISM	
1600	1650	1700	1750	

1627 Vouet returns from Italy and is made court painter by Louis XIII. Vouet revived a dismal period in the fortunes of French painting

1667 First Salon, France's official art exhibition; originally held annually, later every two years

Philippe de Champaigne's Last Supper *(about 1652). His style slowly became more Classical in his later years (Louvre)*

1793 Louvre opens as first national public gallery

1648 Foundation of the Académie Royale de Peinture et de Sculpture, which had a virtual monopoly on art teaching

Vouet's The Presentation in the Temple *(1641) with typically Baroque contrasts of light and shade (Louvre)*

NEO-CLASSICAL ARTISTS

David, Jacques-Louis (1748–1825)
Gros, Antoine Jean (1771–1835)
Ingres, Jean-Auguste-Dominique (1780–1867)
Vigée-Lebrun, Elizabeth (1755–1842)

David's The Oath of the Horatii *(1784), in the Neo-Classical style (Louvre)*

ROMANTIC AND REALIST ARTISTS

Courbet, Gustave (1819–77)
Daumier, Honoré (1808–79)
Delacroix, Eugène (1798–1863)
Géricault, Théodore (1791–1824)
Rude, Francois (1784–1855)

Courbet's The Burial at Ornans
(1850) which showed Courbet to
be the foremost exponent of
Realism (Musée d'Orsay)

Rude's Departure of
the Volunteers in
1792 (1836), a
tribute to the French
Revolution (see p209)

MODERN ARTISTS

Arp, Jean (1887–1966)
Balthus (1908–2001)
Brancusi, Constantin (1876–1957)
Braque, Georges (1882–1963)
Buffet, Bernard (1928–1999)
Chagall, Marc (1887–1985)
Delaunay, Robert (1885–1941)
Derain, André (1880–1954)
Dubuffet, Jean (1901–85)
Duchamp, Marcel (1887–1968)
Epstein, Jacob (1880–1959)
Ernst, Max (1891–1976)
Giacometti, Alberto (1901–66)
Gris, Juan (1887–1927)
Léger, Fernand (1881–1955)
Matisse, Henri (1869–1954)
Miró, Joan (1893–1983)
Modigliani, Amedeo (1884–1920)
Mondrian, Piet (1872–1944)
Picasso, Pablo (1881–1973)
Rouault, Georges (1871–1958)
Saint-Phalle, Niki de (1930–2002)
Soutine, Chaim (1893–1943)
Stael, Nicolas de (1914–55)
Tinguely, Jean (1925–91)
Utrillo, Maurice (1883–1955)
Zadkine, Ossip (1890–1967)

1904 Picasso
settles in Paris

1886 Van
Gogh moves
to Paris

1874 First
Impressionist
exhibition

1905 Birth of Fauvism, the first
of the "isms" in modern art

Giacometti's Standing
Woman II (1959), one of
his many tall, thin bronze
figures (see p112)

1800	1850	1900	1950
ROMANTICISM/REALISM		IMPRESSIONISM	MODERNISM
1800	1850	1900	1950

1863 Manet's Le
Déjeuner sur l'Herbe
causes a scandalous
sensation at the Salon
des Refusés, both for
"poor moral taste",
and for its broad
brushstrokes. The
artist's Olympia was
thought just as
outrageous, but it was
not exhibited until
1865 (see p144)

Monet's Impression: Sunrise (1872),
which led to the name Impressionism

1938
International
Surrealist
exhibition in
Paris

1977
Pompidou
Centre opens

IMPRESSIONIST AND POST-IMPRESSIONIST ARTISTS

Bonnard, Pierre (1867–1947)
Carpeaux, Jean-Baptiste (1827–75)
Cézanne, Paul (1839–1906)
Degas, Edgar (1834–1917)
Gauguin, Paul (1848–1903)
Manet, Edouard (1832–83)
Monet, Claude (1840–1926)
Pissarro, Camille (1830–1903)
Renoir, Pierre-Auguste (1841–1919)
Rodin, Auguste (1840–1917)
Rousseau, Henri (1844–1910)
Seurat, Georges (1859–91)
Sisley, Alfred (1839–99)
Toulouse-Lautrec, Henri de (1864–1901)
Van Gogh, Vincent (1853–90)
Vuillard, Edouard (1868–1940)
Whistler, James Abbott McNeill (1834–1903)

Delacroix's Liberty Leading the
People (1830) romantically
celebrates victory in war (Louvre)

1819 Géricault paints The Raft of the
Medusa, one of the greatest works of
French Romanticism (see p124)

Tinguely and Saint-Phalle's
Fontaine Igor Stravinsky
(1980), a modern kinetic
sculpture (Pompidou Centre)

PARIS THROUGH THE YEAR

Paris's pulling power is strongest in spring – the season for chestnuts in blossom and tables under trees. From June Paris is slowly turned over to tourists; the city almost comes to a standstill for the French Tennis Open, and the major race tracks stage the big summer races. Next comes the 14 July Bastille Day parade down the Champs-Elysées; towards the end of the month the Tour de France ends here.

The end of July also sees the end of Paris' three-month Jazz Festival, after which most Parisians abandon the city to visitors until *la rentrée*, the return to school and work in September. Dates of events listed on the following pages may vary. For details consult the listings magazines, or contact Paris Infos Mairie *(see p357)*. The Office du Tourisme *(see p367)* also produces an annual calendar of events.

French Tennis Open, Stade Roland Garros

SPRING

A good many of the city's annual 20 million visitors arrive in the spring. It is the season for fairs and concerts, when the marathon street race is held and the outdoor temperature is pleasant. Spring is also the time when hoteliers offer weekend packages, often with tickets for jazz concerts and with museum passes included.

MARCH

Spring flower shows
at Parc Floral (Bois de Vincennes, *p233)* and Bagatelle Gardens (Bois de Boulogne, *pp254–5)*.
Banlieues Bleues Festival *(mid-Feb–early Apr)*, Paris suburbs. Jazz, blues, soul and funk.
Salon International d'Agriculture *(1st week)*, Paris-Expo, Porte de Versailles. Vast farming fair.
Jumping International de Paris *(3rd week)*, Palais Omnisports de Paris-Bercy

Paris International Marathon

(pp358–9). International show jumping.
Foire du Trône *(late Mar–May)*, Bois de Vincennes *(p233)*. Large funfair.
Chemin de la Croix *(Good Friday)*. Beautiful Stations of the Cross procession, from Montmartre to Sacré Coeur.

APRIL

Six Nations Trophy *(early Apr)*, Stade de France *(p358)*. International rugby.
Shakespeare Garden Festival *(until Oct)*, Bois de Boulogne *(pp254–5)*. Classic plays performed outdoors.
Paris International Marathon *(April)*, from Place de la Concorde to Avenue Foch.
Foire de Paris *(end Apr–1st week May)*, Paris Expo, Porte de Versailles. Food, wine, homes and gardens and tourism show.

MAY

Carré Rive Gauche *(one week, mid-month)*. Exhibits

at antiques dealers near the Grand Louvre *(p135)*.
Football Cup Final *(2nd week)*, Stade de France.
Grands Eaux Musicales *(Apr–Oct: Sundays; Jul–Sep: Saturdays)*, Versailles *(p248)*. Open-air concerts.

Spring colour, Jardin du Luxembourg

French Tennis Open *(last week May–1st week Jun)*, Stade Roland Garros *(p358)*. Parisian society meets sport!
Le Printemps des Rues *(3rd w/end)*. Concerts and free street theatre in Bastille/République area.

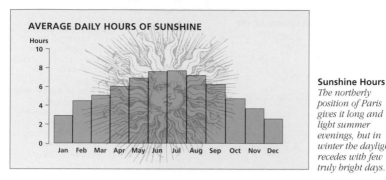

AVERAGE DAILY HOURS OF SUNSHINE

Sunshine Hours
The northerly position of Paris gives it long and light summer evenings, but in winter the daylight recedes with few truly bright days.

SUMMER

Summer begins with the French Tennis Open, and there are many events and festivities until July. Thereafter the French begin thinking of their own annual holiday, but there are big celebrations on Bastille Day (14 July) with military displays for the president and his guests.

Final lap of the Champs-Elysées during the Tour de France

Jardin du Luxembourg in summer

JUNE

Festival St-Denis, Basilique St-Denis. Concerts with emphasis on large-scale choral works *(p346)*.
Fête du Cinéma, films shown all over Paris for €2 nominal entry fee *(p354)*.

Fête de la Musique
(21 Jun), all over Paris. Nightlong summer solstice musical celebrations.
Flower show, Bois de Boulogne *(pp254–5)*. Rose season in the Bagatelle Gardens.
Gay Pride *(end Jun)*. Lively parade around the Bastille.
Paris Jazz Festival *(May–Jul)*, Parc Floral de Paris. Jazz musicians come to play in Paris *(pp349–50)*.
Paris Air and Space Technology Show *(mid-Jun)*, Le Bourget Airport.
Prix de Diane-Hermès
(2nd Sun), Chantilly. French equivalent of the British Ascot high society horse racing event.

JULY

Festival du cinéma en plein air *(mid-Jul–Aug)*, Parc de la Villette *(pp234-5)*.
Paris Quartier d'Eté *(mid-Jul–mid-Aug)*. Dance, music, theatre, ballet.
Tour de France *(late Jul)*. The last stage of the world's greatest cycle race comes to a climax in the Champs-Elysées.
Fêtes de Nuit *(Jul–mid-Sep: Saturdays)*, Versailles. Son et lumiere with music, dance and theatre *(p249)*.
Paris-Plage *(mid-Jul–mid-Aug)*. Sand and palm trees are deposited on the Right Bank of the Seine to create a temporary beach.

March past of troops on Bastille Day (14 July)

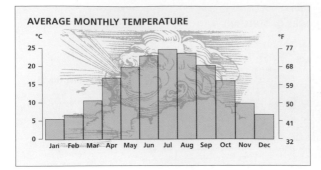

AVERAGE MONTHLY TEMPERATURE

Temperature
The chart shows the average minimum and maximum temperatures for each month. It is hottest in July and August and coolest between December and February, though Paris is rarely freezing cold. Temperatures are pleasant in the spring and autumn.

AUTUMN

September sees the start of the social season, with gala performances of new films, and parties in big houses on the Ile St-Louis. Paris is the world's largest congress centre and there are a rush of shows in September, ranging from children's clothes and gifts to leisure and music. The pace barely slackens in October and November when Parisians begin to indulge their great love for the cinema. French and Hollywood stars frequently make appearances at premiers staged on the Champs-Elysées.

SEPTEMBER

Festival d'Automne à Paris *(mid-Sep–end Dec)*, throughout Paris. Music, dance, theatre *(pp346–7)*.
La Villette Jazz Festival *(mid-Sep)*. Jazz artists come blow their horns with gusto throughout the Cité de la Musique *(p234)*.

The Prix de l'Arc de Triomphe (October)

OCTOBER

Nuit Blanche *(one Sat in Oct)*. Museums stay open all night.
Prix de l'Arc de Triomphe *(1st week)*, Longchamp. An international field competes for the richest prize in European horse-racing.
Salon de l'Automobile *(1st fortnight, alternate years)*, Paris-Expo, Porte de Versailles. Commercial motor show, alternated annually with a motorcycle show.
Journées du Patrimoine *(usually 3rd week)*. Historic buildings, monuments and museums are open free to the public for two days, following an all-night party to kick off proceedings.

Foire Internationale d'Art Contemporain (FIAC) *(last week)*, Paris-Expo, Porte de Versailles. Paris' biggest international modern and contemporary art fair.

Jazz fusion guitarist Al di Meola playing in Paris

NOVEMBER

BNP Paribas Masters *(usually Nov)*, Palais Omnisports de Paris-Bercy *(pp358–9)*.
Festival d'Art Sacré *(Nov–24 Dec)*, at St-Sulpice, St-Eustache and St-Germain-des-Prés churches. Religious art festival.
Mois de la Photo *(Oct–Nov)*. Numerous photography shows.
Beaujolais Nouveau *(3rd Thursday Nov)*. Bars and cafés are crowded on this day, in a race to taste the new vintage.

Autumn in the Bois de Vincennnes

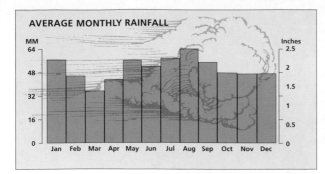

AVERAGE MONTHLY RAINFALL

MM

| 64 |
| 48 |
| 32 |
| 16 |
| 0 |

Jan Feb Mar Apr May Jun Jul Aug Sep Oct Nov Dec

Inches
2.5
2
1.5
1
0.5
0

Rainfall
*August is the wettest
month in Paris as
well as the hottest. In
August and Septem-
ber you risk getting
caught in storms.
Sudden showers,
sometimes with hail,
can occur between
January and April –
notoriously in March.
There is occasional
snow in winter.*

WINTER

Paris rarely sees snow; winter
days tend to be invigorating
rather than chilly. There are
jazz and dance festivals,
candlelit Christmas church
services and much
celebrating in the streets over
the New Year. After New
Year, the streets seem to
become slightly less
congested and on bright days
the riverside quays are used
as the rendezvous point of
strollers and lovers.

Snow in the Tuileries, a rare occurrence

DECEMBER

Christmas illuminations
(until Jan) in the Grands
Boulevards, Opéra, Ave
Montaigne, Champs-Elysées
and the Rue du Faubourg
St-Honoré.
Crèche *(early Dec–early
Jan)*, under a canopy in
Place de l'Hôtel de Ville,
Marais *(p102)*. Lifesize
Christmas crib from a
different country each year.

January fashion show

Horse & Pony Show *(1st
fortnight)*, Paris-Expo,
Porte de Versailles.
**Paris International Boat
Show** *(1st fortnight)*,
Paris-Expo, Porte de
Versailles.

JANUARY

Fête des Rois (Epiphany).
(6 Jan). The *boulangeries*
are full of *galettes des rois*.
Prix d'Amérique *(mid-Jan)*.
Europe's most famous
trotting race, Hippodrome
de Vincennes.
Fashion shows, summer
collections. *(See* Haute
Couture *p324)*

FEBRUARY

Carnaval *(2nd half month)*,
Quartier de St-Fargeau.
Floraisons *(all month)*,
Parc Floral de Paris, Bois
de Vincennes *(p233)* and
Parc de Bagatelle, Bois
de Boulogne *(pp254–5)*.
Say farewell to winter with
these colourful displays of
crocuses and snowdrops.

Eiffel Tower Christmas decorations

A RIVER VIEW OF PARIS

Sculpture on the Pont Alexandre III

The remarkable French music-hall star Mistinguett described the Seine as a "pretty blonde with laughing eyes". The river most certainly has a beguiling quality, but the relationship that exists between it and the city of Paris is far more than one of flirtation.

No other European city defines itself by its river in the same way as Paris. The Seine is the essential point of reference to the city: distances are measured from it, street numbers determined by it, and it divides the capital into two distinct areas, with the Right Bank on the north side of the river and the Left Bank on the south side. These are as well defined as any of the supposedly official boundaries. The city is also divided historically, with the east more closely linked to the city's ancient roots and the west more closely linked to the 19th and 20th centuries.

Practically every building of note in Paris is either along the river or within a stone's throw. The quays are lined by fine bourgeois apartments, magnificent town houses, great museums and striking monuments.

Above all, the river is very much alive. For centuries fleets of small boats used it, but motorized land traffic stifled this once-bustling scene. Today, the river is busy with commercial barges and massive *bateaux mouches* pleasure boats cruising sightseers up and down the river.

The octagonal lake, in the Jardin de Luxembourg, is a favourite spot for children to sail their toy boats. The Seine is host to larger craft, including many pleasure cruisers.

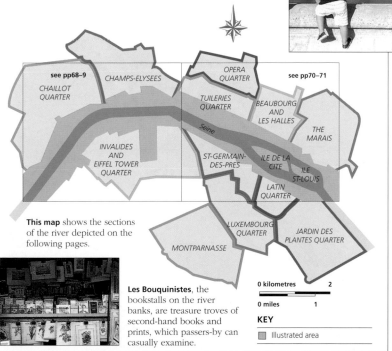

This map shows the sections of the river depicted on the following pages.

Les Bouquinistes, the bookstalls on the river banks, are treasure troves of second-hand books and prints, which passers-by can casually examine.

KEY
Illustrated area

◁ Pont Alexandre III, encrusted with exuberant statuary

From Pont de Grenelle to Pont de la Concorde

The soaring monuments and grand exhibition halls along this stretch of the river are remnants of the Napoleonic era and the Industrial Revolution with its great exhibitions. The exhilarating self-confidence of the Eiffel Tower, the Petit Palais and the Grand Palais is matched by more recent buildings, such as the Palais de Chaillot, the Maison de Radio-France and the skyscrapers of the Left Bank.

Palais de Chaillot
The curved wings and arching fountains make this a spectacular setting for three museums (p198).

Palais de Tokyo
Figures by Bourdelle adorn this museum (p201).

Bateaux Parisiens
Tour Eiffel

Vedettes de Paris
Ile de France

Trocadéro **M**

Passerelle
Debilly

The Statue of Liberty was given to the city in 1885. It faces west, towards the original Liberty in New York.

Pont
d'Iéna

M Passy

Maison de Radio-France
Studios and a radio museum are housed in this imposing circular building (p200).

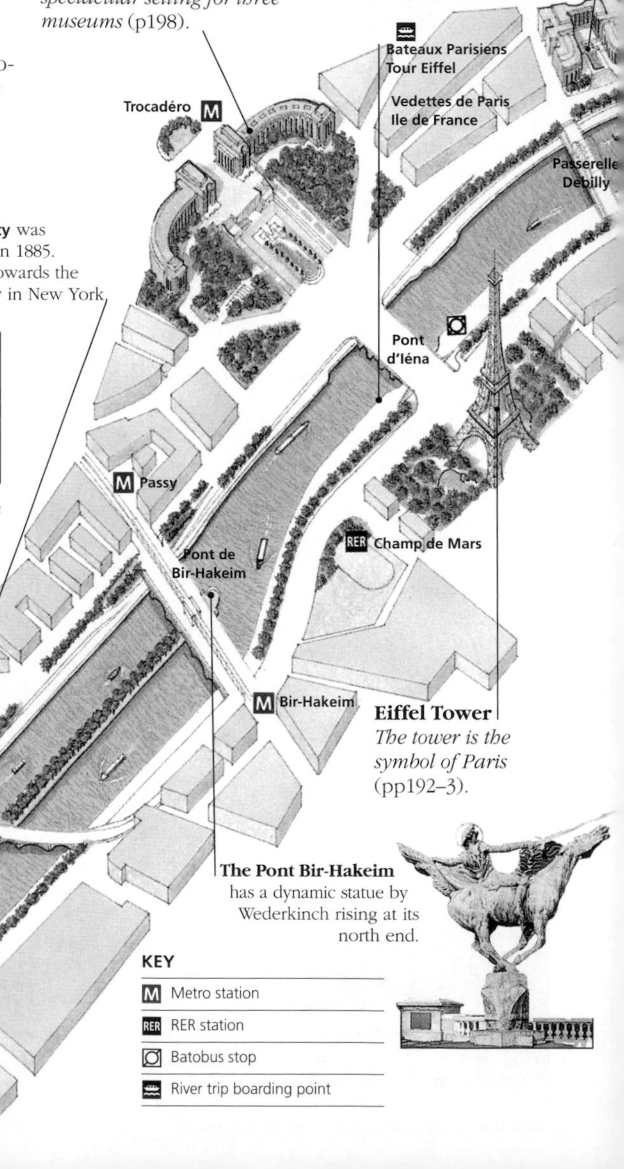

Pont de
Bir-Hakeim

RER Champ de Mars

RER Prés. Kennedy
Radio France

M Bir-Hakeim

Eiffel Tower
The tower is the symbol of Paris (pp192–3).

The Pont Bir-Hakeim
has a dynamic statue by Wederkinch rising at its north end.

Pont de Grenelle

KEY

M	Metro station
RER	RER station
◻	Batobus stop
🚢	River trip boarding point

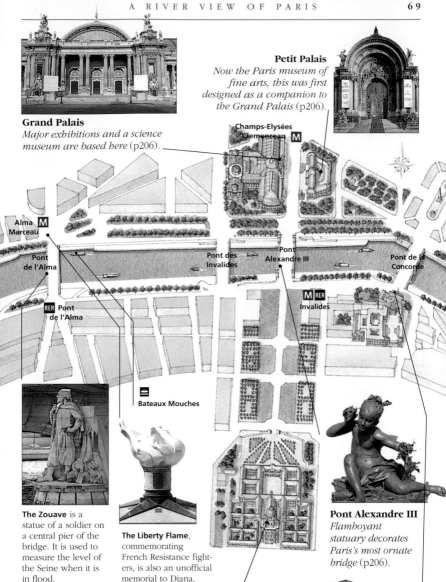

Grand Palais
Major exhibitions and a science museum are based here (p206).

Petit Palais
Now the Paris museum of fine arts, this was first designed as a companion to the Grand Palais (p206).

Champs-Elysées Clemenceau Ⓜ

Alma Marceau Ⓜ

Pont de l'Alma

Pont des Invalides

Pont Alexandre III

Pont de la Concorde

Ⓜ RER Invalides

RER Pont de l'Alma

Bateaux Mouches

The Zouave is a statue of a soldier on a central pier of the bridge. It is used to measure the level of the Seine when it is in flood.

The Liberty Flame, commemorating French Resistance fighters, is also an unofficial memorial to Diana, Princess of Wales.

Pont Alexandre III
Flamboyant statuary decorates Paris's most ornate bridge (p206).

Assemblée Nationale Palais-Bourbon
Louis XIV's daughter once owned this palace, which is now used by the Chambre des Députés as the national forum for political debate (p190).

Dôme Church
The majestic gilded dome (p188–9) *is here seen from Pont Alexandre III.*

From Pont de la Concorde to Pont de Sully

The historic heart of Paris lies on the banks and islands of the east river. At its centre is the Ile de la Cité, a natural stepping stone across the Seine and the cultural core of medieval Paris. Today it is still vital to Parisian life.

Jardin des Tuileries
These are in the formal style (p130).

Musée du Louvre
Before becoming the world's greatest museum and home to the Mona Lisa, *this was Europe's largest royal palace* (pp122–9).

Pont de la Concorde

Assemblée Nationale

Passerelle Solférino

Quai d'Orsay

Pont Royal

Pont du Carrousel

Passerelle des Arts

Musée de l'Orangerie
An important collection of 19th-century paintings are on display here (p131).

The Passerelle des Arts
is a steel reconstruction of Paris's first cast-iron bridge (1804), and was inaugurated in 1984.

Bâteaux Vedettes du Pont Neuf

Musée d'Orsay
Paris's most important collection of Impressionist art is housed in this converted railway station (pp144–7).

Hôtel des Monnaies
Built in 1768–85, this former Mint has a fine coin collection in its old milling halls (p141).

Ile de la Cité

The medieval identity of this small island was almost completely erased in the 19th century by Baron Haussmann's grand scheme. Sainte-Chapelle and parts of the Conciergerie are the only buildings of the period that remain today (pp76–89).

Conciergerie

During the Revolution this building, with its distinctive towers, became notorious as a prison (p81).

Ile St-Louis

This has been a desirable address since the 17th century (p87).

The Tour de l'Horloge, a 14th-century clock tower, features the first public clock in Paris. Germain Pilon's fine carvings continue to adorn the clock face.

St-Gervais–St-Protais

The oldest organ in Paris, dating from the early 17th century, is in this church (p99).

Pont Neuf
 M

nt Neuf

M Châtelet

Hôtel de Ville
M

Pont au Change

Pont Notre Dame

Cité

M

Pont d'Arcole

RER M
St-Michel

Petit Pont

Pont au Double

Pont Louis Philippe

Pont St Louis

M Pont Marie

Pont Marie

Pont de l'Archevêché

Pont de la Tournelle

Sully Morland
 M

Pont de Sully

Notre-Dame

This towering cathedral surveys the river (pp82–5).

 Bâteaux Parisiens

How to Take a River or Canal Trip

River Seine cruises on a variety of pleasure boats operate along the main sightseeing reaches of the river, taking in many of the city's famous monuments. The Batobus river service operates as a shuttle or bus service, allowing you to get on and off anywhere along the route. The main city canal trips operate along the old industrial St-Martin canal in the east of the city.

Pleasure-cruise boats passing under the Pont Alexandre III

Types of Boats
Bateaux mouches, *the largest of the pleasure-cruise boats, are a spectacular sight with their passenger areas enclosed in glass for excellent all round viewing. At night floodlights are used to pick out river bank buildings. A more luxurious version of these is used on the Bateaux Parisien cruises. The* vedettes *are smaller and more intimate boats, with viewing through glass walls. The Canauxrama canal boats are flat-bottomed.*

SEINE CRUISES AND SHUTTLE SERVICES
The Seine cruises and shuttle services information below includes the location of boarding points, the nearest metro and RER stations, and the nearest bus routes. Lunch and dinner cruises must be booked in advance, and passengers must board them 30 minutes before departure.

Vedettes de Paris Seine Cruise
Passengers are carried in comfort and style on a cruise encompassing all major sights along the river. The boarding point is:

Port de Suffren
Map 10 D3. **Tel** 01 44 18 19 50. **M** Bir Hakeim. **RER** Champs de Mars. **🚌** 22, 30, 32, 44, 63, 69, 72, 82, 87.

Departures 10am–10pm (7pm winter) daily (every 30 min). **Duration** 1 hr. **Dinner cruise** 8pm Sat (phone to reserve). **Duration** 2 hr 30 min. **www**.vedettesdeparis. com

Paris Ports Cruise
An educational journey along the city's little-known urban ports (commentary in French). The boarding point is:

Port de la Rapée
Map 18 D1. **Tel** 01 44 18 19 50. **M** Quai de la Rapée. **Departures** 3pm first Sun of month Mar–Oct (exc Jul, Aug). **Duration** 1 hr. **www**. vedettesdeparis.com

Bateaux Parisiens Tour Eiffel Cruise
This company has a fleet of seven boats with a carrying capacity of 1,255 passengers. A commentary is provided in 13 languages. The boarding point is:

Port de la Bourdonnais
Map 10 D2. **Tel** 08 25 01 01 01. **M** Trocadéro, Bir Hakeim. **RER** Champs de Mars. **🚌** 42, 82, 72. **Departures** 10am–10.30pm (10pm Oct–Mar) daily (every 30 min).

Duration 1 hr. **Lunch cruise** 12.15pm daily. **Duration** 2 hr 15 min. **Dinner cruise** 7.45pm. **Duration** 3 hr. Jacket & tie required. **www**. bateauxparisiens.com

Bateaux Parisiens Notre-Dame Cruise
This trip follows the same route as the Tour Eiffel Cruise, but in the opposite direction. The boarding point is:

Quai de Montebello Map 13 B4. **Tel** 08 25 01 01 01. **M** Maubert-Mutualite, St-Michel. **RER** St-Michel. **🚌** 24, 27, 47. **Departures** 24 Mar–6 Apr, 18 Sep–5 Nov: 5 daily (1.30–6.10pm); 7–28 Apr: 7 daily (2–10pm); 29 Apr–2 Jun: 9 daily (11am–9.50pm); 3 Jun–26 Aug: 10 daily (11am–11pm); 27 Aug–17 Sep: 9 daily (11am–10pm). **Duration** 1 hr.

Boarding Points

The boarding points for the river cruises and the Batobus services are easy to find

along the river. Here you can buy tickets, and there are amenities such as snack-bars. Major cruise companies also have foreign exchange booths. There is limited parking around the points, but none near the Pont Neuf.

River boarding point

Shuttle service. 1–2 day passes available. **Tel** 08 25 05 01 01. **Departures** daily. Nov–mid-Mar: 10.30am–4.30pm; mid-Mar–Oct: 10am–7pm (9.30pm Jun–Aug). Board at: **Eiffel Tower: Map** 10 D3. M Bir Hakeim. **Champs-Elysées: Map** 11 B1. M Champs-Elysées-Clemenceau. **Musée d'Orsay: Map** 12 D2. M Solferino. **Louvre: Map** 12 E2. M Louvre. **St-Germain-de-Prés: Map** 12 E3. M St-Germain-de-Prés. **Notre-Dame: Map** 13 B4. M Cité. **Hôtel de Ville: Map** 13 B4. M Hôtel de Ville. **www**.batobus.com

BATEAUX-MOUCHES

Bateaux Mouches Cruise

This well-known pleasure boat company's fleet of 11 boats carries between 600 and 1,400 passengers at a time. The boarding point is:

Pont de l'Alma
Map 10 F1. **Tel** 01 42 25 96 10. M Alma-Marceau. RER Pont de l'Alma. 🚌 28, 42, 49, 63, 72, 80, 83, 92.
Departures Apr–Sep: 10am–11pm daily (every 30 min); Oct–Mar: 11am–9pm (every 45 min).
Duration 1 hr 15 min.
Lunch cruise 1pm daily (embark from 12.15pm).
Duration 1 hr 45 min. Under-12s half price.
Dinner cruise 8.30pm daily (embark from 7.30pm).
Duration 2 hr 15 min. Jacket and tie required.
www.bateaux-mouches.fr

Vedettes du Pont Neuf

Bateaux Vedettes Pont Neuf Cruise

This company runs a fleet of six 80-passenger boats. The boats are of an older style, for a quainter cruise. The boarding point is:

Square du Vert-Galant
(Pont Neuf). **Map** 12 F3.
Tel 01 46 33 98 38. M Pont Neuf. RER Châtelet.
🚌 24, 27, 58, 67, 70, 72, 74, 75. **Departures** Mar–Oct: 10am, 11.15am, noon; 1.30–10.30pm daily (every 30 min); Nov–Feb: 10.30am, 11.15am, noon, 2–6.30pm (every 45 min), 8pm, 10pm Mon–Fri; 10.30am, 11.15am, noon, 2–6.30pm, 8pm, 9–10.30pm (every 30 min) Sat, Sun. **Duration** 1 hr. Snacks available on board. **www**.vedettesdupontneuf.com

CANAL TRIPS

The Canauxrama company operates boat cruises along the city's Canal St-Martin and along the banks of the river Marne. The St-Martin journey passes along the tree-lined canal, which has nine locks, two swing bridges and eight romantic footbridges. The Bords de Marne cruise travels well into the suburbs, as far as Bry-sur-Marne. The **Paris Canal Company** (01 42 40 96 97; **www**.pariscanal.com) also has a St-Martin canal trip, from Parc de la Villette and extending beyond the canal, passing into the River Seine and as far as the Musée d'Orsay.

CANAUXRAMA

Canal St-Martin

The Canauxrama company offers many different trips along this canal, but it has two 125-passenger boats that operate regularly between the Bassin de la Villette and the Port de l'Arsenal. The boarding points are: **Bassin de la Villette. Map** 8 E1. M Jaurès. **Port de l'Arsenal. Map** 14 E4. M Bastille. **Tel** 01 42 39 15 00. **Departures** Apr–Nov, times may vary so phone to check and to make a reservation: Bassin de la Villette 9.45am and 2.45pm; Port de l'Arsenal 9.45am and 2.30pm daily. On weekday mornings there are concessions for students, pensioners and children under 12. Children under six travel free. Concert cruises are available on chartered trips on the Canal St-Martin and the Seine. **Duration** 2 hr 30 min.

Bords de Marne Croisière

This all-day cruise extends westwards out of Paris down the river Marne. The trip includes a commentary, stories and dancing. The boarding point is: **Porte de l'Arsenal. Map** 14 E4. M Bastille. **Tel** 01 42 39 15 00. **Departures** 8.30am all-year-round. Reservations necessary. **Duration** 9 hr.

Canal-cruise boat in the Bassin de la Villette

PARIS AREA
BY AREA

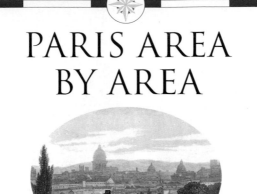

ILE DE LA CITE AND ILE ST-LOUIS

The history of the Ile de la Cité is the history of Paris. This island on the Seine was no more than a primitive village when the conquering Julius Caesar arrived in 53 BC. Ancient kings later made it the centre of political power and in medieval times it became the home of church and law. It no longer has such power, except to draw armies of tourists to the imposing Palais de Justice and to its Gothic masterpiece, Notre-Dame.

The medieval huddles of tiny houses and narrow streets that so characterized the island at one time

The motto of the city of Paris

were swept away by the spacious thoroughfares built in the 19th century. But there are still small areas of charm and relief, among them the colourful bird and flower market, the romantic Square du Vert-Galant and the ancient Place Dauphine.

At the eastern end of the island the St-Louis bridge connects it to the smaller Ile St-Louis. This former swampy pastureland was transformed into an elegant 17th-century residential area, with picturesque, tree-lined quays. More recently, rich artists, doctors, actresses and heiresses have lived here.

SIGHTS AT A GLANCE

Historic Buildings
Hôtel Dieu ❻
Conciergerie ❽
Palais de Justice ❿
Hôtel de Lauzun ⓰

Bridges
Pont Neuf ⓬

Monuments
Paris Mémorial
de la Déportation ❹

Markets
Marché aux Fleurs and Marché
aux Oiseaux ❼

Squares and Gardens
Square Jean XXIII ❸
Place Dauphine ⓫
Square du Vert-Galant ⓭

Museums and Galleries
Musée de Notre-Dame de
Paris ❷
Crypte Archéologique ❺

Société Historique et Littéraire
Polonaise ⓮

Churches and Cathedrals
Notre–Dame pp82–5 ❶
Sainte-Chapelle pp88–9 ❾
St-Louis-en-l'Ile ⓯

GETTING THERE
This area is served by the metro station at Cité and the RER at St-Michel. The bus routes 21, 38, 47, 85 and 96 cross the Ile de la Cité, and 67, 86 and 87 cross the Ile St-Louis.

SEE ALSO

• *Street Finder,* map 12–13
• *St-Louis Walk* pp262–3
• *Where to Stay* p284
• *Restaurants* p300

| 0 metres | 400 |
| 0 yards | 400 |

KEY

▨ Street-by-Street map

Ⓜ Metro station

◁ View of the Conciergerie and the Pont au Change, previous page St-Sulpice church and rooftops

Street-by-Street: Ile de la Cité

The origins of Paris are here on the Ile de la Cité, the boat-shaped island on the Seine first inhabited over 2,000 years ago by Celtic tribes. One tribe, the Parisii, eventually gave its name to the city. The island offered a convenient river crossing on the route between northern and southern Gaul and was easily defended. In later centuries the settlement was expanded by the Romans, the Franks and the Capetian kings to form the nucleus of today's city.

There is no older place in Paris, and remains of the first buildings can still be seen today in the archaeological crypt under the square in front of Notre-Dame, the great medieval cathedral and place of pilgrimage for millions of visitors each year. At the other end of the island is another Gothic masterpiece, Sainte-Chapelle – a miracle of light.

★ Conciergerie
A grisly ante-chamber to the guillotine, this prison was much used in the Revolution ❽

The Cour du Mai
is the impressive main courtyard of the Palais de Justice.

Metro Cité

★ Sainte-Chapelle
A jewel of Gothic architecture and one of the most magical sights of Paris, Sainte-Chapelle is noted for the magnificence of its stained glass ❾

To Pont Neuf

The Quai des Orfèvres
owes its name to the goldsmiths *(orfèvres)* who frequented the area from medieval times onwards.

Palais de Justice
With its ancient towers lining the quays, the old royal palace is today a massive complex of law courts. Its history extends back over 16 centuries ❿

0 metres   100
0 yards   100

The Préfecture de Police
is the headquarters of the police and was the scene of intense battles during World War II.

The Statue of Charlemagne
commemorates the King of the Franks, who was crowned emperor in 800. He united all the Christian peoples of the West.

★ **Marché aux Fleurs et Oiseaux**
The flower and bird market is a colourful, lively island sight. Paris was once famous for its flower markets but this is now one of the last ❼

LOCATOR MAP
See Central Paris Map pp14–15

Hôtel Dieu
Once an orphanage, this is now a city hospital ❻

★ **Crypte Archéologique**
Deep under the square, there are remains of houses from 2,000 years ago ❺

STAR SIGHTS

★ Notre-Dame

★ Sainte-Chapelle

★ Conciergerie

★ Marché aux Fleurs et Oiseaux

★ Crypte Archéologique

KEY

– – – Suggested route

The Rue Chanoinesse has had many famous residents, such as the 17th-century playwright Racine.

Musée Notre-Dame
Many exhibits tracing the cathedral's history are in this museum ❷

Point Zéro
is a mark from which all distances are measured in France.

The Square Jean XXIII
is a peaceful square close to the river ❸

★ **Notre-Dame**
This cathedral is a superb example of French medieval architecture ❶

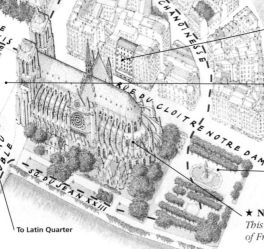

To Latin Quarter

Notre-Dame from the Left Bank

Notre-Dame ❶

See pp82–5.

Musée de Notre-Dame de Paris ❷

10 Rue du Cloître-Notre-Dame 75004.
Map 13 B4. *Tel 01 43 25 42 92.* Ⓜ
Cité. ⓇⒺⓇ St-Michel. ◯ 2.30pm–6pm
Wed, Sat, Sun (last adm: 5.40pm). 🎦

Founded in 1951, this museum has exhibits and documents that commemorate and illustrate the great events in Notre-Dame's history. The displays include Gallo-Roman objects, old engravings, works of art and the city of Paris's oldest extant Christian relic, a fine 4th-century glass cup.

A Gallo-Roman coin

Square Jean XXIII ❸

Rue du Cloître-Notre-Dame 75004.
Map 13 B4. Ⓜ Cité.

Notre-Dame's St Stephen's door (porte St-Etienne) opens on to this pleasant garden square, dedicated to Pope John XXIII. The garden runs alongside the river and is an excellent place for enjoying the sculptures, rose windows and flying buttresses of the east end of the cathedral.

From the 17th century, the square was occupied by the archbishop's palace, which was ransacked by rioters in 1831 and later demolished. A square was conceived to replace the Prefect of Paris, Rambuteau. The Gothic-style fountain of the Virgin standing in the centre of the square has been there since 1845.

Paris Mémorial de la Déportation ❹

Sq de l'Ile de France 75004. **Map** 13 B4.
Tel 01 46 33 87 56. Ⓜ Cité. ⓇⒺⓇ St-Michel. ◯ 10am–6pm Tue–Sun.

The simple, modern memorial to the 200,000 French men, women and children deported to Nazi concentration camps in World War II (often via Drancy, just a few miles to the north of Paris) is covered with a roll-call of names of the camps to which they were deported. Earth from these camps has been used to form small tombs and the interior walls are decorated with poetry. At the far end is the tomb dedicated to the Unknown Deportee.

Inside the Paris Mémorial de la Déportation

The Square Jean XXIII behind Notre-Dame

Gallo-Roman ruins in the Crypte Archéologique

Crypte Archéologique ❺

Pl du Parvis Notre-Dame 75004. **Map** 13 A4. **Tel** 01 55 42 50 10. Ⓜ Cité. ◯ Tue–Sun 10am–6pm (last adm: 30 min before closing). ● 1 May, 8 May, 1 & 11 Nov, 25 Dec, 1 Jan. 🖼 free for children under 12. ⚪

Situated on the main square (the *parvis*) in front of Notre-Dame and stretching 120 m (393 ft) underground, this crypt exhibits the remains of foundations and walls that pre-date the cathedral by several hundred years. There are traces of a sophisticated underground heating system in a house from Lutèce, the settlement of the Parisii, the Celtic tribe who inhabited the island 2000 years ago, giving their name to the present city.

Hôtel Dieu ❻

1 Pl du Parvis Notre-Dame 75004. **Map** 13 A4. ● to the public for visits. Ⓜ Cité.

On the north side of the place du Parvis Notre-Dame is the Hôtel Dieu, the hospital serving central Paris. It was built on the site of an

Hôtel Dieu, central Paris's hospital

orphanage between 1866 and 1878. The original Hôtel Dieu, built in the 12th century and stretching across the island to both banks of the river, was demolished in the 19th century to make way for one of Baron Haussmann's urban-planning schemes.

It was here in 1944 that the Paris police courageously resisted the Germans; the battle is commemorated by a monument in Cour de 19-Août.

Paris's main flower market

Marché aux Fleurs and Marché aux Oiseaux ❼

Pl Louis-Lépine 75004. **Map** 13 A3. Ⓜ Cité. ◯ 8am–7.30pm Mon–Sat; 8am–7pm Sun.

The year-round flower market adds colour and scent to an area otherwise dominated by administrative buildings. It is the most famous and unfortunately one of the last remaining flower markets in the city of Paris, offering a wide range of specialist varieties such as orchids. Each Sunday it makes way for the cacophony of the caged bird market.

Conciergerie ❽

1 Quai de l'Horloge 75001. **Map** 13 A3. 📞 01 53 40 60 93. Ⓜ Cité. ◯ 9.30am–6pm daily (last adm: 30 min before closing). ● 1 Jan, 1 May, 25 Dec. 🖼 (combined ticket with Ste-Chapelle, pp88–9, available.) ⚪ phone to check. 🖥 www.monum.fr

Occupying the north part of the old Capetian palace, the Conciergerie was under the administration of the palace "concierge", the keeper of the King's mansion. When the King moved to the Marais (in 1417), the palace remained the seat of royal administration and law; and the Conciergerie became a prison, with the "concierge" as its chief gaoler. Henry IV's assassin, Ravaillac, was imprisoned and tortured here.

During the Revolution it housed over 4,000 prisoners, including Marie-Antoinette, who was held in a tiny cell until her execution, and Charlotte Corday, who stabbed Revolutionary leader Marat as he lay in his bath. Ironically, the Revolutionary judges Danton and Robespierre also became "tenants" before being sent to the guillotine.

The Conciergerie has a superb four-aisled Gothic Salle des Gens d'Armes (Hall of the Men-at-Arms), where guards of the royal household once lived. The building, renovated in the 19th century, retains the 11th-century torture chamber, the Bonbec Tower and the 14th-century public clock tower on the Tour de l'Horloge (Palais de Justice). It is the city's oldest and is still operating.

A portrait of Marie-Antoinette in the Conciergerie, awaiting her execution at the guillotine

Notre-Dame ●

No other building is so associated with the history of Paris as Notre-Dame. It stands majestically on the Ile de la Cité, cradle of the city. Pope Alexander III laid the first stone in 1163, marking the start of 170 years of toil by armies of Gothic architects and medieval craftsmen. Ever since, a procession of the famous has passed through the three main doors below the massive towers.

The cathedral is a Gothic masterpiece, standing on the site of a Roman temple. At the time it was finished, in about 1330, it was 130 m (430 ft) long and featured flying buttresses, a large transept, a deep choir and 69-m (228-ft) high towers.

★ West Front
Three main doors with superb statuary, a central rose window and an openwork gallery are important details.

The south tower houses the cathedral's famous Emmanuel bell.

★ Galerie des Chimères
The cathedral's legendary gargoyles (chimères) hide behind a large upper gallery between the towers.

★ West Rose Window
This window depicts the Virgin in a medallion of rich reds and blues.

STAR FEATURES

- ★ West Front and Portals
- ★ Flying Buttresses
- ★ Rose Windows
- ★ Galerie des Chimères

The Kings' Gallery features 28 Kings of Judah gazing down on the crowds.

Portal of the Virgin
The Virgin surrounded by saints and kings is a fine composition of 13th-century statues.

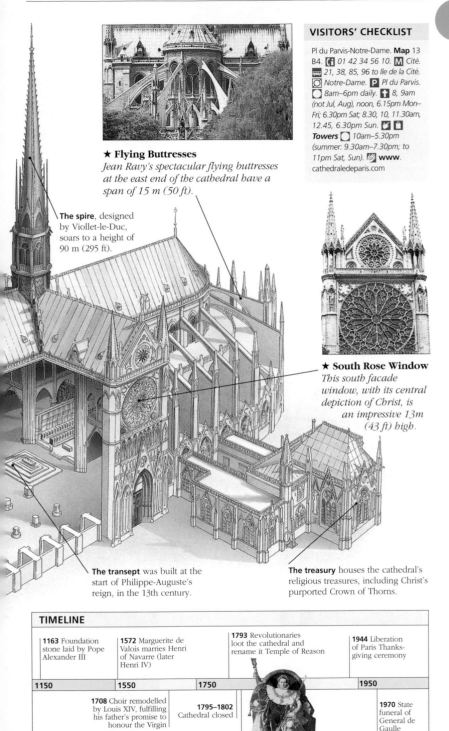

★ **Flying Buttresses**
Jean Ravy's spectacular flying buttresses at the east end of the cathedral have a span of 15 m (50 ft).

The spire, designed by Viollet-le-Duc, soars to a height of 90 m (295 ft).

★ **South Rose Window**
This south facade window, with its central depiction of Christ, is an impressive 13m (43 ft) high.

The transept was built at the start of Philippe-Auguste's reign, in the 13th century.

The treasury houses the cathedral's religious treasures, including Christ's purported Crown of Thorns.

TIMELINE

1163 Foundation stone laid by Pope Alexander III	**1572** Marguerite de Valois marries Henri of Navarre (later Henri IV)	**1793** Revolutionaries loot the cathedral and rename it Temple of Reason		**1944** Liberation of Paris Thanks-giving ceremony
1150	**1550**	**1750**		**1950**
	1708 Choir remodelled by Louis XIV, fulfilling his father's promise to honour the Virgin	**1795–1802** Cathedral closed		**1970** State funeral of General de Gaulle
	1804 Napoleon crowns himself Emperor of France		*Napoleon I*	

A Guided Tour of Notre-Dame

Notre-Dame's interior grandeur is instantly apparent on seeing the high-vaulted central nave. This is bisected by a huge transept, at either end of which are medieval rose windows, 13 m (43 ft) in diameter. Works by major sculptors adorn the cathedral. Among them are Jean Ravy's old choir screen carvings, Nicolas Coustou's *Pietà* and Antoine Coysevox's Louis XIV statue. In this majestic setting kings and emperors were crowned and royal Crusaders were blessed. But Notre-Dame was also the scene of turmoil. Revolutionaries ransacked it, banished religion, changed it into a temple to the Cult of Reason, and then used it as a wine store. Napoleon restored religion in 1804 and architect Viollet-le-Duc later restored the buildings, replacing missing statues, as well as raising the spire and fixing the gargoyles.

A jewelled chalice of Notre-Dame

⑨ **North Rose Window**
This 13th-century stained-glass window depicts the Virgin encircled by figures from the Old Testament.

⑩ **View and Gargoyles**
The 387 steps up the north tower lead to sights of the famous gargoyles and magnificent views of Paris.

Stairs to the tower

Entrance

① **View of Interior**
From the main entrance, the view takes in the high-vaulted central nave looking down towards the huge transept, the choir and the high altar.

KEY

▬ ▬ ▬   Suggested route

② **Le Brun's "May" Paintings**
These religious paintings by Charles Le Brun hang in the side chapels. In the 17th and 18th centuries, the Paris guilds presented a painting to the cathedral on May Day each year.

⑧ **Carved Choir Stalls**
Noted for their early 18th-century carved woodwork, the choir stalls were commissioned by Louis XIV, whose statue stands behind the high altar. Among the details carved in bas-relief on the back of the high stalls are scenes from the life of the Virgin.

⑦ **Louis XIII Statue**
After many years of childless marriage, Louis XIII pledged to erect a high altar and to redecorate the east chancel to honour the Virgin if an heir was born to him. The future Louis XIV was born in 1638, but it took 60 years before the promises were made good. One of the surviving features from that time is the carved choir stalls.

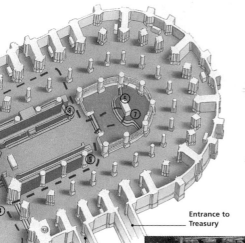

Entrance to
Treasury

Entrance to
Sacristy

⑥ **Pietà**
Behind the high altar is Nicolas Coustou's Pietà, *standing on a gilded base sculptured by François Girardon.*

⑤ **Chancel Screen**
A 14th-century high stone screen enclosed the chancel and provided canons at prayer with peace and solitude from noisy congregations. Some of it has survived to screen the first three north and south bays.

③ **South Rose Window**
Located at the south end of the transept, this window retains some of its original 13th-century stained glass. The window depicts Christ in the centre, surrounded by virgins, saints and the 12 Apostles.

④ **Statue of the Virgin and Child**
Against the southeast pillar of the transept stands the 14th-century statue of the Virgin and Child. It was brought to the cathedral from the chapel of St Aignan, and is known as Notre-Dame de Paris (Our Lady of Paris).

The Pont Neuf, extending to the north and south of the Ile de la Cité

Sainte-Chapelle ❾

See pp88–9.

A Sainte-Chapelle decoration of angels with the Crown of Thorns

Palais de Justice ❿

4 Blvd du Palais (entrance by the Cour de Mai) 75001. **Map** 13 A3.
Tel *01 44 32 50 00.* Ⓜ *Cité.*
◯ *9am–6.30pm Mon–Fri.*
Ⓧ Ⓓ Ⓗ

This huge block of buildings making up the law courts stretches the entire width of the Ile de la Cité. It is a splendid sight with its old towers lining the quays. The site has been occupied since Roman times and was the seat of royal power until Charles V moved the court to the Marais in the 14th century. In April 1793 the Revolutionary Tribunal began dispensing justice from the Première Chambre (gilded chamber). Today the site embodies Napoleon's great legacy – the French judicial system.

Place Dauphine ⓫

75001 (enter by Rue Henri-Robert).
Map 12 F3. Ⓜ *Pont Neuf, Cité.*

East of Pont Neuf is this ancient square, laid out in 1607 by Henri IV and named after the Dauphin, the future Louis XIII. No. 14 is one of the few buildings to have avoided any subsequent restoration. This haven of 17th-century charm is popular with *pétanque* (boules) players and employees of the adjoining Palais de Justice.

Pont Neuf ⓬

75001. **Map** 12 F3. Ⓜ *Pont Neuf, Cité.*

Despite its name (New Bridge), this bridge is the oldest in Paris and has been immortalized by major literary and artistic figures since it was built. The first stone was laid by Henri III in 1578, but it was Henri IV who inaugurated it and gave it its name in 1607. The bridge has 12 arches and spans 275 m (912 ft). The first stone bridge to be built without houses, it heralded a new era in the relationship between the Cité and the river and has been popular ever since. Fittingly, Henri IV's statue stands in the central section.

A sculptured relief on the Palais de Justice

Henri IV in Square du Vert-Galant

Square du Vert-Galant ⓭

75001. **Map** 12 F3. Ⓜ Pont Neuf, Cité.

One of the magical spots of Paris, this square bears the nickname of Henri IV. This amorous and colourful monarch did much to beautify Paris in the early 17th century, and his popularity has lasted to this day. From here there are splendid views of the Louvre and the Right Bank of the river, where Henri was assassinated in 1610. This is also the point from which the Vedettes de Paris pleasure boats depart (see pp72–3).

Société Historique et Littéraire Polonaise ⓮

6 Quai d'Orléans 75004. **Map** 13 C4. **Tel** 01 55 42 83 83. Ⓜ Pont Marie. ◯ 2.15–5.15pm Thu, 9am–noon Sat. 🖼 🎞 every 45 min Thu, on the hour Sat; phone to book.

The Polish Romantic poet Adam Mickiewicz, who lived in Paris in the 19th century, was a major force in Polish cultural and political life, devoting his writing to helping his countrymen who were oppressed at home and abroad. His life is the focal point of the museum, which was founded in 1903 by the poet's son. Part of the famous

Polish library has moved to 74 rue Lauriston, but the archives remain. They form the finest Polish collection outside Poland: paintings, books, maps, emigration archive and Frédéric Chopin memorabilia, including his death mask.

St-Louis-en-l'Ile ⓯

19 bis Rue St-Louis-en-l'Ile 75004. **Map** 13 C4. **Tel** 01 46 34 11 60. Ⓜ Pont Marie. ◯ 9am–noon, 3pm–7pm Tue–Sun. 🔵 public hols. **Concerts.**

The construction of this church was begun in 1664 from plans by the royal architect Louis Le Vau, who lived on the island. It was completed and consecrated in 1726. Among its outstanding exterior features are the 1741 iron clock at the entrance and the pierced iron spire.

The interior, in the Baroque style, is richly decorated with gilding and marble. There is a statue of St Louis holding a crusader's sword. A plaque in the north aisle, given in 1926, bears the inscription "in grateful memory of St Louis in whose honour the City of St Louis, Missouri, USA is named". The church is also twinned with Carthage cathedral in Tunisia, where St Louis is buried.

A bust of Adam Mickiewicz

The interior of St-Louis-en-l'Ile

Hôtel de Lauzun ⓰

17 Quai d'Anjou 75004. **Map** 13 C4. Ⓜ Pont Marie. ◯ Tue, Thu for conferences. Call 01 43 54 27 14 for details.

This splendid mansion was built by Louis Le Vau in the mid-1650s for Charles Gruyn des Bordes, an arms dealer. It was sold in 1682 to the French military commander Duc de Lauzun, who was a favourite of Louis XIV. It later became a focus for Paris's Bohemian literary and artistic life. It now belongs to the city of Paris and, for those lucky enough to see inside, offers an unsurpassed insight into wealthy lifestyles in the 17th century. Charles Le Brun worked on the decoration of its magnificent panelling and painted ceilings before moving on to Versailles.

The poet Charles Baudelaire (1821–67) lived on the third floor and wrote the major part of his controversial masterpiece Les Fleurs du Mal here in a room packed with antiques and bric-a-brac. The celebrated French Romantic poet, traveller and critic, Théophile Gautier (1811–72), had apartments here in 1848. Meetings of the Club des Haschischines (the Hashish-Eaters' Club) took place on the premises.

Other famous residents were the Austrian poet Rainer Maria Rilke, the English artist Walter Sickert and the German composer Richard Wagner. Nowadays it is used for public receptions by the mayor of Paris.

Sainte-Chapelle ❾

Ethereal and magical, Sainte-Chapelle has been hailed as one of the greatest architectural master-pieces of the Western world. In the Middle Ages the devout likened this church to "a gateway to heaven". Today no visitor can fail to be transported by the blaze of light created by the 15 magnificent stained-glass windows, separated by the narrowest of columns that soar 15 m (50 ft) to the star-studded, vaulted roof. The windows portray over 1,000 religious scenes in a kaleidoscope of red, gold, green, blue and mauve. The chapel was built in 1248 by Louis IX to house Christ's purported Crown of Thorns (now housed in the Notre-Dame treasury).

The spire
rises 75 m (245 ft) into the air. It was erected in 1853 after four previous spires burned down.

The Crown of Thorns
decorates the pinnacle as a symbol of the first relic bought by Louis IX.

★ Rose Window
Best seen at sunset, the religious story of the Apocalypse is told in 86 panels of stained glass. The window was a gift from Charles VIII in 1485.

STAR FEATURES

★ Rose Window

★ Window of Christ's Passion

★ Apostle Statues

★ Window of the Relics

Main Portal
The two-tier structure of the portal, the lower half of which is shown here, echoes that of the chapel.

ST LOUIS' RELICS

Louis IX was extremely devout, and was canonized in 1297, not long after his death. In 1239 he acquired the Crown of Thorns from the Emperor of Constantinople and, in 1241, a fragment of Christ's Cross. He built this chapel as a shrine to house them. Louis paid nearly three times more for the relics than for the construction of Sainte-Chapelle. The Crown of Thorns is now kept at Notre-Dame.

VISITORS' CHECKLIST

4 Blvd du Palais. **Map** 13 A3. ⛪ 01 53 40 60 80. Ⓜ Cité. 🚌 21, 38, 85, 96 to Ile de la Cité. RER St-Michel. 🅾 Notre-Dame. 🅿 Palais de Justice. ⬜ daily. Mar–Oct: 9.30am–6pm; Nov–Feb: 9am–5pm. Last adm 30 mins before closing. ⬤ 1 Jan, 1 May, 1 Nov, 11 Nov, 25 Dec. 🎫 (combined ticket with Conciergerie, p81, is available.) 📷 🎥 🏛

The angle

once revolved so that its cross could be seen from anywhere in Paris.

UPPER CHAPEL WINDOWS

1 Genesis
2 Exodus
3 Numbers
4 Deuteronomy: Joshua
5 Judges
6 *left* Isaiah *right* Rod of Jesse
7 *left* St John the Evangelist *right* Childhood of Christ
8 Christ's Passion
9 *left* St John the Baptist *right* Story of Daniel
10 Ezekiel
11 *left* Jeremiah *right* Tobiah
12 Judith and Job
13 Esther
14 Book of Kings
15 Story of the Relics
16 Rose Window: The Apocalypse

Upper Chapel
The windows are a pictorial Bible, showing scenes from the Old and New Testaments.

★ Window of Christ's Passion
The Last Supper is shown here in one of the most beautiful windows in the upper chapel.

★ Apostle Statues
These magnificent examples of medieval stone carving adorn the 12 pillars of the upper chapel.

★ Window of the Relics
This shows the journey of the True Cross and the nails of the Crucifixion to Sainte-Chapelle.

Lower Chapel
Servants and commoners worshipped here, while the chapel above was reserved for the use of the king and the royal family.

THE MARAIS

A place of royal residence in the 17th century, the Marais was all but abandoned during the Revolution, later descending into an architectural wasteland. Sensitive restoration brought the area to life again; some of Paris's most popular museums are now housed in its elegant mansions, while the main streets and narrow passageways bustle with smart boutiques, galleries and restaurants. Many traders have been driven out by high prices, but enough artisans, bakers and small cafés survive, as does the ethnic mix of Jews, former Algerian settlers, Asians and others. Today, the Marais is also the centre of the Parisian gay scene.

SIGHTS AT A GLANCE

Historic Buildings and Streets
Hôtel de Lamoignon **2**
Rue des Francs-Bourgeois **3**
Rue des Rosiers **8**
Hôtel de Ville **19**
Hôtel de Rohan **22**

Churches
St-Paul–St-Louis **15**
St-Gervais–St-Protais **18**
Cloître des Billettes **20**
Notre-Dame-des-Blancs-Manteaux **21**

Museums and Galleries
Musée Carnavalet pp96–7 **1**
Musée Cognacq-Jay **4**
Maison de Victor Hugo **6**
Hôtel de Sully **7**
Hôtel de Coulanges **9**
Hôtel Libéral Bruand **10**
Musée Picasso pp100–1 **11**
Hôtel de Sens **16**
Hôtel de Soubise **23**
Hôtel Guénégaud (Musée de la Chasse et de la Nature) **24**
Musée des Arts et Métiers **25**
Musée d'Art et d'Histoire du Judaïsme **27**

Monuments and Statues
Colonne de Juillet **13**
Mémorial du Martyr Juif Inconnu **17**

Opera Houses
Opéra National de Paris Bastille **12**

Squares
Place des Vosges **5**
Place de la Bastille **14**
Square du Temple **26**

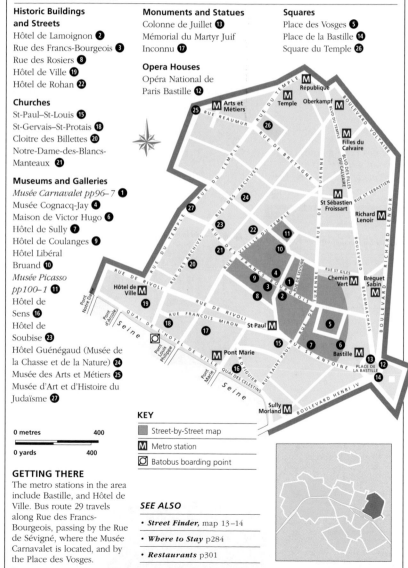

KEY
- Street-by-Street map
- **M** Metro station
- Batobus boarding point

| 0 metres | 400 |
| 0 yards | 400 |

GETTING THERE
The metro stations in the area include Bastille, and Hôtel de Ville. Bus route 29 travels along Rue des Francs-Bourgeois, passing by the Rue de Sévigné, where the Musée Carnavalet is located, and by the Place des Vosges.

SEE ALSO
- **Street Finder,** map 13–14
- **Where to Stay** p284
- **Restaurants** p301

◁ Lunchtime at a Marais park café

Street by Street: The Marais

Once an area of marshland as its name suggests (*marais* means swamp), the Marais grew steadily in importance from the 14th century, by virtue of its proximity to the Louvre, the preferred residence of Charles V. Its heyday was in the 17th century, when it became the fashionable area for the monied classes. They built many grand and sumptuous mansions (*hôtels*) that still dot the Marais today. Many of these *hôtels* have recently been restored and turned into museums. Once again fashionable with the monied classes, designer boutiques, trendy restaurants and cafés now line the streets.

To the Pompidou Centre

RUE BARBETTE

RUE DE TEZETOUR

RUE PAYENNE

RUE DES HOSPITALIERS ST GERVAIS

RUE

RUE DES

RUE

DES

ROSIERS

RUE PAVÉE

RUE MALHER

Rue des Francs-Bourgeois
This ancient street is lined with important museums ❸

Hôtel Libéral Bruand
Named after the architect who built it for his own use, this mansion is now used for temporary art exhibitions ❿

Rue des Rosiers
The smell of hot pastrami and borscht wafts from restaurants and shops in the heart of the Jewish area ❽

Musée Cognacq-Jay
An exquisite collection of 18th-century paintings and furniture is shown in perfect period setting ❹

STAR SIGHTS

★ Musée Picasso

★ Musée Carnavalet

★ Place des Vosges

KEY

— — — Suggested route

0 metres	100
0 yards	100

Hôtel de Lamoignon
Behind the ornate doorway of this fine mansion is Paris's historical library ❷

★ **Musée Picasso**
The palatial home of a 17th-century salt-tax collector is the setting for the largest collection of Picassos in the world, the result of a family bequest to the state ⑪

LOCATOR MAP
See Central Paris Map pp14–15

The Hôtel le Peletier de St-Fargeau adjoins the Hôtel Carnavalet to form the museum of Paris History.

★ **Musée Carnavalet**
The statue of Louis XIV in Roman dress by Coysevox is in the courtyard of the Hôtel Carnavalet ❶

Maison de Victor Hugo
Author of Les Misérables, *Victor Hugo lived at No. 6 Place des Vosges, where his house is now a museum of his life and work* ❻

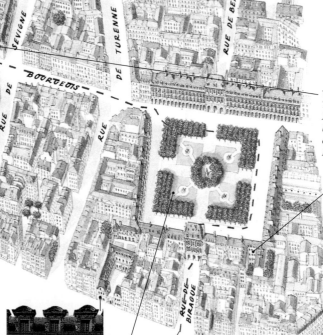

To Metro Sully Morland

★ **Place des Vosges**
Once the site of jousting and tournaments, the historic Place des Vosges, in the very heart of the Marais, is a square of perfect symmetry ❺

Hôtel de Sully
This Renaissance hôtel was built for a notorious gambler ❼

Musée Carnavalet ❶

See pp96–7.

Hôtel de Lamoignon ❷

24 Rue Pavée 75004. **Map** 14 D3.
Tel 01 44 59 29 40. Ⓜ *St-Paul.*
◯ *1–6pm Mon–Sat.* ● *public hols*
& 1–15 Aug. Ⓘ

The imposing Hôtel de Lamoignon is home to the historical library of the city of Paris. This mansion was built in 1585 for Diane de France, also known as the Duchesse d'Angoulême, daughter of Henri II. The building is noted for six high Corinthian pilasters topped by a triangular pediment and flourishes of dogs' heads, bows, arrows and quivers – recalling Diane's passion for hunting. The collection includes documents from the French Revolution and 80,000 prints covering the history of Paris.

Rue des Francs-Bourgeois ❸

75003, 75004. **Map** 14 D3.
Ⓜ *Rambuteau, Chemin-Vert.*

This street is an important thoroughfare in the heart of the Marais, linking the Rue des Archives and the Place

Courtyard of the Musée Carnavalet

des Vosges, with the imposing Hôtel de Soubise at one end and the Musée Carnavalet at the other. The street got its name from the *francs* (free from taxes) – almshouses built for the poor in 1334 at Nos. 34 and 36. These were later closed because of illegal financial activities, although the state kept its pawnshop nearby, still there today.

Musée Cognacq-Jay ❹

Hôtel Donon, 8 Rue Elzévir 75004.
Map 14 D3. *Tel 01 40 27 07 21.*
Ⓜ *St-Paul.* ◯ *10am–6pm Tue–Sun.*
● *public hols.* ▣ *pre-book.* Ⓘ
www.cognac-jay.paris.fr

This fine small collection of French 18th-century works of art and furniture was formed

by Ernest Cognacq and his wife, Louise Jay, founder of the Art Deco La Samaritaine, Paris's largest department store *(see p115).* The private collection was bequeathed to the city and is now housed in the heart of the Marais at the Hôtel Donon – an elegant building dating from 1575 with an 18th-century extension and facade.

Place des Vosges ❺

75003, 75004. **Map** 14 D3.
Ⓜ *Bastille, St-Paul.*

This square is considered among the most beautiful in the world by Parisians and visitors alike *(see pp24–5).* Its impressive symmetry – 36 houses, nine on each side, of brick and stone, with deep slate roofs and dormer windows over arcades – is still intact after 400 years. It has been the scene of many historic events over the centuries. A three-day tournament was held here to celebrate the marriage of Louis XIII to Anne of Austria in 1615. The famous literary hostess, Madame de Sévigné, was born here in 1626; Cardinal Richelieu, pillar of the monarchy, stayed here in 1615; and Victor Hugo, the writer, lived here for 16 years.

A 19th-century engraving of the Place des Vosges

Maison de Victor Hugo **6**

6 Pl des Vosges 75004. **Map** 14 D3.
Tel 01 42 72 10 16. Ⓜ Bastille.
◯ 10am–6pm Tue–Sun.
⬤ public hols. 🎨 🖾 **Library**.
www.musee-hugo.paris.fr

The French poet, dramatist and
novelist lived on the second
floor of the former Hôtel
Rohan-Guéménée from 1832 to
1848. It was here that he wrote
most of *Les Misérables* and
completed many other famous
works. On display are some
reconstructions of the rooms in
which he lived, pen-
and-ink drawings,
books and
mementos from
the crucially
important
periods in his
life, from his
childhood to
his exile between
1852 and 1870.
Temporary exhibi-
tions on Hugo take
place regularly.

**Marble bust of Victor Hugo by
Auguste Rodin**

Hôtel de Sully **7**

62 Rue St-Antoine 75004. **Map** 14
D4. *Tel* 01 42 74 47 75. Ⓜ St-Paul.
◯ noon–7pm Tue–Fri (to 9pm Tue);
10am–7pm Sat, Sun. ⬤ public hols.
🎨 🖾 **www**.jeudepaume.org

This fine 17th-century
mansion on one of Paris's
oldest streets has been
extensively restored, using
old engravings and drawings
as reference. It was built in
1624 for a notorious gambler,
Petit Thomas, who lost his
whole fortune in one night.
The Duc de Sully, Henri IV's
chief minister, purchased the
house in 1634 and added
some of the interior decoration
as well as the Petit Sully
orangery in the gardens. The
Hôtel de Sully has now joined
forces with the Tuileries' Jeu
de Paume museum *(see p131)*,
showcasing contemporary
works on photography,
film and the moving arts.

Late-Renaissance facade of the Hôtel de Sully

Rue des Rosiers **8**

75004. **Map** 13 C3. Ⓜ St-Paul.

The Jewish quarter in and
around this street is one of the
most colourful areas of Paris.
The street's name refers to the
rosebushes within the old city
wall. Jews first settled here in
the 13th century, with a
second wave in the 19th
century from Russia, Poland
and central Europe. Sephardic
Jews arrived from Algeria,
Tunisia, Morocco and Egypt
in the 1950s and 1960s. Some
165 students were rounded
up and deported from the old
Jewish Boys' school nearby at
10 rue de Hospitalières-St-
Gervais. *N'Oubliez pas* (Lest
we forget) is engraved on the
wall. Today this area contains
synagogues, bakeries and
kosher restaurants, the most
famous being Jo Goldenberg's
(see p333).

**Orthodox Jews in
the Marais**

Hôtel de Coulanges **9**

35 rue des Francs Bourgeois, 75004.
Map 13 C3. *Tel* 01 44 61 85 85.
Ⓜ St-Paul. ◯ 10am–1pm, 2–6pm
Mon–Fri. ⬤ public hols.
www.paris-europe.com

This hôtel is a magnificent
example of the architecture of
the early 18th century. The
right wing of the building,
separating the courtyard from
the garden, dates from the
early 17th century. The hôtel
was given in 1640 to Phillipe
II de Coulanges, the King's
counsellor. Renamed the "Petit
hôtel Le Tellier" in 1662 by its
new owner Le Tellier, this is
where the children of Louis
XIV and Madame de Montespan
were raised in secrecy. It is
home to the Maison de
L'Europe, with exhibitions on
themes relating to Europe.

Musée Carnavalet ●

Carnavalet entrance

Devoted to the history of Paris, this vast museum occupies two adjoining mansions, with entire decorated rooms with panelling, furniture and *objets d'art;* many works of art such as paintings and sculptures of prominent personalities; and engravings showing Paris being built. The main building is the Hôtel Carnavalet, built as a town house in 1548 and transformed in the mid-17th century by François Mansart. The neighbouring 17th-century mansion, Hôtel Le Peletier, features superb early 20th-century interiors, and the newly-restored Orangery is devoted to Prehistory and Gallo-Roman Paris.

Marie Antionette in Mourning *(1793) Alexandre Kucharski painted her at the Temple prison after the execution of Louis XVI.*

Memorabilia in this room is dedicated to 18th-century philosophers, in particular Jean-Jacques Rousseau and Voltaire.

★ **Charles Le Brun Ceiling**
Magnificent works by the 17th-century artist decorate the former study and great hall from the Hôtel de la Rivière.

★ **Mme de Sévigné's Gallery**
The gallery includes this portrait of Mme de Sévigné, the celebrated letter-writer, whose beloved home this was for the 20 years up to her death.

STAR EXHIBITS

- ★ Mme de Sévigné's Gallery

- ★ Charles Le Brun Ceiling

- ★ Hôtel d'Uzès Reception Room

- ★ Ballroom of the Hôtel de Wendel

★ **Hotel d'Uzès Reception Room**
The room was created in 1761 by Claude Nicolas Ledoux. The gold-and-white panelling is from a Rue Montmartre mansion.

Entrance
the museu

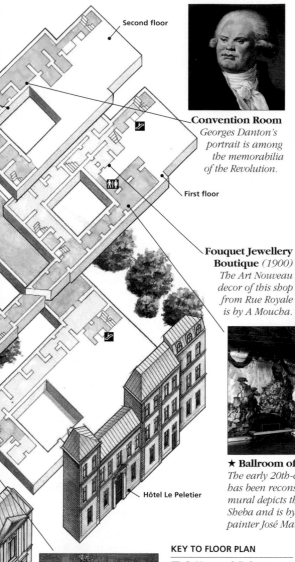

Second floor

First floor

Hôtel Le Peletier

Convention Room
Georges Danton's portrait is among the memorabilia of the Revolution.

Fouquet Jewellery Boutique *(1900)*
The Art Nouveau decor of this shop from Rue Royale is by A Moucha.

VISITORS' CHECKLIST

23 Rue de Sévigné 75003. **Map** 14 D3. *Tel* 01 44 59 58 58. M St-Paul. 29, 69, 76, 96 to St-Paul, Pl des Vosges. P Hôtel de Ville, Rue St-Antoine. ◯ 10am–6pm Tue–Sun (last adm: 5.30pm. Rooms open in rotas; phone to check). ◯ public hols. ◯ ◯ phone for times. ◯ www.carnavalet.paris.fr

★ **Ballroom of the Hôtel de Wendel**
The early 20th-century ballroom interior has been reconstructed. This immense mural depicts the retinue of the Queen of Sheba and is by the Catalan designer and painter José María Sert y Badia.

Louis XV Room
This delightful room contains art from the Bouvier collection and panelling from the Hôtel de Broglie.

KEY TO FLOOR PLAN

- ▢ Prehistory to Gallo-Roman
- ▢ Medieval Paris
- ▢ Renaissance Paris
- ▢ 17th-Century Paris
- ▢ Louis XV's Paris
- ▢ Louis XVI's Paris
- ▢ Revolutionary Paris
- ▢ 19th Century
- ▢ 20th Century
- ▢ Temporary exhibitions
- ▢ Non-exhibition space

GALLERY GUIDE
The collection is mainly arranged chronologically. It covers the history of Paris up to 1789. The Renaissance is on the ground floor, and the exhibits covering the 17th century to the Revolution are on the first floor. In the Hôtel le Peletier the ground floor covers the First–Second Empires, with the new Pre-history–Gallo-Roman departments in the Orangery; from the Second Empire to the present day is on the first floor, and the second floor is devoted to the Revolution.

Hôtel Libéral Bruand ⑩

1 Rue de la Perle 75003. **Map** 14
D3. **Tel** 01 42 77 96 74. Ⓜ St-Paul,
Chemin-Vert. **Museum** ◯ for
temporary exhibitions; phone to
check. ● Aug & public hols. 🖼

This small private house,
built by the architect Libéral
Bruand for himself in 1685,
is far removed, with its
elegant Italianate touches,
from his most famous work,
the gilded Hôtel des Invalides
(see p187).
    The building is usually
closed to the public but
contains an art gallery that
hosts temporary art exhibitions from time to time.

Musée Picasso ⑪

See pp100–1.

Opéra National de Paris Bastille ⑫

120 Rue de Lyon 75012.
Map 4 E4. 🎫 08 92 89 90 90.
Ⓜ Bastille. ◯ phone for details.
● certain public hols.
🖼 ♿ 🎥 compulsory.
See **Entertainment** pp332–5.
www.operadeparis.fr

The controversial "people's
opera" was officially opened
on 14 July 1989 to coincide
with the bicentennial
celebrations of the fall

The "genius of liberty" on top of
the Colonne de Juillet

of the Bastille. Carlos Ott's
imposing building is a notable
break with 19th-century
opera-house design,
epitomized by Garnier's
opulent Opéra in the heart
of the city (see pp214–15).
It is a massive, modern,
curved, glass building. The
main auditorium seats an
audience of 2,700; its design
is functional and modern
with black upholstered seats
contrasting with the granite
of the walls and the
impressive glass ceiling.
With its five moveable
stages, this opera house is
certainly a masterpiece of
technological wizardry.

Colonne de Juillet ⑬

Pl de la Bastille 75004. **Map** 14 E4.
Ⓜ Bastille. ● to the public.

Topped by the statue of the
"genius of liberty", this
column of hollow bronze
reaches 51.5 m (170 ft) into
the sky. It is a memorial to
those who died in the street
battles of July 1830 that led
to the overthrow of the
monarch (see pp32–33). The
crypt contains the remains of
504 victims of the violent
fighting and others who died
in the 1848 revolution.

Place de la Bastille ⑭

75004. **Map** 14 E4. Ⓜ Bastille.

Nothing is now left of the
prison stormed by the
revolutionary mob on 14 July
1789 (see pp30–31) –an event
celebrated annually by the
French at home and abroad –
although the stones were used
for the Pont de la Concorde. A
line of paving stones from Nos.
5 to 49 Blvd Henri IV traces the
former towers and fortifications.
Until recently, the large, traffic-
clogged square which marks
the site, was the border
between central Paris and the
eastern working-class areas
(faubourgs). Gentrificat-ion,
however, is well under-way,
with a new marina, the Port de
Plaisance de l'Arsenal, and
attractive cafés and shops.

The glass facade of the Bastille
Opéra

St-Paul–St-Louis ⑮

99 Rue St-Antoine 75004. **Map** 14 D4. **Tel** 01 42 72 30 32. M St-Paul. 🅾 8am–8pm daily. **Concerts**

A Jesuit church, St-Paul–St-Louis was an important symbol of the influence which the Jesuits held from 1627, when Louis XIII laid the first stone, to 1762 when they were expelled from France. The Gesù church in Rome served as the model for the nave, while the 60-m high (180-ft) dome was the forerunner of those of the Invalides and the Sorbonne. Most of the church's treasures were removed during periods of turmoil, but Delacroix's masterpiece, *Christ in the Garden of Olives*, can still be seen. The church stands on one of the main streets of the Marais, but can also be approached by the ancient Passage St-Paul.

Hôtel de Sens ⑯

1 Rue du Figuier 75004. **Map** 13 C4. **Tel** 01 42 78 14 60. M Pont-Marie. 🅾 1.30–7pm Tue–Sat. 🅾 public hols. 🖾 for exhibitions. 🖾 by appointment only.

This is one of the few medieval buildings left in Paris. It now houses the Forney fine arts library. In the 16th century, at the time of the Catholic League, it was turned into a fortified mansion and occupied by the Bourbons, the Guises and Cardinal de Pellevé, whose religious fervour led

The Hôtel de Sens, now home to a fine arts library

Christ in the Garden of Olives by Delacroix in St-Paul–St-Louis

him to die of rage in 1594 on hearing that the Protestant Henri IV had entered Paris. Marguerite de Valois, lodged here by her ex-husband, Henri IV, led a life of breathtaking debauchery and scandal. This culminated in the beheading of an ex-lover, who had dared to assassinate her current favourite.

The memorial to the unknown Jewish martyr, dedicated in 1956

Mémorial du Martyr Juif Inconnu ⑰

17 Rue Geoffroy-l'Asnier 75004. 75004. **Map** 13 C4. **Tel** 01 42 77 44 72. M Pont-Marie. 🅾 10am–6pm Sun–Fri (10am–10pm Thu). 🖾 🖾 🖾 www.memorial-cdjc.org

The eternal flame burning in the crypt here is the simple memorial to the unknown Jewish martyr of the Holocaust. Its striking feature is a large cylinder that bears the names of the concentration camps where Jewish victims of the Holocaust died. In 2005 a stone wall, engraved with the names of 76,000 Jews – 11,000 of them children – who were deported from France to the Nazi death camps, was also erected here.

St-Gervais–St-Protais ⑱

Pl St-Gervais 75004. **Map** 13 B3. **Tel** 01 48 87 32 02. M Hôtel de Ville. 🅾 5.30am–10pm daily.

Named after Gervase and Protase, two Roman soldiers who were martyred by Nero, this remarkable church dates from the 6th century. It has the oldest Classical facade in Paris, which is formed of a three-tiered arrangement of columns: Doric, Ionic and Corinthian. Behind its facade lies a beautiful Gothic church renowned for its association with religious music. It was for the church's fine organ that François Couperin (1668–1733) composed his two masses. The church currently has a Roman Catholic monastic community whose liturgy attracts people from all over the world.

The facade of St-Gervais–St-Protais with its Classical columns

Musée Picasso ⑪

On the death of the Spanish-born artist Pablo Picasso (1881–1973), who lived most of his life in France, the French State inherited many of his works in lieu of death duties. It used them to establish the Musée Picasso, which opened in 1985. The museum is housed in a large 17th-century mansion, the Hôtel Salé, in the Marais. The original character of the Hôtel, which was built in 1656 for Aubert de Fontenay, a salt-tax collector (*salé* means "salty"), has been preserved. The breadth of the collection reflects both the full extent of Picasso's artistic development, including his Blue, Pink and Cubist periods, and his use of so many different materials.

★ Self-Portrait
Poverty, loneliness and the onset of winter all made the end of 1901, when this picture was painted, a particularly difficult time for Picasso.

Violin and Sheet Music
This collage (1912) is from the artist's Synthetic Cubist period.

★ The Two Brothers
During the summer of 1906 Picasso returned to Catalonia in Spain, where he painted this picture.

★ The Kiss (1969)
Picasso married Jacqueline Roque in 1961, and at around the same time he returned to the familiar themes of the couple and of the artist and model.

Basement

GALLERY GUIDE
The collection is mainly presented in chronological order, starting on the first floor with the Blue and Pink periods, Cubist and Neo-Classical works. Exhibitions change regularly – not all paintings are on show at any one time. On the ground floor there is a sculpture garden and works from the late 1920s to late 1930s, and from the mid-1950s to 1973.

KEY TO FLOORPLAN
- ☐ Paintings
- ☐ Illustrations
- ☐ Sculpture garden
- ☐ Ceramics
- ☐ Non-exhibition space

Woman with a Mantilla (1949)
Picasso extended his range when he began working in ceramics in 1948.

Painter with Palette and Easel (1928)
This Post-Cubist portrait in oils was painted at a time when Picasso's work was verging on Surrealism.

First floor

VISITORS' CHECKLIST

Hôtel Salé, 5 Rue de Thorigny.
Map 14 D2. 01 42 71 25 21. St-Sébastien, St-Paul.
29, 69, 75, 96 to St-Paul, Bastille, Pl des Vosges.
Châtelet-Les-Halles.
Rue St-Antoine, Bastille.
Apr–Sep: 9.30am–6pm Wed–Mon; Oct–Mar: 9.30am–5.30pm Wed–Mon. 1 Jan, 25 Dec. groups by appointment only.
www.musee-picasso.fr

★ **Two Women Running on the Beach** (1922)
In 1924 this was used for the stage curtain design for Diaghilev's ballet The Blue Train. *It proved to be his last major design work for any theatre.*

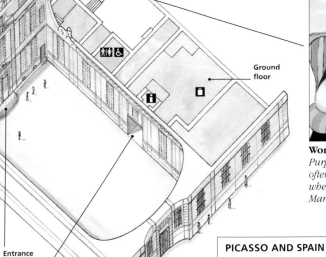

Ground floor

Woman Reading (1932)
Purples and yellows were often used by Picasso when painting his model Marie-Thérèse Walter.

Entrance

STAR PAINTINGS

★ Self-Portrait

★ The Two Brothers

★ Two Women Running on the Beach

★ The Kiss

Entrance

PICASSO AND SPAIN

After 1934, Picasso never returned to his homeland due to his rejection of Franco's regime. However, throughout his life in France he used Spanish themes in his art, such as the bull (often in the form of a minotaur) and the guitar, which he associated with his Andalusian childhood.

The town hall (Hôtel de Ville), overlooking a delightful square

Hôtel de Ville ⓳

Pl de l'Hôtel de Ville 75004. **Map** 13 B3. **Tel** 0820 007 575. Ⓜ Hôtel-de-Ville. ⬤ groups: by arrangement. ⬤ public hols, official functions. ♿ 🎦

Home of the city council, the town hall is a 19th-century reconstruction of the 17th-century town hall that was burned down in 1871. It is highly ornate, with elaborate stonework, turrets and statues overlooking a pedestrianized square which is a delight to stroll in, especially at night when the fountains are illuminated.

The square was once the main site for hangings, burnings and other executions. It was here that Ravaillac, Henri IV's assassin, was quartered alive, his body ripped to pieces by four strong horses.

Inside the Hôtel de Ville, a notable feature is the long Salles des Fêtes (ballroom), with adjoining salons devoted to science, literature and the arts. The impressive staircase, the decorated coffered ceilings with their chandeliers and the numerous statues and caryatids all add to the air of ceremony and pomp – a fitting power base for mayors of the city to hold elaborate banquets and receptions for foreign dignitaries in the building's grand halls. It is also the official residence of the Mayor of Paris, though the current mayor, Bertrand Delanoë, lives elsewhere in the Marais.

Cloître des Billettes ⓴

26 Rue des Archives 75004. **Map** 13 B3. **Tel** 01 42 72 37 08. Ⓜ Hôtel-de-Ville. ⬤ **Cloister** noon–7pm daily; **church** 6.30–8pm Thu, 9.30am–4pm Sun.

This is the only remaining medieval cloister in Paris. It was built in 1427 for the Brothers of Charity, or *Billettes*, and three of its four original galleries are still standing. The adjoining church is a simple Classical building which replaced the monastic original in 1756.

The oldest cloister in Paris

Notre-Dame-des-Blancs-Manteaux ㉑

12 Rue des Blancs-Manteaux 75004. **Map** 13 C3. **Tel** 01 42 72 09 37. Ⓜ Rambuteau. ⬤ 10am–noon, 3pm–7pm daily. **Concerts.**

This church, built in 1685, takes its name from the white habits worn by the Augustinian friars who founded a convent on the site in 1258. It has a magnificent 18th-

century Rococo Flemish pulpit, and its famous organ is best appreciated at one of its regular concerts of religious music.

Hôtel de Rohan ㉒

87 Rue Vieille-du-Temple 75003. **Map** 13 C2. **Tel** 01 40 27 60 09. Ⓜ Rambuteau. ⬤ for temporary exhibitions only.

Although not resembling it in appearance, the Hôtel de Rohan forms a pair with the Hôtel de Soubise. It was built by the same architect, Delamair, for Armand de Rohan-Soubise, a cardinal and Bishop of Strasbourg. The *hôtel* has been home to a part of the national archives since 1927. In the courtyard over the doorway of the stables is the 18th-century sculpture *Horses of Apollo* by Robert Le Lorrain.

Horses of Apollo by Le Lorrain

Hôtel de Soubise ㉓

60 Rue des Francs-Bourgeois 75003.
Map 13 C2. **Tel** 01 40 27 64 19.
Ⓜ Rambuteau. ◐ accessible for
research only 9am–4.45pm Mon–Sat;
phone for appointment.

The Hôtel de Soubise

This imposing mansion, built
from 1705 to 1709 for the
Princesse de Rohan, is one of
two main buildings housing
the national archives. (The
other is the Hôtel de Rohan.)
The Hôtel de Soubise displays
a majestic courtyard and a
magnificent interior decoration dating from 1735 to 1740
by some of the most gifted
painters of the day: Carl Van
Loo, Jean Restout, Natoire
and François Boucher.
Natoire's *rocaille* work on
the Princess's bedroom, the
Oval Salon, forms part of the
museum of French history –
which is unfortunately only
accessible to academics and
researchers. Other exhibits
include Napoleon's will, in
which he asks for his remains
to be returned to France.

Hôtel Guénégaud ㉔

60 Rue des Archives 75003.
Map 13 C2. **Tel** 01 53 01 92 40.
Ⓜ Hôtel de Ville. ◐ 11am–6pm
Tue–Sun. ● public hols. 🎦 🏠 📷

The celebrated architect
François Mansart built this
superb mansion in the mid-
17th century for Henri de
Guénégaud des Brosses, who
was Secretary of State and
Keeper of the Seals. One wing
now contains the Musée

de la Chasse et de la Nature
(Hunting Museum) inaugur-
ated by André Malraux in 1967
and reopened after renovation
in 2006. The exhibits include
a fine collection of hunting
weapons from the 16th to the
19th centuries, many from
Germany and Central Europe.
There are also animal trophies
from around the world, along
with drawings and paintings
by Oudry, Rubens, Rembrandt,
Monet and other artists.

Musée des Arts et Métiers ㉕

60 Rue Réaumur 75003. **Map** 13 B1-
C1. **Tel** 01 53 01 82 00. Ⓜ Arts et
Métiers. ◐ 10am–6pm Tue–Sun (to
9.30pm Thu). ● public hols. 🎦 📷
♿ 💻 📷 www.arts-et-metiers.net

Housed within the old
Abbey of Saint-Martin-des-
Champs, the Arts and Crafts
museum was founded in
1794 and closed down two
centuries later for interior
restructuring and renovation.
It reopened in 2000 as a high-
quality museum of science
and industry displaying 5,000
items (it has 75,000 other items
in store available to academics
and researchers). The theme
is man's ingenuity and the
world of invention and
manufacturing, covering such
topics as textiles, photography
and machines. Among the most
entertaining displays are ones
of musical clocks, mechanical
music instruments and
automata (mechanical figures),
one of which, the "Joueuse
de Tympanon", is said to
represent Marie-Antoinette.

Square du Temple ㉖

75003. **Map** 13 C1. Ⓜ Temple.

A quiet and pleasant square
today, this was once a
fortified centre of the medieval
Knights Templars. A state within a state, the area contained a
palace, a church and shops
behind high walls and a draw-
bridge, making it a haven for
those who were seeking to
escape from royal jurisdiction.
Louis XVI and Marie-Antoinette
were held here after their
arrest in 1792 (see pp30–31).
The king left from here for his
execution on the guillotine.

Musée d'Art et d'Histoire du Judaïsme ㉗

Hôtel de St-Aignan, 71 rue du Temple
75003. **Map** 13 B2. **Tel** 01 53 01 86
60. Ⓜ Rambuteau. ◐ 11am–6pm
Mon–Fri, 10am–6pm Sun.
● Jewish hols. 🎦 ♿ 🏠 💻 📷
www.mahj.org

Housed in an elegant Marais
mansion, the museum unites
collections formerly scattered
around the city, and commemorates the culture of French
Jewry from medieval times to
the present. There has been a
sizeable Jewish community in
France since Roman times, and
some of the world's greatest
Jewish scholars were French.
Much exquisite craftsmanship
is displayed, with elaborate
silverware, Torah covers,
items of fine Judaica and religious objects. There are also
historical documents, photographs, paintings and cartoons.

"Being a Jew in Paris in 1939", a display in the Jewish Museum

BEAUBOURG AND LES HALLES

This Right Bank area is dominated by the modernistic Forum des Halles and the Pompidou Centre. These two spectacular undertakings are thriving public areas of contact for shoppers, art lovers, students and tourists. Literally millions flow between the two squares. The Halles is for street fashion, with most of the shops underground, and the clientele strolling under the concrete and glass bubbles is young. The surrounding streets, coloured by popular cheap shops and bars, are undergoing refurbish-

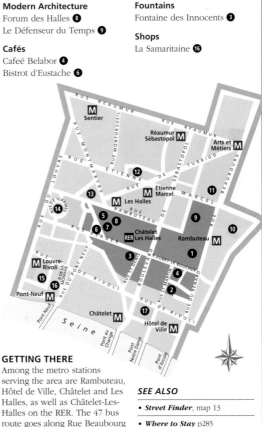

Fountain in the Place Igor Stravinsky

ment to combat their seedy image, and there are still enough specialist food shops, butchers and small markets to recall what Les Halles must have been like in its prime as the city's thriving market. All roads round Les Halles lead to the Beaubourg area and the Pompidou Centre, an avantgarde assembly of vast pipes, ducts and cables, renovated in the 1990s to cope with its 20,000 daily visitors. The adjoining streets, such as Rue St-Martin and Rue Beaubourg, house small contemporary art galleries in crooked, gabled buildings.

SIGHTS AT A GLANCE

Historic Buildings and Streets
No. 51 Rue de Montmorency ⑪
Tour de Jean Sans Peur ⑫
Bourse du Commerce ⑭
Tour St-Jacques ⑰

Churches
St-Merry ②
St-Eustache ⑬
St-Germain l'Auxerrois ⑮

Museums and Galleries
Pompidou Centre pp110–13 ①
Pavillon des Arts ⑤
Forum des Images ⑦
Musée de la Poupée ⑩

Modern Architecture
Forum des Halles ⑧
Le Défenseur du Temps ⑨

Cafés
Cafeé Belabor ④
Bistrot d'Eustache ⑥

Fountains
Fontaine des Innocents ③

Shops
La Samaritaine ⑯

0 metres 400
0 yards 400

KEY

	Street-by-Street map
M	Metro station
RER	RER station

GETTING THERE
Among the metro stations serving the area are Rambuteau, Hôtel de Ville, Châtelet and Les Halles, as well as Châtelet-Les-Halles on the RER. The 47 bus route goes along Rue Beaubourg past the Pompidou Centre and along Boulevard Sebastopol.

SEE ALSO
• *Street Finder*, map 13
• *Where to Stay* p285
• *Restaurants* pp302–303

◁ St-Eustache and sculptured head, *l'Ecoute*, by Henri de Miller

Street-by-Street: Beaubourg and Les Halles

When Emile Zola described Les Halles as the "belly of Paris" he was referring to the meat, vegetable and fruit market that had thrived here since 1183. Traffic congestion in the 1960s forced the market to move to the suburbs and Baltard's giant umbrella-like market pavilions were pulled down, despite howls of protest, and replaced by a shopping and leisure complex, the Forum. The conversion worked: today, Les Halles and the Pompidou Centre, which lies in the Beaubourg quarter and has been Paris's main tourist attraction ever since it opened in 1977, draw the most mixed crowds in Paris.

Pavillon des Arts
This is one of the mushroom-shaped pavilions overlooking the Forum. It houses changing exhibitions ⑤

Bistrot d'Eustache
This lively café is a favourite venue for enthusiasts of both classic and modern jazz ⑥

★ Forum des Halles
Beneath the shops, restaurants, cinemas and swimming pool is the world's busiest underground station ⑧

Forum des Images
Visitors watch videos in the Salle de Consultation ⑦

STAR SIGHTS

- ★ Pompidou Centre
- ★ Le Défenseur du Temps
- ★ Fontaine des Innocents
- ★ Forum des Halles

To Metro Châtelet

Rue de la Ferronnerie was where, in 1610, the religious fanatic Ravaillac assassinated Henri IV while his carriage was caught in the traffic.

★ Fontaine des Innocents
This is the last Renaissance fountain left in Paris. It was designed by the sculptor and architect Jean Goujon ③

IRCAM is an underground research centre dedicated to pioneering new ways of making music.

KEY

– – – Suggested route

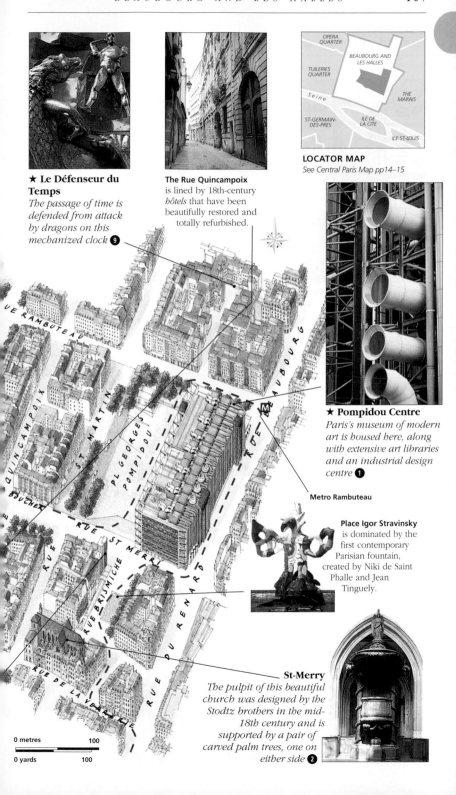

★ **Le Défenseur du Temps**
The passage of time is defended from attack by dragons on this mechanized clock ❾

The Rue Quincampoix is lined by 18th-century *hôtels* that have been beautifully restored and totally refurbished.

LOCATOR MAP
See Central Paris Map pp14–15

OPERA QUARTER

BEAUBOURG AND LES HALLES

TUILERIES QUARTER

Seine

THE MARAIS

ST-GERMAIN-DES-PRES

ILE DE LA CITE

ILE ST-LOUIS

★ **Pompidou Centre**
Paris's museum of modern art is housed here, along with extensive art libraries and an industrial design centre ❶

Metro Rambuteau

Place Igor Stravinsky is dominated by the first contemporary Parisian fountain, created by Niki de Saint Phalle and Jean Tinguely.

St-Merry
The pulpit of this beautiful church was designed by the Stodtz brothers in the mid-18th century and is supported by a pair of carved palm trees, one on either side ❷

0 metres 100
0 yards 100

Pompidou Centre ❶

See pp110–13.

A Nativity scene from the stained-glass windows in St-Merry

St-Merry ❷

76 Rue de la Verrerie 75004. **Map** 13 B3. **Tel** 01 42 71 93 93. Ⓜ Hôtel-de-Ville. ◯ 3–7pm daily.
📷 1st & 3rd Sun, pm. **Concerts.**

The site of this church dates back to the 7th century. St Médéric, the abbot of St-Martin d'Autun, was buried here at the beginning of the 8th century. The saint's name, which was eventually corrupted to Merry, was given to a chapel built nearby. The building of the church – in the Flamboyant Gothic style – was not completed until 1552. The west front is particularly rich in decoration, and the northwest turret contains the oldest bell in Paris, dating from 1331. It was the wealthy parish church of the Lombard moneylenders, who gave their name to the nearby Rue des Lombards.

Fontaine des Innocents ❸

Sq des Innocents 75001. **Map** 13 A2. Ⓜ Les Halles.
🚇 Châtelet-Les-Halles.

This carefully-restored Renaissance fountain stands in the Square des Innocents, the area's main crossroads.

Erected in 1549 on the Rue St-Denis, it was moved to its present location in the 18th century, when the square was constructed on the site of a former graveyard. Popular with the city's youth as a meeting place, the fountain is one of the landmarks of Les Halles.

Decoration on the Fontaine des Innocents

Café Beaubourg ❹

100 Rue St-Martin, 75004. **Map** 13 B2. **Tel** 01 48 87 63 96. Ⓜ Les Halles.
🚇 Châtelet-Les-Halles. ◯ 8am–1am Mon–Thu, Sun; 8am–2am Fri, Sat.

Interior of the Café Beaubourg

Opened by Gilbert Costes in 1987, this stylish café was designed and decorated by one of France's star architects, Christian de Portzamparc, who created the impressive Cité de la Musique in the Parc de la Villette (see p234). Its vast terrace is lined with comfortable red and black wicker chairs. The spacious and coolly elegant interior is decorated with rows of books which soften its severely Art Deco ambience. The café is a favourite meeting point for art dealers from the surrounding galleries and Pompidou Centre staff. It serves light meals and brunch. If the crush gets too much around Les Halles, the Café Beaubourg is the ideal place to soothe the nerves.

Pavillon des Arts ❺

101 Rue Rambuteau, Terrasse Lautréamont 75001. **Map** 13 A2. **Tel** 01 42 33 82 50. Ⓜ Les Halles. 🚇 Châtelet-Les-Halles. ◯ 11.30am–6.30pm Tue–Sun (times may vary). ◯ public hols. 📷 📷
🖥 www.pavillondesarts.paris.fr

In creating this exhibition centre in 1983, Paris opened up the newly revitalized quarter of Les Halles to the arts. Housed in the futuristic glass and steel of the Baltard Pavilion, its programme of changing exhibitions often focuses on unusual or rarely seen subjects and works, drawn together from French and foreign museums. Past exhibitions have included Russian history as portrayed by Soviet photographers, Surrealists recalled through their collections of Indian dolls, or the Seine through the eyes of Turner.

Exterior of the Pavillon des Arts

Bistrot d'Eustache ❻

37 Rue Berger, 75001. **Map** 13 A2.
Tel *01 40 26 23 20.* Ⓜ *Les Halles.*
🆁🅴🆁 *Châtelet-Les-Halles.* ◯
noon–2am daily. **Live jazz, flamenco/
gypsy:** *phone for details.*

This compact café, decorated
with old wood panelling and
attractive mirrors, retains a
feeling of Paris as it was in
the 1930s and 1940s – a period
when jazz venues flourished
throughout the city. It is
always packed for live music
shows, when musicians
squeeze into a handkerchief-
sized space to play racy
guitar-led gypsy jazz. The
café serves a variety of traditional French food, at all
times throughout the day
and at very reasonable prices.

Terrace of the Bistrot d'Eustache

Forum des Images ❼

2 Grande Galerie, Forum des Halles
75001. **Map** 13 A2. ***Tel*** *01 53 01
96 96.* Ⓜ *Les Halles.* 🆁🅴🆁 *Châtelet-
Les-Halles.* ◯ *1–9pm Tue–Sun.*
◯ *public hols.* 🎞 🅑 🖵
www.forumdesimages.net

At the forum you can choose
from thousands of cinema,
television, and amateur films.
All feature the city of Paris.
There is footage on the
history of Paris since 1895
including a remarkable news-
reel of General de Gaulle
avoiding sniper fire during the
Liberation of Paris in 1944.
There are countless movies
such as Truffaut's *Baisers Volés*.
Admission includes two hours'
viewing of your chosen film in

the Salle de Consultation
(*see p106*) and entry to two
auditoriums showing films
linked by a theme.

François Truffaut's *Baisers Volés*

Forum des Halles ❽

75001. **Map** 13 A2. Ⓜ *Les Halles.*
🆁🅴🆁 *Châtelet-Les-Halles.*

The present Forum des
Halles, known simply as Les
Halles, was built in 1979,
amid much controversy, on
the site of the famous old
fruit and vegetable market.
The present complex occupies
7 ha (750,000 sq ft), above
and below ground. The
underground levels 2 and 3
are occupied by a varied array
of shops, from chic boutiques
to megastores. Above ground
there are well-tended gardens,
pergolas and mini-pavilions.
Also outside are the

Pygmalion by Julio
Silva in the
Forum des
Halles

palm-shaped buildings of
metal and glass which house
the Pavillon des Arts and the
Maison de la Poésie, cultural
centres for contemporary art
and poetry respectively. Sadly,
the area has recently become
rather seedy, and is not
recommended at night.

Le Défenseur du Temps ❾

Rue Bernard-de-Clairvaux 75003.
Map 13 B2. Ⓜ *Rambuteau.*

The modern Quartier de
l'Horloge (Clock Quarter) is
the location of Paris's newest
public clock, "The Defender
of Time" by Jacques
Monastier. An impressive
brass-and-steel mechanical
sculpture, it stands 4 m (13 ft)
high and weighs 1 tonne. The
defender battles against the
elements: air, earth and water.
In the shape of savage beasts,
they attack him at the approach
of each hour, to the
accompanying sound of
earthquakes, hurricanes and
rough seas. At 2pm and 6pm
he overcomes
all three, as
watching
children cheer.

Pompidou Centre

The Pompidou is like a building turned inside out: escalators, lifts, air and water ducts and even the massive steel struts that are the building's skeleton have all been placed on the outside. This allowed the architects, Richard Rogers, Renzo Piano and Gianfranco Franchini, to create an uncluttered and flexible space within it for the Musée National d'Art Moderne and for the Pompidou's other activities. Among the schools represented in the museum are Fauvism, Cubism and Surrealism. Outside in the piazza, large crowds gather to watch the street performers. The Pompidou also houses temporary exhibitions that thrust it into the heart of Paris's art scene.

The escalator that rises step by step up the facade overlooking the piazza runs through a glass conduit. From the top there is a spectacular view over Paris that includes Montmartre, La Défense and the Eiffel Tower.

KEY

☐ Exhibition space

▨ Non-exhibition space

GALLERY GUIDE

The permanent collections are on Levels 5 & 4: works from 1905 to 1960 are on the former, with the latter reserved for contemporary art. Levels 1 & 6 are for major exhibitions, while Levels 1, 2 & 3 house an information library. The lower levels make up "The Forum", the focal public area, which include a performance centre for dance, theatre and music, a cinema and children's workshop.

Portrait of the Journalist Sylvia von Harden *(1926)*
The surgical precision of Dix's style makes this a harsh caricature.

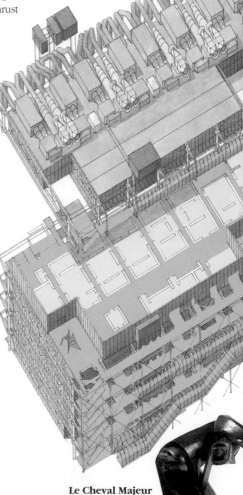

Le Cheval Majeur
This bronze horse (1914–16) by Duchamp-Villon is one of the finest examples of Cubist sculpture.

To Russia, the Asses and the Others *(1911)*
Throughout his life Chagall drew inspiration from the small Russian town of Vitebsk, where he was born.

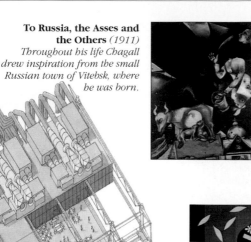

VISITORS' CHECKLIST

Pl Georges Pompidou. **Map** 13 B2. **Tel** 01 44 78 12 33. M Rambuteau, Châtelet, Hôtel de Ville. 🚌 21, 29, 38, 47, 58, 69, 70, 72, 74, 75, 76, 81, 85, 96. RER Châtelet-Les-Halles. ⬚ MNAM & temp exhibs: 11am–9pm Wed–Mon; Library: noon–10pm Wed–Mon (from 11am Sat, Sun & pub hols); Atelier Brancusi: 2–6pm Wed–Mon. 🅿 ♿ 🖼 📷 🎬 🍴 🖥 🌐 www.centrepompidou.fr

Basin and Sculpture Terrace

Sorrow of the King *(1952)*
Towards the end of his life, Matisse produced a number of collages using gouache-painted paper cut-outs.

Le Duo *(1937)*
Georges Braque, like Picasso, developed the Cubist technique of representing different views of a subject in a single picture.

Basin and Sculpture Terrace

COLOUR-CODING

The coloured pipes that are the most striking feature at the back of the Pompidou, on the rue du Renard, moved one critic to compare the building to an oil refinery. Far from being merely decorative, the colours serve to distinguish the pipes' various functions: air-conditioning ducts are blue, water pipes green and electricity lines are painted yellow. The areas through which people move vertically (such as escalators) are red. The white funnels are ventilation shafts for the underground areas, and structural beams are clad in stainless steel. The architects' idea was to help the public understand the way the dynamics of a building function.

Exploring the Pompidou's Modern Art Collection

With a collection of over 50,000 works of art from more than 42,000 artists, the Pompidou encompasses all of the fine arts. Since its renovation, classic disciplines – painting, sculpture, drawing and photography – have been integrated with other media such as cinema, architecture, design, and visual and sound archives. The collections now represent a complete overview of modern and contemporary creation.

The Two Barges (1906) by André Derain

FROM 1905–60

The "historical" collections bring together the great artistic movements of the first half of the 20th century, from Fauvism to Abstract Expressionism to the changing currents of the 1950s. The rich collection of Cubist sculptures, of which the *Cheval Majeur* by Duchamp-Villon (1914–1916) is a fine example, is displayed, as well as examples of the great masters of the 20th century. Matisse, Picasso, Braque, Duchamp, Kandinsky, Léger, Miro, Giacometti and Dubuffet command large

areas at the heart of the collection. Towards the end of his life, Matisse made several collages from cut up large sheets of paper. Among others, the museum possesses *La Tristesse du Roi* (Sorrow of the King) which he created in 1952. With *Homme à la Guitare* (Man with a Guitar), Braque demonstrates his command of the Cubist technique which he pioneered along with Picasso. Considered as one of the first, if not

the first, Abstract painter, Kandinsky transformed works inspired by nature into constructions of colour and form. The museum has a large collection of the Russian painter's works, of which the Impressions (*Impressions V, Parc*, 1911) mark the end of his Expressionist period before his plunge into Abstract art with *Improvisations XIV* or *Avec l'Arc Noir* (With the Black Arc) both dating from 1912 compositions.

The collection also shows the groups and the movements on which the history of modern art is based, or by which it has been affected, including Dada, Abstract Art and Informal. A pioneer of Informal art, Jean Fautrier is represented in the collections with *Otages* (Hostages), a commemoration of the suffering of the resistance fighters.

At the heart of this chronological progression, some newly opened spaces are a revelation. One set shows the Union des Artistes Modernes (Modern Artists Union) where architects, visual artists and designers met in the 1920s. Another room recreates the atmosphere of André Breton's workshop in which the works of his Surrealist friends are also shown. Silent pauses have also been allowed for: the room reserved for Miro's three huge *Bleus* (Blues) gives time and space for visitors to meditate on the explosion and revolutions of modern art.

BRANCUSI'S STUDIO

The Atelier Brancusi, on the rue Rambuteau side of the piazza, is a reconstruction of the workshop of the Romanian born artist Constantin Brancusi (1876-1957), who lived and worked in Paris from 1904. He bequeathed his entire collection of works to the French state on condition that his workshop be rebuilt as it was on the day he died. The collection includes sculptures and plinths, photographs and a selection of his tools. Also featured are some of his more personal items such as documents, pieces of furniture and his book collection.

Miss Pogany (1919–20) by Constantin Brancusi

With the Black Arc (1912) by Vassily Kandinsky

The Good-bye Door (1980) by Joan Mitchell

ART SINCE 1960

The contemporary department opens with the 1960s and pays homage to Jean Tinguely. This sculptor/engineer was creator of the Stravinsky fountain situated near the Centre, along with Niki de Saint-Phalle. The display is organized around a central aisle from which the rooms holding the museum's collections lead off.

The 1960s saw the rise of Pop Art in America, which introduced advertising and mass-media images, along with objects from the consumer society, into art. Works by Jasper Johns, Andy Warhol and Claes Oldenburg are in the collection. In the Rauschenberg *Oracle*, for example, products become abstract shapes. Among other works of importance are *Ghost Drums Set* by Claes Oldenburg and *Electric Chair* by Andy Warhol.

In France, the New Realists, a heterogenous group including Yves Klein, César, Arman and others, were also interested in contemporary objects. They believed that by choosing mundane things from everyday life the artist could imbue them with artistic significance. Arman makes "accumulations",

Mobile on Two Planes (1955)
by Alexander Calder

Raymond Hains collects wall posters in order to make abstract canvases, while Jean Tinguely builds machines using materials collected.

The subtle eroticism of Balthus (Count Balthasar Klossowski de Rola) glows through *The Painter and His Model* (1980–81). In another area are ink drawings by poet-painter Henri Michaux.

Homogenous Infiltration (1966)
by Joseph Beuys

The work of Herbin, who founded the Abstraction-Création group, a loosely-based association of non-figurative painters, is the focus for the work of the Geometric Abstractionists, while the Hard Edge Abstraction movement in America, which specializes in flat-coloured, well-defined shapes, is represented by Ellsworth Kelly and Frank Stella, among others. Richard Serra's *Corner Prop No. 7 (For Natalie)* (1983) and Carl André's *144 Tin Square* (1975) are just two of the several Minimalist sculptures in the collection.

The museum has a selection of figurative art by Georg Baselitz, Gilbert and George, and Anselm Kiefer, as well as art from the abstract landscape painter Joan Mitchell.

Kinetic Art, Poor Art and Conceptual Art, and new trends in figurative and

abstract painting, punctuate the route of the contemporary department's galleries.

Since the Pompidou's reopening, certain areas have been designated to bring together different disciplines around a theme and no longer around a school or movement. For example, the use of plastic materials in contemporary art is shown in the works of Jean Dubuffet, César or Claes Oldenburg and compared against the work of architects such as Richard Buckminster or Hans Hollein and designers such as Ettore Sottsass.

In its new arrangement the fourth floor offers areas allowing different aspects of the museum's collections to be discovered. They often reflect the museum's preference for the more ironic and conceptual forms. One display offered such works as Joseph Beuys's *Plight* (1985), which included a grand piano and wall and ceiling covered with about 7 tonnes of thick felt, and the video artist Nam June Paik's *Video Fish* (1979–85), in which video screens flashed manic sequences of images from behind aquaria populated by indifferent fish.

The museum gallery allows temporary exhibitions to be mounted from works held in reserve. A graphic arts exhibition room and a video area complete the arrangement. A screening room gives access to the museums' entire collection of videotapes and audio recordings of a wide range of modern artists.

Ben's Store (1973) by Ben (Vautier Benjamin)

Musée de la Poupée ⑩

Impasse Berthaud 75003. **Map** 13 B2. *Tel 01 42 72 73 11.* M *Rambuteau.* 🕐 *10am–6pm Tue–Sun.* 🈺 🎫 *for groups, by appt.* **www**.museedelapoupeeparis.com

An impressive collection of hand-made dolls, from the mid-19th century to the present day, are on show in this charming museum. Thirty-six of the displays contain French dolls with porcelain heads ranging from 1850 to 1950. Another 24 display windows are devoted to themed exhibitions of dolls from around the world.

Father and son, Guido and Samy Odin, who own the museum, are at your service if your doll needs medical care. The museum shop stocks everything you need to preserve and maintain these unique works of art. The Odins also offer comprehensive classes on doll-making for both adults and children.

A 19th-century French doll with porcelain head

No. 51 Rue de Montmorency ⑪

75003. **Map** 13 B1. M *Réaumur-Sébastopol.* 🕐 *to the public.*

This house is considered to be the oldest in Paris. No. 51 was built in 1407 by Nicolas Flamel, a book-keeper and alchemist. His house was always open to the poor, from whom he asked nothing more than that they should pray for those who were dead. Today, the house is a French restaurant.

The interior of St-Eustache in the 1830s

Tour de Jean Sans Peur ⑫

20 Rue Etienne-Marcel 75002. **Map** 13 A1. *Tel 01 40 26 20 28.* M *Etienne-Marcel.* 🕐 *1.30–6pm Wed, Sat, Sun.* 🈺 🎫 **www**.tourjeansanspeur.com

After the Duc d'Orléans was assassinated on his orders in 1408, the Duc de Bourgogne feared reprisals. To protect himself, he had this 27-m (88-ft) tower built on to his home, the Hôtel de Bourgogne. He moved his bedroom up to the fourth floor of the tower (which was reached by a flight of 140 steps) to sleep safe from the plots of his enemies.

No. 51 Rue de Montmorency, the oldest house in Paris

St-Eustache ⑬

Pl du Jour 75001. **Map** 13 A1. *Tel 01 40 26 47 99.* M *Les Halles.* RER *Châtelet-Les-Halles.* 🕐 *9.30am–7pm daily.* P ⓕ *12.30pm Mon–Fri; 6pm Mon & Sat; 9.30am, 11am, 6pm Sun.* ***Organ recitals 5.30pm Sun.***

With its gothic plan and Renaissance decoration, St-Eustache is one of the most beautiful churches in Paris. Its interior plan is modelled on Notre-Dame, with five naves and side and radial chapels. The 105 years (1532–1637) it took to complete the church saw the flowering of the Renaissance style, which is evident in the magnificent arches, pillars and columns. The stained-glass windows in the chancel are created from cartoons by Philippe de Champaigne.

The church has associations with many famous figures: Molière was buried here; the Marquise de Pompadour, official mistress of Louis XV, was baptized here, as was Cardinal Richelieu.

Entrance to the Bourse du Commerce, the old corn exchange

Bourse du Commerce ⑭

2 Rue de Viarmes 75001.
Map 12 F2. **Tel** 01 55 65 55 65.
Ⓜ Les Halles. 🚉 Châtelet-Les-Halles. ◯ 9am–1pm, 2–5pm Mon–Fri. 🖼 groups by appt. ♿

Compared by Victor Hugo to a jockey's cap without a peak, the old corn exchange building was constructed in the 18th century and remodelled in 1889.
Today its huge, domed hall is filled with the hustle and bustle of the com-modities market for coffee and sugar. It houses a World Trade Centre and the offices of the Chambre de Commerce et d'Industrie de Paris.

St-Germain l'Auxerrois ⑮

2 Pl du Louvre 75001.
Map 12 F2. **Tel** 01 42 60 13 96.
Ⓜ Louvre, Pont-Neuf.
◯ 8am–7pm daily.
Musical Hour 4–5pm Sun.

After the Valois Court decamped to the Louvre from the Ile de la Cité in the 14th century, this became the favoured church of kings, who attended mass here.
Its many historical associations include the horrific St Bartholomew's Day Massacre on 24 August 1572, the eve of the royal wedding of Henri of Navarre and Marguerite de Valois.

Thousands of Huguenots who had been lured to Paris for the wedding were murdered as the church bell tolled. Later, after the Revolution, the church was used as a barn. Despite many restorations, it is a jewel of Gothic architecture.

La Samaritaine ⑯

19 Rue de la Monnaie 75001.
Map 12 F2. **Tel** 01 40 41 20 20.
Ⓜ Pont-Neuf. ◯ for renovation.
🍴 🖥 Ⓟ See **Shopping** p313.

Currently closed due to renovation, this fashionable department store was founded in 1900 by Ernest Cognacq. Built in 1926 with a framework of iron and wide expanses of glass, La Samaritaine is an outstanding example of the Art Deco style. The interior has a fine Art Nouveau ironwork staircase and hanging galleries under a large dome.
Cognacq was also a collector of 18th-century art, and his collection is now on display in the Musée Cognacq-Jay in the Marais quarter (see p94).

The stylish Art Deco interior of La Samaritaine

The Tour St-Jacques with its ornate decoration

Tour St-Jacques ⑰

Square de la Tour St-Jacques 75004. **Map** 13 A3. Ⓜ Châtelet.
◯ for renovation.

This imposing late Gothic tower, dating from 1523, is all that remains of an ancient church that was a rendezvous for pilgrims setting out on long journeys. The church was destroyed after the Revolution. Earlier, Blaise Pascal, the 17th-century mathematician, physicist, philosopher and writer, used the tower for barometrical experiments. There is a memorial statue to him on the ground floor of the tower. Queen Victoria passed by on her state visit in 1854, giving her name to the nearby Avenue Victoria.

The St Bartholomew's Day Massacre (c. 1572–84) by François Dubois

TUILERIES QUARTER

The Tuileries area is bounded by the vast expanse of the Concorde square at one end and the Grand Louvre at the other. This was a place for kings and palaces. The Sun King (Louis XIV) lives on in the Place des Victoires, which was designed solely to show off his statue. In Place Vendôme, royal glitter has been replaced by the precious stones of Cartier, Boucheron and Chaumet, and the fine cut of Arab, German and Japanese bankers, not to mention the chic ladies visiting the luxurious Ritz. The area is crossed by two of Paris's most magnificent shopping streets – the long Rue de Rivoli, with its arcades, expensive boutiques, bookshops and luxury hotels, and the Rue St-Honoré, another extensive street, bringing together the richest and humblest in people and commerce.

Ornate lamppost on Place de la Concorde

SIGHTS AT A GLANCE

Historic Buildings
Palais Royal ❸
Banque de France ⓴

Museums and Galleries
Musée du Louvre pp122–9 ❶
Musée de la Mode et du Textile ❾
Musée de la Publicité ❿
Musée des Arts Décoratifs ⓫
Galerie Nationale du Jeu de Paume ⓯
Musée de l'Orangerie ⓰
Village Royal ⓲

Monuments and Fountains
Fontaine Molière ❻
Arc de Triomphe du Carrousel ⓬

Squares, Parks and Gardens
Jardin du Palais Royal ❺
Place des Pyramides ❽
Jardin des Tuileries ⓮
Place de la Concorde ⓱
Place Vendôme ⓳
Place des Victoires ㉑

Theatres
Comédie Française ❹

Shops
Louvre des Antiquaires ❷
Rue de Rivoli ⓭

Churches
St-Roch ❼

GETTING THERE
This area is well served by the metro system, with stations at Tuileries, Pyramides, Palais Royal and Louvre. There are frequent buses through the area. Routes 24 and 72 travel along the quayside passing the Jardin des Tuileries and the Musée du Louvre.

0 metres   400
0 yards   400

KEY
Street-by-Street map
M Metro station
i Tourist information

SEE ALSO
• *Street Finder*, map 6, 11–12
• *Where to Stay* pp285–286
• *Restaurants* pp303–304

◁ **View of the Place de la Concorde and the Obelisk**

Street by Street: Tuileries Quarter

Elegant squares, formal gardens, street arcades and courtyards give this part of Paris its special character. Monuments to monarchy and the arts coexist with contemporary luxury: sumptuous hotels, world-famous restaurants, fashion emporiums and jewellers of international renown. Sandblasting and washing have given a new glow to the facades of the Louvre and the Palais Royal square, where Cardinal Richelieu's creation, the royal palace, is now occupied by government offices. From here the Ministry of Culture surveys the cleaning and restoration of the city's great buildings. The other former royal palace, the Louvre, is now one of the great museums of the world.

St-Roch
The papal statue stands in this remarkably long 17th-century church, unusually set on a north-south axis. St-Roch is a treasure house of religious art ❼

Metro Pyramides

The Paris Convention and Visitors' Bureau

The Normandy is an elegant hotel in the Belle Epoque style, a form of graceful living that prevailed in Paris at the turn of the 20th century.

★ **Jardin des Tuileries**
Pony rides are a popular attraction in these formal gardens, which were designed by the royal gardener André Le Nôtre in the 17th century ⓫

Place des Pyramides
Frémiet's gilded statue of Joan of Arc is the focus of pilgrimage for royalists ❽

To the Quai du Louvre

Musée de la Mode et du Textile
The haute couture collections that are kept in this museum have given the Louvre a new role ❾

Musée des Arts Décoratifs
A highlight of the museum's displays of art and design is the Art Nouveau collection ⓫

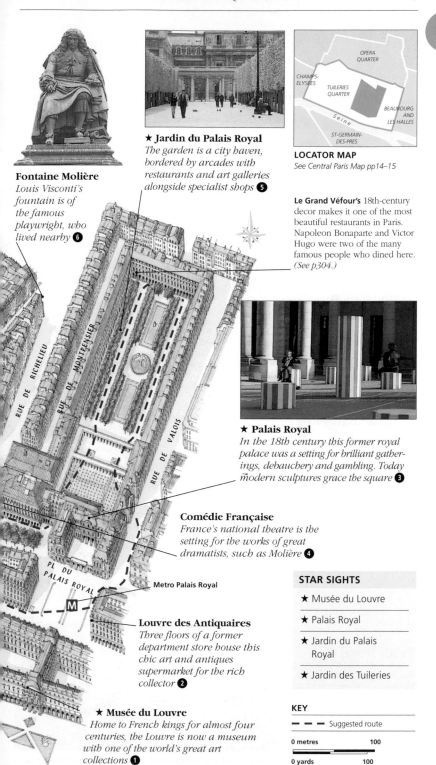

Fontaine Molière
Louis Visconti's fountain is of the famous playwright, who lived nearby 6

★ **Jardin du Palais Royal**
The garden is a city haven, bordered by arcades with restaurants and art galleries alongside specialist shops 5

LOCATOR MAP
See Central Paris Map pp14–15

Le Grand Véfour's 18th-century decor makes it one of the most beautiful restaurants in Paris. Napoleon Bonaparte and Victor Hugo were two of the many famous people who dined here. *(See p304.)*

★ **Palais Royal**
In the 18th century this former royal palace was a setting for brilliant gatherings, debauchery and gambling. Today modern sculptures grace the square 3

Comédie Française
France's national theatre is the setting for the works of great dramatists, such as Molière 4

Metro Palais Royal

Louvre des Antiquaires
Three floors of a former department store house this chic art and antiques supermarket for the rich collector 2

★ **Musée du Louvre**
Home to French kings for almost four centuries, the Louvre is now a museum with one of the world's great art collections 1

STAR SIGHTS

★ Musée du Louvre

★ Palais Royal

★ Jardin du Palais Royal

★ Jardin des Tuileries

KEY

− − − Suggested route

0 metres   100

0 yards   100

The five-arched Pont Royal linking the Louvre with the Left Bank

Musée du Louvre ❶

See pp122–9.

Louvre des Antiquaires ❷

2 Pl du Palais Royal 75001. **Map** 12 E2.
Tel 01 42 97 27 27. ⬛ 11am–7pm
Tue–Sun (Jul & Aug: Tue–Sat). ⬤ 1 Jan,
25 Dec. 🔟 🖥 See **Shopping**
pp336–7. **www**.louvre-antiquaires.com

One of the shops in the Louvre des Antiquaires market

A large department store – the Grands Magasins du Louvre – was converted at the end of the 1970s into this three-floor collection of art galleries and antique shops. Few bargains are found here, but the 250 shops of this chic market provide clues about what nouveaux riches collectors are seeking.

Palais Royal ❸

Pl du Palais Royal 75001. **Map** 12 E1.
Ⓜ Palais Royal. **Buildings not open**
to public.

This former royal palace has had a turbulent history. Starting out in the early 17th century as Richelieu's Palais Cardinale, it passed to the Crown on his death and became the childhood home of Louis XIV. Under the control of the 18th-century royal dukes of Orléans it was the scene of brilliant gatherings, interspersed with periods of debauchery and gambling. The cardinal's theatre, where Molière had performed, burned down in 1763, but was replaced by the Comédie Française. After the Revolution, the palace became a gambling house. It was reclaimed in 1815 by the future King Louis-Philippe, one of whose librarians was Alexandre Dumas. The building narrowly escaped the flames of the 1871 uprising.

After being restored again, between 1872 and 1876, the palace reverted to the state, and it now houses both the Council of State, the supreme legal body for administrative matters, and its more recent "partner", the Constitutional Council. Another wing of the palace is occupied by the Ministry of Culture.

Comédie Française ❹

1 Place Colette 75001. **Map** 12 E1. 📠
0825 101 680. Ⓜ Palais Royal. ⬤
for performances. ⬛ 9.30am, 10am,
10.30am Sat, Sun (01 44 58 13 16). 📷
📷 See **Entertainment** pp342–4.

A stone plaque to Pierre Corneille

Overlooking two charming, if traffic-choked, squares named after the writers Colette and André Malraux, sits France's national theatre. The company has its roots partly in Molière's 17th-century players. In the foyer is the armchair in which Molière collapsed, dying, on stage in 1673 (ironically while he was performing Le Malade Imaginaire – The Hypochondriac). Since the company's founding in 1680 by Louis XIV, the theatre has enjoyed state patronage as a centre of national culture, and it has been based in the present building since 1799. The repertoire includes works of Corneille, Racine, Molière and Shakespeare, as well as those of modern playwrights.

Daniel Buren's stone columns (1980s) in the Palais Royal courtyard

Jardin du Palais Royal ❺

Pl du Palais Royal 75001. **Map** 12 F1.
Ⓜ *Palais Royal.*

The present garden is about a third smaller than the original one, laid out by the royal gardener for Cardinal Richelieu in the 1630s. This is due to the construction, between 1781 and 1784, of 60 uniform houses bordering three sides of the square. Today restaurants, art galleries and specialist shops line the square, which maintains a strong literary history – Jean Cocteau, Colette and Jean Marais are among its famous recent residents.

Statue in the Jardin du Palais Royal

Fontaine Molière ❻

Rue de Richelieu 75001. **Map** 12 F1.
Ⓜ *Palais Royal.*

France's most famous playwright lived near here, in a house on the site of No. 40 Rue de Richelieu. The 19th-century fountain is by Louis Visconti, who also designed Napoleon's tomb at Les Invalides (*see pp188–9*).

St-Roch ❼

296 Rue St-Honoré 75001. **Map** 12 E1.
Tel *01 42 44 13 20.* Ⓜ *Tuileries.*
◯ *8am–7pm daily.* ● *non-religious public hols.* ✝ *Daily, times vary.*
Concerts. 📷

This huge church was designed by Lemercier, archi-tect of the Louvre, and its foundation stone was laid by

Vien's *St Denis Preaching to the Gauls* (1767) in St-Roch

Louis XIV in 1653. Jules Hardouin-Mansart added the large Lady Chapel with its richly decorated dome and ceiling in the 18th century and two further chapels extended the church to 126 m (413 ft), just short of Notre-Dame. It is a treasure house of religious art, much of it from now-vanished churches and monasteries. It also contains the tombs of the playwright Pierre Corneille, the royal gardener André Le Nôtre and the philosopher Denis Diderot. The facades reveal marks of Napoleon's attack, in 1795, on royalist troops who were defending the church steps.

Place des Pyramides ❽

75001. **Map** 12 E1. Ⓜ *Tuileries, Pyramides.*

Joan of Arc, wounded nearby fighting the English in 1429, is commemorated by a 19th-century equestrian statue by the sculptor Emmanuel Frémiet. The statue is a rallying point for royalists.

Musée de la Mode et du Textile ❾

107 Rue de Rivoli 75001. **Map** 12 E1.
Tel *01 44 55 57 50.* Ⓜ *Palais Royal, Tuileries.* ◯ *11am–6pm Tue–Fri; 10am–6pm Sat, Sun.* 📷 📷
www.ucad.fr

Set in the Louvre's Pavillon de Marsan, this museum promotes one of the city's oldest and most famous industries – fashion.

It houses an impressive collection of *haute couture* costumes and accessories and has become an important venue for temporary exhibitions of costumes.

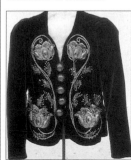

Schiaparelli jacket in the museum

Musée du Louvre **❶**

The Musée du Louvre, containing one of the most important art collections in the world, has a history extending back to medieval times. First constructed as a fortress in 1190 by King Philippe-Auguste to protect Paris against Viking raids, it lost its imposing keep in the reign of François I, who replaced it with a Renaissance-style building. Thereafter, four centuries of French kings and emperors improved and enlarged it. One of the more recent additions is a glass pyramid in the main courtyard from which all the galleries are reached.

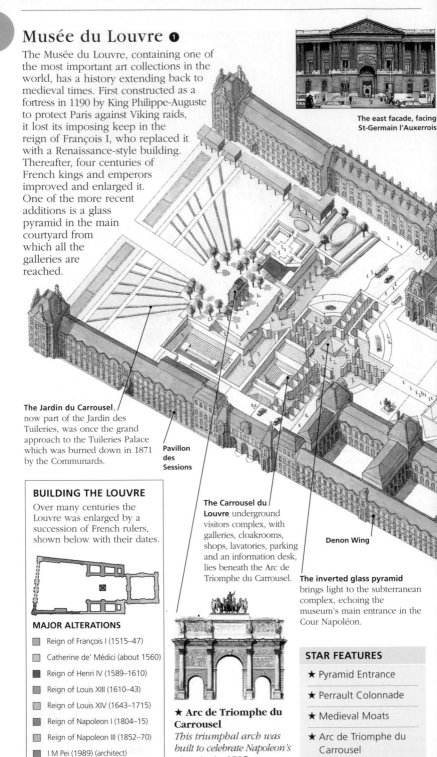

The east facade, facing St-Germain l'Auxerrois

The Jardin du Carrousel, now part of the Jardin des Tuileries, was once the grand approach to the Tuileries Palace which was burned down in 1871 by the Communards.

Pavillon des Sessions

The Carrousel du Louvre underground visitors complex, with galleries, cloakrooms, shops, lavatories, parking and an information desk, lies beneath the Arc de Triomphe du Carrousel.

Denon Wing

The inverted glass pyramid brings light to the subterranean complex, echoing the museum's main entrance in the Cour Napoléon.

BUILDING THE LOUVRE

Over many centuries the Louvre was enlarged by a succession of French rulers, shown below with their dates.

MAJOR ALTERATIONS

- ☐ Reign of François I (1515–47)
- ☐ Catherine de' Médici (about 1560)
- ☐ Reign of Henri IV (1589–1610)
- ☐ Reign of Louis XIII (1610–43)
- ☐ Reign of Louis XIV (1643–1715)
- ☐ Reign of Napoleon I (1804–15)
- ☐ Reign of Napoleon III (1852–70)
- ☐ I M Pei (1989) (architect)

★ **Arc de Triomphe du Carrousel**
This triumphal arch was built to celebrate Napoleon's victories in 1805.

STAR FEATURES

- ★ Pyramid Entrance
- ★ Perrault Colonnade
- ★ Medieval Moats
- ★ Arc de Triomphe du Carrousel

Pavillon Richelieu
This imposing 19th-century pavilion is part of the Richelieu Wing, once home to the Ministry of Finance but now converted into magnificent galleries.

VISITORS' CHECKLIST

Map 12 E2. Automatic ticket booths are located in the Carrousel du Louvre (99 Rue de Rivoli). 01 40 20 50 50. Palais Royal, Musée du Louvre. 21, 24, 27, 39, 48, 68, 69, 72, 81, 95. Châtelet-Les-Halles. Louvre. Carrousel du Louvre (entrance via Ave du General Lemonnier); Pl du Louvre, Rue St-Honoré. 9am–6pm Wed–Mon (to 10pm Wed, Fri). 1 Jan, 1 May, 25 Dec. (free 1st Sun of each month for under-18s, and Fri after 6pm for under-26s). partial (01 40 20 59 90). phone 01 40 20 52 09. **Lectures, films, concerts** (01 40 20 55 55). www.louvre.fr

Cour Marly is the glass-roofed courtyard that now houses the Marly Horses *(see p125).*

Richelieu Wing

★ Pyramid Entrance
The popular new main entrance, designed by the architect I M Pei, was opened in 1989.

Cour Puget

Cour Khorsabad

Sully Wing

Cour Carrée

★Perrault's Colonnade
The east facade with its majestic rows of columns was built by Claude Perrault, who worked on the Louvre with Louis Le Vau in the mid-17th century.

Cour Napoléon

The Salle des Caryatides
takes its name from the statues of women created by Jean Goujon in 1550 to support the upper gallery.

The Louvre of Charles V
In about 1360, Charles V transformed Philippe-Auguste's robust old fortress into a royal residence.

★ Medieval Moats
The base of the twin towers and the drawbridge support of Philippe-Auguste's fortress can be seen in the excavated area.

The Louvre's Collection

The Louvre's treasures can be traced back to the collection of François I (1515–47), who purchased many Italian paintings including the *Mona Lisa (La Gioconda)*. In Louis XIV's reign (1643–1715) there were a mere 200 works, but donations and purchases augmented the collection. The Louvre was first opened to the public in 1793 after the Revolution, and has been continually enriched ever since.

The Lacemaker
In this exquisite picture from about 1665, Jan Vermeer gives us a glimpse into everyday domestic life in Holland. The painting came to the Louvre in 1870.

The Raft of the Medusa *(1819)*
Théodore Géricault derived his inspiration for this gigantic and moving work from the shipwreck of a French frigate in 1816. The painting shows the moment when the few survivors sight a sail on the horizon.

Cour Marly

Richelieu Wing

Main entrance

GALLERY GUIDE

The main entrance is beneath the glass pyramid. From here corridors radiate out to the museum's wings. The works are displayed on four floors: the painting and sculpture collections are arranged by country of origin. There are separate departments for Oriental, Egyptian, Greek, Etruscan and Roman anti-quities, objets d'art and prints and drawings.

Underground visitors' complex

Pavillon des Sessions

Denon Wing

★ **Venus de Milo**
Found in 1820 on the island of Milo in Greece, this ideal of feminine beauty was made in the Hellenistic Age at the end of the 2nd century BC.

KEY TO FLOORPLAN

- ☐ Painting
- ☐ Objets d'art
- ☐ Sculpture
- ☐ Antiquities
- ☐ Non-exhibition space

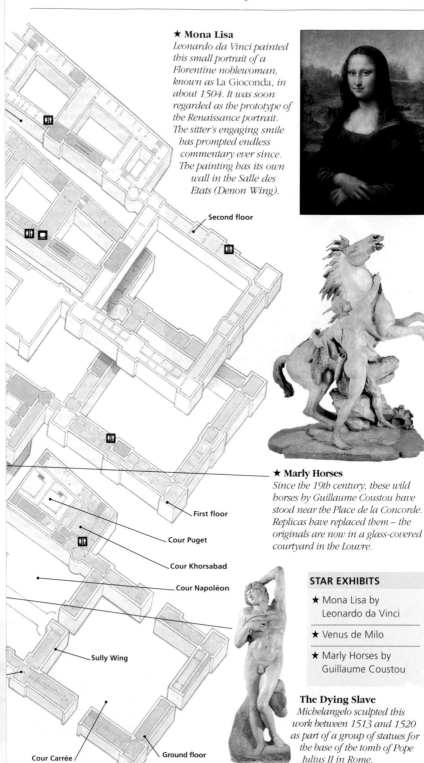

★ Mona Lisa

Leonardo da Vinci painted this small portrait of a Florentine noblewoman, known as La Gioconda, *in about 1504. It was soon regarded as the prototype of the Renaissance portrait. The sitter's engaging smile has prompted endless commentary ever since. The painting has its own wall in the Salle des Etats (Denon Wing).*

Second floor

First floor

Cour Puget

Cour Khorsabad

Cour Napoléon

Sully Wing

Cour Carrée

Ground floor

★ Marly Horses

Since the 19th century, these wild horses by Guillaume Coustou have stood near the Place de la Concorde. Replicas have replaced them – the originals are now in a glass-covered courtyard in the Louvre.

STAR EXHIBITS

★ Mona Lisa by Leonardo da Vinci

★ Venus de Milo

★ Marly Horses by Guillaume Coustou

The Dying Slave

Michelangelo sculpted this work between 1513 and 1520 as part of a group of statues for the base of the tomb of Pope Julius II in Rome.

ORIENTAL, EGYPTIAN, GREEK, ETRUSCAN AND ROMAN ANTIQUITIES

The range of antiquities in the Louvre is impressive. There are objects from the Neolithic period (about 6000 BC) to the fall of the Roman Empire. Important works of Mesopotamian art include the seated figure of Ebih-iI, from 2400 BC, and several portraits of Gudea, Prince of Lagash, from about 2255 BC. A black basalt block bearing the code of the Babylonian King Hammurabi, from about 1700 BC, is one of the world's oldest legal documents.

The warlike Assyrians are represented by delicate carvings and a spectacular reconstruction of part of Sargon II's (722–705 BC) palace with its huge, winged bulls. A fine example of Persian art is the enamelled brickwork depicting the king of Persia's personal guard of archers (5th century BC). It decorated his palace at Susa.

Most Egyptian art was made for the dead, who were provided with the things that they needed for the after-life. It often included vivid images of daily life in ancient Egypt. One example is the tiny funeral chapel built for a high official in about 2500 BC. It is covered with exquisite carvings: men in sailing ships, catching fish, tending cattle and fowl.

It is also possible to gain insights into family life in ancient Egypt through a number of life-like funeral portraits, like the squatting scribe, and several sculptures of married couples. The

Winged Victory of Samothrace (Greece, late 3rd–early 2nd century BC)

Etruscan Sarcophagus (6th century BC)

earliest sculpture dates from 2500 BC, the latest from 1400 BC.

From the New Kingdom (1555–1080 BC) a special crypt dedicated to the god Osiris contains some colossal sarcophagi, and a large number of mummified animals.

Some smaller objects of considerable charm include a 29-cm (11-inch) headless body of a woman, sensually outlined by the transparent veil of her dress and thought to be Queen Nefertiti (about 1365–1349 BC).

The department of Greek, Roman and Etruscan antiquities contains a vast array of fragments, among them some exceptional pieces. There is a large, geometric head from the Cyclades (2700 BC) and an elegant, swan-necked bowl, quite modern in its unadorned simplicity. It is hammered out of a single gold sheet and dates from about 2500 BC. The Archaic Greek period, from the 7th to the 5th century BC, is represented by the *Auxerre Goddess,* one of the earliest-known pieces of Greek sculpture, and the *Hera of Samos* from the Ionian Islands. From the height of the Classical Greek period (about the 5th century BC)

Winged Bull with Human Head from 8th century BC, found in Khorsabad, Assyria

there are several fine male torsos and heads such as the *Laborde Head.* This head has been identified as part of the sculpture that once decorated the west pediment of the Parthenon in Athens.

The two most famous Greek statues in the Louvre, the *Winged Victory of Samothrace* and the *Venus de Milo (see p 124),* belong to the Hellenistic period (late 3rd to 2nd century BC) when more natural-looking human forms were beginning to be produced.

The undisputed star of the Etruscan collection is the terracotta *Sarcophagus of the Cenestian Couple,* who appear

as though they are attending an eternal banquet.

The sculptures in the Roman section demonstrate the great debt owed to the art of ancient Greece. There are many fine pieces: a bust of Agrippa, a basalt head of Livia, the wife of Augustus, and a splendid, powerful bronze head of Emperor Hadrian from the 2nd century AD. This has the look of a true portrait, unlike so many Imperial heads which are uninspired and impersonal.

Squatting Scribe (Egyptian, about 2500 BC)

OBJETS D'ART

The term *objets d'art* (art objects) covers a vast range of "decorative art" objects: jewellery, furniture, clocks, watches, sundials, tapestries, miniatures, silver and glassware, cutlery, small French and Italian bronzes, Byzantine and Parisian carved ivory, Limoges enamels, porcelain, French and Italian stoneware, rugs, snuffboxes, scientific instruments and armour. The Louvre has well over 8,000 items, from many ages and regions.

Many of these precious objects were in the Abbey of St-Denis, where the kings of France were crowned. Long before the Revolution, a regular flow of visitors had made it something of a museum. After the Revolution all the objects were removed and presented to the nation. Much was lost or stolen during the move but what remains is still outstanding.

The treasures include a serpentine stone plate from the 1st century AD with a 9th-century border of gold and precious stones. (The plate itself is inlaid with eight golden dolphins.) There is also a porphyry vase which Suger, Abbot of St-Denis, had mounted in gold in the shape of an eagle, and the golden sceptre made for King Charles V in about 1380.

The French crown jewels include the coronation crowns of Louis XV and Napoleon, sceptres, swords and other accessories of the coronation ceremonies. On view is also the Regent, one of the purest diamonds in the world. It was bought in 1717 and worn by Louis XV at his coronation in 1722.

One whole room is taken up with a series of tapestries called the *Hunts of Maximilian,* which were originally executed for Emperor Charles V

The Eagle of Suger (mid-12th century)

in 1530 after drawings by Bernard Van Orley.

The large collection of French furniture ranges from the 16th to the 19th centuries and is assembled by period, or in rooms devoted to donations by distinguished collectors such as Isaac de Camondo. On display are important pieces by exceptionally prominent furniture-makers such as André-Charles Boulle, cabinet-maker to Louis XIV, who worked at the Louvre in the late 17th to mid-18th centuries. He is noted for his technique of inlaying copper and tortoiseshell. From a later date, the curious inlaid steel and bronze writing desk, created by Adam Weisweiler for Queen Marie-Antoinette in 1784, is one of the more unusual pieces in the museum's collection.

THE GLASS PYRAMID

Plans for the modernization and expansion of the Louvre were first conceived in 1981. They included the transfer of the Ministry of Finance from the Richelieu wing of the Louvre to new offices elsewhere, and a new main entrance to the museum. A Chinese-American architect, I M Pei, was chosen to design the changes. He designed the pyramid as both the focal point and new entrance to the Louvre. Made out of glass, it enables the visitor to see the historic buildings that surround it while allowing light down into the underground visitors' reception area.

Colonnaded entrance to the
Village Royale

Village Royal ⑱

75008. **Map** 5 C5. **M** *Madeleine.*
Galerie Royale ◯ *10am–7pm*
Tue–Sat. ◑ *public hols.*

This delightful enclave of
18th-century town houses sits
discreetly between the Rue
Royale and the Rue Boissy
d'Anglas. The Galerie Royale
is the former home of the
Duchess d'Abrantès. It was
converted in 1994 by architect
Laurent Bourgois who has
combined classical and
modern in superb style,
reflecting both the antique
glass- and silverware on
display and the contemporary
glassworkers and goldsmiths

who occupy the vaults. Beneath the original glass roof
in the central courtyard, a
statue of the goddess Pomona
is lit by fibre-optics and coloured with blue cabochons of
Bohemian crystal. There is also
a quiet, elegant Bernardaud
Porcelain tearoom.

Place Vendôme ⑲

75001. **Map** 6 D5 **M** *Tuileries.*

Perhaps the best example
of 18th-century elegance in
the city, the architect Jules
Hardouin-Mansart's royal
square was begun in 1698.
The original plan was to
house academies and
embassies behind the arcaded
facades. However, bankers
moved in and created opulent
homes. Miraculously the
square has remained virtually
intact, and is home to
jewellers and bankers. Among
the famous, Frederic Chopin
died here in 1848 at No. 12
and Cèsar Ritz established his
famous hotel at the turn of
the 20th century at No. 15.

Banque de France ⑳

39 Rue Croix des Petits Champs 75001.
Map 12 F1. **M** *Palais Royal.* ◯ *for
details phone 01 42 92 42 92.*

Founded by Napoleon in
1800, France's central bank is
housed in a building intended
for quite different purposes.
The 17th-century architect
François Mansart designed
this mansion for Louis XIII's
wealthy Secretary of State,

**Napoleon's
statue in Place
Vendôme**

FORMAL GARDENS IN PARIS

The South Parterre at Versailles *(see pp248–9)*

For the past 300 years the
main formal gardens in Paris
have been open to the public
and are a firm fixture in the
city's life. The Jardin des
Tuileries *(see p130)* will soon
be undergoing extensive
renovation and replanting;
the Jardin du Luxembourg
(see p172), the private
garden of the French Senate,
is still beloved of Left
Bankers; and the Jardin
du Palais Royal *(see p121)*
is enjoyed by those who
seek peace and privacy.
   French landscaping was
raised to an art form in the
17th century, thanks to Louis
XIV's talented landscaper
André Le Nôtre, who created
the gardens of Versailles *(see
pp248–9)*. He achieved a
brilliant marriage between the
traditional Italian Renaissance
garden and the French love
of rational design.
   The role of the French
garden architect was not to
tend nature but to transform
it, pruning and planting to

The long Galerie Dorée in the Banque de France

Louis de la Vrillière, with the sumptuous 50-m (164-ft) long Galerie Dorée specially created for hanging his great collection of historical paintings. The house was later sold to the Comte de Toulouse, son of Louis XIV and Madame de Montespan. The building was extensively reconstructed in the 19th century after the ravages of the Revolution. The bank's most famous modern alumnus is Jacques Delors, president of the European Commission 1985–1994.

Place des Victoires ㉑

75002. **Map** 12 F1. M *Palais Royal.*

This circle of elegant mansions was built in 1685 solely to offset the statue of Louis XIV by Desjardins, which was placed in the middle, with torches burning day and night. The proportions of the buildings and even the arrangement of the surrounding streets were all designed by the architect and courtier Jules Hardouin-Mansart to display the statue to its best advantage.

Unfortunately, the 1792 mobs were less sycophantic and tore down the statue. A replacement, of a different style, was erected in 1822, to the detriment of the whole system of proportions of buildings to statue. Yet the square retains much of the original design, and today it is the address of major names in the fashion business, most notably Thierry Mugler, Cacharel and Kenzo.

Louis XIV on Place des Victoires

A Bagatelle garden with floral colour *(see p255)*

create leafy sculptures out of trees, bushes and hedges. Complicated geometrical designs that were created in beds and paths were interspersed with pebbles and carefully thought-out splashes of floral colour. Symmetry and harmony were the landscaper's passwords, a sense of grandeur and magnificence his ultimate goal.

In the 17th century, as now, French formal gardens served two purposes: as a setting or backdrop for a château or palace, and for enjoyment. The best view of a formal garden was from the first floor of the château, from which the combination of boxwood hedges, flowers and gravel came together in an intricate, abstract pattern, a blossoming tapestry which complemented the château's interior. Paths of trees drew the eye into infinity, reminding the onlooker of how much land belonged to his host, and therefore establishing his undoubted wealth. So, early on the formal garden became a

status symbol, and it still is. This is obvious in both private gardens and in grand public projects. Napoleon Bonaparte completed his vista from the Jardin des Tuileries with a triumphal arch. The late President Mitterrand applied the principle in building his Grand Arc de la Défense *(see pp40–41, 255)* along the same axis as the Tuileries and Arc de Triomphe.

But formal gardens were also made to be enjoyed. People in the 17th century believed that walking in the fresh air kept them in good health. What more perfect spot than a formal garden bedecked with statues and fountains for additional entertainment. The old and infirm could be pushed around in sedan chairs and people could meet one another around a boxwood hedge or on a stone bench under the marbly gaze of the goddess Diana.

ST-GERMAIN-DES-PRES

This Left Bank area is fuller and livelier, its streets and cafés more crowded than when it was at the forefront of the city's intellectual life in the 1950s. The leading figures of the time have now gone, and the rebellious disciples have retreated to their bourgeois backgrounds. But the new philosophers are there, the radical young thinkers who emerged from the 1960s upheavals, and the area still has its major publishing houses, whose executives entertain treasured writers and agents at the celebrated cafés. But they now share the area with the smart set, those who patronize Yves St-Laurent's opulent premises and the elegant Rue Jacob's smart interior designers. On the south side of Boulevard St-Germain the streets are quiet and quaint, with lots of good restaurants, and at the Odéon end there are brassy cafés and a profusion of cinemas.

Musée d'Orsay clock

SIGHTS AT A GLANCE

Historic Buildings and Streets
Palais Abbatial ❷
Boulevard St-Germain ❼

Rue du Dragon ❽
Rue de l'Odéon ❿
Cour de Rohan ⓬
Cour du Commerce St-André ⓭
Institut de France ⓯
Ecole Nationale Supérieure des Beaux-Arts ⓰
Ecole Nationale d'Administration ⓱
Quai Voltaire ⓲

Churches
St-Germain-des-Prés ❶

Museums and Galleries
Musée Eugène Delacroix ❸
Musée de la Monnaie de Paris ⓮
Musée d'Orsay pp144–7 ⓳
Musée Nationale de la Légion d'Honneur ⓴

Theatres
Odéon Théâtre de L'Europe ⓫

Cafés and Restaurants
Les Deux Magots ❹
Café de Flore ❺
Brasserie Lipp ❻
Le Procope ❾

GETTING THERE
Metro stations St-Germain-des-Prés and Odéon and the RER station at Musée d'Orsay serve the area. Bus route 63 travels down Boulevard St-Germain, and 48 and 95 go along Rue Bonaparte. Routes 58 and 70 pass along Rue Mazarine.

KEY

▨	Street-by-Street map
Ⓜ	Metro station
▣	Batobus boarding point
RER	RER station

0 metres 400
0 yards 400

SEE ALSO

◁ **Les Deux Magots café beside the church of St-Germain-des-Prés**

Street-by-Street: St-Germain-des-Prés

Organ grinder in St-Germain

After World War II, St-Germain-des-Prés became synonymous with intellectual life centred around bars and cafés. Philosophers, writers, actors and musicians mingled in the cellar nightspots and brasseries, where existentialist philosophy co-existed with American jazz. The area is now smarter than in the heyday of Jean-Paul Sartre and Simone de Beauvoir, the haunting singer Juliette Greco and the New Wave film-makers.

The writers are still around, enjoying the pleasures of sitting in Les Deux Magots, Café de Flore and other haunts. The 17th-century buildings have survived, but signs of change are evident in the plethora of affluent shops dealing in antiques, books and fashion.

Les Deux Magots
The café is famous for the patronage of celebrities such as Hemingway ❹

Café de Flore
In the 1950s, French intellectuals wrestled with new philoso-phical ideas in the Art Deco interior of the café ❺

RUE DU DRAGON

RUE DU SABOT

RUE DE RENNES

RUE BONAPARTE

BOULEVARD ST

M

RUE BONAPARTE

RUE DU FOUR

Metro St-Germain-des-Prés

Brasserie Lipp
Colourful ceramics decorate this famous brasserie frequented by politicians ❻

★ **St-Germain-des-Prés**
Descartes and the king of Poland are among the notables buried here in Paris's oldest church ❶

★ **Boulevard St-Germain**
Café terraces, boutiques, cinemas, restaurants and bookshops characterize the central section of the Left Bank's main street ❼

Picasso's sculpture *Homage to Apollinaire is a tribute to the artist's friend, the poet Guillaume Apollinaire. It was erected in 1959, near the Café de Flore, where the poet held court.*

★ Musée Delacroix
Here, Delacroix created the splendid mural, Jacob Wrestling, *for St-Sulpice (see p172)* ❸

Rue de Fürstenberg is a tiny square with old-fashioned street lamps and shady trees. It is often used as a film setting.

LOCATOR MAP
See Central Paris Map pp14–15

STAR SIGHTS

★ St-Germain-des-Prés

★ Boulevard St-Germain

★ Musée Delacroix

KEY

– – – Suggested route

0 metres   100
0 yards   100

Rue de Buci was for centuries an important Left Bank street and the site of some Real Tennis courts. It now holds a lively market every day.

Palais Abbatial
This was the residence of abbots from 1586 till the 1789 Revolution ❷

Metro Odéon

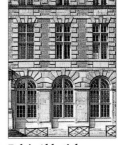

Metro Mabillon

Marché St-Germain is an old covered food market which was opened in 1818, taking over the site of a former fairground. *(See p334.)*

Danton's statue *(1889), by Auguste Paris, is a tribute to the Revolutionary leader.*

St-Germain-des-Prés ❶

3 Pl St-Germain-des-Prés 75006. **Map**
12 E4. **Tel** 01 55 42 81 33. Ⓜ St-
Germain-des-Prés. ◯ 8am–7pm
daily. **Concerts** 8pm Tue, Thu 🎫 🚻

This is the oldest church in
Paris, originating in 542
when King Childebert built
a basilica to house holy relics.
This became an immensely
powerful Benedictine abbey,
which was suppressed during
the Revolution, when most of
the buildings were destroyed
by a fire in 1794. One of the
Revolution's most horrific
episodes took place in a
nearby monastery when 318
priests were hacked to death
by the mob on 3
September 1792.
The present
church dates from
about the 11th
century and was
heavily restored
in the 19th
century. One of
the three original
towers survives,
housing one of
the oldest belfries
in France. The
interior of the
church is an
interesting mix of
architectural styles,
with some 6th-
century marble
columns, Gothic
vaulting and
Romanesque
arches. Famous tombs include
those of the 17th-century
philosopher René Descartes,
the poet Nicolas Boileau and
John Casimir, king of Poland,
who later became abbot of St-
Germain-des-Prés in 1669.

**Our Lady of
Consolation statue
in St-Germain-
des-Prés**

Palais Abbatial ❷

1–5 Rue de l'Abbaye 75006.
Map 12 E4. Ⓜ St-Germain-des-Prés.
Not open to the public.

This brick and stone palace
was built in 1586 for Charles
of Bourbon who was
cardinal-abbot of St-Germain
and, very briefly, king of
France. Ten more abbots
lived there until the Revolution, when the building was

**An ironwork detail from the
facade of the Palais Abbatial**

sold. James Pradier, the 19th-
century sculptor who was
famous for his female figures,
established a studio here.
The palace is now noted
for its mixture of building
materials and its splendid
vertical windows.

Musée Eugène Delacroix ❸

6 Rue de Fürstenberg 75006.
Map 12 E4. **Tel** 01 44 41 86 50.
Ⓜ St-Germain-des-Prés. ◯ 9.30am–
5pm Wed–Mon (last adm: 4.30pm).
🎫 🚻 **www**.musee-delacroix.fr

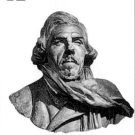
Eugène Delacroix

The leading non-conformist
Romantic painter, Eugène
Delacroix, known for his
passionate and highly-
coloured canvases, lived and
worked here from 1857 to his
death in 1863. Here he
painted *The Entombment
of Christ* and *The Way to
Calvary* (which now hang in
the museum). He also created
superb murals for the Chapel
of the Holy Angels in the
nearby St-Sulpice church,
which is part of the reason
why he moved to this area.

The first-floor apartment and
garden studio now form a
national museum, where
regular exhibitions of
Delacroix's work are held.
The apartment has a portrait
of George Sand, self-portraits,
studies for future works and
artistic memorabilia.
The charm of Delacroix's
garden is reflected in the tiny
Fürstenberg square. With its
pair of rare catalpa trees and
old-fashioned street lamps,
the square is one of Paris's
most romantic corners.

Les Deux Magots ❹

6 Pl St-Germain-des-Prés 75006.
Map 12 E4. **Tel** 01 45 48 55 25.
Ⓜ St-Germain-des-Prés.
◯ 7.30am–1am daily.
⏺ for one week in Jan.
www.lesdeuxmagots.com

The café still trades on its
reputation as the meeting place
of the city's literary and
intellectual elite. This derives
from the patronage of
Surrealist artists and writers
including Ernest Hemingway
in the 1920s and 1930s, and
existentialist philosophers and
writers in the 1950s.
The present clientele is
more likely to be publishers
or people-watchers than the
new Hemingway. The café's
name comes from the two
wooden statues of Chinese
commercial agents *(magots)*
that adorn one of the pillars.
This is a good place for
enjoying an old-fashioned hot
chocolate and watching the
world go by.

The interior of Les Deux Magots

Facade of the Café de Flore, former meeting-place of existentialists

Café de Flore ❺

172 Blvd St-Germain 75006.
Map 12 D4. **Tel** 01 45 48 55 26.
Ⓜ St-Germain-des-Prés. ◯ 7.30am–
1.30am daily. ♿ restricted.
www.cafe-de-flore.com

The classic Art Deco interior
of this café, all-red seating,
mahogany and mirrors, has
changed little since the war.
Like its rival Les Deux
Magots, Café de Flore has
hosted most of the French
intellectuals during the post-
war years. Jean-Paul Sartre
and Simone de Beauvoir
developed their philosophy
of existentialism here.

A waiter at the Brasserie Lipp

Brasserie Lipp ❻

151 Blvd St-Germain 75006.
Map 12 E4. **Tel** 01 45 48 72 93.
Ⓜ St-Germain-des-Prés.
◯ 11.45am–2am daily. (See p305.)
www.brasserie-lipp.fr

Third of the famous cafés
around St-Germain-des-Prés,
Brasserie Lipp combines
Alsatian beer, sauerkraut and
sausages (it was founded by
a refugee from Alsace) with
excellent coffee to produce a
Left Bank fixture popular with

French politicians and fashion
gurus as well as visitors.
Originally opened in the late
19th century, it is regarded by
many as the quintessential
Parisian brasserie, although
the experience is more
atmospheric than culinary
these days. The interior is
bright with ceramic tiles
of parrots and cranes.

Boulevard St-Germain ❼

75006, 75007. **Map** 11 C2 &
13 C5. Ⓜ Solférino, Rue du Bac, St-
Germain-des-Prés, Mabillon, Odéon.

The left bank's most
celebrated thoroughfare, over
3 km (2 miles) long, curves
across three districts from the
Ile St-Louis to the Pont de la
Concorde. The architecture
is homogeneous because
the boulevard was another
of Baron Haussmann's bold
strokes of 19th-century urban
planning, but it encompasses
a wide range of different
lifestyles as well as a number
of religious and cultural
institutions. From the east
(the low street numbers) the

boulevard passes the late
François Mitterrand's private
town residence in the Rue de
Bièvre, as well as the
Maubert-Mutualité market
square, the Musée de Cluny
and the Sorbonne university,
before crossing the lively
Boulevard St-Michel.

It continues past the Ecole
de Médecine and the Place de
l'Odéon to St-Germain-des-
Prés, with its historic church
and café terraces. Fashion
boutiques, cinemas, restaurants
and bookshops give this
central portion its distinctive
character. It is also here that
one is most likely to see a
celebrity. The area is active
from midday to the early
morning hours.

Continuing further, beyond
this section the boulevard
becomes more exclusively
residential and then distinctly
political with the Ministry of
Defence and the National
Assembly buildings.

Rue du Dragon ❽

75006. **Map** 12 D4.
Ⓜ St-Germain-des-Prés.

This short street, between the
Boulevard St-Germain and the
Carrefour de la Croix Rouge,
dates back to the Middle Ages
and still has houses from the
17th and 18th centuries.
Notice their large doors, tall
windows and ironwork
balconies. A group of Flemish
painters lived at No. 37 before
the Revolution. The novelist
Victor Hugo rented a garret
at No. 30 when he was a
19-year-old bachelor.

A plaque at No. 30 Rue du Dragon commemorating Victor Hugo's house

THE CELEBRATED CAFES OF PARIS

One of the most enduring images of Paris is the café scene. For the visitor it is the romantic vision of great artists, writers or eminent intellectuals consorting in one of the Left Bank's celebrated cafés. For the Parisian the café is one of life's constants, an everyday experience, providing people with a place to tryst, drink and meet friends, or to conclude business deals, or to simply watch the world go by.

The first café anywhere can be traced back to 1686, when the café Le Procope *(see p140)* was opened. In the following century cafés became a vital part of Paris's social life. And with the widening of the city's streets, particularly during the 19th century and the building of Haussmann's Grands Boulevards, the cafés spread out on to the pavements, evoking Emile Zola's comment as to the "great silent crowds watching the street live".

The nature of a café was sometimes determined by the interests of its patrons. Some were the gathering places for those interested in playing chess, dominoes or billiards. Literary gents gathered in Le Procope during Molière's time in the 17th century. In the 19th century, First Empire Imperial guards officers were drawn to the Café d'Orsay and Second Empire financiers gathered in the cafés along the Rue de la Chaussée d'Antin. The smart set patronized the Café de Paris and Café Tortini, and theatre-goers met at the cafés around the Opéra, including the Café de la Paix *(see p213)*.

Newspaper reading is still a typical café pastime

Ecole Nationale d'Administration ⑰

13 Rue de l'Université 75007.
Map 12 D3. **Tel** *01 49 26 45 45.*
Ⓜ *Rue du Bac.* ◯ *to the public.*

This fine 18th-century mansion was originally built as two houses in 1643 by Briçonnet. In 1713 they were replaced by a *hôtel,* built by Thomas Gobert for the widow of Denis Feydeau de Brou. It was passed on to her son, Paul-Espirit Feydeau de Brou, until his death in 1767. The *hôtel* then became the residence of the Venetian ambassador. It was occupied by Belzunce in 1787 and became a munitions depot during the Revolution until the restoration of the monarchy in 1815.

Until recently it housed the Ecole Nationale d'Administration (now in Strasbourg), where a high percentage of the elite in politics, economics and science were once students.

Plaque marking the house in Quai Voltaire where Voltaire died

Quai Voltaire ⑱

75006 and 75007. **Map** 12 D3.
Ⓜ *Rue du Bac.*

Formerly part of the Quai Malaquais, then later known as the Quai des Théatins, the Quai Voltaire is now home to some of the most important antiques dealers in Paris. It is also noted for its attractive 18th-century houses and for the famous people who lived in many of them, making it an especially interesting and pleasant street to walk along.

The 18th-century Swedish ambassador Count Tessin lived at No. 1, as did the sculptor James Pradier, famed for his statues and for his wife, who swam naked across the Seine. Louise de Kérouaille, spy for Louis XIV and created Duchess of Portsmouth by the infatuated Charles II of England, lived at Nos. 3–5.

Famous past residents of No. 19 included the composers Richard Wagner and Jean Sibelius, the novelist Charles Baudelaire and the exiled Irish writer and wit Oscar Wilde.

The French philosopher Voltaire died at No. 27, the Hôtel de la Villette. St-Sulpice, the local church, refused to accept his corpse (on the grounds of his atheism) and his body was rushed into the country to avoid a pauper's grave.

Entertainment in the Claude Alain café in the Rue de Seine during the 1950s

The most famous cafés are on the Left Bank, in St-Germain and Montparnasse, where the literati of old used to gather and where the glitterati of today love to be seen. Before World War I, Montparnasse was haunted by hordes of Russian revolutionaries, most eminently Lenin and Trotsky, who whiled away their days in the cafés, grappling with the problems of Russia and the world over a *petit café*. Cultural life flourished in the 1920s, when Surrealists, like Salvador Dalí and Jean Cocteau, dominated café life, and later when American writers led by Ernest Hemingway and Scott Fitzgerald talked, drank and worked in various cafés, among them La Coupole *(see p178)*, Le Sélect and La Closerie des Lilas *(see p179)*.

After the end of World War II, the cultural scene shifted northwards to St-Germain. Existentialism had become the dominant creed and Jean-Paul Sartre its tiny charismatic leader. Sartre and his intellectual peers and followers, among them the writers Simone de Beauvoir and Albert Camus, the poet Boris Vian and the enigmatic singer Juliette Greco, gathered to work and discuss their ideas in Les Deux Magots *(see p138)* and the nearby rival Café de Flore *(see p139)*. The traditional habitué of these cafés is still to be seen, albeit mixing with the international jet-set and with self-publicizing intellectuals hunched over their notebooks.

Works by one of St-Germain's elite, Albert Camus (1913–60)

Musée d'Orsay ⑲

See pp144–7.

Musée Nationale de la Légion d'Honneur ⑳

2 Rue de Bellechasse (2 Rue de la Légion d'Honneur) 75007. **Map** 11 C2. *Tel* 01 40 62 84 25. Ⓜ Solférino. RER Musée d'Orsay. ◯ call for opening times. **www**.legiondhonneur.fr

Next to the Musée d'Orsay is the truly massive Hôtel de Salm. It was one of the last great mansions to be built in the area (1782). The first owner was a German count, Prince de Salm-Kyrbourg, who was guillotined in 1794.

Napoleon III's Great Cross of the Legion of Honour

The Musée d'Orsay, converted from a railway station into a museum

Today the building contains a museum where one can learn all about the Legion of Honour, a decoration launched by Napoleon I and so cherished by the French (and foreigners). Those awarded the honour wear a small red rosette in their buttonhole. The impressive displays of medals and insignia are complemented by paintings. In one of the rooms, Napoleon's Legion of Honour is on display with his sword and breastplate.

The museum also covers decorations from most parts of the world, among them the British Victoria Cross and the American Purple Heart.

Musée d'Orsay ⑲

In 1986, 47 years after it had closed as a mainline railway station, Victor Laloux's superb turn-of-the-century building was reopened as the Musée d'Orsay. Commissioned by the Orléans railway company to be its Paris terminus, it avoided demolition in the 1970s following the outcry over the destruction of Baltard's pavilions at Les Halles food market. During the conversion much of the original architecture was retained. The museum, which is currently undergoing extensive renovation, was set up to present each of the arts of the period from 1848 to 1914 in the context of the contemporary society and all the forms of creative activity happening at the time.

The Museum, from the Right Bank
Victor Laloux designed the building for the Universal Exhibition in 1900.

Chair by Charles Rennie Mackintosh
The style developed by Mackintosh was an attempt to express ideas in a framework of vertical and horizontal forms, as in this tearoom chair (1900).

★ **The Gates of Hell** *(1880–1917)*
Rodin included figures that he had already created, such as The Thinker and The Kiss, in this famous gateway.

★ **Le Déjeuner sur l'Herbe** *(1863)*
Manet's painting, first exhibited in Napoleon III's Salon des Refusés, is presently on display in the first area of the upper level.

KEY TO FLOORPLAN

- ☐ Architecture & Decorative Arts
- ☐ Sculpture
- ☐ Painting before 1870
- ☐ Impressionism
- ☐ Neo-Impressionism
- ☐ Naturalism and Symbolism
- ☐ Art Nouveau
- ☐ Temporary exhibitions
- ☐ Non-exhibition space

GALLERY GUIDE

The collection occupies three levels. On the ground floor there are works from the mid to late 19th century. The middle level features Art Nouveau decorative art and a range of paintings and sculptures from the second half of the 19th century to the early 20th century. The upper level has an outstanding collection of Impressionist and Neo-Impressionist art.

The Dance *(1867–8)*
Carpeaux's sculpture caused a scandal when first exhibited.

★ Dancing at the Moulin de la Galette
To capture the dappled light filtering through the trees, Renoir painted this colourful picture (1876) out in the open in Montmartre.

VISITORS' CHECKLIST

Quai Anatole France.
Map 12 D2. **Tel** *01 40 49 48 14 (groups 01 53 63 04 50).*
M *Solférino.* 🚌 *24, 68, 69, 84 to Quai A. France; 73 to Rue Solférino; 63, 83, 84, 94 to Blvd St-Germain.*
RER *Musée d'Orsay.*
🅿 *Rue du Bac, Blvd St-Germain.*
🕐 *9am–6pm Tue–Sun (to 9.45pm Thu).* ● *1 Jan, 1 May, 25 Dec.* 🖼 🔊 🛗 ✎ 🎧
Concerts. 🍴 📷 📱
www.musee-orsay.fr

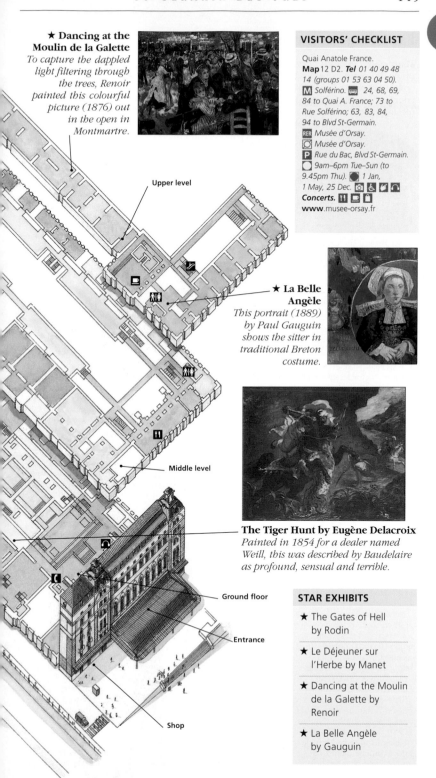

★ La Belle Angèle
This portrait (1889) by Paul Gauguin shows the sitter in traditional Breton costume.

Upper level

Middle level

The Tiger Hunt by Eugène Delacroix
Painted in 1854 for a dealer named Weill, this was described by Baudelaire as profound, sensual and terrible.

Ground floor

Entrance

Shop

STAR EXHIBITS

★ The Gates of Hell by Rodin

★ Le Déjeuner sur l'Herbe by Manet

★ Dancing at the Moulin de la Galette by Renoir

★ La Belle Angèle by Gauguin

Exploring the Orsay

Many of the exhibits now in the Musée d'Orsay originally came from the Louvre, and the superb collection of Impressionist art that was housed in the cramped Jeu de Paume until it closed in 1986 has been rehung here. In addition to the main exhibition, there are displays that explain the social, political and technological context in which the art was created, including exhibits on the history of cinematography.

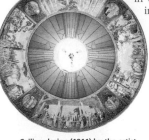

Ceiling design (1911) by the artist and designer Maurice Denis

ART NOUVEAU

The Belgian architect and designer Victor Horta was among the first to give free rein to the sinuous line that gave Art Nouveau its French sobriquet of *Style Nouille* (noodle style). Taking its name from a gallery of modern design that opened in Paris in 1895, Art Nouveau flourished throughout Europe until World War I.

In Vienna, Otto Wagner, Koloman Moser and Josef Hoffmann combined high craft with the new design, while the School of Glasgow, under the impetus of Charles Rennie Mackintosh, developed a more rectilinear approach which anticipated the work of Frank Lloyd Wright in the United States.

René Lalique introduced the aesthetics of Art Nouveau into jewellery and glassware, while Hector Guimard, inspired by Horta, is most famous today for his once-ubiquitous Art Nouveau entrances to the Paris metro.

One exhibit not to be missed is the carved wooden bookcase by Rupert Carabin (1890), with its proliferation of allegorical seated female nudes, bronze palm fronds and severed bearded heads.

SCULPTURE

The museum's central aisle overflows with an oddly-assorted selection of sculptures. These illustrate the eclectic mood around the middle of the 19th century when the Classicism of Eugène Guillaume's *Cenotaph of the Gracchi* (1848–53) co-existed with the Romanticism of François Rude. Rude created the relief on the Arc de Triomphe (1836), often referred to as *La Marseillaise (see p209).*

There is a wonderful series of 36 busts of members of parliament (1832) – bloated, ugly, unscrupulous and self-important – by the satirist Honoré Daumier, and work by the vital but short-lived genius Jean-Baptiste Carpeaux, whose first major bronze, *Count Ugolino* (1862), was a character from Dante. In 1868 he produced his Dionysian delight, *The Dance,* which caused a storm of protest: it was "an insult to public morals". This contrasts with the derivative and mannered work of such sculptors as Alexandre Falguière and Hyppolyte Moulin.

Edgar Degas' famous *Young Dancer of Fourteen* (1881) was displayed during his lifetime, but the many bronzes on show were made from wax sculptures found in his

studio after his death. In contrast, the sculpture of Auguste Rodin was very much in the public eye, and his sensuous and forceful work makes him pre-eminent among 19th-century sculptors. The museum contains many of his works, including the original plaster of *Balzac* (1897). Rodin's talented companion, Camille Claudel, who spent much of her life in an asylum, is represented by a grim allegory of mortality, *Maturity* (1899–1903).

The turn of the 20th century is marked by the work of Emile-Antoine Bourdelle and Aristide Maillol.

PAINTING BEFORE 1870

The surprising diversity of styles in 19th-century painting is emphasized by the close juxtaposition on the ground floor of all paintings prior to 1870 – the crucial year in which Impressionism first made a name for itself. The raging colour and almost Expressionistic vigour of Eugène Delacroix's *Lion Hunt* (1854) stands next to Jean-Dominiques Ingres' cool Classical *The Spring* (1820–56). As a reminder of the academic manner that dominated the century up to that point, the uninspired waxwork style of Thomas Couture's monumental *The Romans in the Age of Decadence* (1847) dominates the central aisle. In a class of their own are Edouard Manet's provocative *Olympia* and *Le Déjeuner sur l'Herbe* (1863), while works painted around the same time by his friends, Claude Monet, Pierre-Auguste Renoir, Frédéric Bazille and Alfred Sisley, give a glimpse of the Impressionists before the Impressionist movement began.

Young Dancer of Fourteen (1881) by Edgar Degas

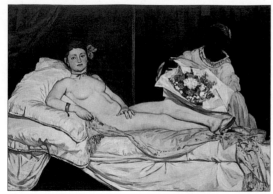

Olympia (1863) by Edouard Manet

IMPRESSIONISM

Rouen Cathedral caught at various moments of the day (1892–3) is one of the many works on show by Claude Monet, the leading figure of the Impressionist movement. Pierre-Auguste Renoir's plump nudes and his young people *Dancing at the Moulin de la Galette* (1876) were painted at the high point of his Impressionist period. Other artists on display include Camille Pissarro, Alfred Sisley and Mary Cassatt.

Edgar Degas, Paul Cézanne and Vincent Van Gogh are included here although their techniques differed from those of the Impressionists. Degas often favoured crisp Realism, though he was quite capable of using the sketchy manner of the Impressionists, as, for instance, in *L'Absinthe* (1876). Cézanne was more concerned with substance than light, as can be seen in his *Apples and*

Oranges (1895–1900). Van Gogh was momentarily influenced by the movement but then went his own way, illustrated here by works from the collection of Dr Gachet.

Breton Peasant Women (1894) by Paul Gauguin

NEO-IMPRESSIONISM

Although labelled Neo-Impressionism, the work of Georges Seurat (which includes *The Circus* from 1891) was quite unrelated to the older movement. He, along with Maximilien Luce and Paul Signac, painted by applying small dots of colour that blended together when viewed from a distance. *Jane Avril Dancing* (1892) is just one of many pictures by Henri de Toulouse-Lautrec on display. The work Paul Gauguin did at Pont-Aven in Brittany is shown next to that of younger artists who

Blue Waterlilies (1919) by Claude Monet

knew him at the time, such as Emile Bernard and the Nabis group. There are also a number of paintings from his Tahitian period.

The Nabis (which included Pierre Bonnard) tended to treat the canvas as a flat surface out of which a sense of depth emerged as the viewer gazed upon it.

The dream-like visions of Odilon Redon are in the Symbolist vein, while the naïve art of Henri (Douanier) Rousseau is represented by *War* (1894) and *The Snake Charmer* (1907).

NATURALISM AND SYMBOLISM

Three large rooms are devoted to paintings that filled the Salons from 1880 to 1900. The work of the Naturalists was sanctioned by the Third Republic and widely reproduced at the time. Fernand Cormon's figure of *Cain* was highly acclaimed when it first appeared in the 1880 Salon. Jules Bastien-Lepage's interest lay in illustrating peasant life, and in 1877 he painted *Haymaking*, which established him as one of the leading Naturalists. His fairly free handling of paint was influenced by what he had learned from Manet and his friends. More sombrely (and effectively) naturalistic is Lionel Walden's view of *The Docks of Cardiff* (1894).

Symbolism developed as a reaction against Realism and Impressionism and tended to be dominated by images of dreams and thoughts. This resulted in a wide variety of subjects and modes of expression. There is the over-sweet vision of levitating harpists, *Serenity* by Henri Martin (1899), Edward Burne-Jones' monumental work *Wheel of Fortune* (1883) and Jean Delville's *School of Plato* (1898). One of the most evocative paintings in this section is Winslow Homer's lyrical *Summer Night* (1890).

LATIN QUARTER

15th-century stained glass in Musée de Cluny

Student book shops, cafés, cinemas and jazz clubs fill this ancient, riverside quarter between the Seine and the Luxembourg Gardens. Famous institutes of learning abound, among them the two most prestigious *lycées*, Henri IV and Louis le Grand, through which passes a large percentage of the future French elite.

As the leaders of the 1968 revolt *(see pp40–41)* disappeared into the mainstream of French life, so the Boulevard St-Michel, the area's spine, turned increasingly to commerce, not demonstrations. Today, there are cheap shops and fast-food outlets, and the maze of narrow, cobbled streets off the boulevard are full of inexpensive ethnic shops, quirky boutiques and avant-garde theatres and cinemas. But the area's 800 years of history are difficult to efface. The Sorbonne retains much of its old character and the eastern half of the area has streets dating back to the 13th century. And the Rue St-Jacques still remains, the long Roman road stretching out of the city, and the forerunner of all the city's streets.

A young musician playing music under the Pont St-Michel is part of the Latin Quarter's long tradition as a focus for the young from all walks of life.

SIGHTS AT A GLANCE

Historic Buildings and Streets
Boulevard St-Michel ❷
La Sorbonne ❼
Collège de France ❽

Museums and Galleries
Musée National du Moyen Age pp154–7 ❶
Musée de la Préfecture de Police ❻

GETTING THERE
Metro stations in the area include those at St-Michel and Cluny La Sorbonne. The Balabus and routes 24 and 87 travel along Blvd St-Germain, and 38 travels along Blvd St-Michel, passing the Sorbonne and the Musée National du Moyen Age.

Churches and Temples
St-Séverin ❸
St-Julien-le-Pauvre ❹

Squares
Place Maubert ❺

Eglise de la Sorbonne ❾
St-Etienne-du-Mont ❿
Panthéon pp158–9 ⓫

KEY

	Street-by-Street map
M	Metro station
⊡	Batobus boarding point
RER	RER station

SEE ALSO

• *Street Finder*, map 12, 13, 17
• *Where to Stay* p287
• *Restaurants* p306

◁ A peaceful spot along a Latin Quarter quay

Street-by-Street: Latin Quarter

Since the Middle Ages this riverside quarter has been dominated by the Sorbonne, and acquired its name from the early Latin-speaking students. It dates back to the Roman town across from the Ile de la Cité; at that time the Rue St-Jacques was one of the main roads out of Paris. The area is generally associated with artists, intellectuals and the bohemian way of life; it also has a history of political unrest. In 1871, the Place St-Michel became the centre of the Paris Commune, and in May 1968 it was the site of the student uprisings. Today the eastern half has become sufficiently chic, however, to contain the homes of some of the Establishment.

Place St-Michel contains a fountain by Davioud. The bronze statue by Duret shows St Michael killing the dragon.

Metro St-Michel

Little Athens is a lively place in the evening, especially at the weekend, when the Greek restaurants situated in the picturesque streets around St-Séverin are at their busiest.

Metro Cluny La Sorbonne

★ **Boulevard St-Michel**
The northern end of the Boul'Mich, as it is affectionately known, is a lively mélange of cafés, book and clothes shops, with nightclubs and experimental cinemas nearby ❷

★ **Musée National du Moyen Age**
One of the finest collections of medieval art in the world is kept here in a superb late 15th-century building ❶

No. 22 Rue St-Séverin is the narrowest house in Paris and used to be the residence of Abbé Prévost, author of *Manon Lescaut*.

★ **St-Séverin**
*Begun in the 13th century,
this beautiful church took
three centuries to build and
is a fine example of the
flamboyant Gothic style* ❸

Rue du Chat qui Pêche is a
narrow pedestrianized street
which has changed little in its
200-year history.

LOCATOR MAP
See Central Paris Map pp14–15

Shakespeare & Co *(see
pp331-2)* at No.37 Rue
de la Bûcherie is a
delightful, if chaotic,
bookshop. Any books
purchased here are
stamped with
*Shakespeare & Co
Kilomètre Zéro Paris.*

★ **St-Julien-le-Pauvre**
*Rebuilt in the 17th
century, this church was
used to store animal feed
during the Revolution* ❹

Rue de Fouarre
used to host
lectures in the
Middle Ages. The
students sat on straw
(fouarre) in the street.

M Metro
Maubert
Mutualité

Rue Galande was home
to the rich and chic
in the 17th century,
but subsequently
became notorious for
its taverns.

STAR SIGHTS

★ Musée de Cluny

★ St-Séverin

★ St-Julien-le-Pauvre

★ Boulevard
St-Michel

KEY

 Suggested route

0 metres   100

0 yards   100

Musée National du Moyen Age **1**

See pp154–7.

Boulevard St-Michel **2**

75005 & 75006. **Map** 12 F5 & 16 F2.
M *St-Michel, Cluny-La Sorbonne.*
RER *Luxembourg.*

Cut through the area in 1869, the boulevard initially gained fame from its many literary cafés, but nowadays many have been replaced by clothes shops. Nos. 60–64 house the Ecole Nationale Supérieure des Mines, one of France's leading engineering schools *(see p173)*. In the Place St-Michel, marble plaques commemorate the many students who died here in 1944 fighting the Nazis.

Gargoyles adorning St-Séverin

St-Séverin **3**

1 Rue-des-Prêtres-St-Séverin 75005.
Map 13 A4. **Tel** 01 42 34 93 50.
M *St-Michel.* 11am–7.30pm daily.
Concerts.

One of the most beautiful churches in Paris, St-Séverin is a perfect example of the Flamboyant Gothic style. It is named after a 6th-century hermit who lived in the area and persuaded the future St Cloud, grandson of King Clovis, to take holy orders. Construction finished in the early 16th century and included a remarkable double ambulatory circling the chancel. In 1684 the Grande

Inside St-Julien-le-Pauvre

Mademoiselle, cousin to Louis XIV, adopted St-Séverin after breaking with her parish church of St-Sulpice and had the chancel modernized.

The burial ground here, which is now a garden, was the site of the first operation for gall stones in 1474. An archer who had been condemned to death was offered his freedom by Louis XI if he consented to the operation and lived. (It was a success, and the archer went free.) In the garden stands the church's medieval gable-roofed charnel house.

St-Julien-le-Pauvre **4**

1 Rue St-Julien-le-Pauvre 75005.
Map 13 A4. **Tel** 01 43 54 52 16.
M *St-Michel.* 9.30am–1.30pm, 3pm–6pm daily. **Concerts.**
See **Entertainment** p336.

At least three saints can claim to be patron of this church, but the most likely is St Julian the Hospitaller. The church, together with St-Germain-des-Prés, is one of the oldest in Paris, dating from between 1165 and 1220. The university held its official meetings in the church until 1524, when a student protest created so much damage that university meetings were barred from the church by parliament. Since 1889 it has belonged to the Melchite sect of the Greek Orthodox Church, and it is now the setting for chamber and religious music concerts.

Place Maubert **5**

75005. **Map** 13 A5.
M *Maubert-Mutualité.*

From the 12th to the middle of the 13th century, "La Maub" was one of Paris's scholastic centres, with lectures given in the open air. After the scholars moved to the new colleges of the Montagne St-Geneviève, the square became a place of torture and execution, including that of the philosopher Etienne Dolet, who was burnt at the stake in 1546.

So many Protestants were burnt here in the 16th century that it became a place of pilgrimage for the followers of the new faith. Its dark reputation has been replaced by respectability and a notable street market.

Musée de la Préfecture de Police **6**

4 Rue de la Montagne Ste-Geneviève 75005. **Map** 13 A5.
Tel 01 44 41 52 50. M *Maubert-Mutualité.* 9am–5pm Mon–Fri; 10am–5pm Sat (last adm: 4.30pm).
public hols.

Weapons in the police museum

A darker side to Paris's history is illustrated in this small, rather old-fashioned museum. Created in 1909, the collection traces the development of the police in Paris from the Middle Ages to the 20th century. Curiosities on show include arrest warrants for figures such as the famous revolutionary Danton, and a rather sobering display of weapons and tools used by famous criminals. There is also a section on the part the police played in the Resistance and subsequent liberation of Paris.

La Sorbonne ❼

47 Rue des Ecoles 75005.
Map 13 A5. **Tel** 01 40 46 22 11.
Ⓜ Cluny-La Sorbonne, Maubert-Mutualité. 🕘 9am–5pm Mon–Fri.
⚫ public hols. 📷 only, by appt: write to Service des Visites.

The Sorbonne, seat of the University of Paris, was established in 1253 by Robert de Sorbon, confessor to Louis IX, for 16 poor students to study theology. From these modest beginnings the college soon became the centre of scholastic theology. In 1469 the rector had three printing machines brought over from Mainz, thereby founding the first printing house in France. The college's opposition to liberal 18th-century philosophy led to its suppression during the Revolution. It was re-established by Napoleon in 1806. The buildings built by Richelieu in the early 17th century were replaced by the ones seen today, with the exception of the chapel.

Statues outside the college

Collège de France ❽

11 Pl Marcelin-Berthelot 75005.
Map 13 A5. **Tel** 01 44 27 12 11.
Ⓜ Maubert-Mutualité. 🕘 Oct–Jun: 9am–6pm Mon–Fri.

One of Paris's great institutes of research and learning, the college was established in 1530 by François I. Guided by the great humanist Guillaume Budé, the king aimed to counteract the intolerance and dogmatism of the Sorbonne. A statue of Budé stands in the west courtyard, and the unbiased approach to learning is reflected in the inscription on the entrance to the old college: *docet omnia* (all are taught here). Lectures are free and open to the public.

Chapelle de la Sorbonne ❾

Pl de la Sorbonne 75005.
Map 13 A5. **Tel** 01 40 46 22 11.
Ⓜ Cluny-La Sorbonne, Maubert-Mutualité. 🚆 Luxembourg.
🕘 for temporary exhibitions only. 📷

Designed by Lemercier and built between 1635 and 1642, this chapel is, in effect, a monument to Richelieu, with his coat of arms on the dome supports and his white marble tomb, carved by Girardon in 1694, in the chancel. The chapel's attractive lateral facade looks on to the main courtyard of the Sorbonne.

Eglise de la Sorbonne clock

St-Etienne-du-Mont ❿

Pl Ste-Geneviève 75005. **Map** 17 A1.
Tel 01 43 54 11 79. Ⓜ Cardinal Lemoine. 🕘 8.45am–7.30pm Tue–Fri, noon–7.30pm Mon; w/e closed midday. ⚫ Mon in Jul–Aug. 📷 🚻

This remarkable church houses not only the shrine of Sainte Geneviève, patron saint of Paris, but also the remains of the great literary figures Racine and Pascal. Some parts are in the Gothic style and others date from the Renaissance, including a magnificent rood screen. The stained glass windows are also of note.

Panthéon ⓫

See pp158–9.

16th-century belfry tower

ST-ETIENNE-DU-MONT

Medieval window

Rood screen

Exploring the Cluny's Collection

Alexandre du Sommerard took over the Hôtel de Cluny
in 1833 and installed his art collection with great sensitivity to the surroundings and a strong sense of the
dramatic. After his death the Hôtel and its contents were
sold to the State and turned into a museum.

The Grape Harvest tapestry

TAPESTRIES

The museum's tapestries are
remarkable for their quality,
age and state of preservation.
The images present a sur-
prising mixture of the naive
with more complex notions.
One of the earliest, *The
Offering of the Heart* (early
15th century), shows a man
who is literally proffering his
heart to a seated medieval
beauty. More everyday scenes
are shown in the magnificent
series *The Noble Life* (about
1500). Upstairs is the
mysterious *Lady with the
Unicorn* series.

CARVINGS

The diverse techniques of
medieval European wood-
carvers are well represented.
From the Nottingham work-
shops in England, there are
wood as well as alabaster
works which were widely
used as altarpieces all over
Europe. Among the smaller
works of this genre are *The
School*, which is touchingly
realistic and dates from the
early 16th century.
    Upstairs there are some fine
Flemish and south German
woodcarvings. The multi-
coloured figure of St John is
typical. Two notable altarpieces on display are the
intricately carved and painted
*Lamentation of
Christ* (about 1485)
from the Duchy of
Clèves, and the
Averbode altarpiece,
which was made in
1523 in Antwerp, and
depicts three scenes
including the Last
Supper. Not to be
missed is a beautiful
full-length figure
of Mary
Magdalene.

STAINED GLASS

Most of the Cluny's glass from
the 12th and 13th centuries is
French. The oldest examples
were originally installed in
the Basilique St-Denis in
1144. There are also three
fragments from the Troyes
Cathedral, destroyed by fire,
two of which illustrate the life
of St Nicholas while the third
depicts that of Christ.
    Numerous panels came to
the Cluny from Sainte-
Chapelle *(see pp88–9)*,
during its mid-19th-century
restoration, and were never
returned, including five
scenes from the story of
Samson dating from 1248.
    The technique of
contrasting coloured glass
with surrounding grisaille
(grey-and-white panels)
developed in the latter half of
the 13th century. Four panels
from the royal château at
Rouen illustrate this.

Stained-glass scenes from Brittany (1400)

The School woodcarving (English,
early 16th century)

Head of a queen from St-Denis from before 1120

SCULPTURE

The highlight here is the Gallery of the Kings, a display of heads and decapitated figures from Notre-Dame. There is also an very graceful statue of Adam, sculped in the 1260s.

In the vaulted room opposite are displays of fine Romanesque sculpture retrieved from French churches. Among the earliest are the 12 capitals from the nave of St-Germain-des-Prés, from the early 11th century. Retrieved from the portal of St-Denis is a boldly sculpted head of a queen (c.1140) which, though badly mutilated, is still compelling.

Other Romanesque and early Gothic capitals include six finely sculpted works from Catalonia and four of the museum's most famous statues, early 13th-century apostles made for Sainte-Chapelle.

EVERYDAY OBJECTS

Household goods show another side to medieval life, and this large collection is grouped in a sensitive way to illustrate their use – from wallhangings and caskets to kitchenware and clothing. Children's toys bring a very human aspect to the display, while travel cases and religious emblems evoke journies of exploration and pilgrimage.

PRECIOUS METALWORK

The Cluny has a fine collection of jewellery, coins, metal and enamelwork from Gallic times to the Middle Ages. The showcase of Gallic jewellery includes gold torques, bracelets and rings, all of a simple design. In between these is one of the Cluny's most precious exhibits, the Golden Rose of Basel, a delicately wrought piece from 1330 and the oldest known of its kind.

The earliest enamelwork on display is the late Roman and Byzantine *cloisonné* pieces, culminating in the remarkable Limoges enamels, which flourished in the late 12th century. There are also two exceptional altarpieces, the Golden Altar of Basel and the Stavelot altarpiece.

Cross from Italy (late 15th century)

LADY WITH THE UNICORN TAPESTRIES

This series of six tapestries was woven in the late 15th century in the southern Netherlands. It is valued for its fresh harmonious colours and the poetic elegance of the central figure. Allegories of the senses are illustrated in the first five: sight (gazing into a mirror), hearing (playing a portable organ), taste (sampling sweets), smell (sniffing carnations) and touch (the lady holding the unicorn's

The Pillar of the Nautes

GALLO-ROMAN RUINS

One of the main reasons for visiting the Musée de Cluny is to see the scale and layout of its earliest function, the Gallo-Roman baths. The vaulted *frigidarium* (cold bath room) was the largest of its kind in France. Here there is another of the Cluny's highlights, the recently restored Pillar of the Nautes (boatmen), unearthed during excavations beneath Notre-Dame in 1711. Composed of five carved stone blocks representing Gallic and Roman divinities, its crowning element is presumed to depict the Seine's boatmen. There are also the ruins of the *caldarium* and *tepidarium* (hot and tepid baths), and visitors can tour the underground vaults.

Unicorn on the sixth tapestry

horn). The enigmatic sixth tapestry (showing jewels being placed in a box) includes the words "to my only desire" and is now thought to represent the principle of free choice.

Panthéon ⓫

When Louis XV recovered from
desperate illness in 1744, he was so
grateful to be alive that he conceived
a magnificent church to honour Sainte
Geneviève. The design was entrusted
to the French architect Jacques-Germain
Soufflot, who planned the church in
Neo-Classical style. Work began in 1764
and was completed in 1790, ten years
after Soufflot's death, under the control
of Guillaume Rondelet. But with the
Revolution underway the church was
soon turned into a pantheon – a location
for the tombs of France's good and great.
Napoleon returned it to the Church in
1806, but it was secularized and then
desecularized once more before finally
being made a civic building in 1885.

The Facade
*Inspired by the
Rome Pantheon,
the temple portico
has 22 Corinthian
columns.*

The arches of the dome show a renewed
interest in the lightness of Gothic
architecture and were designed by
Rondelet. They link four pillars supporting
the dome, which weighs 10,000 tonnes and
is 83 m (272 ft) high.

Pediment Relief
*David d'Angers' pediment
bas-relief depicts the
mother country (France)
granting laurels to her
great men.*

The Panthéon Interior
*The interior has four
aisles arranged in the
shape of a Greek cross,
from the centre of which
the great dome rises.*

Entrance

STAR FEATURES

★ Iron-Framed Dome

★ Frescoes of Sainte
  Geneviève

★ Crypt

**★ Frescoes of Sainte
Geneviève**
*Murals along the south wall of
the nave depict the life of
Sainte Geneviève. They are by
Pierre Puvis de Chavannes, the
19th-century fresco painter.*

The dome lantern allows only a little light to filter into the church's centre. Intense light was thought inappropriate for the place where France's heroes rested.

VISITORS' CHECKLIST

Pl du Panthéon. **Map** 17 A1. **Tel** 01 44 32 18 00. Ⓜ Jussieu, Cardinal-Lemoine. 🚌 84 to Panthéon; 21, 27, 38, 85 to Gare du Luxembourg. 🚉 Luxembourg. 🅿 Pl Edmond Rostand. ⬜ Apr–Sep: 10am–6.30pm daily; Oct–Mar: 10am–6pm daily. ⬤ 1 Jan, 1 May, 11 Nov, 25 Dec. 🎫 📷 ♿

★ Iron-Framed Dome
The tall dome, with its stone cupolas and three layers of shells, was inspired by St Paul's in London and the Dôme Church (see pp188–9).

The dome galleries afford a magnificent panoramic view of France's capital.

Colonnade
The colonnade encircling the dome is both decorative and part of an ingenious supporting system.

Monument to Diderot
This is Alphonse Terroir's statue (1925) to the political writer Denis Diderot.

★ Crypt
Covering the entire area under the building, the crypt divides into galleries flanked by Doric columns. Many French notables rest here.

THE PANTHEON'S ENSHRINED

The first of France's great men to be entombed was the popular orator Honoré Mirabeau. (Later, under the revolutionary leadership of Maximilien Robespierre, he fell from grace and his body was removed.) Voltaire followed. A statue of Voltaire by Jean-Antoine Houdon stands in front of his tomb. In the 1970s the remains of the wartime Resistance leader Jean Moulin were reburied here. Pierre and Marie Curie's remains were transferred here in 1995, and Malraux's followed in 1996. Others here include Jean-Jacques Rousseau, Victor Hugo and Emile Zola.

JARDIN DES PLANTES QUARTER

This area, traditionally, has been one of the most tranquil corners of Paris. It takes its character from the 17th-century botanical gardens where the kings of the *ancien régime* grew medicinal herbs and where the National Natural History Institute stands today. The many hospitals in the area, notably Paris's largest, Pitié-Salpêtrière, add to the atmosphere. A colourful market takes over much of Rue Mouffetard every day, and the streets off Mouffetard are redolent of life in medieval times.

SIGHTS AT A GLANCE

Museums and Galleries
Musée de la Sculpture en Plein Air ❷
Collection des Minéraux de l'Université ❹
Muséum National d'Histoire Naturelle ❿
La Manufacture des Gobelins ⓭

Modern Architecture
Institut du Monde Arabe ❶

Churches and Temples
St-Médard ❽
Mosquée de Paris ❾

Squares, Parks and Gardens
Ménagerie ❸
Place de la Contrescarpe ❻
Jardin des Plantes ⓫

Historic Buildings and Streets
Arènes de Lutèce ❺
Rue Mouffetard ❼
Groupe Hospitalier Pitié-Salpêtrière ⓬

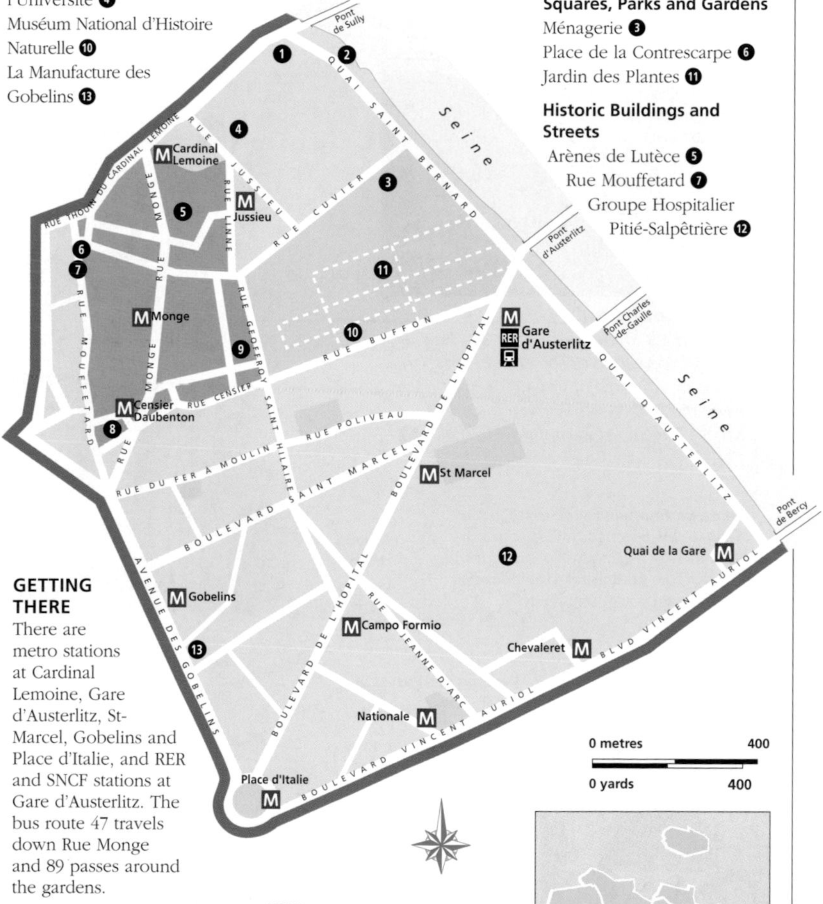

GETTING THERE

There are metro stations at Cardinal Lemoine, Gare d'Austerlitz, St-Marcel, Gobelins and Place d'Italie, and RER and SNCF stations at Gare d'Austerlitz. The bus route 47 travels down Rue Monge and 89 passes around the gardens.

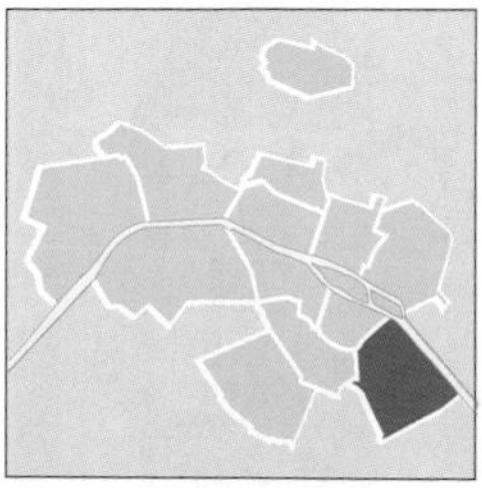

SEE ALSO

• *Street Finder,* map 17–18
• *Restaurants* p307

KEY

- Street-by-Street map
- **M** Metro station
- **RER** RER station
- **R** SNCF (train) station

| 0 metres | 400 |
| 0 yards | 400 |

◁ Market scene on the Rue Mouffetard

Street-by-Street: Jardin des Plantes Quarter

Two physicians to Louis XIII, Jean Hérouard and Guy de la Brosse, obtained permission to establish the royal medicinal herb garden in the sparsely populated St-Victor suburb in 1626. The herb garden and gardens of various religious houses gave the region a rural character. In the 19th century the population and thus the area expanded and it became more built up, until it gradually assumed the character it has today: a well-to-do residential patchwork of 19th- and early 20th-century buildings interspersed with much older and some more recent buildings.

Metro Cardinal Lemoine

Place de la Contrescarpe
This village-like square filled with restaurants and cafés buzzes with student life after dusk ❻

★ Rue Mouffetard
Locals flock to the daily open-air market here which is one of the oldest Paris street markets. A hoard of louis d'or *gold coins from the 18th century were found at No. 53 during its demolition in 1938* ❼

Pot de Fer fountain is one of 14 that Marie de Médicis had built on the Left Bank in 1624 as a source of water for her palace in the Jardin du Luxembourg. The fountain was rebuilt in 1671.

Metro Monge

Passage des Postes is an ancient alley which was opened in 1830. Its entrance is in the Rue Mouffetard.

St-Médard
This church was started in the mid-15th century and completed by 1655. In 1784 the choir was made Classical in style, and the nave's 16th-century windows were replaced with contemporary stained glass ❽

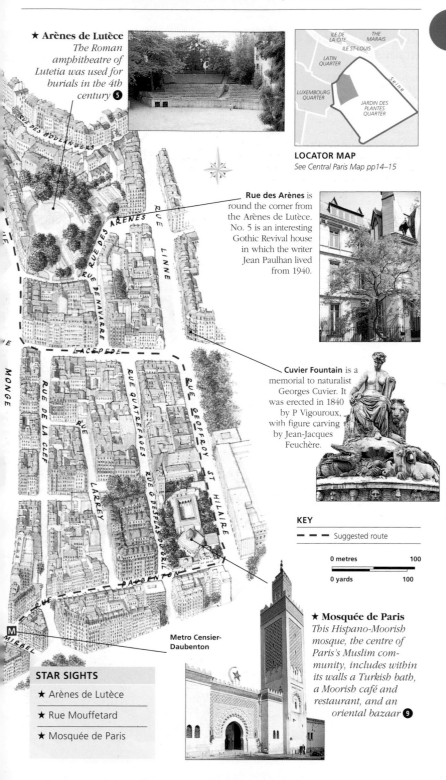

★ **Arènes de Lutèce**
The Roman amphitheatre of Lutetia was used for burials in the 4th century ❺

LOCATOR MAP
See Central Paris Map pp14–15

Rue des Arènes is round the corner from the Arènes de Lutèce. No. 5 is an interesting Gothic Revival house in which the writer Jean Paulhan lived from 1940.

Cuvier Fountain is a memorial to naturalist Georges Cuvier. It was erected in 1840 by P Vigouroux, with figure carving by Jean-Jacques Feuchère.

KEY

– – – Suggested route

| 0 metres | 100 |
| 0 yards | 100 |

Metro Censier-Daubenton

★ **Mosquée de Paris**
This Hispano-Moorish mosque, the centre of Paris's Muslim community, includes within its walls a Turkish bath, a Moorish café and restaurant, and an oriental bazaar ❾

STAR SIGHTS

★ Arènes de Lutèce

★ Rue Mouffetard

★ Mosquée de Paris

Institut du Monde Arabe ❶

1 Rue des Fossées St-Bernard 75005.
Map 13 C5. **Tel** 01 40 51 38 38.
🅼 Jussieu, Cardinal-Lemoine.
⬤ **Museum & temp exhibs:** 10am–
6pm Tue–Sun. **Library:** 1pm–8pm
Tue–Sat. 🎞 ♿ 🎦 **Lectures.**
🍴 🖥 www.imarabe.org

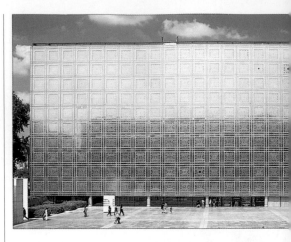

This cultural institute was founded in 1980 by France and 20 Arab countries with the intention of fostering cultural links between the Islamic world and the West. It is housed in a magnificent modern building designed by the French architect Jean Nouvel (also responsible for the Musée du Quai Branly, *see p190*), that combines modern materials with the spirit of traditional Arab architecture. The white marble book tower, which can be seen through the glass of the west wall, spirals upwards bringing to mind the minaret of a mosque. The emphasis that is traditionally placed on interior space in Arab architecture has been used here to create an enclosed courtyard reached by a narrow gap splitting the building in two.

From floors four to seven, there is a fascinating display of Islamic works of art from the 9th to the 19th centuries, including glassware, ceramics, sculpture, carpets and astrolabes. There is also a library and media archive.

Musée de la Sculpture en Plein Air ❷

75004/75005. **Map** 13 C5. 🅼
Gare d'Austerlitz, Sully-Morland.

Butting up to the left hand corner of the Institut du Monde Arabe, the Pont de Sully links the Ile St Louis with both banks of the Seine. Opened in 1877 and built of cast iron, the Pont de Sully is not an especially beautiful structure. Despite this, it is well worth pausing for a moment on the bridge for a fabulous view of Notre-Dame rising dramatically behind the wonderfully graceful Pont Marie.

Running along the river from the Pont de Sully as far as the Pont d'Austerlitz is the peaceful Quai St-Bernard. Not always so sedate, Quai St-Bernard was famous during the 17th century as a spot for nude bathing, until scandalized public opinion made it illegal. The grassy slopes adjoining the quai make a perfect spot to enjoy a picnic. Opened in 1975, they are known as the Jardin Tino Rossi in honour of the celebrated Corsican singer. The garden has a display of open-air sculpture known as the Musée de la Sculpture en Plein Air. Vandalism and other problems have unfortunately necessitated the removal of some of the exhibits.

Ménagerie ❸

57 Rue Cuvier 75005.
Map 17 C1. **Tel** 01 40 79 30 00.
🅼 Jussieu, Austerlitz.
⬤ 9am–5pm daily. 🎞 🍴 🖥

France's oldest public zoo is situated in the lovely surroundings of the Jardin des Plantes. It was set up during the Revolution to house survivors from the Royal menagerie at Versailles – all four of them. The state then rounded up animals from circuses and exotic creatures were sent from abroad. Unfortunately, during the Prussian siege of Paris (1870–71), most of them were slaughtered to feed the hungry citizens (*see p224*). Today the zoo specializes in small mammals, insects, birds, primates and reptiles, and it is a great favourite with children as it is possible for them to get quite close to the animals. The lion house contains an impressive number of large cats, including panthers from China. Other attractions include a large monkey house, bear pits, a large waterfowl aviary and wild sheep and goats.

The displays in the vivarium (enclosures of live animals in natural habitat) are changed at regular intervals and there is a permanent exhibition of micro-arthropods (also known as creepy-crawlies!).

Child playing at the zoo

Light Screens

The south elevation is made up of 1,600 high-tech metal screens which filter the light entering the building. Their design is based on moucharabiyahs *(carved wooden screens found on the outsides of buildings from Morocco to Southeast Asia).*

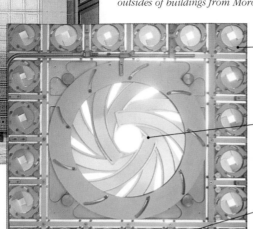

Each screen contains 21 irises which are controlled electronically, opening and closing in response to the amount of sunlight falling on photosensitive screens.

The central iris is made up of interlocking metal blades which move to adjust the size of the central opening.

The peripheral irises are linked to one another and to the central iris. They open and close in unison forming a delicate pattern of light and shade inside the institute.

Collection des Minéraux de l'Université ❹

Paris VI-Jussieu, 4 Pl Jussieu 75005. **Map** 17 B1. **Tel** *01 44 27 52 88.* Ⓜ *Jussieu.* ◯ *1pm–6pm Wed–Mon.* ● *1 Jan, Easter, 1 May, 14 Jul, 1 Nov, 25 Dec.* 🏷 🖥 🎥 *groups Tue pm.* ♿

This fascinating small museum is housed in the main university building, named after the distinguished scientists. The collection comprises cut and uncut gemstones and rock crystal from all over the world, shown to maximum advantage through the expert use of specialized lighting.

Topaz

Arènes de Lutèce ❺

Rue de Navarre 75005. **Map** 17 B1. Ⓜ *Jussieu. See p21.*

The remains of this vast Roman arena (Lutetia was the Roman name for Paris) date from the late 2nd century. Its

destruction began towards the end of the 3rd century at the hands of the Barbarians, and later, parts of it were used to build the walls of the Ile de la Cité. The arena was then gradually buried and its exact location preserved only in old documents and the local name Clos des Arènes. It was rediscovered in 1869 during the construction of the Rue Monge and the allocation of building plots nearby.

Action towards its restoration began with the campaigning of Victor Hugo (among others) in the 19th century but work did not get really underway until 1918.

With a seating capacity of 15,000, arranged in 35 tiers, the original arena was used both for theatrical performances and as an amphitheatre for the more gruesome spectacle of gladiator fights. This type of combined use was peculiar to Gaul (France), and the arena is similar to the other French ones in Nîmes and Arles.

The public park at the Arènes de Lutèce

BUFFON AND THE JARDIN DES PLANTES

At the age of 32 Georges Louis Leclerc, Comte de Buffon (1707–88), became the curator of the Jardin des Plantes at a time when the study of natural history was at the forefront of contemporary thought – Charles Darwin's *The Origin of Species* was to be published 120 years later. Buffon masterminded the reorganization of the Jardin, propelling it to a pre-eminent position within the scientific world. He was elected to the Académie Française in 1752 following the publication of his two main works, *Natural History* and *The Epoques of Nature*. He died in his house in the Jardin.

Illustration of a primate from Buffon's *Natural History*

Place de la Contrescarpe ⑥

75005. **Map** 17 A1. Ⓜ *Place Monge.*

At one time this site lay outside the city walls. It gets its name from the backfilling of the moat that ran along Philippe-Auguste's wall. The present square was laid out in 1852. At No. 1 there is a memorial plaque to the old "pine-cone club" immortalized in the writings of Rabelais; here a group of writers known as *La Pléiade* (named after the constellation of The Pleiades) used to meet in the 16th century.

The area has always been used for meetings and festivals. Today it is extremely lively at weekends, and on Bastille Day *(see p65)* a delightful ball is held here.

Part of the medieval city wall

Cheese in the Mouffetard market

Rue Mouffetard ⑦

75005. **Map** 17 B2. Ⓜ *Censier-Daubenton, Place Monge.* ◯ **Market** *Place Maubert: 7am–2.30pm Tue, Thu, Sat (to 3pm Sat); Place Monge: 7am–2.30pm Wed, Fri, Sun (to 3pm Sun).* See **Shops and Markets** p339.

A major thoroughfare since Roman times, when it linked Lutetia (Paris) and Rome, this street is one of the oldest in the city. In the 17th and 18th centuries it was known as the Grande Rue du Faubourg St-Marcel, and many of its buildings date from that time. Some of the small shops still have ancient painted signs, and some houses have mansard roofs. No. 125 has an attractive, restored Louis XIII facade, and the entire front of No. 134 has beautiful decoration of wild beasts, flowers and plants.

The area is known for its open-air markets, especially those in Place Maubert, Place Monge, and Rue Daubenton, a side street where a lively African market takes place.

St-Médard ⑧

141 Rue Mouffetard 75005. **Map** 17 B2. **Tel** 01 44 08 87 00. Ⓜ *Censier-Daubenton.* ◯ *8am–noon, 2.30–7pm Tue–Sat; 4–7pm Sun.* ⓞ ⓰

The origins of this charming church go back to the 9th century. St Médard, counsellor to the Merovingian kings, was known for his custom of giving a wreath of white roses to young girls noted for their virtue. The churchyard, now a garden, became notorious in the 18th century as the centre of the cult of the Convulsionnaires, whose hysterical fits were brought on by the contemplation of miracle cures. The interior has many fine paintings, including the 17th-century *St Joseph Walking with the Christ Child* by Francisco de Zurbarán.

Mosquée de Paris ⑨

2 bis Pl du Puits de l'Ermite 75005. **Map** 17 C2. **Tel** 01 45 35 97 33; 01 43 31 38 20 (tearoom); 01 43 31 18 14 (Turkish baths). Ⓜ *Place Monge.* ◯ *9am–noon, 2pm–6pm Sat–Thu.* ⬤ *Muslim hols.* ⓞ ⓰ ▢ ⓰ **Library.** www.mosquee-de-paris.com

Built in the 1920s in the Hispano-Moorish style, this group of buildings is the spiritual centre for Paris's Muslim community and the home of the Grand Imam. The complex comprises religious, educational and commercial sections; at its heart is a mosque. Each of the mosque's

Decoration inside the mosque

domes is decorated differently, and the minaret stands nearly 33 m (100 ft) high. Inside is a grand patio with mosaics on the walls and tracery on the arches.

Once used only by scholars, the mosque's place in Parisian life has grown over the years. The Turkish baths can be enjoyed by both men and women, but on alternate days. There is also a tearoom serving Moorish specialities.

Muséum National d'Histoire Naturelle ⑩

2 Rue Buffon 75005. **Map** 17 C2. **Tel** 01 40 79 54 79. Ⓜ Jussieu, Austerlitz. ◯ 10am–6pm Wed–Mon (to 5pm winter). ● 1 May. ▨ ♿ restricted. ▦ ◨ **Library**. www.mnhn.fr

Skull of the reptile dimetrodon

The highlight of the museum is the Grande Galerie de l'Evolution. There are also four other departments: palaeontology, featuring skeletons, casts of various animals and an exhibition showing the evolution of the vertebrate skeleton; palaeo-botany, devoted to plant fossils; mineralogy, including gemstones; and entomology, with some of the oldest fossilized insects on earth. The bookshop is in the house that was occupied by the naturalist Buffon, from 1772 until his death in 1788.

Jardin des Plantes ⑪

57 Rue Cuvier 75005. **Map** 17 C1. **Tel** 01 40 79 56 01. Ⓜ Jussieu, Austerlitz. ◯ 8am–7.30pm (to 5pm winter) daily.

The botanical gardens were established in 1626, when Jean Hérouard and Guy de la Brosse, Louis XIII's physicians,

obtained permission to found a royal medicinal herb garden here and then a school of botany, natural history and pharmacy. The garden was opened to the public in 1640 and flourished under Buffon's direction. Now one of Paris's great parks, it includes a natural history museum, botanical school and zoo.

As well as beautiful vistas and walkways flanked by ancient trees and punctuated with statues, the park has a remarkable alpine garden with plants from Corsica, Morocco, the Alps and the Himalayas and an unrivalled display of herbaceous and wild plants. It also has the first Cedar of Lebanon to be planted in France, originally from Britain's Kew Gardens.

Groupe Hospitalier Pitié-Salpêtrière ⑫

47 Blvd de l'Hôpital 75013. **Map** 18 D3. Ⓜ St-Marcel, Austerlitz. ⓇⒺⓇ Gare d'Austerlitz. ◯ **Chapel** 8.30am–6.30pm daily. ✝ 3.30pm daily. ◙ ♿

The vast Salpêtrière Hospital stands on the site of an old gunpowder factory and derives its name from the saltpetre used in the making of explosives. It was founded by Louis XIV in 1656 to help sick or socially-disadvantaged women and children and later became renowned for its pioneering humane treatment of the insane. It was here that Princess Diana died in 1997, following an automobile accident in a Paris underpass.

The Cedar of Lebanon in the Jardin

Outside the Hôpital Salpêtrière

La Manufacture des Gobelins ⑬

42 Ave des Gobelins 75013. **Map** 17 B3. **Tel** 01 44 08 52 00. Ⓜ Gobelins. ◯ **guided tours only** 2.15pm and 2.30pm Tue–Thu (arrive 15 mins earlier). Groups by appt. ▨ ● public hols.

Versailles tapestry by Le Brun

Originally a dyeing workshop set up in about 1440 by the Gobelin brothers, the building became a tapestry factory early in the 17th century. Louis XIV took it over in 1662 and gathered together the greatest crafts-men of the day – carpet weavers, cabinet makers and silversmiths – to furnish his new palace at Versailles (see pp248–53). Working under the direction of court painter Charles Le Brun, 250 Flemish weavers laid the foundations for the factory's international reputation. Today weavers continue to work in the traditional way but with modern designs, including those of Picasso and Matisse.

LUXEMBOURG QUARTER

Many a Parisian dreams of living in the vicinity of the Luxembourg Gardens, a quieter, greener and somehow more reflective place than its neighbouring areas. Luxembourg is one of the most captivating places in the capital. Its charm is in its old gateways and streets, its bookshops, and in the sumptuous yet intimate gardens. Though writers of the eminence of Paul Verlaine and André Gide no longer stroll in its groves, the paths, lawns and avenues are still full of charm, drawing to them the numerous students from the nearby *grandes écoles* and *lycées*. And on warm days old men meet under the chestnut trees to play chess or the traditional game of *boules*.

To the west the buildings are public and official, and on the east the houses are shaded by the tall chestnut trees of the Boulevard St-Michel.

Sailing boats are hired by children and adults to sail in the *grand bassin* (ornamental pond) in the Luxembourg Gardens.

SIGHTS AT A GLANCE

Museums
Musée du Service de Santé des Armées ⑩
Ecole Nationale Supérieure des Mines ⑪

Historic Buildings
Palais du Luxembourg ③
Institut Catholique de Paris ⑥

Churches
St-Sulpice ②
St-Joseph-des-Carmes ⑦
Val-de-Grâce ⑨

Squares and Gardens
Place St-Sulpice ①
Jardin du Luxembourg ⑤

Fountains
Fontaine de Médicis ④
Fontaine de l'Observatoire ⑧

GETTING THERE
The area is served by the metro, with stations at Mabillon and St-Sulpice, and by the RER, with a station at Luxembourg. Several bus routes pass through the area. Route 38 travels along Boulevard St-Michel on the east side of the Gardens and 58 and 89 pass along the Rue de Rennes on the north side. Route 82 passes along the southern end.

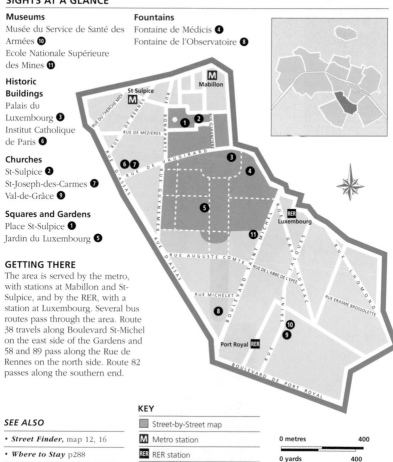

SEE ALSO
- **Street Finder,** map 12, 16
- **Where to Stay** p288

KEY
■ Street-by-Street map
Ⓜ Metro station
RER RER station

0 metres   400
0 yards   400

◁ Playing chess in the Jardin du Luxembourg

Street-by-Street: Luxembourg Quarter

Situated only a few steps from the bustle of St-Germain-des-Prés, this graceful and historic area offers a peaceful haven in the heart of a modern city. The Jardin du Luxembourg and Palais du Luxembourg dominate the vicinity. The gardens became fully open to the public in the 19th century under the ownership of the Comte de Provence (later Louis XVIII), when for a small fee visitors could come in and feast on fruit from the orchard. Today the gardens, palace and old houses on the streets to the north remain unspoilt and attract many visitors.

★ St-Sulpice
This Classical church was built over 134 years to Daniel Gittard's plans. It has a facade by the Italian architect Giovanni Servandoni ❷

To St-Germain-des-Prés

Place St-Sulpice
The Fontaine des Quatre Points Cardinaux depicts four church leaders at the cardinal points of the compass. Point also means "never": the leaders were never made cardinals ❶

The Monument to Delacroix
(1890) by Jules Dalou is situated near the private gardens of the French Senate. Beneath the bust of the leading Romantic painter Eugène Delacroix are the allegorical figures of Art, Time and Glory.

STAR SIGHTS

★ St-Sulpice

★ Jardin du Luxembourg

★ Palais du Luxembourg

★ Fontaine de Médicis

★ Jardin du Luxembourg
Many fine statues were erected in the Luxembourg gardens in the 19th century during the reign of Louis-Philippe ❺

The Rue de Tournon is full of elegant architecture, boutiques and old bookshops. At No. 12 is the Grand Hôtel d'Entragues, reconstructed by Neveu in the 18th century during Louis XVI's reign.

★ Palais du Luxembourg
In 1794, during the Revolution, the painter Jacques-Louis David was imprisoned here and made sketches for the Intervention of the Sabine Women ❸

LOCATOR MAP
See Central Paris Map pp14–15

KEY

— — — Suggested route

0 metres   100
0 yards   100

★ Fontaine de Médicis
The 17th-century fountain is in the style of an Italian grotto and is thought to have been designed by Salomon de Brosse ❹

Sainte Geneviève, the patron saint of Paris, was a wealthy 5th-century Gallo-Roman landowner. When Paris was invaded by the Huns in AD 451, she prayed with women friends that the city would be spared – their prayers were answered. This statue by Michel-Louis Victor (1845) pays homage to her.

The Octagonal Lake (Grand Bassin), attributed to Jean-François Chalgrin, is surrounded by formal terraces where visitors to the gardens often sunbathe.

MONTPARNASSE

In the first three decades of the 20th century, Montparnasse was a thriving artistic and literary centre. Many modern painters and sculptors, new novelists and poets, the great and the young were drawn to this area. Its ateliers, conviviality and renowned Bohemian lifestyle made it a magnet for genius, some of it French, much of it foreign. The great epoch ended with World War II, and change continued with the destruction of many ateliers and the construction of the soaring Tour Montparnasse, Paris's tallest office tower, which heralded the more modern *quartier*. But the area has not lost its appeal. The great cafés remain very much in business and attract a lively international crowd. Small café-theatres have opened and the area springs to life at the weekends with cinema crowds.

Monument to Charles Augustin Ste-Beauve in the Cimetière du Montparnasse

SIGHTS AT A GLANCE

Historic Buildings and Streets
Rue Campagne-Première ❸
Catacombes ❿
Observatoire de Paris ⓫

Cafés and Restaurants
La Coupole ❶
La Closerie des Lilas ⓬

Museums and Galleries
Musée Zadkine ❷
Musée Antoine Bourdelle ❻
Musée de la Poste ❼

Modern Architecture
Tour Montparnasse ❺

Musée Montparnasse ❽
Fondation Cartier ❾

Cemeteries
Cimetière du Montparnasse pp180–81 ❹

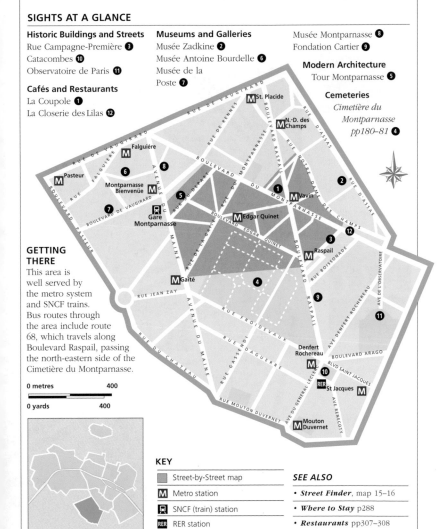

GETTING THERE

This area is well served by the metro system and SNCF trains. Bus routes through the area include route 68, which travels along Boulevard Raspail, passing the north-eastern side of the Cimetière du Montparnasse.

| 0 metres | 400 |
| 0 yards | 400 |

KEY

	Street-by-Street map
M	Metro station
🚊	SNCF (train) station
RER	RER station

SEE ALSO

- *Street Finder*, map 15–16
- *Where to Stay* p288
- *Restaurants* pp307–308

◁ **View of Tour Montparnasse from the Cimetière du Montparnasse**

Street-by-Street: Montparnasse

Renowned for its mix of art and high living, Montparnasse continues to live up to its name: Mount Parnassus was the mountain dedicated by the ancient Greeks to Apollo, god of poetry, music and beauty. That mix was especially potent in the 1920s and 1930s, when such artists and writers as Picasso, Hemingway, Cocteau, Giacometti, Matisse and Modigliani were to be seen in the local bars, cafés and cabarets.

★ La Coupole
This traditional brasserie-style café, with its large enclosed terrace, opened in 1927 and became a famous meeting place for artists and writers ❶

★ Cimetière du Montparnasse
This fine sculpture, The Separation of a Couple *by de Max, stands in the smallest of the city's major cemeteries* ❹

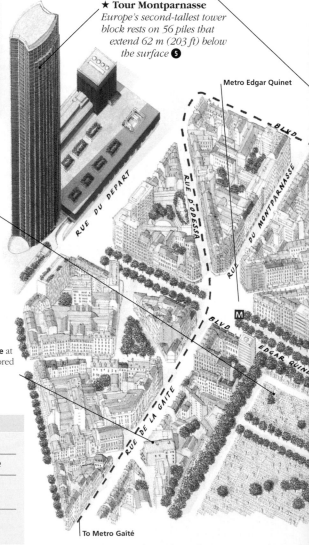

★ Tour Montparnasse
Europe's second-tallest tower block rests on 56 piles that extend 62 m (203 ft) below the surface ❺

Metro Edgar Quinet

The Théâtre Montparnasse at No. 31, with its fully-restored original 1880's decor.

STAR SIGHTS

★ La Coupole

★ Tour Montparnasse

★ Rue Campagne-Première

★ Cimetière du Montparnasse

To Metro Gaîté

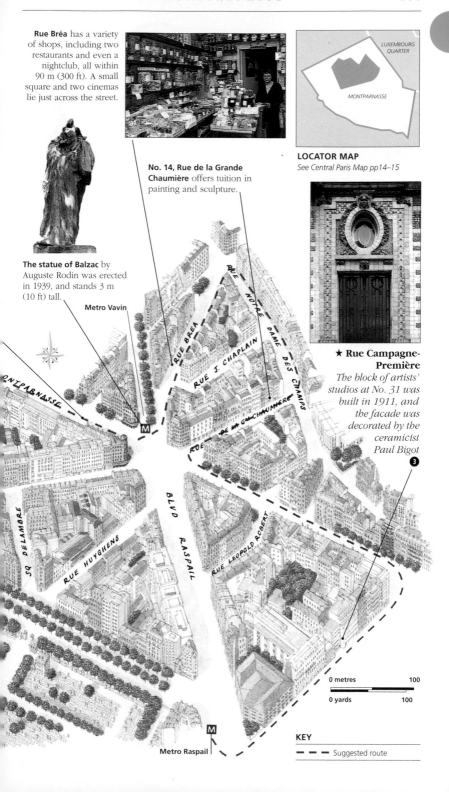

Rue Bréa has a variety of shops, including two restaurants and even a nightclub, all within 90 m (300 ft). A small square and two cinemas lie just across the street.

No. 14, Rue de la Grande Chaumière offers tuition in painting and sculpture.

LOCATOR MAP
See Central Paris Map pp14–15

LUXEMBOURG QUARTER

MONTPARNASSE

The statue of Balzac by Auguste Rodin was erected in 1939, and stands 3 m (10 ft) tall.

Metro Vavin

★ **Rue Campagne-Première**
The block of artists' studios at No. 31 was built in 1911, and the facade was decorated by the ceramicist Paul Bigot

❸

RUE NOTRE DAME DES CHAMPS

RUE BRÉA

RUE J. CHAPLAIN

RUE DE LA Gd CHAUMIÈRE

ONTPARNASSE

SQ DELAMBRE

RUE HUYGHENS

BLVD RASPAIL

RUE LEOPOLD ROBERT

| 0 metres | 100 |
| 0 yards | 100 |

Metro Raspail

KEY

– – – Suggested route

The interior of La Coupole

La Coupole ❶

102 Blvd du Montparnasse 75014.
Map 16 D2. *Tel* 01 43 20 14 20. Ⓜ
Vavin, Montparnasse. ⭕ *8am–1am
Mon–Thu, 8.30am–1.30am Fri–Sun.*
*See **Restaurants and Cafés** p307.*
www.flobrasseries.com

Established in 1927, this historic
café-restaurant and dance hall
underwent a face-lift in the
1980s. Its red velvet seats and
famous columns, decorated by
various artists, have survived.
Among its clientele have been
Jean-Paul Sartre, Josephine
Baker and Roman Polanski.

The museum's *Les Trois Belles*
(1950) by Ossip Zadkine

Musée Zadkine ❷

100 bis Rue d'Assas 75116.
Map 16 E1. *Tel* 01 55 42 77 20.
Ⓜ *Notre-Dame-Les Champs.*
⭕ *10am–6pm Tue–Sun.*
⬤ *public hols.* 📷 🎞 📷 *by appt.*
♿ *limited.* **www.**zadkine.paris.fr

The Russian-born sculptor
Ossip Zadkine lived here

from 1928 until his death in
1967. The small house, studio
and daffodil-filled garden
contain his works. Here he
produced his great commemorative sculpture, *Ville Détruite*,
commissioned by Rotter-
dam after World War II,
and two monuments to
Vincent Van Gogh, one for
Holland and one for Auvers-
sur-Oise, where Van Gogh
died. The museum's works
span the development of
Zadkine's style, from his Cubist beginnings to Expressionism and Abstractionism.

Rue Campagne-
Première ❸

75014. **Map** 16 E2. Ⓜ *Raspail.*

This street has some interesting Art Deco buildings and a
long artistic tradition. Modigliani, ravaged by opium and
tuberculosis, lived at No. 3
during his last years. Between
the wars many artists resided
here, including Picasso, Joan
Miró and Kandinsky.

Cimetière du
Montparnasse ❹

See pp180–1.

Tour
Montparnasse ❺

Pl Raoul Dautry 75014. **Map** 15 C2.
Ⓜ *Montparnasse-Bienvenüe. Tel* 01
45 38 52 56. ⭕ *Apr–Sep: 9.30am–
11.30pm daily; Oct–Mar: 9.30am–
10.30pm daily (to 11pm Fri, Sat).*
🎞 🏢 💻 📷 🎞

This was Europe's largest office
block when it was built in 1973
as the focal point of a new
business sector meant
to revitalize a run-
down area. It stands
210 m (690 ft) high,
is made of curved
steel and smoked
glass, and totally
dominates the area's
skyline. The views
from the 59th floor
are spectacular. The
tower also boasts
Europe's fastest lift (56
floors in 38 seconds).

The Archer (1909) by Antoine
Bourdelle

Musée Antoine
Bourdelle ❻

18 Rue Antoine Bourdelle 75015.
Map 15 B1. *Tel* 01 49 54 73 73.
Ⓜ *Montparnasse-Bienvenüe.*
⭕ *10am–6pm Tue–Sun.*
⬤ *public hols.* 📷 ♿ *limited.*
www.bourdelle.paris.fr

The prolific sculptor, Antoine
Bourdelle, lived and worked
in the studio here from 1884
until his death in 1929. The
house, studio and garden are
now a museum devoted to
his life and work. Among the
900 sculptures on display are
the original plaster casts of
his monumental works
planned for wide public
squares. They are housed in
the Great Hall in an extension
and include the group of
sculptures for the relief
decoration of the Théâtre
des Champs-Elysées.

Musée de la
Poste ❼

34 Blvd de Vaugirard 75015.
Map 15 B2. 🆔 01 42 79 23 00.
Ⓜ *Montparnasse-Bienvenüe.* ⭕
10am–6pm Mon–Sat.
⬤ *public hols.* 📷 📷
♿ *Library.* **www.**
museedelaposte.fr

Every conceivable
aspect of the history
of the French postal
service and methods
of transportation is
covered in this well
laid out collection.
There is even a
room devoted to

A view of the tower

mail delivery in times of war – carrier pigeons were used during the Franco-Prussian War with postmarks stamped on their wings. Postage stamp art is displayed in the gallery.

A Miró-designed postage stamp

Musée du Montparnasse **8**

21 Ave du Maine 75015. **Map** 15 C1. **Tel** 01 42 22 91 96. M *Montparnasse-Bienvenüe, Falguière.* ◑ *1–7pm Wed–Sun.* ▨

During World War I, this was a canteen for needy artists which, by its status as a private club, was not subject to curfew, and so the likes of Picasso, Braque, Modigliani and Léger could eat for 65 centimes and then party until late at night. This symbolic place is now a museum that recalls, through paintings and photos, how at the Vavin crossroads Western art turned some of the most beautiful pages of its modern history.

Fondation Cartier **9**

261 Blvd Raspail 75014. **Map** 16 E3. **Tel** 01 42 18 56 50. M *Raspail.* ◑ *noon–8pm Tue–Sun.* ◑ *1 Jan, 25 Dec.* ▨ ▤ www.fondation.cartier.fr

This foundation for contemporary art is housed in a building designed by architect Jean Nouvel. He has created an air of transparency and light, as well as incorporating a cedar of Lebanon planted in 1823 by François-René de Chateaubriand. The structure complements the nature of the exhibitions of progressive art, which showcase personal, group or thematic displays, often including works by young unknowns.

Catacombes **10**

1 Ave du Colonel Henri Rol-Tanguy 75014. **Map** 16 E3. **Tel** 01 43 22 47 63. M *Denfert-Rochereau.* ◑ *10am–5pm Tue–Sun (last adm: 4pm).* ● *public hols.* ▨ ▢ ▤ www.catacombes.paris.fr

In 1786 a monumental project began here: the removal of the millions of skulls and bones from the unsanitary city cemetery in Les Halles to the ancient quarries formed by excavations at the base of the three "mountains": Montparnasse, Montrouge and Montsouris. It took 15 months to transport the bones and rotting corpses across the city in huge carts to their new resting place; the transportation was carried out at night.

Just before the Revolution, the Comte d'Artois (later Charles X) threw wild parties in the catacombs, and during World War II the French Resistance set up its headquarters here. Above the door outside are the words "Stop! This is the empire of death."

Observatoire de Paris **11**

61 Ave de l'Observatoire 75014. **Map** 16 E3. **Tel** 01 40 51 21 70. M *Denfert-Rochereau.* **Visits** *(2 hrs) apply 2 mths ahead: 1st Sat of mth: 2.30pm; groups by appt.* ● *Aug.* ▨ ▤ www.obspm.fr

In 1667 Louis XIV was persuaded by his scientists and astronomers that France needed a royal observatory. Building began on 21 June,

the day of the summer solstice, and took five years to reach completion.

Astronomical research undertaken here included the calculation of the exact dimensions of the solar system in 1672, calculations of the dimensions of longitude, the mapping of the moon in 1679 and the discovery of the planet Neptune in 1846.

The facade of the Observatoire

La Closerie des Lilas **12**

171 Blvd du Montparnasse 75014. **Map** 16 E2. **Tel** 01 40 51 34 50. M *Vavin.* RER *Port Royal.* ◑ *Bar: 11– 2am, brasserie: noon–1am daily.*

Lenin, Trotsky, Hemingway and Scott Fitzgerald all frequented the numerous bars and cafés of Montparnasse, but the Closerie was their favourite. Much of Hemingway's novel *The Sun Also Rises* takes place here. Hemingway wrote it on the terrace in just six weeks. Today the terrace is ringed with trees and the whole place is more elegant in appearance, but much of the original decor remains *(see pp38–9)*.

Skulls and bones stored in the catacombs

Cimetière du Montparnasse ❹

The Montparnasse Cemetery was planned by Napoleon outside the city walls to replace the numerous, congested small cemeteries within the old city, viewed as a health hazard at the turn of the 19th century. It was opened in 1824 and became the resting place of many illustrious Parisians, particularly Left Bank personalities. Like all French cemeteries it is divided into rigidly aligned paths forming blocks or divisions. The Rue Emile Richard cuts it into two parts, the Grand Cimetière and the Petit Cimetière.

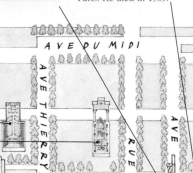

★ Charles Baudelaire Cenotaph
This is a monument to the great poet and critic (1821–67), author of The Flowers of Evil.

Samuel Beckett, the great Irish playwright renowned for *Waiting for Godot*, spent most of his life in Paris. He died in 1989.

The Pétain tomb contains the family of the marshal who collaborated with the Germans during World War II. Pétain himself is buried on Ile d'Yeu, where he was imprisoned.

Guy de Maupassant was a 19th-century novelist.

Alfred Dreyfus was a Jewish army officer whose unjust trial for treason in 1894 provoked a political and social scandal.

Frédéric Auguste Bartholdi was the sculptor of the Statue of Liberty (1886) in New York.

André Citroën, an engineer and industrialist who died in 1935, founded the famous French car firm.

AVE DU MIDI
AVE THIERRY
RUE EMILE RICHARD
AVE DE L'EST

★ Charles Pigeon Family Tomb
This wonderfully pompous Belle Epoque tomb depicts the French industrialist and inventor in bed with his wife.

FAMILLE CHARLES PIGEON

STAR FEATURES

★ Charles Baudelaire Cenotaph

★ Charles Pigeon Family Tomb

★ Jean-Paul Sartre and Simone de Beauvoir

★ Serge Gainsbourg

The Kiss by Brancusi
This is the famous Primitivo-Cubist sculpture (a response to Rodin's Kiss) by the great Romanian artist, who died in 1957 and is buried just off the Rue Emile Richard.

Charles-Augustin Sainte-Beuve was a critic of the French Romantic generation, and is generally described as the "father of modern criticism".

Camille Saint-Saëns, the pianist, organist and composer who died in 1921, was one of France's great post-Romantic musicians.

★ Serge Gainsbourg
The French singer, composer and pop icon of the 1970s and 1980s is best known for his wistful and irreverent songs. He was married to the actress Jane Birkin.

VISITORS' CHECKLIST

3 Blvd Edgar Quinet. **Map** 16 D3. **Tel** 01 44 10 86 50. Ⓜ Edgar Quinet. 🚌 38, 83, 91 to Port Royal. RER Port Royal. 🅿 Rue Campagne-Première, Blvd St-Jacques. ☐ Mid-Mar–Oct: 8am–5.45pm daily (from 8.30am Sat, from 9am Sun); Nov–mid-Mar closes 5.15pm. **Adm free.** 📷 ♿

The Tower is all that remains of a 17th-century windmill. It was part of the old property of the Brothers of Charity on which the cemetery was built.

Génie du Sommeil Eternel
Horace Daillion's wistful bronze angel of Eternal Sleep (1902) is the cemetery's centrepiece.

Tristen Tzara, the Romanian writer, was leader of the literary and artistic Dada movement in Paris in the 1920s.

Henri Laurens
The French sculptor (1885–1954) was a leading figure in the Cubist movement.

Man Ray was an American photographer who immortalized the Montparnasse artistic and café scene in the 1920s and 1930s.

Charles Baudelaire, the 19th-century poet, is buried here in his detested step-father's family tomb, along with his beloved mother.

Chaïm Soutine, a poor Jewish Lithuanian, was a Montparnasse Bohemian painter of the 1920s. He was a friend of the Italian artist Modigliani.

Jean Seberg
The Hollywood actress, chosen by François Truffaut as the star for his film A bout de souffle, *was the epitome of American blonde beauty, youth and candour.*

JEAN PAUL SARTRE
1905 - 1980
SIMONE DE BEAUVOIR
1908 - 1986

★ Jean-Paul Sartre and Simone de Beauvoir
The famous existentialist couple, undisputed leaders of the post-war literary scene, lie here close to their Left Bank haunts.

INVALIDES AND EIFFEL TOWER QUARTER

Musée de l'Armée cannon

Everything in the area of Invalides is on a monumental scale. Starting from the sprawling 18th-century buildings of the Ecole Militaire on the corner of the Avenue de la Motte Piquet, the Parc du Champ de Mars stretches down to the Eiffel Tower and the Seine. The avenues around the Tower are lined with luxurious buildings, some in the Art Nouveau style, and numerous embassies. The area was already highly prized between the World Wars when the noted actor Sacha Guitry lived there. Even earlier, in the 18th century, wealthy residents of the Marais moved to this part of the city, building the aristocratic town houses that line the Rue de Varenne and Rue de Grenelle.

SIGHTS AT A GLANCE

Historic Buildings and Streets
Hôtel des Invalides **6**
Hôtel Matignon **8**
Assemblée Nationale Palais-Bourbon **11**
Rue Cler **12**
Les Egouts **13**
Champ-de-Mars **15**
No. 29 Avenue Rapp **17**
Ecole Militaire **19**

Museums and Galleries
Musée de l'Ordre de la Libération **3**
Musée de l'Armée **4**
Musées des Plans-Reliefs **5**

Musée Rodin **7**
Musée Maillol **9**
Musée du Quai Branly **14**

Churches and Temples
Dôme Church pp188–9 **1**
St-Louis-des-Invalides **2**
Sainte-Clotilde **10**

Monuments and Fountains
Eiffel Tower pp192–3 **16**

Modern Architecture
Village Suisse **18**
UNESCO **20**

GETTING THERE
The metro system serves this area well, with stations at Invalides, Solferino, Sèvres Babylone, Varenne, Latour Maubourg and Ecole Militaire. There are also several bus routes through the area. Route 69 passes along Rue St-Dominique heading east and along Rue de Grenelle on the way back. Route 82 travels along the Avenue de Suffren and 28 along Avenue de la Motte Picquet.

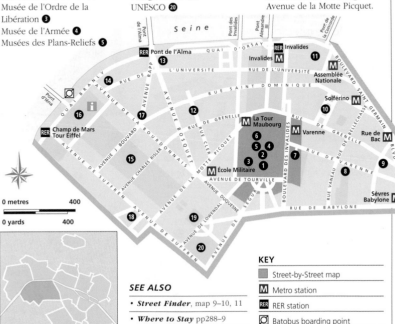

0 metres 400
0 yards 400

SEE ALSO

KEY
Street-by-Street map
M Metro station
RER RER station
Batobus boarding point
i Tourist information

◁ **View of the Eiffel Tower**

Street-by-Street: Invalides

The imposing Hôtel des Invalides, from which the area takes its name, was built from 1671 to 1676 by Louis XIV for his wounded and homeless veterans and as a monument to his own glory. At its centre lies the glittering golden roof of the Sun King's Dôme Church, which marks the final resting place of Napoleon Bonaparte. The emperor's body was brought here from St Helena in 1840, 19 years after he died, and placed inside the majestic red sarcophagus, designed by Joachim Visconti, that lies at the centre of the Dôme's circular glass-topped crypt. Just to the east of the Hôtel on the corner of the Boulevard des Invalides, the superb Musée Rodin offers artistic relief from the pomp and circumstance of the surrounding area.

Mounted military policeman

Metro La Tour Maubourg

The facade of the Hôtel is 196 m (645 ft) long and is topped by dormer windows, each decorated in the shape of a different trophy. A head of Hercules sits above the central entrance.

★ Musée de l'Armée
This vast museum covers military history from the Stone Age to World War II. It contains the third-largest collection of armoury in the world **4**

STAR SIGHTS

- ★ Dôme Church and Napoleon's Tomb
- ★ St-Louis-des-Invalides
- ★ Musée de l'Armée
- ★ Musée Rodin

Musée de l'Ordre de la Libération
The Order was set up to honour feats of heroism during World War II **3**

AVE DE TOURVILLE

Musées des Plans-Reliefs
This museum contains military models of forts and towns, as well as a display on model-making **5**

KEY

– – – Suggested route

| 0 metres | 100 |
| 0 yards | 100 |

General de Gaulle's Liberation Order and compass

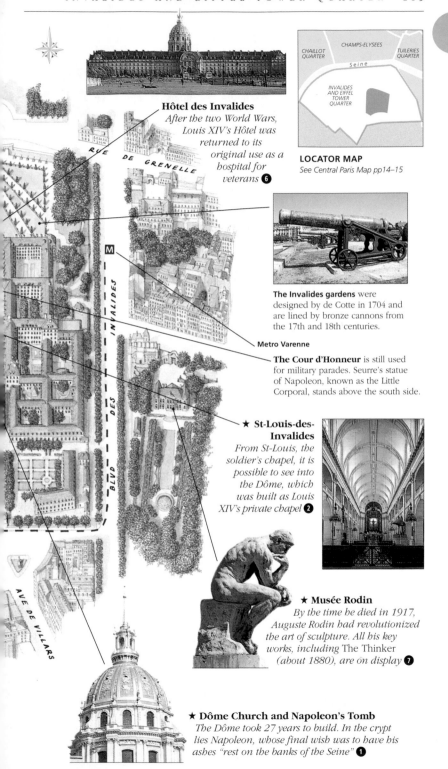

Hôtel des Invalides
After the two World Wars, Louis XIV's Hôtel was returned to its original use as a hospital for veterans ❻

LOCATOR MAP
See Central Paris Map pp14–15

The Invalides gardens were designed by de Cotte in 1704 and are lined by bronze cannons from the 17th and 18th centuries.

Metro Varenne

The Cour d'Honneur is still used for military parades. Seurre's statue of Napoleon, known as the Little Corporal, stands above the south side.

★ **St-Louis-des-Invalides**
From St-Louis, the soldier's chapel, it is possible to see into the Dôme, which was built as Louis XIV's private chapel ❷

★ **Musée Rodin**
By the time he died in 1917, Auguste Rodin had revolutionized the art of sculpture. All his key works, including The Thinker *(about 1880), are on display* ❼

★ **Dôme Church and Napoleon's Tomb**
The Dôme took 27 years to build. In the crypt lies Napoleon, whose final wish was to have his ashes "rest on the banks of the Seine" ❶

Dôme Church ❶

See pp188–9.

St-Louis-des-Invalides ❷

Hôtel des Invalides 75007. **Map** 11
A3. Ⓜ *Varenne, Latour-Maubourg.*
Tel *01 44 42 37 65.* ◯ *Apr–Sep:*
10am–5.30pm daily; Oct–Mar:
10am–4.30pm daily.

Also known as the "soldiers' church", this is the chapel of the Hôtel des Invalides. It was built from 1679 to 1708 by Jules Hardouin-Mansart from the original designs by Libéral Bruand, architect of the Hôtel des Invalides. The imposing, but stark, interior is decorated with banners seized in battle.

The fine 17th-century organ was built by Alexandre Thierry. The first performance of Berlioz's *Requiem* was given on it in 1837, with an orchestra accompanied by a battery of outside artillery.

Musée de l'Ordre de la Libération ❸

51 bis Blvd de Latour-Maubourg
75007. **Map** 11 A4. **Tel** *01 47 05 04*
10. Ⓜ *Latour-Maubourg.* ◯ *10am–*
6pm (to 5pm in winter) daily. ● *1st*
Mon of mth, pub hols. 🎦 ⓞ 🎟
(groups should apply 1 mth before).

This museum is devoted to the wartime Free French and their leader, General Charles

The altar of St-Louis-des-Invalides

The facade of the Musée de l'Ordre de la Libération

de Gaulle. The Order of Liberation was created by de Gaulle at Brazzaville in 1940. It is France's highest honour and was eventually bestowed on those who made an outstanding contribution to the final victory in World War II. The *companions* who received the honour were French civilians and members of the armed forces, plus some overseas leaders, including King George VI, Winston Churchill and General Dwight Eisenhower.

Cannons at the Musée de l'Armée

Musée de l'Armée ❹

Hôtel des Invalides 75007. **Map** 11
A3. **Tel** *01 44 42 38 77.* Ⓜ *Latour-Maubourg, Varenne.* ◯ *10am–6pm (to 5pm winter) daily*
(last adm: 45 mins before closing
time). ● *1 Jan, 1 May, 1 Nov, 25*
Dec. 🎦 *(ticket includes entry to the*
Musée de l'Ordre de la Libération
and the Musée des Plans-Reliefs.)
ⓞ ♿ *ground floor only.* 🎟 ▯
🎬 *Film.* www.*invalides.org*

This is one of the most comprehensive museums of military history in the world, with exhibits ranging from the Stone Age to the final days of World War II. The third-largest collection of armoury in the world is housed here. The whole place is being revamped, so some sections may be closed at the time of your visit.

Situated in the north-east refectory, the Ancient Armoury department is worth visiting for the collection on display as much as for the

17th-century murals adorning the walls. Visible for the first time in 200 years after extensive restoration, the murals by Joseph Parrocel celebrate Louis XIV's military conquests.

In the Coeur de Valeur is an educational display (open from summer 2007) on the life of former war-time president Charles de Gaulle and the role he played in 20th-century politics.

Napoleon's mementoes have been moved to a temporary display in an adjacent chapel in the Dôme church.

Musées des Plans-Reliefs ❺

Hôtel des Invalides 75007. **Map** 11
B3. **Tel** *01 45 51 95 05.* Ⓜ *Latour-Maubourg, Varenne.* RER *Invalides.*
◯ *10am–5.45pm (4.45pm in winter)*
daily. ● *1st Mon of mth, 1 Jan, 1*
May, 1 & 11 Nov, 25 Dec. 🎦 ⓞ 🎟

A map of Alessandria, Italy (1813)

The detailed models of French forts and fortified towns, some dating back to Louis XIV's reign, were considered top secret until the 1950s, when they were put on public display. The oldest model is that of Perpignan, dating to 1686. It shows the fortifications drawn up by the legendary 17th-century military architect Vauban, who built the defences around several French towns, including Briançon.

Hôtel des Invalides ❻

75007. **Map** 11 A3. **Tel** 01 44 42 37 72.
Ⓜ Latour-Maubourg, Varenne.
◯ 10am–6pm daily (5pm winter).
⬤ public hols. www.invalides.org

The Invalides main entrance

Founded by Louis XIV, this was the first military hospital and home for French war veterans and disabled soldiers who had hitherto been reduced to begging. The decree for building this vast complex was signed in 1670, and construction, following the designs of Libéral Bruand, was finished five years later.

Today the harmonious Classical facade is one of the most impressive sights in Paris, with its four storeys, cannon in the forecourt, garden and tree-lined esplanade stretching to the Seine. The south side leads to St-Louis-des-Invalides, the soldiers' church, which backs on to the magnificent Dôme church of Jules Hardouin-Mansart. The dome was re-gilded in 1989 and now glitters anew.

Musée Rodin ❼

77 Rue de Varenne 75007. **Map** 11 B3.
Tel 01 44 18 61 10. Ⓜ Varenne.
◯ Apr–Sep: 9.30am–5.45pm Tue–Sun; Oct–Mar: 9.30am–4.45pm (gdn 1 hr later) Tue–Sun. ⬤ 1 Jan, 1 May, 25 Dec. 🖼 📷 ♿ restricted. ⬚
🚻 📷 occas. www.musee-rodin.fr

Auguste Rodin, widely regarded as the greatest 19th-century French sculptor, lived and worked in the Hôtel

Biron, an elegant 18th-century mansion, from 1908 until his death in 1917. In return for a state-owned flat and studio, Rodin left his work to the nation, and it is now exhibited here. Some of his most celebrated sculptures are on display in the garden: *The Burghers of Calais*, *The Thinker*, *The Gates of Hell and Balzac*. The garden has a stunning array of 2,000 rose bushes.

The indoor exhibits are arranged in chronological order, spanning the whole of Rodin's career, with highlights such as *The Kiss* and *Eve*.

Hôtel Matignon ❽

57 Rue de Varenne 75007.
Map 11 C4. Ⓜ Solférino, Rue du Bac. ⬤ to the public.

One of the most beautiful mansions in the Faubourg area, this was built by Jean Courtonne in 1721 and has been substantially remodelled since. Former owners include Talleyrand, the statesman and diplomat who held legendary parties and receptions here, and several members of the nobility. It has been the official residence of the French Prime Minister since 1958 and has the largest private garden in Paris.

Rodin's *The Kiss* (1886) at the Musée Rodin

Musée Maillol ❾

61 Rue de Grenelle 75007. **Map** 11 C4. **Tel** 01 42 22 59 58. Ⓜ Sèvres-Babylone, Rue du Bac. ◯ 11am–6pm Wed–Mon (last adm: 5.15pm).
⬤ pub hols. ♿ 📱 🚻
www.museemaillol.com

Once the home of novelist Alfred de Musset, this museum was created by Dina Vierny, former model of Aristide Maillol. All aspects of the artist's work are here: drawings, engravings, paintings, sculpture and decorative objects. Also displayed is Vierny's private collection, in which naïve art sits alongside works by Matisse, Dufy, Picasso and Rodin.

Large allegorical figures of the city of Paris and the four seasons decorate Bouchardon's fountain in front of the house.

Sculptured figures at Ste-Clotilde

Sainte-Clotilde ❿

12 Rue de Martignac 75007.
Map 11 B3. 📞 01 44 18 62 60.
Ⓜ Solférino, Varenne, Invalides.
◯ 9am–7pm daily. ⬤ non-religious public hols. 🚻 🚻

Designed by the German-born architect François-Christian Gau and the first of its kind to be built in Paris, this Neo-Gothic church was inspired by the mid-19th-century enthusiasm for the Middle Ages, made fashionable by such writers as Victor Hugo. The church is noted for its imposing twin towers, visible from across the Seine. The interior decoration includes sculpted stations of the cross by James Pradier and stained-glass windows with scenes relating to the patron saint of the church. The composer César Franck was the church organist here for 32 years.

Neo-Classical facade of the Assemblée Nationale Palais-Bourbon

Assemblée Nationale Palais-Bourbon ⓫

126 Rue de l'Université 75007. **Map** 11 B2. **Tel** 01 40 63 60 00. Ⓜ Assemblée-Nationale. RER Invalides. ⬜ to group visits only. Call the above number for more information. 🖪 🖥 www.assemblee-nat.fr

Built in 1722 for the Duchesee de Bourbon, daughter of Louis XIV, the Palais-Bourbon was confiscated during the Revolution. It has been home to the lower house of the French Parliament since 1830.

During World War II, the palace became the Nazi administration's seat of government. The public can enter to watch parliament in action. The grand neo-Classical facade with its fine columns was added to the palace in 1806, partly to mirror the facade of La Madeleine church facing it across the Seine. The adjacent Hôtel de Lassay, built by the Prince de Condé, is now the residence of the president of the National Assembly.

Rue Cler ⓬

75007. **Map** 10 F3. Ⓜ Ecole-Militaire, Latour-Maubourg. **Market** ⬜ Tue–Sat. See **Shops and Markets** p338.

This is the street market of the seventh arrondissement, the richest in Paris, for here live the bulk of senior civil servants, captains of industry and many diplomats. The market area occupies a pedestrian precinct stretching south from the Rue de Grenelle. It is colourful, but very much an exclusive market, with the best-dressed shoppers in town. As one would expect, the produce is excellent, the pâtisserie and cheese shops in particular.

Les Egouts ⓭

93 Quai d'Orsay 75007. **Map** 10 F2. 🖪 01 53 68 27 81. Ⓜ Alma-Marceau. RER Pont de l'Alma. ⬜ 11am–5pm (4pm in winter) Sat–Wed. ● last 3 wks Jan. 🖼 🖸 🖥

One of Baron Haussmann's finest achievements, the majority of Paris's sewers (égouts) date from the Second Empire (see pp32–3). If laid end to end the 2,100 km (1,300 miles) of sewers would stretch from Paris to Istanbul. In the 20th century the sewers became a popular tourist attraction. All tours have been limited to a small area around the Quai d'Orsay entrance and are on foot. A sewer museum has been established here where visitors can discover the mysteries of underground Paris. There are displays of machinery used in the past and in the sewers of today.

Musée du Quai Branly ⓮

22 Rue de l'Université 75007. **Map** 10 E2. **Tel** 01 56 61 70 00. Ⓜ Alma-Marceau. RER Pont de l'Alma. ⬜ 10am–6.30pm Tue–Sun. 🖼 🛅 🖪 **Exhibitions, theatre, film, library.** www.quaibranly.fr

Built to give the arts of Africa, Asia, Oceania and the Americas a platform as shining as that reserved for western art, this museum boasts a collection of more than 300,000 objects. It is particularly strong on Africa, with stone, wooden and ivory masks, as well as ceremonial tools. The Jean Nouvel-designed building, raised on stilts, is a sight in itself: the ingenious use of glass allows the surrounding greenery to act as a natural backdrop for the collection.

The fruit and vegetable market in the Rue Cler

Doorway at No. 29 Avenue Rapp

Champ-de-Mars ⓯

75007. **Map** 10 E3. Ⓜ *Ecole-Militaire.*
Ⓡ *Champ-de-Mars–Tour-Eiffel.*

The gardens stretching from the Eiffel Tower to the Ecole Militaire were originally a parade ground for the officer cadets of the Ecole Militaire. The area has since been used for horse-racing, balloon ascents and the mass celebrations for 14 July, the anniversary of the Revolution.

The first ceremony was held in 1790 in the presence of a glum, captive Louis XVI. Vast exhibitions were held here in the late 19th century, including the 1889 World Fair for which the Eiffel Tower was erected. *Le Mur de la Paix*, Jean-Michel Wilmotte's monument to world peace, stands at one end.

A Paris balloon ascent

Eiffel Tower ⓰

See pp192–3.

No. 29 Avenue Rapp ⓱

75007. **Map** 10 E2. Ⓜ *Pont-de-l'Alma.*

A prime example of Art Nouveau architecture is No. 29 and it won its designer, Jules Lavirotte, first prize at the Concours des Facades de la Ville de Paris in 1901. Its ceramics and brickwork are decorated with animal and flower motifs intermingling with female figures. These are superimposed on a multi-coloured sandstone base to produce a facade that is deliberately erotic, and was certainly subversive in its day. Also worth visiting is Lavirotte's building, complete with watchtower, which can be found in the Square Rapp.

Village Suisse ⓲

38-78 Ave de Suffren 75015.
Map 10 E4. Ⓜ *Dupleix.*
◯ *10.30am–7pm Thu–Mon.*

The Swiss government built a mock-Alpine village for the 1900 Universal Exhibition held in the Champ-de-Mars nearby. It was later used as a centre for dealing in secondhand goods. In the 1950s and 1960s antique dealers moved in, and everything became more fashionable and expensive. The village was renovated in the late 1960s.

Ecole Militaire ⓳

1 Pl Joffre 75007. **Map** 10 F4.
Ⓜ *Ecole-Militaire.* **Visits** *by special permission only – contact the Commandant in writing.* 📷

The Royal Military Academy of Louis XV was founded in 1751 to educate 500 sons of impoverished officers. It was designed by architect Jacques-Ange Gabriel, and one of the features is the central pavilion. This is a magnificent example of the French Classical style, with eight Corinthian pillars and a quadrangular dome. The interior is decorated in Louis XVI style; of main interest are the chapel and a superb Gabriel-designed wrought-iron banister on the main staircase.

An early cadet at the academy was Napoleon, whose passing-out report stated that "he could go far if the circumstances are right".

A 1751 engraving showing the planning of the Ecole Militaire

UNESCO ⓴

7 Pl de Fontenoy 75007. **Map** 10 F5.
Tel *01 45 68 10 00.* 📱 *01 45 68 10 60 (in English).* Ⓜ *Ségur, Cambronne.* ◯ *guided visits 3pm Tue (English) & 3pm Wed (French).* ⬤ *public hols & during conference sessions.* 📷 ♿ 🎬 🍽 📚 ***Exhibitions, films.*** **www**.unesco.org

This is the headquarters of the United Nations Educational, Scientific and Cultural Organization (UNESCO). The organization's stated aim is to contribute to international peace and security through education, science and culture.

UNESCO is a trove of modern art, notably a huge mural by Picasso, ceramics by Joan Miró and sculptures by Henry Moore.

Moore's *Reclining Figure* **at UNESCO (erected 1958)**

Eiffel Tower ⑯

Eiffel Tower from the Trocadéro

Originally built to impress visitors to the Universal Exhibition of 1889, the Eiffel Tower (Tour Eiffel) was meant to be a temporary addition to the Paris skyline. Designed by the engineer Gustave Eiffel, it was fiercely decried by 19th-century aesthetes. The author Guy de Maupassant lunched there to avoid seeing it. The world's tallest building until 1931, when New York's Empire State Building was completed, the tower is now the symbol of Paris. Since its recent renovation and installation of new lighting it has never looked better.

Ironwork Pattern
According to Eiffel, the complex pattern of pig-iron girders came from the need to stabilize the tower in strong winds. But Eiffel's design quickly won admirers for its pleasing symmetry.

Lift Engine Room
Eiffel emphasized safety over speed when choosing the lifts for the tower.

STAR FEATURES

★ Eiffel Bust

★ Cineiffel

★ Hydraulic Lift Mechanism

★ Viewing Gallery

★ Cineiffel
This small museum tells the history of the tower through a short film. It includes footage of famous personalities who have visited the tower, including Charlie Chaplin, Josephine Baker and Adolf Hitler.

THE DARING AND THE DELUDED

The tower has inspired many crazy stunts. It has been climbed by mountaineers, cycled down by a journalist, and used by trapeze artists and as a launch pad by parachutists. In 1912 a Parisian tailor, Reichelt, attempted to fly from the parapet with only a modified cape for wings. He plunged to his death in front of a large crowd. According to the autopsy, he died of a heart attack before even touching the ground.

Birdman Reichelt

★ Hydraulic Lift Mechanism
Still in working order, this part of the original 1900 mechanism was automated in 1986.

The third level, 276 m (905 ft) above the ground, can hold 800 people at a time.

VISITORS' CHECKLIST

Champ de Mars. **Map** 10 D3. *Tel* *01 44 11 23 23*. Ⓜ *Bir Hakeim*. 🚌 *42, 69, 72, 82, 87, 91 to Champ de Mars*. 🚃 *Champ de Mars*. 🅾 *Tour Eiffel*. 🅿 *on site*. ⬜ *Sep–mid-Jun: 9.30am–11pm daily (6.30pm for stairs); mid-Jun– Aug: 9am–midnight (last adm 1hr before)*. 📷 🅾 ♿ *limited*. 🍴 📷 *Films.* **www**.tour-eiffel.fr

★ **Viewing Gallery**
On a clear day it is possible to see for 72 km (45 miles), including a distant view of Chartres Cathedral.

Double-Decker Lifts
During the tourist season, the limited capacity of the lifts means that it can take up to a couple of hours to reach the top. Queuing for the lifts requires patience and a good head for heights.

THE TOWER IN FIGURES
- the top (including the antennae) is 324 m (1,063 ft) high
- the top can move in a curve of 18 cm (7 in) under the effect of heat
- 1,665 steps to the third level
- 2.5 million rivets hold the tower together
- never sways more than 7 cm (2.5 in)
- 10,100 tonnes in weight
- 60 tonnes of paint are used every seven years

A workman building the tower

The second level is at 115 m (376 ft), separated from the first level by 359 steps, or a few minutes in the lift.

Jules Verne Restaurant is one of the best restaurants in Paris, offering superb food and panoramic views (see p304).

The first level, at 57 m (187 ft) high, can be reached by lift or by 360 steps. There is a post office here.

★ **Eiffel Bust**
Eiffel's (1832–1923) achievement was crowned with the Légion d'Honneur in 1889. Another honour was the bust by Antoine Bourdelle, placed beneath the tower in 1929.

Gilded bronze
statues by a number
of sculptors
decorating the
central square of the
Palais de Chaillot

Porte
Dauphine M
Avenue Foch RER 10

BLVD FLANDRIN
RUE DE LA FAISANDERIE
AVE VIC

Avenue
Henri Martin
RER
AVE HENRI MARTIN

RUE DE

M La Mu
RUE DE P

RER
Boulainvilliers-
La Muette

RUE DES VIG

RUE DE BOULAINVILLIERS

CHAILLOT QUARTER

The village of Chaillot was absorbed into Paris in the 19th century and transformed into an area rich in grand Second Empire avenues *(see pp34–5)* and opulent mansions. Some of the avenues converge on the Place du Trocadéro, renowned for its elegant cafés, which leads on to the Avenue du Président Wilson, with

Sculptures at the base of the Chaillot pool

a greater concentration of museums than any other street in Paris. Many of the area's private mansions are occupied by embassies, including the imposing Vatican embassy, and by major company headquarters. To the west is the territory of the *haute bourgeoisie*, one of Paris's most exclusive, if staid, residential neighbourhoods.

SIGHTS AT A GLANCE

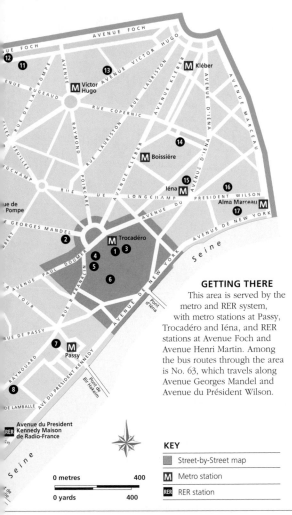

Museums and Galleries
Cimetière de Passy ❷
Cité de l'Architecture et du Patrimoine ❸
Musée de l'Homme ❹
Musée de la Marine ❺
Musée du Vin ❼
Maison de Balzac ❽
Musée de Radio-France ❾
Musée de la Contrefaçon ❿
Musée National d'Ennery ⓫
Musée Arménien ⓬
Musée Dapper ⓭
Musée du Cristal de Baccarat ⓮
Musée National des Arts Asiatiques Guimet ⓯
Musée Galliera ⓰
Musée d'Art Moderne de la Ville de Paris ⓱

Gardens
Jardins du Trocadéro ❻

Modern Architecture
Palais de Chaillot ❶

GETTING THERE
This area is served by the metro and RER system, with metro stations at Passy, Trocadéro and Iéna, and RER stations at Avenue Foch and Avenue Henri Martin. Among the bus routes through the area is No. 63, which travels along Avenue Georges Mandel and Avenue du Président Wilson.

KEY

▨	Street-by-Street map
Ⓜ	Metro station
RER	RER station

SEE ALSO

• *Street Finder*, map 3, 9–10
• *Where to Stay* pp289–290
• *Restaurants* pp309–310

0 metres   400
0 yards   400

Street-by-Street: Chaillot

The Chaillot hill, with its superb position overlooking the Seine, was the site chosen by Napoleon for "the biggest and most extraordinary" palace that was to be built for his son – but by the time of his downfall only a few ramparts had been completed. Today, the monumental Palais de Chaillot, with its two massive curved wings, stands on the site. From the terrace in front of the Palais there is a magnificent view over the Trocadéro gardens and the Seine to the Eiffel Tower.

The statue of Marshal Ferdinand Foch, who led the Allies to victory in 1918, was unveiled on 11 November 1951. It was built by Robert Wlérick and Raymond Martin to commemorate the centenary of Foch's birth and the 33rd anniversary of the 1918 Armistice.

Metro Trocadéro

The Place du Trocadéro was created for the Universal Exhibition of 1878. Initially it was known as the Place du Roi-de-Rome, in honour of Napoleon's son.

★ **Musée de la Marine**
While concentrating on France's maritime history, this museum also has exhibits of navigational instruments ⑤

Palais de Chaillot
This Neo-Classical building was constructed for the World Fair of 1937. It replaced the Palais du Trocadéro, which was built in 1878 ①

★ **Musée de l'Homme**
The Vénus de Lespugue, dating from around 25,000 BC, is one of the many artifacts housed in this museum ④

The Théâtre National de Chaillot, beneath the terrace, includes a multi-purpose cultural centre and a modern 1,200-seat theatre. *(See pp342–4.)*

Jardins du Trocadéro
The present layout of the gardens was created by R Lardat after the World Fair of 1937 **6**

LOCATOR MAP
See Central Paris Map pp14–15

Cité de l'Architecture et du Patrimoine
This vast complex houses an Architecture Museum, a school, library and archive, and various heritage organizations **3**

The Trocadéro fountains are operated in sequence, culminating in the massive water cannons in the centre firing towards the Eiffel Tower. They are illuminated at night.

The Pont d'Iéna was built by Napoleon to celebrate his victory in 1806 over the Prussians at Jena (Iéna) in Prussia. It was widened in 1937 to complement the building of the Palais de Chaillot.

KEY

— — — Suggested route

| 0 metres | 100 |
| 0 yards | 100 |

STAR SIGHTS

★ Musée de l'Homme

★ Musée de la Marine

Trocadéro fountains in front of the Palais de Chaillot

Palais de Chaillot ❶

17 Pl du Trocadéro 75016.
Map 9 C2. **Tel** 01 44 05 39 10.
Ⓜ Trocadéro. ◯ 9.45am–5.15pm
Wed–Mon. 🍴 🖥 🛗

The Palais, with its huge, curved colonnaded wings each culminating in an immense pavilion, was designed in Neo-Classical style for the 1937 Paris Exhibition by Léon Azéma, Louis-Hippolyte Boileau and Jacques Carlu. It is adorned with sculptures and bas-reliefs. On the walls of the pavilions there are gold inscriptions by the poet and essayist Paul Valéry.

The *parvis* or square, situated between the two pavilions is decorated with large bronze sculptures and ornamental pools. On the terrace in front of the *parvis* stand two bronzes, *Apollo* by

Henri Bouchard and *Hercules* by Albert Pommier. Stairways lead from the terrace to the Théâtre National de Chaillot (*see pp342–3*), which, since World War II, has enjoyed huge fame for its avant-garde productions.

Cimetière de Passy ❷

2 Rue du Commandant-Shloesig 75016. **Map** 9 C2. **Tel** 01 47 27 51 42. Ⓜ Trocadéro. ◯ 8am–5.45pm Mon–Fri; 8.30am–5.45pm Sat; 9am–5.45pm Sun.

Located in the elegant 16th arrondissement, this small cemetery is packed with the mortal remains of eminent Parisians – there are more famous people per square metre here than in any other cemetery in Paris. You can find composers Claude

Debussy and Gabriel Fauré, painter Edouard Manet, and many politicians and aristocrats. Opened in 1820, the cemetery is worth a visit just to admire the striking statuary on the tombs.

Church model from Bagneux, Cité de l'Architecture et du Patrimoine

Cité de l'Architecture et du Patrimoine ❸

Palais de Chaillot, Pl du Trocadéro 75016. **Map** 9 C2. **Tel** 01 58 51 52 00. Ⓜ Trocadéro. ◯ from February 2007. 9.30am–5.30pm Tue–Sun, but call ahead to confirm. 🖼 📷 🍴 🛗

In the east wing of the Palais de Chaillot, this museum charts the development of French architecture through the ages. Among the unmissable displays is the Galerie des Moulages, which covers the period between the Middle Ages and the Renaissance. Here you will find three-dimensional models of great French cathedrals, such as Chartres. Also worth a look is the Galerie Moderne et Contemporaine, with a reconstruction of a Le Corbusier-designed apartment.

A tomb in the Cimetière de Passy, in the shadow of the Eiffel Tower

Musée de l'Homme ④

Palais de Chaillot, 17 Pl du Trocadéro 75016. **Map** 9 C2. **Tel** 01 44 05 72 72. ⓜ Trocadéro. ◯ 9.45am–5.15pm Mon, Wed–Fri; 10am–6.30pm Sat, Sun. ◯ public hols. **Exhibitions, films.** ⓘ ◻ ◻ www.mnhn.fr

Situated in the west wing of the Chaillot palace, this museum traces the process of human evolution, from prehistoric times to the present, through a series of anthropological exhibits from around the world.

The museum is currently undergoing extensive renovations that will ultimately lead to its housing one of the most comprehensive prehistoric collections in the world, as well as permanent displays on anatomy and the environment.

Gabon mask at Musée de l'Homme

Musée de la Marine ⑤

Palais de Chaillot, 17 Pl du Trocadéro 75016 **Map** 9 C2. **Tel** 01 53 65 69 69. ⓜ Trocadéro. ◯ 10am–6pm Wed–Mon. ◯ 1 Jan, 1 May, 25 Dec. **Films, videos.** www.musee-marine.fr

French maritime history from the days of the royal wooden warships to today's aircraft carriers and nuclear submarines is told through wonderfully exact scale models (most of them two centuries old), mementoes of naval heroes, paintings and navigational instruments. The museum was set up by Charles X in

Relief outside the Maritime Museum

1827, and was then moved to the Chaillot palace in 1943. Exhibits include Napoleon's barge, models of the fleet he assembled at Boulogne-sur-Mer in 1805 for his planned invasion of Britain, and displays on underwater exploration and fishing vessels.

Jardins du Trocadéro ⑥

75016. **Map** 10 D2. ⓜ Trocadéro.

These lovely gardens cover 10 ha (25 acres). Their centrepiece is a long rectangular ornamental pool, bordered by stone and bronze-gilt statues, which look spectacular at night when the fountains are illuminated. The statues include *Man* by P Traverse and *Woman* by G Braque, *Bull* by P Jouve and *Horse* by G Guyot. On either side of the pool, the slopes of the Chaillot hill gently lead down to the Seine and the Pont d'Iéna. There is a freshwater aquarium in the northeast corner of the gardens, which are richly laid out with trees, walkways, small streams and bridges.

Musée du Vin ⑦

Rue des Eaux, 5 Sq Charles Dickens 75016. **Map** 9 C3. **Tel** 01 45 25 63 26. ⓜ Passy. ◯ 10am–6pm Tue–Sun. ◯ 24 Dec–1 Jan. ◻ ⊘ ◻ groups only. ⓘ lunchtime only. www.museeduvinparis.com

Waxwork figures and cardboard cut-outs graphically illustrate the history of wine-making in these atmospheric vaulted medieval cellars, which were once used by the monks of Passy. The exhibits include a collection of old wine bottles, glasses and cork screws, as well as an array of scientific instruments that were used in the wine-making and bottling processes. There is also an excellent restaurant, wine for sale and tours which include a wine-tasting session.

Bridge in the Trocadéro gardens

Maison de Balzac ⑧

47 Rue Raynouard 75016. **Map** 9 B3. **Tel** 01 55 74 41 80. ⓜ Passy, La Muette. ◯ 10am–6pm Tue–Sun (last adm: 5.30pm). ◯ public hols. ◻ ◻ ◻ ◻ www.balzac.paris.fr

The novelist Honoré de Balzac lived here from 1840 to 1847 under a false name, Monsieur de Brugnol, to avoid his numerous creditors. During this time he wrote many of his most famous novels, among them *La Cousine Bette* (1846).

The house now contains a reference library, with some of his original works, and a museum with memorabilia from his life. Many of the rooms have drawings and paintings portraying Balzac's family and close friends. The Madame Hanska room is devoted to the memory of the Russian woman who corresponded with Balzac for 18 years and was his wife for the five months before his death in 1850.

The house has a back entrance leading into the Rue Berton, which was used to evade unwelcome callers. Rue Berton, with its ivy-covered walls, has retained much of its old, country-like charm.

Plaque marking Balzac's house

Radio (1955) in radio museum

Musée de Radio-France ❾

116 Ave du Président-Kennedy 75016. **Map** 9 B4.
Tel 01 56 40 15 16. **M** Ranelagh.
⭘ for tours only, Mon–Sat.
⬤ public hols. 🖼 🗙 ♿
🎫 10–11am, 2.30–4pm Mon–Fri.
www.radiofrance.fr

Radio-France House is an impressive building designed by Henri Bernard in 1963 as the headquarters of the state-run Radio-France. The largest single structure in France, it is made up of three incomplete concentric circular constructions with a rectangular tower. The building covers an area of 2 ha (5 acres).
Here, in the 70-odd studios and main public auditorium, French radio programmes are produced. The museum traces the history of communications from the first Chappe telegraph, which took place in 1793, to the latest multimedia developments in radio-listening via the internet. It also gives a fascinating insight into how radio programmes are made.

Musée de la Contrefaçon ❿

16 Rue de la Faisanderie 75016.
Map 3 A5. **Tel** 01 56 26 14 00.
M Porte Dauphine. ⭘ 2–5.30pm
Tue–Sun. ⬤ public hols. 🖼 🗙
www.unifab.com

French cognac and perfume producers, and the luxury trade in general, have been plagued for years by counter-

feiters operating around the world. This museum was set up by the manufacturers' union and illustrates the history of this type of fraud, which has been going on since Roman times. Among the impressive display of forgeries are copies of Louis Vuitton luggage, Cartier watches and fake wine from the Narbonne region. The museum also has a display on the fate that awaits anyone who may be tempted to imitate a product.

Musée National d'Ennery ⓫

59 Ave Foch 75016. **Map** 3 B5.
Tel 01 45 53 57 96.
M Porte Dauphine.
⭘ usually 10am–6pm Wed–Mon
but subject to change. Call ahead
to confirm. 🗹

This mansion, which dates from the Second Empire period, houses an intriguing collection of Chinese and Japanese items assembled by Adolphe d'Ennery, the 19th-century dramatist. Dating from the 17th to 19th centuries, the display includes human and animal figures, Japanese ceramic boxes, furniture and hundreds of

Chinese vase (circa 18th century), Musée d'Ennery

netsuke – small, carved belt ornaments made of bone, wood or ivory.

Musée Arménien ⓬

59 Ave Foch 75016. **Map** 3 B5.
Tel 01 45 56 15 88. **M** Porte
Dauphine. ⬤ for renovation until
further notice.

The ground floor of No. 59 Avenue Foch houses the Armenian museum, founded after World War II. Despite its small size the collection has many fascinating treasures, including church plates, exquisite miniatures, silverware, ceramics, carpets and contemporary paintings.

Khmer art in the Musée National des Arts Asiatiques Guimet

Musée Dapper ⓭

35 bis Rue Paul-Valéry, 75116.
Tel 01 45 00 01 50. **M** Victor-Hugo.
⭘ 11am-7pm Wed–Mon. 🖼

Not just a museum, but a world-class ethnographic research centre called the Dapper Foundation, this is France's premier showcase of African art and culture. Located in an attractive building with an "African" garden, it is a treasure house of vibrant colour and powerful, evocative work from the black nations. The emphasis is on pre-colonial folk arts, with sculpture, carvings, and tribal work, but there is later art too. The highlight is tribal masks, with a dazzling, extraordinary array of richly carved religious, ritual and funerary masks, as well as theatrical ones used for comic, magical or symbolic performances, some dating back to the 12th century. Anthropologists, locals and tourists mingle here for the themed exhibitions and events.

Armenian crown (19th century)

Musée du Cristal de Baccarat

11 Place des Etats Unis 75016.
Map 4 D5. **Tel** *01 40 22 11 00.*
Ⓜ *Boissière.* ☐ *10am–6.30pm
Mon–Sat.* ● *public hols.* 🅿️ 📷
📷 🎫 www.baccarat.fr

The Musée du Cristal, also
known as the Galerie-Musée
Baccarat, has on display over
1,200 articles made by the
Baccarat company, which
was founded in 1764 in
Lorraine. These include
services created for the royal
and imperial courts of Europe
and the finest pieces created
in the workshops.

Musée National des Arts Asiatiques Guimet

6 Pl d'Iéna 75116. **Map** 10 D1. **Tel**
01 56 52 53 00. Ⓜ *Iéna.* ☐ *10am–
6pm Wed–Mon (last adm: 5.30pm).*
🅿️ 🚫 ♿ 🎫 🍴 🛍️ 📷 *Panthéon
Bouddhique (additional galleries) at
19 Ave d'Iéna* **Tel** *01 40 73 88 11.*
www.museeguimet.fr

The Musée Guimet has the
finest collection of Khmer
(Cambodian) art in the West.
It was originally set up in Lyon
in 1879 by the industrialist
and orientalist Emile Guimet.
Moved to Paris in 1884, it
meticulously represents every
artistic tradition from Afghani-

Gabriel Forestier's sculpted doors,
Musée d'Art Moderne

stan to India, to China and
Japan, to Korea and Vietnam
and the rest of south-east
Asia. With over 45,000
artworks, the museum is
acclaimed for some especially
unusual collections, including
the Cambodian Angkor Wat
sculptures and 1600 displays
of Himalayan Art. Other highlights include Chinese bronzes
and lacquerware, and many
statues of Buddha.

Musée Galliera

10 Ave Pierre 1er de Serbie 75116.
Map 10 E1. **Tel** *01 56 52 86 00.*
Ⓜ *Iéna, Alma Marceau.* ☐ *for
exhibitions only, 10am–6pm
Tue–Sun (from 2pm on some public
hols).* 🅿️ **Children's room.**
www.galliera.paris.fr

Devoted to the evolution of
fashion, this museum is housed
in the Renaissance-style
palace built for the Duchesse

Maria de Ferrari Galliera in
1892. The collection comprises
more than 100,000 outfits,
from the 18th century to the
present day. Some, from more
recent times, have been
donated by such fashionable
women as Baronne Hélène
de Rothschild and Princess
Grace of Monaco. The various
garments are displayed in
rotation twice per year.

Musée d'Art Moderne de la Ville de Paris

Palais de Tokyo, 11 Ave du Président-
Wilson 75016. **Map** 10 E1. **Tel** *01 53
67 40 00.* Ⓜ *Iéna, Alma Marceau.*
☐ *10am–6pm Tue–Sun (to 10pm
Wed).* 🅿️ *temporary exhibitions.* ♿
🎫 🛍️ 📷 *Films.* www.mam.paris.fr

This large, lively museum is
the municipality's own renowned collection of modern
art, covering all major 20th
century trends (the 21st
century will be included). The
museum occupies the vast
east wing of the Palais de
Tokyo, built for the 1937 World
Fair. One of the highlights is
Raoul Dufy's gigantic mural
La Fée Electricité. Also
notable are the Cubists,
Amadeo Modigliani, and The
Fauves, especially Henri
Matisse, whose *La Danse*
is here in both versions.

Garden and rear facade of the Musée Galliera

CHAMPS-ELYSEES

Two great streets dominate this area – the Avenue des Champs-Elysées and the Rue St-Honoré. The former is the capital's most famous thoroughfare. Its breadth is spectacular. The pavements are wide and their cafés, cinemas and shops attract throngs of people, who come to eat and shop, but also to see and to be seen. Rond Point des Champs-Elysées is the pretty end, with shady chestnut trees and pavements colourfully bordered by flower beds. Luxury and political power are nearby. Five-star hotels, fine restaurants and upmarket shops line the nearby streets and avenues. And along Rue St-Honoré are the impressive, heavily guarded Palais de l'Elysée, the sumptuous town mansions of business chiefs, and the many embassies and consulates.

Ornate lamp-post on Pont Alexandre III

SIGHTS AT A GLANCE

Historic Buildings and Streets
Palais de l'Elysée ⑤
Avenue Montaigne ⑥
Avenue des Champs-Elysées ⑧
Place Charles de Gaulle
(l'Etoile) ⑨

Monuments
Arc de Triomphe pp208–9 ⑩

Bridges
Pont Alexandre III ①

Museums and Galleries
Grand Palais ②
Palais de la Découverte ③
Petit Palais ④
Musée Jacquemart-André ⑦

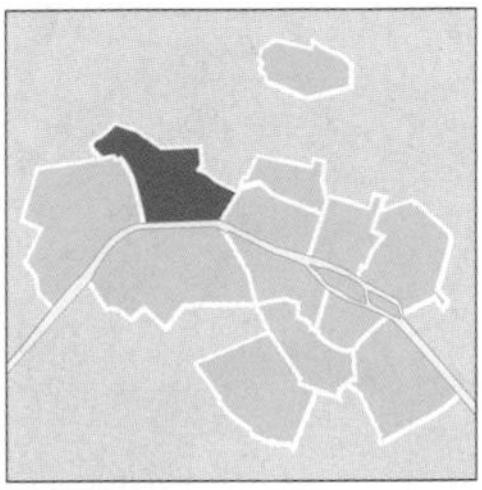

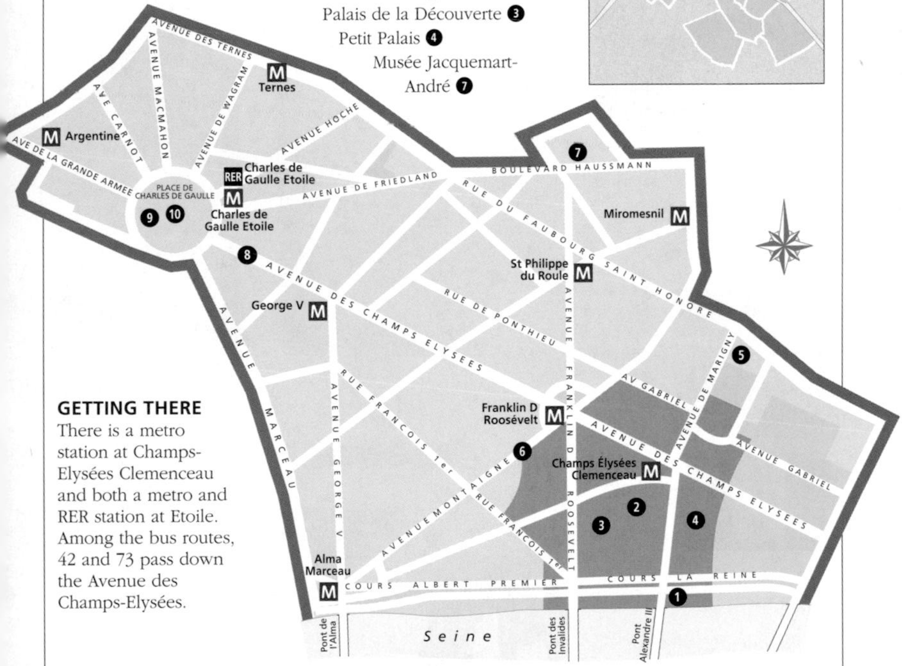

GETTING THERE

There is a metro station at Champs-Elysées Clemenceau and both a metro and RER station at Etoile. Among the bus routes, 42 and 73 pass down the Avenue des Champs-Elysées.

KEY

▨	Street-by-Street map
Ⓜ	Metro station
RER	RER station

SEE ALSO

- *Street Finder,* map 3–4, 5, 11
- *Where to Stay* pp290–291
- *Restaurants* pp310–311

0 metres		400
0 yards		400

◁ **View of the Arc de Triomphe at night**

Street-by-Street: Champs-Elysées

The formal gardens that line the Champs-Elysées from the Place de la Concorde to the Rond-Point have changed little since they were laid out by the architect Jacques Hittorff in 1838. They were used as the setting for the World Fair of 1855, which included the Palais de l'Industrie, Paris's response to London's Crystal Palace. The Palais was later replaced by the Grand Palais and Petit Palais, which were created as a showpiece of the Third Republic for the Universal Exhibition of 1900. They sit on either side of an impressive vista that stretches from the Place Clémenceau across the elegant curve of the Pont Alexandre III to the Invalides.

The Théâtre du Rond-Point was the home of the Renaud-Barrault Company. There are plaques on the back door of the theatre representing Napoleon's campaigns.

Metro Franklin D Roosevelt Ⓜ

Avenue Montaigne
Christian Dior and other haute couture *houses are based in this chic avenue* ❻

★ **Grand Palais**
Designed by Charles Girault, this grand 19th-century building is still used for major exhibitions ❷

The Lasserre restaurant is decorated in the style of a luxurious ocean liner from the 1930s.

RUE JEAN GOUJON

RUE FRANÇOIS PREMIER

AVE GL. EISENHOWER

PL DU CANADA

COURS LA

PONT DES INVALIDES

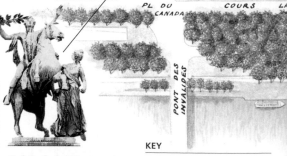

STAR SIGHTS

★ Avenue des Champs-Elysées

★ Grand Palais

★ Petit Palais

★ Pont Alexandre III

Palais de la Découverte
Outside this museum of scientific discoveries is a pair of equestrian statues ❸

KEY

– – – Suggested route

0 metres 　　　　100

0 yards 　　　　100

★ **Avenue des Champs-Elysées**
This was the setting for the victory parades following the two World Wars, and for the bicentennial parade in 1989 **8**

LOCATOR MAP
See Central Paris Map pp14–15

CHAMPS-ELYSEES

CHAILLOT QUARTER

Seine

INVALIDES AND EIFFEL TOWER QUARTER

Metro Champs-Elysées-Clemenceau

The Jardins des Champs-Elysées, with their fountains, flowerbeds, paths and pleasure pavilions, became very popular towards the end of the 19th century. Fashionable Parisians, including Marcel Proust, often came here.

To the Place de la Concorde

★ **Petit Palais**
Lit by natural light, this palace is as much a work of art as the 19th-century items it contains, such as sculptures and Impressionist paintings **4**

To the Invalides

★ **Pont Alexandre III**
The bridge's four columns help to anchor the piers that absorb the immense forces generated by such a large single-span structure **1**

Pont Alexandre III ❶

75008. **Map** 11 A1. Ⓜ *Champs-Elysées-Clemenceau.*

This is Paris's prettiest bridge with its exuberant Art Nouveau decoration of lamps, cherubs, nymphs and winged horses at either end. It was built between 1896 and 1900, in time for the Universal Exhibition and it was named after Tsar Alexander III (father of Nicholas II) who laid the foundation stone in October 1896.

The style of the bridge reflects that of the Grand Palais, to which it leads on the Right Bank. The construction of the bridge is a marvel of 19th-century engineering, consisting of a 6-m (18-ft) high single-span steel arch across the Seine. The design was subject to strict controls that prevented the bridge from obscuring the view of the Champs-Elysées or the Invalides. So today you can still enjoy magnificent views from here.

Pont Alexandre III

Grand Palais ❷

Porte A, Ave Général Eisenhower 75008. **Map** 11 A1. **Tel** *01 44 13 17 30.* Ⓜ *Champs-Elysées-Clemenceau.* ◯ *for temporary exhibitions (usually 10am–8pm Thu–Mon,10am–10pm Wed, but phone to check).* ⬤ *1 May, 25 Dec.* 🎫 🚫 ♿ 🎧 *10am–1pm daily, Wed pm & Sat pm.* ⓣ 🖥 🚻 **www**.rmn.fr

Built at the same time as the Petit Palais and the Pont Alexandre III, the exterior of this massive palace combines an imposing Classical stone

facade with a riot of Art Nouveau ironwork. It has a splendid glass roof, and Récipon's colossal bronze statues of flying horses and chariots at its four corners. The enormous glass roof (15,000 sq metres/160,000 sq ft) has recently been restored to its former glory. The metal structure supporting the glass weighs 8,500 tonnes, some 500 tonnes more than the Eiffel Tower.

Temporary exhibitions are held in the Galeries Nationales du Grand Palais. The basement houses a major police station.

Palais de la Découverte

Palais de la Découverte ❸

Ave Franklin D Roosevelt 75008. **Map** 11 A1. 📞 *01 56 43 20 21.* Ⓜ *Franklin D Roosevelt.* ◯ *9.30am–6pm Tue–Sat; 10am–7pm Sun.* ⬤ *1 Jan, 1 May, 14 Jul, 15 Aug, 25 Dec.* 🚫 📷 *by permission.* ⓣ 🖥 **www**.palais-decouverte.fr

Opened in a wing of the Grand Palais for the World Fair of 1937, this museum of scientific discoveries was an immediate success and has continued to be very popular ever since. The displays help to explain the basics of all the sciences.

Entrance to the Petit Palais

Petit Palais ❹

Ave Winston Churchill 75008. **Map** 11 B1. **Tel** *01 53 43 40 00.* Ⓜ *Champs-Elysées-Clemenceau.* ◯ *10am–6pm Tue–Sun (to 8pm Tue during exhibitions).* ⬤ *public hols.* 🎫 📷 🎧 *for exhibitions.* 🖥

Built for the Universal Exhibition in 1900, to stage a major display of French art, this jewel of a building now houses the Musée des Beaux-Arts de la Ville de Paris. Arranged around a pretty semi-circular courtyard and garden, the palace is similar in style to the Grand Palais, and has Ionic columns, a grand porch and a dome which echoes that of the Invalides across the river.

The Cours de la Reine wing, nearest the river, is used for temporary exhibitions, while the Champs-Elysées side of the palace houses the permanent collections. These are divided into sections: Greek and Roman; medieval and Renaissance ivories and sculptures; Renaissance clocks and jewellery; and 17th-, 18th- and 19th-century art and furniture. There are also many works by the Impressionists.

GRAND PALAIS

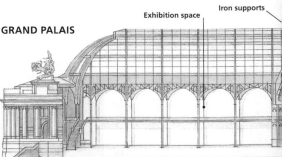
Exhibition space   Iron supports

Palais de l'Elysée ❺

55 Rue du Faubourg-St-Honoré
75008. **Map** 5 B5. **M** St-Philippe-
du-Roule. **Not open** to the public.

Set amid splendid English-
style gardens, the Elysée
Palace was built in 1718 for
the Comte d'Evreux and has
been the official residence
of the President of the
Republic since 1873.
From 1805 to 1808 it
was occupied by
Napoleon's sister,
Caroline, and her
husband, Murat.
Two charming
rooms have been
preserved from this
period: the Salon
Murat and the Salon
d'Argent. General de
Gaulle used to give
press conferences
in the Hall of
Mirrors. Today,
the President's

Elysée guard

modernized apartments can
be found on the first floor
opposite the Rue de l'Elysée.

Avenue Montaigne ❻

75008. **Map** 10 F1. **M** Franklin D
Roosevelt.

In the 19th century this
avenue was famous for its
dance halls and its Winter
Garden, where Parisians went
to hear Adolphe Sax play his
newly-invented saxophone.
Today it is still one of Paris's
most fashionable
streets, bustling with
restaurants, cafés,
hotels and designer
boutiques.

Glass cupola

Inside the Musée Jacquemart-André

Musée Jacquemart-André ❼

158 Blvd Haussmann 75008.
Map 5 A4. **Tel** 01 45 62 11 59.
M Miromesnil, St-Philippe-du-Roule.
⬤ 10am–6pm daily. 🎫 🚫 🔲 📷 📹 🖥
www.musee-jacquemart-andre.com

This museum is known for
its fine collection of Italian
Renaissance and French 18th-
century works of art, as well
as its beautiful frescoes by
Tiepolo. Highlights include
works by Mantegna, Uccello's
masterpiece St George and
the Dragon (about 1435),
paintings by Boucher and
Fragonard and 18th-century
tapestries and furniture.

Avenue des Champs-Elysées ❽

75008. **Map** 5 A5. **M** Franklin D
Roosevelt, George V.

Paris's most famous and
popular thoroughfare had its
beginnings in about 1667,
when the landscape garden
designer, André Le Nôtre,
extended the royal view from
the Tuileries by creating a
tree-lined avenue which
eventually became known as
the Champs-Elysées (Elysian
Fields). It has been the
"triumphal way" (as the
French call it) ever since the
home-coming of Napoleon's
body from St Helena in 1840.
With the addition of cafés and
restaurants in the second half
of the 19th century, the
Champs-Elysées became the
place in which to be seen.

Place Charles de Gaulle (l'Etoile) ❾

75008. **Map** 4 D4. **M** Charles de
Gaulle-Etoile.

Known as the Place de
l'Etoile until the death of
Charles de Gaulle in 1969,
the area is still referred to
simply as l'Etoile, the star.
The present place was laid
out in accordance with Baron
Haussmann's plans of 1854
(see pp34–5). For motorists,
it is the ultimate challenge.

Arc de Triomphe from the west

Arc de Triomphe ❿

See pp208–9.

Quadriga (chariot
and four horses)
by Récipon

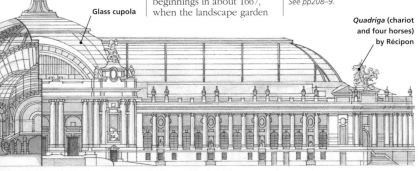

Arc de Triomphe ❿

The east facade of the Arc de Triomphe

After his greatest victory, the Battle of Austerlitz in 1805, Napoleon promised his men, "You shall go home beneath triumphal arches." The first stone of what was to become the world's most famous triumphal arch was laid the following year. But disruptions to architect Jean Chalgrin's plans and the demise of Napoleonic power delayed the completion of this monumental building until 1836. Standing 50 m (164 ft) high, the Arc is now the customary starting point for victory celebrations and parades.

The Battle of Aboukir, a bas-relief by Seurre the Elder, depicts a scene of Napoleon's victory over the Turkish army in 1799.

Triumph of Napoleon
J P Cortot's high-relief celebrates the Treaty of Vienna peace agreement of 1810.

Thirty shields just below the Arc's roof each bear the name of a victorious Napoleonic battle fought in either Europe or Africa.

East facade

The frieze was executed by Rude, Brun, Jacquet, Laitié, Caillouette and Seurre the Elder. This east facade shows the departure of the French armies for new campaigns. The west side shows their return.

STAR FEATURES

★ Departure of the Volunteers in 1792

★ Tomb of the Unknown Soldier

★ **Tomb of the Unknown Soldier**
An unknown French soldier from World War I is buried here.

TIMELINE

1806 Napoleon commissions Chalgrin to build triumphal Arc	**1885** Victor Hugo's body lies in state under the Arc	
	1836 Louis-Philippe completes the Arc	**1944** Liberation of Paris. De Gaulle leads the crowd from the Arc

1800	1850	1900	1950

1840 Napoleon's cortège passes under the Arc

1815 Downfall of Napoleon. Work on Arc ceases

1919 Victory parade of Allied armies through the Arc

NAPOLEON'S NUPTIAL PARADE

Napoleon divorced Josephine in 1809 because she was unable to bear him children. A diplomatic marriage was arranged in 1810 with Marie-Louise, daughter of the Austrian emperor. Napoleon was determined to impress his bride by going through the Arc on their way to the wedding at the Louvre, but work had barely been started. So Chalgrin built a full-scale mock-up of the arch on the site for the couple to pass beneath.

VISITORS' CHECKLIST

Pl Charles de Gaulle. **Map** 4 D4.
Tel 01 55 37 73 77. **M** **RER** Charles
de Gaulle–Etoile. 22, 30, 31,
73, 92 to Pl C de Gaulle. **P** off Pl
C de Gaulle. **Museum** Apr–
Sep: 10am–11pm daily; Oct–Mar:
10am–10.30pm daily (last adm:
30 mins earlier). 1 Jan, 1 May,
8 May, 14 Jul, 11 Nov, 25 Dec.
www.monum.fr

The viewing platform affords one of the best views in Paris, overlooking the grand Champs-Elysées on one side. Beyond the other side is La Défense.

General Marceau's Funeral
Marceau defeated the Austrians in 1795, only to be killed the following year, still fighting them.

The Battle of Austerlitz by Gechter shows Napoleon's army breaking up the ice on the Satschan lake in Austria to drown thousands of enemy troops.

Officers of the Imperial Army are listed on the walls of the smaller arches.

Entrance to museum

★ Departure of the Volunteers in 1792
François Rude's work shows citizens leaving to defend the nation.

Place Charles de Gaulle
Twelve avenues radiate from the Arc at the centre. Some bear the names of important French military leaders, such as Avenues Marceau and Foch. (See pp34–5.)

OPERA QUARTER

The Opéra quarter bustles with bankers and stockbrokers, newspapermen and shoppers, theatre-goers and sightseers. Much of its 19th-century grandeur survives in the Grands Boulevards of Baron Haussmann's urban design. These are still a favourite with thousands of Parisian and foreign promenaders, drawn by the profusion of shops and department stores, which range from the exclusively expensive to the popular.

Much more of the area's older character is found in the many *passages*, delightful narrow shopping arcades with steel and glass roofs. Fashion's bad boy, Jean-Paul Gaultier, has a shop in the smartest

Les Coulisses de l'Opéra (1889) by J Beraud

one, Galerie Vivienne. But more authentically old-style Parisian are the Passage des Panoramas and the Passage Jouffroy, the Passage Verdeau, with its old cameras and comics, and the tiny Passage des Princes. Two of Paris's finest food shops are in the area. Fauchon and Hédiard are noted for mouthwatering mustards, jams, pâtés and sauces. The area still has a reputation as a press centre, although *Le Monde* has moved out, and a history of cinema and theatre – the Lumière brothers held the world's first public film show here in 1895, and the Opéra National de Paris Garnier is famed for its ballet and opera.

SIGHTS AT A GLANCE

Historic Buildings and Streets
Place de la Madeleine ❷
Les Grands Boulevards ❸
Palais de la Bourse ❾
Avenue de l'Opéra ⓬

Churches
La Madeleine ❶

Opera Houses
Opéra National de Paris Garnier ❹

Museums and Galleries
Musée de l'Opéra ❺
Grévin ❼
Cabinet des Médailles et des Antiques ❿
Bibliothèque Nationale ⓫

Shops
Drouot (Hôtel des Ventes) ❻
Les Passages ❽

GETTING THERE

This area is served by the metro and RER systems. Metro lines 3, 7 and 8 serve the station at the Opéra, line 14 stops at Madeleine and the RER Line A stops at Auber. Among the bus routes passing through the area, 42 and 52 travel along Boulevard Madeleine, and 21, 27 and 29 along Avenue de l'Opéra.

0 metres 400
0 yards 400

KEY

Street-by-Street map
M Metro station
RER RER station

SEE ALSO

• *Street Finder*, map 5–6
• *Where to Stay* p291
• *Restaurants* pp311–312

◁ Lamppost statues of the vestal virgins outside the Opéra National de Paris Garnier

Street-by-Street: Opéra Quarter

It has been said that if you sit for long enough at the Café de la Paix (opposite the Opéra National de Paris Garnier) the whole world will pass by. During the day, the area is a mixture of commerce – France's top three banks are based here – and tourism. A profusion of shops, ranging from the chic, exclusive and expensive to the popular department stores, draw the crowds. In the evening, the theatres and cinemas attract a totally different crowd, and the cafés along the Boulevard des Capucines throb with life.

Statue by Gumery on the Opéra

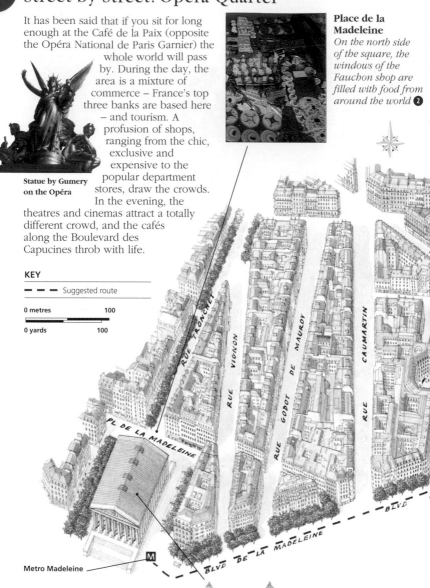

Place de la Madeleine
On the north side of the square, the windows of the Fauchon shop are filled with food from around the world ❷

KEY

‑ ‑ ‑ Suggested route

0 metres 100
0 yards 100

RUE TRONCHET
RUE VIGNON
RUE GODOT DE MAUROY
RUE CAUMARTIN
RUE

PL DE LA MADELEINE
BLVD DE LA MADELEINE
BLVD

Metro Madeleine
M

STAR SIGHTS

★ La Madeleine

★ Boulevard des Capucines

★ Opéra National de Paris Garnier

★ La Madeleine
The final design of this church, which is dedicated to Mary Magdalene, differs from this original model, now in the Musée Carnavalet (see pp96–7) ❶

★ **Opéra National de Paris Garnier**
With a mixture of styles ranging from Classical to Baroque, this building from 1875 has come to symbolize the opulence of the Second Empire ❹

LOCATOR MAP
See Central Paris Map pp14–15

Metro Chaussée d'Antin

PL DIAGHILEV
RUE GLUCK
HALEVY
SCRIBE
PL J ROUCHE
PL CH GARNIER
RUE
PL DE
L'OPERA
INES
RUE DAUNOU
AVE DE L'OPERA
Metro Opéra

Musée de l'Opéra
Famous artists' work is often shown in temporary exhibition rooms ❺

The Place de l'Opéra was designed by Baron Haussmann and is one of Paris's busiest intersections.

The Café de la Paix maintains its old-fashioned ways and still has its 19th-century decor, designed by Garnier. The café is under renovation at present *(See p319.)*

Harry's Bar was named after Harry MacElhone, a bartender who bought the bar in 1913. Past regulars have included F Scott Fitzgerald and Ernest Hemingway.

★ **Boulevard des Capucines**
At No. 14 a plaque tells of the world's first public screening of a movie, by the Lumière brothers in 1895; it took place in the Salon Indien, a room in the Grand Café ❸

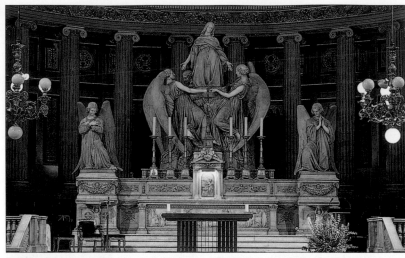

Charles Marochetti's *Mary Magdalene Ascending to Heaven* (1837) behind the high altar of La Madeleine

La Madeleine ❶

Pl de la Madeleine 75008.
Map 5 C5. **Tel** 01 44 51 69 00.
Ⓜ *Madeleine.* ◯ *9am–7pm daily.*
🚌 *frequent.* **Concerts.** 📷 🅿️
See **Entertainment** pp346–7.

This church, which is dedicated to Mary Magdalene, is one of the best-known buildings in Paris because of its prominent location and great size. It stands at one end of the curve of the Grands Boulevards and is the architectural counterpoint of the Palais-Bourbon (home of the Assemblée Nationale, the French parliament) across the river. It was started in 1764 but not consecrated until 1845. There were proposals to convert it into a parliament, a stock exchange or a public library for the nation.

Napoleon decided to build a temple dedicated to military glory and he commissioned Pierre Vignon to design it, after the battle of Jena (Iéna) in 1806. A colonnade of 64 ft high (20 m) Corinthian columns encircles the building and supports a sculptured frieze. The bas-reliefs on the bronze doors are by Henri de Triqueti and show the Ten Commandments.

The inside is decorated with marble and gilt, and has some fine sculpture, notably François Rude's *Baptism of Christ.*

Place de la Madeleine ❷

75008. **Map** 5 C5. Ⓜ
Madeleine. **Flower market**
◯ *8am–7.30pm Tue–Sun.*

The place de la Madeleine was created at the same time as the Madeleine church. It is a food lover's paradise, with many shops specializing in luxuries such as truffles, champagne, caviar and handmade

Fauchon tin

chocolates. Fauchon, the millionaires' supermarket, is situated at No. 26 and stocks more than 20,000 items *(see pp333–5).* The large house at No. 9 is where Marcel Proust spent his childhood. To the east of La Madeleine is a small flower market *(see p338)* and some excellently preserved 19th-century public toilets.

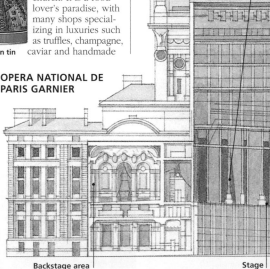

Scenery backdrop operated by pulley

OPERA NATIONAL DE PARIS GARNIER

Backstage area   **Stage**

Les Grands Boulevards ❸

75002 & 75009. **Map** 6 D5–7C5.
Ⓜ️ *Madeleine, Opéra, Richelieu-Drouot, Grands Boulevards.*

Eight broad boulevards – Madeleine, Capucines, Italiens, Montmartre, Poissonnière, Bonne Nouvelle, St-Denis and St-Martin – run from around La Madeleine to the Place de la République. They were constructed in the 17th century to turn obsolete city fortifications into fashionable promenades – *boulevard* came from the Middle Dutch *bulwerc*, which means bulwark or rampart. The boulevards became so famous in the 19th century that the name *boulevardier* was coined for one who cuts a figure on the boulevards.

Around the Madeleine church and the Opéra it is still possible to gain an impression of what the Grands Boulevards looked like in their heyday, lined with cafés and chic shops. Elsewhere, most of the cafés and restaurants have long since gone, and the old facades are now hidden by neon

advertising. However, the Grands Boulevards and the nearby department stores on the Boulevard Haussmann still attract large crowds.

Boulevard des Italiens

Opéra National de Paris Garnier ❹

Pl de l'Opéra 75009. **Map** 6 E4.
📠 *01 40 01 22 63.* Ⓜ️ *Opéra.*
🕐 *10am–4.30pm daily.* ⬤ *public hols.* 🎫 📷 *See **Entertainment** pp345–7.* **www**.operadeparis.fr

Sometimes compared to a giant wedding cake, this sumptuous building was designed by Charles Garnier for Napoleon III; construction started in 1862. Its unique appearance is due to a mixture of materials (including stone, marble and bronze) and styles, ranging from Classical to Baroque, with a multitude of

columns, friezes and sculptures on the exterior. The building was not completed until 1875; work was interrupted by the Prussian War and 1871 uprising.

In 1858 Orsini had attempted to assassinate the emperor outside the old opera house. This prompted Garnier to include a pavilion on the east side of the new building, with a curved ramp leading up to it so that the sovereign could safely step out of his carriage into the suite of rooms adjoining the royal box.

The functions performed by each part of the building are reflected in the structure. Behind the flat-topped foyer, the cupola sits above the auditorium, while the triangular pediment that rises up behind the cupola marks the front of the stage. Underneath the building is a small lake, which provided inspiration for the phantom's hiding place in Paul Leroux's *Phantom of the Opera*.

Both the interior and the exterior have been recently refurbished. Don't miss the magnificent Grand Staircase, made of white marble with a balustrade of red and green marble, and the Grand Foyer, with its domed ceiling covered with mosaics. The five-tiered auditorium is a riot of red velvet, plaster cherubs and gold leaf, which contrast with the false ceiling painted by Marc Chagall in 1964.

Most operas are performed in the new Opéra Nationale de Paris Bastille *(see p98)*, but the ballet remains here.

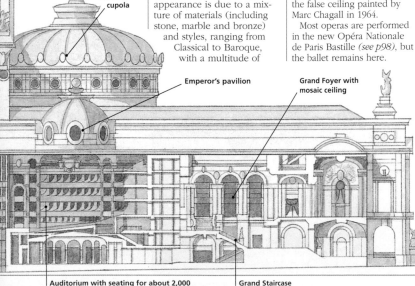

Statue by Millet

Copper-green roofed cupola

Emperor's pavilion

Grand Foyer with mosaic ceiling

Auditorium with seating for about 2,000

Grand Staircase

Sign outside the Grévin waxwork museum

Musée de l'Opéra ⑤

Pl de l'Opéra 75009. **Map** 6 E5. **Tel** 01 40 01 24 93. Ⓜ *Opéra.* ◯ *10am–4.30pm daily (to 1pm Sun).* ● *1 Jan, 1 May.* 🖼 🎟 *01 41 10 08 10.* 🚻

The entrance to this small, charming museum was originally the emperor's private entrance to the Opéra. The museum relates the history of opera through a large collection of musical scores, manuscripts, photographs and artists' memorabilia, such as the Russian dancer Waslaw Nijinsky's ballet slippers and tarot cards. Other exhibits include models of stage sets and busts of major composers. The museum also houses a superb library, containing books and manuscripts on theatre, dance and music, as well as more memorabilia.

Drouot (Hôtel des Ventes) ⑥

9 Rue Drouot 75009. **Map** 6 F4. **Tel** 01 48 00 20 20. Ⓜ *Richelieu Drouot.* ◯ *11am–6pm Mon–Sat.* 🚫 🎟 🚻 See **Shops and Markets** pp336–7. **www**.gazette-drouot.com

This is the leading French auction house (Hôtel des Ventes) and it takes its name from the Comte de Drouot who was Napoleon's aide-de-camp. There has been an auction house on the site since 1858, and in 1860 Napoleon III visited the Hôtel and purchased a couple of earthenware pots. It has been known as the Nouveau Drouot ever since the 1970s, when the existing building was demolished and replaced with today's rather dull structure.

Although overshadowed internationally by Christie's and Sotheby's, auctions at the Nouveau Drouot nevertheless provide a lively spectacle and involve a fascinating range of rare objects. Its presence in the area has attracted many antique and stamp shops.

Grévin ⑦

10 Blvd Montmartre 75009. **Map** 6 F4. **Tel** 01 47 70 85 05. Ⓜ *Grands Boulevards* ◯ *10am–6:30pm Mon–Fri, 10am–7pm Sat & Sun. (last admission 1 hour before closing).* 🖼 🚻 **www**.grevin.fr

This waxwork museum was founded in 1882 and is now a Paris landmark, on a par with Madame Tussauds in London.

Model of a set for *Les Huguenots* (1875) in the Musée de l'Opéra

It contains tableaux of vivid historical scenes (such as Louis XIV at Versailles and the arrest of Louis XVI), distorting mirrors and the Cabinet Fantastique, which includes regular conjuring shows given by a live magician. Famous figures from the worlds of art, sport and politics are also on show, with new celebrities replacing faded and forgotten stars.

Galerie Vivienne

Les Passages ⑧

75002. **Map** 6 F5. Ⓜ *Bourse.*

The early 19th-century Parisian shopping arcades (known as *passages* or *galeries*) are located between the Boulevard Montmartre and the Rue St-Marc (the extensive Passage des Panoramas). Other arcades are found between the Rue du Quatre Septembre and the Rue des Petits Champs.

At the time of their construction, the Passages represented a new traffic-free area for commerce, workshops and apartments. They fell into disuse, but were dramatically revamped in the 1970s and now house an eclectic mixture of small shops selling anything from designer jewellery to rare books. They have high, vaulted roofs of iron and glass. One of the most charming is the Galerie Vivienne (off the Rue Vivienne or the Rue des Petits Champs) with its mosaic floor and excellent tearoom.

The colonnaded Neo-Classical facade of the Palais de la Bourse

Palais de la Bourse ⑨

(Bourse des Valeurs) 4 Pl de la Bourse 75002. **Map** 6 F5. **Tel** 01 49 27 55 54 (tours). Ⓜ Bourse. ◯ by appt only. ⬛ ⬛ ⬛ compulsory (01 49 27 55 50). **Films.**

This neo-classical temple of commerce was commissioned by Napoleon and was home to the French Stock Exchange from 1826 to 1987. Today the French stock market is located at 29 Rue Cambon (not open to visits). The hectic floor trading of the Palais de la Bourse has been considerably reduced and is limited to the Matif (the futures market) and the Monep (the traded options market).

Sainte-Chapelle cameo in the Cabinet des Médailles

Cabinet des Médailles et des Antiques ⑩

58 Rue de Richelieu 75002. **Map** 6 F5. **Tel** 01 53 79 83 30. Ⓜ Bourse. ◯ 1–5.45pm Mon–Sat (to 4.45pm Sat); noon–6pm Sun. ⬛ public hols. ⬛ ⬛ www.bnf.fr

This valuable collection of coins, medals, jewels and Classical objects is part of the Bibliothèque Nationale. Exhibits include the Berthouville Treasure (1st-century Gallo-Roman silverware) and the Grand Camée (cameo) from Sainte-Chapelle.

Bibliothèque Nationale ⑪

58 Rue de Richelieu 75002. **Map** 6 F5. **Tel** 01 53 79 59 59. Ⓜ Bourse. ◯ 9am–6pm Mon–Sat. www.bnf.fr

The Bibliotheque Nationale (National Library) originated with the manuscript collections of medieval kings, to which a copy of every French book printed since 1537, has, by law, been added. The collection, which includes two Gutenberg bibles, is partially housed in this complex,

Bibliothèque Nationale

created in the 17th century by Cardinal Mazarin. Despite the recent removal of the printed books, periodicals and CD Roms to the newly-built Bibliothèque Nationale de France (see p246) at Tolbiac, the rue Richelieu buildings still contain a huge variety of items, including original manuscripts by Victor Hugo and Marcel Proust, among others. The library also has the richest collection of engravings and photographs in the world, and departments for maps and plans, theatrical arts, and musical scores. Sadly, the 19th-century reading room is not open to the public.

Avenue de l'Opéra ⑫

75001 & 75002. **Map** 6 E5. Ⓜ Opéra, Pyramides.

This broad avenue is a notable example of Baron Haussmann's dramatic modernization of Paris in the 1860s and 1870s (see pp34–5). Much of the medieval city (including a mound from which Joan of Arc began her crusade against the English) was cleared to make way for the wide thoroughfares of today. The Avenue de l'Opéra, running from the Louvre to the Opéra de Paris Garnier, was completed in 1876. The uniformity of the five-storey buildings that line it contrast with those found in nearby streets, which date from the 17th and 18th centuries. Nearby, in the Place Gaillon, is the Café and Restaurant Drouant where the prestigious Goncourt Prize for literature is decided. The avenue is dominated by travel and luxury shops. At No. 27 there is the National Centre for the Visual Arts, which has a false entrance.

Avenue de l'Opéra

MONTMARTRE

Montmartre and art are inseparable. By the end of the 19th century the area was a mecca for artists, writers, poets and their disciples, who gathered to sample the bordellos, cabarets, revues and other exotica which made Montmartre's reputation as a place of depravity in the eyes of the city's more sober up-standing citizens. Many of the artists and writers have long since left the area and the lively night life no longer has the same charm.

But the hill of Montmartre (the Butte) still has its physical charms and the village atmosphere remains

Street theatre in Montmartre

remarkably intact. Mobs of eager tourists ascend the hill, most of them gathering in the most spacious parts, particularly where quick portrait artists and souvenir sellers thrive, as in the old village square, the Place du Tertre. Elsewhere there are tiny, exquisite squares, winding streets, small terraces, long stairways, plus the Butte's famous vineyard where the few grapes are harvested in an atmosphere of revelry in early autumn. And there are spectacular views of the city from various points, most especially from the monumental Sacré-Coeur.

SIGHTS AT A GLANCE

Historic Buildings and Streets
Bateau-Lavoir ⑪
Moulin de la Galette ⑭
Avenue Junot ⑮

Churches
Sacré-Coeur pp224–5 ①
St-Pierre de Montmartre ②
Chapelle du Martyre ⑧
St-Jean l'Evangéliste de Montmartre ⑩

Museums and Galleries
Espace Dalí Montmartre ④
Musée de Montmartre ⑤
Musée d'Art Naïf Max Fourny ⑦

Squares
Place du Tertre ③
Place des Abbesses ⑨

Cemeteries
Cimetière de Montmartre ⑬

Theatres and Nightclubs
Au Lapin Agile ⑥
Moulin Rouge ⑫

GETTING THERE
This area is served by several metro stations, including Abbesses and Pigalle. The Montmartrobus leaves Pigalle for the village area and bus route 80 passes Montmartre's cemetery. Route 85 passes along Rue de Clignancourt.

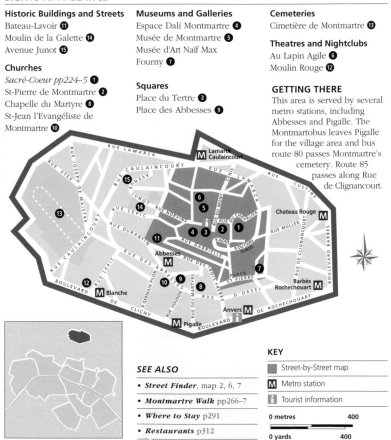

KEY

▨	Street-by-Street map
Ⓜ	Metro station
ℹ	Tourist information

0 metres   400
0 yards   400

SEE ALSO

- *Street Finder*, map 2, 6, 7
- *Montmartre Walk* pp266–7
- *Where to Stay* p291
- *Restaurants* p312

◁ The narrow Rue St-Rustique winding up the hill to Sacré-Coeur

Street-by-Street: Montmartre

The steep butte (hill) of Montmartre has been associated with artists for 200 years. Théodore Géricault and Camille Corot came here at the start of the 19th century, and in the 20th century Maurice Utrillo immortalized the streets in his works. Today street painters thrive on a lively tourist trade as travellers flock to this picturesque district which in places still preserves the atmosphere of prewar Paris. The name of the area is ascribed to local martyrs tortured in Paris around AD 250, hence *mons martyrium*.

Streetside painter

Montmartre vineyard is the the last surviving vineyard in Paris. On the first Saturday in October the start of the grape harvest is celebrated.

Metro Lamarck Caulaincourt

★ Au Lapin Agile
Literary meetings have been held in this rustic nightclub ("The Agile Rabbit") since 1910 **6**

A La Mère Catherine was a favourite eating place of Russian Cossacks in 1814. They would bang on the table and shout *"Bistro!"* (Russian for "quick") – hence the bistro was named.

Espace Dalí Montmartre
The exhibition pays homage to the eclectic artist Dalí. Some of the works are on public display for the first time in France **4**

★ Place du Tertre
The square is the tourist centre of Montmartre and is full of portraitists. No. 3 commemorates local children, as popularized in the artist Poulbot's drawings **3**

STAR SIGHTS

★ Sacré-Coeur

★ Place du Tertre

★ Musée de Montmartre

★ Au Lapin Agile

KEY

- - - Suggested route

0 metres	100
0 yards	100

★ **Musée de Montmartre**
The museum includes the work of artists who lived in the area: this Portrait of a Woman *(1918) is by the Italian painter and sculptor Amedeo Modigliani* **5**

LOCATOR MAP
See Central Paris Map pp14–15

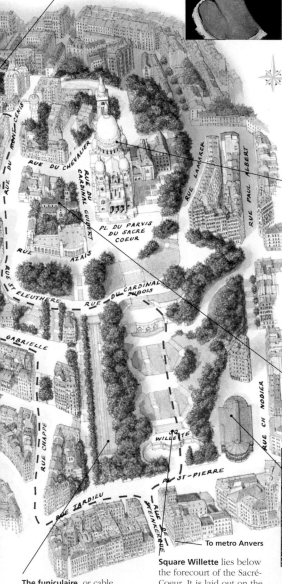

★ **Sacré-Coeur**
This Romano-Byzantine church, started in the 1870s and completed in 1914, has many treasures, such as this figure of Christ by Eugène Benet (1911) **1**

St-Pierre de Montmartre
This church became the Temple of Reason during the Revolution **2**

To metro Anvers

Musée d'Art Naïf Max Fourny
The museum houses 580 examples of naïve art. This oil painting, L'Opéra de Paris *(1986), is by L Milinkov* **7**

The funiculaire, or cable railway, at the end of the Rue Foyatier takes you to the foot of the basilica of the Sacré-Coeur. Metro tickets are valid on it.

Square Willette lies below the forecourt of the Sacré-Coeur. It is laid out on the side of the hill in a series of descending terraces with lawns, shrubs, trees and flowerbeds.

Montmartre streetside paintings

Sacré-Coeur ❶

See pp224–5.

St-Pierre de Montmartre ❷

2 Rue du Mont-Cenis 75018. **Map** 6 F1.
Tel 01 46 06 57 63. Ⓜ *Abbesses.*
◯ *8.45am–7pm daily.* 🔔 *frequent.*
📷 ♿ **Concerts.**

Situated in the shadow of
Sacré-Coeur, St-Pierre de
Montmartre is one of the
oldest churches in Paris. It is
all that remains of the great
Benedictine Abbey of
Montmartre, founded in 1133
by Louis VI and his wife,
Adelaide of Savoy, who, as its
first abbess, is buried here.

Inside are four marble
columns supposedly from
a Roman temple which
originally stood on the site.
The vaulted choir dates from
the 12th century, the nave
was remodelled in the 15th
century and the
west front in the
18th. During the
Revolution the
abbess was
guillotined, and
the church fell into
disuse. It was
reconsecrated in
1908. Gothic-style
stained-glass
windows replace
those destroyed by
a stray bomb in
World War II. The
church also has a   **Doors to St-Pierre church**
tiny cemetery,
which is open to the public
only on 1 November.

Place du Tertre ❸

75018. **Map** 6 F1. Ⓜ *Abbesses.*

Tertre means "hillock", or
mound, and this picturesque
square is the highest point in
Paris at some 130 m (430 ft).
It was once the site of the
abbey gallows but is associated with artists, who began
exhibiting paintings here in
the 19th century. It is lined
with colourful restaurants –
La Mère Catherine dates back
to 1793. The house at No. 21
was formerly the home of the
irreverent "Free Commune",
founded in 1920 to perpetuate
the Bohemian spirit of the
area. It is now the site of
the Old Montmartre infor-
mation office.

The Spanish artist Salvador Dalí

Espace Dalí Montmartre ❹

11 Rue Poulbot 75018.
Map 6 F1. **Tel** 01 42
64 40 10. Ⓜ *Abbesses.*
◯ *10am–6pm daily.*
📷 🎟 *groups by appt.*
www.daliparis.com

A permanent exhi-
bition of 330 works
of the painter and
sculptor Salvador
Dalí is on display
here at the heart of
Montmartre. Inside,
the vast, dark
setting reflects the
dramatic character of this
20th-century genius as

moving lights grace first one,
then another, of his Surrealist
works. This in turn is
counterpointed with the
rhythm of Dalí's recorded
voice. There is an art gallery
as well as a library housed
in this original museum.

Musée de Montmartre ❺

12 Rue Cortot 75018. **Map** 2 F5.
Tel 01 46 06 61 11. Ⓜ *Lamarck-
Caulaincourt.* ◯ *10am–6pm
Tue–Sun.* 📷 🚫 📷
www.museedemontmartre.com

During the 17th century this
charming home belonged to
the actor Roze de Rosimond
(Claude de la Rose), a member
of Molière's theatre company
who, like his mentor Molière,
died during a performance of
Molière's play *Le Malade
Imaginaire*. From 1875 the
big white house, undoubtedly
the finest in Montmartre,
provided living and studio
space for numerous artists,
including Maurice Utrillo and
his mother, Suzanne Valadon,
a former acrobat and model
who became a talented
painter, as well as Raoul Dufy
and Pierre-Auguste Renoir.

The museum recounts the
history of Montmartre from
the days of the abbesses to
the present, through artefacts,
documents, drawings and
photographs. It is particularly
rich in memorabilia of
Bohemian life, and even has
a reconstruction of the Café
de l'Abreuvoir, Utrillo's
favourite watering hole.

Café de l'Abreuvoir reconstructed

The deceptively rustic exterior of Au Lapin Agile, one of the best-known nightspots in Paris

Au Lapin Agile ❻

22 Rue des Saules 75018. **Map**
2 F5. **Tel** *01 46 06 85 87.* **M**
Lamarck-Caulaincourt. ☐ *9pm–*
2am Tue–Sun. See **Entertainment**
pp342–3. **www**.au-lapin-agile.com

The former Cabaret des
Assassins derived its current
name from a sign painted by
the humorist André Gill. His
picture of a rabbit escaping
from a pot *(Le Lapin à Gill)*
became known as the nimble
rabbit *(Lapin Agile)*. The club
enjoyed popularity with
intellectuals and artists at the
turn of the 20th century.
Here in 1911 the novelist
Roland Dorgelès' hatred for
modern art, as practised by
Picasso and the other painters
at the "Bateau-Lavoir" (No. 13
Place Emile-Goudeau), led
him to play an illuminating
practical joke on one of the
customers, Guillaume
Apollinaire, who was a poet,
art critic and champion of
Cubism. He tied a paintbrush
to the tail of the café-owner's
donkey, and the resulting
daub was shown at a Salon
des Indépendants exhibition
under the enlightening title
Sunset over the Adriatic.
In 1903 the premises were
bought by the cabaret
entrepreneur Aristide Bruand
(painted in a series of posters
by Toulouse-Lautrec). Today
it manages to retain much of
its original atmosphere.

Musée d'Art Naïf
Max Fourny ❼

Halle St-Pierre, 2 Rue Ronsard 75018.
Map 7 A1. **Tel** *01 42 58 72 89.*
M *Anvers.* ☐ *10am–6pm daily.*
🖼 🗹 ♿ ☐ 🛍
www.hallesaintpierre.org

Naive art is usually characterized by simple themes,
bright, flat colours and a
disregard for perspective. Max
Fourny's publishing activities
brought him into contact with
many naïve-style painters and
this unusual museum, located
in the Halle St-Pierre, contains
his collection of paintings and
sculptures from more than 30
countries, with exhibitions on

The Wall by F Tremblot (1944)

selected themes. Many of the
paintings shown here are
rarely seen in museums.
The museum also organizes
temporary exhibitions of
outsider art, folk art and work
by self-taught artists, as well
as conducting children's
workshops. The building
itself is a 19th-century iron-
and-glass structure which was
once part of the St-Pierre
fabrics market.

Chapelle du
Martyre ❽

9 Rue Yvonne-Le-Tac 75018.
Map 6 F1. **M** *Pigalle.*
☐ *10am–noon, 3pm–5pm Fri–Wed.*

This 19th-century chapel
stands on the site of a
medieval convent's chapel,
which was said to mark the
place where the early Christian martyr and first bishop of
Paris, Saint Denis, was
beheaded by the Romans in
AD 250. It remained a major
pilgrimage site throughout the
Middle Ages. In the crypt of
the original chapel in 1534
Ignatius de Loyola, founder of
the Society of Jesus (the mighty
Jesuit order designed to save
the Catholic Church from the
onslaught of the Protestant
Reformation), took his Jesuit
vows with six companions.

Sacré-Coeur ❶

South-east rose window (1960)

At the outbreak of the Franco Prussian War in 1870, two Catholic businessmen made a private religious vow. It was to build a church dedicated to the Sacred Heart of Christ should France be spared the impending Prussian onslaught. The two men, Alexandre Legentil and Hubert Rohault de Fleury, lived to see Paris saved from invasion despite the war and a lengthy siege – and the start of what is the Sacré-Coeur basilica. The project was taken up by Archbishop Guibert of Paris. Work began in 1875 to Paul Abadie's designs. They were inspired by the Romano-Byzantine church of St-Front in Périgueux. The basilica was completed in 1914, but the German invasion forestalled its consecration until 1919, when France was victorious.

The Facade
The best view of the domed and turreted Sacré-Coeur is from the gardens below.

The belltower (1895) is 83 m (252 ft) high and contains one of the heaviest bells in the world. The bell itself weighs 18.5 tonnes and the clapper 850 kg (1,900 lb).

★ **Great Mosaic of Christ**
The colossal mosaic (1912–22) dominating the chancel vault was designed by Luc Olivier Merson and Marcel Magne.

Virgin Mary and Child *(1896)*
This Renaissance-style silver statue is one of two in the ambulatory by P Brunet.

THE SIEGE OF PARIS

Prussia invaded France in 1870. During the four-month siege of Paris, instigated by the Prusso-German statesman Otto von Bismarck, Parisians became so hungry that they ate all the animals in the city.

★ **Crypt Vaults**
A chapel in the basilica's crypt contains Legentil's heart in a stone urn.

STAR FEATURES

★ Great Mosaic of Christ

★ Bronze Doors

★ Ovoid Dome

★ Crypt Vaults

VISITORS' CHECKLIST

Parvis de Notre Dame 75018.
Map 6 F1.
Tel 01 53 41 89 00.
Ⓜ Abbesses (then take the funiculaire to the steps of the Sacré-Coeur), Anvers, Barbès-Rochechouart, Lamarck-Caulaincourt.
🚌 30, 54, 80, 85.
🅿 Blvd de Clichy, Rue Custine.
Basilica ◯ 6am–8.30pm daily.
Dome and crypt ◯ 9am–6pm daily. 🖼 **for crypt and dome**.
✝ 11.15am, 6.30pm, 10pm Mon–Thu; 3pm Fri; 10pm Sat; 11am, 6pm, 10pm Sun.
🚫 ♿ restricted. 📷
www.sacre-coeur-montmartre.com

★ Ovoid Dome
This is the second-highest point in Paris, after the Eiffel Tower.

Spiral staircase

The inner structure supporting the dome is made from stone.

The stained-glass gallery affords a view of the whole of the interior.

Statue of Christ
The basilica's most important statue is symbolically placed above the two bronze saints.

Equestrian Statues
The statue of Joan of Arc is one of a pair by H Lefèbvre. The other is of Saint Louis.

★ Bronze Doors
Relief sculptures on the doors in the portico entrance illustrate scenes from the life of Christ, such as the Last Supper.

Main entrance

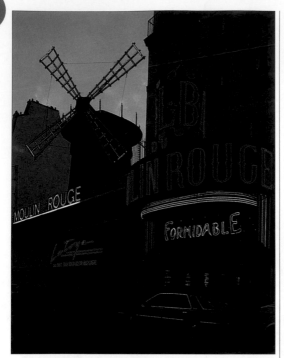

The famous silhouette of the Moulin Rouge nightclub

Place des Abbesses ❾

75018. **Map** 6 F1. **M** *Abbesses*.

This is one of Paris's most picturesque squares. It is sandwiched between the rather dubious attractions of the Place Pigalle with its strip clubs and the Place du Tertre which is mobbed with hundreds of tourists. Be sure not to miss the Abbesses metro station with its unusual green wrought-iron arches

Entrance to the Abbesses metro

and amber lights. Designed by the architect Hector Guimard, it is one of the few original Art Nouveau stations.

St-Jean l'Evangéliste de Montmartre ❿

19 Rue des Abbesses 75018. **Map** 6 F1. **Tel** *01 46 06 43 96.* **M** *Abbesses.* ⬤ *9am–noon, 3pm–7pm Mon–Sat; 2pm–7pm Sun.* ✝ *frequent.* 📷 ✔ *once a month.*

Designed by Anatole de Baudot and completed in 1904, this church was the first to be built from reinforced concrete. The flower motifs on the interior are typical of Art Nouveau, while its interlocking arches suggest Islamic architecture. The red-brick facing has earned it the nickname St-Jean-des-Briques.

Detail of St-Jean l'Evangéliste facade

Bateau-Lavoir ⓫

13 Pl Emile-Goudeau 75018. **Map** 6 F1. **M** *Abbesses.* ⬤ *to public.*

This artistic and literary mecca was an old piano factory. Its name comes from its resemblance to the laundry boats that used to travel along the River Seine. Between 1890 and 1920 it was home to some of the most talented artists and poets of the day. They lived in squalid conditions with only one tap and took it in turns to sleep in the beds. The artists Picasso, Van Dongen, Marie Laurencin, Juan Gris and Modigliani were just a few of the residents. It was here that Picasso painted *Les Demoiselles d'Avignon* in 1907, usually regarded as the painting that inspired Cubism. The shabby building burned down in 1970, but a concrete replica has been built – with studio space for up-and-coming artists.

Moulin Rouge ⓬

82 Blvd de Clichy 75018. **Map** 6 E1. **Tel** *01 53 09 82 82.* **M** *Blanche.* ⬤ *Dinner: 7pm; shows: 9pm and 11pm daily.* 🎭 *See **Entertainment** p343–4.* **www**.moulinrouge.com

Built in 1885, the Moulin Rouge was turned into a dance hall as early as 1900. The cancan originated in Montparnasse, in the polka gardens of the Rue de la Grande-Chaumière, but it will always be associated with the Moulin Rouge where the wild and colourful dance shows were immortalized in the posters and drawings of Henri de Toulouse-Lautrec. The high-kicking routines of famous Dorriss dancers such as Yvette Guilbert and Jane Avril continue today in a glittering, Las Vegas-style revue that includes computerized lights and displays of magic.

place, conveying some of the heated energy and artistic creativity of Montmartre a century ago.

Nearby, close to Square Roland Dorgeles, there is another, smaller, often overlooked Montmartre cemetery – **Cimetière St-Vincent.** Here lie more of the great artistic names of the district, including the Swiss composer Arthur Honegger and the writer Marcel Aymé. Most notable of all at St-Vincent is the grave of the great French painter Maurice Utrillo, the quintessential Montmartre artist, many of whose works are now some of the most enduring images of the area.

Waslaw Nijinsky lies in Montmartre

Cimetière de Montmartre ⑬

20 Ave Rachel 75018. **Map** 2 D5.
Tel 01 53 42 36 30. Ⓜ *Place de Clichy, Blanche.* ◯*8am–5.30pm daily (opens 8.30am Sat, 9am Sun; closes 6pm daily in summer).* ♿

This has been the resting place for many artistic luminaries since the beginning of the 19th century. The composers Hector Berlioz and Jacques Offenbach (who wrote the famous cancan tune), are buried here, alongside many other celebrities such as La Goulue (stage name of Louise Weber, the high-kicking danceuse who was the cancan's first star performer and Toulouse-Lautrec's model), the painter Edgar Degas, writer Alexandre Dumas *fils*, German poet Heinrich Heine, Russian dancer Waslaw Nijinsky, and film director François Truffaut. It's an evocative, atmospheric

Moulin de la Galette ⑭

T-junction at Rue Tholoze and Rue Lepic 75018. **Map** 2 E5.
Tel 01 46 06 84 77.
Ⓜ *Lamarck-Caulaincourt.*

Once more than 30 windmills dotted the Montmartre skyline and were used for grinding wheat and pressing grapes. Now only two remain: the Moulin du Radet, which stands further along the Rue Lepic, and the rebuilt Moulin de la Galette, now converted into a fine restaurant. The latter was built in 1622 and is also known as the Blute-fin; one of its mill owners, Debray, was supposedly crucified on the windmill's sails during the 1814 Siege of Paris. He had been trying to repulse the invading Cossacks. At the

turn of the 20th century the mill became a famous dance hall and provided inspiration for many artists, notably Pierre-Auguste Renoir and Vincent Van Gogh.

The steep Rue Lepic is a busy shopping area with a good market *(see p339)*. The Impressionist painter Armand Guillaumin once lived on the first floor of No. 54, and Van Gogh inhabited its third floor.

Moulin de la Galette

Avenue Junot ⑮

75018. **Map** 2 E5. Ⓜ *Lamarck-Caulaincourt.*

Opened in 1910, this broad, peaceful street includes many painters' studios and family houses. No. 13 has mosaics designed by its former illustrator resident Francisque Poulbot, famous for his drawings of urchins. He is credited with having invented a bar billiards game. At No. 15 is Maison Tristan Tzara, named after its previous owner, the Romanian Dadaist poet. Its eccentric design by the Austrian architect Adolf Loos aimed to complement the poet's character. No. 23 bis is the Villa Léandre, a group of perfect Art Deco houses.

Just off the Avenue Junot up the steps of the Allée des Brouillards is an 18th-century architectural folly, the Château des Brouillards. In the 19th century it was the home of the French symbolist writer Gérard de Nerval, who committed suicide in 1855.

Sacré-Coeur, Montmartre, by Maurice Utrillo

FURTHER AFIELD

Many of the great châteaux outside Paris originally built as country retreats for the aristocracy and post-revolutionary bourgeoisie are now preserved as museums. Versailles is one of the finest, but if your tastes are Modernist, there's also Le Corbusier architecture to see. There are two theme parks – Disneyland Resort Paris and Parc de la Villette – to amuse adults and children alike, and excellent parks to relax in when the bustle of the city gets too much.

SIGHTS AT A GLANCE

Museums and Galleries
Musée Nissim de Camondo ❸
Musée Cernuschi ❹
Musée Gustave Moreau ❺
Musée Edith Piaf ⓲
Musée Marmottan-Claude
Monet ㉙
Musée des Années 30 ㉛
Palais de la Porte Dorée ⓰

Churches
St-Alexandre-Nevsky
Cathedral ❶
Basilique Saint-Denis ❼
Notre-Dame du Travail ㉓

Historic Buildings and Streets
Bercy ⓲
Bibliothèque Nationale de
France ⓳
13th Arrondissement ⓴
Cité Universitaire ㉒
Institut Pasteur ㉔
Versailles pp248–53 ㉖
Rue de la Fontaine ㉗
Fondation Le Corbusier ㉘
La Défense ㉜
Château de Malmaison ㉝

Markets
Marché aux Puces de St-Ouen ❻
Portes St-Denis et St-Martin ❽
Marché d'Aligre ⓯

Parks, Gardens and Canals
Parc Monceau ❷
Canal St-Martin ❾
Parc des Buttes-Chaumont ❿
Château et Bois de
Vincennes ⓱
Parc Montsouris ㉑
Parc André Citroën ㉕
Bois de Boulogne ㉚

Cemeteries
*Cimetière du Père Lachaise
pp240–41* ⓭

Theme Parks
Parc de la Villette pp234–9 ⓫
*Disneyland Resort Paris
pp242–5* ⓮

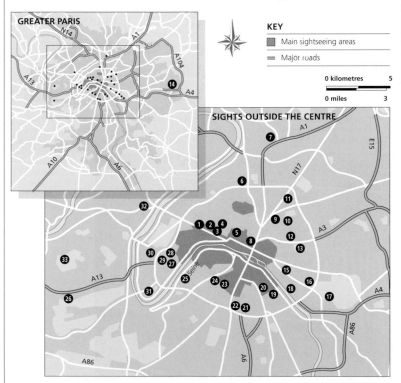

GREATER PARIS

KEY

▢ Main sightseeing areas

▬ Major roads

0 kilometres 5

0 miles 3

SIGHTS OUTSIDE THE CENTRE

North of the City

St-Alexandre-Nevsky Cathedral

St-Alexandre-Nevsky Cathedral **❶**

12 Rue Daru 75008. **Map** 4 F3.
Tel 01 42 27 37 34. Ⓜ *Courcelles.*
◯ *3pm–5pm Tue, Fri, Sun.*
✝ *6pm Sat, 10.30am Sun.* 🚫 ☑

This imposing Russian Orthodox cathedral with its five golden-copper domes signals the presence of a large Russian community in Paris. Designed by members of the St Petersburg Fine Arts Academy and financed jointly by Tzar Alexander II and the local Russian community, the cathedral was completed in 1861. Inside, a wall of icons divides the church in two. The Greek-cross plan and the rich interior mosaics and frescoes are Neo-Byzantine in style, while the exterior and gilt domes are traditional Russian Orthodox in design.

The Russian population in the city increased dramatically following the Bolshevik Revolution of 1917, when thousands of Russians fled to Paris for safety. The Rue Daru, in which the cathedral stands, and the surrounding area form "Little Russia", with its Russian schools and the many dance academies, and delightful tea shops and bookshops where visitors can browse.

Parc Monceau **❷**

Blvd de Courcelles 75017. **Map** 5 A3.
Tel 01 42 27 08 64. Ⓜ *Monceau.*
◯ *7am–8pm daily (to 10pm summer).*
See **Eight Guided Walks** pp258–9.

This green haven dates back to 1778 when the Duc de Chartres (later Duc d'Orléans) commissioned the painter-writer and amateur landscape designer Louis Carmontelle to create a magnificent garden. Also a theatre designer, Carmontelle created a "garden of dreams", an exotic landscape full of architectural follies in imitation of English and German fashion of the time. In 1783 the Scottish landscape gardener Thomas Blaikie laid out an area of the garden in English style. The park was the scene of the first recorded parachute landing, made by André-Jacques Garnerin on 22 October 1797. Over the years the park changed hands and in 1852 it was acquired by the state and half the land sold off for property development. The remaining 9 ha (22 acres) were made into public gardens. These were restored and new buildings erected by Adolphe Alphand, architect of the Bois de Boulogne and the Bois de Vincennes.

Today the park remains one of the most chic in the capital but has unfortunately lost many of its early features. A *naumachia* basin flanked by Corinthian columns remains. This is an ornamental version of a Roman pool used for simulating naval battles. There are also a Renaissance arcade, pyramids, a river and the Pavillon de Chartres, a charming rotunda designed by Nicolas Ledoux which was once used as a tollhouse. Just south of here is a huge red pagoda, which now houses a gallery devoted to Asian art.

Musée Nissim de Camondo **❸**

63 Rue de Monceau 75008.
Map 5 A3. 🖬 01 53 89 06 40.
Ⓜ *Monceau, Villiers.* ◯ *10am–5.30pm Wed–Sun (last adm: 4.30pm).* ● *public hols.* 🏷 ☑
11am Sun (01 44 55 59 26). 📷

Comte Moïse de Camondo, a leading Jewish financier, commissioned this mansion in 1914 to be designed in the style of the Petit Trianon, at Versailles *(see pp248–9)*, to house a rare collection of 18th-century furniture, tapestries, paintings and other precious objects. The museum has been faithfully and lovingly restored to recreate an aristocratic town house of the Louis XV and XVI eras. In the museum there are Savonnerie carpets, Beauvais tapestries and the Buffon service

Colonnade beside the *naumachia* basin in Parc Monceau

(Sèvres porcelain). The very latest gadgets, for the period, are now displayed in the restored kitchen and service quarters, equipped with the utmost efficiency, taste and forethought by their owner.

Musée Nissim de Camondo

Musée Cernuschi ❹

7 Ave Vélasquez 75008. **Map** 5 A3. *Tel 01 53 96 21 50.* Ⓜ *Villiers, Monceau.* ◯ *10am–6pm Tue–Sun.* ◗ *public hols.* 🖉 🗷 📷 🏠
www.cernuschi.paris.fr

This mansion near Parc Monceau contains an intriguing private collection of late East Asian art which was amassed by the Milanese-born politician and banker Enrico Cernuschi (1821–96). The original bequest of 5,000 lacquered, ceramic, bronze and ivory items has been augmented by donations and acquisitions over the years. The wide-ranging collection, now about ten thousand items, includes a 5th-century seated Bodhisattva (Buddhist divine being) from Yunkang; *La Tigresse* (a 12th-century BC bronze vase); and *Horses and Grooms*, an 8th-century T'ang painting on silk attributed to the era's greatest horse painter, court artist Han Kan.

Bodhisattva in the Musée Cernuschi

Musée Gustave Moreau ❺

14 Rue de la Rochefoucauld 75009. **Map** 6 E3. *Tel 01 48 74 38 50.* Ⓜ *Trinité.* ◯ *10am–12.45pm, 2–5.15pm Wed–Mon.* ◗ *1 Jan, 1 May, 25 Dec.* 🖉 📷 🏠
www.museemoreau.fr

The symbolist painter Gustave Moreau (1825–98), known for his vivid, imaginative works depicting biblical and mythological fantasies, left to the French state a vast collection of more than 1,000 oils, watercolours and some 7,000 drawings in his town house. One of Moreau's best-known and most outstanding works, *Jupiter and Semele*, can be seen here. There is also a superb collection of his unfinished sketches.

Marché aux Puces du St-Ouen, a large antique market

Marché aux Puces de St-Ouen ❻

Rue des Rosiers, St-Ouen 75018. **Map** 2 F2. Ⓜ *Porte-de-Clignan-court.* ◯ *9am–6pm Sat–Mon.* See *Markets p335.* **www**.les-puces.com

This is the oldest and largest of the Paris flea markets, covering 6 ha (15 acres). In the 19th century, rag merchants and tramps would gather outside the city limits and offer their wares for sale. By the 1920s there was a proper market here, where masterpieces could sometimes be purchased cheaply

Angel Traveller by Gustave Moreau, in the Musée Gustave Moreau

from the then-unknowing sellers. Today it is divided into specialist markets. Known especially for its profusion of furniture and ornaments from the Second Empire (1852– 70), few bargains are to be found these days, yet some 150,000 bargain-hunters, tourists and dealers still flock here to browse among more than 2,000 open or covered stalls.

Basilique Saint-Denis ❼

2 Rue de Strasbourg, 93200 St-Denis. *Tel 01 48 09 83 54.* Ⓜ *St-Denis-Basilique.* 🆁 *St-Denis.* ◯ *Apr–Sep: 10am–7pm Mon–Sat, noon–7pm Sun; Oct–Mar: 10am–5pm Mon–Sat, noon–5pm Sun (last adm: 15 mins before closing).* 🚻 *8.30am, 10am Sun.* 🖉 📷 🗷 🏠

Constructed between 1137 and 1281, the Basilica is on the site of the tomb of St Denis, the first bishop of Paris, who was beheaded in Montmartre in AD 250. The building was the original influence for Gothic art. From Merovingian times it was a burial place for rulers of France. During the Revolution many tombs were desecrated and scattered, but the best were stored, and now represent a collection of funerary art. Memorials include those of Dagobert (died 638), Henri II (died 1559) and Catherine de' Medici (died 1589), and Louis XVI and Marie-Antoinette (died 1793).

Western arch of the Porte St-Denis, once the entrance to the city

Haussmann worked with the landscape architect/designer Adolphe Alphand, who organized a vast programme to furnish the new pavement-lined avenues with benches and lampposts. Others involved in the creation of this park were the engineer Darcel and the landscape gardener Barillet-Deschamps. They created a lake, made an island with real and artificial rocks, gave it a Roman-style temple and added a waterfall, streams, footbridges leading to the island and beaches. Today visitors will also find boating facilities and donkey rides.

Parc de la Villette ⓫

See pp234–9.

Musée Edith Piaf ⓬

5 Rue Crespin du Gast 75011. **Tel** *01 43 55 52 72.* Ⓜ *Ménilmontant.* ⬜ *1–6pm Mon–Wed, 10am–noon Thu (last adm: 30 mins before closing time), by appointment only.* ⬤ *public hols.* 📷 🚫 📹 📱

Edith Piaf – "the little sparrow" (1915–63)

Born Edith Gassion in the working-class east end of Paris in 1915, Edith Piaf took her stage name from her nickname meaning "the little sparrow". She started her career as a torch singer in local cafés and bars before becoming an international star in the late 1930s.

She never lived at the address of this museum, which was founded in 1967 by an association of fans, Les Amis d'Edith Piaf. Since then, they have collected a host of

Portes St-Denis et St-Martin ⓭

Blvds St-Denis & St-Martin 75010. **Map** 7 B5. Ⓜ *St-Martin, Strasbourg-St-Denis.*

These gates give access to the two ancient and important north–south thoroughfares whose names they bear. They once marked the entrance to the city. The Porte St-Denis is 23 m (76 ft) high and was built in 1672 by François Blondel. It is decorated with figures by Louis XIV's sculptor, François Girardon. They commemorate victories of the king's armies in Flanders and the Rhine that year. Porte St-Martin is 17 m (56 ft) tall and was built in 1674 by Pierre Bullet. It celebrates Besançon's capture and the defeat of the Triple Alliance of Spain, Holland and Germany.

Boats berthed at Port de l'Arsenal

East of the City

Canal St-Martin ⑨

Map 8 E2. Ⓜ *Jaurès, J Bonsergent, Goncourt. See pp260–61.*

The 5-kilometre (3-mile) canal, opened in 1825, provides a short-cut for river traffic between loops of the Seine. It has long been loved by novelists, film directors and tourists alike. It is dotted with barges and pleasure boats that leave from the Port de l'Arsenal. At the north end of the canal is the Bassin de la Villette waterway and the elegant Neo-Classical Rotonde de la Villette, spectacularly floodlit at night.

Parc des Buttes-Chaumont ⑩

Rue Manin 75019 (main access from Rue Armand Carrel). Ⓜ *Botzaris, Buttes-Chaumont.* ⬜ *7am–8.15pm daily (1 Jun–15 Aug: to 10.15pm; May, 16 Aug–30 Sep: to 9.15pm) .* ⓫ *See pp268–9.*

For many this is the most pleasant and unexpected park in Paris. The panoramic hilly site was converted in the 1860s by Baron Haussmann from a rubbish dump and quarry with a gallows below.

memorabilia and squeezed it
into this small apartment.
It contains many photographs
and portraits, lithographs by
Charles Kiffer, intimate letters,
clothes and books – gifts
from Piaf's parents-in-law or
bequests from other singers.
Records by the singer, who
died in 1963 and lies in Père
Lachaise cemetery *(see
pp240–41)*, are played in the
museum on request (visits are
by appointment only).

Cimetière du Père Lachaise ⑬

See pp240–41.

Disneyland Paris ⑭

See pp242–5.

Marché d'Aligre ⑮

Place d'Aligre 75012. **Map** 14 F5.
Ⓜ *Ledru-Rollin.* ◯ *7.30am–
12.30pm daily.*

On Sunday mornings this
lively market offers one of
the most colourful sights in
Paris. French, Arab and
African traders hawk fruit,
vegetables, flowers and
clothing on the streets, while
the adjoining covered market,
the Beauveau St-Antoine,
offers meats, cheeses, pâtés
and many intriguing
international delicacies.
   Aligre is where old and new
Paris meet. Here the established
community of this old artisan
quarter coexists with a more

**Exterior relief on Palais de la
Porte Dorée**

recently established group of
up-and-coming young people.
They have been lured here to
live and work by the recent
transformation of the nearby
Bastille area *(see p98)*.

Palais de la Porte Dorée ⑯

293 Ave Daumesnil 75012. *Tel 01 44
74 84 80.* Ⓜ *Porte Dorée.* ◯ *10am–
5.15pm Wed–Mon.* ✖ ♿ *restricted.*
🖥 www.palais-portedoree.org

This museum and aquarium
is housed in a beautiful Art
Deco building that was
designed especially for the
1931 Colonial Exhibition. The
impressive facade has a vast
frieze by A Janniot, depicting
the contributions of France's
overseas territories.
   Formerly the home of
the Musée National des
Arts d'Afrique et d'Océanie
(whose collection has now
been moved to the Musée
du Quai Branly, *see p190)*,
the Palais de la Porte Dorée
now houses the Cité
Nationale de l'Histoire de
l'Immigration. This acts as
both a museum and a cultural
centre, with regular live
performances and films on
the subject of immigration.
   The magnificent 1930s
Hall d'Honneur and the
Salle des Fêtes (ballroom)
are also open to the public.
In the basement there is a
magnificent tropical aquarium
filled with colourful fish, as
well as terrariums containing
tortoises and crocodiles.

The imposing Château de Vincennes

Château et Bois de Vincennes ⑰

Ⓜ *Château de Vincennes.*
ℝℰℝ *Vincennes.* **Château** Ave
de Paris 94300 Vincennes.
Tel 01 48 08 31 20. ◯ *10am–noon,
1–5pm (to 6pm May–Aug) daily.*
● *public hols.* 🎟 📷 ✔
compulsory in keep & chapel. 🏠
Bois de Vincennes ◯ *dawn
to dusk daily.* www.chateau-
vincennes.fr

The Château de Vincennes,
enclosed by a defensive
wall and a moat, was once
a royal residence. It was here
that Henry V of England died
painfully of dysentery in 1422.
His body was boiled in the
Château's kitchen to prepare
it for shipping back to
England. Abandoned when
Versailles was completed, the
château was converted into
an arsenal by Napoleon.
   The 14th-century keep is
a fine example of medieval
military architecture and
houses the Château's
museum. The Gothic chapel
was finished around 1550,
with beautiful stone rose
windows and a magnificent
single aisle. Two 17th-century
pavilions house a museum of
army insignia.
   Once a royal hunting
ground, the forest of
Vincennes was given to the
City of Paris by Napoleon III
in 1860. Baron Haussman's
landscape architect added
ornamental lakes and
cascades. Among its main
attractions is the largest
funfair in France (from Palm
Sunday to end of May).

Parc de la Villette ⑪

The old slaughterhouses and livestock market of Paris have been transformed into this Bernard Tschumi-designed urban park. Its vast facilities stretch across 55 ha (136 acres) of a previously run-down part of the city. The plan is to revive the tradition of parks for meetings and activities and to stimulate interest in the arts and sciences. Work began in 1984, and the park has grown to include a science museum, a concert hall, an exhibition pavilion, a spherical cinema, a circus and a music centre. Linking them all is the park itself, with its *folies*, walkways, gardens and playgrounds. In the summer the park holds an open-air film festival.

The *Folies*
These red cubes punctuate the park and provide a variety of services, such as a café and a children's workshop.

Children's Playground
A dragon slide, sand pits and colourful play equipment in a maze-like setting make the playground a paradise for young children.

★ Grande Halle
The old cattle hall has been transformed into a flexible exhibition space with mobile floors and auditorium.

Entrance

STAR BUILDINGS

- ★ Cité des Sciences et de l'Industrie
- ★ Grande Halle
- ★ Cité de la Musique
- ★ Zénith Theatre

★ Cité de la Musique
This quirky but elegant all-white complex holds the music conservatory, a concert hall, library, studios and a museum.

Maison de la Villette regularly holds shows and exhibitions.

Entrance

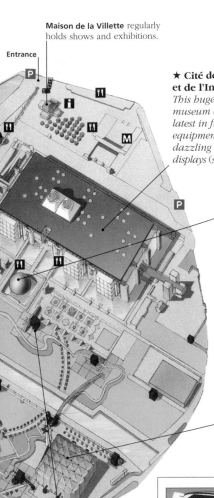

★ **Cité des Sciences et de l'Industrie**
This huge science museum boasts the latest in futurist equipment and has dazzling hands-on displays (see pp236–9).

La Géode
The cinema's gigantic 180° movie screen combines visual and sound effects to create fantastic experiences, such as the sense of travelling in space.

★ **Zénith Theatre**
This vast polyester tent was built as a venue for pop concerts with a capacity to seat more than 6,000 spectators.

L'Argonaute
The exhibit consists of a 1950s submarine and a nearby navigation museum.

Musicians from Guadeloupe performing outside the Museum

LE MUSEE DE LA MUSIQUE

This museum brings together a collection of over 4,500 instruments, objects, tools and works of art covering the history of music since the Renaissance. The permanent collection of over 900 items is displayed chronologically and can be traced using infrared audio headphones.

La Villette: Cité des Sciences et de l'Industrie

This immense science and technology museum occupies the largest of the old Villette slaughterhouses. The building soars 40 m (133 ft) high and stretches over 3 ha (7 acres). Architect Adrien Fainsilber has created an imaginative interplay between the building and three natural themes: water surrounds the structure; vegetation penetrates through the greenhouse; and light flows in through the cupolas. The museum is on five levels. Its heart are the exhibits on levels 1 and 2, where lively and entertaining displays of equipment and activities promote an interest in science and technology. Visitors can actively engage in computerized games on space, computers and sound. On other levels there are cinemas, a Children's Science City, a library, restaurants and shops.

Ayoung visitor at La Villette

Cupolas
The two glazed domes, 17 m (56 ft) in diameter, filter the flow of natural light into the main hall.

★ Planetarium
In this 260-seat auditorium, you can watch eclipses and fly over Martian landscapes thanks to the Allsky video system.

Main Hall
A soaring network of shafts, bridges escalators and balconies creates a cathedral-like atmosphere here.

STAR EXHIBITS

★ Planetarium

★ Ariane Rocket

★ La Géode

★ Ariane Rocket
The fascinating displays of rockets explain how astronauts are launched into outer space, and include an example of the European rocket Ariane.

The moat was designed by Fainsilber at 13 m (43 ft) below the level of the park, so that natural light could penetrate into the lower levels of the building. The sense of the building's massiveness is enhanced by reflections in the water.

Mirage Aircraft
A full-scale model of the French-built jet fighter plane is just one of the exhibits illustrating dramatic advances in technology.

Children's Science City
In this lively, extensive area children can experiment and play with interactive machines that show them how scientific principles work.

The greenhouse
is a square hothouse, 32 m (105 ft) high and wide, linking the park to the building.

To the Géode

Walkways
The walkways cross the encircling moat to link the various floors of the museum to the Géode and the park.

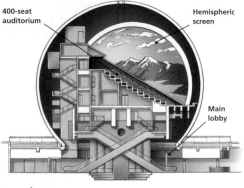

400-seat auditorium

Hemispheric screen

Main lobby

LA GÉODE

This giant entertainment sphere, 36 m (116 ft) in diameter, has a "skin" composed of 6,500 stainless-steel triangles, which reflect the surroundings and the sky. Inside, a huge hemispherical cinema screen, 1,000 sq m (11,000 sq ft), shows films on nature, travel and space.

Cité des Sciences et de l'Industrie

The exhibits on levels 1 and 2 of the Cité are a fascinating guide to the worlds of science and technology. Our understanding of computers, space, ocean, earth, sound and film is heightened by bold, imaginative presentations of multimedia displays, interactive computer exhibits and informative models. Children and adults can learn while playing with light, space and sound. Young children can walk through the sound sponge, experience optical illusions, see how astronauts live in outer space, whisper to one another through the parabolic sound screen, and listen to talking walls. Older children can learn more about how man lives and works under water, how special effects are made in films, listen to the story of a star, and see the birth of a mountain.

Sound Dishes
These parabolic sound screens transmit a conversation between people standing 17m (54ft) apart.

★ **Planetarium**
An "Inspace" simulator shows which stars are visible at any given moment, while a 3-D video allows audiences to travel into the Milky Way.

Level 2

The Nautile
One of the country's most recent scientific exploration submarines, the Nautile is one of the most sophisticated machines in the world and a technological marvel.

Level 1

The self-service media library contains books, magazines and CD-Roms on all fields of science and technology (level 0 for children, levels -1 and -2 for adults).

KEY TO FLOORPLAN

- ☐ Permanent exhibitions
- ☐ Temporary exhibitions
- ☐ Planetarium
- ☐ Future exhibition space
- ☐ Non-exhibition space

STAR EXHIBITS

★ Star Display

★ Man and His Genes

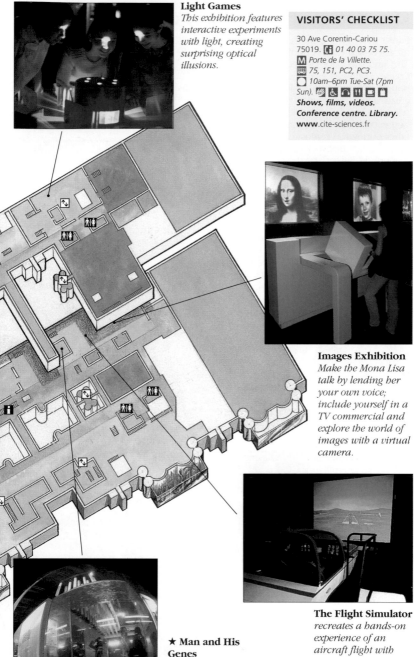

Light Games
This exhibition features interactive experiments with light, creating surprising optical illusions.

VISITORS' CHECKLIST

30 Ave Corentin-Cariou 75019. 🛂 *01 40 03 75 75.*
Ⓜ *Porte de la Villette.*
🚌 *75, 151, PC2, PC3.*
⏰ *10am–6pm Tue-Sat (7pm Sun).* 🎦 🚻 🎦 🍴 🛍 🎦
**Shows, films, videos.
Conference centre. Library.**
www.cite-sciences.fr

Images Exhibition
Make the Mona Lisa talk by lending her your own voice; include yourself in a TV commercial and explore the world of images with a virtual camera.

The Flight Simulator
recreates a hands-on experience of an aircraft flight with feed-in and feed-back computer data.

★ Man and His Genes
Chromosomes are here magnified in a bubble as part of a study of genes, the evolution of the species, reproduction and the bioethics debate.

Cimetière du Père Lachaise ⑬

Paris's most prestigious cemetery is set
on a wooded hill overlooking the city.
The land was once owned by Père de la
Chaise, Louis XIV's confessor, but it was
bought by order of Napoleon in 1803 to
create a new cemetery. The cemetery
became so popular with the Paris
bourgeoisie that it was expanded six
times during the century. Here were
buried celebrities such as the writer
Honoré de Balzac and the composer
Frédéric Chopin, and more recently, the
singer Jim Morrison and the actor Yves
Montand. Famous graves and striking
funerary sculpture make this a pleasant
place for a leisurely, nostalgic stroll.

The Columbarium was built at the end of the 19th
century. The American dancer Isadora Duncan is
one of the many celebrities whose ashes
are housed here.

Marcel Proust
*Proust brilliantly
chronicled the Belle Epoque
in his novel* Remembrance
of Things Past.

**★ Simone Signoret and
Yves Montand**
*France's most famous post-
war cinema couple were
renowned for their left-
wing views and long
turbulent relationship.*

Allan Kardec was the founder of a 19th-
century spiritual cult, which still has a
strong following. His tomb is forever
covered in pilgrims' flowers.

Sarah Bernhardt
*The great French
tragedienne, who
died in 1923 aged
78, was famous for
her portrayal of
Racine heroines.*

Monument aux Morts
by Paul Albert Bartholmé
is one of the best
monumental sculptures in
the cemetery. It dominates the central avenue.

Entrance

Frédéric Chopin, the great Polish
composer, belonged to the
French Romantic generation.

Théodore Géricault
*The French Romantic
painter's masterpiece,* The
Raft of Medusa *(see p124), is
depicted on his tomb.*

★ Oscar Wilde
The Irish dramatist, aesthete and great wit was cast away from virtuous Britain to die of drink and dissipation in Paris in 1900. Jacob Epstein sculpted the monument.

The remains of Molière, the great 17th-century actor and dramatist, were transferred here in 1817 to add historic glamour to the new cemetery.

VISITORS' CHECKLIST

16 Rue du Repos. *Tel 01 55 25 82 10.* Ⓜ *Père Lachaise, Alexandre Dumas.* 🚌 *62, 69, 26 to Pl Gambetta.* Ⓟ *Pl Gambetta.* ⬜ *8am–5.30pm daily (from 8.30am Sat, 9am Sun; mid-Mar–Oct: to 6pm).* 📷 ♿ ℹ️

Mur des Fédérés is the wall against which the last Communard rebels were shot by government forces in 1871. It is now a place of pilgrimage for left-wing sympathizers.

★ Edith Piaf
Known as "the little sparrow" because of her size, Piaf was the 20th century's greatest French popular singer. In her tragic voice she sang of the sorrows and love woes of the Paris working class.

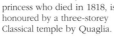

Victor Noir
The life-size statue of this 19th-century journalist shot by Pierre Bonaparte, a cousin of Napoleon III, is said to have fertility powers.

George Rodenbach, the 19th-century poet, is depicted as rising out of his tomb with a rose in the hand of his outstretched arm.

Elizabeth Demidoff, a Russian princess who died in 1818, is honoured by a three-storey Classical temple by Quaglia.

★ Jim Morrison
The death of The Doors' *lead singer in Paris in 1971 is still a mystery.*

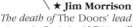

François Raspail
The tomb of this much-imprisoned partisan of the 1830 and 1840 revolutions is in the form of a prison.

Disneyland Resort Paris ⓫

Disneyland Resort Paris is built on a massive scale – the 2,000-ha (5,000-acre) site encompasses two theme parks; seven hotels (several with swimming pools), a shopping, dining and entertainment village; a seasonal ice skating rink; lakes; two convention centres; and a golf course. One stop down the line from their very own train station lies Val d'Europe, a huge new shopping mall with more than 180 shopping outlets, including 60 discount stores, and a Sea World centre.

Unbeatable for complete escapism, combined with vibrant excitement and sheer energy, the Parks offer extreme rides and gentle experiences, all accompanied by phenomenal visual effects.

The Queen of Hearts' Castle, in Alice's Curious Labyrinth

THE PARKS

Disneyland Resort Paris consists of Disneyland Park and Walt Disney Studios Park. Disneyland Park is based on the Magic Kingdom of California and has more than 40 rides or attractions. The newest park is the Walt Disney Studios Park, where interactive exhibits and live shows bring alive the artistic and technical wizardry that has made the movie and television industry so enthralling. Find out more at: www.disneylandparis.com.

GETTING THERE

By Car
Disneyland Resort Paris lies 32 km (20 miles) to the east of Paris, and has its own link (exit 14) from the A4 westbound from Paris and eastbound A4, from Strasbourg. Simply follow the signs to Marne la Vallée (Val d'Europe) until you see the Disneyland signs. (The Davy Crockett Ranch is exit 13.)

By Air
Both Orly and Charles de Gaulle Airports have a shuttle bus which runs every 30 minutes (45 in the low season). No booking is necessary. The fare is about 12€ per person.

By Train
The Paris RER runs directly to the parks, as does the TGV which has connections throughout Europe.

PARKING

There is space for over 12,000 vehicles, and an efficient moving sidewalk conveys you to the exit. Parking costs 8€ per day for cars, and 10€ for campers and coaches. Parking at Disneyland Resort Paris hotels is free to guests, and the Disneyland and New York hotels offer valet parking.

OPENING HOURS

The Parks tend to open at 9am in high season and 10am otherwise. Disneyland Park closes at 11pm in high season and 8pm in low season. The Walt Disney Studios Park closes at 8pm in high season and 6pm in low season. Special events, such as Hallowe'en, can mean extended hours.

WHEN TO VISIT

The busiest times are Christmas and New Year, mid-February to early April and July to early September, and mid-October. Busiest days are Saturday–Monday; Tuesday and Wednesday are quietest.

LENGTH OF VISIT

To experience everything Disneyland Resort Paris has to offer you really need to spend three or four days at the resort. Although it is possible to tour the Parks in one day each, to enjoy them at less than breakneck pace you need at least two days for Disneyland Park alone, and if you want to include Buffalo Bill's Wild West show or visit some of the

EATING AND DRINKING

There's no need to leave the park to eat during the day. **Au Chalet de la Marionnette** (Fantasyland) is excellent for kids (and almost deserted at 3pm) as is the **Cowboy Cookout Barbecue** (Frontierland), which tends to be rather more crowded. **Colonel Hathi's Pizza Outpost** (Adventureland) is worth a visit just to see the authentic colonial gear, whilst **Café Hyperion – Videopolis** (Discoveryland) offers good food plus excellent entertainment, but service is very slow.

You pay a premium for full-service restaurants but the experience of eating in **Blue Lagoon Restaurant** (Adventureland) is one you will remember. You dine on the "shore" of a Caribbean Pirate hideaway while the boats from Pirates of the Caribbean glide past. **Walt's**, on Main Street, USA, is also a good but pricey restaurant offering American fare. If you're lucky, they'll seat you so that you can watch the afternoon Main Street parade in comfort from an upstairs window.

In Disney Village Annette's Diner is staffed by roller-skating waitresses against a background of '50s records. **Planet Hollywood** is another good option, and the **Rainforest Cafe** provides an interestingly animated meal. The **Steakhouse** is excellent, although a little pricey, while a giant **McDonald's** serves the usual fare. The hotel restaurants are more expensive the nearer they are to the park.

nightclubs in Disney Village, then you'll be pushed to manage it all in under four days. Locals turn up on a daily basis from Paris, which is only 35 minutes away on the RER, but most guests from further afield will stay in hotels. Disney offer several packages for those who wish to stay on site. These include passes for the Parks, and accommodation with continental breakfast included. All inclusive packages can also be booked.

TICKETS

If you book a package, tickets will be included in the price. Tickets for both Parks can be bought from any Disney Store before you leave home, or at the Park upon arrival – though this means queuing at a ticket booth. One-, 2- or 3-day tickets are available, and prices vary according to season. The Hopper ticket allows entry to both Parks on the same day. The Paris transport system RATP also sells tickets that combine travel on the RER and entry to the Parks.

GETTING AROUND

Disney provide an efficient transport system between the Parks and the hotels (excluding Davy Crockett Ranch) with buses on the half hour. In summer, a fleet of little open-top buses drive slowly around Lake Disney, ferrying guests between the three lakeside hotels and Disney Village. If you're staying at any of the on-site hotels it's only a short walk (20 minutes at most) to the Park gates.

Sleeping Beauty Castle, the centrepiece of the Park

WHICH HOTEL?

There are six hotels on site, and one in woodland 2 km (3 miles) away. The best hotels are the closest to the Parks.

Hotel Santa Fe: basic, small and reasonably inexpensive. The only hotel offering parking immediately outside your room.
Hotel Cheyenne: a Wild West theme hotel, about 17 minutes walk from the park. Small rooms (with bunks for the kids), a Native American village play area. Inexpensive and a great experience. Kids love this hotel.
Sequoia Lodge: a lakeside "hunter's lodge", moderately priced with more than 1,000 rooms. Ask for a room in the main building. Rooms at the front have great views.
Newport Bay Club: a huge, nautically-themed, hotel on the lakeside. Moderately priced, this massive hotel has a huge convention centre, magnificent swimming pool and three floors offering extra services for a supplement.
Hotel New York: expensive and business-oriented; not a lot for the kids. This hotel also has a large convention centre, and there's an ice-skating rink from October to March.
Disneyland Hotel: the Jewel in the crown. Expensive, but right at the entrance to the Disneyland Park. Full of delightful touches, such as grandfather clocks and ever-present Disney characters. The Castle Club is a 50-room hotel-within-a-hotel. If you can afford it, a week of decadent fawning and unrestrained hedonism can be yours!
Davy Crockett Ranch: log cabins sleeping 4–6 are grouped around a woodland trail, as well as traditional camping facilities. Some excellent facilities: the pool ranks as one of the best in Disneyland Resort Paris.

MONEY

Credit cards are accepted everywhere within the resort. ATMs and commission-free foreign exchange are available immediately inside the Park entrances and at reception in all the hotels.

DISABLED TRAVELLERS

City hall (immediately within Disneyland Park) has a brochure outlining the facilities for the disabled, and a Disabled Guest Guide can be pre-ordered (free) from the Disneyland Resort Paris website. The complex is designed very much with the disabled in mind, but note that cast members are not allowed to assist with lifting people or moving wheelchairs.

STAYING IN A DISNEY HOTEL

The on-site hotels offer rooms at a wide range of prices, with the rule of thumb being that those closest to the Parks are the most expensive. Advantages include virtually

---

The runaway mine-train track of Big Thunder Mountain

no travelling to reach the Parks, and "early bird" entry to the parks on selected dates (usually at peak times).

If you stay at a Disney Hotel you will be given a hotel ID card. This unprepossessing little item is very important. As well as being used to charge anything you buy back to your hotel room (and have it delivered there), it also allows you entry to the Disneyland hotel grounds early in the morning while they're still shut to day trippers (the grounds also act as an entrance to the Park).

For children (of any age), one of the most exciting bonuses of staying in an on-site hotel is the chance to dine with Disney characters.

Exploring Disneyland Resort Paris

The resort is comprised of two large entertainment areas, the Disneyland Park and the Walt Disney Studios Park. The former celebrates lands from a past strongly coloured by Hollywood folklore, and the latter highlights the ingenuity of the production processes involved in cinema, animation and television.

The resort offers a plethora of attractions and themed parades chosen from the "Wonderful World Of Disney".

DISNEYLAND PARK

MAIN STREET, USA

Main Street represents a fantasy small-town America, right down to the traffic, which includes horse-drawn rail cars, a paddy wagon and other vintage transport in a system that runs between Town Square and Central Plaza. The Victorian facades offer a wealth of detail, and hide several interesting stores. The Emporium is the place for gifts. Further along, you can snack at Casey's Corner or succumb to the aromas from Cookie Kitchen or the Cable Car Bake Shop. Either side of the shops are the Discovery and Liberty Arcades, offering a covered route to the Central Plaza and hosting displays and cute small stalls.

At night, thousands of lights set Main Street's paving a-glow. Disney's Fantillusion, a fantasy of music, live action and illuminated floats, begins at Town Square. From Main Street you can ride a 19th century "steam" engine. Do note that boarding elsewhere than Main Street is not always possible before noon.

FRONTIERLAND

This homage to America's Wild West hosts some of the Park's most popular attractions. Big Thunder Mountain, a rollercoaster ride, is circled by two paddle steamers that take a musical cruise around America's finest natural monuments. Phantom Manor is a ghost ride, and at the outdoor Chaparral Theatre you can see some amazing stage performances.

Pocahontas Indian Village and Critter Corral are both popular with younger children.

ADVENTURELAND

Enjoy the wild rides and Audio-Animatronics™ of Adventureland. Indiana Jones™ and the Temple of Peril hurtles you through a derelict mine. The ride has torches, steep drops and tight 360° loops.

Pirates of the Caribbean is a great boat ride through underground prisons and past 16th-century fighting galleons. *La Cabane des Robinson*, based on Jonathan Wyss's *Swiss Family Robinson*, starts with a shaky climb up a 27-m (88-ft) Banyan Tree. From here you explore the rest of the island, including the caves of Ben Gunn from *Treasure Island* and the awe-inspiring suspension bridge near Spyglass Hill. The children's playground, Pirates' Beach, is also well worth a visit.

FANTASYLAND

The buildings here are modelled on those in animated movies. Many attractions are for younger children, such as Snow White and the Seven Dwarfs, and Pinocchio's Fantastic Journey. The very young will love Dumbo the Flying Elephant. Peter Pan's Flight is a triumph of imagination and technology, flying you high over the streets of London. A popular diversion is Alice's Curious Labyrinth.

Hourly, there's a musical parade of clockwork figures at "it's a small world". Aboard a boat, you meander through lands of animated models to the strains of the eponymous song. Le Pays des Contes des Fées (Storybook Land) is another boat ride. Next, hop aboard Casey Jr for a train ride circling the boats.

DISCOVERYLAND

Science fiction and the future are the themes here. The multi-loop ride Space Mountain draws crowds from the outset, but at the end of the day you can often walk straight on. Les Mystères du Nautilus takes you right into the submarine from *20,000 Leagues Under the Sea*. Autopia, where you can drive a real, petrol-engined car, is a magnet for youngsters. Orbitron features spaceships and soon gets crowded, but is worth experiencing. Star Tours makes you a passenger in a star shuttle on a breathtaking journey of narrow escapes.

The best shows are in Videopolis, a cavernous café showing cartoons between shows. Honey, I Shrunk the Audience is a masterpiece of total sensory stimulation.

WALT DISNEY STUDIOS PARK

FRONT LOT

Inside the giant studio gates, the central feature of Front Lot is a fountain in the shape of Mickey Mouse as he appears in *The Sorceror's Apprentice*. It's also hard to miss 'Earful Tower', a massive studio icon based on the water tower at the Disney Studios in California. Disney Studio 1 houses a film set boulevard, complete with facades that front a street and represent stylised locations such as the 1930's-style Club Swankedero, the Liki Tiki tropical bar and the ultra cool rat-packesque Hep Cat Club.

ANIMATION COURTYARD

Celebrating the key art that facilitated Disney's great success, the courtyard is made up of three areas. A huge *Sorcerer's Apprentice* hat marks the entrance to the Art of Disney Animation, an interactive attraction tracing the entire history of moving imagery. Animagique is a show that brings together some of the greatest moments from the Disney corpus. In Flying Carpets over Agrabah, the genie from *Aladdin* invites spectators to participate in an astonishing magic carpet ride all around a magical set whose amazing centrepiece is a giant genie's bottle. Participants even get to be the stars of a film directed by the magical man himself.

PRODUCTION COURTYARD

Here the emphasis is on the production process. At the Walt Disney Television Studios you can see behind the scenes of television production, while Ciné-Magique is a must for film buffs, as it covers the history of both American and European cinema. The Studio Tram Tour gives you a tour of the studio premises, including a visit to Catastrophe Canyon, where you can enjoy the fun of a spectacular film shoot.

BACKLOT

This area concentrates its focus on the topics of special effects, film music recording and crazy dare-devil stunts. Armageddon Special Effects presents a tour of film trickery, while Rock 'n' Roller Coaster is a high-speed attraction (in fact, it is the fastest ride in any Disney theme park) that combines a once-in-a-lifetime ride set against a pulsating musical soundtrack provided by rock legends Aerosmith.

RIDES AND ATTRACTIONS

This chart is designed to help you make the best use of your time at Disneyland Paris, decide on which rides and tours are best for you, and choose when to visit them.

	Queues	Height / Age Restriction	Best Time to Ride or Visit	Fastpass	Scary Rating	May Cause Motion Sickness	Rating Overall
Phantom Manor	◗		Any		❷		★
Rivers of the Far West	○		Any		❶		▼
Big Thunder Mountain	●	1.2m	FT	✔	❷		★
Pocohantas Indian Village	○		Any		❶		▼
Indiana Jones & the Temple of Peril	●	1.4m	LT	✔	❸	✔	★
Adventure Isle	○		Any		❶		▼
La Cabane des Robinson	○		Any		❶		▼
Pirates of the Caribbean	○		Any		❶		★
Peter Pan's Flight	●		FT	✔	❶		◆
Snow White & the Seven Dwarfs	●		➤11		❶		◆
Pinocchio's Fantastic Journey	●		➤11		❶		◆
Dumbo the Flying Elephant	●		FT		❶		◆
Mad Hatter's Teacups	◗		➤12		❶		▼
Alice's Curious Labyrinth	○		Any		❶		▼
"It's a Small World"	○		Any		❶		◆
Casey Jr – Le Petit Train du Cirque	○		➤11		❶		◆
Le Pays des Contes des Fees	○		Any		❶		◆
Star Tours	○	1.3m	Any	✔	❶		★
Space Mountain	●	1.4m	LT	✔	❸	✔	★
Honey, I Shrunk the Audience	○		Any		❶		★
Autopia	●		FT		❶		▼
Orbitron	●	1.2m	FT		❶		▼
Disney Studio 1	◗		Any		❶		◆
Art of Disney Animation	◗		Any		❶		▼
Animagique	●		Any		❶		◆
Flying Carpets Over Agrabah	●	1.2m	FT		❶	✔	◆
Walt Disney Television Studios	●		Any		❶		◆
CinéMagique	◗		Any		❶		◆
Studio Tram Tour	●		FT		❶		★
Armageddon Special Effects	●		Any		❶		▼
Rock 'n' Roller Coaster	●	1.2m	Any		❸	✔	★

Short - ○   Medium - ◗   Long - ●   Anytime - Any   Before 11 - ➤11   First thing - FT   Last thing - LT
Not Scary - ❶   Slightly - ❷   Very - ❸   Quite good - ▼   Very good - ◆   Outstanding - ★

The Palace and Gardens of Versailles 26

Visitors passing through the rich interior of this colossal palace, or strolling in its vast gardens, will understand why it was the glory of the Sun King's reign. Starting in 1668 with his father's modest hunting lodge, Louis XIV built the largest palace in Europe, housing 20,000 people at a time. Architects Louis Le Vau and Jules Hardouin-Mansart designed the

Garden statue of a flautist

buildings, Charles Le Brun did the interiors, and André Le Nôtre, the great landscaper, redesigned the gardens. The gardens are formally styled into regular patterns of paths and groves, hedges and flowerbeds, pools of water and fountains.

★ Formal Gardens
Geometric paths and shrubberies are features of the formal gardens.

The Orangery was built beneath the Parterre du Midi to house exotic plants in winter.

The South Parterre's shrubbery and ornate flowerbeds overlook the Swiss pond.

★ The Château
Louis XIV made the château into the centre of political power in France (see pp250–53).

The Water Parterre's vast pools of water are decorated with superb bronze statues.

Fountain of Latona
Marble basins rise to Balthazar Marsy's statue of the goddess Latona.

Dragon Fountain
The fountain's centrepiece is a winged monster.

The King's Garden with Mirror Pool are a 19th-century English garden and pool created by Louis XVIII.

Colonnade
Mansart designed this circle of marble arches in 1685.

The Grand Canal was the setting for Louis XIV's many boating parties.

Petit Trianon
Built in 1762 as a retreat for Louis XV, this small château became a favourite of Marie-Antoinette.

Fountain of Neptune
Groups of sculptures spray spectacular jets of water in Le Nôtre and Mansart's 17th-century fountain.

★ **Grand Trianon**
Louis XIV built this small palace of stone and pink marble in 1687 to escape the rigours of court life, and to enjoy the company of his mistress, Madame de Maintenon.

STAR SIGHTS

★ The Château

★ Formal Gardens

★ Grand Trianon

The Main Palace Buildings of Versailles

Gold crest from the Petit Trianon

The present palace grew as a series of envelopes enfolding the original hunting lodge, whose low brick front is still visible in the centre. In the 1660s, Louis Le Vau built the first envelope, a series of wings which expanded into an enlarged courtyard. It was decorated with marble busts, antique trophies and gilded roofs. On the garden side, columns were added to the west facade and a great terrace was created on the first floor. Mansart took over in 1678 and added the two immense north and south wings and filled Le Vau's terrace to form the Hall of Mirrors. He designed the chapel, which was finished in 1710. The Opera House (*L'Opéra*) was added by Louis XV in 1770.

South Wing
The wing's original apartments for great nobles were replaced by Louis-Philippe's museum of French history.

The Royal Courtyard was separated from the Ministers' Courtyard by elaborate grillwork during Louis XIV's reign. It was accessible only to royal carriages.

Louis XIV's statue, erected by Louis Philippe in 1837, stands where a gilded gateway once marked the beginning of the Royal Courtyard.

STAR SIGHTS

★ Marble Courtyard

★ L'Opéra

★ Chapelle Royale

Ministers' Courtyard

Main Gate
Mansart's original gateway grille, surmounted by the royal arms, is the entrance to the Ministers' Courtyard.

TIMELINE

1667 Grand Canal begun	*Louis XV*	**1793** Louis XVI and Marie-Antoinette executed	**1833** Louis-Philippe turns the château into a museum
1668 Construction of new château by Le Vau	**1722** 12-year-old Louis XV occupies Versailles		

1650	1700	1750	1800	1850

1671 Interior decoration by Le Brun begun	**1715** Death of Louis XIV. Versailles abandoned by court	**1789** King and queen forced to leave Versailles for Paris	**1919** Treaty of Versailles signed on 28 June
1661 Louis XIV enlarges château	**1682** Louis XIV and Marie-Thérèse move to Versailles	**1774** Louis XVI and Marie-Antoinette live at Versailles	

The Clock
Hercules and Mars flank the clock overlooking the Marble Courtyard.

★ **Marble Courtyard**
The courtyard is decorated with marble paving, urns, busts and a gilded balcony.

North Wing
The chapel, Opéra and picture galleries occupy this wing, which originally housed royal apartments.

★ **L'Opéra**
Built for the 1770 marriage of the future Louis XVI and Marie-Antoinette, the Opéra is usually closed to the public.

★ **Chapelle Royale**
Mansart's last great work, this two-storey Baroque chapel, was Louis XIV's last addition to Versailles.

Inside the Château of Versailles

The sumptuous main apartments are on the first floor of the vast château complex. Around the Marble Courtyard are the private apartments of the king and the queen. On the garden side are the state apartments where official court life took place. These were richly decorated by Charles Le Brun with coloured marbles, stone and wood carvings, murals, velvet, silver and gilded furniture. Beginning with the Salon d'Hercule, each state room is dedicated to an Olympian deity. The climax is the Hall of Mirrors, where 17 great mirrors face tall arched windows.

STAR SIGHTS

★ Chapelle Royale

★ Salon de Venus

★ Hall of Mirrors

★ Queen's Bedroom

KEY

☐	South wing
☐	Coronation room
☐	Madame de Maintenon's apartments
☐	Queen's apartments and private suite
☐	State apartments
☐	King's apartments and private suite
☐	North wing
☐	Non-exhibition space

★ Queen's Bedroom
In this room the queens of France gave birth to the royal children in full public view.

Entrance

Louis XVI's library features Neo-Classical panelling and the king's terrestrial globe.

The Salon du Sacre is adorned with huge paintings of Napoleon by Jacques-Louis David.

Entrance

★ Salon de Venus
A Louis XIV statue stands amidst the rich marble decor of this room.

★ Chapelle Royale
The chapel's first floor was reserved for the royal family and the ground floor for the court. The interior is richly decorated in white marble, gilding and Baroque murals.

★ Hall of Mirrors
Great state occasions were held in this multi-mirrored room along the west façade. The Treaty of Versailles was ratified here in 1919, ending World War I. During restoration in 2007, only parts of it will be open.

Oeil-de-Boeuf

The King's Bedroom
is where Louis XIV died in 1715, aged 77.

Salon de la Guerre
The room's theme of war is dramatically reinforced by Antoine Coysevox's stuccoed relief of Louis XIV riding to victory.

The Cabinet du Conseil is where the king received his ministers and his family.

Salon d'Apollon
Designed by Le Brun and dedicated to the god Apollo, this was Louis XIV's throne room. A copy of Hyacinthe Rigaud's famous portrait of the king (1701) hangs here.

Salon d'Hercule

Stairs to ground floor reception area

PURSUIT OF THE QUEEN

On 6 October 1789, a Parisian mob invaded the palace seeking the despised Marie-Antoinette. The queen, roused in alarm from her bed, fled towards the king's rooms through the anteroom known as the Oeil-de-Boeuf. As the mob tried to break into the room, the queen beat on the door of the king's bedroom. Once admitted she was safe, at least until morning, when she and the king were removed to Paris by the cheering and triumphant mob.

EIGHT GUIDED WALKS

Paris is a city for walking. It is more compact and easier to get around than many other great capitals. Most of its great sights are within walking distance of one another and they are close to the heart of the city, the Ile de la Cité.

There are 14 classic tourist areas described in the *Area by Area* section of this book, each with a short walk marked on its *Street-by-Street* map, taking you past many of the most interesting sights. Yet Paris offers a wealth of lesser known but equally remarkable areas, whose special history, architecture and local customs reveal other facets of the city.

The eight walks around the following neighbourhoods take in the main sights and also introduce visitors to their subtle details, such as street markets, quirky churches, canals, gardens, old village streets and bridges. And the literary, artistic and historical associations allow the past and present to blend into the changing and vibrant life of the modern city.

Parc Monceau statue

Auteuil is renowned for its luxury modern residential architecture, Monceau for its sumptuous Second Empire mansions and St-Louis for its *ancien régime* town houses, narrow streets and literati residents. The old-fashioned charm of the iron footbridges survives along Canal St-Martin, and steep village streets that were once home to famous artists still enrich Montmartre. A tranquil village atmosphere also pervades two lesser-known hilltop districts – Buttes-Chaumont, with one of Paris's loveliest parks, and Butte-aux-Cailles, whose quaint, cobbled alley-ways belie its association with the ill-fated Paris Commune of 1871, while the once working-class area of Faubourg St-Antoine has been given a new lease of life as a pleasure-boat harbour and artisans' quarter.

All the walk areas are readily accessible by public transport and the nearest metro stations and bus routes are listed in the *Tips for Walkers* boxes. For each walk there are suggestions on convenient resting points, such as cafés and squares, along the route.

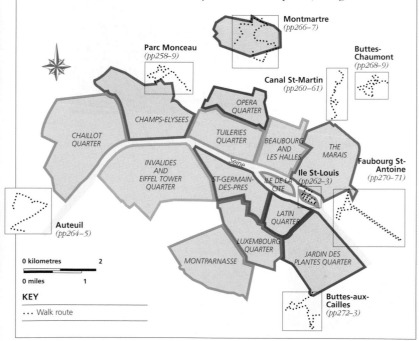

Montmartre *(pp266–7)*

Parc Monceau *(pp258–9)*

Buttes-Chaumont *(pp268–9)*

Canal St-Martin *(pp260–61)*

OPERA QUARTER

CHAMPS-ELYSEES

CHAILLOT QUARTER

TUILERIES QUARTER

BEAUBOURG AND LES HALLES

THE MARAIS

Faubourg St-Antoine *(pp270–71)*

INVALIDES AND EIFFEL TOWER QUARTER

Seine

ST-GERMAIN-DES-PRES

ILE DE LA CITE

Ile St-Louis *(pp262–3)*

Auteuil *(pp264–5)*

LATIN QUARTER

LUXEMBOURG QUARTER

MONTPARNASSE

JARDIN DES PLANTES QUARTER

Buttes-aux-Cailles *(pp272–3)*

0 kilometres 2

0 miles 1

KEY

••• Walk route

◁ **Bridge over the canal St-Martin**

A 90-Minute Walk around Parc Monceau

This leisurely walk passes through the exquisite late-18th-century Parc Monceau, the centrepiece of a smart Second Empire district. It then follows a route along surrounding streets, where groups of opulent mansions stunningly convey the magnificence in which some Parisians live, before ending at Place St-Augustin. For details on Monceau sights, see pages 230–31.

Ruysdaël gate

Parc Monceau to Avenue Velasquez

The walk starts at the Monceau metro station ① on the Boulevard de Courcelles. Enter the park where Nicolas Ledoux's 18th-century tollhouse ② stands. On

Parc Monceau's tollhouse ②

either side are sumptuously gilded 19th-century wrought-iron gates which support ornate lampposts.

Take the second path on the left past the monument to Guy de Maupassant ③ (1897). This is only one of a series of six Belle Epoque monuments of prominent French writers and musicians which are picturesquely scattered throughout the park. Most of them feature a solemn bust of a great man who is accompanied by a swooning muse.

Straight ahead is the most important remaining folly, a moss-covered Corinthian colonnade ④ running around the edge of a charming tiny lake with the requisite island in the centre. Walk around the colonnade and under a 16th-century arch ⑤ transplanted from the old Paris Hôtel de Ville (see p102), which burned down in 1871.

Turn left on the Allée de la Comtesse de Ségur and go into Avenue Velasquez, a

wide tree-lined street with 19th-century Neo-Classical mansions. At No. 7 is the splendid Cernuschi museum ⑥, which houses a collection of Far Eastern art.

Colonnade in Parc Monceau ④

Ambroise Thomas statue ⑧

Avenue Velasquez to Avenue Van Dyck

Re-enter the park and turn left into the second small winding path, which is bordered by an 18th-century mossy pyramid ⑦, antique tombs, a stone arcade, an obelisk and a small Chinese stone pagoda. The romantically melancholy tone of these false ruins suits the spirit of the late 18th century.

Turn right on the first path past the pyramid and walk back to the central avenue. Straight ahead a Renaissance bridge fords the little stream running from the lake. Turn left and walk past the

monument (1902) to the musician Ambroise Thomas ⑧. Immediately behind there is a lovely artificial mountain with cascade. Turn left on the next avenue and walk to the monument (1897) to the composer Charles Gounod ⑨ on the left. From here follow the first winding path to the right towards the Avenue Van Dyck exit. Ahead to the right, in the corner of the park, is the Chopin monument ⑩ (1906), and looking along the Allée de la Comtesse de Ségur, the monument to the 19th-century French poet Alfred de Musset.

Avenue Van Dyck to Rue de Monceau

Leave the park and pass into Avenue Van Dyck. No. 5 on the right is an impressive Parc Monceau mansion ⑪, a Neo-Baroque structure built by chocolate manufacturer Emile Menier; No. 6 is in the French Renaissance style that came back into favour in the 1860s. Straight ahead, beyond the ornate grille, there is a fine view of Avenue Hoche and in the distance the Arc de Triomphe. Walk past the gate

The mountain cascade ⑧

and turn left into Rue de Courcelles and left again into Rue Murillo, bordered by more elaborate town houses in 18th-century and French Renaissance styles ⑫. At the crossing of Rue Rembrandt, on the left, is another gate into the park and on the right a massive apartment building from 1900 (No. 7) and an elegant French Renaissance house with an elaborately carved wooden front door (No. 1). At the corner of the Rue Rembrandt and the Rue de Courcelles is the oddest of all the neighbourhood buildings, a striking five-storey red Chinese pagoda ⑬. It is an exclusive emporium of Chinese art.

Turn left on to the Rue de Monceau, walk past Avenue Ruysdaël and continue to the Musée Nissim de Camondo at No. 63 Rue de Monceau ⑭. Some nearby buildings worth having a look at are Nos. 52, 60 and 61 ⑮.

Boulevard Malesherbes

At the junction of Rue de Monceau and Boulevard Malesherbes turn right. This long boulevard with dignified six-storey apartment buildings is typical of the great avenues cut through Paris by Baron Haussmann, Prefect of the Seine during the Second Empire (*see pp34–5*). They

greatly pleased the Industrial Age bourgeoisie, but horrified sensitive souls and writers who compared them with the buildings of New York.

No. 75 is the posh marble front of Benneton, the most fashionable Paris card and stationery engraver ⑯. On the left, approaching the Boulevard Haussmann, looms the greatest 19th-century Paris church, St-Augustin ⑰, built by Victor-Louis Baltard. Enter the church through the back door on Rue de la Bien-faisance. Walk through the church and leave by the main door. On the left is the massive stone building of the French Officers' club, the Cercle Militaire ⑱. Straight ahead is a bronze statue of Joan of Arc ⑲. Continue on to Place St-Augustin to St-Augustin metro station.

Joan of Arc statue ⑲

TIPS FOR WALKERS

Starting point: Blvd de Courcelles.
Length: 3 km (2 miles).
Getting there: The nearest metro is Monceau, reached by bus No. 30; No. 84 goes to metro Courcelles and No. 94 stops between Monceau & Villiers metros.
St Augustin church: Open 8.30am–7pm daily (closed 12.30–3.30pm public hols).
Stopping-off points: Near the Renaissance bridge in the Parc Monceau there is a kiosk serving coffee and sandwiches. There are two cafés at Place de Rio de Janeiro and several brasseries around Place St-Augustin. The Square M Pagnol is a pleasant place to relax and take in the beauty of the park at the end of the walk.

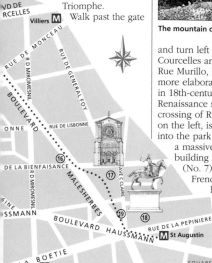

KEY

••• Walk route

🔆 Good viewing point

Ⓜ Metro station

| 0 metres | 250 |
| 0 yards | 250 |

Chinese pagoda emporium ⑬

A 90-Minute Walk along the Canal St-Martin

The walk along the quays on either side of the Canal St-Martin is an experience of Paris very different from that of smarter districts. Here, the older surviving landmarks of the neighbourhood – the factories, warehouses, dwellings, taverns and cafés – hint at life in a thriving 19th-century industrial, working-class world. But there are also the softer charms of the old iron footbridges, the tree-lined quays, the inevitable fishermen, the river barges, and the still waters of the broad canal basins. A walk along the canal, which connects the Bassin de la Villette with the Seine, will evoke images of the Pernod-drinking, working-class Paris of Jean Gabin and Edith Piaf.

The 18th-century
Barrière de la Villette ②

Bassin de la Villette looking north ③

Place de Stalingrad to Avenue Jean-Jaurès

From the Stalingrad metro station ①, follow Boulevard de la Villette to the new square in front of the Barrière de la Villette ②. This is one of the few remaining 18th-century tollhouses in Paris, designed by the celebrated Neo-Classical architect Nicolas Ledoux in the 1780s. The fountains, square and terraces were designed in the 1980s to provide an attractive setting and fine views of the Bassin de la Villette ③ to the north.

Walk towards Avenue Jean-Jaurès. On the left is the first lock ④ leading down to the canal, as well as the art-house cinema chain MK2's landmark complexes, which are linked together by a boat.

View from Rue E Varlin bridge ⑦

KEY

∙∙∙ Walk route

☆ Good viewing point

Ⓜ Metro station

| 0 metres | 500 |
| 0 yards | 500 |

Courtyard garden of Hôpital St-Louis ⑭

Iron footbridges over the canal ⑤

Quai de Valmy to Rue Bichat

Cross over to the Quai de Jemmapes, which runs the length of the east side of the canal and down to the first bridge on Rue Louis Blanc ⑤. Cross the bridge to the Quai de Valmy. From the corner there is a glimpse of the oblique granite and glass front of the new Paris Industrial Tribunal ⑥ on the Rue Louis Blanc.

Continue along Quai de Valmy. At Rue E Varlin cross the bridge ⑦, from where there is an attractive view of the second canal lock, lock-keeper's house, public gardens and old lampposts. At the other side of the bridge and slightly to the left, go along the pedestrianized Rue Haendel, which provides a

good view of the towering buildings of a social housing estate ⑧. Nearby is the French Communist Party headquarters ⑨ on Place du Colonel Fabien, with its curving glazed tower.

Return to the Quai de Jemmapes, where at No. 134 ⑩ stands one of the few surviving brick-and-iron industrial buildings that used to line the canal in the 19th century. At No. 126 ⑪ is another notable modern building, a residence for the aged, with monumental concrete arches and glazed bay windows. Further along, at No. 112 ⑫, is an Art Deco apartment building with bay windows, decorative iron balconies and tiles. On the ground floor there is a typical 1930s proletarian café. Here the canal curves gracefully into the third lock, spanned by a charming transparent iron footbridge ⑬.

Hôpital St-Louis to Rue Léon Jouhaux

Turn left into Rue Bichat, which leads to the remark-able 17th-century Hôpital St-Louis ⑭. Enter through the hospital's old main gate with its high-pitched roof and massive stone arch. Pass into the courtyard. The hospital was founded in 1607 by Henri IV, the first Bourbon king, to care for the victims of the plague. Leave the courtyard from the central gate on the wing on your left. Here you pass by the 17th-century hospital chapel ⑮ and out into the Rue de la Grange aux Belles.

Turn left and walk back to the canal. At the junction of Rue de la Grange Batelière and the Quai de Jemmapes stood, until 1627, the notorious Montfaucon gallows ⑯, one of the chief public execution spots of medieval Paris. Turn into the Quai de Jemmapes. At No. 101 ⑰ is the original front of the Hôtel du Nord, made famous in the eponymous 1930s film. In front is another iron footbridge and a draw-bridge ⑱ for traffic, providing a charming setting with views of the canal on either side. Cross over and continue down the Quai de Valmy until the last footbridge ⑲ at the corner of the Rue Léon Jouhaux. From here the canal can be seen disappearing under the surface of Paris, to continue its journey, through a great stone arch.

Entrance to Hôpital St-Louis ⑭

Square Frédéric Lemaître to Place de la République

Walk along Square Frédéric Lemaître ⑳ to the start of Boulevard Jules Ferry, which has a public garden stretching down its centre. The garden was built over the canal in the 1860s. At its head stands a charmingly nostalgic statue of a flower girl of the 1830s, *La Grisette* ㉑. On the left is a busy working-class street, Rue du Faubourg du Temple ㉒, with flourishing ethnic shops and restaurants. Follow the street to the right and on to the metro station in the Place de la République.

Shop, Rue du Faubourg du Temple ㉒

A 90-Minute Walk around the Ile St-Louis

The walk around this charming tiny island passes along the enchanting, picturesque tree-lined quays from Pont Louis-Philippe to Quai d'Anjou, taking in the sumptuous 17th-century *hôtels* that infuse the area with such a powerful sense of period. It then penetrates into the heart of the island along the main street, Rue St-Louis-en-l'Ile, enlivened by chic restaurants, cafés, art galleries and boutiques, before returning to the north side of the island and back to Pont Marie. For more information on the main sights, see pages 77 and 87.

Left Bank view of the Ile St-Louis

Fishing on a St-Louis quayside

Metro Pont Marie to Rue Jean du Bellay

From the Pont Marie metro station ① walk down Quai des Celestins and Quai de l'Hôtel de Ville, lined with traditional bookstands, from where there is a good view of Ile St-Louis. Turn left at Pont Louis-Philippe ② and, having crossed it, take the steps down to the lower quay immediately to the right. Walk around the tree-shaded west point of the island ③, then up the other side to the Pont St-Louis ④. Opposite the bridge, on the corner of Rue Jean du Bellay, is Le Flore en l'Ile ⑤, the smartest café-cum-tea salon on the island.

Quai d'Orléans

From the corner of the Quai d'Orléans and the Rue Jean du Bellay there are fine views of the Panthéon's dome and Notre-Dame. Along the quay, Nos. 18–20, the Hôtel Rolland, has unusual Hispano-Moorish windows. No. 12 ⑥ is one of several stately 17th-century houses with handsome wrought-iron balconies. At No. 6 the former Polish library,

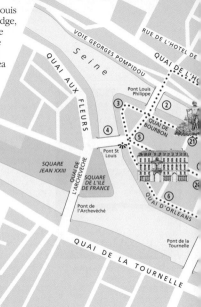

KEY

••• Walk route

☀ Good viewing point

Ⓜ Metro station

0 metres	250
0 yards	250

founded in 1838, now houses the Société Historique et Littéraire Polonaise, focusing on the life of Polish poet Adam Mickiewicz ⑦; it also contains some Chopin scores and autographs by George Sand and Victor Hugo. On the right, the Pont de la Tournelle ⑧ links the island to the Left Bank.

Seine barge passing a St-Louis quay

Quai de Béthune to Pont Marie

Continue beyond the bridge and into Quai de Béthune, where the Nobel-laureate Marie Curie lived at No. 36 ⑨, and where beautiful wrought-iron balconies gracefully decorate Nos. 34 and 30. The Hôtel Richelieu ⑩ at No. 18 is one of the island's most beautiful houses.

St-Louis church door ⑰

It features a fine garden where it has retained its original Classical blind arcades.

If you turn left down Rue Bretonvilliers there is an imposing 17th-century house ⑪, with a high-pitched roof resting on a great Classical arch spanning the street. Back on the Quai de Béthune, proceed to the Pont de Sully ⑫, a late 19th-century bridge joining the river banks. Ahead is the charming 19th-century Square Barye ⑬, a shady public garden at the east point of the island, from where there are fine river views. From here travel towards the Quai d'Anjou as far as the corner of Rue St-Louis-en-l'Ile to see the most famous house on

Gargoyle at No. 51 Rue St-Louis-en-l'Ile ⑳

small, chic, bistro-style restaurants with pleasantly old-fashioned decors. No. 31 is the original Berthillon shop ⑱, No. 60 an art gallery ⑲ with an original 19th-century window front, and at No. 51 is one of the few 18th-century *hôtels* on the island, Hôtel Chernizot ⑳, with a superb Rococo balcony which rests on leering gargoyles.

Turn right into Rue Jean du Bellay and along to Pont Louis-Philippe. Turn right again into the Quai de Bourbon, which is lined by one of the island's finest rows of *hôtels*, the most notable being Hôtel Jassaud at No. 19 ㉑. Continue to the 17th-century Pont Marie ㉒ and cross it to the Pont Marie metro on the other side.

The 17th-century Pont Marie ㉒

the island, the Hôtel Lambert ⑭ (*see pp26–7*). Continue into the Quai d'Anjou where Hôtel de Lauzun ⑮ at No. 17 has a severe Classical front and a beautiful gilded balcony and drain-pipes. Now turn left into Rue Poulletier and note the convent of the Daughters of Charity ⑯ at No. 5 bis. Further on, at the corner of Rue Poulletier and Rue St-Louis-en-l'Ile, is the island church, St-Louis ⑰, with its unusual tower, projecting clock and carved main door. Proceed along Rue St-Louis-en-l'Ile, which abounds in

Windows of the Hôtel Rolland

TIPS FOR WALKERS

Starting point: Pont Marie metro.
Length: 2.6 km (1.6 miles).
Getting there: The walk starts from the Pont Marie metro. How-ever, bus route 67 takes you to Rue du Pont Louis-Philippe and also crosses the island along Rue des Deux Ponts and Blvd Pont de Sully; routes 86 and 87 also cross the island along Blvd Pont de Sully.
Stopping-off points: There are cafés, such as Flore en l'Ile and the Berthillon shops for ice cream (see p317). Restaurants on the Rue St-Louis-en-l'Ile include Auberge de la Reine Blanche (No. 30) and Le Fin Gourmet (No. 42), as well as a pâtisserie and a cheese shop. Good resting-points are the tree-shaded quays and Square Barye to the eastern end of the island.

A 90-Minute Walk in Auteuil

Part of the fascination of the walk around this bastion of bourgeois life in westernmost Paris lies in the contrasting nature of the area's streets. The old village provincialism of Rue d,Auteuil, where the walk begins, leads on to the masterpieces of luxurious modern architecture along Rue La Fontaine and Rue du Docteur Blanche. The walk ends at the Jasmin metro station. For more on the sights of Auteuil, see page 254.

Rue d'Auteuil

The walk begins at Place d'Auteuil ①, a leafy village square with a striking Guimard-designed metro station entrance, an 18th-century funerary obelisk, and the 19th-century Neo-Romanesque Notre Dame d'Auteuil. Walk down Rue d'Auteuil, the main street of the old village, and take in the sense of a past provincial world. The Auberge du Mouton Blanc brasserie at No. 40 ② now occupies the premises of the area's oldest tavern, favoured by Molière and his actors in the 1600s. The house at Nos. 45–47 ③ was the residence of American presidents John Adams and his son John Quincy Adams. Move on to the pleasantly shaded Place Jean Lorrain ④, the site of the local market. Here there is a Wallace drinking fountain,

Wallace fountain ④

donated by the English millionaire, Richard Wallace in the 19th century. On the right, down Rue Donizetti, is the Villa Montmorency ⑤, a private enclave of luxury villas, built on the former country estate of the Comtesse de Boufflers.

Rue La Fontaine

Continue the walk along Rue La Fontaine, renowned for its many Hector Guimard buildings. Marcel Proust was born at No.96. Henri Sauvage's ensemble of artists' studios at No. 65 ⑥ is one of the most original Art Deco buildings in Paris. No. 60 is a Guimard Art Nouveau house ⑦ with elegant cast-iron balconies. Further along there is a small Neo-Gothic chapel at No. 40 ⑧ and Art Nouveau apartment buildings at Nos. 19 and 21 ⑨. No. 14 is Guimard's most spectacular building, the Castel Béranger ⑩, with a superb iron gate.

Obelisk, Place d'Auteuil ①

TIPS FOR WALKERS

Starting point: Place d'Auteuil.
Length: 3 km (2 miles).
Getting there: The nearest metro station to the starting point is Eglise d'Auteuil, and buses that take you there are Nos. 22, 52 and 62.
Stopping-off points: Along Rue d'Auteuil is the inexpensive trendy brasserie, L'Auberge du Mouton Blanc, with 1930s decor. No. 17 Rue La Fontaine is a tiny 1900 Art Nouveau café with old tiled floors and original zinc-covered bar. Place Jean Lorrain is a pleasantly shaded square where walkers can rest, and on Rue La Fontaine there is a small park in front of the Neo-Gothic chapel at No. 40. Further on at Place Rodin there is a pleasant public garden.

Doorway of No. 28 Rue d'Auteuil.

KEY

••• Walk route

🔆 Good viewing point

Ⓜ Metro station

0 metres	250
0 yards	250

Rue de l'Assomption to Rue Mallet Stevens

At the corner of Rue de l'Assomption there is a view of the massive Maison de Radio-France ⑪ built in 1963 to house French radio and television (see p200). It was one of the first modern postwar buildings in the city. Turn left into Rue de l'Assomption and walk to the fine 1920s apartment building at No. 18 ⑫. Turn left into Rue du Général Dubail and follow the street to Place Rodin, where the great sculptor's bronze

Shuttered bay window at No. 3 Square Jasmin ⑲

nude, The Age of Bronze (1877) ⑬, occupies the centre of the roundabout.

Take the Avenue Théodore Rousseau back to Rue de l'Assomption and turn left

were altered dramatically by the addition of an extra three storeys in the 1960s.

Continue on Rue du Docteur Blanche until coming to Villa du Docteur Blanche on the left. At the end of this small cul de sac is the most celebrated modern house in Auteuil, Le Corbusier's Villa Roche ⑰. Together with the adjoining Villa Jeanneret, it is now part of the Corbusier Foundation (see pp38–9). Built for an art collector in 1924 using the new technique of reinforced concrete, the house, with its geometric forms and lack of ornamentation, is a model of early Modernism.

No. 18 Rue de l'Assomption, detail ⑫

Rue du Docteur Blanche to Rue Jasmin

Walk back to Rue du Docteur Blanche and turn right into Rue Henri Heine. No. 18 bis ⑱ is a very elegant Neo-Classical 1920s apartment building offering a good contrast to one of Guimard's last creations from 1926 next door – an Art Nouveau facade much tamer than that at Castel Béranger but still employing brick, and with projecting bay windows and a terraced roof. Turn left on Rue Jasmin. In the second cul de sac on the left there is another Guimard house at No. 3 Square Jasmin ⑲. Towards the end of Rue Jasmin is the metro station.

towards Avenue Mozart. Cut through in the 1880s, this is the principal artery of the 16th arrondissement, linking north and south and lined with typical bourgeois apartment buildings of the late 19th century. Cross the avenue and continue to the Avenue des Chalets where there is a typical collection of weekend villas ⑭ recalling the quieter suburban Auteuil of the mid-19th century. Further along Rue de l'Assomption, Notre- Dame de l'Assomption ⑮ is a Neo-Renaissance 19th-century church. Turn left into Rue du Docteur Blanche. At No. 9 and down the adjoining Rue Mallet Stevens ⑯ there is a row of celebrated modern houses in the International Modern style by the architect Robert Mallet Stevens. In this expensive, once avant-garde enclave lived architects, designers, artists and their modern-minded clients. The original proportions, however,

Courtyard of No. 14 Rue La Fontaine

The Age of Bronze ⑬

A 90-Minute Walk in Montmartre

The walk begins at the base of the sandstone *butte* (hill), where old theatres and dance halls, once frequented and depicted by painters from Renoir to Picasso, have now been taken over by rock clubs. It continues steeply uphill to the original village, along streets which still retain the atmosphere caught by artists like Van Gogh, before winding downhill to end at Place Blanche. For more on the main sights of Montmartre and the Sacré-Coeur, see pages 218–27.

Montmartre seen from a distance

Place Pigalle to Rue Ravignan

The walk starts at the lively Place Pigalle ① and follows Rue Frochot to the Rue Victor Massé. At the corner is the ornate entrance to an exclusive private street bordered by turn-of-the-century chalets ②. Opposite, at No. 27 Rue Victor Massé, is an ornate mid-19th-century apartment building, and No. 25 is where Vincent Van Gogh and his brother Theo

lived in 1886 ③. The famous Chat Noir ④, Montmartre's most renowned artistic cabaret in the 1890s, flourished at No. 12. At the end of the street begins the wide tree-lined Avenue Trudaine. Take Rue Lallier on the left to Boulevard de Rochechouart. Continue east. No. 84 is the first address of the Chat Noir and No. 82 was the Grand Trianon ⑤, Paris's oldest-surviving cinema, from the early 1890s. It is now

Entrance gate to Avenue Frochot

TIPS FOR WALKERS

Starting point: Place Pigalle.
Length: 2.3 km (1.4 miles). The walk goes up some very steep streets to the top; if you do not feel like the climb, consider taking the Montmartrobus, which covers most of the walk and starts at Place Pigalle.
Getting there: The nearest metro is Pigalle; buses that take you there are Nos. 30, 54 and 67.
Stopping-off points: There are many cafés and shops in Rue Lepic and the Rue des Abbesses. Le Saint Jean (16 Pl des Abbesses) remains a locals' haunt and serves well-priced brasserie food. For shade and a rest, Place Jean-Baptiste Clément and Square S Buisson at Avenue Junot are charming public squares.

a theatre. Further along, No. 74 is the original front of Montmartre's first great cancan dance hall, the Elysée-Montmartre ⑥. Today it is a nightclub and concert hall.

Turn left on to Rue Steinkerque, which leads to Sacré-Coeur gardens, and then left into Rue d'Orsel, which leads to the leafy square, Place Charles Dullin, where the small early 19th-century Théâtre de l'Atelier ⑦ stands. Continue up the hill on Rue des Trois Frères and turn left on Rue Yvonne le Tac, which leads to Place des Abbesses ⑧. This is one of the most pleasant and liveliest squares in the area. It has conserved its entire canopied Art Nouveau metro entrance by Hector Guimard. Opposite is St-Jean l'Evangéliste ⑨, an

Rue André Antoine ⑩

unusual brick and mosaic Art Nouveau church. To the right of the church a flight of steep steps leads to the tiny Rue André Antoine, where the Pointillist painter Georges Seurat lived at No. 39 ⑩. Continue along Rue des Abbesses and turn right at Rue Ravignan.

Rue Ravignan
From here there is a sweeping view of Paris. Climb the steps straight ahead to the deeply shaded Place Emile Goudeau ⑪. To the left, at No. 13, is the original entrance to the Bateau-Lavoir, the most important cluster of artists'

St-Jean l'Evangéliste, detail ⑨

studios in Montmartre. Here Picasso lived and worked in the early 1900s. Further up, at the corner of Rue Orchampt and Rue Ravignan, there is a row of picturesque 19th-century artists' studios ⑫.

Rue Ravignan to Rue Lepic
Continue up the hill along the small public garden, Place Jean-Baptiste Clément ⑬. At the top, cross Rue Norvins. Opposite is an old Monmartois restaurant, Auberge de la Bonne Franquette ⑭, which used to be a favourite gathering place for 19th-century artists. Continue along the narrow Rue St-Rustique, from where Sacré-Coeur can be seen. At the end and to the right is Place du Tertre ⑮, the main village square. From here go north on Rue du Mont Cenis and turn left to Rue Cortot. Erik Satie, the eccentric composer, lived in No. 6 ⑯, and at No. 12 is the Musée de Montmartre ⑰. Turn right on Rue des Saules and walk past the very pretty Montmartre vineyard ⑱ to the Au Lapin Agile ⑲ at the corner

of Rue St-Vincent. Go back down Rue des Saules and right on Rue de l'Abreuvoir, an attractive street of turn-of-the-century villas and gardens. Continue into l'Allée des Brouillards, a leafy pedestrian alley. No. 6 ⑳ was Renoir's last house in Montmartre. Take the steps down into the Rue Simon Dereure and immediately turn left into a small park, which can be crossed to reach Avenue Junot. Here, No. 15 ㉑ was the house of Dadaist Tristan Tzara in the early 1920s. Continue up Avenue Junot, turn right on Rue Girardon and right again on Rue Lepic.

Au Lapin Agile nightclub ⑲

Rue Lepic to Place Blanche
At the corner is one of the area's few surviving windmills, the Moulin du Radet ㉒. Continue along Rue Lepic: to the right at the top of a slope is another windmill survivor, the Moulin de la Galette ㉓, now a restaurant. Turn left on Rue de l'Armée d'Orient, with its picturesque artists' studios ㉔, and left again into Rue Lepic. Van Gogh lived at No. 54 ㉕ in June 1886. Continue to Place Blanche, and on Boulevard de Clichy to the right is one of the area's great landmarks, the Moulin Rouge ㉖.

Artist selling his work at Place du Tertre ⑮

RUE SAINT VINCENT

⑰ ⑯

⑮

ELLE

FRERES

Y LE TAC

PLACE
C DULLIN

⑦

⑤ ⑥

RUE DANCOURT

RUE DE ROCHECHOUART

•Anvers M

BD DE ROCHECHOUART

RUE BOCHART DE SARON

KEY
••• Walk route

☆ Good viewing point

Ⓜ Metro station

0 metres 250

0 yards 250

Moulin Rouge nightclub near the Place Blanche ㉖

A 90-Minute Walk in Buttes-Chaumont

This area in the east of the city is little known to many visitors, yet it contains one of Paris' biggest and most beautiful parks and some fascinating architecture. The walk is quite strenuous with many steps, and takes in a charming micro-village, the Butte Bergeyre, which is perched high above the city and has rare houses in contrasting styles. After descending from the village, the walk continues in Buttes-Chaumont park, a vast hill complete with a lake with a huge island and folly, rocky outcrops and a wonderful variety of trees and plants.

a small garden ⑩. This is owned by the city but tended by local residents who can often be found working here.

Head back down the Rue Georges Lardennois to the Rue Michel Tagrine and take the ivy-draped steps back down to the main road ⑪. Continue straight and then turn right onto the Avenue Mathurin-Moreau, noting the fine Art Deco building ⑫ at 42 with its glittering gold-coloured tile detail. At the end of the road, cross the Rue Manin to the entrance to the park.

View across city towards Sacré-Coeur ⑧

The Butte Bergeyre

From the metro Buttes-Chaumont ① take the Rue Botzaris, turning right onto the Avenue Simon Bolivar until you reach the stairs at 54 ②, which lead up into the Butte Bergeyre. At the top of the stairs pause to absorb the enchanting atmosphere of this micro-village of five little streets. Construction started in the 1920s but there are also some modern buildings. Carry on into the Rue Barrelet de Ricou ③ to admire the ivy-covered house at 13 ④, then continue to the end of the road to take a left into the Rue Philippe Hecht ⑤ where the chalet-style house at 7 ⑥ is an interesting contrast to the creeper-covered Art Deco gem at 13 ⑦. At the end of the street take a left up to the corner of the Rue Georges Lardennois and the Rue Rémy-de-Gourmont for a wonderful view across the city ⑧ of Montmartre with its wedding-cake Sacré-Coeur on top. Be sure to admire the tiny patch of grapevines ⑨ in the residents' garden below. Close to this mini-vineyard is

Some of the lovely mature trees in the park

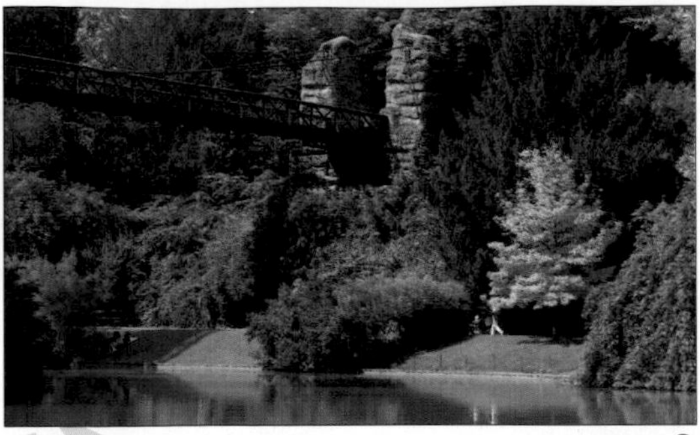

The suspension bridge, for the best view of the park ⑯

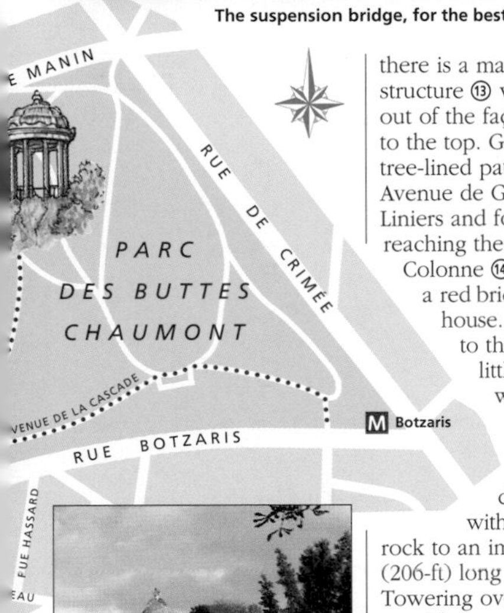

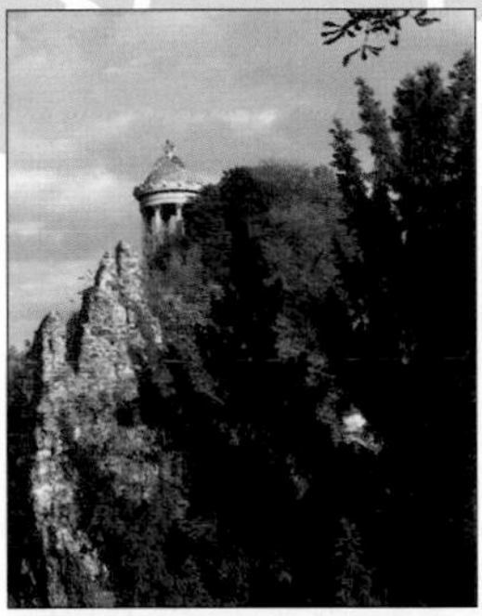

Clifftop folly, the park's summit ㉒

The Buttes-Chaumont Park

Commissioned by Napoleon III and Baron Haussman in 1864, the park covers 25 ha (61 acres) and took four years to complete. It was built by the engineer Adolphe Alphand and the architect Gabriel Davioud. Today, the hilly park is popular with joggers as it provides a fierce work-out. It is packed with mature trees including planes, poplars, ash, maples, chestnuts, sequoias and beautiful magnolias.

At the entrance to the park there is a man-made rock structure ⑬ with steps carved out of the façade; climb them to the top. Go on along a tree-lined path to join the Avenue de General Puebla Liniers and follow this until reaching the Carrefour de la Colonne ⑭ where there is a red brick mansion house. With your back to this go ahead to a little bridge lined with terracotta tiles. Take the bridge ⑮ then branch left down the steps within man-made rock to an impressive 63-m (206-ft) long bridge ⑯. Towering over the lake, this provides wonderful views of the park. Cross the bridge and follow the path down to the lake. The lake ⑰ is encircled by weeping willows and benches for breaks to admire the 50-m (164-ft) high man-made island ⑱. Follow the lake round until you hear rushing water. One of the park's most impressive features is the 32-m (105-ft) high waterfall ⑲ hidden inside a grotto. Walk right up to the waterfall looking up to see a patch of sky and some glorious man-made stalactites. Take a stepping-stone to the other side of the cave and then exit and rejoin the path round the lake, heading left. Ascend the few steps, then veer to the left and up the hill ⑳. Bear left over the terracotta-tiled bridge. Take the right branch of steps and head up to the top of the cliff. Cross a tiny bridge ㉑ and turn left up some steps to the folly ㉒, a copy of the Temple of Sibylle near Rome. This is the highest point in the park providing views across the city all the way to the Sacré-Coeur. Now take the path on the right back to the Carrefour de la Colonne. Turn left and continue along the Avenue de la Cascade all the way to the exit ㉓. From here you can take the metro from station Botzaris.

KEY

• • • Walk route

Good viewing point

M Metro station

0 metres 200

0 yards 200

TIPS FOR WALKERS

Starting point: *Metro Buttes-Chaumont.*
Length: *2.5 km (1.5 miles). Note: Very steep walk in parts, with many steps.*
Getting there: *Go to Buttes-Chaumont metro station, on line 7bis. Or take buses Nos. 26, 60 and 75 to the stop for Buttes Chaumont park.*
Stopping off points: *The park is full of lovely spots to rest, and the benches near the lake are good if bringing your own refreshments. Le Kaskade café opposite the park (at 2 Place Armand-Carrel) is a fashionable spot for snacks and drinks with a terrace that is ideal on a sunny day.*

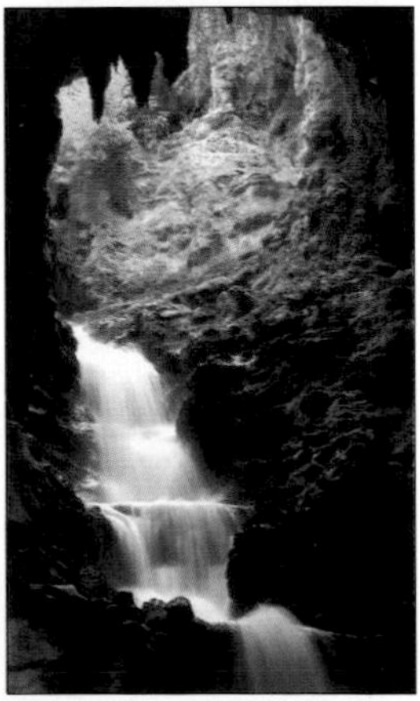

Man-made waterfall, inside the grotto ⑲

A 90-Minute Walk in Faubourg St-Antoine

In the east of the city a few steps away from the bustle of the Bastille lies the Faubourg St-Antoine district, traditionally a working-class neighbourhood full of furniture designers, carpenters and artisans and this legacy can still be seen today. From the Place de la Bastille, the walk takes in Paris' pleasure-boat port, the artisan area around the Viaduc des Arts – a former bridge with arts and crafts studios nestling in the arches – and onto the Promenade Plantée for a fascinating tree-filled stroll.

Les Grandes Marches, Place de la Bastille

The Port de Plaisance, with many leisure boats ④

Port de Plaisance

Tucked away near the traffic of Place de La Bastille ① lies an area of tranquillity that's of interest to boat-lovers and landlubbers alike. The Port de Plaisance and Paris-Arsenal garden ② was inaugurated in 1983 to provide a harbour for pleasure craft. Linking the Seine to the Canal St-Martin, the harbour was previously where commercial barges loaded and unloaded cargo. Today, it's a pretty spot full of with yachts, dingies and Parisians out for a stroll. The cobbled stones on the quayside and old-fashioned lamp posts add to the port's atmosphere. The lawns are perfect for a picnic and the children's play areas, while small, are well stocked with rocking chairs, slides and climbing apparatus ③. Continue to the end of the marina to the lock ④. Cross over the lock bridge, observing the pedestrian crossing sign, and head down on the other quayside turning back towards the Place de La Bastille. Just before the grey

steel bridge ⑤, take the stairs up and then the bridge over to the Boulevard de la Bastille ⑥. Cross the Boulevard and take a right and then left onto the Rue Jules César ⑦ all the way to the end of the street, turn left and then cross the Rue de Lyon turning right onto the Avenue Daumesnil and the start of the Viaduc des Arts ⑧.

Viaduc des Arts

In 1859 the Paris Viaduct was built to take a railway line that linked the Faubourg St-Antoine district with the suburbs. In 1994 the restored and revamped Viaduc des Arts opened with 50 shops and studios nestling in the bridge's rose stone archways.

In keeping with the tradition of the area, the ateliers are all linked to the arts, and some of the city's master crafters call the arches home. The superb window

Place de la Bastille with the impressive Opéra de Paris Bastille ①

displays at the first studio "Fleur d'Art Guillet" ⑨ give a hint of the quality of craftsmanship to come. Guillet specializes in providing silk flowers for Paris' top theatre and fashion houses. The "Ateliers du Temps Passé" ⑩ at 5 is a restorer of paintings, while Lorenove at 11 restores period glass. Number 13 is the base for hot interior designer Cherif, and the whimsical "Au Bonheur des Dames" ⑪ at 17 provides all sorts of materials for embroidery fans. For refreshment, stop at the Viaduc Café at 43 ⑫, which dishes up simple meals and hearty salads to the area's hip creatives. The SEMAEST

One of the arts and crafts shop fronts under the Viaduc des Arts ⑧

gallery space at 55/57 ⑬ hosts temporary exhibitions. Moving on past the metal furniture-maker Baguès at 73, the antique lace restorers Marie Lavande at 83, the Atelier Le Tallec 93/95, which specializes in hand-painted porcelain, it is clear that the spirit of the old artisans' area is alive and well. For those of a musical bent, Allain Cadinot repairs and sells Boehm flutes at 99, while Roger Lanne is a violin- and cello-maker at 103. With the coppersmith at 111, the terracotta tile specialist at 113 and the frame-maker at 117, you are close to the end of the viaduct, where the last atelier Jean-

Vincennes woods. For a longer walk, turn right here and go through tunnels to the city's edge and the woods. Or turn left and head back towards the Bastille. This narrow walkway offers wonderful views of the rooftops, and you can also see into some apartments. With bamboo, roses, lavender and maples, the walkway is a delight. At the end ⑰, take the steps down to the Rue de Lyon ⑱ leading to the Bastille metro, pausing only to admire the splendid Opéra de Paris Bastille ⑲ (see p98).

Promenade Plantée, a lovely rooftop walkway ⑯

Charles Brosseau-Licences ⑮ perhaps sums up the street's diversity specializing in making hats, scent and cutlery.

Promenade Plantée

Turn left, follow the signs and take the steps up to the Promenade Plantée ⑯, a walkway on top of the viaduct. It is 4.5km (2.8 miles) long and goes all the way to the

TIPS FOR WALKERS

Starting point: Bastille Metro
Length: 2.6 km (1.6 miles)
Getting there: Bastille Metro is served by lines 1, 8 and 5. Bus Nos. 29, 65, 69, 76, 86, 87, 91 and more. Get off at "Place de la Bastille" stop.
Stopping off points: The area is full of great cafés, bars and restaurants. Les Grandes Marches (Place de la Bastille) is a chic place for lunch, dinner or just coffee before you start or afterwards. Nearby Rue de Lappe is lined with some fun bars. During the walk, take a break at the Viaduc Café (43 Viaduc des Arts).

KEY

••• Walk route

••• Detour route

🌿 Good viewing point

Ⓜ Metro station

A 90-Minute Walk in Butte-aux-Cailles

This walk takes place in and around the Butte-aux-Cailles, a lovely "village" set on a hill that is all quiet streets, leafy squares and buzzy local bistrots. The area made history in 1783 when the first manned balloon flight touched down here. In the 1800s it was home to many workers from the small factories in the area and was one of the first areas to fight during the Paris Commune. However, it only really developed after 1910 and the architecture reflects the social ideals of the day – that individual houses and green spaces aid health.

Quiet, cobbled streets typify the Butte-aux-Cailles ⑪

de la Butte-aux-Cailles ⑪. Head up the street to the Place de la Commune de Paris ⑫, which today looks unremarkable yet was the site of a major battle in May 1871. Continue up the Rue de la Butte-aux-Cailles. Les Abeilles at 21 ⑬ is a curious store dedicated to bee-keeping and a delight for honey lovers. Pancakes in the old-fashioned crêperie Des Crêpes et des Cailles at 13 may satisfy if you are just peckish, but further down at 20 is the area's best-known restaurant Les Temps de Cerises ⑭. Fittingly, as it's only a few minutes' walk from the Place de la

Buttes-aux-Cailles

Take the "Auguste Blanqui" exit out of the Place d'Italie metro station ①, noting the Guimard decoration. Follow the bustling Rue Bobillot until you reach the Rue Paulin-Méry ② and take your first steps into the peace of the Butte-aux-Cailles. The contrast is surprising as you walk the quiet, narrow, cobbled streets with their old-fashioned street lamps. Note the lovely lilac painted shutters on 5 ③ and the trees in the small garden in front of the house opposite. Continue straight ahead, cross over the Rue du Moulin-des-Près and turn left into the Rue Gérard past the red brick terraces and plant-decked villas ④. Keep on into the Rue Samson and then turn right onto the Rue Jonas and left onto the Rue des Cinq Diamants ⑤. The charming theatre at 10 performs well-reviewed shows, while at 43 ⑥ Hansel et Gretel is a quaint old sweet shop with a few tables and chairs. Those

RUE DE LA BUTTE AUX CAILLES

13ᵉ Arrᵗ

Road sign in the Butte aux Cailles area

interested in history may appreciate the Association des Amis de la Commune de Paris at 46 ⑦, which sells T-shirts, books and pamphlets on that bloody episode in Parisian history. Turn right into the Passage Barrault, a cobbled alleyway with ivy-covered walls and a countryside feel ⑧. At the end of the passage, turn left onto the Rue Barrault and continue up the street until the right turn into the Rue Daviel. At 10 Rue Daviel the row of cottages known as "Little Alsace" ⑨ because of their chalet style are, in fact, one of the first public housing schemes in Paris. Opposite, walk down the Villa Daviel ⑩, a tiny street of terraces with small front gardens overflowing with greenery. Retrace your steps back up to the Rue Barrault, turn left and then right onto the artery of the area, the Rue

Theatre, Rue des Cinq-Diamants ⑤

Le Temps des Cerises, full of bohemian atmosphere ⑭

Commune, it's run as a co-operative and is also the unofficial neighbourhood HQ. At the end of the road is the Place Paul Verlain ⑮. On the other side of the square is the red brick Art Nouveau swimming pool ⑯. Built in 1924, it houses one indoor pool and two lovely outdoor swimming areas. Take the steps in front of the building to find the modern fountain on the Place ⑰.

Crêpes from Des Crêpes et des Cailles

This is supplied by a local well 580 m (1,902 ft) deep, dating from 1863, and was refurbished in 2000. You may see locals queuing to fill plastic bottles here. Exit the square, take a right and then another right past the chic restaurant Chez Nathalie with its flowery terrace, which is always packed in summer, into the Rue Vandrezanne, continuing down this pedestrianized street into the passage Vandrezanne, a steep cobbled alleyway with antiquated lampposts ⑱. Cross over the Rue Moulinet and take the Rue Moulin des Pres until you come to the Rue Tolbiac. Cross this busy road then take a right stepping back into another time at the Square des Peupliers ⑲. Built in 1926, each house is different, reflecting the ideals of the time. All have pretty little gardens, most have lovely Art Nouveau porches and the ornate gilded lamp posts are

very special. Leave the Square des Peupliers and take a right back onto the Rue du Moulin-des-Pres. Head down the street, noting the interesting rough stone houses ⑳, straight past an unusual purple Art Nouveau-style house at 104 ㉑. Take a right onto the Rue Damesme, turn right into the Rue du Docteur Leray and then right again onto Rue Dieulafoy ㉒. Here are several unique, colourful cottages. At the end of the row, take a right onto the Rue Henri Pape, a left onto the Rue Damesme, walk up to the Rue Tolbiac and back out into modern, busy, Paris. Turn right and walk up to the metro Tolbiac ㉓.

Square des Peupliers, with its unique houses ⑲

KEY

••• Walk route

Ⓜ Metro station

0 metres   200

0 yards   200

TRAVELLERS' NEEDS

WHERE TO STAY

Paris has more guest rooms than any other city in Europe. Its hotels vary from magnificent luxurious places like the Ritz (the French call them *palaces*) and exclusive establishments like L'Hôtel, where Oscar Wilde died beyond his means, to much simpler hotels in charming older parts of Paris. It is worth noting that *hôtel* does not always mean "hotel". It can also mean a town hall *(hôtel de ville)*, hospital *(Hôtel-Dieu)* or a mansion.

We have inspected hotels in all price brackets and have selected a broad range, all of which are good value for money. The listings on pp284–91 are organized by area, as in the sightseeing section of the guide, and according to hotel price. Other types of accommodation such as bed and breakfast rooms, self-catering apartments and hostels *(see pp278–9)* are also well worth considering, especially for visitors who are on a tight budget.

WHERE TO LOOK

Hotels in Paris tend to cluster by type in particular areas, with the river separating the business and leisure districts. Luxury hotels tend to be on the north side and *hôtels de charme* on the south side.

In the fashionable districts near the Champs-Elysées and the Opéra Garnier lie many of the grandest hotels in Paris, including the Royal Monceau, the Bristol, the Four Seasons George V, the Meurice and the Plaza Athénée. Several less well known but elegant hotels can be found in the residential and ambassadorial quarter near the Palais de Chaillot.

To the east, still on the Right Bank, in the regenerated Marais, a number of the old mansions and palaces have been converted into exceptionally attractive small hotels at reasonable prices. The nearby areas around Les Halles and the Rue St-Denis, however, attract prostitutes and drug addicts. Just south of the Marais across the Seine, the Ile St-Louis and Ile de la Cité have several charming hotels.

The Left Bank covers some of the most popular tourist areas and has an excellent range of small hotels of great character. The atmosphere subtly changes from the much upgraded Latin Quarter and the chic and arty areas north and south of Boulevard St-Germain, to the rather tatty Boulevard itself and the staid institutional area towards Les Invalides and the Eiffel Tower. The hotels tend to reflect this.

Further from the centre, Montparnasse has several large business hotels in high-rise blocks, and the Porte de Versailles area to the south is usually packed with trade fair participants. The station areas around Gare du Nord and Gare de Lyon offer a number

Hôtel de Crillon *(see pp282, 285)*

of basic hotels (choose carefully). Montmartre has one or two pleasant hotels if you don't mind the hilly location, but beware of hotels allegedly in Montmartre but actually in the red-light, sex-show district of Pigalle. If you are looking for a hotel in person, the best times for inspecting are late morning or mid-afternoon. If the hotels are fully booked, try again after 6pm, when unclaimed provisional bookings become free. Don't rely on the impression of a hotel given by reception: ask to see the room offered, and if it isn't acceptable, ask to be shown another, if available. (For airport hotels *see p379.)*

HOTEL PRICES

Hotel prices aren't always cheaper in low season (mid-November to March or July and August) because fashion shows and other major events

The Hôtel du Louvre *(see p285)*, between the Louvre and the Palais Royal

◁ River view of Notre-Dame

throughout the year can pack rooms, raising prices. However, in the older hotels differences in the size and position of rooms can have a marked effect on cost. Small rooms tend to be cheapest.

Twin rooms are slightly more expensive than doubles; single occupancy rates as high or nearly as high as for two people sharing (tariffs are nearly always quoted per room, not per person). Single rooms are rare and many are extremely poky or poorly equipped. Rooms without a bath tend to be about 20% cheaper than those with. You might find a half-board arrangement unnecessary with such a wide choice of good restaurants around.

It's always worth asking for a discount: you may get a corporate rate, for instance. In some hotels special deals are offered for students, families or senior citizens.

HIDDEN EXTRAS

By law, tax and service must be included in the price quoted or displayed at the reception desk or in the rooms. Tips are unnecessary other than for exceptional service – if the concierge books you a show, for instance, or if the maid does some washing for you. However, before you make a reservation you should always establish whether breakfast is included in the price or not. Beware of extras such as drinks or snacks from

The Hôtel Meurice *(see p285)* in the Tuileries Quarter

a mini-bar, which will probably be pricy, as will laundry services, garage parking or telephone calls from your room – especially telephone calls made through the switchboard.

Exchange rates in hotels invariably tend to be lower than in a bank, so make sure you have enough cash to pay your bill unless you are paying by credit card or using traveller's cheques.

HOTEL GRADINGS

French hotels are classified by the tourist authorities into five broad categories: one to four stars, plus a four-star deluxe rating. Some very simple places are unclassified. Star ratings indicate something about the level of facilities you can expect (for example, any hotel with more than three stars should have a lift). But the French rating system is no reliable guide to friendliness, cleanliness or tastefulness of the decor.

FACILITIES

Few Parisian hotels below a four-star rating have a restaurant, although there is nearly always a breakfast room. Quite a few hotel restaurants close in August. Many of the older hotels also lack a public lounge area. More modern or expensive hotels have correspondingly better facilities and generally some kind of bar. Inexpensive hotels may not have a lift – significant when you are dragging suitcases upstairs. Usually only the more expensive hotels have parking facilities. For exceptions to this rule, see the listings on pages 284–91. If you are driving you may prefer to stay in one of the peripheral motel-style chain hotels *(see pp279–80)*.

All but the very simplest of city hotels will have a telephone in the bedroom; many also have television. Business facilities (fax and internet) are now available in the grander hotels. Double beds *(grands lits)* are common, but you must specify whether or not you want one.

Four Seasons George V *(see p290)*

Statue in the Hôtel Relais Christine *(see pp283, 287)*

The Plaza Athénée *(see p291)* in Champs-Elysées

WHAT TO EXPECT

Many hotel beds still stick to the time-honoured French bolster, a sausage-shaped headrest that can be uncomfortable if you are unused to it. If you prefer pillows, ask for *oreillers*. If you want to make sure you get a toilet, specify a *WC,* and if you want a bath, ask for a *bain*. Otherwise, a *cabinet de toilette* is just a basin and bidet, and *eau courante* means simply a basin with hot and cold running water. A duplex room is a suite on two floors.

The traditional French hotel breakfast of fresh coffee, croissants, jam and orange juice is in Paris gradually changing into an elaborate buffet breakfast with cold meats and cheeses. Some of the luxury hotels are now such popular venues for breakfast that it is worth reserving a place in the breakfast area if you don't want to eat in your room. A pleasant alternative is to head for the nearest

café, where French workers are enjoying breakfast over a newspaper.

Check-out time is usually noon and if you stay longer you will pay for an extra day.

SPECIAL BREAKS

Because Paris is such a popular destination with leisure as well as business travellers, weekend packages are often available via travel agents or the Internet. Providing there are no major events taking place, you can reduce costs by visiting in low season and negotiating a discount, or by seeking out an all-inclusive package.

TRAVELLING WITH CHILDREN

Families with young children will often find they can share a room at no or very little extra cost, and some operators offer packages with this in mind. Few hotels refuse to accept children, though facilities specifically for children are not universal. Some hotels will arrange baby-sitting.

DISABLED TRAVELLERS

Our information about wheelchair access to hotels was gathered by questionnaire and therefore relies on the hotels' own assessment of their suitability. Not many are well geared for use by disabled visitors. The **Association des Paralysés de France** and the **Groupement pour l'Insertion des Personnes Handicapées Physiques (GIHP)** have pertinent information *(For addresses see p367.)*

SELF-CATERING

A scheme called **Résidence Internationale de Paris** provides apartments in specially-run self-catering blocks. Some hotel-type facilities are available, but you pay extra for them. Prices vary from around 90€ a night for a small studio to over 300€ a night for an apartment for several people. Either contact

The quiet Hôtel des Grands Hommes *(see p287)*

Paris-Séjour-Réservation or get in touch with each *résidence* directly. The **Office du Tourisme et des Congrès de Paris** also provides a full list of *résidences*.

Self-catering accommodation is an increasingly popular alternative for staying in Paris. The better known agencies include **Allo Logement Temporaire, At Home In Paris, ASLOM, Paris Appartements Services** and **France Appartements. Good Morning Paris** and **France-Lodge** also arrange self-catering apartments, as well as being B&B agencies (see Directory p280). All provide furnished apartments for stays from one week to six months, sometimes in the apartment of a Parisian who is abroad. Prices are comparable to the Résidence Internationale de Paris, sometimes slightly cheaper for the larger apartments.

STAYING IN PRIVATE HOMES

Bed and breakfast, that typically-British phenomenon, is known as *chambre d'hôte* or *café-couette* ("coffee and a quilt"). B&B accommodation is available at moderate prices, between 35€ and 75€ for a double room per night. **Alcôve & Agapes** offers rooms in some enviable districts of Paris, all within walking distance of a metro station. It is worth enquiring about suites and rooms with a private lounge, kitchen or terrace. All homes are routinely inspected.

France-Lodge is a good-value agency specialising in long-stay room rentals and apartments. A registration fee of 15€ a year is payable but rentals are generally cheaper than with other agencies.

Good Morning Paris provides guest rooms and tourist information. A two-night minimum stay is required when booking *(for details see* Directory p280).

CHAIN HOTELS

A mushroom crop of motel-style establishments on the outskirts of Paris now take large numbers of both business and leisure visitors.

The garden of the Relais Christine *(see p287)*

The very cheapest chains such as Formule 1, Première Class and Fast Hotel, really have nothing except price to recommend them. Further up the ladder are **Campanile, Ibis** and **Primevère**. These places are practical, relatively inexpensive and useful if you have a car, but lack any real

The Hôtel Prince de Galles Sheraton *(see p291)*

Parisian atmosphere or character. Many are in charmless locations on busy roads and may suffer from traffic noise. The newer motels of these chains are better equipped and more smartly decorated than the older ones. Several chains (**Sofitel**, **Novotel** and **Mercure**) are especially geared to business travellers, providing better facilities at higher prices; indeed some of the more central ones are positively luxurious. Reductions can make these hotels good value at

weekends. Many of the hotels have restaurants attached. Most of the chains produce their own brochures, often with useful maps detailing the motel's precise location *(see* Directory p280).

HOSTELS AND DORMITORY ACCOMMODATION

There are several hostel networks in Paris. **Maisons Internationales de la Jeunesse et des Etudiants (MIJE)** provides dormitory accommodation for the 18–30s in three splendid mansions in the Marais. There is no advance booking (except for groups) – call at the central offices on the day.

The **Bureau Voyage Jeunesse (BVJ)** has two 'hotels' with double rooms and dormitory accommodation (23–28€ and 25€ respectively), with breakfast and nearly private bathrooms. Bookings cannot be made more than a fortnight in advance.

La Maison de l'UCRIF (Union des Centres de Rencontres Internationales de France) has nine centres around Paris with individual, shared and dormitory rooms. No age limit is imposed. Cultural and sporting activities are available at some centres.

Fédération Unie des Auberges de Jeunesse (FUAJ) is a member of the International Youth Hostels Federation. There is no age limit at their two Paris hostels. *(For addresses see* Directory p280.)

The Hôtel Atala terrace *(see p290)*

DIRECTORY

OFFICE DU TOURISME

25 Rue des Pyramides 75001.
Tel 08 92 68 30 30.
See also p367.
www.parisinfo.com

AGENCIES

Ely 12 12
182 Rue du Faubourg St-Honoré 75008.
Tel 01 43 59 12 12.
www.ely1212.com

Paris-Séjour-Réservation
90 Ave des Champs-Elysées 75008.
Tel 01 53 89 10 50.
www.psryourhomein paris.com

SELF-CATERING

Allo Logement Temporaire
64 Rue du Temple 75003.
Tel 01 42 72 00 06.
www.allo-logement-temporaire.asso.fr

ASLOM
75–77 Ave Parmentier 75011.
Tel 01 43 49 67 79.
www.aslom.com

At Home in Paris
16 Rue Médéric 75017.
Tel 01 42 12 40 40.
Fax 01 42 12 40 48.

France Appartements
97 Ave des Champs-Elysées 75008.
Tel 01 56 89 31 00.
www.rentapart.com

Paris Appartements Services
20 Rue Bachaumont 75002.
Tel 01 40 28 01 28.
www.paris-apts.com

RESIDENCES DE TOURISME

Les Citadines
Tel 0825 333 332.
www.citadines.com

Pierre et Vacances
Tel 0825 040 608.
www.pierre-vacances.fr

Résidence Internationale de Paris
44 Rue Louis Lumière 75020. *Tel* 01 40 31 45 45. www.residence-inter-paris.com

Résidence du Roy
8 Rue François-1er 75008.
Tel 01 42 89 59 59.
www.hroy.com

BED & BREAKFAST

Alcôve & Agapes
8bis Rue Coysevox 75018.
Tel 01 44 85 06 05.
Fax 01 44 85 06 14.
www.bed-and-breakfast-in-paris.com

France-Lodge
2 Rue Meissonier 75017.
Tel 01 56 33 85 85.
Fax 01 56 33 85 89.
www.apartments-in-paris.com

Good Morning Paris
43 Rue Lacépède, 75005.
Tel 01 47 07 28 29.
Fax 01 47 07 44 45.
www.goodmorningparis.fr

CHAIN HOTELS

Campanile
Tel 0825 003 003
(central reservations).
www.campanile.fr

Hilton
18 Ave de Suffren 75015.
Tel 01 44 38 56 00.
www.hilton.com

Holiday Inn République
10 Pl de la République 75011.
Tel 0800 910 850.
www.holiday-inn.com

Holiday Inn St-Germain-des-Prés
Tel 0800 911 617 or 01 49 54 87 00.
www.holiday-inn.com

Ibis
Tel 0892 686 686
(central reservations).
www.accor.com

Mercure Paris Austerlitz
6 Blvd Vincent Auriol 75013.
Tel 01 45 82 48 00.
www.mercure.com

Mercure Paris Bercy
77 Rue de Bercy 75012.
Tel 01 53 46 50 50.
www.mercure.com

Mercure Paris Montparnasse
20 Rue de la Gaîté 75014.
Tel 01 43 35 28 28.
www.mercure.com

Mercure Paris Porte de Versailles
69 Blvd Victor 75015.
Tel 01 44 19 03 03.
www.mercure.com

Mercure Paris Tour-Eiffel
64 Blvd de Grenelle 75015.
Tel 01 45 78 90 00.
www.mercure.com

Méridien Montparnasse
19 Rue du Commandant René Mouchotte 75014.
Tel 01 44 36 44 36.
www.lemeridien.fr

Novotel Paris Bercy
85 Rue de Bercy 75012.
Tel 01 43 42 30 00.
www.novotel.com

Novotel Paris Les Halles
8 Pl Marguerite de Navarre 75001.
Tel 01 42 21 31 31.
www.novotel.com

Novotel Tour Eiffel
61 Quai de Grenelle 75015.
Tel 01 40 58 20 00.
www.novotel.com

Primevère
Tel 08 00 12 12 12
(central reservations).
www.choicehotels.com

Royal Garden St-Honoré
218 Rue du Faubourg St-Honoré 75008.
Tel 01 49 53 03 03.
www.gtshparis.com

Hotel Sofitel Scribe
1 Rue Scribe 75009.
Tel 01 44 71 24 24.
www.sofitel.com

Sofitel Paris Forum Rive Gauche
17 Blvd St-Jacques 75014.
Tel 01 40 78 79 80.
www.sofitel.com

Sofitel Paris La Défense Centre
34 Cours Michelet, 92060.
Tel 01 47 76 44 43.
www.sofitel.com

Sofitel Le Faubourg
15 Rue Boissy d'Anglas 75008.
Tel 01 44 94 14 14.
www.sofitel.com

Warwick Champs-Elysées
5 Rue de Berri 75008.
Tel 01 45 63 14 11.

HOSTELS

BVJ
20 Rue Jean-Jacques Rousseau 75001.
Tel 01 53 00 90 90.
Fax 01 53 00 90 91.

FUAJ – Centre National
27 Rue Pajol 75018.
Tel 01 44 89 87 27.
Fax 01 44 89 87 10.
www.fuaj.org

La Maison de l'UCRIF
27 Rue de Turbigo 75002.
Tel 01 40 26 57 64.
Fax 01 40 26 58 20.
www.ethic-etapes.fr

MIJE
Head Office: 11 Rue du Fauconnier 75004.
Tel 01 42 74 23 45.
Fax 01 42 74 08 93.
www.mije.com

CAMPING

Camping du Bois de Boulogne/Ile de France
Allée du Bord de l'Eau 75016.
Tel 01 45 24 30 00.
Fax 01 42 24 42 95.
www.campingparis.fr

Camping International de Jablines
Jablines-Annet 77450.
Tel 01 60 26 09 37.
Fax 01 60 26 43 33.

FFCC
78 Rue de Rivoli 75004.
Tel 01 42 72 84 08.
Fax 01 42 72 70 21.
www.ffcc.fr

CAMPING

The only campsite in Paris itself is the **Camping du Bois de Boulogne/Ile de France** (around 12€–35€ per night). This well-equipped site next to the Seine is open all year round but is usually fully booked during the summer. Pitches for tents, caravans as well as rental of mobile homes are available. There are many other campsites in the surrounding region, some close to an RER line. The **Camping International de Jablines** (around 20€–25€ per night) is conveniently located just 9km (5.5 miles) from Disneyland Paris and a 25-minute RER train ride from central Paris. Details of other sites can be obtained from the Paris tourist office or from a booklet produced by the **Fédération Française de Camping-Caravaning (FFCC)** *(see Directory p280)*.

HOW TO BOOK

The busiest tourist seasons are May, June, September and October, but special events such as fashion shows, trade fairs or major exhibitions can fill most rooms in Paris throughout the year. Disney-land Resort Paris has further increased the pressure to find accommodation, as many visitors choose to stay in the capital and commute to the park on the RER. July and August are quieter, as many Parisians are on their annual holiday.

If you have decided on a hotel, it is vital to book ahead by at least a month as Paris is a popular destination. The hotels in the listings are among the best in their category and will fill particularly fast. Make a reservation six weeks in advance between May and October. The best way is to book directly with the hotel. If you make your initial inquiry by telephone, ring during the day if possible – you are more likely to find staff authorized to take bookings. You should send confirmation of your reservation (websites or email addresses are provided where

Tourist information desk, Charles de Gaulle airport

available); credit card details are often required to guarantee your booking.

If you prefer to use an agency, **Ely 12 12** and **Paris-Séjour-Réservation** can book hotels and other kinds of accommodation, sometimes even a barge along the Seine.

If you aren't too fussy about where you stay, or if all the hotels are reportedly full, you can book via the **Office du Tourisme et des Congrès de Paris**, which offers an on-the-spot booking service for a reasonable fee.

DEPOSITS

If you make a reservation by telephone you will be asked for either your credit card number (from which any cancellation fee may be deducted) or a deposit (*arrhes*). These *arrhes* can be as much as the price of a night's stay, but usually cost only about 15% of this. Pay your deposit by credit card or by sending an international money order. You can sometimes send an ordinary cheque for an amount equivalent to the deposit as evidence of your intention to keep the booking. Usually the hotel will simply keep your foreign cheque as security until you arrive, then return it to you and give you one total bill when you leave. But do check with the hotel before sending an ordinary cheque. It's also quite acceptable in France to specify your choice of room when you book.

Try to arrive at your hotel by 6pm on the day you have booked, or at least telephone

to say you will be late, otherwise you may well lose the room. A hotel that breaks a confirmed, prepaid booking is breaking a contract, and the client is entitled to compensation of at least twice any deposit paid. Alternatively, the hotel must offer you equivalent or better accommodation elsewhere. If you have any problems, consult the Office du Tourisme.

TOURIST INFORMATION DESKS

You can book hotels at all airport information desks but only in person and for the same day. The Gare de Lyon and the Tour Eiffel (seasonal) information desks provide a similar booking arrangement for all forms of accom-modation. Many Paris information desks also keep a complete list of city hotels and some book entertain-ment, excursions etc *(see Practical Information p367)*.

Paris's Best: Hotels

Paris is famous for its hotels. It excels in all categories from the glittering opulent *palaces* (the top luxury hotels) to the *hôtels de charme*, full of character and romantic appeal, to the simpler good-value family hotels in quiet back streets. As a centre of culture and fashion, the city has long been a mecca for the rich and famous, great and good from all walks of life. Not surprisingly, therefore, it can boast some of the most magnificent hotels in the world and has more than a thousand hotels in the inner city alone. Whatever the price level, however, the hotels in our listings *(see pp284–91)* all show that inimitable style and taste that Parisians bring to everything they do. These are a selection of the very best.

Bristol
In the chic heart of Paris, this epitomizes luxury. (See p290.)

Champs-Elysées

Chaillot Quarter

R I V E R   S E I

Invalides and Eiffel Tower Quarter

Balzac
Small but stylish, this hotel exudes period charm. The restaurant, Pierre Gagnaire, is highly rated. (See p290.)

Hôtel de Crillon
One of the great palace *hotels, this was built for Louis XV.* (See p285.)

Plaza Athénée
In the heart of haute couture *Paris, this is the favourite haunt of the fashion world. Magnificent decor and a superb restaurant are the main attractions.* (See p291.)

Duc de St-Simon
Bedrooms overlook a leafy garden in this comfortable and peaceful hôtel de charme *situated in an 18th-century mansion south of the Seine.* (See p289.)

Le Grand Hôtel Intercontinental
Built for Napoleon III in 1862, this historic hotel has been patronized by the rich and famous from Mata Hari to Winston Churchill. (See p291.)

L'Hôtel
Best known as the last home of Oscar Wilde, this stylish hotel boasts rooms both impressive and slightly bizarre. One room was furnished and occupied by the music hall star Mistinguett. (See p287.)

Relais Christine
An oasis of calm in the hub of the city, this charming hotel offers traditional comforts such as a welcoming open fire in the drawing room. (See p287.)

Opéra Quarter

uileries Quarter

Beaubourg and Les Halles

St-Germain-des-Prés

The Marais

Ile de la Cité

Ile St-Louis

Luxembourg Quarter

Latin Quarter

Jardin des Plantes Quarter

Hôtel du Jeu de Paume
This cleverly converted hotel was once a court for playing real tennis – jeu de paume. (See p284.)

| 0 kilometres | 1 |
| 0 miles | 0.5 |

Lutétia
This was decorated by top designer Sonia Rykiel. (See p287.)

Hotel de l'Abbaye
A pleasant garden and courtyard and attractive rooms are features of this small secluded hotel near the Jardins du Luxembourg. (See p286.)

Choosing a Hotel

The choice of hotels listed in the following pages have all been individually inspected and assessed specially for this guide. The list covers all the areas and price categories with additional information to help you choose a hotel that best meets your needs. Hotels within the same category are listed alphabetically.

PRICE CATEGORIES
For a standard double room per night including breakfast and necessary charges:

€ under 90 euros
€€ 91–140 euros
€€€ 141–180 euros
€€€€ 181–260 euros
€€€€€ over 260 euros

ILE DE LA CITÉ AND ILE ST-LOUIS

Hôtel des Deux-Iles   €€€
59 Rue St-Louis-en-l'Ile, 75004 **Tel** *01 43 26 13 35* **Fax** *01 43 29 60 25* **Rooms** *17*   **Map** *13 C4*

Its a privilege to be able to stay on the Ile St-Louis, and this converted 17th-century mansion offers an affordable way to do so. Here the atmosphere is peaceful, the small bedrooms are attractive and the lounge has a real fire. **www.deuxiles-paris-hotel.com**

Hôtel du Jeu de Paume   €€€€
54 Rue St-Louis-en-l'Ile, 75004 **Tel** *01 43 26 14 18* **Fax** *01 40 46 02 76* **Rooms** *30*   **Map** *13 C4*

Standing on the site of a former real tennis court, the hotel has been skilfully converted into a warm, elegant place to stay. Features include a glass-walled lift, wooden beams, old terracotta paving, a sauna and several charming duplex rooms. **www.hoteljeudepaume.com**

THE MARAIS

Hôtel de la Bretonnerie   €€
22 Rue Ste-Croix de la Bretonnerie, 75004 **Tel** *01 48 87 77 63* **Fax** *01 42 77 26 78* **Rooms** *29*   **Map** *13 C3*

Carved stone walls and an arched dining room in the basement are some of the charming features of Hôtel de la Bretonnerie, housed in a 17th-century mansion. One of the most comfortable hotels in the area, it has spacious bedrooms with wooden beams and antique furniture. Service is warm and friendly. **www.bretonnerie.com**

Hôtel du Septieme Art   €€
20 Rue St-Paul, 75004 **Tel** *01 44 54 85 00* **Fax** *01 42 77 69 10* **Rooms** *23*   **Map** *14 D4*

A film buff's dream, this charming little spot is stuffed full with mementoes of the movies. The rooms are clean and all have a cinematic touch, from advertising posters to mini-statuettes of Marilyn Monroe. Staff are very friendly too. An ideal place to retire after a long day of sightseeing. **www.hotel7art.com**

Hôtel du Bourg Tibourg   €€€
19 Rue du Bourg Tibourg, 75004 **Tel** *01 42 78 47 39* **Fax** *01 40 29 07 00* **Rooms** *30*   **Map** *13C*

This stylish spot was decorated by top interior designer Jacques Garcia and is extremely popular with fashionable visitors to Paris. Rooms are opulent and all bathrooms are fully clad in black marble. The beautiful interior courtyard is a pleasant surprise. **www.hotelbourgtibourg.com**

St-Merry   €€€
78 Rue de la Verrerie, 75004 **Tel** *01 42 78 14 15* **Fax** *01 40 29 06 82* **Rooms** *12*   **Map** *13 B3*

A historic hotel which, was the presbytery of the adjoining church in the 17th century and later became a bordello, is today a simply lovely place to stay. Furnished in Gothic style, note the flying buttresses crossing room 9. **www.hotelmarais.com**

St-Paul-le-Marais   €€€
8 Rue de Sévigné, 75004 **Tel** *01 48 04 97 27* **Fax** *01 48 87 37 04* **Rooms** *28*   **Map** *14 D3*

Close to the historic Place des Vosges, this hotel has wooden beams and old stone, although the furnishings are simple and modern. Ask for bedrooms facing the courtyard to avoid the noise of traffic coming from the Rue de Sévigné. **www.hotelsaintpaullemarais.com**

Pavillon de la Reine   €€€€€
28 Pl des Vosges, 75003 **Tel** *01 40 29 19 19* **Fax** *01 40 29 19 20* **Rooms** *56*   **Map** *14 D3*

Set back from the marvellous Place des Vosges, the Pavillon de la Reine is the best hotel in the Marais. Incredibly romantic, the courtyard is a haven of peace and the bedrooms are sumptuous and furnished with excellent reproduction antiques. **www.pavillon-de-la-reine.com**

Key to Symbols *see back cover flap*

BEAUBOURG AND LES HALLES

Hôtel Roubaix ⬚ €
6 Rue Grenetta, 75003 **Tel** *01 42 72 89 91* **Fax** *01 42 72 58 79* **Rooms** *53* **Map** *13B*

Hôtel Roubaix is pleasantly old-fashioned and inexpensive in an area with few good places to stay. The owners are exceptionally friendly and the rooms are clean, if a little shabby. The hotel is popular with return guests, so be sure to book a room in advance. **www.hotel-de-roubaix.com**

TUILERIES QUARTER

Hôtel St-Honoré €
85 Rue St-Honoré, 75001 **Tel** *01 42 36 20 38* **Fax** *01 42 21 44 08* **Rooms** *29* **Map** *12 F2*

Close to Concorde, Tuileries, Louvre and Palais-Royal, the St-Honoré has an attractive green façade. The rooms, recently renovated and equipped with all modern amenities, are extremely well kept. Very good value for money considering the excellent location. A few rooms have been designed for families. **www.parishotel.com**

Brighton ⬚▤ €€€
218 Rue de Rivoli, 75001 **Tel** *01 47 03 61 61* **Fax** *01 42 60 41 78* **Rooms** *65* **Map** *12 D1*

A real insiders' location, the Brighton provides a much-sought after Rivoli address without the sky-high prices. The bedrooms have beautiful, high ceilings and large windows that look out either on to the Jardin des Tuileries or on to the courtyard. **www.esprit-de-france.com**

Clarion St-James et Albany ⬚▣⑪▦▥▤ €€€€€
202 Rue de Rivoli, 75001 **Tel** *01 44 58 43 21* **Fax** *01 44 58 43 11* **Rooms** *200* **Map** *12 E1*

This quiet and tidy hotel is currently undergoing a much-needed renovation to do away with its aura of faded grandeur. It is perfectly situated in the heart of Paris, opposite the Tuileries gardens, and boasts a charming spa and swimming pool area. **www.clarionsaintjames.com**

Hôtel Costes ⬚▣⑪▦▥▤ €€€€€
239 Rue St Honoré, 75001 **Tel** *01 42 44 50 00* **Fax** *01 42 44 50 01* **Rooms** *82* **Map** *12 D1*

One of the most fashionable places to stay in Paris, the Costes is a favourite with models and film stars. A sumptuous affair, it is designed to resemble a Second Empire palace. The balcony rooms are the most in demand. In summer, eat in the Italianate courtyard. **www.hotel costes.com**

Hôtel de Crillon ⬚▣⑪▥▤ €€€€€
10 Pl de la Concorde, 75008 **Tel** *01 44 71 15 00* **Fax** *01 44 71 15 02* **Rooms** *147* **Map** *11 C1*

With its magnificent location on the glittering Place de la Concorde, the Crillon offers unsurpassed elegance. The hotel has a fine Royal Suite and terrace, a sublime dining room and a fashionable bar designed by Sonia Rykiel. **www.crillon.com**

Hôtel du Louvre ⬚▣⑪▨▥▤ €€€€€
Pl André Malraux, 75001 **Tel** *01 44 58 38 38* **Fax** *01 44 58 38 01* **Rooms** *177* **Map** *12 E1*

The first luxury hotel in France was built in 1855 by order of Napoleon III. The lavish rooms have spectacular views: the Pissarro Suite is where the artist painted his view of Place du Théâtre Français, while if you book room 551 you can admire the opera house from your bath! **www.hotel dulouvre.com**

Meurice ⬚▣⑪▥▤ €€€€€
228 Rue de Rivoli, 75001 **Tel** *01 44 58 10 10* **Fax** *01 44 58 10 15* **Rooms** *160* **Map** *12 D1*

The Meurice is a perfect example of successful restoration, with excellent replicas of the original plasterwork and furnishings. The staff here are unstintingly helpful and the hotel offers personalised shopping and art buying tours. There is also a top spa. **www.meuricehotel.com**

Regina ⬚⑪▤ €€€€€
2 Pl des Pyramides, 75001 **Tel** *01 42 60 31 10* **Fax** *01 40 15 95 16* **Rooms** *120* **Map** *12 E1*

Surprisingly, the Regina is not known to many tourists, even though it is popular with the media. The wood detail in the lounge is stunning Art Nouveau and many films have been shot here. Some of the Rooms have superb views. **www.regina-hotel.com**

Ritz ⬚▣⑪▦▨▥▤ €€€€€
15 Pl Vendôme, 75001 **Tel** *01 43 16 30 30* **Fax** *01 43 16 45 38* **Rooms** *162* **Map** *6 D5*

A legendary address, the Ritz still lives up to its reputation, combining elegance and decadence. The Louis XVI furniture and chandeliers are all originals, and the floral arrangements are works of art. The Hemingway Bar is home to the glitterati. **www.ritzparis.com**

The Westin Paris
3 Rue de Castiglione, 75001 **Tel** *01 44 77 11 11* **Fax** *01 44 77 14 60* **Rooms** *438*   **Map** *12 D1*

This elegant late 19th-century hotel is situated between the Jardin des Tuileries and the Place Vendôme. It was designed by Charles Garnier, architect of the Paris Opéra. Bedrooms are quiet – the best overlook one of the courtyards. **www.westin.com**

ST-GERMAIN-DES-PRÈS

Grand Hôtel des Balcons
3 Rue Casimir Delavigne, 75006 **Tel** *01 46 34 78 50* **Fax** *01 46 34 06 27* **Rooms** *50*   **Map** *12 F5*

Embellished with Art Nouveau features, this hotel has a beautiful hall with stained-glass windows and striking 19th-century-style lamps and wood panelling. Most guestrooms, quiet and well-decorated, enjoy a balcony. High-speed Internet access with Wi-Fi available. **www.balcons.com**

Hôtel du Globe
15 Rue des Quatre-Vents, 75006 **Tel** *01 43 26 35 50* **Fax** *01 46 33 62 69* **Rooms** *14*   **Map** *12 F4*

A 17th-century building right by the Jardin du Luxembourg, with excellent accommodation. Antique furniture and colourful fabrics liven up the guestrooms. Breakfast is brought to your room. Extremely popular, so book in advance. **www.globe-paris-hotel.com**

Hôtel de Lille
40 Rue de Lille, 75007 **Tel** *01 42 61 29 09* **Fax** *01 42 61 53 97* **Rooms** *20*   **Map** *12 D2*

The jewel-like Hôtel de Lille is situated near the Orsay and Louvre museums in the heart of Faubourg St-Germain. The modern, standard bedrooms are small and the bar is minute. Breakfast is served in the charming arched basement. **www.hotel-paris-lille.com**

Hôtel du Quai Voltaire
19 Quai Voltaire, 75007 **Tel** *01 42 61 50 91* **Fax** *01 42 61 62 26* **Rooms** *33*   **Map** *12 D2*

Overlooking the river, this hotel was once the favourite of Blondin, Baudelaire and Pissarro, and has featured in several films. Bedrooms on the quay are better avoided, as they suffer from traffic noise. Higher floors are quieter, though, and the views are superb. **www.quaivoltaire.fr**

Hôtel des Marronniers
21 Rue Jacob, 75006 **Tel** *01 43 25 30 60* **Fax** *01 40 46 83 56* **Rooms** *37*   **Map** *12 E3*

Situated between a courtyard and a garden, this hotel provides perfect peace. The decor is homely, with lots of textured fabrics, and bedrooms on the fourth floor, garden side, provide very special views over the Parisian rooftops and the St-Germain-des-Prés church steeple. **www.paris-hotel-marronniers.com**

Hôtel des Sts-Pères
65 Rue des Sts-Pères, 75006 **Tel** *01 45 44 50 00* **Fax** *01 45 44 90 83* **Rooms** *39*   **Map** *12 E3*

The hotel occupies one of the old aristocratic mansions of St-Germain-des-Prés. The lounge bar is very popular with authors from the publishing houses nearby. The bedrooms are quiet and roomy – the best has an outstanding ceiling fresco. **www.espritfrance.com**

Lenox
9 Rue de l'Université, 75007 **Tel** *01 42 96 10 95* **Fax** *01 42 61 52 83* **Rooms** *34*   **Map** *12 D3*

The charm of the Lenox lies in its simplicity and literary history – T.S. Elliot, Ezra Pound and James Joyce all lived here. The staff are extremely friendly and the cocktail bar is lovely. The rooms are impeccably decorated. The hotel enjoys a great location in the heart of St-Germain-des-Prés. **www.lenoxsaintgermain.com**

Hôtel de Fleurie
32/34 Rue Grégoire de Tours, 75006 **Tel** *01 53 73 70 00* **Fax** *01 53 73 70 20* **Rooms** *29*   **Map** *12 F4*

The statue-filled façade is enough to make one want to stay in this welcoming, family-run hotel. Inside, the woodwork and white stone create the same light feel, as do the bedrooms, all of which are beautifully decorated, with well-equipped bathrooms. **www.hotel-de-fleurie.tm.fr**

Hôtel de l'Abbaye St-Germain
10 Rue Cassette, 75006 **Tel** *01 45 44 38 11* **Fax** *01 45 48 07 86* **Rooms** *44*   **Map** *12 D5*

A 17th-century abbey, just steps from the Jardin du Luxembourg, this charming hotel has been a preferred hideout for artists and writers. Its finely furnished guestrooms and apartments have been tastefully done up and provided with modern facilities. **www.hotel-abbaye.com**

Hôtel d'Angleterre
44 Rue Jacob, 75006 **Tel** *01 42 60 34 72* **Fax** *01 42 60 16 93* **Rooms** *27*   **Map** *12 E3*

Once the British Embassy, the Hôtel d'Angleterre has retained many of the original features, including the fine old staircase (listed), the exquisite garden and the salon mantelpiece. Bedrooms are individually decorated, many have exposed beams and wonderful four-poster beds. **www.hotel-dangleterre.com**

Key to Price Guide *see p284* **Key to Symbols** *see back cover flap*

L'Hôtel

€€€€€

13 Rue des Beaux-Arts, 75006 **Tel** *01 44 41 99 00* **Fax** *01 43 25 64 81* **Rooms** *20* **Map** *12 E3*

A riot of exuberance and opulence, this Jacques Garcia designed hotel is gloriously decadent. Each room is different, the hotel's most famous one is the Oscar Wilde suite, where the author died and which boasts period furnishings. There's also a beautiful spa. **www.l-hotel.com**

Lutétia

€€€€€

45 Blvd Raspail, 75006 **Tel** *01 49 54 46 46* **Fax** *01 49 54 46 00* **Rooms** *230* **Map** *12 D4*

The Lutétia is a mainstay of glamour on the south side of the river. The building is partly Art Nouveau and partly Art Deco, and has been restored throughout. Publishers and chic shoppers are regular customers in the restaurant. Convenient location. **www.lutetia-paris.com**

Montalembert

€€€€€

3 Rue de Montalembert, 75007 **Tel** *01 45 49 68 68* **Fax** *01 45 49 69 49* **Rooms** *56* **Map** *12 D3*

Situated in the heart of the publishing district, this fashionable hotel combines modernity and timeless elegance. The bedrooms boast fine wood and designer fabrics with excellent quality linen sheets, towels and bathrobes. The eighth-floor suites have good views. Wi-Fi facilities are provided. **www.montalembert.com**

Relais Christine

€€€€€

3 Rue Christine, 75006 **Tel** *01 40 51 60 80* **Fax** *01 40 51 60 81* **Rooms** *51* **Map** *12 F4*

Always full, the Relais Christine is the epitome of the *hôtel de charme*. It is part of the cloister of a 16th-century abbey and is a romantic haven of peace. The bedrooms are bright and spacious, especially the duplex rooms. Wi-Fi is available, as are spa and sauna facilities. **www.relais-christine.com**

LATIN QUARTER

Esmeralda

€

4 Rue St-Julien-le-Pauvre, 75005 **Tel** *01 43 54 19 20* **Fax** *01 40 51 00 68* **Rooms** *19* **Map** *13 A4*

The much-loved bohemian Esmeralda lies in the heart of the Latin Quarter. With old stone walls and beamed ceilings, its charm has seduced the likes of Terence Stamp and Serge Gainsbourg. The best rooms overlook Notre-Dame. No breakfast available.

Hôtel des Grandes Ecoles

€€

75 Rue Cardinal Lemoine, 75005 **Tel** *01 43 26 79 23* **Fax** *01 43 25 28 15* **Rooms** *51* **Map** *13 B5*

This hotel is a cluster of three small houses around a beautiful garden, where you can breakfast in good weather. The rooms are all comfortable and furnished with traditional 18th-century-style floral wallpaper, some open onto the courtyard. Internet access available. **www.hotel-grandes-ecoles.com**

Hôtel des Grands Degrès de Notre Dame

€€

10 Rue des Grands Degrès, 75005 **Tel** *01 55 42 88 88* **Fax** *01 40 46 95 34* **Rooms** *10* **Map** *13 B4*

An exceptionally friendly place to stay. The staff are genuinely welcoming and the wood-panelling and oak beams around the building make it even more special. Lovely, very clean bedrooms with Internet access available. The Bar Restaurant and Tea Room serves great food at a low price. **www.lesdegreshotel.com**

Hôtel des Grands Hommes

€€€

17 Pl du Panthéon, 75005 **Tel** *01 46 34 19 60* **Fax** *01 43 26 67 32* **Rooms** *31* **Map** *17 A1*

Teachers at the Sorbonne frequent this quiet family hotel close to the Jardin du Luxembourg. It boasts a great view of the Panthéon from the attic rooms on the upper floor. The bedrooms are comfortable. Wi-Fi services available. **www.hoteldesgrandshommes.com**

Hôtel de Notre-Dame

€€€

19 Rue Maître Albert, 75006 **Tel** *01 43 26 79 00* **Fax** *01 46 33 50 11* **Rooms** *34* **Map** *13 B5*

The picturesque Hôtel de Notre-Dame overlooks Notre-Dame cathedral and the Seine on one side and the Panthéon on the other. The furnishings are functional, but some rooms have beams or an old stone wall. The main appeal here is the location. The hotel has its own sauna and Wi-Fi access. **www.hotel-paris-notredame.com**

Hôtel du Panthéon

€€€

19 Pl du Panthéon, 75005 **Tel** *01 43 54 32 95* **Fax** *01 43 26 64 65* **Rooms** *36* **Map** *17 A1*

This hotel is managed by the same family as the Hôtel des Grands Hommes: the welcome is equally warm and the decor similarly Classical. Extra romance and luxury can be found in room 33 with its divine four-poster bed. Wi-Fi available in the reception room only. **www.hoteldupantheon.com**

Hôtel Residence Hotel IV

€€€€

50 Rue des Bernadins, 75005 **Tel** *01 44 41 31 81* **Fax** *01 46 33 93 22* **Rooms** *13* **Map** *13 B5*

Overlooking a pretty park square and with window boxes full of geraniums in season, this hotel is a real jewel. Bedrooms are bright andairy, some of the larger rooms have attached kitchens and there is also a flat for four people available. Wi-Fi services provided. Very quiet for the area. **www.residencehenri4.com**

LUXEMBOURG QUARTER

Hôtel Récamier

🖩 €€

3 bis Pl St-Sulpice, 75006 **Tel** *01 43 26 04 89* **Fax** *01 46 33 27 73* **Rooms** *30* **Map** *12 E4*

Hotel Récamier, which is situated on the quiet Place St-Sulpice, is a family hotel with an air of old-fashioned Parisian charm. The hotel was constructed in 1905 and remains a favourite both with writers and Left Bank tourists. Bedrooms overlooking the square have lovely views.

Aviatic

🖩 P 🗐 €€€

105 Rue de Vaugirard, 75006 **Tel** *01 53 63 25 50* **Fax** *01 53 63 25 55* **Rooms** *43* **Map** *12 E5*

True to its Parisian past and long-standing family hotel tradition, the much-loved Aviatic combines bohemian style with modern comforts. The rooms are individually decorated with charming pieces found at local flea markets and warm, bright textiles. Parking is available for 23 euros per day. **www.aviatic.fr**

MONTPARNASSE

Hôtel Apollon Montparnasse

🖩 P 🗐 €€

91 Rue Ouest, 75014 **Tel** *01 43 95 62 00* **Fax** *01 43 95 62 10* **Rooms** *33* **Map** *15 C3*

Close to the Parc des Expositions of the Porte de Versailles, the Apollon Montparnasse is decorated with Grecian statues, fine furnishings and lots of peach. You can get simple, well-equipped guestrooms. Parking is available for 12 euros per day. The hotel also provides Wi-Fi facilities. **www.apollon-montparnasse.com**

Hôtel Delambre

🖩 🗐 €€

35 Rue Delambre, 75014 **Tel** *01 43 20 66 31* **Fax** *01 45 38 91 76* **Rooms** *30* **Map** *16 D2*

Located a few steps away from Montparnasse cemetery, and close to the Jardin de Luxembourg and Latin Quarter, this hotel stylishly mixes modern and classical styles. Guestrooms are simply furnished with all mod cons. **www.hoteldelambre.com**

Ferrandi

🖩 P 🗐 €€€

92 Rue du Cherche-Midi, 75006 **Tel** *01 42 22 97 40* **Fax** *01 45 44 89 97* **Rooms** *42* **Map** *15 C1*

The Rue du Cherche-Midi is well-known to lovers of antiques. The Hôtel Ferrandi is a quiet hotel with a fireplace in the lounge and comfortable bedrooms filled with dark wood and decorated in warm tones. Four-poster beds in some rooms. **www.123france.com**

Ste-Beuve

🖩 🗐 €€€

9 Rue Ste Beuve, 75006 **Tel** *01 45 48 20 07* **Fax** *01 45 48 67 52* **Rooms** *22* **Map** *16 D1*

The Ste-Beuve is a small, carefully restored hotel for aesthetes and habitués of the Rive Gauche galleries. There is a fireplace in the hall, the rooms are pleasantly decorated in pastel shades and there are several classic, contemporary paintings. **www.paris-hotel-charme.com**

Villa des Artistes

🖩 🗐 €€€

9 Rue de la Grande Chaumière, 75006 **Tel** *01 43 26 60 86* **Fax** *01 43 54 73 70* **Rooms** *59* **Map** *16 D2*

The Villa des Artistes aims to recreate Montparnasse's artistic heyday when Modigliani, Beckett and Fitzgerald were all visitors here. The bedrooms are clean, but the main draw is the large patio garden and fountain, where you can breakfast in peace. **www.villa-artistes.com**

Le Saint-Grégoire

🖩 🗐 €€€€

43 Rue de l'Abbé Grégoire, 75006 **Tel** *01 45 48 23 23* **Fax** *01 45 48 33 95* **Rooms** *20* **Map** *11 C5*

Le Saint-Grégoire is a fashionable townhouse hotel with immaculately-decorated bedrooms and 19th-century furnishings. At the centre of the drawing room is a charming fireplace with a real fire. Book a room with a delightful private terrace. Parking costs 13 euros a day. **www.lesaintgregoire.com**

INVALIDES AND EIFFEL TOWER QUARTER

Grand Hôtel Levêque

🖩 🗐 €€

29 Rue Cler, 75007 **Tel** *01 47 05 49 15* **Fax** *01 45 50 49 36* **Rooms** *50* **Map** *10 F3*

On a street with a quaint fruit-and-vegetable market, the Levêque lies between the Eiffel Tower and the Invalides. The great location isn't the only attraction – guestrooms are well-kept and the hotel also provides Internet facilities. **www.hotel-leveque.com**

Key to Price Guide *see p284* **Key to Symbols** *see back cover flap*

Hôtel de Varenne

€€

44 Rue de Bourgogne, 75007 **Tel** *01 45 51 45 55* **Fax** *01 45 51 86 63* **Rooms** *24* **Map** *11 B2*

Beyond its severe façade, this hotel conceals a narrow courtyard garden where guests breakfast in the summer. The bedrooms, recently refurbished in elegant Louis XVI or Empire style, are impeccable. The hotel is popular with French government officials. **www.hoteldevarenne.com**

Eiffel Park Hôtel

€€€

17 bis Rue Amélie, 75007 **Tel** *01 45 55 10 01* **Fax** *01 47 05 28 68* **Rooms** *36* **Map** *10 F3*

In the heart of the Champs de Mars, the charming Eiffel Park Hôtel has been entirely renovated. It offers individually designed guestrooms with intricate wallpaper in some and exotic furniture in others. On the top floor is a breakfast terrace. Wi-Fi facilities provided. **www.eiffelpark.com**

Hôtel de Suède St-Germain

€€€

31 Rue Vaneau, 75007 **Tel** *01 47 05 00 08* **Fax** *01 47 05 69 27* **Rooms** *40* **Map** *11 B4*

Located near the Orsay and Rodin museums, the Hôtel de Suède St-Germain offers elegant rooms, decorated in late 18th-century styles in pale colours and the owners' welcome is exceptionally warm. Deluxe rooms offer a view over the park. A lovely little garden to breakfast in completes the picture. **www.hoteldesuede.com**

Hôtel Bourgogne et Montana

€€€€

3 Rue de Bourgogne, 75007 **Tel** *01 45 51 20 22* **Fax** *01 45 56 11 98* **Rooms** *32* **Map** *11 B2*

Situated in front of the Assemblée Nationale, the hotel has an air of sobriety. Features include a mahogany bar, an old lift and a circular hall with pink marble columns. The bedrooms were recently refurbished in an aristocratic style. Extremely stylish. **www.paris-hotel-montana.com**

Duc de St-Simon

€€€€€

14 Rue de St-Simon, 75007 **Tel** *01 44 39 20 20* **Fax** *01 45 48 68 25* **Rooms** *34* **Map** *11 C3*

The Hôtel Duc de St-Simon is justifiably one of the most sought-after hotels on the south side of the Seine. A charming 18th-century mansion furnished with antiques, it lives up to its aristocratic pretensions. **www.hotelducdesaintsimon.com**

CHAILLOT QUARTER

Hameau de Passy

€€

48 Rue de Passy, 75016 **Tel** *01 42 88 47 55* **Fax** *01 42 30 83 72* **Rooms** *32* **Map** *9 B3*

In the heart of the residential quarter of Passy, a stone's throw from the Eiffel Tower and the Trocadero, Hameau de Passy lies in a private lane, which is an oasis of greenery. Rooms overlook the garden. Breakfast can be served in your room upon request. **www.hameaudepassy.com**

Hôtel Keppler

€€

12 Rue Keppler, 75016 **Tel** *01 47 20 65 05* **Fax** *01 47 23 02 23* **Rooms** *49* **Map** *4 E5*

Within walking distance from the Champs-Elysées, this is an excellent budget hotel located in a quiet street of the elegant 16th arrondissement. Its decor is unremarkable, but the rooms are clean and spacious, with high ceilings. **www.hotel-keppler-paris.federal-hotel.com**

Hôtel du Bois

€€€

11 Rue du Dôme, 75016 **Tel** *01 45 00 31 96* **Fax** *01 45 00 90 05* **Rooms** *41* **Map** *4 D5*

Two minutes from the Arc de Triomphe and the Champs Elysées, Hôtel du Bois is ideal for haute-couture boutique lovers. Behind a typically Parisian façade, is an interior exuding British charm – Georgian furniture in the lounge, thick patterned carpeting and fine prints in the bedrooms. **www.hoteldubois.com**

Concorde La Fayette

€€€€€

3 Pl du Général Koenig, 75017 **Tel** *01 40 68 50 68* **Fax** *01 40 68 50 43* **Rooms** *950* **Map** *3 C2*

The formulaic Concorde La Fayette with its fascinating egg-shaped tower is thoroughly high-tech. It has numerous facilities, including a fitness club, a bar on the 33rd floor, restaurants, a shopping gallery, and identical bedrooms with some absolutely splendid views. **www.concorde-lafayette.com**

Costes K

€€€€

81 Ave Kléber, 75016 **Tel** *01 44 05 75 75* **Fax** *01 44 05 74 74* **Rooms** *83* **Map** *4 D5*

This hotel, not to be confused with the more expensive Hôtel Costes, is situated steps from the Eiffel Tower. A piece of modern art by Spanish architect Ricardo Bofill, who used sycamore, stucco, marble and stainless steel in the construction. Cool Asian interiors for the guestrooms. **www.hotelcostesk.com**

Raphaël

€€€€€

17 Ave Kléber, 75016 **Tel** *01 53 64 32 00* **Fax** *01 53 64 32 01* **Rooms** *85* **Map** *4 D4*

The epitome of discreet elegance, film stars come here to be sheltered from the paparazzi. The decor is opulent and the roof terrace bar is the loveliest in Paris and extremely popular with the jet set. There are amazing views of the city and its principal monuments illuminated at night. **www.raphael-hotel.com**

Square €€€€€

3 Rue de Boulainvilliers, 75016 ***Tel*** *01 44 14 91 90* ***Fax*** *01 44 14 91 99* ***Rooms*** *22* ***Map*** *9 A4*

An exceptional hotel, the curvy granite façade hides 22 rooms and suites furnished with exotic fabrics and woods. The hotel boasts a fashionable restaurant and night club and, most unusually, a small but well-stocked modern art gallery. **www.hotelsquare.com**

St-James €€€€€

43 Ave Bugeaud, 75016 ***Tel*** *01 44 05 81 81* ***Fax*** *01 44 05 81 82* ***Rooms*** *48* ***Map*** *3 B5*

The St-James occupies a mansion with a small park near the Avenue Foch and the Bois de Boulogne. Reminiscent of a gentleman's club, guests here become "temporary members" and a token fee is included in the room price. Aristocratic atmosphere. **www.saint-james-paris.com**

Villa Maillot €€€€€

143 Ave de Malakoff, 75016 ***Tel*** *01 53 64 52 52* ***Fax*** *01 45 00 60 61* ***Rooms*** *42* ***Map*** *3 C4*

Conveniently situated for Porte Maillot and La Défense, the hotel was once an embassy and remains suitably refined with delightful Art-Deco style furnishings. The rooms have large beds, concealed kitchenettes and marble bathrooms. A new spa area offers massages. **www.lavillamaillot.fr**

CHAMPS-ELYSÉES

Résidence Lord Byron €€€

5 Rue Chateaubriand, 75008 ***Tel*** *01 43 59 89 98* ***Fax*** *01 42 89 46 04* ***Rooms*** *31* ***Map*** *4 E4*

Close to the Etoile, the Résidence Lord Byron is a discreet, small hotel with a courtyard garden for breakfast. Its bright bedrooms are quiet but small; if you want more space, ask for a salon bedroom or a ground-floor room. **www.escapade-paris.com**

Atala €€€€

10 Rue Chateaubriand, 75008 ***Tel*** *01 45 62 01 62* ***Fax*** *01 42 25 66 38* ***Rooms*** *48* ***Map*** *4 E4*

Situated in a quiet street near the Champs-Elysées, the Atala's rooms overlook a tranquil garden with tall trees. The bedrooms are functional rather than charming, so book a room on the eighth floor with spectacular views of the Eiffel Tower. **www.hotelatala.com**

Balzac €€€€€

6 Rue Balzac, 75008 ***Tel*** *01 44 35 18 00* ***Fax*** *01 44 35 18 05* ***Rooms*** *70* ***Map*** *4 F4*

This calm and luxurious hotel in a typically Parisian Belle Epoque building has just been refurbished. Its trendy address is nothing compared to its bar; designed by Philippe Starck in violets and electric blues, it is a favourite destination for fashionable night owls. **www.hotelbalzac.com**

Bristol €€€€€

112 Rue du Faubourg-St-Honoré, 75008 ***Tel*** *01 53 43 43 00* ***Fax*** *01 53 43 43 01* ***Rooms*** *180* ***Map*** *5 A4*

One of Paris's finest hotels, the Bristol's large rooms are sumptuously decorated with antiques and magnificent marble bathrooms. The period dining room, with its Flemish tapestries and glittering crystal chandeliers, has been winning rave reviews. Wonderful swimming pool. **www.lebristolparis.com**

Claridge-Bellman €€€€€

37 Rue François 1er, 75008 ***Tel*** *01 47 23 54 42* ***Fax*** *01 47 23 08 84* ***Rooms*** *42* ***Map*** *4 F5*

The Claridge-Bellman is a miniature version of the old Claridge Hotel and is managed by its former directors. The hotel has a truly traditional feel. It is quiet, sober and efficiently run, and is furnished throughout with tapestries and antiques. **www.hotel-claridge-bellman.com**

Four Seasons George V €€€€€

31 Ave George V, 75008 ***Tel*** *01 49 52 70 00* ***Fax*** *01 49 52 71 10* ***Rooms*** *246* ***Map*** *4 E5*

This legendary hotel, dotted with salons, old furniture and art, lost a little of its charm when it was renovated. But it gained a stunning restaurant, Le Cinq, which boasts the world's top sommelier and an award-winning chef. Great spa. **www.fourseasons.com/paris**

Hôtel de la Trémoille €€€€€

14 Rue de la Trémoille, 75008 ***Tel*** *01 56 52 14 00* ***Fax*** *01 40 70 01 08* ***Rooms*** *93* ***Map*** *10 F1*

The Hôtel de la Trémoille is an impressive, yet relaxed, establishment. Rooms are decorated with comfortable antiques and the bathrooms are extremely luxurious. A fashionable restaurant, Senso, by Terence Conran is now a hit with Paris's beautiful people. **www.hotel-tremoille.com**

Hôtel Franklin Roosevelt €€€€€

18 Rue Clément Marot, 75008 ***Tel*** *01 53 57 49 50* ***Fax*** *01 53 57 49 59* ***Rooms*** *48* ***Map*** *4 F5*

Chic interior throughout, complete with period furniture, old paintings and a fireplace in the lounge. The bedrooms are generally very large. Cosy atmosphere at the Lord's bar, though the cafés of the Champs-Elysées are also nearby. **www.hroosevelt.com**

Key to Price Guide *see p284* **Key to Symbols** *see back cover flap*

Hôtel Vernet

26 Rue Vernet, 75008 **Tel** *01 44 31 98 00* **Fax** *01 44 31 85 69* **Rooms** *51* **Map** *4 E4*

Gustave Eiffel, architect of the Eiffel Tower, created the dazzling glass roof of the dining room here. The hotel lobby is impressive with Persian rugs, precious woods, antiques and parquet flooring. The large, quiet bedrooms are pleasantly furnished and guests have free use of the Royal Monceau's fitness club. **www.hotelvernet.com**

Plaza Athénée

25 Ave Montaigne, 75008 **Tel** *01 53 67 66 65* **Fax** *01 53 67 66 66* **Rooms** *188* **Map** *10 F1*

The legendary Plaza Athénée is popular with honeymooners, aristocracy and haute couture shoppers. The restaurant by Alain Ducasse is wonderfully romantic, while Le Bar du Plaza is now the hottest address in Paris for cocktails. The last word in luxury. **www.plaza-athenee-paris.com**

Prince de Galles

33 Ave George V, 75008 **Tel** *01 53 23 77 77* **Fax** *01 53 23 78 78* **Rooms** *168* **Map** *4 E5*

Less prestigious than its neighbour the Four Seasons George V, the Prince de Galles most definitely has its own identity and charm. The marble and chandelier filled lobby gives way to subdued elegance in the bedrooms. Wi-Fi facilities available. **www.luxurycollection.com/princedegalles**

Royal Monceau

37 Ave Hoche, 75008 **Tel** *01 42 99 88 00* **Fax** *01 42 99 89 90* **Rooms** *180* **Map** *4 F3*

The Royal Monceau champions subtle luxury. The breakfast room is unusual – a striking glass gazebo with curved walls. Its health club is one of the most fashionable in Paris. The bedrooms are elegant – book a room overlooking the courtyard. **www.royalmonceau.com**

San Régis

12 Rue Jean Goujon, 75008 **Tel** *01 44 95 16 16* **Fax** *01 45 61 05 48* **Rooms** *44* **Map** *11 A1*

Since it opened in 1923 the San Régis has been popular with the jet set, who enjoy its quiet but central location. This particularly welcoming, intimate luxury hotel is full of excellent antiques, overstuffed sofas and a distinctly opulent air. **www.hotel-sanregis.fr**

OPÉRA QUARTER

Ambassador

16 Blvd Haussmann, 75009 **Tel** *01 44 83 40 40* **Fax** *01 42 46 19 84* **Rooms** *300* **Map** *6 E4*

One of the best of Paris's Art Deco hotels, it has been restored to its former glory and has deep carpeting and antique furniture. The ground floor has pink marble columns, Baccarat crystal chandeliers and Aubusson tapestries. The restaurant, 16 Haussmann, is extremely popular with Parisian gourmets. **www.hotelambassador-paris.com**

Edouard VII Hotel

39 Ave de l'Opéra, 75002 **Tel** *01 42 61 56 90* **Fax** *01 42 61 47 73* **Rooms** *69* **Map** *6 E5*

The only hotel on the impressive Avenue de l'Opéra, the Edouard VII is centrally located between the Louvre and the Opéra Garnier, which makes it perfect for sightseeing. Ask for a room at the front for a breathtaking view over the Opéra House, and book a table at the excellent hotel restaurant, Angl'Opera. **www. edouard7hotel.com**

Le Grand Hôtel Intercontinental

2 Rue Scribe, 75009 **Tel** *01 40 07 32 32* **Fax** *01 40 07 32 02* **Rooms** *478* **Map** *6 D5*

Directly next to the Opéra Garnier, the hotel is a sumptuous example of good taste. The bedrooms all have pictures with a musical theme reflecting the hotel's location. The renowned restaurant, the Café de La Paix, is an opulent affair in Opéra Quarter. **www.paris.intercontinental.com**

MONTMARTRE

Regyn's Montmartre

18 Pl des Abbesses, 75018 **Tel** *01 42 54 45 21* **Fax** *01 42 23 76 69* **Rooms** *22* **Map** *6 E1*

Near Sacré-Coeur, this is an impeccably kept hotel. Top-floor guestrooms have views of the Eiffel Tower. Round the corner from here is Tabac des Deux Moulins on 15 Rue le Pic where Amelie worked in the film Amelie. **www.regynsmontmartre.com**

Terrass Hôtel

12-14 Rue Joseph-de-Maistre, 75018 **Tel** *01 46 06 72 85* **Fax** *01 42 52 29 11* **Rooms** *100* **Map** *6 E1*

Montmartre's most luxurious hotel, the rooms here are comfortably, if unremarkably, furnished. A few bedrooms retain the original Art-Deco woodwork. The big draw is the rooftop restaurant, where in the summer fashionable Parisians take in a world-class view. **www.terrass-hotel.com**

RESTAURANTS, CAFES AND BARS

The French national passion for good cuisine makes eating out one of the greatest pleasures of a visit to Paris. Everywhere in the city you see people eating – in restaurants, bistros, tea salons, cafés and wine bars.

Most restaurants serve French food but there is a range of Chinese, Vietnamese and North African eateries in many areas as well as Italian, Greek, Lebanese and Indian places. The restaurants in the list-

ings *(see pp300–315)* have been selected from the best that Paris can offer across all price ranges. The listings are organized by area, as in the sightseeing section of the guide, and by price. Most places will serve lunch from noon until around 2pm, and the menu often includes fixed-price meals. Parisians usually start to fill restaurants for dinner around 8.30pm and most places serve from around 7.30pm until 11pm. *(See also Light Meals and Snacks pp316–19.)*

WHAT TO EAT

A tremendous range of food is available in Paris, from the rich meat dishes and perfect pâtisserie for which France is most famous to simpler French regional cuisines *(see pp296–7)*. The latter are available in brasseries and bistros – the type usually depends on the birthplace of the chef. At any time of day simple, tasty meals can be had in cafés, wine and beer bars, and brasseries, bistros and cake shops – or pâtisseries – abound. Some cafés, like the Bar du Marché *(see p318)* in St-Germain-des-Prés, are known for their excellent cold food and don't offer hot meals at lunchtime.

The best ethnic food comes from France's former colonies: Vietnam and North Africa. North African places are known as *couscous* restaurants and serve filling, somewhat spicy, inexpensive food that

varies in quality. Vietnamese restaurants are also good value and provide a light alternative to rich French food. Paris also has some good Japanese restaurants, notably around Rue Monsieur le Prince (6th arrondissement); Rue Ste-Anne (2nd) and Rue de Belleville (19th) have others.

WHERE TO FIND GOOD RESTAURANTS AND CAFES

You can eat well in almost any part of Paris. Wherever you are, as a rule of thumb you will find that the most outstanding restaurants and cafés are those that cater predominantly to a French clientele.

The Left Bank probably has the greatest concentration of restaurants, especially in tourist areas like St-Germain-des-Prés and the Latin Quarter. The quality of food varies, but there are some commendable bistros, outdoor cafés and

The prim Mariage Frères shop and tea room *(see p318)*

Beauvilliers restaurant *(see p312)*

wine bars – see pages 316–19 for a selection of the best places to go in Paris for light meals and snacks. The Latin Quarter also has a high concentration of Greek restaurants centred chiefly around Rue de la Huchette.

In the Marais and Bastille areas, small bistros, tea salons and cafés are plentiful, some new and fashionable. There are also many good, traditional long-established bistros and brasseries.

In the Champs-Elysées and Madeleine area it is difficult to find inexpensive good food. Sadly, this area tends to be overrun with fast food joints and pricy but not very good cafés. There are, however, some very good expensive restaurants here.

Montparnasse still has some great cafés from the 1920s, including Le Sélect and La Rotonde, on the Boulevard du Montparnasse *(see p319)*. Sensitive renovation has recaptured much of their old splendour. There are excellent bistros in this area as well.

There are many noteworthy restaurants, bistros and cafés in the Louvre-Rivoli area, competing with tourist-oriented, overpriced cafés. Just to the east, Les Halles is choc-a-bloc with fast food joints and mediocre restaurants but there are few places of note.

Good Japanese food can be found near the Opéra together with some fine brasseries, but otherwise the area around the Opéra and Grands Boulevards is not the best for restaurants. Near the Bourse are a number of reputable restaurants and bistros frequented by stockbrokers.

Montmartre has a predictable number of tourist restaurants, but it also has a few very pleasant small bistros. One expensive and luxurious exception is Beauvilliers (see p312), a Montmartre landmark tucked on the far side of the Butte.

Quiet neighbourhoods in the evening, the Invalides, Eiffel Tower and Palais de Chaillot tend to have less noisy, more serious restaurants than areas with lively nightlife. Prices can be high.

Two Chinatowns, one in the area south of the Place d'Italie, the other in the traditionally working-class, hill-top area of Belleville, have concentrations of ethnic food but few French restaurants of note. There are a number of Vietnamese eating places as well as large, inexpensive Chinese ones, and Belleville is also packed with small North African restaurants.

Le Grand Véfour in the Palais Royal *(see p304)*

TYPES OF RESTAURANTS AND CAFES

One of the most enjoyable aspects of eating in Paris is the diversity of places to eat. Bistros are small, often moderately priced restaurants with a limited selection of dishes. Those from the Belle Epoque era are particularly beautiful, with zinc bars, mirrors and attractive tiles. The food is generally, but not always, regional and traditional. Many chefs from the smartest restaurants have now also opened bistros and these can be very good value.

Brasseries are generally large bustling eateries, many with an Alsatian character serving carafes of Alsatian wine and platters of sauerkraut and sausage. They have immense menus, and most serve food throughout the day and are open late. Outside you may well see impressive pavement displays of shellfish, with apron-clad oyster shuckers working late into the night.

Cafés open early in the morning, and apart from the large tourist cafés, the majority close by around 10pm. They serve drinks and food all day long from a short menu of salads, sandwiches and eggs. At lunch most also offer a small choice of hot daily

A typical bistro menu

specials. Café prices vary from area to area, in direct proportion to the number of tourists. Smarter cafés, like Café de Flore and Les Deux Magots serve food until late at night. Those cafés specializing in beer almost always include onion tarts, French fries and hearty bowls of steamed mussels on the menu. Brunch is now served in many places at weekends, from around 17€.

Wine bars are informal. They usually have a moderately priced, simple lunch menu and serve wine by the glass. They serve snacks at any time of day – such as marvellous open sandwiches *(tartines)* made with sourdough Poilâne bread topped with cheese, sausage or pâté – until around 10pm, but a few stay open for dinner.

Tea salons open for breakfast or mid-morning until the early evening. Many offer lunch, as well as a selection of sweet pastries for afternoon tea. They are at their best in the middle of the afternoon and offer coffee and hot chocolate as well as fine teas. Some, like Le Loir dans la Théière, are casual with sofas and big tables, while Mariage Frères is more formal. Angélina on the Rue de Rivoli is famous for its hot chocolate, and Ladurée has excellent macaroons. *(For addresses see pp318–19.)*

Tour d'Argent decoration *(see p306)*

VEGETARIAN FOOD

Vegetarian restaurants in Paris are few, and non-vegetarian restaurant menus are usually firmly oriented towards meat and fish. However, you can get a good salad almost anywhere and you can often fare well by ordering two courses from the list of *entrées* (first courses). The North African restaurants will serve you *couscous nature* – which doesn't have meat.

Never be timid about asking for a change in a dish. If you see a salad with ham, bacon or *foie gras*, ask the waiter for it without the meat. If you are going to a smart restaurant, telephone ahead and ask the manager if it is possible to prepare a special meal for you. Most restaurants will be happy to oblige.

Organic produce is starting to be used in French cuisine.

HOW MUCH TO PAY

Prices for meals in Paris range from extremely economic to astronomical. You can still enjoy a hearty restaurant or café lunch for 15€, but a typical good bistro, brasserie or restaurant meal in central Paris will average 30€–38€ with wine. (Remember that the better French wines will increase the size of your bill significantly.) More expensive restaurants begin at about 45€ with wine and go up to 200€ for the top places. Many places offer a *formule* or *prix-fixe* (fixed price) menu, especially at

Le Carré des Feuillants *(see p304)*

lunch, and this will almost always offer the best value. Some restaurants feature menus for under 15€ – a few at this price include wine. Coffee usually carries an extra charge.

All French restaurants are obliged by law to display their menu outside. The posted rates include service but a tip for particularly good service will always be appreciated (any amount from one Euro to 5% of the total).

The most widely accepted credit card is Visa. Few restaurants accept American Express, and some bistros do not accept credit cards at all, so it is wise to enquire when you book. Traveller's cheques are not widely accepted either, and cafés require cash.

MAKING RESERVATIONS

It is best to reserve a table in all restaurants, brasseries and bistros. Although you can usually get into a brasserie without a reservation, you may have to wait for a table.

DRESS CODE

Except for some three-star restaurants which can be rather formal, you can dress up or down in Parisian restaurants – within reason. The restaurant listings *(see pp300–319)* indicate which places require formal dress.

READING THE MENU AND ORDERING

Menus in small restaurants and bistros, and even in big brasseries, are often handwritten and can be difficult to decipher, so ask for help if necessary.

The waiter usually takes your choice of *entrée* (first course), then the *plat* (main course). Dessert is ordered after you have finished your main course, unless there are some hot desserts which have to be ordered at the start of

The Angélina restaurant, also known for its tea room *(see p318)*

the meal. The waiter will tell you this, or the dessert section of the menu will be marked *à commander avant le repas*.

The first course generally includes a choice of seasonal salads or vegetables, pâté and small hot or cold vegetable dishes or tarts. Small fish dishes like smoked salmon, grilled sardines, herring, fish salads and tartares are also offered. Brasseries have shellfish such as oysters, which can also be eaten as a main course. (The French tend to eat shellfish only when the month ends in 're'!)

Main dishes usually include a selection of meat, poultry and fish and upmarket restaurants offer game in

Le Pavillon Montsouris near the Parc Montsouris *(see p315)*

Le Train Bleu station restaurant in the Gare de Lyon *(see p315)*

autumn. Most restaurants also offer daily specials *(plats du jour)*. These dishes will incorporate fresh, seasonal produce and are usually good value.

Cheese is eaten either as a dessert or as a pre-dessert course. Some people have a green salad with their cheese. Coffee is served after, not with, dessert. You will need to ask specifically if you want it *au lait* (with milk). Decaffeinated coffee *(décaféiné)* and herbal teas *(tisanes)* are also popular after-dinner beverages.

In most restaurants you will be asked if you would like a drink before ordering food. A typical apéritif is *kir* (white wine with a drop of crème de cassis, a blackcurrant liqueur) or *kir royal* (champagne with crème de cassis). Beer, how-ever, is rarely drunk before a

An elegant Parisian restaurant

meal in France *(see* What to Drink in Paris *pp298–9)*.

Bistros and brasseries usually include the wine list with the menu. The more expensive restaurants have separate wine lists, which are generally brought to the table by the wine waiter after you have seen the meal menu.

SERVICE

As eating is a leisurely pas-time in France, although the general standard of service in Paris restaurants is high, it is not always fast. In small restaurants in particular don't expect rapid attention: there may be only one waiter, and dishes are cooked to order.

CHILDREN

Children are usually very welcome, but there may be little room in a busy restaurant for push-chairs or prams. Nor are special facilities like high-chairs or baby seats commonly provided in eating places.

SMOKING

France has passed strict legislation forcing restaurants to provide no-smoking tables. These are often not the best tables in the house, and while most restaurants abide by the

regulation, cheaper eating places, specially cafés, still tend to be very smoky.

WHEELCHAIR ACCESS

Parisian restaurants are generally accommodating, and a word when you book should ensure that you are given a more conveniently situated table when you arrive. It is always worth checking that toilets can also be used by wheelchair users, since access can be restricted.

USING THE LISTINGS
Key to symbols used in the restaurant listings on pp300–315.

🏃	children's portions
♿	wheelchair access
👔	formal dress required
⛲	outside tables
📄	no credit cards accepted
🅿	parking

Price categories for a three-course meal including a half-bottle of house wine, tax and service:

€	under 25 euros
€€	26–35 euros
€€€	36–50 euros
€€€€	51–75 euros
€€€€€	over 75 euros

The Flavours of Paris

From the glittering temples of haute cuisine to the humblest neighbourhood bistro, Paris is a paradise for food lovers, whether you dine on foie gras and truffles or steak-frîtes, a seafood platter or a perfumed Moroccan couscous. France is immensely proud of its cuisine, from its classic origins to the most rustic of regional dishes. All are available in the capital and, though the French themselves will debate endlessly about the ideal sauce to complement meat or fish, or the right wine to accompany them, they will always be in total agreement that theirs is the best food in the world.

Girolles (chanterelles) on a stall in rue Mouffetard market

the season. Even if you are not shopping for food to cook, the markets are worth browsing and, after an hour or so in the crowded, narrow streets of the rue de de Buci or rue Moufettard you will be more than ready for lunch.

The food of the French provinces, once despised for its rusticity, is now celebrated and almost every region is represented in the capital,

from the rich, bourgeois cuisines of Burgundy and Lyon to the celebrated healthy Mediterranean diet of Provence. Paris itself is surrounded by top quality market gardens which supply young peas, carrots and potatoes. Salmon, asparagus, and wild mushrooms come from the Loire; Normandy brings salt-marsh lamb, apples and Camembert.

What all French chefs agree on is the importance of using the finest quality ingredients, and there is no better place to appreciate the quality of French produce than in the markets of Paris. Here, top chefs may be spied early in the morning, alongside local shoppers, seeking inspiration and the prize ingredients of

Comté

Brie de Meaux

Tomme de chevre

Ami du Chambertin

Roquefort

Selection of fine French cheeses in perfect condition

CLASSIC FRENCH CUISINE

What is usually thought of as classic French cuisine developed in kings' palaces and noble châteaux, with the emphasis on luxury and display, not frugality or health. Dishes are often bathed in rich sauces of butter or cream, enhanced with luxurious ingredients like truffles, foie gras, rare mushrooms and alcohol. Meat is treated with reverence, and you will usually be asked how you want your beef, lamb or duck cooked; the French tend to like their beef rare (*bleu* or *saignant*) and their lamb and duck pink (*rose*). For well-cooked meat, ask for *"bien cuit"* but still expect at least a tinge of pinkness. The most famous country classics include slowly cooked casseroles like *coq au vin* and *boeuf à la bourguignonne*, as well as the bean, sausage and duck baked dish *cassoulet*, from the southwest.

Escargots à la Bourguignonne *are plump Burgundy snails served in their shells with garlic, butter and parsley.*

Salers beef and lentils come from the Auvergne; beef and Bresse chickens from Burgundy; not forgetting Basque ham, Collioure anchovies, lamb from the Pyrenees, or fragrant Provençal melons.

THE NEW STYLE

In recent years, innovative chefs have developed new styles of cooking, reacting against the richness of traditional cookery, and using fresh ingredients, lightly cooked to retain their flavour.

Mouthwatering display in a Parisian patisserie

Sealed jars of whole duck-liver foie gras, a luxury item

Sauces are made of light reductions to enhance, not obscure, the main ingredient of a dish. A wave of invention and originality has resulted in a plethora of unusual ingredients, fresh twists on the classics, and sometimes wonderful new combinations and flavours, such as sea bass with bean purée and red wine sauce, or with fermented grape juice; sole with quince juice and tarragon; tempura of langoustines with cinnamon beurre blanc; rabbit with Indian spices and tomato polenta; and rosemary ice cream or lavender sorbet.

FOREIGN FOOD

Paris can also offer diners an amazing selection of world flavours, especially those of France's former colonies – for example, Moroccan tajines and Cambodian fish with coconut milk. Most fascinating of all is to observe how these cuisines are developing, as young chefs adapt and combine traditional ingredients and culinary styles with those of France.

ON THE MENU

Andouillettes Sausages made of pork intestines

Blanquette de veau Veal stew with eggs and cream

Crottin chaud en salade Goat's cheese on toast with salad

Cuisses de grenouille Frogs' legs in garlic butter

Iles flottantes Meringues floating in creamy sauce

Plateau de fruits de mer Platter of raw and cooked seafood

Ris de veau Veal sweetbreads

Rognons à la moutarde Kidneys in mustard sauce

Salade frisée aux lardons Endive salad with fried bacon

Sole meunière Fried sole with melted butter

Moules marinière *are mussels steamed in a fragrant sauce of white wine, garlic, parsley and sometimes cream.*

Coq au vin *is a male chicken braised with red wine, herbs, garlic, baby onions and button mushrooms.*

Tarte tatin *is a caramelized upside-down buttery apple tart, created at the hotel Tatin in the Loire Valley.*

What to Drink in Paris

Paris is the best place in France to sample a wide range of the country's many different wines. It's cheapest to order wine by the carafe, normally referred to by size: 25cl *(quart)*, 33cl *(fillette)*, 50cl *(demi)* or 75cl *(pichet,* equivalent to a bottle*).* Cafés and wine bars always offer wine by the glass – *un petit blanc* is a small glass of white, a larger glass of red, *un ballon rouge*. House wine is nearly always reliable.

Paris's last vineyard, near Sacré-Coeur *(see p220)*

RED WINE

Some of the world's finest red wines come from the Bordeaux and Burgundy regions, but for everyday drinking choose from the vast range of basic Bordeaux or Côtes du Rhône wines. Or try one of the Beaujolais *crus,* such as Morgon or Fleurie, situated in the southern end of Burgundy, or Beaujolais Villages, which is light enough to serve chilled.

Distinctive bottle shapes for Bordeaux and Burgundy

Bordeaux châteaux include Margaux, which makes some of the world's most elegant red wines.

Burgundy includes some big, strong red wines from the village of Gevrey-Chambertin in the Côte de Nuits.

Beaujolais Nouveau, the fruity first taste of the year's new wine, is released on the third Thursday of November.

The Loire has very good red wines from the area around Chinon. They are usually quite light and very dry.

Southern Rhône is famous for its dark, rich red wines from Châteauneuf-du-Pape, north of Avignon.

Northern Rhône has some dark, spicy red wines, best aged for at least 10 years, from Côte-Rôtie near Vienne.

FINE WINE VINTAGE CHART

	2005	2004	2003	2002	2001	2000	1999	1998	1997
BORDEAUX									
Margaux, St-Julien, Pauillac, St-Estèphe	9	7	8	6	7	8	7	7	7
Graves, Pessac-Léognan (red)	9	7	6	6	7	8	7	8	7
Graves, Pessac-Léognan (white)	9	8	7	6	7	8	8	7	8
St-Emilion, Pomerol	9	7	6	5	8	8	7	7	7
BURGUNDY									
Chablis	9	8	7	8	8	8	8	8	9
Côte de Nuits (red)	9	7	7	6	7	7	7	7	8
Côte de Beaune (white)	9	8	7	8	8	7	7	8	9
LOIRE									
Bourgueil, Chinon	9	7	7	8	7	8	8	7	9
Sancerre (white)	9	8	7	7	8	8	8	7	9
RHONE									
Hermitage (red)	9	7	7	4	7	7	8	8	7
Hermitage (white)	9	7	6	4	8	9	7	8	8
Côte-Rôtie	9	7	6	4	7	8	9	8	7
Châteauneuf-du-Pape	9	7	6	3	7	8	7	8	7

The quality scale from 1 to 10 represents an overall rating for the year and is only a guideline

WHITE WINE

The finest white Bordeaux and Burgundy are best with food, but for everyday drinking try a light dry wine such as Entre-Deux-Mers from Bordeaux, or Anjou Blanc or Sauvignon de Touraine from the Loire. Alsace makes some more reliable white wines. Sweet wines such as Sauternes, Barsac or Coteaux du Layon are delicious with *foie gras*.

Alsace Riesling and Burgundy

Alsace wines are usually labelled by grape variety. Gewürztraminer is one of the most distinctive.

Loire wines include Pouilly-Fumé, from the east of the region. It is very dry, often with a slightly smoky perfume.

Burgundy wines include Chablis, a fresh, full-flavoured dry wine from the northernmost vineyards.

The Loire has the perfect partner for seafood dishes in Muscadet, a dry white wine from the Atlantic Coast.

SPARKLING WINE

In France champagne is the first choice for a celebration drink, and styles range from non-vintage to deluxe. Many other wine regions make sparkling wines by the champagne method which tend to be a lot cheaper. Look out for Crémant de Loire, Crémant de Bourgogne, Vouvray Mousseux, Saumur Mousseux and Blanquette de Limoux.

Champagne

Champagne vineyards east of Paris produce the famous sparkling wine. Billecart-Salmon is a light, pink Champagne.

Sweet Bordeaux are luscious, golden-coloured dessert wines, the most famous being Barsac and Sauternes.

APERITIFS AND DIGESTIFS

Kir, white wine mixed with a small amount of blackcurrant liqueur or *crème de cassis*, is the ubiquitous apéritif. Also common is aniseed-flavoured *pastis* which is served with ice and a pitcher of water and can be very refreshing. Vermouths, especially Noilly-Prat, are also common apéritifs. *Digestifs*, or after-dinner drinks, are often ordered with coffee and include *eaux-de-vie*, the strong colourless spirits infused with fruit, and brandies such as Cognac, Armagnac and Calvados.

Kir: white wine with cassis

BEERS

Beer in France is sold either by the bottle or, more cheaply, on tap by the glass – *un demi*. The cheapest is lager-style *bière française*, and the best brands are Meteor and Mutzig, followed by "33", "1664" and Kronenbourg. A maltier beer is Leffe, which comes as *blonde* (lager) or *brune* (darker, more fully flavoured). Pelforth makes very good dark beer and lager. Some bars and cafés specialize in foreign beers, especially from Belgium, and these are very malty and strong; others brew their own beer. (For beer bars see p317.)

OTHER DRINKS

The brightly-coloured drinks consumed in cafés all over Paris are mixtures of flavoured syrups and mineral waters, called *sirops à l'eau*. The emerald-green drinks use mint syrup, the red ones grenadine. Fruit juices and tomato juice are sold in bottles unless you specify *citron pressé* or *orange pressée* (freshly-squeezed lemon or orange), which is served with a pitcher of water and with sugar or sugar syrup for you to dilute and sweeten to taste. If you ask for water, you will be served mineral water, sparkling (*gazeuse*) or still (*naturelle*); if you don't want to be charged, ask for tap water (*eau de robinet*).

Fresh lemon juice is served with water and sugar

Choosing a Restaurant

The restaurants listed on the following pages have been selected for their good value or exceptional food. The chart below lists restaurants in Paris by area, and the entries are alphabetical within each price category. Details on snack and sandwich bars are in Light Meals and Snacks on pages 316–319.

PRICE CATEGORIES
For a three-course meal per person, with a half-bottle of house wine, including tax and service.
€ under 25 euros
€€ 26–35 euros
€€€ 36–50 euros
€€€€ 51–75 euros
€€€€€ over 75 euros

ILE DE LA CITÉ AND ÎLE SAINT-LOUIS

Au Rendez-Vous des Camionneurs   €
72 Quai des Orfèvres, 75001 **Tel** *01 43 54 88 74*   **Map** *12 F3*

There aren't many *camionneurs* (lorry drivers) on picturesque Ile de la Cité, but this restaurant can satisfy the biggest appetite. Veal stew in white sauce is the house speciality, along with *foie gras* terrine and puff pastry filled with tomato, basil and mozzarella. Extra charges for evenings.

L'Ane et la Mule   €€
74 Quai des Orfèvres, 75001 **Tel** *01 43 54 16 71*   **Map** *12 F3*

Formerly called Ristorante il Delfino, this is a comfortable and stylish Italian restaurant, complete with fireplace and 17th-century cellar, and well suited to a romantic dinner. Pasta, tiramisu and the Delfino escalope (breaded veal cutlet) deserves its place as house speciality.

La Rose de France   €€€
24 Pl Dauphine, 75001 **Tel** *01 43 54 10 12*   **Map** *12 F3*

Majestic setting, looking onto a 17th-century square. The cooking updates French classics, with specialities like the John Dory with rhubarb, ginger and Basmati rice. More traditional is the duck fillet in ratatouille. A *cuisine du marché* restaurant, La Rose uses the freshest produce from the day's market.

Nos Ancêtres les Gaulois   €€€
39 Rue St-Louis en l'Ile, 75004 **Tel** *01 46 33 66 07*   **Map** *13 C4*

This restaurant has a jolly atmosphere and caters to big appetites. Only one set menu, which includes assorted salads, a buffet of cooked meats, one grilled meat, cheeseboard, fruit, dessert and plenty of wine. Satisfying and entertaining. Children's menu available for 10 euros.

Le Vieux Bistro   €€€€
14 Rue du Cloître-Notre-Dame, 75004 **Tel** *01 43 54 18 95*   **Map** *13 B4*

This authentic bistro is popular with many Paris restaurateurs and entertainers. The slightly rundown decor suits the place and the rendition of favourites like *boeuf bourguignon, gratin dauphinois* (sliced potatoes baked in cream), *tarte tatin* (upside-down apple tart) and profiteroles are good.

THE MARAIS

Galerie 88   €
88 Quai de l'Hotel de Ville, 75004 **Tel** *01 42 72 17 58*   **Map** *13 B4*

The bare-walled decor in this tiny restaurant on the banks of the Seine, appeals to students and people on a budget. Prices are low, service is friendly if slow, and you really know you are in Paris. The food is old-fashioned, and includes terrines and a selection of delicious homemade tarts. A few vegetarian dishes too.

Il Piccolo Teatro   €
6 Rue des Ecouffes, 75004 **Tel** *01 42 72 17 79*   **Map** *13 C3*

Established in the 1970s, Il Piccolo Teatro is one of Paris's first vegetarian restaurants. Delicious cuisine, with a Mediterranean accent, is served here. Specialities include moussaka, lasagne and stuffed aubergines (eggplant). Lots of organic produce is used.

Le Baracane   €
38 Rue des Tournelles, 75004 **Tel** *01 42 71 43 33*   **Map** *14 E3*

A tiny restaurant with good quality food at reasonable prices. The fixed-price menu is particularly good value. The Southwestern cuisine includes a delicious rabbit *confit*, braised oxtail, pears poached in Madeira and Cassis (blackcurrant liqueur), and superb homemade chestnut bread.

Key to Symbols *see back cover flap*

Le Passage des Carmagnoles
🏃 €

18 Passage de la Bonne Graine, 75011 **Tel** *01 47 00 73 30*   **Map** 14 F4

A short walk from the Place de la Bastille, the proprietor Soizik may personally greet you. Although it calls itself a wine bar (and the selection of wines by the glass and bottle is excellent), it offers a full menu including five styles of *andouillette* (tripe sausage) and a variety of daily specials. Excellent cheeses; desserts include a vast chocolate éclair.

Aux Vins des Pyrénées
🏃♿🖼 €€

25 Rue Beautrellis, 75004 **Tel** *01 42 72 64 94*   **Map** 13 C3

A very old bistro with a friendly and typically Parisian atmosphere. The day's menu, written up on a blackboard, typically offers a selection of grilled meats. There is an excellent selection of wines by the glass (particularly good value Bordeaux and lesser-known wines from Southwest France). Extra charges for a menu *à la carte.*

Brasserie Bofinger
🏃 €€

3 Rue de la Bastille, 75004 **Tel** *01 42 72 87 82*   **Map** 14 E4

Established in 1864, Bofinger claims to be the oldest brasserie in Paris. It is certainly one of the prettiest, with stained glass, leather banquettes, brass decorations and murals by the Alsatian artist Hansi. It serves good shellfish, as well as respectable *choucroute,* and grilled meats.

Chez Jenny
🏃♿🖼 €€

39 Blvd du Temple, 75003 **Tel** *01 44 54 39 00*   **Map** 14 D1

This huge brasserie on the Place de la République has been a bastion of Alsatian cooking since it was founded over 60 years ago. Service by women in Alsatian dress adds to the atmosphere. The *choucroute* (sauerkraut) *spéciale Jenny* makes a hearty meal with a fruit tart or sorbet, served with a fruit liqueur for dessert.

Le Colimaçon
🏃 €€

44 Rue Vieille du Temple, 75004 **Tel** *01 48 87 12 01*   **Map** 13 C3

Le Colimaçon (snail) refers to the restaurant's centrepiece: a corkscrew staircase. A listed building dating to 1732, it has period wooden beams in the ceiling. Snails are also on the menu along with frogs' legs in parsley and tomato sauce and *gigot de sept heures.*

Trésor
🏃♿🖼 €€

5–7 Rue du Trésor, 75004 **Tel** *01 42 71 35 17*   **Map** 13 C3

The decor of the tiny and trendy Trésor is defined by a contemporary elegance, with a touch of kitsch. Lasagne, grilled steak in wine sauce and tiramisu show the blending of French and Italian cooking. A wide selection of wines, whiskeys and cocktails available. Service is not always with a smile, but the dining room opens on to a pleasant terrace.

Auberge Nicolas Flamel
🏃 €€€

51 Rue de Montmorency, 75003 **Tel** *01 42 71 77 78*   **Map** 13 B1

Located in Paris's oldest house (1407) and named after the famous alchemist who lived here. The restaurant's specialities include *Tatin de foie gras poellé* and *Gala au pain d'épices,* while the *tour de force* here is *gigot de sept heures* following a medieval recipe. Comprehensive wine list.

La Guirlande de Julie
🖼 €€€

25 Pl des Vosges, 75003 **Tel** *01 48 87 94 07*   **Map** 14 D3

Consummate restaurant professional Claude Terrail of the Tour d'Argent (see p306) has employed a good chef here, and the decor is fresh and appealing. For the best views, ask for a table near the window in the first dining room. In good weather meals are served under the cool vaulted stone arcades.

Le Bar à Huîtres
🅿🏃♿🖼 €€€

33 Blvd Beaumarchais, 75003 **Tel** *01 48 87 98 92*   **Map** 14 E3

Oysters predominate in Paris's three Bars à Huêtres (the others are in Montparnasse and St-Germain-des-Prés). You can compose your own seafood platter to start, followed by a choice of hot fish dishes, with meat on offer for carnivores. Convenient for the Place de la Bastille and the Marais.

Le Dôme du Marais
€€€

53bis Rue des Francs-Bourgeois, 75004 **Tel** *01 42 74 54 17*   **Map** 14 D3

Come here for serious French cuisine: sweetbreads, pig's trotters and *tête de veau* are all regulars on the menu. Other, more delicate, features include fillet of sea bream with a spiced crust, and cod cooked in Champagne. Decent service and the remarkable domed building contribute to a truly memorable dining experience. Book ahead.

Le Repaire de Cartouche
🏃♿ €€€

8 Blvd des Filles du Calvaire, 75011 **Tel** *01 47 00 25 86*   **Map** 14 D2

Like its "sister" establishment, Le Villaret, this restaurant is run by former employees of Astier, to the same excellent standards. It too has a changing seasonal menu, which includes roast pigeon with leeks in a vinegar sauce and rabbit terrine with chocolate. Its decor is reassuringly traditional.

L'Ambroisie
🅿🏃♿🖼🅣 €€€€€

9 Pl des Vosges, 75004 **Tel** *01 42 78 51 45*   **Map** 14 D3

Housed in a former jewellery shop restored by Chef Mousieur Pacaud, this is one of only seven Michelin three-star restaurants in Paris. The cuisine includes a mousse of sweet red peppers, *truffle feuilleté* (layered pastry) and langoustines. Reservations are accepted one month in advance.

BASTILLE

Boca Chica 🏃🍴🍷 €€
58 Rue de Charonne, 75011 **Tel** *01 43 57 93 13* **Map** *14 F4*

The upbeat Boca Chica boasts a funky decor, trendy tunes and Spanish fare. Tapas, paella, grilled sardines, pork ribs and *gâteau Basque* are all on the menu. On Mondays, there's a clairvoyance night here, while salsa is featured every Tuesday night.

Barrio Latino 🅿🏃♿🍷 €€€
46 Rue du Faubourg St-Antoine, 75012 **Tel** *01 55 78 84 75* **Map** *14 F4*

Three floors of exuberant and luxurious South American decor in a building designed by Gustave Eiffel. Exotic food includes *guacamole, quesadillas* (grilled cheese-filled tortillas), Brazilian grilled pork and Uruguayan-style scallops on a skewer with salsa. Cheaper lunch. Children are not allowed into the restaurant after 10pm. Discotheque and salsa.

China Club 🏃🍷 €€€
50 Rue de Charenton, 75012 **Tel** *01 43 43 82 02* **Map** *14 F5*

Chinese restaurants can be kitsch, but this one is revolutionary in an extremely glamorous way. China Club has a Colonial chic decor as well as superior Asian cuisine. Specialities include five-spice crispy pigeon and sautéed sole with ginger-plum sauce. Jazz and world-music concerts are also regular fixtures.

Blue Elephant 🏃♿ €€€€
43 Rue de la Roquette, 75011 **Tel** *01 47 00 42 00* **Map** *14 F3*

An island of refinement in the trendy Bastille area, with a tropical decor of lush plants, gurgling fountains and Thai woodwork. Superbly presented Thai cuisine: *som tam* (green papaya, dried shrimp and lime salad) and cashew nut chicken served in a fresh pineapple. Sunday brunch.

BEAUBOURG AND LES HALLES

Au Crocodile 🏃🍴 €
28 Rue Léopold Bellan, 75002 **Tel** *01 42 36 92 44* **Map** *13 A1*

The limited menu of this welcoming neighbourhood restaurant is seasonal, with dishes such as marinated sardines, salmon profiteroles and sea trout with basil. Natural products used. The varnished ivory-coloured ash wood decor with abundant flowers is refreshing.

La Victoire Suprême du Coeur 🏃♿🍴 €
41 Rue des Bourdonnais, 75001 **Tel** *01 40 41 93 95* **Map** *13 A2*

Comforting vegetarian fare served in a bright blue and white dining room. Mushrooms are a speciality here, as in mushroom pâté or roast mushrooms with blackberry sauce. Desserts include a famous berry crumble. No alcohol served except cider; try the biodynamic carrot juice.

Le Bistrot Beaubourg 🏃♿🍴 €
25 Rue Quincampoix, 75004 **Tel** *01 42 77 48 02* **Map** *13 B2*

This arty but chic establishment serves classic French food. Skate with "black" butter sauce and rib-eye steak with green pepper sauce are typical of their excellent menus, changed daily. Lingering over one's meal is no sin here. Equally pleasurable inside, or outside on the sunny terrace.

Aux Tonneau des Halles 🏃♿🍴 €€
28 Rue Montorgueil, 75001 **Tel** *01 42 33 36 19* **Map** *13 A1*

A genuine Parisian bistro, Aux Tonneau des Halles is one of the last of its kind, with its real zinc bar, smoky interior and one of the tiniest kitchens in Paris. Service is not quick, but when the food is this good, who cares! The wines are original and good value.

Café Beaubourg 🏃🍴 €€
43 Rue Saint-Merri, 75004 **Tel** *01 48 87 63 96* **Map** *13 B2*

With views of the animated piazza of the Beaubourg museum, Café Beaubourg has an elegant and contemporary decor. Simple and reliable, if slightly overpriced, fare is guaranteed – a variety of tartares, grilled meats and fish. The menu even offers a Thai salad.

Le Grizzli 🏃🍴 €€
7 Rue St-Martin, 75004 **Tel** *01 48 87 77 56* **Map** *13 B3*

A change of ownership has breathed new life into the Grizzli, founded in 1903 when it was one of the last Parisian places to have dancing bears! The owner orders much produce from his native Southwest including local ham, lamb chops, cooked on a sizzling slate, cheeses and wines made by his family.

Key to Price Guide *see p300* **Key to Symbols** *see back cover flap*

Le Louchebem 🚹 🔲 €€
31 Rue Berger, 75001 **Tel** *01 42 33 12 99*   **Map** *12 F2*

A former butcher's shop (*louchebem* means "butcher" in old French slang). Meat is what this no-nonsense eatery is all about, with portions designed more for rugby players than ballet dancers. *L'assiette du rôtisseur* is a classic (3-meat roast platter, each with its own sauce), and the *aiguillette à la ficelle* are still prepared in the traditional manner.

Le Tire-bouchon 🚹 🔲 €€
22 Rue Tiquetonne, 75002 **Tel** *01 42 21 95 51*   **Map** *13 A1*

The chef elaborates on various regional classics adding a gourmet touch. Confit de canard, prawns in puff pastry with saffron sauce and roast pigeon with morels. One of the popular dishes served at the restaurant is the honey-roasted *Magret de canard au miel*.

Au Pied de Cochon 🚹 ♿ 🔲 €€€
6 Rue Coquillière, 75004 **Tel** *01 40 13 77 00*   **Map** *12 F1*

This colourfully restored brasserie was once popular with high society, who came to observe the workers in the old market and to relish the onion soup. Although touristy, this gigantic place is fun, and has a menu with something for everyone (including excellent shellfish). Still one of the best places after a night out.

Joe Allen 🚹 ♿ 🔲 €€€
30 Rue Pierre Lescot, 75001 **Tel** *01 42 36 70 13*   **Map** *13 A2*

Known to offer some of the best burgers in Paris, Joe Allen's boasts an American menu, with chicken wings, grilled tuna with pesto and cheesecake. Chilled but chic atmosphere, candlelit in the evening. The restaurant serves an excellent brunch on Sunday. Midweek lunchtimes also see some special deals.

Le 404 ♿ €€€
69 Rue Gravilliers, 75003 **Tel** *01 42 74 57 81*   **Map** *13 B1*

Magnificently located in the *hôtel particulier* built for Gabrielle d'Estrées (Henri IV's mistress) in 1737, Le 404 is impeccably run by debonair actor Smaïn, who also owns London's Momo restaurant. The food is deeply rooted in his native Morocco: genuine-tasting *couscous*, tajine and vegetarian delicacies. Cheaper lunches.

Le Pharamond 🚹 ♿ 🔲 €€€
24 Rue de la Grand-Truanderie, 75001 **Tel** *01 40 28 45 18*   **Map** *13 A1*

Founded in 1870, this bistro is a charming remnant of its age, with tiles and mosaics, handsome woodwork and mirrors. Specialities include *tripes à la mode de Caen* (tripe cooked with onions, leeks, cider and Calvados) and *boeuf en daube* (beef stew). The Normandy cider is strongly recommended.

Saudade 🚹 €€€
34 Rue des Bourdonnais, 75001 **Tel** *01 42 36 03 65*   **Map** *13 A2*

This is probably Paris's finest Portuguese restaurant, with all the tiles you except to see along the Tajo not the Seine. The staple salt cod is prepared in fritters, with tomato and onion or with potatoes and eggs. Roast suckling pig and *cozido* (Portuguese stew) are other dishes. A good selection of wines and ports.

Georges 🅿 🚹 ♿ 🔲 €€€€
19 Rue Beaubourg, 75004 **Tel** *01 44 78 47 99*   **Map** *13 B2*

On the top floor of the Pompidou Centre, the Georges offers stunning views. Light and inspired cuisine, such as cherry tomato and goat's cheese cake, *sole meunière*, lamb with chutney and macaroons. Roasted scallops with lemon butter is a hit. Terrace seating too. Decor is minimalist, with lots of steel and aluminium.

Benoît 🚹 €€€€€
20 Rue St-Martin, 75004 **Tel** *01 42 72 25 76*   **Map** *13 B2*

A gem of a Parisian bistro. The owner has retained the faux-marbre, polished-brass and lace-curtain decor created by his grandfather in 1912. The menu includes *saladiers* (assorted cold salads), house *foie gras, boeuf à la mode* and *cassoulet* (white bean and meat stew). The wine list is outstanding.

TUILERIES QUARTER

Salon de Thé Angélina €
226 Rue de Rivoli, 75001 **Tel** *01 42 60 82 00*   **Map** *11 C1*

The speciality of this smart tearoom is the *Mont Blanc*: a soft, chewy meringue topped with whipped cream and chestnut cream. The hot chocolate is also one of the best in town, and the Belle Epoque setting is the ideal background for a quick lunch or a sticky treat.

Toraya 🚹 ♿ €
10 Rue St-Florentin, 75001 **Tel** *01 42 60 13 00*   **Map** *11 C1*

One of the oldest Japanese pâtisseries in Paris, Toraya offers a slice of Japan to Parisians. Dark wood contrasts with the vivid colours of the leather armchairs. Beautifully crafted Japanese pastries are on the menu: red-bean or green-tea-flavoured macaroons and many authentic, delicate rice dishes.

Lapérouse
P ♿ T €€€€€

51 Quai des Grands Augustins, 75006 **Tel** *01 43 26 68 04*

Map *12 F4*

This famous establishment from the 19th century was once one of the glories of Paris. Under the impeccable management of owner-chef Alain Hacquard, this is still the case. The series of salons have kept their 1850s decor. The best tables are by the window. Valet parking available.

LATIN QUARTER

Le Grenier de Notre Dame
P ♿ ♿ ♿ €

18 Rue de la Bûcherie, 75005 **Tel** *01 43 29 98 29*

Map *13 A4*

Le Grenier de Notre Dame opened in the 1970s and still exudes its original hippie atmosphere. Mostly organic ingredients are used to make the filling meals such as fish gratin, vegetarian casserole or vegetarian escalope in breadcrumbs. The wine list offers a good choice of reasonably priced labels, including Château Chaurignac Bordeaux.

Loubnane
♿ ♿ €€

29 Rue Galande, 75005 **Tel** *01 43 26 70 60 or 01 43 54 21 27*

Map *9 A4*

A Lebanese restaurant where specialities include delicious and generous *mezzes*, served under the watchful eye of a patron whose main aim in life actually seems to be the happiness of his customers. Live Lebanese music is often performed in the basement.

La Truffière
€€€

4 Rue Blainville, 75005 **Tel** *01 46 33 29 82*

Map *17 A1*

This classic Latin Quarter address is best in winter, when you can warm up under a medieval vaulted ceiling, in front of a roaring fire. The *prix-fixe* lunch menu is by far the best value for money; but if you like your truffles, then there are plenty of dishes to splash out on.

Le Balzar
♿ ♿ €€€

49 Rue des Ecoles, 75005 **Tel** *01 43 54 13 67*

Map *13 A5*

There's a fair choice of brasserie food here but the main attraction is the ambience. It's typically Left Bank: traditionally-dressed waiters weave their way amongst the hustle and bustle providing express service, with archetypal brasserie decor to match: there are large mirrors and comfortable leather seats.

Le Petit Pontoise
♿ ♿ €€€

9 Rue Pontoise, 75005 **Tel** *01 43 29 25 20*

Map *13 B5*

Popular neighbourhood venue. Inventive use of herbs and spices: pan-fried quail with honey, dried fruits and nuts and prawns Provençal. A perfect menu will probably be composed of a *Risotto à la Truffe*, followed by a duck *parmentier* and stir-fried *foie gras* and, finally, a hot vanilla *soufflé*. Reservations recommended.

Les Bouchons du 5ème
€€€

12 Rue de l'Hôtel Colbert, 75005 **Tel** *01 43 54 15 34*

Map *13 A4*

A comprehensive wine list with vintages offered at wine growers' prices complements dishes such as marrow-flavoured roast beef with potato gratin and Morello cherry soufflé. The chef recommends pan-fried scallops, lentils with foie gras sauce or a pan-roasted beef of *bavière* with bone marrow and ground pepper.

Moissonnier
🍽 ♿ ♿ €€€

28 Rue des Fossés St-Bernard, 75005 **Tel** *01 43 29 87 65*

Map *13 B5*

This family-run bistro serves favourites which have Lyonnais overtones, such as *saladiers* (assorted salads), *tablier de sapeur* (ox tripe), *quenelles de brochet* (pike dumplings) and chocolate cake. Beaujolais wines are traditionally served in a small bottle known as a pot. Ask to be seated downstairs.

Rôtisserie du Beaujolais
♿ €€€

19 Quai de la Tournelle, 75005 **Tel** *01 43 54 17 47*

Map *13 B5*

Facing the Seine and owned by Claude Terrail of the Tour d'Argent next door, the restaurant has a large rôtisserie for roasting poultry and meats. Many of the meats and cheeses are ordered specially from the best suppliers in Lyon. A Beaujolais is, of course, the wine you should order here.

L'Atelier Maître Albert
P ♿ ♿ €€€€

1 Rue Maître Albert, 75005 **Tel** *01 56 81 30 01*

Map *13 B5*

The antique fireplace is purely decorative, yet dishes from the rôtisserie are this restaurant's speciality. Traditional fare such as veal kidneys and mouthwatering chocolate cake are the chief attractions. Other specialities include veal, mixed salad *du moment* and chicken livers. Owned by Guy Savoy *(see p311)*.

La Tour d'Argent
P ♿ ♿ T €€€€€

15–17 Quai de la Tournelle, 75005 **Tel** *01 43 54 23 31*

Map *13 B5*

Established in 1582, the Tour appears to be eternal. Patrician owner Claude Terrail has hired young chefs who have rejuvenated the classic menu. The ground-floor bar is also a gastronomic museum; from here take a lift to the luxurious panoramic cellars. One of the finest wine cellars. Lunch menu is much cheaper than dinner.

JARDIN DES PLANTES QUARTER

Les 5 Saveurs d'Anada 🖾🖾 €

72 Rue du Cardinal Lemoine, 75005 **Tel** *01 43 29 58 54* **Map** *17 A1*

Les 5 Saveurs d'Anada offers a small menu, featuring high-class macrobiotic, organic and (mostly) vegetarian food. Inventive soups are flavoured with butternut squash or cinnamon; mains include fish bento or seitan (gluten) curry. Good choice of organic wines, plus fruit cocktails.

Marty Restaurant 🅿🖾🖾🖾 €€€

20 Ave des Gobelins, 75005 **Tel** *01 43 31 39 51* **Map** *17 B3*

Authentic Art Deco interior but the cuisine steals the show. Serves a hearty fare, such as roast duck or rabbit casserole. Insist on seasonal dishes such as gazpacho. Excellent *crème brûlée*. The Marty was established by E Marty in 1913 and is still family-run.

Mavromatis 🖾🖾🖾 €€€€

42 Rue Daubenton, 75005 **Tel** *01 43 31 17 17* **Map** *17 B2*

With an elegant decor, this restaurant is manned by the Mavrommatis brothers, one in the kitchen, the other welcomes guests. Its Greek specialities include roast lamb and *moussaka*. The Hellenic excursion continues with Greek yogurt and *baklava* for dessert.

MONTPARNASSE

Aux Petits Chandeliers 🖾 €

62 Rue Daguerre, 75014 **Tel** *01 43 20 25 87* **Map** *16 D3*

Unpretentious bistro, established in 1962 and still featuring the small chandeliers after which it was named. This was the first restaurant in Paris to serve cuisine from the island of Réunion. On the menu are Creole-style pudding, exotic fruit sorbets and coconut-and-vanilla punch.

La Bretonne 🖾🖾🖾 €

56 Rue du Montparnasse, 75014 **Tel** *01 43 20 89 58* **Map** *16 D2*

La Bretonne is a little piece of Brittany, complete with antique furniture and decorative plates. Tasty pancakes such as Provençal (mushrooms and snail butter), *Guéménée* (with chitterling sausages), and a large choice of flambéed varieties for dessert.

La Régalade 🖾 €€

49 Ave Jean Moulin, 75014 **Tel** *01 45 45 68 58* **Map** *15 C5*

Gourmet fare for a bargain at this traditional bistro. Duck *foie gras* casserole and pan-fried cod with leek vinaigrette are main courses. Grand Marnier soufflé is the chef's speciality dessert. The seasonal menu, based on a *cuisine du marché*, is often renewed, depending on market. Reservations essential.

Natacha €€

17bis Rue Campagne Première, 75014 **Tel** *01 43 20 79 27* **Map** *16 E2*

Long drapes by the entrance and theatre seats bring drama to an otherwise simple interior of the Natacha restaurant. You can get a hint of the exotic on the menu, which includes chicken terrine with pistachios and glazed kumquats and steamed fish with herb dressing. Brunch on Sundays.

Wadja 🖾 €€€

10 Rue de la Grande-Chaumière, 75006 **Tel** *01 46 33 02 02* **Map** *16 D2*

This is a favourite hangout for local families and arty types on a budget, thanks to its excellent-value *menu du jour*. Game, meat and fish are permanent fixtures, the wine list is suitably eclectic, and the waiters are always ready to advise on the right wine to go with the dishes you have chosen.

Contre-Allée 🖾🖾 €€€

83 Ave Denfert-Rochereau, 75014 **Tel** *01 43 54 99 86* **Map** *16 E3*

Sylvain Pineau (former chef at Le Crillon) conjures up mouth-watering dishes such as lamb steak in a herb crust with potatoes sautéed in goose fat, and scallops in parsley butter. The decor is minimalist, with lots of dark woods; the service is friendly.

La Cagouille 🖾🖾 €€€

10–12 Pl Constantin Brancusi, 75014 **Tel** *01 43 22 09 01* **Map** *15 C3*

This large venue, on the stark new Place Brancusi in the rebuilt Montparnasse district, is one of Paris's best fish restaurants. Big fish are served simply with few fancy sauces or adornments. You might also find unusual seasonal delicacies like black bay scallops and *vendangeurs* (tiny red mullet).

L'Astrance
P   €€€€€
4 Rue de Beethoven, 75016 **Tel** *01 40 50 84 40*   **Map** *9 C3*

The inventive cuisine of L'Astrance's two chefs have made it so popular that you must book at least a month ahead. Dishes include sautéed pigeon with a caramelized hazelnut sauce and apple and celery minestrone with roasted spice ice cream. The Menu Surprise is as lovely as the mountain flower this restaurant is named after.

Le Relais du Parc
€€€€€
55–57 Ave Raymond Poincaré, 75016 **Tel** *01 47 27 59 59*   **Map** *9 C1*

In this historic townhouse, Alain Ducasse and Joel Robuchon create France's great "classic" dishes. Each culinary region is featured, and dishes include *turbot de Bretagne, chevreuil (venison) d'Alsace* and *fois gras de canard des Landes*. The enviable wine list highlights the Bordeaux region. The restaurant has just received a Michelin star.

CHAMPS-ELYSÉES

Ladurée
€
75 Ave des Champs-Elysées, 75008 **Tel** *01 40 75 08 75*   **Map** *4 F5*

Celebrated as one of the best tearooms in town since 1862, Ladurée hasn't lost any of its class. This elegant tearoom, famous for its Renaissance-style interior, still serves its renowned macaroons, which come in all sorts of inventive flavours: aniseed, caramel, chestnut, lime and basil.

Le Stübli
€
11 Rue Poncelet, 75017 **Tel** *01 42 27 81 86*   **Map** *4 E3*

A little corner of Germany with a patisserie, deli and tearoom. For lunch, try the great classics, such as sauerkraut. Their apple *strudel, linzertorte* and authentic Viennese hot chocolate make for a fine afternoon tea. Lunch is served on the terrace. German beer and wine is available.

L'Ascot
€€€
66 Rue Pierre Charron, 75008 **Tel** *01 43 59 28 15*   **Map** *4 F5*

The present restaurant is an offshoot of the original Sébillon based in the bourgeois suburb of Neuilly since 1913. The menu specializes in meat-based dishes, and puddings are traditionally French. The decor is stately, with red banquettes and lots of dark woods.

Le Boeuf sur le Toit
P   €€€
34 Rue du Colisée, 75008 **Tel** *01 53 93 65 55*   **Map** *5 A4*

Highly inspired by the 1930s – *Les Années Folles* – the building (The Ox on the Roof) was formerly a venue hosting cabarets. Exemplifying the classic Paris Art-Deco brasserie, its changing menu can include sole meunière, snails, *foie gras* and *crème brûlée*.

Verre Bouteille
€€€
85 Ave des Ternes, 75017 **Tel** *01 45 74 01 02*   **Map** *3 C2*

Verre Bouteille proves that simple can be tasty. The house speciality is steak tartare, but goat's cheese ravioli, *foie gras* and chocolate cake are also superb. Lunch is much cheaper than dinner. If you liked what you ate here, and feel audacious enough to try the recipe, you can find it on their website: **www.leverrebouteille.com**

Flora Danica
€€€€
142 Ave des Champs-Elysées, 75008 **Tel** *01 44 13 86 26*   **Map** *4 E4*

On the ground floor of the House of Denmark, this venue is more relaxed and less pricey than Copenhague upstairs. Original Scandinavian cuisine, with just a touch of France. Specialities include grilled salmon and strawberries with mulled wine. Interiors are prettily done in Danish style. Valet parking available.

La Fermette Marbeuf 1900
€€€€
5 Rue Marbeuf, 75008 **Tel** *01 53 23 08 00*   **Map** *4 F5*

Fabulous Belle Époque mosaics, tiles and ironwork were discovered beneath the formica walls of this Champs-Elysées bistro. La Fermette Marbeuf also serves good brasserie-style food including a commendable set menu with many *appellations contrôlées* wines – a measure of their quality.

L'Avenue
€€€€
41 Ave Montaigne, 75008 **Tel** *01 40 70 14 91*   **Map** *10 F1*

Located at the hub of *couture* fashion, L'Avenue attracts an elegant crowd. The unusual Neo-1950s decor is fresh and colourful. Service can get a bit hectic at peak lunch and dinner times, but then this is a brasserie. The cuisine is varied and supper is served until late.

Man Ray
€€€€
34 Rue Marbeuf, 75008 **Tel** *01 56 88 36 36*   **Map** *4 F5*

A hip resto-bar filled with golden Buddhas, Chinese lanterns and Oriental artefacts. French-Asian fusion cuisine features citrus and ginger tuna and wok-fried scampi with oyster mushrooms. Great selection of sushi. A live orchestra plays Mozart on occasional Monday evenings.

Sens

☐P☐ €€€€

23 Rue de Pontieux, 75008 **Tel** *01 42 25 95 00* **Map** *5 A5*

This new concept restaurant, clad in soft greys and silvers, makes clever use of lighting to create the urban-chic feel that attracts the trendy crowds. Plastic tree trunk-like pillars prop up the mezzanine and young chef Christophe Fluck serves interesting Mediterranean-influenced dishes.

Guy Savoy

☐ €€€€€

18 Rue Troyon, 75017 **Tel** *01 43 80 40 61* **Map** *4 D3*

A handsome dining room and professional service further compliment the remarkable cuisine of Guy Savoy himself. The three-starred Michelin menu includes oysters in aspic, Bresse chicken with a sherry vinegar glaze, poached or grilled pigeon with lentils, and then an extraordinary dessert.

La Maison Blanche

☐P☐☐☐☐ €€€€€

15 Ave Montaigne, 75008 **Tel** *01 47 23 55 99* **Map** *10 F1*

The popular Maison Blanche restaurant affixed 15 Avenue Montaigne to its name when it moved here. Although the decor is modern, the restaurant is almost opulently vast. The cuisine, with its Provençale and Southwestern influences, is flavoursome and is the main attraction for its worldly clientele.

Pavillon Ledoyen

☐P☐☐ €€€€€

1 Ave Dutuit, 75008 **Tel** *01 53 05 10 02* **Map** *11 B1*

The refined cuisine at Pavillon Ledoyen mainly features turbot breast and mashed potatoes with truffle butte (a sea fish recipe) and *mille-feuilles de Krampouz croustillante avec crème de citron*. Ask for a table in the dining room – a re-creation of a 1950s grill room – or on the terrace.

OPÉRA QUARTER

Chartier

☐☐ €

7 Rue du Faubourg Montmartre, 75009 **Tel** *01 47 70 86 29* **Map** *6 F4*

Despite its impressive, listed 1900s decor, Chartier still caters to people on a budget, mostly students and tourists, though some of the old habitués still come for the basic cuisine (hard-boiled eggs with mayonnaise, house pâté, roast chicken and pepper steak). No frills, and expect to wait: the waiters are very busy.

Chez Clément

☐ €€

17 Blvd des Capucines, 75002 **Tel** *01 53 43 82 00* **Map** *6 E5*

Just two minutes' walk from the Opéra, this comfortable bistro (part of a chain) serves its signature dishes of roast meats until well after midnight every day of the year. The dish of the day is always good value and, unusually, is available for both lunch and dinner.

La Vaudeville

☐☐ €€

29 Rue Vivienne, 75002 **Tel** *01 40 20 04 62* **Map** *6 F5*

This is one of seven brasseries owned by Paris's reigning brasserie king, Jean-Paul Bucher. Good shellfish, Bucher's famous smoked salmon, many different fish dishes as well as classic brasserie standbys like pig's trotters and *andouillette*. A quick, friendly service and noisy ambience make it lots of fun.

Le Noces de Jeanette

☐☐ €€

14 Rue Favart, 75002 **Tel** *01 42 96 36 89* **Map** *6 F5*

A typical Parisian bistro, named for the one-act curtain-raising opera performed at the Opera Comique across the street. An ornate interior belies the cosy atmosphere. The fixed-price menu offers a wide choice of classic dishes. Try the vichyssoise or *terrine de crustacés à la crème d'Oseille*. Menu changes regularly.

Angl'Opéra

☐☐ €€€

39 Ave de l'Opéra, 75002 **Tel** *01 42 61 86 25* **Map** *6 E5*

In this chic, informal restaurant, top chef Gilles Choukroun flexes his culinary muscles with his trademark cooking of blending and marrying flavours in ways quite unlike anywhere else in Paris's food circuit. Expect iconoclastic dishes such as *crème brulée* of foie gras.

Le Grand Colbert

€€€

2–4 Rue Vivienne, 75002 **Tel** *01 42 86 87 88* **Map** *6 F5*

Situated in the restored Galérie Colbert owned by the Bibliothèque Nationale, this must be one of the prettiest brasseries in Paris. The menu offers classic brasserie fare – herring fillets with potatoes or cream, snails, onion soup, classic whiting Colbert (in breadcrumbs) and grilled meats.

Les Alchimistes

☐ €€€

16 Rue Favart, 75002 **Tel** *01 42 96 69 86* **Map** *6 F5*

In the shadow of the Opéra Comique, this friendly restaurant offers dishes such as veal parmentier with oyster mushrooms, and warm chocolate tart with white-chocolate ice cream. The decor is a mix of old and new, with red walls and dark furniture.

Willi's Wine Bar
🏃 €€€

13 Rue des Petits-Champs, 75001 **Tel** *01 42 61 05 09*

Map *12 F1*

Original wine posters cover the walls and over 250 vintages are in the cellar at Willi's Wine Bar. The menu includes onion tart with a salad topped with pine nuts, beef *fricassée* with braised chicory (endive) and rosemary sauce and bitter chocolate terrine.

Café Drouant
P🏃♿🔲T €€€€

18 Rue Gaillon, 75002 **Tel** *01 42 65 15 16*

Map *6 E5*

Founded in the 19th century, this is one of Paris's most historic restaurants. The café, not to be confused with the more expensive restaurant, is a fashionable spot which serves excellent food until late and has an extremely good value menu at dinner. The interior has a famous shellfish-motif ceiling.

La Fontaine Gaillon
P🏃🔲 €€€€€

1 Rue de la Michodière, 75002 **Tel** *01 47 42 63 22*

Map *6 E5*

In a 17th-century mansion, Fontaine Gaillon is partly owned by legendary film actor, Gérard Depardieu. The menu showcases sautéed John Dory, Merlan Colbert with sorrel purée, *confit de canard* and lamb chops. Comfortable interiors and a good wine list.

Senderens
♿T €€€€€

9 Pl de la Madeleine, 75008 **Tel** *01 42 65 22 90*

Map *5 C5*

Super-chef Alain Senderens has just given up the Michelin stars of his Lucas Carton restaurant to open this more informal eatery, on the same spot as its famous predecessor. His legendary creations include *foie gras* with cabbage, spicy duck Apicius and a mango *mille-feuille vanille*. The Belle-Époque decor is stunning and the crowd glamorous.

MONTMARTRE

Au Grain de Folie
📋🏃 €

24 Rue la Vieuville, 75018 **Tel** *01 42 58 15 57*

Map *6 F1*

Paris has only a handful of vegetarian restaurants, and Au Grain de Follie has a truly cosy feel. Main courses consist of salads with interesting combinations of vegetables and grains (most of which are organic). The apple crumble is highly recommended.

Musée de la Halle St-Pierre
📋🏃♿ €

2 Rue Ronsard, 75018 **Tel** *01 42 58 72 89*

Map *7 A1*

Formerly a covered market, this venue now hosts a library, the Max Fourny primitive art museum and a restaurant. This is a popular spot for afternoon tea and pastries. At lunch, the menu is more substantial with savoury bites such as quiche, pies and tarts. Children's activities provided.

Le Restaurant
🏃 €€

32 Rue Véron, 75018 **Tel** *01 42 23 06 22*

Map *6 E1*

Almost invisible from the main road, this place teems with locals every night of the week. Its original distressed-chic decor provides a unique setting, while the kitchen offers French food with a twist. The split-pea soup with giant *gambas* (prawns) is a must, as is the delicious chocolate tart.

Le Wepler
P🏃♿🔲 €€€

14 Pl de Clichy, 75018 **Tel** *01 45 22 53 24*

Map *6 D1*

Retro-style brasserie open until late into the night. Good for afternoon tea, early evening cocktails and pre- or post-show suppers. Large shellfish platters as well as sauerkraut, *andouillette* and *confit de canard*. An institution, established in 1892.

Beauvilliers
🔲T €€€€€

52 Rue Lamarck, 75018 **Tel** *01 42 54 54 42*

Map *2 E5*

Montmartre's best and one of the most festive in Paris, this is where effusive chef Edouard Carlier delves into old cookbooks for ideas. Favourites are *escabèche* of red mullet (the fish is cooked and marinated), veal *rognonnade* (part of a loin of veal with the kidney) and a very lemony lemon tart.

FURTHER AFIELD

Beyrouth
€

16 Rue de la Vacquerie, 75011 **Tel** *01 43 79 27 46*

In a residental street near the cemetery of Père Lachaise, this is a wonderful Lebanese restaurant frequented by a mixture of locals, media types (from the TV studio next door) and drama students. The food is as copious and delicious as it is well priced, and the service is friendly.

Key to Price Guide *see p300* **Key to Symbols** *see back cover flap*

Chez Gladines

30 Rue des Cinq Diamantes, 75013 **Tel** *01 45 80 70 10*   **Map** *17 C4*

In the villagey Butte-aux-Cailles quarter, hidden behind the high rises of Place d'Italie, this is a haven of decent, no-frills food. The place is so popular, it is always busy. Giant salads are among the favourite items on the menu: they are served in massive bowls and are often covered in sautéed potatoes.

Favela Chic

18 Rue Fbg du Temple, 75011 **Tel** *01 40 21 38 14*   **Map** *8 D5*

Not much of Brazil is missing from this lively haven, run by Jerome and Roseanne. The *caipirinha* (fresh lime, cane-sugar alcohol and lots of crushed ice) has lost none of its buzz, and the *feijoada* tastes just as it does back in Salvador Bahia. The place gets noisy as the evening progresses, so come early.

La Boulangerie

15 Rue des Panoyaux, 75020 **Tel** *01 43 58 45 45*

Set in a converted bakery, this is a real neighbourhood bistro that fills up quickly with locals and regulars. The atmosphere is friendly and the food is excellent value for money. Try the crab ravioli in lobster cream sauce or the tender steaks.

Le Baron Rouge

1 Rue Théophile Roussel, 75012 **Tel** *01 43 43 14 32*   **Map** *14 F5*

Right next to the lively Marché d'Aligre (see p338), Parisians rush here at weekends to sample the divine oysters, brought straight from Cap Ferret on the Atlantic coast. These can be eaten out on the pavement, standing round large wine barrels. Also a good wine bar during the week.

Le Volant

13 Rue Beatrix Dussane, 75015 **Tel** *01 45 75 27 67*   **Map** *10 D5*

The owner of Le Volant (The Steering Wheel) is fanatical about motorcar racing. There's nothing racy, however, about the cooking: it is simple, traditional French cuisine at its best; *boeuf bourguignon*, mouth-watering homemade fruit tarts and the never-to-be-forgotten chocolate mousse.

L'Occitanie

96 Rue Oberkampf, 75011 **Tel** *01 48 06 46 98*   **Map** *14 F1*

As the name indicates, the cuisine here is deeply rooted in the Southwest, as is the welcome from the Occitan-speaking *bon-viveur* owner. *Cassoulet, confit or potage à rouzole* (soup with sausage-meat and herb dumplings) are some of the typical dishes served here. Helpings are generous.

Piston Pélican

15 Rue de Bagnolet, 75020 **Tel** *01 43 70 35 00*

A long bar, wooden benches and a collection of old advertisements adorn this quaint venue. Salads served in hollowed-out bread, salmon tartare with sesame oil and caramel-centred chocolate cake exemplify the menu's twist on classic dishes.

Astier

44 Jean-Pierre Timbaud, 75011 **Tel** *01 43 57 16 35*   **Map** *14 E1*

Quality here is among the best for the price in Paris, and the dining rooms are always full in this hugely popular bistro. The food is very good, including mussel soup with saffron, rabbit in mustard sauce, duck breast with honey, and good cheeses and wines.

Chez Prune

36 Rue Beaurepaire, 75010 **Tel** *01 42 41 30 47*   **Map** *8 D4*

With wonderful views of Canal Saint-Martin, this is a top spot for brunch on Sundays, with a choice of smoked salmon or ham with croissants. Upmarket cuisine for lunch: saffron and lime fish and three-cheese ravioli. Platters of cold meats and cheeses in the evening. Daily food based on *cuisine du marché*.

La Mère Lachaise

78 Bd de Menilmontant, 75020 **Tel** *01 47 97 61 60*

This is a friendly bistro with a split personality. A great terrace and two dining rooms – one traditional and the other plastered in aluminium. Uncomplicated food includes asparagus and citrus fruit salad, beef with potato gratin, *charcuterie* and crumble with seasonal fruit.

Le Bistro des Deux Théâtres

18 Rue Blanche, 75009 **Tel** *01 45 26 41 43*   **Map** *6 D3*

If you are on a strict budget this formula restaurant in the theatre district is a real find. The reasonable set menu includes an apéritif, a choice of first and main courses, cheese or dessert and a half bottle of wine. The food is reliably good, including duck *foie gras* and smoked salmon with *blinis* (small savoury pancakes).

Le Clos Morillons

50 Rue des Morillons, 75015 **Tel** *01 48 28 04 37*

This discreet family-run restaurant's menu evolves constantly. The Far Eastern travels of chef, Philippe Delacourcelle, are evident in specialities such as cod roasted with cinnamon, pigeon with sesame and monkfish and lobster with ginger. Other dishes are more French. Respectable Loire wines compliment the set menu which changes regularly.

Les Allobroges   🚶   €€
71 Rue des Grands-Champs, 75020 **Tel** *01 43 73 40 00*

It's worth the trip out to taste chef Olivier Pateyron's fresh and innovative cooking. Specialities include *Canettes aux épices* (duck with spices) and *Souris d'agneau ail en chemise et purée de poix* (lamb with garlic and bean mash). A complementary *amuse-gueule*, different every day of the year, is offered.

Les Zygomates   €€
7 Rue Capri, 75012 **Tel** *01 40 19 93 04*

This former butcher's shop is now a popular eatery – surprising, given its out-of-town-centre address. The ceiling is painted tin and the dining room is filled with other interesting touches. Food is plentiful and wonderfully innovative, with dishes such as turkey in a salted rosemary crust or snail and mushroom ravioli.

Ma Pomme/Colimaçon   🚶   €€
107 Rue de Ménilmontant, 75020 **Tel** *01 40 33 10 40*

It is worth the 10-minute walk up steep Rue de Ménilmontant to get to this well-kept secret. Excellent food is served with a smile in a bright-yellow dining room with temporary art collections on the walls. Expect unusual dishes with ingredients such as ostrich and kangaroo.

Pause Café   🚶 ♿ 🍴   €€
41 Rue de Charonne, 75011 **Tel** *01 48 06 80 33*   **Map** *14 F4*

Since the shooting of *Chacun Cherche son Chat*, this has been a top spot to be seen. Luckily this has not ruined the friendly ambience nor the fine cuisine: light dishes such as steak tartare, tarts with salads and excellent homemade pastries. The stone and glass interior lends a rustic-elegant charm

Brasserie Flo   🅿 🚶 ♿ 🍴   €€€
7 Cour des Petites-Ecuries, 75010 **Tel** *01 47 70 13 59*   **Map** *7 B4*

This authentic Alsatian brasserie is situated in a passageway in a slightly unsavoury neighbourhood. But it is worth the effort to find it: the rich wood and stained-glass decor is unique and very pretty and the straightforward brasserie menu includes good shellfish and *choucroute* (sauerkraut).

Brasserie Julien   🅿 🚶   €€€
16 Rue du Faubourg St-Denis, 75010 **Tel** *01 47 70 12 06*   **Map** *7 B5*

With its superb 1880s decor, Julien is upmarket but reasonable. Under the same ownership as Brasserie Flo, it has the same friendly service and wide dessert variety. The imaginative brasserie cuisine includes hot *foie gras* with lentils, breaded pig's trotter and Julien's version of *cassoulet*.

Faucher   🍴   €€€
123 Ave de Wagram, 75017 **Tel** *01 42 27 61 50*   **Map** *4 E2*

Monsieur and Mme Faucher take a great interest in their restaurant and guests. The big dining room with large windows is pretty and the terrace a delight in fine weather. The original food includes *mille-feuille* of spinach and sliced raw beef, truffle-stuffed egg, turbot with caviar cream and a good selection of desserts.

La Marine   🚶 🍴   €€€
55 Quai Valmy, 75010 **Tel** *01 42 39 69 81*   **Map** *8 D5*

For several years now this establishment has been the headquarters of the Internet trade, and as such, is usually packed, so book ahead. The main courses are good and mainly fishy, such as red mullet in puff pastry, fish steak with a creamy nettle sauce, or fish stew. The desserts aren't so highly recommended.

L'Auberge du Bonheur   🅿 🚶 ♿ 🍴   €€€
Allée de Longchamps, Bois de Boulogne, 75016 **Tel** *01 42 24 10 17*   **Map** *3 A3*

This is probably the only affordable restaurant in the Bois. In summer you can sit on the gravel terrace under chestnut and plane trees, surrounded by wisteria and bamboo. It's also delightful in cool weather inside the cosy chalet. The simple service complements cuisine that emphasizes grilled meats.

Le Bistro d'à Côté Flaubert   🚶 🍴   €€€
10 Rue Gustave Flaubert, 75017 **Tel** *01 42 67 05 81*   **Map** *4 E2*

This was the first and remains the most appealing of star-chef Michel Rostang's boutique bistros. Many Lyonnais dishes are served including lentil salad, *cervelas* or *sabodet* sausage, *andouillette*, and macaroni gratin. Popular with executives at lunch and with the upper layers of the bourgeoisie at night.

Le Chardenoux   🚶 ♿ 🍴   €€€
1 Rue Jules Vallès, 75011 **Tel** *01 43 71 49 52*

This classic bistro is one of the prettiest in Paris. Both fish and meat feature on the traditional French menu, with dishes such as roasted cod, preserved duck and fricasée of kidney. The wine list covers all of France's wine regions. The menu changes depending on the market.

Le Clou   🚶 ♿ 🍴   €€€
132 Rue Cardinet, 75017 **Tel** *01 42 27 36 78*   **Map** *5 A1*

Traditional bistro, complete with a collection of old advertisements and blackboard menus. Scallops, grilled beef and desserts such as glazed nougat and chocolate cake never leave the menu. The well-priced wine list features a great range of French wines from various regions.

Key to Price Guide *see p300* **Key to Symbols** *see back cover flap*

Le Paprika

28 Ave Trudaine, 75009 **Tel** *01 44 63 02 91*

€€€

Map *6 F2*

Gourmet Hungarian cuisine and live gypsy music (October–April and June). A dish such as the *csáky bélszin* (beef with morels and *foie gras*) is familiar to the French palate, but desserts such as apple and cinnamon strudel offer a taste of Central Europe. Occasional live music.

Le Train Bleu

Pl Louis Armand, 75012 **Tel** *01 43 43 09 06*

€€€

Map *18 E1*

Train station restaurants were once grand places for a meal. Today this is not usually so, but the Train Bleu (named after the fast train that once took the élite to the Riviera) in the Gare de Lyon is a pleasant exception. Upmarket brasserie cuisine such as hot Lyonnais sausage, with excellent pastries. The Belle Époque decor is a landmark.

Les Amognes

243 Rue du Faubourg St-Antoine, 75011 **Tel** *01 43 72 73 05*

€€€

Chef Thierry Coué has worked under Alain Senderens (see p312), and his small restaurant is not pretty, but the food is original and good. The cod fritters with tomatoes and basil, tuna with artichokes and bell pepper, sea bream with a chilli-oil and pineapple soup with Pina Colada are worth the trip. Seasonal menu.

Le Villaret

13 Rue Ternaux, 75011 **Tel** *01 43 57 89 76*

€€€

Map *14 E2*

Tucked away on the Oberkampf district's northern fringes, this restaurant is run by the former staff from Astier closeby. Well-known for its *cuisine du marché* (using the freshest ingredients from the day's market), carefully chosen and prepared meat and big cheese selection. Packed at weekends.

Le Chalet des Îles

14 Chemin Ceinture du Lac Inférieur du Bois de Boulogne, 75116 **Tel** *01 42 88 04 69*

€€€€

Map *3 A4*

Idyllic setting, nestled on an island in the middle of a lake. The country-style interior suits the bucolic environment, but the cuisine showcases a modern approach: pan-fried sole with a Creole-style sauce, coconut and lemon chicken with red rice and chocolate cake with a red berry *coulis*.

Le Pavillon Montsouris

20 Rue Gazan, 75014 **Tel** *01 43 13 29 00*

€€€€

This restored building once counted Trotsky, Mata Hari and Lenin among its clientele. Today the attractive interior and terrace make fine surroundings for a good value set menu. Specialities include fish tartar, wild boar with bacon and wine sauce, and *crème brulée à la vanille Bourbon*.

L'Oulette

15 Pl Lachambeaudie, 75012 **Tel** *01 40 02 02 12*

€€€€

L'Oulette's vast new premises may lack intimacy, but Chef Marcel Baudis's cuisine, reflecting his native Quercy, remains excellent. Dishes include duck *foie gras* cooked en terrine and jurancon sauce, lamb from the Pyrenées, and *pain d'épices* (a kind of spiced cake).

Tante Jeanne

116 Blvd Pereire, 75017 **Tel** *01 43 80 88 68*

€€€€

Map *4 E1*

The late Bernard Loiseau opened this place where a smart crowd now enjoys *croustillant de langoustine et pied de cochon jus iodé* (pig's trotters in a fish-flavoured sauce), *filet de bar grille au fenouil "confit-purée-jus"* (anis-flavoured grilled fish), and *rafraichi de pamplemousse, gelée de Campari* (grapefruit, Campari sauce).

Augusta

98 Rue de Tocqueville, 75017 **Tel** *01 47 63 39 97*

€€€€€

Map *5 A1*

This reliable restaurant serves excellent fish and a few meat dishes. The *salade augusta* is generously garnished with shellfish and the house speciality *bouillabaise* with potatoes must be one of the best in Paris. An unusual dish is langoustines flavoured with tarragon and saffron.

Au Trou Gascon

40 Rue Taine, 75012 **Tel** *01 43 44 34 26*

€€€€€

This authentic 1900s bistro owned by star-chef Alain Dutournier (of Carré des Feuillants) is one of Paris's most popular places. The delicious Gascon food includes ham from the Chalosse region, great *foie gras*, lamb from the Pyrenees and local poultry. Dutournier's desserts are also worth finding room for.

Dessirier

9 Pl du Maréchal Juin, 75017 **Tel** *01 42 27 82 14*

€€€€€

Map *4 E1*

Dedicated to seafood since 1883, this is one of Paris's best-known fish restaurants. Oyster risotto, whole grilled sea bass and langoustine salad feature. A combination of fish brasserie and wet-fish market, it offers a variety of fish-based dishes, depending on the season. Affordable wine list available. Valet parking.

Le Pré Catelan

Route de Suresnes, Bois de Boulogne, 75016 **Tel** *01 44 14 41 14*

€€€€€

This elegant Belle Époque restaurant in the Bois is a delight, either in midsummer when you can dine on the terrace, or in midwinter when the lights inside are magical. The menu is luxurious, with huge langoustines, special Duclair duck with spices and sea urchin soufflé. Divine desserts. There is a cheaper menu at lunchtime.

Light Meals and Snacks

Good food and drink is so much a part of everyday life in Paris that you can eat and drink well without ever going to a restaurant. Whether you want to enjoy a meal or casual drink at a café, wine bar or tearoom, buy a crêpe from a street stand or a quiche or crusty *baguette* sandwich from a bakery, or put together a picnic from cheeses, breads, salads and *pâtés*, informal eating is one of the city's great gastronomic strengths.

Paris is also a wonderful city for drinking. Wine bars in every quarter offer various wines by the glass. Beer bars have astounding selections, and Irish pubs are much-loved spots which serve Guinness in a relaxed, sometimes rowdy atmosphere. Or choose from chic hotel bars or fun late-night bars. *(See also pp298–9.)*

CAFES

Paris is famous for its cafés, and rightly so. You can't walk far in this city without passing one. They range in size from tiny to huge, some with pinball machines, a tobacconist and betting stations, some with elegant Belle Epoque decorations and immaculately attired waiters. Every Parisian has their favourite local café and these establishments function as the heart of any neighbourhood. The life of a café changes throughout the day and it's always fascinating to check out the locals at leisure, sipping their morning espresso, tucking into a hearty lunch or drinking an *apéritif* after work. Most cafés will serve you light food and drink at any time of day.

Breakfast definitely is one of the busiest times and fresh croissants and *pains au chocolat* (chocolate-filled pastries) sell fast. The French often eat these dipped in a bowl or large cup of milky coffee or hot chocolate. Eating breakfast out at a café, or at least grabbing a quick caffeine fix in the morning is a fundamental part of the French lifestyle.

The café lunch usually includes *plats du jour* (daily specials) and, in the smaller cafés, is one of the great Parisian bargains, rarely costing more than 12€ for two courses with wine. The specials are often substantial meat dishes such as *sauté d'agneau* (sautéed lamb) or *blanquette de veau* (veal with

a white sauce), with fruit tarts for dessert. For a simpler lunch, salads, sandwiches and omelettes are usually available at any time of day. One of the best places for this kind of food is **Le Bourdonnec Pascal** in St-Germain-des-Prés. **Le Rostand** by the Luxembourg Gardens is also an excellent place to eat as is **Le Café du Marché** in the Invalides district.

Most museums have reliable cafés, but those at the Pompidou Centre *(see pp110–11)* and the Musée d'Orsay *(see pp144–5)* are especially good. When visiting the Louvre, it is worth waiting till you re-emerge from the galleries and stopping at the upmarket **Café Marly** in front of the glass pyramid for an expensive, yet memorable drink or meal. Should you find yourself in the department store **Galeries Lafayette** *(see p321)*, it's worth going to the café for the fabulous views over Paris.

Cafés in the main tourist and nightlife areas (Boulevard St-Germain, Avenue des Champs-Elysées, Boulevard Montparnasse, the Opéra and Bastille) generally stay open late – some until 2am.

It is important to note that prices change depending on where in the café you choose to enjoy your drink. Standing at the bar with a glass of beer is usually a little cheaper than sitting at one of the tables and heading outside to the terrace will normally cost you more again.

TEA SALONS

Tearooms have become increasingly popular in Paris over the last few years and the selection of teas is normally impressive. Some tea salons also offer light lunches, as well as breakfast and afternoon tea, including **Angélina**, with its Belle Epoque decor. **Mariage Frères** in the Marais is well known for its exhaustive drink list and also sells loose tea and lovely teapots to take home. **Ladurée** on the Champs Elysées is a Parisian institution where well-heeled ladies sip tea and nibble the house speciality macaroons. For another type of tea, visit the mosaic-tiled **Café de la Mosquée**, at Paris's mosque in the Jardin des Plantes area, for sticky pastries and excellent mint tea.

WINE BARS

Most Parisian wine bars are small, convivial neighbourhood places. They open early, many doubling as cafés for breakfast, and offer a small, good-quality lunch menu. It's best to get there early or after 1.30pm if you want to avoid the crowd. Most wine bars are usually closed by 9pm.

Wine bar owners tend to be passionate about wine, most of them buying directly from producers. Young Bordeaux wines and those from the Loire, Rhône and the Jura can be surprisingly good, and wine bar owners usually seek out interesting tipples. The **L'Ecluse** chain specializes in Bordeaux, but for the most part you will find delicious lesser-known wines at very reasonable prices. Serious oenophiles might like to visit wine bars which form part of wine shops so that any interesting vintages tasted can be ordered by the caseload and enjoyed at home. There are several examples of this type of place in Paris – **Juveniles**, **Lavinia** and **Legrand Filles et Fils** in the Opéra district are among the finest. Juveniles is a small shop with a zinc bar run by a Scotsman. The selection is very good, especially for wines from the New World and great food is also served here. Lavinia is Europe's largest wine store, the choice is vast, there are regular tastings and the sleek bar serves many wines by the glass. The climate-controlled fine wines section is also worth a visit. Legrand is an old-fashioned vintner which is extremely popular with Parisian wine buffs. The bar has a lovely selection and knowlegable staff. The most fashionable wine bar of this type is **Wine and Bubbles** in the Beaubourg and Les Halles district. This is a great place to spend a whole evening.

BEER BARS AND PUBS

Paris has both pubs and beer bars. Whereas pubs are simply for drinking, beer bars also serve a particular style of food and are larger. *Moules-frites* (a generous bowl of steamed mussels served with French fries), *tarte aux poireaux* (leek tart) and *tarte aux oignons* (onion tart) are classic examples of the food they serve. The chief reason for going to a beer bar, however, is for the beer. The lists are often vast: some specialize in Belgian *gueuze* (heavy, malty, very alcoholic beer), others have beers from all around the world.

Some beer bars are open from noon, whereas pubs open later in the afternoon. Pubs are usually open every day, often until 1 or 2am. The pubs in Paris have a good mix of expatriate and French clients. Some pubs are also micro-breweries serving beer brewed on the premises. The **Frog and Princess** and the **Frog and Rosbif** are good examples of this type of pub, serving several types of home-brewed beer. The bar staff are very friendly and will happily help you choose the pint that's right for you. Aside from traditionally English pubs such as **The Bombardier** in the Latin Quarter, Paris has

dozens of Irish pubs and a few Scottish pubs. The best Irish pubs include **Coolin** and **Corcoran's** in St-Germain-des-Prés, **Kitty O'Sheas** and **Carrs** in the Tuileries district and **O'Sullivans by the Mill** in Montmartre. A Highland fling and good whisky can be found in the **Highlander** in St-Germain-des-Prés and **The Auld Alliance** in the Marais.

BARS

Being such an elegant city, it's no surprise that Paris has more than its share of cocktail and late-night bars too. Some pretty Paris brasseries, such as **La Coupole**, **La Rotonde** and **La Closerie des Lilas**, have long wooden or zinc bars, accomplished bartenders, a glamorous ambience and a sense of distinguished times past. Hotel bars are some of the loveliest places for cocktails in Paris. **The Hemingway Bar** at the Ritz *(see p286)* is the most famous hotel bar in Paris. It is full of nostalgia, small, intimate, lined with heavy wood and has the official Best Bartender in the World, Colin Peter Field. The cocktails here are wonderful and each drink for a lady comes complete with a fresh flower. Other hotel bars of note include the bar at the hotel Four Seasons George V *(see p290)* where the bartenders will shake your martini at your table and present it in an individual silver shaker, the rooftop terrace at the Hôtel Raphaël *(see p289)* and the fashionable bar at the hotel Plaza Athénée *(see p291)*.

La Mezzanine de l'Alcazar is one of Paris' most fashionable bars, while **Le Rosebud** and the **China Club** are young and trendy. Other hip bars include **Le Fumoir** next to the Louvre with its long elegant bar and excellent cocktails, **Andy Wahloo** which is tiny with a Moroccan design, **De LaVille** café which is popular as a pre-club destination, **Rhubarb** which has a wonderful martini menu and **The Lizard Lounge**, which attracts a noisy, young crowd. The

Philippe Starck designed bar and restaurant **Kong**, on top of the Kenzo store near the Pont Neuf, is currently Paris's trendiest place for drinks.

Bars which are less trendy but great for a relaxing drink include the tiny, stone-clad **Stolly's** in the Marais and **Harry's Bar**, a legendary American bar which claims to have invented the Bloody Mary.

TAKE-AWAY FOOD

Crêpes are the traditional Parisian street food. Although there are fewer good crêpe stands than there used to be, they still exist. Sandwich bars provide *baguettes* with a wide range of fillings, a Parisien – a type of *baguette* – is normally Emmental cheese with ham, Camembert-filled sandwichs tend to be delicious, but beware the misguidingly named *crudités* (salad) which normally includes tuna and mayonnaise along with the *crudités*. The best fast food in Paris is freshly-baked flat *focaccia* bread sprinkled with savoury flavourings. It is sold fresh from a wood-burning oven and filled with one or more fillings of your choice. You can buy it at **Cosi** in Rue de Seine. Busy tourist areas also have their share of *kebab* shops, if this is what appeals.

Ice-cream stands open around noon, and stay open late in summer. It's worth queuing for the city's best ice-cream at **Maison Berthillon**. Seasoned gourmets come from across the city to queue around the block for a scoop or two of their delicious concoctions. Chocoholics will be delighted with their intense cocoa ice-cream, whilst fruit fans can expect sorbets packed with flavour. There are several branches of Berthillon in the city but the Ile St Louis store is recommended: nothing beats strolling along the Seine catching the drips from a divine ice-cream cone. Ice-cream obsessives might also like to head to **Amorino** which makes Italian-style *gelati*. Don't miss the *amaretto gelato* which comes sprinkled with crushed *amaretti* biscuits.

DIRECTORY

ILE DE LA CITÉ AND ILE ST-LOUIS

WINE BARS
Jazz Club de l'Ile Saint-Louis
1 Quai de Bourbon 75004.
Map 13 C4.

TEA SALONS
Le Flore en l'Isle
42 Quai d'Orléans 75004.
Map 13 B4.

ICE-CREAM PARLOURS
Amorino
47 Rue St-Louis-en-l'Ile 75004.
Map 13 C4.

Maison Berthillon
31 Rue St-Louis-en-l'Ile 75004. **Map** 13 C4.

TUILERIES QUARTER

CAFÉS
Café Marly
93 Rue de Rivoli
Cour Napoleon du Louvre 75001.
Map 12 F1.

WINE BARS
La Cloche des Halles
28 Rue Coquillière 75001.
Map 12 E2.

Juveniles
47 Rue de Richelieu 75001.
Map 12 E1.

TEA SALONS
Angélina
226 Rue de Rivoli 75001.
Map 12 D1.

Ladurée
16 Rue Royale 75008.
Map 5 C5.

PUBS
Carrs
1 Rue Mont Thabor 75001.
Map 12 D1.

Kitty O'Sheas
10 Rue des Capucines 75002.
Map 6 D5.

BARS
Bars du Ritz
15 Pl Vendôme 75001.
Map 6 D5.

Le Comptoir
37 Rue Berger 75001.
Map 12 F2.

Le Fumoir
6 Rue de l'Amiral-de-Coligny 75001.
Map 12 F2.

Harry's Bar
5 Rue Danou 75002.
Map 6 E5.

THE MARAIS

CAFÉS
Au Petit Fer à Cheval
30 Rue Vielle du Temple 75004. **Map** 13 C3

L'Etoile Manquante
34 Rue Vieille du Temple 75004. **Map** 13 C3.

Feria Café
4 Rue du Bourg Tibourg 75004. **Map** 13 C3.

Ma Bourgogne
19 Pl des Vosges 75004.
Map 14 D3.

Le Trésor
5 Rue du Trésor 75004.
Map 13 C3.

TEA SALONS
Le Loir dans la Théière
3 Rue des Rosiers 75004.
Map 13 C3.

Mariage Frères
30–32 Rue du Bourg-Tibourg 75004.
Map 13 C3.

BEER BARS
Café des Musées
49 Rue de Turenne 75003.
Map 14 D3.

WINE BARS
La Belle Hortense
31 Rue Vieille du Temple 75004. **Map** 13 C3.

Le Coude Fou
12 Rue du Bourg-Tibourg 75004.
Map 13 C3.

Le Passage des Carmagnoles
18 Passage de la Bonne-Graine 75011.
Map 14 F4.

PUBS
The Auld Alliance
80 Rue François Miron 75004.
Map 13 C3.

BARS
L'Apparement Café
18 Rue des Coutures St-Gervais 75004.
Map 14 D2.

Chez Richard
37 Rue Vieille du Temple 75004.
Map 13 C3.

China Club
50 Rue de Charenton 75012. **Map** 14 F5.

Le Connetable
55 Rue des Archives 75004.
Map 13 C2.

Les Etages
35 Rue Vieille du Temple 75004.
Map 13 C3.

The Lizard Lounge
18 Rue du Bourg-Tibourg 75004. **Map** 13 C3.

Les Philosophes
28 Rue Vieille du Temple 75004.
Map 13 C3.

Stolly's
16 Rue Cloche Perce 75004. **Map** 13 C3.

BEAUBOURG AND LES HALLES

CAFÉS
Bistrot d'Eustache
(See p109).

Café Beaubourg
100 Rue St Martin 75004.
Map 13 B2.
(See p108).

WINE BARS
Wine and Bubbles
3 Rue Français 75001.
Map 13 A1.

PUBS
Flann O'Brien
6 Rue Bailleul 75001.
Map 12 F2.

Frog and Rosbif
116 Rue Saint-Denis 75001. **Map** 13 B1.

BARS
Andy Wahloo
69 Rue des Gravilliers 75003.
Map 13 B1.

Kong
1 Rue Pont Neuf 75001.
Map 13 A2.

ST-GERMAIN-DES-PRÉS

CAFÉS
Le Bourdonnec Pascal
75 Rue de Seine 75006.
Map 12 E4.

Café de Flore
(See p139).

Café de la Mairie
8 Place St-Sulpice 75006.
Map 12 E4.

Les Deux Magots
(See p138).

La Palette
43 Rue de Seine 75006.
Map 12 E4.

SANDWICH BARS
Cosi
54 Rue de Seine 75006.
Map 12 E4.

WINE BARS
Au Sauvignon
80 Rue des Sts-Pères 75007.
Map 12 D4.

Bistro des Augustins
39 Quai des Grands-Augustins 75006.
Map 12 F4.

PUBS
Coolin
15 Rue Clément 75006.
Map 12 E4.

Corcoran's
28 Rue Saint-André des Arts 75006.
Map 12 F4.

Frog and Princess
9 Rue Princesse 75006.
Map 12 E4.

Highlander
8 Rue de Nevers 75006.
Map 12 F3.

The Moosehead
16 Rue des Quatre-Vents 75006.
Map 12 F4.

BARS
Le Bar Dix
10 Rue de l'Odéon 75006.
Map 12 F4.

Birdland
8 Rue Guisarde 75006. **Map** 12 E4.

DIRECTORY

Café Mabillion
164 Blvd St-Germain 75006.
Map 12 E4.

Don Carlos
66 Rue Mazarine 75006.
Map 12 F4.

Fu Bar
5 Rue St Sulpice 75006.
Map 12 F4.

La Mezzanine de l'Alcazar
62 Rue Mazarine 75006.
Map 12 F4.

Zéro de Conduite
14 Rue Jacob 75006.
Map 12 E3.

LATIN QUARTER

CAFÉS
Panis
21 Quai Montebello 75005.
Map 13 A4.

WINE BARS
Les Pipos
2 Rue de l'Ecole Polytechnique 75005.
Map 13 A5.

BEER BARS
La Gueuze
19 Rue Soufflot 75005.
Map 12 F5.

PUBS
The Bombardier
2 Place du Panthéon 75005.
Map 17 A1.

BARS
Le Caveau des Oubliettes
52 Rue Galande 75005.
Map 13 A4.

Rhubarb
8 Rue Laplace 75005.
Map 13 A5.

JARDIN DES PLANTES

CAFÉS
Café Egyptien
112 Rue Mouffetard 75005.
Map 17 B2.

TEA SALONS
Café de la Mosquée
39 Rue Geoffroy St-Hilaire 75005.
Map 17 C2.

PUBS
Finnegan's
9 Rue des Boulangers 75005.
Map 17 B1.

ICE-CREAM PARLOURS
Häagen-Dazs
3 Pl de la Contrescarpe 75005.
Map 17 A1.

LUXEMBOURG QUARTER

CAFÉS
Au Petit Suisse
16 Rue de Vaugirard 75006.
Map 21 F5.

Le Rostand
6 Place Edmond Rostand 75006.
Map 12 F5.

BEER BARS
L'Académie de la Bière
88 Blvd de Port-Royal 75005. **Map** 17 B3.

MONTPARNASSE

CAFÉS
Café de la Place
23 Rue d'Odessa 75014.
Map 15 C2.

La Rotonde
7 Pl 25 Août 1944 75014.
Map 16 D2.

Le Sélect Montparnasse
99 Blvd du Montparnasse 75006.
Map 16 D2.

WINE BARS
Le Rallye
6 Rue Daguerre 75014.
Map 16 D4.

TEA SALONS
Max Poilâne
29 Rue de l'Ouest 75014.
Map 15 C3.

BARS
La Closerie des Lilas
171 Blvd du Montparnasse 75014.
Map 16 D2.

La Coupole (Café Bar)
102 Blvd du Montparnasse 75014.
Map 16 D2.
(See p178).

Cubana Café
45 Rue Vavin 75006.
Map 12 F5.

Le Rosebud
11 bis Rue Delambre 75014.
Map 16 D2.

INVALIDES AND EIFFEL TOWER QUARTER

CAFÉS
Café Constant
139 Rue St-Dominique 75007.
Map 11 B2.

PUBS
O'Brien's
77 Rue Saint-Dominique 75007.
Map 10 F3.

BARS
Café Thoumieux
4 Rue de la Comète 75007.
Map 11 A3.

CHAMPS-ELYSÉES

WINE BARS
L'Ecluse
64 Rue François Premier 75008.
Map 4 F5.

Ma Bourgogne
133 Blvd Haussmann 75008.
Map 5 B4.

TEA SALONS
Ladurée
75 Ave des Champs-Elysées 75008.
Map 4 F5.

BARS
Le Bar du Plaza at the Plaza Athénée
(See p291).

Hôtel Raphaël
(See p289).

Le V at Four Seasons George V
(See p290).

OPÉRA QUARTER

CAFÉS
Café de la Paix
12 Blvd des Capucines 75009. **Map** 6 E5.
(See p213).

WINE BARS
Bistro du Sommelier
97 Blvd Haussmann 75008.
Map 5 C4.

Lavinia
3-5 Blvd de la Madeleine 75008.
Map 6 D5.

Legrand Filles et Fils
1 Rue de la Banque 75002.
Map 12 F1.
Tel 01 42 60 07 12.

MONTMARTRE

CAFÉS
Le Saint Jean
16 Place des Abbesses 75018.
Map 6 F1.

Le Sancerre
35 Rue des Abbesses 75018.
Map 6 E1.

PUBS
O'Sullivans by the Mill
92 Blvd de Clichy 75018.
Map 6 E21.

FURTHER AFIELD

WINE BARS
Le Verre Volé
67 Rue de Lancry 75010.
Map 8 D4.

BARS
L'Autre Café
62 Rue Jean-Pierre Timbaud 75011.
Map 8 F5.

Café Charbon
109 Rue Oberkampf 75011. **Map** 14 E1.

Chez Prune
36 Rue Beaurepaire 75010. **Map** 8 D4.

Pause Café
41 Rue de Charonne 75011.
Map 14 F4.

SHOPS AND MARKETS

Paris seems to be the very definition of luxury and good living. Beautifully dressed people sip wine by the banks of the Seine against a backdrop of splendid architecture, or hurry down gallery-lined streets carrying parcels from specialist shops. The least expensive way of joining the chic set is to create French style with accessories or costume jewellery.

Alternatively, splash out on the fashion, or the wonderful food and related items from kitchen gadgets to tableware. Remember too that Parisian shops and markets are the ideal place to indulge in the French custom of strolling through the streets, seeing and being seen. For high fashion there's the exquisite *couture* house window displays on Avenue Montaigne or browse around the bookstalls along the Seine. A survey of some of the most famous places to shop follows.

OPENING HOURS

Shops are usually open from 10am to 7pm, Monday to Saturday, but hours can vary. Many department stores stay open late on Thursday, while boutiques may shut for an hour or two at midday. Markets and local neighbourhood shops close on Mondays. Some places shut for the summer, usually in August, but they may leave a note on the door suggesting an open equivalent nearby.

HOW TO PAY

Cash is readily available from the ATMs in most banks, which accept both credit and bank debit cards. Visa and MasterCard are the most widely accepted credit cards.

VAT EXEMPTION

A sales tax (TVA) from 5.5–19.6 per cent is imposed on most goods and services in EU countries. Non-EU residents shopping in France are entitled to a refund of this if they spend a minimum of 175€ in one shop in one day. You must have been resident in France for less than six months and either carry the goods with you out of the country within three months of purchase or get the shop to forward them to you. If shopping in a group, you can usually buy goods together in order to reach the minimum.

Larger shops will generally supply a form (*bordereau de détaxe or bordereau de vente*) and help you to fill it in. When you leave France or the EU you present the form to Customs, who either permit you to be reimbursed straight away, or forward your claim to the place where you bought the merchandise; the shop eventually sends you a refund. If you know someone in Paris it may be quicker if they can pick up the refund for you at the

Shopping in Avenue Montaigne

shop. Alternatively at large airports such as Orly and Roissy some banks may have the facilities to refund you on the spot. Though the process involves a lot of paperwork, it can be worth it. There is no refund on food, drink, tobacco, cars and motorbikes. Bicycles, however, can be reimbursed.

SALES

The best sales (*soldes*) are held in January and July, although you can sometimes find sale items before Christmas. If you see goods labelled *Stock*, it means that they are stock items. *Dégriffé* means designer labels marked down, frequently from the previous year's collections. *Fripes* indicates that the clothes are second-hand. The sales tend to occupy prime floor space for the first month and are then relegated to the back of the store.

Au Printemps, the grand dame of Parisian department stores

DEPARTMENT STORES

Much of the pleasure of shopping in Paris is derived from going to the small specialist shops. But if time is short, try the *grands magasins* (department stores). Some still operate a ticket system for selling goods. The shop assistant writes up a ticket for goods from their own boutique which you take to one of the cashiers. You then return with your validated ticket to pick up your purchase. This can be time-consuming, so go early in the morning and don't shop on Saturdays. The French don't pay much attention to queues, so be assertive! One peculiarity of a visit is that the security guards may ask to inspect your bags as you leave. These are random checks and should not be taken as an implication of theft.

Though department stores have different emphases, all have places to eat. **Au Printemps** is noted for its exciting and innovative household goods section, and large menswear store. The clothes departments for women and children are well-stocked. The lovely domed restaurant in the cupola often hosts chic after-hours parties;

Apolonia Poilâne's bread bears her trademark "P" (see pp333–5)

Kenzo designerwear in the Place des Victoires (see pp324–25)

Snails from the *charcuterie*

these are private, but do visit the restaurant during shopping hours.

BHV (Le Bazar de l'Hôtel de Ville) is a DIY enthusiast's paradise. It also sells a host of other items related to home decor. The Left Bank **Le Bon Marché** was Paris's first department store and today is its chicest. The designer clothing sections are well-sourced, the high-end accessories are excellent and the own-brand linen has a good quality to price ratio. The prepared food sections serve restaurant quality fare to take away.

Galeries Lafayette is perhaps the best-known department store and has a wide range of clothes available at all price levels. Its first-floor trends section plays host to lots of innovative designers. Having taken over the old Marks & Spencer, Galeries Lafayette also boasts a wonderful food hall, Lafayette Gourmet, which offers a vast array of mouthwatering goodies.

Virgin Megastore is open until late and has an excellent record selection and an impressive book section. **FNAC** sells records, books (foreign editions can be found at Les Halles) and electronic equipment. The branch on the Champs-Elysées specializes in music, videos and DVDs and concert tickets. **FNAC Digitale** sells a wide range of the latest technological equipment.

ADDRESSES

Au Printemps
64 Blvd Haussman 75009.
Map 6 D4. **Tel** 01 42 82 50 00.

BHV
52–64 Rue de Rivoli 75004.
Map 13 B3. **Tel** 01 42 74 90 00.

Le Bon Marché
24 Rue de Sèvres 75007.
Map 11 C5. **Tel** 01 44 39 80 00.

Bookstall, Vanves market (see p339)

FNAC
Forum des Halles, 1 Rue Pierre Lescot 75001. **Map** 13 A2.
Tel 01 40 41 40 00.
74 Ave des Champs-Elysées 75008.
Map 4 F5. **Tel** 01 53 53 64 64.

FNAC Digitale
77–81 Blvd St-Germain 75006.
Map 13 A5. **Tel** 01 53 10 44 44.

Galeries Lafayette
40 Blvd Haussmann 75009.
Map 6 E4. **Tel** 01 42 82 34 56.

Virgin Megastore
52–60 Ave des Champs-Elysées 75008. **Map** 4 F5.
Tel 01 49 53 50 00.

Paris's Best: Shops and Markets

Old-fashioned and conservative yet full of surprises, Paris is a treasure trove of quality shops and boutiques. Time-honoured emporia mix with modern precincts in a city that buzzes with life in its inner quarters, not least in the markets. Here you can buy everything from exotic fruit and vegetables to fine china and antiques. Whether you're shopping for handmade shoes, perfectly-cut clothes or traditionally-made cheeses, or simply soaking in the atmosphere, you won't be disappointed.

Place de la Madeleine
Top-class groceries and delicacies are sold on the north side of this square.
(See p214.)

THE CENTRE OF PARIS COUTURE

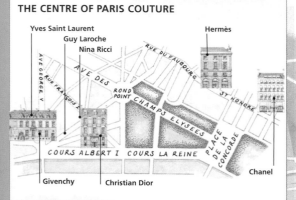

Yves Saint Laurent
Guy Laroche
Nina Ricci
Hermès
Givenchy
Christian Dior
Chanel

Chanel
Coco Chanel (1883–1971) reigned over the fashion world from No. 31 Rue Cambon. The main boutique is in the Avenue Montaigne. (See p325.)

See inset map

Champs-Elysées

R I V E R

Invalides and Eiffel Tower Quarter

Rue de Rivoli
Inexpensive mementos like this Paris snow shaker can be found in the shops on the Rue de Rivoli. (See p130.)

Marché de la Porte de Vanves
This charming and relaxed market sells old books, linen, postcards, china and musical instruments. (weekends only – see p339.)

Kenzo
The Japanese designer has colourful apparel for men, women and children in his clothes shops. (See p327.)

Cartier
The early Cartier jewellery designs with their beautifully-cut stones are still highly sought after. This shop in the Rue de la Paix sells all the Cartier lines. (See p329.)

Rue de Paradis
You can buy porcelain and crystal at reduced prices at the company showrooms on this street. Look out for Porcelainor, Baccarat and Lumicristal. (See pp330–2.)

Passage des Panoramas
This once-prosperous arcade at Les Galeries has an old engraving house. (See p216.)

Opéra Quarter

0 kilometres 1

0 miles 0.5

Tuileries Quarter

Beaubourg and Les Halles

The Marais

S E I N E

St-Germain-des-Prés

Ile de la Cité

Ile St-Louis

Latin Quarter

Rue des Francs-Bourgeois
Stylish fashion stores such as A-Poc (see pp324–5) line this thoroughfare in the Marais.

Luxembourg Quarter

Jardin des Plantes Quarter

Montparnasse

St Marcellin
06 F 80

Rue Mouffetard
The market sells cheeses and other quality foods. (See p339.)

Forum des Halles
This modern glass arcade has many shops. (See p109.)

Clothes and Accessories

For many people Paris is synonymous with fashion and Parisian style is the ultimate in chic. More than anywhere else in the world, women in Paris seem to be in tune with current trends and when a new season arrives appear, as one, to don the look. Though less trend-conscious generally, Parisian men are aware of style and mix and match patterns and colours with élan. Finding the right clothes at the right price means knowing where to shop. For every luxury boutique on the Avenue Montaigne, there are ten young designers' shops waiting to become the next Jean-Paul Gaultier – and hundreds more selling imitations.

HAUTE COUTURE

Paris is the home of *haute couture*. The original *couture* garments, as opposed to the imitations and adaptations, are one-off creations, designed by one of the nine *haute couture* houses listed with the Fédération Française de la Couture. The rules for being classified are fairly strict, and many of the top designers are not included. Astronomical prices put *haute couture* beyond the reach of all but a few immensely deep pockets, but it's still the lifeblood of the fashion industry providing inspiration for the mass market.

The fashion seasons are launched with the *couture* shows in January and July. Most shows are held in the Carrousel du Louvre *(see p123)*. If you want to see a show, you stand a much better chance of getting a seat at the private *couture* shows (the main shows are for buyers and the press). To do this call the press offices of the *haute couture* houses a month in advance. You can only be sure you have a place when you receive the ticket. For the private shows, telephone the fashion house or, if you're in Paris, try going to the boutique and asking if there's a show – and do remember to dress the part.

Most *couture* houses make *prêt-à-porter* clothes as well – ready-to-wear clothes fitted on a standard model. They're still not cheap, but give you an idea of some of the designer elegance and creativity at a fraction of the cost.

WOMEN'S CLOTHES

The highest concentration of *couture* houses is on the Right Bank. Most are on or near the Rue du Faubourg-St-Honoré and the classier Avenue Montaigne: **Christian Dior**, **Pierre Cardin**, **Chanel**, **Christian Lacroix**, **Marcel Marongiu**, **Givenchy**, **Louis Féraud**, **Nina Ricci** and **Yves Saint Laurent**. This is where you will rub shoulders with the rich and famous.

Hermès has classic country chic. **MaxMara's** Italian elegance is quite popular in France and no one can resist a **Giorgio Armani** suit. **Karl Lagerfeld** has a shop where the latest creations from his own line, Lagerfeld Gallery, are exhibited.

The theatrical **Paco Rabanne** has also stuck to the Right Bank, but many other fine fashion houses prefer the Left Bank. Try **Sonia Rykiel** for knitwear, **Junko Shimada** for sporty casuals and **Barbara Bui** for soft, feminine clothes.

Many designers have a Left Bank branch in addition to their Right Bank bastions, and they all have ready-to-wear shops here. For sheer quality there's **Georges Rech**, but don't forget Yves Saint Laurent or **Jil Sander** for their exquisite tailoring. Try Armani's St-Germain temple of fashion, or Prada's affordable boutique, **Miu Miu**, in the Rue de Grenelle. Onward Kashiyama France has its cult following for some imaginative clothes, and **Irié** is the place for reasonably-priced clothes which are trendy but will

stand the test of time. Also in the Saint-Germain-des-Près district, the **Comptoir des Cotonniers** stocks excellent basics, **Maje** has everything from boho chic to stylish cuts, and **Vanessa Bruno** is extremely popular for feminine flair. Quirky looks can be found at **Corinne Sarut**, who has a growing following amongst French fashionistas.

Ready-to-wear shops blanket Paris, and in the beautiful Place des Victoires they thrive off shoppers visiting the Rue du Faubourg-St-Honoré. The **Victoire** boutique offers one of the best collections of current designer labels with Michael Klein, Helmut Lang and Thierry Mugler among many others. **Kenzo** is here (although a new flagship store now exists near the Pont Neuf), along with fellow Japanese designers **Comme des Garçons**, with its avant-garde, quirky fashion for both sexes, and **Yohji Yamamoto** just down the street, near Ventilo. The nearby Rue Jean-Jacques-Rousseau has now become one of the city's prime shopping stops.

Moving east to the Rue du Jour, **Agnès B** and **Claudie Pierlot's** clothes have timeless elegance. There are also many shops selling inexpensive copies of new designs in the centre. **Martin Margiela** carries excellent quality basics with a twist.

The Marais is a haven for up-and-coming designers and is always busy on Saturdays. One of the best streets is the Rue des Rosiers, which includes Issey Miyake's **Pleats Please**, **L'Eclaireur** and a branch of **Tehen** for clothes. **Nina Jacob** is on the neighbouring Rue des Francs-Bourgeois, and daring designer **Azzedine Alaïa's** shop is just around the corner. **Plein Sud** stocks sexy creations, **A-Poc** is an offshoot of Issey Miyake and has daring designs.

The Bastille area has trendy boutiques, as well as some more established names.

DIRECTORY

WOMEN'S CLOTHES

Agnès B
2–3–6–19 Rue du Jour 75001. **Map** 13 A1.
Tel 01 45 08 56 56.
One of several branches.

A-Poc
47 Rue des Francs-Bourgeois 75006.
Map 14 D3.
Tel 01 44 54 07 05

Azzedine Alaïa
7 Rue de Moussy 75004.
Map 13 C3.
Tel 01 42 72 19 19.

Barbara Bui
23 Rue Etienne-Marcel 75001. **Map** 13 A1.
Tel 01 40 26 43 65.
www.barbarabui.com
One of two branches.

Chanel
42 Ave Montaigne 75008.
Map 5 A5.
Tel 01 47 23 47 12.
www.chanel.com
One of several branches.

Christian Dior
30 Ave Montaigne 75008.
Map 10 F1.
Tel 01 40 73 73 73.
www.doir.com

Christian Lacroix
73 Rue du Faubourg-St-Honoré 75008.
Map 5 B5.
Tel 01 42 68 79 00.
www.christian-lacroix.com

Claudie Pierlot
1 Rue Montmartre 75001.
Map 13 A1.
Tel 01 42 21 38 38.
www.claudie-pierlot.com
One of three branches.

Colette
213 Rue St-Honoré 75001.
Map 12 D1.
Tel 01 55 35 33 90.
www.colette.fr

Comme des Garçons
54 Rue du Faubourg St-Honoré 75008.
Map 4 E3.
Tel 01 53 30 27 27.

Comptoir des Cotonniers
59 Rue Bonaparte 75006.
Map 12 E3.
Tel 01 43 26 07 56.

Corrine Sarut
4 Rue Pré aux Clercs 75007.
Map 12 D3.
Tel 01 42 61 71 60.

L'Eclaireur
3 ter Rue des Rosiers 75004. **Map** 13 C3.
Tel 01 48 87 10 22.

Eres
2 Rue Tronchet 75008.
Map 5 C5.
Tel 01 47 42 28 82.
One of two branches.

Gaëlle Barré
17 Rue Keller 75011.
Map 14 F4.
Tel 01 43 14 63 02.

Georges Rech
54 Rue Bonaparte 75006.
Map 12 E3.
Tel 01 43 26 84 11.
www.georges-rech.fr
One of several branches.

Giorgio Armani
6 Pl Vendôme 75001.
Map 6 D5.
Tel 01 42 61 55 09
www.giorgioarmani.com

Givenchy
3 Ave Georges V 75008.
Map 4 E5.
Tel 01 44 31 50 00.
www.givenchy.com

Hennes
15 Rue Commerce 75015.
Map 10 E5.
Tel 01 40 57 24 60.
One of several branches.

Hermès
24 Rue du Faubourg-St-Honoré 75008.
Map 5 C5.
Tel 01 40 17 47 17.
www.hermes.com
One of several branches.

Irié
8 Rue du Pré-aux-Clercs 75007. **Map** 12 D3.
Tel 01 42 61 18 28.

Isabel Marant
16 Rue de Charonne 75011. **Map** 14 F4.
Tel 01 49 29 71 55.

Jean-Paul Gaultier
6 Rue Vivienne 75002.
Map 12 F1.
Tel 01 42 86 05 05.
One of several branches.

Jil Sander
52 Ave Montaigne 75008.
Map 10 F1.
Tel 01 44 95 06 70.

Junko Shimada
13 Rue St-Florentin 75008.
Map 11 C1.
Tel 01 42 60 94 12.
One of two branches.

Kenzo
3 Pl des Victoires 75001.
Map 12 F1.
Tel 01 40 39 72 00.
One of several branches.

Kookaï
82 Rue Reaumur 75002.
Map 13 B1.
Tel 01 45 08 93 69.
One of several branches.

LA City
141 Rue de Rennes 75006.
Map 16 D1.
Tel 01 45 44 71 18.
One of several branches.

Lolita Lempicka
46 Ave Victor Hugo 75016. **Map** 3C5.
Tel 01 45 02 14 46.

Louis Féraud
2 Place Porte Maillot 75017. **Map** 3 B3.
Tel 01 40 68 21 34.

Mac Douglas
9 Rue de Sèvres 75006.
Map 12 D4.
Tel 01 45 48 14 09.
One of several branches.

Maje
42 Rue du Four 75006.
Map 12 E4.
Tel 01 42 22 43 69.

Marcel Marongiu
203 Rue St-Honoré 75001.
Map 13 A2.
Tel 01 49 27 96 38.

Martin Margiela
25 Rue de Montpensier 75001. **Map** 12 E1.
Tel 01 40 15 07 55.

MaxMara
37 Rue du Four 75006.
Map 12 D4.
Tel 01 43 29 91 10.
One of several branches.

Miu Miu
16 Rue de Grenelle 75007.
Map 12 D4.
Tel 01 53 63 20 30.
www.miumiu.com

Morgan
165 Rue de Rennes 75006.
Map 16 D1.
Tel 01 45 48 96 77.
One of several branches.

Nina Jacob
23 Rue des Francs-Bourgeois 75004.
Map 14 D3.
Tel 01 42 77 41 20.

Nina Ricci
39 Ave Montaigne 75008.
Map 10 F1.
Tel 01 40 88 67 60.
www.ninaricci.fr

Onward Kashiyama France
147 Blvd St-Germain 75006. **Map** 12 E4.
Tel 01 55 42 77 55.

Paco Rabanne
Lobato, 6 Rue Malher 75004. **Map** 13 C3.
Tel 01 48 87 68 14.

Pierre Cardin
27 Ave de Marigny 75008.
Map 5 B5.
Tel 01 42 66 68 98.
www.pierrecardin.com
One of two branches.

Pleats Please
3 bis Rue des Rosiers 75004. **Map** 13C3.
Tel 01 40 29 99 66.
One of several branches.

Plein Sud
2 Rue Vide Gousset 75002.
Map 12 F1.
Tel 01 42 36 75 02.

Promod
60 Rue Caumartin 75009.
Map 6 D4.
Tel 01 45 26 01 11.
One of several branches.

Ragtime
23 Rue de l'Echaudé 75006. **Map** 12 E4.
Tel 01 56 24 00 36.

Sinequanone
16 Rue Four 75006.
Map 12 E4.
Tel 01 56 24 27 74.
One of several branches.

Designer **Jean-Paul Gaultier** has a boutique in the Rue du Faubourg St-Antoine. His "senior" and "junior" collections reflect price and attitude. **Isabel Marant's** boutique is renowned for its originality, and **Gaëlle Barré** is a stylist with a fast-growing reputation. The swimsuit store is **Eres**, while for leather, it's **Mac Douglas**.

Young designers' clothes are found at **Colette**, **Stella Cadente** and **Zadig &Voltaire**, while **Zucca** now has several boutiques. For fabulous, if somewhat pricey, clothes from the 1920s to the 1950s, try **Ragtime**.

Not all Parisians have pocketbooks that allow them to shop on the Avenue Montaigne, but those on smaller budgets still manage to look chic in clothes from high street stores. There are many large chain stores here which have branches in other European cities. Chain stores tend to stock each store differently, depending on the desires and buying patterns of the local clientele. Because of this it is possible to find quintessentially French fashion in large chains such as **Zara**, particularly at the branches in Passy and near the Opera.

Mighty Swedish retailer **Hennes** has an exciting concept store for young fashion in Paris's 15th arrondissement and stocks designs by Karl Lagerfeld in some of its larger shops. French high street stores are also numerous. Well-known names such as **Kookaï** and **Morgan** stock fresh and funky items. **Sinéquanone** and **LA City**, on the other hand, are rather classic in their designs, while **Promod** is a very cheap store for fun merchandise.

CHILDREN'S CLOTHES

Lots of options for children exist in various styles and many price ranges. Many top designers of adult clothes also have boutiques for children. These include **Kenzo**, **Baby Dior**, **Agnès B**, **Sonia Rykiel** and **Teddy's**. Ready-to-wear shops such

as **Jacadi** and **Du Pareil au Même** are serviceable and wide-ranging, while **Tartine et Chocolat's** best-selling garments are overalls. **Bonpoint** stocks adorably chic clothing for mini-Parisians. **Petit Bateau** is coveted as much by grown-ups as it is by children. The inevitable has finally happened – children now have their own concept store in **Bonton**.

For little feet, **Froment-Leroyer** probably offers the best all-round classics. **Six Pieds Trois Pouces** has a vast choice of styles.

MEN'S CLOTHES

Men don't have the luxury of *haute couture* dressing and their choice is limited to ready-to-wear. Still, some men's clothes, mostly by womens-wear designers, can be very expensive.

On the Right Bank, there's **Giorgio Armani**, **Pierre Cardin**, **Kenzo**, **Lanvin** (also good for accessories) and **Yves Saint Laurent**. On the Left Bank, **Michel Axael** and **Jean-Charles de Castelbajac** are known for their ties and **Francesco Smalto's** elegant creations are worn by some of the world's leading movie stars. **Yohji Yamamoto's** clothes are for those who are intent on making a serious fashion statement, while **Gianni Versace** is classic, suave and Italian in style. **APC**, **Paul Smith** and **Ron Orb** garments are rather more contemporary, and **Olivier Strelli**, **Polo by Ralph Lauren** and **Loft Design By** are chic without being overtly trendy, and thus are likely to have a longer shelf-life.

The ultimate in Parisian elegance for men is a suit, custom-made shirt or silk tie from **Charvet**. A trip to the **Place Vendôme** store is a pleasure in itself. Be sure to ask the charming and friendly staff for a tour around their atelier for an insight into how such exquisite creations are crafted. **Madelios** is a great shopping mall for men which mixes designer and high-street brands.

LIFESTYLE STORES

Since **Colette** first burst on to the Parisian shopping scene six years ago, the fad for lifestyle shops has shown no sign of slowing down. Concept stores tend to be high-end affairs crammed with designer labels, some obscure, some household names, all grouped together to kit you out with everything you could possibly need. From fashionable books to shoes, beauty products, household goods, music and furniture via designer mineral water, handbags, trainers and evening gowns, the one-stop shopping experience provides the ultimate in retail therapy.

Spree in Montmartre mixes fashion, art and design so that you can buy a great outfit and some interesting art at the same time, whilst **View on Fashion** in the Bastille focuses on designer street wear. **Gravity Zero** brings music, photography and fashion together over three floors.

VINTAGE AND SECOND-HAND STORES

The vintage craze hit Paris some time back and there are some wonderful shops to plunder for a retro look. The best of the bunch is **Didier Ludot**, where an Alladin's Cave of chic *haute couture* is elegantly displayed. From vintage Courrèges dresses to excellent condition Chanel suits, this is the place for top of the range retro. The **Depôt-Vente de Buci-Bourbon** is another good place to bargain hunt. A cheaper option and a way to access more recent looks is to head for one of the many second-hand or consignment stores in the city. Chic Parisians discard their outfits with the seasons so it is very easy to pick up some quality items which are normally in top condition from places such as **Réciproque** in Passy or **Alternatives** in the Marais. Sample pieces, sale stock and last season's collection pieces can be found at **Le Mouton à Cinq Pattes**.

DIRECTORY

Sonia Rykiel
175 Blvd St-Germain
75006. **Map** 12 D4.
Tel 01 49 54 60 60.
One of several branches.

Stella Cadente
4 Quai des Célestins
75004. **Map** 13 C4.
Tel 01 44 78 05 95.
www.stella-cadente.com

Vanessa Bruno
25 Rue St-Sulpice 75006.
Map 12 E5.
Tel 01 43 54 41 04.

Ventilo
27 bis Rue du Louvre
75002. **Map** 12 F2.
Tel 01 44 76 83 00.
One of six branches.

Victoire
2 Rue du Mail 75002.
Map 12 F1.
Tel 01 42 96 46 76.
One of several branches.

Yohji Yamamoto
25 Rue du Louvre 75001.
Map 12 F1.
Tel 01 42 21 42 93.

Yves Saint Laurent
38 Rue du Faubourg-St-
Honoré 75008. **Map** 5 C5.
Tel 01 42 65 74 59.
One of several branches.

Zadig & Voltaire
9 Rue du 29 Juillet 75001.
Map 12 D1.
Tel 01 42 92 00 80.

Zara
53 Rue Passy 75016.
Map 9 B3.
Tel 01 45 25 07 00.
One of several branches.

Zucca
8 Rue St-Roch 75001.
Map 12 E1.
Tel 01 44 58 98 88.

CHILDREN'S CLOTHES

Agnès B
(See p325).

Baby Dior
(See p325 Christian Dior).

Bonpoint
320 Rue St-Honoré 75001.
Map 13 A2.
Tel 01 49 27 94 82.
www.bonpoint.com
One of several branches.

Bonton
82 rue de Grenelle 75007.
Map 10 F3.
Tel 01 44 39 09 20.

Du Pareil au Même
1 Rue St-Denis 75001.
Map 13 A3.
Tel 01 42 36 07 57.

Froment-Leroyer
7 Rue Vavin 75006.
Map 16 E1.
Tel 01 43 54 33 15.
www.froment-leroyer.fr
One of several branches.

Jacadi
17 Rue Tronchet 75008.
Map 5 C5.
Tel 01 42 65 84 98.
www.jacadi.fr

Kenzo
(See p325).

Petit Bateau
116 Ave des Champs
Elysées 75008.
Map 4 E4.
Tel 01 40 74 02 03.

**Six Pieds Trois
Pouces**
78 Ave de Wagram
75017. **Map** 4 E2.
Tel 01 46 22 81 64.
One of several branches.

Tartine et Chocolat
105 Rue du Faubourg-St-
Honoré 75008. **Map** 5 B5.
Tel 01 45 62 44 04.

Teddy's
38 Rue François-1er
75008. **Map** 10 F1.
Tel 01 47 20 79 79.

MEN'S CLOTHES

APC
45 Rue Madame 75006.
Map 12 E5.
Tel 01 45 48 43 71.

Celio
26 Rue du Faubourg St-
Antoine 75012. **Map** 14
E4. *Tel* 01 43 42 31 68.

Charvet
28 Place Vendôme 75001.
Map 6 D5.
Tel 01 42 60 30 70.

Francesco Smalto
44 Rue François-1er
75008. **Map** 4 F5.
Tel 01 47 20 96 04.
www.smalto.com

**Jean-Charles de
Castelbajac**
10 Rue de Vauvilliers
75001.
Tel 01 55 34 10 10.
www.jedecastelbajac.com

Gianni Versace
62 Rue du Faubourg
St-Honoré 75008.
Map 5 C5.
Tel 01 47 42 88 02.
www.versace.com

Giorgio Armani
(See p325).

Kenzo
(See p325).

Lanvin
15 Rue du Faubourg
St-Honoré 75008.
Map 14 F4.
Tel 01 44 71 31 33.
www.lanvin.com
One of several branches.

Loft Design By
175 Blvd Pereire 75017.
Map 3 C3.
Tel 01 46 22 44 20.
One of several branches.

Michel Axael
121 Blvd St-Germain
75006.
Map 12 E4.
Tel 01 43 26 01 96.

Olivier Strelli
7 Blvd Raspail 75007.
Map 12 D4.
Tel 01 45 44 62 21.
www.strelli.be
One of two branches.

Paul Smith
22 Blvd Raspail 75007.
Map 12 D4.
Tel 01 42 84 15 30.

Pierre Cardin
(See p325).

Ron Orb
147 Rue Temple 75003.
Map 13 B2.
Tel 01 40 28 09 33.

Yohji Yamamoto
47 Rue Etienne
Marcel 75001.
Tel 01 45 08 82 45.

Yves Saint Laurent
12 Pl St-Sulpice 75006.
Map 12 D4.
Tel 01 43 26 84 40.

LIFESTYLE STORES

Colette
(See p325).

Gravity Zero
1 Rue Keller 75011.
Tel 01 43 57 97 62.

Spree
16 Rue de La Vieuville
75018. **Map** 6 F1.
Tel 01 42 23 41 40.

View on Fashion
27 Rue des Taillandiers
75011. **Map** 6 F1.
Tel 01 43 55 05 03.

VINTAGE AND SECOND-HAND STORES

Alternatives
18 Rue du Roi-de-Sicile
75004. **Map** 13 C3.
Tel 01 42 78 31 50

**Depôt-Vente de
Buci-Bourbon**
6 Rue de Bourbon-le-
Château 75006.
Map 12 E4.
Tel 01 46 34 45 05.

Didier Ludot
19-24 Galerie
Montpensier 75001.
Map 12 E1.
Tel 01 42 96 06 56.

**Le Mouton à
Cinq Pattes**
19 Rue Grégoire-de-
Tours 75006.
Map 12 F4.
Tel 01 43 29 73 56.
One of several branches.

Réciproque
95 Rue de la Pompe
75016.
Map 9 A1.
Tel 01 47 04 30 28.

JEWELLERY

Agatha
97 Rue de Rennes 75006.
Map 12 D5.
Tel 01 45 48 81 30.
www.agatha.fr
One of several branches.

JEWELLERY

The *couture* houses probably stock some of the best jewellery and scarves. **Chanel's** jewels are classics and **Christian Lacroix's** are fun. **Boutique YSL** is a great place for accessories.

Among the main expensive Paris jewellery outlets are **Boucheron**, **Mauboussin** and **Poiray**. They are for the serious jewellery buyer. Other top retailers include **Harry Winston** and **Cartier**. **Dinh Van** has some quirky pieces, whilst **Mikimoto** is a must for pearls and **H Stern** has some innovative designs using semi-precious and precious stones. For a range of more unusual jewellery and accessories, try the **Daniel Swarovski Boutique**, which is owned by the Swarovksi crystal family.

Trends and imitations can be found around the Marais, the Bastille and Les Halles, in that order for quality. Those of note include **Scooter**, where chic young Parisians shop, **Métal Pointu's**, which sells great fantasy jewellery, and **Agatha** for copies of Chanel designs and basics.

Imitations in precious metals are available at **Verlor**, a cheap jeweller where one can find copies of pieces by top jewellers using genuine stones. Another reasonably priced Parisian jeweller is **Chaput**, where decent jewellery, especially the pieces made with semi-precious stones, can be found at good prices.

SHOES, BAGS AND BELTS

For sheer luxury **Harel** has a wide range of exotic leather footwear. Go to **Charles Jourdan** for a big selection of colours or to **Sidonie Larizzi** who will make up shoes from one of numerous leather swatches. Current favourites with the fashion set include **Michel Perry**, **Bruno Frisoni** and **Robert Clergerie**. **Rodolphe Ménudier** and **Christian Louboutin** are mainstays for sexy stilettos. **Carel** stocks smart basics, **Mosquitos** make comfortable

but trendy shoes and **Jonak** is a must for good imitations of designer footwear. **Bowen** has a selection of traditional men's shoes and **Fenestrier** creates chic versions of classics. **J M Weston** or **Berluti** are the last words in elegance for many Parisian men.

Christian Lacroix makes wonderful handbags and belts. Beautifully made leather goods can also be found at **Longchamp**, **Gucci** and **Hermès**. For ladies handbags, nothing beats **Chanel** or **Dior** at the top end of the scale, although **Goyard** comes close. Mid-range bags from **Furla** are a great compromise, as are the colourful bags from **Karine Dupont**. Fabric bags from **Jamin Puech**, **Vanessa Bruno** or **Hervé Chapelier** are a feature in every chic Parisian closet. For a great range of shoes, boots and bags at reasonable prices, try **Jet-Set**. Cheap, cheerful and very stylish bags can be found at **Lollipops**.

HATS

One of Paris's favourite milliners is **Marie Mercié**. **Anthony Peto** now creates men's hats at her old shop in Rue Tiquetonne. **Manon Martin** is offbeat and imaginative and **Philippe Model** is one of the most creative and stylish hatmakers in Paris.

LINGERIE

For modern lingerie go to **Fifi Chachnil**, whose shop is filled with colourful underwear. **La Boite à Bas** sells fine French stockings, whereas **Princesse Tam Tam** offers quality items at reasonable prices, whilst divine designer underwear can be found at cult store **Sabbia Rosa**. The ultimate in Parisian lingerie can be bought off the peg or made to order at **Cadolle**, the store which invented the bra. For a more raunchy number, go to **Yoba**.

SIZE CHART

For Australian sizes follow the British and American conversions.

Children's clothing

French	2–3	4–5	6–7	8–9	10–11	12	14	14+ (years)
British	2–3	4–5	6–7	8–9	10–11	12	14	14+ (years)
American	2–3	4–5	6–6x	7–8	10	12	14	16 (size)

Children's shoes

French	24	25½	27	28	29	30	32	33	34
British	7	8	9	10	11	12	13	1	2
American	7½	8½	9½	10½	11½	12½	13½	1½	2½

Women's dresses coats and skirts

French	34	36	38	40	42	44	46
British	6	8	10	12	14	16	18
American	2	4	6	8	10	12	14

Women's blouses and sweaters

French	81	84	87	90	93	96	99 (cms)
British	31	32	34	36	38	40	42 (inches)
American	6	8	10	12	14	16	18 (size)

Women's shoes

French	36	37	38	39	40	41
British	3	4	5	6	7	8
American	5	6	7	8	9	10

Men's suits

French	44	46	48	50	52	54	56	58
British	34	36	38	40	42	44	46	48
American	34	36	38	40	42	44	46	48

Men's shirts

French	36	38	39	41	42	43	44	45
British	14	15	15½	16	16½	17	17½	18
American	14	15	15½	16	16½	17	17½	18

Men's shoes

French	39	40	41	42	43	44	45	46
British	6	7	7½	8	9	10	11	12
American	7	7½	8	8½	9½	10½	11	11½

DIRECTORY

Boucheron
26 Pl Vendôme 75001.
Map 6 D5.
Tel 01 42 61 58 16.
www.boucheron.com

Boutique YSL
38 Rue du Faubourg-St-Honoré 75008.
Map 5 C5.
Tel 01 42 65 74 59.

Cartier
13 Rue de la Paix 75002.
Map 6 D5.
Tel 01 42 18 53 70.
One of several branches.

Chanel
(See p325).

Chaput
53 Rue Passy 75016.
Map 9 B3.
Tel 01 42 24 50 40.
One of several branches.

Christian Lacroix
(See p325).

Daniel Swarovski Boutique
7 Rue Royale 75008.
Map 5 C5. *Tel* 01 40 17 07 40. www.daniel-swarovski.com

Dinh Van
15 Rue de la Paix 75002. **Map** 6 D5.
Tel 01 42 86 02 66.
One of several branches.

H Stern
3 Rue Castiglione 75001.
Map 12 D1.
Tel 01 42 60 22 27.
One of several branches.

Harry Winston
29 Ave Montaigne 75008.
Map 10 F1.
Tel 01 47 20 03 09.
www.harrywinston.com

Mauboussin
20 Pl Vendôme 75001.
Map 6 D5.
Tel 01 44 55 10 00.
www.mauboussin.com

Métal Pointu's
2 Rue du Marché
St-Honoré 75001.
Map 12 D1.
Tel 01 42 60 01 42.

Mikimoto
8 Pl Vendôme 75001.
Map 6 D5.
Tel 01 42 60 33 55.

Poiray
1 Rue de la Paix 75002.
Map 6 D5.
Tel 01 42 61 70 58.

Scooter
10 Rue de Turbigo 75001.
Map 13 A1.
Tel 01 45 08 50 54.
One of several branches.

Verlor
187 Rue du Temple
75003.
Map 13 C1.
Tel 01 48 87 96 26.

SHOES, BAGS AND BELTS

Bowen
97 Rue St-Lazare 75009.
Map 6 D3.
Tel 01 53 32 32 40.

Berluti
26 Rue Marbeuf 75008.
Map 4 F5.
Tel 01 53 93 97 97.

Bruno Frisoni
34 Rue de Grenelle 75007.
Map 12 D4.
Tel 01 42 84 12 30.

Carel
4 Rue Tronchet 75008.
Map 6 D4.
Tel 01 43 12 37 00.
One of several branches.

Charles Jourdan
23 Rue François-1er 75008.
Tel 01 47 20 81 28.
www.charles-jourdan.com
One of several branches.

Christian Louboutin
38-40 Rue de Grenelle
75007. **Map** 10 F3.
Tel 01 42 22 33 07.

Eden Shoes
8 Rue de Marignan
75008.
Map 4 F5.
Tel 01 42 25 76 26.

Fenestrier
23 Rue du Cherche-Midi
75006. **Map** 12 D5.
Tel 01 42 22 66 02.

Furla
8 Rue de Sèvres 75006.
Map 11 C5.
Tel 01 40 49 06 44.
One of several branches.

Goyard
233 Rue St-Honoré
75001.
Map 5 C5.
Tel 01 42 60 57 04.

Gucci
23 Rue Royale 75001.
Map 5 C5.
Tel 01 44 94 14 70.
www.gucci.com

Harel
7 Rue Tournon 75006.
Map 12 E5.
Tel 01 43 54 16 16.

Hermès
(See p325).

Hervé Chapelier
1 Rue du Vieux-Colombier
75006. **Map** 12 D4.
Tel 01 44 07 06 50.

Jamin Puech
61 Rue de Hauteville
75010. **Map** 7 B4.
Tel 01 43 54 16 16.

Jet-Set
85 Rue de Passy 75016.
Map 9 B3.
Tel 01 42 88 21 59.
One of two branches.

Jonak
70 Rue de Rennes 75006.
Map 16 D1.
Tel 01 45 48 27 11.

Karine Dupont
16 Rue du Cherche-Midi
75006.
Map 12 D4.
Tel 01 42 84 06 30.

Lollipops
60 Rue Tiquetonne 75002.
Map 13 A1.
Tel 01 42 33 15 72.
www.lollipops.fr

Longchamp
404 Rue St-Honoré 75001.
Map 5 C5.
Tel 01 43 16 00 18.
www.longchamp.com

Michel Perry
243 Rue St-Honoré 75001.
Map 5 C5.
Tel 01 42 44 10 07.

Mosquitos
25 Rue du Four 75006.
Map 12 E4.
Tel 01 43 25 25 16.

Robert Clergerie
5 Rue du Cherche-Midi
75006. **Map** 12 D1.
Tel 01 42 71 02 82.

Rodolphe Ménudier
14 Rue de Castiglione
75001. **Map** 12 D1.
Tel 01 42 60 86 27.

Vanessa Bruno
(See p327).

HATS

Anthony Peto
56 Rue Tiquetonne 75002.
Map 13 A1.
Tel 01 40 26 60 68.

Manon Martin
19 Rue de Turenne 75004.
Map 14 D3.
Tel 01 48 04 00 84.

Marie Mercié
23 Rue St-Sulpice 75006.
Map 12 E4.
Tel 01 43 26 45 83.

Philippe Model
33 Pl du Marché
St-Honoré 75001.
Map 12 D1.
Tel 01 42 96 89 02.

LINGERIE

La Boête à Bas
27 Rue Boissy-d'Anglas
75008. **Map** 5 C5.
Tel 01 42 66 26 85.

Cadolle
4 Rue Cambon 75001.
Map 6 D5.
Tel 01 42 60 94 20.

Fifi Chachnil
26 Rue Cambon 75001.
Map 6 D5.
Tel 01 42 60 38 86.
One of several branches.

Princesse Tam Tam
52 Blvd St-Michel 75006.
Map 12 F5.
Tel 01 42 34 99 31.
One of several branches.

Sabbia Rosa
73 Rue des Sts-Pères
75006.
Map 12 D4.
Tel 01 45 48 88 37.

Yoba
11 Rue Marché St-Honoré
75001.
Map 12 D1.
Tel 01 40 41 04 06.

Gifts and Souvenirs

Paris has a wealth of stylish gifts and typical souvenirs, from designer accessories and perfume to French delicacies and Eiffel Tower paperweights. Shops on the Rue de Rivoli and around major tourist attractions such as Nôtre Dame or Sacré Coeur offer a range of cheap holiday paraphernalia, or go to some of the souvenir shops such as **Les Drapeaux de France**. Mementos can often be found in museum shops, including reproductions and creations by young designers. Try **Le Musée du Louvre, Musée d'Orsay** or **Musée Carnavalet**.

GIFTS

Au Printemps has excellent own-brand accessories, especially ladies handbags. The luxury floor is ideal for window-shopping or high-end purchases such as Tiffany jewellery or Cartier watches. It also stocks small, reasonably-priced items.

For those looking to take home gastronomic tasters, the famed food hall at **Le Bon Marché**, La Grande Epicerie, offers anything and everything you might need for a gourmet feast or quick snack.

Galeries Lafayette now boasts the world's biggest lingerie department.

PERFUME AND COSMETICS

Many shops advertise discounted perfume and cosmetics. Some even offer duty-free perfume to shoppers outside the EU, with discounts on the marked prices when you show your passport. They include **Eiffel Shopping** near the Eiffel Tower. The **Sephora** chain has a big selection, or try the department stores for a range of designers' perfumes. In particular, the beauty department at **Au Printemps** is one of Europe's biggest with one of the world's largest perfume selections. It stocks many beauty brands which are hard to find elsewhere.

If you fancy stepping back in time, **Detaille 1905** is the place for you. Everything here rings true to the early 20th century, and there are six main fragrances on offer – three for women and three

for men – all made up using original recipes. **Parfums Caron** also has many scents created at the turn-of-the-19th century, which are unavailable elsewhere; so this is the place to find exclusive presents that you will almost certainly decide to keep for yourself. Beautifully packaged perfumes made from natural essences are available from **Annick Goutal**. **Guerlain** has the ultimate in beauty care, while the elegant shops of **L'Artisan Parfumeur** specialize in exquisitely packaged scents which evoke specific memories. They have also re-issued favourites from the past, including perfume made to exactly the same formula as one that was worn at the court of Versailles. **Frédéric Malle** is another big name in top-of-the-range scent. Exclusive perfumes can also be found in the beautiful surroundings of the **Salons du Palais Royal**, an upscale Shiseido store. Serge Lutens, the company's creative director and a renowned parfumier creates exquisite and exotic scents which can only be bought in this store. **Lunx** is another designer perfumery where you can choose between one of their ten exclusive fragrances.

Paris is also home to several *haute* cosmetics designers. One of the most renowned is Terry de Gunzberg, whose store **By Terry** stocks fantastic products. Personalize your gift by having a message inscribed on the sleek, silver packaging. Further bespoke beauty products can be found at the **Galerie Noemi**, where lipstick can be mixed up just for you.

HOUSEHOLD GOODS

Though certain items are obviously rather delicate to carry home, it is difficult to ignore some of the world's most elegant tableware, found in Paris's chic shops. If you are wary of loading up your hold-all with breakable pieces, many shops will arrange to ship crockery overseas. Luxury household goods can be found on the Rue Royale, where many of the best shops are located. They sell items such as rustic china and reproduction and modern silverware. **Lalique's** Art Nouveau and Art Deco glass sculptures are collected all over the world. Impeccable silverware including fine photograph frames and even chopsticks comes from **Christofle**.

For significant savings on porcelain and crystal, try **Lumicristal**, which stocks Baccarat, Daum and Limoges crystal, or go to **Baccarat** itself. Baccarat also has a boutique on the Place de la Madeleine. The interior designer **Pierre Frey** has an upstairs showroom displaying fabrics which have been made into a fabulous array of cushions, bedspreads and tablecloths. Excellent quality bed linen can also be found at **Yves Delorme**.

La Chaise Longue has a selection of well-designed *objets*, along with fun gift ideas. **Bô** is contemporary, while **La Tuile à Loup** carries more traditional French handicrafts. **DOM** and **Why** stock an excellent range of cheap, kitsch home accessories for funky flats. A newly opened interior design store at **Galeries Lafayette** has everything from fancy mops to cutting-edge, three-piece suites. The **Sentou Gallery** is a clutch of stores full of chic pieces for Parisian living. One shop carries interesting tableware, whilst another focuses on practical purchases, with the final store dedicated to high-end furniture.

Kitchen equipment which can't be beaten comes from

E. Dehillerin. A must-have item in many Parisian homes is a scented candle from **Diptyque**. Figuier is their most popular fragrance.

The basement at **BHV** *(see p321)* is full of all sorts of tools and equipment for doing up your house and garden.

BOOKS, MAGAZINES AND NEWSPAPERS

Many English and American publications can be found at large magazine stands or at some of the bookshops listed. If French is no obstacle the weeklies *Pariscope, L'Officiel des Spectacles* and *Zurban* have the most comprehensive listings of what's going on around town.

The *International Herald Tribune*, an English-language daily newspaper, is published in Paris and contains good American news coverage. Two periodicals, *Paris Free Voice* and the bi-weekly *France–US Contacts*, are also published in English.

Some of the large department stores have a book section *(see Department Stores p321)*. There is a large branch of **W H Smith** and a useful **Galignani**, or try **Brentano's**. A small, somewhat disorganized, but cosy and convivial bookshop is **Shakespeare & Co**. The American-influenced **Village Voice** has a good literary and intellectual selection of new books, while **The Abbey**

Bookshop does the same for second-hand books. **Tea and Tattered Pages** is a British second-hand bookshop.

French-language bookshops include **La Hune**, specializing in art, design, architecture, photography, fashion and cinema; **Gibert Joseph**, selling general and educational books; and **Le Divan** which has social science, psychology, literature and poetry sections. French food lovers and cooks will adore browsing at **Food**, a cornucopia of cookbooks in several languages, edible goodies and tableware.

FLOWERS

Some Parisian florists such as **Christian Tortu** are very well known, so be sure to buy one of Tortu's signature vases. **Art Nature Harmonie** and **Monceau Fleurs** offer a good selection at reasonable prices; and **Mille Feuilles** is the place to go to in the Marais. *(See* also Specialist Shops *p332.)* Stunning silk flowers can be found at **Hervé Gambs**, whose chic store is brimming over with beautiful artifical blooms.

SPECIALIST SHOPS

For cigars, **A La Civette** is perhaps Paris's most beautiful tobacconist. It is also probably the most devoted to its wares and has humidified shop windows to keep its merchandise in top condition.

Go to **A L'Olivier** in the Rue de Rivoli for a wonderful selection of exotic oils and vinegar. Or, if honey is your favourite condiment, try **La Maison du Miel** where you can buy all sorts of fine honeys, including those made from the flowers of lavender and acacia. You can also buy refreshing beeswax soap and candles here. **Mariage Frères** has become a cult favourite for its 350 varieties of tea; it also sells teapots.

Couture fabrics can be purchased from a range at **Wolff et Descourtis**. For an unusual gift of traditional French card games or tarot cards, go to **Jeux Descartes**.

One of the world's most famous and delightful toyshops is **Au Nain Bleu**, while the name **Cassegrain** is synonymous with high-quality stationery and paper products. **Calligrane** sells a tempting range of high-quality desk accessories and paper products.

The **La Maison de la Fausse Fourrure** offers just about everything made in fake fur. From floor-length coats to shopping trolleys, via hot-water bottle covers and tactile lampshades, an unusual gift is sure to result from a trip here.

However, the ultimate in eccentric shopping can be found at **Deyrolle**, Paris's most famous taxidermist, which provides gifts for the person who truly has everything.

DIRECTORY

SOUVENIR AND MUSEUM SHOPS

Les Drapeaux de France
1 Place Colette 75001.
Map 12 E2.
Tel 01 40 20 00 11.

Le Musée
Niveau 2, Forum des Halles, Porte Berger 75001.
Map 13 A2.
Tel 01 40 39 97 91.

Musée Carnavalet
(See p97).

Le Musée du Louvre
(See p123).

Musée d'Orsay
(See p145).

GIFTS

Au Printemps
64 Blvd Haussman 75009.
Map 6 D4.
Tel 01 42 82 50 00.

Le Bon Marché
24 Rue de Sèvres 75007.
Map 11 C5.
Tel 01 44 39 80 00.

Galeries Lafayette
40 Blvd Haussmann 75009.
Map 6 E4.
Tel 01 42 82 34 56.
One of two branches.

PERFUME AND COSMETICS

Annick Goutal
16 Rue de Bellechasse 75007.
Map 11 C3.
Tel 01 45 51 36 13.
One of several branches.

L'Artisan Parfumeur
24 Blvd Raspail 75007.
Map 16 D1.
Tel 01 42 22 23 32.
One of several branches.

By Terry
36 Passage Véro-dodat 75001.
Map 12 F2.
Tel 01 44 76 00 76.

Detaille 1905
10 Rue St-Lazare 75009.
Map 6 D3.
Tel 01 48 78 68 50.

DIRECTORY

Eiffel Shopping
9 Ave de Suffren 75007.
Map 10 D3.
Tel 01 45 66 55 30.

Frédéric Malle
21 Rue Mont Thabor
75001.
Map 12 D1.
Tel 01 42 22 74 10.

Galerie Noemi
92 Ave des Champs
Elysées 75008.
Map 4 F5.
Tel 01 45 62 78 27.

Guerlain
68 Ave des Champs-
Elysées 75008.
Map 4 F5.
Tel 01 45 62 52 57.
One of several branches.
www.guerlain.com

Lunx
48–50 Rue de l'Université
75007. **Map** 12 D3.
Tel 01 45 44 05 46.

Parfums Caron
34 Ave Montaigne 75008.
Map 10 F1.
Tel 01 47 23 40 82.

Sephora
70 Ave des Champs-
Elysées 75008.
Map 11 B1.
Tel 01 53 93 22 50.
www.sephora.fr
One of several branches.

**Salons du Palais
Royal**
25 Rue de Valois 75001.
Map 12 F1.
Tel 01 49 27 09 09.

HOUSEHOLD GOODS

Baccarat
11 Pl de la Madeleine
75008. **Map** 5 C5.
Tel 01 42 65 36 26.
(See also p201)

Bô
8 Rue St-Merri 75004.
Map 13 B3.
Tel 01 42 74 55 10.

La Chaise Longue
30 Rue Croix-des-Petits-
Champs 75001.
Map 12 F1.
Tel 01 42 96 32 14.
One of several branches.

Christofle
24 Rue de la Paix 75002.
Map 6 D5.
Tel 01 42 65 62 43.
One of several branches.

Diptyque
34 Bld St Germain 75006.
Map 13 B5.
Tel 01 43 26 45 27.

DOM
21 Rue Ste-Croix de la
Bretonnerie 75004.
Map 13 B3.
Tel 01 42 71 08 00.

E. Dehillerin
18 Rue Coquillière 75001.
Map 12 F1.
Tel 01 42 36 53 13.

Lalique
11 Rue Royale 75008.
Map 5 C5.
Tel 01 53 05 12 12.

Lumicristal
22 bis Rue de Paradis
75010. **Map** 7 B4.
Tel 01 42 46 96 25.

Pierre Frey
22 Rue Royale 75008.
Map 5 C5.
Tel 01 49 26 04 77.

Point à la Ligne
67 Ave Victor Hugo
75116. **Map** 3 B5.
Tel 01 45 00 87 01.

Sentou Gallery
18 & 24 Rue Pont
Louis-Philippe 75004.
Map 13 C3.
Tel 01 42 71 00 01.

La Tuile à Loup
35 Rue Daubenton 75005.
Map 17 B2.
Tel 01 47 07 28 90.

Why
93 Rue Rambuteau 75001.
Map 13 A2.
Tel 01 40 26 39 56.

Yves Delorme
8 Rue Vavin 75006.
Map 16 D1.
Tel 01 44 07 23 14.

BOOKS, MAGAZINES AND NEWSPAPERS

Abbey Bookshop
29 Rue de la Parcheminerie
75005. **Map** 13 A4.
Tel 01 46 33 16 24.

Brentano's
37 Ave de l'Opéra 75002.
Map 6 E5.
Tel 01 42 61 52 50.
www.brentanos.fr

Le Divan
203 Rue de la Convention
75015. **Map** 12 E3.
Tel 01 53 68 90 68.

Food
58 Rue Charlot 75003.
Map 14 D2.
Tel 01 42 72 68 97.

Galignani
224 Rue de Rivoli 75001.
Map 13 A2.
Tel 01 42 60 76 07.

Gibert Joseph
26 Blvd St-Michel 75006.
Map 12 F5.
Tel 01 44 41 88 88.

La Hune
170 Blvd St-Germain
75006. **Map** 12 D4.
Tel 01 45 48 35 85.

Shakespeare & Co
37 Rue de la Bûcherie
75005. **Map** 13 A4.
Tel 01 43 26 96 50.

**Tea and Tattered
Pages**
24 Rue Mayet 75006.
Map 15 B1.
Tel 01 40 65 94 35.

Village Voice
6 Rue Princesse 75006.
Map 12 E4.
Tel 01 46 33 36 47.
www.villagevoicebookshop.
com

W H Smith
248 Rue de Rivoli 75001.
Map 11 C1.
Tel 01 44 77 88 99.

FLOWERS

**Art Nature
Harmonie**
1 Rue Abbé de l'Epée
75005. **Map** 16 F1.
Tel 01 44 07 15 00.

Christian Tortu
6 Carrefour de l'Odéon
75006. **Map** 12 F4.
Tel 01 43 26 02 56.

Hervé Gambs
9 Bis Rue des Blancs
Manteaux 75004.
Map 13 C3.
Tel 01 44 59 88 88.

Monceau Fleurs
84 Blvd de Raspail 75006.
Map 12 D4.
Tel 01 45 48 70 10.
One of several branches.

SPECIALIST SHOPS

A La Civette
157 Rue St-Honoré 75001.
Map 12 F2.
Tel 01 42 96 04 99.

A L'Olivier
23 Rue de Rivoli 75004.
Map 13 C3.
Tel 01 48 04 86 59.

Au Nain Bleu
408 Rue St-Honoré 75008.
Map 5 C5.
Tel 01 42 60 39 01.
www.aunainbleu.com
One of several branches.

Calligrane
4 Rue du Pont-Louis-
Philippe 75004. **Map** 13
B4. *Tel* 01 48 04 31 89.

Cassegrain
422 Rue St-Honoré 75008.
Map 5 C5.
Tel 01 42 60 20 08.
www.cassegrain.fr

Deyrolle
46 Rue du Bac 75007.
Map 12 D3.
Tel 01 42 22 30 07.

Jeux Descartes
52 Rue des Écoles 75005.
Map 13 A5.
Tel 01 43 26 79 83.
One of three branches.

**La Maison de la
Fausse Fourrure**
34 Boulevard Beaumarchais
75011. **Map** 14 E3.
Tel 01 43 55 24 21.

La Maison du Miel
24 Rue Vignon 75009.
Map 6 D5.
Tel 01 47 42 26 70.

Mariage Frères
30 Rue du Bourg-Tibourg
75004. **Map** 13 C3.
Tel 01 42 72 28 11.
www.mariagefreres.com
One of several branches.
(See p286).

Wolff et Descourtis
18 Galerie Vivienne
75002. **Map** 12 F1.
Tel 01 42 61 80 84.

Food and Drink

Paris is as famous for food as it is for fashion. Gastronomic treats include *foie gras*, cold meats from the *charcuterie*, cheese and wine. Certain streets are so overflowing with food shops that you can put together a picnic for 20 in no time: try the Rue Montorgueil *(see p339)*. The Rue Rambuteau, running on either side of the Pompidou Centre, has a marvellous row of fishmongers, cheese delicatessens and shops selling prepared foods. *(See also* What to Eat and Drink in Paris *pp296–99* and Light Meals and Snacks *pp316–19.)*

BREAD AND CAKES

There is a vast range of breads and pastries in France's capital. The *baguette* is often translated as "French bread"; a *bâtard* is similar but thicker, while a *ficelle* is thinner. A *fougasse* is a crusty, flat loaf made from *baguette* dough, often filled with onions, cheese, herbs or spices. Since most French bread contains no fat it goes stale quickly: the sooner you eat it, the better. The French would never eat day-old bread so be sure to be up in time to make it to the bakery for breakfast!

Croissants can be bought *ordinaire* or *au beurre* – the latter is flakier and more buttery. *Pain au chocolat* is a chocolate-filled pastry eaten for breakfast and *chausson aux pommes* is filled with apples. There are also pear, plum and rhubarb variations. A *pain aux raisins* is a bread-like wheel filled with custard and raisins.

Poilâne sells perhaps the only bread in Paris known by the name of its baker (the late Lionel, brother of Max) and his hearty wholewheat loaves are tremendously popular, with freshly baked loaves being jetted around the world to satisfy the cravings of certain film stars. There are always big queues at the weekend and around 4pm when a fresh batch comes out of the oven.

Many think **Ganachaud** bakes the best bread in Paris. Thirty different kinds, including ingredients such as walnuts and fruit, are made in the old-fashioned ovens.

Although **Les Panetons** is part of a larger chain, it is one of the best of its kind with a broad range of breads. Favourites here include five-grain bread, sesame rolls and *mouchoir aux pommes*, a variation on the traditional *chausson*.

It is very important to remember that every Parisian has a favourite neighbourhood bakery, so when you are buying bread locally simply plump for the shop with the longest queues.

Many of the Jewish delicatessens have the best ryes and the only pumpernickels in town. One of the best known is **Sacha Finkelsztajn**.

Le Moulin de la Vierge uses a wood fire to bake organic breads and rich pound cakes. **Boulangerie de l'Ouest** is second only to **Max Poilâne** in the Montparnasse area with *baguettes, fougasses*, cakes and pastries. **J L Poujauran** is known for his black-olive bread and nut-and-raisin wholegrain breads. **Pierre Hermé** is to cakes what Chanel is to fashion, while **Ladurée** macaroons are legendary.

CHOCOLATE

Like all food in France, chocolate is to be savoured. **Christian Constant's** low-sugar creations are made with pure cocoa and are known to connoisseurs. **Dalloyau** makes all types of chocolate and is not too expensive (it's also known for its pâtisserie and cold meats). **Fauchon** is world famous for its luxury food products. Its chocolates are excellent, as is the pâtisserie. **Lenôtre** makes classic truffles and pralines. Robert Linxe at **La Maison du Chocolat** is constantly inventing fresh, rich chocolates with mouth-watering exotic ingredients. **Richart** boasts beautifully presented and hugely-expensive chocolates, which are usually coated with dark chocolate or liqueur-filled. **Debauve & Gallais** are best known for their wonderful and delicious glacé chestnut treats *(marron glacés)*.

CHARCUTERIE AND FOIE GRAS

Charcuteries often sell cheese, snails, truffles, smoked salmon, caviar and wine as well as cold meats. **Fauchon** has a good grocery, as does the department store **Le Bon Marché**. **Hédiard** is a luxury shop similar to Fauchon, and **Maison de la Truffe** sells *foie gras* and sausages as well as truffles. For Beluga caviar, Georgian tea and Russian vodka go to **Petrossian**.

The Lyon and Auvergne regions of France are the best known for their *charcuterie*. Examples can be bought from **Chretienne Jean-Jacques**. **Aux Vrais Produits d'Auvergne** has a number of outlets where you can stock up on dried and fresh sausages and delicious Cantal cheese (rather like Cheddar). **Pou** is a sparklingly clean and popular shop selling *pâté en croute* (pâté baked in pastry), *boudins* (black and white puddings), Lyonnais sausages, ham and *foie gras*. Just off the Champs-Elysées, **Vignon** has superb *foie gras* and Lyonnais sausages as well as popular prepared foods.

Together with truffles and caviar, *foie gras* is the ultimate in gourmet food. The quality (and price) depends upon the percentage of liver used. Though most specialist food shops sell *foie gras*, you can be sure of quality at **Comtesse du Barry**, which has six outlets in Paris. **Divay** is relatively inexpensive and will ship overseas. **Labeyrie** has a range of beautifully-packaged *foie gras* suitable for giving as presents.

CHEESE

Although Camembert is undoubtedly a favourite, there is an overwhelming range of cheeses available.

A friendly *fromager* will help you choose. **Marie-Anne Cantin** is one of the leading figures in the fight to protect traditional production methods, and her fine cheeses are available from the shop that she inherited from her father. Some say that **Alléosse** is the best cheese delicatessen in Paris – the façade may be in need of renovation, but all the cheeses are made according to traditional methods. **Fromagerie Quatrehomme** sells farm-made cheeses, many of which are in danger of becoming extinct, these include a rare and delicious truffle Brie (when in season). **Boursault** is one of the best shops in Paris for all types of cheese – the *chèvre* (goat's cheese) is particularly good, and outside on the pavement the daily specials are offered at remarkably reasonable prices. **Barthelemy** in the Rue de Grenelle has a truly exceptional Roquefort. **Androuet** is a Parisian institution with several branches across the city. Try a pungent Munster or a really ripe Brie. A charming cheese shop on the bustling Rue Montorgeuil market street, **La Fermette**, offers a dazzling array of dairy products, which the helpful and friendly staff will happily encase in plastic for the journey home. This is imperative when bringing cheese through customs, so don't forget to ask your *fromager* to wrap it for you. Well-heeled locals queue in the street to buy oozing *livarot* and sharp *chèvre* from **La Fromagerie d'Auteuil**.

WINE

The chain store which has practically cornered the every-day tippling market is **Nicolas** – there's a branch in every neighbourhood with a range of wines to suit all pockets. As a rule, the sales-people are knowledgeable

and helpful. Try the charming **Legrand Filles et Fils** *(see p319)* for a carefully chosen selection. **Caves Taillevent** on the Rue du Faubourg-St-Honoré is worth a sightseeing tour. It is an enormous, overwhelming cellar with some of the most expensive wine. **Cave Péret** on the Rue Daguerre has a vast selection of wines and can offer personal advice to help you with your purchase. The beautiful **Ryst-Dupeyron**, in the St-Germain quarter, displays whiskies, wines, ports, and Monsieur Ryst's own Armagnac. He will even personalize a bottle for that special occasion.

Other great wine stores include **Lavinia** *(see p319)*, which is the largest in Europe, and **Renaud Michel** at Nation, whose small boutique is well stocked and well connected. The staff in **Les Caves Augé** are also very knowledgeable and friendly.

CHAMPAGNE

Fabulous fizz can be found at most wine stores, but some know their bubbles better than others. The **Nicolas** chain, mentioned above, frequently has great offers on well-known brands so this is a good place to come and stock up on your favourite famous tipple. **La Cave des Martyrs** on the Rue Martyrs is a friendly and well-stocked wine shop with charming staff to help you with your selection. The **Repaire du Bachus** on the Rue d'Auteuil is a good place to go for hard-to-find vintages. The *sommelier* here is very knowledgable and able to provide excellent alternative advice if your preferred brand is out of stock. **Legrand Filles et Fils** on the Rue de la Banque, is one of the few shops in Paris to stock Salon, a rare high-end champagne. They also sell champagne by Jacques Selosse which is little-known but well-loved by champagne connoisseurs. **Les Caves du Panthéon** on the Rue Saint Jacques, is a small, but lovely wine shop which has a particularly

interesting selection of champagnes. Close by is **Ex Cellar France**, a corner wine-shop which is distinguished both by its charming and helpful staff and also by its frequent deals on champagne. The climate-controlled section of **Hédiard** at the Place de la Madelaine is a good place to find rare, fine sparkling wines. **Caprices de l'Instant** is a fashionable wine store which stocks good quality champagne including bottles by some lesser-known producers. A stroll along the Boulevard St-Germain can be enhanced with a visit to **La Maison du Millesimes**, a wonderful store carrying excellent vintages of household name champagnes.

OYSTERS

The ultimate aphrodisac for some, a slippery sea creature for others, there is no doubt that the once humble oyster can cause heated debate. In Paris, the argument tends to be over the best place to purchase these creatures, with every seafood fan worth his platter claiming a favourite spot and it is, of course, important to get it right. A deciding factor for some is the grace with which your fishmonger will agree to open them for you. In general, a polite request will be honoured, although sometimes you may have to wait a while before being presented with a platter perfect for a picnic. The fishmonger on the Rue Cler market street, **La Sablaisse Poissonerie**, has an excellent reputation as does the **Poissonerie du Dôme** in the city's 14th arrondissement. Over in the traditionally rough-and-ready area around the Rue Oberkampf, you can find excellent oysters at the **Poissonerie Lacroix**. If you prefer to eat your oysters on the spot then head to an *huitrerie* (oyster shop) such as the **Huiterie Garnier** on the Avenue Mozart in the chic 16th arrondissement, where you can tuck in to your shellfish straight away at the few tables tucked into the corner of the store.

DIRECTORY

BREAD AND CAKES

Boulangerie de l'Ouest
4 Pl Constantin Brancusi 75014. **Map** 15 C3.
Tel 01 43 21 76 18.

Ganachaud
226 Rue des Pyrénées 75020.
Tel 01 43 58 42 62.

J L Poujauran
20 Rue Jean-Nicot 75007.
Map 10 F2.
Tel 01 43 17 35 20.

Max Poilâne
29 Rue de l'Ouest 75014.
Map 15 B3.
Tel 01 43 27 24 91.

Le Moulin de la Vierge
105 Rue Vercingétorix 75014.
Map 15 A4.
Tel 01 45 43 09 84.
One of several branches.

Les Panetons
113 Rue Mouffetard 75005. **Map** 17 B2.
Tel 01 47 07 12 08.

Pierre Hermé
72 Rue Bonaparte 75006.
Map 12 E4.
Tel 01 43 54 47 77.

Poilâne
8 Rue du Cherche-Midi 75006. **Map** 12 D4.
Tel 01 45 48 42 59.

Sacha Finkelsztajn
27 Rue des Rosiers 75004.
Map 13 C3.
Tel 01 42 72 78 91.
www.laboutiquejaune.fr

CHOCOLATE

Christian Constant
37 Rue d'Assas 75006.
Map 16 E1.
Tel 01 53 63 15 15.

Dalloyau
101 Rue du Faubourg-St-Honoré 75008.
Map 5 B5.
Tel 01 42 99 90 00.

Debauve & Gallais
30 Rue des Saints-Pères 75007.
Map 12 D4.
Tel 01 45 48 54 67.
One of two branches.

Fauchon
26 Pl de la Madeleine 75008. **Map** 5 C5.
Tel 01 47 42 91 10.
www.fauchon.fr

Lenôtre
40 Rue Cler 75007.
Map 10 F3.
Tel 01 45 87 86 65.

La Maison du Chocolat
225 Rue du Faubourg-St-Honoré 75008. **Map** 4 E3. *Tel* 01 42 27 39 44.

Richart
258 Blvd St-Germain 75007. **Map** 11 C2.
Tel 01 45 55 66 00.

CHARCUTERIE AND FOIE GRAS

Chretienne Jean-Jacques
58 Rue des Martyrs 75009.
Map 6 F2.
Tel 01 48 78 96 45.

Comtesse du Barry
1 Rue de Sèvres 75006.
Map 12 D4.
Tel 01 45 48 32 04.
One of several branches.

Divay
4 Rue Bayen 75017.
Map 4 D2.
Tel 01 43 80 16 97.

Fauchon
26 Pl de la Madeleine 75008. **Map** 5 C5.
Tel 01 47 42 60 11.

Hédiard
21 Pl de la Madeleine 75008. **Map** 5 C5.
Tel 01 43 12 88 88.

Labeyrie
11 Rue d'Auteuil 75016.
Tel 01 42 24 17 62.

Maison de la Truffe
19 Pl de la Madeleine 75008. **Map** 5 C5.
Tel 01 42 66 10 01.

Petrossian
18 Blvd Latour-Maubourg 75007. **Map** 11 A2.
Tel 01 44 11 32 22.

Pou
16 Ave des Ternes 75017.
Map 4 D3.
Tel 01 43 80 19 24.

Vignon
14 Rue Marbeuf 75008.
Map 4 F5.
Tel 01 47 20 24 26.

CHEESE

Alléosse
13 Rue Poncelet 75017.
Map 4 E3.
Tel 01 46 22 50 45.

Androuët
134 Rue Mouffetard 75005. **Map** 17 B1.
Tel 01 45 87 86 65.

Barthelemy
51 Rue de Grenelle 75007.
Map 12 D4.
Tel 01 45 48 56 75.

Boursault
71 Ave du Général-Leclerc 75014. **Map** 16 D5.
Tel 01 43 27 93 30.

La Fermette
86 Rue Montorgueil 75002. **Map** 13 A1.
Tel 01 42 36 70 96.

La Fromagerie d'Auteuil
58 Rue d'Auteuil 75016.
Tel 01 45 25 07 10.

Fromagerie Quatrehomme
62 Rue de Sèvres 75007.
Map 11 C5.
Tel 01 47 34 33 45.

Marie-Anne Cantin
12 Rue du Champ-de-Mars 75007. **Map** 10 F3.
Tel 01 45 50 43 94.

WINE

Les Caves Augé
116 Blvd Haussman 75008. **Map** 5 C4.
Tel 01 45 22 16 97.

Cave Péret
6 Rue Daguerre 75014.
Map 16 D4.
Tel 01 43 22 08 64.

Caves Taillevent
199 Rue du Faubourg-St-Honoré 75008.
Map 4 F3.
Tel 01 45 61 14 09.

Nicolas
35 Blvd Malesherbes 75008. **Map** 5 C5.
Tel 01 42 65 00 85.

Renaud Michel
12 Pl de la Nation 75012.
Map 9 A3.
Tel 01 43 07 98 93.

Ryst-Dupeyron
79 Rue du Bac 75007. **Map** 12 D3. *Tel* 01 45 48 80 93.

CHAMPAGNE

Caprices de l'Instant
12 Rue Jacques Couer 75004. **Map** 14 E4.
Tel 01 40 27 89 00.

La Cave des Martyrs
39 Rue Martyrs 75009.
Map 6 F3.
Tel 01 40 16 80 27.

Les Caves du Panthéon
174 Rue St Jacques 75005. **Map** 13 A5.
Tel 01 46 33 90 35.

Ex Cellar France
25 Rue des Ecoles 75005.
Map 13 A5.
Tel 01 43 26 99 43.

Hédiard
2 Place de la Madeleine 75008. **Map** 5 C5.
Tel 01 43 12 88 88.

La Maison de Millesimes
137 Boulevard St-Germain 75006. **Map** 12 F4.
Tel 01 40 46 80 01.

Repaire du Bacchus
1 Rue de Maistre 75018.
Tel 01 46 06 80 84.

OYSTERS

Huiterie Garnier
114 Avenue Mozart 75016. **Map** 9 A3.
Tel 01 40 50 17 27.

Poissonerie du Dôme
4 Rue Delambre 75014.
Map 16 D2.
Tel 01 43 35 23 95.

Poissonerie Lacroix
44 Rue Oberkampf 75011.
Map 14 E1.
Tel 01 47 00 93 13.

La Sablaise Poissonerie
28 Rue Cler 75007.
Map 10 F3.
Tel 01 45 51 61 78.

Art and Antiques

In Paris you can either buy art and antiques from shops and galleries with established reputations, or from flea markets and avant-garde galleries. Many of the prestigious antiques shops and galleries are located around the Rue du Faubourg-St-Honoré and are worth a visit even if you can't afford to buy. On the Left Bank is Le Carré Rive Gauche, an organization of 30 antiques dealers. *Objets d'art* over 50 years old, worth more than a given amount (values vary for all categories of art object), will require a *Certificat pour un bien culturel* to be exported anywhere in the world (provided by the vendor), plus a *licence d'exportation* for non-EU countries. Seek professional advice from the large antique shops.

EXPORTING

The Ministry of Culture designates *objets d'art*. Export licences are available from the **Centre Français du Commerce Extérieur**. The **Centre des Renseignements des Douanes** has a booklet, *Bulletin Officiel des Douanes*, with all the details.

MODERN CRAFTS AND FURNITURE

One of the best places for furniture and *objets d'art* by up-and-coming designers is **Sentou**, where you can find objects and textiles, as well as furniture by contemporary designers. Another essential venue is the showroom of the Italian designer, **Giulio Cappellini**. **Le Viaduc des Arts** is a railway viaduct, each arch of which has been transformed into a shop front and workshop space. Stroll along this street for a great show of contemporary metalwork, tapestry, sculpture, ceramics and much more.

ANTIQUES AND OBJETS D'ART

If you wish to buy antiques, you might like to stroll around the areas that boast many galleries – in Le Carré Rive Gauche around Quai Malaquais, try **L'Arc en Seine** and **Anne-Sophie Duval** for Art Nouveau and Art Deco. Rue Jacob is still one of the best places to seek beautiful objects, antique or modern.

Close to the Louvre, the **Louvre des Antiquaires** (see *p120*) sells expensive, quality furniture. On the Rue du Faubourg-St-Honoré you will find **Didier Aaron**, expert on furniture from the 17th and 18th centuries. **Village St-Paul** between the Quai des Célestins, the Rue Saint Paul and the Rue Charlemange, is the most charming group of antiques shops and is also open on Sundays.

La Calinière has a superb range of *objets d'art* and old lighting fixtures. Glassware from the 19th century to the 1960s is sold at **Verreglass**. **La Village Suisse** in the south of the city also groups many art and antiques dealers.

REPRODUCTIONS, POSTERS AND PRINTS

A beautiful, contemporary art gallery called **Artcurial** on the Place des Champs-Elysées has one of the best selections of international art periodicals, books and prints. On the Boulevard Saint Germain, **La Hune** is a popular bookshop, particularly for art publications. The museum bookshops, especially those in the Musée d'Art Moderne (see *p201*), Louvre (see *p123*), Musée d'Orsay (see *p145*) and Pompidou Centre (see *p111*) are good for recent art books and prints.

Galerie Documents on the Rue de Seine sells original antique posters. Or leaf through the second-hand book stalls along the banks of the Seine.

ART GALLERIES

Established art galleries are located on or around the Avenue Montaigne. The **Louise Leiris** gallery was founded by D H Kahnweiler, the dealer who "discovered" both Georges Braque and Pablo Picasso. The gallery still shows Cubist masterpieces.

Artcurial holds many exhibitions and has an impressive permanent collection of 20th-century art, including works by Joan Miró, Picasso, Alberto Giacometti and Max Ernst. **Galerie Lelong** is devoted to contemporary artists.

On the Left Bank **Adrian Maeght** has a tremendous stock of paintings at prices to suit most budgets; he also publishes fine art books. **Galerie 1900–2000** specializes in works by Surrealist and Dada artists, and **Galerie Jeanne Bucher** represents post-war Abstraction with artists like Nicolas de Staël and Vieira da Silva. **Dina Vierny** is a bastion of Modernism, founded by sculptor Aristide Maillol's famous model of the same name. **Rue Louise-Weiss** has become an area for cutting-edge creativity and innovation known as "Scène Est". The **Air de Paris** gallery is also popular. In the Marais try **Yvon Lambert**, **Galerie Templon** – specializing in American art, **Galerie Emmanuel Perrotin** and **Galerie du Jour Agnès B**, and in the Bastille, **Levignes-Bastille** and **L et M Durand-Dessert**, also a fashionable place to buy catalogues on new artists, if not their actual works.

AUCTIONS AND AUCTION HOUSES

The great Paris auction centre, in operation since 1858, is **Drouot-Richelieu** (see *p216*). Bidding can be intimidating since most of it is done by dealers. Beware of the auctioneer's high-speed patter. *La Gazette de L'Hôtel Drouot* tells you what auctions are coming up when. Drouot-Richelieu has its own auction catalogue as well. The house only accepts cash and French cheques, but there is an exchange desk in house. A 10–15 per cent commission to the house is charged, so add it on to any price you hear. You may view from 11am to 6pm on the day before the sale, and from 11am to noon on the morning of the sale. Items considered not good enough for the main house are sold at **Drouot-Nord**. Here auctions take place from 9am to noon and viewing is just 5 minutes before the sales begin. The most prestigious auctions are held at **Drouot-Montaigne**.

The **Crédit Municipal** holds around 12 auctions a month, and almost all the items on sale are small objects and furs off-loaded by rich Parisians. The rules follow those at Drouot. Information can also be found in *La Gazette de L'Hôtel Drouot.*

Service des Domaines sells all sorts of odds and ends, and here you can still find bargains. Many of the wares come from bailiffs and from Customs and Excise *(see p374)* confiscations. Viewing is from 10am to 11.30am on the day of the sale.

DIRECTORY

EXPORTING

Centre Français du Commerce Extérieur
22 Ave Franklin Roosevelt 75008.
Map 5 A4.
Tel 01 53 83 92 92.
www.cfce.fr

Centre des Renseignements des Douanes
84 Rue d'Hauteville 75010.
Tel 08 25 30 82 63.
www.douane.gouv.fr

MODERN CRAFTS AND FURNITURE

Cappellini
4 Rue des Rosiers 75004.
Map 13 C4.
Tel 01 42 78 39 39.
www.cappellini.it

Sentou
18 Rue du Pont-Louis-Philippe 75004.
Map 13 C3.
Tel 01 42 77 44 79.

Le Viaduc des Arts
Ave Daumesnil 750012.
Map 14 F5.
Tel 01 43 40 75 75.
This comprises a series of shops on the Avenue.

ANTIQUES AND OBJETS D'ART

Anne-Sophie Duval
5 Quai Malaquais 75006.
Map 12 E3.
Tel 01 43 54 51 16.

L'Arc en Seine
31 Rue de Seine 75006.
Map 12 E3.
Tel 01 43 29 11 02.

La Calinière
68 Rue Vieille-du-Temple 75003. **Map** 13 C3.
Tel 01 42 77 40 46.

Didier Aaron
118 Rue du Faubourg-St-Honoré 75008.
Map 5 C5.
Tel 01 47 42 47 34.

Louvre des Antiquaires
2 Pl du Palais Royal 75001.
Map 12 E2.
Tel 01 42 97 27 27.

Verreglass
32 Rue de Charonne 75011. **Map** 14 F4
Tel 01 48 05 78 43.

Village St-Paul
Between the Quai des Célestins, the Rue St-Paul and the Rue Charlemagne 75004. **Map** 13 C4.

La Village Suisse
78 Ave de Suffren 75015.
Map 10 E4.
www.levillagesuisseparis.com

REPRODUCTIONS, POSTERS, PRINTS

Artcurial
7 Pl des Champs-Elysées M. Dassault 75008.
Map 5 A5.
Tel 01 42 99 16 16.

Galerie Documents
53 Rue de Seine 75006.
Map 12 E4.
Tel 01 43 54 50 68.

La Hune
170 Blvd St-Germain 75006.
Map 12 D4.
Tel 01 45 48 35 85.

ART GALLERIES

Adrian Maeght
42 Rue du Bac 75007.
Map 12 D3.
Tel 01 45 48 45 15.

Air de Paris
32 Rue Louise-Weiss 75013.
Map 18 E4.
Tel 01 44 23 02 77.

Dina Vierny
36 Rue Jacob 75006.
Map 12 E3.
Tel 01 42 86 00 87.

Galerie 1900–2000
8 Rue Bonaparte 75006.
Map 12 E3.
Tel 01 43 25 84 20.

Galerie Emmanuel Perrotin
76 Rue de Turenne 75003.
Map 14 D2.
Tel 01 42 16 79 79.

Galerie Jeanne Bucher
53 Rue de Seine 75006.
Map 12 E4.
Tel 01 44 41 69 55.

Galerie du Jour Agnès B
44 Rue Quincampoix 75004.
Map 13 B2.
Tel 01 44 54 55 90.

Galerie Lelong
13 Rue de Téhéran 75008.
Map 5 A3.
Tel 01 45 63 13 19.

Galerie Templon
30 Rue Beaubourg 75003.
Map 13 B1.
Tel 01 42 72 14 10.
Open by appt only.

L et M Durand-Dessert
28 Rue de Lappe 75011.
Map 14 F4.
Tel 01 48 06 92 23.

Levignes-Bastille
27 Rue de Charonne 75011. **Map** 14 F4.
Tel 01 47 00 88 18.

Louise Leiris
47 Rue de Monceau 75008.
Map 5 A3.
Tel 01 45 63 28 85.

Rue Louise Weiss
75013.

Yvon Lambert
108 Rue Vieille-du-Temple 75003. **Map** 14 D2.
Tel 01 42 71 09 33.

AUCTION HOUSES

Crédit Municipal
55 Rue des Francs-Bourgeois 75004.
Map 13 C3.
Tel 01 44 61 64 00.
www.creditmunicipal.fr

Drouot-Montaigne
15 Ave Montaigne 75008.
Map 10 F1.
Tel 01 48 00 20 20.
www.drouot.fr

Drouot-Nord
64 Rue Doudeauville 75018.
Tel 01 48 00 20 20.

Drouot-Richelieu
9 Rue Drouot 75009.
Map 6 F4.
Tel 01 48 00 20 20.

Service des Domaines
Tel 01 44 64 50 00.

Markets

For eye-catching displays of wonderful food or a lively shopping atmosphere, there is no better place than a Paris market. There are large covered food markets; markets where stalls change regularly; and permanent street markets with a mixture of shops and stalls which are open on a daily basis. Each has its own personality reflecting the area in which it is located. A list of some of the more famous markets, with approximate opening times, follows. For a complete list of markets contact the Paris Office du Tourisme *(see p280)*. And while you're enjoying browsing round the stalls remember to keep an eye on your money – and be prepared to bargain.

FRUIT AND VEGETABLE MARKETS

The French treat food with the kind of reverence usually reserved for religion. Most still shop on a daily basis to be sure of buying the freshest produce possible, so food markets tend to be busy. The majority of fruit and vegetable markets are open from around 8am to 1pm and from 4pm to 7pm Tuesday to Saturday, and from 9am to 1pm Sunday.

Watch what you buy in the food markets or you may find you have purchased a kilo of fruit or vegetables from a marvellous display only to discover later that all the produce hidden underneath is rotten. To avoid this, try to buy produce loose rather than in boxes. Most outdoor stalls prefer to serve you rather than allow you to help yourself, but you can point to the individual fruit and vegetables of your choice. A little language is useful for specifying *pas trop mûr* (not too ripe), or *pour manger ce soir* (to be eaten tonight). If you go to the same market every day you'll become familiar to the stall holders and are far less likely to be cheated. You will also get to know the stalls worth buying from and the produce worth buying. Seasonal fruit and vegetables are, of course, usually a good buy, tending to be fresher and cheaper than at other times of the year. Finally, go early in the day when the food is freshest and the queues are shortest.

FLEA MARKETS

It's often said that you can no longer find bargains at the Paris flea markets. Though this may be true, it's still worth going to one for the sheer fun of browsing. And bear in mind that the price quoted is not the one that you are expected to pay – it's generally assumed that you will bargain. Most flea markets are located on the city's boundaries. Whether you pick up any real bargains has as much to do with luck as with judgement. Often the sellers themselves have little or no idea of the true value of their goods – which can work either for or against you. The biggest and most famous market, incorporating several smaller ones, is the Marché aux Puces de St-Ouen. Keep your eye on your wallet, as pickpockets frequent these markets.

SPECIALIST MARKETS

Try the Marché aux Fleurs Madeleine in the Opéra, the Marché aux Fleurs on the Ile de la Cité *(see p81)* or the Marché aux Fleurs Ternes in the Champs-Elysées district for fresh flowers. On the Ile de la Cité on Sundays the Marché aux Oiseaux bird market replaces the flower market. Stamp collectors will enjoy the permanent Marché aux Timbres where you can also buy old postcards. In Montmartre the Marché St-Pierre, famous for cheap fabrics, is patronized by professional designers.

Marché d'Aligre

(See p233.)

Reminiscent of a Moroccan bazaar, this must be the cheapest and liveliest market in the city. Here traders hawk ingredients such as North African olives, groundnuts and hot peppers and there are even a few halal butchers. The noise reaches a crescendo at weekends when the cries of the market boys mingle with those of militants of all political persuasions as the latter petition and protest in the Place d'Aligre. The stalls on the square sell mostly second-hand clothes and bric-à-brac. This is a less affluent area of town with few tourists and many Parisians.

Rue Cler

(See p190.)

This high-class, pedestrianized food market is patronized mainly by the politicians and captains of industry who live and work in the vicinity, so it's good for people-spotting! The produce is excellent – there's a Breton delicatessen and some good cheese delicatessens.

Marché Enfant Rouges

39 Rue de Bretagne 75003. **Map** 14 D2. Ⓜ️ *Temple, Filles-du-Calvaire.* ⏱ *8.30am–1pm, 4–7.30pm Tue–Sat (to 8pm Fri, Sat); 8.30am–2pm Sun.*

This long-established, charming fruit and vegetable market on the Rue de Bretagne is part covered, part outdoors and dates from 1620. The items on sale are famous for their freshness, and on Sunday mornings street singers, performers and accordionists sometimes enliven the proceedings.

Marché aux Fleurs Madeleine

Pl de la Madeleine 75008. **Map** 5 C5. Ⓜ️ *Madeleine.* ⏱ *7am–8pm Tue–Sun.*

Marché aux Fleurs Ternes

Pl des Ternes 75008. **Map** 4 E3. Ⓜ️ *Ternes.* ⏱ *8am–8pm Tue–Sun.*

Marché St-Pierre

Pl St-Pierre 75018. **Map** 6 F1. Ⓜ️ *Anvers.* ⏱ *2–7pm Mon, 9am–7pm Tue–Sat.*

Marché aux Timbres

Cour Marigny 75008. **Map** 5 B5. Ⓜ️ *Champs-Elysées.* ⏱ *8am–7pm Thu, Sun & public hols.*

Marché St-Germain

4–8 Rue Lobineau 75006.
Map 12 E4. M *Mabillon.*
⬤ 8.30am–1pm, 4–7.30pm
Tue–Sat; 8.30am–1pm Sun.

St-Germain is one of the few covered markets left in Paris and has been enhanced by renovation. Here you can buy Italian, Mexican, Greek, Asian and organic produce and other goods.

Rue Lepic

75018. **Map** 6 F1. M *Blanche,*
Lamarck-Caulaincourt.
⬤ 8am–2pm Tue–Sun.

The Rue Lepic fruit and vegetable market is situated conveniently close to the sights of Montmartre in this refreshingly unspoilt winding old quarry road. The market is at its liveliest at the weekend.

Rue de Lévis

Blvd des Batignolles 75017. **Map** 5 B2.
M *Villiers.* ⬤ 8am–1pm, 4pm–7pm
Tue–Sat; 9am–2pm Sun.

Rue de Lévis is a bustling, popular food market near the Parc Monceau with a number of good pâtisseries, an excellent cheese delicatessen and a *charcuterie* which is known for its savoury pies. The part of the street that leads to the Rue Legendre sells haberdashery and fabrics.

Rue Montorgueil

75001 & 75002. **Map** 13 A1. M *Les*
Halles. ⬤ usually 9am–7pm Tue–Sun.

The Rue Montorgueil is what remains of the old Les Halles market. The street has now been repaved and restored to its former glory. Here you can buy exotic fruit and vegetables like green bananas and yams from the market gardeners' stalls, or sample offerings from the delicatessens or from the Stohrer pastry shop. Alternatively pick up some of the pretty Moroccan pottery for sale.

Rue Mouffetard

(See p166.)

Rue Mouffetard is one of the oldest market streets in Paris. Although it has become touristy and somewhat overpriced, it's still a charming winding street full of quality food products. It's worth queueing for the freshly-made bread at Les Panetons bakery at No. 113 *(see pp333–5).* There is also a lively African market down the nearby side street of Rue Daubenton.

Rue Poncelet

75017. **Map** 4 E3. M *Ternes.*
⬤ 8am–noon, 4pm–7.30pm
Tue–Sat; 8am–12.30pm Sun.

The Rue Poncelet food market is situated away from the main tourist areas of Paris but is worth visiting for its authentic French atmosphere. Choose from the many bakeries, pâtisseries and *charcuteries* or enjoy authentic Auvergne specialities from Aux Fermes d'Auvergnes.

Marché de la Porte de Vanves

Ave Georges-Lafenestre & Ave Marc-Sangnier 75014. M *Porte-de-Vanves.*
⬤ 7am–6pm Sat & Sun.

Porte de Vanves is a small market selling good-quality bric-à-brac and junk as well as some second-hand furniture. It's best to get to the market early on Saturday morning for the best choice of wares. Artists exhibit nearby in the Place des Artistes.

Marché Président-Wilson

Situated in Ave du Président-Wilson, between Pl d'Iéna & Rue Debrousse 75016. **Map** 10 D1. M *Alma-Marceau.*
⬤ 7am–2.30pm Wed, 7am–3pm Sat.

This very chic food market on Avenue Président-Wilson is close to the Musée d'Art Moderne and the Palais Galliera fashion museum. It has become important because there are no other food shops nearby. It is best for meat.

Marché aux Puces de Montreuil

Porte de Montreuil, 93 Montreuil 75020. M *Porte-de-Montreuil.*
⬤ 8am–6pm Mon, Sat & Sun.

Go early to the Porte de Montreuil flea market, where you'll have a better chance of picking up a bargain. The substantial second-hand clothes section attracts many young people. There's also a wide variety of items including used bicycles, bric-à-brac and an exotic spices stand.

Marché aux Puces de St-Ouen

(See p231.)

This is the most well known, the most crowded and the most expensive of all the flea markets, situated on the northern outskirts of the city. Here you'll find a range of markets, locals dealing from their car boots and a number of extremely large buildings packed with stalls. Some of them are very

upmarket, others sell junk. The flea market is a 10–15 minute walk from Clignancourt metro – don't be put off by the somewhat sleazy Marché Malik which you have to pass through on your way from the metro. *A Guide des Puces* (guide to the flea markets) can be obtained from the information kiosk in the Marché Biron on the Rue des Rosiers. The more exclusive markets will take credit cards and arrange for goods to be shipped home. New stock arrives on Friday, the day when professionals come from all over the world to sweep up the best buys.

Among the markets here the Marché Jules Vallès is good for turn-of-the-19th century *objets d'art.* Marché Paul-Bert is more expensive, but charming. Items on sale include furniture, books and prints. Both markets deal in second-hand goods rather than antiques.

In a different league, Marché Biron sells elegant, expensive antique furniture of very high quality. Marché Vernaison is the oldest and biggest market, good for collectables such as jewellery as well as lamps and clothes. No information about the Marché aux Puces is complete without mentioning Chez Louisette in the Vernaison market. This café is always full of locals enjoying the home cooking and the well-intentioned renditions of Edith Piaf songs. Marché Cambo is a fairly small market with beautifully-displayed antique furniture. Marché Serpette is popular with the dealers: everything sold here is in mint condition.

Marché Raspail

Situated on Blvd Raspail between Rue du Cherche-Midi & Rue de Rennes 75006. **Map** 12 D5. M *Rennes (closed Sun, use Sevres Babylone).*
⬤ 7am–2.30pm Tue, Fri.

The Raspail market sells typical French groceries as well as Portuguese produce on Tuesdays and Fridays. But Sunday is the day for which it's famous, when health-conscious Parisians turn up in droves for the organically-grown produce. Marché Raspail is not a cheap market, but it is very good.

Rue de Seine and Rue de Buci

75006. **Map** 12 E4. M *Odéon.*
⬤ 8am–1pm, 4–7pm Tue–Sat; 9am–1pm Sun.

The stalls here are expensive and crowded but sell quality fruit and vegetables. There is also a large florist's and two excellent pâtisseries.

ENTERTAINMENT IN PARIS

Whether you prefer classical drama or cabaret, leggy show-girls or ballet, opera or jazz, cinema or dancing the night away, Paris has it all. Free entertainment is aplenty as well, from the street performers outside the Pompidou Centre to musicians busking in the metros. Parisians themselves enjoy strolling along the boulevards or sitting at a pavement café, and nursing a drink. Of course, for the ultimate "oh-la-la!" experience, showgirls await you at celebrated cabarets while supermodels pose in nightclubs. For fans of spectator sports there is tennis, the Tour de France, horse racing, football or rugby. Recreation centres and gyms cater to the more active, while the municipal swimming pools delight waterbabies. And for those disposed either way, there's always the popular type of bowls played in Paris, *pétanque*.

PRACTICAL INFORMATION

For the visitor in Paris there is no shortage of information about what's on offer.

The **Office du Tourisme** near the Tuileries and Opera is the city's main tourism distribution point for leaflets and schedules of events. It has a recorded information telephone service giving details of free concerts and exhibitions along with information on transport to the venues. Its website is also extremely useful. Your hotel reception desk or concierge should also be able to help you with any such information. They usually keep a wide range of brochures and leaflets for guests, and will generally be more than happy to make reservations for you.

BOOKING TICKETS

Depending on the event, tickets can be bought at the door, but for blockbuster concerts it is necessary to book well in advance. For most major events, including some classical music concerts and museum shows, tickets can be purchased at the **FNAC** chain or **Virgin Megastore**. For popular events be sure to book well in advance, Parisians can be very quick off the draw for hot tickets. However, for theatre, opera and dance performances, you can often buy inexpensive tickets at the last minute. If the tickets are marked *sans visibil-ité* you will be able to see the stage only partially, or perhaps not at all. Often, obliging ushers

Ballerina of the Ballet de l'Opéra

Nightclubbing in Paris

will put you in a better seat, depending on availability, but don't forget to tip.

Theatre box offices are open daily from approximately 11am–7pm. Most box offices accept credit card bookings made by phone or in person. But you may have to arrive early to pick up your tickets if you booked by telephone, as they may be sold to someone else at the last minute. If you

Concert at Opéra National de Paris Garnier *(see p348)*

LISTINGS MAGAZINES

Paris has several good listings magazines. Among them are *Pariscope*, the simplest to use, *L'Officiel des Spectacles* and *Zurban*. They are published every Wednesday and are widely available. *Le Figaro* also has a good listings section on Wednesdays. Two English publications, *Paris Voice* and the quarterly *The City*, are both available at newsstands or **WH Smith** *(see p332)*.

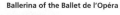

Buying tickets at the box office of a comedy club

are really keen and can't get hold of tickets, you can always turn up at the box office just before the performance in case there are unclaimed or returned tickets.

TICKET TOUTS

If you must have a ticket to a sold-out performance, do as the French do: stand at the entrance with a sign that says *cherche une place (or deux,* etc). Many people have an extra ticket to sell. Often the people selling the extra tickets are simply doing so because a person in their party has stood them up and they will simply sell the ticket on at face value. It is fine to buy these tickets, but do watch out for touts and be sure you don't buy a counterfeit or overpriced ticket.

Pétanque players

CUT-PRICE TICKETS

Half-price tickets to current plays are sold on the day of performance at **Kiosque Théâtre**. Credit cards are not accepted and a small commission is charged per ticket. There is a booth on the Place de la Madeleine *(see p214),* open 12.30–8pm, Tuesday– Saturday, 12.30–4pm Sunday, and in the Parvis de la Gare Montparnasse 12.30–6pm Tuesday–Saturday. This is a great way to buy tickets without booking weeks or even months in advance and, of course, has the added benefit of costing less. The *kiosque* is a Parisian institu-tion and often has passes for the season's top shows.

DISABLED VISITORS' FACILITIES

Where facilities do exist, they are either very good or dreadful. Many venues have wheelchair space, but always phone in advance to make sure it's properly equipped. As far as public transport is concerned, the metro, with its long stairways, is completely inaccessible to wheelchairs. Some bus lines are equipped with ramps to make them accessible to wheelchairs, check with the city's transport authority, the RATP, to find out which lines have facilities.

USEFUL ADDRESSES

FNAC
Forum des Halles, 1 Rue Pierre-Lescot 75001. **Map** 13 A2.**Tel** *01 40 41 40 00.*

The Grand Rex cinema *(see p354)*

FNAC
26 Ave des Ternes 75017.
Map 4 D3. **Tel** *01 44 09 18 00.*

G7 Taxis
Tel *01 47 39 47 39.*

Office du Tourisme
25 Rue des Pyramides 75001.
Map 12 E1. **Tel** *08 92 68 30 00.*
www.*parisinfo.com*

Taxis Bleus
Tel *01 49 36 10 10.*

Virgin Megastore
52–60 Ave des Champs-Elysées 75008. **Map** 4 F5.
Tel *01 49 53 50 00.*

Theatre

From the grandeur of the Comédie Française to slap-stick farce and avant-garde drama, theatre is flourishing in Paris and the suburbs – the training ground for the best young actors and directors. The city also has a long tradition of playing host to visiting companies, and it attracts many foreign productions, often in the original languages.

There are theatres scattered throughout the city and the theatre season runs from September to July; national theatres close during August but many commercial ones stay open. For complete listings of what's on read *Pariscope*, *Zurban* or *L'Officiel des Spectacles (see p340)*.

NATIONAL THEATRES

Founded in 1680 by royal decree, the **Comédie Française** *(see p120)*, with its strict conventions regarding the style of acting and interpretation, is the bastion of French theatre. Its aim is to keep classical drama in the public eye and also to perform works by the best modern playwrights.

The Comédie Française (inextricably linked in the national consciousness to Molière) is the oldest national theatre in the world and one of the few institutions of *ancien-régime* France to have survived the Revolution. It settled into its present home after players occupied the Palais-Royal during the Revolution. The traditionally-styled red velvet auditorium has a vast stage equipped with the latest technology.

The majority of the repertoire is classical, dominated by Corneille, Racine and Molière, followed by second strings Marivaux, Alfred de Musset and Victor Hugo. The company also performs modern plays by French and foreign playwrights.

The **Odéon Théâtre de l'Europe**, also known as the Théâtre National de l'Odéon *(see p140)*, was at one time the second theatre of the Comédie Française. It now has two sites and specializes in performing plays from other countries in their original languages.

Next door the **Petit Odéon** features new plays and those in foreign languages.

The **Théâtre National de Chaillot** is a huge under-ground auditorium in the Art Deco Palais de Chaillot *(see p198)*. It stages lively productions of mainstream European classics and, occasionally, musical revues. The theatre also contains a studio, the **Salle Gémier**, for more experimental work.

The **Théâtre National de la Colline** has two performance spaces and specializes in contemporary dramas.

FURTHER AFIELD

A thriving multi-theatre complex in the Bois de Vincennes, the **Cartoucherie** houses five separate avant-garde theatres, including the internationally famous **Théâtre du Soleil**.

INDEPENDENT THEATRES

Among the most important of the serious independents are the **Comédie des Champs-Elysées**, the **Hébertot** and the **Atelier**, which aims to be experimental. Other notable venues include the **Théâtre Marigny**, for excellent modern French drama, the **Montparnasse** and the **Théâtre Antoine** which pioneered the use of realism on stage. The **Madeleine** maintains consistently high standards and the **Huchette** specializes in Ionesco plays. The avant-garde producer/director Peter Brook has a loyal following at the **Bouffes-du-Nord**.

For over a hundred years the **Palais Royal** has been the temple of risqué farce. With fewer French Feydeau-style farce writers these days, translations of English and American sex comedies are filling the gap. Other notable venues include the **Bouffes-Parisiens**, **La Bruyère**, the **Michel** and the **St-Georges**. The **Théâtre Marie Bell** presents popular one-man comedy shows.

CAFE-THEATRES AND CHANSONNIERS

There is a long tradition of entertainment in cafés, but the café-theatres of today have nothing in common with the "café-concerts" of the turn-of-the-19th century. These modern entertainments have originated because young actors and new playwrights could not find work, while drama students were unable to pay to hire out established theatres. Don't be surprised if there is an element of audience participation, or alternatively, in small venues, if the actors can sometimes seem a little too close for comfort. This form of theatre is now so popular in Paris that one can often see posters advertising classes for café-theatre or notices inviting people to join small troupes. Café-theatres rose to prominence during the 1960s and 70s, when unknowns such as Coluche, Gérard Depardieu and Miou-Miou made their debut at the **Café de la Gare** before going on to success on the screen, so who knows who you might see at your local café.

Good venues for seeing new talent include the **Théâtre d'Edgar** and **Au Bec Fin**, while **Chez Michou** is an old-fashioned spot which is very popular and tends to specialize in broad caricature. Traditional *chansonniers* – cabarets where ballads, folk songs and humour abound – include **Au Lapin Agile** *(see p223)*, in the heart of Mont-martre. Political satire is on offer at the **Caveau de la République** and the **Deux Anes**, also in Montmartre. Another form of café entertainment that often veers towards the theatrical is café-philosophique. These are philosophical discussions or debates, held on topics such as justice, war or love, in which skilled orators take to the floor to declaim their positions. Audience participation is encouraged. Such evenings are held in many locations, but the best known are held at **Le 7 Lézards**. The debates take place in French, English language events also exist: the monthly play-reading at the **Café de Flore** is a fine example of the genre.

CHILDREN'S THEATRE

Some Paris theatres, such as the **Gymnase-Marie Bell**, the **Porte St-Martin** and the **Café d'Edgar**, have children's matinees on Wednesdays and weekends. In the city parks there are several tiny puppet theatres (marionnettes), which are sure to delight children and adults alike. *(See* Independent Theatres *p344.)* The **Lido** also has a new show for children.

OPEN-AIR THEATRE

During the summer, weather permitting, open-air performances of Shakespeare in French and classic French plays are held in the Shakespeare Garden in the Bois de Boulogne. There are also occasional performances in the Tuileries and in Montmartre as part of Paris's summer festival, check listings magazines for these events.

ENGLISH-LANGUAGE THEATRE IN PARIS

The On Stage Theatre Company and The Dear Conjunction Theatre are both Paris-based companies who perform in English (details in listings magazines). There are also several English language poetry societies which host poetry and play readings, the best is the Live Poets Society. **Kilometre Zero** is an interesting English language arts collective that performs plays, publishes a magazine and hosts open-mike recital evenings. **La Java** puts on excellent stand-up comedy acts in English each month, courtesy of Anything Matters.

An historic venue, it is much-loved by expatriates and plays host to some of the finest comic talent on the circuit at the moment.

STREET THEATRE

Street theatre thrives during the summer. Jugglers, mime artists, fire-eaters and musicians can be seen mainly in tourist areas such as the Pompidou Centre *(see pp110–11)*, St-Germain-des-Prés and Les Halles.

CABARET

The music hall revue is the entertainment form most associated with turn-of-the-19th-century Paris. It evokes images of bohemian artists and champagne-induced debauchery. Today, most of the girls are likely to be American and the audience is made up mainly of foreign businessmen and tour groups.

When it comes to picking a cabaret the rule of thumb is simple: the better-known places are the best. Lesser-known shows resemble nothing so much as Grade-B strip shows. All the cabarets listed here guarantee topless women sporting outrageous feather- and sequin-encrusted headpieces, an assortment of vaudeville acts and, depending on your point of view, spectacularly entertaining evening or an exercise in high kitsch.

The **Lido** is the most Las Vegas-like of the cabarets and stars the legendary Bluebell Girls. The **Folies-Bergères** is renowned for lively entertainment. It is the oldest music hall in Paris and probably the most famous in the world.

The **Crazy Horse** features some of the more risqué costumes and performances, and dancers with names such as Betty Buttocks, Fila Volcana and Nouka Bazooka. It has been transformed from its Wild West bar-room into a jewel-box theatre with a champagne bucket fastened to each seat. Here, the lowly striptease of burlesque shows has been refined into a vehicle for comedy sketches and international beauties.

Paradis Latin is the most "French" of all the city's cabaret shows. It has variety acts with remarkable special effects and scenery in a beautiful, old Left Bank theatre, partially designed by Gustave Eiffel.

The **Don Camillo Rive Gauche** has more elegant, less touristy shows, with excellent *chanson* singers, comedians and all sorts of other variety acts. The **Moulin Rouge** *(see p226)*, once the haunt of Toulouse-Lautrec, is the birthplace of the cancan. Today, the Moulin Rouge is less extravagant than the screen version portrayed in the famous film, but cabaret fans can still be certain of an evening of glamour, glitz and good times. Outrageously camp, transvestite parodies of these showgirl reviews can be seen at **Chez Madame Arthur**.

BOOKING TICKETS

Tickets can be bought at the box office, by telephone or through theatre agencies. Box offices are open daily from about 11am–7pm; some accept credit card bookings by telephone or in person.

TICKET PRICES

Ticket prices range from 7€–30€ for the national theatres and 8€–38€ for the independent. Reduced-price tickets and student stand-bys are available in some theatres 15 minutes before curtain-up. For cabaret, expect to pay from 23€–60€; 68€–105€ including dinner.

The **Kiosque Théâtre** offers half-price tickets on the day-of-performance: credit cards are not accepted and a small commission is charged for each ticket sold. There is a ticket booth in the Place de la Madeleine and one in front of Gare Montparnasse.

DRESS

These days, evening clothes are only worn to gala events at the Opéra National de Paris Garnier, the Comédie Française or the premiere of an up-market play.

DIRECTORY

NATIONAL THEATRES

Comédie Française
Salle Richelieu, 1 Pl Colette 75001. **Map** 12 E1.
Tel 08 25 10 16 80.
www.comedie-francaise.fr

Odéon Théâtre de l'Europe
Ateliers Berthier, 8 Blvd Berthier 75017. **Map** 12 F5. *Tel 01 44 85 40 40.*
Théâtre de l'Odéon, Pl de l'Odéon 75006.
Map 12 F4.
www.theatre-odeon.fr

Théâtre National de Chaillot
Pl du Trocadéro 75016.
Map 9 C2.
Tel 01 53 65 31 00.

Théâtre National de la Colline
15 Rue Malte-Brun 75020.
Tel 01 44 62 52 52.
www.colline.fr

FURTHER AFIELD

Cartoucherie
Route du Champ-de-Manoeuvre 75012.
Tel 01 43 74 24 08.

Théâtre de l'Aquarium
Tel 01 43 74 72 74.

Théâtre de l'Epée de Bois
Bois de Vincennes
Tel 01 48 08 39 74.

Théâtre de la Tempête
Tel 01 43 28 36 36.

Théâtre du Chaudron
Tel 01 43 28 97 04.

Théâtre du Soleil
Tel 01 43 74 24 08.

INDEPENDENT THEATRES

Bouffes-du-Nord
37 bis Blvd de la Chapelle 75010.
Map 7 C1.
Tel 01 46 07 34 50.

Bouffes-Parisiens
4 Rue Monsigny 75002.
Map 6 E5.
Tel 01 42 96 92 42.

La Bruyère
5 Rue La Bruyère 75009.
Map 6 E3.
Tel 01 48 74 76 99.

Cinq Diamants
10 Rue des Cinq Diamants 75013. **Map** 17 B5.
Tel 01 45 80 51 31.

Comédie des Champs-Elysées
15 Ave Montaigne 75008. **Map** 10 F1.
Tel 01 53 23 99 10.

Gaiété Montparnasse
26 Rue de la Gaiété 75014. **Map** 15 C2.
Tel 01 43 20 60 56.

Hébertot
78 bis Blvd des Batignolles 75017.
Map 5 B2.
Tel 01 43 87 23 23.

Madeleine
19 Rue de Surène 75008.
Map 5 C5.
Tel 01 42 65 07 09.

Marigny
7 Ave de Marigny 75008.
Map 5 A5.
Tel 01 53 96 70 30.

Michel
38 Rue des Mathurins 75008.
Map 5 C4.
Tel 01 42 65 35 02.

Montparnasse
31 Rue de la Gaîté 75014. **Map** 15 C2.
Tel 01 43 22 77 30.

Palais Royal
38 Rue Montpensier 75001.
Map 12 E1.
Tel 01 42 97 59 81.

Porte St-Martin
16 Blvd St-Martin 75010.
Map 7 C5.
Tel 01 42 08 00 32.

St-Georges
51 Rue St-Georges 75009.
Map 6 E3.
Tel 01 48 78 63 47.

Théâtre Antoine
14 Blvd de Strasbourg 75010.
Map 7 B5.
Tel 01 42 08 77 71 & 01 42 08 76 58.

Théâtre de l'Atelier
Pl Charles Dullin 75018.
Map 6 F2.
Tel 01 46 06 49 24.

Théâtre de la Huchette
23 Rue de la Huchette 75005.
Map 13 A4.
Tel 01 43 26 38 99.

Théâtre Marie Bell
38 Blvd Bonne-Nouvelle 75010.
Map 7 A5.
Tel 01 42 46 79 79.

Théâtre Sudden
14 bis Rue Sainte-Isaure 75018.
Map 2 F4.
Tel 01 42 62 35 00.

CAFE-THEATRES AND CHANSONNIERS

Au Bec Fin
6 bis Rue Thérèse 75001.
Map 12 E1.
Tel 01 42 96 29 35.

Au Lapin Agile
22 Rue des Saules 75018.
Map 2 F5.
Tel 01 46 06 85 87.

Café de Flore
See 139.

Café de la Gare
41 Rue du Temple 75004.
Map 13 B2.
Tel 01 42 78 52 51.

Caveau de la République
23 Place République 75003.
Map 8 D5.
Tel 01 42 78 44 45.

Chez Michou
80 Rue des Martyrs 75018.
Map 6 F3.
Tel 01 46 06 16 04.

Deux Anes
100 Blvd de Clichy 75018.
Map 6 D1.
Tel 01 46 06 10 26.

La Java
105 Rue du Faubourg du Temple 75010. **Map** 8 E5.
Tel 01 53 19 98 88.
www.anythingmatters.com

Le Point Virgule
7 Rue St-Croix-de-la-Bretonnerie 75004.
Map 13 C3.
Tel 01 42 78 67 03.

Le 7 Lézards
10 Rue des Rosiers 75004.
Map 13 C3.
Tel 01 48 87 08 97.

Théâtre d'Edgar
58 Blvd Edgar-Quinet 75014.
Map 16 D2.
Tel 01 42 79 97 97.

CABARET

Chez Madame Arthur
75 bis Rue des Martyrs 75018.
Map 6 F2.
Tel 01 42 54 40 21.

Crazy Horse
12 Ave George V 75008.
Map 10 E1.
Tel 01 47 23 32 32.

Don Camillo Rive Gauche
10 Rue des Sts-Pères 75007. **Map** 12 E3.
Tel 01 42 60 82 84.

Folies-Bergères
32 Rue Richer 75009.
Map 7 A4.
Tel 01 44 79 98 98.

Lido
116 bis Ave des Champs-Elysées 75008.
Map 4 E4.
Tel 01 40 76 56 10.
www.lido.fr

Moulin Rouge
82 Blvd de Clichy 75018.
Map 6 E1.
Tel 01 53 09 82 82.
www.moulinrouge.fr

Classical Music

The music scene in Paris has never been so busy and exciting. Government spending has ensured that there are many first-class venues with an excellent range of opera, and classical and contemporary music productions. There are also numerous concerts in churches and many music festivals.

Information about what's on is listed in *Pariscope*, *Zurban* and *L'Officiel des Spectacles*. A free monthly listing of musical events is given out at most concert halls. Also, try the Office du Tourisme in the Rue des Pyramides *(see pp340–41)* for details of many free and open-air classical music performances.

OPERA

Opera lovers will find themselves well catered for, with many productions mounted at the Bastille and the beautifully renovated **Opéra National de Paris Garnier**. Opera is also an important part of the programming at the Théâtre du Châtelet, as well as being produced intermittently by a variety of small organizations, and there are occasional large-scale lavish productions at the **Palais Omnisports de Bercy** or POB *(see p359)*.

The Opéra de Paris's ultra-modern home is the **Opéra National de Paris Bastille** *(see p98)*, where performances have finally begun to make full use of the house's mind-boggling array of high-tech stage mechanisms. There are 2,700 seats, all with a good view of the stage, and the accoustics are excellent.

Productions feature classic and modern operas, and its interpretations are often avant-garde: Philippe Mamoury's *K...*; Bob Wilson's production of *The Magic Flute*, done in the style of Japanese Noh, with some of the cast delivering their lines while balancing on one leg; Messiaen's *St Francis of Assissi*, with video screens and neon added to bring the story up to date. At Thursday lunchtimes they also offer free concerts, lectures and films as part of a programme known as *Casse-Croûte à l'Opéra*.

There are also occasional dance performances, when the Bastille plays host to the ballet company from the Opéra National de Paris Garnier *(see*

p215). The house includes two smaller spaces, the **Auditorium** (500 seats) and the **Studio** (200 seats) for smaller-scale events connected to the current productions on the main stages here and at the Opera Garnier.

The **Opéra Comique** (also known as the Salle Favart), now run by Jérôme Savary, no longer has opera, but stages a wide range of eccentric, light-weight productions, including some popular music-hall-style work and operetta. Savary is also behind several large-scale musicals at the Palais des Congrès exhibtion space and some municipal events (such as a public ball held to cele-brate the 50th anniversary of the liberation of Paris.)

CONCERTS

Paris is the home of three major symphony orchestras, and a good half-dozen other orchestras; it is also a major venue for touring European and American orchestras. Chamber music is also flour-ishing, either as part of the programming of the major venues, or in smaller halls and churches.

The **Salle Pleyel** is Paris's principal concert hall. After extensive renovation, it has become part of the Cité de la Musique and now houses the Orchestre de Paris, directed by Christoph Eschenbach, as well as Radio France's Philharmonic Orchestra, led by Myung-Whun Chung. Guest orchestras and jazz and world-music ensembles complete the concert season, which tends to run from September to July. Over the

next few years, the Salle's owner will invest a further 23 million euros in the refurbishment of the hall (in lieu of tax payments); then, in 2056, this legendary concert hall will become property of the French state.

The **Théâtre du Châtelet** has become one of the city's principal venues for all kinds of concerts, opera and dance. The high-quality programme includes opera classics from Mozart's *Così fan tutte* to Verdi's *La Traviata*, and more modern works, such as Boessman's *Contes d'Hiver*, and occasional concerts by international opera stars. Great attention is also devoted to 20th-century music here, and throughout the season there are lunchtime concerts and recitals in the foyer.

The beautiful Art Deco **Théâtre des Champs-Elysées** is a celebrated classical music venue which also produces some opera and dance. Radio-France is part-owner of the theatre, and its Orchestre National de France gives concerts here, as do many touring orchestras and soloists. The Orchestre des Champs-Elysées, directed by Philippe Herreweghe, is in residence here, and gives period-instrument performances.

Radio-France is the biggest single concert organizer in Paris, with a musical force that includes two major symphony orchestras: the Orchestre National de France and the Orchestre Philharmonique. Many of its concerts are given in Paris's other concert halls, but the **Maison de Radio-France** has a large hall and several smaller studios that are used for concerts and broadcasts open to the public *(see p200, Musée de Radio France)*.

The **Cité de la Musique** is a massive cultural centre devoted entirely to music – of all genres and from all eras. Classical music features heavily on its programme, with lots of chamber music and recitals, as well as more ambitious orchestral concerts.

Dance

When it comes to dance, Paris is more a cultural crossroads than a cultural centre. Due to a deliberate government policy of decentralization, many of the top French dance companies are based in the provinces, although they frequently visit the capital. In addition, the greatest dance companies from all over the world perform here. Paris has a well-deserved reputation as a centre of excellence for modern and experimental dance, and has numerous workshops and places in which to learn its many forms.

CLASSICAL BALLET

The opulent **Opéra National de Paris Garnier** (see p215) is the home of the Ballet de l'Opéra de Paris, which is earning a reputation as one of the world's best classical dance companies.

Since the Opéra National de Paris Bastille opened in 1989, the Opéra National de Paris Garnier has been used almost exclusively for dance. It is one of the largest theatres in Europe, with performance space for 450 artists and a seating capacity of 2,200.

Modern dance companies such as the Martha Graham Company, Paul Taylor, Merce Cunningham, Alvin Ailey, Jerome Robbins and Roland Petit's Ballet de Marseille also regularly perform here.

The Opéra National de Paris Garnier, extensively restored both inside and out, now shares operatic productions with the **Opéra National de Paris Bastille**.

MODERN DANCE

Government support has helped the **Théâtre de la Ville** (once run by Sarah Bernhardt) to become Paris's most important venue for modern dance, with subsidies keeping ticket costs relatively low. Through performances at the Théâtre de la Ville, modern choreographers such as Jean-Claude Gallotta, Regine Chopinot, Maguy Marin and Anne Teresa de Keersmaeker have gained international recognition. Here you may also see troupes such as Pina Bausch's Wuppertal Dance Theatre, whose tormented, existential choreography may not be to everyone's taste, but is always popular with Parisian audiences.

Music performances also run throughout the season and include chamber music, recitals, world music and jazz.

The **Maison des Arts de Créteil** presents some of the most interesting dance works in Paris. It is located in the Paris suburb of Créteil, where the local council gives strong support to dance. Créteil's company choreographer, Maguy Marin, has won consistent praise for her darkly expressive work.

The Maison des Arts also brings in such innovative companies as the Sydney Ballet, and the Kirov from St Petersburg, which is more inclined towards the classical.

Set amid the opulent *couture* shops and embassies, the elegant Art Deco **Théâtre des Champs-Élysées** has 1,900 seats. It is frequented by an upmarket audience who watch major international companies perform here. It was here that Nijinsky first danced Stravinsky's iconoclastic *The Rite of Spring*, which led to rioting among the audience.

The theatre is more famous as a classical music venue, but recent visitors have included the Harlem Dance Company and London's Royal Ballet, and it is here that Mikhail Baryshnikov and American choreographer Mark Morris perform when they are in Paris. It also sponsors the popular *Géants de la Danse* series, an evening-length sampling of international ballet. The lovely old **Théâtre du Châtelet** is a renowned opera and classical music venue, but it is also host to international contemporary dance companies such as the Tokyo Ballet and the Birmingham Royal Ballet.

Experimental dance companies perform in the **Théâtre de la Bastille**, where innovative theatre is also staged. Many directors and companies start here, then go on to international fame.

New companies to look out for include La P'tit Cie and L'Esquisse, but they have no fixed venue.

EVENTS LISTINGS

To find out what's on, read the inexpensive weekly entertainment guides *Pariscope* and *L'Officiel des Spectacles*. Posters advertising dance performances are widely displayed in the metros and on the streets, especially on the green advertisement columns, the *colonnes Morris*.

TICKET PRICES

Expect to pay 10€–100€ for tickets to the Opéra de Paris Garnier (5€–60€ for a ballet), 6€–75€ for the Théâtre des Champs-Élysées, and anything from 9€–30€ for other venues.

DANCE VENUES

Maison des Arts et de la Culture de Créteil
Pl Salvador Allende 94000 Créteil.
Tel 01 45 13 19 19.

Opéra National de Paris Garnier
See p214-5.

Opéra National de Paris Bastille See p98.

Théâtre de la Bastille
76 Rue de la Roquette 75011.
Map 14 F3.
Tel 01 43 57 42 14.

Théâtre de la Ville
See p334.

Théâtre des Champs-Elysées
See p334.

Théâtre du Châtelet
See p334.

Rock, Jazz and World Music

Music lovers will find every imaginable form of music in Paris and its enviorns, from international pop stars in major venues to buskers of varying degrees of talent in the metro. There's a huge variety of styles on offer, with reggae, hip-hop, world music, blues, folk, rock and jazz – Paris is said to be second only to New York in the number of jazz clubs and jazz recordings and there is always an excellent selection of bands and solo performers.

On the summer solstice (21 June) each year, the Fête de la Musique takes place, when anyone can play any form of music, anywhere, without a licence, and when the whole city parties all night. Ears may be assailed by a heavy metal rock band or lulled by an accordionist playing traditional French songs.

For complete listings of what's happening, buy *Zurban* or *Pariscope* (published every Wednesday) at any kiosk. For jazz fans there's the monthly *Jazz* magazine for schedules and in-depth reviews.

MAJOR VENUES

The top international acts are often at the enormous arenas: **Palais Omnisports** at Bercy, **Stade de France** at St-Denis or the **Zénith**. Other venues such as the legendary *chanson* centre of the universe, the **Olympia**, or the **Grand Rex** (also a cinema), have assigned seating and a more intimate atmosphere. They host everyone from bewigged and cosmetically enhanced iconic first ladies of country to acid jazz stars. *(See Directories p350 & p359).*

ROCK AND POP

Until recently, Paris's indigenous rock groups (Les Négresses Vertes are probably the best-known, and are still going strong) drew foreign attention precisely because they were French. For too long, Paris pop meant Johnny Hallyday and insipid covers of US and UK hits, or Serge Gainsbourg and his brand of faintly naughty decadence. Paris rock traditionally (and deservedly) attracted either patronizing praise or outright mockery.

That is no longer the case. The international success of the groups Daft Punk and Air and the contribution to the music scene of producer, songwriter and musician

Bertrand Burgalat have led to a growth in confidence in the local music scene. The phrase French Touch often describes hip producers, writers or singers, now in demand all over the world. Banlieue- (suburb-) based rap, rai and reggae no longer sound like French versions of imported forms, instead they now have their own identity.

There is no shortage of gigs. The latest bands usually play at **La Cigale** and its downstairs den of din, **La Boule Noire**, the **Divan du Monde** and the **Elysée-Montmartre**, while the **Bataclan** and the **Rex** club are the best places for R&B. The **Olympia** is the city's most famous rock venue, attracting top acts. Many nightclubs also double up as live music venues *(see pp351–3)*.

JAZZ

Paris is still jazz-crazy. Many American musicians have made the French capital their home because of its receptive atmosphere. All styles, from free-form to Dixieland and swing, and even hip-hop-jazz crossover, are on offer. Clubs range from quasi-concert halls to piano bars and pub-like venues. One of the most

popular places, though not the most comfortable, is the **New Morning**. It's hot and smoky, and the table service can be a little erratic, but all the great jazz musicians continue to perform here, as they have in the past. Arrive early to ensure a good seat. **Le Duc des Lombards** is a lively jazz club in Les Halles, which also features salsa.

Many jazz clubs are also cafés, bars or restaurants. The latter includes the intimate **Bilboquet**, with its Belle Epoque interior. This stylish place is favoured by film stars. Dining might not be a requirement, but it's always wise to check first.

Other hotspots are **Le Petit Journal Montparnasse** for modern jazz, **Le Petit Journal St-Michel** for Dixieland and the **Sunset**. A trendy crowd is drawn to the **7 Lézards**, in the Marais. **Caveau de la Huchette** looks like the archetypal jazz joint, but today, it favours swing and big-band music, and is popular with students. The **Caveau des Oubliettes** has a growing reputation for cutting-edge jazz.

For a change, try the local talent at small, friendly bars such as the less expensive **Bistrot d'Eustache**, or the trendy **China Club**, with its 1940s *film noir* decor. The **Jazz-Club Lionel Hampton** in the Méridien hotel is a well-respected venue which features Sunday jazz brunch. On the other side of town, the renovated **Trabendo** has an intriguing mix of up-and-comers and down-and-outers.

Paris does not neglect blues fans either. The **Quai du Blues** is the best-known haunt, hosting concerts by established performers.

Paris has two international jazz festivals in summer: the Paris Jazz Festival *(see p63)* which is the mainstay of the summer calendar, and the JVC Halle That Jazz at the **Grande Halle de la Villette** in July, with films on jazz, debates and discussions and *boeufs* (jam sessions).

WORLD MUSIC

With its large populations from West Africa and the countries of the Maghreb, the Antilles and Latin America, Paris is a natural centre for world music. The **Chapelle des Lombards** has played host to top acts; it also has jazz, salsa and Brazilian music. **Aux Trois Maillets** is a medieval cellar with everything from blues to tango and rock and roll covers, while **Kibélé** is a great place for North African sounds. Many jazz clubs intersperse their programmes with ethnic music. These include **New Morning**, which also has shows with South American artists, and **Baiser Salé**, for popular acts including Makossa, Kassav, Malavoi and Manu Dibango.

World music in a stunning setting can be found at the Institut du Monde Arabe, a wonderful architectural feat (see p164) which draws stars from the Arab music world to its concert hall.

TICKET PRICES

Prices at jazz clubs can be steep, and there may be a cover charge of over 15€ at the door, which usually includes the first drink. If there is no cover charge, the drinks will be expensive and at least one must be bought.

Tickets can be bought from FNAC outlets and Virgin Megastore (see p341), or directly from venue box offices and at the door of the clubs themselves.

DIRECTORY

MAJOR VENUES

Grand Rex
1 Blvd Poissonnière 75002.
Map 7 A5.
Tel 01 45 08 93 89.

Olympia
28 Blvd des Capucines 75009.
Map 6 D5.
Tel 08 92 68 33 68.
www.olympiahall.com

Palais Omnisports de Paris-Bercy
8 Blvd de Bercy 75012.
Map 18 F2.
Tel 08 92 69 23 00.

Zénith
211 Ave de Jean-Jaurès 75019.
Tel 01 42 08 60 00.

ROCK AND POP

Bataclan
50 Blvd Voltaire 75011.
Map 14 E1.
Tel 01 43 14 35 35.

La Cigale/ La Boule Noire
120 Blvd Rochechouart 75018.
Map 6 F2.
Tel 01 49 25 81 73.

Divan du Monde
75 Rue des Martyrs 75018.
Map 6 F2.
Tel 01 42 52 02 46.

Elysée-Montmartre
72 Blvd Rochechouart 75018.
Map 6 F2.
Tel 01 42 23 46 50.

Rex Club
5 Blvd Poissonnière 75002.
Map 7 A5.
Tel 01 42 36 83 98.

JAZZ

Baiser Salé
58 Rue des Lombards 75001.
Map 13 A2.
Tel 01 42 33 37 71.

Bilboquet
13 Rue St-Benoêt 75006.
Map 12 E3.
Tel 01 45 48 81 84.

Bistrot d'Eustache
37 Rue Berger, Carré des Halles 75001.
Map 13 A2.
Tel 01 40 26 23 20.

Caveau de la Huchette
5 Rue de la Huchette 75005.
Map 13 A4.
Tel 01 43 26 65 05.

Caveau des Oubliettes
52 Rue Galande 75005.
Map 13 A4.
Tel 01 46 34 23 09.

China Club
50 Rue de Charenton 75012. **Map** 14 F5.
Tel 01 43 43 82 02.

Le Duc des Lombards
42 Rue des Lombards 75001.
Map 13 A2.
Tel 01 42 33 22 88.

La Grande Halle de la Villette
211 Ave Jean-Jaurès 75019.
Map 8 F1
Tel 01 40 03 75 75.

Jazz-Club Lionel Hampton
Hôtel Méridien, 81 Blvd Gouvion-St-Cyr 75017.
Map 3 C3.
Tel 01 40 68 34 34.
www.jazzclub-paris.com

New Morning
7–9 Rue des Petites-Écuries 75010.
Map 7 B4.
Tel 01 45 23 51 41.

Paris Jazz Festival
Parc Floral Bois de Vincennes 75012.
Tel 01 55 94 29 29.

Le Petit Journal Montparnasse
13 Rue du Commandant-Mouchotte 75014.
Map 15 C2.
Tel 01 43 21 56 70.

Le Petit Journal St-Michel
71 Blvd St-Michel 75005.
Map 16 F1.
Tel 01 43 26 28 59.

7 Lézards
10 Rue des Rosiers 75004.
Map 13 C3.
Tel 01 48 87 08 97.

Sunset
60 Rue des Lombards 75001.
Map 13 A2.
Tel 01 40 26 46 60.

Trabendo
211 Ave Jean-Jaurès 75019.
Map 8 F1.
Tel 01 42 01 12 12.

WORLD MUSIC

Aux Trois Maillets
56 Rue Galande 75005.
Map 13 A4.
Tel 01 43 54 42 94.

Baiser Salé
See Jazz.

Chapelle des Lombards
19 Rue de Lappe 75011. **Map** 14 F4.
Tel 01 43 57 24 24.

Institut du Monde Arabe
See p164.

Kibélé
12 Rue de l'Echiquier 75010. **Map** 7 B5.
Tel 01 48 24 57 74.

New Morning
7 Rue des Petites-Ecuries 75010.
Map 7 B4
Tel 01 45 23 51 41

Quai du Blues
17 Blvd Vital-Bouhot 92200.
Neuilly sur Seine.
Tel 01 46 24 22 00.
www.quaidublues.com

Nightclubs

The club scene in Paris is now somewhat under siege as government legislation on noise levels slightly hampers establishments' *modus operandi*. The city council is waging war on noise pollution and whilst this suits those with neighbours who possess large stereos, it's bad news for people who like to dance till dawn. They carry on regardless, albeit with fewer decibels, and you will still find every type of sound (and a great deal of creativity) on the club scene. There are clubs to suit every taste and it's worth noting that bouncers often treat foreign would-be entrants preferentially, so be sure to stand proud, ditch the attempts at French and speak English when you get near the door. The magazine *Zurban* lists up-to-the-minute information, with opening times and brief descriptions of club nights. Alternatively, read the posters at the Bastille metro station or listen to Radio NOVA 101.5 FM, which gives details of the night's best raves. Flyers advertising what's on at which clubs can be found on café, bar and shop counters. Popular nighttime options for the more mature set include ballroom dancing and visits to suave piano bars. If you're wondering about what to wear, the smart side of the smart-casual approach is usually the safest bet. Attire for nightclubs varies, for upscale venues be sure to put your designer-labelled best foot forward, whilst more relaxed ones will accept an urban look, but generally, tracksuits, jeans and trainers are definite no-nos.

MAINSTREAM

A vast yet convivial venue, **Le Bataclan** is a showcase for current bands. After the show on Saturday nights, it becomes one of the best nightclubs in Paris, legendary for its mouth-watering choice of funk, soul and new jack swing.

Les Etoiles gives salsa lessons, while the inexpensive **La Scala** attracts a large, young crowd, and has recently played host to ultra-fashionable party producers la Johnson. Linked to the **Alcazar**, which is a fashionable Terence Conran bar and restaurant very popular with a pre-club crowd, **WAGG** just next door is a wonderful spot for some uninhibited dancing. WAGG is unpretentious although the door staff are discriminating, and the disco and soul played in the stone cellars make for a great night out.

Les Bains, a former Turkish bath, may have lost some of its glitterati appeal but it is still a place to go to be seen. Its upstairs restaurant, now serving Thai food, is a popular place for private dinner parties. This is the place to be, so book a table for dinner if you're concerned about gaining entry and getting a much-coveted seat. The dance floor is tiny and music is mainly house, with 1970s and 80s disco on Mondays, and R&B on Wednesdays. Gay night is *Café con Leche* on Sundays. Legendary promoters and Parisian nightowls David and Cathy Guetta left Les Bains a while ago and took some of their regulars with them, but the club is still a flash place to be and there is always the possibility of spotting a film star. Advertising executives and filmmakers frequent the **Rex Club**. Despite the essentially conservative nature of the clientele, the music on different nights ranges from glam rock and house to "exotique" – funk, reggae and world music. Sounds are mainly rock

and roll at the smart and non-ageist **Zed Club**. The vast **La Locomotive** caters to mainstream tastes most nights, with rock, house, groove and dance music each occupying a different floor.

Utterly unpretentious, **Club Med World** is the place to go for 1980s classics and unselfconscious dancing.

EXCLUSIVE

Being rich, beautiful and famous may not be enough to get you into **Castel's**, but it could help. It is a strictly private club and the happy few who make it, dine in one of two very good restaurants before heading down to the dance floor.

Regine's is mostly full of besuited executives and wealthy foreigners who dine and dance to the easy-listening music. However, it is now enjoying something of a renaissance, especially on ladies nights, when a trained physiognomist picks out only the best looking women to come in for a girls-own session for a few hours, complete with male strip show. Predictably, when the doors open to men later in the evening, it becomes one of Paris's top nightspots for seeing and being seen.

The wood-panelled, cosy **Ritz Club** in the legendary Ritz hotel is open only to members and hotel guests, though the chic and elegant are welcome. The ambience is upmarket and the music makes for easy listening. A younger, glamourous set have recently begun to make the Ritz Club their home, attracted, no doubt, by its old-fashioned star quality.

La Suite is currently one of the hardest places to get into in Paris. Run by the Guettas formerly of Les Bains, the smooth decor sets off the expensive tans sported by the jetsetters, supermodels and film stars who come here. Booking a table at the expensive, but decent, restaurant is a good way to ensure access. Equally, posh, **Le VIP** is populated by wannabes attracted by the name. Private parties are often held here, so it's a good idea to call ahead.

Nirvana Lounge is an opulent affair with a designer music soundtrack compiled by Claude Challe. The bar is open all day and stays busy with party-goers on the dance floor until four in the morning. Another extremely upscale spot is **L'Etoile** situated near the Arc de Triomphe. Be prepared to make the effort to look your best (and most-solvent) to get in here.

The most popular of the posh clubs and the most laid-back and friendly once you're inside, is **Le Cab** (formerly known as Cabaret). The interior has recently been redesigned by Ora Ito, and today, anybody who's any-body comes here to dance like crazy or lay back and take it all in on one of the sumptuous mattresses in the chillout area.

TRENDY

Once a working-class music hall frequented by famous Parisians Edith Piaf and Jean Gabin, **Balajo** has now gone upmarket although it still emits a friendly vibe and remains one of the best clubs in Paris for dancing; they even hold ballroom dancing nights. It's also one of the few clubs open on Mondays.

An ultra-hip young crowd (and a few drag queens) flock to the small and cosy **Folie's Clubbing**, one-time strip joint and present-day venue for live music. Its original theme nights make for some of the best fun clubbing around. For a top dancing night out, try the fortnightly "Bal" with live big band at the **Elysée Montmartre**. Here too, look out for "Return to the Source", Goa-trance nights that come all the way from London's Fridge.

Paris's trendy clubs seem to have a longer shelf-life than those in some other cities and another hip venue that's still going strong is **Le**

Gibus which offers different dance styles throughout the week. Check the flyers to pick your own style of party.

The **Batofar**, the scarlet lighthouse ship moored on the Seine in the 13th arrondissement, is now a mainstay of the Paris club scene. The music here varies from underground techno to reggae depending on the night of the week, but the crowd are always friendly and relaxed. In the summer, try not to miss their wonderfully chilled-out afternoon sessions on the quayside.

The **Nouveau Casino** behind the ever trendy Café Charbon (see p319) in Oberkampf pulls in an eclectic crowd for events varying from dub to air-guitar competitions. Newcomer **Le Triptyque** has made an impressive mark on the Paris club scene with its mixed programming and excellent live music agenda. Old-timer **La Flêche d'Or** also offers an eclectic array of concerts, DJ nights and concept evenings. Whilst if it's just a large dance floor that's needed, then Johnny Hallyday's club **L'Amnesia** should suffice.

WORLD MUSIC

A stylish and expensive African-Antillean club, **Keur Samba** is popular with the jetset. Things get going after 2am and last long into the night. **Le Casbah** is exclusive, jazzy and one of the best established venues on the Paris club scene. Its African-Middle Eastern decor has always been a magnet for models and trendies who, in between dances, do a little nocturnal shopping in the club's downstairs boutique. Le Casbah is currently enjoying something of a renaissance of its 'chicest of the chic' reputation.

If your nervous system responds favourably to the heaving rhythms and throbbing beat of authentic Latin music, you should head for **La Java**, which combines

glorious sounds with the quaint appeal of a Belleville dance hall. **Les Etoiles** is the place to go for salsa with soul. The **Latina Café**, on the other hand, is a more upmarket venue for Latin music. Other lively world music nights are held at **Trottoirs de Buenos-Aires**, **Chapelle des Lombards** and the cellar bar at **Aux Trois Maillets** (see Rock, Jazz and World Music pp349–50).

GAY AND LESBIAN

The gay scene in Paris is thriving. **Le Queen** boasts a great line-up of DJs. Monday is disco night, Friday and Saturday are garage and soul and the rest of the week is drum and bass and house. Some of the raunchier events are men-only. Girls should go with pretty boys. Sunday nights at **La Locomotive** are the Gay Tea Dance. Wednesday is Respect, formally of Le Queen. **Le Champmeslé**, one of the most venerable fixtures of Paris's ever more upfront and confi-dent lesbian scene, continues to evolve and attract a new clientele. **Pulp** is the city's biggest and best lesbian club. Men are admitted in the week, but the weekend is strictly for ladies. For a pre-club venue, lesbian bars **Bliss Kfé** and **Le Troisième Lieu** are the hippest and busiest. Scream is the gay night at the **Elysée Montmartre**. **Le Depôt** is rumoured to be one of the most fun gay clubs in Paris, with a much-talked about backroom. Their Gay Tea Dance, held every Sunday, is legendary.

ADMISSION CHARGES

Some clubs are strictly private, others have a more generous admission policy. Prices can range from 12€ to 15€ or 30€, or more, and may be higher after midnight and on week-ends. But quite often there are concessions for women.

In general, one drink (une consommation) is included in the entry price; thereafter it can become an extremely expensive evening.

DIRECTORY

DISCO AND CLUB VENUES

Alcazar
62 Rue Mazarine 75006.
Map 12 F4.
Tel 01 53 10 19 99.

L'Amnesia
33 Ave Maine 75015.
Map 15 C3.
Tel 01 56 80 37 37.

Les Bains
7 Rue du Bourg-
L'Abbé 75003.
Map 13 B1.
Tel 01 48 87 01 80.

Balajo
9 Rue de Lappe 75011.
Map 14 E4.
Tel 01 47 00 07 87.

Le Bataclan
50 blvd Voltaire 75011.
Map 13 E1.
Tel 01 43 14 35 35.

Batofar
Moored opposite 11
Quai Francois Mauriac
75013.
Tel 01 56 29 10 00.

Le Cab
2 Pl de Palais Royale
75001.
Map 12 E1.
Tel 01 58 62 56 25.

**Le Cabaret
Milliardaire**
68 rue Pierre Charon
75008.
Map 4 F5.
*Tel 01 42 89 44 14 &
01 53 5 49 49.*

Castel's
15 Rue Princesse 75006.
Map 12 E4.
Tel 01 40 51 52 80.

Club Med World
39 Cour St-Emilion
75012.
Tel 08 10 81 04 10.

**Dancing de la
Coupole**
102 Boulevard
Montparnasse 75014.
Map 15 C1
Tel 01 43 27 56 00.

Le Duplex
2 Bis Avenue Foch 75002.
Map 4 D4.
Tel 01 45 00 45 00.
www.leduplex.fr

Elysée Montmartre
72 Blvd Rochechouart
75018.
Map 6 F2.
Tel 01 44 92 45 38.

L'Etoile
12 Rue de Presbourg
75016.
Map 4 D4.
Tel 01 45 00 78 70.

Les Etoiles
61 Rue du Château d'Eau
75010.
Map 7 C5.
Tel 01 47 70 60 56.
www.etoiles-salsa.com

La Flèche d'Or
102 bis Rue de Bagnolet
75002.
Tel 01 44 64 01 02.

Folie's Clubbing
11 Pl Pigalle 75009.
Map 6 E2.
Tel 01 48 78 55 25.

Le Gibus
18 Rue du Faubourg-du-
Temple 75011.
Map 8 E15.
Tel 01 47 00 78 88.

Hammam Club
94 Rue d'Amsterdam
75009.
Map 6 D2.
Tel 01 55 07 80 00.

La Locomotive
90 Blvd de Clichy 75018.
Map 4 E4.
Tel 01 53 41 88 88.

Nouveau Casino
109 Rue Oberkampf
75011.
Map 14 E1.
Tel 01 43 57 57 40.

Nirvana Lounge
3 Ave Matignon 75008.
Map 5 A5.
Tel 01 53 89 18 91.

Les Plances
40 Rue de Colisée 75008.
Map 5 A4.
Tel 01 42 25 11 68.

Pulp
25 Blvd Poissonière
75002.
Map 7 A5.
Tel 01 40 26 01 93.

Regine's
49–51 Rue Ponthieu
75008.
Map 5 A5.
Tel 01 43 59 21 13.

Rex Club
5 Blvd Poissonière
75002.
Map 7 A5.
Tel 01 42 36 10 96.

Ritz Club
Hôtel Ritz, 15 Pl
Vendôme 75001.
Map 6 D5.
Tel 01 43 16 30 30.
www.ritzparis.com

La Scala
188 bis Rue de Rivoli
75001.
Map 12 E2.
Tel 01 42 61 64 00.

La Suite
40 Ave George V 75008.
Map 4 E5.
Tel 01 53 5 49 49.

Triptyque
142 rue Montmartre
75002.
Map 13 A1.
Tel 01 40 28 05 55.

VIP
78 Ave des Champs-
Elysées 75008.
Map 4 E4.
Tel 01 56 69 16 66.

WAGG
62 Rue Mazarine 75006.
Map 12 F4.
Tel 01 55 42 22 00.

Zed Club
2 Rue des Anglais 75005.
Map 13 A5.
Tel 01 43 54 93 78.

WORLD MUSIC

Le Casbah
18-20 Rue de la Forge-
Royale 75011.
Tel 01 43 71 04 39.

Les Etoiles
61 Rue Château d'Eau
75010.
Map 7 C5.
Tel 01 45 00 78 70.

La Java
105 Rue du Faubourg-du-
Temple 75010.
Map 8 E5.
Tel 01 42 02 20 52.

Latina Café
114 Ave des Champs-
Elysées 75008.
Map 4 E4.
Tel 01 42 89 98 89.

Keur Samba
79 Rue de la Boétie
75008.
Map 5 A4.
Tel 01 43 59 03 10.

GAY AND LESBIAN VENUES

Bliss Kfé
30 Rue du Roi de Sicile
75004.
Map 13 C3.
Tel 01 42 78 49 36.

La Champmeslé
4 Rue Chabanais 75001.
Map 12 E1.
Tel 01 42 96 85 20.

Le Depôt
10 Rue aux Ours 75003.
Map 13 B2.
Tel 01 44 54 96 96.

Le Queen
102 Ave des Champs-
Elysées 75008.
Map 4 E4.
Tel 01 53 89 08 90.

Le Troisième Lieu
62 Rue Quincampoix
75004.
Map 13 B2.
Tel 01 48 04 85 64.

Cinema

Paris is the world's capital of film appreciation. With more than 370 screens within the city limits, distributed among over 100 cinemas and multiplexes, a fabulous cornucopia of films are screened, both brand-new and classic. Although American movies dominate the market more than ever, virtually every filmmaking industry in the world has found a niche in the city's art houses. Cinemas change their programmes on Wednesdays. The cheapest practical guides to what's on are *Pariscope* and *L'Officiel des Spectacles (see p340)* with complete cinema listings and timetables for some 300 films. *Zurban* also has features on current releases. Films shown in subtitled original language versions are coded "VO" *(version originale)*; dubbed films are coded "VF" *(version française)*. The Fête du Cinéma is held for three days in June. The system is that you pay full price for one film and then every film seen subsequently in any cinema on that day costs around 2€. Film buffs think nothing of taking in six or seven screenings on the day.

MOVEMENTS IN CINEMA

Paris was the cradle of the cinematograph over 100 years ago, when Auguste and Louis Lumière invented the early film projector. Their screening of *L'Arrivée d'un Train en Gare de la Ciotat* ('Arrival of a Train at la Ciotat Station) in Paris in 1895, is considered by many to mark the birth of the medium. The French reverence for film as a true art form is based on a theory of one of the world's first film critics, Ricciotto Canudo, an Italian intellectual living in France, who dubbed cine-matography "the Seventh Art" in 1922. The title holds true even today. The city was of course also the incubator of that very Parisian vanguard movement, the New Wave, when film directors such as Claude Chabrol, François Truffaut, Jean-Luc Godard and Eric Rohmer in the late 1950s and early 60s revolutionized the way films were made and perceived. The exploration of existential themes, the use of long tracking shots and the rejection of studios for outside locations are some of the characteristics of New Wave film. In 2001, the success of *Amélie Poulain* revitalized the Parisian filmmaking scene; many of its locations are easy to spot as you walk around town. The same is true of *The Da Vinci Code*, also featuring *Amelie* star Audrey Tautou.

CINEMA ZONES

Most Paris cinemas are concentrated in several cinema belts, which enjoy the added appeal of nearby restaurants and shops.

The Champs-Elysées remains the densest cinema strip in town, where you can see the latest Hollywood smash hit or French *auteur* triumph, as well as some classic re-issues, in subtitled original language versions. Cinemas in the Grands Boulevards, in the vicinity of the Opéra de Paris Garnier, show films in both subtitled and dubbed versions. The Place de Clichy is the last Parisian stronghold of Pathé, which operates no less than 13 screens there, all showing dubbed versions. A major hub of Right Bank cinema activity is in the Forum des Halles shopping mall.

The Left Bank, historically associated with the city's intel-lectual life, remains the centre of the art and repertory cine-mas. Yet, it has equally as many of the latest block-busters. Since the 1980s, many cinemas in the Latin Quarter have closed down and the main area for Left Bank theatres is now the Odéon-St-Germain-des-Prés area. The Rue Champollion is an exception. It has enjoyed a revival as a mini-district for art and repertory films.

Further to the south, Mont-parnasse remains a lively district of new films in both dubbed and subtitled prints.

BIG SCREENS AND PICTURE PALACES

Among surviving landmark cinemas are two Grands Boulevards venues, the 2,800-seat **Le Grand Rex** with its Baroque decor, and the **Max Linder Panorama**, which was refurbished by a group of independent film buffs in the 1980s for both popular and art film programming.

The massive new 14-screen **MK2 Bibliothèque** cinema (plus bar, shops and exhibition space), recently opened up in the revitalised 13th arrondisse-ment, just across the river, the **Bercy** cinema complex is well worth a visit too.

In the Cité des Sciences et de l'Industrie at La Villette, scientific films are shown at **La Géode** *(see p235)*. This has a hemispheric screen (once the world's largest) and an "omnimax" projector which uses 70-mm film shot horizon-tally to project an image which is nine times larger than the standard 35-mm print. Along the Canal St-Martin, **MK2**'s twin cinema complexes – **Quai de la Loire** and **Quai de la Seine** – are linked by a canal boat.

REVIVAL AND REPERTORY HOUSES

Each week, more than 150 titles representing the best of world cinema can be seen. For old Hollywood films, the independent **Grand Action** mini-chain can't be beaten. Other active and thoughtful repertory and re-issue venues include the excellent **Reflets Médicis** screens in the Rue Champollion and the **Pagode**. The latter is particularly striking, the Oriental pagoda was constructed in 1895 and has been recently renovated.

The **Studio 28** in Montmartre is a lovely old movie house with lights in the theatre designed by Jean Cocteau and a charming garden bar full of fairy lights and kitsch cut-outs of old film stars. Opened in the 1920s, Studio 28 claims to be the first ever avant-garde cinema and once played host to film greats such as Luis Buñuel and Abel Gance. They screen everything from the latest releases through to Fellini festivals and documentary shows. There are at least ten films screened here each week, including art-house classics and pre-releases. The cinema also holds regular debates with well-known directors and actors. Another Parisian institution, the **Studio Galande** has shown the *Rocky Horror Picture Show* to costumed movie-goers every Friday night for over 20 years.

CINÉMATHÈQUE FRANÇAISE

The private "school" of the New Wave generation, this famous film archive and repertory cinema was created by Henri Langlois in 1936 *(see p198)*. It has lost its monopoly on classic film screenings, but it is still a must for cinephiles in search of that rare film no longer in theatrical circulation or, perhaps, recently restored or rescued. The association is now housed at 51 Rue de Bercy in a wonderfully futuristic-looking building designed by Frank Gehry. The sail-like façade has given the building its nickname: "dancer revealing her tutu". The film library has more than 18,000 digitalized movies, and there are enough exhibitions, projections, lectures and workshops to satisfy the appetite of any film enthusiast.

NON-THEATRICAL VENUES

In addition to the Cinémathèque Française, film programmes and festivals are integral parts of two highly popular Paris cultural institutions, the Musée d'Orsay *(see pp144–5)* and

the Pompidou Centre *(see pp110–11)* with its **Salle Garance**. The Musée d'Orsay regularly schedules film programmes to complement current art exhibitions and is usually restricted to silent films. The Pompidou Centre organizes vast month-long retrospectives, devoted to national film industries and on occasion to some of the major companies.

Finally, the **Forum des Images** *(see p109)* in the heart of Les Halles is a hi-tech film and video library with a vast selection of films and documentaries featuring the city of Paris from the late 19th century to the present day. The archives here are amazing and include newsreels and advertisements featuring Paris alongside the feature films and documentaries. The Forum has three cinemas, all of which run daily screenings of feature films, beginning at 2.30pm. One ticket allows the visitor access to both the video library and to the cinema screenings. In the video library it is possible to search the database of over 6,000 films and then watch your choice on your own personal screen. The cinema screenings are frequently grouped according to theme or director, making it possible to spend several hours enjoying a mini-retrospective.

TICKET PRICES

Expect to pay around 9€ at first-run venues or even more for films of unusual length or special media attention. However, exhibitors practise a wide array of collective discount incentives, including cut-rate admissions for students, the unemployed, the elderly, old soldiers and large families. Wednesday is discount day for everybody at some cinemas – prices are slashed to as low as 4€.

France's three exhibition giants, Gaumont, UGC and MK2, also sell special discount cards and accept credit card reservations for their flagship houses, while repertory houses issue "fidelity" cards.

FILMS WITH STRONG IMAGES OF PARIS

Historical Paris (studio-made)
An Italian Straw Hat
(René Clair, 1927)

Sous les toits de Paris
(René Clair, 1930)

Les Misérables
(Raymond Bernard, 1934)

Hôtel du Nord
(Marcel Carné, 1937)

Les Enfants du Paradis
(Marcel Carné, 1945)

Casque d'Or
(Jacques Becker, 1952)

La Traversée de Paris
(Claude Autant-Lara, 1956)

Playtime
(Jacques Tati, 1967)

New Wave Paris (location-made)
Breathless
(Jean-Luc Godard, 1959)

Les 400 coups
(François Truffaut, 1959)

Documentary Paris
Paris 1900
(Nicole Vedrès, 1948)

La Seine a rencontré Paris
(Joris Ivans, 1957)

Paris as seen by Hollywood
Seventh Heaven
(Frank Borzage, 1927)

Camille
(George Cukor, 1936)

An American in Paris
(Vincente Minnelli, 1951)

Gigi
(Vincente Minnelli, 1958)

Irma La Douce
(Billy Wilder, 1963)

Le Divorce
(James Ivory, 2003)

The Bourne Identity
(Doug Liman, 2002)

Frantic
(Roman Polanski, 1988)

French Kiss
(Lawrence Kasdan, 1995)

Moulin Rouge
(Baz Luhrmann, 2001)

Before Sunset
(Richard Linklater, 2004)

The Ninth Gate
(Roman Polanski, 1999)

Paris when it Sizzles
(Richard Quine, 1964)

Cinema Festivals

Film festivals are a way of life for Parisian movie buffs, there are several major events each year and lots of small themed festivals happening at any given time around the city. The annual Paris Film Festival, held at the end of March, may be dwarfed by its glitzier sister in Cannes, but the capital's version is a far friendlier event for the public to attend – and there are still more than enough opportunities to spot celebrities.

OPEN AIR FESTIVALS

There are several outdoor cinema festivals throughout the summer, including the Festival Silhouette which shows short films in the lovely Buttes Chaumont (see p232), the Cinema au Clair du Lune festival which has projections of films at Parisian sites which are relevant to the movie and Le Cinema en Plein Air which draws crowds to a lawn in La Villette (see pp234-35), where a giant inflatable screen shows old and contemporary classics. This is one of the summer's most popular events so be sure to get there early and don't forget to take a hamper full of goodies to nibble on throughout the movie.

INDOOR FESTIVALS

During the annual Paris Film Festival, over 100 films are shown at the Gaumont Marignon on the Champs-Elysées. The city's gay and lesbian film festival at the Forum des Images usually takes place in November. Paris Tout Court is an impressive short film festival held at the Arlequin in St-Germain which also stages lectures and meetings with renowned directors and artists. Other film festivals include the Les Etranges festival which shows weird and wonderful offbeat films from around the world to enthusiastic audiences.

DIRECTORY

CINEMAS

Action Christine Odeon
4 Rue Christine 75006.
Map 12 F4.
Tel 01 43 29 11 30.

Action Ecoles
23 Rue des Ecoles 75005.
Map 13 A5.
Tel 01 43 25 72 07.

Arelquin
76 Rue de Rennes 75006.
Map 12 E4.
Tel 01 45 44 28 80.

Le Balzac
1 Rue Balzac 75008.
Map 4 E4.
Tel 08 92 68 31 23.

Le Champo
51 Rue des Ecoles 75005.
Map 13 A5.
Tel 01 43 29 79 89.

Cinémathèque Française
51 Rue de Bercy 75013.
Tel 01 71 19 33 33.
www.cinemateque.fr

Cinema Studio Galande
42 Rue Galande 75005.
Map 13 A4.
Tel 08 92 68 06 24.

Forum des Images
Porte St-Eustache,
Forum des Halles 75001.
Map 13 A2.
Tel 01 44 76 62 00.

Gaumont Marignan
27 Ave Champs-Elysées 75008.
Map 5 A5.
Tel 01 42 89 12 74.

La Géode
26 Ave Corentin-Cariou 75019.
Tel 08 92 68 45 40.
www.cite-sciences.fr

Goethe Institut
17 Ave d'Iena 75016.
Map 10 D1.
Tel 01 44 43 92 30.

Grand Action
Action Rive Gauche,
5 Rue des Ecoles 75005.
Map 13 B5.
Tel 01 43 54 47 62.

Le Grand Rex
1 Blvd Poissonnière 75002.
Map 7 A5.
Tel 08 92 68 70 23.

Images d'Ailleurs
21 Rue de la Clef 75005.
Map 13 B2.
Tel 01 45 87 18 09.

Latina
20 Rue du Temple 75004.
Map 7 C2.
Tel 08 92 68 07 51.

Lucenaire
53 Rue Notre-Dame-des-Champs 75006.
Map 16 E2.
Tel 01 45 44 57 34.

Max Linder Panorama
24 Blvd Poissonnière 75009. **Map** 7 A5.
Tel 08 92 68 00 31.

Majestic Bastille
4 Blvd Richard Lenoir 75011.
Map 14 E4.
Tel 01 47 00 02 48.

MK2 Beaubourg
50 Rue Rambuteau 75003.
Map 7 B2.
Tel 08 92 69 84 84.

MK2 Bibliothèque
128-162 Ave de France 75015. **Map** 18 F4.
Tel 08 92 69 84 84.

MK2 Quai de la Seine/Quai de la Loire
Map 8 F1.
Tel 08 92 69 84 84.

Pagode
57 bis Rue de Babylone 75007. **Map** 11 C4.
Tel 01 45 55 48 48.

Quartier Latin
9 Rue Champollion 75005.
Map 13 A5.
Tel 01 43 26 84 65.

Racine Odeon
6 Rue de l'Ecole de Medecine 75006.
Map 12 F4.

Reflets Médicis
3-7 Rue Champollion 75005.
Map 12 F5.
Tel 01 46 33 25 97.

Salle Garance
Centre Georges Pompidou, 19 Rue Beaubourg 75004.
Map 13 B2.

St-Andre des Arts
30 Rue St Andre des Arts 75006.
Map 12 F4.
Tel 01 43 26 48 18.

Studio 28
10 Rue Tholozé 75018.
Map 6 E1.
Tel 01 46 06 36 07.

UGC Ciné Cité Bercy
2 Cour St-Emilion 75012.
Tel 08 36 68 68 58.

UGC Cine-Cite les Halles
7 Place de la Rotonde 75001.
Map 7 A2.
Tel 08 92 70 00 00.

Sport and Fitness

There is no end of sporting activities in Paris. Certain events such as the Roland Garros tennis tournament and the Tour de France bicycle race are national institutions. The only drawback is that many of the facilities are on the outskirts of the city.

For details regarding all sporting events in and around Paris contact **Paris Infos Mairie** – a free information service run by the Town Hall. The weekly entertainment guides *L'Officiel des Spectacles*, *Pariscope* and the Wednesday edition of *Le Figaro* also have good listings of the week's sporting events *(see p340)*. For in-depth sports coverage there is the daily paper *L'Equipe*. See also *Children's Paris* on page 362.

OUTDOOR SPORTS

The annual Tour de France bicycle race finishes in July in Paris to city-wide frenzy, when the French president awards the coveted *maillot jaune* (yellow jersey) to the winner. For over twenty years now the final stage of the tour has taken place on the Champs-Elysées with the riders racing up the famous avenue. Traffic across the city grinds to a halt and sports fans and couch potatoes alike flock to cheer on the cyclists. Finding a spot to watch can be extremely tough, it's best to hunt down your speck several hours before the riders are expected.

For those brave enough to tackle cycling through the city traffic, bikes may be hired throughout Paris, including at **Paris Vélo** in the Rue du Fer-à-Moulin and **Maison Roue Libre** in Passage Mondétour, headquarters of the RATP's bicycle rental service, Roue Libre *(see p359)*. In summer (weekends and bank holidays only), old RATP buses hire out bicycles from five locations (Place de la Concorde, Stalingrad, Place du Châtelet, Porte d'Auteil and Parc Floral de Vincennes). The **Fédération Française de Cyclotourisme** in the Rue Louis Bertrand will give you information on over 300 cycling clubs around Paris. Things are gradually improving for those who favour pedal power, all year round, the city council shuts down some of the quaysides on Sundays and national holidays to allow cyclists freewheeling next to the Seine. The city has also undertaken a programme of expansion for its cycle lanes. Be aware though that Paris traffic is heavy and Parisian drivers not especially two-wheel friendly. Those who can't wait for the quais along the Seine to be closed on Sundays should head over to the Bois de Vincennes or the Bois de Boulogne for a leisurely bike ride through the woods. The more ambitious can pick up a copy of the free Paris à Vélo map from a tourist office to find details of all the city's cycle lanes. If you'd prefer to take an organized cycle tour through the city, there are several organizations who run fun trips. **Fat Tire Bike Tours** in the Rue Edgar Faure have daily trips in spring and summer in which knowledgeable guides shepherd cyclists around the streets whilst imparting interesting information on the city's landmarks. **Paris à Vélo c'est Sympa** runs multilingual tours to offbeat parts of the city.

Roller bladers can enjoy parades through the city on Friday nights. The police close off boulevards around the city allowing thousands of skate fans to join the trip every week. The parade usually starts at Place de la Bastille at 10pm, but you can join the route at any point if the whole circuit seems a little much. Contact www.pari-roller.com for details of the route. Beginners can enjoy free tuition prior to the departure of the parade if they arrive at the start point at 8pm. There are many good outlets in the city for roller-blade rental. The parade's website provides useful links to recommended outlets. As a safety precaution the trip is cancelled if the weather is inclement and the roads wet.

Parisians enjoy Sunday afternoon boating in the Bois de Vincennes *(see p233)*, the Bois de Boulogne *(see p254)* and the Parc des Buttes-Chaumont *(see p232)*. Just queue up to hire a boat.

All the golf courses are outside Paris. Many are private clubs, but some will admit non-members – for further information contact the **Fédération Française du Golf** in the Rue Anatole-France. Otherwise try the **Golf de Chevry, Golf de St-Pierre du Perray, Golf de St-Quentin en Yvelines** or the **Golf de Villennes**. Expect to pay at least 25€ each time you want to play.

You can go horse-riding in both the Bois de Boulogne and the Bois de Vincennes. For details, contact the **Ligue Equestre de Paris** in the Rue Laugier.

Tennis can be played at municipal courts such as the **Tennis Luxembourg** in the Jardin du Luxembourg. Courts are available every day on a first-come first-served basis. **Tennis de la Faluère** in the Bois de Vincennes has some of the better courts, but these must be booked at least 24 hours in advance.

INDOOR SPORTS

There are plenty of gyms in Paris which you can use with a day pass. Expect to pay 20€ or more, depending on the facilities.

Club Med Gym is a well-equipped, popular chain of gyms with more than twenty sites in Paris and the suburbs. Good choices include the branches in Rue de Berri and Rue de Rennes. **Club Jean de Beauvais** in the Rue Jean de Beauvais, is a state-of-the-art

CHILDREN'S PARIS

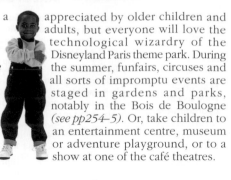

It's never too early to instil a lifelong taste for this magical city in your children. A trip to Disneyland Resort Paris *(see pp242–5)* or down the Seine *(see pp72–3)*, the dizzy heights of the Eiffel Tower *(see pp192–3)* or a visit to Notre-Dame *(see pp82–5)* are fun at any age, and with children in tow you will see old haunts through new eyes. The historic parks are probably best

appreciated by older children and adults, but everyone will love the technological wizardry of the Disneyland Paris theme park. During the summer, funfairs, circuses and all sorts of impromptu events are staged in gardens and parks, notably in the Bois de Boulogne *(see pp254–5)*. Or, take children to an entertainment centre, museum or adventure playground, or to a show at one of the café theatres.

La Cité des Enfants at La Villette

PRACTICAL ADVICE

Paris welcomes young families in hotels *(see p278)* and most restaurants *(see p295)*. Many sights and attractions offer child reductions, while infants under three or four enter free. The upper age limit for reductions is usually about 12 but can vary considerably. Many museums are free on Sundays; others allow children under 18 in free at any time. Ask at the Office du Tourisme

(see p280) for full details of child reductions, or check in the weekly entertainment guides such as *Pariscope, L'Officiel des Spectacles, Paris Mômes* and *Zurban*.

A lot of the children's activities are geared to end-of-school times, including Wednesday afternoons when French children have time off. For information on museum workshops, contact the **Ministère de la Culture** or visit **www.paris-frimousse.com**, which has information on events for 2–12-year olds.

Cots and baby-buggies can be hired from major baby-sitting agencies like **Home Service**. **Mamynoo** and **Kid Services** are other specialist baby-sitting organizations.

MUSEUMS

Top of the museum list for children is undoubtedly the Cité des Sciences et de l'Industrie *(see pp234–9)* at Parc de la Villette. Hands-on activities and changing exhibitions illuminate many aspects of science and modern technology in this immense

complex. There are sections for children called La Cité des Enfants and Techno Cité. In central Paris, the Palais de la Découverte, within the Grand Palais *(see p206)*, is an old-fashioned but lively science museum where staff adopt the role of mad inventors.

The Louvre *(see pp122–9)* organizes special sessions designed to introduce children to various aspects of art, while the Galerie des Enfants at the Pompidou Centre *(see pp110–13)* does the same with modern art.

Other enjoyable museums for children include the Musée de la Marine *(see p199)* and the Musée de la Poupée *(see p114)*. The former covers the history of the French maritime tradition and includes scale models. The latter displays hand-made dolls dating from the mid-19th century, and also offers doll-making classes for both adults and children.

USEFUL CONTACTS

Home Service

Tel 08 73 04 40 36.

www.homeserviceidf.com

Kid Services

Tel 08 20 00 02 30.

Mamynoo

Tel 08 20 00 07 82.

www.mamynoo.com

Ministère de la Culture

www.culture.gouv.fr

The Café d'Edgar theatre

The Guignol marionnettes

PARKS, ZOOS AND ADVENTURE PLAYGROUNDS

The best children's park within Paris is the Jardin d'Acclimatation in the Bois de Boulogne *(see pp254–5)*, with a children's theatre and circus, a pony club, a mini railway and boats. The Musée en Herbe *(see p254)* is a museum created especially for children offering entertaining educational activities.

Pony rides, Jardin d'Acclimatation

France Miniature recreates France on a small scale, complete with all its monuments.

The Bois de Vincennes *(see p233)* has simple amusements for children in the inexpensive Parc Floral. It also has the largest funfair in France, open from Palm Sunday through to the end of May. Perhaps the most appealing zoo is the small Ménagerie in the Jardin des Plantes *(see p164)*.

ENTERTAINMENT CENTRES

There are many supervised children's activity centres in Paris. The Atelier des Enfants in the Pompidou Centre *(see pp110–11)* has a workshop on Wednesday and Saturday afternoons from 2.30 to 4pm. The medium of instruction is French but the circuses, mime-shows, marionnettes and craft or museum workshops focus on actions rather than words.

Several café-theatres, including Café d'Edgar *(see p343)* and Au Bec Fin *(see p342)*, offer children's shows where mime, dance or music form part of the content. The most spectacular cinematic experience is in La Géode at the Cité des Sciences et de l'Industrie (see p237). The cinema **Le Saint Lambert** specializes in children's films and comic strips in French, though most films for children

Lion in the Bois de Vincennes zoo

will not have English subtitles. Cinema tickets are cheaper on Wednesdays, with no child reductions at weekends.

The **Cirque de Paris** offers children a day's entertainment when they can meet the animals, put on clown make-up or practise tightrope walking. Shows are in the afternoon, after lunch with the *artistes*.

The Guignol marionnette puppet shows are a summer tradition in Paris. The themes are similar to the traditional English Punch and Judy shows. Most of the main parks hold Guignol shows in summer on Wednesday afternoons and at weekends. One or two shows are free. Consult the entertainment guides such as *Pariscope*, *L'Officiel des Spectacles* and *Paris Mômes*.

ADDRESSES

Cirque de Paris
115 Blvd Charles de Gaulle, 92390 Ville-neuve-la-Garenne. *Tel* 01 47 99 40 40.

France Miniature
25 Route du Mesnil, 78990 Elancourt. *Tel* 01 30 16 16 30. **www**.franceminiature.com

Le Saint Lambert
6 Rue Peclet 75015. *Tel* 01 45 32 91 68.

Circus acrobats training at the Cirque de Paris

Fireworks over Sleeping Beauty Castle, Disneyland Resort Paris

Old-fashioned fairground carousels are situated near Sacré-Coeur *(see pp224–5)* and Forum des Halles *(see p109)*. A great way of inspiring interest in the city's history, and great fun too, is a boat trip. Several companies compete *(see pp72– 3)* from different departure points, and pass a host of waterfront sites including Notre-Dame, the Louvre and the Musée d'Orsay. Boats departing from La Villette travel along the Paris canal system. Radio-controlled model boats are popular on the ponds of the Jardin du Luxembourg *(see p172)*. Or, take the family boating on the lakes of the Bois de Boulogne *(see pp254–5)* or the Bois de Vincennes *(see p233)*. Riding is also popular in these parks *(see p357 Directory)*.

THEME PARKS

The two parks of Disneyland Resort Paris *(see pp242–5)* are the biggest and most spectacular of the Paris theme parks. Six hotels, each with a different, imaginative theme, and a campsite provide on-site accommodation. The complex also includes a golf course, shops and restaurants.

Parc Asterix is a French theme park centring around the legendary world of Asterix the Gaul. Here six themed "worlds" feature gladiators, slave auctions and rides among the many attractions. The park is situated 38 km (24 miles) northeast of Paris. Take the RER line B to Charles de Gaulle Airport then the shuttle bus to Parc Asterix.

SPORTS AND RECREATION

The giant waterpark **Aquaboulevard** is one of the best places to take energetic youngsters. Also good is the indoor pool at **Forum des Halles**. The weekly entertainment guide *Pariscope* lists the swimming pools in and around Paris. Remember that it is compulsory to wear a swimming cap. Accomplished rollerskaters and skateboarders practise outside the Palais de Chaillot *(see p198)*. On Sundays, in summer, the roads along the Seine (between Chatelêt and Bercy) are closed to traffic. Bikers and rollerbladers descend en masse. Disneyland Resort Paris *(see pp242–5)* has ice-skating rinks and a range of other sports facilities.

Donald Duck

ADDRESSES

Aquaboulevard
4 Rue Louis Armand 75015.
Tel *01 40 60 10 00.* ⬜ *9am–11pm Mon–Thu, 9am–midnight Fri, 8am–midnight Sat, 8am–11pm Sun.*

La Piscine des Halles
Forum des Halles, 10 Pl de la Rotonde, Les Halles 75001. **Map** 12 F2. **Tel** *01 42 36 98 44.* ⬜ *11.30am–10pm Mon–Fri, 9am–7pm Sat–Sun.*

Parc Asterix
BP8 Plailly 60128. 📠 *08 26 3010 40, 08 26 68 30 10.* ⬜ *Apr–mid-Oct: 10am–6pm Mon–Fri, 9am–7pm w/e & hols.* **www**.parcasterix.fr

Apache
56 Rue du Commerce 75015.
Map 10 E5. **Tel** *01 40 43 10 04.* *One of several branches.*

CHILDREN'S SHOPS

There is no shortage of chic children's fashion in Paris. A good place to start is the Rue du Jour in Beaubourg and Les Halles which has a number of children's boutiques. The city has many appealing toy shops such as Au Nain Bleu *(see p331)* or the branches of Apache *(see Addresses)*, but, like the clothes shops, they can be prohibitively expensive. *(See also p326.)*

Characters from the book *Tintin*, in Au Nain Bleu toy shop

Roller-skaters near the Eiffel Tower

Carousel near Sacré-Coeur

STREET LIFE AND MARKETS

Outside the Pompidou Centre (see pp110–11) street entertainers draw the crowds on sunny afternoons. Musicians, conjurors, fire-eaters and artists of all kinds perform here. In Montmartre there is a tradition of street-painting, predominantly in the Place du Tertre (see p222) where

Model boats for hire in the Jardin du Luxembourg

someone will always be willing to draw your child's portrait. It's also fun to take the funicular up the hill to Sacré-Coeur (see pp224–5), then walk down through the pretty streets.

Parisian markets are colourful and animated. Try taking children to the Marché aux Fleurs on the Ile de la Cité (see p81) or to the food markets on the Rue Mouffetard, in the Jardin des Plantes Quarter (see p166 and p339), or the Rue de Buci in St-Germaindes-Prés. The biggest flea market, Marché aux Puces de St-Ouen, is at weekends (see p231 and p339).

Alternatively take children to the quiet Ile de la Cité or Ile St-Louis on the Seine.

VIEWPOINTS AND SIGHTSEEING

Top of the sightseeing list for children is a trip up the Eiffel Tower (see pp192–3). On a clear day spectacular views over Paris will enable you to point out a number of sights, and at night the city is magically lit up. Lifts run until 11pm and queues are much shorter in the evenings. If you are pushing a baby buggy, bear in mind that the ascent is in three stages, using two separate lifts.

Other interesting sights for children include Sacré-Coeur (see pp224–5) with its ovoid dome – the second highest point in Paris after the Eiffel Tower – and Notre-Dame cathedral (see pp82–3) on the Ile de la Cité. Children will enjoy feeding the pigeons in the cathedral square, counting the 28 kings of Judah on the West Front and listening to you recount the story of the hunchback of Notre-Dame. There are incomparable views from the towers. Children and adults alike will appreciate the enchanting Sainte-Chapelle (see pp88–9), also on the Ile de la Cité. There are reductions for children under the age of 18.

Contrast ancient and modern Paris with a visit to the Pompidou Centre (see pp110–13) and enjoy a ride on the caterpillar-like escalators outside, or go to the café on the roof terrace for the views. There is also the 56-storey Montparnasse Tower (see p178) with some spectacular telescopic views from the top terrace; and there is the huge arch at La Défense (see p255) which has lifts to exhibition platforms where visitors can overlook the whole complex.

OTHER INTERESTS

Children are quick to see the funny side of unusual spectacles. Les Egouts, Paris's sewers, now welcome apprehensive visitors for a

Escalators at the Pompidou Centre

short tour of the city's sewerage system (see p190). Display boards in several languages explain the processes.

The Catacombes (see p179) are a long series of quarry tunnels built in Roman times, now lined with ancient skulls.

On the Ile de la Cité is the Conciergerie (see p81), a turreted prison where many hapless aristocrats spent their final days. The Grévin waxworks are in Boulevard Montmartre (see p216). The museum's Revolution rooms will especially appeal to older children, with gruesome scenes and grisly sound effects, demonstrating the reality of social upheaval.

EMERGENCIES

Enfance et Partage is a free 24-hour child helpline, (also for adults). One of Paris's largest children's hospitals is **Hôpital Necker**.

Enfance et Partage
Tel 08 00 05 12 34.

Hôpital Necker 149 Rue de Sèvres 75015. **Map** 15 B1. *Tel* 01 44 49 40 00.

A young visitor to Paris

SURVIVAL GUIDE

PRACTICAL INFORMATION

As in most large cities, it's easy to waste your limited sightseeing time in Paris on transport and in queues. A little forward planning can minimize this. Ring in advance to confirm the sight is open, and isn't closed for refurbishment or holidays – a phonecard, or *télécarte,* is a wise investment *(see p372).* Purchase a *carnet* or travel pass to economize and simplify transport on the buses and metro *(see pp384–7).* Buying a *Paris Museum Pass* will give unlimited

access to museums and monuments, and cuts down on queues. Beware the Paris lunch break (around 1–3pm), since many essential services shut down, as well as some museums. Guided tours are often the best way to see the essential sights before you get your bearings. If you're on a tight budget, admission prices are sometimes lower at certain times of day, or on Sundays; card-carrying students can obtain discounts on some tickets and admissions *(see p374).*

MUSEUMS AND MONUMENTS

There are more than 170 museums and monuments open to the public in Paris. Most are open Monday (or Tuesday) to Sunday, and from 10am to 5.40pm. Some offer evening visits. The national museums are closed on Tuesdays, except Versailles and the Musée d'Orsay, which are closed on Mondays. The municipal museums, such as those run by the city of Paris (Ville de Paris) are usually closed on Mondays.

An admission fee is usually charged, or a donation is expected. The entrance fee to some national museums is waived on the first Sunday of each month. Those under 18 are usually admitted free, and those 18–25 and over 60 often pay a reduced rate. The municipal museums, and some other museums, do not charge a fee to see their permanent collections on Sundays. Those under 7 and over 60 are admitted free at all times. To obtain the discounts you will have to provide absolute proof of who you are and how old you are.

Train station sign for information services

The *Paris Museum Pass* gives the bearer unlimited access to more than 60 museums and monuments for 2, 4 or 6 days, without having to queue – a significant advantage. It does not allow entry to temporary exhibitions. The pass can be purchased at any of the city's museums as well as main metro stations, Batobus stops, FNAC ticket counters and at the headquarters of the **Office du Tourisme** or **Paris Convention and Visitors' Bureau.**

OPENING HOURS

Most Paris shops and businesses are open from 9am to 7pm. While many stay open all day, others close for an hour or two from noon or 12.30. Some smaller food shops open earlier, around 7am, and take a longer midday break. Most business is closed on Sunday, and many shops close Monday too. Some restaurants close at least one day a week. Many shops close for a month or more during summer. Banks are open from around 9am to 4.30–5.15pm Mon–Fri, 9am–noon Sat. Some

close noon–2pm. The day before a public holiday some close at noon.

TOURIST INFORMATION

The main tourist office in Paris, the **Office du Tourisme et des Congrès de Paris,** is near the Tuileries garden. It provides the latest maps, information and brochures, and gives a comprehensive picture of events in the city. It is well worth a visit.
- There are also tourist offices at the Eiffel Tower, the Carrousel du Louvre, at Place du Tertre in Montmartre, at the Gare du Nord and Gare de Lyon, in the Opéra quarter, in front of Anvers metro station and at the Paris Expo exhibition centre (Porte de Versailles).

PARIS Convention and Visitors Bureau
Tourist Office logo

ENTERTAINMENT

The main listings magazines in Paris, available at all newsagents, are *Pariscope* and *L'Officiel des Spectacles (see p340).* Each Wednesday they present full information on the week's current theatre, cinema and exhibits, as well as on cabarets, dinner clubs and some restaurants.

Paris museum pass, for saving time and money

◁ **River view of Pont Neuf and the Ile de la Cité**

Paris sightseeing tour bus

FNAC ticket agencies book all the entertainment venues, including temporary museum shows. There are FNAC branches throughout Paris. For more information call one of their branches *(see p341)*.

For booking the theatre only, the Kiosque Théâtre sells same-day tickets at 50% discount. The two locations are Place de la Madeleine and the Parvis de la Gare Montparnasse *(see p341)*.

Visitors should be aware that smoking is generally not allowed in theatres or cinemas.

Kiosque Théâtre booking kiosk

GUIDED TOURS

Double-decker bus tours with commentaries in English, Italian, Japanese and German are organized by **France Tourisme**, **Cityrama** and **Paris**

Vision. The tours begin from the city centre and take about two hours. They pass the main sights but do not stop at all of them. Departure times vary. **Les Cars Rouges** runs British double-decker bus tours, stopping at many of the sights in Paris, which allow you to leave the bus at any of the stops and to continue later (ticket valid for 2 days). **Paris Balades** (www.paris balades.com) offers guided walking tours.

DISABLED ACCESS

Services for disabled people in Paris are still comparatively limited. Although most pavements are contoured to allow wheelchairs an easier passage, many restaurants, hotels, and even museums

are poorly equipped (they may claim otherwise). However, better facilities are being incorporated into all renovated and new buildings, and the French are usually more than ready to help disabled people who are having difficulty. For up-to-date information on public facilities for the disabled, contact the **Groupement pour l'Insertion des Personnes Handicapées Physiques (GIHP)**.

DISABILITY INFORMATION

Les Compagnons du Voyage
163 bis Ave de Clichy 75017.
Tel 01 53 11 11 12.
⬡ 7am–8pm Mon–Fri; 9.30am–6pm Sat; 9.30am–9pm Sun (to 5.30pm Jul & Aug). 7-day escort services on all transport. Costs vary.
www.compagnons.com

Association des Paralysés de France
17 Blvd August Blanqui 75013.
Map 17 B5. *Tel 01 40 78 69 00.*
Fax 01 45 89 40 57.
www.apf.asso.fr

GIHP
10 Rue Georges de Porto-Riche 75014. *Tel 01 43 95 66 36.*
Fax 01 45 40 40 26.
www.gihpnational.org

DIRECTORY

CITY CENTRE TOURIST OFFICES	Eiffel Tower	FOREIGN FRENCH TOURIST OFFICES	BUS TOUR OPERATORS
	Champ de Mars 75007. **Map** 10 F3. ⬡ *11am–6.40pm daily.*		
Office du Tourisme et des Congrès de Paris 25 Rue des Pyramides 75001. **Map** 12 E1. *Tel 08 92 68 30 00.* ⬡ *10am–7pm daily (from 11am Sun).* www.parisinfo.com	**Gare de Lyon** 20 Blvd Diderot 75012. **Map** 18 F1. ⬡ *8am–6pm Mon–Sat.*	**Australia** Level 13, 25 Bligh St, Sydney NSW 2000. *Tel (2) 92 31 52 44.*	**Cityrama** 2 Rue des Pyramides 75001. **Map** 12 E1. *Tel 01 44 55 60 00.* www.graylineparis.com
	Gare du Nord 18 Rue de Dunkerque 75010. **Map** 7 B2. ⬡ *8am–6pm daily.*	**Canada** 1981 Ave McGill College, Suite 490, Montréal QUE H3A 2W9. *Tel 514 288 2026.* @ canada@ franceguide.com	**France Tourisme** 33 Quai des Grands Augustins 75006. **Map** 12 F4. *Tel 01 45 02 88 05.* www.francetourisme.com
Anvers 72 Blvd Rochechouart 75018. **Map** 7 A2. ⬡ *10am–6pm daily.*	**Montmartre** 21 Place du Tertre 75018. **Map** 6 F1. ⬡ *10am–7pm daily.*	**United Kingdom** 178 Piccadilly, London W1V OAL. *Tel (0906) 8244 123 (within UK).* @ info.uk@ franceguide.com	**Les Cars Rouges** 17 Quai de Grenelle 75015. **Map** 9 C4. *Tel 01 53 95 39 53.* www.carsrouges.com
Carrousel du Louvre 99 Rue de Rivoli 75001. **Map** 13 A2. ⬡ *10am–6pm daily.*	**Opéra** 11 Rue Scribe 75009. **Map** 6 D4. ⬡ *9am–6.30pm Mon–Sat.*	**United States** 444 Madison Ave, New York, NY 10022. *Tel (212) 514 288 1904.*	**Paris Vision** 214 Rue de Rivoli 75001. **Map** 12 D1. *Tel 01 42 60 30 01.* www.parisvision.com

Personal Security and Health

Paris is as safe or as dangerous as you make it – common sense is usually sufficient to stay out of trouble. If, on the other hand, you fall sick during your visit, pharmacists are an excellent source of advice. In France pharmacists can diagnose many health problems and suggest appropriate treatment. For more serious medical help, someone at the emergency numbers below will be able to deal with most enquiries. There are many specialist services available, including a general advice line for English-speakers in crisis, an English-speaking Alcoholics Anonymous group, and a phoneline for psychiatric help.

French pharmacy sign

Emergency button at metro stations

EMERGENCY NUMBERS

SAMU (ambulance)
Tel 15 (freecall).

Police
Tel 17 (freecall).

**Pompiers
(fire department)**
Tel 18 (freecall).

European Emergency Call
Tel 112 (freecall).

**SOS Medecin
(doctor, house calls)**
Tel 01 47 07 77 77.

SOS Dentaire (dentist)
Tel 01 43 37 51 00.

Burn Specialists
Hôpital Cochin 75014.
Tel 01 58 41 41 41.

**SOS Help (English
language crisis line)**
Tel 01 46 21 46 46.

**SOS Dépression
(for psychiatric help)**
Tel 01 40 47 95 95.

Sexual Disease Centre
Tel 01 40 78 26 00.

Family Planning Centre
Tel 01 48 88 07 28/0800 803 803.

Anti Poison Centre
Tel 01 40 05 48 48.

PERSONAL SECURITY

For a city of over 2 million people, Paris is surprisingly safe. The centre of the city in particular has little violent crime. Muggings and brawls do occur, but they are rare compared to many other world capitals. However, do try to avoid poorly lit or isolated places. Beware of pickpockets, especially on the metro during the rush hour. Keep all valuables securely concealed and if you carry a handbag or case, never let it out of your sight.

When travelling late at night, avoid long transfers in metro stations, such as Montparnasse and Châtelet-Les Halles. Generally, areas around RER train stations tend to attract groups of youths from outlying areas who come to Paris for entertainment, and may become unruly. The last runs each night of RER trains to and from outlying areas should also be avoided. In an emergency in the metro, call the station agent by using the yellow telephone marked *Chef de Station* on all metro and RER platforms, or go to the ticket booth at the entrance. Most metro stations also have emergency buttons. Carriages also have alarm pulls. If there is a problem outside stations, or at bus stops, telephone the police by dialling 17.

PERSONAL PROPERTY

Take great care with your personal property at all times. Make sure you insure your possessions before arrival. On sightseeing or entertainment trips do not carry valuables with you. Also, only take as much cash as you think you will need. Most places accept credit cards. Traveller's cheques are the safest method

Paris fireman   **Policewoman**   **Policeman**

Typical Paris police car

Paris fire engine

Paris ambulance

of carrying large sums of money. You should never leave your luggage unattended in metro or train stations – it may be stolen or cause a bomb scare. For missing persons, or in the case of robbery or assault, call the police or go to the nearest police station *(Commissariat de Police)*. For lost or stolen passports call your consulate *(see p375)*.

MEDICAL TREATMENT

All European Union nationals are entitled to French Social Security coverage. However, treatment must be paid for, and hospital rates vary widely. Reimbursements may be obtained if you are carrying Form E111 (available free to EU citizens), but the process is long and involved. All travellers should consider purchasing travel insurance, and obtain a Form E111 in case of emergencies. Non-EU nationals must carry their own medical insurance.

In the case of a medical emergency, call **SAMU** *(see box on facing page)* or the **Pompiers** (fire department). Fire department ambulances are often the quickest to arrive at an emergency. In addition, first-aid and emergency treatment is provided at all fire stations.

Hospitals with casualty departments are shown on the Street Finder *(see p390)*. For English-language visitors, there are two hospitals with English-speaking staff and doctors: the **American Hospital** and the **British Hospital**.

There are many pharmacies throughout the city, and a short list is provided here. Pharmacies are recognized by the green crosses on the shop front. At night and on Sundays, pharmacies hang in their doorway the address of the nearest one open.

DIRECTORY

LOST PROPERTY BUREAU

Service des Objets Trouvés, 36 Rue des Morillons 75015.
☐ *8.30am–5pm Mon–Thu, 8.30am–4.30pm Fri.*
***Tel** 08 21 00 25 25.*

MEDICAL CENTRES

American Hospital
63 Blvd Victor-Hugo, 92200 Neuilly sur Seine.
***Tel** 01 46 41 25 25.*
Private hospital. Enquire about insurance and costs.

British Hospital
3 Rue Barbés 92300 Levallois-Perret.
Tel 01 46 39 22 22.
A private hospital.

Centre Médical Europe
44 Rue d'Amsterdam 75009.
Map 6 D3. ***Tel** 01 42 81 93 33.*
For dentists ***Tel** 01 42 81 80 00.*
☐ *8am–8pm Mon–Sat.*
An inexpensive private clinic. Appointments, or walk-in.

PHARMACIES

British and American Pharmacy
1 Rue Auber 75009.
Map 6 D4. ***Tel** 01 42 65 88 29.*
☐ *8.30am–8.30pm Mon–Fri, 10am–8pm Sat.*

Pharmacie Bader
12 Blvd St-Michel 75006.
Map 12 F5.
Tel 01 43 26 92 66.
☐ *9am–9pm Mon–Sat, 11am–9pm Sun.*

Pharmacie Anglo-Americaine
37 Ave Marceau 75116.
Map 10 E1.
Tel 01 47 20 57 37.
☐ *8.30am–7.30pm Mon–Fri, 9am–5pm Sat.*

Pharmacie des Halles
10 Blvd Sebastopol 75004.
Map 13 A3.
Tel 01 42 72 03 23.
☐ *9am– midnight Mon–Sat, 9am–10pm Sun.*

Pharmacie Dhery
84 Ave des Champs-Elysées 75008. **Map** 4 F5.
Tel 01 45 62 02 41.
☐ *24 hours daily.*

Banking and Local Currency

Visitors to Paris will find that the banks usually offer them the best rates of exchange. Privately owned bureaux de change, on the other hand, have variable rates, and care should be taken to check small print details relating to commission and minimum charges before any transaction is completed.

BANKING

There is no restriction on the amount of money or currency you may bring into France. It is wise to carry large sums in the form of travellers' cheques. To exchange travellers' cheques or cash, bureaux de change are located at airports, large railway stations, and in some hotels and shops.

Many bank branches in central Paris have their own bureaux de change. They generally offer the best exchange rates but also charge a commission for doing the exchange.

Many independent, non-bank exchange offices do not charge commission, but they offer poorer rates of exchange. Central Paris non-bank exchanges are usually open 9am–6pm Mon–Sat, and are found along the Champs-Elysées, around the Opéra and Madeleine, and near some tourist attractions and monuments. They can also be found at all main railway stations, open 8am–9pm daily. Note that the bureaux located at Gare St-Lazare and Gare d'Austerlitz are closed on Sunday. Airport offices tend to open 7am–11pm daily.

CHANGE
CAMBIO-WECHSEL

Sign at bureau de change

CARDS AND CHEQUES

Travellers' cheques can be obtained from **American Express, Travelex** or from your bank. If you know that you will spend most of them, it is best to have them issued in Euros. American Express

cheques are widely accepted in France and, if the cheques are exchanged at an Amex office, no commission will be charged. In the case of theft, your cheques will be replaced at once.

Because of the high commissions charged, many French businesses do not accept the American Express credit card. The most commonly used credit card is Carte Bleue/Visa. Eurocard/Mastercard is also widely accepted.

Credit card cash dispenser

French credit cards are now "smart cards", with a *puce* (a microchip capable of storing data) as well as a magnetic strip on the back. Many retailers have machines designed to read both smart cards and magnetic strips. Conventional non-French cards cannot be read in the smart card slot. Ask the cashier to swipe the card through the magnetic reader *(bande magnétique).* You may also be asked to tap in your PIN code *(code confidentiel)* and press the green key *(validez)* on a small keypad by the cash desk.

CONVERSION CHART

The following is a rough guide to equivalent currency values, rounded up or down for ease of use.

Euros	Francs
1	6.5
5	33
20	130
50	330
100	650

DIRECTORY

AFTER-HOURS BUREAUX DE CHANGE

Le Comptour des Tuileries
27 Rue de l'Arbre Sec 75001.
Map 12 F2.
Tel 01 42 60 17 16.
◯ 10am–7.30pm Mon–Fri, 1–8pm Sat.

Global Change
134 Blvd St-Germain 75006.
Map 12 F4.
Tel 01 40 46 87 75.
◯ 9am–10.30pm daily.

HSBC
123 Ave des Champs-Elysées 75008. **Map** 4 E4.
Tel 01 40 70 16 50 or 01 40 70 19 54.
◯ 9am–7.15pm Mon–Fri, 9.45am–6.15pm Sat.

Travelex
Gare du Nord
(opposite Eurostar arrivals).
Map 7 B2.
Tel 01 42 80 11 50.
◯ 6.30am–11.30pm daily (to 11.15pm Sat).

FOREIGN BANKS

American Express
11 Rue Scribe 75009.
Map 6 D5.
Tel 01 47 14 50 00.

Barclays
24 bis Ave de l'Opéra 75001.
Map 6 E5.
Tel 01 44 86 00 00.
One of several branches.

HSBC
22 Pl de la Madeleine 75008.
Map 5 C5.
Tel 01 44 71 10 00.

Travelex
8 Place de l'Opéra 75009.
Tel 01 47 42 46 52.

LOST CARDS AND TRAVELLERS' CHEQUES

American Express
Tel 01 47 77 70 00 **Cards**.
Tel 08 00 90 86 00 **Cheques**.

Mastercard
Tel 01 45 67 53 53 **Cards**.

Visa/Carte Bleue
Tel 08 92 70 57 05 **Cards**.

THE EURO

The euro (€), the single European currency, is now operational in 12 of the 25 member states of the EU. Austria, Belgium, Finland, France, Germany, Greece, Ireland, Italy, Luxembourg, Netherlands, Portugal and Spain all chose to join the new currency; Denmark, the UK and Sweden chose to stay out, with an option to review their decision. France's Overseas Departments (Réunion etc) also all now use the euro.

Euro notes are identical throughout all 12 countries, bearing architectural drawings of fictitious monuments. The coins, however, have one side identical (the value side), and one side unique to each country. Both notes and coins are valid and interchangeable within each of the 12 countries.

Bank Notes

Euro bank notes have seven denominations. The 5€ note (grey in colour) is the smallest, followed by the 10€ note (pink), 20€ note (blue), 50€ note (orange), 100€ note (green), 200€ note (yellow) and 500€ note (purple). All notes show the stars of the European Union.

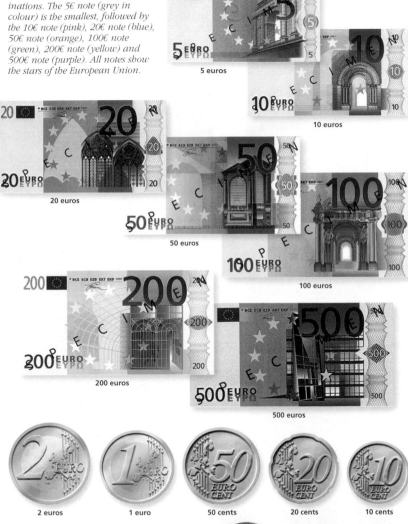

5 euros

10 euros

20 euros

50 euros

100 euros

200 euros

500 euros

2 euros

1 euro

50 cents

20 cents

10 cents

Coins

The euro has eight coin denominations: 1€ and 2€; 50 cents, 20 cents, 10 cents, 5 cents, 2 cents and 1 cent. The 1€ and 2€ coins are both silver and gold in colour. The 50-, 20- and 10-cent coins are gold. The 5-, 2- and 1-cent coins are bronze.

5 cents

2 cents

1 cent

Telephone and Postal Service

The French telecommunications agency is called France Télécom, the postal service is La Poste. Both work efficiently, though the customer services of the post offices may not. So, be prepared to wait in queues. There are many *bureaux des postes* scattered throughout the city. These are identified by the blue-on-yellow La Poste sign *(see p373)*. Public telephones are located in most public places, including on the streets and in railway and metro stations. If you are dialling abroad from Paris, the best way is to purchase a telephone card *(télécarte)*, then find a quiet location to call from.

Telephone Boxes
Coin-operated telephone boxes are now rare. Card-operated telephones are cheap and easy to use, but you must buy a télécarte *first.*

Modern, card-operated phonebox

Older-style phonebox

USING A PHONECARD (TELECARTE) TELEPHONE

1 Lift the receiver and wait for a dialling tone.

2 Holding the *télécarte* with the arrow side up, insert it into the slot in the direction that the arrow is pointing.

3 Wait for the display screen to indicate how many units are stored on the card. The screen will then tell you to dial.

4 Dial the number and wait to be connected.

5 If you want to make another call do not replace the receiver, simply press the green follow-on call button.

6 When you have finished the call, replace the receiver. The card will emerge from the slot. Remove it.

FRANCE TELECOM
600 AGENCES
PARTOUT
EN FRANCE
TELECARTE 50

FRANCE TELECOM

Télécarte phonecard

USING THE TELEPHONE

To use a Paris payphone, you generally need a phone card (*télécarte*), though some accept credit cards. Sold in *tabacs*, post offices and some newsagents, *télécartes* are available in 50 or 120 telephone units. Remember to buy a new card before the old one runs out! Coin telephones have virtually disappeared from the streets of Paris. Reverse charge calls are known as *PCV* in France. Most telephone boxes can be rung from anywhere. The telephone box number is displayed above the telephone unit.

French telephone numbers have ten digits. The first two digits indicate the region: 01 for Paris and the Ile de France; 02, the northwest; 03, the northeast; 04, the southeast; and 05, the southwest. Do not dial the initial zero when phoning from abroad.

Most new mobile phones brought from another European or Mediterranean country can be used in France. Alert your network in good time that you plan to use the phone abroad so that they can enable it. However, US-based mobiles need to be "triple band" to be used in France. Remember that the making and receiving of international mobile calls can be very expensive.

INTERNET ACCESS

Internet access is widely available in Paris, including in many hotels. The French modem socket is incompatible with US and UK plugs, although adaptors are available. Internet cafés are recognisable by an @ sign.

REACHING THE RIGHT NUMBER

- **In the case of emergencies,** dial 17.

- **Directory enquiries** dial 118 712.

- **International directory enquiries,** for all countries, dial 32 12.

- **International telegrams** dial 0800 33 44 11; for telegrams in France, dial 36 55.

- **Home Direct** (reverse charge), dial 0800 99, then the country code (preceded by 00).

- To make direct international calls, dial 00, wait for the tone, then dial the country code, area code (omit the intital 0) and the number.

- The country codes for the following are: **Australia**: 61; **Canada and USA**: 1; **Eire**: 353; **New Zealand**: 64; **UK**: 44.

- **Low-rate period** (for most places): 7pm–8am Mon–Fri, all day Sun and public holidays.

- The middle pages of the telephone directory give the cost of calls per minute for each country and list their country codes, Home Direct codes, etc.

- To telephone **France** from your home country, dial: from the UK 00 33; from the US 011 33; from Australia: 00 11 33. Omit the first 0 of the French area code.

Mail and Postal Services – Using La Poste

LA POSTE

Post office sign

In addition to all normal services – telegrams, postage stamps, registered letters, special delivery, delivery of packages and books – the post office also sells collectors' stamps, and will cash or send international money orders. Fax and telex services, as well as public telephones and Minitel, are available in all main offices.

Paris-Champs Elysées
71 Ave des Champs Elysées 75008.
Map 4 F5.
Tel 01 53 89 05 80.
Fax 01 42 56 13 71.
◯ 9am–7.30pm Mon–Fri,
10am–7pm Sat.

SENDING A LETTER

Common postage stamps *(timbres)* are sold singly or in *carnets* of ten. These are valid for letters and postcards up to 20 g (approximately an ounce) to most EU countries. Stamps can often be bought in *tabacs.* Paris post office hours are 8am–7pm (or 8pm) Mon–Fri, 8am–noon Sat. At post offices you can consult the phone book *(annuaire),* buy phonecards *(télécartes),* send or receive money orders *(mandats)* and call anywhere in the world.

Letters are dropped into yellow mail boxes.

For poste restante (mail holding), the sender should write the recipient's name in block letters, then "Poste Restante", then the address of the Paris-Louvre post office.

Paris Arrondissements

The districts or arrondissements of Paris are numbered from 1 to 20 (see p390). The first three numbers of the postcode – 750 (sometimes 751) – indicate Paris; the last two give the arrondissement number. The first arrondissement's postcode is 75001.

When sending a letter poste restante, it is wise to underline the surname, as French officials otherwise sometimes assume the first name is the family name.

MAIN POST OFFICES

Paris-Louvre
52 Rue de Louvre 75001. **Map** 12
F1. **Tel** 01 40 28 76 00. **Fax** 01 40
28 21 47. ◯ 24 hrs daily.

Paris-Forum des Halles
Forum des Halles 75001. **Map**
13 A2. **Tel** 01 44 76 84 60. ◯
8am–6pm Mon–Fri, 8am–noon Sat.

Destinations

Paris letter box

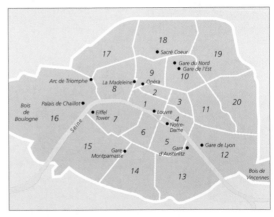

CUSTOMS AND IMMIGRATION

For travellers coming from within the EU's "Schengen" zone (ie. those that agreed to the Schengen Treaty), no documentation at all is needed to enter France. For "non-Schengen" nationals, includ-ing the UK, a passport (or similar) is required. Visitors from the US, Canada, Australia and New Zealand do not need a visa if staying under 3 months. However, for a trip over 3 months, a visa must be applied for from the French consulate in the visitor's own country before leaving. It is always advisable to double-check visa requirements as these can be subject to change at any time.

TAX-FREE GOODS

The purchase of goods "Duty Free" for export to another EU country is no longer possible. Visitors resident outside the European Union can reclaim the sales tax (TVA, or VAT; *see p320*) they pay on French goods if they spend more than 175€ in the same shop in one day and take the goods out of France.

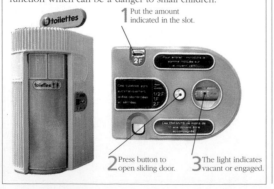

Bottle of scent

Détaxe receipts can be issued on purchase to reclaim the tax paid, and reimbursements are collected when exiting the EU, which must be within 3 months of purchase. There are some goods you cannot claim a rebate on, namely food and drink, medicines, tobacco, cars and motorbikes.

DUTY-PAID AND DUTY-FREE GOODS

There are no longer any restrictions on the quantities of duty-paid and VAT-paid goods you can take from one EU country to another, as long as they are for your own use and not for resale. You may be asked to prove the goods are for your own use if they exceed the EU suggested quantities. If you cannot do so, the entire amount of the goods (not just the deemed excess) may be confiscated. The suggested limits are: 10 litres of spirits (i.e. drinks over 22° proof), 90 litres of wine (of which a maximum of 60 litres can be sparkling), 110 litres of beer and five multipacks of cigarettes. Some dangerous goods are illegal. Visitors under the age of 17 are not allowed to import duty-paid tobacco or alcohol.

IMPORTING OTHER GOODS

In general, all personal goods (eg. car or bicycle) may be imported to France if they are obviously for personal use and not for sale. The brochure *Voyagez en toute liberté* clarifies this. It is available from the **Centre** below, which also gives advice on import regulations (usually in French).

CUSTOMS INFORMATION

Centre des Renseignements des Douanes
84 Rue d'Hauteville 75010. *Tel 08 20 02 44 44.* ☐ *8.30am–6pm Mon–Fri.* **www**.douane.gouv.fr

ELECTRICAL ADAPTORS

The voltage in France is 220 volts. Plugs have two small round pins; heavier-duty installations have two large round pins. Better hotels offer built-in adaptors for shavers only or will lend you an adaptor. Adaptors can be bought at department stores, such as BHV *(see p321)*.

French two-pin electrical plug

STUDENT INFORMATION

Students with valid ID cards benefit from discounts of 25–50% at theatres, museums, cinemas and many public monuments. An ISIC card (the International Student ID card) may be purchased from main travel agencies, Office de Tourisme de l'Université offices (**OTU**) and the Centre d'Information et de Documen-tation Jeunesse (**CIDJ**). CIDJ provides information on student life in Paris and can furnish a list of inexpensive accommodation, including the Bureau Voyage Jeunesse (**BVJ**), which has 2 hostels in central Paris with double rooms and dormitory accommodation at reasonable prices *(see pp279-80 and 375)*.

PUBLIC TOILETS IN PARIS

Most old-fashioned urinals and toilets have been replaced by modern pay toilets. They are found on pavements all over the city. In some units, classical music is played. It is crucial that children under 10 are not allowed into these toilets on their own. They have an automatic cleaning function which can be a danger to small children.

1 Put the amount indicated in the slot.

2 Press button to open sliding door.

3 The light indicates vacant or engaged.

INTERNATIONAL BOOKSHOPS

Brentano's
37 Ave de l'Opéra 75002.
Map 6 E5. **Tel** *01 42 61 52 50.*
◯ *10am–7.30pm Mon–Sat.*

Gibert Jeune
5 Place St-Michel 75005.
Map 13 A4. **Tel** *01 56 81 22 22.*
◯ *9.30am–7.30pm Mon–Sat.*

WH Smith
248 Rue de Rivoli 75001. **Map** 11
C1. **Tel** *01 44 77 88 99.* ◯ *9am–7.30pm Mon–Sat, 1–7.30pm Sun.*

TV, RADIO, PRESS

British and other European papers can be bought on the day of publication at *maisons*

Foreign newspapers from kiosks

de la presse (newsagents) or *kiosques* (news-stands) throughout the city. Some are European or international editions, such as *The Sun, Financial Times Europe* and the *Guardian International, The Weekly Telegraph, USA Today, The Economist,* and *The International Herald Tribune.*

The main French national dailies are – from right to left on the political spectrum – *Le Figaro, France Soir, Le Monde, Libération* and *L'Humanité.* The weeklies include satirical *Le Canard Enchaîné,* news magazines *Marianne, Le Nouvel Observateur* and *L'Express,* and numerous titles devoted to fashion, gossip and gastronomy.

The French TV channels are *TF1* and *France 2,* both with a lightweight mix, *France 3,* with documentaries, debate and classic films, *5*ᵉ ("La Cinquième") and the Franco-German high-culture *ARTE,* which share a channel special-ising in arts, classical music and films, and *M6* which devotes a lot of time to pop and rock. Cable and satellite channels include CNN, Sky and a variety of BBC channels.

BBC Radio 4 can be picked up during the day, while at

night, *BBC World Service* uses the same channel (648AM or 198 Long Wave). *Radio France International* (738AM) gives excellent daily news in English on their web site www.rfi.fr.

PARIS TIME

Paris is, conveniently, one hour ahead of Greenwich Mean Time (GMT) all year round. The French use the 24-hour clock, therefore, 9am is 09.00, 9pm is 21.00. New York is some 6 hours behind Paris, Los Angeles 9 hours behind and Auckland 11 hours ahead.

CONVERSION CHART

Imperial to metric
1 inch = 2.54 centimetres
1 foot = 30 centimetres
1 mile = 1.6 kilometres
1 ounce = 28 grams
1 pound = 454 grams
1 pint = 0.6 litre
1 gallon = 4.6 litres

Metric to imperial
1 millimetre = 0.04 inch
1 centimetre = 0.4 inch
1 metre = 3 feet 3 inches
1 kilometre = 0.6 mile
1 gram = 0.04 ounce
1 kilogram = 2.2 pounds
1 litre = 1.8 pints

DIRECTORY

STUDENT INFO

OTU Voyages
119 Rue St-Martin 75004.
Map 13 B2. **Tel** *01 40 29 12 22.*

1 Pl du M.al de Lattre de Tassigny 75016. **Map** 3 A4. **Tel** *01 47 55 03 01.*

39 Ave Georges Bernanos 75005. **Map** 16 F2.
Tel *01 44 41 38 50.*

CIDJ
101 Quai Branly 75015.
Map 10 E2. **Tel** *01 44 49 12 00.* ◯ *9.30am–6pm Mon–Fri (7pm Tue & Thu), 9.30am–1pm Sat.*

BVJ
20 Rue Jean-Jacques Rousseau 75001. **Map** 12 F2. **Tel** *01 53 00 90 90.*

44 Rue des Bernardins 75005. **Map** 13 B5.
Tel *01 43 29 34 80.*

EMBASSIES

Australia
4 Rue Jean Rey 75015.
Map 10 D3.
Tel *01 40 59 33 00.*

Canada
35 Ave Montaigne 75008.
Map 10 F1.
Tel *01 44 43 29 00.*

Great Britain
35 Rue du Faubourg St-Honoré 75008.
Map 5 C5.

Consulate (visas) 18bis Rue d'Anjou 75008.
Tel *01 44 51 31 01.*

Ireland (Eire)
12 Ave Foch 75016. **Map** 3 B4. **Tel** *01 44 17 67 00.*

New Zealand
7 ter, Rue Léonard de Vinci 75116. **Map** 3 C5.
Tel *01 45 01 43 43.*

USA
2 Ave Gabriel 75008.
Map 5 B5.
Tel *01 43 12 22 22.*

RELIGIOUS SERVICES

PROTESTANT

American Church
65 Quai d'Orsay 75007.
Map 10 F2.
Tel *01 40 62 05 00.*

Church of Scotland
17 Rue Bayard 75008.
Map 10 F1.
Tel/Fax *01 48 78 47 94.*

St George's Anglican Church
7 Rue Auguste Vacquerie 75116. **Map** 4 E5.
Tel *01 47 20 22 51.*

CATHOLIC

Basilique du Sacré-Coeur
35 Rue du Chevalier de la Barre 75018.
Map 6 F1.
Tel *01 53 41 89 00.*

Cathédrale de Notre-Dame
Pl du Parvis Notre-Dame 75004. **Map** 13 A4.
Tel *01 42 34 56 10.*

JEWISH

Synagogue Nazareth
15 Rue Notre Dame de Nazareth 75003. **Map** 7 C5. **Tel** *01 42 78 00 30.*

MOSLEM

Grande Mosquée de Paris
Place du Puits de l'Ermite 75005. **Map** 17 B2.
Tel *01 45 35 97 33.*

GETTING TO PARIS

Paris is a major hub of European air, road and rail travel. Direct flights from around the world serve the French capital's two main international airports. Paris is also at the centre of Europe's growing high-speed rail network, with arrivals throughout the day of Eurostar from London, Thalys from Brussels, Amsterdam and Cologne, and TGVs from Marseille and Geneva. Approaching by road, *autoroutes* (motorways) converge on Paris from all directions, including – via Eurotunnel's Channel rail shuttle – the UK.

Boeing 737 passenger jet

ARRIVING BY AIR

The main British airlines with regular flights to Paris are **British Airways** and **British Midland**. The main French airline is **Air France**. From the United States there are regular flights direct to Paris mainly on **American**, **United**, **Northwest**, **Continental**, **Delta**, **Virgin** and **British Airlines**. From Canada, **Air France** and **Air Canada** fly direct to Paris. **Qantas** is one of the few providing connecting flights from Australia and New Zealand.

Easyjet (from Liverpool, Luton, Newcastle and Belfast), **BmiBaby** (Durham, East Midlands, Cardiff, Leeds and London) and **Jet2** (Leeds Bradford) offer an inexpensive CDG service. **Ryanair** flies from Dublin and Glasgow (Prestwick) to Beauvais, an hour's bus journey west of Paris. **Airwales** also flies from Cardiff to Beauvais. For airline offices in Paris, see page 379.

The peak summer season in Paris is from July to September. Airline fares are at their highest during this time. Different airlines, however, may have slightly different high summer season periods, so check with the airlines or an agent as to which months are covered by these fares.

If you are prepared to look around for the best deals, there are very good ones on offer from reputable discount agents. If you book a cheap deal with a discount agent, check whether you will get a refund if the agent or operator ceases trading, and don't part with the full fare until you actually see the ticket.

Addresses of reputable discount agencies in Paris are listed on page 379. These offer charters and regular scheduled flights at competitive prices. Many of them have representatives in other countries. Note that children can travel more cheaply than adults.

Flight Times
Here are some flight times to Paris from cities in different parts of the world: London 1 hour; Dublin 90 minutes; Montreal 7.5 hours; New York 8 hours; Los Angeles 12 hours; Sydney 23 hours.

CHARLES DE GAULLE AIRPORT

The terminals CDG1, CDG2 and T3 are linked by shuttle buses. The main transport services to Paris are shown below. Check door numbers as they are subject to change.

CDG1 is used for international flights, except those of Air France (see CDG2).

CDG2 is used for all Air France flights and for short-hop international flights by other carriers.

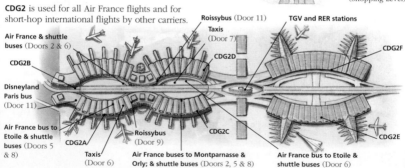

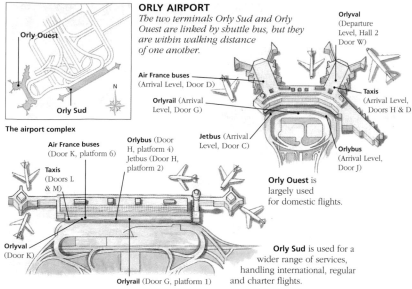

ORLY AIRPORT

The two terminals Orly Sud and Orly Ouest are linked by shuttle bus, but they are within walking distance of one another.

Orly Ouest

Orly Sud

The airport complex

Orlyval (Departure Level, Hall 2 Door W)

Air France buses (Arrival Level, Door D)

Orlyrail (Arrival Level, Door G)

Taxis (Arrival Level, Doors H & D)

Air France buses (Door K, platform 6)

Taxis (Doors L & M)

Orlybus (Door H, platform 4) Jetbus (Door H, platform 2)

Jetbus (Arrival Level, Door C)

Orlybus (Arrival Level, Door J)

Orly Ouest is largely used for domestic flights.

Orlyval (Door K)

Orly Sud is used for a wider range of services, handling international, regular and charter flights.

Orlyrail (Door G, platform 1)

CHARLES DE GAULLE (CDG) AIRPORT

Paris's main airport lies 30 km (19 miles) north of the city. It has two main terminals, CDG1 and CDG2, and a charter flight terminal, T3. CDG2 straddles the TGV-RER station and comprises six linked halls: CDG2A, CDG2B, CDG2C, CDG2D, CDG2E and CDG2F.

Getting into Town

Buses, trains and taxis all run to central Paris. Air France operates two services from CDG1 and CDG2: one goes to Porte Maillot and Charles de Gaulle-Etoile (about every 12mins; journey time about 40mins); the other to the Gare de Lyon and Montparnasse TGV train station (every 30mins; journey time about 50mins). From T3 it is a short walk to the RER station, where you can catch a train to central Paris. The RATP Roissybus, serving all three terminals, takes travellers to Opéra (every 20mins 6am–11pm; journey time about 50mins).

Disneyland Paris runs the VEA bus service (8.30am–7.45pm daily, to 10pm Fri, to 9.30pm Sun) every 30–45 minutes from CDG1 and CDG2.

The TGV station is in CDG2, and there are RER train stations (Line B) at

CDG1 (linked via a shuttle bus) and CDG2. Trains leave every 5–15 minutes and take about 35 minutes to reach the city centre, at the Gare du Nord, Châtelet, St-Michel, Luxembourg and Port Royal.

Airport Shuttle (Tel: 01 53 39 18 18) provides door-to-door service in a small minibus for both airports, for 25€ for one person, or 16€–19€ each for two or more (book at least 48 hours ahead, then call them after landing to confirm your journey). Normal taxis to the centre run between 36€ (daytime) and 45€, often with long queues.

ORLY AIRPORT (ORY)

This is Paris's second airport, which is located 15 km (9 miles) south of the capital. It has two terminals, Orly Sud and Orly Ouest.

Getting into Town

Transport services go to the southern part of the city, and a special bus (VEA shuttle) links the airport with Disneyland Resort Paris (every 45mins 8.30am–7.30pm).

Travellers arriving at Orly can take a taxi, bus or train to central Paris. The bus services are run by Air France and RATP (Orlybus). Air France buses take about 30 minutes

to reach the city centre, stopping at Les Invalides and Gare de Montparnasse. The Orlybus (every 12–20mins) takes about 25 minutes to reach the city centre at Denfert-Rochereau. The Jet Bus service takes travellers from the airport to Villejuif-Louis Aragon metro station every 15–20 minutes.

A bus called Orlyrail links the airport with RER Line C at Pont de Rungis, from where trains leave every 15 minutes (half hour after 9pm), taking 25 minutes to reach the Gare d'Austerlitz. An automatic train, Orlyval, links the airport with RER Line B at Antony station, from where trains leave every 4–8 minutes for Châtelet (35-minute total journey).

Taxis to the city centre take 25–45 minutes, depending on the traffic, and cost 20€–30€.

Orlyval train leaving Orly Airport

CROSSING THE CHANNEL

Travellers coming to Paris from Britain by road will need to cross the English Channel. The simplest and most popular way is on the vehicle-carrying train shuttles through the Channel Tunnel. Operated by **Eurotunnel**, these run between the terminals at Folkestone and Calais. You are directed onto the trains and remain with your vehicle, though you may get out of your car and walk about inside the train.

The journey through the Tunnel takes about 30 minutes, is unaffected by sea conditions or weather, and trains depart every 15–30 minutes, depending on demand. On both the English and the French side, the Tunnel terminal has direct motorway access.

There are also several ship or catamaran car ferries across the Channel. On the short Dover–Calais route alone, there are up to 100 crossings per day, operated by several operators running frequent, fast services. **SeaFrance** takes 90 minutes to cross, for example. **Transmanche Ferries**, part of Corsica Ferries, runs the route between Newhaven and Dieppe, which takes nearly 4 hours. **Norfolkline** has a 2-hour Dover to Dunkerque crossing.

Two companies ply the longer western routes across the Channel. **Brittany Ferries** crossings from Plymouth to Roscoff take up to 8 hours, and from Poole to Cherbourg they take 4¼ hours on conventional ferry, or 3 hours on the Condor Vitesse (fast ferry). From Portsmouth, Brittany take 6 hours to Caen, and 11 hours overnight to St-Malo. **P&O** has reduced its ferry routes to just Dover–Calais. **LD Lines** now runs from Portsmouth to Le Havre in 5½ hours. Driving to Paris from Cherbourg takes 4–5 hours; from Dieppe or Le Havre, about 2½–3 hours; from Calais, 2 hours.

ARRIVING BY COACH

The main coach operator to Paris is **Eurolines**, based at the Gare Routière Internationale in eastern Paris. Its coaches travel to Belgium, Holland, Ireland, Germany, Scandinavia, United Kingdom, Italy and Portugal.

Their terminus in London is Victoria Coach Station, from where there are between three and five daily departures for Paris, depending on the season. The journey from London to Paris takes between 8 and 9 hours.

A long-haul coach

USEFUL CONTACTS

Eurostar
Tel 08705 186 186.
www.eurostar.com

Eurotunnel
Tel 08705 35 35 35.

Brittany Ferries
Tel 08703 66 53 33.

LD Lines
Tel 0825 304 304.
www.ldlines.com

Norfolkline
Tel 03 28 28 95 50.

P&O
Tel 0825 120 156.

SeaFrance
Tel 0825 082 505.

Transmanche Ferries
Tel 0800 650 100.

Eurolines
Ave de Général de Gaulle, Bagnolet.
Tel 08 92 89 90 91.
Victoria Coach Station, London SW1.
Tel 08705 143 219.

ARRIVING BY RAIL

Eurostar trains travel directly from central London (Waterloo) and Ashford (Kent) to central Paris (Gare du Nord) in 2hrs and 35mins. There are up to 24 departures daily. Other high-speed services into Paris

The high-speed TGV train

THE TGV

Trains à Grande Vitesse, or TGV high-speed trains, travel at speeds up to 300 km/h (186mph). TGVs for northern France leave from the Gare du Nord, for the Atlantic Coast and Brittany from Gare Montparnasse, and for Provence and the southeast from Gare de Lyon. The network serves a large number of stations on routes to these destinations, and the number of stations served is growing all the time, making this an ever-more convenient form of transport (*see pp380–81*).

include **Thalys**, from Brussels, Amsterdam and Cologne, and **TGVs** from throughout France. These services must be pre-booked, though reservations can be made up to the last moment. Prices are much cheaper booked ahead.

As the railway hub of France and the Continent, Paris has five major international railway stations operated by the French state railways, known as SNCF (see p388). The Gare de Lyon in eastern Paris is the city's main station, serving the south of France, the Alps, Italy and Switzerland. The Gare de l'Est serves eastern France, Austria, Switzerland and Germany.

Arriving at the Gare du Nord are trains from Britain, Holland, Belgium and Scandinavia. Trains from some Channel ports arrive at the Gare St-Lazare. The termini for trains from Spain, as well as from the Brittany ports, are the Gare Montparnasse and Gare d'Austerlitz. The other main stations are: Massy-Palaiseau (SW of city); Marne-la-Vallée for Disneyland Resort Paris (E); Aeroport Charles-de-Gaulle (NE).

There is a tourist office at the Gare de Lyon where you can book accommodation (see p367). All the railway stations are served by city buses, the metro and RER trains. Directional signs show where to make connections to the city transport system.

ARRIVING BY CAR

Paris is an oval-shaped city. It is surrounded by an outer ring road called the Boulevard Périphérique. All motorways leading to the capital link in to the Périphérique, which separates the city from the suburbs. Each former city gate, called a *porte*, now corresponds to an exit from (or entrance to) the Périphérique. Arriving motorists should check their destination address and consult a map of central Paris to find the closest correspond-ing *porte*. For example, a motorist who wants to get to the Arc de Triomphe should exit at Porte Maillot.

DIRECTORY

MAIN AIRLINES SERVING PARIS

Aer Lingus
Tel 01 70 20 00 72.
www.aerlingus.com

Air Canada
Tel 0825 880 881.
www.aircanada.ca

Air France
49 Ave de l'Opéra 75002.
Map 6 E5.
Tel 0820 820 820.
www.airfrance.fr

Airwales
Tel 0870 777 3131 (UK).
Tel 1 800 654 193
(Ireland).
Tel +44 1792 633 200
(overseas).
www.airwales.com

American Airlines
Charles de Gaulle airport.
Tel 0810 872 872.
www.aa.com

British Airways
Tel 0825 825 400.
www.ba.com

British Midland
Tel 01 41 91 87 04.
www.flybmi.com

Delta Airlines
Aérogare des Invalides,
2 Rue Robert Esnault-
Pelterie 75007. **Map** 11
B2. Tel 0811 640 005.
www.delta.com

Easyjet
Tel 08 25 08 25 08.
www.easyjet.com

Jet2
Tel 0871 226 17 37 (UK).
Tel 0818 200 017
(Ireland).
Tel +44 207 17 00 737
(overseas).
www.jet2.com

Qantas Airways
Tel 0820 820 500.
www.qantas.com

Ryanair
Tel 0892 232 375 (France).
www.ryanair.com

DISCOUNT TRAVEL AGENCIES

Directours
90 Ave des Champs-
Elysées 75008. **Map** 4 E4.
Tel 01 45 62 62 62.
www.directours.com

Forum Voyages
1 Rue Cassette 75006.
Map 12 D5.
Tel 01 45 44 38 61.
www.forumvoyages.com

Jet Tours
29 Ave de la Motte Picquet
75007. **Map** 10 F4.
Tel 01 47 05 01 95.
www.jettours.com

Nouvelles Frontières
12 Rue Auber 75009.
Map 6 D4. Tel 08 25 00
08 25. www.nouvelles-
frontieres.fr

USIT Voyages
85 Blvd St-Michel 75005.
Tel 08 25 08 25 25 or 01
43 29 69 50.
www.usitconnections.fr

AIRPORT INFORMATION

www.adp.fr

Information/paging
Tel 01 48 62 22 80 (CDG).
Tel 01 49 75 15 15 (Orly).
Tel 0892 681 515 (CDG &
Orly: same day flight info).

Disabled Assistance
To order free guide *Guide
Passager à mobilité réduite*
and further information:
Tel 01 48 62 22 80 (CDG).
Tel 01 49 75 15 15 (Orly).

Air France Buses
Tel 0892 350 820.

**RATP (Roissybus/
Orlybus)**
Tel 08 92 68 77 14
(French);
08 92 68 41 14 (English).
www.ratp.fr

RER Trains
Tel 0892 687 714.

TGV & SNCF
Tel 36 35.
www.sncf.com

Airport Shuttle
Tel 01 53 39 18 18.
www.parishuttle.fr

CDG Airport Hotels

Ibis
Tel 01 49 19 19 20.
@ H1404@accor.com
www.accorhotels.com

Holiday Inn
Tel 01 34 29 30 00.
@ hiroissy@alliance-
hospitality.com

Novotel
Tel 01 49 19 27 27.
@ H1014@accor.com
www.accorhotels.com

Sofitel
Tel 01 49 19 29 29.
@ H0577@accor.com

ORLY SUD AIRPORT HOTELS

Ibis
Tel 01 56 70 50 50.
@ H1413@accor.com

Hilton Hotel
Tel 01 45 12 45 12.
@ oryhitwRM@hilton.
com. www.hilton.com

Mercure
Tel 01 49 75 15 50.
@ H1246@accor.com
www.accorhotels.com

Arriving in Paris

This map depicts the bus and rail services between the two main airports and the city. It shows the ferry-rail links from the UK, the main railway links from other parts of France and Europe, and the long-haul coach services from other European countries. It also shows the main city railway and coach termini, the airport shuttle connections and the airport bus and rail stops. The frequency of services and journey times from the airport are provided, as are the approximate times of rail journeys from other cities. Metro and RER line connections to other parts of Paris are indicated at the termini and route stops.

⚓ CALAIS
Ferry and Eurotunnel links with Dover and Folkestone. Eurostar train from London to Paris Gare du Nord (3 hrs) passes through here but cannot be boarded at Calais. SNCF train to Gare du Nord (2 hrs– 2 hrs 45 mins).

⚓ LE HAVRE
Ferry links with Portsmouth. SNCF train to Gare St-Lazare (2 hrs).

⚓ DIEPPE
Ferry links with Newhaven (summer). SNCF train to Gare St-Lazare (2 hrs 20 mins).

⚓ CAEN
Ferry links with Portsmouth. SNCF train to Gare St-Lazare (1 hr 50 mins).

⚓ CHERBOURG
Ferry links with Portsmouth and Poole. SNCF train to Gare St-Lazare (3 hrs).

GARE ST-LAZARE
Rouen (1 hr 30 mins).

GARE MONTPARNASSE
Bordeaux (3 hrs 30 mins)
Brest (4 hrs 30 mins)
Lisbon (21 hrs)
Madrid (16 hrs)
Nantes (2 hrs 15 mins)
Rennes (2 hrs 20 mins)

Porte Maillot
M ①
RER Ⓐ Ⓒ

Charles de Gaulle-Etoile
M ① ② ⑥
RER Ⓐ

Champs-Elysées

Chaillot Quarter

Gare St-Lazare
M ③ ⑫

Invalides
M ⑧ ⑬
RER Ⓒ

Invalides and Eiffel Tower Quarter

Montparnasse

Gare Montparnasse
M ④ ⑥ ⑫ ⑬

Porte de Orléans
M ④

Antony

KEY

▬▬▬	SNCF see pp378–9
▬▬▬	Coaches see p378
▬▬▬	Roissybus see p377
▬▬▬	Air France bus see p377
▬▬▬	RER B see p377
▬▬▬	Orlyrail see p377
▬▬▬	Orlyval see p377
▬▬▬	Orlybus see p377
▬▬▬	Jet Bus see p377
M	Metro station
RER	RER station

0 kilometres 1
0 miles 0.5

GARE TGV DE MASSY-PALAISEAU
Bordeaux (3 hrs 30 mins)
Lille (1 hr 40 mins)
London (3 hrs 40 mins)
Lyon (2 hrs)
Nantes (2 hrs 30 mins)
Rennes (2 hrs 10 mins)

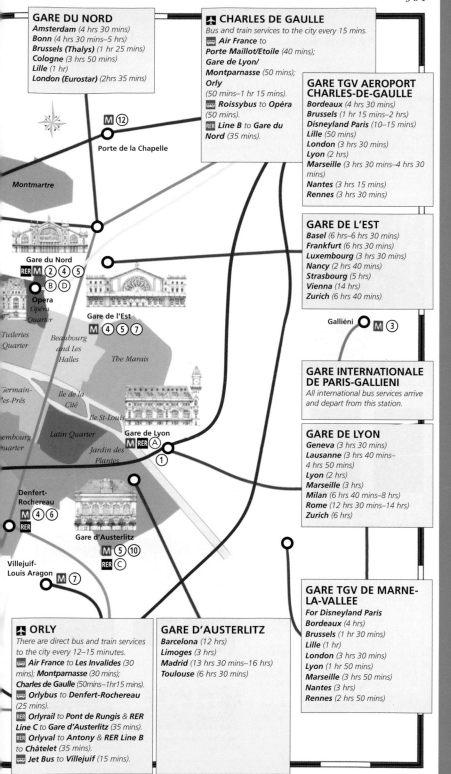

GARE DU NORD
Amsterdam (4 hrs 30 mins)
Bonn (4 hrs 30 mins–5 hrs)
Brussels (Thalys) (1 hr 25 mins)
Cologne (3 hrs 50 mins)
Lille (1 hr)
London (Eurostar) (2hrs 35 mins)

✈ CHARLES DE GAULLE
Bus and train services to the city every 15 mins.
🚌 **Air France** to
Porte Maillot/Etoile (40 mins);
**Gare de Lyon/
Montparnasse** (50 mins);
Orly
(50 mins–1 hr 15 mins).
🚌 **Roissybus** to **Opéra**
(50 mins).
RER **Line B** to **Gare du
Nord** (35 mins).

GARE TGV AEROPORT CHARLES-DE-GAULLE
Bordeaux (4 hrs 30 mins)
Brussels (1 hr 15 mins–2 hrs)
Disneyland Paris (10–15 mins)
Lille (50 mins)
London (3 hrs 30 mins)
Lyon (2 hrs)
Marseille (3 hrs 30 mins–4 hrs 30 mins)
Nantes (3 hrs 15 mins)
Rennes (3 hrs 30 mins)

GARE DE L'EST
Basel (6 hrs–6 hrs 30 mins)
Frankfurt (6 hrs 30 mins)
Luxembourg (3 hrs 30 mins)
Nancy (2 hrs 40 mins)
Strasbourg (5 hrs)
Vienna (14 hrs)
Zurich (6 hrs 40 mins)

GARE INTERNATIONALE DE PARIS-GALLIENI
All international bus services arrive and depart from this station.

GARE DE LYON
Geneva (3 hrs 30 mins)
Lausanne (3 hrs 40 mins–
4 hrs 50 mins)
Lyon (2 hrs)
Marseille (3 hrs)
Milan (6 hrs 40 mins–8 hrs)
Rome (12 hrs 30 mins–14 hrs)
Zurich (6 hrs)

GARE TGV DE MARNE-LA-VALLEE
For Disneyland Paris
Bordeaux (4 hrs)
Brussels (1 hr 30 mins)
Lille (1 hr)
London (3 hrs 30 mins)
Lyon (1 hr 50 mins)
Marseille (3 hrs 50 mins)
Nantes (3 hrs)
Rennes (2 hrs 50 mins)

✈ ORLY
There are direct bus and train services to the city every 12–15 minutes.
🚌 **Air France** to **Les Invalides** (30 mins); **Montparnasse** (30 mins);
Charles de Gaulle (50mins–1hr15 mins).
🚌 **Orlybus** to **Denfert-Rochereau** (25 mins).
RER **Orlyrail** to **Pont de Rungis** & **RER Line C** to **Gare d'Austerlitz** (35 mins).
RER **Orlyval** to **Antony** & **RER Line B** to **Châtelet** (35 mins).
🚌 **Jet Bus** to **Villejuif** (15 mins).

GARE D'AUSTERLITZ
Barcelona (12 hrs)
Limoges (3 hrs)
Madrid (13 hrs 30 mins–16 hrs)
Toulouse (6 hrs 30 mins)

Porte de la Chapelle

Montmartre

Gare du Nord

Opéra
*Opéra
Quarter*

*Tuileries
Quarter*

Gare de l'Est

*Beaubourg
and Les
Halles*

The Marais

*Germain-
es-Prés*

*Ile de la
Cité*

Ile St-Louis

*embourg
uarter*

Latin Quarter

Gare de Lyon

*Jardin des
Plantes*

Denfert-
Rochereau

Gare d'Austerlitz

Villejuif-
Louis Aragon

Galliéni

GETTING AROUND PARIS

Central Paris is compact. The best way to get around is to walk. Cycling and roller-blading are increasingly popular with Parisians and tourists alike but they are not without risk. Visitors unfamiliar with the motoring code and undisciplined French driving need to take care.

Driving a car in the city centre is not fun. Traffic is often heavy, there are many one-way streets, and parking is notoriously difficult and expensive. The bus, metro and RER train system operated by the RATP makes getting around cheap and easy. The city is divided into five travel zones: zones 1 and 2 corresponding to the centre and zones 3, 4 and 5 to the suburbs and the airport. The city is also divided into 20 arrondissements, which will help visitors in their search for addresses (see p373).

Parisian drivers do not always respect pedestrian crossings.

Stop sign   **Walk sign**

WALKING IN PARIS

Australian, British, Irish and New Zealand visitors need to remember that cars drive on the right-hand side of the road. There are many two-stage road crossings where pedestrians wait on an island in the centre of the road before proceeding. These are marked *piétons traversez en deux temps*.

Walking tours are cited in the weekly listings magazines (see p340).

CYCLING IN PARIS

Paris is an excellent city for cyclists. It's reasonably flat, manageably small, has many backstreets where car traffic is restricted, and about 150 km (103 miles) of cycle lanes (*pistes cyclables*). Parisian motorists are increasingly respectful of cyclists as more

and more of their fellow citizens turn to two wheels.

The RATP's own cycling centre, the **Maison Roue Libre**, in the heart of Paris, is most helpful for rental and organized tours, as well as for repairs and storage. The free map *Paris à Vélo* (Paris by Bike), available here and in most RATP metro, RER and bus stations, is a useful starting point. Bicycles may be taken on SNCF trains, and

A Parisian cyclist

TICKETS AND TRAVEL PASSES

The tickets and passes on offer in Paris will suit most tourists. Tickets can be purchased at all main metro and RER stations, at the airports and several tourist offices. Individual tickets are relatively cheap and you can buy a block of ten (*carnet*) at a discount. The *Paris Visite* pass for one, two, three or five days includes discounted entry to some sights but is comparatively expensive unless you intend to travel fairly extensively. To get a *Carte Orange*, you will need ID and a passport photo. Write your French address on the back of the main card and then the number of the card on the ticket. Visitors can also buy a one-day *Mobilis* card or a Monday–Sunday weekly (*hebdomadaire*) or monthly *Carte Orange* for selected zones.

Paris Visite pass and one-day ticket

Tickets for use on metro, RER or bus

Mobilis card

Carte Orange

Carte Orange one-month travel ticket for zones 1 and 2

some suburban train stations rent bicycles.

There are now bicycle shops throughout Paris, most of them renting bikes from about 14€ a day, and many also organize guided tours. **Fat Tire Bike Tours** offers tours in English, departing from near the Eiffel Tower, as do **Paris Vélo** and others (*see Directory*).

DRIVING IN PARIS

Though driving and parking can be difficult in central Paris, a hire car can be useful for visiting outlying areas. To hire a car, a valid driving licence and passport are required (most firms also require one major credit card). For payment by cheque or cash, additional ID may be required (including air tickets and credit cards). International driving licences are not needed for drivers from the EU, North America, Australia and New Zealand.

Cars drive on the right-hand side of the road and must yield to traffic merging from the right, even on thoroughfares, unless marked by a *priorité* sign, which indicates right of way. Cars on a roundabout usually have right of way, though one exception is the Arc de Triomphe where cars yield to traffic from the right – one of Paris's most hair-raising experiences!

No entry sign

INTERDIT
SUR TOUTE LA LONGUEUR
DE LA VOIE

Parking Interdit (no parking)

Speed limit sign in km/h

Tow-away zone

PARKING

Parking in Paris is difficult and expensive. Never park where there are *Parking (Stationnement) Interdit* signs. Park only in areas with a large "P" or a *Parking Payant* sign on the pavement or road, and pay at the *horodateur* machine. For towed or clamped cars, phone or go to the nearest police station (*Commissariat de Police*). For towing away there is a fine, plus a fee for each day the car is held. There are 7 car pounds (*perfourrières*) in Paris, where cars are kept for 48 hours, then sent to outlying long-term garages (*fourrières*).

USING AN HORODATEUR MACHINE

Horodateurs (parking metres) operate from 9am–7pm Mon–Fri. Unless otherwise indicated, parking is free Sat–Sun, public holidays and in August.

Card-only machine

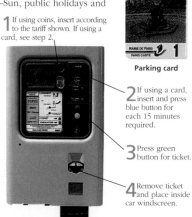

1 If using coins, insert according to the tariff shown. If using a card, see step 2.

Parking card

2 If using a card, insert and press blue button for each 15 minutes required.

3 Press green button for ticket.

4 Remove ticket and place inside car windscreen.

BICYCLE HIRE/REPAIR & TOURS

Fat Tire Bike Tours
Ave Gustave Eiffel 75007 & 22 Rue Edgar Foure 75015.
Map 10 D3.
Tel 01 56 58 10 54.
www.fattiretoursparis.com
English-language bicycle tours.

Maison Roue Libre
1 Passage Mondétour 75001.
Map 13 B2.
Tel 0810 44 15 34.
www.rouelibre.fr
Bicycle rental, storage, repair.

Paris à vélo c'est sympa!
22 Rue Alphonse Baudin 75011.
Tel 01 48 87 60 01.
www.parisvelosympa.com
Bicycle rental and tours.

Paris Vélo
2 Rue du Fer-à-Moulin 75005.
Map 17 C2. **Tel** 01 43 37 59 22.
www.paris-velo-rent-a-bike.fr
Bicycle rental, tours.

RATP Information
Tel 08 92 68 77 14.
www.ratp.fr

SNCF Information
Tel 36 35.
www.sncf.fr

CAR HIRE AGENCIES

Car hire agencies abound in Paris. Here is a list of major firms with agencies at Charles de Gaulle and Orly airports, main railway stations and city-centre locations. Telephone for reservations and pick-up and drop-off information.

ADA
Tel 08 92 68 40 02.

Avis
Tel 0820 05 05 05.

Budget
Tel 0825 003 564.

Europcar
Tel 0825 358 358.

Hertz
Tel 0825 861 861.

National Citer
Tel 0825 161 212.

Sixt-Eurorent
Tel 0820 007 498.

Travelling by Metro

The RATP (Paris transport company) operates 14 metro lines, referred to by their number and terminus names, criss-crossing Paris and its suburbs. This is often the fastest and cheapest way to get across the capital, as there are dozens of stations scattered around the city. Metro stations are easily identified by their logo, a large circled "M", and sometimes their elegant Art Nouveau entrances. Neighbourhood maps are found in all stations, near the exits. The metro and RER (Paris rail network) systems operate in much the same way, though RER carriages are slightly larger. The first trains leave their termini at 5.30am and the last return at 1.15am.

RATP logo

Art Nouveau metro sign

Modern metro sign

Reading the Metro Map

Metro and RER lines are shown in various colours on the metro map. Metro lines are identified by a number, which is located on the map at either end of a line. Some metro stations serve only one line, others serve more than one. There are stations sharing both metro and RER lines and some are linked to one another by interconnecting passages.

Metro and RER stations with inter-connecting passage

RER and metro station serving the same lines

Metro line

Metro station serving one line

Metro station serving two lines

RER line

Metro line identification number

USING THE RER

The RER is a system of commuter trains, travelling underground in central Paris and above ground in outlying areas. Both metro tickets and passes are valid on it. There are five lines, known by their letters: A, B, C, D and E. Each line forks. For example, Line C has six forks, labelled C1, C2 etc. All RER trains bear names (for example, ALEX or VERA) to make it easier to read RER timetables in the station halls and on platforms. Digital panels on all RER platforms indicate train name, direction of travel (terminus) and upcoming stations.

RER stations are identified by a large circled logo. The main city stations are: Charles de Gaulle-Etoile, Châtelet-Les-Halles, Gare de Lyon, Nation, St-Michel-Notre-Dame, Auber-Haussmann St-Lazare and the Gare du Nord-Magenta.

The RER and metro systems overlap in central Paris. It is often quicker to take an RER train to a station served by both, as in the case of La Défense and Nation. However, getting into the RER stations, which are often linked to the metro by a maze of corridors, can be very time-consuming.

The RER is particularly useful for getting to Paris airports and to many of the outlying towns and tourist attractions. Line B3 serves Charles de Gaulle airport; Lines B4 and C2 serve Orly airport; Line A4 goes to Disneyland Resort Paris; and Line C5 runs to Versailles.

RER logo

BUYING A TICKET

Ordinary metro and RER tickets can be bought either singly or as a *carnet* of 10, from ticket booths or ticket machines in the booking halls (carry some 1 and 2 Euro coins). The useful **Paris Visite** bus, metro and RER pass (*see p382*) is widely available, and you can also buy it in advance at certain travel agencies and rail ticket agents abroad (eg. Rail Europe in London). One metro ticket "section urbaine" entitles you to travel anywhere on the metro, and on RER trains in central Paris. RER trips outside the centre (such as to airports) require special tickets. Fares to suburbs and nearby towns vary. Consult the fare charts posted in all RER stations. Passengers on all city transport must retain their tickets during the trip, as regular inspections are made and fines can be imposed for not having a ticket.

MAKING A JOURNEY BY METRO

1 To determine which metro line to take, travellers should first find their destination on a metro map. (Maps can be found inside stations and also on the inside back cover of this book.) Trace the metro line by following the colour coding and the number of the line. At the end of the line you will see the number of the terminus – remember this, as it will help you to find the correct train.

Insert the train ticket in the first barrier.

Remove the ticket from the second barrier.

2 Metro tickets are sold at all stations. Some stations are equipped with coin-operated automatic machines. All metro tickets are second class. One ticket allows the bearer travel for one journey and any transfers on the metro system.

3 To enter the platform area, insert the metro ticket, with the magnetic strip facing down, into the first barrier slot. Remove the ticket from the second slot, then push through the turnstile, or step through the barrier if automatic.

4 At the entrance to each station platform, or in the station corridors, there is a list of upcoming stations corresponding to a given terminus. Terminus names are also indicated on the platform and should be checked before boarding the train.

5 To change lines, get off at the appropriate transfer station and follow the *correspondance* (connections) signs on the platform indicating the appropriate direction.

6 On older trains there are door handles which have to be lifted to open the door. On more modern trains there is a release button which you press to open the door. Before the doors open and close, a single tone will sound.

7 Inside the trains are charts of the line being served by the train. The station stops are plotted on the chart, so travellers can track their journeys.

8 The "Sortie" sign indicates the way out. At all metro exits there are neighbourhood maps.

Travelling by Bus

The bus is an excellent way to see the great sights of Paris. The bus system is run by the RATP, as is the metro, so you can use the same tickets for both. There are over 200 bus lines in greater Paris and over 3,500 buses in daily circulation at rush hour. This is often the fastest way to travel short distances. However, buses can get caught up in heavy traffic and are often crowded during peak hours. Visitors should check the times for the first and last buses as they vary widely, depending on the line. Most buses run from Monday to Saturday, from early morning to mid-evening (6am–8.30pm).

Ticket-cancelling machine

Bus Stop Signs
Signs at bus stops display route numbers. A white background indicates a service every day all year; a black one means no service on Sundays or public holidays.

Bus terminus sign

Night bus sign

Bus stop

TICKETS AND PASSES

A single bus ticket entitles the bearer to a single journey on a single line. If you want to make a change, you'll need another ticket. (Exceptions to this rule are the buses Balabus, Noctambus, Orlybus and

Roissybus, and lines 221, 297, 299, 350 and 351.) Children under four travel for free, and those aged between four and ten may travel at half price.

You can purchase a *carnet* of 10 tickets, each of them valid for a single bus or metro journey. However, a *carnet* can only be obtained at the metro stations, not on the buses. Metro tickets may be used for bus travel. Bus-only tickets are purchased from the bus driver and must be cancelled to be valid. To do this, insert the ticket into the cancelling machine inside the bus. Hold on to your ticket until the end of the journey. Inspectors do make

Red exit button

Cancelling a Bus Ticket
Insert the ticket into the machine in the direction of the arrow, then withdraw it.

random checks and are empowered to levy on-the-spot fines if you cannot produce a valid cancelled ticket for your journey.

Travel passes are a good idea if you are planning a number of journeys during your stay. For a set fee, you can enjoy unlimited travel on Paris buses (*see p382*). Never cancel these as it will render them invalid. They should be shown to the bus driver whenever you board a bus, and to a ticket inspector on request. If you have a *Carte Orange*, attach a passport photograph and write the card number on the ticket.

Paris's Buses
Passengers can identify the route and destination of a bus from the information on the panels at the front. Some buses have open rear platforms, although these are becoming more rare.

Bus route number

Bus destination

Gare du Nord

Passengers enter the bus at the front door

Bus front displaying information

Bus route number on rear of bus

Open rear platform

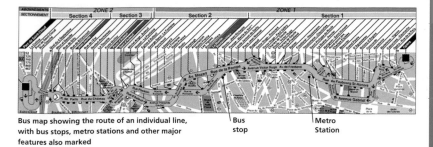

Bus map showing the route of an individual line, with bus stops, metro stations and other major features also marked

Bus stop

Metro Station

USING THE BUSES

Bus stops and shelters are identified by the number shields of the buses that stop at them, and by the distinctive RATP logo. Route maps at bus stops indicate transfers and nearby metro and RER stops. Bus stops also display timetables, and show first and last buses. Neighbourhood maps are also displayed at most bus shelters.

Most buses must be flagged down. Some models have multiple doors which must be opened by pressing a red button inside the bus to exit, or outside the bus to enter. All buses have buttons and bells to signal for a stop. Some buses do not go all the way to their terminus; in that case, there will be a slash through the name of the destination on the front panel.

Buses are gradually being equipped with access for wheelchairs, and all buses already have some seats reserved for disabled and elderly persons. These seats are identified by a sign and must be given up on request.

NIGHT AND SUMMER BUSES

There are 35 night bus lines, called Noctilien, for Paris and its suburbs (running 1–5.30am daily). The terminus for most lines is Châtelet, at Avenue Victoria or Rue St-Martin. Noctilien stops are identified by a letter "N" set in a white circle on a blue background. Noctilien must be flagged down. Travel passes are valid, as are normal metro tickets, which must be cancelled on board. Fares vary according to destination. Travellers may buy tickets on board the bus.

The RATP also operates buses in the Bois de Vincennes and Bois de Boulogne during the summer. The **RATP Information** is extremely helpful on these services and on the best and cheapest ways to get around the city.

RATP Information
54 Quai de la Rapée 75012.
Tel *08 92 68 77 14*
www.ratp.fr
www.noctilien.fr

USEFUL BUS ROUTES

Here is a selection of the best sightseeing bus routes around the centre of Paris, taking in some of the great sights of the city. The routes show the major bus stops, the nearest metro stations and locations of some of the notable sights.

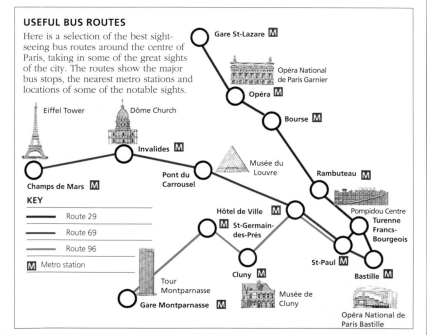

Gare St-Lazare M

Opéra National de Paris Garnier

Opéra M

Bourse M

Eiffel Tower

Dôme Church

Invalides M

Pont du Carrousel

Musée du Louvre

Rambuteau M

Champs de Mars M

KEY

Hôtel de Ville M

St-Germain-des-Prés M

Pompidou Centre

Turenne Francs-Bourgeois

Route 29

Route 69

Route 96

M Metro station

St-Paul M

Cluny M

Bastille M

Tour Montparnasse

Gare Montparnasse M

Musée de Cluny

Opéra National de Paris Bastille

Using the SNCF Trains

The French state railway, Société Nationale des Chemins de Fer (**SNCF**), has two kinds of service in Paris: the Banlieue suburban service and the Grandes Lignes, or long-distance service. The suburban services all operate within the five-zone network (*see p382*). The long-distance services operate throughout France. These services allow visitors to visit parts of France close to Paris in a day round trip. The TGV high-speed service is particularly useful for such journeys, as it is capable of travelling about twice as fast as the normal trains (*see pp378–9*).

Gare de l'Est railway station in 1920

RAILWAY STATIONS

As the railway hub of France, Paris boasts six major international railway stations operated by the SNCF: the Gare du Nord, Gare de l'Est, Gare de Lyon, Gare d'Austerlitz, Gare St-Lazare and Gare Montparnasse.

All the main train stations have long-distance and suburban destinations. Some of the main suburban locations, such as Versailles and Chantilly, are served by both long-distance and suburban trains.

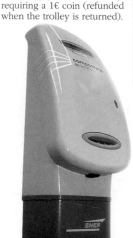

Rail traveller with luggage trolley

The stations have departures and arrivals boards showing the train number, departure and arrival time, delay, platform number, provenance, and main stops en route. For those with heavy luggage, there are trolleys, requiring a 1€ coin (refunded when the trolley is returned).

TICKETS

Tickets to suburban destinations can often be purchased at coin-operated automatic machines located inside station halls, so it is useful to carry coins (the machines give change; some also take credit cards). Otherwise you can buy tickets at the ticket counters.

Before boarding a train, travellers must time-punch (*composter*) their tickets and reservations in a *composteur* machine. Inspectors do check travellers' tickets and anyone who fails to time-punch their ticket can be fined.

Ticket booths are marked with panels indicating the kind of tickets (*billets*) sold: *Banlieue* for suburban tickets, *Grandes Lignes* for mainline tickets, and *Internationale* for international tickets.

Substantial fare discounts of 25-50% are offered to the over 60s (*Découverte Senior*), those under 26s (*Découverte 12-25*), up to four adults

Composteur Machine

The composteur machines are located in station halls and at the head of each platform. Tickets and reservations must be inserted face up.

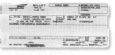

A time-punched ticket

travelling with a child under the age of 12 (*Découverte Enfant Plus*), or anyone booking more than 30 days in advance.

Advance Internet bookings also offer a limited number of cheaper tickets called *prems*. Payment for these tickets (which you print from your computer) must be made online. Be aware that these tickets are not covered by an exchange or reimbursement policy.

Some last-minute offers are also available online. Visit **www**.voyages-sncf.com for more information.

SUBURBAN TRAINS

Suburban lines are found at all main Paris train stations and are clearly marked Banlieue. Tickets for city

A double-decker Banlieue train

transport cannot be used on Banlieue trains, with the exception of some RER tickets to stations with both SNCF and RER lines. Several tourist destinations are served by Banlieue trains, including Chantilly, Chartres, Fontaine-bleau, Giverny and Versailles (*see pp248–53*). Telephone the SNCF for details on 36 35 or try their website: **www**.sncf.fr

Travelling by Taxi

Taxis are more expensive than trains or buses, but they are an advantage after 1am, when the metro has stopped running. There are taxi ranks (*station de taxis*) throughout the city; a short list is provided below.

A Paris taxi rank sign

CATCHING A TAXI

There are over 10,000 taxis operating in central Paris. Yet there never seem to be enough of them to meet demand, particularly during rush hours and on Friday and Saturday nights.

Taxis can be hailed in the street, but not within 50 m (165 ft) of a taxi rank. Since ranks always take priority over street stops, the easiest way to get a cab is to find a rank and join the queue. Ranks are found at many busy cross-roads, at main metro and RER stations, and at all hospitals, train stations and airports. An illuminated white light on the roof shows that the taxi is available. A small light lit below means that the taxi is occupied. If the white light is covered the taxi is off duty. Taxis on their last run can refuse to take passengers.

The meter should have a specified initial amount showing at the taxi rank, or when it is hailed. Initial charges on radio taxis vary widely, depending on the distance the taxi covers to arrive at the pick-up point. Payment by cheque is not accepted but some cars take credit cards.

Rates vary with the part of the city and the time of day. Rate A, in the city centre, is charged per kilometre. The higher rate B applies in the city centre on Sundays, holidays and at night (7pm–7am), or daytime in the suburbs or airports. Even higher rate C applies to the suburbs and airports at night. Taxis charge for each piece of luggage. There's no need to give a tip.

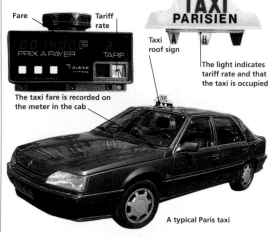

The taxi fare is recorded on the meter in the cab

The light indicates tariff rate and that the taxi is occupied

A typical Paris taxi

DIRECTORY

TAXI RANKS

Charles de Gaulle-Etoile
1 Ave Wagram 75017.
Map 4 D4.
Tel 01 43 80 01 99.

Eiffel Tower
Quai Branly 75007.
Map 10 D3.
Tel 01 45 55 85 41.

Metro Concorde
252 Rue de Rivoli 75001.
Map 11 C1.
Tel 01 42 61 67 60.

Place de Clichy
Pl de Clichy 75009.
Map 6 D1.
Tel 01 42 85 00 00.

Place Denfert-Rochereau
297 Blvd Raspail 75014.
Map 16 E3.
Tel 01 43 35 00 00.

Place de la Madeleine
8 Blvd Malesherbes 75008.
Map 5 C5.
Tel 01 42 65 00 00.

Place de la République
1 Ave de la République 75011.
Map 14 D1.
Tel 01 43 55 92 64.

Place St-Michel
29 Quai St-Michel 75005.
Map 13 A4.
Tel 01 43 29 63 66.

Place du Trocadéro
1 Ave D'Eylau 75016.
Map 9 C1.
Tel 01 47 27 00 00.

Rond Point des Champs-Elysées
7 Ave Matignon 75008.
Map 5 A5.
Tel 01 42 56 29 00.

St-Paul
10 Rue de Rivoli 75004.
M *St-Paul.* **Map** 13 C3.
Tel 01 48 87 49 39.

TAXIS BOOKED BY TELEPHONE

Alpha
Tel 01 45 85 85 85.

Artaxi
Tel 01 42 03 50 50.

G7
Tel 01 47 39 47 39, 01 47 39 00 91 (special needs).

Les Taxis Bleus
Tel 08 25 16 10 10.

SNCF INFORMATION

General Information and Ticket Reservations
Tel 36 35.
www.sncf.fr

Autotrain (Car trains)
Tel 36 35 (within France) or +33 892 35 35 33 (from abroad).

STREET FINDER

The map references given with all sights, hotels, restaurants, shops and entertainment venues described in this book refer to the maps in this section (*see* How the Map References Work *opposite*). A complete index of street names and all the places of interest marked on the maps can be found on the following pages. The key map shows the area of Paris covered by the *Street Finder*, with the arrondissement numbers for each district. The maps include not only the sightseeing areas (which are colour-coded), but the whole of central Paris with all the districts important for hotels, restaurants, shopping and entertainment venues. The symbols used to represent sights and features on the *Street Finder* maps are listed opposite.

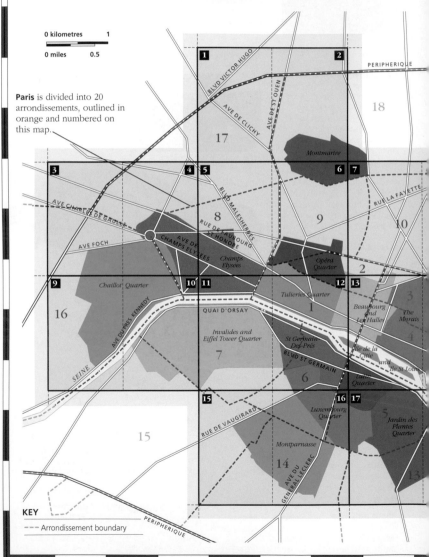

0 kilometres 1

0 miles 0.5

Paris is divided into 20 arrondissements, outlined in orange and numbered on this map.

PERIPHERIQUE

1 2 3 4 5 6 7 9 10 11 12 13 15 16 17

18

17

Montmartre

BLVD VICTOR HUGO

AVE DE ST OUEN

AVE DE CLICHY

AVE CHARLES DE GAULLE

BLVD MALESHERBES

RUE LA FAYETTE

8

9

10

2

AVE FOCH

AVE DES CHAMPS ELYSEES

RUE DU FAUBOURG ST HONORE

Champs Elysees

Opéra Quarter

16

Chaillot Quarter

QUAI D'ORSAY

Tuileries Quarter

1

Beaubourg and Les Halles

The Marais

AVE DU PRES KENNEDY

Invalides and Eiffel Tower Quarter

7

St Germain Des-Prés

BLVD ST GERMAIN

Ile de la Cité and Ile St Louis

Latin Quarter

SEINE

6

15

RUE DE VAUGIRARD

Luxembourg Quarter

Jardin des Plantes Quarter

5

Montparnasse

14

AVE DU GENERAL LECLERC

13

KEY

PERIPHERIQUE

- - - Arrondissement boundary

HOW THE MAP REFERENCES WORK

The first figure tells you which *Street Finder* map to turn to.

Hôtel de Ville ⑲

4 Pl de l'Hôtel-de-Ville 75004.
[Map]13 [B3]. **Tel** 01 42 76 50 49.
Ⓜ *Hôtel de Ville.* ◯ *groups: by arrangement.* ⬤ *public hols, official functions* ♿ 📷

The letter and number give the grid reference. Letters go across the map's top and bottom; figures on its sides.

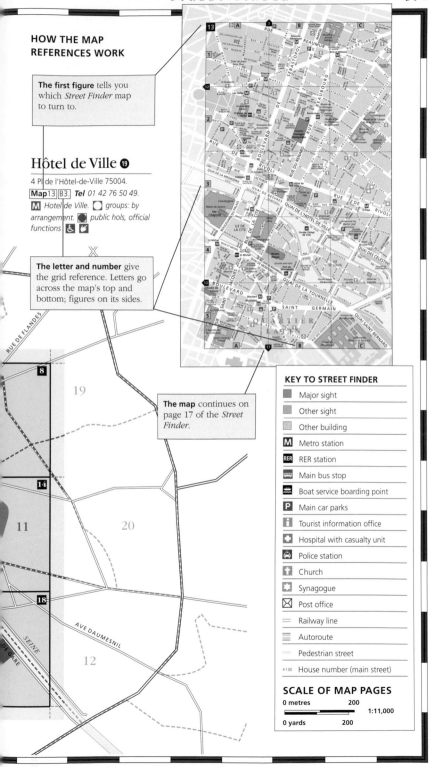

The map continues on page 17 of the *Street Finder.*

KEY TO STREET FINDER

▪	Major sight
▪	Other sight
▫	Other building
Ⓜ	Metro station
RER	RER station
🚌	Main bus stop
🚢	Boat service boarding point
🅿	Main car parks
ℹ	Tourist information office
✛	Hospital with casualty unit
🚓	Police station
✝	Church
✡	Synagogue
⊠	Post office
═	Railway line
▬	Autoroute
─	Pedestrian street
K130	House number (main street)

SCALE OF MAP PAGES

0 metres   200
                            1:11,000
0 yards   200

Street Finder Index

Each place name is followed by its arrondissement number, and then by its Street Finder reference.

Each place name is followed by its arrondissement number, and then by its Street Finder reference.

Each place name is followed by its arrondissement number, and then by its Street Finder reference.

Each place name is followed by its arrondissement number, and then by its Street Finder reference.

Each place name is followed by its arrondissement number, and then by its Street Finder reference.

Each place name is followed by its arrondissement number, and then by its Street Finder reference.

Each place name is followed by its arrondissement number, and then by its Street Finder reference.

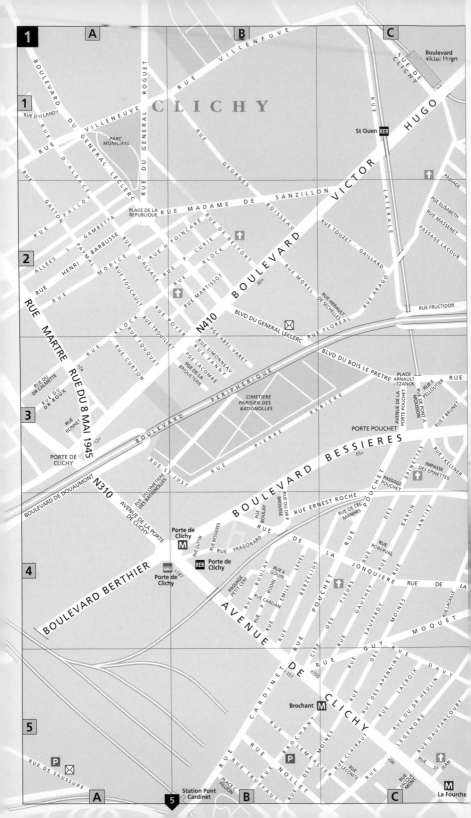

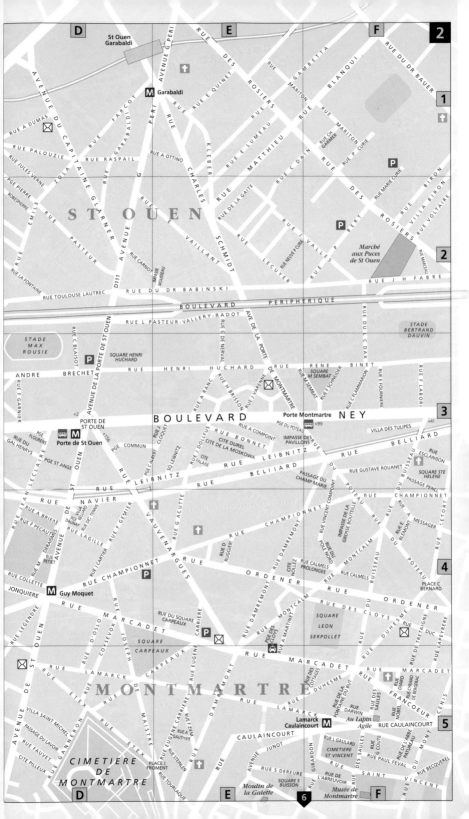

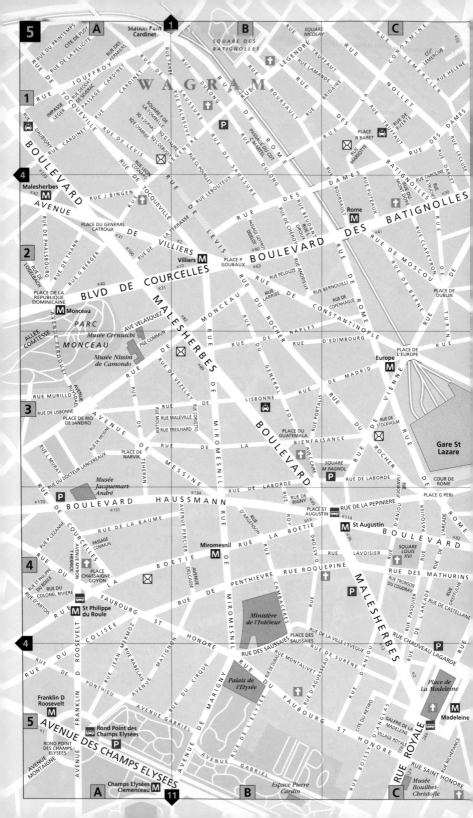

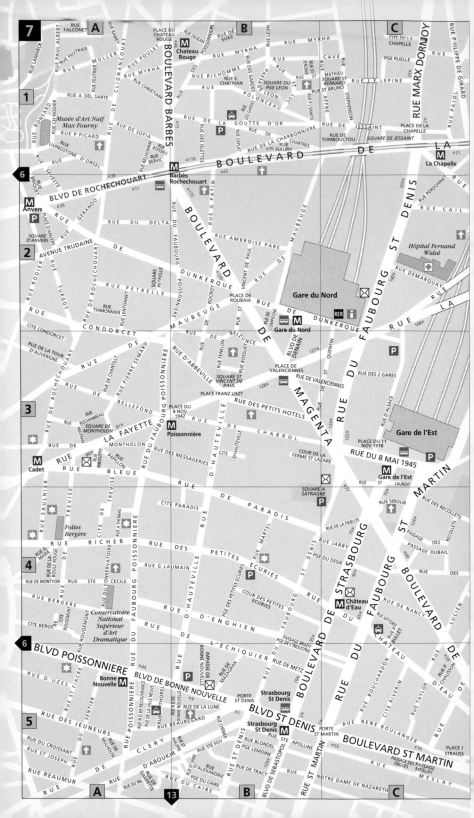

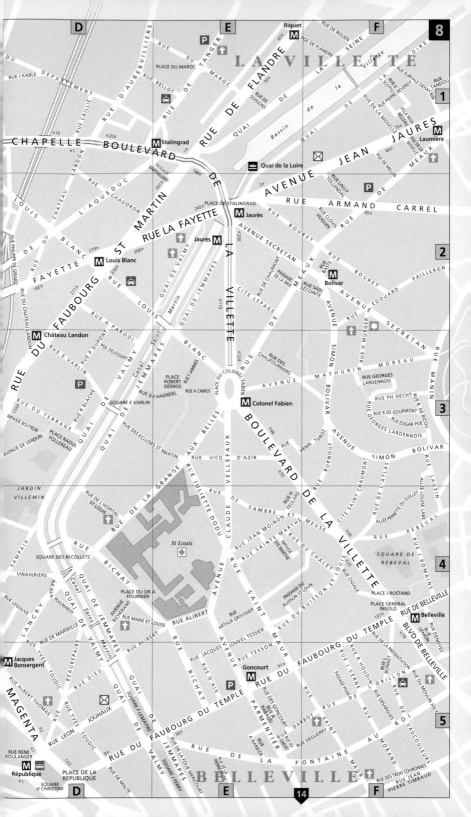

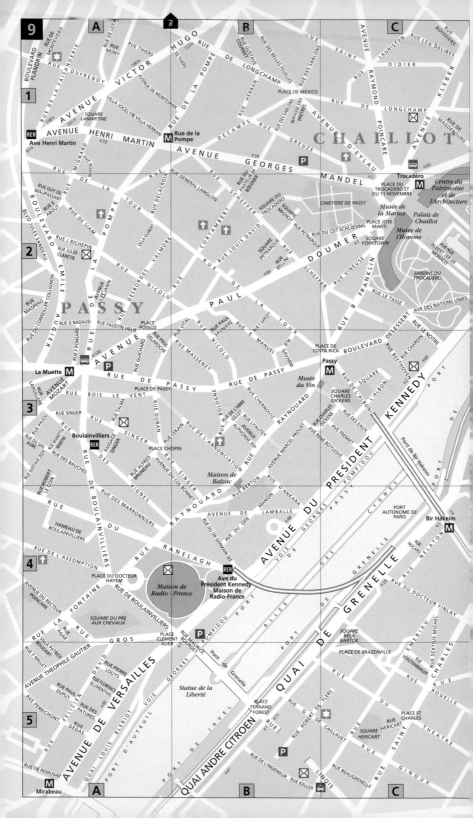

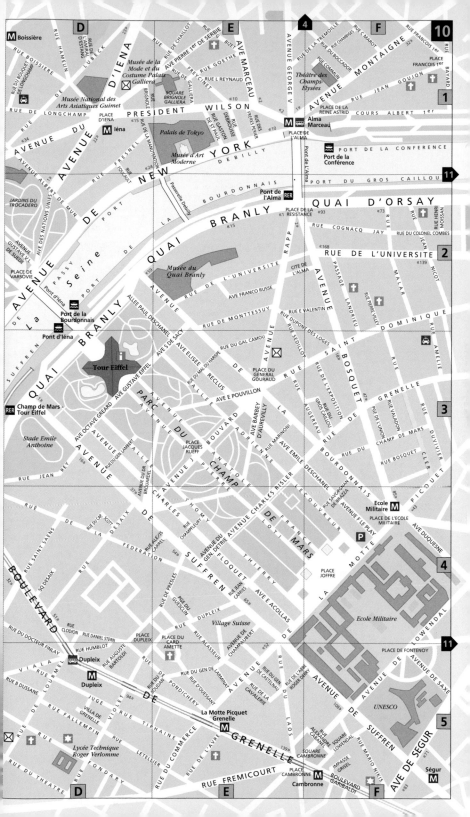

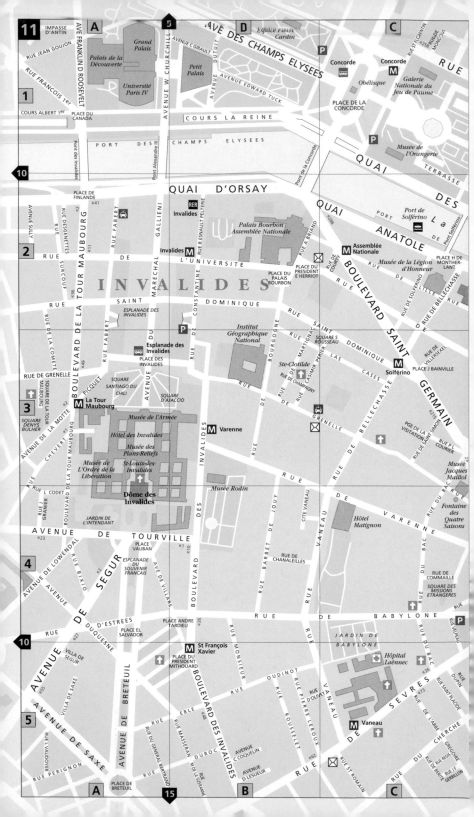

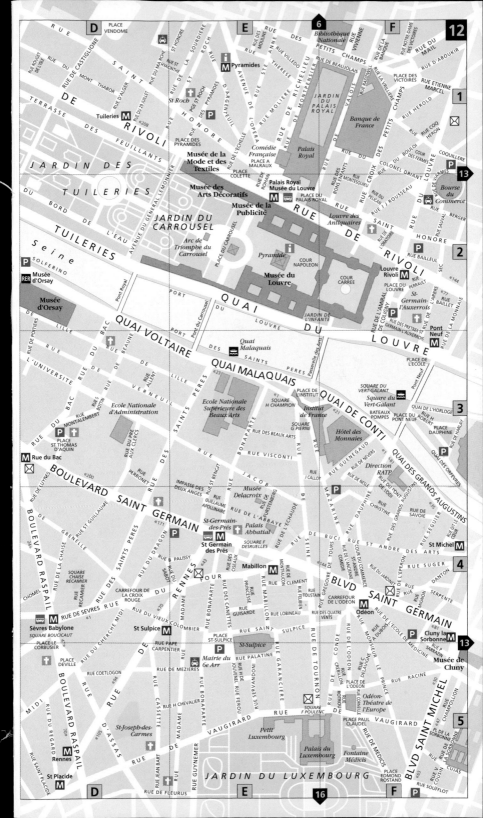

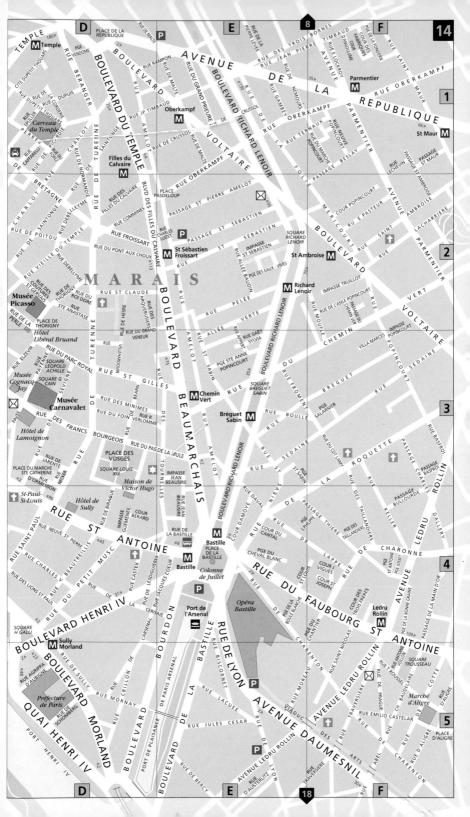

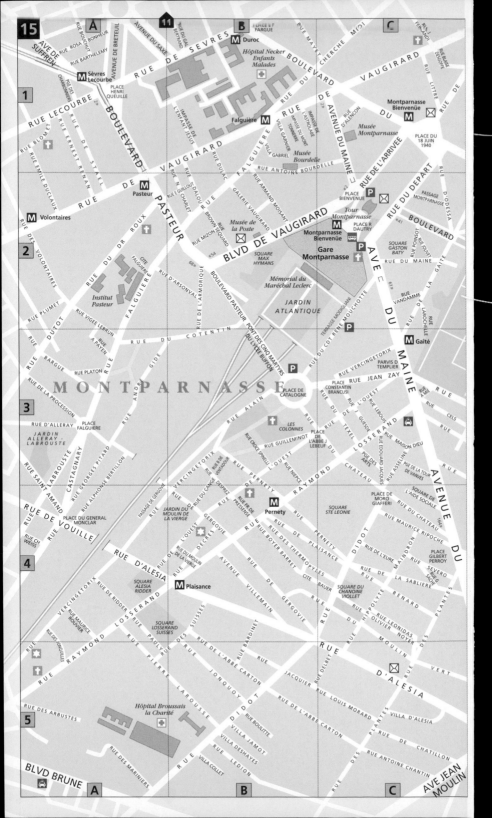

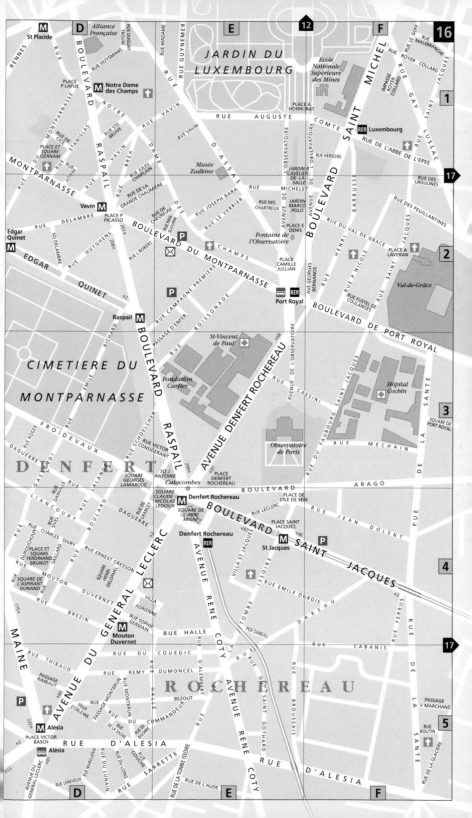

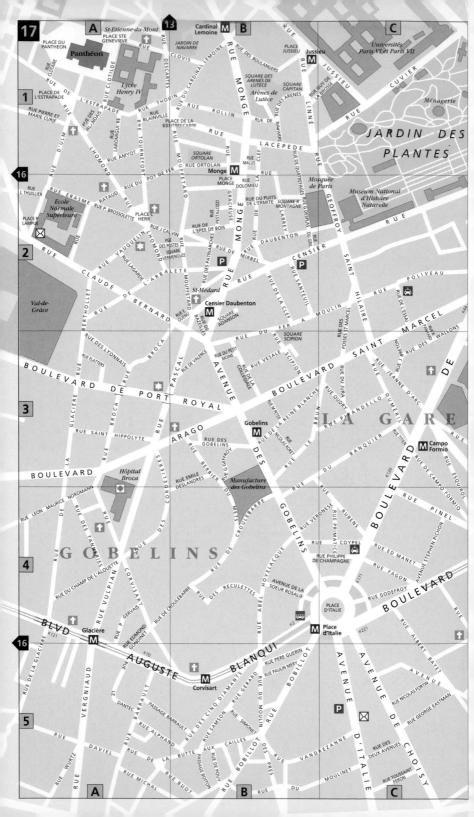

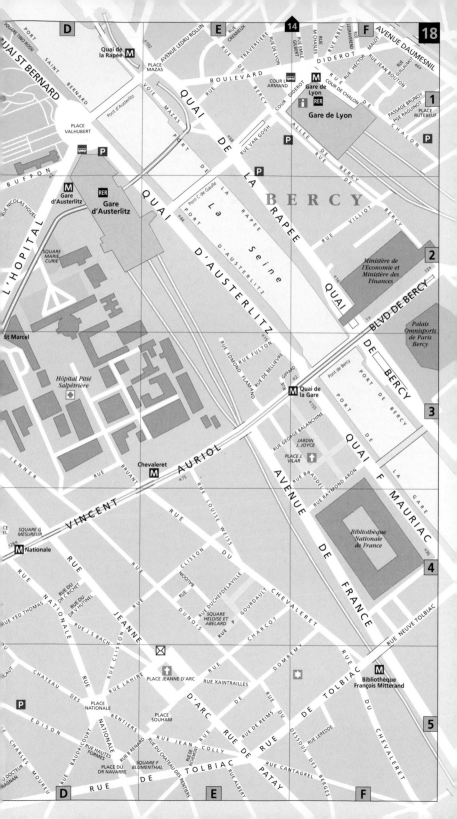

General Index

Acknowledgments

Dorling Kindersley would like to thank the many people whose help and assistance contributed to the preparation of this book.

Main Contributor
Alan Tillier has lived in all the main areas of Paris for 25 years, during which time he has been Paris correspondent for several journals including Newsweek, The Times and the International Herald Tribune. He is the author of several Herald Tribune guides for business travellers to Europe.

Contributors
Lenny Borger, Karen Burshtein, Thomas Quinn Curtiss, David Downie, Fiona Dunlop, Heidi Ellison, Alexandre Lazareff, Robert Noah, Andrew Sanger, Martha Rose Shulman, David Stevens, Ian Williams, Jude Welton.

Dorling Kindersley wishes to thank the following editors and researchers at Websters International Publishers: Sandy Carr, Siobhan Bremner, Valeria Fabbri, Gemma Hancock, Sara Harper, Annie Hubert, Celia Woolfrey.

Additional Photography
Andy Crawford, Michael Crockett, Lucy Davies, Mike Dunning, Philip Gatward, Steve Gorton, Alison Harris, Andrew Holligan, Chas Howson, Britta Jaschinski, Dave King, Ranald MacKechnie, Oliver Knight, Eric Meacher, Neil Mersh, Ian O'Leary, Stephen Oliver, Poppy, Susannah Price, Tim Ridley, Philippe Sebert, Steve Shott, Peter Wilson, Steven Wooster.

Additional Illustrations
John Fox, Nick Gibbard, David Harris, Kevin Jones Associates, John Woodcock.

Cartography
Andrew Heritage, James Mills-Hicks, Suresh Kumar, Alok Pathak, John Plumer, Chez Picthall (DK Cartography). Advanced Illustration (Cheshire), Contour Publishing (Derby), Euromap Limited (Berkshire). Street Finder maps: ERA-Maptec Ltd (Dublin) adapted with permission from original survey and mapping by Shobunsha (Japan).

Cartographic Research
Roger Bullen, Tony Chambers, Paul Dempsey, Ruth Duxbury, Ailsa Heritage, Margaret Hynes, Jayne Parsons, Donna Rispoli, Andrew Thompson.

Design and Editorial
Managing Editor Douglas Amrine
Managing Art Editor Geoff Manders
Senior Editor Georgina Matthews
Series Design Consultant Peter Luff
Editorial Director David Lamb
Art Director Anne-Marie Bulat
Production Controller Hilary Stephens
Picture Research Naomi Peck
DTP Designer Andy Wilkinson
Janet Abbott, Emma Ainsworth, Vandana Bhagra, Hilary Bird, Vanessa Courtier, Maggie Crowley, Lisa Davidson, Guy Dimond, Elizabeth Eyre, Simon Farbrother, Fay Franklin, Eric Gibory, Paul Hines, Fiona Holman, Gail Jones, Nancy Jones, Stephen Knowlden, Chris Lascelles, Rebecca Milner, Fiona Morgan, Lyn Parry, Shirin Patel, Pamposh Raina, Philippa Richmond, Philippe Rouin, Sands Publishing Solutions, Andrew Szudek, Alka Thakur, Dora Whitaker.

Special Assistance
Miranda Dewer at Bridgeman Art Library, Editions Gallimard, Lindsay Hunt, Emma Hutton at Cooling Brown, Janet Todd at DACS.

Photographic Reference
Musée Carnavalet, Thomas d'Hoste.

Photography Permissions
Dorling Kindersley would like to thank the following for their kind permission to photograph at their establishments: Aéroports de Paris, Basilique du Sacré-Coeur de Montmartre, Beauvilliers, Benoit, Bibliothèque Historique de la Ville de Paris, Bibliothèque Polonaise, Bofinger, Brasserie Lipp, Café de Flore, Caisse Nationale des Monuments Historiques et des Sites, Les Catacombes, Centre National d'Art et de Culture Georges Pompidou, Chartier, Chiberta, La Cité des Sciences et de l'Industrie and L'EPPV, La Coupole, Les Deux Magots, Fondation Cousteau, Le Grand Colbert, Hôtel Atala, Hôtel Liberal Bruand, Hôtel Meurice, Hôtel Relais Christine, Kenzo, Lucas-Carton, La Madeleine, Mariage Frères, Memorial du Martyr Juif Inconnu, Thierry Mugler, Musée Armenien de France, Musée de l'Art Juif, Musée Bourdelle, Musée du Cabinet des Medailles, Musée Carnavalet, Musée Cernuschi: Ville de Paris, Musée du Cinema Henri Langlois, Musée Cognacq-Jay, Musée de Cristal de Baccarat, Musée d'Ennery, Musée Grévin, Musée Jacquemart-André, Musée de la Musique Méchanique, Musée National des Châteaux de Malmaison et Bois-Préau, Collections du Musée National de la Légion d'Honneur, Musée National du Moyen Age-Thermes de Cluny, Musée de Notre-Dame de Paris, Musée de l'Opéra, Musée de l'Ordre de la

Libération, Musée d'Orsay, Musée de la Préfecture de la Police, Musée de Radio France, Musée Rodin, Musée des Transports Urbains, Musée du Vin, Musée Zadkine, Notre-Dame du Travail, A l'Olivier, Palais de la Découverte, Palais de Luxembourg, Pharamond, Pied de Cochon, Lionel Poilaêne, St Germain-des-Prés, St Louis en l'Ile, St Médard, St Merry, St Paul–St-Louis, St-Roch, St-Sulpice, La Société Nouvelle d'Exploitation de La Tour Eiffel, La Tour Montparnasse, Unesco, and all the other museums, churches, hotels, restaurants, shops, galleries and sights too numerous to thank individually.

Picture Credits

t=top; tc=top centre; tr=top right; cla=centre left above; ca=centre above; cra=centre right above; cl=centre left; c=centre; cr=centre right; clb=centre left below; cb=centre below; crb=centre right below; bl=bottom left; bc=bottom centre; br=bottom right.

Works of art have been reproduced with the permission of the following copyright holders: © Succession H Matisse/DACS 1993: 111ca; © ADAGP/SPADEM, Paris and DACS, London 1993: 44cl; © ADAGP, Paris and DACS, London 1993: 61br, 61tr, 105tc, 107cb, 109b, 111ttc, 111cb, 112bl, 112t, 112br, 113bl, 113br, 119c, 120b, 179tl, 180bc, 181cr, 211tc; © DACS 1993: 38tl, 45cr, 50br, 55cr, 57tl, 100t, 100br, 100clb, 100cl, 100ca, 101t, 101ca, 101cr, 101bl, 104, 107cra, 113c, 137tl, 178cl, 178ca, 208br.

Christo–The Pont Neuf wrapped, Paris, 1975-85: 40cla; © Christo 1985, by kind permission of the artist. Photos achieved with the assistance of the EPPV and the CSI pp 234-9; Courtesy of Erben Otto Dix: 110bl; Photos of Disneyland ® Paris: 242tr, 243bl, 243cr. The characters, architectural works and trademarks are the property of The Walt Disney Company. All rights reserved; Fondation Le Corbusier: 59t, 254b; Courtesy of The Estate of Joan Mitchell: 113t; © Henry Moore Foundation 1993: 191b. Reproduced by kind permission of the Henry Moore Foundation; Beth Lipkin: 241t; Courtesy of the Maison Victor Hugo, Ville de Paris: 95cl; Courtesy of the Musée d'Art Naïf Max Fourny Paris: 221b, 223b; Musée Carnavalet: 212b; Musée de L'Histoire Contemporaine (BDIC), Paris: 208br; Musée de L'Orangerie: 130tr; Musée du Louvre: 125br, 128c; Musée National des ChÂteaux de Malmaison et Bois-Préau: 255cr; Musée Marmottan: 58c, 58cb, 59c, 60tl, 131tr; Musée de la Mode et du Costume Palais Galliera: 57br; Musée de Montmartre, Paris: 221t; Musée des Monuments Français: 197tc, 198cr; Musée National de la Légion d'Honneur: 32bc, 143bl; Musée de la Ville de Paris: Musée du Petit Palais: 54cl, 205cb; © Sundancer: 362bl.

The Publishers are grateful to the following individuals, companies and picture libraries for permission to reproduce their photographs:

ADP: 377b; Alamy: Bertrand Collet 269cl; Glenn Harper 212tl; Image State 270br; Allsport UK: Sean Botterill 41br; Allvey & Towers: 378bl; The Ancient Art and Architecture Collection: 22clb; James Austin: 88t.

Banque de France: 133t; Nelly Bariand: 165c; Gérard Boullay: 84tl, 84tr, 84bl, 84br, 85t, 85cra, 85crb, 85br, 85bl; Bridgeman Art Library, London: (detail) 21br, 22cr, 23cl, 30cr–31cl, (detail) 35br; British Library, London (detail) 18br, (detail) 23bl, (detail) 24tl, (detail) 31tl; B N, Paris 19bl, (detail) 23tc, (detail) 23cr; Château de Versailles, France 19tr, 19bc, (detail) 19br, (detail) 30br, (detail) 155b; Christie's, London 8–9, (detail) 24cb, 34cla, 36tl, 44c; Delomosne, London 32clb; Giraudon 16, (detail) 26bl, (detail) 26clb, (detail) 27br, (detail) 30bl, (detail) 30cla, (detail) 31bl, 33cb, 58br, (detail) 60bl, 60ca, 60c; Lauros– Giraudon 23tr; Louvre, Paris 56t, 60br, 61bl, 61tl; Roy Miles Gallery 27tr; Musée de L'Armée, Paris (detail) 83br; Musée Condé, Chantilly (detail) 4tr, 18bl, 19tcl, (detail) 19tcr, (detail) 19c, (detail) 22tl, (detail) 26bc; Musée Crozatier, Le Puy en Velay, France (detail) 25bl; Musée Gustave Moreau, Paris 56b, 231tr; National Gallery (detail) 29tl, (detail) 44b; Musée de la Ville de Paris, Musée Carnavalet (detail) 30bc, (detail) 31tr, 31crb, 97t. Collection Painton Cowen 40cla; Palais du Tokyo, Paris 59b; Temples Newsham House, Leeds 25cr; Uffizi Gallery, Florence (detail) 24br; © The British Museum; 31tc

Cité de la Musique: Eric Mahondieu 235br; Cité des Sciences et de l'Industrie: Christophe Foubert Alcaline 239bl; Michel Lamoureux 236cb, 236b, 237tl, 237tr, 238clb, 238t, 239cra, 239crb; Pascal Prieur 238cla; Natacha Soury 236tl; Michel Virad 236clb, 237tl, 238br, 239tl; Corbis: Burnstein Collection 227b; Ray Juno 10cl; Richard List 11cl; Sylvain Saustier 268b; Tom Craig: 273t, 273br.

R Doisneau: Rapho 143t Espace Montmartre: 220bl; European Commission 371; Mary Evans Picture Library: 38bl, 81br, 89tl, 94b, 130b, 141cl, 191c, 192cr, 193crb, 209b, 224bl, 247br, 251t, 253b, 388t.

Giraudon: (detail) 22bl, (detail) 23crb; Lauros– Giraudon (detail) 33bl; Musée de la Ville de Paris: Musée Carnavalet (detail) 211t; Le Grand Véfour: 293t.

Robert Harding Picture Library: 22br, 26tl, 29ca, 29br, 36cla, 38tl, 41tl, 45cr, 65br, 240cb, 381cr; B M 27ca; B N 191tr, 208bc; Biblioteco Reale, Turin 127t; Bulloz 208cb; P Craven 380b; R Francis

82clb; I Griffiths 376t; H Josse 208br; Musée National des Châteaux de Malmaison et Bois-Préau 33tc; Musée de Versailles 26cl; R Poinot 361b; P Tetrel 251crb; Explorer 12bl; F. Chazot 341b; Girard 65c; P Gleizes 62bl; F Jalain 378b; J Moatti 340bl, 340cl; Walter Rawlings 43bc; A Wolf 123br, 123tl; Alison Harris: Musée de Montparnasse 179cl; Pavillon des Arts 108br; Le Village Royale 132tl; John Heseltine Photography: 174; Hulton Getty: 45cl, 101br, 181tc, 231bl, 232c; Charles Hewitt 40clb; Lancaster 181tc.

© IGN Paris 1990 Authorisation N° 90–2067: 13b; Institut du Monde Arabe: Georges Fessey 165tr.

The Kobal Collection: 44t, 140b; Columbia Pictures 181br; Société Générale de Films 38tc; Les Films du Carrosse 109t; Kong: Patricia Bailer 10b.

The Lebrecht Collection: 227br; François Lequeux 194cl.

Magnum: Bruno Barbey 64b; Philippe Halsmann 45b; Ministère de L'Economie et des Finances: 371c; Ministère de L'Intérieur SGAP de Paris: 368bc, 368br, 369t; Collections du Mobilier National-Cliché du Mobilier National: 167cr; © photo Musée de L'Armée, Paris: 189cr; Musée des Arts Décoratifs, Paris: L Sully Jaulmes 54t; Musée des Arts de la Mode-Collection UCAD–UFAC: 121b; Musée Bouilhet-Christofle: 57tr, 132t; Musée Cantonal des Beaux-Arts, Lausanne: 115b; Musée Carnavalet: Dac Karin Maucotel 97t; Musée d'Art et d'Histoire du Judaïsme/Christophe Fouin 103br; Musée National de L'Histoire Naturelle: D Serrette 167cl; Musée de L'Holographie: 109cl; © Musée de L'Homme, Paris: D Ponsard 196cb, 199c; © Photo Musée de la Marine, Paris: 32bl, 196cl; Musée National d'Art Modern– Centre Georges Pompidou, Paris: 61tr, 110br, 110bl, 111t, 111ca, 111cb, 112t, 112bl, 112br, 113t, 113c, 113bl, 113br; Musée des Plans-Reliefs, Paris: 186crb; Musée de la Poste, Paris: 179tl; Musée de la Seita, Paris: D Dado 190t.

© Paris Tourist Office: Catherine Balet 270cl; David Lefranc 268c, 269t, 269br, 270tr, 271t, 271br, 272cl, 272bl, 272br; Philippe Perdereau: 132b, 133b; Cliché Photothèque des Musées de la Ville

de Paris –© DACS 1993: 21ca, 21crb, 28cr–29cl, 96tr; courtesy of Poilâne: 321bl; Popperfoto: 227t.

Paul Raferty 246b; RATP.SG/G.I.E. Totheme 54; 386; Redferns: W Gottlieb 38clb; © Photo Réunion des Musées Nationaux: Grand Trianon 26crb; Musée Guimet 54cb, 200tr; Musée du Louvre: 27cb, (detail) 32cr–33cl, 55tl, 123bl, 124t, 124c, 124b, 125t, 125c, 126c, 126bl, 126br, 127b, 128t, 128b, 129t, 129c; Musée Nationaux d'Art Moderne © DACS/ADAGP 111crb; Musée Picasso 55cr, 100t, 100c, 100cl, 100clb, 100br, 101bl, 101cr, 101ca, 101t; Roger- Viollet: (detail) 24clb, (detail) 39bl, (detail) 192bc, (detail) 209t; Ann Ronan Picture Library: 173cr; Philippe Ruault: Fondation Cartier 179bl.

La Samaritaine, Paris: 115c; Sealink Plc: 378cl; Sipapress: 222c; SNCF – Service Presse Voyages France Europe: 388bl; Frank Spooner Pictures: F Reglain 64ca; P Renault 64c; Sygma: 35crb, 240cl; F Poincet 40tl; Keystone 40bc, 241cra; J Langevin 41br; Keler 41crb; J Van Hasselt 41tr; P. Habans 62c; A Gyori 63cr; P Vauthey 65bl; Y Forestier 188t; Sunset Boulevard 241br; Water Carone 340t.

Tallandier: 25cb, 25tl, 28cl, 28clb, 28bl, 29bl, 30tl, 31cr, 31ca, 32tl, 32cb, 32br, 38cla, 39ca, 39br, 40cb, 52cla; B N 28br, 32crb, 38bc; Brigaud 39crb; Brimeur 34bl; Charmet 36cb; Dubout 17b, 20br, 24ca, 25br, 26br, 30c, 33cr, 33tr, 34br, 35bl, 36clb, 36bl, 36br, 37bl, 37br, 37clb, 37tl, 37crb; Josse 20cla, 20tc, 20c, 20clb, 21tl, 36bc; Josse-B N 20bl; Joubert 38c; Tildier 37ca; Vigne 34clb; Le Train Bleu: 295t.

Vidéothèque de Paris: Hoi Pham Dinh 106lb
Agence Vu: Didier Lefèvre 340cr.

Front Endpaper: John Heseltine Photography br. © DACS 1993: cra. Back endpaper: RATP CML Agence Cartographique.

Jacket:
Front - DK Images: Eric Meacher bl; Tips Images: Chad Ehlers main image.
Back - DK Images: Max Alexander tl, clb, bl; Le Grand Vefour: cla.
Spine - DK Images: b; Tips Images: Chad Ehlers t.

SPECIAL EDITIONS OF DK TRAVEL GUIDES

Phrase Book

In Emergency

Help!	**Au secours!**	*oh sekoor*
Stop!	**Arrêtez!**	*aret-ay*
Call a doctor!	**Appelez un médecin!**	*apuh-lay uñ medsañ*
Call an ambulance!	**Appelez une ambulance!**	*apuh-lay oon oñboo-loñs*
Call the police!	**Appelez la police!**	*apuh-lay lah poh-lees*
Call the fire brigade!	**Appelez les pompiers!**	*apuh-lay leh poñ-peeyay*
Where is the nearest telephone?	**Où est le téléphone le plus proche?**	*oo ay luh tehlehfon luh ploo prosh*
Where is the nearest hospital?	**Où est l'hôpital le plus proche?**	*oo ay l'opeetal luh ploo prosh*

Communication Essentials

Yes	**Oui**	*wee*
No	**Non**	*noñ*
Please	**S'il vous plaît**	*seel voo play*
Thank you	**Merci**	*mer-see*
Excuse me	**Excusez-moi**	*exkoo-zay mwah*
Hello	**Bonjour**	*boñzhoor*
Goodbye	**Au revoir**	*oh rub-vwar*
Good night	**Bonsoir**	*boñ-swar*
Morning	**Le matin**	*matañ*
Afternoon	**L'après-midi**	*l'apreh-meedee*
Evening	**Le soir**	*swar*
Yesterday	**Hier**	*eeyehr*
Today	**Aujourd'hui**	*oh-zhoor-dwee*
Tomorrow	**Demain**	*dubmañ*
Here	**Ici**	*ee-see*
There	**Là**	*lah*
What?	**Quoi, Quel, quelle?**	*kwah, kel, kel*
When?	**Quand?**	*koñ*
Why?	**Pourquoi?**	*poor-kwah*
Where?	**Où?**	*oo*

Useful Phrases

How are you?	**Comment allez-vous?**	*kom-moñ talay voo*
Very well, thank you.	**Très bien, merci.**	*treb byañ, mer-see*
Pleased to meet you.	**Enchanté de faire votre connaissance.**	*oñshoñ-tay duh fehr votr kon-ay-sans*
See you soon.	**A bientôt.**	*byañ-toh*
That's fine	**Voilà qui est parfait**	*vualah kee ay par-fay*
Where is/are...?	**Où est/sont...?**	*oo ay/soñ*
How far is it to...?	**Combien de kilomètres d'ici à...?**	*kom-byañ duh keelo-metr d'ee-see ab*
Which way to...?	**Quelle est la direction pour...?**	*kel ay lah deer-ek-syoñ poor*
Do you speak English?	**Parlez-vous anglais?**	*par-lay voo oñg-lay*
I don't understand.	**Je ne comprends pas.**	*zhuh nuh kom-proñ pah*
Could you speak slowly please?	**Pouvez-vous parler moins vite s'il vous plaît?**	*poo-vay voo par-lay mwañ veet seel voo play*
I'm sorry.	**Excusez-moi.**	*exkoo-zay mwah*

Useful Words

big	**grand**	*groñ*
small	**petit**	*pub-tee*
hot	**chaud**	*show*
cold	**froid**	*frwah*
good	**bon/bien**	*boñ/byañ*
bad	**mauvais**	*moh-veh*
enough	**assez**	*assay*
well	**bien**	*byañ*
open	**ouvert**	*oo-ver*
closed	**fermé**	*fer-meh*
left	**gauche**	*gohsh*
right	**droit**	*drwah*
straight on	**tout droit**	*too drwah*
near	**près**	*preb*
far	**loin**	*lwañ*
up	**en haut**	*oñ oh*
down	**en bas**	*oñ bab*
early	**de bonne heure**	*dub bon urr*
late	**en retard**	*oñ rub-tar*
entrance	**l'entrée**	*l'on-tray*
exit	**la sortie**	*sor-tee*
toilet	**les toilettes, le WC**	*twab-let, vay-see*
free, unoccupied	**libre**	*leebr*
free, no charge	**gratuit**	*grah-twee*

Making a Telephone Call

I'd like to place a long-distance call.	**Je voudrais faire un appel á l'étranger.**	*zhub voo-dreh febr uñ apel a laytroñ-zhay*
I'd like to make a reverse charge call.	**Je voudrais faire une communication en PCV.**	*zhub voo-dreh febr oon komoonikah-syoñ oñ peh-seh-veh*
I'll try again later.	**Je rappelerai plus tard.**	*zhub rapel-eray ploo tar*
Can I leave a message?	**Est-ce que je peux laisser un message?**	*es-keb zhub pub leh-say uñ mebsazh*
Hold on.	**Ne quittez pas, s'il vous plaît.**	*nuh kee-tay pah seel voo play*
Could you speak up a little please?	**Pouvez-vous parler un peu plus fort?**	*poo-vay voo par-lay uñ pub ploo for*
local call	**la communication locale**	*komoonikah-syoñ low-kal*

Shopping

How much does this cost?	**C'est combien s'il vous plaît?**	*say kom-byañ seel voo play*
I would like...	**je voudrais...**	*zhub voo-dray*
Do you have?	**Est-ce que vous avez?**	*es-kub voo zavay*
I'm just looking.	**Je regarde seulement.**	*zhub rubgar sublmoñ*
Do you take credit cards?	**Est-ce que vous acceptez les cartes de crédit?**	*es-kub voo zaksept-ay leh kart duh kreb-dee*
Do you take traveller's cheques?	**Est-ce que vous acceptez les chèques de voyages?**	*es-kub voo zaksept-ay leh shek dub vvayazh*
What time do you open?	**A quelle heure vous êtes ouvert?**	*ah kel urr voo zet oo-ver*
What time do you close?	**A quelle heure vous êtes fermé?**	*ah kel urr voo zet fer-may*
This one.	**Celui-ci.**	*subl-wee-see*
That one.	**Celui-là.**	*subl-wee-lah*
expensive	**cher**	*shebr*
cheap	**pas cher, bon marché**	*pab shebr, boñ mar-shay*
size, clothes	**la taille**	*tye*
size, shoes	**la pointure**	*pwañ-tur*
white	**blanc**	*bloñ*
black	**noir**	*nwabr*
red	**rouge**	*roozb*
yellow	**jaune**	*zhobwn*
green	**vert**	*vebr*
blue	**bleu**	*bluh*

Types of Shop

antique shop	**le magasin d'antiquités**	*maga-zañ d'oñteekee-tay*
bakery	**la boulangerie**	*booloñ-zhuree*
bank	**la banque**	*boñk*
book shop	**la librairie**	*lee-brebree*
butcher	**la boucherie**	*boo-shebree*
cake shop	**la pâtisserie**	*patee-sree*
cheese shop	**la fromagerie**	*fromazh-ree*
chemist	**la pharmacie**	*farmab-see*
dairy	**la crémerie**	*krem-ree*
department store	**le grand magasin**	*groñ maga-zañ*
delicatessen	**la charcuterie**	*sharkoot-ree*
fishmonger	**la poissonnerie**	*pwasson-ree*
gift shop	**le magasin de cadeaux**	*maga-zañ duh kadob*
greengrocer	**le marchand de légumes**	*mar-shoñ dub lay-goom*
grocery	**l'alimentation**	*alee-moñta-syoñ*
hairdresser	**le coiffeur**	*kwafubr*
market	**le marché**	*marsh-ay*
newsagent	**le magasin de journaux**	*maga-zañ duh zhoor-no*
post office	**la poste, le bureau de poste, le PTT**	*pobst, booroh dub pobst, peh-teb-teb*
shoe shop	**le magasin de chaussures**	*maga-zañ dub show-soor*
supermarket	**le supermarché**	*soo pebr-marshay*
tobacconist	**le tabac**	*tabah*
travel agent	**l'agence de voyages**	*l'azhoñs dub vwayazh*

Sightseeing

abbey	**l'abbaye**	*l'abay-ee*
art gallery	**la galerie d'art**	*galer-ree dart*
bus station	**la gare routière**	*gabr roo-tee-yebr*

cathedral	la cathédrale	katay-dral
church	l'église	l'aygleez
garden	le jardin	zhar-dañ
library	la bibliothèque	beebleeo-tek
museum	le musée	moo-zay
railway station	la gare (SNCF)	gabr (es-en-say-ef)
tourist information office	les renseignements touristiques, le syndicat d'initiative	roñsayn-moñ toorees-teek, sandee-ka d'eenee-syateev
town hall	l'hôtel de ville	l'obtel dub veel
closed for public holiday	fermeture jour férié	febrmeb-tur zhoor febree-ay

Staying in a Hotel

Do you have a vacant room?	Est-ce que vous avez une chambre?	es-kuh voo-zavay oon shambr
double room, with double bed	la chambre à deux personnes, avec un grand lit	shambr ab dub pebr-son avek un gronñ lee
twin room	la chambre à deux lits	shambr ab dub lee
single room	la chambre à une personne	shambr ab oon pebr-son
room with a bath, shower	la chambre avec salle de bains, une douche	shambr avek sal dub bañ, oon doosh
porter	le garçon	gar-soñ
key	la clef	klay
I have a reservation.	J'ai fait une réservation.	zhay fay oon rayzebrva-syoñ

Eating Out

Have you got a table?	Avez-vous une table ce libre?	avay-voo oon tabbl dub leebr
I want to reserve a table.	Je voudrais réserver une table.	zhuh voo-dray rayzebr-vay oon tabbl
The bill please.	L'addition s'il vous plaît.	l'adee-syoñ seel voo play
I am a vegetarian.	Je suis végétarien.	zhuh swee vezhay-tebryañ
Waitress/ waiter	Madame, Mademoiselle/ Monsieur	mah-dam, mah-demwahzel/ muh-syub
menu	le menu, la carte	men-oo, kart
fixed-price menu	le menu à prix fixe	men-oo ab pree feeks
cover charge	le couvert	koo-vebr
wine list	la carte des vins	kart-deb vañ
glass	le verre	vebr
bottle	la bouteille	boo-tay
knife	le couteau	koo-toh
fork	la fourchette	for-shet
spoon	la cuillère	kwee-yebr
breakfast	le petit déjeuner	pub-tee deb-zhub-nay
lunch	le déjeuner	deb-zhub-nay
dinner	le dîner	dee-nay
main course	le plat principal	plab prañsee-pal
starter, first course	l'entrée, le hors d'oeuvre	l'oñ-tray, or-dubvr
dish of the day	le plat du jour	plab doo zhoor
wine bar	le bar à vin	bar ah vañ
café	le café	ka-fay
rare	saignant	say-noñ
medium	à point	ab pwañ
well done	bien cuit	byañ kwee

Menu Decoder

apple	la pomme	pom
baked	cuit au four	kweet ob foor
banana	la banane	banan
beef	le boeuf	buhf
beer, draught	la bière, bière à la pression	bee-yebr, bee-yebr ah lab pres-syoñ
beer		
boiled	bouilli	boo-yee
bread	le pain	pan
butter	le beurre	burr
cake	le gâteau	gab-toh
cheese	le fromage	from-azh
chicken	le poulet	poo-lay
chips	les frites	freet
chocolate	le chocolat	shoko-lab
cocktail	le cocktail	cocktail
coffee	le café	kab-fay
dessert	le dessert	deb-ser
dry	sec	sek
duck	le canard	kanar

egg	l'oeuf	l'uf
fish	le poisson	pwab-ssoñ
fresh fruit	le fruit frais	fruee freb
garlic	l'ail	l'eye
grilled	grillé	gree-yay
ham	le jambon	zboñ-boñ
ice, ice cream	la glace	glas
lamb	l'agneau	l'anyob
lemon	le citron	see-troñ
lobster	le homard	omabr
meat	la viande	vee-yand
milk	le lait	leb
mineral water	l'eau minérale	l'ob meeney-ral
mustard	la moutarde	moo-tard
oil	l'huile	l'weel
olives	les olives	leb zoleev
onions	les oignons	leb zonyoñ
orange	l'orange	l'oroñzh
fresh orange juice	l'orange pressée	l'oroñzh press-eb
fresh lemon juice	le citron pressé	see-troñ press-eb
pepper	le poivre	pwavr
poached	poché	posb-ay
pork	le porc	por
potatoes	les pommes de terre	pom-dub tebr
prawns	les crevettes	kruh-vet
rice	le riz	ree
roast	rôti	row-tee
roll	le petit pain	pub-tee pañ
salt	le sel	sel
sauce	la sauce	sobs
sausage, fresh	la saucisse	sobsees
seafood	les fruits de mer	fruee dub mer
shellfish	les crustaces	kroos-tas
snails	les escargots	leb zes-kar-gob
soup	la soupe, le potage	soop, pob-tazh
steak	le bifteck, le steack	beef-tek, stek
sugar	le sucre	sookr
tea	le thé	tay
toast	pain grillé	pan greeyay
vegetables	les légumes	lay-goom
vinegar	le vinaigre	veenaygr
water	l'eau	l'ob
red wine	le vin rouge	vañ roozh
white wine	le vin blanc	vañ bloñ

Numbers

0	zéro	zeb-rob
1	un, une	uñ, oon
2	deux	dub
3	trois	trwab
4	quatre	katr
5	cinq	sañk
6	six	sees
7	sept	set
8	huit	weet
9	neuf	nerf
10	dix	dees
11	onze	oñz
12	douze	dooz
13	treize	trebz
14	quatorze	katorz
15	quinze	kañz
16	seize	sebz
17	dix-sept	dees-set
18	dix-huit	dees-weet
19	dix-neuf	dees-nerf
20	vingt	vañ
30	trente	tront
40	quarante	karoñt
50	cinquante	sañkoñt
60	soixante	swasoñt
70	soixante-dix	swasoñt-dees
80	quatre-vingts	katr-vañ
90	quatre-vingt-dix	katr-vañ-dees
100	cent	soñ
1,000	mille	meel

Time

one minute	une minute	oon mee-noot
one hour	une heure	oon urr
half an hour	une demi-heure	oon dub-mee urr
Monday	lundi	luñ-dee
Tuesday	mardi	mar-dee
Wednesday	mercredi	mehrkruh-dee
Thursday	jeudi	zhub-dee
Friday	vendredi	voñdruh-dee
Saturday	samedi	sam-dee
Sunday	dimanche	dee-moñsh

Paris Metro and Regional Express Railway (RER)

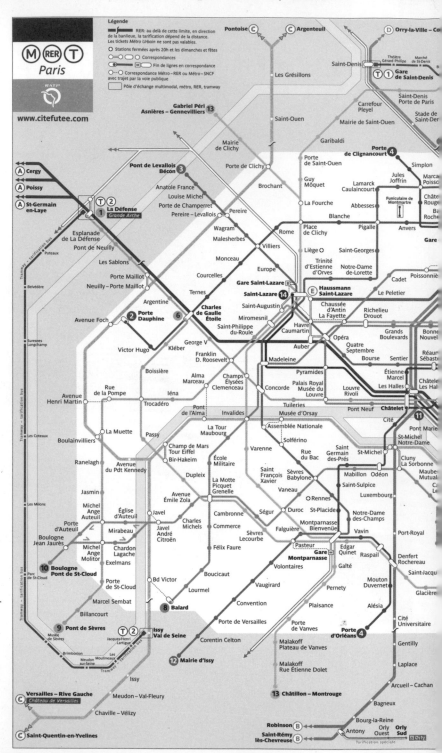

Vatican City is the world's second-smallest independent state. Here you can see its center, St. Peter's Basilica and part of the Vatican Palace, with Bernini's glorious St. Peter's Square beyond. See chapter 6. © Guido Rossi/The Image Bank.

Frommer's®

POSTCARDS

FROM

ROME

To "ensure" your return to the Eternal City, come and throw a coin in Rome's most famous fountain, the Trevi, where a triumphant Neptune is flanked by Tritons. See chapter 6.
© David Barnes/The Stock Market.

The Colosseum could seat some 50,000 Romans for its bloody spectacles (even mock naval battles when it was flooded). On one side, part of the original four tiers remains; the first three levels were constructed in Doric, Ionic, and Corinthian styles to lend variety. See chapter 6. © Dave G. Houser Photography.

The Capitoline Museums' sculptures and paintings are housed in two Michelangelo palaces: the Palazzo Nuovo and the Palazzo dei Conservatori. The latter's courtyard contains the remains (head, hands, a foot, a kneecap) of an ancient colossal statue of Constantine the Great. See chapter 6. © Dave Bartruff Photography.

The Spanish Steps—adorned in spring with azaleas—and Piazza di Spagna take their names from the Spanish Embassy that used to be here. Designed by Francesco de Sanctis in the 1720s, the steps were funded mostly by the French as a preface to their church of Trinità dei Monti at the top. See chapter 6. © Robert Frerck/Odyssey.

The always-crowded Spanish Steps are a great place to people-watch—you'll see Romans and visitors alike, street performers, poseurs, and even a sidewalk artist or two perhaps working on a Madonna and bambino. See chapter 6. © Dave Bartruff Photography.

You can't say you've tasted pizza until you've tried the genuine article made with fresh local ingredients in an Italian oven. In Rome you'll find many pizzerie and trattorie serving delicious pies, but our favorite is Da Vittorio. See chapters 1 and 5. © *Dave Bartruff Photography.*

When it came to buying a harlot or conducting other important business, the Roman Forum was the place to go. What you'll find today are only bits of temples and arches—the Forum was used for years as a quarry. This is what's left of the Arch of Septimius Severus. See chapter 6. © RAGA/The Stock Market.

At Tivoli, 20 miles east of Rome, you'll find the ruins of Hadrian's Villa. He spent the last 3 years of his life in grand style here, enjoying acres of palaces, temples, gardens, and theaters built for a vast royal entourage and their servants and guards. See chapter 10. © Sheila McKinnon/Dave G. Houser Photography.

Of all ancient Rome's great buildings, only the Pantheon remains intact, standing on Piazza della Rotunda. The Pantheon, built in 27 B.C. by Marcus Agrippa and rebuilt by Hadrian in the early 2nd century, is among the world's architectural wonders because of its dome and concept of space. See chapter 6. © John Lawrence/Tony Stone Images.

Animals were sacrificed and burned in the center of the Pantheon, and the smoke escaped through the only means of light, the 18-foot oculus at the top. Michelangelo studied this dome before designing the one at St. Peter's. Raphael and monarchs Vittorio Emanuele II and Umberto I are interred here. See chapter 6. © RAGA/The Stock Market.

Ocher-colored Piazza Navona features vendors and street performers and pricey cafes as well as several baroque fountains. The Fountain of Neptune is a 19th-century addition, restored after a 1997 attack by two men who broke off the tail of one of its sea creatures. See chapter 6. © *Dave Bartruff Photography.*

Part of Rome's inner core is pedestrian-only, but in many areas you have to deal with heavy traffic. Where sidewalks don't exist, it becomes a free-for-all as pedestrians compete for space with vehicles—watch out for those Vespas! See chapter 3 for tips. © Andrea Pistolesi Photography.

When should I travel to get the best airfare?
Where do I go for answers to my travel questions?
What's the best and easiest way to plan and book my trip?

frommers.travelocity.com

Frommer's, the travel guide leader, has teamed up with **Travelocity.com**, the leader in online travel, to bring you an in-depth, easy-to-use resource designed to help you plan and book your trip online.

At **frommers.travelocity.com**, you'll find free online updates about your destination from the experts at Frommer's plus the outstanding travel planning and purchasing features of Travelocity.com. Travelocity.com provides reservations capabilities for 95 percent of all airline seats sold, more than 47,000 hotels, and over 50 car rental companies. In addition, Travelocity.com offers more than 2,000 exciting vacation and cruise packages. Travelocity.com puts you in complete control of your travel planning with these and other great features:

> **Expert travel guidance from Frommer's** - over 150 writers reporting from around the world!

> **Best Fare Finder** - an interactive calendar tells you when to travel to get the best airfare

> **Fare Watcher** - we'll track airfare changes to your favorite destinations

> **Dream Maps** - a mapping feature that suggests travel opportunities based on your budget

> **Shop Safe Guarantee** - 24 hours a day / 7 days a week live customer service, and more!

Whether traveling on a tight budget, looking for a quick weekend getaway, or planning the trip of a lifetime, Frommer's guides and Travelocity.com will make your travel dreams a reality. You've bought the book, now book the trip!

Other Great Guides for Your Trip:

Frommer's Italy

Frommer's Tuscany & Umbria

Frommer's Italy from $70 a Day

Frommer's Portable Venice

Here's what the critics say about Frommer's:

"Amazingly easy to use. Very portable, very complete."
—*Booklist*

♦

"The only mainstream guide to list specific prices. The Walter Cronkite of guidebooks—with all that implies."
—*Travel & Leisure*

♦

"Complete, concise, and filled with useful information."
—*New York Daily News*

♦

"Hotel information is close to encyclopedic."
—*Des Moines Sunday Register*

♦

"Detailed, accurate and easy-to-read information for all price ranges."
—*Glamour Magazine*

Rome
2001

by Darwin Porter &
Danforth Prince

IDG Books Worldwide, Inc.
An International Data Group Company
Foster City, CA • Chicago, IL • Indianapolis, IN • New York, NY

ABOUT THE AUTHORS

A native of North Carolina, **Darwin Porter** was a bureau chief for the *Miami Herald* when he was 21 and later worked in television advertising. A veteran travel writer, he wrote Frommer's first-ever guide to Italy and has been a frequent traveler in Italy ever since. He's joined by **Danforth Prince,** formerly of the Paris bureau of the *New York Times,* who has lived and traveled in Italy extensively. This team writes a number of best-selling Frommer's guides, notably to England, France, and Germany.

IDG BOOKS WORLDWIDE, INC.

An International Data Group Company
909 Third Avenue
New York, NY 10022

Find us online at **www.frommers.com**

ISBN: 0-7645-6169-3
ISSN: 1068-9338

Editor: Lisa Renaud/Dog-Eared Pages
Production Editor: Todd A. Siesky
Photo Editor: Richard Fox
Design by Michele Laseau
Staff Cartographers: John Decamillis, Roberta Stockwell, Elizabeth Puhl
Production by IDG Books Indianapolis Production Department

SPECIAL SALES

For general information on IDG Books Worldwide's books in the U.S., please call our Consumer Customer Service department at 1-800-762-2974. For reseller information, including discounts, bulk sales, customized editions, and premium sales, please call our Reseller Customer Service department at 1-800-434-3422.

Manufactured in the United States of America

5 4 3 2

Contents

List of Maps

An Invitation to the Reader

In researching this book, we discovered many wonderful places—hotels, restaurants, shops, and more. We're sure you'll find others. Please tell us about them, so we can share the information with your fellow travelers in upcoming editions. If you were disappointed with a recommendation, we'd love to know that, too. Please write to:

Frommer's Rome 2001
IDG Books Worldwide, Inc.
909 Third Avenue
New York, NY 10022

An Additional Note

Please be advised that travel information is subject to change at any time—and this is especially true of prices. We therefore suggest that you write or call ahead for confirmation when making your travel plans. The authors, editors, and publisher cannot be held responsible for the experiences of readers while traveling. Your safety is important to us, however, so we encourage you to stay alert and be aware of your surroundings. Keep a close eye on cameras, purses, and wallets, all favorite targets of thieves and pickpockets.

What the Symbols Mean

✪ Frommer's Favorites

Our favorite places and experiences—outstanding for quality, value, or both.

The following abbreviations are used for credit cards:

AE	American Express	EC	Eurocard
CB	Carte Blanche	JCB	Japan Credit Bank
DC	Diners Club	MC	MasterCard
DISC	Discover	V	Visa
ER	EnRoute		

Find Frommer's Online

www.frommers.com offers up-to-the-minute listings on almost 200 cities around the globe—including the latest bargains and candid, personal articles updated daily by Arthur Frommer himself. No other Web site offers such comprehensive and timely coverage of the world of travel.

The Best of Rome

Rome is a city of vivid and unforgettable images: the view of the city's silhouette from Janiculum Hill at dawn; the array of broken marble columns and ruins of temples of the Roman Forum; St. Peter's Dome against a pink-and-red sunset, capping a gloriously decorated basilica.

Rome is also a city of sounds, beginning early in the morning with the peal of church bells calling the faithful to mass. As the city awakens and comes to life, the sounds multiply and merge into a kind of urban symphony. The streets fill with cars, taxis, and motor scooters, all blaring their horns as they weave in and out of traffic; the sidewalks become overrun with bleary-eyed office workers rushing to their desks after stealing into crowded cafes for the first cappuccino of the day. The shops lining the streets open for business by raising their protective metal grilles as loudly as possible, seeming to delight in their contribution to the general din. Before long, fruit-and-vegetable stands are abuzz with activity as homemakers, maids, cooks, and others arrive to purchase their day's supply of fresh produce, haggling over prices and clucking over quality.

By 10am the tourists are on the streets, battling crowds and traffic as they wind their way from Renaissance palaces and baroque buildings to the famous ruins of antiquity. Indeed, Rome often appears to have two populations: one of Romans and one of visitors. During the summer months especially, the city plays host to a horde of countless sightseers who converge on it with guidebooks and cameras in hand. To all of them—Americans, Europeans, Japanese—Rome extends a warm and friendly welcome, wining, dining, and entertaining them in its inimitable fashion. (Of course, if you visit in August, you may see only tourists, not Romans, as the locals flee the summer heat of the city. Or as one Roman woman once told us, "Even if we're too poor to go on vacation, we close the shutters and pretend we're away so neighbors won't find out we couldn't afford to leave the city.")

The traffic, unfortunately, is worse than ever, and as the capital, Rome remains at the center of the major political scandals and corruption known as *Tangentopoli* (bribe city), which sends hundreds of government bureaucrats to jail each year.

Despite all this chaos, Romans still know how to live the good life. After you've done your duty to culture by wandering through the Colosseum and being awed by the Pantheon, after you've traipsed through St. Peter's Basilica and thrown a coin in the Trevi Fountain, you can pause to experience the charm of the Roman evening. Find a cafe at summer twilight and watch the shades of pink turn to gold and copper before night finally falls. That's when another Rome comes alive; restaurants and cafes grow more animated, especially if you've found one on an ancient hidden piazza or along a narrow alley deep in Trastevere. After dinner, you can stroll by the fountains or through Piazza Navona, have a gelato (or an espresso in winter), and the night is yours.

In chapters 6 and 7, we'll tell you all about the ancient monuments and basilicas. But monuments are only a piece of the whole. Below we've tried to capture a snapshot of the special experiences that might be the highlights of your visit.

1   Frommer's Favorite Rome Experiences

- **Walking Through Ancient Rome:** A vast, almost unified archaeological park cuts through the center of Rome. For those who want specific guidance, we have a walking tour in chapter 7 that will lead you through these haunting ruins. But it's fun to wander on your own and let yourself get lost on the very streets where Julius Caesar or Lucrezia Borgia once tread. A slice of history unfolds at every turn: an ancient fountain, a long-forgotten statue, a ruined temple dedicated to some long-faded cult. A narrow street suddenly opens, and you'll have a vista of a triumphal arch. The Roman Forum and the Palatine Hill are the highlights, but the glory of Rome is hardly confined to these dusty fields. If you wander long enough, you'll eventually emerge onto Piazza della Rotunda to stare in awe at one of Rome's most glorious sights, the Pantheon.

- **Hanging Out at the Pantheon:** The world's best-preserved ancient monument is now a hot spot—especially at night. Find a cafe table out on the square and take in the action, which all but awaits a young Fellini to record it. The Pantheon has become a symbol of Rome itself, and we owe our thanks to Hadrian for leaving it to the world. When you tire of people-watching and cappuccino, you can go inside to inspect the tomb of Raphael, who was buried here in 1520. (His mistress, La Fornarina, wasn't allowed to attend the services.) Nothing is more dramatic than being in the Pantheon during a rainstorm, watching the sheets of water splatter on the colorful marble floor. It enters through the oculus on top, which provides the only light for the interior.

- **Taking a Sunday Bike Ride in Rome:** Only a daredevil would try this on city streets on a weekday, but on a clear Sunday morning, while Romans are still asleep, you can rent a bike and discover Rome with your own two wheels. The Villa Borghese is the best place to bike. Its 4-mile borders contain a world unto itself, with museums and galleries, a riding school, an artificial lake, and a grassy amphitheater. Another choice place for Sunday biking is the Villa Doria Pamphilj, an extensive park lying above the Janiculum. Laid out in the mid-1600s, this is Rome's largest park, with numerous fountains and some summer houses.

- **Strolling at Sunset in the Pincio Gardens:** Above the landmark Piazza del Popolo, this terraced and lushly planted hillside is the most romantic place for a twilight walk. A dusty orange-rose glow often colors the sky, giving an otherworldly aura to the park's umbrella pines and broad avenues. The ancient Romans turned this hill into gardens, but today's look came from the design of Giuseppe Valadier in the 1800s. Pause at the main piazza, Napoleone I, for a spectacular view of the city stretching from the Janiculum to Monte Mario. The Egyptian-style obelisk here was erected by Emperor Hadrian on the tomb of his great love, Antinous, a beautiful male slave who died prematurely.

- **Enjoying Roma di Notte:** At night, ancient monuments like the Forum are bathed in a theatrical white light; it's thrilling to see the glow of the Colosseum with the moon rising behind its arches. Begin your evening with a Roman *passeggiata* (early-evening stroll) along Via del Corso or Piazza Navona. There's plenty of action going on inside the clubs too, from Via Veneto to Piazza Navona. Clubbers flock to the colorful narrow streets of Trastevere, the area around the Pantheon, and the even more remote Testaccio. The jazz scene is especially good, and big names often pop in. A little English-language publication, *Info Rome,* will keep you abreast of what's happening, or check *Time Out's* listings on the Web at www.timeout.co.uk.

- **Exploring Campo de' Fiori at Mid-Morning:** In an incomparable setting of medieval houses, this is the liveliest fruit and vegetable market in Rome, where peddlers offer their wares as they've done for centuries. The market is best viewed after 9am any day but Sunday. By 1pm the stalls begin to close. Once the major site for the medieval inns of Rome (many of which were owned by Vanozza Catanei, the 15th-century courtesan and lover of Pope Alexander VI Borgia), this square maintains some of its old bohemian atmosphere. We often come here when we're in Rome for a lively view of local life that no other place provides. Often, you'll spot your favorite *trattoria* chef bargaining for the best and freshest produce, everything from fresh cherries to the perfect vine-ripened tomato.

- **Attending the Opera:** The Milanese claim that Roman opera pales in comparison with La Scala, but Roman opera buffs, of course, beg to differ. At Rome's Teatro dell'Opera, the season runs between December and June and programs concentrate on the classics: Bellini, Donizetti, Puccini, and Rossini. No one seems to touch the Romans' operatic soul more than Giuseppe Verdi (1813–1901), who became a national icon in his support for Italian unification. His *Aida* used to be performed at the Baths of Caracalla, but these days you're more likely to catch his *La Traviata,* which remains a perennial favorite, even though the reviewer for *The Times* of London, on first hearing it at its debut, found it filled "with foul and hideous horrors."

- **Touring the Janiculum:** On the Trastevere side of the river, where Garibaldi held off the attacking French troops in 1849, the Janiculum Hill was always strategic in Rome's defense. Today a walk in this park at the top of the hill can provide an escape from the hot, congested streets of Trastevere. Filled with monuments to Garibaldi and his brave men, the hill is no longer peppered with monasteries, as it was in the Middle Ages. A stroll will reveal monuments and fountains, plus panoramic views over Rome. The best vista is from Villa Lante, a Renaissance summer residence. The most serene part of the park is the 1883 Botanical Gardens, with palm trees, orchids, bromeliads, and sequoias—more than 7,000 plant species from all over the world.

- **Strolling Along the Tiber:** Without the Tiber River, there might have been no Rome at all. A key player in the city's history for millennia, the river flooded the capital every winter until it was tamed in 1870. The massive *lungotevere* embankments on both sides of the Tiber keep it in check and make a perfect place for a memorable stroll. You not only get to walk along the river from which Cleopatra made her grand entrance into Rome, but you'll also see the riverside life of Trastevere and the Jewish Ghetto. Start at Piazza della Bocca della Verità in the early evening; from there, you can go for some 2 or more miles.

- **Picnicking on Isola Tiberina:** In ancient times this boat-shaped island stood across from the port of Rome and from 293 B.C. was home to a temple dedicated to Aesculapius, the god of healing. A church was constructed in the 10th century on the ruins of this ancient temple. You can reach the island from the Jewish Ghetto by a footbridge, Ponte Fabricio, the oldest original bridge over the Tiber River, which dates from 62 B.C. Romans come here to sunbathe, sitting along the river's banks, and to escape the traffic and the crowds. Arrive with the makings of a picnic, and the day is yours.

- **Following in the Footsteps of Bernini:** One of the most enjoyable ways to see Rome is to follow the trail of Giovanni Lorenzo Bernini (1598–1680), who left a greater mark on the city than even Michelangelo. Under the patronage of three different popes, Bernini "baroqued" Rome. Start at Largo di Santa Susanna, north of the Stazione Termini, at the Church of Santa Maria della Vittoria, which houses one of Bernini's most controversial sculptures, the *Ecstasy of St. Teresa* from 1646. Walk from here along Via Barberini to Piazza Barberini, in the center of which stands Bernini's second most dramatic fountain, the Fontana del Tritone. From the piazza, go along Via delle Quattro Fontane, bypassing (on your left) the Palazzo Barberini designed by Bernini and others for Pope Urban VIII. At the famous crossroads of Rome, Le Quattro Fontane, take Via del Quirinale to see the facade of Sant'Andrea, one of the artist's greatest churches. Continue west, bypassing the Pantheon, to arrive eventually at Piazza Navona, which Bernini remodeled for Pope Innocent X. The central fountain, the Fontana dei Fiumi, is Bernini's masterpiece, though the figures representing the four rivers were sculpted by others to his plans.

- **Spending a Day on the Appian Way:** Dating from 312 B.C., the Appian Way (Via Appia) once traversed the whole peninsula of Italy and was the road on which Roman legions marched to Brindisi and their conquests in the East. One of its darkest moments was the crucifixion in 71 B.C. of the rebellious slave army of Spartacus, whose bodies lined the road from Rome to Capua. Fashionable Romans were buried here, and early Christians dug catacombs through which to flee their persecutors. Begin at the Tomb of Cecilia Metella and proceed up Via Appia Antica past a series of tombs and monuments (including a monument to Seneca, the great moralist who committed suicide on the orders of Nero, and one to Pope St. Urban, who reigned from A.D. 222 to 230). The sights along Via Appia Antica are among the most fascinating in Rome. You can go all the way to the Church of Domine Quo Vadis.

- **Enjoying a Taste of the Grape:** While in Rome, do as the Romans do and enjoy a carafe of dry white wine from the warm climate of Lazio. In restaurants and *trattorie* you'll find the most popular brand, Frascati, but try some of the other wines from the Castelli Romani, too, including Colli Albani, Velletri, and Marino. All these wines come from one grape: Trebbiano. Sometimes a dash of Malvasia is added for greater flavor and an aromatic bouquet. Of course, you don't have to wait until dinner to drink wine, but can sample it at any of hundreds of wine bars throughout the city, which offer a selection of all the great reds and whites of Italy.

- **Savoring Gelato on a Summer Night:** Sampling gelato on a hot summer day is worth the wait through the long winter. Tubs of homemade ice cream await you in a dazzling array of flavors: everything from candied orange peels with chocolate to watermelon to rice. *Gelaterie* offer *semifreddi* concoctions (made with cream instead of milk) in such flavors as almond, *marengo* (a type of meringue), and *zabaglione* (eggnog). Seasonal fresh fruits are made into ice creams of blueberry, cherry, and peach. *Granite* (crushed ice) flavored with sweet fruit are another cool delight on a sultry night. Tre Scalini at Piazza Navona is the most fabled spot for enjoying *divino tartufo,* a chocolate concoction with a taste to match its name.

- **Dining on a Hidden Piazza:** If you're in Rome with that special someone, you'll appreciate the romance of discovering your own little neighborhood trattoria that opens onto some forgotten square deep in the heart of ancient Rome. And if your evening dinner extends for 3 or 4 hours, who's counting? The waiters won't rush you out the door even when you've overstayed your time at the table. This is a special experience, and Rome has dozens of these little restaurants. Two in particular come to mind: **Montevecchio,** Piazza Montevecchio 22 (☎ 06-6861319), on the square near Piazza Navona where both Raphael and Bramante had studios and Lucrezia Borgia was a frequent visitor. Try the pasta of the day or the roebuck with polenta. Or sample the menu at **Vecchia Roma,** Piazza Campitella 18 (☎ 06-6864604), with a theatrical setting on a lovely square. Order spaghetti with double-horned clams and enjoy the old-fashioned ambience while you rub elbows with savvy local foodies.

- **Hearing Music in the Churches:** Artists like Plácido Domingo and Luciano Pavarotti have performed around Rome in halls ranging from churches to ancient ruins. Churches often host concerts, though by decree of Pope John Paul II, it must be sacred music—no hip-grinding, body-slamming stuff. When church concerts are performed, programs appear not only outside the church but also on various announcements posted throughout Rome. The top professionals play at the "big-name" churches, but don't overlook those smaller, hard-to-find churches on hidden squares. Some of the best music we've ever heard has been by up-and-coming musicians getting their start in these little-known churches. The biggest event is the RAI (national broadcasting company) concert on December 5 at St. Peter's—even the pope attends. Other favorite locations for church music include Sant'Ignazio di Loyola, on Piazza di Sant'Ignazio, and San Paolo Fuori le Mura, at Via Ostiense 186.

- **Walking from Fountain to Fountain:** Romans—especially those who live in crowded ghetto apartments without air-conditioning—are out on summer nights walking from fountain to cooling fountain. It's an artistic experience for the visitor as well. Everybody makes at least one trip to Bernini's fountain on Piazza Navona, after stopping off at the Trevi Fountain to toss in a coin (thus ensuring their return to Rome), but there are hundreds more. One hidden gem is the Fontana delle Tararughe, in tiny Piazza Mattei. It has stood there since 1581, a jewel of Renaissance sculpture showing youths helping tortoises into a basin. Our favorite Bernini fountain is at Piazza Barberini; his Fontana del Tritone is a magnificent work of art from 1642 showing the sea god blowing through a shell. If you think you can still jump into these fountains and paddle around as Anita Ekberg did in *La Dolce Vita,* forget it. That's now against the law.

- **Hanging Out in the Campidoglio at Night:** There is no more splendid place to be at night than Piazza del Campidoglio, where Michelangelo designed both the geometric paving and the facades of the buildings. A broad flight of steps, the Cordonata, takes you up to this panoramic site, a citadel of ancient Rome from which traitors to the empire were once tossed to their deaths. Home during the

Rome Today

As the scaffolding throughout Rome came down at the dawn of the Papal Jubilee 2000, the city hailed its "second Renaissance." Italy greeted the new millennium with a burst of energy for protecting its heritage and mining its tourism potential.

Christian pilgrims in record numbers are streaming into Rome to mark the birth of Jesus in the Roman province of Judea. This onslaught has dwarfed the previous invasions of Etruscans, Vandals, and Normans. Most journalists are giving an "A" to Rome for the way in which it has carried out the Jubilee celebrations. Perhaps thousands were afraid to visit because of all the advance hype about the size of the crowds, but at least as of press time, the crowds have been massive but have not matched the wildest expectations of city officials. Because the city's infrastructure wasn't taxed to the degree it was feared, the progress of the Jubilee has been running fairly smoothly up till now.

Most foreign visitors interviewed have told the press that it's like visiting "one of the world's great open-air museums." After a dismal beginning, where progress was slow, Romans rallied and managed to wrap up massive restoration projects at the 11th hour. Some projects were finished with only minutes to spare, but the city is up and running to receive visitors to its newly restored historic district.

During Easter celebration in 2000, the streets of the capital were almost deserted, as visitors crammed historic squares, monuments, and museums. St. Peter's Square alone was filled with some 129,000 people who listened to the Pope's celebration of Easter Mass. At some of the more popular attractions, like the Colosseum, waits of 2 hours or more are not unheard of, but at most attractions crowds moved well during the early months of 2000.

New millennium or not, political chaos remains part of everyday life on the Roman landscape. At least until recently, it was sometimes assumed that anyone entering politics was doing so for personal gain. Some of that changed in the mid-1990s, when stringent penalties and far-reaching investigations were instituted by a controversial public magistrate, Antonio Di Pietro, who operated with a widespread public approval bordering on adoration. The "Clean Hands" (*Mani Pulite*) campaign he began mandated stiff penalties and led to reams of negative publicity for any politician accused of accepting bribes or campaign contributions that could be interpreted in any way as influence peddling.

Besides soccer (*calcio*), family, and affairs of the heart, the primal obsession of Rome as it moves into the millennium is *il sorpasso,* a term that describes Italy's surpassing of its archrivals, France and Britain, in economic indicators. (Italy ranks fifth among world economic powers, third among European countries.) Economists disagree about whether or not *il sorpasso* has happened, and statistics vary

day to the Capitoline Museums, it takes on a different aura at night, when it's dramatically lit, the measured Renaissance facades glowing like jewel boxes. The views of the brilliantly lit Forum and Palatine at night are also worth the long trek up those stairs. There's no more stunning cityscape view at night than from this hill.

- **Shopping in the Flea Markets:** We have never discovered an original Raphael at Rome's Porta Portese flea market (which locals call *mercato delle pulci*). But we've picked up some interesting souvenirs over the years. The market, the largest

widely from source to source. Italy's true economy is difficult to measure because of the vast Mafia-controlled underground economy (*economia sommersa*) that competes on a monumental scale with the official economy. Almost every Roman has some unreported income or expenditure, and people at all levels of Italian society are engaged to some degree in withholding funds from the government.

Another complicating factor is the surfeit of laws passed in Rome and their effect on the citizens. Before they get thrown out of office, politicians pass laws and more laws, adding to the seemingly infinite number already on the books. Italy not only has more laws on its books than any other nation of Western Europe but also suffers from a bloated bureaucracy. Something as simple as cashing a check or paying a bill can devour half a day. To escape red tape, Romans have become marvelous improvisers and corner-cutters. Whenever possible, they bypass the public sector and negotiate private deals *fra amici* (among friends).

There's also a lot of talk in Rome today about the introduction of the euro, though visitors needn't worry about dealing with it for a while. Though the new currency took effect on paper on January 1, 1999—at which time the exchange rates of participating countries were locked in together and are now fluctuating against the dollar in sync—this change will apply mostly to financial transactions between businesses in Europe. Euros won't be issued as banknotes and coins until January 1, 2002, and won't fully replace national currencies until July 1, 2002. Until then, you're likely to see prices displayed in euros as well as in lire, and you may see the euro used for purchases you make with credit cards.

A new millennium, a new currency, and Rome remains a city of contradictions. This simultaneously strident, romantic, and sensual city has forever altered the Western world's religion, art, and government. Despite the traffic, pollution, overcrowding, crime, and barely controlled chaos of modern Rome, the city endures and thrives.

In all the confusion of their city, Romans still manage to live a relatively relaxed way of life. Along with their southern cousins in Naples, they are specialists in *arte di arrangiarsi,* the ability to cope and survive with style. The Romans have humanity if not humor, a 2,000-year-old sense of cynicism, and a strong feeling of belonging to a particular place. The city's attractions seem as old as time itself, and despite the frustrations of daily life, Rome will continue to lure new visitors every year, with or without a millennium celebration. As the Jubilee celebration passes into history, the city will endure to greet yet another millennium. After all, Rome is "The Eternal City."

in Europe, began after World War II when black marketers needed an outlet for illegal wares. Today the authentic art and antiques once sold here have given way to reproductions, but the selection remains enormous: World War II cameras, caviar from immigrant Russians, luggage (fake Gucci), spare parts, Mussolini busts, and so on. Near Porta Sublicio in Trastevere, the market has some 4,000 stalls, but it's estimated that only 10% of them have a license. Sunday from 5am to 2pm is the best time to visit, and beware of pickpockets at all times.

2 Best Hotel Bets

See chapter 4 for complete reviews of all these hotels.

- **Best Historic Hotel:** The truly grand **St. Regis Grand,** Via Vittorio Emanuele Orlando 3 (☎ 06-47-091), was created by César Ritz in 1894, with the great chef Escoffier presiding over a lavish banquet. Its roster of guests has included some of the greatest names in European history, including royalty, naturally, but also such New World moguls as Henry Ford and J. P. Morgan.
- **Best New Hotel:** Opening to media acclaim in 2000, the brilliantly restored **Hotel de Russie,** Via del Babuino 9 (☎ 800/323-7500 in the U.S., or 06/ 328-881), was a retreat for artists, including Picasso and Stravinsky. Reclaiming its 1890s style, it is both opulent and well located, lying right off the Piazza del Popolo.
- **Best for Business Travelers:** On the west side of the Tiber River, about 6 short blocks northeast of the Vatican, the **Hotel Atlante Star,** Via Vitelleschi 34 (☎ 06-687-3233), operates in conjunction with the **Atlante Garden,** a block away and under the same management. Together they share a conference room and a well-run business center. Many young executives check into these hotels and find a helpful staff composed of multilingual European interns eager to help visitors with their problems in the Eternal City. All the latest business equipment is available, and the reception desk is excellent at receiving messages.
- **Best for a Romantic Getaway:** A private villa in the exclusive Parioli residential area, the **Hotel Lord Byron,** Via G. de Notaris 5 (☎ 06-322-0404), is a chic hideaway. It has a clubby ambience, and everybody is oh, so very discreet here. You get personal attention in subdued opulence, and the staff definitely respects that DO NOT DISTURB sign on the door. You don't even have to leave the romantic premises for dinner, as the Relais Le Jardin is among the finest restaurants in Rome.
- **Best Renovation:** Ernest Hemingway and Ingrid Bergman don't hang out here anymore, but the **Hotel Eden,** Via Ludovisi 49 (☎ 800/225-5843 in the U.S., or 06-478-121), remains grand and glamorous. After a $20-million renovation by Forte, it's better than ever, with a parade of rich and famous guests. Everything looks as if it's waiting for photographers from *Architectural Digest* to arrive.
- **Most Opulent Lobby:** In the "Hollywood on the Tiber" heyday of the 1950s, you might have encountered Elizabeth Taylor in the lobby here, accompanied by her husband of the moment—usually Richard Burton or Eddie Fisher. They're gone now, but the grandeur of **The Excelsior,** Via Vittorio Veneto 125 (☎ 800/ 325-3589 in the U.S, or 06-47-081), lives on. The city's most posh hotel is *the* place to meet someone you're trying to impress (even if you're not a guest). Its sprawling lounges are formal, with glittering chandeliers, lots of marble, and high ceilings.
- **Best for Families:** Near the Stazione Termini (in one of the safer areas), the **Hotel Venezia,** Via Varese 18, near Via Marghera (☎ 06-445-7101), has rooms large enough to accommodate you and the kids. Some have balconies for checking out the action on the street below. The housekeeping is superb, and the management is caring. Extra beds for children can be brought into the room.
- **Best Moderately Priced Hotel:** On an ancient street in the old quarter of Rome, the **Albergo Cesàri,** Via di Pietra 89A (☎ 06-679-2386), lies between the Trevi Fountain and the Pantheon. Since 1787, it has welcomed everybody from Garibaldi to Stendhal. Recently renovated in 1998, the hotel is better than

ever. Some rooms are triples and quads; all have furnishings that are solidly comfortable.

- **Best Friendly Pensione:** You can't get much simpler than the **Pensione Papà Germano,** Via Calatafimi 14A (☎ **06-486-919**), but it's a favorite budget choice, and warm and welcoming to boot. A high-turnover clientele of European and American students check in here, backpacks in hand, as the address is passed around by word of mouth. The energetic family owners may not speak the Queen's English, but they are receptive to your needs and happy to share their home.
- **Best Service:** Both management and staff at the **Hotel Star de la Ville Inter-Continental Roma,** Via Sistina 67–69 (☎ **800/327-0200** in the U.S. and Canada, or 06-67-331), are highly professional and exceedingly hospitable. The staff is particularly adept at taking messages, giving you helpful hints about what to see and do in Rome, and fulfilling any special room service requests. Their general attentiveness to your needs, quick problem-solving, good manners, and friendly helpfulness make this place exceptional. Room service is available 24 hours daily.
- **Best Location:** Right at the top of the Spanish Steps, directly across the small piazza from the deluxe Hassler, is the **Hotel Scalinata di Spagna,** Piazza Trinità dei Monti 17 (☎ **06-679-3006**). Could there be any more desirable location in all of Rome? The interior is like an old inn; the public rooms are small with bright print slipcovers, old clocks, and low ceilings. You can soak up the atmosphere inside or head for the roof garden with its sweeping view of the dome of St. Peter's across the Tiber. When you step out your door, the heart of Rome is at your feet, including the best shopping streets, at the bottom of the Spanish Steps.
- **Best Views:** From its perch atop Monte Mario, on 15 acres of landscaped grounds, the deluxe **Cavalieri Hilton,** Via Cadlolo 101 (☎ **800/445-8667** in the U.S. and Canada, or 06-35-091), opens onto panoramic views of the Eternal City's skyline. Many Romans themselves drive up here to linger over a drink at night just to take in the lights of the city. Another great place to book a room with a view is the **Albergo del Sole al Pantheon,** Piazza della Rotonda 63 (☎ **06-678-0441**), where you can gaze out at the Pantheon from your bedroom window, just as Simone de Beauvoir and Jean-Paul Sartre did when they checked in long ago.
- **Best for Understated Elegance:** Of course, it's not as elegant or as grand as the Excelsior, Eden, or Hassler, but the **Hotel d'Inghilterra,** Via Bocca di Leone 14 (☎ **06-69-981**), has its own unique brand of low-key opulence. Two blocks west of the Spanish Steps, its public rooms feature black-and-white checkerboard marble floors and its upholstered lounges are filled with antiques. The fifth floor has some of the loveliest terraces in Rome, and the romantic restaurant below has trompe l'oeil clouds that give the impression of a courtyard terrace open to the sky.
- **Best in a Roman Neighborhood:** You can't get more Roman than the **Teatro di Pompeo,** Largo del Pallaro 8 (☎ **06-6830-0170**). The hotel is actually built on top of the ruins of the Theater of Pompey, where Caesar met his fate. It's on a quiet piazzetta near the Palazzo Farnese and Campo de' Fiori, whose open-air market makes this one of Rome's most colorful neighborhoods. Shopping and nightlife abound in this fascinating section of Renaissance Rome, and restaurants and pizzerie keep the area lively at all hours.

- **Best Value:** Rated three stars by the government, the **Hotel delle Muse,** Via Tommaso Salvini 18 (☎ **06-808-8333**), lies half a mile north of the Villa Borghese. It's run by the efficient, English-speaking Giorgio Lazar. The furnishings are modern and come in a wide range of splashy colors. In summer, Mr. Lazar operates a garden restaurant serving a reasonably priced fixed-price menu, and the bar is open 24 hours a day. This is one of Rome's best bargains, and you should consider checking in before he wises up and raises his rates.

3 Best Dining Bets

See chapter 5 for complete reviews of all these restaurants.

- **Best for Romance:** A great place to pop the question or just enjoy a romantic evening is **Relais Le Jardin,** in the Hotel Lord Byron, Via G. de Notaris 5 (☎ **06-361-3041**), a stunner of a place that also just happens to serve the best Italian cuisine in town. The decor is as romantic as the atmosphere; it's all white lattice and bold Italian colors highlighted by masses of fresh flowers. The setting is in a Relais & Châteaux–member hotel, an art deco villa set on a residential hilltop in Parioli, an area of embassies and exclusive town houses at the edge of the Villa Borghese.
- **Best for a Business Lunch:** The location of **George's,** Via Marche 7 (☎ **06-4208-4575**), right off Via Veneto, is central (not far from the heartbeat Piazza Barberini), and the discreet staff and clubby atmosphere are just perfect for cutting a deal—and for dining well. Here, one of the most professional and best-trained staffs in Rome will serve you in elegantly decorated dining rooms. If the weather is fair, you may want to request a table in the lovely garden. Making those deals go down even easier is one of Rome's finest wine cellars.
- **Best for a Celebration:** Romans have been flocking to **Checchino dal 1887,** Via di Monte Testaccio 30 (☎ **06-574-3816**), since the early 19th century for fun and hearty food. With a bountiful array of wine and foodstuffs, every night seems like a party. The tables are packed nightly, and the place is a local legend. You'll have fun while still enjoying some of the best cuisine in town.
- **Best Decor:** By night chic Romans and savvy foreign visitors alike show up at **El Toulà** (The Hayloft), Via della Lupa 29B (☎ **06-687-3498**), an elegant establishment set near the fabled Caffè Greco and some of the chicest boutiques in Rome. It's no bargain, but once you see the sumptuous setting and, more important, enjoy the cuisine, you'll think you've gotten your money's worth. Haute cuisine is served in a subdued, tasteful setting of antiques, paintings, ever-so-discreet lighting, and to-die-for flower arrangements.
- **Best View:** The stars really do come out at night at **Les Etoiles** (The Stars), in the Hotel Atlante Star, Via Vitelleschi 34 (☎ **06-687-3233**), which has been called "the most beautiful rooftop in Italy." This restaurant is a virtual garden in the sky, with a 360-degree view of Roman landmarks, including the floodlit dome of St. Peter's. Try for a table alfresco in summer, but even in winter the same incredible view can be seen through picture windows. Fortunately, the food—delicately prepared Mediterranean cuisine using the freshest of ingredients—lives up to the setting.
- **Best Pizzeria:** Even the hardest-to-please Roman pizza lovers head for **Pizzeria Baffetto,** Via del Governo Vecchio 114 (☎ **06-686-1617**). This is a popular and fun place, drawing a young crowd. The crusts are delightfully thin.

- **Best Wine List:** The food is only secondary at the **Trimani Wine Bar,** Via Cernaia 37B (☎ 06-446-9630), but the wine list is fabulous, a deluxe tour through the vineyards of Italy. One of the best tasting centers in Rome for both French and Italian vintages, this elegant wine bar offers a dazzling array of wines at reasonable prices. The Trimani family has had a prestigious name in the wine business since 1821; simply sit down at one of their tables and let the pouring begin. If you like what you've tasted, you can buy bottles at the wine shop on the premises.
- **Best Value:** A mere $20 gets you one of the finest fixed-price menus in Rome at the **Ristorante del Pallaro,** Largo del Pallaro 15 (☎ 06-6880-1488). Each dish is lovingly prepared by the chef-owner, Paola Fazi, who urges her diners to *Mangia! Mangia!* The moment you're seated at the table, the dishes start to arrive—first a selection of antipasto, then the homemade, succulent pastas of the day, which in turn are followed by such meat courses as tender roast veal. Everything's included, even a carafe of the house wine.
- **Best for the Kids:** After their tour of the Vatican or St. Peter's, many savvy Roman families head for the **Ristorante Il Matriciano,** Via dei Gracchi 55 (☎ 06-321-2327). It's not fancy, but the price is right, and in summer you can opt for a sidewalk table. Let your kids feast on good, reasonably priced, homemade fare that includes such crowd pleasers as ricotta-stuffed ravioli. At the next table you're likely to see some priests from the Vatican dining. It's a safe, wholesome environment, and the food really is tasty.
- **Best Continental Cuisine:** The city's finest restaurant is now **La Terrazza,** in the Hotel Eden, Via Ludovisi 49 (☎ 06-478-121), edging out a position long held by Sans Souci. In the newly and fabulously restored Hotel Eden, you can dine on continental cuisine that is both bold and innovative. The seasonal menu offers the most polished, sophisticated cuisine in Rome; perhaps you'll choose a "symphony" of seafood or a warm salad of grilled vegetables.
- **Best Italian Cuisine:** Italian food as you've (almost) never had it before is served at the **Relais Le Jardin,** in the Hotel Lord Byron, Via G. de Notaris 5 (☎ 06-361-3041), a refined citadel of haute cuisine. In a luxurious setting, you'll feast on traditional fare prepared with a light, innovative touch, with specialties from such regions as Lazio and Abruzzi. The most demanding Roman palates wine and dine here and enjoy the freshest of seasonal produce, beginning with the bright zucchini blossoms of spring.
- **Best Emilia-Romagna Cuisine:** The area around Bologna has long been celebrated for serving the finest cuisine in Italy, and the little trattoria **Colline Emiliane,** Via Avignonesi 22 (☎ 06-481-7538), maintains that stellar reputation among Romans. The pastas here are among the best in Rome, especially the handmade tortellini alla panna (with cream sauce) with truffles. You can order less expensive pastas as well, all of them good. Their prosciutto comes from a small town near Parma and is reputedly the best in the world.
- **Best Neapolitan Cuisine:** It's so cornball that you'll think we've sent you to a tourist trap. But the food that emerges from the Neapolitan kitchen at **Scoglio di Frisio,** Via Merulana 256 (☎ 06-487-2765), is the best of its kind in the city. You get not only the crunchy, oozy, and excellent Neapolitan pizzas here but also an array of dishes ranging from chicken cacciatore to veal scaloppine that's perfectly prepared. Near the Stazione Termini, the trattoria has been a longtime favorite of visitors to Rome in spite of its somewhat sleazy location.

- **Best Roman Cuisine:** The tempting selection of antipasti is enough of a treat to lure you to **Al Ceppo** (The Log), Via Panama 2 (☎ 06-841-9696). Try such appetizers as stuffed yellow or red peppers or finely minced cold spinach blended with ricotta. Only 2 blocks from the Villa Borghese, this is a dining address jealously guarded by Romans, who often take their friends from out of town here. They feast on the succulent lamb chops, charcoal-grilled to perfection, or other grilled meats, such as quail, liver, and bacon.
- **Best Tuscan Cuisine:** For the most tender and delicious *bistecca alla fiorentina* (beefsteak Florentine style) in Rome, head for **Girarrosto Toscano,** off Via Veneto at Via Campania 29 (☎ 06-482-3835). The chefs grill the meats to perfection, using only virgin olive oil, salt, and pepper for seasoning. You get an array of other dishes as well, including one of the best selections of antipasti in town, everything from vine-ripened melon with prosciutto to a delectable Tuscan salami. Oysters and fresh fish from the Adriatic are also served.
- **Best Seafood:** The best and most beautiful seafood restaurant in Rome is **Alberto Ciarla,** Piazza San Cosimato 40 (☎ 06-581-8668). This place was among the first to create new and innovative preparations of seafood, which Romans traditionally have either fried or put into soups. Overcooked seafood is definitely not on the agenda; some Romans even tried raw fish for the first time here. Although this restaurant doesn't enjoy the fame it did when it first opened, it's just as good as ever. Dishes are perfectly seasoned and designed to bring out the natural flavor of the sea.
- **Best Nuova Cucina:** Near the Vittorio Emanuele monument, the well-decorated **Agata e Romeo,** Via Carlo Alberto 45 (☎ 06-446-6115), prepares one of Rome's most inventive new-style cuisines. If you'd like a sampling of the best selections of the day, you can order one of the fixed-price menus, available with or without wine. The menu reflects the agrarian bounty of Italy, with ample choices for everyone: meat eaters, fish fanciers, and vegetarians.
- **Best in the Jewish Ghetto:** For centuries, Romans have flocked to the Jewish Ghetto to sample Jerusalem artichokes. No one prepares them better than **Piperno,** Via Monte de' Cenci 9 (☎ 06-6880-6629), which serves savory (though nonkosher) Roman food. Of course, you can order more than these deep-fried artichokes here. A full array of delights includes everything from stuffed squash blossoms to succulent pastas.
- **Best Wild Game:** The best selection of unusual meat specialties in Rome is served at **Da Mario,** Via della Vite 55–56 (☎ 06-678-3818), although you can order other excellently prepared dishes as well if your dining partner isn't game. You could begin with pappardelle, which comes with a game sauce known as caccia, or the roast quail with polenta (the best this side of Lombardy in Milan). Wild game dishes are served in autumn; unusual, delectable offerings from both field and stream are always available.
- **Best Desserts:** It's a bit of an exaggeration to say that people fly to Rome just to sample the tartufo at **Tre Scalini,** Piazza Navona 30 (☎ 06-687-9148), but we'd consider it. The dessert is fabled, consisting of a grated bitter chocolate–covered chocolate ice-cream ball swathed in whipped cream. It's named for its resemblance to the knobby truffle. There are other desserts as well, and on almost any night you'll find people lined up three deep at the ice-cream counter outside. If you can take your mind off the tartufo, you'll have a ringside seat at Rome's most beautiful square, Piazza Navona, facing Bernini's Fontana dei Fiumi.

- **Best for Lingering over a 4-Hour Lunch:** On the historic Appian Way, only a short walk from the catacombs of St. Sebastian, the family-run **Antica Hostaria l'Archeologia,** Via Appia Antica 139 (☎ 06-788-0494), which looks like an 18th-century village tavern, is a place for lingering. If the day is sunny, you can sit late into the afternoon enjoying the wines of Lazio after a robust and satisfying Roman-style meal. Opt for the garden out back and find a table shaded from the sun by the spreading wisteria, and you may end up lingering until the waiters start closing down the joint. The wines emerge from a cellar that used to be a Roman tomb. You never know what might happen after a long meal here; we once took travel guru and founder of this travel series, Arthur Frommer, here for lunch, and before it was over he'd proposed that we write a guide to Italy.
- **Best Late-Night Pastry Shop:** Right on Piazza del Popolo, where young men and women drive up in their Maseratis and Porsches, the **Café Rosati,** Piazza del Popolo 5A (☎ 06-322-5859), heats up as the night wears on. Although you can order whisky, many come for the delectable Italian pastries. A sidewalk table makes an ideal spot to enjoy an ice-cream dish.
- **Best Alfresco Dining:** In Trastevere, Piazza Santa Maria comes alive at night. If you reserve a sidewalk table at **Sabatini,** Piazza Santa Maria in Trastevere 13 (☎ 06-581-2026), you'll have a view of all the action, including the floodlit golden mosaics of the church on the piazza, Santa Maria in Trastevere. At the next table you're likely to see . . . well, just about anybody (on our most recent visit, Roman Polanski). In addition to the view, you get some of the best grilled fish and Florentine steaks here.
- **Best for People-Watching:** Join the beautiful people—young actors, models, and artists from nearby Via Margutta—who descend at night on Piazza del Popolo. Young men with their silk shirts unbuttoned alight from sports cars to go on the prowl. At **Dal Bolognese,** Piazza del Popolo 1–2 (☎ 06-361-1426), you can not only take in this fascinating scene but also enjoy fine Bolognese cuisine as enticing as the people-watching. In the 1950s, during the heyday of *la dolce vita,* Via Veneto was the place to be for Elizabeth Taylor, Frank Sinatra, and other Hollywood types. Today the celebs are long gone, and Via Veneto is more about overpriced tourist traps than genuine hip. But lots of folks like to stroll this strip anyway, and enjoy the passing parade from a table at the **Caffè de Paris,** Via Vittorio Veneto 90 (☎ 06-488-5284).
- **Best for a Cappuccino with a View:** Perhaps the best-located cafe in Rome is **Di Rienzo,** Piazza della Rotonda 8–9 (☎ 06-686-9097), which stands directly on Piazza della Rotonda, fronting the Pantheon. On a summer night there's no better place to be than "the living room" of Rome, as the square before you has been dubbed, as you sit and slowly sip your cappuccino.
- **Best *Tavola Calda*:** One of the best *tavola caldas* (hot tables) in Rome is at **Bar Cottini,** Via Merulana 286–287 (☎ 06-474-0768), which is convenient for those staying in hotels around the Stazione Termini. The food is artfully displayed, and the selection is bountiful—not only freshly made salads but also hot pastas and just-prepared main courses. Portions are very generous, and you can fill up fast on the cornucopia of agrarian Latium's bounty. Tempting desserts such as a melt-in-your-mouth chocolate cake are prepared by the in-house bakery.
- **Best Picnic Fare:** When the weather is cool and the day is sunny, it's time for an alfresco meal, and there's no better place to purchase the makings of a picnic than the **Campo de' Fiori** open-air market, between Corso Vittorio Emanuele II and the Tiber. The luscious produce of Lazio is on display here right in the heart of

the old city. If you wish, you can purchase vegetables already chopped and ready to be dropped into the minestrone pot. Romans are particular about their food—you'll see some people inspecting cherries or other items one by one by one. There are also several excellent delicatessen shops on the square. Visit one of the shops selling freshly baked Roman bread, pick up a bottle of wine, and a companion—and off you go.

- **Best Ristorante:** With one dining room decorated in the style of an 18th-century tavern and another occupying Pompey's ancient theater, the **Ristorante da Pancrazio,** Piazza del Biscione 92 (☎ 06-686-1246), isn't just an architectural curiosity—it's a national monument that happens to serve good food. Here you sample one of the widest selections of Roman dishes, including the kitchen's fabled mixed fish fry. There's also a savory risotto made with a medley of fruits of the sea.

- **Best Trattoria:** In the heart of the old Jewish Ghetto, a short walk from Michelangelo's Campodoglio, is **Vecchia Roma,** Via della Tribuna di Campitelli 18 (☎ 06-686-4604), a landmark trattoria that's been feeding savvy Roman foodies for years. The antipasto selection is prepared fresh daily and is one of the finest in the area. The pasta and risotto dishes are succulent, and the meats (especially the lamb roasted in Roman ovens to crispy perfection) are from excellent cuts.

- **Best Restaurant for Celebrity-Spotting:** Glitz and glamour reign supreme at **Sans Souci,** Via Sicilia 20 (☎ 06-482-1814), Rome's flashiest dining room. You'll rarely find a Roman here, but those on the hipster international circuit show up. If you had to invite Madonna to dinner during a visit to Rome, this is where you'd take her.

Planning Your Trip: The Basics

This chapter is devoted to the where, when, and how of your trip—the advance planning required to get it together and take it on the road. Doing a little homework before you go leaves you more able to relax once you're actually on vacation.

1 Visitor Information

For information before you go, contact the **Italian Government Tourist Board.**

In the United States: 630 Fifth Ave., Suite 1565, New York, NY 10111 (☎ **212/245-4822;** fax 212/586-9249); 500 N. Michigan Ave., Suite 2240, Chicago, IL 60611 (☎ **312/644-0990;** fax 312/644-3019); 12400 Wilshire Blvd., Suite 550, Los Angeles, CA 90025 (☎ **310/820-0098;** fax 310/820-6367).

In Canada: 1 place Ville-Marie, Suite 1914, Montréal, PQ H3B 2C3 (☎ **514/866-7667;** fax 514/392-1429).

In the United Kingdom: 1 Princes St., London W1R 8AY (☎ **020/7408-1254;** fax 020/7493-6695).

On the Web, the Italian National Tourist Board sponsors the sites **www.italiantourism.com** and **www.enit.it**.

Among the best Web sites specifically for Rome is **Travelocity** (**www.travelocity.com**). From the home page, click on the "Destinations Guide" button, then navigate your way to "Rome and Environs." It has hundreds of listings, plus an excellent festivals and events calendar. For information on the **Vatican,** check out its Web site (**www. vatican.va**), where in 1998 the pope made his first live Internet appearance. **In Italy** (**www.lainet.com/~initaly**) not only contains solid information on Italy and Rome presented in a very personal and friendly way, but also has one of the best sets of links to other Italy-related sites on the Web. Another good site, **www.enjoyrome.com**, contains information about walking tours, accommodations, restaurants, side trips from Rome, useful links, and maps.

Note: For more Web sites, and general advice on how to use the Web for your trip-planning needs, see "Planning Your Trip: An Online Directory" on p. 32.

2 Entry Requirements & Customs

ENTRY REQUIREMENTS

U.S., Canadian, U.K., Irish, Australian, and New Zealand citizens with a **valid passport** don't need a visa to enter Italy if they don't expect to stay more than 90 days and don't expect to work there. If after entering Italy you find you want to stay more than 90 days, you can apply for a permit for an extra 90 days, which as a rule is granted immediately. Go to the nearest *questura* (police headquarters) or your home country's consulate. If your passport is lost or stolen, head to your consulate as soon as possible for a replacement.

CUSTOMS

WHAT YOU CAN BRING INTO ITALY   Foreign visitors can bring along most items for personal use duty-free, including fishing tackle, a pair of skis, two tennis racquets, a baby carriage, two hand cameras with 10 rolls of film, and 200 cigarettes or a quantity of cigars or pipe tobacco not exceeding 250 grams (0.05). There are strict limits on importing alcoholic beverages. However, limits are much more liberal for alcohol bought tax-paid in other countries of the European Union.

There are no restrictions as to how much foreign currency you can bring into Italy, though you should declare the amount. This proves to the Italian Customs office that the currency came from outside the country and, therefore, you can take out the same amount or less. Italian currency taken into or out of Italy may not exceed 200,000L in denominations of 50,000L or lower.

WHAT YOU CAN BRING HOME   Check with your country's Customs or Foreign Affairs department for the latest guidelines—including information on items that are not allowed to be brought in to your home country—just before you leave home, since regulations frequently change.

Returning **U.S. citizens** who've been away for 48 hours or more are allowed to bring back, once every 30 days, $400 worth of merchandise duty-free. You'll be charged a flat rate of 10% duty on the next $1,000 worth of purchases. Be sure to have your receipts handy. On gifts, the duty-free limit is $100. You can't bring fresh foodstuffs into the United States; tinned foods, how-ever, are allowed. For more information, contact the **U.S. Customs Service,** 1301 Constitution Ave. (P.O. Box 7407), Washington, DC 20044 (☎ **202/ 927-6724**), and request the free pamphlet "Know Before You Go." It's also available on the Web at **www.customs.ustreas.gov/travel/travel.htm**.

U.K. citizens should contact HM Customs & Excise Passenger Enquiries (☎ **0181/910-3744**) or visit **www.open.gov.uk**.

For a clear summary of **Canadian** rules, visit the comprehensive Web site of the **Canada Customs and Revenue Agency** at **www.ccra-adrc.gc.ca**.

Citizens of **Australia** should request the helpful Australian Customs brochure *Know Before You Go,* available by calling ☎ **1-300/363-263** from within Australia, or 61-2/6275-6666 from abroad. For additional information, go online to **www.dfat.gov.au** and click on HINTS FOR AUSTRALIAN TRAVELLERS.

For New Zealand customs information, contact the **New Zealand Customs Service** at ☎ **09/359-6655,** or go online to **www.customs.govt.nz**.

CURRENCY

The basic unit of Italian currency is the **lira** (plural: **lire**), which you'll see abbreviated as **L.** Coins are issued in denominations of 10L, 20L, 50L, 100L, 200L, 500L, and 1,000L, and bills come in denominations of 1,000L, 2,000L, 5,000L, 10,000L, 50,000L, 100,000L, and 500,000L. Coins for 50L and 100L come in two sizes each (the newer ones both around the size of a dime). The most common coins are the 200L and 500L ones, and the most common bills are the 1,000L, 5,000L, and 10,000L.

With the arrival of the euro, things will change considerably. Until then, interbank exchange rates are established daily and listed in most international newspapers. To get a transaction as close to this rate as possible, pay for as much as possible with credit cards. ATMs and bank cards offer close to the same rate, plus an added-on fee for cash transaction.

THE EURO

The **euro,** the new single European currency, became the official currency of Italy and 10 other participating countries on **January 1, 1999.** But you needn't worry about dealing with it for a while.

Though the euro took effect on paper in 1999—at which time the exchange rates of participating countries were locked in together and are now fluctuating against the dollar in sync—this change applies mostly to financial transactions between banks and businesses in Europe. The Italian lira remains the only currency in Italy for cash transactions. That is, until **December 21, 2001,** when more and more businesses will start posting their prices in euros alongside those in Italian lire, which will continue to exist (you'll already see some stores listing euro prices). Currently, the euro can be used in noncash transactions, such as with checks and credit cards.

On **January 1, 2002,** euro banknotes and coins will be introduced. Over a maximum 6-month transition period, Italian lire banknotes and coins will be withdrawn from circulation and the euro will become the official currency of Italy. The symbol of the euro is €. Its official abbreviation is "EUR."

For more details on the euro, check out **www.europa.eu.int/euro**.

Though exchange rates are more favorable at the point of arrival, it's often helpful to exchange at least some money before going abroad (standing in line at the Milan or Rome airport's *cambio* may make you miss the next bus leaving for downtown). Check with any of your local American Express or Thomas Cook offices or major banks. Or order Italian lire in advance from the following: **American Express** (☎ **800/221-7282;** cardholders only), **Thomas Cook** (☎ **800/223-7373**), or **International Currency Express** (☎ **888/842-0880**).

It's best to exchange currency or traveler's checks at a bank, not a *cambio* (exchange bureau), hotel, or shop. Currency and traveler's checks (for which you'll receive a better rate than cash) can be changed at all principal airports and some travel agencies, such as American Express and Thomas Cook. Note the rates and ask about commission fees; it can sometimes pay to shop around and ask the right questions.

TRAVELER'S CHECKS

Traveler's checks once were the only sound alternative to traveling with dangerously large amounts of cash—they were as reliable as currency, unlike

For American Readers   At this writing $1 U.S. = approximately 1,800L (or 100L = 5¢), and this was the rate of exchange used to calculate the dollar values given throughout this book (amounts over $5 have been rounded to the nearest dollar). The rate fluctuates from day to day and might not be the same when you travel to Italy.

For British Readers   The ratio of the British pound to the lira fluctuates constantly. Currently, £1 = approximately 3,007L (or 100L = 0.03 pence).

Regarding the Euro   Though it isn't yet in widespread use, the euro will become an increasingly important international currency during the lifetime of this edition. At press time, the euro was fixed at 1,936.27L, a rate that's likely to remain constant throughout the lifetime of this edition. As regards the U.S. dollar, however, the euro fluctuates from time to time. At press time, the euro equaled approximately US$1.10 (or US$1 = 91 eurocents). For up-to-date conversion ratios at the time of your trip, check with any international bank.

Lira	U.S.$	U.K.£	Euro	Lira	U.S.$	U.K.£	Euro
50	.03	0.02	0.03	10,000	5.50	3.33	5.20
100	0.05	0.03	0.05	20,000	11.00	6.65	10.40
300	0.16	0.10	0.16	25,000	13.75	8.31	13.00
500	0.27	0.17	0.26	30,000	16.50	9.98	15.60
700	0.38	0.23	0.36	35,000	19.25	11.65	18.20
1,000	0.55	0.33	0.52	40,000	22.00	13.30	20.80
1,500	0.82	0.50	0.78	45,000	24.75	15.00	23.40
2,000	1.10	0.67	1.04	50,000	27.50	16.63	26.00
3,000	1.65	1.00	1.56	100,000	55.00	33.25	52.00
4,000	2.20	1.33	2.08	150,000	82.50	49.90	78.00
5,000	2.75	1.66	2.60	200,000	110.00	66.50	104.00
7,500	4.10	2.50	3.90	500,000	275.00	66.30	260.00

personal checks, but could be replaced if lost or stolen, unlike cash. But these days they seem less necessary because most larger cities have 24-hour ATMs allowing you to withdraw small amounts of cash as needed. Many banks, however, impose a fee every time you use a card at an ATM in a different city or bank. If you plan to withdraw money every day, you might be better off with traveler's checks—provided you don't mind showing ID every time you want to cash a check.

You can get traveler's checks at almost any bank. **American Express** offers checks in denominations of $10, $20, $50, $100, $500, and $1,000. You'll pay a service charge ranging from 1 to 4%. You can also get American Express traveler's checks over the phone by calling ☎ **800/221-7282** or 800/721-9768; you can also purchase checks online at **www.americanexpress.com**. AmEx gold or platinum cardholders can avoid paying the fee by ordering over the telephone; platinum cardholders can also purchase checks fee-free in person at AmEx Travel Service locations (check the Web site for the office nearest you). American Automobile Association members can obtain checks fee-free at most AAA offices.

Visa offers traveler's checks at Citibank branches and other financial institutions nationwide; call ☎ **800/227-6811** to locate the purchase location near you. **MasterCard** also offers traveler's checks through **Thomas Cook Currency Services;** call ☎ **800/223-9920** for a location near you.

If you carry traveler's checks, be sure to keep a record of their serial numbers (separately from the checks, of course), so you're ensured a refund in case they're lost or stolen.

ATMS

ATMs are linked to a national network that most likely includes your bank at home. Both the **Cirrus** (☎ 800/424-7787; www.mastercard.com/atm) and the **PLUS** (☎ 800/843-7587; www.visa.com) networks have automated ATM locators listing the banks in Italy that'll accept your card. Or just search out any machine with your network's symbol emblazoned on it.

You can also get a cash advance through Visa or MasterCard (contact the issuing bank to enable this feature and get a PIN), but note that the credit-card company will begin charging you interest immediately and many have begun assessing a fee every time. American Express card cash advances are usually available only from AMEX offices.

Important Note: Make sure the PINs on your bank cards and credit cards will work in Italy. You'll need a **four-digit code** (six digits won't work), so if you have a six-digit code you'll have to go into your bank and get a new PIN for your trip. If you're unsure about this, contact Cirrus or PLUS (above). Be sure to check the daily withdrawal limit at the same time.

CREDIT CARDS

Credit cards are invaluable when traveling—a safe way to carry money and a convenient record of all your expenses. You can also withdraw cash advances from your cards at any bank (though you'll start paying hefty interest the moment you receive the cash and you won't receive frequent-flyer miles on an airline credit card). At most banks, you don't even need to go to a teller; you can get a cash advance at an ATM with your PIN.

Note, however, that many banks, including Chase and Citibank, have begun to charge a 2% service fee for transactions in a foreign currency (3% or a minimum of $5 on cash advances).

Almost every credit card company has an emergency toll-free number you can call if your wallet or purse is stolen. They may be able to wire you a cash advance off your credit card immediately, and in many places, they can deliver an emergency card in a day or two. The issuing bank's number is usually on the back of the credit card (though that doesn't help you much if the card was stolen). A toll-free **information directory** at ☎ 800/555-1212 will provide the number for you. Citicorp Visa's U.S. emergency number is ☎ **800/ 336-8472. American Express** cardholders and traveler's check holders should call ☎ **800/221-7282,** and **MasterCard** holders should call ☎ **800/ 307-7309.**

4 When to Go

April to June and **late September to October** are the best months for touring Italy—temperatures are usually mild and the crowds aren't quite so intense. Starting in mid-June, the summer rush really picks up, and from **July to mid-September** the country teems with visitors. **August** is the worst month: Not only does it get uncomfortably hot, muggy, and crowded, but the entire country goes on vacation at least from August 15 to the end of the month, and a good percentage of Italians take off the entire month. Many hotels, restaurants, and shops are closed (except at the spas, beaches, and islands, which are where 70% of the Italians head). From **late October to Easter**, most attractions go on shorter winter hours or are closed for renovation; many hotels and restaurants take a month or two off between **November and February**, spa and beach destinations become padlocked ghost towns, and it can get much colder than you'd expect (it may even snow).

High season on most airlines' routes to Rome usually stretches from June to the beginning of September. This is the most expensive and most crowded time to travel. **Shoulder season** is from April to May, early September to October, and December 15 to 24. **Low season** is November 1 to December 14 and December 25 to March 31.

WEATHER

It's warm all over Italy in summer; it can be very hot in the south, especially inland. The high temperatures (measured in Italy in degrees Celsius) begin in Rome in May, often lasting until sometime in October.

For the most part, it's drier in Italy than in North America, so high temperatures don't seem as bad since the humidity is lower. In Rome, temperatures can stay in the 90s for days, but nights are most often comfortably cooler. The average high temperatures in Rome are 82°F (27.8°C) in June, 87°F (30.5°C) in July, and 86°F (30°C) in August; the average lows are 63°F (17.2°C) in June and 67°F (19.4°C) in July and August.

HOLIDAYS

Offices and shops in Italy are closed on the following **national holidays:** January 1 (New Year's Day), Easter Monday, April 25 (Liberation Day), May 1 (Labor Day), August 15 (Assumption of the Virgin), November 1 (All Saints' Day), December 8 (Feast of the Immaculate Conception), December 25 (Christmas Day), and December 26 (Santo Stefano). Many offices and business also close on June 29, for the feast day of Sts. Peter and Paul, the city's patron saints.

Rome Calendar of Events

For more information about these and other events, contact the Rome tourist office, **Ente Provinciale per il Turismo,** Via Parigi 11, Roma 00185 (☎ **06-4889-9253**). Dates may vary from year to year.

January
- **Carnevale.** This festival, centered around the Piazza Navona, marks the last day of the children's market and lasts until dawn of the following day. Usually January 4 to 5.
- **Epiphany celebrations,** nationwide. All cities, towns, and villages in Italy stage Roman Catholic Epiphany observances. One of the most festive celebrations is the Epiphany Fair at the Piazza Navona. Usually January 5 to 6.
- **Festa di Sant'Agnese,** Sant'Agnese Fuori le Mura. During this ancient ceremony, two lambs are blessed and shorn, and their wool is used later for palliums (vestments). Usually January 17.

March

- **Festa di Santa Francesca Romana,** Piazzale del Colosseo near Santa Francesco Romana in the Roman Forum. A blessing of cars is performed at this festival. Usually March 9.
- **Festa di San Giuseppe,** the Trionfale Quarter, north of the Vatican. The heavily decorated statue of the saint is brought out at a fair with food stalls, concerts, and sporting events. Usually March 19.

April

- **Holy Week observances.** The most notable procession is led by the pope, passing the Colosseum and the Roman Forum up to Palatine Hill; a torchlit parade caps the observance. Beginning 4 days before Easter Sunday.
- **Easter Sunday.** In an event broadcast around the world, the pope gives his blessing from the balcony of St. Peter's. April 15 in 2001.
- **Festa della Primavera,** Rome. The Spanish Steps are decked out with banks of azaleas and other flowers and later, orchestral and choral concerts are presented in Trinità dei Monti. Dates vary.

May

- **Concorso Ippico Internazionale (International Horse Show),** Piazza di Siena in the Villa Borghese. Usually May 1 to 10, but the dates can vary.

June

- **Son et Lumière,** Rome. The Roman Forum and Tivoli areas are dramatically lit at night. Early June to end of September.
- **Festa di San Pietro,** St. Peter's Basilica, Rome. This most significant Roman religious festival is observed with solemn rites. Usually around June 29.

July

- **Festa di Nolantri.** Trastevere, Rome's most colorful neighborhood, becomes a gigantic outdoor restaurant, with tables lining the streets and merrymakers and musicians providing the entertainment. After reaching the area, find the first empty table and try to get a waiter—but keep a close eye on your valuables. For details, contact the **Ente Provinciale per il Turismo,** Via Parigi 11, 00185 Roma (☎ **06-4889-9253** or 06-4889-9255). Mid-July.

August

- **Festa delle Catene.** The relics of St. Peter's captivity go on display in the church of San Pietro in Vincoli. August 1.
- **Ferragosto.** Most city residents not directly involved with the tourist trade take a 2-week vacation (many restaurants are closed as well). This is a good time *not* to be in Rome. Beginning on August 15.

September

- **Sagra dell'Uva,** Basilica of Maxentius, the Roman Forum. At this harvest festival, musicians in ancient costumes entertain and grapes are sold at reduced prices. Dates vary, usually early September.

December

- **Christmas Blessing of the Pope,** Piazza di San Pietro, Rome. Delivered at noon from the balcony of St. Peter's Basilica. It's broadcast around the world. December 25.
- **New Year's Eve 2000.** At press time, no official festivities for the *real* turn of the millennium have been announced, but you can be assured of major parties all over Italy, particularly in Rome. And of course there'll be a special Mass at St. Peter's.

5 Health & Insurance

Planning Basics

STAYING HEALTHY

If you worry about getting sick away from home, you may want to consider **medical travel insurance** (see "Insurance," below). In most cases, however, your existing health plan will provide all the coverage you need. Be sure to carry your identification card in your wallet.

If you suffer from a chronic illness, consult your doctor before your departure. For conditions like epilepsy, diabetes, or heart problems, wear a **Medic Alert Identification Tag** (☎ **800/ID-ALERT;** www.medicalert.org), which will immediately alert doctors to your condition and give them access to your records through Medic Alert's 24-hour hotline.

Pack prescription medications in your carry-on luggage. Carry written prescriptions in generic, not brand-name form, and dispense all prescription medications from their original labeled vials. If you wear contact lenses, pack an extra pair in case you lose one.

Contact the **International Association for Medical Assistance to Travelers** (**IAMAT;** ☎ **716/754-4883** or 416/652-0137; www.sentex.net/~iamat). This organization offers tips on travel and health concerns in the countries you'll be visiting and lists many local English-speaking doctors. In Canada call ☎ **519/836-0102.**

INSURANCE

There are three kinds of travel insurance: trip-cancellation, medical, and lost-luggage coverage. **Trip-cancellation insurance** is a good idea if you have paid a large portion of your vacation expenses up front (say, by purchasing a package deal). Make sure you buy it from an outside vendor, though, not from your tour operator; you don't want to put all your eggs in one basket.

Rule number one: Check your existing policies before you buy any additional coverage you may not need.

Your existing health insurance should cover you if you get sick while on vacation—though if you belong to an HMO, you should check to see whether you are fully covered when away from home. For independent travel health-insurance providers, see below.

Your homeowner's or renter's insurance should cover stolen luggage. The airlines are responsible for only a very limited amount if they lose your luggage on an overseas flight, so if you plan to carry anything really valuable, keep it in your carry-on bag.

The differences between **travel assistance** and insurance are often blurred, but in general, the former offers on-the-spot assistance and 24-hour hot lines (mostly oriented toward medical problems), while the latter reimburses you for travel problems (medical, travel, or otherwise) after you have filed the paperwork. The coverage you should consider will depend on how much protection is already contained in your existing health insurance or other policies. Some credit- and charge-card companies may insure you against travel accidents if you buy plane, train, or bus tickets with their cards. Before purchasing additional insurance, read your policies and agreements over carefully. Call your insurers or credit-card companies if you have any questions.

If you do require additional insurance, try one of the companies listed below. But don't pay for more than you need. If you need only trip-cancellation insurance, don't purchase coverage for lost or stolen property, which should be covered by your homeowner's or renter's policy. Trip-cancellation insurance costs approximately 6 to 8% of the total value of your vacation.

Among the reputable issuers of travel insurance are **Access America** (☎ 800/284-8300; www.accessamerica.com) and **Travel Guard International** (☎ 800/826-1300; www.travel-guard.com). One company specializing in accident and medical care is **Travel Assistance International** (Worldwide Assistance Services; ☎ 800/821-2828 or 202/828-5894).

6 Tips for Travelers with Special Needs

FOR TRAVELERS WITH DISABILITIES

Laws in Italy have compelled rail stations, airports, hotels, and most restaurants to follow a stricter set of regulations about **wheelchair accessibility** to rest rooms, ticket counters, and the like. Even museums and other attractions have conformed to the regulations, which mimic many of those presently in effect in the United States. Always call ahead to check on the accessibility in hotels, restaurants, and sights you wish to visit.

Moss Rehab ResourceNet (www.mossresourcenet.org) is a great source for information, tips, and resources relating to accessible travel. You'll find links to a number of travel agents who specialize in planning trips for disabled travelers here and through **Access-Able Travel Source (www.access-able.com)**, another excellent online source. You'll also find relay and voice numbers for hotels, airlines, and car-rental companies on Access-Able's user-friendly site, as well as links to accessible accommodations, attractions, transportation, tours, local medical resources and equipment repairers, and much more.

You can join **The Society for the Advancement of Travelers with Handicaps** (SATH), 347 Fifth Ave., Suite 610, New York, NY 10016 (☎ 212/447-7284; fax 212-725-8253; www.sath.org), to gain access to their vast network of connections in the travel industry. They provide information sheets on destinations and referrals to tour operators that specialize in traveling with disabilities. Their quarterly magazine, *Open World,* is full of good information and resources.

A World of Options, a 658-page book of resources for disabled travelers, covers everything from biking trips to scuba outfitters. It costs $35 ($30 for members) and is available from **Mobility International USA** (☎ 541/343-1284, voice and TDD; www.miusa.org). Annual membership for Mobility International is $35, which includes their quarterly newsletter, "Over the Rainbow."

You may also want to join a tour catering to travelers with disabilities. One of the best operators is **Flying Wheels Travel** (☎ 800/535-6790; www.flyingwheels.com), offering various escorted tours and cruises, with an emphasis on sports, as well as private tours in minivans with lifts. Other reputable operators are **Accessible Journeys** (☎ 800/TINGLES or 610/521-0339; www.disabilitytravel.com), for slow walkers and wheelchair travelers; **The Guided Tour** (☎ 215/782-1370); and **Directions Unlimited** (☎ 800/533-5343).

For British travelers, the **Royal Association for Disability and Rehabilitation (RADAR),** Unit 12, City Forum, 250 City Rd., London EC1V 8AF (☎ 020/7250-3222), publishes three holiday "fact packs" for £2 each or £5 for all three. The first provides general information, including planning and booking a holiday, insurance, and finances; the second outlines transportation available when going abroad and equipment for rent; the third deals with specialized accommodations. Another good resource is the **Holiday Care Service,** Imperial Building, 2nd Floor, Victoria Road, Horley, Surrey RH6 7PZ (☎ 01293/774-535; fax 01293/784-647), a national charity advising on accessible accommodations for the elderly and persons with disabilities. Annual membership is £30.

FOR GAYS & LESBIANS

Since 1861, Italy has had liberal legislation regarding homosexuality, but that doesn't mean it has always been looked on favorably in a Catholic country. Homosexuality is much more accepted in the north than in the south, especially in Sicily, though Taormina has long been a gay mecca. (The World Pride celebrations in Rome in the summer of 2000 went off smoothly, but were preceded by months of denouncements by church officials and conservative politicians.) However, all major towns and cities have an active gay life, especially Florence, Rome, and Milan, which considers itself the "gay capital" of Italy and is the headquarters of **ARCI Gay,** the country's leading gay organization with branches throughout Italy. Capri is the gay resort of Italy, rivaled only by the gay beaches of Venice.

As a companion to this guide, you may want to pick up *Frommer's Gay & Lesbian Europe,* with helpful chapters on Rome, Florence, Venice, and Milan.

If you want help planning your trip, **The International Gay & Lesbian Travel Association** (IGLTA; ☎ **800/448-8550** or 954/776-2626; www.iglta.org), can link you up with the appropriate gay-friendly service organization or tour specialist. With around 1,200 members, it offers quarterly newsletters, marketing mailings, and a membership directory that's updated quarterly. Members are kept informed of gay and gay-friendly hoteliers, tour operators, and airline and cruise-line representatives.

Out and About (☎ **800/929-2268** or 212/645-6922; www. outandabout. com) has been hailed for its "straight" reporting about gay travel. It offers a monthly newsletter packed with good information on the global gay and lesbian scene. Out and About's guidebooks are available at most major bookstores and through **A Different Light Bookstore,** 151 W. 19th St. (☎ **800/343-4002** or 212/989-4850; www.adlbooks.com), while its Web site features links to gay and lesbian tour operators and other gay-themed travel links.

General U.S. gay and lesbian travel agencies include **Family Abroad** (☎ **800/999-5500** or 212/459-1800); and **Above and Beyond Tours** (☎ **800/397-2681**). In the United Kingdom, try **Alternative Holidays** (☎ **020/7701-7040;** fax 020/7708-5668; e-mail: info@alternativeholidays.com).

FOR SENIORS

One of the benefits of age is that travel often costs less. Always bring an ID card, especially if you've kept your youthful glow. Also mention the fact that you're a senior when you first make your travel reservations, since many airlines and hotels offer discount programs for senior travelers.

Members of the **American Association of Retired Persons** (AARP; ☎ **800/424-3410;** www.aarp.org), get discounts on hotels, airfares, and car rentals. The AARP offers members a wide range of special benefits, including *Modern Maturity* magazine and a monthly newsletter. If you're not already a member, do yourself a favor and join.

SAGA International Holidays, 222 Berkeley St., Boston, MA 02116 (☎ **800/343-0273**), offers inclusive tours and cruises for those 50 and older. SAGA also sponsors the more substantial **"Road Scholar Tours"** (☎ **800/621-2151**), which are fun-loving but with an educational bent.

If you want something more than the average vacation or guided tour, try **Elderhostel** (☎ 877/426-8056; www.elderhostel.org) or the University of New Hampshire's **Interhostel** (☎ 800/733-9753), both variations on the same theme: educational travel for senior citizens. On these escorted tours, the days are packed with seminars, lectures, and field trips, and the sightseeing is all led by academic experts. The courses in both programs are ungraded, involve no homework, and often focus on the liberal arts. They're not luxury vacations but are fun and fulfilling.

FOR STUDENTS

The best resource for students is the **Council on International Educational Exchange (CIEE).** It can set you up with an ID card (see below), and its travel branch, **Council Travel Service (CTS),** 205 E. 42nd St., New York, NY 10017 (☎ 800/226-8624 in the United States to find your local branch, or 212/822-2700; www.counciltravel.com), is the world's biggest student travel agency operation. It can get you discounts on plane tickets, rail passes, and the like. Ask them for a list of CTS offices in major cities so you can keep the discounts flowing (and aid lines open) as you travel.

From CIEE you can obtain the $18 **International Student Identity Card (ISIC),** the only officially acceptable form of student ID, good for cut rates on rail passes, plane tickets, and other discounts. It also provides you with basic health and life insurance and a 24-hour help line. If you're no longer a student but are still under 26, you can get a **GO 25 card** from the same people; it'll get you the insurance and some of the discounts (but not student admission prices in museums). CTS also sells **EurailPasses** and **YHA (Youth Hostel Association)** passes and can book hostel or hotel accommodations.

CTS's **U.K. office** is at 28A Poland St. (Oxford Circus), London WIV 3DB (☎ 020/7437-7767); the **Italy office** is at Via Genova 16, 00184 Roma (☎ 06-46791). In Canada, **Travel CUTS,** 200 Ronson St., Ste. 320, Toronto, ONT M9W 5Z9 (☎ 800/667-2887 or 416/614-2887; www.travelcuts.com), offers similar services. **Usit Campus,** 52 Grosvenor Gardens, London SW1W 0AG (☎ 020/7730-3402; www.campustravel.co.uk), opposite Victoria Station, is Britain's leading specialist in student and youth travel.

7 Getting There

BY PLANE

FROM NORTH AMERICA   Fares to Italy are constantly changing, but you can expect to pay somewhere in the range of $400 to $800 for a direct round-trip ticket from New York to Rome in coach class. **Flying time** to Rome from New York, Newark, and Boston is 8 hours, from Chicago 10 hours, and from Los Angeles 12½ hours.

American Airlines (☎ 800/433-7300; www.aa.com) offers daily nonstop flights to Rome from Chicago's O'Hare, with flights from all parts of American's vast network making connections into Chicago. **TWA** (☎ 800/892-4141; www.twa.com) offers daily nonstop flights from New York's JFK to Rome, as does **Delta** (☎ 800/241-4141; www.delta.com). **United** (☎ 800/538-2929; www.ual.com) has service only to Milan only from Dulles in Washington, D.C. **US Airways** (☎ 800/428-4322; www.usairways.com) offers one flight daily to Rome out of Philadelphia (you can connect through Philly from most major U.S. cities). And **Continental** (☎ 800/525-0280; www.flycontinental.com) flies twice daily to Rome from its hub in Newark.

Canadian Airlines International (☎ 800/426 7000; www.cdnair.ca) flies daily from Toronto to Rome. Two of the flights are nonstop; the others touch down en route in Montréal, depending on the schedule.

British Airways (☎ 800/AIRWAYS; www.british-airways.com), Virgin Atlantic Airways (☎ 800/862-8621; www.fly.virgin.com), Air France (☎ 800/237-2747; www.airfrance.com), Northwest/KLM (☎ 800/374-7747; www.klm.nl), and Lufthansa (☎ 800/645-3880; www.lufthansa-usa. com) offer some attractive deals for anyone interested in combining a trip to Italy with a stopover in, say, Britain, Paris, Amsterdam, or Germany along the way.

Alitalia (☎ 800/223-5730 in the United States, 514/842-8241 in Canada; www.alitalia.it/english/index.html) is the Italian national airline, with nonstop flights to Rome from New York (JFK), Newark, Boston, Chicago, and Miami. Alitalia can easily book connecting domestic flights to other cities in Italy. Alitalia participates in the frequent-flyer programs of other airlines, including Continental and US Airways.

FROM THE UNITED KINGDOM Operated by the European Travel Network, **www.discount-tickets.com** is a great online source for regular and discounted airfares to destinations around the world. You can also use this site to compare rates and book accommodations, car rentals, and tours. Click on "Special Offers" for the latest package deals. Students should also try **Campus Travel** (☎ 0171/730-2101; www.usitcampus.co.uk).

British newspapers are always full of classified ads touting slashed fares to Italy. One good source is *Time Out.* London's *Evening Standard* has a daily travel section, and the Sunday editions of almost any newspaper will run many ads. Though competition is fierce, one well-recommended company that consolidates bulk ticket purchases and then passes the savings on to its consumers is **Trailfinders** (☎ 020/7937-5400 in London). It offers access to tickets on such carriers as SAS, British Airways, and KLM.

CEEFAX, a British TV information service included on many home and hotel TVs, runs details of package holidays and flights to Italy and beyond. Just switch to your CEEFAX channel and you'll find a menu of listings that includes travel information.

Both **British Airways** (☎ 0345/222-111 in the U.K.; www.british-airways.com) and **Alitalia** (☎ 020/7602-7111; www.alitalia.it/english/index.html) have frequent flights from London's Heathrow to Rome. BA also has one direct flight a day from Manchester to Rome. **Virgin Atlantic** doesn't serve Italy at all at press time.

FLY FOR LESS: TIPS FOR GETTING THE BEST AIRFARES

- **Take advantage of APEX fares.** Advance-purchase booking is often the key to getting the lowest fare. You generally must be willing to make your plans and buy your tickets as far ahead as possible. Be sure you understand cancellation and refund policies before you buy.
- **Watch for sales.** You'll almost never see them during July and August or the Thanksgiving or Christmas seasons, but at other times you can get great deals. In the last couple of years, there have been amazing deals on winter flights to Rome. If you already hold a ticket when a sale breaks, it may even pay to exchange it, which usually incurs a $50 to $75 charge. Note, however, that the lowest-priced fares are often nonrefundable, require advance purchase of 1 to 3 weeks and a certain length of stay, and

carry penalties for changing dates of travel. So, when you're quoted a fare, make sure you know exactly what the restrictions are before you commit.

- If your schedule is flexible, ask if you can secure a cheaper fare by **staying an extra day** or by **flying midweek.** (Many airlines won't volunteer this information, so ask lots of questions.)
- **Consolidators,** also known as bucket shops, are a good place to find low fares, often below even the airlines' discounted rates. There's nothing shady about the reliable ones—basically, they're just big travel agents that get discounts for buying in bulk and pass some of the savings on to you. Before you pay, however, ask for a confirmation number from the consolidator and then call the airline itself to confirm your seat. Be prepared to book your ticket with a different consolidator—there are many to choose from—if the airline can't confirm your reservation. Also be aware that consolidator tickets are usually non-refundable or come with stiff cancellation penalties.

    We've gotten great deals on many occasions from ✪ **Cheap Tickets** (☎ 800/377-1000; www.cheaptickets.com). **Council Travel** (☎ 800/226-8624; www.counciltravel.com) and **STA Travel** (☎ 800/ 781-4040; www.sta.travel.com) cater especially to young travelers, but their bargain-basement prices are available to people of all ages. Other reliable consolidators include **Lowestfare.com** (☎ 888/278-8830; www.lowestfare. com); **1-800-AIRFARE** (www.1800airfare.com); **Cheap Seats** (☎ 800/ 451-7200; www.cheapseatstravel.com); and **1-800-FLY-CHEAP** (www.flycheap.com).

- Search the **Internet** for cheap fares—though it's still best to compare your findings with the research of a dedicated travel agent, if you're lucky enough to have one—especially when you're booking more than just a flight. A few of the better-respected virtual travel agents are **Travelocity** (**www.travelocity.com**) and **Microsoft Expedia** (**www.expedia.com**).

    Smarter Living (**www.smarterliving.com**) is a great source for great last-minute deals. Take a moment to register, and every week you'll get an e-mail summarizing the discount fares available from your departure city. The site also features concise lists of links to hotel, car rental, and other hot travel deals.

    See **"Planning Your Trip: An Online Directory"** on p. 32 for further discussion on this topic and other recommendable sites.

BY TRAIN

If you plan to travel heavily on the European rails, get yourself a copy of the latest edition of the *Thomas Cook European Timetable of Railroads.* This 500-plus-page timetable accurately documents all of Europe's mainline passenger rail services. It's available from **Forsyth Travel Library,** 226 Westchester Ave., White Plains, NY 10604 (☎ 800/367-7984; www.forsyth.com), for $27.95 (plus $4.95 shipping in the U.S. and $5.95 in Canada), or at travel specialty stores like **Rand McNally,** 150 E. 52nd St., New York, NY 10022 (☎ 212/758-7488).

New electric trains have made travel between France and Italy faster and more comfortable than ever before. **France's TGVs** travel at speeds of up to 185 miles per hour and have cut travel time between Paris and Turin from 7 to 5½ hours and between Paris and Milan from 7½ to 6¾ hours. **Italy's ETRs** travel at speeds of up to 145 miles per hour and currently run between Milan and Lyon (5 hours), with a stop in Turin.

EUROPEAN-WIDE RAIL PASSES

EURAILPASS Many travelers to Europe take advantage of one of the greatest travel bargains, the **EurailPass,** which permits unlimited first-class rail travel in any country in western Europe (except the British Isles) and Hungary in eastern Europe. Oddly, it doesn't include travel on the rail lines of Sardinia, which are organized independently of the rail lines of the rest of Italy.

The advantages are tempting: There are no tickets; simply show the pass to the ticket collector, then settle back to enjoy the scenery. Seat reservations are required on some trains. Many of the trains have couchettes (sleeping cars), for which an extra fee is charged. Obviously, the 2- or 3-month traveler gets the greatest economic advantages. To obtain full advantage of a 15-day or 1-month pass, you'd have to spend a great deal of time on the train.

EurailPass holders are entitled to considerable reductions on certain buses and ferries as well. You'll get a 20% reduction on second-class accommodations from certain companies operating ferries between Naples and Palermo or for crossings to Sardinia and Malta.

A **EurailPass** is $554 for 15 days, $718 for 21 days, $890 for 1 month, $1,260 for 2 months, and $1,558 for 3 months. Children 3 and under travel free providing they don't occupy a seat (otherwise they're charged half fare); children 4 to 11 are charged half fare. If you're under 26, you can buy a **Eurail Youthpass,** entitling you to unlimited second-class travel for $388 for 15 days, $499 for 21 days, $623 for 1 month, $882 for 2 months, and $1,089 for 3 months.

The **Eurail Saverpass,** valid all over Europe for first class only, offers discounted 15-day travel for groups of three or more people traveling together April to September or two people traveling together October to March. The price is $470 for 15 days, $610 for 21 days, and $756 for 1 month, $1,072 for 2 months, $1,324 for 3 months.

The **Eurail Flexipass** allows you to visit Europe with more flexibility. It's valid in first class and offers the same privileges as the EurailPass. However, it provides a number of individual travel days you can use over a much longer period of consecutive days. That makes it possible to stay in one city and yet not lose a single day of travel. There are two passes: 10 days of travel in 2 months for $654 and 15 days of travel in 2 months for $862.

With many of the same qualifications and restrictions as the previously described Flexipass is a **Eurail Youth Flexipass.** Sold only to travelers under 26, it allows 10 days of travel within 2 months for $458 and 15 days of travel within 2 months for $599.

EUROPASS The **Europass** is more limited than the EurailPass but may offer better value for visitors traveling over a smaller area. It's good for 2 months and allows 5 days of rail travel within three to five European countries (Italy, France, Germany, Switzerland, and Spain) with contiguous borders. For individual travelers, 5 days of travel costs $348 in first class, $233 in second; 6 days of travel $368 in first class, $253 in second; 8 days of travel $448 in first class, $313 in second; 10 days of travel $528 in first class, $363 in second; and 15 days of travel $728 in first class, $513 in second.

For travelers under 26, a **Europass Youth** is available. The fares are 35% to 55% off those quoted above, and the pass is good only for second-class travel. Unlike the adult Europass, there's no discount for a companion.

Where to Buy a Pass

In **North America,** you can buy these passes from travel agents or rail agents in major cities like New York, Montréal, and Los Angeles. EurailPasses are also available from the North American offices of **Rail Europe** (☎ **800/ 438-7245;** www.raileurope.com). No matter what everyone tells you, you can buy EurailPasses in Europe as well as in America (at the major train stations), but they're more expensive. Rail Europe can also give you information on the rail/drive versions of the passes.

For details on the rail passes available in the **United Kingdom,** stop in at or contact the **International Rail Centre,** Victoria Station, London SW1V 1JZ (☎ **0990/848-848**). The staff can help you find the best option for the trip you're planning. Some of the most popular are the **Inter-Rail** and **Under 26** passes, entitling you to unlimited second-class travel in 26 European countries.

Under 26 tickets are a worthwhile option for travelers under 26. They allow you to move leisurely from London to Rome, with as many stopovers en route as you want, using a different route southbound (through Belgium, Luxembourg, and Switzerland) from the return route northbound (exclusively through France). All travel must be completed within 1 month of the departure date. Under 26 tickets from London to Rome cost from £133 for the most direct route or from £209 for a roundabout route through the south of France.

Wasteels, adjacent to Platform 2 in Victoria Station, London SW1V 1JZ (☎ **020/7834-7066**), will sell a **Rail Europe Senior Pass** to U.K. residents for £5. With it, a British resident over 60 can buy discounted tickets on many of Europe's rail lines. To qualify, you must present a valid British Senior Citizen rail card, available for £16 at any BritRail office on presentation of proof of age and British residency.

RAIL PASSES WITHIN ITALY

If you'll be traveling beyond Rome by rail, you'll need to know a bit about the Italian train system. As a rule of thumb, second-class travel usually costs about two-thirds the price of an equivalent first-class trip. A couchette (a private fold-down bed in a communal cabin) requires a supplement above the price of first-class travel. Children ages 4 to 11 receive a discount of 50% off the adult fare and children 3 and under travel free with their parents.

If you don't buy the Eurailpass (see above), you might consider an **Italian Railpass** (known in Italy as a **BTLC Pass**), which allows non-Italian citizens to ride as much as they like on Italy's entire rail network. Buy the pass in the United States or at main train stations in Italy, have it validated the first time you use it at any rail station, and ride as frequently as you like within the time validity. An 8-day pass is $273 first class and $182 second, a 15-day pass $341 first class and $228 second, a 21-day pass $396 first class and $264 second, and a 30-day pass $478 first class and $318 second. All passes have a $15 issuing fee per class.

With the Italian Railpass and each of the other special passes, a supplement must be paid to ride on certain rapid trains, designated **ETR-450** or **Pendolino trains.** The rail systems of Sardinia are administered by a separate entity and aren't included in the Railpass or any of the other passes.

Another option is the **Italian Flexirail Card,** which entitles you to a predetermined number of days of travel on any rail line in a certain time period. It's ideal for passengers who plan in advance to spend several days sightseeing before boarding a train for another city. A pass giving 4 possible travel days out of a block of 1 month is $216 first class and $144 second, a pass for 8 travel days stretched over a 1-month period $302 first class and $202 second, and a pass for 12 travel days within 1 month $389 first class and $259 second.

You can buy these passes from any travel agent or by calling ☎ 800/ 248-7245. You can also call ☎ 800/4-EURAIL or 800/EUROSTAR.

BY CAR

If you're already on the Continent, particularly in a neighboring country such as France or Austria, you may want to drive to Italy. However, you should make arrangements in advance with your car-rental company.

U.S. and Canadian drivers don't need an **International Driver's License** to drive a rented car in Italy. However, if driving a private car, they need such a license. You can apply for an International Driver's License at any **American Automobile Association (AAA)** branch (☎ 800/222-4357 or 407/ 444-4240 for the national headquarters; www.aaa.com). You must be at least 18 and have two 2-by-2-inch photos and a photocopy of your U.S. driver's license with an AAA application form. The actual fee for the license can vary, depending on where it's issued. In Canada, you can get the address of the **Canadian Automobile Association** closest to you by calling ☎ 613/ 247-0117.

The **Automobile Club d'Italia (ACI)** is at Via Marsala 8, 00185 Roma (☎ 06-4998-2389), open Monday to Friday 8am to 2pm. The ACI's 24-hour **Information and Assistance Center (CAT)** is at Via Magenta 5, 00185 Roma (☎ 06-4477). Both offices are near the main rail station (Stazione Termini).

It's possible to drive from London to Rome, a distance of 1,124 miles (1,810km), via Calais/Boulogne/Dunkirk, or 1,085 miles (1,747km) via Oostende/Zeebrugge, not counting channel crossings by Hovercraft, ferry, or the Chunnel. Milan is some 400 miles (644km) closer to Britain than is Rome. If you cross over from England and arrive at one of the continental ports, you still face a 24-hour drive. Most drivers play it safe and budget 2 to 3 days for the journey.

Most of the roads from Western Europe leading into Italy are toll-free, with some notable exceptions. If you use the Swiss superhighway network, you'll have to buy a special tax sticker at the frontier. You'll also pay to go through the St. Gotthard Tunnel into Italy. Crossings from France can be through the Mont Blanc Tunnel, for which you'll pay, or you can leave the French Riviera at Menton and drive directly into Italy along the Italian Riviera toward San Remo.

If you don't want to drive such distances, ask a travel agent to book you on a Motorail arrangement where the train carries your car. This service, however, is good only to Milan, as there are no car and sleeper expresses running the 400 miles (644km) south to Rome.

8 Escorted Tours & Independent Package Tours

The biggest operator of escorted tours is **Perillo Tours** (☎ 800/431-1515 or 201/307-1234 in the United States; www.perillotours.com), family operated for three generations—perhaps you've seen the TV commercials featuring the "King of Italy," Mario Perillo, and his son. Since it was founded in 1945, it has sent more than a million travelers to Italy on guided tours. Perillo's escorted tours cost much less than you'd spend if you arranged a comparable trip yourself. Accommodations are in first-class hotels, and guides tend to be well qualified and well informed.

Another contender is **Italiatour,** a company of the Alitalia Group (☎ 800/ 845-3365 or 212/765-2183; www.italiatour.com), offering a wide variety of tours through all parts of Italy, including Rome. It specializes in packages for independent travelers (not tour groups) who ride from one destination to another by train or rental car. In most cases, the company sells pre-reserved accommodations, which are usually less expensive than if you had reserved them yourself. Because of the company's close link with Alitalia, the prices quoted for air passage are sometimes among the most reasonable on the retail market.

Trafalgar Tours (☎ 800/854-0103; www.trafalgartours.com) is one of Europe's largest tour operators, offering affordable guided tours with lodgings in unpretentious hotels. Check with your travel agent for more information on these tours (Trafalgar only takes calls from agents).

One of Trafalgar's leading competitors is **Globus/Cosmos Tours** (☎ 800/221-0090; www.globusandcosmos.com). Globus has first-class escorted coach tours of various regions lasting from 8 to 16 days. Cosmos, a budget branch of Globus, sells escorted tours of about the same length. Tours must be booked through a travel agent, but you can call the 800 number for brochures.

Abercrombie & Kent (☎ 800/323-7308 in the U.S., or 020/7730-9600 in the U.K.; www.abercrombiekent.com) offers a variety of luxurious premium packages. Your overnight stays will be in meticulously restored castles and exquisite Italian villas, most of which are four- and five-star accommodations. Several trips are offered, including tours of the Lake Garda region and the southern territory of Calabria.

Planning Your Trip: An Online Directory

Frommer's Online Directory will help you take better advantage of the travel-planning information available online. Part 1 lists general Internet resources that can make any trip easier, such as sites for obtaining the best possible prices on airline tickets. In Part 2 you'll find some top sites specifically for Rome.

This is not a comprehensive list, but a discriminating selection to get you started. Recognition is given to sites based on their content value and ease of use. Inclusion here is not paid for—unlike some Web-site rankings, which are based on payment. Finally, remember this is a press-time snapshot of leading Web sites; some undoubtedly will have evolved, changed, or moved by the time you read this.

1 The Top Travel-Planning Web Sites

by Lynne Bairstow

Lynne Bairstow is the co-author of *Frommer's Mexico,* and the editorial director of *e-com* magazine.

WHY BOOK ONLINE?

Online agencies have come a long way over the past few years, now providing tips for finding the best fare, and giving you suggested dates or times to travel that yield the lowest price if your plans are at all flexible. Other sites even allow you to establish the price you're willing to pay, and they check the airlines' willingness to accept it. However, in some cases, these sites may not always yield the best price. Unlike a travel agent, for example, they may not have access to charter flights offered by wholesalers.

Online booking sites aren't the only places to reserve airline tickets—all major airlines have their own Web sites and often offer incentives (bonus frequent flyer miles or Net-only discounts, for example) when you buy online or buy an e-ticket.

The new trend is toward conglomerated booking sites. By June 2001, a consortium of U.S. and European-based airlines is planning to launch a Web site called **Orbitz.com** that will offer fares lower than those available through travel agents. United, Delta, Northwest, American, and Continental have initiated this effort, based on their success at selling airline seats on their own sites.

Check Out Frommer's Site

We highly recommend **Arthur Frommer's Budget Travel Online** (**www. frommers.com**) as an excellent travel-planning resource. Of course, we're a little biased, but you'll find indispensable travel tips, reviews, monthly vacation giveaways, and online booking. Among the most popular features of this site are the regular "Ask the Expert" bulletin boards, which feature Frommer's authors answering your questions via online postings.

Subscribe to Arthur Frommer's Daily Newsletter (**www.frommers. com/newsletters**) to receive the latest travel bargains and inside travel secrets in your e-mailbox every day. You'll read daily headlines and articles from the dean of travel himself, highlighting last-minute deals on airfares, accommodations, cruises, and package vacations.

Search our Destinations archive (**www.frommers.com/destinations**) of more than 200 domestic and international destinations for great places to stay and dine, and tips on sightseeing. Once you've researched your trip, the online reservation system (**www.frommers.com/booktravelnow**) takes you to Frommer's favorite sites for booking your vacation at affordable prices.

The best of the travel planning sites are now highly personalized; they store your seating preferences, meal preferences, tentative itineraries, and credit-card information, allowing you to quickly plan trips or check agendas.

In many cases, booking your trip online can be better than working with a travel agent. It gives you the widest variety of choices, control, and the 24-hour convenience of planning your trip when you choose. All you need is some time—and often a little patience—and you're likely to find the fun of online travel research will greatly enhance your trip.

WHO SHOULD BOOK ONLINE?

Online booking is best for travelers who want to know as much as possible about their travel options, for those who have flexibility in their travel dates, and for bargain hunters.

One of the biggest successes in online travel for both passengers and airlines is the offer of last-minute specials, such as American Airlines' weekend deals or other Internet-only fares that must be purchased online. Another advantage is that you can cash in on incentives for booking online, such as rebates or bonus frequent-flyer miles.

Business and other frequent travelers also have found numerous benefits in online booking, as the advances in mobile technology provide them with the ability to check flight status, change plans, or get specific directions from handheld computing devices, mobile phones, and pagers. Some sites will even e-mail or page a passenger if their flight is delayed.

Online booking is increasingly able to accommodate complex itineraries, even for international travel. The pace of evolution on the Net is rapid, so you'll probably find additional features and advancements by the time you visit these sites. The future holds ever-increasing personalization and customization for online travelers.

TRAVEL-PLANNING & BOOKING SITES

Below are listings for sites for planning and booking travel. The following sites offer domestic and international flight, hotel, and rental-car bookings, plus news, destination information, and deals on cruises and vacation packages. Free (one-time) registration is required for booking.

Travelocity (incorporates Preview Travel). www.travelocity.com; www.previewtravel.com; www.frommers.travelocity.com

Travelocity is Frommer's online travel-planning and booking partner. Travelocity uses the SABRE system to offer reservations and tickets for more than 400 airlines, plus reservations and purchase capabilities for more than 45,000 hotels and 50 car-rental companies. An exclusive feature of the SABRE system is its **Low Fare Search Engine,** which automatically searches for the three lowest-priced itineraries based on a traveler's criteria. Last-minute deals and consolidator fares are included in the search. If you book with Travelocity, you can select specific seats for your flights with online seat maps, and also view diagrams of the most popular commercial aircraft. Its hotel finder provides street-level location maps and photos of selected hotels. With the **Fare Watcher** e-mail feature, you can select up to five routes and receive e-mail notices when the fare changes by $25 or more.

Travelocity's **Destination Guide** includes updated information on some 260 destinations worldwide—supplied by Frommer's.

Note to AOL Users: You can book flights, hotels, rental cars, and cruises on AOL at keyword: Travel. The booking software is provided by Travelocity/Preview Travel and is similar to the Internet site. Use the AOL "Travelers Advantage" program to earn a 5% rebate on flights, hotel rooms, and car rentals.

Expedia. www.expedia.com

Expedia is Travelocity's major competitor. It offers several ways of obtaining the best possible fares: **Flight Price Matcher** service allows your preferred airline to match an available fare with a competitor; a comprehensive **Fare Compare** area shows the differences in fare categories and airlines; and **Fare Calendar** helps you plan your trip around the best possible fares. Its main limitation is that like many online databases, Expedia focuses on the major airlines and hotel chains, so don't expect to find too many budget airlines or one-of-a-kind B&Bs here.

TRIP.com. www.trip.com

TRIP.com began as a site geared toward business travelers, but its innovative features and highly personalized approach have broadened its appeal to leisure travelers as well. It is the leading travel site for those using mobile devices to access Internet travel information.

TRIP.com includes a trip-planning function that provides the average and lowest fare for the route requested, in addition to the current available fare. An on-site "newsstand" features breaking news on airfare sales and other travel specials. Among its most popular features are Flight TRACKER and intelliTRIP. **Flight TRACKER** allows users to track any commercial flight en route to its destination anywhere in the U.S., while accessing real-time FAA-based flight monitoring data. **intelliTRIP** is a travel search tool that allows users to identify the best airline, hotel, and rental-car rates in less than 90 seconds.

In addition, the site offers e-mail notification of flight delays, plus city resource guides, currency converters, and a weekly e-mail newsletter of fare updates, travel tips, and traveler forums.

Online Directory

More people still look online than book online, partly due to fear of putting their credit-card numbers out on the Net. Secure encryption, and increasing experienced buying online, has removed this fear for most travelers. In some cases, however, it's simply easier to buy from a local travel agent who can deliver your tickets to your door (especially if your travel is last-minute or if you have special requests). You can find a flight online and then book it by calling a toll-free number or contacting your travel agent, though this is somewhat less efficient. To be sure you're in secure mode when you book online, look for a little icon of a key or a padlock at the bottom of your Web browser.

Yahoo Travel. www.travel.yahoo.com

Yahoo is currently the most popular of the Internet information portals, and its travel site is a comprehensive mix of online booking, daily travel news, and destination information. The **Best Fares** area offers what it promises, plus provides feedback on refining your search if you have flexibility in travel dates or times. There is also an active section of Message Boards for discussions on travel in general and specific destinations.

LAST-MINUTE DEALS & OTHER ONLINE BARGAINS

There's nothing airlines hate more than flying with lots of empty seats. The Net has enabled airlines to offer last-minute bargains to entice travelers to fill those seats. Most of these are announced on Tuesday or Wednesday and are valid for travel the following weekend, but some can be booked weeks or months in advance. You can sign up for weekly e-mail alerts at the airlines' own sites (see the box below listing the airlines' Web addresses) or check sites that compile lists of these bargains, such as **Smarter Living** or **WebFlyer** (see below). To make it easier, visit a site that will round up all the deals and send them in one convenient weekly e-mail.

Important Note: See "Getting There" in chapter 2 for the Web addresses of airlines serving Italy. These sites offer schedules and flight booking, and most have pages where you can sign up for e-mail alerts for weekend deals and other late-breaking bargains.

Cheap Tickets. www.cheaptickets.com

Cheap Tickets has exclusive deals that aren't available through more mainstream channels. One caveat about the Cheap Tickets site is that it will offer fare quotes for a route and later show this fare is not valid for your dates of travel—most other Web sites, such as Expedia, consider your dates of travel before showing what fares are available. Despite its problems, Cheap Tickets can be worth the effort because its fares can be lower than those offered by its competitors.

✪ 1travel.com. www.1travel.com

Here you'll find deals on domestic and international flights and hotels. 1travel.com's **Saving Alert** compiles last-minute air deals so you don't have to scroll through multiple e-mail alerts. A feature called "Drive a little using low-fare airlines" helps map out strategies for using alternate airports to find lower fares. And **Farebeater** searches a database that includes published fares, consolidator bargains and special deals exclusive to 1travel.com. *Note:* The travel agencies listed by 1travel.com have paid for placement.

Bid for Travel. www.bidfortravel.com

Bid for Travel is another of the travel auction sites, similar to Priceline (see below), which are growing in popularity. In addition to airfares, Internet users can place a bid for vacation packages and hotels.

LastMinuteTravel.com. www.lastminutetravel.com

Suppliers with excess inventory come to this online agency to distribute unsold airline seats, hotel rooms, cruises, and vacation packages. It's got great deals, but an excess of advertisements and slow-loading graphics.

Moment's Notice. www.moments-noticc.com

As the name suggests, Moment's Notice specializes in last-minute vacation deals. You can browse for free, but if you want to purchase a trip you have to join Moment's Notice, which costs $25.

✪ Priceline.com. www.travel.priceline.com

Priceline lets you "name your price" for domestic and international airline tickets and hotel rooms. You select a route and dates, guarantee with a credit card, and make a bid for what you're willing to pay. If one of the airlines in Priceline's database has a fare lower than your bid, your credit card will automatically be charged for a ticket.

But you can't say when you want to fly—you have to accept any flight leaving between 6am and 10pm on the dates you selected, and you may have to make a stopover. No frequent-flyer miles are awarded, and tickets are non-refundable and can't be exchanged for another flight. So if your plans change, you're out of luck. Priceline can be good for travelers who have to take off on short notice (and who are thus unable to qualify for advance purchase discounts). But be sure to shop around first, because if you overbid, you'll be required to purchase the ticket—and Priceline will pocket the difference between what it paid for the ticket and what you bid.

Priceline says that over 35% of all reasonable offers for domestic flights are being filled on the first try, with much higher fill rates on popular routes (New York to San Francisco, for example). They define "reasonable" as not more than 30% below the lowest generally available advance-purchase fare for the same route.

Smarter Living. www.smarterliving.com

Best known for its e-mail dispatch of weekend deals on 20 airlines, Smarter Living also keeps you posted about last-minute bargains.

SkyAuction.com. www.skyauction.com

An auction site with categories for airfare, travel deals, hotels, and much more.

Travelzoo.com. www.travelzoo.com

At this Internet portal, more than 150 travel companies post special deals. It features a Top 20 list of the best deals on the site, selected by its editorial staff each Wednesday night. This list is also available via an e-mailing list, free to those who sign up.

WebFlyer. www.webflyer.com

WebFlyer is a comprehensive online resource for frequent flyers and also has an excellent listing of last-minute air deals. Click on "Deal Watch" for a round-up of weekend deals on flights, hotels, and rental cars from domestic and international suppliers.

ONLINE TRAVELER'S TOOLBOX

Exchange Rates. www.x-rates.com

See what your dollar or pound is worth in Italian lire.

Check Your E-mail While You're on the Road

You don't have to be out of touch just because you don't carry a laptop while you travel. Web browser–based free e-mail programs make it much easier to stay in e-touch.

Just open a freemail account at a browser-based provider, such as **MSN Hotmail** (**www.hotmail.com**) or **Yahoo! Mail** (**www.mail.yahoo.com**).

AOL users should check out **AOL Netmail,** and **USA.NET** (**www. usa.net**) comes highly recommended for functionality and security. You can find hints, tips and a mile-long list of freemail providers at www. emailaddresses.com.

Be sure to give your freemail address to the family members, friends, and colleagues with whom you'd like to stay in touch while you're in Italy. All you'll need to check your freemail account while you're away from home is a Web connection, easily available at Internet cafes, copy shops, and cash- and credit-card Internet-access machines (often available in hotel lobbies or business centers). After logging on, just point the browser to **www.hotmail.com**, **www.yahoo.com**, or the address of any other service you're using. Enter your user name and password, and you'll have access to your mail, both for receiving and sending messages to friends and family back home, for just a few dollars an hour.

The Net Café Guide (**www.netcafeguide.com/mapindex.htm**) will help you locate Internet cafes at hundreds of locations around the globe. Cybercafes come and go, and are becoming more widespread, so you're likely to find them in more and more cities across Italy by the time you travel. You can log onto the Web in central Rome at **Thenetgate,** Piazza Firenze 25 (☎ **06-689-3445;** Bus: 116). Summer hours are Monday to Saturday 10:30am to 12:30pm and 3:30 to 10:30pm, and winter hours daily 10:40am to 8:30pm. A 20-minute visit costs 5,000 lire ($2.50), with 1 hour (including mailbox) at 10,000 lire ($5). Access is free Saturdays 10:30 to 11am and 2 to 2:30pm. You can kill two birds with one stone just north of Stazione Termini at **Splash,** Via Varese 33 (☎ **06-4938-2073;** Metro: Termini), a do-it-yourself Laundromat with a satellite TV and four computers hooked up to the Net (5,000 lire/$2.50 per half hour).

Online Directory

✪ **Foreign Languages for Travelers. www.travlang.com**
Learn basic terms in more than 70 languages and click on any underlined phrase to hear what it sounds like. (*Note:* Free audio software and speakers are required.) They also offer hotel and airline finders with excellent prices and a simple system to get the listings you are looking for.

U.S. Customs Service Traveler Information. www.customs.ustreas.gov/ travel/index.htm
HM Customs & Excise Passenger Enquiries. www.open.gov.uk
Canada Customs and Revenue Agency. www.ccra-adrc.gc.ca
Australian Customs. www.dfat.gov.au
New Zealand Customs Service. www.customs.govt.nz
Planning a shopping spree and wondering what you're allowed to bring home? Check the latest regulations at these thorough sites.

Visa ATM Locator. www.visa.com/pd/atm/
MasterCard ATM Locator. www.mastercard.com/atm
Find ATMs in hundreds of cities around the world. Both include maps for some locations and both list airport ATM locations, some with maps.

The Weather Channel. www.weather.com
Weather forecasts for cities around the world.

2 The Top Web Sites for Rome

Updated by Matthew Garcia

Many of the following sites give users the option of using English or Italian. Though some will first come up in Italian, you can follow the icons for English versions. If it's not evident at first, scroll down to find an American or British flag.

The major problem with Web sites that cover Italy (and, I'm sure, many other destinations) is updating—or rather, the lack thereof. Many people think that Web sites must be more up to date than guidebooks, but so far, that's definitely not true. One way to check on how stale information might be is to use a search engine that tells you when each site was updated—I like AltaVista for this, but there are others. If you run across a description or listing of an establishment or event that you know will make or break your trip, *always* double-check that information; call ahead before you block out time for an activity or destination that might turn out to be closed.

Christus Rex. www.christusrex.org
This site is heavily religious, with a fantastic photo tour of the Vatican Museums and their art treasures.

Comune di Roma. www.informaroma.it
Written delightfully in "English as a second language," this site directs you to everything you might need to feel at home in Rome. Find shops, restaurants, museums, monuments, sporting events, and parks alongside such practicalities as post offices, embassies, emergency services, and hotels, which are ranked on a scale of one to four stars.

Nerone: The Insider's Guide. www.nerone.cc
Get tips on everything from museums to Roman public toilets. Check the site's events menu to see what arts and entertainment highlights will coincide with your visit to the Eternal City. Sort through archives of the *Nerone* newspaper as well.

Roma Online. www.romaonline.net/eng
This online tourist guide has pictures, QuickTime video, and virtual renderings of Roman monuments and sights around the city. There is also information on getting around, enjoying the city's parks, sports, and shopping.

Roma 2000: Museums of Rome. www.roma2000.it
Though it clearly promotes the Roma 2000 shopper's discount-card program and participating merchants, this site also provides a thorough guide to Rome's many museums and monuments. Each attraction entry includes a photo, a brief history, a map, transportation info, and, if applicable, hours and admission fees.

Rome Guide. www.romeguide.it
Click on the British flag for the English version of this site, which is so chockful of information you'll need a pickax to excavate it. Each click of the mouse

Online Directory

A Place to Stay in Rome

These directories can help you find (and often book) a hotel, an apartment, a B&B, or a furnished home.

- **Apartments in Rome:** www.guestinitaly.com/apart.htm
- **Bed and Breakfast Association of Rome:** www.b-b.rm.it/frame.htm
- **Hotels in Italy:** www.italyincoming.com
- **ItalyHotelLink:** www.italyhotelink.com
- **Italy Hotel Reservation:** www.italyhotel.com
- **Roman Homes:** www.romanhomes.com
- **Villas and Apartments in Rome:**
  www.villavacations.com/italy/latium/rome

reveals multiple new layers of tourist information, extending beyond the typical hotel/restaurant listings and into ecotourism opportunities, walking tours, nightclubs, airfares, and other specifics. One unique feature is the ability to search for upcoming cultural events by venue.

Time Out Rome. www.timeout.co.uk
Download the latest issue of *Time Out Rome,* which offers great up-to-date listings of events and exhibits.

Tour Rome. www.tourome.com/tourrome.htm
Here you'll find information on day tours of Rome's sights and attractions, led by local tour leaders who'll pick you up and drop you off at your hotel.

✪ Traveling with Ed and Julie. www.twenj.com/romevisit.htm
Seasoned travelers advise first-timers on what to do when in Rome. Musing romantically about the ancient city, the pair will guide you to hotels, restaurants, excursions, quiet spots, tips on seeing Rome with kids, and, of course, attractions such as the Vatican and the Colosseum.

Vatican: The Holy See. www.vatican.va
The official site of the Vatican offers audio and video programs in multiple languages to accompany profiles of all the popes, the Vatican museum, the Roman Curia, and the Vatican library.

COUNTRY GUIDES TO ALL OF ITALY

Dolce Vita. www.dolcevita.com
The self-proclaimed "insider's guide to Italy" is all about style—as it pertains to fashion, cuisine, design, and travel. A scrolling bulletin at the site shares factoids, survey results, and other bits of Italian news, and the events section brims with major performing arts, music, and museum happenings. While clearly driven by consumers and advertisers, Dolce Vita is a good place to stay up to date on trends in modern Italian culture.

✪ In Italy Online. www.initaly.com
This extensive site helps you find all sorts of accommodations (including country villas, historic homes, and gay-friendly hotels) and includes tips on shopping, dining, driving, and viewing works of art. In Italy Online, there's an information-packed section dedicated to each region of Italy, plus a section on books and movies to help you enjoy the Italian experience at home. Join the mailing list for monthly updates.

Online Directory

Italian Tourist Web Guide. www.itwg.com

Need help planning your travel schedule? Be sure to check out the Italian Tourist Web Guide, which each month recommends new itineraries for art lovers, nature buffs, wine enthusiasts, and other Italiophiles. The site features a searchable directory of accommodations, transportation tips, and city-specific lists of restaurants and attractions.

Italy in a Flash. www.italyflash.com

This site offers hotel information, railway and airline schedules, the latest exchange rates, weather, and current news.

ItalyTour.com. www.italytour.com

Search ItalyTour.com for all things Italian. This vast directory covers arts, culture, business, tours, entertainment, restaurants, lodging, real estate, news and media, shopping, sports, transportation, and major Italian cities. It's not the most excitingly designed site, but it does include photo collections and videos in the Panorama section.

✪ Wandering Italy. www.wandering.com

Amid lyrical travel stories of language mishaps and cobblestone streets, penned by an international brood of tourists, Wandering Italy takes you on virtual reality tours of spots such as the village of Marciana Marina and the Piazza San Marco. This site's slide shows reveal views of stunning scenery and artwork from more than 25 of Italy's cities.

GETTING AROUND

Autostrade S.P.A. www.autostrade.it

This site is a valuable resource for anyone brave enough to drive in Italy. The interactive Motorway Map helps you plan your route and prepare for the toll booths you'll encounter along the way. The site also offers traffic forecasts, safety tips, and lists of service stations.

CIT Tours. www.cittours.com

This tour company specializes in trips to Italy. Even if you're not interested in one of their group tours, you can buy all kinds of European rail passes online on this site. The Italian Flexirail Card, in particular, entitles holders to a pre-determined number of days on any rail line of Italy within a certain period. It must be purchased before you arrive in Italy, making CIT Tours a valuable contact.

Rail Europe. www.raileurope.com

Rail Europe lets you buy Eurail, Europass, and Brit Rail railroad passes online, as well as rail and drive packages and point-to-point travel in 35 European countries. Even if you don't want a rail pass, the site offers invaluable first- and second-class fare and schedule information to the most popular European rail routes.

Rail Pass Express. www.eurail.com

A good source for Eurail pass information, purchasing, and deals.

Getting to Know Rome 3

In this chapter, you'll find all the details to help you settle into Rome, from arriving at the airport to how to get around. There's a quick breakdown of neighborhoods to help you figure out where you'll want to base yourself, and that will help organize and orient all the hotels, restaurants, and sights in the following chapters. We'll round it off with a list of "Fast Facts"—everything from cybercafes and embassies to where to find English-speaking doctors and how to make a phone call.

1 Essentials

ARRIVING

BY PLANE   Chances are you'll arrive at Rome's **Leonardo da Vinci International Airport** (☎ **06-65-951** or 06-6595-3640), popularly known as **Fiumicino,** 18½ miles (30km) from the city center. (If you're flying by charter, you might wing into Ciampino Airport; see below.)

After you leave Passport Control, you'll see two **information desks** (one for Rome, one for Italy; ☎ **06-6595-6074**). At the Rome desk you can pick up a general map and some pamphlets Monday to Saturday 8:30am to 7pm; the staff can also help you find a hotel room if you haven't reserved ahead. A *cambio* (money exchange) operates daily 7:30am to 11pm, offering surprisingly good rates. **Luggage storage** is available 24 hours in the main arrivals building daily, costing 5,000 lire ($2.50) per bag.

There's a **train station** in the airport. To get into the city, follow the signs marked TRENI for the 30-minute shuttle to Rome's main station, **Stazione Termini** (arriving on Track 22). It runs 7:30am to 10pm for 16,000 lire ($8) one-way. On the way you'll pass a machine dispensing tickets automatically, or you can buy them in person near the tracks if you don't have small bills on you. When you arrive at Termini, get out of the train quickly and grab a baggage cart. It's a long schlep from the track to the exit or to the other train connections, and there never seem to be enough baggage carts available.

A **taxi** from Da Vinci to the city costs 75,000 lire ($37.50) and up for the 1-hour trip, depending on traffic. The expense may be worth it if you have a lot of luggage or just don't want to be bothered with the train trip. Call ☎ **06-6645,** 06-3570, or 06-4994 for information.

A Few Train Station Warnings

In Stazione Termini, you'll almost certainly be approached by touts claiming to work for a tourist organization. They really work for individual hotels (not always the most recommendable) and will say almost anything to sell you a room. Unless you know something about Rome's layout and are savvy, it's best to ignore them.

Be aware of all your belongings at all times and keep your wallet and purse away from professionally experienced fingers. Never ever leave your bags unattended for even a second, and while making phone calls or waiting in line, make sure your attention doesn't wander from any bags you've set by your side or on the ground. Be aware if someone asks *you* for directions or information—it's likely meant to distract you and easily will.

Ignore the taxi drivers soliciting passengers right outside the terminal; they can charge as much as triple the normal amount. Instead, line up at the official taxi stand in Piazza dei Cinquecento.

If you arrive on a charter flight at **Ciampino Airport** (☎ 06-794-941), you can take a COTRAL bus, departing every 30 minutes or so for the Anagnina stop of Metropolitana (subway) Line A. Take Line A to Stazione Termini, where you can make your final connections. Trip time is about 45 minutes, costing 1,500 lire (75¢). A **taxi** from this airport to Rome costs the same as the one from the Da Vinci airport (above), but the trip is shorter (about 40 minutes).

BY TRAIN OR BUS   Trains and buses (including trains from the airport) arrive in the center of old Rome at the silver **Stazione Termini,** Piazza dei Cinquecento (☎ 1478-880-88); this is the train, bus, and subway transportation hub for all of Rome and is surrounded by many hotels (especially cheaper ones).

If you're taking the **Metropolitana** (subway), follow the illuminated red-and-white M signs. To catch a **bus,** go straight through the outer hall and enter the sprawling bus lot of Piazza dei Cinquecento. You'll also find **taxis** there.

The station is filled with services. At a branch of the **Banca San Paolo di Torino** (between Tracks 8 to 11 and Tracks 12 to 15) you can exchange money. **Informazioni Ferroviarie** (in the outer hall) dispenses information on rail travel to other parts of Italy. There's also a **tourist information booth** here, along with baggage services, newsstands, and snack bars.

BY CAR   From the north, the main access route is the **Autostrada del Sole (A1),** cutting through Milan and Florence, or you can take the coastal route, **SSI Aurelia,** from Genoa. If you're driving north from Naples, you take the southern lap of the **Autostrada del Sole (A2).** All the autostrade join with the **Grande Raccordo Anulare,** a ring road encircling Rome, channeling traffic into the congested city. Long before you reach this road, you should study a map carefully to see what part of Rome you plan to enter and mark your route accordingly. Route markings along the ring road tend to be confusing.

Warning: Return your rental car immediately, or at least get yourself to a hotel, park your car, and leave it there until you leave Rome. Don't even try to drive in Rome— the traffic is just too nightmarish.

VISITOR INFORMATION

Information is available at three locations maintained by the Azienda Provinciale di Turismo (APT). They include a kiosk at **Leonardo da Vinci International Airport**

(☎ 06-6595-6074); a kiosk in **Stazione Termini** (☎ 06-487-1270); and a kiosk and **administrative headquarters** at Via Parigi 5 (☎ **06-4889-9253**). The headquarters are open Monday to Friday 8:15am to 7:15pm (Saturday to 2pm). The office at the airport and the one at the Stazione Termini are open daily 8:15am to 7:15pm. However, don't expect much help from these offices.

More helpful, and stocking maps and brochures, are the offices maintained by the **Comune di Roma** at various sites around the city with red-and-orange or yellow-and-black signs saying COMUNE DI ROMA—PUNTI DI INFORMAZIONE TURISTICA. They're staffed daily 9am to 6pm, except the one at Termini (daily 8am to 9pm). Here are the addresses and phone numbers: in Stazione Termini (☎ **06-4890-6300**); in Piazza dei Cinquecento, outside Termini (☎ **06-4782-5194**); in Piazza Pia, near the Castel Sant'Angelo (☎ **06-6880-9707**); in Piazza San Giovanni in Laterano (☎ **06-7720-3598**); along Largo Carlo Goldoni (☎ **06-6813-6061**), near the intersection of Via del Corso and Via Condotti; on Via Nazionale, near the Palazzo delle Esposizioni (☎ **06-4782-4525**); on Largo Corrado Ricci, near the Colosseum (☎ **06-6992-4307**); on Piazza Sonnino in Trastevere (☎ **06-5833-3457**); on Piazza Cinque Lune, near Piazza Navona (☎ **06-6880-9240**); and on Piazza Santa Maria Maggiore (☎ **06-4788-0294**).

Enjoy Rome, Via Varese 39, near the train station (☎ **06-445-1843;** fax 06-445-0734; www.enjoyrome.com; e-mail: info@enjoyrome.com), was begun by a wonderful young English-speaking couple, Fulvia and Pierluigi. They dispense information about just about everything in Rome and are far more pleasant and organized than the Board of Tourism. They'll also help you find a hotel room, with no service charge (in anything from a hostel to a three-star hotel). Summer hours are Monday to Friday 8:30am to 7pm and Saturday 8:30am to 1:30pm; winter hours are Monday to Friday 8:30am to 1:30pm and 3:30 to 6pm.

CITY LAYOUT

Arm yourself with a detailed street map, not the general overview handed out free at tourist offices. Most hotels hand out a pretty good version at their front desks.

The bulk of ancient, Renaissance, and baroque Rome (as well as the train station) lies on the east side of the **Tiber River (Fiume Tevere),** which meanders through town. However, several important landmarks are on the other side: **St. Peter's Basilica** and the **Vatican,** the **Castel Sant'Angelo,** and the colorful **Trastevere** neighborhood.

The city's various quarters are linked by large boulevards (large at least in some places) that have mostly been laid out since the late 19th century. Starting from the **Vittorio Emanuele Monument,** a controversial pile of snow-white Brescian marble that's often compared to a wedding cake, there's a street running practically due north to **Piazza del Popolo** and the city wall. This is **Via del Corso,** one of the main streets of Rome—noisy, congested, always crowded with buses and shoppers, called simply "Il Corso." To its left (west) lie the Pantheon, Piazza Navona, Campo de' Fiori, and the Tiber. To its right (east) you'll find the Spanish Steps, the Trevi Fountain, the Borghese Gardens, and Via Veneto.

Back at the Vittorio Emanuele monument, the major artery going west (and ultimately across the Tiber to St. Peter's) is **Corso Vittorio Emanuele.** Behind you to your right, heading toward the Colosseum, is **Via del Fori Imperiali,** laid out in the 1930s by Mussolini to show off the ruins of the imperial forums he had excavated, which line it on either side. Yet another central conduit is **Via Nazionale,** running from **Piazza Venezia** (just in front of the Vittorio Emanuele Monument) east to **Piazza della Repubblica** (near Stazione Termini). The final lap of Via Nazionale is called **Via Quattro Novembre.**

Finding an address in Rome can be a problem because of the narrow streets of old Rome and the little, sometimes hidden *piazze* (squares). Numbers usually run consecutively, with odd numbers on one side of the street and even numbers on the other. However, in the old districts the numbers will sometimes run consecutively up one side of the street to the end, then back in the opposite direction on the other side. Therefore, no. 50 could be opposite no. 308.

For the 2½ millennia before the modern wide boulevards were built, the citizens had to make their way through narrow byways and curves that defeated all but the best senses of direction. These streets—among the most charming aspects of the city—still exist in large numbers, mostly unspoiled by the advances of modern construction. However, this tangled street plan has one troublesome element: automobiles. The traffic in Rome is awful! When the claustrophobic street plans of the Dark Ages open unexpectedly onto a vast piazza, every driver accelerates full throttle for the horizon, while pedestrians flatten themselves against marble fountains in fear or stride with firm jaws right into the thick of the howling traffic.

The Neighborhoods in Brief

This section will give you some idea of where you may want to stay and where the major attractions are located. It may be hard to find a specific address, though, because of the narrow streets of old Rome and the little, sometimes hidden *piazze* (squares).

Near Stazione Termini   The main train station, **Stazione Termini,** adjoins **Piazza della Repubblica,** and most likely this will be your introduction to Rome. Much of the area is seedy and filled with gas fumes from all the buses and cars, but it has been improving. If you stay here, you may not get a lot of atmosphere, but you'll have a lot of affordable options and a very convenient location, near the transportation hub of the city and not too far from ancient Rome. There's a lot to see here, like the **Basilica di Santa Maria Maggiore** and the **Baths of Diocletian.** Some high-class hotels are sprinkled in the area, including the **Grand,** but many are long past their heyday.

The neighborhoods on either side of Stazione Termini have improved greatly recently, and some streets are now attractive. The best-looking area is ahead and to your right as you exit the station on the Via Marsala side. Most budget hotels here occupy a floor or more of a palazzo, and the entries are often drab, though upstairs they're often charming or at least clean and livable. In the area to the left of the station, as you exit, the streets are wider, the traffic is heavier, and the noise level is higher. This area off Via Giolitti is being redeveloped, and now most streets are in good condition. There are a few that still need improvement, and caution at night is a given.

Via Veneto & Piazza Barberini   In the 1950s and early 1960s, **Via Veneto** was the haunt of the *dolce vita* set, as the likes of King Farouk and Swedish actress Anita Ekberg paraded up and down the boulevard to the delight of the paparazzi. The street is still here, still the site of luxury hotels and elegant cafes and restaurants, though it's no longer the happening place to be. It's lined with restaurants catering to those tourists who've heard of this famous boulevard from decades past, but they're mostly overpriced and overcrowded. Rome city authorities would like to restore this legendary street to some of its former glory by banning vehicular traffic on the top half. It makes for a pleasant stroll in any case.

To the south, Via Veneto comes to an end at **Piazza Barberini,** dominated by the 1642 **Triton Fountain (Fontana del Tritone),** a baroque celebration with four dolphins holding up an open scallop shell in which sits a triton blowing into a conch. Overlooking the square is the **Palazzo Barberini.** In 1623, when Cardinal Maffeo Barberini became Pope Urban VIII, he ordered Carlo Maderno to build a palace here; it was later completed by Bernini and Borromini.

Ancient Rome   Most visitors explore this area first, taking in the **Colosseum, Palatine Hill, Roman Forum, Imperial Forums,** and **Circus Maximus.** It forms part of the *centro storico* (historic district)—along with **Campo de' Fiori** and **Piazza Navona** and the **Pantheon,** which are described below (we've considered them separately for the purposes of helping you locate hotels and restaurants). Because of its narrow streets, airy piazzas, antique atmosphere, and great location, this is a good place to stay. If you base yourself here, you can walk to the monuments and avoid the hassle of Rome's inadequate public transportation.

Campo de' Fiori & The Jewish Ghetto   South of Corso Vittorio Emanuele and centered around **Piazza Farnese** and the market square of **Campo de' Fiori,** many buildings in this area were constructed in Renaissance times as private homes. Stroll along **Via Giulia** Rome's most fashionable street in the 16th century with its antiques stores, interesting hotels, and modern art galleries.

West of Via Arenula lies one of the city's most intriguing districts, the old **Jewish Ghetto,** where the dining options far outnumber the hotel options. In 1556, Pope Paul IV ordered the Jews, about 8,000 at the time, to move into this area. The walls weren't torn down until 1849. Though we think ancient and medieval Rome have a lot more atmosphere, this area is close to many attractions and makes a great place to stay. Nevertheless, hoteliers still sock it to you on prices.

Piazza Navona & The Pantheon   One of the most desirable areas of Rome, this district is a maze of narrow streets and alleys dating from the Middle Ages and is filled with churches and palaces built during the Renaissance and baroque eras, often with rare marble and other materials stripped from ancient Rome. The only way to explore it is on foot. Its heart is **Piazza Navona,** built over Emperor Domitian's stadium and bustling with sidewalk cafes, palazzi, street artists, musicians, and pickpockets. There are several hotels in the area and plenty of *trattorie.* Rivaling it—in general activity, the cafe scene, and nightlife—is the area around the **Pantheon,** which remains from ancient Roman times and is surrounded by a district built much later (this "pagan" temple was turned into a church and rescued, but the buildings that once surrounded it are long gone). If you'd like to stay in medieval Rome, you face the same 30% to 50% increase in hotel prices as you do for ancient Rome.

Piazza del Popolo & The Spanish Steps   **Piazza del Popolo** was laid out by Giuseppe Valadier and is one of Rome's largest squares. It's characterized by an obelisk brought from Heliopolis in lower Egypt during the reign of Augustus. At the end of the square is the **Porta del Popolo,** the gateway in the 3rd-century Aurelian wall. In the mid–16th century this was one of the major gateways into the old city. If you enter the piazza along Via del Corso from the south, you'll see twin churches, **Santa Maria del Miracoli** and **Santa Maria di Montesanto,** flanking the street. But the square's major church is **Santa Maria del Popolo** (1442–47), one of the best examples of a Renaissance church in Rome.

Ever since the 17th century, the **Spanish Steps** (former site of the Spanish ambassador's residence) have been a meeting place for visitors. Keats lived in a house opening onto the steps, and some of Rome's most upscale shopping streets fan out from it, including **Via Condotti.** The elegant **Hassler,** one of Rome's grandest hotels, lies at

Rome Orientation

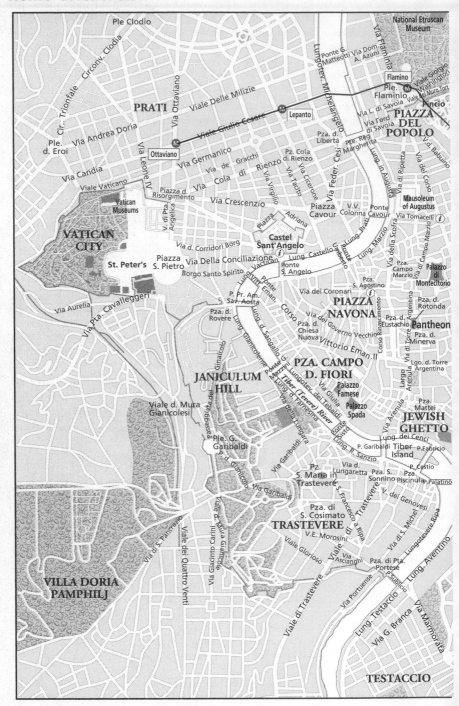

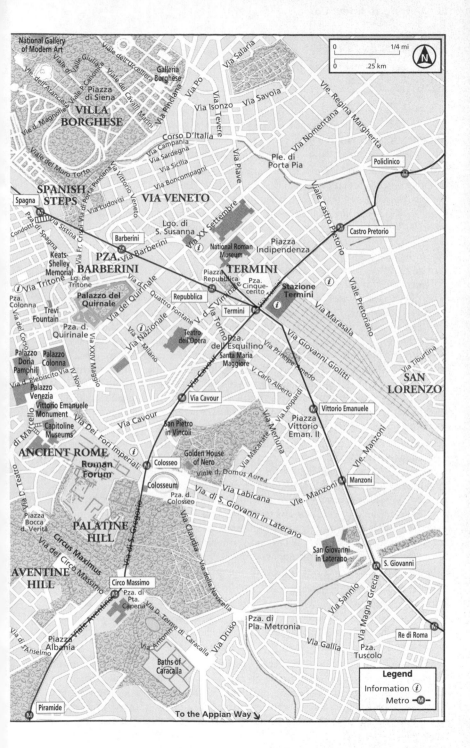

Rome has *four* daily rush hours: to work, to home for lunch *(riposo),* back to work, to home in the evening.

the top of the steps. If you want to stay in this part of town, you must be willing to part with a lot of extra lire. This area charges some of the city's highest prices, not only for hotels but also for restaurants, designer silk suits, and leather loafers.

Around Vatican City   Across the Tiber, **Vatican City** is a small city-state, but its influence extends around the world. The **Vatican Museums, St. Peter's,** and the **Vatican Gardens** take up most of the land area, and the popes have lived here for 6 centuries. Though the neighborhood contains some good hotels (and several bad ones), it's somewhat removed from the more happening scene of ancient and Renaissance Rome, and getting to and from it can be time consuming. And the area is rather dull at night and contains few if any of Rome's finest restaurants. Vatican City and its surrounding area are best for exploring during the day.

Trastevere   Rome's most authentic district, **Trastevere** is a place to see how real people live away from the touristy areas. It lies across the Tiber; its people are of mixed ancestry, including Jewish, Roman, and Greek, and they speak their own dialect. The area centers around the ancient churches of **Santa Cecilia** and **Santa Maria in Trastevere.** Home to many young expatriates, the district became a gathering place for hedonists and bohemians after World War II. There are those who speak of it as a "city within a city"—or at least a village within a city. It's said that the language is rougher and the cuisine spicier, and though Trastevere doesn't have the glamorous hotels of central Rome, it does have some of the last remaining authentic Roman dining. This used to be a great hunting ground for budget travelers, but foreigners from virtually everywhere have been buying real estate en masse here, so change is in the air.

Testaccio   In A.D. 55, Nero ordered that Rome's thousands of broken amphoras and terra-cotta roof tiles be stacked in a carefully designated pile to the east of the Tiber, just west of Pyramide and today's Ostia Railway Station. Over the centuries, the mound grew to a height of around 200 feet, then was compacted to form the centerpiece for one of the city's most unusual neighborhoods, **Testaccio.** Eventually, houses were built on the terra-cotta mound and caves dug into its mass to store wine and foodstuffs. Bordered by the Protestant cemetery, Testaccio is home to restaurants with very Roman cuisine. However, don't wander around here alone at night; the area still has a way to go before regentrification.

The Appian Way   **Via Appia Antica** is a 2,300-year-old road that has witnessed much of the history of the ancient world. By 190 B.C. it extended from Rome to Brindisi on the southeast coast, and its most famous sight today is the **catacombs,** the graveyards of patrician families (despite what it says in *Quo Vadis,* they weren't used as a place for Christians to hide out while fleeing persecution). This is one of the most historically rich areas of Rome to explore but not a viable place to stay.

Prati   The little-known **Prati** district is a middle-class suburb north of the Vatican. It's been discovered by budget travelers because of its affordable *pensioni,* though it's not conveniently located for much of the sightseeing you'll want to do. The **Trionfale flower-and-food market** itself is worth the trip. The area also abounds in shopping streets less expensive than those found in central Rome, and street crime isn't much of a problem.

Parioli   Rome's most elegant residential section, **Parioli** is framed by the green spaces of the **Villa Borghese** to the south and the **Villa Glori** and **Villa Ada** to the north. It's a setting for some of the city's finest restaurants, hotels, and nightclubs. It's not exactly central, however, and can be a hassle if you're dependent on public transportation. Parioli lies adjacent to Prati, but across the Tiber to the east, and, like Prati, is one of the safer districts.

Monte Mario   On the northwestern precincts of Rome, **Monte Mario** is the site of the deluxe **Cavalieri Hilton,** an excellent stop to take in a drink and the panorama of Rome. If you plan to spend a lot of time shopping and sightseeing in the heart of Rome, it's a difficult and often expensive commute. The area lies north of Prati, away from the hustle and bustle of central Rome. Bus no. 913 runs from Piazza Augusto Imperator near Piazza del Popolo to Monte Mario.

2 Getting Around

Rome is excellent for walking, with sites of interest often clustered together. Much of the inner core is traffic-free, so you'll need to walk whether you like it or not. However, in many parts of the city it's hazardous and uncomfortable because of the crowds, heavy traffic, and narrow sidewalks. Sometimes sidewalks don't exist at all, and it becomes a sort of free-for-all with pedestrians competing for space against vehicular traffic (the traffic always seems to win). Always be on your guard. The hectic crush of urban Rome is considerably less during August when many Romans leave town for vacation.

BY SUBWAY

The **Metropolitana,** or **Metro** for short, is the fastest means of transportation, operating daily 5:30am to 11:30pm. It has two underground lines: **Line A** goes between Via Ottaviano (near St. Peter's) and Anagnina, stopping at Piazzale Flaminio (near Piazza del Popolo), Piazza di Spagna, Piazza Vittorio Emanuele, and Piazza San Giovanni in Laterano. **Line B** connects the Rebibbia District with Via Laurentina, stopping at Via Cavour, Stazione Termini, the Colosseum, the Circus Maximus, the Pyramid, St. Paul's Outside the Walls, and E.U.R. A big red letter "M" indicates the entrance to the subway.

Tickets are 1,500 lire (75¢) and are available from *tabacchi* (tobacco shops), many newsstands, and vending machines at all stations. These machines accept 50-lire, 100-lire, and 200-lire coins, and some will take 1,000-lire notes. Some stations have managers, but they won't make change. Booklets of tickets are available at tabacchi and in some terminals. You can also buy a **tourist pass** on either a daily or a weekly basis (see below).

Building a subway system for Rome hasn't been easy, since every time workers start digging, they discover an old temple or other archaeological treasure and heavy earth-moving has to cease for a while.

BY BUS & TRAM

Roman buses and trams are operated by an organization known as **ATAC (Azienda Tramvie e Autobus del Comune di Roma)**, Via Volturno 65 (☎ **06-46-951** for information).

For 1,500 lire (75¢) you can ride to most parts of Rome, though it can be slow going in all that traffic, and the buses are often very crowded. Your ticket is valid for 75 minutes, and you can get on many buses and trams during that time using the same

Rome Metropolitana

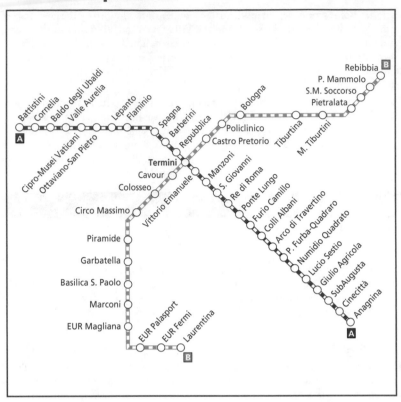

ticket. Ask about where to buy bus tickets, or buy them in tabacchi or bus terminals. You must have your ticket before boarding, as there are no ticket-issuing machines on the vehicles.

At Stazione Termini, you can buy a special **tourist pass,** costing 6,000 lire ($3) for a day or 24,000 lire ($12) for a week. This allows you to ride on the ATAC network without bothering to buy individual tickets. The tourist pass is also valid on the subway—but never ride the trains when the Romans are going to or from work or you'll be mashed flatter than fettuccine. On the first bus you board, you place your ticket in a small machine that prints the day and hour you boarded before you withdraw it. And you do the same on the last bus you take during the validity of the ticket.

Buses and trams stop at areas marked FERMATA. At most of these, a yellow sign will display the numbers of the buses that stop there and a list of all the stops along each bus's route in order, so you can easily search out your destination. In general, they're in service daily 6am to midnight. After that and until dawn, you can ride on special night buses (they have an "N" in front of their bus number), which run only on main routes. It's best to take a taxi in the wee hours—if you can find one.

At the **bus information booth** at Piazza dei Cinquecento, in front of the Stazione Termini, you can purchase a directory complete with maps summarizing the routes.

Though routes change often, a few old reliable routes have remained valid for years, such as **no. 27** from Stazione Termini to the Colosseum, **nos. 75** and **170** from Stazione Termini to Trastevere, and **no. 492** from Stazione Termini to the Vatican. But

Two Bus Warnings

Any map of the Roman bus system will likely be outdated before it's printed. Many buses listed on the "latest" map no longer exist; others are enjoying a much-needed rest, and new buses suddenly appear without warning. There's also talk of completely renumbering the whole system soon, so be aware the route numbers we've listed may have changed by the time you travel.

Take extreme caution when riding Rome's overcrowded buses—pickpockets abound! This is particularly true on bus no. 64, a favorite of visitors because of its route through the historic districts and, thus, also a favorite of Rome's vast pickpocketing community. This bus has earned various nicknames, like the "Pickpocket Express" and "Wallet Eater."

if you're going somewhere and are dependent on the bus, be sure to carefully check where the bus stop is and exactly what bus goes there—don't assume it'll be the same bus the next day.

BY TAXI

If you're accustomed to hopping a cab in New York or London, then do so in Rome. If not, take less expensive means of transport or walk. Avoid paying your fare with large bills—invariably, taxi drivers claim they don't have change, hoping for a bigger tip (stick to your guns and give only about 10%). Don't count on hailing a taxi on the street or even getting one at a stand. If you're going out, have your hotel call one. At a restaurant, ask the waiter or cashier to dial for you. If you want to phone for yourself, try one of these numbers: ☎ 06-6645, 06-3570, or 06-4994.

The meter begins at 4,500 lire ($2.25) for the first 3 kilometers, then rises 1,300 lire (65¢) per kilometer. Every suitcase is 2,000 lire ($1), and on Sunday a 2,000 lire ($1) supplement is assessed. There's another 5,000 lire ($2.50) supplement 10pm to 7am.

BY BICYCLE, MOTOR SCOOTER & MOTORCYCLE

At track 1 inside Stazione Termini, **Treno e Scooter** (☎ 06-4890-5823; Metro: Termini) rents bikes and scooters (pick up bikes outside the station on the right). Rates begin at 4,000 lire ($2) per hour or 10,000 to 13,000 lire ($5 to $6.50) per day for a regular bike and 30,000 to 70,000 lire ($15 to $35) for 4 hours or 35,000 to 100,000 lire ($17.50 to $50) for a day with a scooter (depending on engine size). Scooters come with a *casco* (helmet) and lock. **I Bike Rome,** Via Vittorio Veneto 156 (☎ 06-322-5240; Metro: Barberini), rents bicycles from the underground parking garage at the Villa Borghese. Most bikes cost 4,000 lire ($2) per hour or 10,000 lire ($5) per day. Mountain bikes rent for 7,000 lire ($3.50) per hour or 18,000 lire ($9) per day. It's open daily 9am to 7pm. Bring an ID card with you.

For mopeds, try **Happy Rent,** Via Farimi 3 (☎ 06-481-8185; Metro: Termini), 300 yards from Stazione Termini and open daily 9am to 7pm. Most mopeds cost 20,000 lire ($10) for 1 hour or 70,000 lire ($35) for the day. Happy Rent also offers several guided moped tours of Rome and environs. Open Monday to Saturday from 9am to 7pm.

Bike riders are permitted anywhere in the city, including pedestrian-only zones and traffic-free areas, such as St. Peter's Square, where you can ride within the arcaded confines of what's been called the world's most magnificent oval. Also appealing is a 30-kilometer (18.5-mile) bike lane beside the Tiber that extends from central Rome north, to the industrial suburb of Castel Jubileo.

BY CAR

All roads may lead to Rome, but you don't want to drive once you get here. Since the reception desks of most Roman hotels have at least one English-speaking person, call ahead to find out the best route into Rome from wherever you're starting out. You're usually allowed to park in front of the hotel long enough to unload your luggage. You'll want to get rid of your rental car as soon as possible or park in a garage.

To the neophyte, Roman driving will appear like the chariot race in *Ben-Hur.* When the light turns green, go forth with caution. Many Roman drivers at the other part of the intersection will still be going through the light even though it has turned red. Roman drivers in traffic gridlock move bravely on, fighting for every inch of the road until they can free themselves from the tangled mess. To complicate matters, many zones, such as that around Piazza di Spagna, are traffic-free.

You may want to rent a car to explore the countryside around Rome or drive on to another city. You'll save the most money if you reserve before leaving home. But if you want to book a car here, know that **Hertz** is at Via Vittorio Veneto 156, near the parking lot of the Villa Borghese (☎ **06-321-6831;** Metro: Barberini); **Italy by Car** at Via Ludovisi 60 (☎ **06-482-0966;** Bus: 95 or 116); and **Avis** at Stazione Termini (☎ **06-428-24-728;** Metro: Termini). **Maggiore,** an Italian company, has an office at Via di Tor Cervara 225 (☎ **06-229-351**). There are also branches of the major rental agencies at the airport.

Fast Facts: Rome

American Express   The Rome offices are at Piazza di Spagna 38 (☎ **06-67-641;** Metro: Spagna). The travel service is open Monday to Friday 9am to 5:30pm and Saturday 9am to 12:30pm. Hours for the financial and mail services are Monday to Friday 9am to 5pm. The tour desk is open during the same hours as those for travel services and also Saturday 2 to 2:30pm (May to October).

Baby-Sitters   Most hotel desks in Rome will help you secure a baby-sitter. Inquire as far in advance as possible and also make another request for an English-speaking sitter. You won't always get one but it pays to ask. A good choice is **Angels Baby Sitting Services** at Via delle Quattro Fontane (☎ **06-420-13-080** or 06-329-56-95), which offers British, American, or Australian baby-sitters, available for a few hours or even for 1 or more days. Rates range from 12,000 to 25,000 lire ($6 to $12.50) per hour.

Banks   In general, banks are open Monday to Friday 8:30am to 1:30pm and 3 to 4pm. Some banks keep afternoon hours 2:45 to 3:45pm. There's a branch of **Citibank** at Via Abruzzi 2 (☎ **06-478-171;** Metro: Barberini). The bank office is open Monday to Friday 8:30am to 1:30pm.

Currency Exchange   There are exchange offices throughout the city, and they're also at all major rail and air terminals, including Stazione Termini, where the *cambio* (exchange booth) beside the rail information booth is open daily 8am to 8pm. At some *cambi* you'll have to pay commissions, often $1\frac{1}{2}$%. Banks, likewise, often charge commissions.

Dentists   To find a dentist who speaks English, call the **U.S. Embassy** in Rome at ☎ **06-46-741.** You may have to call around in order to get an appointment. There's also the 24-hour **G. Eastman Dental Hospital,** Viale Regina Elena 287 (☎ **06-844-831;** Metro: Policlinico).

Doctors   For a doctor, call the U.S. Embassy (see "Dentists," above), which will provide a list of doctors who speak English. All big hospitals have a 24-hour first-aid service (go to the emergency room—*Pronto Soccorso*). You'll find English-speaking doctors at the privately run **Salvator Mundi International Hospital,** Viale delle Mura Gianicolensi 67 (☎ **06-588-961;** Bus: 41). For medical assistance, the **International Medical Center** is on 24-hour duty at Via Giovanni Amendola 7 (☎ **06-488-2371;** Metro: Termini). You could also contact the **Rome American Hospital,** Via Emilio Longoni 69 (☎ **06-22-551**), with English-speaking doctors on duty 24 hours. A more personalized service is provided 24 hours by **MEDI-CALL,** Studio Medico, Via Salaria 300, Palazzina C, interno 5 (☎ **06-884-0113;** Bus: 3, 4, or 57). It can arrange for qualified doctors to make a call to your hotel or anywhere in Rome. In most cases, the doctor will be a GP who can refer you to a specialist if needed. Fees begin at around $100 per visit and can go higher if a specialist or specialized treatments are necessary.

Drugstores   A reliable pharmacy is **Farmacia Internazionale,** Piazza Barberini 49 (☎ **06-487-1195;** Metro: Barberini), open day and night. Most pharmacies are open 8:30am to 1pm and 4 to 7:30pm. In general, pharmacies follow a rotation system so several are always open on Sunday.

Electricity   It's generally 220 volts, 50 Hz AC, but you might find 125-volt outlets, with different plugs and sockets for each. Pick up a transformer either before leaving home or in any appliance shop in Rome if you plan to use electrical appliances. Check the exact local current at your hotel. You'll also need an adapter plug.

Embassies/Consulates   The Embassy of the **United States** is at Via Vittorio Veneto 119A (☎ **06-46741;** fax 06-488-2672; Metro: Barberini), open Monday to Friday 8:30am to 12:30pm and 2 to 4:30pm. The consular and passport services are also at Via Vittorio Veneto 119A (same phone); for **Canada,** it's at Via Zara 30 (☎ **06-445-981;** fax 06-4459-8750; Metro: Policlinico), open Monday to Friday from 10am to 12:30pm. For the **United Kingdom,** consular offices are at Via XX Settembre 80A (☎ **06-482-5441;** fax 06-487-3324; Metro: Barberini), open Monday to Friday from 9:15am to 1:30pm. For **Australia,** the embassy is at Via Alessandria 215 (☎ **06-852-721;** fax 06-8527-2300; Metro: Policlinico), open Monday to Thursday from 8:30am to noon and 2 to 4pm, and on Friday from 8:30am to 1:15pm. The Australian consulate is around the corner in the same building at Corso Trieste 25 (☎ **06-852-721**). For **New Zealand,** the consular office is at Via Zara 28 (☎ **06-441-7171;** fax 06-440-2984; Metro: Policlinico), and it's open Monday to Friday from 8:30am to 12:45pm and 1:45 to 5pm. The embassy of **Ireland** in Rome is at Piazza di Campitelli 3 (☎ **06-697-912;** fax 06-679-2354; Bus: 46). For consular queries, dial ☎ **06-6979-1211.** Open Monday to Friday from 9:30am to 12:30pm and 2 to 4pm. The embassy for **South Africa** is at Via Tanaro 14 (☎ **06-852-541;** fax 06-8525-4300; Bus: 56 or 910), open Monday to Friday from 9:30am to 4pm. In case of emergency, embassies have a 24-hour referral service.

Emergencies   Dial ☎ **113** for an ambulance or to call the police; to report a fire, call ☎ **115.**

Eyeglasses   Try **Vasari,** Piazza della Repubblica 61 (☎ **06-488-2240;** Metro: Termini), adjacent to the St. Regis Grand Hotel, a very large shop with lots of choices. They serve wearers of contact lenses and conventional eyeglasses. Open Monday to Tuesday 9:30am to 1pm and 4 to 8pm.

Hospitals   See "Doctors," above.

Hot Lines   Dial ☎ **113,** which is a general SOS, to report any kind of danger, such as rape. You can also dial ☎ **112,** the police emergency number. For an ambulance call ☎ **118.**

Information   See "Visitor Information," earlier in this chapter.

Internet Access   You can log onto the Web in central Rome at **Thenetgate,** Piazza Firenze 25 (☎ **06-689-3445;** Bus: 116). Summer hours are Monday to Saturday 10:30am to 12:30pm and 3:30 to 10:30pm, and winter hours daily 10:40am to 8:30pm. A 20-minute visit costs 5,000 lire ($2.50), with 1 hour (including mailbox) at 10,000 lire ($5). Access is free Saturdays 10:30 to 11am and 2 to 2:30pm. You can kill two birds with one stone just north of Stazione Termini at **Splash,** Via Varese 33 (☎ **06-4938-2073;** Metro: Termini), a do-it-yourself Laundromat (13,000 lire/$6.50 per load, including soap) with a satellite TV and four computers hooked up to the Net (5,000 lire/$2.50 per half hour).

Legal Aid   The consulate of your country is the place to turn. Although consular officials cannot interfere in the Italian legal process, they can inform you of your rights and provide a list of attorneys. You'll have to pay for the attorney out of pocket—there's no free legal assistance. If you're arrested for a drug offense, about all the consulate will do is notify a lawyer and perhaps inform your family.

Liquor Laws   Wine with meals has been a normal part of Italian family life for hundreds of years. There is no legal drinking age for buying or ordering alcohol, and alcohol is sold day and night throughout the year.

Luggage Storage/Lockers   These are available at the Stazione Termini along Tracks 1 and 22 daily from 5am to 1am. The charge is 5,000 lire ($2.50) per piece of luggage per 12-hour period.

Mail   It's easiest just to buy stamps and mail letters and postcards at your hotel's front desk. Stamps (*francobolli*) can also be bought at *tabacchi* (tobacco shops/newsstands). You can buy special stamps at the **Vatican City Post Office,** adjacent to the information office in St. Peter's Square; it's open Monday to Friday 8:30am to 7pm and Saturday 8:30am to 6pm. Letters mailed at Vatican City reach North America far more quickly than does mail sent from within Rome for the same cost.

Newspapers/Magazines   You can get the *International Herald Tribune, USA Today,* the *New York Times,* and *Time* and *Newsweek* magazines at most newsstands. The expatriate magazine (in English) *Wanted in Rome* comes out monthly and lists current events and shows. If you want to try your hand at reading Italian, the Thursday edition of the newspaper *La Repubblica* contains "Trova Roma," a magazine supplement full of cultural and entertainment listings, and *Time Out* now has a Rome edition.

Police   The police hot line number is ☎ **112.** To report a fire or to summon an ambulance, call ☎ **113,** reserved for general SOS calls and for English-speaking members of the state police.

Radio/TV   Major radio and television broadcasts are on RAI, the Italian state radio and TV network. Occasionally during the tourist season it will broadcast special programs in English; look in the radio and TV guide sections of local newspapers. Vatican Radio also carries foreign-language religious news programs, often in English. Shortwave transistor radios pick up broadcasts from the BBC (Britain), Voice of America (United States), and CBC (Canada). More expensive hotels often have TVs in the bedrooms with CNN.

Rest Rooms   Facilities are found near many of the major sights, often with attendants, as are those at bars, clubs, restaurants, cafes, and hotels, plus the airports and the rail station. (There are public rest rooms near the Spanish Steps, or you can stop at the McDonald's there—one of the nicest branches of the golden arches you'll ever see!) You're expected to leave 200 to 500 lire (10¢ to 25¢) for the attendant. It's not a bad idea to carry some tissues in your pocket when you're out and about.

Safety   Pickpocketing is the most common problem. Men should keep their wallets in their front pocket or inside jacket pocket. Purse snatching is also commonplace, with young men on Vespas who'll ride past you and grab your purse. To avoid trouble, stay away from the curb and keep your purse on the wall side of your body and the strap across your chest. Don't lay anything valuable on tables or chairs where it can be grabbed up. Gypsy children have long been a particular menace, though the problem isn't as severe as in years past. If they completely surround you, you'll often virtually have to fight them off. They'll often approach you with pieces of cardboard hiding their stealing hands. Just keep repeating a firm *no!*

Taxes   As a member of the European Union, Italy imposes a **value-added tax** (called **IVA** in Italy) on most goods and services. The tax most affecting visitors is the one imposed on hotel rates, which ranges from 9% in first- and second-class hotels to 19% in deluxe hotels.

Non-EU (European Union) citizens are entitled to a **refund of the IVA** if they spend more than 300,000 lire ($150) at any one store, before tax. To claim your refund, request an invoice from the cashier at the store and take it to the Customs office (*dogana*) at the airport to have it stamped before you leave. *Note:* If you're going to another EU country before flying home, have it stamped at the airport Customs office of the last EU country you'll be in (for example, if you're flying home via Britain, have your Italian invoices stamped in London). Once back home, mail the stamped invoice (keep a photocopy for your records) back to the original vendor within 90 days of the purchase. The vendor will, sooner or later, send you a refund of the tax you paid at the time of your original purchase. Reputable stores view this as a matter of ordinary paperwork and are businesslike about it. Less honorable stores might lose your dossier. It pays to deal with established vendors on large purchases. You can also request that the refund be credited to the credit card with which you made the purchase; this is usually a faster procedure.

Many shops are now part of the **"Tax Free for Tourists"** network (look for the sticker in the window). Stores participating in this network issue a check along with your invoice at the time of purchase. After you have the invoice stamped at Customs, you can redeem the check for cash directly at the Tax Free booth in the airport (past Customs in the Rome airport) or mail it back in the envelope provided within 60 days.

Telephone   A **local phone call** in Italy costs around 220 lire (10¢). **Public phones** accept coins, precharged phone cards (*scheda* or *carta telefonica*), or both. You can buy a *carta telefonica* at any *tabacchi* (tobacconists; most display a sign

Calling Italy

To call Italy from the United States, dial the **international prefix, 011;** then Italy's **country code, 39;** then the city code (**06** for Rome), which is now built into every number; then the actual **phone number.**

Note that numbers in Italy range from four to eight digits in length. Even when you're calling within the same city, you must dial that city's area code—including the zero. A Roman calling another Rome number must dial 06 before the local number.

with a white "T" on a brown background) in increments of 5,000 lire ($2.50), 10,000 lire ($5), and 15,000 lire ($7.50). To make a call, pick up the receiver and insert 200 lire or your card (break off the corner first). Most phones have a digital display that'll tell you how much money you've inserted (or how much is left on the card). Dial the number, and don't forget to take the card with you after you hang up.

To **call from one city code to another,** dial the city code, complete with initial zero, then the number.

To **dial direct internationally,** dial **00,** then the country code, the area code, and the number. **Country codes** are as follows: the United States and Canada 1, the United Kingdom 44, Ireland 353, Australia 61, New Zealand 64. Make international calls from a public phone if possible, because hotels almost invariably charge ridiculously inflated rates for direct dial, but bring plenty of *schede* to feed the phone. Calls dialed directly are billed on the basis of the call's duration only. A reduced rate is applied 11pm to 8am on Monday to Saturday and all day Sunday. Direct-dial calls from the United States to Italy are much cheaper, so arrange for whomever to call you at your hotel.

Italy has recently introduced a series of **international phone cards** (*scheda telefonica internazionale*) for calling overseas. They come in increments of 50 (12,500 lire/$6.25, 100 (25,000 lire/$12.50), 200 (50,000 lire/$25), and 400 (100,000 lire/$50) *unita* (units), and they're usually available at tabacchi and bars. Each *unita* is worth 250 lire (15¢) of phone time; it costs 5 *unita* (1,250 lire/65¢) per minute to call within Europe or to the United States or Canada and 12 *unita* (3,000 lire/$1.50) per minute to call Australia or New Zealand. You don't insert this card into the phone; merely dial ☎ **1740,** then "*2" for instructions in English when prompted.

To call for free **national telephone information** (in Italian) in Italy, dial ☎ **12. International information** is available at ☎ **176** but costs 1,200 lire (60¢) a shot.

To make **collect or calling card calls,** drop in 200 lire (10¢) or insert your card, dial one of the numbers below, and an American operator will be on shortly to assist you (as Italy has yet to discover the joys of the touch-tone phone, you'll have to wait for the operator to come on). The following calling-card numbers work all over Italy: **AT&T ☎ 172-1011, MCI ☎ 172-1022, Sprint ☎ 172-1877.** To make collect calls to a country besides the United States, dial ☎ **170** (free) and practice your Italian counting in order to relay the number to the Italian operator. Tell him or her you want it *a carico del destinatario.*

Don't count on all Italian phones having touch-tone service! You may not be able to access your voice mail or answering machine if you call home from Italy.

Time   In terms of standard time zones, Italy is 6 hours ahead of eastern standard time in the United States. Daylight saving time goes into effect in Italy each year from the end of March to the end of September.

Tipping   This custom is practiced with flair in Italy—many people depend on tips for their livelihoods. In **hotels,** the service charge of 15% to 19% is already added to a bill. In addition, it's customary to tip the chambermaid 1,000 lire (50¢) per day; the doorman (for calling a cab) 1,000 lire (50¢); and the bellhop or porter 3,000 to 5,000 lire ($1.50 to $2.50) for carrying your bags to your room. A concierge expects about 15% of his or her bill, as well as tips for extra services performed, which could include help with long-distance calls. In expensive hotels these lire amounts are often doubled.

In **restaurants and cafes,** 15% is usually added to your bill to cover most charges. If you're not sure whether this has been done, ask *"È incluso il servizio?"* (ay een-*cloo*-soh eel sair-*vee*-tsoh?). An additional tip isn't expected, but it's nice to leave the equivalent of an extra couple of dollars if you've been pleased with the service. Checkroom attendants expect 1,500 lire (75¢), and washroom attendants should get 500 to 700 lire (25¢ to 35¢). Restaurants are required by law to give customers official receipts.

Taxi drivers expect at least 15% of the fare.

Water   Though most Italians take mineral water with their meals, tap water is safe everywhere, as are public drinking fountains. Unsafe sources will be marked ACQUA NON POTABILE. If tap water comes out cloudy, it's only the calcium or other minerals inherent in a water supply that often comes untreated from fresh springs.

4 Accommodations

The good news is that Rome's hotels are in better shape than they've been in years; dozens upon dozens of properties have undergone major renovations.

The bad news is that with the huge surge in tourism the city has experienced in the last couple of years, finding a hotel room at any time of the year is harder than ever. *Make your reservations as far ahead as possible*—we're talking months here, especially in the last few months of the Jubilee! If you like to gamble and arrive without a reservation, head quickly to the **airport information desk** or, once you get into town, to the offices of **Enjoy Rome** (see "Visitor Information" in section 1 of chapter 3)—their staff can help reserve you a room, if any are available.

Rome's poshest hotels are among the most luxurious in Europe. The bulk of this chapter, however, concerns moderately priced hotels, where you'll find comfortable, charming lodgings with private bathrooms. Even our inexpensive choices are clean and cheerful, and they offer more in services and facilities than you might expect from the prices. In the less expensive categories, you'll find a few *pensiones,* the Roman equivalent of a boardinghouse.

The Italian government controls the prices of its hotels, designating a minimum and a maximum rate. The difference between the two may depend on the season, the location of the room, and even its size. The government also classifies hotels with star ratings that indicate their category of comfort: five stars for deluxe, four for first class, three for second class, two for third class, and one for fourth class. Most former pensiones are now rated as one- or two-star hotels. The distinction between a pensione hotel (where some degree of board was once required along with the room) and a regular hotel is no longer officially made, although many smaller, family-run establishments still call themselves pensiones. Government ratings don't depend on sensitivity of decoration or frescoed ceilings, but on facilities, such as elevators and the like. Many of the finest hotels in Rome have a lower rating because they serve only breakfast.

In Rome, B&Bs are common, and they offer the best accommodation value. Finding a suitable one, however, may be tricky. Often B&Bs are family homes or apartments, so don't count on hotel services or even private bathrooms. Sometimes, however, B&Bs are in beautiful private homes, lovely guest houses, or restored mansions. Prices range from $35 to $65 or more per person nightly, including breakfast. Sometimes you can arrange to order an evening meal. Tourist offices and the Web sites listed in the online directory on p. 32 can help you find even more options than we can list in this guide.

All the hotels listed serve breakfast (often a buffet with coffee, fruit, rolls, and cheese), but you can't take for granted that it's included in the room rate. That used to be universal, but it's not anymore, so check the listing carefully and ask the hotel to confirm what's included.

Nearly all hotels are heated in the cooler months, but not all are air-conditioned in summer, which can be vitally important during a stifling July or August. The deluxe and first-class ones are, but after that it's a toss-up. Be sure to check the listing carefully before you book a stay in the dog days of summer!

All Italian hotels impose an IVA (Imposta sul Valore Aggiunto), or value-added tax. This tax is in effect throughout the European Union countries. It replaces some 20 other taxes and is an effort to streamline the tax structure. What does this mean for you? A higher hotel bill. Deluxe hotels will slap you with a whopping 13% tax, whereas first-class, second-class, and other hotels will impose a mere 9%. Most hotels will quote a rate inclusive of this tax, but others prefer to add it on when you go to pay the bill. To avoid unpleasant surprises, ask to be quoted an all-inclusive rate—that is, with service, even a continental breakfast (which is often obligatory)—when you check in.

See "Best Hotel Bets" in chapter 1 for a quick-reference list of our favorite hotels in a variety of categories. See also "The Neighborhoods in Brief" in chapter 3 for a quick summary of each area that will help you decide if you'd like to stay there.

1 Near Stazione Termini

VERY EXPENSIVE

Empire Palace Hotel. Via Aureliana 39, 00187 Roma. ☎ **06-421-281.** Fax 06-4212-8400. www.empirepalacehotel.com. E-mail: gold@empirepalacehotel.com. 115 units. A/C MINIBAR TV TEL. 610,000 lire ($305) double; 910,000 lire ($455) suite. Rates include breakfast. AE, DC, MC, V. Metro: Repubblica or Termini.

Like many of its nearby competitors, this hotel combines a historic core (in this case, a palazzo built around 1870) with modern amenities that, jointly, create a very comfortable and appealing ambience. The exterior's vaguely Gothic theme derived from the original builders, an aristocratic Venetian family who requested an astral theme (i.e., ceiling frescoes showing the heavens) in azure blue on some of the ceilings. Some of the striking combinations of the original core with unusual modern paintings are show-stoppers. Opened as a hotel in 1999, it's classified four stars by the Italian government. Bedrooms have marble bathrooms, conservative and traditional-looking cherrywood furnishings, and textured fabrics of blue and off-white with touches of gold.

Dining/Diversions: The building's courtyard is outfitted with a splashing fountain and a verdant garden. Immediately adjacent, with tables spilling into the courtyard during clement weather, is the Aureliano Restaurant, which is outfitted with Murano chandeliers and lots of pale, full-grained paneling. It's open Monday to Saturday for both lunch and dinner. There's also an American-style bar on the premises.

Amenities: Concierge, room service, laundry/valet, baby-sitting.

Mecenate Palace Hotel. Via Carlo Alberto 3, 00185 Roma. ☎ **06-4470-2024.** Fax 06-446-1354. www.mecenatepalace.com. E-mail: info@mecenate.com. 62 units. A/C MINIBAR TV TEL. 600,000 lire ($300) double; 1,400,000 lire ($700) suite. Rates include buffet breakfast. AE, DC, MC, V. Parking 45,000 lire ($22.50). Metro: Termini or Vittorio Emanuele.

The hotel is composed of two adjacent buildings. One of them was designed by Rinaldi in 1887, the second one (on Via Carlo Alberto) much later on. The hotel rises five floors above a neighborhood near the rail station. The pastel-colored guest rooms, where traces of the original detailing mix with contemporary furnishings, overlook the city rooftops or Santa Maria Maggiore. They range from small to medium but boast high ceilings and extras like private safes and luxury mattresses. The marble bathrooms are sumptuous—with makeup mirrors, hair dryers, and deluxe toiletries. Bedrooms range from medium to large in size. The three suites are named after the poets/philosophers Virgilio, Orazio, and Properzio, and they offer superior comfort, authentic 19th-century antiques, and a fireplace.

Dining/Diversions: The hotel's formal La Terraza Papi restaurant serves a refined Italian cuisine every day except Sunday. There's also a bar, Caffè di Papa Sisto, and a roof garden with sweeping views over the rooftops.

Amenities: Concierge, room service, dry cleaning/laundry, twice-daily maid service, baby-sitting, secretarial services.

✪ St. Regis Grand. Via Vittorio Emanuele Orlando 3, 00185 Roma. ☎ **06-47-091.** Fax 06-474-7307. www.luxurycollection.com. 170 units. A/C MINIBAR TV TEL. 1,210,000–1,265,000 lire ($605–$632.50) double; from 2,970,000 lire ($1,485) suite. AE, DC, MC, V. Parking 50,000–60,000 lire ($25–$30). Metro: Repubblica.

When César Ritz founded this outrageously expensive hotel in 1894, it was the first to offer a private bathroom and two electric lights in every room. Today, it has been vastly improved following a $35 million restoration. Restored to its former glory, it is a magnificent Roman palazzo in the heart of the city, combining Italian and French styles in decoration and furnishings. The lobby is decked out with Murano chandeliers, columns, and marble busts and cherubs. Guest rooms, most of which are exceedingly spacious, are luxuriously furnished with everything from sumptuous mattresses to Murano chandeliers. Hand-painted frescoes are installed above each headboard, and the bathrooms are done in fabulous marble.

Dining/Diversions: The formal restaurant, Vivendo, serves a refined international and Italian cuisine, one of the most elegant hotel dining rooms in Rome with superior food and deluxe service. There is also the less formal Grand Hall Café, plus Rome's most elegant hotel bar, the aptly named Le Grand Bar.

Amenities: 24-hour butler service, fitness center, massage rooms, laundry/valet, baby-sitting.

EXPENSIVE

Hotel Artemide. Via Nazionale 22, 00184 Roma. ☎ **06-489-911.** Fax 06-4899-1700. www.travel.it/roma/artemide/artemide.html. E-mail: hotel.artemide@agora.it. 79 units. A/C MINIBAR TV TEL. 490,000–540,000 lire ($245–$270) double; 630,000 lire ($315) suite. Rates include breakfast. AE, MC, DC, V. Parking 30,000 lire ($15). Metro: Piazza Repubblica.

The Artemide was transformed from a 19th-century palazzetto into a four-star hotel. Near the train station, it combines stylish simplicity with modern comforts against a backdrop of art nouveau motifs. The original stained-glass skylight dome was retained in the lobby. The guest rooms are furnished in natural colors and have good furnishings, like elegantly comfortable beds, and such extras as safes and spacious marble bathrooms with hair dryers. No-smoking units are available.

Dining/Diversions: Caffè Caffeteria Nazionale serves a Mediterranean cuisine along with light buffets for both dinner and lunch, afternoon tea, and mid-afternoon snacks. There's also an American bar open daily from 7am to midnight.

Amenities: Concierge, room service, laundry/dry cleaning.

Accommodations Near Via Veneto & Termini

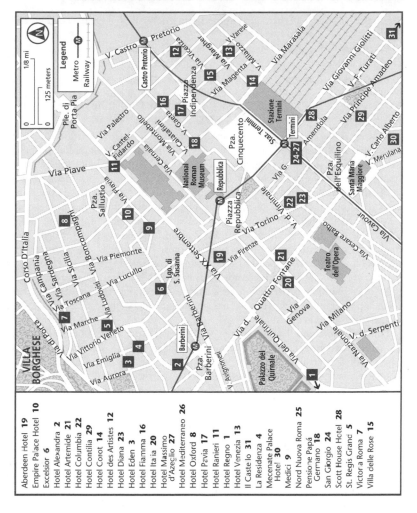

Legend
Ⓜ Metro
Railway

Aberdeen Hotel **19**
Empire Palace Hotel **10**
Excelsior **6**
Hotel Alexandra **21**
Hotel Artemide **22**
Hotel Columbia **29**
Hotel Contilia **14**
Hotel Corot **14**
Hotel des Artistes **12**
Hotel Diana **23**
Hotel Eden **3**
Hotel Fiamma **16**
Hotel Ita ia **20**
Hotel Massimo d'Azeclio **27**
Hotel Mediterraneo **26**
Hotel Oxford **8**
Hotel Pevia **17**
Hotel Ranieri **11**
Hotel Regno **1**
Hotel Venezia **13**
Il Caste lo **31**
La Residenza **4**
Mecenate Palace Hotel **30**
Medici **9**
Nord Nuova Roma **25**
Pensione Papà Germano **18**
San Giorgio **24**
Scott House Hctel **28**
St. Regis Granc **5**
Victor a Roma **7**
Villa delle Rose **15**

Hotel Massimo d'Azeglio. Via Cavour 18, 00184 Roma. ☎ **800/783-6904** in the U.S., or 06-487-0270. Fax 06-482-7386. www.bettojahotels.it. E-mail: hb@bettojahotels.it. 198 units. A/C MINIBAR TV TEL. 475,000 lire ($237.50) double. Rates include breakfast. DC, MC, V. Parking 35,000–45,000 lire ($17.50–$22.50). Metro: Termini.

This up-to-date hotel was opened as a small restaurant by one of the founders of an Italian hotel dynasty more than a century ago. During World War II, it was a refuge for the king of Serbia and a favorite with Italian generals. Today, this centrally located hotel is the flagship of the Bettoja chain. Run by Angelo Bettoja and his charming wife, it offers a well-trained staff. The rooms are brighter and better furnished than those at the Mediterraneo nearby. Each is tasteful, with parquet floors, 18th-century reproductions, and generously sized beds. Extras include bedside controls, double-glazed windows, marble bathrooms (more than half with tubs), hair dryers, and thick towels. The hotel boasts one of the area's most elegant neoclassical facades.

Dining: For many decades, the hotel restaurant, Massimo d'Azeglio, was a neighborhood fixture. It's no longer *the* place to go around here, but if you're too tired to venture out, it's still a safe bet for good food with market-fresh ingredients. There's also a bar.

Amenities: Concierge, 24-hour room service, dry cleaning/laundry, baby-sitting, car-rental desk.

Hotel Mediterraneo. Via Cavour 15, 00184 Roma. ☎ **800/223-9832** in the U.S., or 06-488-4051. Fax 06-474-4105. www.bettojahotels.it. E-mail: hb@bettojahotels.it. 274 units. A/C MINIBAR TV TEL. 520,000 lire ($260) double; from 580,000 lire ($290) suite. Rates include buffet breakfast. AE, DC, MC, V. Parking 35,000 lire ($17.50). Metro: Termini.

The Mediterraneo sports vivid Italian art deco styling. Because it's beside what Mussolini planned as his triumphant passageway through Rome, local building codes were violated and approval was granted for the creation of this 10-floor hotel. Its height, coupled with its position on one of Rome's hills, provides panoramic views from the most expensive rooms on the highest floors (some with lovely terraces) and from its roof garden/bar (open May to October), which is especially charming at night.

Mario Loreti, one of Mussolini's favorite architects, designed an interior sheathing of gray marble, the richly allegorical murals of inlaid wood, and the art deco friezes ringing the ceilings of the enormous public rooms. The lobby is also decorated with antique busts of Roman emperors. Recent renovations have upgraded the guest rooms, most in art deco and all with comfortable mattresses and bedside controls, and the large marble bathrooms offer hair dryers. The most luxurious accommodations are the seven top-floor suites (even the phones are antique). Double glazing and excellent maintenance are other pluses.

Dining/Diversions: Though it's not well known, the hotel restaurant, Ristorante 21, serves excellent and affordable Roman and Italian cuisine. The gracefully curved bar is crafted from illuminated cut crystal. La Cantina in the cellar is ideal for a romantic dinner, and La Terrazza on the top floor serves lovely cocktails.

Amenities: Concierge, room service, dry cleaning/laundry, baby-sitting, car-rental desk.

San Giorgio. Via Giovanni Amendola 61, 00185 Roma. ☎ **800/783-6904** in the U.S., or 06-482-7341. Fax 06-488-3191. www.bettohahotels.it. E-mail: hb@bettojahotels.it. 186 units. A/C MINIBAR TV TEL. 400,000 lire ($200) double; from 570,000 lire ($285) suite. Rates include breakfast. AE, DC, MC, V. Parking 35,000–45,000 lire ($17.50–$22.50). Metro: Termini.

A four-star hotel built in 1940, the San Giorgio is constantly being improved by its founders, the Bettoja family (it was the first air-conditioned hotel in Rome, and is now also soundproof). The hotel is ideal for families, as many of its corner rooms can accommodate extra people. Behind wood-veneer doors, the bedrooms are middle of the road—clean, well maintained, and functional. All units are spacious except some on the upper floor.

Dining/Diversions: Breakfast is served in a light and airy room, and the staff is most attentive. The hotel doesn't have a restaurant of its own, but sends guests to its sibling hotels (both described elsewhere in this chapter), the Massimo d'Azeglio or the nearby Hotel Mediterraneo, with its summer-only roof garden and cafe.

Amenities: Car-rental desk, concierge, room service, dry cleaning/laundry, baby-sitting.

MODERATE

Aberdeen Hotel. Via Firenze 48, 00184 Roma. ☎ **06-482-3920.** Fax 06-482-1092. www.travel.it/aberdeen/rome. E-mail: hotel.aberdeen@travel.it. 36 units. A/C MINIBAR TV TEL. 300,000 lire ($150) double. Rates include buffet breakfast. AE, DC, MC, V. Parking 40,000 lire ($20). Metro: Repubblica. Bus: 64 or 170.

This completely renovated hotel near the opera and the train station is in a fairly safe area—in front of the Ministry of Defense. The guest rooms, ranging from small to medium, were renovated in 1998, with new Italian mattresses added to all the comfortable beds, usually queen size or twins. The marble bathrooms are rather small but nicely appointed, each with a hair dryer. The breakfast buffet is the only meal served, but many inexpensive trattorie lie nearby.

Hotel Columbia. Via del Viminale 15, 00184 Roma. ☎ **06-474-4289** or 06-488-3509. Fax 06-474-0209. www.venere.it/roma/columbia. E-mail: columbia@flashnet.it. 45 units. A/C MINIBAR TV TEL. 325,000–345,000 lire ($162.50–$172.50) double. Rates include buffet breakfast. AE, DC, MC, V. Parking nearby 35,000 lire ($17.50). Metro: Repubblica.

This is one of the train station neighborhood's newest hotels, a three-star choice with a hardworking multilingual staff. It's a well-done radical renovation (1997) of a hotel built around 1900. The interior contains Murano chandeliers and conservatively modern furniture. The guest rooms are compact and cozy and can hold their own with some of the best of the three-star hotels nearby. Each contains a comfortable bed with a quality mattress and fine linen, plus a tiled bathroom with medium-sized towels and adequate shelf space. The appealing roof garden has a bar and a view over surrounding rooftops.

Under the same management, on the opposite side of the rail station, is the Columbia's sibling, the **Hotel Venezia** (below), which sometimes accommodates the Columbia's overflow.

Hotel des Artistes. Via Villafranca 20, 00185 Roma. ☎ **06-445-4365.** Fax 06-446-2368. www.hoteldesartistes.com. E-mail: info@hoteldesartistes.com. 45 units. TV TEL. 260,000–270,000 lire ($130–$135) double; 320,000–330,000 lire ($160–$165) triple; 380,000–390,000 lire ($190–$195) quad. Rates include buffet breakfast. AE, DC, MC, V. Parking 25,000–35,000 lire ($12.50–$17.50) nearby. Metro: Castro Pretorio. Bus: 310.

This no-smoking hotel was completely renewed in 1997. A few steps from Termini Station, it offers good quality accommodation at a moderate price. One part of the hotel is a hostel with dormitory-style rooms with bathrooms in the corridors, and a TV in each room; rates for those accommodations range from 170,000 lire ($85) for a triple to 220,000 lire ($110) for a quad. Regular rooms range from small to medium in size, some of them decorated with Oriental rugs. The furniture is simple but classic and the maid service is excellent. The hotel's rooms have private bathrooms, small but neat and just renovated, offering hair dryers and small shower stalls. Breakfast is the only meal served, but an intimate bar is open daily from 7am to 2am. The roof garden, open 24 hours, is an ideal place to socialize with other visitors or local people as well.

Amenities include a concierge; baby-sitting; car, scooter, and bicycle rental; plus tour desk.

Hotel Diana. Via Principe Amedeo 4, 00185 Roma. ☎ **06-482-7541.** Fax 06-486-998. www.hoteldianaroma.com. E-mail: diana@venere.it. 186 units. A/C MINIBAR TV TEL. 330,000 lire ($165) double; 450,000 lire ($225) suite. Rates include breakfast. AE, DC, MC, V. Parking 35,000 lire ($17.50).

In the heart of 19th-century Rome, the Diana has been totally renovated in an inviting art deco style, recapturing its early 1900s heyday. It offers an elegant yet comfortable atmosphere, as evoked by the spacious lobby and welcoming lounges. The guest rooms are tastefully furnished in floral fabrics, the walls covered in English-style striped tapestry in soft greens and creamy tones. The beds boast luxury mattresses and first-rate linens. The bathrooms are tiled with attractive ceramics, offering hair dryers and heated towel racks. No-smoking units are available. Amenities include concierge, room service, and laundry/dry cleaning.

The hotel's restaurant offers a menu of classic Italian dishes and daily seasonal specialties. The American Bar in summer moves to the rooftop terrace, where lunch and dinner can be served; shaded by tents and surrounded by plants, you'll have sweeping views over the ancient roofs.

Hotel Fiamma. Via Gaeta 61, 00185 Roma. ☎ **06-481-8436.** Fax 06-488-3511. www.travel.it/roma/ianr. E-mail: fiamma.travel@travel.it. 78 units. A/C MINIBAR TV TEL. 300,000–320,000 lire ($150–$160) double. Rates include breakfast. AE, DC, MC, V. Parking 35,000 lire ($17.50) nearby. Metro: Termini.

On the far side of the Baths of Diocletian, the Fiamma is in a renovated building, with five floors of shuttered windows and a ground floor faced with marble and plate-glass windows. The hotel is an enduring favorite, if a bit past its prime. The lobby is long and bright, filled with a varied collection of furnishings, like overstuffed chairs and blue enamel railings. On the same floor is an austere marble breakfast room. Some of the comfortably furnished guest rooms, ranging from small to medium-sized, are air-conditioned. The mattresses are a bit worn but still comfortable, and the small bathrooms are tiled, with adequate shelf space.

Hotel Ranieri. Via XX Settembre 43, 00187 Roma. ☎ **06-420-145-31.** Fax 06-420-145-43. www.hotelranieri.com. E-mail: hotel.ranieri@italyhotel.com. 47 units. A/C MINIBAR TV TEL. 220,000–300,000 lire ($110–$150) double. Rates include breakfast. AE, DC, MC, V. Parking 30,000–45,000 lire ($15–$22.50). Metro: Repubblica.

The Ranieri is a winning three-star hotel in a restored old building. The guest rooms received a substantial renovation in 1995, adding new furniture, carpets, wall coverings, and even new bathrooms. They're a bit small but reasonably comfortable for two persons, with mattresses that are still firm. The bathrooms aren't very big but are well equipped with hair dryers. The public rooms, the lounge, and the dining room are attractively decorated, in part with contemporary art. You can arrange for a home-cooked meal in the dining room, offering five different fixed-price menus ranging from 30,000 to 50,000 lire ($15 to $25) per person.

✪ **Hotel Venezia.** Via Varese 18 (near Via Marghera), 00185 Roma. ☎ **06-445-7101.** Fax 06-495-7687. www.hotelvenezia.com. E-mail: info@hotelvenezia.com. 61 units. A/C MINIBAR TV TEL. 325,000–345,000 lire ($162.50–$172.50) double; 465,000 lire ($232.50) triple. Rates include buffet breakfast. AE, DC, MC, V. Parking 35,000 lire ($17.50). Metro: Termini.

Just when you've decided the whole city was full of overpriced hotels, the cheerful Venezia will restore your faith in affordable rooms. The location is good—3 blocks from the rail station, in a relatively quiet business/residential area with a few old villas. Its public rooms are charming. Some guest rooms are furnished in 17th-century style, though a few are beginning to look worn (the last renovation was in 1991); the rest are in modern style. All units are spacious, boasting Murano chandeliers, first-rate beds and mattresses, and bathrooms with hair dryers; some have balconies for surveying the street action. The management really cares, and the helpful staff speaks English.

Medici. Via Flavia 96, 00187 Roma. ☎ **06-482-7319.** Fax 06-474-0767. www. hotelmedici.com. 69 units. MINIBAR TV TEL. 260,000–330,000 lire ($130–$165) double. Rates include breakfast. AE, DC, MC, V. Parking 35,000–40,000 lire ($17.50–$20). Metro: Piazza della Repubblica.

The Medici, built in 1906, is near the rail station and the shops along Via XX Settembre. Many of its better guest rooms overlook an inner patio garden with Roman columns and benches. All rooms were renovated in 1997 in classic Roman style, with a generous use of antiques and first-class Italian mattresses. The cheapest are a good buy, for they're only slightly smaller than the others (but they have older furnishings and no air-conditioning). The bathrooms are small but well organized, and hair dryers are available on request. Breakfast is the only meal served.

Nord Nuova Roma. Via Giovanni Amendola 3, 00185 Roma. ☎ **800/223-9832** in the U.S., or 06-488-5441. Fax 06-481-7163. www.bettojahotels.it. 158 units. A/C MINIBAR TV TEL. 320,000 lire ($160) double. Rates include breakfast. AE, DC, MC, V. Parking 35,000–45,000 lire ($17.50–$22.50). Metro: Termini or Repubblica.

Although rather plain, this is the best bargain in the Bettoja chain and a good choice for families. This hotel was built in 1935; it's in a convenient position near Stazione Termini and the Baths of Diocletian. Rooms are quite spacious and bright. The standard rooms range from small to spacious and are well furnished, though the pieces are often aging. Nonetheless, the beds are comfortable, most often twins or doubles. Each bathroom is fairly roomy. You can arrange a savory lunch or dinner at the nearby Massimo d'Azeglio Restaurant, and there's an intimate bar.

Villa delle Rose. Via Vicenza 5, 00185 Roma. ☎ **06-445-1788.** Fax 06-445-1639. www.venere.it/roma/villadellerose. E-mail: villadellerose@flashnet.it. 37 units. TV TEL. 180,000–300,000 lire ($90–$150) double. Rates include continental breakfast. AE, DC, MC, V. Free parking (only 4 cars). Metro: Termini or Castro Pretorio.

Less than 2 blocks north of the rail station, this hotel began in the late 1800s as a villa with a dignified cut-stone facade inspired by the Renaissance. Despite many renovations, the ornate trappings of the original are still visible, like the lobby's Corinthian-capped marble columns and the flagstone-covered terrace filling part of the verdant back garden. Much of the interior has been recently redecorated and upgraded with traditional wall coverings, new carpets, new mattresses, and tiled bathrooms. Breakfasts in the garden do a lot to add country flavor to an otherwise very urban and noisy location. The English-speaking staff is helpful and tactful.

INEXPENSIVE

Hotel Contilia. Via Principe Amadeo 79d–81, 00185 Roma. ☎ **06-446-6942.** Fax 06-446-6904. E-mail: contilia@tin.it. 40 units. A/C TV TEL. 150,000–300,000 lire ($75–$150) double. Rates include breakfast. AE, DC, MC, V. Parking 30,000 lire ($15); free on street. Metro: Termini.

As the automatic doors part to reveal a stylish marble lobby with Persian rugs and antiques, you might step back to double-check the address. The popular old-fashioned Pensione Tony Contilia of yesteryear has taken over this building's other small hotels and upgraded itself into one of the best choices in the neighborhood. The guest rooms have been redone in modern midscale comfort, with perfectly firm beds and built-in units. The double-glazed windows keep out traffic noise, and the rooms overlooking the cobblestone courtyard are even more quiet. Oddly, the smallish contemporary bathrooms lack shower curtains.

Hotel Corot. Via Marghera 15–17, 00185 Roma. ☎ **06-4470-0900.** Fax 06-4470-0905. www.venere.it/roma/corot. E-mail: hotel.corot@mclink.it. 28 units. A/C MINIBAR TV TEL. 190,000–230,000 lire ($95–$115) double; 240,000–270,000 lire ($120–$135) triple; 250,000–300,000 lire ($125–$150) quad. Rates include breakfast. AE, DC, MC, V. Parking 30,000 lire ($15) for 1st night, 19,000 lire ($9.50) for the 2nd. Metro: Termini.

This modernized hotel (renovated in 1997) occupies the second and third floors of an early 1900s building that contains a handful of apartments and another, somewhat inferior hotel. The Corot is a safe, if not thrilling, bet north of the train station. You register in a small paneled street-level area, then take an elevator to your high-ceilinged guest room. Each room has simple but traditional furniture, including a good bed, and a modern bathroom with a hair dryer. There's a bar near a sunny window in one of the public rooms.

Hotel Italia. Via Venezia 18, 00184 Roma. ☎ **06-482-8355.** Fax 06-474-5550. www.hotelitaliaroma.com. E-mail: hitalia@pronet.it. 31 units. TV TEL. 200,000 lire ($100) double. Rates include buffet breakfast. AE, DC, MC, V. Parking nearby 25,000–40,000 lire ($12.50–$20). Metro: Repubblica. Bus: 64.

This turn-of-the-century building and its eight-room annex across the street have functioned as a hotel for at least 20 years, but have never been as well managed as they are now under the stewardship of the Valentini family. Both buildings employ a night porter/security guard, and both offer their guests a breakfast buffet that's one of the most appealing in the neighborhood—it even includes pizza. Midsize bedrooms are well maintained, are conservatively decorated with comfortable, yet simple, furniture and often have parquet floors. Eleven rooms are equipped with air-conditioning. Only one room (no. 6) doesn't have direct access to its bathroom, although a full bathroom that's reserved for the exclusive use of room no. 6 lies just across the hallway. All other rooms in the hotel have direct access to a private bathroom.

Hotel Pavia. Via Gaeta 83, 00185 Roma. ☎ **06-483-801.** Fax 06-481-9090. www.travel.it/roma/hotelpavia. E-mail: hotelpavia@hotmail.com. 25 units. A/C MINIBAR TV TEL. 250,000 lire ($125) double. Rates include breakfast. AE, DC, MC, V. Parking 25,000 lire ($12.50). Metro: Termini.

The Pavia, in a much-renovated 100-year-old villa, is a popular choice on this quiet street near the gardens of the Baths of Diocletian. You take a wisteria-covered passage to reach the recently modernized reception area and tasteful public rooms, where the staff is friendly. The front guest rooms tend to be noisy, but that's the curse of all Termini hotels. All the rooms are comfortable and fairly attractive, with mattresses that've just been replaced. The maids keep everything beautifully maintained, including the medium-sized bathrooms with new plumbing and hair dryers. You don't get grand style, but the quality of the rooms makes this an exceptional bargain.

Il Castello. Via Vittorio Amedo II, no. 9, 00185 Roma. ☎ **06-7720-4036.** Fax 06-7049-0068. www.ilcastello.com. E-mail: info@ilcastello.com. 18 units, 3 with private bathroom. TEL. 100,000 lire ($50) double without bathroom; 160,000 lire ($80) double with bathroom. MC, V. Metro: Manzoni.

Simple, unassuming, and often filled with backpackers, this three-floor hotel was built in the 1950s. It has a small garden, and well-scrubbed, no-frills rooms. You don't get anything fancy—just good value, a clean bed, and a bit more space, at least in some of the rooms, than you might have expected.

✪ **Pensione Papà Germano.** Via Calatafimi 14A, 00185 Roma. ☎ **06-486-919.** Fax 06-478-81281. www.hotelpapagermano.it. E-mail: info@hotelpapagermano.it. 17 units, 7 with private bathroom. TV TEL. 70,000–90,000 lire ($35–$45) double without bathroom, 110,000–140,000 lire ($55–$70) double with bathroom; 100,000 lire ($50) triple without bathroom, 150,000 lire ($75) triple with bathroom. AE, DC, MC, V. Metro: Termini.

Papà Germano is about as basic as anything in this book, but it's clean and decent. This 1892 building, on a block-long street immediately east of the Baths of Diocletian, has undergone some recent renovations, yet retains its modest ambience. The pensione offers clean accommodations with plain furniture, good mattresses, hair dryers, and well-maintained showers, and you'll find a high-turnover crowd of European and North American students. The energetic English-speaking owner, Gino Germano, offers advice on sightseeing. No breakfast is served, but dozens of cafes nearby open early.

Scott House Hotel. Via Gioberti 30, 00185 Roma. ☎ **06-446-5379.** Fax 06-446-4986. www.scotthouse.com. 36 units. A/C TV TEL. 150,000–170,000 lire ($75–$85) double. Rate includes breakfast. AE, DC, MC, V. Metro: Termini.

Simple but adequate for anyone who's not too high-maintenance, this hotel occupies the fourth and fifth floors of a building originally constructed in the 18th-century. Bedrooms are high-ceilinged, freshly painted, and compact; most have comfortable beds and at least one upholstered armchair. Each was completely renovated and freshened up in 1999.

2 Near Via Veneto & Piazza Barberini

To locate the hotels in this section, see the "Accommodations Near Via Veneto & Termini" map on p. 61.

VERY EXPENSIVE
The Excelsior. Via Vittorio Veneto 125, 00187 Roma. ☎ **800/325-3589** in the U.S., or 06-47-081. Fax 06-482-6205. www.luxurycollection.com. 321 units. A/C MINIBAR TV TEL. 700,000–800,000 lire ($350–$400) double; 1,350,000–2,400,000 lire ($675–$1,200) suite. AE, DC, DISC, MC, V. Parking 70,000 lire ($35). Metro: Piazza Barberini.

If money is no object, here's a good place to spend it. This limestone palace's baroque corner tower, looking over the U.S. Embassy, is a landmark in Rome. You enter a string of cavernous reception rooms with thick rugs, marble floors, gilded garlands decorating the walls, and Empire furniture. Everything looks just a tad dowdy today, but The Excelsior endures, seemingly as eternal as Rome itself. In no small part that's because of the exceedingly hospitable staff.

The guest rooms come in two varieties: new (the result of a major renovation) and traditional. The old ones are a bit worn, while the newer ones have more imaginative color schemes and plush carpeting. All are spacious and elegantly furnished, always with deluxe mattresses and often with antiques and silk curtains. Most rooms are unique, though many have sumptuous Hollywood-style marble bathrooms with hair dryers and bidets.

Dining/Diversions: The Excelsior Bar (daily 10:30am to 1am) is the most famous on Via Vittorio Veneto, and La Cupola is known for its national and regional cuisine, with spa cuisine and kosher food prepared on request. The Gran Caffè Doney, with sidewalk tables, is a perfect place for excellent drinks, appetizers, and Sunday brunch.

Amenities: Room service, laundry/valet, baby-sitting, beauty salon, barbershop.

✪ **Hotel Eden.** Via Ludovisi 49, 00187 Roma. ☎ **800/225-5843** in the U.S., or 06-478-121. Fax 06-482-1584. www.hotel-eden.it. E-mail: reservations@hotel-eden.it. 119 units. A/C MINIBAR TV TEL. From 1,100,000 lire ($550) double; from 2,600,000 lire ($1,300) suite. AE, DC, MC, V. Parking 50,000 lire ($25). Metro: Piazza Barberini.

For several generations after its 1889 opening, this hotel near the top of the Spanish Steps reigned over one of the world's most stylish shopping neighborhoods. Hemingway, Callas, Ingrid Bergman, Fellini—all checked in during its heyday. It was bought by Trusthouse Forte in 1989 and reopened in 1994 after 2 years (and $20 million) of renovations that enhanced its grandeur and added the amenities its five-star status calls for. The Eden's hilltop position guarantees a panoramic city view from most guest rooms, and its rates guarantee that all those rooms are elegantly appointed and spacious, with a decor harking back to the late 19th century, plus marble-sheathed bathrooms with deluxe toiletries and makeup mirrors. Amenities include fax machines, dual-line phones with data ports, safes, TVs with VCRs, and ample closet space. Some of the front rooms open onto balconies with views of Rome.

Dining/Diversions: There is a piano bar and a glamorous restaurant, La Terrazza (see chapter 5).

Amenities: Concierge, 24-hour room service, dry cleaning/laundry, newspaper delivery on request, secretarial service (prior notification), gym and health club.

EXPENSIVE

Hotel Alexandra. Via Vittorio Veneto 18, 00187 Roma. ☎ **06-488-1943.** Fax 06-487-1804. www.venere.it/roma/alexandra. E-mail: alexandra@venere.it. 64 units. A/C MINI-BAR TV TEL. 390,000 lire ($195) double; 600,000 lire ($300) suite. Rates include buffet breakfast. AE, DC, MC, V. Parking 30,000 lire ($15). Metro: Piazza Barberini.

This is one of your few chances to stay on Via Veneto without going broke (though it's not exactly cheap). Set behind the dignified stone facade of what was a 19th-century mansion, the Alexandra offers immaculate guest rooms. Those facing the front are exposed to roaring traffic and street life; those in back are quieter but with less of a view. The rooms range from rather cramped to medium-sized, but each has been recently redecorated, filled with antiques or tasteful contemporary pieces. They have extras like swing-mirror vanities and brass or wood bedsteads with frequently renewed mattresses. The bathrooms are small to medium. Breakfast is the only meal served, though a staff member can carry drinks to you in the reception area. The breakfast room is especially appealing: Inspired by an Italian garden, it was designed by noted architect Paolo Portoghesi.

Victoria Roma. Via Campania 41, 00187 Roma. ☎ **06-473-931.** Fax 06-487-1890. E-mail: hotel.victoria@flashnet.it. 108 units. A/C MINIBAR TV TEL. 400,000 lire ($200) double. Rates include breakfast. AE, DC, MC, V. Parking 40,000–50,000 lire ($20–$25). Metro: Barberini. Bus: 52, 53, 490, 495, or 910.

It may not be as hip as it was decades ago, but this hotel still keeps abreast of changing times. The location overlooking the Borghese Gardens remains one of its most desirable assets; you can sit in the roof garden drinking your cocktail amidst palm trees and potted plants, imagining you're in a country villa. The lounges and living rooms retain a country-house decor, with soft touches that include high-backed chairs, large oil paintings, bowls of freshly cut flowers, provincial tables, and Oriental rugs. You don't get opulence here, but you do get a 1950s kind of class—a sort of dowdy charm—plus good maintenance. Rooms range from standard to spacious; each is comfortably equipped with good beds, and most units were renovated during the late 1990s. Furnishings like Oriental carpets are common, and the bathrooms are generally spacious, with dual basins, phones, hair dryers, and scales. Some of the tubs are extra-long. Floor number five has the best views of the Villa Borghese.

Dining: Meals can be taken à la carte in the elegant grill room, which serves the best of Italian cuisine.

Amenities: Concierge, dry cleaning/laundry, room service, massage, twice-daily maid service, car-rental and tour desk. Plentiful shopping is a short walk from the hotel.

MODERATE

Hotel Oxford. Via Boncompagni 89, 00187 Roma. ☎ **06-4282-8952.** Fax 06-4281-5349. www.hoteloxford.com. E-mail: info@hoteloxford.com. 59 units. A/C MINIBAR TV TEL. 250,000–320,000 lire ($125–$160) double; 300,000–360,000 lire ($150–$180) triple; 330,000–420,000 lire ($165–$210) suite. Rates include buffet breakfast. AE, DC, MC, V. Parking 35,000–40,000 lire ($17.50–$20). Metro: Barberini. Bus: 53 or 63.

The Oxford is a solid if not spectacular choice adjacent to the Borghese Gardens. Recently renovated, it's now centrally heated and fully carpeted throughout. There's a pleasant lounge and Tony's Bar (serving snacks), plus a dining room offering good

Italian cuisine. The guest rooms, which were recently freshened up, contain modern furnishings, including excellent mattresses on twin beds. Each bathroom is tiled, with adequate shelf space and a shower/tub combination.

Hotel Regno. Via del Corso 330, 00186 Roma. ☎ **06-679-2162.** Fax 06-678-9239. www.hotelregno.com. E-mail: info@hotelregno.com. 46 units. A/C MINIBAR TV TEL. 270,000–340,000 lire ($135–$170) double; 460,000 lire ($230) suite. AE, DC, MC, V. Metro: Barberini.

Set in a great shopping area, this hotel has a severe stone facade. It was originally a library in the 1600s. In the 1960s, its six-story premises were transformed into a simple hotel, and in 1999, it was upgraded into a well-managed three-star hotel. Bedrooms are relatively small, but comfortably appointed with good mattresses and a nondescript collection of conservative modern furniture. The staff is friendly and hard-working. There's a simple breakfast room, and a sundeck on the building's roof.

La Residenza. Via Emilia 22–24, 00187 Roma. ☎ **06-488-0789.** Fax 06-485-721. www. italyhotel.com/roma/la_residenza. E-mail: hotel.la.residenza@italyhotel.com. 29 units. A/C MINIBAR TV TEL. 310,000–350,000 lire ($155–$175) double; 350,000–410,000 lire ($175–$205) suite. Rates include buffet breakfast. AE, MC, V. Parking (limited) 10,000 lire ($5). Metro: Piazza Barberini.

La Residenza, in a superb but noisy location, successfully combines the intimacy of a town house with the elegance of a four-star hotel. It's a bit old-fashioned and homelike but still a favorite of international travelers. The converted villa has an ivy-covered courtyard and a series of upholstered public rooms with Empire divans, oil portraits, and rattan chairs. Terraces are scattered throughout. The guest rooms are generally spacious, containing bentwood chairs and built-in furniture, including beds with quality mattresses. The dozen or so junior suites boast balconies. The bathrooms have hair dryers, robes, even ice machines.

3 Near Ancient Rome

EXPENSIVE

Hotel Forum. Via di Tor de Conti 25–30, 00184 Roma. ☎ **06-679-2446.** Fax 06-678-6479. www.hotelforum.com. E-mail: info@hotelforum.com. 80 units. A/C TV TEL. 420,000–510,000 lire ($210–$255) double; 650,000 lire ($325) triple; 800,000 lire ($400) suite. Rates include breakfast. AE, CB, DC, MC, V. Parking 40,000 lire ($20). Bus: 75, 117, 85, 87, or 40.

Back in the 1950s, this former convent was converted into a hotel. Built around a medieval bell tower off the Fori Imperiali, the Hotel Forum offers old-fashioned elegance and accommodations that range from tasteful to opulent. The midsize rooms, which look out on the sights of the ancient city, are well appointed with antiques, mirrors, quality mattresses, and Oriental rugs.

   Dining/Diversions: The hotel's lounges are conservatively conceived as a country estate, with paneled walls and furnishings that combine Italian and French provincial styles. Dining is an event in the roof-garden restaurant. Reserve well in advance.

   Amenities: Twice-daily maid service, baby-sitting, concierge, dry cleaning/laundry, 24-hour room service, in-room massage, secretarial and business services, conference rooms, car-rental and tour desk.

MODERATE

Colosseum Hotel. Via Sforza 10, 00184 Roma. ☎ **06-482-7228.** Fax 06-482-7285. www.venere.it/home/roma/colosseum/colosseum.html. E-mail: colosseum@venere.it. 47 units. TV TEL. 239,000–245,000 lire ($119.50–$122.50) double. Rates include breakfast. AE, DC, MC, V. Parking 35,000 lire ($17.50). Metro: Cavour.

Two short blocks southwest of Santa Maria Maggiore, this hotel offers affordable and comfortable (yet small) rooms. Someone with flair and lots of lire designed the public areas and upper halls, which hint at baronial grandeur. The drawing room, with its long refectory table, white walls, red tiles, and provincial armchairs, invites lingering. The guest rooms are furnished with well-chosen antique reproductions (beds of heavy carved wood, dark-paneled wardrobes, leatherwood chairs), and all have stark white walls and sometimes old-fashioned plumbing in the bathrooms. Most rooms have air-conditioning.

Hotel Duca d'Alba. Via Leonina 14, 00184 Roma. ☎ **06-484-471.** Fax 06-488-4840. www.italyhotel.com/roma/duca_dalba. E-mail: duca_dalba@venere.it. 27 units. A/C MINIBAR TV TEL. 200,000–370,000 lire ($100–$185) double; 300,000–400,000 lire ($150–$200) suite. Rates include breakfast. AE, DC, MC, V. Parking 40,000–50,000 lire ($20–$25). Metro: Cavour.

A bargain near the Roman Forum and the Colosseum, this hotel lies in the Suburra neighborhood, which was once pretty seedy but is being gentrified. Though completely renovated, the Duca d'Alba retains an old-fashioned air (it was built in the 19th century). The guest rooms have elegant Roman styling, with soothing colors, light wood pieces, luxurious beds and bedding, safes, and bathrooms with hair dryers. The most desirable rooms are the four with private balconies.

Hotel Nerva. Via Tor di Conti 3, 00184 Roma. ☎ **06-678-1835.** Fax 06-699-22204. 19 units. A/C MINIBAR TV TEL. 230,000–360,000 lire ($115–$180) double. Rates include breakfast. AE, MC, V. Metro: Colosseo.

Some of the Nerva's walls and foundations date from the 1500s, others from a century later, but the modern amenities date only from 1997. The site, above and a few steps from the Roman Forum, will appeal to any student of archaeology and literature, and the warm welcome from the Cirulli brothers will appeal to all. The decor is accented with wood panels and terra-cotta tiles; some guest rooms even retain the original ceiling beams. The furniture is contemporary and comfortable, with excellent beds and mattresses. The tiled bathrooms have adequate shelf space.

INEXPENSIVE

Casa Kolbe. Via San Teodoro 44, 00186 Roma. ☎ **06-679-4974.** Fax 06-699-41550. 65 units. TEL. 140,000 lire ($70) double. AE, MC, V. Metro: Circo Massimo.

Occupying an 1800 building, the Casa Kolbe (often full of bus tour groups from North America and Germany) has a great position between the Palatine and the Campidoglio. The guest rooms, painted in old-fashioned tones of deep red and brown, are simple and well kept, even if some are a bit battered from use. The mattresses may be thin but they still have comfort in them, and the bathrooms are small. Many rooms overlook a small garden. The hotel dining room, open only to guests, serves affordable set menus.

4 Near Campo de' Fiori

MODERATE

✪ **Casa di Santa Brigida.** Via Monserato 54 (off Piazza Farnese). Postal address: Piazza Farnese 96, 00186 Roma. ☎ **06-6889-2596.** Fax 06-6889-1573. www.brigidine.org. E-mail: brigida@mclink.it. 20 units. TEL. 250,000 lire ($125) double. Rates include breakfast. DC, MC, V. Bus: 46, 62, or 64.

Across from the Michelangelo-designed Palazzo Farnese on a quiet square a block from Campo de' Fiori, Rome's best (and poshest) convent hotel is run by the friendly sisters of St. Bridget in the house where that Swedish saint died in 1373. Rooms where

Accommodations Near the Spanish Steps & Ancient Rome

Casa Kolbe **18**

Colosseum Hotel **17**

Grand Hotel Plaza **3**

The Hassler **11**

Hotel Condotti **4**

Hotel d'Inghilterra **5**

Hotel de la Ville Inter-
Continental Roma **12**

Hotel de Russie **1**

Hotel Duca d'Alba **16**

Hotel Forum **14**

Hotel Gregoriana **10**

Hotel Madrid **8**

Hotel Margutta **2**

Hotel Nerva **15**

Hotel Parlamento **6**

Hotel Piazza
di Spagna **7**

Hotel Scalinata
di Spagna **9**

Hotel Trinità
dei Monti **13**

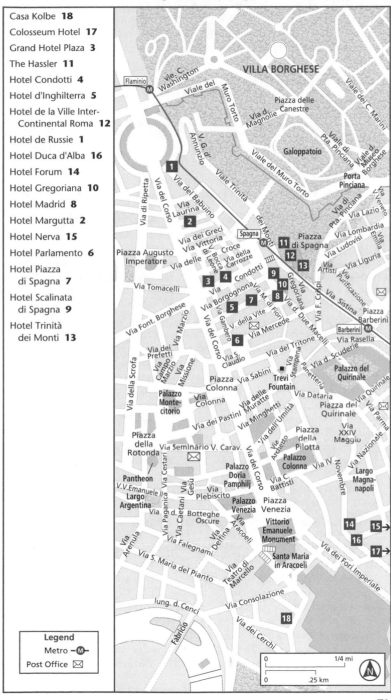

Legend
Metro –Ⓜ–
Post Office ✉

Santa Brigida lived and died are on the first floor. The library is quite large. This convent hotel accepts people of every age and creed. The rates are justified by the comfy and roomy old-world guest rooms with antiques or reproductions on parquet (lower level) or carpeted (upstairs) floors. The bathrooms are a little old but at least have shower curtains, and the beds are heavenly firm. There's a roof terrace, library, and church.

○ **Teatro di Pompeo.** Largo del Pallaro 8, 00186 Roma. ☎ **06-6830-0170.** Fax 06-6880-5531. 13 units. A/C TV TEL. 350,000 lire ($175) double. Rates include breakfast. AE, DC, MC, V. Bus: 64.

Built atop the ruins of the Theater of Pompey, from about 55 B.C., this small charmer lies near the spot where Julius Caesar met his end on the Ides of March. Intimate and refined, it's on a quiet piazzetta near the Palazzo Farnese and Campo de' Fiori. The rooms are decorated in an old-fashioned Italian style with hand-painted tiles, and the beamed ceilings date from the days of Michelangelo. The guest rooms range from small to medium, each with a good mattress and a tidy but cramped tiled bathroom.

5 Near Piazza Navona & the Pantheon

VERY EXPENSIVE

○ **Albergo del Sole al Pantheon.** Piazza della Rotonda 63, 00186 Roma. ☎ **06-678-0441.** Fax 06-6994-0689. www.italyhotel.com/roma/solealpantheon. E-mail: hotsole@flashnet.it. 25 units. A/C MINIBAR TV TEL. 570,000 lire ($285) double; 750,000 lire ($375) junior suite. Rates include buffet breakfast. AE, DC, MC, V. Bus: 64.

You're obviously paying for the million-dollar view, but you may find it's worth it to be across from the Pantheon, one of antiquity's great relics. (Okay, so you're above a McDonald's, but one look at the Pantheon at sunrise and you won't think about Big Macs.) This building was constructed in 1450 as a home, and the first records of it as a hostelry appeared in 1467, making it one of the world's oldest hotels. The layout is amazingly eccentric and on various levels—prepare to walk up and down a lot of three- or four-step staircases. The guest rooms vary greatly in decor, none award-winning and much of it hit or miss, with compact tiled bathrooms. The windows are double-glazed, but the rooms opening onto the piazza still tend to be noisy at all hours. The quieter rooms overlook the courtyard but are sans the view.

Dining: Breakfast is the only meal served, but there are dozens of trattorie in the neighborhood.

Amenities: Room service, laundry/dry cleaning, baby-sitting (not always available), twice-daily maid service.

Albergo Nazionale. Piazza Montecitorio 131, 00186 Roma. ☎ **06-69-5001.** Fax 06-678-6677. E-mail: nazionale@micanet.it. A/C MINIBAR TV TEL. 550,000 lire ($275) double; 1,300,000 lire ($650) suite. Rates include breakfast. AE, DC, MC, V. Parking 45,000 lire ($22.50). Bus: 52, 53, 58, 85, or 95.

The Albergo Nazionale faces the Piazza Colonna, with its Column of Marcus Aurelius, the Palazzo di Montecitorio, and the Palazzo Chigi. Because it's next to the parliament buildings, the Albergo is often full of government officials and diplomatic staff. The lobbies are wood-paneled, and there are many antiques throughout. The guest rooms are high-ceilinged, comfortably proportioned, and individually decorated in a late-19th-century style. They either have carpet or marble floors, and some offer interesting views over the ancient square outside. Beds and mattresses are luxurious, and maintenance is good.

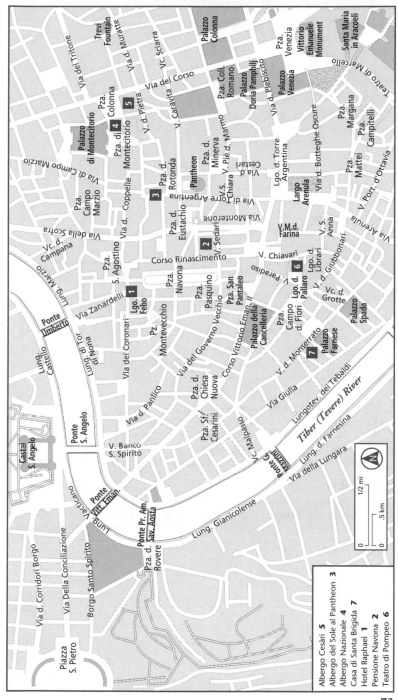

ⓘ Family-Friendly Hotels

Cavalieri Hilton *(see p. 84)* This hotel is like a resort, with a pool, gardens, and plenty of grounds for children to run and play. It's only 15 minutes from the center of Rome, which you can reach via the hotel shuttle bus.

Nord Nuova Roma *(see p. 65)* For the family on a budget who wants to be near the rail station, this is a good choice because many of the rooms are quite spacious and extra beds can be added. It's also near a family-friendly restaurant run by the same people.

Hotel Ranieri *(see p. 64)* This hotel offers a family-style atmosphere, with some rooms large enough to comfortably house families of three or four. Baby cots are on hand as well.

Hotel Venezia *(see p. 64)* At this good, moderately priced family hotel near Stazione Termini, the rooms have been renovated and most are large enough to hold extra beds for children.

San Giorgio *(see p. 62)* Near the train station, this family-owned hotel is ideal for parents traveling with children. Many of its corner rooms can be converted into larger quarters by using connecting doors.

Hotel Raphael. Largo Febo 2, 00186 Roma. ☎ **06-682-831.** Fax 06-687-8993. www.raphaelhotel.com. E-mail: info@raphaelhotel.com. 72 units. A/C MINIBAR TV TEL. 500,000–600,000 lire ($250–$300) double; 700,000–800,000 lire ($350–$400) suite. Breakfast 35,000 lire ($17.50). AE, DC, MC, V. Parking 45,000 lire ($22.50). Bus: 70, 81, 87, or 115.

Adjacent to Piazza Navona, the Raphael is within easy walking distance of many sites. The ivy-covered facade invites you to enter the lobby, decorated with antiques that rival the cache in local museums (even a Picasso ceramics collection). The guest rooms (some quite small) were recently refurbished with a Florentine touch and contain quality mattresses on double or twin beds. Some of the suites have private terraces.

   Dining: The elegant restaurant/bar, Café Picasso, serves a French/Italian cuisine. From the hotel's rooftop garden terrace, Bramante, you can enjoy a panoramic view over the ancient city while you dine in summer.

   Amenities: Room service, fitness room, baby-sitting, laundry, currency exchange.

MODERATE

❍ Albergo Cesàri. Via di Pietra 89A, 00186 Roma. ☎ **06-679-2386.** Fax 06-679-0882. www.venere.it/roma/cesari/cesari.html. E-mail: cesari@venere.it. 48 units. A/C MINIBAR TV TEL. 300,000–340,000 lire ($150–$170) double; 400,000 lire ($200) triple; 450,000 lire ($225) quad. Rates include buffet breakfast. AE, DC, MC, V. Parking 50,000 lire ($25). Bus: 492 from Stazione Termini.

The Cesàri, on an ancient street, has occupied its desirable location between the Trevi Fountain and the Pantheon since 1787. Its well-preserved exterior harmonizes with the Temple of Neptune and many little antiques shops nearby. The guest rooms (some suitable for the disabled) have mostly functional modern pieces, but there are a few traditional trappings as well to maintain character; the mattresses are fine and firm. In 1998, all the accommodations and the breakfast room were completely renovated.

INEXPENSIVE

Pensione Navona. Via dei Sediari 8, 00186 Roma. ☎ **06-686-4203.** Fax 06-6880-3802. 35 units, 30 with bathroom. 130,000 lire ($65) double without bathroom, 180,000–220,000 lire ($90–$110) double with bathroom; 230,000 lire ($115) triple with bathroom. Rates include breakfast. No credit cards. Bus: 70, 81, 87, or 115.

This pensione is on a small street radiating from Piazza Navona's southeastern tip. The rooms aren't as glamorous as the exterior, but the Navona offers decent accommodations, many of which have been renovated and some of which open to views of the central courtyard. Run by an Australian-born family of Italian descent, it boasts ceilings high enough to help relieve the midsummer heat and an array of architectural oddities (the legacy of the continual construction this palace has undergone since 1360). The beds, most often twins or doubles, have fine linens and good mattresses. You can get an air-conditioned room by request for 40,000 lire ($20) per night (only in the doubles with bathroom).

6 Near the Spanish Steps & Piazza del Popolo

To locate the hotels in this section, see the "Accommodations Near the Spanish Steps & Ancient Rome" map on p. 71.

VERY EXPENSIVE

Grand Hotel Plaza. Via del Corso 126, 00186 Roma. ☎ **06-6992-1111.** Fax 06-6994-1575. www.venere.it/roma/plaza. E-mail: plaza@grandhotelplaza.com. A/C MINIBAR TV TEL. 580,000–900,000 lire ($290–$450) double; 980,000–2,500,000 lire ($490–$1,250) suite. AE, DC, MC, V. Parking 45,000 lire ($22.50). Metro: Piazza di Spagna.

Pietro Mascagni composed his *Nerone* in one of the guest rooms here and Vincent Price stayed here while making "all those bad movies." When you see the very grand decor, you'll understand why. Renovated in 1999 and 2000, this hotel's public rooms are vintage 19th century and contain stained-glass skylights, massive crystal chandeliers, potted palms, inlaid marble floors, and a life-size stone lion guarding the ornate stairway. The theatrical grandeur of the lobby carries over into the suites, where the furnishings mimic the gilded-age splendor of the public rooms on a smaller scale. But the standard guest rooms are just that—standard, contemporary, midsized, and streamlined, with efficient but comfortable furniture (including excellent mattresses).

Dining: The hotel does not have a full-fledged restaurant, but sandwiches, salads, pastas, and platters are served informally, in the hotel bar, every day from 7:30am to 1am.

Amenities: Concierge, 24-hour room service, baby-sitting, laundry/dry cleaning, conference rooms.

The Hassler. Piazza Trinità dei Monti 6, 00187 Roma. ☎ **800/223-6800** in the U.S., or 06-699-340. Fax 06-678-9991. www.hotelhasslerroma.com. E-mail: hasslerroma@inclink.it. 100 units. A/C MINIBAR TV TEL. 790,000–950,000 lire ($395–$475) double; from 2,600,000 lire ($1,300) suite. Breakfast 40,000–70,000 lire ($20–$35). AE, CB, DC, MC, V. Parking 50,000 lire ($25). Metro: Piazza di Spagna.

The Hassler, rebuilt in 1944 to replace the 1885 original, uses the Spanish Steps as its grand entrance. Its crown has become a bit tarnished, but it possesses such a mystique from tradition and the one-of-kind-location it can get away with charging astronomical rates. The lounges and the guest rooms, with their "Italian Park Avenue" trappings, all strike a faded, if still glamorous, 1930s note.

The guest rooms range from small singles to some of the most spacious suites in town. High ceilings make them appear larger than they are, and many of them open onto private balconies or terraces. The mattresses are deluxe and the beds suitable for a president or king (you'll likely see one or two of each). Only medium in size, the bathrooms are classy, complete with hair dryers and a range of deluxe body and hair products. The front rooms, though dramatically overlooking the Spanish Steps, are often noisy at night, but the views are worth it. For panoramas of the Rome rooftops, ask for a room on the top floor.

Dining/Diversions: The Hassler Roof Restaurant is a favorite with visitors and Romans alike for its fine cuisine and view. Its Sunday brunch is a popular rendezvous time. The Hassler Bar is ideal, if a little formal, for cocktails; in the evening it has piano music.

Amenities: Room service, laundry, limousine, in-room massages, nearby fitness center, tennis court (summer), free bicycles.

✪ Hotel de Russie. Via del Babuino 9, 00187 Roma. ☎ **800/323-7500** in North America or 06-328-881. Fax 06-328-8888. www.rfhotels.com. E-mail: reservations@hotelderussie.it. 129 units. A/C MINIBAR TV TEL. 800,000–1,100,000 lire ($400–$550) double; 1,500,000–2,000,000 lire ($750–$1,000) suite. Rates include breakfast. AE, DC, MC, V. Metro: Flaminia.

Just off the Piazza del Popolo, this five-star deluxe hotel has a pedigree partially based on the success of the Forte family, Britain's most prominent hotel family. It opened in the spring of 2000 to media acclaim for its opulent furnishings and choice location. In its previous reincarnation, it was a favorite of Russian dignitaries (hence its name), and it's also hosted Jean Cocteau, Stravinsky, and Picasso. In World War II, it was used by the Italian government as a secret military center for spy secrets. The hardworking, multilingual staff works hard to make stays here memorable and comfortable. Public areas are glossy and contemporary. About 30% of the bedrooms are conservative, with traditional furniture, while the remaining 70% are more minimalist, with a stark and striking style. Each is equipped with every conceivable electronic amenity, and offers lots of deeply upholstered comforts and views over a verdant garden.

Dining/Diversions: Le Jardin de Russie offers upscale Italian cuisine with a view opening onto the gardens. The Stravinskij Bar serves stiff drinks in a formal *moderno* setting.

Amenities: 24-hour room service, concierge, health club, laundry/dry cleaning. One of the hotel's most memorable features, aside from a location adjacent to the Piazza del Popolo, is a very large (¾ acre) garden, studded with venerable magnolias, palms, orange trees, and rosebushes.

✪ Hotel d'Inghilterra. Via Bocca di Leone 14, 00187 Roma. ☎ **06-69-981.** Fax 06-679-8601. www.charminghotels.it/inghilterra. E-mail: hir@charminghotel.it. 106 units. A/C MINIBAR TV TEL. 540,000 lire ($270) double; from 1,050,000 lire ($525) suite. Breakfast 34,000 lire ($17). AE, DC, MC, V. Parking 40,000 lire ($20). Metro: Piazza di Spagna.

The Inghilterra holds onto its traditions and heritage, even though it has been renovated. Situated between Via Condotti and Via Borgogna, this hotel in the 17th century was the guest house of the Torlonia princes. If you're willing to spend a king's ransom, Rome's most fashionable small hotel is up there with the Hassler and Inter-Continental. The rooms have mostly old pieces (gilt and lots of marble, mahogany chests, and glittery mirrors), complemented by modern conveniences. Some, however, are just too cramped, though all boast quality mattresses and fine linen. The preferred rooms are higher up, opening onto a tile terrace, with a balustrade and a railing covered with flowering vines and plants. The bathrooms have been refurbished and offer deluxe toiletries and hair dryers.

Dining/Diversions: The Roman Garden serves excellent Roman dishes. The English-style bar with its paneled walls, tip-top tables, and old lamps is a favorite gathering spot in the evening. The Roman Garden Lounge offers light lunches and snacks.

Amenities: Concierge, room service, dry cleaning/laundry, baby-sitting, car-rental desk, secretarial services, gym.

☼ Hotel de la Ville Inter-Continental Roma. Via Sistina 67–69, 00187 Roma. ☎ **800/ 327-0200** in the U.S. and Canada, or 06-67-331. Fax 06-678-4213. www.interconti.com. E-mail: rome@interconti.com. 192 units. A/C MINIBAR TV TEL. 700,000–810,000 lire ($350–$405) double; from 1,110,000 lire ($555) suite. Rates include continental breakfast. AE, DC, MC, V. Parking 45,000 lire ($22.50). Metro: Piazza di Spagna or Barberini.

We prefer this place, designed in 1924 by Hungarian architect Jozef Vago, to the overpriced glory of the Hassler next door. The hotel looks deluxe (it's officially rated first class) from the minute you walk through the revolving door, where a smartly uniformed doorman greets you. Once inside this palace, built in the 19th century on the site of the ancient Gardens of Lucullus, you'll find Oriental rugs, marble tables, brocade furniture, and an English-speaking staff. There are endless corridors leading to what at first seems a maze of ornamental lounges. Some of the public rooms have a sort of 1930s elegance and others are strictly baroque, and in the middle of it all is an open courtyard.

The guest rooms and the public areas have been renovated in a beautifully classic and yet up-to-date way. The higher rooms with balconies have panoramic views of Rome, and you're free to use the roof terrace with the same view. Most units are small but boast chintz-covered fabrics, fine beds with quality mattresses, and concealed minibars. The bathrooms have built-in hair dryers and generous shelf space.

Dining/Diversions: La Piazzetta de la Ville Restaurant, overlooking the garden, serves an Italian/international cuisine. Inside you'll find two bars, La Saletta and I Due Murano.

Amenities: Room service, baby-sitting, laundry/valet, car-rental desk, beauty salon, barber shop.

EXPENSIVE

☼ Hotel Scalinata di Spagna. Piazza Trinità dei Monti 17, 00187 Roma. ☎ **06- 679-3006.** Fax 06-6994-0598. www.italyhotel.com/home/roma/scalinata/scalinata.html. 16 units. A/C MINIBAR TV TEL. 400,000–500,000 lire ($200–$250) double; 600,000 lire ($300) triple. Rates include breakfast. AE, MC, V. Parking 45,000 lire ($22.50). Metro: Spagna.

The Scalinata di Spagna has always been one of Rome's top choices, at the top of the steps, across from the Hassler. Its delightful little building—only two floors are visible from the outside—is nestled between much larger structures, with four relief columns across the facade and window boxes with bright blossoms. The recently redecorated interior is like an old inn's—the public rooms are small, with bright print slipcovers, old clocks, and low ceilings.

The decorations vary radically from one guest room to the next. Some have low beamed ceilings and ancient-looking wood furniture; others have loftier ceilings and more run-of-the-mill furniture. The tiled bathrooms range from small to medium but offer hair dryers and state-of-the-art plumbing. The best units are any overlooking the steps, but the best of the best are room nos. 10 and 12. Everything is spotless and pleasing to the eye.

Dining: Breakfast is the only meal served, but you'll enjoy it on one of the most panoramic terraces in all Rome.

Amenities: Concierge, dry cleaning/laundry, baby-sitting.

MODERATE

Hotel Condotti. Via Mario de' Fiori 37, 00187 Roma. ☎ **06-679-4661.** Fax 06-679-0457. www.venere.it/roma/condotti. 16 units. A/C MINIBAR TV TEL. 310,000–490,000 lire ($155– $245) double; 350,000–520,000 lire ($175–$260) minisuite. Rates include buffet breakfast. AE, DC, MC, V. Metro: Piazza di Spagna.

The Condotti is small, choice, and terrific for shoppers intent on being near the tony boutiques. The mostly English-speaking staff is cooperative and hardworking. The mostly blue-and-white modern rooms may not have much historic charm, but they're comfortable and soothing. Renovated in 1991, each is decorated with traditional furnishings, including excellent beds—usually twins. Room 414 is often requested because it has a geranium-filled terrace. There's no bar or restaurant, but dry cleaning/laundry, a car rental, and a tour desk are extras.

Hotel Gregoriana. Via Gregoriana 18, 00187 Roma. ☎ **06-679-4269.** Fax 06-678-4258. 20 units. A/C TV TEL. 380,000 lire ($190) double. Rates include breakfast. AE, DC, V. Parking 30,000–40,000 lire ($15–$20). Metro: Spagna.

The intimate Gregoriana has many fans, including guests from the Italian fashion industry. The matriarch of an aristocratic family left the building to an order of nuns in the 19th century, but they eventually retreated to other quarters. (There might be an elevated spirituality in Room C, as it used to be a chapel.) The elevator cage is a black-and-gold art deco fantasy. The smallish guest rooms provide comfort and fine Italian design, and the door to each bears a reproduction of an Erté print whose fanciful characters indicate the letter designating that room. Each has a queen or double bed, with a firm mattress. The bathrooms are a bit small but always spotless, with hair dryers.

Hotel Madrid. Via Mario de' Fiori 93–95, 00187 Roma. ☎ **06-699-1511.** Fax 06-679-1653. www.hotel-madrid.net. 26 units. A/C MINIBAR TV TEL. 350,000 lire ($175) double; 500,000 lire ($250) suite. Rates include breakfast. AE, DC, MC, V. Parking 40,000–45,000 lire ($20–$22.50) nearby. Metro: Piazza di Spagna.

Despite modern touches in the comfortable, if minimalist, guest rooms, the interior of the Madrid manages to evoke fin-de-siècle Roma. Guests often take their breakfast amid ivy and blossoming plants on the roof terrace with a panoramic view of rooftops and the distant dome of St. Peter's. Some of the doubles are large, with scatter rugs, veneer armoires, and shuttered windows, but others are quite small, so make sure you know what you're getting before you check in. Each bed (usually doubles or twins) is fitted with a good mattress. The bathrooms were renovated in 1998.

Hotel Piazza di Spagna. Via Mario de' Fiori 61, 00187 Roma. ☎ **06-679-6412.** Fax 06-679-0654. www.hotelpiazzadispagna.it. E-mail: info@hotelpiazzadispagna.it. 17 units. A/C MINIBAR TV TEL. 280,000–380,000 lire ($140–$190) double. Rates include breakfast. AE, MC, V. Parking 24,000 lire ($12) nearby. Metro: Piazza di Spagna. Bus: 590.

About a block from the downhill side of the Spanish Steps, this hotel was once just a run-down pensione until new owners took it over in the 1990s and substantially upgraded it. It's small but classic, with an inviting atmosphere. The guest rooms (some very small) boast a functional streamlined decor; some even have Jacuzzis in the tiled bathrooms. Dry cleaning, laundry, and room service (7am to 6pm) are available.

Hotel Trinità dei Monti. Via Sistina 91, 00187 Roma. ☎ **06-679-7206.** Fax 06-699-0111. 25 units. A/C MINIBAR TV TEL. 290,000–340,000 lire ($145–$170) double. Rates include breakfast. AE, DC, MC, V. Metro: Barberini or Piazza di Spagna.

Between two of the most-visited piazzas in Rome (Barberini and Spagna), this is a well-maintained, friendly place. The hotel occupies the second and third floors of an antique building, and its guest rooms come with herringbone-patterned parquet floors and big windows and are comfortable if not flashy. Each has a good mattress and a tidy tiled bathroom. The hotel's social center is a simple coffee bar near the reception desk. Don't expect anything terribly fancy, but the welcome is warm and the location ultraconvenient.

INEXPENSIVE

Hotel Margutta. Via Laurina 34, 00187 Roma. ☎ **06-322-3674.** Fax 06-320-0395. 24 units. 190,000–260,000 lire ($95–$130) double; 250,000 lire ($125) triple. Rates include breakfast. AE, DC, MC, V. Metro: Flaminio.

The Margutta, on a cobblestone street near Piazza del Popolo, offers attractively decorated guest rooms, a helpful staff, and a simple breakfast room. The best rooms are the three on the top floor, offering a great view. Two of these three (nos. 50 and 51) share a terrace, and the larger room has a private terrace. (There's usually a 20% to 35% supplement for these.) Drawbacks? No air-conditioning, no room phones. However, each room comes with a comfortable bed containing a good mattress, plus a small but tidy bathroom.

✪ **Hotel Parlamento.** Via delle Convertite 5 (at the intersection with Via del Corso), 00187 Roma. ☎ **06-679-2082.** Fax 06-6992-1000. 23 units. TV TEL. 200,000 lire ($100) double. Rates include breakfast. AE, DC, MC, V. Parking 28,000–30,000 lire ($14–$15). Metro: Spagna.

The Parlamento has four-star class at two-star prices with a friendly pensione-style reception. The street traffic is so heavy they installed an effective *double set* of double-glazed windows. The furnishings are antiques or reproduction, and the firm beds are backed by carved wood or wrought-iron headboards. Fifteen rooms are air-conditioned, and the bathrooms were recently redone with hair dryers, heated towel racks, phones, and (in a few) even marble sinks. *Note:* It's a three-story hotel with a recently added elevator. Rooms are different in style; the most desirable are no. 82 with its original 1800s furniture, and nos. 104, 106, and 107 because they open onto the roof garden. You can enjoy the chandeliered and tromp l'oeil breakfast room or carry your cappuccino up to the small roof terrace with its view of San Silvestro's bell tower.

7 Near the Vatican

VERY EXPENSIVE

Hotel Columbus. Via della Conciliazione 33, 00193 Roma. ☎ **06-686-5435.** Fax 06-686-4874. 92 units. A/C MINIBAR TV TEL. 570,000 lire ($285) double; 660,000 lire ($330) suite. Rates include buffet breakfast. AE, CB, DC, MC, V. The hotel has a few free parking spaces. Bus: 62 or 64.

An impressive 15th-century palace, the Columbus was once the home of the cardinal who became Pope Julius II and tormented Michelangelo into painting the Sistine Chapel. It looks much as it must have centuries ago: a severe time-stained facade, small windows, and heavy wooden doors leading from the street to the colonnades and arches of the inner courtyard. The cobbled entranceway leads to a reception hall and a series of baronial public rooms. Note the main salon with its walk-in fireplace, oil portraits, battle scenes, and Oriental rugs.

The guest rooms are considerably simpler than the salons, furnished with comfortable modern pieces. All are spacious, but a few are enormous and still have such original details as decorated wood ceilings and frescoed walls. The best and quietest rooms front the garden. The bathrooms are medium in size and offer all the standards, like up-to-date plumbing, hair dryers, and toiletries.

Dining: Many guests like La Veranda so much they prefer to dine here at night instead of roaming the streets looking for a trattoria. Standard Italian cuisine is served: time-tested recipes made with fresh ingredients rather than anything too innovative.

Amenities: Concierge, room service, dry cleaning/laundry, car-rental desk.

✪ Hotel Atlante Star. Via Vitelleschi 34, 00193 Roma. ☎ **06-687-3233.** Fax 06-687-2300. www.atlantehotels.com. E-mail: atlante.star@atlantehotels.com. 90 units. A/C MINIBAR TV TEL. 580,000 lire ($290) double; from 750,000 lire ($375) suite. Rates include buffet breakfast. AE, DC, MC, V. Parking 40,000 lire ($20). Metro: Ottaviano. Bus: 23, 64, or 492.

The Atlante Star is a first-class hotel with striking views of St. Peter's. The tastefully renovated lobby is covered with dark marble, chrome trim, and exposed wood; the upper floors will make you feel as if you're on a luxury ocean liner (no icebergs in sight). This stems partly from the lavish use of curved and lacquered surfaces, walls upholstered in printed fabrics, and wall-to-wall carpeting. Even the door handles are deco. The guest rooms are small but posh, with all the modern comforts, like elegant beds with quality mattresses and modern bathrooms with hair dryers. There's also a royal suite with a Jacuzzi. If there's no room here, the owner will try to accommodate you in his less expensive **Atlante Garden** nearby (see below).

Dining: Les Etoiles is an elegant roof-garden choice at night, with a 360-degree view of Rome and an illuminated St. Peter's in the background. The flavorful cuisine is inspired in part by Venice. There is also a less formal restaurant, Terrazza Paradiso, serving international cuisine.

Amenities: 24-hour room service, laundry/valet, baby-sitting, express checkout, foreign-currency exchange, secretarial services in English, translation services.

EXPENSIVE
✪ Hotel Atlante Garden. Via Crescenzio 78, 00193 Roma. ☎ **06-687-2361.** Fax 06-687-2315. www.atlantehotels.com. E-mail: atlante.garden@atlantehotels.com. 60 units. A/C MINIBAR TV TEL. 395,000–450,000 lire ($197.50–$225) double. Rates include breakfast. AE, DC, MC, V. Parking 40,000 lire ($20). Metro: Ottaviano. Bus: 23, 32, 49, 51, or 492.

The Atlante Garden stands on a tree-lined street near the Vatican. Although not as attractive or well appointed as its sibling, the Atlante Star (see above), it's much more reasonably priced. The entrance takes you through a garden tunnel lined with potted palms, which eventually leads into a series of handsomely decorated public rooms. More classical in its decor than the Atlante Star, the Garden offers freshly papered and painted 19th-century-style midsize rooms that contain tastefully conservative furniture and all the modern accessories, such as quality mattresses and comfortable beds. Each was renovated in 1999. The renovated baths are tiled, each equipped with a Jacuzzi.

Dining: The hotel doesn't have a restaurant. Guests can have meals at the Atlante Star restaurant.

Amenities: Baby-sitting, laundry/dry cleaning, 24-hour room service, concierge, car-rental desk.

Hotel dei Mellini. Via Muzio Clementi 81, 00193 Roma. ☎ **06-324-771.** Fax 06-3247-7801. www.hotelmellini.com. E-mail: info@hotelmellini.com. 80 units. A/C MINIBAR TV TEL. 500,000 lire ($250) double; 780,000 lire ($390) suite. Rates include breakfast. AE, DC, MC, V. Parking 40,000 lire ($20). Metro: Lepanto or Flaminio.

Built as a neoclassical-style home in the early 1900s, this town house in a quiet neighborhood without a lot of traffic was abandoned in 1970 and stood as an empty shell for years. Then it got a radical transformation and opened in 1995 as a four-star hotel. It consists of two interconnected buildings, one with four floors and one with six; the top is graced with a terrace overlooking the baroque cupolas of at least three churches. A small staff, headed by the highly capable Roberto Altezza, maintains the lovely guest rooms, whose decor includes art deco touches, Italian marble, mahogany furniture,

Accommodations Near the Vatican

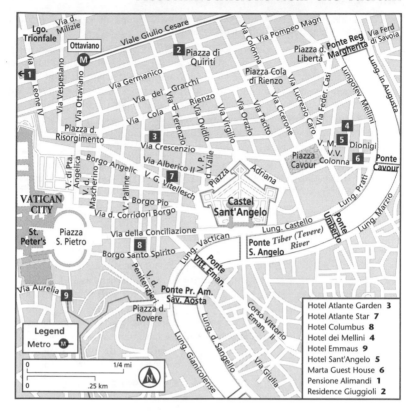

Legend
Metro — Ⓜ

Hotel Atlante Garden	3
Hotel Atlante Star	7
Hotel Columbus	8
Hotel dei Mellini	4
Hotel Emmaus	9
Hotel Sant'Angelo	5
Marta Guest House	6
Pensione Alimandi	1
Residence Giuggioli	2

and beds with fine linen and quality mattresses. The tiled bathrooms have adequate shelf space. No-smoking rooms are available.

Dining/Diversions: Other than a simple platter of food the staff might rustle up on short notice, breakfast is the only meal served. The breakfast room is extremely pleasant, adjoining a small green courtyard. There's also a hospitable American bar.

Amenities: Concierge, room service, dry cleaning/laundry, courtesy car, car-rental desk, nearby gym.

INEXPENSIVE

Hotel Emmaus. Via delle Fornaci 23, 00165 Roma. ☎ **06-638-0370.** Fax 06-635-658. www.venere.it/roma/emmaus. E-mail: hotel.emmaus@flashnet.it. 29 units. MINIBAR TV TEL. 250,000 lire ($125) double. Rates include breakfast. AE, DC, MC, V. Parking 25,000 lire ($12.50) nearby. Metro: Ottaviano. Bus: 64.

Because of its relatively low prices and location near the Vatican, you might share this hotel with Catholic pilgrims from all over the world. Occupying an older building last renovated and upgraded in 1992, it offers unpretentious and basic but comfortable accommodations. The guest rooms have recently been renovated but are still quite small, fitted with good mattresses on twin or double beds. Each comes with a small but efficiently organized bathroom. There's a breakfast area.

Hotel Sant'Angelo. Via Mariana Dionigi 16, 00193 Roma. ☎ **06-322-0758.** Fax 06-320-4451. www.novaera.it/hsa. E-mail: hsa@novaera.it. 31 units. TV TEL. 160,000–270,000 lire ($80–$135) double; 180,000–300,000 lire ($90–$150) triple. Rates include breakfast. MC, V. Parking 35,000 lire ($17.50). Metro: Lepanto.

This hotel, right off Piazza Cavour (northeast of the Castel Sant'Angelo) and a 10-minute walk from St. Peter's, is in a relatively untouristy area. Maintained and operated by several members of the Torre family, it occupies the second and third floors of an imposing 200-year-old building whose other floors house offices and private apartments. The rooms are simple, modern, and clean, with wooden furniture and views of either the street or a rather bleak but quiet courtyard. Rooms are quite small but not cramped, all painted in a different shade of blue. Each has a good mattress resting on a comfortable bed, plus a small tiled bathroom.

Marta Guest House. Via Marianna Dionigi 17, 00193 Roma. ☎ **06-324-0428.** Fax 06-323-0184. 9 units, 2 with private bathroom. 120,000 lire ($60) double without bathroom, 150,000 lire ($75) double with bathroom. Bus: 492 to Piazza Cavour.

Named after one of its owners, Marta Balbi, this is a friendly and well-scrubbed but simple pensione with a good location near Piazza Cavour and the Spanish Steps. It fills the entire second floor of a 10-story apartment house built around 1900. Take an elevator upstairs to the unassuming reception area, where a staff member will lead you to one of the airy and high-ceilinged but utterly plain and unassuming rooms. Bedrooms are small but comfortable, with small bathrooms and fine mattresses on the double beds. No breakfast is served, but the neighborhood is filled with cafes where you can get your morning cappuccino.

In 2000, the owners here invested heavily in an annex guesthouse on the nearby Piazza Cavour. Each of its 10 rooms has a private bathroom and is decorated in the same style, with the same amenities and price structure as the original guest house described above. Overflow from the main house is usually directed toward the annex.

Pension Alimandi. Via Tunisi 8, 00192 Roma. ☎ **06-3972-3948.** Fax 06-3972-3943. 30 units. A/C TV TEL. 220,000 lire ($110) double. AE, MC, V. Parking 30,000 lire ($15). Metro: Ottaviano.

Named after the three brothers who run it (Luigi, Enrico, and Paolo), this friendly guest house was built as an apartment house in 1908 in a bland residential neighborhood. The guest rooms are comfortable, albeit a bit small, with unremarkable contemporary furniture and cramped but modern-looking bathrooms. All have been upgraded and fitted with fine mattresses on the beds, most often doubles. Each of the three upper floors is serviced by two elevators leading down to a simple lobby. The social center and most appealing spot is the roof garden, with potted plants, a bar, and views of St. Peter's dome.

Residence Giuggioli. Via Germanico 198, 00192 Roma. ☎ **06-324-2113.** 5 units, 2 with bathroom. 130,000 lire ($65) double without bathroom, 150,000 lire ($75) double with bathroom. No credit cards. Parking 25,000–40,000 lire ($12.50–$20) in nearby garage. Metro: Ottaviano.

The force behind this place is Sra. Gasparina Giuggioli, whose family founded this guest house in the 1940s. It occupies most of the second floor of a five-story 1870s apartment house, with high-ceilinged rooms that were originally much grander but whose noble proportions are still obvious. Three of the five rooms have balconies overlooking the street; the one with the private bathroom is no. 6. The Giuggioli is always crowded, partly because the owner is so convivial and partly because the rooms are larger than expected and have a scattering of antiques and reproductions (though the mattresses could use replacing). There's no breakfast or other meal service, but there are cafes nearby.

If this place is full, walk a few flights to the similar **Pensione Lady** (☎ 06-324-2112), where up to seven rooms might be available at about the same rates.

8 In Trastevere

INEXPENSIVE

Trastevere Manara. Via L. Manara 24–25, 00153 Roma. ☎ **06-581-4713.** Fax 06-588-1016. 9 units. TV TEL. 130,000 lire ($65) double. AE, MC, V. Free parking on the street. Bus: H. Tram: 8.

Once upon a time, tourists used to avoid Trastevere, but today, though it's off the beaten track, it's sought out as an up-and-coming neighborhood where you can experience a true slice of Roman life. Manara opened its newly restored doors in 1998 to meet the new demand. This little gem has freshly decorated rooms, all gleaming with new tiles and fresh paint. All of the bathrooms have also been renovated, though they're small. The price is hard to beat for those who want to stay in one of the most atmospheric sections of Rome. Most of the rooms open onto the lively Piazza San Cisimato, and all of them have comfortable, albeit functional, furnishings. Breakfast is the only meal served, but many good restaurants lie just minutes outside the door.

9 In Prati

VERY EXPENSIVE

Giulio Cesare. Via degli Scipioni 287, 00192 Roma. ☎ **06-321-0751.** Fax 06-321-1736. www.travel.it/roma/giulioce/giulioce.html. E-mail: giulioce@uni.net. 86 units. A/C MINIBAR TV TEL. 520,000 lire ($260) double. Rates include breakfast. AE, DC, MC, V. Free parking. Metro: Lepanto. Bus: 280.

The tasteful Giulio Cesare, an elegant villa that was the former house of Countess Paterno Solari, lies in a sedate part of Rome across the Tiber from Piazza del Popolo. The guest salon, where the countess once entertained diplomats from all over the globe, is mostly furnished with antiques and Oriental carpets. Tapestries, Persian rugs, mirrors, ornate gilt pieces, and crystal chandeliers grace the public rooms; guests gather for drinks in a smaller salon with fruitwood paneling and 18th-century furniture. The carpeted guest rooms look like part of a lovely private home; some contain needlepoint-covered chairs. As befits a building of this age, rooms come in various dimensions, ranging from small to spacious, but each is comfortably furnished with excellent mattresses and well-maintained tiled bathrooms. Breakfast is served in a garden, and there's also a snack bar and a piano bar.

10 In Parioli

VERY EXPENSIVE

✪ **Hotel Lord Byron.** Via G. de Notaris 5, 00197 Roma. ☎ **06-322-0404.** Fax 06-322-0405. www.lordbyronhotel.com. E-mail: info@lordbyronhotel.com. 37 units. A/C MINIBAR TV TEL. 500,000–750,000 lire ($250–$375) double; from 1,200,000 lire ($600) suite. Rates include breakfast. AE, DC, MC, V. Parking 45,000 lire ($22.50). Metro: Flaminio. Bus: 52.

Lots of sophisticated travelers with hefty wallets are forgetting about the old landmarks (the Grand and Excelsior) and choosing this chic boutique hotel. The Lord Byron exemplifies modern Rome—an art deco villa set on a residential hilltop in Parioli, an area of embassies and exclusive town houses at the edge of the Villa

Borghese. From the curving entrance steps off the staffed parking lot in front, you'll notice striking design touches. Flowers are everywhere, the lighting is discreet, and everything is on an intimate scale. Each guest room is unique, but most have lots of mirrors, upholstered walls, sumptuous beds, spacious bathrooms with gray marble accessories, hair dryers, and big dressing room/closets. Ask for room nos. 503, 602, or 603 for great views.

Dining/Diversions: Relais Le Jardin is one of Rome's best restaurants (see chapter 5). The hotel has a sophisticated bar, Il Salotto, a good place for afternoon tea, drinks, or piano music in the evening.

Amenities: Concierge, room service, laundry/valet, currency exchange.

MODERATE

Hotel degli Aranci. Via Barnaba Oriani 11, 00197 Roma. ☎ **06-808-5250.** Fax 06-807-0202. 55 units. A/C MINIBAR TV TEL. 380,000 lire ($190) double; from 500,000 lire ($250) suite. Rates include breakfast. AE, DC, MC, V. Free parking. Bus: 3 or 53.

This former villa is on a tree-lined street, surrounded by similar villas now often used as consulates and diplomats' homes. Most of the accommodations have tall windows opening onto city views and are filled with provincial furnishings or English-style reproductions, including good beds fitted with fine mattresses and linen, and tiled bathrooms with adequate shelf space. Scattered about the public rooms are memorabilia of ancient Rome, like medallions of soldiers in profile, old engravings of ruins, and classical vases. A marble-topped bar in an alcove off the sitting room adds a relaxed touch. From the glass-walled breakfast room at the rear, you can see the tops of orange trees.

INEXPENSIVE

✪ **Hotel delle Muse.** Via Tommaso Salvini 18, 00197 Roma. ☎ **06-808-8333.** Fax 06-808-5749. www.venere.it/roma/muse. E-mail: hmuse@flashnet.it. 61 units. TV TEL. 160,000–240,000 lire ($80–$120) double; 200,000–290,000 lire ($100–$145) triple. Rates include buffet breakfast. AE, CB, DC, MC, V. Parking 30,000 lire ($15). Bus: 360.

This three-star hotel, half a mile north of the Villa Borghese, is a winning but undiscovered choice run by the efficient English-speaking Giorgio Lazar. Most rooms have been renovated but remain rather minimalist. Nonetheless, there's reasonable comfort here, with good mattresses and tidy bathrooms. In summer, Sr. Lazar operates a restaurant in the garden. A bar is open 24 hours in case you get thirsty at 5am. There's also a TV room, a writing room, and a dining room.

11 In Monte Mario

VERY EXPENSIVE

✪ **Cavalieri Hilton.** Via Cadlolo 101, 00136 Roma. ☎ **800/445-8667** in the U.S. and Canada, or 06-35-091. Fax 06-3509-2241. www.cavalieri-hilton.it. E-mail: info@cavalieri-hilton.it. 376 units. A/C MINIBAR TV TEL. 700,000–900,000 lire ($350–$450) double; from 1,400,000 lire ($700) suite. AE, CB, DC, DISC, MC, V. Parking 40,000 lire ($20). Free shuttle bus to/from city center.

A 15-minute drive from the center of Rome, the Cavalieri Hilton has all the amenities of a resort hotel. Overlooking Rome and the Alban Hills from atop Monte Mario, it's set among 15 acres of trees, flowering shrubs, and stonework. Its facilities are amazingly complete.

The entrance leads into a lavish red-and-gold lobby, whose sculpture and winding staircases are usually flooded with sun from the massive windows. The guest rooms and suites, many with panoramic views, are contemporary and stylish. Soft furnishings in

Staying in J. Paul Getty's Former Villa

La Posta Vecchia, in Palo Laziale, just south of Ladispoli (☎ **06-994-9501;** fax 06-994-9507; www.lapostavecchia.com; e-mail: postavec@caerenet.it), lies 22 miles northwest of Rome and about 14 miles up the coast from Leonardo da Vinci airport. Set on foundations of villas possibly built by Tiberius, this palatial villa was owned between 1960 and 1976 by one of the world's richest men, J. Paul Getty. Set behind iron gates, the stucco-sided building stands amid formal gardens in an 8-acre park.

The villa contains many antiques collected by Getty, as well as many carefully disguised steel doors, escape routes, and security devices installed to protect him from intruders. Following the tragic kidnapping of his son in the early 1970s, Getty declared that the building's access to the sea was an unacceptable security risk. The house was sold and became a private home until 1990, when it was transformed into an exceptionally elegant hotel.

Guests stay in 17 sumptuously decorated suites, which range in price from 775,000 to 2,380,000 lire ($387.50 to $1,190) a night. With discretion and politeness, staff members serve international cuisine at dinner and lunch in a richly formal dining room. The villa is closed from November 15 to April 6. The restaurant is open to non-residents if they phone in advance, but only if there are fewer than 11 guests in the dining room.

Extensive renovations initiated during Getty's ownership revealed hundreds of ancient Roman artifacts, many of which are on display in a mini-museum. There's an indoor pool, plus a staff (some of whom used to work for Getty) adept at maintaining the illusion that clients have arrived as friends of the long-departed billionaire.

pastels are paired with Italian furniture in warm-toned woods, including beds with deluxe mattresses and linen. Each unit has a keyless electronic lock, individually controlled heating and air-conditioning, a color TV with in-house movies, a radio, bedside controls for all the gadgets, and a spacious balcony. The bathrooms, sheathed in Italian marble, come with large mirrors, hair dryers, international electric sockets, vanity mirrors, piped-in music, and phones. There are facilities for travelers with disabilities.

Dining: The stellar La Pergola restaurant boasts one of the best views in Rome; its light Mediterranean menu emphasizes seafood like tagliolini with tiger prawns in pesto. In summer, Il Giardino dell'Uliveto, with a pool veranda, is an ideal choice.

Amenities: Concierge, room service, laundry/valet, tennis courts, jogging paths, indoor shop arcade, outdoor pool. The hotel's health and fitness center could be the setting for a film on late Empire decadence, with its triple-arched Turkish bath, marble, and mosaics; there's a 55-foot indoor pool and a state-of-the-art weight room.

12 Near the Airport

INEXPENSIVE

Cancelli Rossi. Via R. La Valle 54, 00054 Fiumicino. ☎ **06-650-7221.** Fax 06-6504-9168. 50 units. A/C MINIBAR TV TEL. 198,000 lire ($99) double. Rates include breakfast. Free parking. Free bus shuttle from/to the Leonardo Da Vinci airport every day 7–9:45am and 5–8:45pm every 20 min.

Since Rome's airport is close to the heart of the city, most visitors stay in the center of Rome, and just resign themselves to getting up early if they have a morning flight. Because of that, Fiumicino doesn't have any major hotels. But if you're nervous about making your flight, you could book into this very simple motellike inn, which is 1½ miles from the airport. The hotel was built in 1994, and a full renovation was completed in 1999. Two floors are served with an elevator, and the decor is minimal. Rooms range in size from small to medium and are functionally furnished but reasonably comfortable, with good beds, along with perfectly clean, tiled bathrooms with hair dryers and shower stalls. The atmosphere is a bit antiseptic, but this place is geared more for business travelers than vacationers. A restaurant set within an annex nearby serves both Italian and international food.

13 On the Outskirts

EXPENSIVE

✪ **Borgo Paraelios.** Valle Collicchia, 02040 Poggio Cantino, Rieti. ☎ **0765-26-267.** Fax 0765-26-268. www.relaischateaux.fr/borgo. E-mail: borgo@fabaris.it or borgo@relaischateaux.fr. 15 units. A/C MINIBAR TV TEL. 450,000 lire ($225) double; 550,000 lire ($275) junior suite. Rates include continental breakfast. AE, DC, MC, V. Free parking. About 20 miles north of Rome, take autostrada A1, exit at Fiano Romano and follow signs for Passo Corese, take SS313 (on the left) to Terni.

This 19th-century villa, a 45-minute drive from the city center, is surrounded by olive groves and farmlands. It combines the formality and grace of a Relais & Châteaux with a down-home informality and friendliness. Guests are welcomed in a charming lobby decorated with Oriental rugs and Italian paintings, some of them by Canaletto. Rooms are tastefully furnished with Florentine-style antiques and they include all the modern comforts. The large marbled bathrooms have robes, hair dryers, and body care products. The 173-acre park offers the possibility of enjoying the bucolic atmosphere of Roman hills. You can also sip a drink on the edges of the outside pool, framed by Mediterranean flowers.

Dining: The Borgo Paraelios restaurant is a stellar example of high quality Italian cuisine merged with refined service. It's open also to non-guests Wednesday to Monday year-round.

Amenities: Concierge, shuttle bus to Rome, outdoor and indoor pools, games room, tennis court, sauna, Turkish bath, nine-hole golf course.

Dining 5

Rome is one of the world's greatest cities for dining. From elegant, deluxe spots with lavish trappings to little *trattorie* opening onto hidden piazzas deep in the heart of Old Rome, the city abounds in good restaurants in all price ranges.

The better-known restaurants have menus printed in English. Even some of the lesser-known neighborhood restaurants have at least one person on the staff who speaks English a bit to help you get through the menu.

Most Italian restaurants are either called a *trattoria* or a *ristorante*. In theory there's a difference, but in reality it's difficult to discern. Traditionally, trattorie are smaller and less formal, but sometimes in a kind of reverse snobbism the management will call an elegant place a trattoria. A ristorante is supposed to be more substantial, but often the opposite is true.

It's difficult to compile a list of the best restaurants in a city like Rome. Everybody—locals, expatriates, even those who have chalked up only one visit—has favorites. What follows is not a comprehensive list of all the best restaurants of Rome, but simply a personal running commentary on a number of our favorites. For the most part, we've chosen not to review every deluxe spot known to all big spenders. We've chosen the handful of splurge restaurants where you'll really get what you pay for, and then we've reviewed a large selection of moderately priced and affordable restaurants that will give you a wonderful meal, authentic cuisine, and a lovely experience without breaking the bank.

Rome's cooking is not subtle, but it rivals anything the chefs of Florence or Venice can turn out. A feature of Roman restaurants is skill at borrowing—and sometimes improving on—the cuisine of other regions. Throughout the capital you'll come across Neapolitan (*alla neapolitana*), Bolognese (*alla bolognese*), Florentine (*alla fiorentina*), and even Sicilian (*alla siciliana*) specialties. One of the oldest sections of the city, Trastevere, is a gold mine of colorful streets and restaurants with a time-tested cuisine.

Roman meals customarily include at least three separate courses: pasta, a main course (usually a meat dish with vegetables or salad), and dessert. Meats, though tasty, are definitely secondary to the pasta dishes, which are much more generous and filling. The wine is so excellent (especially the white Frascati wine from the nearby Castelli Romani) and moderate in price that you may want to do as the Romans do and have it with both lunch and dinner.

Meal hours are rather confining in Italy. Restaurants generally serve lunch between 1 and 3pm and dinner between about 8 and 10:30pm; at all other times, restaurants are closed. Dinner, by the way, is taken late in Rome, so although the restaurant may open at 7:30, even if you get there at 8pm, you'll often be the only one in the place. What if you're hungry outside those hours? Well, if you don't take continental breakfast at your hotel, you can have coffee and a pastry at any **bar** (really a cafe, although there will be liquor bottles behind the counter) or a *tavola calda* (hot table). These are stand-up snack bar-type arrangements, open all day long and found all over the city. Romans think in terms of "dinner" in the afternoon (*pranzo*) and "supper" in the evening (*cena*). In Rome, as in much of the rest of Europe, a heavier meal is typically eaten at midday and a lighter one in the evening.

We recommend that you leave a few hours free for dinner and go to a restaurant in a different part of town each night. It's a great way to get a real taste of Rome. Romans think of meals as leisurely affairs, so allow yourself enough time and relax—do as the Romans do.

THE CUISINE

Many visitors from North America erroneously think of Italian cuisine as one-dimensional. Of course, everybody's heard of minestrone, spaghetti, chicken cacciatore, and spumoni ice cream. But chefs hardly confine themselves to such a limited repertoire.

Throughout your Roman holiday you'll encounter such savory treats as *zuppa di pesce* (a soup or stew of various fish, cooked in white wine and herbs), *cannelloni* (tube-shaped pasta baked with any number of stuffings), *riso col gamberi* (rice with shrimp, peas, and mushrooms, flavored with white wine and garlic), *scampi alla griglia* (grilled prawns, one of the best-tasting, and most expensive, dishes in the city), *quaglie con risotto e tartufi* (quail with rice and truffles), *lepre alla cacciatore* (hare flavored with tomato sauce and herbs), *zabaglione* (a cream made with sugar, egg yolks, and Marsala), *gnocchi alla romana* (potato-flour dumplings with a sauce made with meat and covered with grated cheese), *stracciatella* (chicken broth with eggs and grated cheese), *abbacchio* (baby spring lamb, often roasted over an open fire), *saltimbocca alla romana* (literally "jump-in-your-mouth"—thin slices of veal with cheese, ham, and sage), *fritta alla romana* (a mixed fry that's likely to include everything from brains to artichokes), *carciofi alla romana* (tender artichokes cooked with mint and garlic, and flavored with white wine), *fettuccine all'uovo* (egg noodles served with butter and cheese), *zuppa di cozze o vongole* (a hearty bowl of mussels or clams cooked in broth), *fritta di scampi e calamaretti* (baby squid and prawns fast-fried), *fragoline* (wild strawberries, in this case from the Alban Hills), and *finocchio* (or fennel, a celerylike raw vegetable, the flavor of anisette, often eaten as a dessert and in salads).

Incidentally, except in the south, Italians do not use as much garlic in their food as most foreigners seem to believe. Most northern Italian dishes are butter based. Virgin olive oil is preferred in the south. Spaghetti and meatballs is not an Italian dish, although certain restaurants throughout the country have taken to serving it for homesick Americans.

WINES & OTHER DRINKS

Italy is the largest wine-producing country in the world; as far back as 800 B.C. the Etruscans were vintners. It's said that more soil is used in Italy for the cultivation of grapes than for growing food. Many Italian farmers produce wine just for their own consumption or for their relatives. It wasn't until 1965, however, that laws were enacted to guarantee regular consistency in wine making. Wines regulated by the government are labeled "DOC" (*Denominazione di Origine Controllata*). If you see "DOCG" on a label (the "G" means *garantita*), that means even better quality control.

Lazio (Rome's region) is a major wine-producing region of Italy. Many of the local wines come from the Castelli Romani, the hill towns around Rome. Horace and Juvenal sang the praises of Latium wines even in imperial times. These wines, experts agree, are best drunk when young, and they are most often white, mellow, and dry (or else demi-sec). There are seven different types, including **Falerno** (yellowish straw in color) and **Cecubo** (often served with roast meat). Try also **Colli Albani** (straw-yellow with amber tints and served with both fish and meat). The golden-yellow wines of **Frascati** are famous, produced in both a demi-sec and a sweet variety, the latter served with dessert.

Romans drink other libations as well. Their most famous drink is **Campari,** bright red in color and herb flavored, with a quinine bitterness to it. It's customary to serve it with ice cubes and soda.

Beer is also made in Italy and, in general, is lighter than German beer. If you order beer in a Roman bar or restaurant, chances are it will be imported unless you specify otherwise, and you'll be charged accordingly. Some famous names in European beer-making now operate plants in Italy, where the brew has been "adjusted" to Italian taste.

High-proof **grappa** is made from the leftovers after the grapes have been pressed. Many Romans drink this before or after dinner (some put it into their coffee). To an untrained foreign palate, it often seems rough and harsh; some say it's an acquired taste.

Italy has many **brandies,** though according to an agreement with France, it is not supposed to use the word *cognac* in labeling them. A popular one is Vecchia Romagna.

Other popular drinks include several **liqueurs.** Try herb-flavored Strega, or perhaps an almond-flavored Amaretto. One of the best known is Maraschino, taking its name from a type of cherry used in its preparation. Galliano is also herb flavored, and Sambuca (anisette) is made of aniseed and is often served with a "fly" (coffee bean) in it. On a hot day the true Roman orders a vermouth, Cinzano, with a twist of lemon, ice cubes, and a squirt of soda water.

1 Restaurants by Cuisine

ABRUZZESE
Abruzzi (Near Ancient Rome, *I*)
Ristorante al Cardello (Near Ancient Rome, *I*)

BOLOGNESE/EMILIA-ROMAGNOLA
Césarina (Near Via Veneto & Piazza Barberini, *M*)
Colline Emiliane (Near Via Veneto & Piazza Barberini, *M*)
Dal Bolognese (Near the Spanish Steps & Piazza del Popolo, *M*)

CALABRESE
Le Maschere (Near Campo de' Fiori & the Jewish Ghetto, *I*)

CONTINENTAL
Trimani Wine Bar (Near Stazione Termini, *I*)

ENGLISH
Babington's Tea Rooms (Near the Spanish Steps & Piazza del Popolo, *M*)

Key to Abbreviations: *VE* = Very Expensive; *E* = Expensive; *M* = Moderate; *I* = Inexpensive

FLORENTINE

Da Mario (Near the Spanish Steps &
Piazza del Popolo, *I*)

FRENCH

L'Eau Vive (Near Piazza Navona &
the Pantheon, *E*)
Sans Souci (Near Via Veneto &
Piazza Barberini, *VE*)

GREEK

Antica Hostaria l'Archeologia
(On the Appian Way, *M*)

INTERNATIONAL

Alfredo alla Scrofa (Near Piazza
Navona & the Pantheon, *M*)
George's (Near Via Veneto & Piazza
Barberini, *VE*)
La Terrazza (Near Via Veneto &
Piazza Barberini, *VE*)
L'Eau Vive (Near Piazza Navona &
the Pantheon, *E*)
Osteria dell'Antiquario (Near Piazza
Navona & the Pantheon, *M*)
Taverna Flavia (Near Stazione
Termini, *M*)

ITALIAN (PAN-ITALIAN)

Al Bric (Near Piazza Navona &
the Pantheon, *I*)
Alvaro al Circo Massimo (Near
Ancient Rome, *E*)
Antico Arco (In Trastevere, *M*)
Arancia Blu (In San Lorenzo, *I*)
Asinocotto (In Trastevere, *M*)
Aurora 10 da Pino il Sommelier
(Near Via Veneto & Piazza
Barberini, *M*)
Boccondivino (Near Piazza Navona
& the Pantheon, *E*)
Café Riccioli (Near Piazza Navona &
the Pantheon, *M*)
'Gusto (Near the Spanish Steps &
Piazza del Popolo, *I*)
Hostaria Nerone (Near Ancient
Rome, *I*)
Il Bacaro (Near the Spanish Steps &
Piazza del Popolo, *M*)
Il Convivio (Near Piazza Navona &
the Pantheon, *M*)

Il Dito e La Luna (In San Lorenzo, *I*)
Il Ristorante 34 (Near the Spanish
Steps & Piazza del Popolo, *I*)
Insalata Ricca 2 (Near Piazza Navona
& the Pantheon, *I*)
La Terrazza (Near Via Veneto &
Piazza Barberini, *VE*)
Montevecchio (Near Piazza Navona
& the Pantheon, *M*)
Myosotis (Near Piazza Navona & the
Pantheon, *M*)
Passetto (Near Piazza Navona & the
Pantheon, *M*)
Quirino (Near Piazza Navona & the
Pantheon, *M*)
Relais Le Jardin (In Parioli, *VE*)
Ristorante Giardinaccio (Near the
Vatican, *I*)
Sans Souci (Near Via Veneto &
Piazza Barberini, *VE*)
Tre Scalini (Near Piazza Navona &
the Pantheon, *M*)
Troiani (Near Piazza Navona & the
Pantheon, *E*)
Vecchia Roma (Near Campo de'
Fiori & the Jewish Ghetto, *M*)

JAPANESE

Café Riccioli (Near Piazza Navona &
the Pantheon, *M*)

JEWISH

Da Giggetto (Near Campo de' Fiori
& the Jewish Ghetto, *M*)
Piperno (Near Campo de' Fiori & the
Jewish Ghetto, *E*)

MEDITERRANEAN

Babington's Tea Rooms (Near the
Spanish Steps & Piazza del
Popolo, *M*)
Les Etoiles (Near the Vatican, *VE*)

MOLISIAN

Ristorante Giardinaccio (Near the
Vatican, *I*)

NEAPOLITAN

Il Quadrifoglio (Near Ancient
Rome, *M*)
Scoglio di Frisio (Near Stazione
Termini, *M*)

PACIFIC RIM

'Gusto (Near the Spanish Steps & Piazzi del Popolo, *I*)

PIZZA

Pizzeria Baffetto (Near Piazza Navona & the Pantheon, *I*)
Scoglio di Frisio (Near Stazione Termini, *M*)

ROMAN

Abruzzi (Near Ancient Rome, *I*)
Agata e Romeo (Near Ancient Rome, *VE*)
Al Ceppo (In Parioli, *M*)
Alfredo alla Scrofa (Near Piazza Navona & the Pantheon, *M*)
Antica Hostaria l'Archeologia (On the Appian Way, *M*)
Bar Cottini (Near Stazione Termini, *I*)
Bramante (Near Piazza Navona & the Pantheon, *M*)
Césarina (Near Via Veneto & Piazza Barberini, *M*)
Checchino dal 1887 (In Testaccio, *M*)
Da Giggetto (Near Campo de' Fiori & the Jewish Ghetto, *M*)
Da Mario (Near the Spanish Steps & Piazza del Popolo, *I*)
El Toulá (Near the Spanish Steps & Piazza del Popolo, *VE*)
Enoteca Corsi (Near the Spanish Steps & Piazza del Popolo, *I*)
Hostaria dei Bastioni (Near the Vatican, *I*)
Hostaria Nerone (Near Ancient Rome, *I*)
Il Miraggio (Near Piazza Navona & the Pantheon, *I*)
Il Ristorante 34 (Near the Spanish Steps & Piazza del Popolo, *I*)
Il Sanpietrino (Near Campo de' Fiori & the Jewish Ghetto, *M*)
La Campana (Near the Spanish Steps & Piazza del Popolo, *M*)
La Cisterna (In Trastevere, *M*)
Monte Arci (Near Stazione Termini, *I*)
Montevecchio (Near Piazza Navona & the Pantheon, *M*)

Osteria dell'Antiquario (Near Piazza Navona & the Pantheon, *M*)
Otello Alla Concordia (Near the Spanish Steps & Piazza de Polopo, *I*)
Pari (In Trastevere, *M*)
Passetto (Near Piazza Navona & the Pantheon, *M*)
Piperno (Near Campo de' Fiori & the Jewish Ghetto, *E*)
Quirino (Near Piazza Navona & the Pantheon, *M*)
Ristorante al Cardello (Near Ancient Rome, *I*)
Ristorante da Pancrazio (Near Campo de' Fiori & the Jewish Ghetto, *M*)
Ristorante del Pallaro (Near Campo de' Fiori & the Jewish Ghetto, *M*)
Ristorante Il Matriciano (Near the Vatican, *M*)
Ristorante Nino (Near the Spanish Steps & Piazza del Popolo, *M*)
Ristorante Pierdonati (Near the Vatican, *I*)
Sabatini (In Trastevere, *E*)
Taverna Flavia (Near Stazione Termini, *M*)
Tre Scalini (Near Piazza Navona & the Pantheon, *M*)
Vecchia Roma (Near Campo de' Fiori & the Jewish Ghetto, *M*)

SARDINIAN

Il Drappo (Near Campo de' Fiori & the Jewish Ghetto, *E*)
Il Miraggio (Near Piazza Navona & the Pantheon, *I*)
Monte Arci (Near Stazione Termini, *I*)

SEAFOOD

Alberto Ciarla (In Trastevere, *E*)
Café Riccioli (Near Piazza Navona & the Pantheon, *M*)
Il Miraggio (Near Piazza Navona & the Pantheon, *I*)
La Rosetta (Near Piazza Navona & the Pantheon, *VE*)
Quinzi & Gabrieli (Near Piazza Navona & the Pantheon, *VE*)
Sabatini (In Trastevere, *E*)

SICILIAN

Il Dito e la Luna (In San Lorenzo, *I*)
Quirino (Near Piazza Navona & the
Pantheon, *M*)

TUSCAN

Girarrosto Toscano (Near Via Veneto
& Piazza Barberini, *M*)
Ristorante Nino (Near the Spanish
Steps & Piazza del Popolo, *M*)

VEGETARIAN

Arancia Blu (In San Lorenzo, *I*)
Insalata Ricca 2 (Near Piazza Navona
& the Pantheon, *I*)

VENETIAN

El Toulà (Near the Spanish Steps &
Piazza del Popolo, *VE*)

2 Near Stazione Termini

VERY EXPENSIVE

✪ **Agata e Romeo.** Via Carlo Alberto 45. ☎ **06-446-6115.** Reservations recommended. Main courses 40,000–50,000 lire ($20–$25). AE, DC, MC, V. Mon–Sat 1–3pm and 8–11:30pm. Metro: Vittorio Emanuele. NEW ROMAN.

One of the most charming places near the Vittorio Emanuele Monument is this striking duplex restaurant in turn-of-the-century Liberty style. You'll enjoy the creative cuisine of Romeo Caraccio (who manages the dining room) and his wife, Agata Parisella (who prepares her own version of sophisticated Roman food). Look for pasta garnished with broccoli and cauliflower and served in skate broth as well as a crisp *sformato* loaded with eggplant, parmigiano, mozzarella, and fresh Italian herbs. Sweet-tasting swordfish might be served thinly sliced as roulade and loaded with capers and olives; beans will probably be studded with savory mussels, clams, and pasta. For dessert, consider Agata's *millefoglie,* puff pastry stuffed with almonds and sweetened cream. In 1998 they added a charming wine cellar offering a wide choice of international and domestic wines.

MODERATE

Il Quadrifoglio. Via del Boschetto 19. ☎ **06-482-6096.** Reservations recommended. Main courses 20,000–30,000 lire ($10–$15). AE, DC, MC, V. Mon–Sat 7pm–midnight. Closed Aug. Metro: Cavour. NEAPOLITAN.

In a grandiose palace, this well-managed restaurant lets you sample the flavors and herbs of Naples and southern Italy. You'll find a tempting selection of antipasti, like anchovies, peppers, capers, onions, and breaded and fried eggplant, all garnished with fresh herbs and virgin olive oil. The pastas are made daily, usually with tomato- or oil-based sauces and always with herbs and aged cheeses. Try a zesty rice dish (one of the best is *sartù di riso,* studded with vegetables, herbs, and meats), followed by a hard-to-resist grilled octopus or a simple but savory *granatine* (meatballs, usually of veal, bound together with mozzarella). Dessert anyone? A longtime favorite is *torta caprese,* with hazelnuts and chocolate.

✪ **Scoglio di Frisio.** Via Merulana 256. ☎ **06-487-2765.** Reservations recommended. Main courses 12,000–32,000 lire ($6–$16). AE, DC, MC, V. Mon–Fri 12:30–3pm; daily 7:30–11pm. Metro: Manzoni. Bus: 714. NEAPOLITAN/PIZZA.

Scoglio di Frisio is the supreme choice for an introduction to the Neapolitan kitchen. Here you can taste a *genuine* plate-sized Neapolitan pizza (crunchy, oozy, and excellent) with clams and mussels. Or perhaps you can start with a medley of savory stuffed vegetables and antipasti before moving on to chicken cacciatore or well-flavored tender veal scaloppini. Scoglio di Frisio also makes for an inexpensive night of slightly

Dining Near Via Veneto & Termini

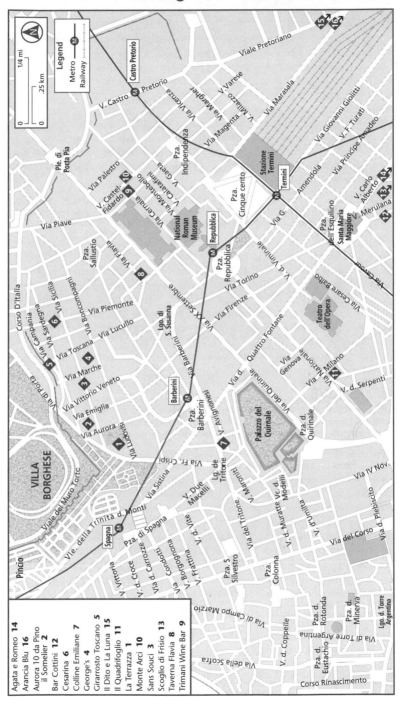

Agata e Romeo **14**
Arancia Blu **16**
Aurora 10 da Pino
il Sommelier **2**
Bar Cottini **12**
Cesarina **6**
Colline Emiliane **7**
George's **4**
Girarrosto Toscano **5**
Il Dito e La Luna **15**
Il Quadrifoglio **11**
La Terrazza **1**
Monte Arci **10**
Sans Souci **3**
Scoglio di Frisio **13**
Taverna Flavia **8**
Trimani Wine Bar **9**

Check, Please

In the cheapest restaurants you may be charged a *pane e coperto* (bread and cover charge) of from 1,000 to 3,000 lire (50¢ to $1.50) per person. Also note that a *servizio* (tip) of 10% to 15% will often be added to your bill or included in the price, although patrons often leave an extra 1,000 to 3,000 lire (50¢ to $1.50) as a token.

---

hokey but still charming entertainment, as cornball "O Sole Mio" renditions and other Neapolitan songs spring forth from a guitar, mandolin, and strolling tenor (Mario Lanza reincarnate). The nautical decor (in honor of the top-notch fish dishes) is complete with a high-ceilinged grotto of fisher's nets, crustaceans, and a miniature three-masted schooner.

Taverna Flavia. Via Flavia 9. ☎ **06-474-5214.** Reservations recommended. Main courses 20,000–35,000 lire ($10–$17.50). AE, DC, MC, V. Mon–Fri 12:30–3pm and 7:30–11pm, Sat 7:30–11:30pm. Metro: Repubblica. ROMAN/INTERNATIONAL.

Taverna Flavia, a block from Via XX Settembre, is a robustly Roman restaurant where movie people used to meet and eat during the heyday of *la dolce vita*. It still serves the food that once delighted the late Frank Sinatra and the "Hollywood on the Tiber" crowd. It's not chic anymore, but you can still enjoy the hearty classics here. Specialties are risotto with scampi, spaghetti with champagne, *osso bucco* (veal shank) with peas, a delectable seafood salad, and a to-die-for fondue with truffles. There's a daily-changing regional dish (it might be Roman-style tripe prepared in such a savory manner it tastes far better than you might expect). A chef always prepares our favorite salad in Rome: Veruska, made with five kinds of lettuce and mushrooms, including fresh truffles.

INEXPENSIVE

✪ **Bar Cottini.** Via Merulana 286–287. ☎ **06-474-0768.** Reservations not accepted. Main courses 11,000–16,000 lire ($5.50–$8) lunch. No credit cards. Restaurant daily noon–3pm, bar daily noon–9pm. Metro: Termini. ROMAN.

Large and bustling, this is the most popular *tavola calda* in this congested neighborhood, feeding hundreds of hungry office workers and shopkeepers every day. At lunch, it's self-service, not unlike an American cafeteria, but with the noteworthy difference that the food represents the bounty of agrarian Italy (and is rather lacking on the tuna-casserole front). Separate areas are devoted to hot pastas—most priced at 5,000 lire ($2.50) per heaping portion—meats, and, to a lesser extent, fish. High turnover ensures a relatively fresh, if not particularly stylish, array of mass-produced, pan-Italian cuisine. For such a bustling food factory, the flavors are very good, as are the seasonings. It's a great way to fill up on good, hearty food at a relatively modest price. Even when it's not serving food, it's a fine choice to visit as a bar, as it has a relaxed pub atmosphere until 9pm each evening.

Monte Arci. Via Castelfirdardo 33. ☎ **06-494-1220.** Reservations recommended. Main courses 15,000–20,000 lire ($7.50–$10); fixed-price menu 50,000 lire ($25). AE, DC, V. Mon–Fri 12:30–3pm and 7–11:30pm, Sat 7–11:30pm. Closed Aug. Metro: Stazione Termini. ROMAN/SARDINIAN.

Monte Arci, on a cobblestone street near Piazza Indipendenza, is set behind a sienna-colored facade. It features low-cost Roman and Sardinian specialties (you'll spend even less for pizza) like *nialoreddus* (a regional form of gnocchetti); pasta with clams, lobster, or the musky-earthy notes of porcini mushrooms; green and white spaghetti with bacon, spinach, cream, and cheese; and delicious lamb sausage flavored with herbs and pecorino cheese. Much of the food is just like Mamma would make, with the strengths and weaknesses that implies.

○ **Trimani Wine Bar.** Via Cernaia 37B. ☎ **06-446-9630.** Reservations recommended. Main courses 12,000–26,000 lire ($6–$13); glass of wine (depending on vintage) 3,500–20,000 lire ($1.75–$10). AE, DC, MC, V. Mon–Sat 11:30am–3:30pm and 6pm–12:30am (Dec open also on Sun). Closed 2 weeks in Aug. Metro: Repubblica or Castro Pretorio. CONTINENTAL.

Opened as a tasting center for French and Italian wines, spumantis, and liqueurs, this elegant wine bar has a lovely decor (stylish but informal) and comfortable seating. More than 30 wines are available by the glass, and to accompany them you can choose from a bistro-style menu, with dishes like salad Niçoise, vegetarian pastas, herb-laden bean soups (*fagiole*), quiche, and Hungarian goulash. They also have a wider menu including meat and fish courses like veal medallions with roasted potatoes and sage, grilled fish (depending on what's fresh at the market) with steamed vegetables, or shell of scampi au gratin filled with salmon. Their specialty is the large choice of little "bruschette" with cheese and prosciutto, since they order every kind of prosciutti and cheese, from all over Italy. The dishes are matched with the appropriate wines. Among the desserts, the specialty deservedly wins many friends: chestnut mousse served with a sauce of white wine (Verduzzo di Ronco di Viere), covered by whipped cream and meringue.

Trimani maintains a well-stocked shop about 40 yards from its wine bar, at V. Goito 20 (☎ **06-446-9661**), where an astonishing array of Italian wines is for sale.

3 In San Lorenzo

INEXPENSIVE

○ **Arancia Blu.** Via dei Latini 55–65 (at Via Arunci). ☎ **06-445-4105.** Reservations highly recommended. Main courses 12,000–16,000 lire ($6–$8). AE, V. Daily 8pm–midnight. Bus: 71. INVENTIVE VEGETARIAN ITALIAN.

Fabio Bassan and Enrico Bartolucci offer Rome's best vegetarian cuisine. Under soft lighting and wood ceilings, surrounded by wine racks and university intellectuals, the friendly waiters will help you compile a menu to fit any dietary need. The dishes at this trendy spot are inspired by peasant cuisines from across Italy and beyond. The appetizers range from hummus and tabouleh to zucchini-and-saffron quiche or salad with apples, gorgonzola, and balsamic vinegar. The main courses change seasonally and may be lasagna with red onions, mushrooms, zucchini, and ginger; *cous cous con verdure* (vegetable couscous); or *ravioli ripieni di patate e menta* (ravioli stuffed with potatoes and mint served under fresh tomatoes and Sardinian sheep's cheese). They offer 250 wines and inventive desserts like pears cooked in wine and juniper, served with orange-honey *semifreddo* or dark chocolate cake with warm orange sauce.

Il Dito e La Luna. Via dei Sabelli 49–51, San Lorenzo. ☎ **06-494-0726.** Reservations recommended. Main courses 19,000–24,000 lire ($9.50–$12). No credit cards. Mon–Sat 8pm–midnight. Metro: Piazza Vittorio. SICILIAN/ITALIAN.

This charming, unpretentious bistro has counters and service areas accented with the fruits of a bountiful harvest. The menu—divided between traditional Sicilian and creative up-to-date recipes prepared with flair—includes orange-infused anchovies served on orange segments, creamy flan of mild onions and mountain cheese, and seafood couscous loaded with shellfish. The pastas are excellent, particularly the square-cut spaghetti (*tonnarelli*) with mussels, bacon, tomatoes, and exotic mushrooms. Even those not particularly enamored with fish might like the *baccalà mantecato* (baked and pulverized salt cod) with lentils. The specialty of the house is *caponata di melanzane*, chopped eggplant stewed in tomato sauce with onions and potatoes.

4 Near Via Veneto & Piazza Barberini

To locate the restaurants in this section, see the "Dining Near Via Veneto & Termini" map on p. 93.

VERY EXPENSIVE

❂ George's. Via Marche 7. ☎ **06-4208-4575.** Reservations required. Main courses 100,000–120,000 lire ($50–$60). AE, DC, MC, V. Mon–Sat 12:30–3pm and 7:30pm–midnight. Closed Aug. Metro: Barberini. INTERNATIONAL.

George's has been a favorite of ours seemingly forever, though its prices have skyrocketed over the years. It's right off Via Veneto, in a classical 18th-century building. Many guests drop in for a before-dinner drink, enjoying the music in the piano bar and the relaxed, clubby atmosphere. Meals are served in a pair of elegant dining rooms with tented ceilings. The kitchen has an uncompromising dedication to quality, as reflected by such dishes as smoked trout with horseradish sauce, grilled scampi with bacon and sliced tomatoes, orange-scented duckling, and all kinds of veal and steak dishes. Regardless of how crowded the place may be, the chefs take special care with each dish, using only the freshest produce, meats, and fish. After years of dining here, we've never had a bad meal. From June to October, in good weather the action shifts to the garden, suitably undisturbed because it's in the garden of a papal villa.

❂ La Terrazza. In the Hotel Eden, Via Ludovisi 49. ☎ **06-478-121.** Reservations recommended. Main courses 50,000–85,000 lire ($25–$42.50); fixed-price menu 130,000 lire ($65). AE, DC, MC, V. Daily 12:30–2:30pm and 7:30–10:30pm. Metro: Barberini. ITALIAN/INTERNATIONAL.

La Terrazza and Relais Le Jardin (under "In Parioli," later in this chapter) serve the city's finest cuisine; at La Terrazza, you also get a sweeping view over St. Peter's. The service manages to be formal and flawless yet not intimidating. Chef Enrico Derfligher, the wizard behind about a dozen top-notch Italian restaurants around Europe, prepares a seasonally changing menu that's among the most polished in Rome. You might start with zucchini blossoms stuffed with ricotta and black olives or lobster medallions with apple purée and black truffles. Main courses may include red tortelli (whose coloring comes from tomato mousse) stuffed with mascarpone cheese and drizzled with lemon, sea bass baked in a crust of black olives and salt with oregano and potatoes, or grilled tagliata of beef with radicchio salad and aniseed sauce. On our last visit, we shared a superb "symphony" of seafood, a platter of perfectly seasoned Mediterranean sea bass, turbot, gilthead, and prawns for two. There's even a macrobiotic fixed-price menu, plus an authentic Roman menu. All the desserts are served with a sweet wine—try the strawberry mousse with mango sauce or the ricotta cheesecake with raisins, rum, and chocolate sauce.

❂ Sans Souci. Via Sicilia 20. ☎ **06-482-1814.** Reservations recommended. Main courses 40,000–70,000 lire ($20–$35). AE, CB, DC, DISC, MC, V. Tues–Sun 8pm–1am. Closed Aug 10–30. Metro: Barberini. FRENCH/ITALIAN.

Not long ago, Sans Souci was getting a little tired, but it's now bounced back, and Michelin has restored its coveted star. As you step into the dimly lit lounge, the maître d' will present you with the menu, which you can peruse while sipping a drink amid tapestries and glittering mirrors. The menu is ever changing, though the classics never disappear. A great beginning is the goose-liver terrine with truffles, one of the chef's signatures. The fish soup is, according to one Rome restaurant critic, "a legend to experience." The soufflés are popular (like artichoke, asparagus, and spinach), as are the succulent truffle-filled ravioli, homemade foie gras, and tender Normandy lamb. Save room for a special dessert soufflé (prepared for two), such as chocolate and Grand Marnier.

MODERATE

Aurora 10 da Pino il Sommelier. Via Aurora 10. ☎ **06-474-2779.** Reservations recommended. Main courses 22,000–35,000 lire ($11–$17.50). AE, DC, MC, V. Tues–Sun noon–3pm and 7–11pm. Metro: Barberini. ITALIAN.

Skip the tourist traps along Via Veneto and walk another block or two for the much better food and lovely service here. The wait staff is welcoming to foreigners, though you'll also dine with regulars from the chic neighborhood. The place is noted for its array of more than 250 wines, representing every province. The linguine with chunky lobster and the *rigatoni alla siciliana* with eggplant, black olives, and tomato sauce are better than your mama made (if your mama was Livia Soprano). The fish is fresh every day, and the chefs grill it to perfection. The exquisite meat dishes include grilled strips of fillet with seasonal vegetables. Among the more delectable desserts are crème brûlée and Neapolitan babba, filled with liqueur.

Césarina. Via Piemonte 109. ☎ **06-488-0828.** Reservations recommended. Main courses 18,000–30,000 lire ($9–$15). AE, DC, MC, V. Mon–Sat 12:30–3pm and 7:30–11pm. Metro: Barberini. Bus: 52, 53, 63 or 80. EMILIANA-ROMAGNOLA/ROMAN.

Specializing in the cuisines of Rome and the region around Bologna, this place has grown considerably since matriarch Césarina Masi opened it around 1960 (many Rome veterans fondly remember her strict supervision of the kitchen and how she'd lecture regulars who didn't finish their tagliatelle). Though Césarina passed away in the mid-1980s, her traditions are kept going. The polite staff roll an excellent *bollito misto* (an array of well-seasoned boiled meats) from table to table on a trolley and often follow with misto Césarina—four kinds of creamy handmade pasta, each with a different sauce. Equally appealing are the *saltimbocca* (veal with ham) and the *cotoletta alla bolognese* (tender veal cutlet baked with ham and cheese). A dessert specialty is *semifreddo* Césarina with hot chocolate, so meltingly good it's worth the 5 pounds you'll gain.

✪ Colline Emiliane. Via Avignonesi 22 (off Piazza Barberini). ☎ **06-481-7538.** Reservations highly recommended. Main courses 35,000–60,000 lire ($17.50–$30). MC, V. Sat–Thurs 12:45–2:45pm and 7:45–10:45pm. Closed Aug. Metro: Barberini. EMILIANA-ROMAGNOLA.

Serving the *classica cucina bolognese,* Colline Emiliane is a small family-run place—the owner is the cook and his wife makes the pasta (about the best you'll find in Rome). The house specialty is an inspired *tortellini alla panna* (with cream sauce and truffles), but the less expensive pastas are excellent too, like *maccheroni al funghetto* and *tagliatelle alla bolognese.* As an opener, we suggest *culatello di Zibello,* a delicacy from a small town near Parma known for the world's finest prosciutto. Main courses include *braciola di maiale* (boneless rolled pork cutlets stuffed with ham and cheese, breaded, and sautéed) and an impressive *giambonnetto* (roast veal Emilian style with roast potatoes).

Take a Gelato Break

If you're craving luscious gelato, our top choice is ✪ **Giolitti,** Via Uffici del Vicario 40 (☎ **06-699-1243**), the city's oldest ice-cream shop, open daily 7am to 2am. You'll find the usual vanilla (*vaniglia*), chocolate (*cioccolato*), strawberry (*fragola*), and coffee (*caffè*), but also flavors you might not have heard of, like *gianduia* (chocolate hazelnut), plus *cassata alla siciliana, zabaglione* (see appendix B), *mascarpone,* and *maron glacé.* The preposterously oversized showpiece sundaes have names like Coppa Olimpico di Roma and Coppa Mondiale. And if you want at least the illusion you're eating healthy, try the Coppa Primanata (ice cream plus lots of fresh fruit). Prices here and at each of the places below range from 2,500 to 16,000 lire ($1.25 to $8).

Close behind is **Tre Scalini,** Piazza Navona 30 (☎ **06-687-9148;** see full entry below under "Near Piazza Navona & the Pantheon"), celebrated for its *tartufo.* It's said you haven't really experienced Rome until you've enjoyed a tartufo here. Another favorite is the **Palazzo del Freddo Giovanni Fassi,** Via Principe Eugenio 65–67 (☎ **06-446-4740**). More than 100 years old, this ice-cream outlet (part of a gelato factory) turns out yummy concoctions and specializes in rice ice cream. It's open Tuesday to Sunday noon to 12:30am.

If you're fond of the frothy *frullati* frappes for which Italy is famous, head to **Pascucci,** Via Torre Argentina 20 (☎ **06-686-4816**), where blenders work all day grinding fresh fruit into delectable drinks. It's open Monday to Saturday noon to 1am. And if you're in the mood for frozen yogurt, try **Yogofruit,** P. G. Travani Arquati 118 (☎ **06-587-972**), near Piazza San Sonnino. It's especially popular with young Romans, who line up to sample the tart frozen yogurt delights blended with fruit from the Latium countryside. It's open daily 6am to 11pm.

✪ **Girarrosto Toscano.** Via Campania 29. ☎ **06-482-3835.** Reservations required. Main courses 25,000–40,000 lire ($12.50–$20). AE, CB, DC, MC, V. Thurs–Tues 12:30–2:30pm and 7:30–11pm. Metro: Barberini. Bus: 95 or 116. TUSCAN.

Girarrosto Toscano, facing the walls of the Borghese Gardens, draws large crowds, so you may have to wait. Under a vaulted cellar ceiling, it serves some of Rome's finest Tuscan fare. Begin by trying the enormous selection of fresh antipasti, from little meatballs and melon with savory prosciutto to *frittate* (omelettes) and delectable Tuscan salami. You're then given a choice of pasta, like creamy fettuccine. Although expensive, the delicately flavored *bistecca alla fiorentina* (grilled steak seasoned with oil, salt, and pepper) is worth every lire if you're in the mood to splurge. Fresh fish from the Adriatic is served daily. Order with care if you're on a budget; both meat and fish are priced according to weight and can run considerably higher than the prices above.

5 Near Ancient Rome

EXPENSIVE

Alvaro al Circo Massimo. Via dei Cerchi 53. ☎ **06-678-6112.** Reservations required. Main courses 20,000–35,000 lire ($10–$17.50). AE, MC, V. Tues–Sun 12:30–3:30pm and 7:30–11pm, Sun 12:30–3:30pm; Tues–Sat 7–11pm. Closed Aug. Metro: Circo Massimo. ITALIAN.

Alvaro, at the edge of the Circus Maximus, is Rome's closest thing to a genuine provincial inn, right down to the hanging corncobs and rolls of fat sausages. The antipasti

Dining Near the Spanish Steps & Ancient Rome

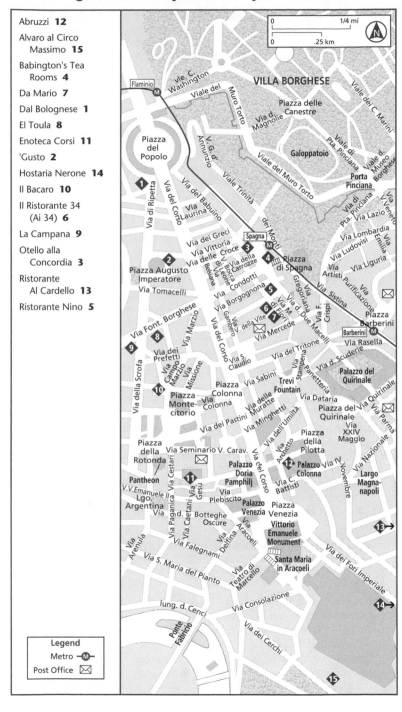

and pastas are fine, the meat courses are even better, and the fresh fish is never overcooked. Other specialties are tagliolini with mushrooms and truffles and briny-flavored roasted turbot with potatoes. They're especially well stocked with exotic seasonal mushrooms, including black truffles rivaling the ones you'd find in Spoleto. A basket of fresh fruit rounds out the meal. The atmosphere is comfortable and mellow.

INEXPENSIVE

Abruzzi. Via del Vaccaro 1. ☎ **06-679-3897.** Reservations recommended. Main courses 10,000–23,000 lire ($5–$11.50). AE, DC, MC, V. Sun–Fri 12:30–3pm and 7:30–10:30pm. Closed 3 weeks in Aug. Bus: 44, 46. ABRUZZESE/ROMANA.

Abruzzi, which takes its name from the region east of Rome, is at one side of Piazza S.S. Apostoli, just a short walk from Piazza Venezia. The good food and reasonable prices make it a big draw for students. The chef offers a satisfying assortment of cold antipasti. With your starter, we suggest a liter of garnet-red wine; we once had one whose bouquet was suggestive of Abruzzi's wildflowers. If you'd like soup as well, you'll find a good *stracciatella* (egg-and-Parmesan soup). A typical main dish is *vitella tonnata con capperi* (veal in tuna sauce with capers). But the menu ranges far wider than that; it's a virtual textbook of classical Italian dishes, everything from a creamy baked eggplant with mozzarella to meltingly tender veal cutlets in the Milanese style (fried with potatoes). No one in Italy does roast lamb better than the Romans, and the selection here is good—tender, grilled to perfection, seasoned with virgin olive oil and fresh herbs, and dished up with roast potatoes.

Hostaria Nerone. Via Terme di Tito 96. ☎ **06-474-5207.** Reservations recommended. Main courses 15,000–20,000 lire ($7.50–$10). AE, DC, V. Mon–Sat noon–3pm and 7–11pm. Metro: Colosseo. Bus: 85, 87, 75, 175, or 117. ROMAN/ITALIAN.

Built atop the ruins of the Golden House of Nero, this trattoria is run by the energetic De Santis family, who cook, serve, and handle the large crowds of hungry locals and visitors. Opened in 1929 at the edge of the Colle Oppio Park, it contains two compact dining rooms, plus a terrace lined with flowering shrubs that offers a view over the Colosseum and the Bathrooms of Trajan. The copious antipasti buffet represents the bounty of Italy's fields and seas. The pastas include savory spaghetti with clams and, our favorite, *pasta fagioli* (with beans). There's also grilled crayfish and swordfish and Italian sausages with polenta. Roman-style tripe is a local favorite, but you may want to skip it for the osso bucco (braised veal shanks) with mashed potatoes and seasonal mushrooms. The wide list of some of the best of Italian wines is priced at reasonably.

Ristorante al Cardello. Via del Cardello 1 (at the corner of Via Cavour). ☎ **06-474-5259.** Reservations recommended. Main courses 14,000–20,000 lire ($7–$10). AE, DC, MC, V. Mon–Sat noon–3pm and 7–11pm. Closed Aug. Metro: Cavour or Colosseo. ROMAN/ABRUZZI.

Conveniently close to the Colosseum, this restaurant has thrived since the 1920s, when it opened in the semicellar of an 18th-century building. We always love the antipasti buffet, where the flavorful marinated vegetables reveal the bounty of the Italian harvest; at 10,000 lire ($5) per person for a good serving, it's a great deal. You might follow with *bucatini* (thick spaghetti) *all'amatriciana;* tender roast lamb with potatoes, garlic, and mountain herbs; or a thick hearty stew. A Roman food critic, dining with us, claimed he always comes here when he wants to eat like a peasant (and that's a compliment).

6 Near Campo de' Fiori & the Jewish Ghetto

EXPENSIVE

Il Drappo. Vicolo del Malpasso 9. ☎ **06-687-7365.** Reservations required. Main courses 20,000–45,000 lire ($10–$22.50); fixed-price menus (including Sardinian wine) 65,000–70,000 lire ($32.50–$35). AE, DC, MC, V. Mon–Sat 7pm–midnight. Closed Aug 15–31. Bus: 46, 62, or 64. SARDINIAN.

Il Drappo, a favorite of the local artsy crowd, is on a narrow street near the Tiber and run by a woman known to her regulars only as "Valentina." You have your choice of two tastefully decorated dining rooms festooned with patterned cotton draped from the ceiling. Flowers and candles are everywhere. Fixed-price dinners reflecting diverse choices may begin with wafer-thin *carte di musica* (sheet-music paper) topped with tomatoes, green peppers, parsley, and olive oil, then follow with fresh spring lamb in season, fish stew made with tuna caviar, or one of the strong-flavored regional specialties. For dessert, try the *seadas* (cheese-stuffed fried cake in special dark honey). Valentina's cuisine is a marvelous change of pace from the typical Roman diet, showing an inventiveness that keeps us coming back again and again.

✪ Piperno. Via Monte de' Cenci 9. ☎ **06-6880-6629.** Reservations recommended. Main courses 30,000–40,000 lire ($15–$20). AE, DC, MC, V. Tues–Sat noon–2:30 and 8–10:30pm, Sun noon–2:30pm. Bus: 23. ROMAN/JEWISH.

This longtime favorite, opened in 1856 and now run by the Mazzarella and Boni families, celebrates the Jerusalem artichoke, incorporating it into a number of recipes. You'll be served by a uniformed crew of hardworking waiters, whose advice and suggestions are worth considering. You might begin with aromatic *fritto misto vegetariano* (artichokes, cheese-and-rice croquettes, mozzarella, and stuffed squash blossoms) before moving on to a fish fillet, veal, succulent beans, or a pasta creation. Many of the foods are fried or deep-fried and benefit from a technique that leaves them flaky and dry, not at all greasy. (The deep-fried artichokes, when submerged in hot oil, open their leaves into a form that's akin to a lotus's and infinitely more delicious.)

MODERATE

Da Giggetto. Via del Portico d'Ottavia 21/A. ☎ **06-686-1105.** Reservations recommended. Main courses 18,000–30,000 lire ($9–$15). AE, DC, MC, V. Tues–Sun 12:30–3pm and 7:30–11pm. Closed Aug 1–15. Bus: 62, 64, 75, 90, or 170. ROMAN/JEWISH.

Da Giggetto is right next to the Theater of Marcellus, and old Roman columns extend practically to its doorway. Romans flock to this bustling trattoria for its special traditional dishes. None is more typical than *carciofi alla giudia,* baby-tender fried artichokes—a true delicacy. The cheese concoction called *mozzarella in carrozza* is another delight, as are the zucchini flowers stuffed with mozzarella and anchovies, our personal favorite. You could also sample shrimp sautéed in garlic and olive oil or one of Rome's best versions of *saltimbocca* (veal with ham).

Il Sanpietrino. Piazza Costaguti 15. ☎ **06-68806471.** Reservations recommended. Main courses 28,000–35,000 lire ($14–$17.50). AE, DC, MC, V. Mon–Sat 8–11pm. Metro: Colosseo or Circo Massimo. ROMAN.

This Jewish Ghetto restaurant, with three formal dining rooms, is stylish but affordable, with a sophisticated selection of both traditional and modern dishes. Chef Marco Cardillo uses market-fresh ingredients to prepare a seasonal cuisine that's varied and inventive at any time of the year. His combinations are often a surprise but generally delightful; for example, cream of fagioli (bean) soup comes not only with the

Quick Bites

At **Dar Filettaro a Santa Barbara,** just off the southeast corner of Campo de' Fiori at Largo dei Librari 88 (☎ **06-686-4018**), you can join the line of people threading to the back of the bare room to order a fillet of *baccalà* (salt cod) fried golden brown *da portar via* (wrapped in paper to eat as you *passeggiata*). It costs 5,000 to 18,000 lire ($2.50 to $9); they're closed Sunday.

Lunchtime offers you the perfect opportunity to savor Roman fast food: *pizza rustica,* by the slice (often called *pizza à taglio*), half-wrapped in waxed paper for easy carrying. Just point to the bubbling, steaming sheet with your preferred toppings behind the counter and hand over a few thousand lire; 4,000 lire ($2) buys a healthy portion of "plain" tomato sauce: basil-and-cheese *pizza margherita*. *Pizza rossa* (just sauce) and *pizza con patate* (with cheese and potatoes) cost even less, as does the exquisitely simple *pizza bianca* (plain dough brushed with olive oil and sprinkled with salt and sometimes rosemary).

A *rosticceria* is a *pizza à taglio* with spits of chickens roasting in the window and a few pasta dishes kept warm in long trays. You can also sit down for a quick pasta or prepared meat dish steaming behind the glass counters at a **tavola calda** (literally "hot table") for about half the price of a *trattoria*. A Roman **bar,** though it does indeed serve liquor, is more what we'd call a cafe, a place to grab a cheap *panino* (flat roll stuffed with meat, cheese, and/or vegetables) or *tramezzino* (large, triangular sandwiches on white bread with the crusts cut off—like giant tea sandwiches).

traditional ingredients, but also with mussels and even octopus. The medley of fish antipasti, some of it smoked, is so tempting that you might want to make a meal of it, enjoying items like savory fresh anchovies baked between layers of well-seasoned eggplant. Also look for asparagus-flavored tortellini with cheese; spaghetti with fresh anchovies and tomatoes; and a delectable version of cream of monkfish soup. Crème brûlée always makes a tempting dessert.

✪ **Ristorante da Pancrazio.** Piazza del Biscione 92. ☎ **06-686-1246.** Reservations recommended. Main courses 18,000–35,000 lire ($9–$17.50); fixed-price menu 50,000 lire ($25). AE, DC, MC, V. Thurs–Tues noon–3pm and 7:30–11:15pm. Closed 2 weeks in Aug (dates vary). Bus: 46, 62, or 64. ROMAN.

This place is popular as much for its archaeological interest as for its food. One of its two dining rooms is gracefully decorated in the style of an 18th-century tavern; the other occupies the premises of Pompey's ancient theater and is lined with carved capitals and bas-reliefs. In this historic setting, you can enjoy time-tested Roman food that's among the finest in the area. Once a simple fishermen's dish, flavorful *risotto alla pescatora* (with seafood) enjoys a certain chic today, and the scampi is grilled to perfection. Pancrazio is another restaurant preparing two classics with great skill: saltimbocca (veal with ham) and tender roast lamb with potatoes. For a superb pasta, opt for the ravioli stuffed with artichoke hearts.

✪ **Ristorante del Pallaro.** Largo del Pallaro 15. ☎ **06-6880-1488.** Reservations recommended. Fixed-price menu 32,000 lire ($16). No credit cards. Tues–Sun 1–3pm and 7:30pm–1am. Bus: 46, 62, or 64. ROMAN.

The cheerful woman in white who emerges with clouds of steam from the bustling kitchen is owner Paola Fazi, running two simple dining rooms where value-conscious

Dining Near Campo de' Fiori & Piazza Navona

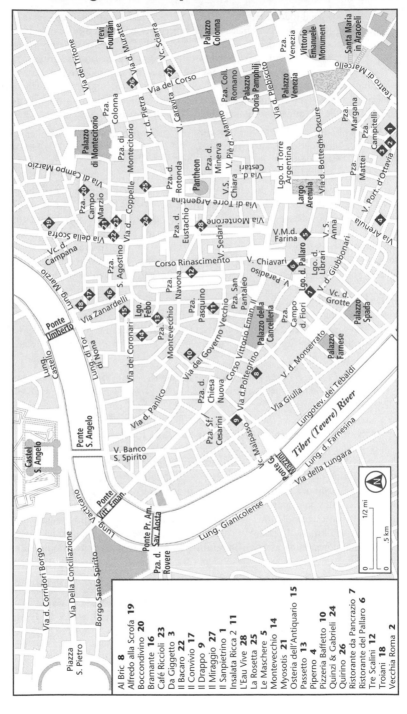

Al Bric **8**
Alfredo alla Scrofa **19**
Boccondivino **20**
Bramante **16**
Café Riccioli **23**
Da Gigetto **3**
Il Bacaro **22**
Il Convivio **17**
Il Drappo **9**
Il Miraggio **27**
Il Sanpietrino **1**
Insalata Ricca 2 **11**
L'Eau Vive **28**
La Rosetta **25**
Le Maschere **5**
Montevecchio **14**
Myosotis **21**
Osteria dell'Antiquario **15**
Passetto **13**
Piperno **4**
Pizzeria Baffetto **10**
Quinzi & Gabrieli **24**
Quirino **26**
Ristorante da Pancrazio **7**
Ristorante del Pallaro **6**
Tre Scalini **12**
Troiani **18**
Vecchia Roma **2**

Romans go for good food at bargain prices. (She also claims—though others dispute it—that Julius Caesar was assassinated on this very site.) The fixed-price menu is the only choice and has made the place famous. Ms. Paolo Fazi prepares everything with love, as if she were feeding her extended family. As you sit down, your antipasto, the first of eight courses, appears. Then comes the pasta of the day, followed by roast veal, white meatballs or (Friday only) dried cod, along with potatoes and eggplant. For your final courses, you're served mozzarella, cake with custard, and fruit in season. The meal also includes bread, mineral water, and half a liter of the house wine.

✪ **Vecchia Roma.** Via della Tribuna di Campitelli 18. ☎ **06-686-4604.** Reservations recommended. Main courses 24,000–40,000 lire ($12–$20). AE, DC. Thurs–Tues 1–3:30pm and 8–11pm. Closed 10 days in Aug. Bus: 64, 90, 90b, 97, or 774. ROMAN/ITALIAN.

Vecchia Roma is a charming moderately priced trattoria in the heart of the Ghetto. Movie stars have frequented the place, sitting at the crowded tables in one of the four small dining rooms (the back room is the most popular). The owners are known for their *frutti de mare* ("fruits of the sea"), a selection of briny fresh seafood. The minestrone is made with fresh vegetables, and an interesting selection of antipasti, including salmon or vegetables, is always available. The pastas and risottos are savory, like *linguine alla marinara* with calamari—the "green" risotto with porcini mushrooms is reliably good. The chef's specialties are lamb and *spigola* (a type of white fish).

INEXPENSIVE

Vegetarians looking for monstrous salads (or anyone who just wants a break from all those heavy meals) can find great food at **Insalata Ricca,** Largo dei Chiavari 85 (☎ **06-6880-3656**). See the review under "Near Piazza Navona & the Pantheon," later in this section.

Le Maschere. Via Monte della Farina 29 (near Largo Argentina). ☎ **06-687-9444.** Reservations recommended. Main courses 14,000–22,000 lire ($7–$11). AE, DC, MC, V. Tues–Sun 7:30–11pm. Closed Aug. Bus: 46, 62, or 64. CALABRESE.

Le Maschere specializes in the fragrant, often-fiery cooking of Calabria's Costa Viola, with lots of fresh garlic and wake-up-your-mouth red peppers. In a cellar from the 1600s decorated with artifacts of Calabria, it has enlarged its kitchen and added three dining rooms, all with fantastic medieval- and Renaissance-inspired murals. Begin with a selection of *antipasti calabresi.* For your first course, try one of the many preparations of eggplant or a pasta—perhaps with broccoli or with devilish red peppers, garlic, bread crumbs, and more than a touch of anchovy. The chef also grills meats and fresh swordfish caught off the Calabrian coast, and does so exceedingly well. If you don't want a full meal, you can visit just for pizza and beer and listen to the music at the piano bar, beginning at 8pm. In summer, you can dine at a small table outside overlooking a tiny piazza.

7 Near Piazza Navona & the Pantheon

To locate the restaurants in this section, see the "Dining Near Campo de' Fiori & Piazza Navona" map on p. 103.

VERY EXPENSIVE

✪ **La Rosetta.** Via della Rosetta 8. ☎ **06-686-1002.** Reservations recommended. Main courses 60,000–100,000 lire ($30–$50). AE, CB, DC, MC, V. Thurs–Fri 12:45–2:45pm and Mon–Sat 8–11:30pm. Bus: 70. Metro: Spagna. SEAFOOD.

You won't find any meat on the menu at this sophisticated choice near Piazza Navona, where the Riccioli family has been directing operations since the late 1960s. If money is no object, there's no better seafood in Rome, except at Quinzi & Gabrieli (below). An excellent start is *insalata di frutti di mare,* studded with squid, lobster, octopus, and shrimp. Menu items include just about every fish native to the Mediterranean, as well as a few from the Atlantic coast of France. There's even a sampling of lobster imported from Maine, which can be boiled with drawn butter or served Catalan style with tomatoes, red onions, and wine sauce. Hake, monkfish, and sole can be grilled or roasted in rock salt and served with potatoes, and calamari is deep-fried (breaded or unbreaded) or stewed. Everyone at our table agreed that the homemade spaghetti garnished with shrimp, squash blossoms, and pecorino cheese, with a drizzling of olive oil and herbs adding a savory zing, was tops.

○ **Quinzi & Gabrieli.** Via delle Coppelle 5–6, 00185 Roma. ☎ **06-687-9389.** Reservations required as far in advance as possible. Main courses 40,000–60,000 lire ($20–$30). AE, DC, MC, V. Mon–Sat 7:30–11:30pm. Closed Aug. Bus: 44, 46, 55, 60, 61, 62, 64, or 65. SEAFOOD.

We've never found better or fresher seafood than that served in this 15th-century building. Don't be put off by the rough-and-ready service, and come for the great taste instead. Be prepared to pay for the privilege, as fresh seafood is extremely expensive in Rome. Alberto Quinzi and Enrico Gabrieli have earned their reputation on their simply cooked and presented *fresh* fish (heavy sauces aren't used to disguise old fish), like sea urchins, octopus, sole, and red mullet. In fact, the restaurant is known for its raw seafood, like a delicate carpaccio of swordfish, sea bass, and deep-sea shrimp. The house specialty is spaghetti with lobster. Sometimes the headwaiters will prepare wriggling crab or scampi right on the grill before you. In summer, French doors lead to a small dining terrace.

EXPENSIVE

○ **Boccondivino.** Piazza in Campo Marzio 6. ☎ **06-68308626.** Reservations recommended. Main courses 25,000–120,000 lire ($12.50–$60). AE, DC, MC, V. Mon–Sat 1–3:30pm and 8pm–midnight. Bus: 87. ITALIAN.

Part of the fun of this restaurant involves wandering through historic Rome to reach it. Inside, you'll find delicious food and an engaging mix of the Italian Renaissance with imperial and ancient Rome, thanks to recycled columns salvaged from ancient monuments by 16th-century builders. Modern art and a hip staff dressed in black and white serve as a tip-off, though, that the menu is completely up-to-date. Dishes vary with the seasons, but you might find fettuccine with shellfish and parsley; carpaccio of beef; various risottos, including a version with black truffles; and grilled steaks and veal. Especially intriguing is whipped codfish resting on spikes of polenta; and tagliolini with cinnamon, prosciutto, and lemon. If you appreciate fish, look for either the marinated and grilled salmon or a particularly subtle blend of roasted turbot stuffed with foie gras. Desserts feature the fresh fruits of the season, perhaps marinated pineapple or fruit-studded house-made ice creams. The restaurant's name, incidentally, translates as "divine mouthful."

○ **L'Eau Vive.** Via Monterone 85. ☎ **06-6880-1095.** Reservations recommended. Main courses 22,000–40,000 lire ($11–$20); fixed-price menus 15,000 lire ($7.50), 30,000 lire ($15), and 50,000 lire ($25). AE, MC, V. Mon–Sat 12:30–2:30pm and 8–10:30pm. Closed Aug 1–20. Bus: 64, 70, 81, 87, or 115. FRENCH/INTERNATIONAL.

Here you'll find an elegant dining experience, with unique food and atmosphere. Fine French cuisine and a daily exotic dish are prepared and served by a lay sisterhood of missionary Christians from five continents who dress in traditional costumes. Nonsmokers can skip the plain stuccoed vaulting downstairs and head to the *piano nobile* of the 16th-century Palazzo Lantante della Rovere, where the high ceilings are gorgeously frescoed. Pope John Paul II dined here when he was archbishop of Krakow, and today some jet-setters have adopted it as their favorite spot. You'll never know until you arrive what the dishes for the evening will be. On previous occasions we've enjoyed beef fillet flambé with cognac, toasted goat cheese coated with mustard and almond slivers, and duck fillet in Grand Marnier sauce with puff-fried potatoes. The homemade pâtés are always flavorful. At 10pm, the recorded classical music is interrupted so the sisters can sing the "Ave Maria of Lourdes," and some evenings they interpret a short Bible story in ballet.

Troiani. Via dei Soldati 28. ☎ **06-6880-5950.** Reservations recommended. All main courses 43,000 lire ($21.50). AE, DC, MC, V. Tues–Sat 1–2:30pm and Tues–Sun 8–10:30pm. Bus: 70, 87, or 90. ITALIAN.

In a new location that's a great improvement over the former cramped setting, Chef Angelo Troiana still is on the A-list of Roman chefs, even though he now has a lot more diners to feed. Seasonal Italian cooking and creative culinary innovation make for solid good taste. Since 1989 Angelo, along with his two brothers, has excited the discriminating palates of Rome. Start off with a warm seafood salad made with clams, mussels, white fish, and a giant prawn with al dente vegetables and a "mayonnaise of the sea," a fragrant lemony sauce. Even the ravioli is stuffed creatively, with ingredients and inspiration that changes with the seasons. Worthy main courses, all of which cost the same, include saddle of rabbit that might be stuffed with porcini mushrooms and served with an onion marmalade, or a boned rack of lamb cooked in an herb and vegetable crust. For dessert consider a slice of almond and bitter chocolate cake accented with fresh currants.

MODERATE

Alfredo alla Scrofa. Via della Scrofa 104. ☎ **06-6880-6163.** Reservations recommended. Main courses 23,000–35,000 lire ($11.50–$17.50). AE, DC, MC, V. Oct–Apr Wed–Mon 1–3pm and 7:30–11pm; May–Nov daily 1–3pm and 7:30–11pm. Bus: 87, 492, or 680. ROMAN/INTERNATIONAL.

Yes, folks, this is one of two places in Rome claiming to be the birthplace of fettuccine Alfredo, which almost seems as well known in America today as it is in Italy. Douglas Fairbanks and Mary Pickford liked this dish so much they presented a golden spoon and fork to the owners when they parted with the recipe. Thus, a culinary legend was born. If you like something buttery and rich, you can still opt to order the dish that delighted these long-departed silent-screen stars. Although the fettuccine remains the best dish on the chef's menu, you can try something a little lighter and healthier, perhaps *tagliolini allo scoglio*, delectably concocted from fresh tomatoes and shellfish. We always enjoy the filet mignons; one is offered with a delectable sauce made from Barolo wine, another with a sauce of wine and Gorgonzola. There's another filet mignon dish named after Casanova, prepared with wine sauce, freshly ground pepper, and foie gras. A final offering is the sautéed breast of turkey covered with thin slices of white truffles from Italy's Piedmont district, a truly delightful dish.

Bramante. Via della Pace 25, Roma. ☎ **06-6880-3916.** Reservations recommended. Main courses 20,000–30,000 lire ($10–$15). AE, DC, MC, V. Mon–Sat 5pm–1am, Sun noon–1am. Closed Dec 24. Bus: 44, 46, 55, 60, 61, 62, 64, or 65. ROMAN.

In an exquisite 18th-century structure on a cobblestone street in back of the Piazza Navona, this cafe-restaurant opens onto a delightful small square of vine-draped taverns. The establishment is named for the 16th-century church on the square, which was designed by the architect Bramante. Behind the ivy-covered facade, the interior is

ⓘ Family-Friendly Restaurants

Césarina *(see p. 97)*   A longtime family favorite, this restaurant offers the most kid-pleasing pastas in town, each handmade and presented with a different sauce. You can request a selection of three kinds of pasta on one plate so finicky young diners can try a little taste of each.

Otello alla Concordia *(see p. 114)*   This place is as good as any to introduce your child to hearty Roman cuisine. If your child doesn't like the spaghetti with clams, then maybe the eggplant parmigiana will do. Families can dine in an arbor-covered courtyard.

Planet Hollywood, Via del Tritone 118 (☎ 06-282-8012). If the kids absolutely insist they can't take another day without a burger or a taco, then head to Rome's Planet Hollywood. Behind its stately neoclassical facade, you'll find all the usual suspects on the menu, as well as a souvenir stand if you want to bring some Americana back to America with you.

Tre Scalini *(see p. 109)*   All families visit Piazza Navona at some point, and this is the best choice if you'd like a dining table overlooking the square. Perhaps a juggler or a fire eater will come by to entertain the crowds. The cookery is Roman and the menu wide enough to accommodate most palates—including children's. The *tartufo* (ice cream with a coating of bittersweet chocolate, cherries, and whipped cream) at the end of the meal is a classic bound to please.

completely hand painted, as white candles illuminate the marble bar, making for a cozy, inviting atmosphere. The owner, Mr. Giuseppe, tries to make visitors appreciate Italian food and traditions, and succeeds admirably. Almost all his dishes are handmade, and the cooks use only the freshest ingredients such as parmigiano, fresh vegetable, and extra virgin olive oil. Recipes are simple but rich in Mediterranean flavor. You can taste wonderful pastas made just with fresh tomato sauce, garlic, and pasta, or else something heavier such as braised beef or tender grilled steak flavored with herbs and served with potatoes. They don't serve fish, however.

Café Riccioli. Piazza delle Coppelle 10A. ☎ 06-6821-0313. Reservations recommended. Main courses 22,000–35,000 lire ($11–$17.50). AE, DC, MC, V. Mon–Sat noon–1am. Tram 8. Bus: 64 or 492. SASHIMI/ITALIAN.

Stylish and hip, this restaurant has built a reputation on its sashimi-style raw fish, plus a menu of sophisticated and upscale Italian cuisine. The setting is a trio of artfully minimalist dining rooms painted in bright primary colors; after lunch and dinner, this place becomes a buzzing late-night cafe. No one will mind if you order just a light meal (we've often spotted models here doing just that). Food, served by one of the most attractive waitstaffs anywhere, includes platters of sashimi, priced at around 33,000 lire ($16.50) each; salads of raw marinated hake with Italian herbs; more substantial fare such as roast beef with green apples, sea bass with mango sauce; and richly textured chocolate tortes laced with marsala wine.

Il Convivio. Via dei Soldati 28. ☎ 06-686-9432. Reservations recommended. Main courses 22,000–46,000 lire ($11–$23). AE, DC, MC, V. Tues–Sat 1–2:30pm and Tues–Sun 8–10:30pm. Bus: 87, 492, 680. ITALIAN.

The well-conceived pan-Italian menu here is definitely daring. The creativity is supplied by the Troiani brothers, who cook, welcome visitors, and compile the sophisticated wine list. We love to begin with *ricotta romanda calda,* warm ricotta dumplings stuffed with crunchy *guanciale* and bits of salt pork and served with sliced porcinis; zesty tomato sauce gives it an extra zing. The chef can sometimes be a little *too* bold, as with his roast rabbit stuffed with mashed potatoes and porcini mushrooms—he intensifies the act by adding a sauce made with fresh anchovies, which unfortunately overpowers the delicate truffles topping the creation. But the seafood salad is a happy blend of squid, mussels, clams, whitefish, and a large prawn, placed on a bed of al dente carrots and zucchini and topped with lemony sauce. The desserts are equally inventive.

Montevecchio. Piazza Montevecchio 22A. ☎ **06-686-1319.** Reservations required. Main courses 24,000–32,000 lire ($12–$16). AE, MC, V. Tues–Sun 7:30pm–midnight. Closed Aug 10–25 and Dec 26–Jan 9. Bus: 60 or 64. Metro: Spagna. ROMAN/ITALIAN.

To visit, you must negotiate the winding streets of one of Rome's most confusing neighborhoods, near Piazza Navona. The heavily curtained restaurant on this Renaissance piazza is where both Raphael and Bramante had studios and where Lucrezia Borgia spun many of her intrigues. The entrance opens onto a high-ceilinged room filled with rural mementos and bottles of wine. Your meal might begin with a strudel of porcini mushrooms followed by the invariably good pasta of the day, perhaps a bombolotti succulently stuffed with prosciutto and spinach. Then you might choose roebuck with polenta, roast Sardinian goat, or veal with salmon mousse. Each of these dishes is prepared with flair and technique, and the food takes advantage of the region's bounty.

○ Myosotis. Vicolo della Vaccarella 3–5. ☎ **06-6865554.** Reservations recommended. Main courses 18,000–42,000 lire ($9–$21). AE, MC, V. Mon–Sat 12:30–3pm and 7:30–11:30pm. Bus: 70, 87, 186, or 492. ITALIAN.

This is the relatively new (ca. 1997) central Roman branch of a restaurant that has flourished in the distant suburbs of the city since the 1960s. Midway between Piazza Navona, the Pantheon, and the Italian Parliament, the building that contains it is relatively modern and nondescript, but as the name promises (translated from Latin, it means "forget-me-not"), you're likely to remember the food for a long time. Menu items include a cornucopia of fresh-baked bread; tagliatelle with an old-fashioned country recipe that substitutes sautéed bread crumbs instead of beef; grilled buffalo steak; grilled, very fresh prawns served as simply as possible, with virgin olive oil and herbs; and a succulent version of baked swordfish that's stuffed with cheese, bread crumbs, and capers. There's also a mixed fish fry (*frittura mista*) that some diners claim is one of the best dishes served here; and flavorful fillet of pork with a sauce of carefully aged pecorino cheese. The array of fresh fish that's available here includes sea bass, gilthead, and the ever-present calamari.

Osteria dell'Antiquario. Piazzetta di S. Simeone 26/27, Via dei Coronari. ☎ **06-687-9694.** Reservations recommended. Main courses 28,000–40,000 lire ($14–$20). AE, DC, MC, V. Tues–Sat 12:30–2:30pm and 8–11pm, Mon 8–11pm. Closed 15 days in mid-Aug, Christmas, Jan 1–15. Bus: 70, 87, or 90. INTERNATIONAL/ROMAN.

This virtually undiscovered osteria has a good location, a few blocks down the Via dei Coronari as you leave the Piazza Navona and head toward St. Peter's. In a stone-built stable from the 1500s, this restaurant has three dining rooms used in winter, although in fair weather diners prefer to retreat outdoors for a table on the terrace. Shaded by umbrellas, tables face a view of the Palazzo Lancillotti. We prefer to begin with a delectable appetizer of sautéed shellfish (usually mussels and clams), although you might opt for the risotto with porcini mushrooms. For a main course, you can go experimental with the fillet of ostrich covered by a slice of ham and grated Parmesan, or else opt for shellfish flavored with saffron. The fish soup with fried bread is excellent, as is an array of freshly made soups and pastas. Veal rolls Roman style and turbot flavored with fresh tomatoes and basil are other excellent choices. This is dining in the classic Roman style.

Passetto. Via Zanardelli 14. ☎ **06-6880-6569.** Reservations recommended. Main courses 24,000–45,000 lire ($12–$22.50). AE, DC, MC, V. Daily noon–3:30pm and 7pm–midnight. Bus: 87. ROMAN/ITALIAN.

Passetto, dramatically positioned at the north end of Piazza Navona, has drawn patrons for a century and a half with excellent food. The stylish interior consists of a trio of high-ceilinged dining rooms, each outfitted with antique furniture and elaborate chandeliers. In summer, however, you'll want to sit outside looking out on Piazza Sant'Apollinare. The pastas are exceptional, including *farfalle passetto* (pasta with shrimp, mushrooms, and fresh tomatoes). One recommended main dish is *orata al cartoccio* (sea bass baked in a paper bag, to seal in the juices and the aroma, with tomatoes, mushrooms, capers, and white wine). Another house specialty is *rombo passetto* (a fish similar to sole) cooked in cognac and pine nuts. An eternal Roman favorite is lamb in the style of Abruzzi (oven-roasted with potatoes). Fresh fish is often priced by its weight, so tabs can soar quickly. Fresh vegetables are abundant in summer, and a favorite dessert is seasonal berries with fresh thick cream.

Quirino. Via delle Muratte 84. ☎ **06-679-4108.** Reservations recommended. Main courses 20,000–35,000 lire ($10–$17.50); fish dishes 25,000–30,000 lire ($12.50–$15). AE, MC, V. Mon–Sat 12:30–3:30pm and 7–11pm. Closed 3 weeks in Aug. Metro: Barberini or Spagna. ROMAN/ITALIAN/SICILIAN.

Quirino is a good place to dine after you've tossed your coin into the Trevi. The atmosphere is typical Italian, with hanging Chianti bottles, a beamed ceiling, and muraled walls. We're fond of the mixed fry of tiny shrimp and squid rings, and the vegetarian pastas are prepared only with the freshest ingredients. The regular pasta dishes are fabulous, especially our favorite—homemade pasta with baby clams and porcini mushrooms. The *pasta alla Norma* with tomatoes and eggplant has won the approval of many a demanding Italian opera star. A variety of fresh and tasty fish is always available and always grilled to perfection. For dessert, try the yummy chestnut ice cream with hot chocolate sauce or homemade cannoli.

Tre Scalini. Piazza Navona 30. ☎ **06-687-9148.** Reservations recommended. Main courses 24,000–32,000 lire ($12–$16). AE, DC, MC, V. Thurs–Tues noon–3pm and 7–11pm. Closed Dec–Feb. Bus: 70, 87, or 90. ROMAN/ITALIAN.

Opened in 1882, this is the most famous restaurant on Piazza Navona—a landmark for ice cream as well as for more substantial meals. Yes, it's crawling with tourists, but its waiters are a lot friendlier and more helpful than those at the nearby Passetto, and the setting can't be beat. The cozy bar on the upper floor offers a view over the piazza, but most visitors opt for the ground-floor cafe or restaurant. During warm weather, try to snag a table on the piazza where the people-watching is extraordinary.

The Lombard specialty of risotto with porcini mushrooms is worthy of the finest restaurants in Milan, the carpaccio of sea bass is worthy of a three-star restaurant in Paris, and the roast duck with prosciutto wins many a devoted fan. One cook confided to us, "I cook dishes to make people love me." If that's the case, try his saltimbocca (veal with ham) and roast lamb Roman style—and you'll fall in love. No one will object if you order just a pasta and salad. Their famous tartufo (ice cream coated with bittersweet chocolate, cherries, and whipped cream) makes a fantastic dessert.

INEXPENSIVE

Al Bric. Via del Pellegrino 51. ☎ **06-687-9533.** Reservations recommended. Main courses 13,000–30,000 lire ($6.50–$15). Tues–Sun 7:30–11:30pm. Closed Aug and 2 weeks in Jan. Bus: 64. ITALIAN.

With four separate and artfully minimalist dining rooms in a 16th-century building close to Campo de' Fiori, this well-managed restaurant combines creative cooks with a polite and efficient waitstaff. Many of the dishes include dollops of some kind of Italian cheese, a flavor that seems to make the wines here taste better. Menu items are based on a combination of traditional and creatively modern cuisine. Examples include house-made, ultra-fresh *bucatini alla matriciana; bucatini* flavored with fresh-ground black pepper and aged *caciocavallo* cheese; tonnarelli pasta with Sicilian broccoli and aged pecorino cheese; and roasted, aromatic rabbit laden with herbs and Camembert cheese and drenched in apple-flavored Calvados liqueur. There's even a delicious roasted shoulder of lamb drizzled with aged pecorino sauce, or a stuffed fillet of veal with French brie and sweet-textured Sicilian broccoli that may have you asking for the recipe.

Il Miraggio. Vicolo Sciarra 59. ☎ **06-678-0226.** Reservations recommended. Main courses 13,000–20,000 lire ($6.50–$10). AE, MC, V. Thurs–Tues 12:30–3:30pm and 7:30–11pm. Closed 15 days in Feb. Metro: Barberini. Bus: 56, 60, 62, 81, 85, 95, 160, 175, 492, or 628. ROMAN/SARDINIAN/SEAFOOD.

You may want to escape the roar of traffic along Via del Corso by ducking into this informal spot on a crooked side street (about midway between Piazza Venezia and Piazza Colonna). It's a cozy neighborhood setting with rich and savory flavor in every dish. The risotto with scampi or the fettuccine with porcini mushrooms will have you begging for more. Some dishes are classic, like roast lamb with potatoes, but others are more inventive, like sliced stew beef with arugula. The grilled scampi always is done to perfection, or you may prefer a steaming kettle of mussels flavored with olive oil, lemon juice, and fresh parsley. We're especially fond of the house specialty, *spaghetti alla bottarga* with roe sauce, especially if it's followed by *spigola alla vernaccia* (sea bass sautéed in butter and vernaccia wine from Tuscany). For dessert, try the typical Sardinian *seadas,* thin-rolled pastry filled with fresh cheese, fried, and served with honey.

Insalata Ricca 2. Piazza Pasquino 72 (southwest of Piazza Navona). ☎ **06-6830-7881.** Reservations recommended. Main courses 8,000–25,000 lire ($4–$12.50); salads 7,000–14,000 lire ($3.50–$7). AE, MC, V. Daily 12:15–3:15pm and 7pm–12:30am. Bus: 46, 62, or 64. ITALIAN/SALADS.

A need for more vegetarian restaurants and lighter low-fat fare in Rome helped a single little trattoria hawking entree-size salads grow into a small chain. Most people call ahead for an outdoor table, though on summer days you may prefer the smoke-free air-conditioning inside. The more popular of the oversized salads are the *baires* (lettuce, rughetta, celery, walnuts, apples, Gorgonzola) and *siciliana* (lettuce, rughetta, sun-dried tomatoes, green olives, corn, hard salted ricotta). Also on the menu are dishes like *gnocchi verdi al gorgonzola* (spinach gnocchi with Gorgonzola sauce) and *pasta integrale* (whole-wheat pasta in tomato-and-basil sauce). The branches near Campo de' Fiori and near the Vatican (mentioned under their respective neighborhoods) offer the same basic menu.

✪ **Pizzeria Baffetto.** Via del Governo Vecchio 114. ☎ **06-686-1617.** Reservations not accepted. Pizza 6,000–10,000 lire ($3–$5). No credit cards. Daily 6:30pm–1am. Closed Aug. Bus: 46, 62, 64. PIZZA.

Our Roman friends always take out-of-towners here when they request the best pizza in Rome. Arguably Pizzeria Baffetto fills the bill and has done so admirably for the past 80 years. Pizzas are sold as *piccolo* or small, *media* or medium, or *grande* (large). Most pizza aficionados order the margherita, which is the simplest version with mozzarella and a delectable tomato sauce, but a wide range of toppings is served. The chef is preening proud of his pizza Baffetto, the house specialty. It comes with a topping of tomato sauce, mozzarella, mushrooms, onions, sausages, roasted peppers, and eggs. The pizza crusts are delightfully thin, and the pies are served piping hot from the intense heat of the ancient ovens.

8 Near the Spanish Steps & Piazza del Popolo

To locate the restaurants in this section, see the "Dining Near the Spanish Steps & Ancient Rome" map on p. 99.

VERY EXPENSIVE

✪ El Toulà. Via della Lupa 29B. ☎ **06-687-3498.** Reservations required for dinner. Main courses 40,000–46,000 lire ($20–$23); 5-course menu degustazione 120,000 lire ($60); 4-course menu *veneto* 100,000 lire ($50). AE, DC, MC, V. Tues–Fri noon–3pm and 7:30–11pm, Mon and Sat 7:30–11pm. Closed Aug. Bus: 81, 90, 90b, 628, or 913. ROMAN/VENETIAN.

El Toulà, offering sophisticated haute cuisine, is the glamorous flagship of an upscale chain that's now gone international. The setting is elegant, with vaulted ceilings, large archways, and a charming bar. The impressive always-changing menu has one section devoted to Venetian specialties, in honor of the restaurant's origins. Items include tender *fegato* (liver) *alla veneziana*, vegetable-stuffed calamari, a robust *baccalà* (codfish mousse with polenta), and *broetto*, a fish soup made with monkfish and clams. Save room for the seasonal selection of sorbets and sherbets (the cantaloupe and fresh strawberry are celestial)—you can request a mixed plate if you'd like to sample several. El Toulà usually isn't crowded at lunchtime. The wine list is extensive and varied, but hardly a bargain.

MODERATE

Babington's Tea Rooms. Piazza di Spagna 23. ☎ **06-678-6027.** Main courses 35,000–55,000 lire ($17.50–$27.50); brunch 48,000 lire ($24). AE, CB, DC, DISC, MC, V. Daily 9am–8:30pm. Metro: Spagna. ENGLISH/MEDITERRANEAN.

When Victoria was on the throne in 1893, an Englishwoman named Anne Mary Babington arrived in Rome and couldn't find a place for "a good cuppa." With stubborn determination, she opened her own tearooms near the foot of the Spanish Steps, and the rooms are still going strong, though the prices are terribly inflated because of its fabulous location. You can order everything from Scottish scones and Ceylon tea to a club sandwich and American coffee. Brunch is served at all hours. Pastries cost 4,000 to 13,000 lire ($2 to $6.50); a pot of tea (dozens of varieties available) goes for 12,000 lire ($6).

✪ Dal Bolognese. Piazza del Popolo 1–2. ☎ **06-361-1426.** Reservations required. Main courses 18,000–30,000 lire ($9–$15). AE, DC, MC, V. Tues–Sun 12:30–3pm and 8:15pm–1am. Closed 20 days in Aug. Metro: Flaminio. BOLOGNESE.

This is one of those rare dining spots that's chic but actually lives up to the hype with truly noteworthy food. Young actors, shapely models, artists from nearby Via Margutta, and even corporate types on expense accounts show up, trying to land one of the few sidewalk tables. To begin, we suggest *misto di pasta:* four pastas, each with a different sauce, arranged on the same plate. A worthy substitute would be thin slices of savory Parma ham or the delectable prosciutto and vine-ripened melon. For your main course, specialties that win hearts year after year are *lasagne verde* and *tagliatelle alla bolognese.* The chefs also turn out the town's most recommendable veal cutlets bolognese topped with cheese. They're not inventive, but they're simply superb.

You may want to cap your evening by dropping into the ✪ **Rosati** cafe next door (or its competitor, the **Canova,** across the street), to enjoy one of the tempting pastries.

Il Bacaro. Via degli Spagnoli 27, near Piazza delle Coppelle. ☎ **06-686-4110.** Reservations recommended. Main courses 18,000–30,000 lire ($11–$18). MC, V. Mon–Sat 8pm–midnight. Metro: Spagna. ITALIAN.

Unpretentious and very accommodating to foreigners, this restaurant contains only about half a dozen tables and operates from an ivy-edged hideaway alley near Piazza di Spagna. The restaurant is well known for its fresh and tasty cheese. This was a palazzo in the 1600s, and some vestiges of the building's former grandeur remain, despite an impossibly cramped kitchen where the efforts of the staff to keep the show moving are nothing short of heroic. The offerings are time-tested and flavorful: home-made ravioli stuffed with mushrooms and parmigiano (in season), grilled beef fillet with roasted potatoes, and an unusual version of warm carpaccio of beef. What dish do we prefer year after year? Admittedly it's an acquired taste, but it's radicchio stuffed with Gorgonzola.

La Campana. Vicolo della Campana 18. ☎ **06-686-7820.** Reservations recommended. Main courses 20,000–29,000 lire ($10–$14.50). AE, DC, MC, V. Tues–Sun 12:30–3pm and 7:30–11pm. Metro: Spagna. ROMAN.

If you opt for a meal in this comfortable but not particularly innovative restaurant, you won't be alone. The place has been dishing up traditional Roman specialties since it began welcoming locals and religious pilgrims in 1518 (unlike those folks, you'll enjoy air-conditioning in summer). Look for a well-stocked antipasti buffet, rich pastas, herb-laden roast lamb with potatoes, aromatic roast hen with roasted vegetables, and perfectly grilled fish or squid. We always start with *vignarola,* a soup made with fresh green peas and artichokes. The welcome is always warm, after all those years and all those thousands of diners.

Ristorante Nino. Via Borgognona 11. ☎ **06-679-5676.** Reservations recommended. Main courses 24,000–55,000 lire ($12–$27.50). AE, DC, MC, V. Mon–Sat 12:30–3pm and 7:30–11pm. Closed Aug. Metro: Spagna. TUSCAN/ROMAN.

Ristorante Nino, off Via Condotti and a short walk from the Spanish Steps, is a mecca for writers, artists, and the occasional model. If you had a Tuscan mama, she might have cooked like the chefs here; hearty, robustly flavored Tuscan home-style dishes that change with the season have made Nino's famous. Beef, shipped in from Florence and charcoal-broiled, is pricier than the rest of the menu items, but it's not as succulent or tender as that served at the better-known (and admittedly more expensive) Girarrosto Toscano (see section 4 of this chapter). A plate of cannelloni Nino (the house version of the popular dish, consisting of meat-stuffed pasta) is one of the chef's specialties. Other good dishes include grilled veal liver, *fagiole cotti al fiasco* (beans boiled in white wine, salt, ground black pepper, and herbs), codfish *alla livornese* (codfish cooked with tomatoes and onions), and zucchini pie. The reasonably priced wine list is mainly Tuscan, with some especially good choices among the Chiantis.

INEXPENSIVE

✪ **Da Mario.** Via della Vite 55–56. ☎ **06-678-3818.** Reservations recommended. Main courses 17,000–26,000 lire ($8.50–$13). AE, DC, MC, V. Mon–Sat 12:30–3pm and 7:30–11pm. Closed Aug. Metro: Spagna. ROMAN/FLORENTINE.

Impressions

In Italy, the pleasure of eating is central to the pleasure of living. When you sit down to dinner with Italians, when you share their food, you are sharing their lives.

— Fred Plotkin, *Italy for the Gourmet Traveler* (1996)

Da Mario is noted for its flavorful game specialties and excellent Florentine-style dishes (meats marinated in olive oil with fresh herbs and garlic and lightly grilled). The rich bounty of meats available during hunting season makes this a memorable choice, but even if you aren't feeling game (sorry, bad pun), you'll find this a convivial and quintessentially Roman trattoria. A good beginning is the wide-noodle pappardelle, best when served with a game sauce (*caccia*) or with chunks of rabbit (*lepre*), available only in winter. *Capretto* (kid), beefsteaks, and roast quail with polenta are other good choices. The wine cellar is well stocked with sturdy reds, the ideal accompaniment for the meat dishes. For dessert we heartily recommend the *gelato misto*, a selection of mixed velvety ice cream. You can dine in air-conditioned comfort at street level or descend to the cellars.

Enoteca Corsi. Via del Gesù 87–88. ☎ **06-679-0821.** Reservations not necessary. Main courses 14,000 lire ($7) each; pastas 8,000 lire ($4); vegetable side dishes 4,000 lire ($2). AE, DC, MC, V. Mon–Sat noon–3pm. Closed Aug. Metro: Spagna or Barberini. ROMAN.

This is a breath of unpretentious fresh air in a pricey neighborhood, an informal wine tavern open for lunch only. Both dining rooms are usually packed and full of festive diners, just as they've always been since 1943. The wine list includes affordable choices from around Italy, to go perfectly with the platters of straightforward cuisine. It's nothing fancy, just hearty fare like bean soup, gnocchi, Roman tripe, and roasted codfish with garlic and potatoes. It's what your Italian mama (assuming you had one) might have prepared for your dinner.

'Gusto. Piazza Augusto Imperatore 9. ☎ **06-322-6273.** Reservations recommended. Main courses in street-level pizzeria 11,000–25,000 lire ($5.50–$12.50); main courses in upstairs restaurant 25,000–55,000 lire ($12.50–$27.50). AE, MC, V. Daily 1–2:30pm and 8–11:45pm. Metro: Flaminio. ITALIAN/PACIFIC RIM.

This restaurant is made up of two separate parts, each aimed at differing degrees of culinary sophistication. The simpler of the two is a street-level pizzeria, where at least a dozen kinds of homemade pastas and pizzas are offered along with freshly made salads and simple platters of such grilled specialties as veal, chicken, steak, and fish. More urbane, and somewhat calmer, is the upstairs restaurant, where big windows, high ceilings, floors of glowing hardwood, and lots of exposed brick create an appropriately minimalist setting for the cutting-edge cuisine. Look for a fusion of Italian and Pacific Rim cuisine in such internationally inspired combinations as spaghetti stir-fried in a Chinese wok with fresh, al dente vegetables; prawns and spring baby vegetables done tempura-style; buffalo mozzarella intriguingly entwined with tuna and arugula; Middle Eastern staples like chickpea paste (*tabouleh*); and stir-fried scallops with Italian herbs.

Il Ristorante 34 (Al 34). Via Mario de' Fiori 34. ☎ **06-679-5091.** Reservations required. Main courses 17,000–30,000 lire ($8.50–$15); fixed-price menu 55,000 lire ($27.50). AE, DC, MC, V. Tues–Sun 12:30–3pm and 7:30–10:30pm. Closed 1 week at Easter and 3 weeks in Aug. Metro: Spagna. ROMAN/ITALIAN.

Il Ristorante 34, very good and increasingly popular, is close to Rome's most famous shopping district. Its long, narrow interior is sheathed in scarlet wallpaper, ringed with modern paintings, and capped with a vaulted ceiling. In the rear, stop to admire a display of *dolce* proudly exhibited near the entrance to the bustling kitchen. The chef might whip caviar and salmon into the noodles to enliven a dish or add generous chunks of lobster into the risotto. He also believes in rib-sticking fare like pasta lentil soup or meatballs in a sauce with "fat" mushrooms. One of his most interesting pastas comes with a pumpkin-flavored cream sauce, and his spaghetti with clams is among the best in Rome.

Otello alla Concordia. Via della Croce 81. ☎ **06-679-1178.** Reservations recommended. Main courses 14,000–30,000 lire ($7–$15); fixed-price menu 40,000 lire ($20). AE, DC, MC, V. Mon–Sat 12:30–3pm and 7:30–11pm. Closed 2 weeks in Feb. Metro: Piazza di Spagna. ROMAN.

On a side street amid the glamorous boutiques near the northern edge of the Spanish Steps, this is one of Rome's most consistently reliable restaurants. A stone corridor from the street leads into the dignified Palazzo Povero. Choose a table in the arbor-covered courtyard or the cramped but convivial dining rooms. Displays of Italian bounty decorate the interior, where you're likely to rub elbows with many of the shopkeepers from the fashion district. The *spaghetti alle vongole veraci* (with clams) is excellent, as are Roman-style saltimbocca, *abbacchio arrosto* (roast baby lamb), eggplant parmigiana, a selection of grilled or sautéed fish dishes (including swordfish), and several preparations of veal.

9 Near the Vatican

VERY EXPENSIVE

✪ **Les Etoiles.** In the Hotel Atlante Star, Via Vitelleschi 34. ☎ **06-687-3233.** Reservations required. Main courses 60,000–120,000 lire ($30–$60). AE, DC, MC, V. Daily 12:30–2:30pm and 7:30–10:30pm. Metro: Ottaviano. MEDITERRANEAN.

Les Etoiles ("The Stars") deserves all the stars it receives. At this garden in the sky you'll have an open window over Rome's rooftops—a 360-degree view of landmarks, especially the floodlit dome of St. Peter's. A flower terrace contains a trio of little towers named Michelangelo, Campidoglio, and Ottavo Colle. In summer, everyone wants a table outside, but in winter almost the same view is available near the picture windows. Savor the textures and aromas of sophisticated Mediterranean cuisine with perfectly balanced flavors, perhaps choosing quail in a casserole with mushrooms and herbs, delectable artichokes stuffed with ricotta and pecorino cheeses, Venetian-style risotto with squid ink, and roast suckling lamb perfumed with mint. The creative chef is justifiably proud of his many regional dishes, and the service is refined, with an exciting French and Italian wine list.

MODERATE

✪ **Ristorante Il Matriciano.** Via dei Gracchi 55. ☎ **06-321-2327.** Reservations required. Main courses 14,000–28,000 lire ($7–$14). DC, MC, V. Daily 12:30–3pm and 8pm–midnight. Closed Aug 5–25. Metro: Ottaviano. ROMAN.

Il Matriciano is a family restaurant with a devoted following and a convenient location near St. Peter's. The food is good but mostly country fare. In summer, try to get one of the sidewalk tables behind a green hedge and under a shady canopy. For openers, you might enjoy a bracing *zuppa di verdura* (vegetable soup) or creamy *ravioli di ricotta.* From many dishes, we recommend *scaloppa alla valdostana* or *abbacchio* (suckling lamb) *al forno,* each evocative of the region's bounty. The specialty, and our personal favorite, is *bucatini matriciana,* a variation on the favorite sauce in the

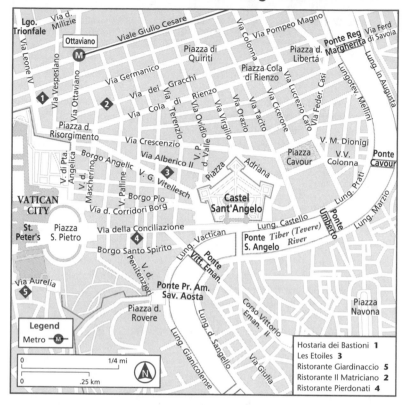

Legend
Metro —Ⓜ—

0   1/4 mi
0   .25 km

Hostaria dei Bastioni **1**
Les Etoiles **3**
Ristorante Giardinaccio **5**
Ristorante Il Matriciano **2**
Ristorante Pierdonati **4**

Roman repertoire, *amatriciana,* richly flavored with bacon, tomatoes, and basil. Dining at the convivial tables, you're likely to see an array of Romans, including prelates and cardinals ducking out of the nearby Vatican for a meal.

INEXPENSIVE

The no. 6 branch of **Insalata Ricca,** the popular chain of salad-and-light-meals restaurants, is across from the Vatican walls at Piazza del Risorgimento 5 (☎ 06-3973-0387). See the review in section 7 of this chapter.

Hostaria dei Bastioni. Via Leone IV 29. ☎ **06-3972-3034.** Reservations recommended Fri–Sat. Main courses 12,000–20,000 lire ($6–$10). AE, DC, MC, V. Mon–Sat noon–3pm and 7–11:30pm. Closed July 15–Aug 1. Metro: Ottaviano. ROMAN.

This simple but well-managed restaurant is about a minute's walk from the entrance to the Vatican Museums and has been open since the 1960s. Although a warm-weather terrace doubles the place's size during summer, many diners prefer the inside room as an escape from the roaring traffic. In a dining room suitable for only 50, you can order from the staples of Rome's culinary repertoire, like fisher's risotto (a broth-simmered rice dish studded with fresh fish, usually shellfish), a vegetarian *fettuccine alla bastione* with orange-flavored creamy tomato sauce, an array of grilled fresh fish, and saltimbocca (veal with ham). The food is first rate, particularly at the prices charged.

Ristorante Giardinaccio. Via Aurelia 53. ☎ **06-631-367.** Reservations recommended, especially on weekends. Main courses 15,000–40,000 lire ($7.50–$20); fixed-price menus 15,000–60,000 lire ($7.50–$30). AE, DC, MC, V. Daily 12:15–3:15pm and 7:15–11:15pm. Bus: 46, 62, or 98. ITALIAN/MOLISIAN/ROMAN.

This popular restaurant, operated by Nicolino Mancini, is only a stone's throw from St. Peter's. Unusual for Rome, it offers Molisian specialties from southeastern Italy. It's rustically decorated in the country-tavern style with dark wood and exposed stone. Flaming grills provide succulent versions of perfectly done quail, goat, and other dishes, but perhaps the mutton goulash would be more adventurous. You can order many pastas, including homemade *taconelle* with lamb sauce. Vegetarians will like the large self-service selection of antipasti made from market-fresh ingredients. This is robust peasant fare, a perfect introduction to the cuisine of an area rarely visited by Americans.

Ristorante Pierdonati. Via della Conciliazione 39. ☎ **06-6880-3557.** Reservations not necessary. Main courses 12,000–29,000 lire ($6–$14.50); fixed-price menu 25,000 lire ($12.50). DC, MC, V. Fri–Wed noon–4pm and 7–10pm. Closed Aug. Bus: 46, 62 or 64. ROMAN.

Ristorante Pierdonati has been serving visitors to the Vatican since 1868. In the same building as the Hotel Columbus, this restaurant was the former home of Cardinal della Rovere. Today it's the headquarters of the Knights of the Holy Sepulchre of Jerusalem and is the best choice for a sit-down lunch after touring St. Peter's. The calves' liver Venetian style is prepared to perfection, tender and sautéed with herb-flavored onions. The stewed veal may be old-fashioned, but it's still a winner here, served with a savory tomato sauce. A cut of tender fillet of beef emerges with a delicious topping of fresh mushrooms, mustard, and brandy. It's robust and filling fare. Given this location, expect a crowd. Tuesday and Friday are fresh-fish days.

10 In Trastevere

EXPENSIVE

✪ **Alberto Ciarla.** Piazza San Cosimato 40. ☎ **06-581-8668.** Reservations required. Main courses 20,000–48,000 lire ($10–$24); fixed-price menus 80,000–120,000 lire ($40–$60). AE, DC, MC, V. Mon–Sat 8:30pm–12:30am. Closed 1 week in Jan and 1 week in Aug. Bus: 44, 75, 170, 280, or 718. SEAFOOD.

The Ciarla, in an 1890 building set in an obscure corner of an enormous square, is Trastevere's best restaurant and one of its most expensive. You'll be greeted with a cordial reception and a lavish display of seafood on ice. A dramatically modern decor plays light against shadow for a Renaissance chiaroscuro effect. The specialties include a handful of ancient recipes subtly improved by Signor Ciarla (an example is the soup of pasta and beans with seafood). Original dishes include a delectable fish in orange sauce, savory spaghetti with clams, and a full array of delicious shellfish. The sea bass fillet is prepared in at least three ways, including an award-winning version with almonds.

✪ **Sabatini.** Piazza Santa Maria in Trastevere 13. ☎ **06-581-2026.** Reservations recommended. Main courses 20,000–60,000 lire ($10–$30); fixed-price menu 110,000 lire ($55). AE, DC, MC, V. Daily noon–3pm and 8pm–midnight. Closed 2 weeks in Aug (dates vary). Bus: 45, 65, 170, 181, or 280. ROMAN/SEAFOOD.

This is a real neighborhood spot in a lively location. (You may have to wait for a table even if you have a reservation.) In summer, tables are placed on the charming piazza

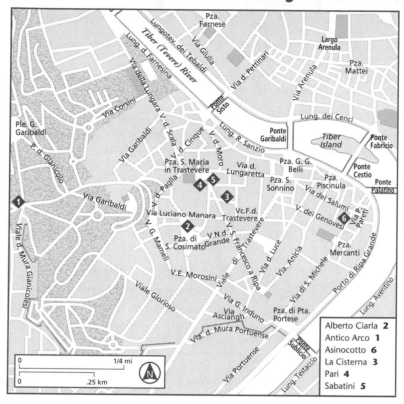

Map labels (partial): Pza. Farnese, Lungotev. dei Tebaldi, Via Giulia, Largo Arenula, Via d. Pettinari, Pza. Mattei, Via Arenula, Tiber (Tevere) River, Lung. d. Farnesina, Via della Lungara, Via Corsini, Ple. G. Garibaldi, Ponte Sisto, Lung. dei Cenci, Via Garibaldi, Via d. Scala, Via d. Cinque, Via d. Moro, Lung. R. Sanzio, Ponte Garibaldi, Tiber Island, Ponte Fabricio, Ponte Cestio, Pza. S. Maria in Trastevere, Via d. Lungaretta, Pza. G. G. Belli, Ponte Palatino, Pza. Piscinula, Via d. Paglia, Via Luciano Manara, Vc.F.d. Trastevere, Pza. S. Sonnino, Via dei Salumi, V. dei Genovesi, Pza. di S. Cosimato, V.N.d.S. Grande, Via S. Francesco a Ripa, Pza. Mercanti, V. G. Manelli, V.E. Morosini, Viale Glorioso, Via di S. Michele, Porto di Ripa Grande, Via G. Induno, Via Asciangh, Pza. di Pta. Portese, Via d. Mura Portuense, Ponte Sublicio, Via Portuense, Lung. Testaccio, Lung. Aventino

0 1/4 mi
0 .25 km

Alberto Ciarla	**2**
Antico Arco	**1**
Asinocotto	**6**
La Cisterna	**3**
Pari	**4**
Sabatini	**5**

and you can look across at the church's floodlit golden frescoes. The dining room sports beamed ceilings, stenciled walls, lots of paneling, and framed oil paintings. The spaghetti with seafood is excellent, and the fresh fish and shellfish, especially grilled scampi, may tempt you as well. For a savory treat, try *pollo con peperoni,* chicken with red and green peppers. The large antipasti table is one of the delights of this district, and the delicious pastas, the superb chicken and veal dishes, and the white Frascati wine or the house Chianti continue to delight year after year. (Order carefully, though; your bill can skyrocket if you choose grilled fish or the Florentine steaks.)

MODERATE

Antico Arco. Piazzale Aurelio 7. ☎ **06-581-5274.** Reservations recommended. Main courses 26,000–34,000 lire ($13–$17). AE, MC, V. Mon–Sat 8pm–midnight. Bus: 44 or 870. ITALIAN.

Named after one of the gates of early medieval Rome (Arco di San Pancrazio), which rises nearby, this place is set on the Janiculum Hill not far from Trastevere and the American Academy. It's a hip restaurant with a young, stylish clientele. It's run by three investors (Maurizio and Patrizia, who are married, and their friend Domenico) who are likely to be on-site themselves, working hard to ensure that food and service flow smoothly. Carefully created menu items include herb-laden versions of onion flan with Parmesan sauce; a palate-awakening truffle and rabbit-meat salad with sliced Parmesan and honey sauce; and a succulent version of spaghetti served with *pecorino romano* cheese, heavenly fried zucchini blossoms, and fresh-ground pepper. A bitter orange sauce and a sesame-flavored chutney are appropriate foils for roasted duck. Macaroni carbonara and *tagliolini con bottarga* (a Sardinian dish composed of pasta flavored with fish roe) are particularly enticing pastas.

Asinocotto. Via dei Vascellari. ☎ **06-589-8985.** Reservations recommended. Main courses 23,000–26,000 lire ($11.50–$13). AE, DC, MC, V. Tues–Sun 8–11pm. Tram 8. ITALIAN.

Within a pair of cramped dining rooms (one on street level, the other upstairs), you'll be served by a cheerful staff that's well versed in hauling steaming platters of food up the steep flight of stairs. The simple decor of white-painted walls accented with dark timbers and panels is an appropriate foil for the flavor-filled dishes that stream from the busy kitchens of Giuliano Brenna. Menu items are more sophisticated than you might have thought, thanks to the owner's stint as a chef at the Hotel Eden, one of Rome's more upscale hotels. Menu items include an antipasto that's been compared to a small portion of bouillabaisse. Also look for whole-wheat pasta garnished with lamb stew, swordfish in pesto sauce, and breast of duckling in green tea sauce with tangerine slices. The restaurant's name, incidentally, translates a "cooked donkey meat," but don't look for that on the menu anytime soon.

La Cisterna. Via della Cisterna 13. ☎ **06-581-2543.** Reservations recommended. Main courses 20,000–32,000 lire ($10–$16). AE, DC, MC, V. Mon–Sat 7pm–1:30am. Bus: 44, 75, 170, 280, or 710. ROMAN.

If you'd like traditional home cooking based on the best regional ingredients, head here. La Cisterna, named for an ancient well from imperial times discovered in the cellar, lies deep in the heart of Trastevere. For more than 75 years it has been run by the wonderful Simmi family. In good weather you can dine at sidewalk tables. If it's rainy or cold you'll be in rooms decorated with murals. In summer you can inspect the antipasti right out on the street before going in. From the ovens emerge Roman-style suckling lamb that's amazingly tender and seasoned with fresh herbs and virgin olive oil. The fiery hot *rigatoni all'amatriciana* is served with red-hot peppers, or you may decide on another delectable pasta dish, *papalini romana,* wide noodles flavored with prosciutto, cheese, and eggs. The shrimp is grilled to perfection, and you can rely on the chef selecting an array of fresh fish for dishes like flaky sea bass baked with fresh herbs.

Pari. Piazza San Calisto 7A. ☎ **06-581-5378.** Reservations recommended. Main courses 20,000–34,000 lire ($10–$17). AE, DC, MC, V. Tues–Sun noon–3pm and Tues–Sat 7:45am–11pm. Tram 8. ROMAN.

For about a century, there's been a restaurant here in this weathered stone building erected about 600 years ago in Trastevere. Over the years, this cramped but convivial place has turned out thousands of platters of authentic Roman cuisine, usually with an emphasis on seafood. Menu items are savory, time-tested, and charmingly archaic; don't look for the latest foodie trends here. Despite that, you're likely to be very happy here, thanks to heaping portions of such dishes as fried fillet of sole; turbot with mushrooms, olive oil, and herbs; several interpretations of scampi; Roman tripe; *coda alla vaccinara* (slow-baked rumpsteak in the Roman style); and succulent grilled baby lamb chops. Vegetarians appreciate one of the house specialties—a beautifully presented platter of fried, very fresh vegetables that's configured as a main course for one diner or as a shared *antipasti* if it's passed around between several people. We especially love the deep-fried zucchini blossoms stuffed with mozzarella and anchovies, when they're available.

You Paid What?

47,000 hotels, 700 airlines,
50 rental car companies. And a few
million ways to save money.

Travelocity.com
A S a b r e C o m p a n y

Go Virtually Anywhere.

Will you have enough stories to tell your grandchildren?

©2000 Yahoo! Inc.

Yahoo! Travel

11 In Testaccio

MODERATE

✪ **Checchino dal 1887.** Via di Monte Testaccio 30. ☎ **06-574-3816.** Reservations recommended. Main courses 20,000–35,000 lire ($10–$17.50). AE, DC, MC, V. Tues–Sat 12:30–3pm and 8–11pm, Sun 12:30–3pm; June–Sept closed on Sun. Bus: 75 from Termini Station. ROMAN.

During the 1800s, a wine shop flourished here, selling drinks to the butchers working in the nearby slaughterhouses. In 1887, ancestors of this restaurant's present owners began serving food, too. Slaughterhouse workers in those days were paid part of their meager salaries with the *quinto quarto* (fifth quarter) of each day's slaughter (the tail, feet, intestines, and other parts not for the squeamish). Following centuries of Roman traditions, Ferminia, the wine shop's cook, somehow transformed these products into the tripe and oxtail dishes that form an integral part of the menu. Many Italian diners come here to relish the *rigatoni con pajata* (pasta with small intestines), *coda alla vaccinara* (oxtail stew), *fagioli e cotiche* (beans with intestinal fat), and other examples of *la cucina povera* (food of the poor). In winter they also serve a succulent wild boar with dried prunes and red wine. Safer and possibly more appetizing is the array of salads, soups, pastas, steaks, cutlets, grills, and ice creams. The English-speaking staff is helpful, tactfully proposing alternatives if you're not ready for Roman soul food.

12 On the Appian Way

MODERATE

✪ **Antica Hostaria l'Archeologia.** Via Appia Antica 139. ☎ **06-788-0494.** Reservations recommended Sat–Sun. Main courses 20,000–30,000 lire ($10–$15); fixed-price menu from 28,000 lire ($14). AE, DC, MC, V. Fri–Wed 12:30–3:30pm and 7:30–11pm. Bus: 218 from San Giovanni or 660 from colli Albani. ROMAN/GREEK.

A short walk from the catacombs of St. Sebastian, the family run Antica Hostaria l'Archeologia is like an 18th-century village tavern with lots of atmosphere, strings of garlic and corn, oddments of copper hanging from the ceiling, earth-brown beams, and sienna-washed walls. In summer, you can dine in the garden out back under the wisteria. From the kitchen emerges an array of first-rate food items, like gnocchi with wild boar sauce and a special favorite of ours—*veal alla massenzio* (with artichokes, olives, and mushrooms). An eternal favorite is braised beef, tender chunks cooked in a Barolo wine sauce. Many Roman families visit on the weekend. Of special interest is the wine cellar, excavated in an ancient Roman tomb, with bottles dating from 1800. (You go through an iron gate, down some stairs, and into the underground cavern. Along the way, you can still see the holes once occupied by funeral urns.)

13 In Parioli

VERY EXPENSIVE

✪ **Relais Le Jardin.** In the Hotel Lord Byron, Via G. de Notaris 5. ☎ **06-361-3041.** Reservations required. Main courses 28,000–60,000 lire ($14–$30). AE, DC, MC, V. Mon–Sat 1–3pm and 8–10:30pm. Closed Aug. Bus: 52. ITALIAN/TRADITIONAL.

Relais Le Jardin is one of the best places to go for both traditional and creative cuisine, and a chichi crowd with demanding palates packs it nightly. There are places in Rome with better views, but not with such an elegant setting, inside one of the capital's most exclusive small hotels. The lighthearted decor combines white lattice with bold colors and flowers. The service is impeccable.

The pastas and soups are among the finest in town. We were particularly taken by the tonnarelli pasta with asparagus and smoked ham with concassé tomatoes. The chef can take a dish once served only to the plebes in ancient times, bean soup with clams, and make it something elegant. For your main course you can choose from a delectable roast loin of lamb with artichoke romana or tender grilled beef sirloin with hot chicory and sautéed potatoes. The chef also creates a fabulous risotto with pheasant sauce, asparagus, black truffle flakes, and a hint of fresh thyme—it gets our vote as the best risotto around.

MODERATE

✪ **Al Ceppo.** Via Panama 2. ☎ **06-841-9696.** Reservations recommended. Main courses 20,000–32,000 lire ($10–$16). AE, DC, MC, V. Tues–Sun 12:30–3pm and 8–11pm. Closed last 2 weeks of Aug. Bus: 4, 52, or 53. ROMAN.

Because the place is somewhat hidden (though only 2 blocks from the Villa Borghese, near Piazza Ungheria), you're likely to rub elbows with more Romans than tourists. It's a longtime favorite, and the cuisine is as good as it ever was. "The Log" features an open wood-stoked fireplace on which the chef roasts lamb chops, liver, and bacon to perfection. The beefsteak, which hails from Tuscany, is also succulent. Other dishes we continue to delight in are *linguine monteconero* (with clams and fresh tomatoes); savory spaghetti with peppers, fresh basil, and pecorino cheese; swordfish fillet filled with grapefruit, parmigiano, pine nuts, and dry grapes; and a fish *carpaccio* (raw sea bass) with a green salad, onions, and green pepper. Save room for dessert, especially the apple cobbler, pear-and-almond tart, or chocolate meringue hazelnut cake.

Exploring Rome   6

Where else but in Rome could you admire a 17th-century colonnade designed by Bernini while resting against an Egyptian obelisk carried off from Heliopolis while Jesus was still alive? Or stand amid the splendor of Renaissance frescoes in a papal palace built on top of the tomb of a Roman emperor? Where else, for that matter, are vestal virgins buried adjacent to the Ministry of Finance?

Rome went all out to spruce up for 2000, and the visitor in 2001 will benefit from all those improvements made at the end of the 20th century. For the Jubilee, decades' worth of grime from car exhaust and other pollution was scrubbed from the city's facades, revealing the original glory of the Eternal City (though Rome could still stand even more work on this front), and ancient treasures like the Colosseum were shored up. Many of the most popular areas (such as the Trevi Fountain and Piazza Navona) are sparkling and inviting again.

Whether they're still time-blackened or newly gleaming, the city's ancient monuments are a constant reminder that Rome was one of the greatest centers of Western civilization. In the heyday of the Empire, all roads led to Rome with good reason. It was one of the first cosmopolitan cities, importing slaves, gladiators, great art—even citizens—from the far corners of the world. Despite its carnage and corruption, Rome left a legacy of law; a heritage of great art, architecture, and engineering; and an uncanny lesson in how to conquer enemies by absorbing their cultures.

But ancient Rome is only part of the spectacle. The Vatican has had a tremendous influence on making the city a tourism center. Though Vatican architects stripped down much of the glory of the past, looting ancient ruins for their precious marble, they created great Renaissance treasures and even occasionally incorporated the old into the new—as Michelangelo did when turning the Baths of Diocletian into a church. And in the years that followed, Bernini adorned the city with the wonders of the baroque, especially his glorious fountains.

Rome Attractions

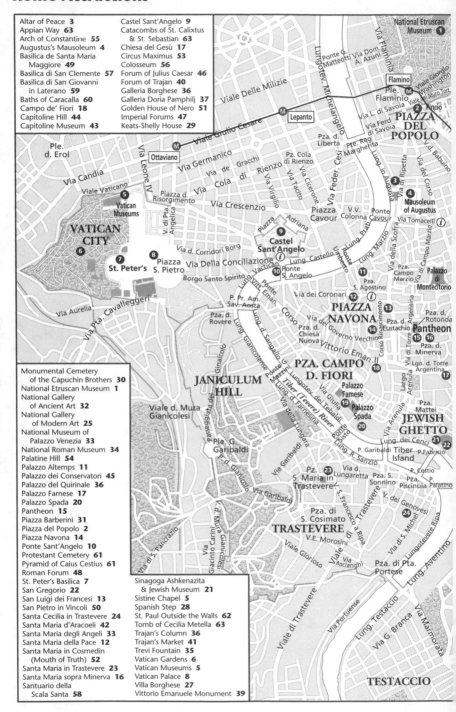

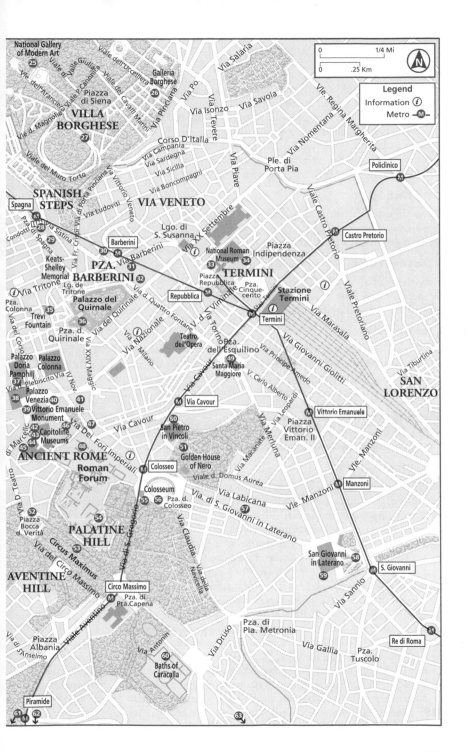

Suggested Itineraries

If You Have 1 Day

Far too brief—after all, Rome wasn't built in a day nor can you see it in one—but you can make the most of your limited time. You'll basically have to choose between the legacy of imperial Rome (mainly the Roman Forum, the Imperial Forum, and the Colosseum) or St. Peter's and the Vatican. Walk along the Spanish Steps at sunset. At night go to Piazza del Campidoglio for a fantastic view of the Forum below. Have a nightcap on Via Veneto, which, although past its prime, is still a lure for first-time visitors. Toss a coin in the Trevi Fountain and promise a return visit to Rome.

If You Have 2 Days

If you elected to see the Roman Forum and the Colosseum on your first day, then spend Day 2 exploring St. Peter's and the Vatican Museums (or vice versa). Have dinner that night in a restaurant in Trastevere.

If You Have 3 Days

Spend your first 2 days as above. In the morning of Day 3, go to the Pantheon in the heart of Old Rome, then try to explore two museums after lunch: the Castel Sant'Angelo and the Etruscan Museum. Have dinner at a restaurant on Piazza Navona.

If You Have 4 Days

Spend your first 3 days as above. On Day 4, head for the environs, either to Tivoli, where you can see the Villa d'Este and Hadrian's Villa, or to Ostia to explore the ruins of Ostia Antica; return to Rome for lunch, and visit the Capitoline Museum and Basilica di San Giovanni in Laterano in the afternoon.

1 St. Peter's & the Vatican

If you want to know more about the Vatican, check out its Web site at **www.vatican.va**.

IN VATICAN CITY

In 1929, the Lateran Treaty between Pope Pius XI and the Italian government created the **Vatican,** the world's second-smallest sovereign independent state. It has only a few hundred citizens and is protected (theoretically) by its own militia, the curiously uniformed (some say by Michelangelo) Swiss guards.

The only entrance to the Vatican for the casual visitor is through one of the glories of the Western world: Bernini's **St. Peter's Square (Piazza San Pietro).** As you stand in the huge piazza, you'll be in the arms of an ellipse partly enclosed by a majestic **Doric-pillared colonnade.** Atop it stands a gesticulating crowd of some 140 saints. Straight ahead is the facade of **St. Peter's Basilica** (Sts. Peter and Paul are represented by statues in front, Peter carrying the Keys to the Kingdom), and to the right, above the colonnade, are the dark brown buildings of the **papal apartments** and the **Vatican Museums.** In the center of the square is an **Egyptian obelisk,** brought from the ancient city of Heliopolis on the Nile delta. Flanking the obelisk are two 17th-century **fountains.** The one on the right (facing the basilica) by Carlo Maderno, who designed the facade of St. Peter's, was placed here by Bernini himself; the other is by Carlo Fontana.

On the left side of Piazza San Pietro is the **Vatican Tourist Office** (☎ **06-6988-4466** or 06-6988-4866), open Monday to Saturday 8:30am to 7pm. It sells maps and guides that'll help you make more sense of the riches you'll be seeing in the museums, accepts reservations for tours of the Vatican Gardens, and tries to answer questions.

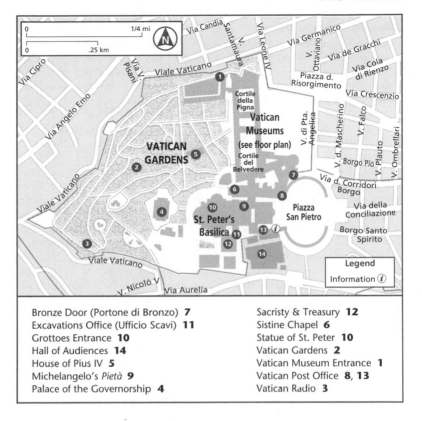

Bronze Door (Portone di Bronzo) **7**
Excavations Office (Ufficio Scavi) **11**
Grottoes Entrance **10**
Hall of Audiences **14**
House of Pius IV **5**
Michelangelo's *Pietà* **9**
Palace of the Governorship **4**

Sacristy & Treasury **12**
Sistine Chapel **6**
Statue of St. Peter **10**
Vatican Gardens **2**
Vatican Museum Entrance **1**
Vatican Post Office **8, 13**
Vatican Radio **3**

Though it had been suspended during renovations of the Vatican grounds, by the time you arrive, a **shuttle bus** should again be running from in front of this office for the entrance to the Vatican Museums; it runs daily every 30 minutes from the museums' opening till an hour before they close and costs 2,000 lire ($1). Take it! It's a long and generally uninteresting walk from the piazza to the museum entrance, and on the bus's route you'll pass through some of the Vatican's lovely gardens.

✪ **Basilica di San Pietro** (St. Peter's Basilica). Piazza San Pietro. ☎ **06-6988-4466** (for information on celebrations). Basilica (including grottoes) free. Guided tour of excavations around St. Peter's tomb, 15,000 lire ($7.50) (children younger than 15 are not admitted). Stairs to the dome 7,000 lire ($3.50); elevator to the dome 8,000 lire ($4); sacristy (with Historical Museum) 9,000 lire ($4.50). Basilica (including the sacristy and treasury) Oct–Mar daily 7am–6pm; Apr–Sept daily 7am–7pm. Grottoes daily 8am–5pm. Dome Oct–Mar daily 8am–5pm; Apr–Sept 8am–6pm. Bus: 46. Metro: Ottaviano/San Pietro, then a long stroll.

In ancient times, the Circus of Nero, where St. Peter is said to have been crucified, was slightly to the left of where the basilica is now located. Peter was buried here in A.D. 64 near the site of his execution, and in 324 Constantine commissioned a basilica to be built over Peter's tomb. That structure stood for more than 1,000 years, until it verged on collapse. The present basilica, mostly completed in the 1500s and 1600s, is predominantly High Renaissance and baroque. Inside, the massive scale is almost too much to absorb, showcasing some of Italy's greatest artists: Bramante, Raphael, Michelangelo, and Maderno. In a church of such grandeur—overwhelming in its

A St. Peter's Warning

St. Peter's has a strict dress code: no shorts, no skirts above the knee, and no bare shoulders. *They will not let you in if you don't come dressed appropriately.* In a pinch, men and women alike can buy a big cheap scarf from a nearby souvenir stand and wrap it around their legs as a long skirt or throw it over their shoulders as a shawl. You also must remain silent and cannot take photographs.

detail of gilt, marble, and mosaic—you can't expect much subtlety. It's meant to be overpowering.

In the nave on the right (the first chapel) stands one of the Vatican's greatest treasures: Michelangelo's exquisite *Pietà,* created while the master was still in his early 20s but clearly showing his genius for capturing the human form. He was contracted to create "the most beautiful work in marble that exists in Rome to this day." Showing an amazing creative power, the execution of the profoundly moving figures, both mother and son, achieves perfection, so much so that Michelangelo's enemies spread a rumor that the work was not his but that of a much older master. Michelangelo added his signature across the Virgin's sash, his only work so marked. (The sculpture has been kept behind reinforced glass since a madman's act of vandalism in the 1970s.) Note the incredibly lifelike folds of Mary's robes and her youthful features (though she would've been middle-aged at the time of the Crucifixion, Michelangelo portrayed her as a young woman to convey her purity).

Much farther on, in the right wing of the transept near the Chapel of St. Michael, rests Canova's neoclassic **sculpture of Pope Clement XIII.** The truly devout stop to kiss the feet of the 13th-century **bronze of St. Peter,** attributed to Arnolfo di Cambio (at the far reaches of the nave, against a corner pillar on the right). Under Michelangelo's dome is the celebrated twisty-columned **baldacchino** (1524) by Bernini, resting over the papal altar. The 96-foot-high ultra-fancy canopy was created in part, so it's said, from bronze stripped from the Pantheon, though that's up for debate.

In addition, you can visit the **treasury,** filled with jewel-studded chalices, reliquaries, and copes. One robe worn by Pius XII strikes a simple note in these halls of elegance. The sacristy now contains a **Historical Museum (Museo Storico)** displaying Vatican treasures, including the large 1400s bronze tomb of Pope Sixtus V by Antonio Pollaiuolo and several antique chalices.

An underground visit to the **Vatican grottoes** reveals both ancient and modern tombs. (Pope John XXIII gets the most adulation.) Along with pillars of an earlier church that stood on this spot, you can view the tombs of such pontiffs as Pius II, Pius XII, Paul VI, John Paul I, and even the only British pope, Nicholas Breakspear, who ruled under the name of Hadrian IV in 1154. One extraordinary gem here: an **angel,** which is all that remains from Giotto's original mosaic from the first church. Behind a wall of glass are what's assumed to be the remains of St. Peter himself.

To go even farther down, to the area around St. Peter's tomb, you must apply several days beforehand to the **excavations office** (you could also stop by first thing in the morning and try to get on the afternoon tour, but don't count on it). Apply in advance (4 or 5 days before you plan to visit, if possible) at the Ufficio Scavi (☎ **06-6988-5318**), through the arch to the left of the stairs up the Basilica. You specify your name, the number in your party, language, and dates you'd like to visit. They'll notify you by phone of your admission date and time. For 15,000 lire ($7.50), you'll take a guided tour of the tombs that were excavated in the 1940s, 23 feet beneath the church floor.

After you leave the grottoes, you'll find yourself in a courtyard and ticket line for the grandest sight: the climb to ✪ **Michelangelo's dome,** about 375 feet high. (*Warning:* Though you can walk up the steps, we recommend taking the elevator for as far as it goes—it'll save you 171 steps, and you'll *still* have 320 to go. The climb isn't recommended if you're not in good shape or are claustrophobic—and there's no turning back once you've started.) After you've made it, you'll have an astounding view over the rooftops of Rome and even the Vatican Gardens and papal apartments. This is a photo op if ever there was one.

Vatican Museums (Musei Vaticani) & the Sistine Chapel (Cappella Sistina). Vatican City, Viale Vaticano (a long walk around the Vatican walls from St. Peter's Square). ☎ **06-6988-3333.** Admission 18,000 lire ($9); free for everyone the last Sun of each month (be ready for a crowd). Mid-Mar to Oct Mon–Fri 8:45am–3:45pm, Sat and last Sun of the month 8:45am–12:45pm. Off-season Mon–Sat and last Sun of the month 8:45–12:45pm. Closed all national and religious holidays (except Easter week) and Aug 15–16. Metro: Ottaviano/San Pietro.

The Vatican Museums boast one of the world's greatest art collections. It's a gigantic repository of treasures from antiquity and the Renaissance, all housed in a labyrinthine series of lavishly adorned palaces, apartments, and galleries leading you to the real gem: the Sistine Chapel. The Vatican Museums occupy a part of the papal palaces built from the 1200s onward. From the former papal private apartments, the museums were created over a period of time to display the vast treasure trove of art acquired by the Vatican.

You'll climb a magnificent spiral ramp to get to the ticket windows. After you're admitted, you can choose your route through the museum from **four color-coded itineraries** (A, B, C, D) according to the time you have (from 1½ to 5 hours) and your interests. You determine your choice by consulting large-size panels on the wall and then following the letter/color of your choice. All four itineraries culminate in the Sistine Chapel. Obviously, 1, 2, or even 20 trips will not be enough to see the wealth of the Vatican, much less to digest it. With that in mind, we've previewed only a representative sampling of the masterpieces on display (in alphabetical order).

Borgia Apartments: Frescoed with biblical scenes by Pinturicchio of Umbria and his assistants, these rooms were designed for Pope Alexander VI (the infamous Borgia pope). They may be badly lit but boast great splendor and style. At the end of the Raphael Rooms (below) is the Chapel of Nicholas V, an intimate room frescoed by Dominican monk Fra Angelico, the most saintly of all Italian painters.

Chiaramonti Museum: Founded by Pope Pius VII, also known as Chiaramonti, the museum includes the Corridoio (corridor), the Galleria Lapidaria, and the Braccio Nuovo (New Side). The Corridor hosts an exposition of more than 800 Greek-Roman works, including statues, reliefs, and sarcophagi. In the Galleria Lapidaria there are about 5,000 Christian and pagan inscriptions. You'll find a dazzling array of Roman sculpture and copies of Greek originals in these galleries. In the Braccio Nuovo, built as an extension of the Chiaramonti, you can admire *The Nile,* a magnificent reproduction of a long-lost Hellenistic original and one of the most remarkable pieces of

Impressions

As a whole St. Peter's is fit for nothing but a ballroom, and it is a little too gaudy even for that.

— John Ruskin, letter to the Rev. Thomas Dale (1840)

Oh for a half-hour of Europe after this sanctimonious icebox.
—Wyndham Lewis, *The Letters of Wyndham Lewis*

sculpture from antiquity. The imposing statue of Augustus of Prima Porta presents him as a regal commander.

Collection of Modern Religious Art: This museum, opened in 1973, represents the American artists' first invasion of the Vatican (the church had previously limited itself to European art from before the 18th century). But Pope Paul VI's hobby changed all that. Of the 55 rooms, at least 12 are devoted to American artists. All the works chosen were judged on their "spiritual and religious values." Among the American works is Leonard Baskin's 5-foot bronze sculpture of *Isaac.* Modern Italian artists like De Chirico and Manzù are also displayed, and there's a special room for the paintings of the Frenchman Georges Rouault. You'll also see works by Picasso, Gauguin, Gottuso, Chagall, Henry Moore, Kandinsky, and others.

Egyptian-Gregorian Museum: Experience the grandeur of the pharaohs by studying sarcophagi, mummies, statues of goddesses, vases, jewelry, sculptured pink-granite statues, and hieroglyphics.

Etruscan-Gregorian Museum: It was founded by Gregory XIV in 1837 and then enriched year after year, becoming one of the most important and complete collections of Etruscan art. With sarcophagi, a chariot, bronzes, urns, jewelry, and terra-cotta vases, this gallery affords remarkable insights into an ancient civilization. One of the most acclaimed exhibits is the Regolini-Galassi tomb, unearthed in the 19th century at Cerveteri (see "Side Trips from Rome: Tivoli, Ostia Antica & More" later in this chapter). It shares top honors with the *Mars of Todi,* a bronze sculpture probably dating from the 5th century B.C.

Ethnological Museum: This is an assemblage of works of art and objects of cultural significance from all over the world. The principal route is a half-mile walk through 25 geographical sections, displaying thousands of objects covering 3,000 years of world history. The section devoted to China is especially interesting.

Historical Museum: This museum, founded by Pope Paul VI, was established to tell the history of the Vatican. It exhibits arms, uniforms, and armor, some dating from the early Renaissance. The carriages displayed are those used by the popes and cardinals in religious processions. Among the showcases of dress uniforms are the colorful outfits worn by the Pontifical Army Corps, which was discontinued by Pope Paul VI.

Pinacoteca (Picture Gallery): The Pinacoteca houses paintings and tapestries from the 11th to the 19th century. As you pass through room 1, note the oldest picture at the Vatican, a keyhole-shaped wood panel of the *Last Judgment* from the 11th century. In room 2 is one of the finest pieces—the *Stefaneschi Triptych* (six panels) by Giotto and his assistants. Bernardo Daddi's masterpiece of early Italian Renaissance art, *Madonna del Magnificat,* is also here. And you'll see works by Fra Angelico, the 15th-century Dominican monk who distinguished himself as a miniaturist (his *Virgin with Child* is justly praised—check out the Madonna's microscopic eyes).

In the Raphael salon (room 8) you can view three paintings by that Renaissance giant: the *Coronation of the Virgin, the Virgin of Foligno,* and the massive *Transfiguration* (completed shortly before his death). There are also eight tapestries made by Flemish weavers from cartoons by Raphael. In room 9, seek out Leonardo da Vinci's masterful but uncompleted *St. Jerome with the Lion,* as well as Giovanni Bellini's *Pietà* and one of Titian's greatest works, the *Virgin of Frari.* Finally, in room 10, feast your eyes on one of the masterpieces of the baroque, Caravaggio's *Deposition from the Cross.*

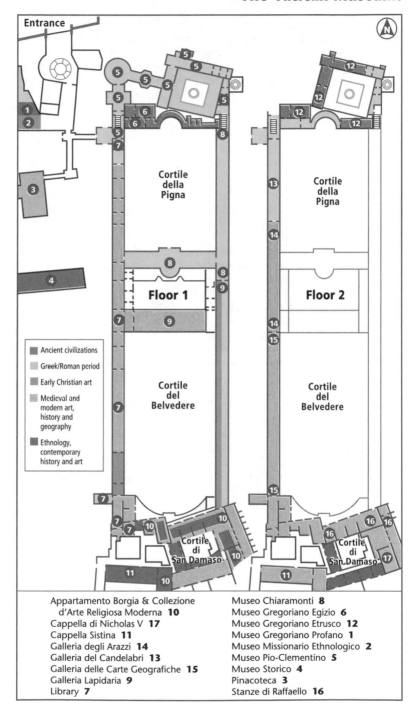

Entrance

Cortile della Pigna

Floor 1

Cortile del Belvedere

Cortile di San Damaso

Cortile della Pigna

Floor 2

Cortile del Belvedere

Cortile di San Damaso

Ancient civilizations

Greek/Roman period

Early Christian art

Medieval and modern art, history and geography

Ethnology, contemporary history and art

Appartamento Borgia & Collezione
    d'Arte Religiosa Moderna **10**
Cappella di Nicholas V **17**
Cappella Sistina **11**
Galleria degli Arazzi **14**
Galleria del Candelabri **13**
Galleria delle Carte Geografiche **15**
Galleria Lapidaria **9**
Library **7**

Museo Chiaramonti **8**
Museo Gregoriano Egizio **6**
Museo Gregoriano Etrusco **12**
Museo Gregoriano Profano **1**
Museo Missionario Ethnologico **2**
Museo Pio-Clementino **5**
Museo Storico **4**
Pinacoteca **3**
Stanze di Raffaello **16**

Pio Clementino Museum: Here you'll find Greek and Roman sculptures, many of which are immediately recognizable. The rippling muscles of the *Belvedere Torso,* a partially preserved Greek statue (1st century B.C.) much admired by the artists of the Renaissance, especially Michelangelo, reveal an intricate knowledge of the human body. In the rotunda is a large gilded bronze of *Hercules* from the late 2nd century. Other major sculptures are under porticoes opening onto the Belvedere courtyard. From the 1st century B.C., one sculpture shows Laocoön and his two sons locked in an eternal struggle with the serpents. The incomparable *Apollo Belvedere* (a late Roman reproduction of an authentic Greek work from the 4th century B.C.) has become the symbol of classic male beauty, rivaling Michelangelo's *David.*

Raphael Rooms: While still a young man, Raphael was given one of the greatest assignments of his short life: the decoration of a series of rooms in the apartments of Pope Julius II. The decoration was carried out by Raphael and his workshop from 1508 to 1524. In these works, Raphael achieves the Renaissance aim of blending classic beauty with realism. In the first chamber, the Stanza dell'Incendio, you'll see much of the work of Raphael's pupils but little of the master—except in the fresco across from the window. The figure of the partially draped Aeneas rescuing his father (to the left of the fresco) is sometimes attributed to Raphael, as is the surprised woman with a jug balanced on her head to the right.

Raphael reigns supreme in the next and most important salon, the Stanza della Segnatura, the first room decorated by the artist, where you'll find the majestic *School of Athens,* one of his best-known works, depicting such philosophers from the ages as Aristotle, Plato, and Socrates. Many of the figures are actually portraits of some of the greatest artists of the Renaissance, including Bramante (on the right as Euclid, bent over and balding as he draws on a chalkboard), Leonardo da Vinci (as Plato, the bearded man in the center pointing heavenward), even Raphael himself (looking out at you from the lower-right corner). While he was painting this masterpiece, Raphael stopped work to walk down the hall for the unveiling of Michelangelo's newly finished Sistine Chapel ceiling. He was so impressed he returned to his *School of Athens* and added to his design a sulking Michelangelo sitting on the steps. Another well-known masterpiece here is the *Disputa del Sacramento.*

The *Stanza d'Eliodoro,* also by the master, manages to flatter Raphael's papal patrons (Julius II and Leo X) without compromising his art (though one rather fanciful fresco depicts the pope driving Attila from Rome). Finally, there's the *Sala di Constantino,* which was completed by his students after Raphael's death. The loggia, frescoed with more than 50 scenes from the Bible, was designed by Raphael, but the actual work was done by his loyal students.

Sistine Chapel: Michelangelo considered himself a sculptor, not a painter. While in his 30s, he was commanded by Julius II to stop work on the pope's own tomb and to devote his considerable talents to painting ceiling frescoes (an art form of which the Florentine master was contemptuous). Michelangelo labored for 4 years (1508–12) over this epic project, which was so physically taxing it permanently damaged his eyesight. All during the task he had to contend with the pope's incessant urgings to hurry up; at one point Julius threatened to topple Michelangelo from the scaffolding— or so Vasari relates in his *Lives of the Artists.*

It's ironic that a project undertaken against the artist's wishes would form his most enduring legend. Glorifying the human body as only a sculptor could, Michelangelo painted nine panels, taken from the pages of Genesis, and surrounded them with prophets and sibyls. The most notable panels detail the expulsion of Adam and Eve from the Garden of Eden and the creation of man; you'll recognize the image of God's

Papal Audiences

When he's in Rome, the pope gives a public audience every Wednesday beginning at 10:30am (sometimes at 10am in summer). It takes place in the Paul VI Hall of Audiences, though sometimes St. Peter's Basilica and St. Peter's Square are used to accommodate a large attendance. Anyone is welcome, but you must first obtain a **free ticket** from the office of the Prefecture of the Papal Household, accessible from St. Peter's Square by the Bronze Door, where the right-hand colonnade (as you face the basilica) begins. The office is open Monday to Saturday 9am to 1pm. Tickets are readily available on Monday and Tuesday, and sometimes you won't be able to get into the office on Wednesday morning. Occasionally, if there's enough room you can attend without a ticket.

You can also write ahead to the **Prefecture of the Papal Household,** 00120 Città del Vaticano (☎ 06-698-83114), indicating your language, the dates of your visit, the number of people in your party, and (if possible) the hotel in Rome to which the cards should be sent the afternoon before the audience. American Catholics, armed with a letter of introduction from their parish priest, should apply to the **North American College,** Via dell'Umiltà 30, 00187 Roma (☎ 06-690-011).

At noon on Sunday, the pope speaks briefly from his study window and gives his blessing to the visitors and pilgrims gathered in St. Peter's Square. From about mid-July to mid-September, the Angelus and blessing take place at the summer residence at Castelgandolfo, some 16 miles (26km) out of Rome and accessible by metro and bus.

---

outstretched hand as it imbues Adam with spirit. (You may want to bring along binoculars so you can see the details better.)

The Florentine master was in his 60s when he began the masterly *Last Judgment* on the altar wall. Again working against his wishes, Michelangelo presents a more jaundiced view of people and their fate; God sits in judgment and sinners are plunged into the mouth of hell.

A master of ceremonies under Paul III, Monsignor Biagio da Cesena, protested to the pope about the "shameless nudes" painted by Michelangelo. Michelangelo showed he wasn't above petty revenge by painting the prude with the ears of a jackass in hell. When Biagio complained to the pope, Paul III maintained he had no jurisdiction in hell. However, Daniele de Volterra was summoned to drape clothing over some of the bare figures—thus earning for himself a dubious distinction as a haberdasher.

On the side walls are frescoes by other Renaissance masters, like Botticelli, Perugino, Signorelli, Pinturicchio, Roselli, and Ghirlandaio. If these paintings had been displayed by themselves in other chapels, they would be the object of special pilgrimages. But since they have to compete unfairly with the artistry of Michelangelo, they're virtually ignored by most visitors.

The restoration of the Sistine Chapel in the 1990s touched off a worldwide debate among art historians. The chapel was on the verge of collapse, from both its age and the weather, and restoration has taken years, as restorers used advanced computer analyses in their painstaking and controversial work. They reattached the fresco and repaired the ceiling, ridding the frescoes of their dark and shadowy look. Critics claim that in addition to removing centuries of dirt and grime—and several of the added "modesty" drapes—the restorers removed a vital second layer of paint as well. Purists argue that many of the restored figures seem flat compared to the original, which had more shadow and detail. Others have hailed the project for saving Michelangelo's masterpiece for future generations to appreciate and for revealing the vibrancy of his color palette.

Vatican Library: The library is richly decorated, with frescos created by a team of Mannerist painters commissioned by Sixtus V.

Vatican Gardens. North and west of the Vatican. See below for tour information.

Separating the Vatican from the secular world on the north and west are 58 acres of lush gardens filled with winding paths, brilliantly colored flowers, groves of massive oaks, and ancient fountains and pools. In the midst of this pastoral setting is a small summer house, Villa Pia, built for Pope Pius IV in 1560 by Pirro Ligorio. The gardens contain medieval fortifications from the 9th century to the present. Profuse waters sprout from a variety of fountains.

To make a reservation to visit the Vatican Gardens, send a fax to **06-698-851-00.** Once the reservation is accepted, you have to go to the Vatican information office (at Piazza San Pietro, on the left side looking at the facade of St. Peter's) and pick up the tickets 2 or 3 days before your visit at the gardens. Tours of the gardens are Monday, Tuesday, Thursday, Friday, and Saturday at 10am; they last for 2 hours and the first half hour is by bus. The cost of the tour is 20,000 lire ($10). For further information, contact the Vatican Tourism office (☎ **06-698-844-66,** or 06-698-848-66).

NEAR VATICAN CITY

Castel Sant'Angelo. Lungotevere Castello 50. ☎ **06-681-9111.** Admission 10,000 lire ($5). Tues–Sun 9am–8pm. Closed 2nd and last Wed of the month. Metro: Ottaviano, then a long stroll. Bus: 23, 46, 49, 62, 87, 98, 280, or 910.

This overpowering castle on the Tiber was built in the 2nd century as a tomb for Emperor Hadrian; it continued as an imperial mausoleum until the time of Caracalla. If it looks like a fortress, it should—that was its function in the Middle Ages, built over the Roman walls and linked to the Vatican by an underground passage that was much used by the fleeing papacy, who escaped from unwanted visitors like Charles V during his 1527 sack of the city. In the 14th century, it became a papal residence, enjoying various connections with Boniface IX, Nicholas V, and Julius II, patron of Michelangelo and Raphael. But its legend rests largely on its link with Pope Alexander VI, whose mistress bore him two children (those darlings of debauchery, Cesare and Lucrezia Borgia).

The highlight here is a trip through the Renaissance apartments with their coffered ceilings and lush decoration. Their walls have witnessed some of the most diabolical plots and intrigues of the High Renaissance. Later, you can go through the dank cells that once echoed with the screams of Cesare's victims of torture. The most famous figure imprisoned here was Benvenuto Cellini, the eminent sculptor/goldsmith, remembered chiefly for his candid *Autobiography.* Now an art museum, the castle halls display the history of the Roman mausoleum, along with a wide-ranging selection of ancient arms and armor. You can climb to the top terrace for another one of those dazzling views of the Eternal City.

2 The Colosseum, the Roman Forum & Highlights of Ancient Rome

THE TOP SIGHTS IN ANCIENT ROME

The Colosseum (Colosseo). Piazzale del Colosseo, Via dei Fori Imperiali. ☎ **06-700-4261.** Admission 10,000 lire ($5) all levels. Oct–Jan 15 daily 9am–3pm; Jan 16–Feb 15 daily 9am–4pm; Feb 16–Mar 17 daily 9am–4:30pm; Mar 18–Apr 16 daily 9am–5pm; Apr 17–Sept

Ancient Rome & Attractions Nearby

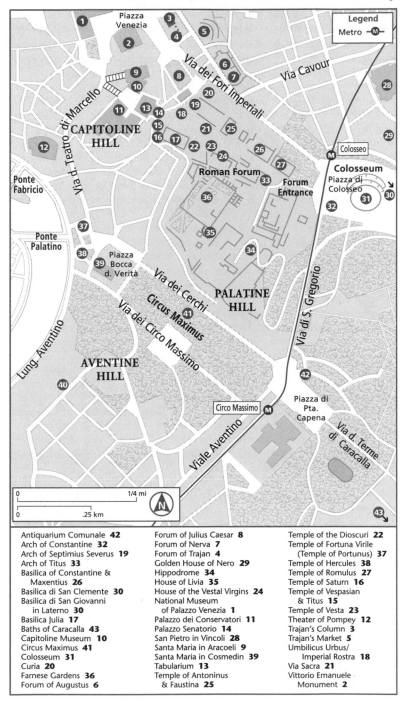

daily 9am–7pm. Guided tours in English with an archaeologist 3 times per morning on Sun and holidays 6,000 lire ($3). Tickets to Palatine Hill also sold at box office for 12,000 lire ($6).

Though it's a mere shell, the Colosseum remains the greatest architectural legacy from ancient Rome, although it remains under almost constant scaffolding because of its deteriorating condition. Vespasian ordered the construction of the elliptical bowl, called the Amphitheatrum Flavium, in A.D. 72; it was inaugurated by Titus in A.D. 80 with a many-weeks-long bloody combat between gladiators and wild beasts. At its peak, under the cruel Domitian, the Colosseum could seat 50,000. The vestal virgins from the temple screamed for blood, as more and more exotic animals were shipped in from the far corners of the Empire to satisfy jaded tastes (lion versus bear, two humans vs. hippopotamus, or whatever). Not-so-mock naval battles were staged (the canopied Colosseum could be flooded), and the defeated combatants might have their lives spared if they put up a good fight. Many historians now believe that one of the most enduring legends about the Colosseum (that Christians were fed to the lions) is unfounded.

Long after it ceased to be an arena to amuse sadistic Romans, the Colosseum was struck by an earthquake. Centuries later it was used as a quarry, its rich marble facing stripped away to build palaces and churches. On one side, part of the original four tiers remains; the first three levels were constructed in Doric, Ionic, and Corinthian styles to lend variety. Inside, the seats are gone, as is the wooden floor. Efforts are currently under way to restore and shore up the Colosseum, but they seem to be dragging. As of this writing, scaffolding still covers one section, but that should be done by the time you arrive. The Colosseum has become the turnstile for Rome's largest traffic circle, around which thousands of cars whip daily, spewing exhaust over this venerable monument. In addition to reinforcing the structure, workers are attempting to clean off a layer of grime. Ambitious plans are also underway to allow visitors to explore the interior more fully by 2002. For now, you can explore on your own or rent an audio guide for 7,000 lire ($3.50).

A highly photogenic memorial next to the Colosseum, the **Arch of Constantine** was erected by the Senate in A.D. 315 to honor Constantine's defeat of the pagan Maxentius (306). Many of the reliefs have nothing whatever to do with Constantine or his works but tell of the victories of earlier Antonine rulers (they were apparently lifted from other, long-forgotten memorials).

Historically, the arch marks a period of great change in the history of Rome and, thus, the history of the world. Converted to Christianity by a vision on the battlefield, Constantine ended the centuries-long persecution of the Christians (during which many devout followers of the new religion had often been put to death in a most

No More Lines

Sun or rain, the endless lines outside Italian museums and attractions are a fact of life. But new reservation services can help you to avoid waiting, at least for some of the major museums.

Select Italy offers the possibility to reserve your tickets for the Colosseum, the Palatine Forum & Museum, Palazzo Altemps, the Domus Aurea, the Galleria Borghese, and more, plus many other museums in Florence and Venice. The cost varies from U.S. $15 to $24, depending on the museum, and several combination passes are available. Select Italy's main office is at 329 Linden Avenue, Wilmette, IL 60091-2788 (☎ **847/853-1661;** fax 847/853-1667). You can buy your tickets from them online at www.selectitaly.com.

gruesome manner). While Constantine didn't ban paganism (which survived officially until the closing of the temples more than half a century later), he espoused Christianity himself and began the inevitable development that culminated in the conquest of Rome by the Christian religion.

After visiting the Colosseum, it's convenient to head over to the recently reopened **Domus Aurea (Golden House of Nero)** on the Esquiline Hill; it faces the Colosseum and is adjacent to the Forum (see below).

Golden House of Nero (Domus Aurea). Via della Domus Aurea. ☎ **06-397-499-07.** Admission 12,000 lire ($6). Daily 9am–7:45pm. Last admission 1 hour before closing. Metro: Colosseo.

"Nero's Folly" finally reopened in 1999 after a 15-year restoration. After the disastrous A.D. 64 fire swept over Rome (it has never been proven that Nero set the fire, much less fiddled while Rome burned), the emperor seized about three-quarters of the burned-out historic core (more than 200 acres) to create in just 4 years one of the most sumptuous palaces in history. Subsequent emperors destroyed much of the golden palace, but what remains is now on view.

The area that's the Colosseum today was a central ornamental lake reflecting the glitter of the Golden House. At the entrance Nero installed a 150-foot statue of himself in the nude. In the words of Suetonius, "all parts of it were overlaid with gold and adorned with jewels and mother-of-pearl." During the Renaissance, painters like Raphael chopped holes in the long-buried ceilings to gain admittance and were inspired by the frescoes and small "grotesques" of cornucopia and cherubs. The word *grotto* came from this palace, as it was believed to have been built underground. Remnants of these almost-2,000-year-old frescoes and fragments of mosaics remain. Out of the original 250 rooms, 30 are now open to the public. Some of the sculptures that survived are also on view.

Practical matters: To visit the Domus Aurea you must make a reservation at Centro Servizi per l'Archeologia, Via Amendola 2 (Metro: Colosseo; open Monday to Saturday 9am to 1pm and 2 to 5pm). But it's easier to book your visit by calling the number above (☎ **06-397-499-07**); where a recorded message both in Italian and English will guide you through the reservation process. Be aware that usually you have to call at least 1 week before the date you've scheduled your visit. The guided tours, both with a guide or with audio-guides, last about 1 hour from 9am to 7pm. Visitors enter in groups of no more than 25, with gaps of 15 minutes between one group and the other.

Of particular interest are the Hall of Hector and Andromache (Sala di Ettore e Andromaca), once illustrated with scenes from Homer's *Iliad;* the Hall of Achilles (Sala di Achille), with a gigantic shell decoration; the Hall of Ninfeo (Sala di Ninfeo), which once had a waterfall; and the Hall of the Gilded Vault (Sala della Volta Dorata), depicting satyrs raping nymphs, plus Cupid driving a chariot pulled by panthers. You'll be amazed by the beauty of the floral frescoes along the *cryptoportici* (long corridors); the longest is about 200 feet. The most spectacular sight is the Octagonal Hall, Nero's banqueting hall, where the menu included casseroles of flamingo tongues and other rare dishes.

When Nero moved in, he shouted, "At last I can start living like a human being!"

✪ Roman Forum (Foro Romano), Palatine Hill (Palatino), and Palatine Museum (Museo Palatino). Via dei Fori Imperiali. ☎ **06-699-0110.** Forum free admission; Palatine Hill 12,000 lire ($6). Apr–Sept daily 9am–8pm; Oct–Mar daily 9am–sunset. Last admission 1 hour before closing. Closed holidays. Metro: Colosseo. Bus: 27, 81, 85, 87, or 186.

When it came to cremating Caesar, purchasing a harlot for the night, sacrificing a naked victim, or just discussing the day's business, the Roman Forum was the place to be. Traversed by **Via Sacra (Sacred Way),** the Broadway of ancient Rome, it was built in the marshy land between the Palatine and Capitoline hills and flourished as the center of Roman life in the days of the Republic, before it gradually lost prestige to the Imperial Forums.

You'll see only ruins and fragments, an arch or two, and lots of overturned boulders, but with some imagination you can feel the rush of history here. That any semblance of the Forum remains today is miraculous, as it was used for years (like the Colosseum) as a quarry. Eventually it reverted to what the Italians call a *campo vaccino* (cow pasture). But excavations in the 19th century began to bring to light one of the world's most historic spots.

By day, the columns of now-vanished temples and the stones from which long-forgotten orators spoke are mere shells. Bits of grass and weed grow where a triumphant Caesar was once lionized. But at night, when the Forum is silent in the moonlight (you can get a dramatic view of the floodlit ruins from the Campidoglio), it isn't difficult to imagine vestal virgins still guarding the sacred temple fire. (The maidens were assigned to keep the temple's sacred fire burning, but to keep their own passions under control. Failure to do the latter sent them to an early grave—alive!)

You can spend at least a morning wandering alone through the ruins of the Forum. If you're content with just looking at the ruins, you can do so at your leisure. But if you want the stones to have some meaning, buy a detailed plan at the gate (the temples are hard to locate otherwise).

Turn right at the bottom of the entrance slope to walk west along the old Via Sacra toward the arch. Just before it on your right is the large brick **Curia** built by Julius Caesar, the main seat of the Roman Senate (pop inside to see the 3rd-century marble inlay floor).

The triumphal **Arch of Septimius Severus** (A.D. 203) displays time-bitten reliefs of the emperor's victories in what are today Iran and Iraq. During the Middle Ages, Rome became a provincial backwater, and frequent flooding of the nearby river helped rapidly bury most of the Forum. This former center of the empire became a cow pasture. Some bits did still stick out above ground, including the top half of this arch, which was used to shelter a barbershop! It wasn't until the 19th century that people really became interested in excavating these ancient ruins to see what Rome in its glory must once have been like.

Just to the left of the arch, you can make out the remains of a cylindrical lump of rock with some marble steps curving off it. That round stone was the **Umbilicus Urbus,** considered the center of Rome and of the entire Roman empire, and the curving steps of the **Imperial Rostra,** where great orators and legislators stood to speak and the people gathered to listen. Nearby, the much-photographed trio of fluted columns with Corinthian capitals supporting a bit of architrave form the corner of the **Temple of Vespasian and Titus** (emperors were routinely turned into gods on dying).

Start heading to your left toward the eight Ionic columns marking the front of the **Temple of Saturn** (rebuilt 42 B.C.), which housed the first treasury of Republican Rome. It was also where they threw one of the Roman year's biggest annual blowout

The Ruins Before & After

To appreciate the Colosseum, the Roman Forum, and other ruins more fully, buy a copy of the small red book called *Rome Past and Present* (Vision Publications), sold in bookstores or by vendors near the Forum. Its plastic overleafs show you the elaborate way things were 2,000 years ago.

festivals, the December 17 feast of *Saturnalia*, which, after a bit of tweaking, we now celebrate as Christmas. Now turn left to start heading back east past the worn steps and stumps of brick pillars outlining the enormous **Basilica Julia,** built by Julius Caesar. Past it are the three Corinthian columns of the **Temple of the Dioscuri,** dedicated to the Gemini twins, Castor and Pollux.

Beyond the bit of curving wall that marks the site of the little round **Temple of Vesta** (rebuilt several times after fires started by the sacred flame housed within), you'll find the partially reconstructed **House of the Vestal Virgins** (A.D. 3rd–4th century) against the south side of the grounds. This was home to the consecrated young women who tended the sacred flame in the Temple of Vesta. Vestals were young girls chosen from patrician families to serve a 30-year priesthood. During their tenure, they were among Rome's most venerated citizens, with unique powers like the ability to pardon condemned criminals. The cult was quite serious about the "virgin" part of the job description—if any of Vesta's earthly servants were found to have "misplaced" their virginity, the miscreant Vestal was summarily buried alive. (Her amorous accomplice was merely flogged to death.) The overgrown rectangle of their gardens has lilied goldfish ponds and is lined with broken, heavily worn statues of senior Vestals on pedestals (and, at any given time when the guards aren't looking, two to six tourists posing as Vestal Virgins on the empty pedestals).

The path dovetails back to join Via Sacra at the entrance. Turn right and then left to enter the massive brick remains and coffered ceilings of the 4th-century **Basilica of Constantine and Maxentius.** These were Rome's public law courts, and their architectural style was adopted by early Christians for their houses of worship (the reason so many ancient churches are called "basilicas").

Return to the path and continue toward the Colosseum, veering right to the second great surviving triumphal arch, the **Arch of Titus** (A.D. 81), on which one relief depicts the carrying off of treasures from Jerusalem's temple—look close and you'll see a menorah among the booty. The war this arch glorifies ended with the expulsion of Jews from the colonized Judea, signaling the beginning of the Jewish Diaspora throughout Europe. From here you can enter and climb the only part of the Forum archaeological zone that still charges admission, the **Palatine Hill** (with the same hours as the Forum).

The Palatine, tradition tells us, was the spot on which the first settlers built their huts, under the direction of Romulus. In later years, the hill became a patrician residential district that attracted such citizens as Cicero. In time, however, the area was gobbled up by imperial palaces and drew a famous and infamous roster of tenants, like Livia (some of the frescoes in the House of Livia are in miraculous condition), Tiberius, Caligula (he was murdered here by members of his Praetorian Guard), Nero, and Domitian.

Only the ruins of its former grandeur remain today, and you really need to be an archaeologist to make sense of them, as they're more difficult to understand than those in the Forum. But even if you're not interested in the past, it's worth the climb for the panoramic view of both the Roman and the Imperial forums, as well as the Capitoline Hill and the Colosseum.

In 1998, the **Palatine Museum (Museo Palatino)** here finally reopened, displaying a good collection of Roman sculpture from the ongoing digs in the Palatine villas. In summer, they run guided tours in English Monday to Sunday at noon for 6,000 lire ($3); call in winter to see if they're still running. If you ask the museum's custodian, he may take you to one of the nearby locked villas and let you in for a peek at surviving frescoes and stuccoes. The entire Palatine is slated for renewed excavations, so be on the lookout for many areas to be roped off at first, but soon even more than before will open to the public.

Imperial Forums (Fori Imperiali). Via de Fori Imperiali. Free admission. Metro: Colosseo.
Keep to the right side of the street.

It was Mussolini who issued the controversial orders to cut through centuries of debris
and junky buildings to carve out Via dei Fori Imperiali, thereby linking the Colosseum
to the grand 19th-century monuments of Piazza Venezia. Excavations under his Fascist
regime began at once, and many archaeological treasures were revealed.

Begun by Julius Caesar as an answer to the overcrowding of Rome's older forums,
the Imperial Forums were at the time of their construction flashier, bolder, and more
impressive than the buildings in the Roman Forum. This site conveyed the unquestioned authority of the emperors at the height of their absolute power. On the street's
north side you'll come to a large outdoor restaurant, where Via Cavour joins the
boulevard. Just beyond the small park across Via Cavour are the remains of the **Forum
of Nerva,** built by the emperor whose 2-year reign (A.D. 96–98) followed that of the
paranoid Domitian. You'll be struck by just how much the ground level has risen in
19 centuries. The only really recognizable remnant is a wall of the Temple of Minerva
with two fine Corinthian columns. This forum was once flanked by that of Vespasian,
which is now gone. It's possible to enter the Forum of Nerva from the other side, but
you can see it just as well from the railing.

The next forum you approach is the **Forum of Augustus,** built before the birth of
Christ to commemorate the emperor's victory over the assassins Cassius and Brutus in
the Battle of Philippi (42 B.C.). Like the Forum of Nerva, you can enter this forum
from the other side (cut across the wee footbridge).

Continuing along the railing, you'll see the vast semicircle of **Trajan's Market,** Via
Quattro Novembre 94 (☎ **06-679-0048**), whose teeming arcades stocked with
merchandise from the far corners of the Roman world long ago collapsed, leaving only
a few cats to watch after things. The shops once covered a multitude of levels, and you
can still wander around many of them. In front of the perfectly proportioned facade
(designed by Apollodorus of Damascus at the beginning of the 2nd century) are the
remains of a great library, and fragments of delicately colored marble floors still shine
in the sun between stretches of rubble and tall grass. Trajan's Market is worth the
descent below street level. To get there, follow the service road you're on until you
reach the monumental Trajan's Column on your left, where you turn right and go up
the steep flight of stairs leading to Via Nazionale. At the top, about half a block
farther on the right, you'll see the entrance. It's open Tuesday to Sunday 9am to
4:30pm. Admission is 4,000 lire ($2).

Before you head down through the labyrinthine passages, you might like to climb
the **Tower of the Milizie,** a 12th-century structure that was part of the medieval headquarters of the Knights of Rhodes. The view from the top (if it's open) is well worth
the climb.

You can enter the **Forum of Trajan** on Via Quattro Novembre near the steps of Via
Magnanapoli. Once through the tunnel, you'll emerge into the newest and most
beautiful of the Imperial Forums, built between A.D. 107 and 113 and designed by
Greek architect Apollodorus of Damascus (who laid out the adjoining market). There
are many statue fragments and pedestals bearing still-legible inscriptions, but more
interesting is the great Basilica Ulpia, whose gray marble columns rise roofless into the
sky. This forum was once regarded as one of the architectural wonders of the world.

Beyond the Basilica Ulpia is **Trajan's Column,** in magnificent condition, with intricate bas-relief sculpture depicting Trajan's victorious campaign (though from your
vantage point you'll be able to see only the earliest stages). The next stop is the **Forum
of Julius Caesar,** the first of the Imperial Forums. It lies on the opposite side of

❓ Did You Know?

- Along with miles of headless statues and acres of paintings, Rome has 913 churches.

- Some Mongol khans and Turkish chieftains pushed westward to conquer the Roman empire after it had ceased to exist.

- At the time of Julius Caesar and Augustus, Rome's population reached one million—it was the largest city in the Western world. Some historians claim that by the year A.D. 500 only 10,000 inhabitants were left.

- Pope Leo III sneaked up on Charlemagne and set an imperial crown on his head, a surprise coronation that launched a precedent of Holy Roman Emperors being crowned by popes in Rome.

- More than 90% of Romans live in private apartments, some of which rise 10 floors and have no elevators.

- The bronze of Marcus Aurelius in the Capitoline Museums, one of the world's greatest equestrian statues, escaped being melted down because the early Christians thought it was of Constantine.

- The Theater of Marcellus incorporated a gory realism in some of its stage plays: Condemned prisoners were often butchered before audiences as part of the plot.

- Christians may not have been fed to the lions at the Colosseum, but in 1 day 5,000 animals were slaughtered (about one every 10 seconds). North Africa's native lions and elephants were rendered extinct.

Via dei Fori Imperiali. This was the site of the Roman stock exchange, as well as of the Temple of Venus.

After you've seen the wonders of ancient Rome, you might continue up Via dei Fori Imperiali to Piazza Venezia, where the white Brescian marble **Vittorio Emanuele Monument** dominates the scene. (You can't miss it.) Italy's most flamboyant landmark, it was built in the late 1800s to honor the first king of Italy. It has been compared to everything from a frosty wedding cake to a Victorian typewriter and has been ridiculed because of its harsh white color in a city of honey-gold tones. An eternal flame burns at the Tomb of the Unknown Soldier. The interior of the monument has been closed for many years, but you'll come to use it as a landmark as you figure your way around the city.

Circus Maximus (Circo Massimo). Between Via dei Cerchi and Via del Circo Massimo. Metro: Circo Massimo.

The Circus Maximus, with its elongated oval proportions and ruined tiers of benches, will remind you of the setting for *Ben-Hur*. Today a formless ruin, the once-grand circus was pilfered repeatedly by medieval and Renaissance builders in search of marble and stone. At one time, 250,000 Romans could assemble on the marble seats, while the emperor observed the games from his box high on the Palatine Hill.

The circus lies in a valley formed by the Palatine on the left and the Aventine on the right. Next to the Colosseum, it was the most impressive structure in ancient Rome, located certainly in one of the most exclusive neighborhoods. For centuries, the pomp and ceremony of imperial chariot races filled this valley with the cheers of thousands.

When the dark days of the 5th and 6th centuries fell, the Circus Maximus seemed a symbol of the complete ruination of Rome. The last games were held in 549 on the orders of Totilla the Goth, who had seized Rome in 547 and established himself emperor. He lived in the still-glittering ruins on the Palatine and apparently thought the chariot races in the Circus Maximus would lend credence to his charade of Empire. It must've been a pretty miserable show, since the decimated population numbered something like 500 when Totilla recaptured the city. The Romans of these times were caught between Belisarius, the imperial general from Constantinople, and Totilla the Goth, both of whom fought bloodily for control of Rome. After the travesty of 549, the Circus Maximus was never used again, and the demand for building materials reduced it, like so much of Rome, to a great dusty field.

✪ **Capitoline Museum (Museo Capitolino) and Palazzo dei Conservatori.** Piazza del Campidoglio. ☎ **06-6710-2071.** Admission (to both) 10,000 lire ($5). Free on last Sun of each month. Tues–Sun 9am–7pm. Bus: 44, 89, 92, 94, or 716.

Of Rome's seven hills, the **Capitoline (Campidoglio)** is the most sacred—its origins stretch way back into antiquity (an Etruscan temple to Jupiter once stood on this spot). The approach is dramatic as you climb the long sloping steps by Michelangelo. At the top is a perfectly proportioned square, **Piazza del Campidoglio,** also laid out by the Florentine artist. Michelangelo positioned the bronze equestrian statue of Marcus Aurelius in the center, but it has now been moved inside to be protected from pollution (a copy was placed on the pedestal in 1997). The other steps adjoining Michelangelo's approach will take you to Santa Maria d'Aracoeli (below).

One side of the piazza is open; the others are bounded by the **Senatorium (Town Council),** the statuary-filled **Palace of the Conservatori (Curators),** and the **Capitoline Museum.** These museums house some of the greatest pieces of classical sculpture in the world.

The **Capitoline Museum** was built in the 17th century based on an architectural sketch by Michelangelo. In the first room is *The Dying Gaul,* a work of majestic skill that's a copy of a Greek original dating from the 3rd century B.C. In a special gallery all her own is the *Capitoline Venus,* who demurely covers herself. This statue was the symbol of feminine beauty and charm down through the centuries (also a Roman copy of a 3rd-century B.C. Greek original). *Amore* (Cupid) and *Psyche* are up to their old tricks near the window.

The famous equestrian statue of Marcus Aurelius, whose years in the piazza made it a victim of pollution, has recently been restored and is now kept in the museum for protection. This is the only bronze equestrian statue to have survived from ancient Rome, mainly because it was thought for centuries that this was a statue of Constantine the Great and papal Rome respected the memory of the first Christian emperor. It's beautiful, though the perspective is rather odd. The statue is housed in a glassed-in room on the street level, the Cortile di Marforio; it's a kind of Renaissance greenhouse, surrounded by windows.

A Tip to a View

Standing on Piazza del Campidoglio, walk around the right side of the Palazzo Senatorio to a terrace overlooking the city's best panorama of the Roman Forum, with the Palatine Hill and the Colosseum as a backdrop. It's great day or night—at night the Forum is dramatically floodlit.

The Palace of the Conservatori, across the way, was also based on a Michelangelo architectural plan and is rich in classical sculpture and paintings. One of the most notable bronzes, a Greek work of incomparable beauty dating from the 1st century B.C., is *Lo Spinario* (a little boy picking a thorn from his foot). In addition, you'll find *Lupa Capitolina* (the *Capitoline Wolf*), a rare Etruscan bronze that may date from the 5th century B.C. (Romulus and Remus, the legendary twins the wolf suckled, were added at a later date). The palace also contains a *Pinacoteca* (Picture Gallery)—mostly works from the 16th and 17th centuries. Notable canvases are Caravaggio's *Fortune-Teller* and his curious *John the Baptist, The Holy Family* by Dosso Dossi, *Romulus and Remus* by Rubens, and Titian's *Baptism of Christ.* The entrance courtyard is lined with the remains (head, hands, foot, and kneecap) of an ancient colossal statue of Constantine the Great.

Baths of Caracalla (Terme di Caracalla). Via delle Terme di Caracalla 52. ☎ **06-575-8626.** Admission 8,000 lire ($4). Oct–Jan daily 9am–4pm; Jan 16–Feb 15 daily 9am–4:30; Feb 16–Mar 15 daily 9am–5pm; Mar 16–31 daily 9am–5:30pm; Apr–Sept daily 9am–7pm. Last admission 1 hour before closing. Closed holidays. Bus: 628.

Named for the emperor Caracalla, the baths were completed in the early 3rd century. The richness of decoration has faded and the lushness can be judged only from the shell of brick ruins that remain. In their heyday, they sprawled across 27 acres and could handle 1,600 bathers at one time. A circular room, the ruined caldarium for very hot baths, had been the traditional setting for operatic performances in Rome, until it was discovered that the ancient structure was being severely damaged. However, there are rumors that operas will again be held here soon—stay tuned.

OTHER ATTRACTIONS NEAR ANCIENT ROME

Santa Maria d'Aracoeli. Piazza d'Aracoeli. ☎ **06-679-8155.** Free admission. Daily 6:30am–5pm. Bus 44, 46, or 75.

On the Capitoline Hill, this landmark church was built for the Franciscans in the 13th century. According to legend, Augustus once ordered a temple erected on this spot, where a sibyl, with her gift of prophecy, forecast the coming of Christ. In the interior are a coffered Renaissance ceiling and a mosaic of the Virgin over the altar in the Byzantine style. If you're enough of a sleuth, you'll find a tombstone carved by the great Renaissance sculptor Donatello. The church is known for its **Bufalini Chapel,** a masterpiece by Pinturicchio, who frescoed it with scenes illustrating the life and death of St. Bernardino of Siena. He also depicted St. Francis receiving the stigmata. These frescoes are a high point in early Renaissance Roman painting. You have to climb a long flight of steep steps to reach the church, unless you're already on neighboring Piazza del Campidoglio, in which case you can cross the piazza and climb the steps on the far side of the Museo Capitolino (above).

National Museum of Palazzo Venezia (Museo Nazionale di Palazzo di Venezia). Via del Plebiscito 118. ☎ **06-679-8865.** Admission 8,000 lire ($4). Tues–Sun 9am–2pm. Bus: 57, 65, 70, or 75.

The Palazzo Venezia, in the geographic heart of Rome near Piazza Venezia, served as the seat of the Austrian Embassy until the end of World War I. During the Fascist regime (1928–43), it was the seat of the Italian government. The balcony from which Mussolini used to speak to the people was built in the 15th century. You can now visit the rooms and halls containing oil paintings, porcelain, tapestries, ivories, and ceramics. No one particular exhibit stands out—it's the sum total that adds up to a major attraction. The State Rooms occasionally open to host temporary exhibits.

Seeing the Sights at Night

Some of Rome's most popular monuments, archaeological sites, and museums have begun not only staying open until 8 or 10pm during summer but also engaging in **Art and Monuments Under the Stars.** For these special summer schedules, they reopen one or more nights from around 8:30 to 11:30pm. The offering includes guided tours (often in English), concerts, or simply general admission to sights for night owls, with tours of some ancient sites usually closed to the public, like the Tomb of Augustus and the Stadium of Domitian (under Piazza Navona). This is a developing phenomenon, so we can't give you many specifics, but keep your eyes peeled in the events guides from mid-June to September.

Santa Maria in Cosmedin. Piazza della Bocca della Verità 18. ☎ **06-678-1419.** Free admission. Summer daily 9am–1pm and 2:30–6pm; winter daily 10am–1pm and 3–5pm. Metro: Circo Massimo.

This little church was begun in the 6th century but was subsequently rebuilt, and a Romanesque campanile was added at the end of the 11th century, though its origins go back to the 3rd century. The church was destroyed several times by earthquakes or by foreign invasions but it has always been rebuilt.

People come not for great art treasures but to see the **"Mouth of Truth,"** a large disk under the portico. As Gregory Peck demonstrated to Audrey Hepburn in the film *Roman Holiday,* the mouth is supposed to chomp down on the hand of liars who insert their paws. (According to local legend, a former priest used to keep a scorpion in back to bite the fingers of anyone he felt was lying.)

The purpose of this disk (which is not of particular artistic interest) is not clear. One hypothesis affirms that it was used to collect the faithful's donations to God that were introduced through the open mouth.

Basilica di San Clemente. Via San Giovanni in Laterano at Piazza San Clemente, Via Labicana 95. ☎ **06-7045-1018.** Basilica free; excavations 4,000 lire ($2). Mon–Sat 9am–12:30pm and 3–6pm, Sun 10am–12:30pm and 3–6pm. Metro: Colosseo.

From the Colosseum, head up Via San Giovanni in Laterano to this basilica. It isn't just another Roman church—far from it. In this church-upon-a-church, centuries of history peel away. In the 4th century, a church was built over a secular house from the 1st century, beside which stood a pagan temple dedicated to Mithras (god of the sun). Down in the eerie grottoes (which you can explore on your own), you'll discover well-preserved frescoes from the 9th to the 11th century. The Normans destroyed the lower church, and a new one was built in the 12th century. Its chief attraction is the bronze-orange mosaic (from that period) adorning the apse, as well as a chapel honoring St. Catherine of Alexandria with frescoes by Masolino.

Basilica di San Giovanni in Laterano. Piazza San Giovanni in Laterano 4. ☎ **06-6988-6433.** Basilica free; cloisters 4,000 lire ($2). Summer daily 7am–6:45pm (off-season to 6pm). Metro: San Giovanni. Bus: 4, 16, 30, 85, 87, or 174.

This church (not St. Peter's) is the cathedral of the diocese of Rome, where the pope comes to celebrate mass on certain holidays. Built in A.D. 314 by Constantine, it has suffered the vicissitudes of Rome, forcing it to be rebuilt many times. Only fragmented parts of the baptistry remain from the original.

The present building is characterized by its 18th-century facade by Alessandro Galilei (statues of Christ and the Apostles ring the top). A 1993 terrorist bomb caused severe damage, especially to the facade. Borromini gets the credit (some say blame) for the interior, built for Innocent X. It's said that in the misguided attempt to redecorate, frescoes by Giotto were destroyed (remains believed to have been painted by Giotto were discovered in 1952 and are now on display against a column near the entrance on the right inner pier). In addition, look for the unusual ceiling and the sumptuous transept and explore the 13th-century cloisters with twisted double columns. The popes used to live next door at the **Palazzo Laterano** before the move to Avignon in the 14th century.

Across the street is the **Santuario della Scala Santa (Palace of the Holy Steps),** Piazza San Giovanni in Laterano (☎ **06-7049-4619**). It's alleged that the 28 marble steps here (now covered with wood for preservation) were originally at Pontius Pilate's villa in Jerusalem and that Christ climbed them the day he was brought before Pilate. According to a medieval tradition, the steps were brought from Jerusalem to Rome by Constantine's mother, Helen, in 326, and they've been in this location since 1589. Today pilgrims from all over the world come here to climb the steps on their knees. This is one of the holiest sites in Christendom, though some historians say the stairs may date only to the 4th century.

✪ **San Pietro in Vincoli (St. Peter in Chains).** Piazza San Pietro in Vincoli 4A (off Via degli Annibaldi). ☎ **06-488-2865.** Free admission. Spring/summer daily 7am–12:30pm and 3:30–7pm (autumn/winter to 6pm). Metro: V. Cavour, then cross the boulevard and walk up the flight of stairs. Turn right and you'll head into the piazza; the church will be on your left.

This recently renovated church was founded in the 5th century to house the chains that bound St. Peter in Palestine (they're preserved under glass). But the drawing card is the tomb of Pope Julius II, with one of the world's most famous sculptures: **Michelangelo's** *Moses.* As readers of Irving Stone's *The Agony and the Ecstasy* know, Michelangelo was to have carved 44 magnificent figures for the tomb. That didn't happen, of course, but the pope was given a great consolation prize—a figure intended to be "minor" that's now numbered among Michelangelo's masterpieces. In the *Lives of the Artists,* Vasari wrote about the stern father symbol of Michelangelo's *Moses:* "No modern work will ever equal it in beauty, no, nor ancient either." *Moses* is badly lit, so bring 500-lire coins to turn on the light box.

3 Attractions Near Piazza Navona & Campo de' Fiori

THE PANTHEON & NEARBY ATTRACTIONS

The Pantheon stands on **Piazza della Rotonda,** a lively square with cafes, vendors, and great people-watching.

✪ **The Pantheon.** Piazza della Rotonda. ☎ **06-6830-0230.** Free admission. Mon–Sat 9am–6pm, Sun 9am–1pm. Bus: 46, 62, 64, 170 or 492 to Largo di Torre.

Of all ancient Rome's great buildings, only the Pantheon ("All the Gods") remains intact. It was built in 27 B.C. by Marcus Agrippa and reconstructed by Hadrian in the early 2nd century A.D. This remarkable building, 142 feet wide and 142 feet high (a perfect sphere resting in a cylinder) and once ringed with white marble statues of Roman gods in its niches, is among the architectural wonders of the world because of its dome and its concept of space. Animals were sacrificed and burned in the center, and the smoke escaped through the only means of light, the oculus, an opening at the top 18 feet in diameter. Michelangelo came here to study the dome before designing the cupola of St. Peter's (whose dome is 2 feet smaller than the Pantheon's). The walls are 25 feet thick, and the bronze doors leading into the building weigh 20 tons each. About 125 years ago, Raphael's tomb was discovered here (fans still bring him flowers). Vittorio Emanuele II, king of Italy, and his successor, Umberto I, are interred here as well.

Galleria Doria Pamphilj. Piazza del Collegio Romano 2 (off Via del Corso). ☎ **06-679-7323.** Gallery 13,000 lire ($6.50) adults, 10,000 lire ($5) students/seniors; apartments 5,000 lire ($2.50). Gallery Fri–Wed 10am–5pm. Apartments Fri–Wed 10:30am–12:30pm. Private visits can be arranged. Metro: Colosseo or Cavour, then a long stroll.

This museum offers a look at what it was like to live in an 18th-century palace. It's been restored to its former splendor and expanded to include four rooms long closed to the public. It's partly leased to tenants (on the upper levels) and there are shops on the street level—but you'll overlook all this after entering the grand apartments of the Doria Pamphilj family, which traces its lines to before the great 15th-century Genoese admiral Andrea Doria. The apartments surround the central court and gallery. The **ballroom, drawing rooms, dining rooms,** and **family chapel** are full of gilded furniture, crystal chandeliers, Renaissance tapestries, and family portraits. The **Green Room** is especially rich, with a 15th-century Tournay tapestry, paintings by Memling and Filippo Lippi, and a seminude portrait of Andrea Doria by Sebastiano del Piombo. The **Andrea Doria Room,** dedicated to the admiral and to the ship of the same name, contains a glass case with mementos of the great 1950s maritime disaster.

Skirting the central court is a **picture gallery** with a memorable collection of frescoes, paintings, and sculpture. Most important are the portrait of Innocent X by Velàzquez, *Salome* by Titian, works by Rubens and Caravaggio, the *Bay of Naples* by Pieter Brueghel the Elder, and a copy of Raphael's portrait of Principessa Giovanna d'Aragona de Colonna (who looks remarkably like Leonardo's *Mona Lisa*). Most of the sculpture came from the Doria country estates: marble busts of Roman emperors, bucolic nymphs, and satyrs.

Santa Maria Sopra Minerva. Piazza della Minerva 42. ☎ **06-6793926.** Free admission. Daily 7am–noon and 4–7pm. Bus: 64 or 119.

Beginning in 1280, early Christian leaders ordained that the foundation of an ancient temple dedicated to Minerva (goddess of wisdom) be reused as the base for Rome's only Gothic church. Architectural changes and redecorations in the 1500s and 1900s stripped it of some of its magnificence, but it still includes an awe-inspiring collection of medieval and Renaissance tombs. You'll find a beautiful chapel frescoed by Fillipino Lippi and, to the left of the apse, a muscular *Risen Christ* carrying a rather small marble cross carved by Michelangelo (the bronze drapery covering Christ's nudity was added later). Under the altar lie the remains of St. Catherine of Siena. After St. Catherine died, her head was separated from her body, and now the head is in Siena, where she was born. In the passage to the left of the choir, surrounded by a small fence, is the floor tomb of the great monastic painter Fra Angelico. The amusing baby elephant carrying a small obelisk in the piazza outside was designed by Bernini.

PIAZZA NAVONA & NEARBY ATTRACTIONS

✪ **Piazza Navona,** one of the most beautifully baroque sites in all Rome, is an ocher-colored gem, unspoiled by new buildings or traffic. Its shape results from the ruins of the Stadium of Domitian, lying underneath. Great chariot races were once held here (some rather unusual—such as the one in which the head of the winning horse was lopped off as it crossed the finish line and carried by runners to be offered as a sacrifice by the Vestal Virgins atop the Capitoline). In medieval times, the popes used to flood the piazza to stage mock naval encounters. Today the piazza is packed with vendors and street performers and lined with pricey cafes where you can enjoy a cappuccino or gelato and indulge in unparalleled people-watching.

Besides the twin-towered facade of 17th-century Santa Agnes, the piazza boasts several baroque masterpieces. The best known, in the center, is Bernini's **Fountain of**

Attractions Near Piazza Navona & Campo de' Fiori

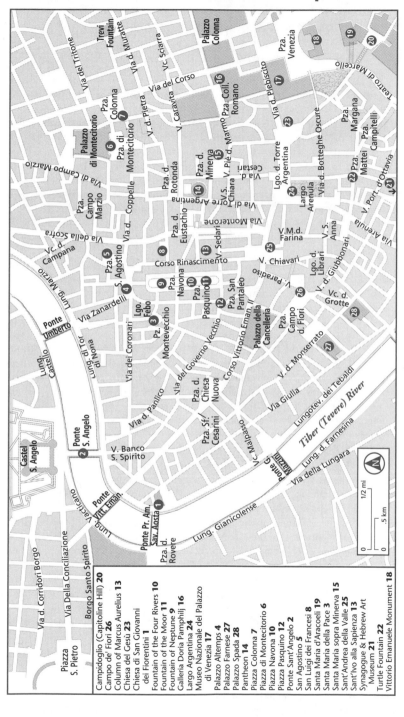

Campidoglio (Capitoline Hill) **20**
Campo de' Fiori **26**
Column of Marcus Aurelius **13**
Chiesa del Gesù **23**
Chiesa di San Giovanni
  dei Fiorentini **1**
Fountain of the Four Rivers **10**
Fountain of the Moor **11**
Fountain of Neptune **9**
Galleria Doria Pamphilj **16**
Largo Argentina **24**
Museo Nazionale del Palazzo
  di Venezia **17**
Palazzo Altemps **4**
Palazzo Farnese **27**
Palazzo Spada **28**
Pantheon **14**
Piazza Colonna **7**
Piazza di Montecitorio **6**
Piazza Navona **10**
Piazza Pasquino **12**
Ponte Sant'Angelo **2**
San Agostino **5**
San Luigi dei Francesi **8**
Santa Maria d'Aracoeli **19**
Santa Maria della Pace **3**
Santa Maria sopra Minerva **15**
Sant'Andrea della Valle **25**
Sant'Ivo alla Sapienza **13**
Synagogue & Hebrew Art
  Museum **21**
Turtle Fountain **22**
Vittorio Emanuele Monument **18**

913 Churches, 1 Synagogue: Jews in the Capital of Christendom

Nestled midway between the Isola Tiberina and the monument to Vittorio Emanuele II, Rome's Jewish ghetto was designated during the administration of Pope Paul IV between 1555 and 1559. At the time, it enclosed several thousand people into a cramped, 2½-acre tract of walled-in, overcrowded real estate that did much to contribute to the oppression of the Jews during the Italian Renaissance.

Jews had played an important part in the life of Rome prior to that time. They migrated to the political center of the known world during the 1st century B.C., and within 200 years their community had grown to a very noticeable minority. Most of it was based in Trastevere, a neighborhood that for many years was referred to as the *Contrada Iudaeorum* (Jewish Quarter). By 1309 ordinances were passed that forced Jews to illustrate their religious and cultural backgrounds with special garments, and their ability to worship as they wished depended on the indulgence of the pope.

In 1363 additional ordinances were passed that limited Jewish cemeteries to an area adjacent to the Tiber, near the present-day Church of San Francesco a Ripa. During the 1400s the Jewish population regrouped onto the opposite side of the Tiber, in an area around the square that's known today as Piazza Mattei.

In 1492 Queen Isabella and King Ferdinand of Spain killed, tortured, forcibly converted, or forced the emigration of thousands of Jews from Spain. Many came to Rome, swelling the ranks of the city. Pope Alexander VI (1492–1503), whose political sympathies lay firmly with the Spanish monarchs, grudgingly admitted the refugees into his city, on condition that each pay a hefty fee in gold. His papal bull, *Cum nimis absurdium,* defined the borders of the Jewish ghetto within the boundaries of the Sant'Angelo district and later enlarged them to include the muddy, frequently flooded banks of the Tiber. Water levels often reached the

---

the Four Rivers (**Fontana dei Quattro Fiumi**), whose four stone personifications symbolize the world's greatest rivers: the Ganges, Danube, della Plata, and Nile. It's fun to try to figure out which is which. (*Hint:* The figure with the shroud on its head is the Nile, so represented because the river's source was unknown at the time.) At the south end is the **Fountain of the Moor (Fontana del Moro),** also by Bernini. The **Fountain of Neptune (Fontana di Nettuno),** which balances that of the Moor, is a 19th-century addition; it has been restored after a demented 1997 attack by two men who broke off the tail of one of its sea creatures.

In summer, there are outdoor art shows in the evening, but visit during the day—that's the best time to inspect the fragments of the original stadium under a building on the north side of the piazza. If you're interested, walk out at the northern exit and turn left for a block. It's astonishing how much the level of the ground has risen since ancient times.

Palazzo Altemps. Piazza San Apollinare 44, near the Piazza Navona. ☎ **06-489-035-00.** Admission 12,000 lire ($6). Tues–Fri 9am–9pm, Sat 9am–midnight, Sun 9am–8pm. Last admission 1 hour before closing. Bus 70, 81, 87, 115, 116, or 492

This branch of the National Roman Museum is housed in a 15th-century palace that was restored and opened to the public in 1997. It is home to the fabled Ludovisi

third floors of the houses of the poorest families, who were forced, by law and economics, to settle here. Piling humiliation on humiliation, the residents of the nearly uninhabitable riverbanks were forced to pay for the construction of the embankments that prevented the neighborhood from flooding. For centuries, no one could enter or leave the ghetto between sundown and sunrise.

In 1848 the walls that had defined and confined the ghetto were demolished under the auspices of the relatively lenient Pope Leo XII. In 1883, during the surge of nationalism that preceded the unification of Italy, the ghetto was abolished altogether.

Tragically, on October 16, 1943, the segregation of Rome's Jews was reestablished when German Nazi soldiers rounded up most of the Jews from throughout Rome into a re-creation of the medieval ghetto and imposed a flabbergastingly high ransom on them. Amazingly, this fee—more than 100 pounds of gold per resident—was eventually collected. Despite having made the payment, the Jews were rounded up and deported to the death camps anyway, one of the most horrible episodes of Italy's participation in the war years.

Today the neighborhood, centered around Piazza Mattei and its elegant Renaissance fountain, lacks any coherent architectural unity; it's a colorful hodgepodge of narrow, twisting streets and sometimes derelict buildings. One of the most unusual streets is Via del Portico d'Ottavia, where medieval houses and pavements adjoin kosher food stores and simple trattorie that almost invariably feature *carciofi alla Giudeai* (deep-fried Jerusalem artichokes).

Although it bears the scars and honors of centuries of occupation by Jews, today this is a Jewish neighborhood mostly in name only. Its centerpiece is the synagogue on Via Catalana.

Collection of Greek and Roman sculpture. Among the masterpieces of the Roman Renaissance, you'll find the *Ares Ludovisi,* a Roman copy of the original dated 330 B.C. and restored by Bernini during the 17th century. In the *Sala delle Storie di Mosè* is the *Ludovisi's Throne,* representing the birth of Venus. The *Sala delle Feste* (The Celebrations' Hall) is dominated by a sarcophagus depicting the Romans fighting against the Ostrogoth Barbarians; this masterpiece, carved from a single block, dates back to the 2nd century A.D. and nowadays is called *Grande Ludovisi* (Great Ludovisi). Other outstanding art from the collection includes a copy of Phidias's celebrated *Athena,* which once stood in the Parthenon in Athens. (The Roman copy here is from the 1st century B.C., as the original *Athena* is lost to history.) The huge *Dionysus with Satyr* is from the 2nd century A.D.

San Luigi dei Francesi. Via Santa Giovanna d'Arco 5. ☎ **06-688271.** Free admission. Fri–Wed 8am–12:30pm and 3:30–7pm, Thurs 8am–12:30pm. Bus: 70, 81, or 87.

This has been the national church of France in Rome since 1589, and a stone salamander (the symbol of the Renaissance French monarch François I) was subtly carved into its facade. Inside, in the last chapel on the left, is a noteworthy series of frescoes by Caravaggio: the celebrated *Calling of St. Matthew* on the left, *St. Matthew and the Angel* in the center, and the *Martyrdom of St. Matthew* on the right.

Santa Maria della Pace. Vicolo del Arco della Pace 5 (off Piazza Navona). ☎ **06-6861156.** Free admission. Tues–Sat 10am–noon and 4–6pm, Sun 9–11am. Bus: 70, 81, or 87.

According to legend, blood flowed from a statue of the Virgin above the altar here after someone threw a pebble at it. This legend motivated Pope Sixtus to rebuild the church in the 1500s on the foundations of an even older sanctuary. For generations after that, its curved porticos, cupola atop an octagonal base, cloisters by Bramante, and frescoes by Raphael helped make it one of the most fashionable churches for aristocrats residing in the surrounding palazzos.

CAMPO DE' FIORI & THE JEWISH GHETTO

During the 1500s, **Campo de' Fiori** was the geographic and cultural center of secular Rome, site of dozens of inns that would almost certainly have been reviewed by this guide. From its center rises a statue of severe-looking monk Giordano Bruno, whose presence is a reminder that religious heretics were occasionally burned at the stake here. Today, ringed with venerable houses, the campo is the site of an **open-air food market** held Monday to Saturday from early in the morning until around noon (or whenever the food runs out).

Built from 1514 to 1589, the **Palazzo Farnese,** on Piazza Farnese, was designed by Sangallo and Michelangelo, among others, and was an astronomically expensive project for the time. Its famous residents have included a 16th-century member of the Farnese family, Pope Paul III, Cardinal Richelieu, and the former Queen Christina of Sweden, who moved to Rome after abdicating. During the 1630s, when the heirs couldn't afford to maintain it, the palazzo became the site of the French Embassy, as it still is (it's closed to the public). For the best view of it, cut west from Via Giulia along any of the narrow streets (we recommend Via Mascherone or Via dei Farnesi).

Palazzo Spada, Capo di Ferro 3 (☎ **06-686-1158**), built around 1550 for Cardinal Gerolamo Capo di Ferro and later inhabited by the descendants of several other cardinals, was sold to the Italian government in the 1920s. Its richly ornate facade, covered in high-relief stucco decorations in the Mannerist style, is the finest of any building from 16th-century Rome. Though the State Rooms are closed, the richly decorated courtyard and a handful of galleries of paintings are open. Admission is 4,000 lire ($2) on Tuesday to Saturday 9am to 7pm and Sunday 9am to 1pm. Bus: 44, 56, 60, 65, 75, 170 or 710.

The best way to see the **Jewish Ghetto** is to go on a free walking tour offered by **Service International de Documentation Judeo-Chrétienne,** Via Plebiscito 112 (☎ **06-6795307**). An interesting remnant from the era of the ghetto is **San Gregorio,** Ponte Quattro Capi, at the end of Via del Portico d'Ottavia; it bears an inscription in both Hebrew and Latin asking Jews to convert to Catholicism.

Also in this neighborhood stands the **Sinagoga Ashkenazita** (☎ **06-6840-061**), open only for services. Trying to avoid all resemblance to a Christian church, the building (1874–1904) evokes Babylonian and Persian details. The synagogue was attacked by terrorists in 1982 and since then has been heavily guarded by *carabinieri* (a division of the Italian army) armed with machine guns. It houses the **Jewish Museum** (☎ **06-6840-061**), open Monday to Thursday 9am to 5pm, Friday 9am to 2pm, and Sunday 9am to 12:30pm. Admission is 10,000 lire ($5). Many rare and even priceless treasures are here, including a Moroccan prayer book from the early 14th century and ceremonial objects from the 17th-century Jewish Ghetto.

4 The Spanish Steps, the Trevi Fountain & Attractions Nearby

ON OR AROUND PIAZZA DI SPAGNA

○ **The Spanish Steps** (Scalinata di Spagna; Metro: Spagna) are filled in spring with azaleas and other flowers, flower vendors, jewelry dealers, and photographers snapping pictures of visitors. The steps and the square (Piazza di Spagna) take their names from the Spanish Embassy, which used to be headquartered here. Designed by Italian architect Francesco de Sanctis and built from 1723 to 1725, they were funded almost entirely by the French as a preface to Trinità dei Monti at the top.

The steps and the piazza below are always packed with a crowd: strolling, reading in the sun, browsing the vendors' carts, and people-watching. Near the steps, you'll also find an American Express office, public rest rooms (near the Metro stop), and the most sumptuous McDonald's we've ever seen (cause for uproar among the Romans when it first opened, and another convenient source for clean bathrooms).

Keats-Shelley House. Piazza di Spagna 26. ☎ **06-678-4235.** Admission 5,000 lire ($2.50). May–Sept Mon–Fri 9am–1pm and 3–6pm; Sat 11am–2pm and 3–6pm. Guided tours on appointment. Metro: Spagna.

At the foot of the Spanish Steps is this 18th-century house where John Keats died of consumption on February 23, 1821, at age 25. Since 1909, when it was bought by well-intentioned English and American literary types, it has been a working library established in honor of Keats and poet Percy Bysshe Shelley, who drowned off the coast of Viareggio with a copy of Keats in his pocket. Mementos range from the kitsch to the immortal and are laden with nostalgia. The apartment where Keats spent his last months, carefully tended by his close friend Joseph Severn, shelters a strange death mask of Keats as well as the "deadly sweat" drawing by Severn.

○ **Trevi Fountain (Fontana dei Trevi).** Piazza di Trevi. Metro: Barberini.

As you elbow your way through the summertime crowds around the Trevi Fountain, you'll find it hard to believe that this little piazza was nearly always deserted before the film *Three Coins in the Fountain* brought the stampede of tour buses. Today this newly restored gem is a must on everybody's itinerary.

Supplied by water from the Acqua Vergine aqueduct and a triumph of the baroque style, it was based on the design of Nicolo Salvi (who's said to have died of illness contracted during his supervision of the project) and was completed in 1762. The design centers around the triumphant figure of Neptunus Rex, standing on a shell chariot drawn by winged steeds and led by a pair of tritons. Two allegorical figures in the side niches represent good health and fertility.

On the southwestern corner of the piazza is a somber, not particularly spectacular-looking church, **S.S. Vincenzo e Anastasio,** with a strange claim to fame. Within it survive the hearts and intestines of several centuries of popes. According to legend, the church was built on the site of a spring that burst from the earth after the beheading of St. Paul, at one of three sites where his head is said to have bounced off the ground.

Palazzo del Quirinale. Piazza del Quirinale. Free admission (but a passport or similar ID is required for entrance). Sun 9am–1pm. Metro: Barberini.

Until the end of World War II, this palace was the home of the king of Italy, and before that it was the residence of the pope. Despite its Renaissance origins (nearly every important architect in Italy worked on some aspect of its sprawling premises), it's rich in associations with ancient emperors and deities. The colossal statues of the dioscuri Castor and Pollux, which now form part of the fountain in the piazza, were found in the nearby great Baths of Constantine, and in 1793 Pius VI had the ancient Egyptian obelisk moved here from the Mausoleum of Augustus. The sweeping view of Rome from the piazza, which crowns the highest of the seven ancient hills of Rome, is itself worth the trip.

AROUND VIA VENETO & PIAZZA BARBERINI

Piazza Barberini lies at the foot of several Roman streets, among them Via Barberini, Via Sistina, and Via Vittorio Veneto. It would be a far more pleasant spot were it not for the heavy traffic swarming around its principal feature, Bernini's **Fountain of the Triton (Fontana del Tritone).** For more than 3 centuries, the strange figure sitting in a vast open clam has been blowing water from his triton. Off to one side of the piazza is the aristocratic side facade of the **Palazzo Barberini,** named for one of Rome's powerful families; inside is the **Galleria Nazionale d'Arte Antica** (below). The Renaissance Barberini reached their peak when a son was elected pope as Urban VIII; he encouraged Bernini and gave him great patronage.

As you go up Via Vittorio Veneto, look for the small fountain on the right corner of Piazza Barberini—it's another Bernini, the small **Fountain of the Bees (Fontana delle Api).** At first they look more like flies, but they're the bees of the Barberini, the crest of that powerful family complete with the crossed keys of St. Peter above them (the keys were always added to a family crest when a son was elected pope).

National Gallery of Ancient Art (Galleria Nazionale d'Arte Antica). Via Quattro Fontane 13. ☎ **06-481-4430.** Admission 10,000 lire ($5). Metro: Barberini.

Palazzo Barberini, right off Piazza Barberini, is one of the most magnificent baroque palaces in Rome. It was begun by Carlo Maderno in 1627 and completed in 1633 by Bernini, whose lavishly decorated rococo apartments, the **Gallery of Decorative Art (Galleria d'Arte Decorativa),** are on view. This gallery is part of the **National Gallery of Ancient Art.**

The bedroom of Princess Cornelia Costanza Barberini and Prince Giulio Cesare Colonna di Sciarra stands just as it was on their wedding night, and many household objects are displayed in the decorative art gallery. In the chambers, boasting frescoes and hand-painted silk linings, you can see porcelain from Japan and Bavaria, canopied beds, and a wooden baby carriage.

On the first floor is a splendid array of paintings from the 13th to the 16th century, most notably *Mother and Child* by Simone Martini and works by Filippo Lippi, Andrea Solario, and Francesco Francia. Il Sodoma has some brilliant pictures here, like *The Rape of the Sabines* and *The Marriage of St. Catherine.* One of the best-known paintings is Raphael's beloved *La Fornarina,* the baker's daughter who was his mistress and who posed for his Madonna portraits. Titian is represented by his *Venus and Adonis.* Also here are Tintorettos and El Grecos. Many visitors come just to see the magnificent Caravaggios, including *Narcissus.*

Monumental Cemetery of the Capuchin Brothers (Cimitero Monumentale dei Padri Cappuccini). Beside the Church of the Immaculate Conception, Via Vittorio Veneto 27. ☎ **06-487-1185.** Donation required. Fri–Wed 9am–noon and 3–6pm. Metro: Barberini.

One of the most horrifying sights in all Christendom, this is a series of chapels with hundreds of skulls and crossbones woven into mosaic "works of art." To make this allegorical dance of death, the bones of more than 4,000 Capuchin brothers were used. Some of the skeletons are intact, draped with Franciscan habits. The creator of this chamber of horrors? The tradition of the friars is that it was the work of a French Capuchin. Their literature suggests you should visit the cemetery keeping in mind the

AT&T Direct® Service

AT&T Access Numbers

Aruba	800-8000	Czech Rep. ▲	00-42-000-101
Australia	**1-800-551-155**	Egypt●(Cairo)+	510-0200
Austria●	0800-200-288	France	0-800-99-0011
Bahamas	1-800-872-2881	Germany	0800-2255-288
Barbados+	1-800-872-2881	Greece●	00-800-1311
Belgium●	0-800-100-10	Guam	1-800-2255-288
Bermuda+	1-800-872-2881	Hong Kong	800-96-1111
Cayman Isl.+	1-800-872-2881	Hungary	06-800-01111
China, PRC▲	10811	India ✕,➤	000-117
Costa Rica	0-800-0-114-114	Ireland ✓	1-800-550-000

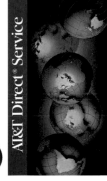

AT&T Direct® Service

AT&T Access Numbers

Aruba	800-8000	Czech Rep. ▲	00-42-000-101
Australia	**1-800-551-155**	Egypt●(Cairo)+	510-0200
Austria●	0800-200-288	France	0-800-99-0011
Bahamas	1-800-872-2881	Germany	0800-2255-288
Barbados+	1-800-872-2881	Greece●	00-800-1311
Belgium●	0-800-100-10	Guam	1-800-2255-288
Bermuda+	1-800-872-2881	Hong Kong	800-96-1111
Cayman Isl.+	1-800-872-2881	Hungary	06-800-01111
China, PRC▲	10811	India ✕,➤	000-117
Costa Rica	0-800-0-114-114	Ireland ✓	1-800-550-000

Israel	1-800-94-94-949	Philippines•	105-11
Italy•	172-1011	Portugal▲	0800-800-128
Jamaica•▲	1-800-872-2881	Singapore	800-0111-111
Japan•▲	005-39-111	Spain	900-99-00-11
Malaysia•	1800-80-0011	Switzerland•	0-800-89-0011
Mexico•▽	01-800-288-2872	Thailand•◄	001-999-111-11
Neth.Ant.○	001-800-872-2881	Turkey•○	00-800-12277
Netherlands•	0800-022-9111	U.K.	0800-89-0011
New Zealand•	000-911	U.K.	0800-013-0011
Panama	800-001-0109	Venezuela	800-11-120

FOR EASY CALLING WORLDWIDE

1. Just dial the AT&T Access Number for the country you are calling from.
2. Dial the phone number you're calling. 3. Dial your card number.

For access numbers not listed ask any operator for **AT&T Direct®** Service.
In the U.S. call 1-800-331-1140 for a wallet guide listing all worldwide
AT&T Access Numbers.

Visit our Web site at: **www.att.com/traveler**
Bold-faced countries permit country-to-country calling outside the U.S.

- • Public phones may require coin or card deposit to place call.
- ♦ Outside of Cairo, dial "02" first.
- ▲ May not be available from every phone/payphone.
- ▽ Public phones and select hotels.
- ✓ Use U.K. access number in N. Ireland.
- ◄ When calling from public phones, use phones marked "Lenso."
- ✕ Not available from public phones.
- ▽ Available from phones with international calling capabilities or from most Public Calling Centers.
- ○ From St. Maarten or phones at Bobby's Marina, use 1-800-872-2881.

When placing an international call *from* the U.S., dial 1 800 CALL ATT.

© 1/2000

Israel	1-800-94-94-949	Philippines•	105-11
Italy•	172-1011	Portugal▲	0800-800-128
Jamaica•▲	1-800-872-2881	Singapore	800-0111-111
Japan•▲	005-39-111	Spain	900-99-00-11
Malaysia•	1800-80-0011	Switzerland•	0-800-89-0011
Mexico•▽	01-800-288-2872	Thailand•◄	001-999-111-11
Neth.Ant.○	001-800-872-2881	Turkey•○	00-800-12277
Netherlands•	0800-022-9111	U.K.	0800-89-0011
New Zealand•	000-911	U.K.	0800-013-0011
Panama	800-001-0109	Venezuela	800-11-120

FOR EASY CALLING WORLDWIDE

1. Just dial the AT&T Access Number for the country you are calling from.
2. Dial the phone number you're calling. 3. Dial your card number.

For access numbers not listed ask any operator for **AT&T Direct®** Service.
In the U.S. call 1-800-331-1140 for a wallet guide listing all worldwide
AT&T Access Numbers.

Visit our Web site at: **www.att.com/traveler**
Bold-faced countries permit country-to-country calling outside the U.S.

- • Public phones may require coin or card deposit to place call.
- ♦ Outside of Cairo, dial "02" first.
- ▲ May not be available from every phone/payphone.
- ▽ Public phones and select hotels.
- ✓ Use U.K. access number in N. Ireland.
- ◄ When calling from public phones, use phones marked "Lenso."
- ✕ Not available from public phones.
- ▽ Available from phones with international calling capabilities or from most Public Calling Centers.
- ○ From St. Maarten or phones at Bobby's Marina, use 1-800-872-2881.

When placing an international call *from* the U.S., dial 1 800 CALL ATT.

© 1/2000

TIMBUKTU

KALAMAZOO

AT&T Direct® Service

The easy way to call home from anywhere.

Global
connection
with the AT&T
Network

AT&T
direct
service

For the easy way to call home, take the attached wallet guide.

Attractions Near the Spanish Steps & Piazza del Popolo

American Express
  Office **12**
Ara Pacis
  (Altar of Peace) **9**
Campidoglio
  (Capitoline Hill) **24**
Cimitero Monumentale
  dei Padri Cappucini
  (Capuchin Crypt) **13**
Fountain of the Bees
  (Fontana dei Api) **15**
Fountain of the Triton
  (Fontana del Tritone) **14**
Galleria Nazionale
  d'Arte Antica **2**
Galleria Borghese **3**
Keats-Shelley
  Memorial House **12**
Pantheon **19**
Piazza Barberini **15**
Piazza Colonna
  (Marcus Aurelius
  Column) **18**
Piazza del Popolo **7**
Piazza del Quirinale **17**
Pincio Gardens **5**
Mausoleo Augusteo
  (Augustus's
  Mausoleum) **8**
Museo Nazionale della
  Villa Giuila
  (Etruscan Museum) **1**
Museo Nazionale del
  Palazzo di Venezia **21**
Roman Forum
  (Foro Romano) **25**
Santa Maria d'Aracoeli **23**
Santa Maria del Popolo **6**
Santa Maria sopra
  Minerva **20**
Spanish Steps
  (Scalinata di Trinita
  dei Monti) **11**
Trevi Fountain
  (Fontana di Trevi) **16**
Via dei Condotti **10**
Villa Borghese Park **4**
Vittorio Emanuele
  Monument **22**

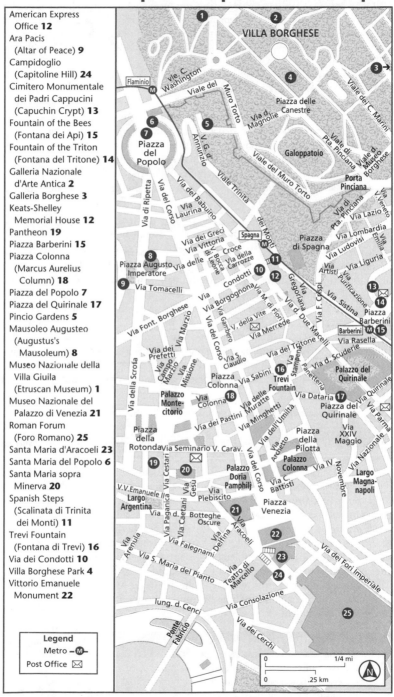

Legend
Metro —Ⓜ—
Post Office ✉

historical moment of its origins, when Christians had a rich and creative cult for their dead, and great spiritual masters meditated and preached with a skull in hand. Those who've lived through the days of crematoriums and other such massacres may view the graveyard differently, but to many who pause to think, this sight has a message. It's not for the squeamish, however. The entrance is halfway up the first staircase on the right of the church.

NEAR PIAZZA DEL POPOLO

The newly restored ✪ **Piazza del Popolo** is haunted with memories. According to legend, the ashes of Nero were enshrined here until 11th-century residents began complaining to the pope about his imperial ghost. The **Egyptian obelisk** dates from the 13th century B.C., removed from Heliopolis to Rome during Augustus's reign (it stood at the Circus Maximus). The piazza was designed in the early 19th century by Valadier, Napoléon's architect. The lovely **Santa Maria del Popolo** (with two Caravaggios) is at its northern curve, and opposite are almost-twin baroque churches, overseeing the never-ending traffic.

Altar of Peace (Ara Pacis). Lungotevere Augusta ☎ **06-3600-3471.** Admission 3,750 lire ($1.90). Tues–Sat 9am–7pm, Sun 9am–1pm. Bus: 70,81,186, or 628.

In an airy glass-and-concrete building beside the eastern banks of the Tiber rests a reconstructed treasure from the reign of Augustus. It was built by the Senate as a tribute to that emperor and the peace he had brought to the Roman world. You can see portraits of the imperial family—Augustus, Livia (his second wife), Tiberius (Livia's son from her first marriage and Augustus's successor), even Julia (Augustus's unfortunate daughter, who divorced her first husband to marry Tiberius and then was exiled by her father for her sexual excesses)—on the marble walls. The altar was reconstructed from literally hundreds of fragments scattered in museums for centuries. A major portion came from the foundations of a Renaissance palace on the Corso. The reconstruction (quite an archaeological adventure story in itself) took place during the 1930s.

Augustus's Mausoleum (Mausoleo Augusteo). Piazza Augusto Imperatore. Bus: 81, 115, or 590. Metro: Spagna.

This seemingly indestructible pile of bricks has been here for 2,000 years and will probably remain for another 2,000. Like the larger tomb of Hadrian across the river, this was once a circular marble-covered affair with tall cypresses, symmetrical groupings of Egyptian obelisks, and some of Europe's most spectacular ornamentation. Many of the 1st-century emperors had their ashes deposited in golden urns inside, and it was probably because of this crowding that Hadrian decided to construct an entirely new tomb (the Castel Sant'Angelo) for himself in another part of Rome. The imperial remains stayed intact here until the 5th century, when invading barbarians smashed the bronze gates and stole the golden urns, emptying the ashes on the ground outside. After periods when it functioned as a Renaissance fortress, a bullfighting ring, and a private garden, the tomb was restored in the 1930s by Mussolini, who might have envisioned it as a burial place for himself. You can't enter, but you can walk along the four streets encircling it.

5 In the Villa Borghese

Villa Borghese, in the heart of Rome, is 3½ miles (6km) in circumference. One of Europe's most elegant parks, it was created by Cardinal Scipione Borghese in the 1600s. Umberto I, king of Italy, acquired it in 1902 and presented it to the city of

Rome. With lovely landscaped vistas, the greenbelt is crisscrossed by roads, but you can escape from the traffic and seek a shaded area under a pine or oak tree to enjoy a picnic or simply relax. On a sunny weekend afternoon, it's a pleasure to stroll here and see Romans at play, relaxing or in-line skating. There are a few casual cafes and some food vendors throughout; you can also rent bikes here. In the northeast of the park is a small zoo; the park is also home to a few outstanding museums.

○ **Galleria Borghese.** Piazza Scipione Borghese 5 (off Via Pinciano). ☎ **06-841-7645** for information. Admission 12,000 lire ($6). Nov–Apr Tues–Sun 9am–7pm; May–Oct, Tues–Sun 9am–7pm. Bus: 56 or 910.

This legendary art gallery shut its doors in 1984 and appeared to have closed forever. However, in early 1997, after a complete restoration, it returned in all its fabulous glory.

This treasure trove includes such masterpieces as Bernini's *Apollo and Daphne,* Titian's *Sacred and Profane Love,* Raphael's *Deposition,* and Caravaggio's *Jerome.* The collection began with the gallery's founder, Scipione Borghese, who by the time of his death in 1633 had accumulated some of the greatest art of all time, even managing to acquire Bernini's early sculptures. Some paintings were spirited out of Vatican museums and even confiscated when their rightful owners were hauled off to prison until they became "reasonable" about turning over their art. The great collection suffered at the hands of Napoléon's notorious sister Pauline, who married Prince Camillo Borghese in 1807 and sold most of the ancient collection (many works are now in the Louvre in Paris). One of the most popular pieces of sculpture in today's gallery, ironically, is Canova's life-size sculpture of Pauline in the pose of *Venus Victorious.* (When Pauline was asked if she felt uncomfortable posing in the nude, she replied, "Why should I? The studio was heated.")

Important Tip: No more than 300 visitors at a time are allowed on the ground floor and no more than 90 on the upper floor. Reservations are essential, so call ☎ **06-32010** (Monday to Friday 9am to 6pm). However, the number always seems to be busy. If you'll be in Rome for a few days, try stopping by in person on your first day to reserve tickets for a later day. Before you leave home, you can also contact **Select Italy** (see page 134 above for more information) to reserve tickets for this museum, and other major museums in Florence and Venice, cutting down on your time spent waiting in line.

○ **National Etruscan Museum (Museo Nazionale di Villa Giulia).** Piazzale di Villa Giulia 9. ☎ **06-320-1951.** Admission 8,000 lire ($4). Tues–Sat 9am–7pm, Sun 9am–2pm. Metro: Flaminio.

This 16th-century papal palace shelters a priceless collection of art and artifacts from the mysterious Etruscans, who predated the Romans. Known for their sophisticated art and design, they left a legacy of sarcophagi, bronze sculptures, terra-cotta vases, and jewelry, among other items. If you have time for only the masterpieces, head for room 7, with a remarkable 6th-century B.C. *Apollo from Veio* (clothed, for a change). The other two widely acclaimed statues here are *Dea con Bambino* (*Goddess with a Baby*) and a greatly mutilated but still powerful *Hercules* with a stag. In room 8, you'll see the lions' sarcophagus from the mid–6th century B.C., which was excavated at Cerveteri, north of Rome.

Finally, one of the world's most important Etruscan art treasures is the bride and bridegroom coffin from the 6th century B.C., also dug out of the tombs of Cerveteri (in room 9). Near the end of your tour, another masterpiece of Etruscan art awaits you in room 33: the Cista Ficoroni, a bronze urn with paw feet, mounted by three figures, dating from the 4th century B.C.

National Gallery of Modern Art (Galleria Nazionale d'Arte Moderna). Viale delle Belle Arti 131. ☎ **06-322-4151.** Admission 12,000 lire ($6). Tues–Sat 9am–7pm, Sun 9am–1pm. Bus: 56 or 910.

This gallery of modern art is a short walk from the Etruscan Museum (above). With its neoclassic and Romantic paintings and sculpture, it makes a dramatic change from the glories of the Renaissance and ancient Rome. Its 75 rooms also house the largest collection in Italy of 19th- and 20th-century works by Balla, Boccioni, De Chirico, Morandi, Manzù, Burri, Capogrossi, and Fontana. Look for Modigliani's *La Signora dal Collaretto* and large *Nudo*. There are also many works of Italian optical and pop art and a good representation of foreign artists, including Degas, Cézanne, Monet, and van Gogh. Surrealism and expressionism are well represented by Klee, Ernst, Braque, Mirò, Kandinsky, Mondrian, and Pollock. You'll also find sculpture by Rodin. Several other important sculptures, including one by Canova, are on display in the museum's gardens. You can see the collection of graphics, the storage rooms, and the Department of Restoration by appointment Tuesday to Friday.

6 The Appian Way & the Catacombs

Of all the roads that led to Rome, **Via Appia Antica** (built in 312 B.C.) was the most famous. It eventually stretched all the way from Rome to the seaport of Brindisi, through which trade with the colonies in Greece and the East was funneled. (According to Christian tradition, it was along the Appian Way that an escaping Peter encountered the vision of Christ, causing him to go back into the city to face subsequent martyrdom.) The road's initial stretch in Rome is lined with the great monuments and ancient tombs of patrician Roman families—burials were forbidden within the city walls as early as the 5th century B.C.—and, beneath the surface, miles of tunnels hewn out of the soft tufa stone.

These tunnels, or **catacombs,** were where early Christians buried their dead and, during the worst times of persecution, held church services discreetly out of the public eye. A few of them are open to the public, so you can wander through mile after mile of musty-smelling tunnels whose soft walls are gouged out with tens of thousands of burial niches (long shelves made for two to three bodies each). In some dank, dark grottoes (never stray too far from your party or one of the exposed light bulbs), you can still discover the remains of early Christian art. The requisite guided tours, hosted by priests and monks, feature a smidgen of extremely biased history and a large helping of sermonizing.

The Appia Antica has been a popular Sunday lunch picnic site for Roman families (following the half-forgotten pagan tradition of dining in the presence of one's ancestors on holy days). This practice was rapidly dying out in the face of the traffic fumes that for the past few decades have choked the venerable road, but a 1990s initiative has closed the Via Appia Antica to cars on Sundays, bringing back the picnickers and bicyclists—along with in-line skaters and a new Sunday-only bus route to get out here.

You can take bus 218 from the San Giovanni Metro stop, which follows the Appia Antica for a bit, then veers right on Via Ardeatina at Domine Quo Vadis? Church. After another long block, the 218 stops at the square Largo M.F. Via d. Sette Chiese to the San Domitilla catacombs; or walk left down Via d. Sette Chiese to the San Sebastiano catacombs.

An alternative is to ride the Metro to the Colli Albani stop and catch bus 660, which wraps up the Appia Antica from the south, veering off it at the San Sebastiano catacombs (if you're visiting all three, you can take the 218 to the first two, walk to

San Sebastiano, then catch the 660 back to the Metro). On Sundays the road is closed to traffic, but bus 760 trundles from the Circo Massimo Metro stop down the Via Appia Antica, turning around after it passes the Tomb of Cecilia Metella.

Of the monuments on the Appian Way, the most impressive is the **Tomb of Cecilia Metella,** within walking distance of the catacombs. The cylindrical tomb honors the wife of one of Julius Caesar's military commanders from the Republican era. Why such an elaborate tomb for such an unimportant person in history? Cecilia Metella happened to be singled out for enduring fame because her tomb has remained and the others have decayed.

Catacombs of St. Callixtus (Catacombe di San Callisto). Via Appia Antica 170. ☎ **06-513-6725.** Admission 8,000 lire ($4) adults, 4,000 lire ($2) children 6–15, children 5 and under free. Apr–Oct Thurs–Tues 8:30am–noon and 2:30–5:30pm (5pm Nov–Mar). Bus: 218 from Piazza San Giovanni in Laterano to Fosse Ardeatine; ask driver to let you off at Catacombe di San Callisto.

"The most venerable and most renowned of Rome," said Pope John XXIII of these funerary tunnels. The founder of Christian archaeology, Giovanni Battista de Rossi (1822–94), called them "catacombs par excellence." This catacomb is often packed with tour-bus groups, and it has perhaps the most cheesy tour, but the tunnels are simply phenomenal. They're the first cemetery of the Christian community of Rome, burial place of 16 popes in the 3rd century. They bear the name of St. Callixtus, the deacon Pope St. Zephyrinus put in charge of them and who was later elected pope (A.D. 217–22) in his own right. The complex is a network of galleries stretching for nearly 12 miles (19km), structured in five levels and reaching a depth of about 65 feet. There are many sepulchral chambers and almost half a million tombs of early Christians. Paintings, sculptures, and epigraphs (with such symbols as the fish, anchor, and dove) provide invaluable material for the study of the life and customs of the ancient Christians and the story of their persecutions.

Entering the catacombs, you see at once the most important crypt, that of the nine popes. Some of the original marble tablets of their tombs are still preserved. The next crypt is that of St. Cecilia, the patron of sacred music. This early Christian martyr received three ax strokes on her neck, the maximum allowed by Roman law, which failed to kill her outright. Farther on, you'll find the famous Cubicula of the Sacraments with its 3rd-century frescoes.

Catacombs of St. Sebastian (Catacombe di San Sebastiano). Via Appia Antica 136. ☎ **06-785-0350.** Admission 8,000 lire ($4) adults, 4,000 lire ($2) children 6–15, children 5 and under free. Mon–Sat 8:30am–noon and 2:30–5pm. Closed Nov.

Today the tomb of St. Sebastian is in the basilica, but his original tomb was in the catacombs under it. From the reign of Valerian to the reign of Constantine, the bodies of St. Peter and St. Paul were hidden in the catacombs, which were dug from tufo, a soft volcanic rock. The big church was built in the 4th century. The tunnels here, if stretched out, would reach a length of 7 miles (11km). In the tunnels and mausoleums are mosaics and graffiti, along with many other pagan and Christian objects from centuries even before the time of Constantine. The tour here is one of the shortest and least satisfying of all the catacomb visits.

۞ Catacombs of St. Domitilla (Catacombe di San Domitilla). Via d. Sette Chiese 283. ☎ **06-511-0342.** Admission 8,000 lire ($4) adults, 4,000 lire ($2) children 6–14. Wed–Mon 8:30am–noon and 2:30–5pm. Closed Jan.

This oldest of the catacombs is also the hands-down winner for most enjoyable catacomb experience. Groups are small, most guides are genuinely entertaining and

Beneath It All: Touring Roma Sotteranea

Talk about the "underground" and a growing legion of Romans will excitedly take up the story, offering tidbits about where to go, who to talk to, what's been seen, and what's allegedly awaiting discovery around the next bend in the sewer. The sewer? That's right. **Roma Sotteranea (Subterranean Rome)** is neither subway nor trendy arts movement but the vast historic ruins of a city that has been occupied for nearly 3,000 years, the first 2 millenniums of which are now largely buried by natural sediment and artificial landfills. Archaeologists estimate these processes have left the streets of ancient Rome as much as 20 yards beneath the surface.

A little too deep for you? Consider this: Each year, an inch of dust in the form of pollen, leaves, pollution, sand, and silt from disintegrating ruins settles over Rome. That silt has really taken a toll in its own right. Archaeologists estimate the ruins of a one-story Roman house will produce debris 6 feet deep over its entire floor plan. When you multiply that by more than 40,000 apartment buildings, 1,800 palaces, and numerous giant public buildings, a real picture of the burial of the ancient city presents itself. You should also take note of the centuries-old Roman tradition of burying old buildings in landfills, which can raise the level of the earth up to several yards all at once. In fact, past builders have often filled up massive stone ruins with dirt or dug down through previous landfills to the columns and vaults of underlying structures, then laid a foundation for a new layer of Roman architecture.

As a result, many buildings on the streets today actually provide direct access to Rome's inner world. Doorways lead down to hidden crypts and shrines—the existence of which are closely guarded secrets. Nondescript locked doors in churches and other public buildings often open on whole blocks of the ancient city, streets still intact. For example, take **San Clemente,** the 12th-century basilica east of the Colosseum, where a staircase in the sacristy leads down to the original 4th-century church. Not only that, but a staircase near the apse goes down to an earlier Roman apartment building and temple, which in turn leads down

personable, and depending on the mood of the group and your guide, the visit may last anywhere from 20 minutes to over an hour. You enter through a sunken 4th-century church. There are fewer "sights" than in the other catacombs—although the 2nd-century fresco of the Last Supper is impressive—but some of the guides actually hand you a few bones out of a tomb niche. (Incidentally, this is only catacomb where you'll still see bones; the rest have emptied their tombs to rebury the remains in ossiaries on the inaccessible lower levels.)

7 More Attractions

AROUND STAZIONE TERMINI

Basilica di Santa Maria Maggiore. Piazza di Santa Maria Maggiore. ☎ **06-488-1094.** Free admission. Daily 7am–7pm. Metro: Termini.

This great church, one of Rome's four major basilicas, was built by Pope Liberius in A.D. 358 and rebuilt by Pope Sixtus III from 432 to 440. Its 14th-century **campanile** is the city's loftiest. Much doctored in the 18th century, the church's facade isn't an accurate reflection of the treasures inside. Restoration of the 1,600-year-old church is scheduled for completion in 2000. The basilica is especially noted for the 5th-century

to a giant public building dating back to the Great Fire (A.D. 64). Another interesting doorway to the past is in the south exterior wall of **St. Peter's,** leading down to an intact necropolis. That crumbling brick entry in the gardens on the east side of Esquiline Hill carries you into the vast **Domus Aurea (Golden House),** Nero's residence, built on the ruins left by the Great Fire (see the entry for the Colosseum).

Don't expect a coherent road map of this subterranean world; it's a meandering labyrinth beneath the streets. A guided tour can be useful, especially those focusing on Roman excavations and anything to do with church crypts. Several tour companies now offer selected subterranean views, lasting 90 to 120 minutes and costing 25,000 to 50,000 lire ($12.50 to $25). The best are provided by **Itinera (☎ 06-275-7323)** and **LUPA (☎ 06-574-1974),** both run by trained archaeologists. **Città Nascosta (☎ 06-321-6059)** offers offbeat tours to less-visited churches and monuments and advertises the week's schedule via a recorded phone announcement that changes every week.

For those who want still more access to this world, the Italian monthly magazine *Forma Urbis* features the photos of Carlo Pavia, who (armed with lights, camera, hip boots, and oxygen mask) slogs through ancient sewage and hordes of jumping spiders, giant rats, and albino insects to record part of the ancient city that has never been seen before. Pavia's most bizarre discovery was a series of plants from North Africa and the Arab world growing in rooms beneath the Colosseum. The theory is they grew from seeds that fell from the coats of exotic animals sent into the arena to battle gladiators.

It's probably true that much of the underground will remain inaccessible to the general public. However, influential citizens like Emanuele Gattis, a retired government archaeologist who oversaw more than 30 years' worth of construction projects in Rome, are urging government leaders to direct money into opening up more of the city's buried past.

Roman mosaics in its nave, as well as for its coffered ceiling, said to have been gilded with gold brought from the New World. In the 16th century, Domenico Fontana built a now-restored "Sistine Chapel." In the following century, Flaminio Ponzo designed the **Pauline (Borghese) Chapel** in the baroque style. The church also contains the tomb of Bernini, Italy's most important baroque sculptor/architect. Ironically, the man who changed the face of Rome with his elaborate fountains is buried in a tomb so simple it takes a sleuth to track it down (to the right near the altar).

MUSEO NAZIONALE ROMANO

Originally, this museum occupied only the Diocletian Baths. Today it is divided into four different sections: Palazzo Massimo alle Terme; Terme di Diocleziano (Diocletian Baths), with the annex Octagonal Hall; and Palazzo Altemps (which is near Piazza Navona; see section 3 of this chapter for a complete listing).

Palazzo Massimo alle Terme. Largo di Villa Peretti 67. ☎ **06-489-035-00.** Admission 12,000 lire ($6); the same ticket will admit you to the Diocletian Baths. Tues–Sun 9am–8pm. Last admission 1 hour before closing. Metro: Termini.

If you'd like to go wandering in a virtual garden of classical statues, head for this palazzo, built during 1883–87 and opened as a museum in 1998. Much of the art here, including the frescoes, stuccoes, and mosaics, was discovered in excavations in the 1800s but has never been put on display before.

If you ever wanted to know what all those emperors from your history books looked like, this museum will make them live again, togas and all. In the central hall are works representing the political and social life of Rome at the time of Augustus Caesar. Note the statue of the emperor with a toga covering his head, symbolizing his role as the head priest of state. Other works include an altar from Ostia Antica, the ancient port of Rome, plus a statue of a wounded Niobid from 440 B.C. that is a masterwork of expression and character. Upstairs, stand in awe at all the traditional art from the 1st century B.C. to the Imperial Age. The most celebrated mosaic is of the *Four Charioteers.* In the basement is a rare numismatic collection and an extensive collection of Roman jewelry.

Terme di Diocleziano (Diocletian Bath) and the Aula Ottagona (Octagonal Hall). Viale E. di Nicola 79. ☎ **06-489-035-00.** Admission to the Baths 12,000 lire ($6), Octagonal Hall free. The same ticket will admit you to Palazzo Massimo alle Terme. Tues–Fri 9am–2pm, Sat–Sun 9am–1pm. Last admission 1 hour before closing. Metro: Termini.

Near Piazza dei Cinquecento, which fronts the rail station, this museum occupies part of the 3rd-century A.D. Baths of Diocletian and part of a convent that may have been designed by Michelangelo. The Diocletian Baths were the biggest thermal baths in the world. Nowadays they host a marvelous collection of funereal art works, such as sarcophagi, and decorations dating back to the Aurelian period. The Baths also have a section reserved for temporary exhibitions.

The Octagonal Hall occupies the southwest corner of the central building of the Diocletian Baths. Here you can see the *Lyceum Apollo,* a copy of the 2nd century A.D. work inspired by the Prassitele. Also worthy of note is the *Aphrodite of Cyrene,* a copy dating back to the second half of the 2nd century A.D. and discovered in Cyrene, Libya.

IN THE TESTACCIO AREA & SOUTH

Protestant Cemetery. Via Caio Cestio 6. ☎ **06-574-1900.** Free admission (but a 1,500–2,000 lire (75¢–$1) offering is customary). Apr–Sept Tues–Sun 9am–6pm (Oct–Mar to 4:30pm). Metro: Piramide. Bus: 23 or 27.

Near Porta San Paola, in the midst of cypress trees, lies the old cemetery where John Keats is buried. In a grave nearby, Joseph Severn, his "deathbed" companion, was

---

Crossing the Ponte Sant'Angelo

The trio of arches in the Tiber River's center has been basically unchanged since the **Ponte Sant'Angelo** was built around A.D. 135; the arches abutting the river's embankments were added late in the 19th century as part of a flood-control program. On December 19, 1450, so many pilgrims gathered on this bridge (which at the time was lined with wooden buildings) that about 200 of them were crushed to death.

Since the 1960s, the bridge has been reserved for pedestrians who can stroll across and admire the statues designed by Bernini. On the southern end is **Piazza Sant'Angelo,** the site of one of the most famous executions of the Renaissance. In 1599, Beatrice Cenci and several members of her family were beheaded on orders of Pope Clement VIII. Their crime? Plotting the successful death of their rich and brutal father. Their tale later inspired a tragedy by Shelley and a novel by a 19th-century Italian politician named Francesco Guerrazzi.

Attractions Near Via Veneto & Termini

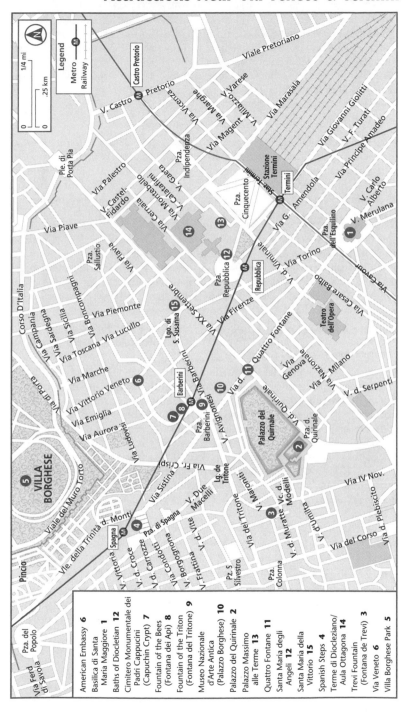

American Embassy **6**

Basilica di Santa
Maria Maggiore **1**

Baths of Diocletian **12**

Cimitero Monumentale dei
Padri Cappucini
(Capuchin Crypt) **7**

Fountain of the Bees
(Fontana dei Api) **8**

Fountain of the Triton
(Fontana del Tritone) **9**

Museo Nazionale
d'Arte Antica
(Palazzo Borghese) **10**

Palazzo del Quirinale **2**

Palazzo Massimo
alle Terme **13**

Quattro Fontane **11**

Santa Maria degli
Angeli **12**

Santa Maria della
Vittorio **15**

Spanish Steps **4**

Terme di Diocleziano/
Aula Ottagona **14**

Trevi Fountain
(Fontana de Trevi) **3**

Via Veneto **6**

Villa Borghese Park **5**

interred beside him 6 decades later. Dejected and feeling his reputation as a poet diminished by the rising vehemence of his critics, Keats asked the following epitaph be written on his tombstone: "Here lies one whose name was writ in water." A great romantic poet Keats certainly was, but a prophet, thankfully not. Percy Bysshe Shelley, author of *Prometheus Unbound,* drowned off the Italian Riviera in 1822, before his 30th birthday, and his ashes rest beside those of Edward John Trelawny, fellow romantic and man of the sea.

Pyramid of Caius Cestius. Piazzale Ostiense. Metro: Piramide.

From the 1st century B.C., the Pyramid of Caius Cestius, about 120 feet high, looks as if it belongs to the Egyptian landscape. It was constructed during the "Cleopatra craze" in architecture that swept across Rome. You can't enter the pyramid, but it's a great photo op. And who was Caius Cestius? He was a rich magistrate in imperial Rome whose tomb is more impressive than his achievements. You can visit at any time.

IN TRASTEVERE

One of the best spots for a memorable vista is the ✪ **Janiculum Hill (Gianicolo),** across the Tiber, not one of the "Seven Hills" but certainly one of the most visited (and a stop on many bus tours). The view is at its best at sundown or at dawn, when the skies are often fringed with mauve. The Janiculum was the site of a battle between Giuseppe Garibaldi and the forces of Pope Pius IX in 1870—an event commemorated with statuary. Take bus no. 41 from Ponte Sant'Angelo.

Galleria Nazionale di Palazzo Corsini. Via della Lungara 10. ☎ **06-6880-2323.** Admission 8,000 lire ($4) adults, 4,000 lire ($2) 17 and under. Tues–Fri 9am–7pm, Sat–Sun 9am–1pm. Bus: 23 or 280.

After you've seen Italy's National Gallery of Art at the Palazzo Barberini, head to Trastevere to view the other half of the collection. This collection is installed in what was the 18th-century mansion of Pope Clemente XII (whose real name was Lorenzo Corsini, of the famous banking family). Before it was damaged by French attacks in 1849, the palace was once the grandest in Rome. Queen Christina died here in her bedroom (room 5) in 1689, and Napoléon's mother, Letizia, once lived here as well. The palace is still rich in neoclassical works of the Napoleonic era.

The gallery hosts a wide array of paintings from the 16th and 17th centuries, although they are bunched together and badly displayed. Nonetheless, this is an outstanding treasure trove of such European masters as Van Dyck, although Italian artists dominate. Seek out, in particular, Caravaggio's *St. John the Baptist,* and also a rendition of the same subject by Guido Reni who painted *Salome with the Head of St. John the Baptist.* Murillo's *Madonna and Bambino* is one of his less saccharine efforts, and some Rubens paintings are a bit overripe, notably a *St. Sebastian* and a *Madonna.* For sheer gore, Salvator Rosa tops them all with his version of *Prometheus.*

Santa Cecilia in Trastevere. Piazza Santa Cecilia 2. ☎ **06-589-9289.** Church free; Cavallini frescoes 3,000 lire ($1.50); excavations 3,000 lire ($1.50). Main church and excavations daily 8am–noon and 3–7pm; frescoes Tues and Thurs 10–11:30am, Sun 11:30am–noon. Bus: 44, 75, 170, or 181.

A cloistered and still-functioning convent with a fine garden, Santa Cecilia contains a difficult-to-visit fresco by Cavallini in its inner sanctums and a late-13th-century baldacchino by Arnolfo di Cambio over the altar. The church is built on the reputed site of Cecilia's long-ago palace, and for a small fee you can descend under the church to inspect the ruins of some Roman houses as well as peer through a gate at the stuccoed grotto beneath the altar.

Attractions in Trastevere

Botanical Gardens **3**
Ex Instituto San
  Michele a Ripa **14**
Folklore Museum **8**
Galleria Nazionale di
  Palazzo Corsini **5**
Gianicolo (Janiculum Hill) **4**
Palazzo Corsini
  (Galleria Nazionale
  d'Arte/Antica) **2**
Piazza Piscinula/Casa
  dei Mattei **10**
Piazza San Cosimato **16**
Porta Portese Market **17**
San Benedetto **11**
San Francesco a Ripa **15**
Santa Cecilia in
  Trastevere **12**
Santa Maria dell'Orto **13**
Santa Maria della Scala **6**
Santa Maria in Trastevere **9**
Santa Sabina **18**
Tempietto **7**
Villa Farnesina **1**

Santa Maria in Trastevere. Piazza Santa Maria in Trastevere. ☎ **06-581-4802.** Free admission. Daily 7am–7pm. Bus: 44, 75, 170, or 181.

This Romanesque church at the colorful center of Trastevere was built around A.D. 350 and is one of the oldest in Rome. The body was added around 1100 and the portico in the early 1700s. The restored mosaics on the apse date from around 1140, and below them are the 1293 mosaic scenes depicting the life of Mary done by Pietro Cavallini. The faded mosaics on the facade are 12th or 13th century, and the octagonal fountain in the piazza is an ancient Roman original restored and added to in the 17th century by Carlo Fontana.

✪ **Villa Farnesina.** Via della Lungara 230. ☎ **06-6880-1767.** Admission 8,000 lire ($4) adults, 6,000 lire ($3) age 14–18, free under 14. Mon–Sat 9am–1pm. Bus: 23, 280.

This is the most impressive of the great Renaissance villas of Rome. It once dominated the little satellite town of Caprarola, which was enveloped by the growing city. Its first owner, the rich Tuscan banker, Agostino Chigi, was a free spender in the early 16th century and entertained lavishly here. Cardinals, princes, artists, and courtesans were wined and dined by him. Servants ostentatiously threw gold and silver plates into the Tiber after each course (though there was a net to secretly retrieve the treasures).

Baldassare Peruzzi built the villa, and such artists as Raphael and Il Sodoma (so named because of his sexual practices) helped decorate the interior. The ceiling painted by Peruzzi himself can still be seen in the Loggia of Galatea, as can Raphael's fresco, *Galatea,* the villa's most famous work of art. It's a gay romp, with a nymph and her companions fleeing on the backs of pug-nosed dolphins trying to escape the attentions of mermen. Lunettes by Sebastiano del Piombo feature scenes from Ovid's *Metamorphosis.*

In time, Chigi's servants must not have retrieved enough gold plates. Overdrawn at the bank, the family sold the property to the Farnese family, for which it is named to this day, even though the villa had other roles, becoming in time a scientific circle of which Galileo was an early member.

In a ground floor room, the Loggia of Cupid and Psyche, Raphael's pupils, including Giulio Romano, painted several scenes from Apuleius's *Golden Ass.* Upstairs can be seen a curious masterpiece of Peruzzi, the Salone delle prospettive. Trompe l'oeil archways encase mock window views of Roman vistas. Although badly damaged, they still provide an insight as to what the Vatican and Trastevere looked like in the 1500s.

THE AVENTINE & SOUTH

Art Center Acea. Via Ostiense 106. ☎ **06-574-8030.** Admission 12,000 lire ($6) adults, 8,000 lire ($4) age 18 and under. Tues–Fri 10am–6pm, Sat–Sun 10am–7pm. Bus: 23 or 702. Metro: Piramide or Garbatella.

Hike out to this old power plant if you want to see some of the finest sculptures in ancient Rome, including many items from the Capitoline Museum stockpile that haven't been displayed in Rome since Mussolini was in power. They're displayed against a backdrop of Industrial Age machinery that once supplied electricity to the area. The prize here is the Togato Barberini, a berobed aristocrat from Rome of 90 B.C. He carries two heads, the symbol of an old custom in Republican Rome when patricians maintained hollow wax portrait busts of their former ancestors. They brought these busts out for special celebrations. By carrying the head, they were signifying that they were the stand-in for their illustrious progenitors.

You'll find everything from a Greek Aphrodite from the 5th century B.C. to an endless array of marble busts and statues, many of which might have come from the area of the Imperial Forum. Many of the statues, especially those in the rooms upstairs, are superb Roman copies of Greek originals. The most stunning of these is a towering goddess statue from 100 B.C. that once graced the Temple of Fortuna in Largo di Teatro Argentina.

Museo della Civiltà Romana (Museum of Roman Civilization). Piazza Giovanni Agnelli 10 (in EUR, south of the city center). ☎ **06-592-6041.** Admission 5,000 lire ($2.50). Mon–Sat 9am–7pm, Sun 9am–1pm. Metro: EUR-Fermi.

Some 3½ miles south of the historic center of Rome is a more modern city conceived by the Fascist-era dictator, Mussolini. At the height of his power, he launched a complex of impersonal modern buildings, many of them in cold marble, to dazzle Europe with a scheduled world's fair in 1942 that never happened. Il Duce got strung up, and EUR—the neighborhood in question—got hamstrung. The new Italian government that followed inherited the unfinished project and turned it into a center of government and administration.

The most intriguing sight here is this Museum of Roman Civilization, in which are housed two fascinating scale models that reproduce Rome in two different epochs: the early Republican Rome, and the city in its imperial heyday in the 4th century A.D. You'll see the then impressive Circus Maximus, the intact Colosseum, the Baths of Diocletian—and lots more. You can also see examples of late Imperial and Paleochristian art, including more than a hundred casts of the reliefs that climb Trajan's Column in the Imperial Forum.

St. Paul Outside the Walls (Basilica di San Paolo Fuori le Mura). Via Ostiense 184.
☎ **06-5410341.** Free admission. Basilica daily 7am–6:30pm; cloisters daily 9am–1pm and 3–6pm. Metro: San Paolo Basilica.

The Basilica of St. Paul, whose origins go back to the time of Constantine, is Rome's fourth great patriarchal church; it's believed to have been erected over the tomb of St. Paul, was burned in 1823, and was subsequently rebuilt. From the inside, its windows may appear to be stained glass, but they're actually translucent alabaster. With its forest of single-file columns and mosaic medallions (portraits of the various popes), this is one of the most streamlined and elegantly decorated churches in Rome. Its most important treasure is a 12th-century candelabra by Vassalletto, who's also responsible for the remarkable cloisters, containing twisted pairs of columns enclosing a rose garden. The Benedictine monks and students sell a fine collection of souvenirs, rosaries, and bottles of Benedictine every day except Sunday and religious holidays.

✪ **Santa Sabina.** Piazza Pietro d'Iliria. ☎ **06-574-3573.** Free admission. Daily 7:30am–12:30pm and 3:30–5:30pm. Bus: 81 or 160.

A rarity in a city of churches, Santa Sabina is the best remaining example of a Paleochristian church, dating from 422 A.D., with its original wooden doors from that time still intact. The doors alone are worth the trek here. They are handsomely carved with Bible scenes, including one that depicts the Crucifixion, one of the earliest examples of this in the art of the Western world. You'll find it carved on a door at the end of a "porch" from the 1400s. The porch itself contains ancient sarcophagi.

Santa Sabina was the site of the temple of Juno Regina, the patroness of Rome's Etruscan arch-rival, Veii, who was seduced into switching sides in 392 B.C. She was martyred to the Christian cause. In 1936 much of the church was restored to its original appearance, and today it is one of Rome's most beautiful churches. The surviving 2 dozen Corinthian columns may have come from the Temple of Juno. The windows of great delicacy were pieced together from 9th-century fragments. In the floor of the nave is Rome's only surviving mosaic, tomb, circa 1300.

8 Organized Tours

Because of the sheer number of sights to see, some first-time visitors like to start out with an organized tour. While few things can really be covered in any depth on these overview tours, they're sometimes useful for getting your bearings.

One of the leading tour operators is **American Express,** Piazza di Spagna 38 (☎ **06-67641;** Metro: Spagna). One popular tour is a 4-hour orientation of Rome and the Vatican, which departs most mornings at 9:30am and costs 70,000 lire ($35) per person. Another 4-hour tour, which focuses on the Rome of antiquity (including visits to the Colosseum, the Roman Forum, the ruins of the Imperial Palace, and San Pietro in Vincoli), costs 60,000 lire ($30). April to October, a popular excursion outside Rome is a 5-hour bus tour to Tivoli, where visits are conducted of the Villa d'Este and its spectacular gardens and the ruins of the Villa Adriana, all for 70,000 lire ($35) per person.

The agency **Enjoy Rome,** Via Varese 39 (☎ **06-445-18-43;** fax 06-445-07-34; www.enjoyrome.com), makes the 1-day sprint from Rome to Pompeii as inexpensive and painless as possible with an 8:30am-to-5:30pm round-trip daily tour by airconditioned minivan (fitting eight passengers), costing 65,000 lire ($32.50). The trip is 3 hours one-way, with an English-speaking driver. You're on your own once you reach the archaeological site and there's no imposed restaurant lunch: That's what keeps their prices the lowest around.

Another option is **Scala Reale,** Via Varese 52 (☎ **888/467-1986** in the U.S., or 06-4470-0898), a cultural association founded by American architect Tom Rankin. He offers small-group tours and excursions focusing on the architectural and artistic significance of Rome. Tours include visits to monuments, museums, and piazzas as well as to neighborhood trattorie. In addition, custom-designed tours are available. Tours begin at 60,000 lire ($30). Children 12 and under are admitted free to walking tours. Tour discounts are available for a group of four.

Strolling Through Rome 7

Rome is a great city for walking—be sure to allow yourself enough time to just wander and let yourself get lost. Those of you who want more guidance in your exploration may enjoy the walking tours we've designed in this chapter. Visitors with very limited time might want to concentrate on Walking Tour 1, "Rome of the Caesars," and Walking Tour 2, "The Heart of Rome." Those with more time can try out "Renaissance Rome" and "Trastevere." Many of the major sights along these routes, especially on Walking Tours 2 to 4, are covered fully in chapter 6. These tours serve both to string the sights together—for those who have limited time or want more structure—and they'll also reveal some lesser-known hidden gems along the way.

Walking Tour 1: Rome of the Caesars

Start: Via Sacra, in the Roman Forum.
Finish: Circus Maximus.
Time: 5½ hours.
Best Times: Any sunny day.
Worst Times: After dark, or when the place is overrun with tour groups.

This tour takes in the most central of the monuments and ruins that attest to the military and architectural grandeur of ancient Rome. As a whole, they make up the most famous and evocative ruins in the world, despite such drawbacks as the roaring traffic that's the bane of the city's civic planners and a general dustiness and heat that might test even the hardiest amateur archaeologists.

After the collapse of Rome and during the Dark Ages, the forums and many of the other sites on this tour were lost to history, buried beneath layers of debris, their marble mined by medieval builders, until Benito Mussolini set out to restore the grandeur of Rome by reminding his compatriots of their glorious past.

THE ROMAN FORUM
The western entrance to the Roman Forum (there are two entrances) is at the corner of Via dei Fori Imperiali and Via Cavour, adjacent to Piazza Santa Maria Nova. The nearest Metro is the Colosseo stop. As you walk down into the Forum along a masonry ramp, you'll be heading for Via Sacra, the ancient Roman road that ran through the Forum

connecting the Capitoline Hill, to your right, with the Arch of Titus (1st century A.D.), off to your left. The Roman Forum is the more dignified and more austere of the two forums you'll visit on this walking tour. Although it consists mostly of artfully evocative ruins scattered confusingly around a sun-baked terrain, it represents almost 1,000 years of Roman power during the severely disciplined period that preceded the legendary decadence of the later Roman emperors.

During the Middle Ages, when this was a cow pasture and all these stones were underground, there was a dual column of elm trees connecting the Arch of Titus with the Arch of Septimius Severus (A.D. 200), to your right.

Arriving at Via Sacra, turn right. The random columns on the right as you head toward the Arch of Septimius Severus belong to the:

1. **Basilica Aemilia,** formerly the site of great meeting halls and shops, all maintained for centuries by the noble Roman family who gave it its name. At the corner nearest the Forum entrance are some traces of melted bronze decoration that was fused to the marble floor during a great fire set by invading Goths in A.D. 410.

The next important building is the:

2. **Curia,** or Senate house—it's the large brick building on the right that still has its roof. Romans had been meeting on this site for centuries before the first structure was erected, and that was still centuries before Jesus. The present building is the fifth (if you count all the reconstructions and substantial rehabilitations) to stand on the site. Legend has it that the original building was constructed by an ancient king with the curious name of Tullus Hostilius. The tradition he began was noble indeed, and our present legislative system owes much to the Romans who met in this hall. Unfortunately, the high ideals and inviolate morals that characterized the early Republican senators gave way to the bootlicking of imperial times, when the Senate became little more than a rubber stamp. Caligula, who was only the third emperor, had his horse appointed to the Senate, which pretty much sums up the state of the Senate by the middle of the 1st century A.D.

The building was a church until 1937, when the fascist government tore out the baroque interior and revealed what we see today. The original floor of Egyptian marble and the tiers that held the seats of the senators have miraculously survived. In addition, at the far end of the great chamber we can see the stone on which rested the fabled golden statue of Victory. Originally installed by Augustus, it was disposed of in the 4th century by a fiercely divided Senate whose Christian members convinced the emperor that it was improper to have a pagan statue in such a revered place.

Outside, head down the Curia stairs to the:

3. **Lapis Niger,** the remains of black marble blocks that reputedly mark the tomb of Romulus. Today, they bask under a corrugated metal roof. Go downstairs for a look at the excavated tomb. There's a stone here with the oldest Latin inscription in existence, which unfortunately is nearly illegible. All that can be safely assumed is that it genuinely dates from the Rome of the kings, an era that ended in a revolution in 510 B.C.

Across from the Curia, the:

4. **Arch of Septimius Severus** was dedicated at the dawn of the troubled 3rd century to the last decent emperor to govern Rome for some time. The friezes on the arch depict victories over Arabs and Parthians by the cold but upright Severus and his two dissolute sons, Geta and Caracalla. Severus died on a campaign to subdue the unruly natives of Scotland. At the end of the first decade of the

Walking Tour: Rome of the Caesars

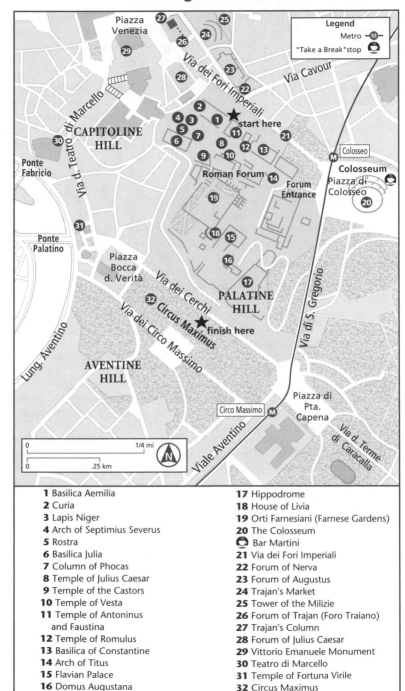

Legend

Metro —Ⓜ—

"Take a Break" stop

1 Basilica Aemilia	**17** Hippodrome
2 Curia	**18** House of Livia
3 Lapis Niger	**19** Orti Farnesiani (Farnese Gardens)
4 Arch of Septimius Severus	**20** The Colosseum
5 Rostra	Ⓒ Bar Martini
6 Basilica Julia	**21** Via dei Fori Imperiali
7 Column of Phocas	**22** Forum of Nerva
8 Temple of Julius Caesar	**23** Forum of Augustus
9 Temple of the Castors	**24** Trajan's Market
10 Temple of Vesta	**25** Tower of the Milizie
11 Temple of Antoninus and Faustina	**26** Forum of Trajan (Foro Traiano)
12 Temple of Romulus	**27** Trajan's Column
13 Basilica of Constantine	**28** Forum of Julius Caesar
14 Arch of Titus	**29** Vittorio Emanuele Monument
15 Flavian Palace	**30** Teatro di Marcello
16 Domus Augustana	**31** Temple of Fortuna Virile
	32 Circus Maximus

3rd century, Rome unhappily fell into the hands of the young Caracalla, chiefly remembered today for the baths he ordered built.

Walk around to the back of the Severus arch, face it, and look to your right. There amid the rubble can be discerned a semicircular stair that led to the famous:

5. **Rostra,** the podium from which dictators and caesars addressed the throngs of the Forum below. One can just imagine the emperor, shining in his white toga, surrounded by imperial guards and distinguished senators, gesticulating grandly like one of the statues on a Roman roofline. The motley crowd falls silent, the senators pause and listen, the merchants put down their measures, even the harlots and unruly soldiers lower their voices in such an august presence. Later emperors didn't have much cause to use the Rostra; they made their policies known through edicts and assassinations instead.

Now, facing the colonnade of the Temple of Saturn, once the public treasury, and going to the left, you'll come to the ruins of the:

6. **Basilica Julia,** again little more than a foundation. The basilica gets its name from Julius Caesar, who dedicated the first structure in 46 B.C. Like many buildings in the Forum, the basilica was burned and rebuilt several times, and the last structure dated from those shaky days after the Gothic invasion of A.D. 410. Throughout its history, it was used for the hearing of civil court cases, which were conducted in the pandemonium of the crowded Forum, open to anyone who happened to pass by. The building was also reputed to be particularly hot in the summer, and it was under these sweaty and unpromising circumstances that Roman justice, the standard of the world for a millennium, was meted out.

Walking back down the ruined stairs of the Basilica Julia and into the broad area whose far side is bounded by the Curia, you'll see the:

7. **Column of Phocas.** Probably lifted from an early structure in the vicinity, this was the last monument to be erected in the Roman Forum, and it commemorates the Byzantine emperor Phocas's generous donation of the Pantheon to the pope of Rome, who almost immediately transformed it into a church.

Now make your way down the middle of the Forum, nearly back to the ramp from which you entered. The pile of brick with the semicircular indentation that stands in the middle of things was the:

8. **Temple of Julius Caesar,** erected some time after the dictator was deified. Judging from the reconstruction, it was quite an elegant building. As you stand facing the ruins, with the entrance to the Forum on your left, you'll see on your right three columns originally belonging to the:

9. **Temple of the Castors.** This temple perpetuated the legend of Castor and Pollux, who appeared out of thin air in the Roman Forum and were observed watering their horses at the fountain of Juturna (still visible today), just as a major battle against the Etruscans turned in favor of Rome. Castor and Pollux, the heavenly twins (and the symbol of the astrological sign Gemini) are a favorite of Rome.

The next major monument is the circular:

10. **Temple of Vesta,** wherein dwelt the sacred flame of Rome and the Atrium of the Vestal Virgins. A vestal virgin was usually a girl of good family who signed a contract for 30 years. During that time she lived in the ruin you're standing in right now. Of course, back then it was an unimaginably rich marble building with two floors. There were only six vestal virgins at a time during the imperial period, and even though they had the option of going back out into the world at the end of their 30 years, few did. The cult of Vesta came to an end in A.D. 394, when a

Christian Rome secularized all its pagan temples. A man standing on this site before then would have been put to death immediately.

Stand in the atrium with your back to the Palatine and look beyond those fragmented statues of the former vestals to the:

11. Temple of Antoninus and Faustina. It's the building with the freestanding colonnade just to the right of the ramp where you first entered the Forum. Only the colonnade dates from imperial times; the building behind it is a much later church dedicated to San Lorenzo.

After you inspect the beautifully proportioned Antoninus and Faustina temple, head up Via Sacra away from the entrance ramp toward the Arch of Titus. Pretty soon, on your left, you'll see the twin bronze doors of the:

12. Temple of Romulus. It's the doors themselves that are really of note here—they're the original Roman doors, swinging on the same massive hinges they were mounted on in A.D. 306. In this case, the temple is not dedicated to the legendary cofounder of Rome, but to the son of its builder, Emperor Maxentius, who named his son Romulus in a fit of antiquarian patriotism. Unfortunately for both father and son, they competed with a general who deprived them of their empire and lives. That man was Constantine, who, while camped outside Rome during preparations for one of his battles against Maxentius, saw the sign of the cross in the heavens with the insignia *In hoc signo vinces* (in this sign shall you conquer). Raising the standard of Christianity above his legions, he defeated Maxentius and became the first Christian emperor.

At the time of Constantine's victory (A.D. 306), the great:

13. Basilica of Constantine (marked by those three gaping arches up ahead on your left) was only half finished, having been started by the unfortunate Maxentius. However, Constantine finished the job and affixed his name to this, the largest and most impressive building in the Forum. To our taste, the more delicate, Greek-influenced temples are more attractive, but you have to admire the scale and the engineering skill that erected this monument. The fact that portions of the original coffered ceiling are still intact is amazing. The basilica once held a statue of Constantine so large that his little toe was as wide as an average man's waist. You can see a few fragments from this colossus—the remnants were found in 1490—in the courtyard of the Conservatory Museum on the Capitoline Hill. As far as Roman emperors went, Christian or otherwise, ego knew no bounds.

From Constantine's basilica, follow the Roman paving stones of Via Sacra to the:

14. Arch of Titus, clearly visible on a low hill just ahead. Titus was the emperor who sacked the great Jewish temple in Jerusalem, and the bas-relief sculpture inside the arch shows the booty of the Jews being carried in triumph through the streets of Rome, while Titus is crowned by Victory, who comes down from heaven for the occasion. You'll notice in particular the candelabrum, for centuries one of the most famous pieces of the treasure of Rome. In all probability it lies at the bottom of the Busento River in the secret tomb of Alaric the Goth.

THE PALATINE HILL

When you've gathered your strength in the shimmering sun, head up the Clivus Palatinus, the road to the palaces of the Palatine Hill, or *Palatino*. With your back to the Arch of Titus, it's the road going up the hill to the left.

It was on the Palatine Hill that Rome first became a city. Legend tells us that the date was 753 B.C. The new city originally consisted of nothing more than the Palatine, which was soon enclosed by a surprisingly sophisticated wall, remains of which can still be seen on the Circus Maximus side of the hill. As time went on and Rome grew in power and wealth, the boundaries were extended and later enclosed by the Servian Wall. When the last of the ancient kings was overthrown (510 B.C.), Rome had already extended over several of the adjoining hills and valleys. As Republican times progressed, the Palatine became a fashionable residential district. So it remained until Tiberius—who, like his predecessor, Augustus, was a bit too modest to call himself "emperor" out loud—began the first of the monumental palaces that eventually covered the entire hill.

It's difficult today to make sense out of the Palatine. First-time viewers might be forgiven for suspecting it to be an entirely artificial structure built on brick arches. Those arches, which are visible on practically every flank of the hill, are actually supports that once held imperial structures. Having run out of building sites, the emperors, in their fervor, simply enlarged the hill by building new sides on it.

The road goes on only a short way, through a small sort of valley filled with lush, untrimmed greenery. After about 5 minutes (for slow walkers), you'll see the ruins of a monumental stairway just to the right of the road. The Clivus Palatinus turns sharply to the left here, skirting the monastery of San Bonaventura, but we'll detour to the right and take a look at the remains of the:

15. **Flavian Palace.** As you walk off the road and into the ruins, you'll be able to discern that there were once three rooms here. But it's impossible for anyone but the most imaginative to comprehend quite how splendid these rooms were. The entire Flavian Palace was decorated in the most lavish of colored marbles and gold. Much of the decoration survived as late as the 18th century, when the greedy duke of Parma removed most of what was left. The room closest to the Clivus Palatinus was called the Lararium and held statues of the divinities that protected the imperial family. The middle room was the grandest of the three. It was the imperial throne room, where sat the ruler of the world, the emperor of Rome. The far room was a basilica and, as such, was used for miscellaneous court functions, among them audiences with the emperor. This part of the palace was used entirely for ceremonial functions. Adjoining these three rooms are the remains of a spectacularly luxurious peristyle. You'll recognize it by the hexagonal remains of a fountain in the middle. Try, if you can, to imagine this fountain surrounded by marble arcades planted with mazes and equipped with mica-covered walls. On the opposite side of the peristyle from the throne room are several other great reception and entertainment rooms. The banquet hall was here; beyond it, looking over the Circus Maximus, are a few ruins of former libraries. Although practically nothing remains except the foundations, every now and then you'll catch sight of a fragment of colored marble floor in a subtle, sophisticated pattern.

    The imperial family lived in the:

16. **Domus Augustana,** the remains of which lie toward the Circus Maximus, slightly to the left of the Flavian Palace. The new building that stands here—it looks old to us, but in Rome it qualifies as a new building—is a museum (usually closed). It stands in the absolute center of the Domus Augustana. In the field adjacent to the stadium well into the present century stood the Villa Mills, a gingerbread Gothic villa of the 19th century. It was quite a famous place, owned by a rich Englishman who came to Rome from the West Indies. The Villa Mills was the scene of fashionable entertainment in Victorian times, and it's

interesting to note, as H. V. Morton pointed out, that the last dinner parties that took place on the Palatine Hill were given by an Englishman. At any of several points along this south-facing gazebo of the Palatine Hill, you'll be able to see the faraway oval walls of the Circus Maximus. Continue with your exploration of the Palatine Hill by heading across the field parallel to the Clivus Palatinus until you come to the north end of the:

17. Hippodrome, or Stadium of Domitian. The field was apparently occupied by parts of the Domus Augustana, which in turn adjoined the enormous stadium. The stadium itself is worth examination, although sometimes it's difficult to get down inside it. The perfectly proportioned area was usually used for private games staged for the amusement of the imperial family. As you look down the stadium from the north end, you can see, on the left side, the semicircular remains of a structure identified as Domitian's private box. Some archaeologists claim that this stadium was actually an elaborate sunken garden.

The aqueduct that comes up the wooded hill used to supply water to the Baths of Septimius Severus, whose difficult-to-understand ruins lie in monumental poles of arched brick at the far end of the stadium.

Returning to the Flavian Palace, leave the peristyle on the opposite side from the Domus Augustana and follow the signs for the:

18. House of Livia. They take you down a dusty path to your left. Although legend says that this was the house of Augustus's consorts, it actually was Augustus's all along. The place is notable for some rather well preserved murals showing mythological scenes. But more interesting is the aspect of the house itself—it's smallish, and there never were any great baths or impressive marble arcades. Augustus, even though he was the first emperor, lived simply compared to his successors. His wife, Livia, was a fiercely ambitious aristocrat who divorced her first husband to marry the emperor (the ex-husband was made to attend the wedding, incidentally) and, according to some historians, the true power behind Roman policy between the death of Julius Caesar and the ascension of Tiberius. She even controlled Tiberius, her son, since she had engineered his rise to power through a long string of intrigues and poisonings.

After you've examined the frescoes in Livia's parlor, head up the steps that lead to the top of the embankment to the north. Once on top, you'll be in the:

19. Farnese Gardens (Orti Farnesiani), the 16th-century horticultural fantasy of a Farnese cardinal. They're constructed on top of the Palace of Tiberius, which, you'll remember, was the first of the great imperial palaces to be built on this hill. It's impossible to see any of it, but the gardens are cool and nicely laid out. You might stroll up to the promontory above the Forum and admire the view of the ancient temples and the Capitoline heights off to the left.

You've now seen the best of the Forum and the Palatine. To leave the archaeological area, you should now continue walking eastward along the winding road that meanders steeply down from the Palatine Hill to Via di San Gregorio. When you reach the roaring traffic of that busy thoroughfare, walk north toward the bulk of what some Romans consider the most potent symbol of their city:

20. The Colosseum. Its crumbling, oval bulk is the greatest monument of ancient Rome, and visitors are impressed with its size, its majesty, and its ability to conjure up the often cruel games that were played out for the pleasure of the Roman masses. Visit it now or return later.

☕ **TAKE A BREAK**　On a hill in back of the landmark Colosseum is the **Bar Martini,** Piazza del Colosseo 3A (☎ **06-700-4431**), surrounded by flowery shrubs. Have your coffee or cool drink outside at one of the tables and absorb one of the world's greatest architectural views: that of the Colosseum itself. A pasta dish costs 12,000 to 25,000 lire ($6 to $12.50); a sandwich, 5,000 to 8,000 lire ($2.50 to $4). Service is daily from 8:30am to midnight. Metro: Colosseo.

THE IMPERIAL FORUMS

Begun by Julius Caesar as an answer to the overcrowding of Rome's older forums during the days of the empire, the imperial forums were at the time of their construction flashier, bolder, and more impressive than the old Roman Forum, and as such represented the unquestioned authority of the Roman emperors at the height of their absolute power. After the collapse of Rome and during the Dark Ages, they, like many other ancient monuments, were lost to history, buried beneath layers of debris. Mussolini, in an egomaniacal attempt to draw comparisons between his fascist regime and the glory of ancient Rome, later helped restore the grandeur of Rome.

With your back to the Colosseum, walk westward along the:

21. **Via dei Fori Imperiali,** keeping to the right side of the street. It was Mussolini who issued the controversial orders to cut through centuries of debris and junky buildings to reveal many archaeological treasures and carve out this boulevard linking the Colosseum to the grand 19th-century monuments of Piazza Venezia. The vistas over the ruins of Rome's imperial forums from the northern side of the boulevard make for one of the most fascinating walks in Rome.

Some of the rather confusing ruins you'll see from the boulevard include the shattered remnants of the colonnade that once surrounded the Temple of Venus and Roma. Next to it, you'll see the back wall of the Basilica of Constantine. Shortly, on the street's north side, you'll come to a large outdoor restaurant, where Via Cavour joins the boulevard. Just beyond the small park across Via Cavour are the remains of the:

22. **Forum of Nerva,** best observed from the railing that skirts it on Via dei Fori Imperiali. It was built by the emperor whose 2-year reign (A.D. 96–98) followed that of the paranoid Domitian. You'll be struck by just how much the ground level has risen in 19 centuries. The only really recognizable remnant is a wall of the Temple of Minerva with two fine Corinthian columns. This forum was once flanked by that of Vespasian, which is now completely gone. It's possible to enter the Forum of Nerva from the other side, but you can see it just as well from the railing.

The next forum you approach is the:

23. **Forum of Augustus,** built to commemorate the emperor's victory over the assassins Cassius and Brutus in the Battle of Philippi (42 B.C.). Fittingly, the temple that once dominated this forum—its remains can still be seen—was that of Mars Ultor, or Mars the Avenger, in which stood a mammoth statue of Augustus that unfortunately has vanished completely. You can enter the Forum of Augustus from the other side (cut across the wee footbridge).

Continuing along the railing, you'll see next the vast semicircle of:

24. **Trajan's Market,** Via IV Novembre 95 (☎ **06-679-0048**), whose teeming arcades stocked with merchandise from the far corners of the Roman world long ago collapsed, leaving only the ubiquitous cats to watch over things. The shops once covered a multitude of levels, and you can still wander around many of them. In front of the perfectly proportioned semicircular facade, designed by Apollodorus of Damascus at the beginning of the 2nd century, are the remains of a great library. Fragments of delicately colored marble floors still shine in the sunlight between stretches of rubble and tall grass.

Although the view from the railing is interesting, it's worth your time to descend below street level. To get here, follow the service road you're on until you reach the monumental Trajan's Column on your left, where you turn right and go up the steep flight of stairs that leads to Via Nazionale. At the top of the stairs, about half a block farther on the right, you'll see the entrance to the market. It's open Tuesday to Sunday from 9am to 4:30pm. Admission is 3,750 lire ($1.90) for adults, 2,500 lire ($1.25) for students, and free for children age 17 and under.

Before you head down through the labyrinthine passageways, you might like to climb the:

25. Tower of the Milizie, a 12th-century structure that was part of the medieval headquarters of the Knights of Rhodes. The view from the top (if it's open) is well worth the climb.

From the tower, you can wander where you will through the ruins of the market, admiring the sophistication of the layout and the sad beauty of the bits of decoration that still remain. When you've examined the brick and travertine corridors, head out in front of the semicircle to the site of the former library; from here, scan the retaining wall that supports the modern road and look for the entrance to the tunnel that leads to the:

26. Forum of Trajan (Foro Traiano), entered on Via IV Novembre near the steps of Via Magnanapoli. Once through the tunnel, you'll emerge in the newest and most beautiful of the imperial forums, designed by the same man who laid out the adjoining market. There are many statue fragments and pedestals that bear still-legible inscriptions, but more interesting is the great Basilica Ulpia, with gray marble columns rising roofless into the sky. You wouldn't know it to judge from what's left, but the Forum of Trajan was once regarded as one of the architectural wonders of the world. Constructed between A.D. 107 and 113, it was designed by the Greek architect Apollodorus of Damascus.

Beyond the Basilica Ulpia is:

27. Trajan's Column, which is in magnificent condition, with intricate bas-relief sculpture depicting Trajan's victorious campaign (although from your vantage point you'll only be able to see the earliest stages). The emperor's ashes were kept in a golden urn at the base of the column. If you're fortunate, someone on duty at the stairs next to the column will let you out there. Otherwise, you'll have to walk back the way you came.

The next stop is the:

28. Forum of Julius Caesar, the first of the imperial forums. It lies on the opposite side of Via dei Fori Imperiali, the last set of sunken ruins before the Victor Emmanuel monument. Though it's possible to go right down into the ruins, you can see everything just as well from the railing. This was the site of the Roman stock exchange, as well as of the Temple of Venus, a few of whose restored columns stand cinematically in the middle of the excavations.

ON TO THE CIRCUS MAXIMUS

From here, retrace your last steps until you're in front of the white Brescian marble monument around the corner on Piazza Venezia, where the:

29. Vittorio Emanuele Monument dominates the piazza. The most flamboyant landmark in Italy (it's been compared to a frosted wedding cake or a Victorian typewriter), it was constructed in the late 1800s to honor the first king of Italy. An eternal flame burns at the Tomb of the Unknown Soldier. The interior of the monument has been closed to the public for many years.

Keep close to the monument and walk to your left, in the opposite direction from Via dei Fori Imperiali. You might like to pause at the fountain that flanks one of the monument's great white walls and splash some icy water on your face. Stay on the same side of the street and just keep walking around the monument. You'll be on Via del Teatro Marcello, which takes you past the twin lions that guard the sloping stairs and on along the base of the Capitoline Hill.

Keep walking along this street until you come to the:

30. Teatro di Marcello, on your right. You'll recognize the two rows of gaping arches, which are said to be the models for the Colosseum. Julius Caesar is credited with starting the construction of this theater, but it was finished many years after his death (in 11 B.C.) by Augustus, who dedicated it to his favorite nephew, Marcellus. A small corner of the 2,000-year-old arcade has been restored to what presumably was the original condition. Here, as everywhere, there are numerous cats stalking around the broken marble.

The bowl of the theater and the stage were adapted many centuries ago as the foundation for the Renaissance palace of the Orsini family. The other ruins belong to old temples. To the right is the Porticus of Octavia, dating from the 2nd century B.C. Note how later cultures used part of the Roman structure without destroying its original character. There's another good example of this on the other side of the theater. Here you'll see a church with a wall that completely incorporates part of an ancient colonnade.

Keep walking along Via del Teatro Marcello away from Piazza Venezia for 2 more long blocks, until you come to Piazza della Bocca della Verità. The first item to notice in the attractive piazza is the rectangular:

31. Temple of Fortuna Virile. You'll see it on the right, a little off the road. Built a century before the birth of Jesus, it's still in magnificent condition. Behind it is another temple, dedicated to Vesta. Like the one in the Roman Forum, it is round, symbolic of the prehistoric huts where continuity of the hearth fire was a matter of survival.

About a block to the south you'll pass the facade of the Church of Santa Maria in Cosmedin, set on Piazza della Bocca della Verità. Even more noteworthy, a short walk to the east, is the:

32. Circus Maximus, whose elongated oval proportions and ruined tiers of benches evoke the setting for *Ben-Hur*. Today a formless ruin, the victim of countless raids on its stonework by medieval and Renaissance builders, the remains of the once-great arena lie directly behind the church. At one time 250,000 Romans could assemble on the marble seats, while the emperor observed the games from his box high on the Palatine Hill.

The circus lies in a valley formed by the Palatine Hill on the left and the Aventine Hill on the right. Next to the Colosseum, it was the most impressive structure in ancient Rome, located certainly in one of the most exclusive neighborhoods. Emperors lived on the Palatine, and the great palaces of patricians sprawled across the Aventine, which is still a nice neighborhood. For centuries the pomp and ceremony of imperial chariot races filled this valley with the cheers of thousands.

When the dark days of the 5th and 6th centuries fell on the city, the Circus Maximus seemed a symbol of the complete ruination of Rome. The last games were held in 549 on the orders of Totilla the Goth, who had seized Rome in 547 and established himself as emperor. He lived in the still-glittering ruins on the Palatine and apparently thought that the chariot races in the Circus Maximus would lend credence to his charade of empire. It must have been a pretty miserable show, as the decimated population numbered something like 500 when Totilla recaptured the city. The Romans of those times were caught between Belisarius, the imperial general from Constantinople, and Totilla the Goth, both of whom fought bloodily for control of Rome. After the travesty of 549, the Circus Maximus was never used again, and the demand for building materials reduced it, like so much of Rome, to a great dusty field.

To return to other parts of town, head for the bus stop adjacent to the Church of Santa Maria in Cosmedin, or walk the length of the Circus Maximus to its far end and pick up the Metro to Termini or anywhere else in the city that appeals to you.

Walking Tour 2: The Heart of Rome

This walking tour will lead you down narrow, sometimes traffic-clogged streets that have witnessed more commerce and religious fervor than any other neighborhood in Rome. Be prepared for glittering and very unusual shops that lie cheek by jowl with churches dating back to A.D. 500.

Start: Palazzo del Quirinale.
Finish: Piazza Santi Apostoli.
Time: 3½ hours.
Best Times: Sunday mornings.
Worst Times: Morning and afternoon rush hours on weekdays.

Begin in the monumental, pink-toned:

1. **Piazza del Quirinale.** Crowning the highest of the seven ancient hills of Rome, this is where Augustus's Temple of the Sun once stood (the steep marble steps that now lead to Santa Maria d'Aracoeli on the Capitoline Hill once serviced this spot), and part of the fountains in the piazza were built from the great Baths of Constantine, which also stood nearby. The palace, today home to the president of Italy, is open to the public only on Sunday mornings.

You can admire a view overlooking Rome from the piazza's terrace, then meander along the curiously lifeless streets that surround it before beginning your westward descent along Via della Dataria and your northerly descent along Via San Vincenzo to one of the most famous waterworks in the world, the:

2. **Trevi Fountain.** Supplied by water from the Acqua Vergine aqueduct, and a triumph of the baroque style, it was based on the design of Nicolo Salvi (who is said to have died of illness contracted during his supervision of the project) and completed in 1762. On the southwestern corner of the fountain's piazza you'll see a somber, not particularly spectacular church (Chiesa S.S. Vincenzo e Anastasio) with a strange claim to fame: In it are contained the hearts and intestines of several centuries' worth of popes. This was the parish church of the popes when they resided at the Quirinal Palace on the hill above, and for many years each pontiff willed those parts of his body to the church. According to legend, the church was

built on the site of a spring that burst from the earth after the beheading of St. Paul, at one of three sites where his head is said to have bounced off the ground.

If you want, throw a coin or two into the fountain to ensure your return to Rome, then walk around to the right of the fountain along streets whose names will include Via di Stamperia, Via del Tritone, and Via F. Crispi. These lead to a charming street, Via Gregoriana, whose relatively calm borders and quiet apartments flank a narrow street that inclines upward to one of the most spectacular public squares in Italy:

3. **Piazza della Trinità dei Monti.** Partly because of its position at the top of the Spanish Steps (which you'll descend in a moment), partly because of its soaring Egyptian obelisk, and partly because of its lavish and perfect baroque symmetry, this is one of the most theatrical piazzas in Italy. Flanking the piazza are buildings that have played a pivotal role in French (yes, French) politics for centuries, including the Church of Trinità dei Monti, begun by the French monarch Louis XII in 1502, and restored during Napoléon's occupation of Rome in the early 1800s. The eastern edge of the square, adjacent to Via Gregoriana, is the site of the 16th-century Palazzetto Zuccaro, built for the mannerist painter Federico Zuccaro with doorways and window openings fashioned into deliberately grotesque shapes inspired by the mouths of sea monsters. (It lies between Via Gregoriana, Via Sistina, and Piazza Trinità dei Monti.) In this building, at the dawn of the French Revolution, David painted the most politicized canvas in the history of France, *The Oath of the Horatii* (1784), which became a symbol of the Enlightenment then sweeping through the salons of Paris. Today the palazzetto is owned by the German Institute for Art History.

Begin your meandering descent of the most famous staircase in the world, the:

4. **Spanish Steps** (Scalinata della Trinità dei Monti), an azalea-flanked triumph of landscape design that takes its name (its English name, at least) from the Spanish Embassy, which was in a nearby palace during the 19th century. The Spanish, however, had nothing to do with the construction of the steps. Designed by Italian architect Francesco de Sanctis between 1723 and 1725, they were funded almost entirely by the French as a preface to the above-mentioned French church, Trinità dei Monti.

The Spanish Steps are at their best in spring, when they're filled with flowers that seem to cascade down into Piazza di Spagna, a piazza designed like two interconnected triangles. It's interesting to note that in the early 19th century the steps were famous for the sleek young men and women who lined the travertine steps, flexing muscles and ankles in hopes of attracting an artist and being hired as a model.

The boat-shaped Barcaccia fountain, in the piazza at the foot of the steps, was designed by Bernini's father at the end of the 16th century.

There are two nearly identical houses at the foot of the steps on either side. One is the home of Babington's Tea Rooms (see "Take a Break," below); the other is the house where the English romantic poet John Keats lived—and died. That building contains the:

5. **Keats-Shelley Memorial** (Casina Rossa), at Piazza di Spagna 26. Keats died here on February 23, 1821, at the age of 25, during a trip he made to Rome to improve his failing health. Since 1909, when well-intentioned English and American aficionados of English literature bought the building, it has been a

Walking Tour: The Heart of Rome

1 Piazza del Quirinale
2 Trevi Fountain
3 Piazza della Trinità
  dei Monti
4 Spanish Steps
  (Scalinata della
  Trinita dei Monti)
5 Keats-Shelley Memorial
  (Casina Rossa)
☕ Babington's Tea Rooms
6 Collegio di
  Propoganda Fide
7 Via Condotti
8 Augustus's Mausoleum
  (Mausoleo Augusteo)
9 Altar of Peace
  (Ara Pacis)
10 Borghese Palace
   (Palazzo Borghese)
11 Via del Corso
12 Palazzo Ruspoli
13 Chiesa di San Lorenzo
   in Lucina
14 Piazza Colonna
15 Piazza di Montecitorio
16 Chiesa San Marcello
   al Corso
17 Chiesa S.S. Apostoli

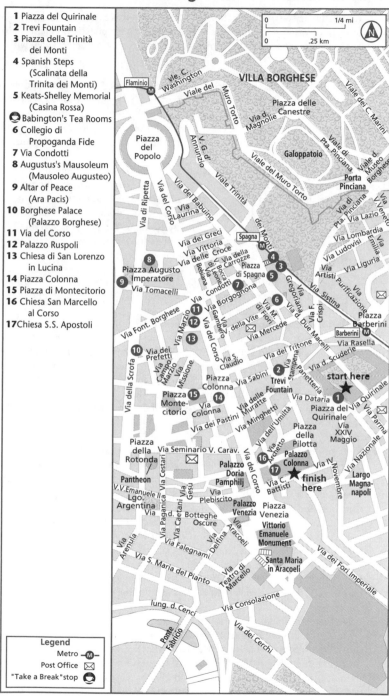

Legend
Metro —Ⓜ—
Post Office ✉
"Take a Break" stop ☕

working library established in honor of Keats as well as Shelley, who drowned off the coast of Viareggio with a copy of Keats's work in his pocket. Mementos inside range from the kitschy to the immortal and are almost relentlessly laden with literary nostalgia.

☕ **TAKE A BREAK**   Opened in 1893 by Miss Anna Maria Babington, **Babington's Tea Rooms,** Piazza di Spagna 23 (☎ **06-678-6027**), has been serving homemade scones and muffins, along with a good cuppa, ever since, based on her original recipes. Celebrities and thousands of tourists have stopped off here to rest in premises inspired by England's Victorian age. Prices are high, however.

In the past, the Piazza di Spagna area was a favorite of English lords, who rented palaces hereabouts and parked their coaches on the street. Americans predominate in the 20th century, especially since the main office of American Express is right on Piazza di Spagna and dispenses all those letters (and money) from home. Much to the dismay of many Romans, the piazza is also home to a **McDonald's,** though it's not your average Golden Arches—we've never seen one so lavish, and it's a good place to duck in if you need a rest room.

To the extreme southern edge of the square—flanked by Via Due Macelli, Via Propaganda, and Piazza di Spagna—is an odd vestige of the Catholic church's sense of missionary zeal, the:

6. **Collegio di Propoganda Fide.** Established in 1627 as the headquarters of a religious organization devoted to the training of young missionaries, it later grew into one of the most important centers for missionary work in the world. Owned and administered by the Vatican, and therefore exempt from most of the laws and legalities of Italy, it contains design elements by two of the 17th century's most bitter artistic rivals, Bernini and Borromini.

The street that runs east-west as the logical continuation of the descent of the Spanish Steps is one of the most celebrated venues for style and materialism in Italy:

7. **Via Condotti,** lined with windows displaying the latest offerings from the Italian fashion industry. Even the least materialistic will enjoy window shopping along this impressive line-up of the most famous names in international design. (Via Condotti is only the most visible of several upscale shopping streets in the neighborhood. For more of the same kind of temptation, detour onto a smaller but equally glamorous parallel street, Via della Croce, 2 blocks to the north, and wander at will you're your platinum card in hand. You'll need to walk to Via Condotti eventually for the continuation of this walking tour.)

Via Condotti ends at a shop-lined plaza, Largo Goldoni, where your path will fork slightly to the right onto Via Tomacelli. Staying on the right-hand (northern) edge of the street, turn right at the second intersection into Piazza Augusto, site of the:

8. **Augustus Mausoleum** (Mausoleo Augusteo). Once covered with marble and cypress trees, this tomb housed the ashes of many of the emperors of the 1st century all the way up to Hadrian (who built what is now Castel Sant'Angelo across the river for his own tomb). The imperial remains stayed intact within this building until the 5th century, when invading barbarians smashed the bronze gates and stole the golden urns, probably emptying the ashes onto the ground outside. The tomb was restored by Mussolini, and although you cannot enter the mausoleum itself, you can walk around it.

At the mausoleum's southwestern corner (Largo San Rocco), veer northwest until you reach the edge of the Tiber, stopping for a view of a bizarre, almost surreal compendium of ancient archaeological remnants restored, and in some cases enhanced, by Mussolini. It sits in an airy glass-and-concrete building beside the eastern banks of the Tiber at Ponte Cavour. Inside is one of the treasures of antiquity, the:

9. **Altar of Peace** (Ara Pacis), built by the Senate as a tribute to Augustus and the peace he had brought to the Roman world. Look closely at the marble walls for portraits of Augustus's imperial family. Mussolini collected the few fragments of this monument that were scattered in museums throughout the world and gave his archaeological engineers a deadline for digging out the bulk of the altar, which remained underground—below the water table and forming part of the foundation of a Renaissance palace on the Corso. Fearful of failing Il Duce, the engineers hit on the idea of chemically freezing the water surrounding the altar and simply chipping the relic out in huge chunks of ice, building new supports for the palace overhead as they went.

After a look at these fragments of another civilization's history, proceed southward along Via Ripetta, cross over Piazza di Porto di Ripetta, then fork left, walking southeast along Via Borghese for a block until you reach the austerely dignified entrance to the:

10. **Borghese Palace** (Palazzo Borghese). Although many of the art treasures that once graced its interior now form part of the Galleria Borghese collections (for details, see "In the Villa Borghese" in chapter 6—you can't just duck in quickly on a whim), this huge and somewhat disjointed palazzo retains its status as the modern-day Borghese family's seat of power and prestige. Bought from another family in 1605 by the cardinal who later became Pope Paul V, it was later occupied by Pauline Borghese, Napoléon's scandalous sister, a noted enemy of opera composer Rossini. Regrettably, the palace, carefully preserving its status as one of the most prestigious private homes in the world, is not open to the public.

From your vantage point, walk in a westerly direction along Via Fontanella Borghese back to a square you've already visited, Largo Goldoni, the western terminus of Via Condotti. The busy avenue on your right is one of the most richly stocked treasure troves of Italian merchandise in Rome:

11. **Via del Corso.** When compared to the many meandering streets with which it merges, the rigidly straight lines of Via del Corso are unusual. In the 18th century, residents of Rome commandeered the street to race everything from horses to street urchins, festooning the windows of buildings on either side of the narrow street with banners and flags. Although today its merchandise is not as chic (nor as expensive) as what you'll find along Via Condotti, it's well worth more than a few glances to see what's up in the world of Italian fashion.

Walk south along Via del Corso's western edge, turning right (west) after 1 block into Piazza San Lorenzo in Lucina. The severely massive building on the piazza's northern edge is the:

12. **Palazzo Ruspoli,** a 16th-century testament to the wealth of the Florentine Rucellai family. Family members commissioned the same architect (Bartolommeo Ammannati) who designed parts of the Pitti Palace in Florence to build their Roman headquarters. Today the building belongs to a private foundation, although it's occasionally open for temporary, infrequently scheduled exhibitions. The entrance is at Via del Corso 418A, although your best vantage point will be from Piazza San Lorenzo in Lucina.

On the piazza's southern edge rises the:

13. Chiesa di San Lorenzo in Lucina. Most of what you'll see today was rebuilt around 1650, although if you look carefully, the portico and most of the bell tower have survived almost unchanged since the 1100s. According to tradition, this church was built on the site of the mansion of Lucina, a prosperous Roman matron who salvaged the corpses of Christian martyrs from prisons and amphitheaters for proper burials. The church was founded by Sixtus III, who reigned for 8 years beginning in A.D. 432. Inside, look for the tomb of the French painter Poussin (1594–1665), which was carved and consecrated on orders of the French statesman Chateaubriand in 1830.

After your visit, retrace your steps back to Via del Corso and walk southward until you reach the venerable perimeter of:

14. Piazza Colonna. Its centerpiece is one of the most dramatic obelisks in town, the Column of Marcus Aurelius, a hollow bronze column rising 83 feet above the piazza. Built between A.D. 180 and 196, and restored (some say "defaced") in 1589 by a pope who replaced the statue of the Roman warrior on top with a statue of St. Paul, it's one of the ancient world's best examples of heroic bas-relief and one of the most memorable sights of Rome. Beside the piazza's northern edge rises the Palazzo Chigi, official residence of the Italian prime minister.

Continue walking west from Piazza Colonna into another square a few steps to the east and you'll find yourself in a dramatic piazza designed by Bernini:

15. Piazza di Montecitorio. This was the site during ancient times of the cremations of the Roman emperors. In 1792 the massive obelisk of Psammetichus II, originally erected in Egypt in the 6th century B.C., was placed here as the piazza's centerpiece. Brought to Rome by barge from Heliopolis in 10 B.C., it was unearthed from a pile of rubble in 1748 at a site close to the Church of San Lorenzo in Lucina. The Palazzo di Montecitorio, which rises from the piazza's northern edge, is the modern-day site of the Italian legislature (the Chamber of Deputies) and is closed to the public.

Retrace your steps back to Via del Corso, then walk south, this time along its eastern edge. Within 6 blocks, just after crossing over Via dell'Umiltà, you'll see the solid stone walls of the namesake church of this famous shopping boulevard:

16. Chiesa San Marcello al Corso. Originally founded in the 4th century and rebuilt in 1519 after a disastrous fire, it was ornamented in the late 1600s with a baroque facade by Carlo Fontana. A handful of ecclesiastical potentates from the 16th and 17th centuries, many resting in intricately carved sarcophagi, are contained inside.

After your visit, return to the piazza in front of the church, then continue walking for half a block south along Via del Corso. Turn left (eastward) onto Via S.S. Apostoli, then turn right onto Piazza S.S. Apostoli, and conclude this tour with a visit to a site that has witnessed the tears of the penitent since the collapse of the Roman empire, the:

17. Chiesa S.S. Apostoli. Because of alterations to the site, especially a not-very-harmonious rebuilding that began in the early 1700s, there's very little to suggest the ancient origins of this church of the Holy Apostles. Pope Pelagius founded it in the dim, early days of the Roman papacy, sometime between A.D. 556 and 561, as a thanksgiving offering for the short-term defeat of the Goths at a battle near Rome. The most interesting parts of this ancient site are the fluted stone columns at the end of the south aisle, in the Cappella del Crocifisso; the building's front portico, added in the 1300s, which managed to incorporate a frieze from ancient Rome; and one of the first works executed by Canova, a painting near the high altar completed in 1787 shortly after his arrival in Rome. The church is open daily from 6:30am to noon and 4 to 7pm.

Walking Tour 3: Renaissance Rome

The threads that unify this tour are the grandiose tastes of Rome's Renaissance popes and the meandering Tiber River that has transported building supplies, armies, pilfered treasures from other parts of Europe, and such famous personages as Cleopatra and Mussolini into Rome. Slower and less powerful than many of Italy's other rivers (such as the mighty Po, which irrigates the fertile plains of Lombardy and the north), the Tiber varies, depending on the season, from a sluggish ribbon of sediment-filled water only 4 feet deep to a 20-foot-deep torrent capable of flooding the banks that contain it.

The last severe flood to destroy Roman buildings occurred in 1870. Since then, civic planners have built mounded barricades high above its winding banks, a development that has diminished the river's visual appeal. The high embankments, as well as the roaring traffic arteries that parallel them, obscure views of the water along most of the river's trajectory through Rome. In any event, the waters of the Tiber are so polluted that many modern Romans consider their concealment something of a plus.

Begin your tour at Piazza Pia. (Don't confuse Piazza Pia with nearby Piazza Pio XII.) Piazza Pia is the easternmost end of Rome's most sterile and impersonal boulevard.

Start: Via della Conciliazione (Piazza Pia).
Finish: Galleria Doria Pamphili.
Time: 4 hours, not counting a tour of the Castel Sant'Angelo and visits to the Palazzo Spada and the Palazzo Pamphil.
Best Times: Early and mid-mornings.
Worst Times: After dark.

Start at:

1. **Via della Conciliazione.** Conceived by Mussolini as a monumental preface to the faraway dome of St. Peter's Basilica, construction required the demolition of a series of medieval neighborhoods between 1936 and 1950, rendering it without challenge the most disliked avenue in Rome.

   Walk east toward the massive and ancient walls of the:

2. **Castel Sant'Angelo.** Originally built by Emperor Hadrian in A.D. 135 as one of the most impressive mausoleums in the ancient world, it was adapted for use as a fortress, a treasure vault, and a pleasure palace for the Renaissance popes. Visit its interior, noting the presence near the entrance of architectural models showing the castle at various periods of its history. Note the building's plan (a circular tower set atop a square foundation), and the dry moats (used today for impromptu soccer games by neighborhood kids), which long ago were the despair of many an invading army.

   After your visit, walk south across one of the most ancient bridges in Rome:

3. **Ponte Sant'Angelo.** The trio of arches in the river's center is basically unchanged since the bridge was built around A.D. 135; the arches that abut the river's embankments were added late in the 19th century as part of a flood-control program. On December 19, 1450, so many pilgrims gathered on this bridge (which at the time was lined with wooden buildings) that about 200 of them were

crushed to death. Today the bridge is reserved exclusively for pedestrians; vehicular traffic was banned in the 1960s. On the southern end of the bridge is the site of one of the most famous executions of the Renaissance:

4. **Piazza Sant'Angelo.** Here, in 1599, Beatrice Cenci and several members of her family were beheaded on the orders of Pope Clement VIII. Their crime? Plotting the successful death of their very rich and very brutal father. Their tale later inspired a tragedy by Shelley and a novel by 19th-century Italian politician Francesco Guerrazzi.

From the square, cut southwest for 2 blocks along Via Paola (crossing the busy traffic of Corso Vittorio Emanuele in the process) onto:

5. **Via Giulia.** Laid out during the reign of Pope Julius II (1503–13), Via Giulia's straight edges were one of Renaissance Rome's earliest examples of urban planning. Designed to facilitate access to the Vatican, it was the widest, straightest, and longest city street in Rome at the time of its construction and was bordered by the 16th-century homes of such artists as Raphael, Cellini, and Borromini and the architect Sangallo. Today the street is lined with some of the most spectacular antiques stores in Rome. At the terminus of Via Paola, the first building on Via Giulia you're likely to see is the soaring dome of the:

6. **Florentine Church** (Chiesa di San Giovanni dei Fiorentini), designated the premier symbol of the city of Florence in papal Rome. Its design is the result of endless squabbling between such artistic rivals as Sansovino, Sangallo, and Maderno, each of whom added embellishments of his own. Michelangelo also submitted a design for the church, although his drawing did not prevail during the initial competition. Although most of the building was completed during the 1620s, Lorenzo Corsini added the facade during the 1700s.

Now walk in a southeasterly direction along Via Giulia, making special note of houses at **no. 82** (built in the 1400s, it was offered by Pope Julius II to the Florentine community), **no. 85** (the land it sits on was once owned by Raphael), and **no. 79** (built in 1536 by the architect Sangallo as his private home, it was later snapped up by a relative of Cosimo de' Medici).

In less than 3 short blocks, on the northwest corner of Vicolo del Cefalo, rises the symmetrical bulk of the:

7. **Palazzo Sacchetti.** Completed by Vasari in the mid-1500s, it was built for the Sacchetti family, a Florence-based clan of bankers and merchants who moved to Rome after they lost an epic power struggle with the Medicis.

Continue walking south along Via Giulia. On your right rises the baroque facade of the unpretentious:

8. **Church of San Biagio.** Although its front was added in the early 1700s, it's actually one of the oldest churches in Rome, rebuilt from an even earlier model dating to around 1070. The property of an Armenian Christian sect based in Venice, the church is named after an early Christian martyr (St. Biagio), a portion of whose throat is included among the sacred objects inside.

Walk another short block south along Via Giulia. Between Via del Gonfalone and Vicolo della Scimia are the barred windows of what was originally built early in the 19th century as a:

9. **Prison for Minors.** This, along with another nearby building (at Via Giulia 52, a few blocks to the south, which was built during the mid-1600s) incarcerated juvenile delinquents, political prisoners, debtors, common rogues, and innocent victims of circumstance for almost a hundred years. During its Industrial

Walking Tour: Renaissance Rome

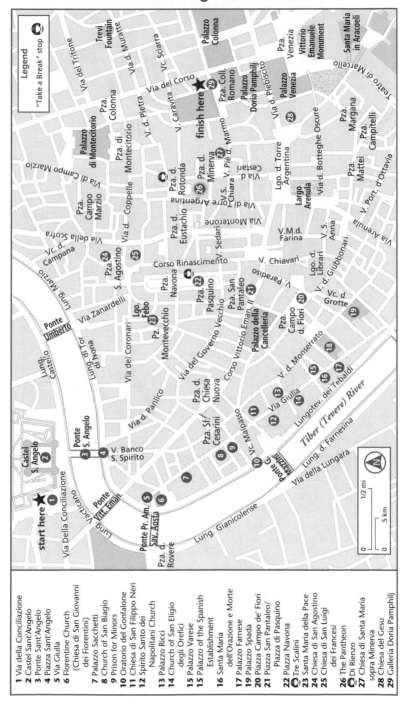

183

Revolution heyday, armed guards supervised all comings and goings along this section of Via Giulia.

Turn right onto Vicolo della Scimia and descend toward the Tiber. On your left, at no. 18, is a building used since the early 1500s as a guildhall for the flag-bearers of Rome, the:

10. Oratorio del Gonfalone. The guild of flag-bearers had, by the time this building was constructed, evolved into a charitable organization of concerned citizens and a rather posh social and religious fraternity. The frescoes inside were painted in 1573 by Zuccari. Restored during the early 1980s, they now form a backdrop for concerts held inside. The building is usually open Monday to Saturday from 9:30am to noon.

Walk to the very end of Vicolo della Scimia and make a hard left onto Vicolo Prigioni, which will eventually lead back to Via Giulia.

At this point, as you continue to walk south along Via Giulia, you'll notice a swath of trees and a curious absence of buildings flanking the corner of Via Moretta. In 1940 Mussolini ordered the demolition of most of the buildings along Via Moretta for the construction of a triumphal boulevard running from east to west. His intention—which was never fulfilled—was to link together the nearby Ponte Mazzini with Corso Vittorio Emanuele. One building that suffered was the:

11. Chiesa di San Filippo Neri, whose baroque facade sits near the corner. Originally funded during the early 1600s by a wealthy but ailing benefactor in hopes of curing his gout, the church retains only its facade—the rest of the building was demolished. Where choirs once sang and candles burned during masses, there is now a market for fruits and vegetables.

About another block to the south, on your right, rises the bulk of the:

12. Spirito Santo del Napolitani Church. Once one of the headquarters of the Neapolitan community in Rome, the version you see today is a product of a rebuilding during the 1700s, although parts of the foundation were originally constructed during the 1300s.

Slightly farther south, at Via Giulia 146, rises the:

13. Palazzo Ricci, one of the many aristocratic villas that once flanked this historic street. For a better view of its exterior frescoes, turn left from Via Giulia into Piazza Ricci to admire this building from the rear.

Returning to Via Giulia, walk south for a block, then turn right onto Via Barchetta. At the corner of Via di San Eligio, notice the:

14. Church of San Eligio degli Orefici, which was designed, according to popular belief, by Raphael in 1516. Completed about 60 years later, it was dedicated to (and funded by) the city's gold- and silversmiths.

Return to Via Giulia and notice, near its terminus, the:

15. Palazzo Varese, Via Giulia 16, built as an aristocratic residence in the Tuscan style; and, at Via Giulia 151, the:

16. Palazzo of the Spanish Establishment. Constructed in anticipation of the 1862 visit of Queen Elizabeth II of Spain, for the occasion of her charitable visit to Rome, it was designed by Antonio Sarti.

Continue walking south along Via Giulia, past the faded grandeur of at least another half-dozen palazzi. These will include the **Palazzo Cisterno** (from about 1560) at no. 163; **Palazzo Baldoca/Muccioli/Rodd** (about 1700) at no. 167; and **Palazzo Falconieri** (about 1510) at no. 1.

Opposite the corner of Via dei Farnesi rise the walls of one of the most macabre buildings in Rome, the church of:

17. **Santa Maria dell'Orazione e Morte.** Built around 1575, and reconstructed about 160 years later, it was the property of an order of monks whose job it was to collect and bury the unclaimed bodies of the indigent. Notice the depictions of skulls decorating the church's facade. During the Renaissance, underground chambers lined with bodies led from the church to the Tiber, where barges carried the corpses away. Although these vaults are not open to the public, the church's interior decoration carries multiple reminders of the omnipresence of death.

After exiting the church, notice the covered passageway arching over Via Giulia. Built in 1603 and designed by Michelangelo, it connected the:

18. **Palazzo Farnese,** whose rear side rises to your left, with the Tiber and a series of then-opulent gardens and villas that no longer exist. The Palazzo Farnese was designed by Sangallo and Michelangelo, among others, and has housed dignitaries ranging from Pope Paul III to Queen Christina of Sweden. Today the French Embassy, it's closed to the public. For the best view of the building, cut west from Via Giulia along any of the narrow streets (Via Mascherone or Via dei Farnesi will do nicely) to reach Piazza Farnese.

To the southwest is a satellite square, Piazza Quercia, at the southern corner of which rises the even more spectacular exterior of the:

19. **Palazzo Spada,** Capo di Ferro 3. Built around 1550 for Cardinal Gerolamo Capo di Ferro, its ornate facade is stuccoed in high-relief in the mannerist style. Although the staterooms are closed to the public, the courtyard and several galleries are open.

From here, walk 2 blocks north along either Vicolo del Grotte or Via Balestrari until you reach one of the most famous squares of Renaissance Rome:

20. **Piazza Campo de' Fiori.** During the 1500s this square was the geographic and cultural center of secular Rome, with inns and the occasional burning at the stake of religious heretics. Today the campo hosts a morning open-air food market every day except Sunday.

After your visit, continue to walk north for 3 meandering blocks along the narrow confines of Via Baullari to:

21. **Piazza San Pantaleo/Piazza di Pasquino,** whose interconnected edges are the site of both the Palazzo Massimo (to the east) and the Palazzo Braschi (Museo di Roma) to the north. The Palazzo Massimo (currently home to, among other things, the Rome campus of Cornell University) was begun as a private home in 1532 and designed with an unusual curved facade that corresponded to the narrow confines of the street. Regrettably, because it's open to the public only 1 day a year (March 17), it's viewed as a rather odd curiosity from the Renaissance by most passersby. More accessible is the **Palazzo Braschi,** built during the late 1700s by Pope Pius IV Braschi for his nephews. Severe and somewhat drab, it was the last palace ever constructed in Rome by a pope. Since 1952 it has contained the exhibits of the Museo di Roma, a poorly funded entity whose visiting hours and future are uncertain.

Continue walking north for 2 blocks until you reach the southernmost entrance of the most thrilling square in Italy:

22. **Piazza Navona.** Originally laid out in A.D. 86 as a stadium by Emperor Domitian, stripped of its marble in the 4th century by Constantine, and then embellished during the Renaissance into the lavish baroque form you'll see today, it has witnessed as much pageantry and heraldic splendor as any other site in

Rome. The fact that it's reserved exclusively for pedestrians adds enormously to its charm, but makes parking in the neighborhood around it almost impossible.

☕ **TAKE A BREAK**   Established in 1882, **Tre Scalini,** Piazza Navona 28 (☎ **06-687-9148**), is the most famous cafe on the square. Literally hundreds of people go here every day to sample its tartufo (ice cream disguised with a coating of bittersweet chocolate, cherries, and whipped cream). There are simpler versions of gelato as well.

After you've perked yourself up with sugar or caffeine or both, head for the piazza's northwestern corner, adjacent to the startling group of heroic fountains at the square's northern edge, and exit onto Via di Lorenesi. Walk westward for 2 crooked blocks, forking to the left onto Via Parione until you reach the edge of one of the district's most charming churches:

23. **Santa Maria della Pace.** According to legend, blood flowed from a statue of the Virgin above the altar after someone threw a pebble at it. This legend motivated Pope Sixtus IV to rebuild the church in the 1500s on the foundations of an even older sanctuary. For generations after that, its curved porticos, cupola atop an octagonal base, and frescoes by Raphael helped make it one of the most fashionable churches for aristocrats residing in the surrounding palazzos.

   After admiring the subtle, counterbalancing curves of the church, retrace your steps to the welcoming confines of Piazza Navona, then exit from it at its northernmost (narrow) end. Walk across the broad expanse of Via Zanardelli to its northern edge, then head east for 2 blocks to Piazza San Agostino, on whose northern flank rises the:

24. **Chiesa di San Agostino.** Built between 1479 and 1483 and originally commissioned by the archbishop of Rouen, France, it was one of the first churches erected in Rome during the Renaissance. Its interior was altered and redecorated in the 1700s and 1800s. A painting by Caravaggio, *Madonna of the Pilgrims* (1605), hangs over the first altar on the left, as you enter.

   After your visit, continue walking east along Via Zanardelli, turning south in about a block onto Via della Scrofe. Be alert to the fact that this street changes its name, in rapid order, to Largo Toniolo and Via Dogana, but regardless of how it's marked, walk for about 2 blocks south until, on the right, you'll see a particularly charming church, the:

25. **Chiesa di San Luigi dei Francesi,** which has functioned as the national church of France in Rome since 1589. Subtly carved into its facade is a stone salamander, the symbol of the Renaissance French monarch François I. Inside are a noteworthy series of frescoes by Caravaggio, *The Martyrdom of St. Matthew.*

   Continue walking south for less than a block along Via Dogana, then turn left for a 2-block stroll along the Salita dei Crescenzi. Suddenly, at Piazza della Rotonda, there will emerge a sweeping view of one of our favorite buildings in all of Europe:

26. **The Pantheon.** Rebuilt by Hadrian around A.D. 125, it's the best-preserved ancient monument in Rome, a remarkable testimony to the skill of ancient masons, whose (partial) use of granite helped ensure the building's longevity. Originally dedicated to all the gods, it was transformed into a church (Santa Maria ad Martyres) by Pope Boniface IV in A.D. 609. Many archaeologists find the building's massive, slightly battered dignity thrilling. Its flattened dome is the widest in the world, exceeding the width of the dome atop St. Peter's by about 2 feet.

☕ **TAKE A BREAK** For contemplating the glory of the Pantheon, **Di Rienzo,** Piazza della Rotunda 8–9 (☎ **06-686-9097**), is the most ideal cafe in Rome. Here you can sit at a table enjoying a pick-me-up while you view not only one of the world's premier ancient monuments but also the lively crowd of people who come and go on this square, one of the most interesting in Rome.

After your coffee, walk southward along the eastern flank (Via Minerva) of the ancient building. That will eventually lead you to Piazza di Minerva. On the square's eastern edge rises the massive and severe bulk of a site that's been holy for more than 3,000 years:

27. **Chiesa di Santa Maria Sopra Minerva.** Beginning in 1280, early Christian leaders ordained that the foundation of an already ancient temple dedicated to Minerva (goddess of wisdom) be reused as the base for Rome's only Gothic church. Unfortunately, architectural changes and redecorations during the 1500s and the 1900s weren't exactly improvements. Despite that, the awe-inspiring collection of medieval and Renaissance tombs inside creates an atmosphere that's something akin to a religious museum.

After your visit, exit Piazza di Minerva from the square's easternmost edge, following Via del Gesù in a path that proceeds eastward, then meanders to the south. Continue walking southward until you eventually cross over the roaring traffic of Corso Vittorio Emanuele II/Via del Plebiscito. On the southern side of that busy avenue, you'll see a church that for about a century after the Protestant Reformation was one of the most influential in Europe, the:

28. **Chiesa del Gesù.** Built between 1568 and 1584 with donations from a Farnese cardinal, this was the most powerful church in the Jesuit order for several centuries. Conceived as a bulwark against the perceived menace of the Protestant Reformation, it's sober, monumental, and historically very important to the history of the Catholic Counter-Reformation. The sheathing of yellow marble that covers part of the interior was added during the 1800s.

After your visit, cross back over the roaring traffic of Via del Plebiscito, walk eastward for 2 blocks, and turn left (north) onto Via de Gatta. Pass through the first piazza (Piazza Grazioli), then continue northward to Piazza del Collegi Romano, site of the entrance to one of Rome's best-stocked museums, the:

29. **Galleria Doria Pamphili,** Piazza del Collegio Romano 1. It's described fully under "Attractions Near Piazza Navona & Campo de' Fiori" in chapter 6.

Walking Tour 4: Trastevere

Not until the advent of the Fellini films did Trastevere make a name for itself. Set on the western bank of the Tiber, away from the main tourist path, Trastevere (whose name translates as "across the Tiber") seems a world apart from the rest of Rome. Its residents have traditionally been considered more insular than the Romans across the river.

Because only a fraction of Trastevere has been excavated, it remains one of Rome's most consistently unchanged medieval neighborhoods, despite a trend toward gentrification. Dotted with ancient and dimly lit churches, crumbling buildings angled above streets barely wide enough for a Fiat, and very articulate inhabitants who have stressed their independence from Rome for many centuries, the district is the most consistently colorful of the Italian capital.

Be warned that street crime, pickpockets, and purse snatchers are more plentiful here than in Rome's more frequently visited neighborhoods, so leave your valuables behind and be alert to what's going on around you.

Start: Isola Tiberina.

Finish: Palazzo Corsini.

Time: 3 hours, not counting museum visits.

Best Times: Daylight hours during weekday mornings, when the outdoor food markets are open, or early on a Sunday, when there's very little traffic.

Worst Times: After dark.

Your tour begins on the tiny but historic:

1. **Tiber Island** (Isola Tiburtina). Despite its location in the heart of Rome, this calm and sun-flooded island has always been a refuge for the sick. The oldest bridge in Rome, the Ponte Fabricio, constructed in 62 B.C., connects the island to the Tiber's eastern bank. The church at the island's eastern end, **San Bartolomeo,** was built during the 900s by Holy Roman Emperor Otto III, although dozens of subsequent renovations have removed virtually everything of the original structure. The complex of structures at the island's western end contain the hospital of Fatebenefratelli, whose foundations and traditions date back to the ancient world (the island was associated with the healing powers of the god Aesculapius, son of Apollo).

Walk south along the bridge (Ponte Cestio) that connects the island to the western bank of the Tiber. After crossing the raging traffic, which runs parallel to the riverbanks, continue south for a few steps. Soon you'll reach:

2. **Piazza Piscinula.** Named after the Roman baths (piscina) that once stood here, the square contains the tiny but ancient Church of San Benedetto, whose facade was rebuilt in a simplified baroque style during the 1600s. It's classified as the smallest Romanesque church in Rome and supposedly is constructed on the site where St. Benedict, founder of the Benedictine order, lived as a boy. Directly opposite the church rises the intricate stonework of the Casa dei Mattei. Occupied during the Renaissance by one of the city's most powerful and arrogant families (the Mattei), it was abandoned as unlucky after several family members were murdered during a brawl at a wedding held inside. In reaction, the family moved to more elegant quarters across the Tiber.

Exit the piazza at the northwest corner, walking west along either the narrow Via Gensola or the somewhat wider Via della Lungaretta. In about 2 jagged blocks you'll reach the first of a pair of connected squares:

3. **Piazza Sidney Sonnino** (named after the Italian minister of foreign affairs during World War I); a few hundred feet to the north, facing the Tiber, is Piazza G. G. Belli, with a statue commemorating Giuseppe Gioacchino Belli (1791–1863), whose more than 2,000 satirical sonnets (written in Roman dialect) on Roman life have made him a particular favorite of the Trasteverans. From one edge of the piazza rise the 13th-century walls of the Torre degli Anguillara and the not-very-famous church of St. Agatha, and on the southern edge, across the street, stand the walls of the Church of San Crisogono. Founded in the 500s and rebuilt in the 1100s (when the bell tower was added), it contains stonework and mosaics that merit a visit.

Now, from a point near the southernmost expanses of these connected squares, cross the traffic-clogged Viale di Trastevere and head southeast into a maze of narrow alleyways. We suggest that you ask a passerby for Via dei Genovesi, as street signs in this maze of piazzas might be hard to find. Walking along Via dei

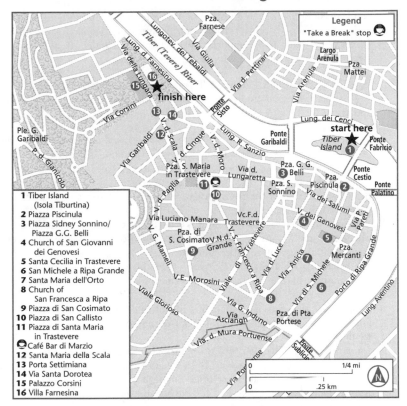

Pza.
Farnese

Legend
"Take a Break" stop

Largo
Arenula

Pza.
Mattei

Lungotev. dei Tebaldi

Via Giulia

Tiber (Tevere) River

Via della Lungara

Via d. Farnesina

Via d. Pettinari

Via Avenula

Via Corsini

16
15
finish here

Ponte
Sisto

Lung. dei Cenci

start here

13
14

Ple. G.
Garibaldi

P. d. Gianicolo

Via Garibaldi

12

V. d. Cinque

V. d. Scala

Lung. R. Sanzio

Ponte
Garibaldi

Ponte
Fabricio

*Tiber
Island* 1

Ponte
Cestio

Pza. S. Maria
in Trastevere

V. d. Moro

Via d.
Lungaretta

Pza. G. G.
Belli 3

Pza.
Piscinula 2

Ponte
Palatino

11

10

Pza. S.
Sonnino

Via dei Salumi

V. d. Paglia

Via Luciano Manara

Vc.F.d.
Trastevere

V. dei Genovesi

Via P.
Pareti

Pza. di
S. Cosimato V.N.D.S.

4

5

Pza.
Mercanti

9

Grande

Via d. Luce

7

Via Anicia

6

V.E. Morosini

V. G. Mameli

Viale di Trastevere

Via Francesco a Ripa

Via di S. Michele

Porto di Ripa Grande

Lung. Aventino

Viale Glorioso

Via G. Induno

8

Pza. di Pta.
Portese

Via
Asciangh

Via d. Mura Portuense

Via Po...nse

Ponte
Sublicio

0   1/4 mi
0   .25 km

1 Tiber Island
   (Isola Tiburtina)
2 Piazza Piscinula
3 Piazza Sidney Sonnino/
   Piazza G.G. Belli
4 Church of San Giovanni
   dei Genovesi
5 Santa Cecilia in Trastevere
6 San Michele a Ripa Grande
7 Santa Maria dell'Orto
8 Church of
   San Francesca a Ripa
9 Piazza di San Cosimato
10 Piazza di San Callisto
11 Piazza di Santa Maria
   in Trastevere
 Café Bar di Marzio
12 Santa Maria della Scala
13 Porta Settimiana
14 Via Santa Dorotea
15 Palazzo Corsini
16 Villa Farnesina

Genovesi, traverse Via della Luce, then turn right onto Via Anicia (which was named after the family that produced the medieval leader Pope Gregory the Great). Then, at Via Anicia 12, on the west side of the street, you'll see the simple but dignified walls of the:

4. **Church of San Giovanni dei Genovesi.** Built during the 1400s for the community of Genoan sailors who labored at the nearby port, it has a tranquil garden on the opposite side of the street, which you may or may not be able to visit according to the whim of the gatekeeper.

   After your visit, look across Via Anicia to the forbidding rear walls and ancient masonry of:

5. **Santa Cecilia in Trastevere.** (To reach its entrance, continue walking another block southeast along Via dei Genovesi, then turn right onto Via Santa Cecilia, which soon funnels into Piazza dei Mercanti.) A cloistered and still-functioning convent with a fine garden, Santa Cecilia contains in its inner sanctum hard-to-visit frescoes by Cavallini. (If you want to see the frescoes, call ☎ **06-589-9289** to make an appointment. Viewing hours are Tuesday or Thursday from 10 to 11:30am.) The church is more easily visited and contains a white marble statue of the saint herself. The church is built on the reputed site of Saint Cecilia's long-ago palace and contains sections dating from the 12th to the 19th century.

   St. Cecilia, who proved of enormous importance in the history of European art as a symbol of the struggle of the early church, was a wealthy Roman aristocrat condemned for her faith by a Roman prefect around A.D. 300. According to legend, her earthly body proved extraordinarily difficult for Roman soldiers to slay, affording the saint ample opportunity to convert bystanders to the Christian cause as she slowly bled to death over a period of 3 days.

☕ **TAKE A BREAK**   About half a dozen cafes are near this famous church. Any of them will serve frothy cups of cappuccino, tasty sandwiches, ice cream, and drinks.

After your snack, take the opportunity to wander randomly down three or four of the narrow streets outward from Piazza dei Mercanti. Of particular interest might be Via del Porto, which stretches south to the Tiber. The largest port in Rome once flourished at this street's terminus (Porto di Ripa Grande). During the 1870s redesign of the riverfront, when the embankments were added, the port was demolished.

Retrace your steps northward along Via del Porto, turning left onto Via di San Michele. At no. 22, inside a stucco-covered, peach-colored building that never manages to lose its bureaucratic anonymity despite its age, you'll see:

6. **San Michele a Ripa Grande.** For many years this was the temporary home of the paintings of the Borghese Gallery until that gallery was restored and reopened.

After your visit, turn north onto Via Madonna dell'Orto, a narrow street that intersects Via di San Michele. One block later, at the corner of Via Anicia, you'll see the baroque:

7. **Santa Maria dell'Orto,** which was originally founded by the vegetable gardeners of Trastevere during the early 1400s, when the district provided most of the green vegetables for the tables of Rome. Famous for the obelisks that decorate its cornices (added in the 1760s) and for the baroque gilding inside, it's one of the district's most traditional churches.

Now walk southwest along Via Anicia. In 2 blocks the street funnels into Piazza di San Francesco d'Assisi. On your left, notice the ornate walls of the:

8. **Church of San Francesco a Ripa.** Built in the baroque style, and attached to a medieval Franciscan monastery, the church contains a mannerist statue by Bernini depicting Ludovica Albertoni. It's Bernini's last known sculpture and supposedly one of his most mystically transcendental.

Exit from Piazza di San Francesco d'Assisi and walk north along Via San Francesco a Ripa. After traversing the feverish traffic of Viale di Trastevere, take the first left onto a tiny street with a long name, Via Natale del Grande Cardinale Merry di Val. (Its name is sometimes shortened to simply "Via Natale," if it's marked at all on your map.) This funnels into:

9. **Piazza di San Cosimato,** known for its busy food market, which operates every weekday from early morning until around noon. On the north side of the square lies the awkwardly charming church of San Cosimato, sections of which were built around A.D. 900; it's closed to the public.

Exit from the piazza's north side, heading up Via San Cosimato (its name might not be marked). This will lead into:

10. **Piazza di San Callisto.** Much of the real estate surrounding this square, including the 17th-century Palazzo San Callisto, belongs to the Vatican. The edges of this piazza will almost imperceptibly flow into one of the most famous squares of Rome:

11. **Piazza di Santa Maria in Trastevere.** The Romanesque church that lends the piazza its name (Santa Maria in Trastevere) is the most famous building in the entire district. Originally built around A.D. 350 and thought to be one of the oldest churches in Rome, it sports a central core that was rebuilt around 1100 and an entrance and portico that were added in the 1840s. The much-restored mosaics on both the facade and in the interior, however, date from around 1200. Its sense of timelessness is enhanced by the much-photographed octagonal fountain in front (and the hundreds of pigeons).

TAKE A BREAK   Try one of the many cafes that line this famous square. Although any would be suitable, a good choice might be the **Café Bar di Marzio,** Piazza di Santa Maria in Trastevere 14B (☎ **06-581-6095**), where rows of tables, both inside and out, offer an engaging view of the ongoing carnival of Trastevere.

After your stop, walk to the church's north side, toward its rear. Stretching from a point beginning at its northwestern edge is an ancient square, Piazza di San Egidio, with its own drab and rather nondescript 16th-century church (Chiesa di San Egidio) set on its western edge. Use it as a point of reference for the left-hand street that funnels from its base in a northeasterly direction, Via della Scalla.

The next church you'll see on your left, just after Via della Scalla, is:

12. **Santa Maria della Scala,** a 17th-century baroque monument that belongs to the Discalced Carmelite order of nuns. The interior contains works by Caravaggio and his pupils. There's also a pharmacological oddity in the annexes associated with the building: They include a modern pharmacy as well as a room devoted to arcane jars and herbal remedies that haven't changed very much since the 18th century.

In about 5 blocks, you'll reach a triumphal archway that marks the site of one of the ancient Roman portals to the city, the:

13. **Porta Settimiana.** During the 3rd century it was a vital link in the Roman defenses of the city, but its partially ruined masonry provides little more than poetic inspiration today. Much of its appearance dates from the age of the Renaissance popes, who retained it as a site marking the edge of the ancient Aurelian wall. The narrow medieval-looking street leading off to the right is:

14. **Via Santa Dorotea.** Site of a rather drab church (Chiesa San Dorotea, a few steps from the intersection with Via della Scala), the street also marks a neighborhood that was, according to legend, the home of La Fornarina, the baker's daughter. She was the mistress of Raphael, and he painted her as the Madonna, causing a scandal in his day.

Return to Via della Scala (which at this point has changed its name to Via della Lungara) and continue walking north. After Via Corsini, the massive palace on your left is the:

15. **Palazzo Corsini,** Via della Lungara 10. Built in the 1400s for a nephew of the pope, it was acquired by Queen Christina of Sweden, the fanatically religious monarch who abdicated the Protestant throne of Sweden for a life of devotion to Catholic causes. Today it houses some of the collection of the **National Gallery of Ancient Art,** plus European paintings of the 17th and 18th centuries. It's open Tuesday to Sunday from 9am to 2pm.

After your visit, cross Via della Lungara, heading east toward the Tiber, for a look at what was once the most fashionable villa in Italy, the:

16. **Villa Farnesina.** It was built between 1508 and 1511 by a Sienese banker, Agostino Chigi (Il Magnifico), who was believed to be the richest man in Europe at the time. After his death in 1520, the villa's frescoes and carvings were partially sacked by German armies in 1527. After years of neglect, the building was bought by the Farnese family, after whom it is named today, and in the 18th century by the Bourbons of Naples. Graced with sculpture and frescoes (some by Raphael and his studio), it now belongs to the Italian government and is the home of the National Print Cabinet (Gabinetto Nazionale delle Stampe), whose collections are open for view only by appointment. The public rooms, however, are open Monday to Saturday from 9am to 1pm, and also on Tuesday afternoon from 3 to 5:30pm.

Shopping 8

Rome offers temptations of every kind. You might find hidden oases of charm and value in lesser-known neighborhoods, but in our limited space below, we've summarized certain streets known throughout Italy for their shops. The monthly rent on these places is very high and those costs are passed on to you. Nonetheless, a stroll down some of these streets presents a cross section of the most desirable wares in Italy.

Though Rome has many wonderful boutiques, you'll find better shopping in Florence and Venice. If you're continuing on to either of these cities, hold off a bit.

Running a sophisticated boutique is considered an art form in Italy. Lack of space usually restricts an establishment's goods to one particular style, so browse at will, and let the allure of the shop window (particularly when shopping for fashions) communicate the mood and style of what you're likely to find inside.

Shopping hours are generally Monday from 3:30 to 7:30pm, and Tuesday to Saturday from 9:30 or 10am to 1pm and from 3:30 to 7 or 7:30pm. Some shops are open on Monday mornings, however, and some shops don't close for the afternoon break.

1 The Shopping Scene

SHIPPING   Shipping can be a problem, but—for a price—any object can be packed, shipped, and insured. For major purchases, you should buy an all-risks insurance policy to cover damage or loss in transit. Because these policies can be expensive, check into whether using a credit or charge card to make your purchase will provide automatic free insurance.

TAX REBATES ON PURCHASES IN ITALY   Visitors are sometimes appalled at the high taxes and add-ons that seem to make so many things expensive in Italy. Those taxes, totaling as much as 19% to 35% for certain goods, apply to big-ticket purchases of more than 300,000 lire ($150), but can be refunded if you plan ahead and perform a bit of sometimes tiresome paperwork. When you make your purchase, be sure to get a receipt from the vendor. When you leave Italy, find an Italian Customs agent at the point of your exit from the country. The agent will want to see the item you've bought, confirm that it's physically leaving Italy, and stamp the vendor's receipt.

You should then mail the stamped receipt (keeping a photocopy for your records) back to the original vendor. The vendor will, sooner or later, send you a check representing a refund of the tax you paid at the time of your original purchase. Reputable stores view this as a matter of ordinary paperwork and are very businesslike about it. Less honorable stores might lose your receipts. It pays to deal with established vendors on purchases of this size.

MAJOR SHOPPING STREETS

VIA BORGOGNONA This street begins near Piazza di Spagna, and both the rents and the merchandise are chic and ultra-expensive. Like its neighbor, Via Condotti, Via Borgognona is a mecca for wealthy well-dressed women and men from around the world. Its storefronts have retained their baroque or neoclassical facades.

VIA COLA DI RIENZO Bordering the Vatican, this long, straight street runs from the Tiber to Piazza Risorgimento. Since the street is wide and clogged with traffic, it's best to walk down one side and then up the other. Via Cola di Rienzi is known for stores selling a wide variety of merchandise at reasonable prices—from jewelry to fashionable clothes and shoes.

VIA CONDOTTI Easy to find because it begins at the base of the Spanish Steps, this is Rome's poshest and most visible upper-bracket shopping street. Even the recent incursion of some less elegant stores hasn't diminished the allure of Via Condotti as a consumer's playground for the rich and super rich. For us mere mortals, it's a great place for window-shopping and people-watching.

VIA DEL CORSO Not attempting the stratospheric image or prices of Via Condotti or Via Borgognona, Via del Corso boasts styles aimed at younger consumers. There are, however, some gems scattered amid the shops selling jeans and sporting equipment. The most interesting stores are nearest the fashionable cafes of Piazza del Popolo.

VIA FRANCESCO CRISPI Most shoppers reach this street by following Via Sistina (below) 1 long block from the top of the Spanish Steps. Near the intersection of these streets are several shops well suited for unusual and less expensive gifts.

VIA FRATTINA Running parallel to Via Condotti, it begins, like its more famous sibling, at Piazza di Spagna. Part of its length is closed to traffic. Here the concentration of shops is denser, though some aficionados claim that its image is slightly less chic and prices are slightly lower than at its counterparts on Via Condotti. It's usually thronged with shoppers who appreciate the lack of motor traffic.

VIA NAZIONALE The layout recalls 19th-century grandeur, but the traffic is horrendous; crossing Via Nazionale requires a good sense of timing and a strong understanding of Italian driving patterns. It begins at Piazza della Repubblica and runs down almost to the 19th-century monuments of Piazza Venezia. You'll find an abundance of leather stores (more reasonable in price than those in many other parts of Rome) and a welcome handful of stylish boutiques.

VIA SISTINA Beginning at the top of the Spanish Steps, Via Sistina runs to Piazza Barberini. The shops are small, stylish, and based on the tastes of their owners. The pedestrian traffic is less dense than on other major streets.

VIA VITTORIO VENETO Via Veneto is filled these days with expensive hotels and cafes and an array of relatively expensive stores selling shoes, gloves, and leather goods.

Rome Shopping

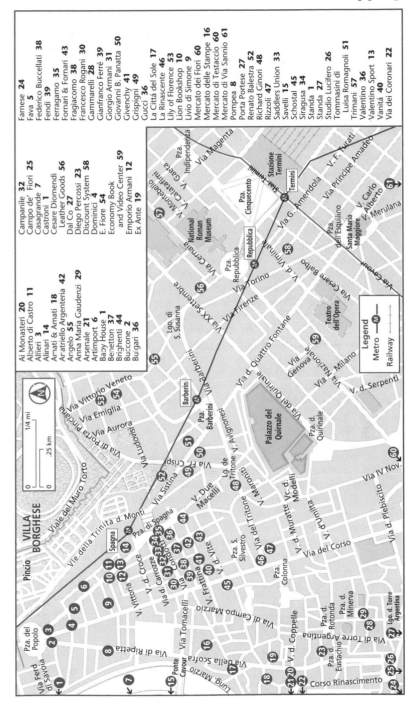

Farnese **24**
Fava **5**
Federico Buccellati **38**
Fendi **39**
Ferragamo **35**
Fornari & Fornari **43**
Fragiacomo **38**
Francesco Rogani **30**
Gammarelli **28**
Gianfranco Ferré **39**
Giorgio Armani **31**
Giovanni B. Panatta **50**
Givenchy **41**
Grispigni **49**
Gucci **36**
La Città di Sole **17**
La Rinascente **46**
Lily of Florence **53**
Lion Bookshop **10**
Livio di Simone **9**
Mercato dei Fiori **60**
Mercato delle Stampe **16**
Mercato di Testaccio **60**
Mercato di Via Sannio **61**
Pompea **8**
Porta Portese **27**
Renato Balestra **52**
Richard Ginori **48**
Rizzoli **47**
Saddlers Union **33**
Savelli **15**
Schostal **45**
Siragusa **34**
Standa **1**
Standa **27**
Studio Lucifero **26**
Tommasini di
  Luisa Romagnoli **51**
Trimani **57**
Valentino **36**
Valentino Sport **13**
Vanità **40**
Via dei Coronari **22**

Campanile **32**
Campo de' Fiori **25**
Casagrande **7**
Castroni **1**
Cesare Diomendi
  Leather Goods **56**
Dal Co **27**
Diego Percossi **23**
Discount System **58**
Dominici **4**
E. Fiore **54**
Economy Book
  and Video Center **59**
Emporio Armani **12**
Ex Ante **19**

Ai Monasteri **20**
Alberto di Castro **11**
Alfieri **3**
Alinari **14**
Amati & Amati **18**
Anatriello Argenteria **42**
Angelo **55**
Anna Maria Gaudenzi **29**
Arsenale **21**
Artimport **6**
Baoy House **1**
Benetton **37**
Brighenti **44**
Buccone **2**
Bulgari **36**

195

BEST BUYS

Because of the Italians' consummate skill as manufacturers and designers, it's no surprise that consumers from all over the world flock to Italy's shops, trade fairs, and design studios to see what's new, hot, and salable back home.

The most obvious draw is **fashion.** Milan may be the center of the fashion industry, but Rome is a principal distribution center. There are literally hundreds of famous designers for both men and women, most of whom make eminently stylish garments. Materials include silks, leathers, cottons, synthetics, and wool, often of the finest quality.

Italian design influences everything from typewriter keyboards to kitchen appliances to furniture. The Italian studios of Memphis-Milan and Studio Alchimia are two of the leaders in this field, and many of their products (and many rip-offs) are now highly visible in machines and furnishings throughout the world. Alessi has become a world-renowned name in witty, innovative houseware design. You can preview many of Italy's new products and designs by reading a copy of *Domus,* a monthly photographic magazine that reports on many different aspects of the country's design scene.

Food and wine never go out of style, and many gourmets bring some of Italy's bounty home with them. Many Roman shops sell chocolates, pastries, liqueurs, wines, and limited-edition olive oils. Be alert to restrictions against importing certain food products into North America, including anything fresh, such as fruit, as well as prosciutto. Italian wines include many excellent vintages, and bottles of liqueurs (which are sometimes distilled from herbs and flowers) make unusual gifts. You can bring home only 1 liter of wine or spirits duty free.

The **glassware** of Italy (and especially of Venice) is famous throughout the world and sold all over Rome. It's fragile enough that you should look into shipping it directly home with insurance.

Italy's **porcelain** may be elegant and sought after, but personally we prefer the hand-painted rustic plates and bowls of thick-edged **stoneware** known as Laveggio. Done in strong and clear glazes and influenced by their rural origins, the bowls and plates are often used at the most formal dinners for their originality and style. The **tiles** and **mosaics** of Italy are virtually without equal in the world, whether used individually as drink coasters or decorative ornaments, or in groups set into masonry walls.

Lace was, for many years, made in convents by nuns. Venice became the country's headquarters. Handmade Italian lace is exquisite and justifiably expensive, crafted into a wide array of tablecloths, napkins, clothing, and bridal veils. Beware of machine-made imitations; although with a bit of practice, you'll soon be able to recognize the shoddy copies.

Paper goods, stationery, elegantly bound books, prints, and engravings are specialties of Italy. The engravings you find amid stacks of dozens of others will invariably look stately when framed and hanging on a wall back home.

Fabrics, especially silk, are made near Lake Como, in the foothills of the Italian Alps. Known for their supple beauty and their ability to hold color for years (the thicker the silk, the more desirable), these silks are rivaled only by the finest of India, Thailand, and China. Their history in Italy goes back to the era of Marco Polo, possibly much earlier.

Finally, Rome is the home to a **religious objects** industry. Centered on the streets near the Church of Santa Maria Sopra Minerva are dozens of shops selling pictures, statues, and reliefs of most of the important saints, the Madonna, Jesus, and John the Baptist.

2 Shopping A to Z

ANTIQUES

Some visitors to Italy consider the treasure trove of antiques for sale the country's greatest treasure. But prices have risen to alarming levels as increasingly wealthy Europeans outbid one another in a frenzy. Any antiques dealer who risks the high rents of central Rome is acutely aware of valuations. So you might find gorgeous pieces, but you're not likely to find any bargains.

Beware of fakes; remember to insure anything you have shipped home; and for larger purchases—anything more than 300,000 lire ($150) at any one store—keep your paperwork in order to obtain your tax refund (see section 1 of this chapter).

Via dei Coronari, buried in a colorful section of the Campo Marzio, is lined with stores offering magnificent vases, urns, chandeliers, chaises, refectory tables, and candelabra. To find the street's entrance, turn left out of the north end of Piazza Navona and pass the excavated ruins of Domitian's Stadium—it will be just ahead. There are more than 40 antiques stores in the next 4 blocks, offering inlaid secretaries, gilded consoles, vases, urns, chandeliers, marble pedestals, chaises, refectory tables—you name it. Bring your pocket calculator and keep in mind that stores are frequently closed between 1 and 4pm.

Via del Babuino is another major street for antiques in Rome, with some of the most prestigious stores found here, including Alberto di Castro (our favorite store for prints—see "Art," below), but many others as well.

Ad Antiqua Domus. Via Paola 25–27. ☎ **06-686-1530.** Bus: 41, 46B, or 98.

This shop practically feels like a museum of Italian furniture design through the ages. You'll find Italian furniture from the days of Caesar through the 19th century for sale here. There's a second location at Via dei Coronari 41 (☎ **06-686-1186**).

ArtImport. Via del Babuino 150. ☎ **06-322-1330.** Metro: Spagna.

An antiques shopper's dream, this bazaar always has something for sale that's intriguing and tasteful—that is, if you can agree on a price. The store's motto is "In the service of the table," so there's an emphasis on silver, although the objects run the gamut. The goblets, elegant bowls, candlesticks, and candelabra sold here are almost without equal in Rome.

ART

✪ **Alberto di Castro.** Via del Babuino 71. ☎ **06-361-3752.** Metro: Spagna.

Alberto di Castro is one of the largest dealers in antique prints and engravings in Rome. You'll find rack after rack of depictions of everything from the Colosseum to the Pantheon, each evocative of the best architecture in the Mediterranean world, priced between $25 and $1,000, depending on the age and rarity of the engraving.

Giovanni B. Panatta Fine Art Shop. Via Francesco Crispi 117. ☎ **06-679-5948.** Metro: Spagna or Barberini.

In business since 1890, this store is up the hill toward the Villa Borghese. Here you'll find excellent prints in color and black-and-white, covering a variety of subjects from 18th-century Roman street scenes to astrological charts. There's a good selection of attractive and reasonably priced reproductions of medieval and Renaissance art as well.

BOOKSTORES

Economy Book and Video Center. Via Torino 136. ☎ **06-474-6877.** Metro: Repubblica.

Catering to the expatriate English-speaking communities of Rome and staffed by native English speakers, this bookstore sells only English-language books (both new and used, paperback and hardcover), greeting cards, and videos.

Libreria Babele. Via dei Banchi Vecchi 116. ☎ **06-6876628.**

This is Rome's only gay and lesbian bookstore. Besides the usual stock, it sells a gay map of the city.

The Lion Bookshop. Via del Greci 33. ☎ **06-3265-4007.** Metro: Spagna.

The Lion Bookshop is the oldest English-language bookshop in town, specializing in both American and English literature. It also sells children's books and photographic volumes on both Rome and Italy. A vast choice of English-language videos is for sale or rent. Closed in August.

Rizzoli. Largo Chigi 15. ☎ **06-6796641.**

Rizzoli has one of the largest collections of Italian-language books in Rome. If your native language happens to be French, English, German, or Spanish, the endless shelves will have a section to amuse, enlighten, and entertain you.

CHINA, PORCELAIN & GLASSWARE

✪ **Richard Ginori.** Piazza Trinità dei Monti 18B. ☎ **06-679-3836.** Metro: Spagna.

One of the city's most prestigious retail outlets for porcelain, both artworks and plates, contains a glittering assortment of the impeccably crafted porcelain of Richard Ginori. Founded in 1735, it offers china and glassware as well. Anything you buy here can be shipped, but if you prefer to buy at Ginori's outlets in North America (which include Tiffany's in New York), you can at least check out the dozens of patterns.

DEPARTMENT STORES

La Rinascente. Piazza Colonna, Via del Corso 189. ☎ **06-679-7691.** Bus: 117.

This upscale department store offers clothing, hosiery, perfume, cosmetics, and other goods. It also has its own line of clothing (Ellerre) for men, women, and children. This is the largest of the Italian department-store chains, and its name is seen frequently on billboards and newspaper ads throughout the country.

Standa. Corso Francia 124. ☎ **06-333-8719.**

Standa isn't super-chic, but it's fun to wander through the racks of department-store staples to see what an average Italian household might buy.

DISCOUNT SHOPPING

Certain stores that can't move their merchandise at any price often consign their unwanted goods to discounters. In Italy, the original labels are usually still inside the garment (and you'll find some very chic labels strewn in with mounds of more generic garments). Know in advance, however, that these pieces couldn't be sold at higher prices in more glamorous shops, and some garments are either the wrong size, are the wrong look, or have a stylistic mistake. If you're willing to sift through a lot, you might find a gem, though.

Discount System. Via del Viminale 35. ☎ **06-482-3917.** Metro: Repubblica.

Discount System sells men's and women's wear by many of the big names (Armani, Valentino, Nino Cerruti, Fendi, and Krizia). Even if an item isn't from a famous designer, it often comes from a factory that produces some of the best quality Italian fashion. If you find something you like, it will be priced at around 50% of its original price tag in its original boutique.

Il Discount dell'Alta Moda. Near the Spanish Steps at Via di Gesù e Maria 16A. ☎ **06-361-3796.** Another branch near Termini at Via Viminale 35 (☎ 06-482-3917).

The honest and genuinely helpful staff here will help you pick through the constantly changing racks of women's and men's clothing, with discounts of up to 50% on such labels as Versace, Donna Karan, Armani, Krizia, and Ferré.

FASHION

See also "Department Stores," "Discount Shopping," "Leather," "Lingerie," and "Shoes."

FOR MEN

Angelo. Via Bissolati 34. ☎ **06-474-1796.** Metro: Barberini.

Angelo is a custom tailor for discerning men and has been featured in *Esquire* and *GQ*. He employs the best cutters and craftspeople, and his taste in style and design is impeccable. Custom shirts, suits, dinner jackets, even casual wear, can be made on short notice. A suit, for instance, takes about 8 days. If you haven't time to wait, Angelo will ship anywhere in the world.

☉ Emporio Armani. Via del Babuino 140. ☎ **06-3600-2197.** Metro: Spagna.

This store stocks relatively inexpensive menswear crafted by the couturier who has dressed perhaps more stage and screen stars than any other designer in Italy. The designer's more expensive line—sold at sometimes staggering prices that are nonetheless up to 30% less than what you'd pay in the United States—is a short walk away at **Giorgio Armani,** Via Condotti 77 (☎ **06-699-1460).**

Schostal. Via del Corso 158. ☎ **06-679-1240.** Bus: 117.

Dating to 1870, this is the clothing store for men who like their garments conservative and well crafted. It features everything from underwear to cashmere overcoats. The prices are more reasonable than you might think, and a devoted staff is both courteous and attentive.

Valentino. Via dei Condotti. ☎ **06-673-9420.** Metro: Spagna.

This is a swank emporium for the men's clothing of the acclaimed designer. Here, if you can afford the high prices, you can become the most fashionable man in town. Valentino's women's haute couture is sold around the corner in an even bigger showroom at Via Bocca di Leone 15 (☎ **06-679-5862).**

FOR WOMEN

Arsenale. Via del Governno Vecchio 64. ☎ **06-686-1380.**

Most of the inventory that's displayed in this shop for women is the creative statement of owner **Patrizia Pieroni.** Her design preferences include lots of ultra-rich fabrics, nothing too frilly or girlish, and a dignified kind of severity that many foreign visitors find captivating. Favorite colors at this place include a spectrum of pinks, pale grays, and lilacs, with accents of bright orange, celadon green, Bordeaux, and off-whites.

Benetton. Via Condotti 18. ☎ **06-679-7982.** Metro: Spagna.

Despite the gracefully arched ceiling and its prized location, this branch of the worldwide sportswear distributor has down-to-earth prices and some of the same stock you'd find at its other branches around the world. Famous for woolen sweaters, tennis wear, blazers, and resort wear, this company has suffered (like every other clothier) from inexpensive copies of its designs. The original, however, is still best for guaranteed quality. Their men's line is also worth a look.

Gianfranco Ferré. Via Borgognona 42B. ☎ **06-679-7445.** Metro: Spagna.

Here you'll find the women's line by this famous designer whose clothes have been called "adventurous."

Givenchy. Via Borgognona 21. ☎ **06-678-4058.** Metro: Spagna.

This is the Roman headquarters of one of the great design houses of France, a company known since World War I for its couture. In its Roman branch, the company emphasizes stylish ready-to-wear garments for women, appropriate for the warm Italian weather. Tasteful shirts and pullovers for men are also featured.

Max Mara. Via Frattina 28 (at Largo Goldoni). ☎ **06-679-3638.** Metro: Spagna.

Max Mara is one of the best outlets in Rome for chic women's clothing. The fabrics are appealing, and the alterations are free.

✪ **Renato Balestra.** Via Sistina 67. ☎ **06-679-5424.**

Rapidly approaching the stratospheric upper levels of Italian fashion is Renato Balestra, whose women's clothing exudes a lighthearted elegance. This branch carries a complete line of the latest Balestra ready-to-wear.

FOR CHILDREN

Baby House. Via Cola di Rienzo 117. ☎ **06-321-4291.** Metro: Spagna.

Baby House offers stylish clothing for the under-15 set. This shop is for the budding young fashion plate, with threads by Valentino, Bussardi, and Biagiotti.

Benetton 012. Via Condotti 59. ☎ 06-679-7982.

Benetton isn't as expensive as you might expect. This store is the famous sportswear manufacturer's outlet for children's clothes (from infants to age 12), as well as adult garments for men and women. You can find rugby shirts, corduroys and jeans, and accessories in a wide selection of colors and styles.

SPORTSWEAR FOR MEN & WOMEN

Valentino Sport. Via del Babuino 61. ☎ **06-3600-1906.**

Specializing exclusively in sportswear for men and women, this is the least expensive line of clothing offered by normally wallet-denting designer Valentino. His easy-to-wear, stylish clothing has warm climates in mind. In summer, there's more emphasis on women's clothes than men's, but the rest of the year, the inventories are about equally divided.

FOOD

✪ **Castroni.** Via Cola di Rienzo 196. ☎ **06-687-4383.** Bus: 32 or 81.

At this old-fashioned store, you'll find an amazing array of unusual foodstuffs from around the Mediterranean. If you want herbs from Apulia, pepperoncino oil, cheese from the Valle d'Aosta, or that strange brand of balsamic vinegar whose name you can never remember, Castroni will have it. Filled to the rafters with the abundance of agrarian Italy, it also carries foods that are exotic in Italy but commonplace in North America, like taco shells, corn curls, and peanut butter. (Remember, there are

Shopping Tips

Remember to bring your pocket calculator with you and keep in mind that stores are often closed between 1 and 4pm. Most important? Save your receipts! See section 1 of this chapter for important money-saving information on obtaining a tax refund.

___

restrictions against importing certain food products into North America, including prosciutto and fresh produce.)

GIFTS

Amati & Amati. Via dei Pianellari 21. ☎ **06-686-4319.**

This intimate shop sells antique jewelry, high-fashion clothing, and exotic handcrafts. Good examples include mirrors framed in assorted seashells and lavishly carved chests from North Africa that might inspire you to store your wedding mementos. And if you're on the hunt for exotic fashion accessories, this is the place for you.

Ex Ante. Largo Toniolo 4. ☎ **06-6880-1107.** Bus: 70, 81, 119, or 170.

You can find some of the most exquisite and exotic gifts in Rome here, though you should expect to find a hefty price tag attached. If you're looking for a gift item from Italy, France, China, the Middle East, or some other faraway land, this is the place for you. Examples include handcrafted silver frames embedded with amber or trunks from Asia. You'll find it near the Pantheon. There's another location at Via Vittoria 13 (☎ **06-3265-0534**), with smaller and more affordable items.

Grispigni. Via Francesco Crispi 59 (at Via Sistina). ☎ **06-679-0290.** Metro: Spagna or Barberini.

Here you'll find a constantly changing array of gifts, including a large assortment of leather-covered boxes, women's purses, compacts, desk sets, and cigarette cases.

HOUSEWARES

Bagagli. Via Campo. Marzio 42. ☎ **06-687-1406.**

Here you'll find a good selection of Alessi, Rose and Tulipani, and Villeroy & Boch china in a pleasantly kitschy old Rome setting that comes complete with cobblestone floors.

c.u.c.i.n.a. Via di Babuino 118A. No phone.

This is a stainless steel shrine to everything you need for a proper Italian kitchen, sporting designs that are as beautiful in their simplicity as they are utilitarian.

✪ **Spazio Sette.** Via D. Barberi, off Largo di Torre Argentina. ☎ **06-686-9747.**

This is far and away Rome's best housewares emporium, a design boutique of department store proportions. It goes way beyond the Alessi tea kettles to fill three huge floors with the greatest names, and latest word, in Italian and international design.

Stock Market. Via D. Banchi Vecchi 51–52. ☎ **06-686-4238.** Another location near the Vatican at Via Tacito 60; ☎ **06-3600-2343.**

Bargain hunters will find mouthwatering prices on last year's models, overstock, slight irregulars, and artistic misadventures in design that the pricier boutiques haven't been able to move. Most is moderately funky household stuff, but you never know when you'll find a gem of design hidden on the shelves.

JEWELRY

Since the days when the ancient Romans imported amethysts and pearls from the distant borders of their empire, and when the great trading ships of Venice and Genoa carried rubies and sapphires from Asia, Italians have collected jewelry. Styles range from the most classically conservative to neo-punk-rock frivolous, and part of the fun is shopping for something you might never before have considered wearing.

✪ **Bulgari.** Via Condotti 10. ☎ **06-696-261.** Metro: Spagna.

Bulgari is the capital's most prestigious jeweler and has been since the 1890s. The shop window, on a conspicuously affluent stretch of Via Condotti, is a visual attraction in its own right. Bulgari designs combine classical Greek aesthetics with Italian taste. Over the years, Bulgari has managed to follow changes in style while still maintaining its tradition. Prices range from affordable to insane.

Diego Percossi Papi. Via Sant'Eustachio 16. ☎ **06-6880-1466.**

Look here for the ornate jewelry Lucrezia Borgia might wear if she were alive, well, and living in 2000. Most of the designs are inspired by Renaissance themes, many of them crafted from colored gemstones, and in some cases, accented with iridescent patches of enameling. Jade, opal, and semi-precious gemstones are heavily featured.

E. Fiore. Via Ludovisi 31. ☎ **06-481-9296.** Bus: 95 or 115.

This store near Via Veneto is as multifaceted as its jewels. You can select a stone and have it set according to your specifications; choose from a rich assortment of charms, bracelets, necklaces, rings, brooches, corals, pearls, cameos, watches, silverware, and goldware; or have Fiore expertly repair your own jewelry and watches. Closed in August.

✪ **Federico Buccellati.** Via Condotti 31. ☎ **06-679-0329.** Metro: Spagna.

At this, one of the best gold- and silversmiths in Italy, neo-Renaissance creations will change your thinking about gold and silver designs. You'll discover the Italian tradition and beauty of handmade jewelry and hollowware whose principles sometimes hark back to the designs of Renaissance gold master Benvenuto Cellini.

LEATHER

Italian leather is among the very best in the world, and at its best, can attain buttersoft textures more pliable than cloth. You'll find hundreds of leather stores in Rome, many of them excellent.

Alfieri. Via del Corso 1–2. ☎ **06-361-1976.** Bus: 117.

You'll find virtually any leather garment imaginable in this richly stocked store. Established in the 1960s, with a somewhat more funky and counterculture slant than Casagrande or Campanile, Alfieri prides itself on leather jackets, boots, bags, belts, shirts, hats, and pants for men and women; shorts reminiscent of German lederhosen; and skirts that come in at least 10 different, sometimes neon colors. Although everything sold is made in Italy, this place prides itself on reasonable prices rather than ultra-high quality. So, although you'll definitely find whimsy, an amazingly wide selection, and affordable prices, check the stitching and zippers carefully before you invest.

Campanile. Via Condotti 58. ☎ **06-678-3041.**

Belying the postmodern sleekness of its premises, this outfit has a pedigree going back to the 1870s and an impressive inventory of well-crafted leather jackets, belts, shoes, bags, and suitcases for both men and women. Quality is relentlessly high (as are prices), and as such, the store might function as the focal point of your window-shopping energies along either side of Rome's most glamorous shopping street.

Casagrande. Via Cola di Rienzo 206. ☎ **06-687-4610.** Bus: 32 or 81.

If famous names in leather wear appeal to you, you'll find most of the biggies here. Names signifying quality include Fendi and its youth-conscious offspring, Fendissime, plus Cerruti, Mosquino, and Valentino. This well-managed store has developed an impressive reputation for quality and authenticity since the 1930s. The prices are more reasonable than those for equivalent merchandise in some other parts of town.

Cesare Diomedi Leather Goods. Via Vittorio Emanuele Orlando 96–97. ☎ **06-488-4822.**

Located in front of the Grand Hotel, this store offers one of the most outstanding collections of leather goods in Rome. And leather isn't all you'll find in this small, two-story shop; many other distinctive items, such as small gold cigarette cases and jeweled umbrellas, make this a good stopping-off point for that last gift. Up the spiral staircase is a wide assortment of elegant leather luggage and accessories.

Fendi. Via Borgognona 36–40. ☎ **06-679-7641.** Metro: Spagna.

The House of Fendi is mainly known for its leather goods, but it also has furs, stylish purses, ready-to-wear clothing, and a new men's line of clothing and accessories. Gift items, home furnishings, and sports accessories are also sold here, all emblazoned with an "F." Closed Saturday afternoons from July to September.

Francesco Rogani. Via Condotti 47. ☎ **06-678-4036.**

Francesco Rogani has become one of Rome's most famous leather stores, offering a wide selection of bags for every occasion. At Rogani, you'll find a good price-quality relation also for wallets, belts, and handmade ties.

Gucci. Via Condotti 8. ☎ **06-679-0405.**

Of course, Gucci has been a legend since 1900. It sells high-class leather goods, such as suitcases, handbags, wallets, shoes, and desk accessories. It also has departments complete with elegant men's and women's wear, including tailored shirts, blouses, and dresses, as well as ties and scarves of numerous designs. *La bella figura* is alive and well at Gucci, and prices have never been higher. Among the many temptations is Gucci's own perfume.

Pompea. Via di Ripetta 150. ☎ **06-687-9165.**

Fine leather, some of it made to order, is the main focus at this store, where leather bags of all shape and sizes are sold in a quality that rivals that of the best stores in Italy. You can buy anything on display, but if you have something of a flair for design, you can specify the size, number of compartments, and color of the leather from which your bag will be crafted. Most of the leather goods involve women's purses and bags, although a selection of men's suitcases, briefcases, and garment bags are also sold.

Saddlers Union. Via Condotti 26. ☎ **06-679-8050.**

This is a great place to look for well-crafted leather accessories, such as bags, belts, wallets, shoes, briefcases, and more.

LINGERIE
Brighenti. Via Frattina 7–8. ☎ **06-6791484.**

Brighenti sells strictly lingerie *di lusso,* or perhaps better phrased, haute corseterie. The shop is amid several famous neighbors on Via Frattina; you may run across a lacy, seductive fantasy you just have to have. Closed 2 weeks in August.

One-of-a-Kind Shops

Alinari, Via Alibert 16A (☎ **06-679-2923;** Metro: Spagna), takes its name from the famed Florentine photographer of the 19th century. Original Alinari prints are almost as prized as paintings in national galleries, and they record the Rome of a century ago.

Fava, Via del Babuino 180 (☎ **06-361-0807;** Metro: Spagna), recaptures the era when Neapolitans sold 17th- and 18th-century pictures of the eruptions of Mount Vesuvius, once highly sought by collectors.

Siragusa, Via delle Carrozze 64 (☎ **06-679-7085;** Metro: Spagna), is more like a museum than a shop, specializing in unusual jewelry, based on ancient carved stones or archaeological pieces mounted in 24K gold. Handmade chains, for example, often hold coins and beads discovered in Asia Minor that date from the 3rd to the 4th century B.C.

Tomassini di Luisa Romagnoli. Via Sistina 119. ☎ **06-488-1909.** Metro: Spagna or Barberini.

This shop offers delicately beautiful lingerie and negligees, all original designs of Luisa Romagnoli. Most of the merchandise sold here is of shimmery Italian silk; other items, to a lesser degree, are of fluffy cotton or frothy nylon. Very revealing garments are sold either ready-to-wear or are custom-made.

Vanità. Via Frattina 70. ☎ **06-679-1743.** Metro: Spagna.

The lingerie selection here spans the spectrum. Yes, you can get black or white, but take the time to browse and you'll find underthings from over, under, and all around the rainbow, including hues you've never dreamed of.

LUGGAGE

Livio di Simone. Via San Giacomo 23. ☎ **06-3600-1732.**

Unusual suitcases in many shapes and sizes, into which hand-painted canvas has been sewn, are sold here. This outlet has one of the most tasteful yet durable collections in Rome.

MARKETS

Piles of fresh vegetables arranged above ancient pavements in the streaming Italian sunshine—well, what visitor can resist? Here's a rundown on the Roman markets known for the freshest produce, the most uninhibited merchants, and the longest-running traditions.

✪ **Campo de' Fiori.** Campo de' Fiori.

During the Renaissance, this neighborhood contained most of the inns that pilgrims and merchants from other parts of Europe used for lodgings. Today its battered and slightly shabby perimeter surrounds about a hundred merchants who arrange their produce artfully every day.

Mercato Andrea Doria. Via Andrea Doria.

After a visit to this open-air festival, you'll never look at the frozen vegetable section in your local supermarket the same way. Set near the Vatican, on a large, sun-baked stretch of pavement between Via Tunisi and Via Santamaura, the merchandise includes meats, poultry, eggs, dairy products, wines, an endless assortment of *frutta e verdura* (fruits and vegetables), and even some scruffy-looking racks of secondhand clothing.

Mercato dei Fiori. Via Trionfale.

Most of the week this vast covered market sells flowers only to retail florists, who resell them to consumers. Every Tuesday, however, the industrial-looking premises open to the public, who crowd in for access to exotic, Mediterranean flowers at bargain-basement prices. Open to the public Tuesday from 10:30am to 1pm.

Mercato delle Stampe. Largo della Fontanella di Borghese.

Virtually everything that's displayed in the dozens of battered kiosks here is dog-eared and evocatively ragtag. You'll find copies of engravings, books, magazines from the 1960s (or before), and prints and engravings that are either worthless or priceless, depending on your taste. If your passion is the printed word, this is your place, and bargaining for value is part of the experience.

Mercato di Testaccio. Piazza Testaccio.

Because their stalls are covered from the wind, rain, and dust of the rest of Rome, the vendors here are able to retain an air of permanence about their set-ups that most out-door markets simply can't provide. Inside you'll find fishmongers, butchers, cheese sellers, a wide array of dairy products, and the inevitable fruits and vegetables of the Italian harvest.

Mercato di Via Sannio. Via Sannio.

If you like street fairs loaded with items that verge on the junky, but that contain occasional nuggets of value or eccentric charm, this is the market for you. Regret-tably, rare or unusual items are getting harder to find here, as every antiques dealer in Italy seems to have combed through the inventories long before your arrival. Despite that, you'll find some ragtag values in the endless racks of clothing that await cost-conscious buyers.

Piazza Vittorio Emanuele. South of Stazione Termini.

Near Santa Maria Maggiore, the largest open-air food market in Rome takes place Monday through Saturday at Piazza Vittorio Emanuele. For browsing Roman style, head here any time between 7am and noon. Most of the vendors at this gigantic square sell fresh fruit, vegetables, and other foodstuffs, although many stalls are devoted to such items as cutlery, clothing, and other merchandise. The place has little to tempt the serious shopper, but it's great for discovering a slice of Roman life.

Porta Portese. Via Portuense and Via Ippolito Nievo.

The mother lode of Roman bazaars is Porta Portese, a flea market off Piazza Ippolito Nievo that is one of Europe's premier permanent garage sales. Vendors sell merchan-dise ranging from secondhand paintings of Madonnas (the Italian market is glutted with these) to termite-eaten wooden Il Duce medallions. There are also pseudo-Etruscan hairpins, bushels of rosaries, television sets that haven't transmitted an image since 1965, books printed early in the 19th century, and rack after rack of secondhand (or never-sold) clothing. Serious shoppers can often ferret out a good buy. You'll find everything from antique credenzas to bootleg CDs, birds that squawk "ciao" to old clothes, all in a carnival atmosphere of haggling and jostling. Brace yourself for crowds and a few beggars, and keep your eyes out for pickpockets. It runs every Sunday from dawn to lunchtime.

MARQUETRY

Farnese. Piazza Farnese 52. ☎ **06-689-6109.**

The entrepreneurs who are the backbone of this outfit are expert restorers of marquetry and inlay work and have been commissioned to help renovate floors as far away as the Kremlin in Moscow. If you want to commission a floor or an entire room sheathed with marquetry crafted from wood, marble, or terra cotta, this place will send out teams of artisans to install one. But if you're merely in the market for a table, an elaborate cigar or jewel box, or a modest wall plaque that's crafted in a dozen hues of hardwood, look no further.

MOSAICS

✪ **Savelli.** Via Paolo VI 27. ☎ **06-830-7017.** Metro: San Paola.

This company specializes in the manufacture and sale of mosaics, an art form as old as the Roman empire itself. Many of the objects in the company's gallery were inspired by ancient originals discovered in thousands of excavations throughout the Italian peninsula, including those at Pompeii and Ostia. Others, especially the floral designs, rely on the whim and creativity of the artists. Objects include tabletops, boxes, and vases. The cheapest mosaic objects begin at around $125 and are unsigned products crafted by students at a school for artists that is partially funded by the Vatican. Objects made in the Savelli workshops that are signed by the individual artists tend to be larger and more elaborate. The outlet also contains a collection of small souvenir items, such as keychains and carved statues.

MURALS

Studio Lucifero. Via Grottapinta 21. ☎ **06-689-6277.**

Chances are that you won't walk away from this store with a minor purchase, as its specialty involves the creation of full-scale, wall-sized murals, each specifically commissioned for the size of the room being decorated and usually based on bucolic or ancient themes. Although the artisans from this shop have actually traveled to execute their works on plaster, the more common motif involves painting a series of large-scale canvas panels, which are then stretched as displays for the room being decorated. The headquarters are within a deconsecrated church near Campo de' Fiori. Here teams of artisans also duplicate such long-ago techniques as trompe l'oeil, gold leafing, and marbelizing techniques known as *faux-marbre*.

RELIGIOUS ART & FASHION

Anna Maria Gaudenzi. Piazza della Minerva 69A. ☎ **06-790-431.** Bus: 116.

Set in a neighborhood loaded with purveyors of religious art and icons, this shop claims to be the oldest of its type in Rome. If you collect depictions of Mary, paintings of the saints, exotic rosaries, chalices, small statues, or medals, you can feel secure knowing that thousands of pilgrims have spent their money here before you. Whether you view this type of merchandise as devotional aid or bizarre kitsch, this shop has it all.

Gamarelli. Via Santa Chiara 34. ☎ **06-6801314.**

Few laypersons ever really think about how or where a clergyman might clothe himself for mass, but in the Eternal City, the problem is almost universal. If you're looking for a gift for your parish priest or a nephew who has decided to take the vows, head to this store that's known as the "Armani" of the priestly garment biz. Established

200 years ago, it employs a battalion of embroiderers, usually devout Catholics in their own right, who wield needles and either purple, scarlet, or gold threads like the legendary swords of the Counter-Reformation. The inventories are so complete that priests, bishops, and cardinals from around the world consider this a worthwhile stopover during their pilgrimages to Rome. The store does not stock any garments for nuns.

SHOES

Dal Co. Via Vittoria 65. ☎ **06-678-6536.**

If you've ever suspected that a shoe fetish might be lurking within the depths of your psyche, a visit to this store will probably unleash it. Everything inside is handmade and usually can be matched to a handbag that, if it doesn't match exactly, at least provides a reasonably close approximation. Most of the shoes are low-key and conservative, but a few are wild, whimsical, and outrageous enough to appeal even to RuPaul for a night on the town. Only women's shoes are stocked.

Dominici. Via del Corso 14. ☎ **06-361-0591.** Bus: 117.

An understated facade a few steps from Piazza del Popolo shelters an amusing and lighthearted collection of men's and women's shoes in a rainbow variety of vivid colors. The style is aggressively young-at-heart, and the children's shoes are adorable.

Ferragamo. Via Condotti 73–74. ☎ **06-679-8402.** Metro: Spagna.

Ferragamo sells elegant and fabled footwear, plus ties, women's clothing, and accessories in an atmosphere full of Italian style. The name became famous in America when such silent-screen vamps as Pola Negri and Greta Garbo began appearing in Ferragamo shoes. There are always many customers waiting to enter the shop; management allows them to enter in small groups. (Wear comfortable shoes for what may well be a 30-minute wait.)

Fragiacomo. Via Condotti 35. ☎ **06-0679-8780.** Metro: Spagna.

Here you can buy shoes for both men and women in a champagne-colored showroom with gilt-touched chairs and big display cases.

Lily of Florence. Via Lombardia 38 (off Via Vittorio Veneto). ☎ **06-474-0262.** Bus: 116.

This famous Florentine shoemaker now has a shop in Rome, with the same merchandise that made the outlet so well known in the Tuscan capital. Colors come in a wide range, the designs are stylish, and leather texture is of good quality. Shoes for both men and women are sold, and American sizes are a feature.

SILVER

Anatriello Argenteria Antica e Moderna Roma. Via Frattina 123. ☎ **06-678-9601.**

This store is known for stocking an inventory of new and antique silver, some of it among the most unusual in Italy. All the new items are made by Italian silversmiths, in designs ranging from the whimsical to the severely formal and dignified. Also on display are antique pieces from England, Germany, and Switzerland.

Fornari & Fornari. Via Frattina 133. ☎ **06-678-0105.**

This two-story showroom is filled with silver, lamps, porcelain, crystal, furniture, and upscale gift items from many different manufacturers throughout Italy and Europe. Virtually anything can be shipped around the world. Closed in August.

TOYS

La Città del Sole. Via della Scrofe 65. ☎ **06-687-5404.**

Other than the branch in Milan, this is the largest and best stocked of any of the stores in its 40-member chain. It specializes in amusements for children and adults, with a wide range of toys and games that don't make beeping noises. Many of the games are configured in English, others in Italian. You'll find role-playing games, battlefield strategy games, family games, and children's games that will challenge a young person's gray matter and probably drive their parents crazy. Also for sale are such rainy-day distractions as miniature billiards tables and tabletop golf sets.

WINES & LIQUORS

Ai Monasteri. Corso Rinascimento 72 (2 blocks from Piazza Navona). ☎ **06-6880-2783.** Bus: 70, 81, or 87.

Italy produces a staggering volume of wines, liqueurs, and after-dinner drinks, and here you'll find a treasure trove of selections: liquors (including liqueurs and wines), honey, and herbal teas made in monasteries and convents all over Italy. You can buy excellent chocolates and other candies here as well. The shop will ship some items home for you. In a quiet atmosphere, reminiscent of a monastery, you can choose your spirits as they move you.

Buccone. Via Ripetta 19. ☎ **06-361-2154.** Bus: 698 or 926.

This is a historic wine shop, right near Piazza del Popolo. Its selection of wines and gastronomic specialties is among the finest in Rome.

Trimani. Via Goito 20. ☎ **06-446-9661.** Metro: Castel Pretorio. Bus: 3, 4, or 36.

Established in 1821, Trimani sells wines and spirits from Italy, with a selection of thousands of bottles. Purchases can be shipped to your home. It collaborates with the Italian wine magazine *Gambero Rosso,* organizing some lectures about wine in which enthusiasts can improve their knowledge and educate their taste buds.

Rome After Dark

When the sun goes down, lights across the city bathe palaces, ruins, fountains, and monuments in a theatrical white light. There are few evening pursuits as pleasurable as a stroll past the solemn pillars of old temples or the cascading torrents of Renaissance fountains glowing under the blue-black sky.

Of these fountains, the **Naiads** (Piazza della Repubblica), the **Tortoises** (Piazza Mattei), and of course, the **Trevi** are particularly beautiful at night. The **Capitoline Hill** is magnificently lit after dark, with its measured Renaissance facades glowing like jewel boxes. Behind the **Senatorial Palace** is a fine view of the illuminated **Roman Forum.** If you're across the Tiber, **Piazza San Pietro** (in front of St. Peter's Basilica) is particularly impressive at night, when the tour buses and crowds have departed. A combination of illuminated architecture, Renaissance fountains, sidewalk stage shows, and art expos enliven **Piazza Navona.** If you're ambitious and have a good sense of direction, try exploring the streets west of Piazza Navona, which resemble a stage set when they're lit at night.

Even if you don't speak Italian, you can generally follow the listings of special events and evening entertainment featured in *La Repubblica,* one of the leading Italian newspapers. *TrovaRoma,* a special weekly entertainment supplement (good for the coming week) is published in this paper on Thursday. The mini-mags *Metropolitan* and *Wanted in Rome* (www.wantedinrome.com) have listings of jazz, rock, and such and give an interesting look at expat Rome. The daily *Il Messaggero* lists current cultural news, especially in its Thursday magazine supplement, *Metro. Un Ospite a Roma,* available free from the concierge desks of top hotels, is full of details on what's happening. There's now a Rome edition of *Time Out,* too, with entertainment and cultural listings available on its Web site at **www.timeout.co.uk.**

1 The Performing Arts

Rome's premier cultural venue is the **Teatro dell'Opera** (see below), which may not be Milan's legendary La Scala, but offers stellar performances nevertheless. The outstanding local troupe is the **Rome Opera Ballet** (see below).

Rome doesn't have a major center for classical music concerts, although performances of the most important orchestra, the **RAI**

Symphony Orchestra, most often take place at the RAI Auditorium, as well as at the Academy of St. Cecilia (see below).

Rome is also a major stopover for international stars. Rock headliners often perform at **Stadio Flaminio, Foro Italico,** and at two different places in the EUR, the **Palazzo della Civiltà del Lavoro** and the **Palazzo dello Sport.** Most of the concerts are at the Palazzo dello Sport.

CLASSICAL MUSIC

Academy of St. Cecilia. Via della Conciliazione 4. ☎ **06-6880-1044.** Tickets 25,000–80,000 lire ($12.50–$40).

Concerts given by the orchestra of the Academy of St. Cecilia usually take place at Piazza di Villa Giulia, site of the Etruscan Museum, from the end of June to the end of July; in winter, they're held in the academy's concert hall on Via della Conciliazione. Sometimes other addresses are selected for concerts, including a handful of historic churches. Performance nights are either Saturday, Sunday, Monday, or Tuesday. Friday nights feature chamber music.

Teatro Olimpico. Piazza Gentile da Fabriano. ☎ **06-323-4890.** Tickets 20,000–80,000 lire ($10–$40), depending on the event.

Large and well publicized, this echoing stage hosts a widely divergent collection of singers, both classical and pop, who perform according to a schedule that sometimes changes at the last minute. Occasionally the space is devoted to chamber orchestras or visits by foreign orchestras.

OPERA

Teatro dell'Opera. Piazza Beniamino Gigli 1 off Via Nazionale. ☎ **06-481-601.** Tickets 25,000–300,000 lire ($12.50–$150).

If you're in the capital for the opera season—usually from the end of December until June—you may want to attend a performance at the historic Rome Opera House, located off Via Nazionale. Nothing is presented here in August; in summer, the venue usually changes. Call ahead or ask your hotel concierge before you go. You can buy tickets at the box office (closed Monday), at any Banca di Roma bank, or by phone at ☎ 147/882-211.

BALLET & DANCE

Performances of the Rome Opera Ballet are given at the **Teatro dell'Opera** (see above). The regular repertoire of classical ballet is supplemented by performances of internationally acclaimed guest artists, and Rome is on the agenda for major troupes from around the world. Watch for announcements in the weekly entertainment guides to see what's happening at the time of your visit and to check on other venues, including the Teatro Olimpico and open-air performances.

A MEAL & A SONG

Da Ciceruacchio. On Piazza dei Mercanti, at Via del Porto 1, in Trastevere. ☎ **06-580-6046.** 40,000–60,000 lire ($20–$30). Tues–Sun 7:30pm–midnight.

This restaurant was once a sunken jail; the ancient vine-covered walls date from the 18th century. Folkloric groups appear throughout the evening, especially singers of Neapolitan songs, accompanied by guitars and harmonicas. It's a rich repertoire of old-time favorites, some with bawdy lyrics. There are charcoal-broiled steaks and chops along with lots of local wine, and bean soup is a specialty. The grilled mushrooms are another harmonious opening, as is the spaghetti with clams.

Da Meo Patacca. Piazza dei Mercanti 30, in Trastevere. ☎ **06-5833-1086.** Daily 8–11:30pm.

Da Meo Patacca would have pleased Barnum and Bailey. On a gaslit piazza from the Middle Ages, it serves bountiful self-styled "Roman country" meals to flocks of tourists. The atmosphere is one of extravaganza—primitive, colorful, and theatrical in a carnival sense. It's touristy, all right, but good fun if you're in the mood. Downstairs is a vast cellar with strolling musicians and singers. Many offerings are as adventurous as the decor (wild boar, wild hare, and quail), but you'll also find corn on the cob, pork and beans, thick-cut sirloins, and chicken on a spit. For 55,000 lire ($27.50) and more, you'll get fun and entertainment—not refined cuisine. In summer, you can dine at outdoor tables.

Fantasie di Trastevere. Via di Santa Dorotea 6. ☎ **06-588-1671.** Cover (including the first drink) 35,000 lire ($17.50), 80,000–120,000 lire ($40–$60) including dinner. Meals daily from 8pm; piano bar music 8:30–9:30pm; show 9:30–10:30pm.

Roman rusticity is combined with theatrical flair at Fantasie di Trastevere, the people's theater where the famous actor Petrolini made his debut. In the 16th century, this restaurant was an old theater built for Queen Cristina of Sweden and her court. The cuisine is bountiful, though hardly subtle. Such dishes as the classic saltimbocca (ham with veal) are preceded by tasty pasta, and everything is helped along by Castelli Romani wines. Accompanying the main dishes is a big basket of warm, country-coarse herb bread. Some two dozen folk singers and musicians in regional attire make it a festive affair.

2 The Club & Music Scene

NIGHTCLUBS/DANCE CLUBS

Alien. Vla Vellertri 13–19. ☎ **06-841-2212.** Cover (including the first drink) 30,000–35,000 lire ($15–$17.50). Tues–Sat 11pm–5am. Bus 3, 4, or 57.

In a setting of high-tech futuristic rows of exposed pipes and ventilation ducts, Alien provides a bizarre space-age dance floor, bathed in strobe lights and rocking to the sounds of house/techno music. Occasionally, a master of ceremonies will interject brief interludes of cabaret or comedy.

Alpheus. Via del Commercio 36. ☎ **06-574-7826.** Cover 10,000–20,000 lire ($5–$10). Tues–Sun 10pm–4am. Bus: 713.

One of Rome's largest and most energetic nightclubs, Alpheus contains three sprawling rooms, each with a different musical sound and an ample number of bars. You'll find areas devoted to Latin music, to rock, and to jazz. Live bands come and go, and there's enough cultural variety in the crowd to keep virtually anyone amused throughout the course of the evening.

Berimbau. Via di Fienaroli 30B. ☎ **06-581-3249** weekends. Cover 15,000–20,000 lire ($7.50–$10), including first drink. Fri–Sat 10:30pm–dawn.

The spirit is South American *latino,* the decor evokes the southern Mediterranean, and the rhythms are pure Caribbean, including Cuban and Dominican sounds.

Black Out. Via Saturnia 18. ☎ **06-704-96791.** Cover (including the first drink) 10,000–15,000 lire ($5–$7.50). Thurs–Sat 10:30pm–4am.

If you're looking for a little counterculture edge, where you might hear the latest indie music from the U.K., head for Black Out, which occupies an industrial-looking site. Whenever it can manage, a live band is presented on Thursday—very late. The

Nightlife Tips

In addition to high charges (all nightclubs in Rome are expensive), many otherwise legitimate clubs have add-on expenses in the form of hookers plying their trade.

Another important warning: During the peak of summer tourism, usually in August, all nightclub proprietors seem to lock their doors and head for the seashore, where they operate alternate clubs. Some of them close at different times each year, so it's hard to keep up-to-date. Always have your hotel check to see whether a club is operating before you trek out to it.

Testaccio may be radical chic personified, but it's also a neighborhood with an edge (you don't want to wander around here alone at night). However, Testaccio is the place to find out what's hot in Rome—ask around.

recorded music includes punk, retro, R&B, grunge, and whatever else happens to be in fashion. There's always one room (with an independent sound system) set aside as a lounge.

Club Picasso. Via Monte di Testaccio 63. ☎ **06-574-2975.** No cover Tues–Thurs, 15,000 lire ($7.50) Fri, 20,000 lire ($10) Sat. Tues–Sun 8pm–4am. Bus: 95.

This high-energy dance spot attracts everyone from teeny-boppers to 50-year-olds (who remember some of the music as original to their college years) and lots of high-energy people-watchers in between. A strict bouncer at the door bars any potential trouble-makers. There's a pizzeria, where you can grab a cheap bite.

Gilda. Via Mario de' Fiori 97. ☎ **06-678-4838.** Cover (including the first drink) 40,000 lire ($20); meals from 45,000 lire ($22.50). Disco Tues–Sun midnight–4am; restaurant from 9:30pm. Metro: Spagna.

Gilda is a combination of nightclub, disco, and restaurant known for its glamorous acts (past performances include Diana Ross and splashy, Paris-type revues). The artistic direction assures first-class shows, a well-run restaurant (featuring international cuisine), and disco music played between the live acts. The disco offers music from the 1960s to the present. The attractive piano bar, Swing, features Italian and Latin music.

Jackie O. Via Boncompagni 11. ☎ **06-4288-5457.** Cover (including the first drink) 40,000 lire ($20). Meals 80,000 lire ($40) without wine. Tues–Sun 8:30pm–4am.

Close to the American Embassy and Via Veneto, Jackie O is a glittery club that draws an affluent, well-dressed, over-30 crowd. If you opt to go dancing here (it's not as frenzied as some might like), you might begin your evening with a drink at the piano bar, then perhaps end it in the restaurant.

Magic Fly. Via Bassanello 15, Cassia-Grottarossa. ☎ **06-3326-8956.** Cover (including the first drink) 10,000–30,000 lire ($5–$15). Wed–Sat 10:30pm–dawn.

Small-scale and somewhat cramped when it really begins to rock, this club is more elegant than the norm and lies about 3 miles to the northeast, outside the ring road that encircles the center of Rome. Music changes nightly; depending on the schedule, you might hear anything from Latin salsa and merengue to American-style rock or British new wave. There's a posh feel throughout (enhanced by the many men in neckties). You'll need to take a taxi to get here.

Radio Londra. Via Monte Testaccio 67. No phone. Cover (including the first drink) 20,000 lire ($10). Club: Wed–Mon 11:30am–4am; pub/pizzeria: Sun–Mon and Wed–Fri 9pm–3am, Sat 9pm–4am. Bus: 95.

Radio Londra revels in the counterculture ambience of punk rock, inspired, as its name implies, by the chartreuse-haired, nose-pierced variety from London. Since Radio Londra is near the popular gay L'Alibi (see below), the downstairs club attracts many brethren, though the crowd is mixed. Upstairs is a pub/pizzeria where bands often appear; you can even order a veggie burger with a Bud.

JAZZ & OTHER LIVE SOUNDS

Alexanderplatz. Via Ostia 9. ☎ **06-3974-2171.** Club membership (valid for 3 months) 12,000 lire ($6). Mon–Sat 9pm–2am, live music from 10:15pm. Bus: 23.

At this leading jazz club you can listen to the music or enjoy the good kitchen, which serves everything from pesto alla genovese to gnocchi alla romana to Japanese cuisine.

✪ **Arciliuto.** Piazza Monte Vecchio 5. ☎ **06-6879419.** Cover (including the first drink) 35,000 lire ($17.50). Mon–Sat 10pm–2am. Closed July 20–Sept 3. Bus: 42, 62, or 64.

This place reputedly once housed Raphael's studio, but now it's home to one of the most romantic candlelit spots in Rome. Guests listen to both a guitarist and a lute player in an intimate setting. The evening's presentation also includes Neapolitan love songs, old Italian madrigals, even current hits from New York's Broadway or London's West End. Highly recommended, it's hard to find, but is within walking distance of Piazza Navona. From the west side of Piazza Navona, take Via di S. Agnese in Agone, which leads to Via di Tor Milliana, then follow this street into Piazza Monte Vecchio.

✪ **Big Mama.** Vicolo San Francesco a Ripa 18. ☎ **06-581-2551.** Cover 20,000–30,000 lire ($10–$15) for big acts (free for minor shows), plus 20,000 lire ($10) seasonal membership fee. Mon–Sat 9pm–1:30am. Closed July–Sept. Bus: 44, 75, or 170.

Big Mama is a hangout for jazz and blues musicians, where you're likely to meet the up-and-coming jazz stars of tomorrow and sometimes even the big names.

Fonclea. Via Crescenzio 82A. ☎ **06-689-6302.** No cover Sun–Fri; 10,000 lire ($5) Sat. Sun–Thurs 7pm–2am, Fri–Sat 7pm–3:30am. Closed July–Aug. Bus: 32 or 39.

Fonclea offers live music every night—jazz, Dixieland, rock, rhythm and blues, and funk. This is basically a cellar jazz bar that attracts folks from all walks of Roman life. There's also a restaurant that features moderately priced grilled meats, salads, and crêpes; if you want dinner it's best to reserve a table. Music usually starts at 9:15pm and lasts until about 12:30am.

Saint Louis Music City. Via del Cardello 13A. ☎ **06-474-5076.** Cover (including club membership) 9,000 lire ($4.50). Tues–Sun 9pm–2am.

This is another leading jazz venue, offering soul and funk sometimes, too. In large, contemporary surroundings, Saint Louis Music City features young and sometimes very talented newcomers. The crowd includes the occasional celeb. You can order a moderately priced meal here.

GAY & LESBIAN CLUBS

Two English-speaking gay and lesbian organizations can be found in Rome: **ARCI-Gay,** Via Primo Acciaresi 7 (☎ **06-862-02-728;** Bus: 71) and **Circolo Mario Mieli,** Via Efeso 2 (☎ **06-54-13-985;** Metro: San Paolo). Both are helpful with political and social information.

Angelo Azzuro. Via Cardinal Merry del Val 13. ☎ **06-580-0472.** Cover, including 1 drink, 20,000 lire ($10). Bus: 44, 75, or 170.

This is a gay hot spot deep in the heart of Trastevere, open Friday, Saturday, and Sunday 11pm to 4am. Men dance with men to recorded music, though women are also invited (Friday is for women only).

◐ The Hangar. Via in Selci 69. ☎ **06-4881397.** No cover. Club membership 5,000 lire ($2.50). Wed–Mon 10:30pm–2:30am. Closed 3 weeks in Aug. Metro: Cavour.

Having survived since 1984, the Hangar is a landmark on the gay nightlife scene. It's on one of Rome's oldest streets, adjacent to the Forum, on the site of the palace once inhabited by Claudius's deranged wife Messalina. Each of the Hangar's two bars has an independent sound system. Women are welcome any night except Monday, when the club features videos and entertainment for men. The busiest nights are Saturday, Sunday, and Monday, when as many as 500 people cram inside.

Joli Coeur. Via Sirte 5. ☎ **06-8621-6240.** Cover (including the first drink) 20,000 lire ($10). Sat–Sun 11pm–5am. Bus: 52 or 56.

This bar caters to lesbians; Saturdays are reserved for women only. A fixture in the city's lesbian night scene, it also attracts women from around Europe. Information about Joli Coeur (pretty heart) can be had by contacting The Hangar (see above), as Joli Coeur can be difficult to reach directly.

L'Alibi. Via Monte Testaccio 44. ☎ **06-574-3448.** Cover 25,000 lire ($12.50). Tues–Sun 11pm–4am. Bus: 95.

L'Alibi, in the Testaccio sector away from the heart of Rome, is a year-round stop on many a gay man's agenda. The crowd, however, tends to be mixed: Roman and international, straight and gay, male and female. One room is devoted to dancing.

3 The Cafe & Bar Scene

It seems there's nothing Romans like better than sitting and talking over their favorite beverage—usually wine or coffee. Unless you're dead set on making the Roman nightclub circuit, try what might be a far livelier and less expensive scene—sitting late at night on **Via Veneto, Piazza della Rotonda, Piazza del Popolo,** or one of Rome's other piazzas, all for the cost of an espresso, a cappuccino, or a Campari.

If you're looking for some scrumptious **ice cream,** see Café Rosati and Giolitti below as well as the box "Take a Gelato Break" in chapter 5.

CAFES
ON VIA VENETO

Back in the 1950s (a decade *Time* magazine gave to Rome, in the way it conceded the 1960s and later the 1990s to London), **Via Vittorio Veneto** rose in fame as the hippest street in Rome, crowded with aspiring and actual movie stars, their directors, and a fast-rising group of card-carrying members of the jet set. Today, the beautiful people wouldn't be caught dead on Via Veneto—it's become touristy. Nevertheless, you may want to check it out for old times' sake.

◐ Caffè de Paris. Via Vittorio Veneto 90. ☎ **06-488-5284.** Metro: Barberini.

This spot has been around for decades. It's popular in summer, when the tables spill right out onto the sidewalk and the passing crowd walks through the maze.

Harry's Bar. Via Vittorio Veneto 150. ☎ **06-484-643.**

Sophisticated Harry's Bar is a perennial favorite. Every major Italian city (like Florence and Venice) seems to have one, and Rome is no exception, though this one has no connection with the others. In summer, tables are placed outside. For those who wish to dine outdoors but want to avoid the scorching sun, there's an air-conditioned sidewalk cafe open May to November. Meals inside cost about double what you'd pay outside. In back is a small dining room serving some of the finest (and priciest) food in central Rome. The restaurant inside is open Monday to Saturday 12:30 to 3pm and 7:30pm to 1am. Outside you can eat from noon to midnight. The bar is open Monday to Saturday 11am to 2am (closed August 1 to 10), and the piano bar is open nightly from 9:30pm, with live music starting at 11pm.

NEAR PIAZZA NAVONA

Bar della Pace. Via della Pace 3–5. ☎ **06-686-1216.** Mon 3pm–3am; Tues–Sun 9am–3am.

Bar della Pace, located near Piazza Navona, has elegant neighbors, such as Santa Maria della Pace, a church with sibyls by Raphael and a cloister designed by Bramante. The bar dates from the beginning of this century and is decorated with wood, marble, and mirrors.

NEAR THE PANTHEON

The **Piazza della Rotonda,** across from the Pantheon, is the hopping place to be after dark, especially in summer.

✪ Caffè Sant'Eustachio. Piazza Sant'Eustachio 82. ☎ **06-686-1309.** Tues–Fri and Sun 8:30am–1am; Sat 8:30am–1:30am. Bus: 116.

Strongly-brewed coffee is liquid fuel to Italians, and many Romans will walk blocks and blocks for what they consider a superior brew. Caffè Sant'Eustachio is one of Rome's most celebrated espresso shops, where the water supply is funneled into the city by an aqueduct built in 19 B.C. Rome's most experienced espresso judges claim the water plays an important part in the coffee's flavor, though steam forced through ground Brazilian coffee roasted on the premises has a significant effect as well. Buy a ticket from the cashier for as many cups as you want, then leave a small tip (about 900 to 1,000 lire/45¢ to 50¢) for the counter-person when you present your receipt. It's open Tuesday to Friday and Sunday 8:30am to 1am and Saturday 8:30am to 1:30am.

Ciampini. Piazza San Lorenzo in Lucina 29. ☎ **06-687-6606.** Mon–Sat 7:30am–9pm. Bus: 116.

This stylish, breezy spot has a staff that's usually hysterically overburdened, with little time for small talk. But despite the fact that service might be slow, a crowd of midday office workers loyally returns for morning shots of espresso; affordable, filling salads at lunch; and tea in the afternoon.

✪ Di Rienzo. Piazza della Rotonda 8–9. ☎ **06-6869097.** Daily 7am–1 or 2am. Bus: 116.

This is the top cafe on this piazza. In fair weather, you can sit at one of the sidewalk tables (if you can find a free one). In cooler weather, you can retreat inside, where the walls are inlaid with the type of marble found on the Pantheon's floor. Many types of pastas appear on the menu, as does *risotto alla pescatora* (fisherman's rice) and several meat courses. You can also order pizzas.

La Caffettiera. Piazza di Pietra 65. ☎ **06-679-8147.** Mon–Sat 7am–9pm. Bus: 116.

In a comfortable, albeit bustling setting, you can enjoy a refreshingly light and easy meal, like a sandwich or a slice of quiche, or just a quick fix of caffeine. Lots of folks drop in for the Neapolitan-style ice-cream confections in the afternoon.

Tazza d'Oro. Piazza della Rotonda, Via degli Orfani 84. ☎ **06-678-2792.** Daily 7:30am–1am. Bus: 116.

This cafe is known for serving its own brand of espresso. Another specialty, ideal on a hot summer night, is *granità di caffè* (coffee that has been frozen, crushed into a velvety slushlike ice, and placed in a glass between layers of whipped cream).

On the Corso & Piazza Colonna

Autogrill. Via del Corso 181. ☎ **06-678-9135.** Daily 7am–10pm.

Autogrill is a monumental cafe that's often filled with busy shoppers. There's a stand-up sandwich bar with dozens of selections and a cafeteria, both self-serve and with a sit-down area. The decor includes high coffered ceilings, baroque wall stencils, globe lights, crystal chandeliers, and black stone floors.

Giolitti. Via Uffici del Vicario 40. ☎ **06-699-1243.** Bus: 116.

Near Piazza Colonna, this is one of the city's most popular nighttime gathering spots and the oldest ice-cream shop. Some of the sundaes look like Vesuvius about to erupt. Many people take gelato out to eat on the streets; others enjoy it in the post-empire splendor of the salon inside. You can have your "coppa" daily 7am to 2am (closed at 1am in winter). There are many excellent, smaller gelaterie throughout Rome, wherever you see the cool concoction advertised as *produzione propria* (homemade). See the box "Take a Gelato Break" in chapter 5.

On or Near Piazza del Popolo

This piazza is haunted with memories. According to legend, the ashes of Nero were enshrined here until 11th-century residents began complaining to the pope about his imperial ghost. The Egyptian obelisk seen here today dates from the 13th century B.C.; it was removed from Heliopolis to Rome during the reign of Augustus (it originally stood at the Circus Maximus). The present piazza was designed in the early 19th century by Valadier, Napoléon's architect. Two almost-twin baroque churches stand on the square, overseeing the never-ending traffic.

✪ Café Rosati. Piazza del Popolo 5A. ☎ **06-322-5859.** Daily noon–11pm. Bus: 117.

Café Rosati, which has been around since 1923, attracts guys and dolls of all persuasions who drive up in Maseratis and Porsches. It's really a combination of sidewalk cafe, ice-cream parlor, candy store, confectionery, and *ristorante* that has been swept up in the fickle world of fashion. The later you go, the more interesting the action.

Canova Café. Piazza del Popolo 16. ☎ **06-361-2231.** Meals 25,000 lire ($12.50). Restaurant daily noon–3:30pm and 7–11pm; bar daily 8am to midnight or 1am. Bus: 117.

Though the management has filled it with boutiques selling expensive gift items, like luggage and cigarette lighters, many Romans still consider Canova Café *the* place to be on the piazza. The Canova has a sidewalk terrace for people-watching, plus a snack bar, a restaurant, and a wine shop. In summer, you'll have access to a courtyard whose walls are covered with ivy and where flowers grow in terra-cotta planters. A buffet meal is 25,000 lire ($12.50) and up. Food is served daily noon to 3:30pm and 7 to 11pm, but the bar is open 8am to midnight or 1am depending on the crowd.

Night & Day. Via dell'Oca 50. ☎ **06-320-2300.** No cover. Drinks 6,000 lire ($3). Daily 5pm–5am.

It sounds like an old Cole Porter song, but it's actually one of the most popular Irish pubs near Piazza del Popolo. It really heats up around 2am, when many dance clubs close for the evening. American music is played as you down your Harps and Guinness. Amazingly, foreigners are issued drink cards, making all their drinks 6,000 lire ($3) instead of the 8,000 lire ($4) usually charged. A young man in his 20s, who introduces himself only as "Simone," is your host and often works behind the bar himself.

NEAR THE SPANISH STEPS

○ Antico Caffè Greco. Via Condotti 84. ☎ **06-679-1700.** Mon–Sat 8am–9pm. Closed 10 days in Aug. Metro: Spagna.

Since 1760, this has been Rome's poshest coffee bar. Stendhal, Goethe, Keats, and D'Annunzio have sipped coffee here before you. Today, you're more likely to see ladies who lunch and American tourists, but there's plenty of atmosphere. In front is a wooden bar and beyond is a series of small salons. You sit at marble-topped tables of Napoleonic design, against a backdrop of gold or red damask, romantic paintings, and antique mirrors. The house specialty is *paradisi,* made with lemon and orange.

La Buvette. Via Vittoria 44–47. ☎ **06-679-0383.** Mon–Sat 7am–8:30pm. Metro: Spagna.

This place is both a cafe and an unpretentious restaurant. No one will mind if you come here just for an espresso, but if you're hungry, consider ordering one of the meal-sized salads, which serious shoppers from the nearby Via Condotti order as a pick-me-up in the heat and humidity of a hot Roman midday. More elaborate platters are also available.

IN TRASTEVERE

Several cafes in Trastevere, across the Tiber, are attracting crowds. Fans who saw Fellini's *Roma* know what **Piazza Santa Maria in Trastevere** looks like at night. The square, filled with milling throngs in summer, is graced with an octagonal fountain and a 12th-century church. Children run and play on the piazza, and occasional spontaneous guitar fests break out when the weather's good.

Café-Bar di Marzio. Piazza di Santa Maria in Trastevere 15. ☎ **06-581-6095.** Daily 7am–2am. Closed Mon in Feb. Bus: 44, 75, or 170.

This warmly inviting place, which is strictly a cafe (not a restaurant), has both indoor and outdoor tables at the edge of the square with the best view of its famous fountain.

Pasquino-Net. Piazza San Egidio, just off Piazza di Santa Maria in Trastevere. ☎ **06-580-3622.** Bus: 44, 75, or 170.

If you want to send or receive e-mails, surf the Web, or flirt with an anonymous stranger online, this place maintains about a dozen computers that they'll rent to you for between 7,500 to 9,900 lire ($3.75 to $4.95) per hour, depending on when you show up. A brief look-see at your e-mail, if you remain online for less than about 10 minutes, goes for 2,000 lire ($1). It's open daily from 4pm to midnight. You can also enjoy drinks and affordable burgers, pastas, salads, and steaks. It's associated with the also-recommended Pasquino Cinema.

WINE BARS

○ Enoteca Fratelli Roffi Isabelli. Via della Croce 76B. ☎ **06-679-0896.** Restaurant daily 12:30–3:30pm and 7:30–11pm; bar daily 11:30am–1am.

Wine has played a prominent role in Roman life since the word *bacchanalian* was first invented (and that was very early indeed). One of the best places to taste the wines of Italy is at the Enoteca Fratelli Roffi Isabelli. A stand-up drink in these darkly antique confines is the perfect ending to a visit to the nearby Spanish Steps. Set behind a discreet facade in a chic shopping district, this is the city's best repository for Italian wines, brandies, and grappa. You can opt for a postage-stamp-sized table in the back or stay at the bar with its impressive display of wines stacked on shelves in every available corner.

Il Goccetto. Via dei Banchi Vecchi 14. ☎ **06-686-4268.** Mon–Sat 11am–2pm and 5–11pm.

Set near Campo de' Fiori, Il Goccetto specializes in French and Italian wines by the glass at prices that range from 5,000 lire ($2.50) for a simple Chianti to as much as 18,000 lire ($9) for a glass of French champagne. Platters of food are on hand to assuage your hunger pangs, but don't expect anything hot, as there are no real kitchen facilities. Instead, you'll be presented with an extensive list of Italian cheeses and processed meats, especially salami and pâtés, as well as an occasional salad. Overall, this place provides an excellent site for the *degustazione* of a wide assortment of unusual Italian wines, many of them from less-well-known small producers.

La Bottega del Vino. Via Santa Maria del Pianto 9A–12. ☎ **06-686-5970.** Lunch Mon–Sat 12:30–3pm; wine bar and snacks Mon–Sat 12:30–3:30pm and 5–8:30pm.

This old-fashioned setting comes complete with terra-cotta floors and long, battered wooden tables. Everything acts as a foil for the Italian and French wines served here. Priced at 5,000 to 13,000 lire ($2.50 to $6.50) per glass, depending on the vintage, they derive from well-known or obscure vineyards throughout Italy. Affordable snacks and cold platters are available as accompaniment. Lunch features more elaborate offerings, like crushed crabmeat served in a roulade of smoked salmon, or a spinach, pear, and walnut salad. In other hours, the snacks are simpler, consisting mostly of salami, bread, and cheese, but always a good foil for the wines.

IRISH PUBS

The two most popular Irish pubs, both near Piazza di Santa Maria Maggiore, draw mostly English-speaking expatriates. You can always see a cluster of disoriented local teenagers here and there, but their Italian is drowned in the sea of English, Scottish, Irish, Canadian, Australian, and sometimes American accents.

Druid's Den. Via San Martino ai Monti 28. ☎ **06-488-0258.** Daily 5pm–12:30am. Metro: Termini.

At the popular Druid's Den you can enjoy a pint of beer while listening to Irish music. One night we saw a group of young Irishmen dancing an Irish jig, much to the delight of the Roman onlookers.

Fiddler's Elbow. Via dell'Olmata 43. ☎ **06-4872110.** Daily 4:30pm–12:30am. Metro: Termini.

Fiddler's Elbow, near Piazza di Santa Maria Maggiore and the railway station, is reputedly the oldest pub in the capital. Sometimes, however, the place is so packed you can't find room to drink.

4 At the Movies

Pasquino Cinema. Piazza San Egidio, just off Piazza di Santa Maria in Trastevere. ☎ **06-580-3622.** Tickets 12,000 lire ($6). Bus: 45, 65, 170, 181, or 280.

Just off the corner of Piazza Santa Maria in Trastevere, the little Pasquino draws faithful English-speaking fans, both Italians and expatriates. You might catch the occasional classic amid the more recent releases. Most are in their original language (usually English) with Italian subtitles. There are three theaters with screenings daily, as well as a bookshop selling videotapes and movie posters, an Internet cafe (Pasquino-Net, which is recommended separately), and a bar. Films usually start at 4pm, with the day's last film usually beginning at 10:30pm.

Side Trips from Rome 10

Most European capitals are surrounded with a number of worthwhile attractions, but Rome tops them all for sheer variety. Just a few miles from Rome, you can go back to the dawn of Italian history and explore the dank tombs the Etruscans left as their legacy or drink the golden wine of the towns in the Alban Hills (Castelli Romani). You can wander the ruins of Hadrian's Villa, the "queen of villas of the ancient world," or be lulled by the music of the baroque fountains in the Villa d'Este. You can turn yourself bronze on the beaches of Ostia di Lido or explore the remarkable ruins of Ostia Antica, Rome's ancient seaport.

If you have time, the attractions in the environs can fill at least 3 days. We've highlighted the best of the lot below.

1 Tivoli

20 miles E of Rome

An ancient town, Tivoli predates Rome itself. At the height of the empire, "Tibur," as it was called, was a favorite retreat for the rich. Horace, Catullus, Sallust, Maecenas, and a few emperors (notably Hadrian) maintained lavish villas here near the woods and waterfalls. It was popular enough to warrant a Roman road, Via Tiburtina; its modern equivalent funnels trucks and tour buses into today's Tivoli. During the Middle Ages, Tivoli achieved a form of independence, which lasted through its rise in fortunes during the Renaissance. This latter period saw real-estate investment by several of the wealthier princes of the church, especially Cardinal Ippolito d'Este. By the late 19th century Tivoli had been incorporated into the new kingdom of Italy, and its former privileges of independence passed into history.

ESSENTIALS

GETTING THERE   Take Metro Linea B to the end of the line, the Rebibbia station. After exiting the station, catch an Acotral bus the rest of the 30-minute ride to Tivoli. Generally buses depart about every 20 minutes and the fare is about 10,000 lire ($5) each way.

If you drive, expect about an hour's drive with traffic on Via Tiburtina.

VISITOR INFORMATION   Check with **Azienda Autonoma di Turismo,** Largo Garibaldi (☎ **0774-334-522**), open Monday to Saturday from 9am to 2:30pm and Tuesday to Friday 9am to 2pm and 3 to 6pm.

EXPLORING THE VILLAS

✪ **Hadrian's Villa (Villa Adriana).** Via di Villa Adriana. ☎ **0774-530-203.** Admission 8,000 lire ($4). Daily 9am–sunset (about 6:30pm in summer, 4pm Nov–Mar). Closed New Year's Day, May Day, and Christmas. Bus: 2 or 4 from Tivoli.

The globe-trotting Hadrian spent the last 3 years of his life in the grandest style. Less than 4 miles (6km) from Tivoli, he built one of the greatest estates ever erected in the world and filled acre after acre with some of the architectural wonders he'd seen on his many travels. A preview of what he envisioned in store for himself, the emperor even created a representation of hell centuries before Dante got around to recording its horrors. Hadrian was a patron of the arts, a lover of beauty, and even something of an architect, and he directed the staggering feat of building much more than a villa: It was a self-contained world for a vast royal entourage and the hundreds of servants and guards they required to protect them, feed them, bathe them, and satisfy their libidos.

Hadrian erected theaters, baths, temples, fountains, gardens, and canals bordered with statuary throughout his estate. He filled the palaces and temples with sculpture, some of which now rests in the museums of Rome. In later centuries, barbarians, popes, and cardinals, as well as anyone who needed a slab of marble, carted off much that made the villa so spectacular. But enough of the fragmented ruins remain for us to piece together the story.

For a glimpse of what the villa used to be, see the plastic reconstruction at the entrance. Then, following the arrows around, look in particular for the **Marine Theater** (ruins of the round structure with Ionic pillars); the **Great Baths,** with some intact mosaics; and the **Canopus,** with a group of *caryatids* (fully draped, sculpted female figures used for support in the place of columns or pilasters) whose images are reflected in the pond, as well as a statue of Mars. For a closer look at some of the items excavated, you can visit the museum on the premises and a museum and visitor center near the villa parking area.

✪ **Villa d'Este.** Piazza Trento, Viale delle Centro Fontane. ☎ **0774-312-070.** Admission 10,000 lire ($5), children age 17 and under and seniors free. Nov–Feb daily 9am–4pm; Mar to mid-Apr daily 9am–4:30pm; mid-Apr to mid-Sept daily 9am–6:30pm; mid-Sept to Oct daily 9am–4:30pm. The bus from Rome stops right near the entrance.

Like Hadrian centuries before, Cardinal Ippolito d'Este of Ferrara believed in heaven on earth, and in the mid–16th century, he ordered this villa built on a hillside. The dank Renaissance structure, with its second-rate paintings, is hardly worth the trek from Rome, but the gardens below (designed by Pirro Ligorio) dim the luster of those at Versailles.

You descend the cypress-studded slope to the bottom and on the way are rewarded with everything from lilies to gargoyles spouting water, torrential streams, and waterfalls. The loveliest fountain is the **Ovato Fountain (Fontana dell Ovato),** by Ligorio. But nearby is the most spectacular achievement: the **Fountain of the Hydraulic Organ (Fontana dell'Organo Idraulico),** dazzling with its water jets in front of a baroque chapel, with four maidens who look tipsy. The work represents the genius of Frenchman Claude Veanard. The moss-covered **Fountain of the Dragons (Fontana dei Draghi),** also by Ligorio, and the so-called **Fountain of Glass (Fontana di Vetro)** by Bernini are the most intriguing. The best walk is along the promenade, with 100 spraying fountains. The garden is worth hours of exploration, but you'll need frequent rests after those steep climbs.

Villa Gregoriana. Largo Sant'Angelo. ☎ **0774-334-522.** Admission 3,500 lire ($1.75), 1,000 lire (50¢) children ages 11 and under. May–Aug daily 10am–7:30pm; Sept daily 9:30am–6:30pm; Oct–Mar daily 9:30am–4:30pm; Apr daily 9:30am–6pm. The bus from Rome stops near the entrance.

Side Trips from Rome

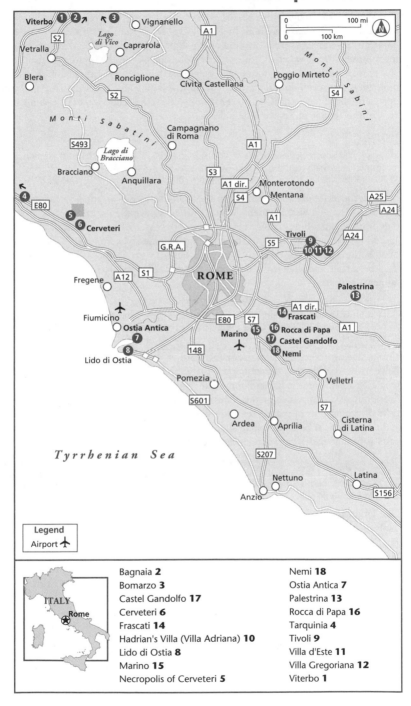

100 mi
100 km

Viterbo ① ② ⟋ ⟍ ③ Vignanello
S2
Vetralla
Blera
Lago di Vico
Caprarola
Ronciglione
Civita Castellana
Campagnano di Roma
A1
Poggio Mirteto
Monti Sabini
S4
S2
Monti Sabatini
S493
Lago di Bracciano
Bracciano
Anquillara
S3
A1 dir.
S4
Monterotondo
Mentana
A25
A24
④ E80
⑤ ⑥ Cerveteri
G.R.A.
A1
Tivoli ⑨ ⑩ ⑪ ⑫
A24
S5
Fregene
A12
S1
ROME
Palestrina ⑬
Fiumicino
Ostia Antica ⑦
⑧ Lido di Ostia
E80
S7
⑭ Frascati
A1 dir.
A1
Marino ⑮ ⑯ Rocca di Papa
⑰ Castel Gandolfo
⑱ Nemi
148
Pomezia
Velletrl
S601
Ardea
Aprília
S7
Cisterna di Latina
Tyrrhenian Sea
S207
Latina
Nettuno
S156
Anzio

Legend
Airport ✈

ITALY
Rome

Bagnaia **2**	Nemi **18**
Bomarzo **3**	Ostia Antica **7**
Castel Gandolfo **17**	Palestrina **13**
Cerveteri **6**	Rocca di Papa **16**
Frascati **14**	Tarquinia **4**
Hadrian's Villa (Villa Adriana) **10**	Tivoli **9**
Lido di Ostia **8**	Villa d'Este **11**
Marino **15**	Villa Gregoriana **12**
Necropolis of Cerveteri **5**	Viterbo **1**

The Villa d'Este dazzles with artificial glamour, but the Villa Gregoriana relies more on nature. The gardens were built by Pope Gregory XVI in the 19th century. At one point on the circuitous walk carved along a slope, you can stand and look out onto the most panoramic waterfall (Aniene) at Tivoli. The trek to the bottom on the banks of the Anio is studded with grottoes and balconies that open onto the chasm. The only problem is that if you do make the full journey, you may need a helicopter to pull you up again (the climb back is fierce). From one of the belvederes, there's a panoramic view of the Temple of Vesta on the hill.

DINING

Albergo Ristorante Adriano. Via di Villa Adriana 194. ☎ **0774-535-028.** Reservations recommended. Main courses 24,000–32,000 lire ($12–$16). AE, DC, MC, V. Mon–Sat 12:30–2:30pm and 8–10pm, Sun 12:30–2:30pm. Bus: 2 or 4 from Tivoli. ITALIAN.

In a stucco-sided villa a few steps from the ticket office sits an idyllic stop for either before or after you visit Hadrian's Villa. It offers terrace dining under plane trees or indoor dining in a high-ceilinged room with terra-cotta walls, neoclassical moldings, and white Corinthian pilasters. The cooking is home-style, and the menu includes roast lamb, saltimbocca (veal cooked with ham), a variety of veal dishes, deviled chicken, salads and cheeses, and simple desserts. They're especially proud of their homemade pastas.

Le Cinque Statue. Via Quintillio Varo 8. ☎ **0774-335-366.** Reservations recommended. Main courses 14,000–26,000 lire ($7–$13). AE, DC, MC, V. Mon and Thurs–Sat 12:30–3pm and 7–11pm; Sun 12:30–3pm. Closed Aug 16–25. The Acotral bus from Rome stops nearby. ROMAN.

This restaurant takes its name from the quintet of old carved statues (like Apollo Belvedere and gladiators) decorating the place. Today, this comfortable place is maintained by a hardworking Italian family that prepares an honest, unpretentious cuisine. Everything is accompanied by the wines of the hill towns of Rome. Begin with a pastiche of mushrooms or make a selection from the excellent antipasti. Try the rigatoni with fresh herbs, tripe fried Roman style, or mixed fry of brains and vegetables. All the pasta is freshly made. They also have a wide array of ice creams and fruits.

2 Palestrina

24 miles E of Rome

Like Tibur, ancient Preneste (as Palestrina was called) was a superb holiday spot. It was the favorite of Horace, Pliny, and even Hadrian, who maintained a villa here.

GETTING THERE

Buses leave every 30 to 45 minutes during the day from Rome; departures are from Via Castro Pretorio (take the Metro to the stop at Castro Pretorio to catch the bus). It takes about an hour to reach Palestrina and costs about 2,500 lire ($1.25).

Take either Via Prenestina (much less trafficked than Via Tiburtina), or the Autostrada (A2) and get off at Valmontana; the latter route is much quicker.

EXPLORING THE TOWN

If you go out of Rome through the Porta Maggiore and travel on Via Prenestina for about 24 miles, you'll eventually come to Palestrina, a medieval hillside town that overlooks a wide valley.

When U.S. airmen flew over in World War II and bombed part of the town, they never imagined their actions would launch Palestrina as an important tourist attraction. After the debris was cleared, a pagan temple (once one of the greatest in the world) emerged: the **Fortuna Primigenia,** rebuilt in the days of the empire but dating from centuries before. In Palestrina you'll also find a **Duomo** dating from 1100, with a mostly intact bell tower.

Palestrina predates the founding of Rome by several hundred years. It resisted conquest by the early Romans and later took the wrong side in the civil war between Marius and Sulla. When Sulla won, he razed every stone in the city except the Temple of Fortune and then built a military barracks on the site. Later, as a favorite vacation spot for the emperors and their entourages, it sheltered some of the most luxurious villas of the Roman empire. Its most famous child was Pier Luigi da Palestrina, recognized as the father of polyphonic harmony.

Colonna-Barberini Palace. Palazzo Barberini. ☎ **06-481-4591.** Admission 12,000 lire ($6) adults, free for children ages 17 and under. Tues–Sat 9am–7pm, Sun 9am–1pm. Follow the signs from the center to the top of the town.

High on a hill overlooking the valley, the palace today houses Roman statuary found in the ruins, plus Etruscan artifacts, such as urns the equal of those in Rome's Villa Giulia. But worth the trip itself is the **Nile Mosaic,** a well-preserved ancient Roman work and the most remarkable ever uncovered. The mosaic details the flooding of the Nile, a shepherd's hunt, mummies, ibises, and Roman warriors, among other things.

ACCOMMODATIONS & DINING

Albergo Ristorante Stella (Restaurant Coccia). Piazza della Liberazione 3, Palestrina, 00036 Roma. ☎ **06-953-8172.** Fax 06-957-3360. 28 units. A/C TV TEL. 100,000 lire ($50) double; 160,000 lire ($80) suite. AE, DC, V. Free parking.

A contemporary hotel and restaurant, the Stella is in the commercial district of town on a cobblestone square filled with parked cars, trees, and a small fountain. The bedrooms remain rather basic, but comfortable. The simple lobby is filled with warm colors and contains curved leather couches and autographed photos of local sports heroes.

The sunny restaurant serves a zesty Roman cuisine. Meals start at 40,000 lire ($20). There's a small bar where you might have an aperitif. The bar and restaurant are open daily from noon to 3pm and 7 to 9pm.

3 The Castelli Romani

For the Roman emperor and the wealthy cardinal in the heyday of the Renaissance, the **Castelli Romani (Roman Castles)** exerted a powerful lure, and they still do. The Castelli aren't castles but hill towns—many of them with an ancient history and several producing well-regarded wines.

The ideal way to explore the hill towns is by car. But you can get a limited review by taking one of the buses (costing 2,500 lire/$1.25) that leaves every 20 minutes from Rome's Subaugusta stop on Metro Line A.

MARINO

Marino, the closest to Rome (only 15 miles away), is about 4½ miles off Via Appia Nuova, quite near Ciampino Airport. Much of Marino's original charm has fallen victim to modern builders, but the town is still the place to go each October during the **grape harvest.** Check with the Rome tourist office for the actual dates, as they vary from year to year. At that time, the town's fountains are switched from water to wine, and everyone drinks for free.

ROCCA DI PAPA

This, the most attractive of the hill towns, lies only some 6 miles from Marino. By car, the best route is 217 to the junction with 218, where you make a left turn. Before the intersection, you'll be high on a ridge above Lake Albano, where the views of the lake, the far woods, and the papal palace of Castel Gandolfo on the opposite mountain are superb.

Just before Rocca di Papa is the entrance to the toll road to **Monte Cavo.** A temple of Jove once stood on top of this mountain, and before that, the tribes of the area met with King Tarquin (the Proud) before Rome was a republic. At the top of the mountain is one of the most dramatic panoramic views in the hill towns, giving you a wide survey of the Alban Hills and the Castelli Romani. Down below, Rocca di Papa is a tangle of old streets and churches. A legend of dubious origin claims that Hannibal once camped just below the town in a wooded hollow.

NEMI

The Romans flock to **Nemi** in droves, particularly from April to June, for the succulent **strawberries** grown here, acclaimed by some gourmets as Europe's finest. In May, there's a strawberry festival.

Nemi was also known to the ancients. A temple to the huntress Diana was erected on **Lake Nemi,** which was said to be her "looking glass." In A.D. 37, Caligula built luxurious barges to float on the lake. The boats, lavishly fitted with bronze and marble, were sunk during Claudius's reign (he succeeded the insane Caligula) and were entirely forgotten until Mussolini drained the lake in the 1930s. Then the barges were found, set up in a lakeside museum, and remained as a wonder of ancient Rome until the Nazis burned them during their retreat.

At the **Roman Ship Museum (Museo delle Navi),** Via di Diana 15 (☎ 06-939-8040), you can see two scale models of the ships destroyed by the Nazis. The major artifacts on display are mainly copies, as the originals now rest in world-class museums. The museum is open daily: October to March 9am to noon, April and May to 5:30pm, and June to September 9am to 7pm. Admission is 4,000 lire ($2). To reach the museum, head from the center of Nemi toward the lake.

The 15th-century **Palazzo Ruspoli,** a private baronial estate, is the focal point of Nemi, but the town itself invites exploration—particularly the alleyways the locals call streets and the houses with balconies jutting out over the slopes.

DINING

✪ **Ristorante Il Castagnone.** In the Diana Park Hotel, Via Nemorense 44. ☎ **06-936-4041.** Reservations recommended. Main courses 20,000–40,000 lire ($10–$20). AE, DC, MC, V. Tues–Sun noon–3pm and 8–10pm. Closed Nov. ROMAN/SEAFOOD.

This well-managed dining room of the town's best hotel takes a definite pride in a Roman-based cuisine emphasizing seafood above meat. The attentive formal service is usually delivered with a kind of gentle humor. Amid neoclassical accessories and marble, you can order delectable veal, chicken, beef, and fish dishes like fried calamari, spaghetti with shellfish in garlicky tomato-based sauce, and roasted lamb with potatoes and Mediterranean herbs. As you dine, expect a sweeping lake view from the restaurant's windows.

Reserving Winery Tours

While exploring the Castelli Romani, the hill towns around Rome, you might want to visit some of the better-known wineries. The region's most famous producers of Frascati are **Fontana Candida,** Via di Fontana Candida, 00040 Monte Porzio Catone, Roma (☎ **06/942-0066**), whose winery, 14 miles southwest of Rome, was built around 1900; and **Gotto D'Oro–Cantina Sociale di Marino,** Via del Divino Amore 115, 00040 Frattocchie, Roma (☎ **06/935-6931** and 06/935-6932). To arrange visits, contact the **Gruppo Italiano Vini,** Villa Belvedere, 37010 Calmasino, Verona (☎ **045/626-0600**).

EN ROUTE TO CASTEL GANDOLFO

The road to Gandolfo leads us through a few worth-a-visit towns on the way. **Genzano,** on the other side of Lake Nemi, has views of the countryside and a 17th-century palace that belonged to the Sforza-Cesarini.

Ariccia is an ancient town that sent representatives to meet with Tarquin the Proud on top of Monte Cavo 2,500 years ago. After many centuries of changing hands, especially between medieval and Renaissance families, it has taken on a suburban look. The palace in the middle of town is still private and belongs to the Chigi family.

Albano practically adjoins Castel Gandolfo. It has a long history; this is the reputed site of Alba Longa, the so-called mother city of Rome, but it's quite built up and modern today. Trains going to Albano leave from Stazione Termini in Rome.

CASTEL GANDOLFO

Now we come to the summer residence of the pope. The papal palace, a 17th-century edifice designed by Carlo Maderno, stands practically on the foundations of another equally regal summer residence, the villa of Emperor Domitian. Unfortunately, the palace, the gardens, and the adjoining Villa Barberini can't be visited. You'll have to content yourself with a visit to **Piazza della Libertà,** the piazza out front with its church, Chiesa di San Tomaso di Villanova, and fountain by Bernini.

If you're here for lunch, as many are, your best bet is **Antico Ristorante Pagnanelli,** Via Gramsci 4 (☎ **06-9360004**), which serves both regional and pan-Italian dishes, with meals starting at 60,000 lire ($30), with a high of 80,000 lire ($40) for the fresh seafood dishes. The restaurant is closed Tuesdays.

FRASCATI

Lying 13 miles southeast of Rome, on Via Tuscolana, this is the best known of the hill towns. Some 1,073 feet above sea level, Frascati is celebrated for its white wines. Golden vineyards cover the surrounding northern slopes of the outer crater ring of the Alban Hills. From its lofty perch you'll see a panoramic view of the countryside and the other small towns.

ESSENTIALS

GETTING THERE   You can take an Acotral bus from the Anagnina station at the end of Metro Linea A in Rome. From there, take the Blue Cotral bus to Frascati; it takes 45 minutes and costs 2,500 lire ($1.25) each way. Remember that the transportation system in Italy is in a constant state of flux, so check your route at the station.

If you're driving, from the ring road around Rome (its southeast section), head southeast along Route 215.

VISITOR INFORMATION Tourist information is available at **Azienda di Soggiorno e Turismo,** at Piazza Marconi 1 (☎ 06-942-0331). It's open Tuesday to Friday from 8am to 2pm and 3:30 to 6:30pm in winter; otherwise Tuesday to Friday 9am to 2pm and 4 to 7pm, and Monday and Saturday 8am to 2pm.

WHAT TO SEE & DO: WINE TASTING, RENAISSANCE GARDENS & ANCIENT RUINS

Though Frascati wine is exported, and served in many of Rome's restaurants and trattorie, tradition holds that it's best near the vineyards from which it came. Romans drive up on Sunday just to drink it. To sample some of the golden white wine, head for **Cantina Comandini,** Via E. Filiberto 1 (☎ 06-942-0915), right off Piazza Roma. The Comandini family welcomes you to the wine cellar, a regional tavern in which they sell Frascati from their own vineyards. You can drink the wine on the spot for 6,000 lire ($3) per liter or 2,000 lire ($1) per glass and can buy sandwiches to go with your vino. The tavern is open Monday to Saturday 4 to 8pm. Reservations are required.

Stand in the heart of Frascati, at Piazza Marconi, to see the most important of the estates: **Villa Aldobrandini,** Via Massala. The finishing touches to this 16th-century villa were added by Maderno, who designed the facade of St. Peter's in Rome, but you can visit only the gardens. Still, with its grottoes, yew hedges, statuary, and splashing fountains, it makes for an exciting outing. The gardens are open Monday to Friday 9am to 1pm and 3 to 5pm (to 6pm in summer), but you must go to the **Azienda di Soggiorno e Turismo,** Piazza Marconi 1 (☎ 06-942-0331), to ask for a free pass. The office is open Monday to Saturday 8am to 2pm and also Tuesday to Friday 3:30 to 6:30pm in winter and 4 to 7pm in summer.

You may also want to visit the bombed-out **Villa Torlonia,** adjacent to Piazza Marconi. Its grounds have been converted into a public park whose chief treasure is the Theater of the Fountains, designed by Maderno.

If you have a car, you can continue about 3 miles (5km) past the Villa Aldobrandini to **Tuscolo,** an ancient spot with the ruins of an amphitheater dating from about the 1st century B.C. It offers what may be one of Italy's most panoramic views.

DINING

Cacciani Restaurant. Via Armando Diaz 13. ☎ 06-942-0378. Reservations required on weekends. Main courses 20,000–35,000 lire ($12–$21). AE, DC, MC, V. Tues–Sun 12:30–3pm and 7:30–10:30pm. Closed Jan 7–19 and Aug 18–27. ROMAN.

Cacciani is the top restaurant in Frascati, where the competition has always been tough. It boasts a terrace commanding a view of the valley, and the kitchen is exposed to the public. To start, we recommend the pasta specialties, such as *pasta cacio e pepe* (pasta with caciocavallo cheese and black pepper) or the original spaghetti with seafood and lentils. For a main course, the baby lamb with a sauce of white wine and vinegar is always fine. There is, of course, a large choice of wine. If you call ahead, the Cacciani family will arrange a visit to several of Frascati's wine-producing villas along with a memorable meal at their restaurant.

4 Ostia

16 miles SW of Rome

Ostia was the port of ancient Rome and a city in its own right. The currents and uneven bottom of the Tiber River prevented Mediterranean shipping from going farther upstream, so merchandise was transferred to barges for the remainder of the trip. Ostia's fate was tied closely to that of the empire. At the peak of Rome's power, the city had 100,000 inhabitants—hard to imagine looking at today's ruins. Ostia was important enough to have had a theater (still standing in reconstructed form), numerous temples and baths, great patrician houses, and a large business complex. Successive emperors, notably Claudius and Trajan, enlarged and improved the facilities, but by Constantine's time (4th century A.D.), the worm had turned. The barbarian sieges of Rome in the 5th century spelled the end of Ostia.

Without the empire to trade with and Rome to sell to, the port quickly withered, reverting in a few centuries to a malarial swamp without a trace of Roman civilization. The excavations, still only partial, were started by the papacy in the 19th century, but the really substantial work took place between 1938 and 1942 under the Mussolini government.

Today, **Ostia Antica** is one of the area's major attractions, particularly of interest to those who can't make it to Pompeii.

GETTING THERE

Take Metro Linea B from the Stazione Termini to the Magliana stop. Change there for the Lido train to Ostia Antica, about 16 miles from Rome. Departures are about every half hour, and the trip takes only 20 minutes. The Metro lets you off across the highway that connects Rome with the coast. From here it's just a short walk to the ruins.

If you're driving, head out Via Ostiense, heading for Route 8 (signposted LIDO DI ROMA OSTIA).

EXPLORING THE RUINS & HITTING THE BEACH

After you've explored the ruins, board the Metro again to visit the **Lido di Ostia,** the beach. Italy may be a Catholic country, but the Romans don't allow religious conservatism to affect their bathing attire. This is the beach where the denizens of the capital frolic on the seashore and at times create a merry carnival atmosphere, with dance halls, cinemas, and pizzerias. The Lido is set off best at Castelfusano, against a backdrop of pinewoods. This stretch of shoreline is referred to as the Roman Riviera.

✪ **Ostia Antica's Ruins.** Viale dei Romagnoli 717. ☎ **06-5635-8099.** Admission 8,000 lire ($4). Tues–Sun 9am–6pm. Metro: Ostia Antica Line Roma-Ostia-Lido.

Ostia, at the mouth of the Tiber, was the port of ancient Rome, serving as the gateway for all the riches from the far corners of the empire. It was founded in the 4th century B.C. and became a major port and naval base primarily under two later emperors, Claudius and Trajan.

A prosperous city developed, full of temples, baths, theaters, and patrician homes. Ostia flourished for about 8 centuries before it began to wither away. Gradually it became little more than a malaria bed, a buried ghost city that faded into history. Though a papal-sponsored commission launched a series of digs in the 19th century, the major work of unearthing was carried out under Mussolini's orders from 1938 to 1942 (the work had to stop because of the war). The city is only partially dug out today, but it's believed that all the chief monuments have been uncovered.

These principal monuments are clearly labeled. The most important spot is **Piazzale delle Corporazioni,** an early version of Wall Street. Near the theater, this square contained nearly 75 corporations, the nature of their businesses identified by the patterns of preserved mosaics. Greek dramas were performed at the **ancient theater,** built in the early days of the empire. The classics are still aired here in summer (check with the tourist office for specific listings), but the theater as it looks today is the result of much rebuilding. Every town the size of Ostia had a forum, and during the excavations, a number of pillars of the ancient **Ostia Forum** were uncovered. At one end is a 2nd-century B.C. temple honoring a trio of gods, Minerva, Jupiter, and Juno (little more than the basic foundation remains). In addition, in the enclave is a well-lit **museum** displaying Roman statuary along with some Pompeii-like frescoes. There are perfect picnic spots beside fallen columns or near old temple walls.

5 Fregene

24 miles N of Rome

The fame of this coastal city north of the Tiber dates back to the 1600s, when the land belonged to the Rospigliosi, a powerful Roman family. Pope Clement IX, a member of that wealthy family, planted a forest of pine that extends along the shoreline for 2½ miles and stands half a mile deep to protect the land from the strong winds of the Mediterranean. Today, the wall of pines makes a dramatic backdrop for the golden sands and luxurious villas of the resort. If you'd like to sample an Italian beach, head here instead of to the more polluted beaches along Ostia's Lido.

GETTING THERE

You can catch the Fregene bus, which leaves from the Lepanto Metro stop in Rome and carries passengers to the center of Fregene. A ticket costs 4,800 lire ($2.40) and travel time is 1 hour.

If you're driving, follow Autostrada 1 (also known as Via Aurelia Malagrotta) heading west, crossing over the bypass that encircles Rome. After Castello di Guido, 14 miles west of Central Rome, exit onto the secondary road marked MACCARESE-FREGENE. Then continue southwest for another 10 miles, following the signs to Fregene. There is no tourist information office.

ACCOMMODATIONS & DINING

La Conchiglia. Lungomare di Ponente 4, Fregene, 00050 Roma. ☎ **06-668-5385.** Fax 06-665-63185. E-mail: conhotel@ats.it. 42 units. A/C MINIBAR TV TEL. 200,000 lire ($100) double. Rates include breakfast. AE, DC, MC, V. Free parking.

La Conchiglia means "The Shell," and it's an appropriate name for this hotel and restaurant right on the beach with views of the water and the pines. It features a circular lounge with built-in curving wall banquettes facing a cylindrical fireplace. The bar in the cocktail lounge, which faces the terrace, is also circular. The guest rooms are comfortable and well furnished, ranging from medium to spacious, each with a fine mattress and quality linen.

It's also possible to stop by just for a good meal. Try, for example, spaghetti with lobster and grilled fish or one of many excellent meat dishes. Meals start at 50,000 lire ($25). The restaurant is open daily 1 to 3pm and 8 to 10pm.

6 Cerveteri & Tarquinia

As Livy's Trojans landed in ancient Italy, so did the Etruscans. Who were they? We still don't know, and the many inscriptions they left behind—mostly on graves—are no help because the Etruscan language has not been completely deciphered. We deduce the date of their arrival on the west coast of Umbria at around 800 B.C.

Two former strongholds of the Etruscans can be visited today, Cerveteri and Tarquinia. (For Etruscan museums in Rome, see the Vatican's Etruscan-Georgian Museum and the National Etruscan Museum of the Villa Giulia, both in chapter 6.)

CERVETERI

28 miles NW of Rome

Cerveteri is older than Rome and stands on the site of a major Etruscan stronghold called Caere. If you drive here, you'll pass through the rolling hills of the Roman countryside and eventually see the city's medieval walls up in the hills on your right. To the left are the modern towers of Ladispoli, a rapidly growing seaside town.

The best way to reach Cerveteri is by car. Head out Via Aurelia, northwest of Rome, for a distance of 28 miles. If you don't have a car, take Metro Linea A in Rome to the Lepanto stop. From Via Lepanto, you can catch an Acotral coach to Cerveteri ☎ 06-324-4724); the trip takes about 1 hour and costs 5,000 lire ($2.50). Once at Cerveteri, it's a 1¼-mile walk to the necropolis—just follow the signs.

EXPLORING THE CITY OF THE DEAD

As you walk through the National Etruscan Museum in Rome (Villa Giulia), you'll often see the word *Caere* written under a figure vase or a sarcophagus. This is a reference to the nearby town known today as Cerveteri, one of the great Etruscan cities of Italy, whose origins may go as far back as the 9th century B.C.

Of course, the Etruscan town has long since faded, but not the **Necropolis of Cerveteri** (☎ 06-994-0001). The effect is eerie; Cerveteri is often called a "city of the dead." When you go beneath some of the mounds, you'll discover the most striking feature of the necropolis: The tombs are like rooms in Etruscan homes. The main burial ground is called the **Necropolis of Banditacca.** Of the graves thus far uncovered, none is finer than the **Tomba Bella** (sometimes called the Reliefs' Tomb), the burial ground of the Matuna family. Articles like utensils and even house pets were painted in stucco relief. Presumably these paintings were representations of items the dead family would need in the world beyond. The necropolis is open Tuesday to Sunday from 9am to 1 hour before sunset. Admission is 8,000 lire ($4).

Relics from the necropolis are displayed at the **Museo Nazionale Cerite,** Piazza Santa Maria Maggiore (☎ 06-9941354). The museum is housed within the ancient walls and crenellations of Ruspoldi Castle. It's open Tuesday to Sunday from 9am to 7pm. Admission is free.

TARQUINIA

60 miles NW of Rome

An even more striking museum is at Tarquinia, near Civitavecchia, which was the port of Rome in the days of Trajan. Tarquinia is commandingly situated atop a rocky cliff with a view of the sea. It's medieval in appearance, with its fortifications and nearly two dozen towers.

ESSENTIALS

GETTING THERE   As for public transportation, the train is the preferred choice; a *diretto* train from the Stazione Termini in Rome takes 50 minutes and costs 9,800 lire ($5.90).

Eight buses a day leave from the Via Lepanto Metro stop in Rome for the 2-hour trip to the neighboring town, Barriera San Giusto, which is 1½ miles from Tarquinia. The cost is 5,000 lire ($2.50). Bus schedules are available by calling ☎ 06-324-4724.

Take Via Aurelia outside Rome and continue on the Autostrada toward Civitavecchia. Bypass Civitavecchia and continue another 13 miles north until you see the exit signs for Tarquinia.

VISITOR INFORMATION   Tourist information is available at the tourist office in Barriera San Giusto (☎ **0766-856-384**). It's open Monday to Saturday from 8am to 2pm.

EXPLORING THE TOWN

Tarquinia has even more striking and more recently excavated tombs than those at Cerveteri. Its medieval turrets and fortifications seem to contradict the Etruscan name of Tarquinia. Actually, Tarquinia is the adopted name of the old medieval community of Corneto, in honor of the major Etruscan city that once stood nearby.

✪ Tarquinia National Museum. Piazza Cavour. ☎ **0776-856036.** Admission 8,000 lire ($4). Tues–Sun 9am–7pm.

This impressive museum is devoted to Etruscan exhibits and sarcophagi excavated from the necropolis a few miles away. The museum is housed in the Palazzo Vitelleschi, a Gothic palace that dates from the mid–15th century. Among the exhibits are gold jewelry, black vases with carved and painted bucolic scenes, and sarcophagi decorated with carvings of animals and relief figures of priests and military leaders. But the biggest attraction is in itself worth the ride from Rome—the almost life-size pair of winged horses from the pediment of a Tarquinian temple. The finish is worn here and there, and the terra-cotta color shows through, but the relief stands as one of the greatest Etruscan masterpieces ever discovered.

✪ Etruscan Necropolis. ☎ **0766-856308.** Admission 8,000 lire ($4). Generally open Tues–Sun 9am–5pm. Take a bus from the Barriera San Giusto to the Cimitero stop; or take the 20-min. walk from the museum (inquire at the museum for directions).

This "city of the dead" covers more than 2½ miles of rough terrain near where the ancient Etruscan city once stood. Thousands of tombs have been discovered, some of which haven't yet been explored. Others, of course, were discovered by looters, but many treasures remain. The paintings on the walls of the tombs have helped historians reconstruct the life of the Etruscans. Many of the paintings—in vivid colors mixed from iron oxide, lapis lazuli dust, and charcoal—depict feasting couples and convey an earthy, vigorous, sexy life among the wealthy Etruscans.

7 Viterbo

61 miles N of Rome

The 2,000 years that have gone into the creation of the city of Viterbo make it one of the most interesting day trips from Rome. Although it traces its history back to the Etruscans, the bulk of its historical architecture dates from the Middle Ages and the Renaissance, when the city was a residence (and hideout) for the popes. The old section of the city is still surrounded by the thick stone walls that once protected the inhabitants from papal (or antipapal, depending on the situation at the time) attacks.

ESSENTIALS

GETTING THERE   From Rome take Metro Linea A to Flaminio. At the Flaminio station, follow the signs pointing to Roma Nord station. Once there, purchase a combined rail and bus ticket to Viterbo, costing 8,000 lire ($4) one-way. The train takes you to Saxa Rubra in just 15 minutes. At Saxa Rubra, take an Acotral bus for the 1½-hour trip to Viterbo. Especially if you're trying to see Viterbo on a day trip, it might be worth the extra money to take a taxi from Saxa Rubra the remainder of the way.

If you're driving, take Autostrada 2 north to the Orte exit.

VISITOR INFORMATION   Tourist information is available at Piazzale dei Caduti 16 (☎ 0761-304795); the office is open Monday to Saturday from 8am to 2pm.

SEEING THE SIGHTS

The only way to see Viterbo properly is to wander through the narrow cobblestone streets of the medieval town, pausing in front of the antiquity-rich structures. **Piazza del Plebiscito,** dominated by the 15th-century town hall, impresses visitors with the fine state of preservation of Viterbo's old buildings. The courtyard and fountain in front of the town hall and the 13th-century governor's palace are favorite meeting places for townsfolk and visitors alike.

Just down Via San Lorenzo is **Piazza San Lorenzo,** the site of Viterbo's cathedral, which sits atop the former Etruscan acropolis. The **Duomo,** dating from 1192, is a composite of architectural styles, from its pagan foundations to its Renaissance facade to its gothic bell tower. Next door is the 13th-century **Palazzo Papale,** built as a residence for the pope, but also serving as a hideout when the pope was in exile. It was the site of three papal elections. The exterior staircase and the colonnaded loggia combine to make up one of the finest examples of civil Roman architecture from the gothic period.

The finest example of medieval architecture in Viterbo is the **San Pellegrino Quarter,** reached from Piazza San Lorenzo by a short walk past Piazza della Morte. This quarter, inhabited by working-class Viterboans, is a maze of narrow streets, arched walkways, towers, steep stairways, and ornamental fountains.

Worth a special visit is the **Convent of Santa Maria della Verità,** dating from 1100. The church contains 15th-century frescoes by Lorenzo da Viterbo, student of Piero della Francesca.

Park of the Monsters (Parco dei Mostri). Villa delle Meraviglie, Bomarzo. ☎ 0761-924029. Admission 15,000 lire ($7.50). Daily 8am–dusk. Bus: 6 from Piazza Martiri d'Ungheria in Viterbo.

About 8 miles east of Bagnaia at Bomarzo lies the Park of the Monsters. Prince Vicino Orsini had it built in a deep valley that's overlooked by the Orsini Palace and the houses of the village. On the other side of the valley are stone cliffs. Prince Orsini's park, Bosco Sacro (sacred wood), is filled with grotesque figures carved from natural rock. Nature and art have created a surrealistic fantasy; the Mouth of Hell (an ogre's face so big that people can walk into its gaping mouth), a crude Hercules slaying an Amazon, nymphs with butterfly wings, a huge tortoise with a statue on its shell, a harpy, a mermaid, snarling dogs, lions, and much, much more.

✪ **Villa Lante.** Bagnaia. ☎ 0761-288-008. Admission 4,500 lire ($2.25). Nov–Feb Tues–Sun 9am–4:30pm; Mar Tues–Sun 9am–5:30pm; mid-Apr and Sept–Oct 9am–6:30pm; mid-Apr to Aug 9am–7:30pm. Bus: 6 from Viterbo.

The English author Sacheverell Sitwell called Villa Lante, located in Bagnaia, a suburb of Viterbo, "the most beautiful garden in Italy." Water from Monte Cimino flows down to the fountains of the villa, running from terrace to terrace until it reaches the central pool of the regal garden, with statues, stone banisters, and shrubbery. Two symmetrical Renaissance palaces make up the villa. The estate is now partly a public park open during the day. The gardens that adjoin the villa, however, can only be visited on a guided tour. (The gatekeeper at the guard house will show you through, usually with a group that has assembled.) The interiors of the twin mansions can't be visited.

Appendix A: Rome in Depth

Rome, according to legend, was built on seven hills. These hills rise from the marshy lowlands of the Campagna and are mostly on the left bank of the Tiber River. They include the Quirinale (seat of the modern Italian government), Esquiline, Viminal, Caelian, and Aventine—and all combine to form a crescent-shaped plateau of great historical fame. In its center rises the Palatine Hill, the all-powerful seat of the imperial residences of ancient Rome, which looks down on the ancient Forum and the Colosseum. To the northwest rises the Capitoline Hill. Some historians have suggested that Rome's geography—set above a periphery of marshy and swelteringly hot lowlands—contributed to the fall of the Roman empire because of its propensity to breed malaria-inducing mosquitoes.

The modern city of Rome is composed of 22 districts, covering an area of nearly 10 square miles. The Tiber makes two distinct bends within Rome, below Ponte Cavour, one of the city's major bridges, and again at the history-rich island of Tiberina.

With bloodlines including virtually every race ever encompassed by the borders of the ancient Roman empire, the people of Rome long ago grew accustomed to seeing foreign influences come and go. Picking their way through the architectural and cultural jumble of Rome, they are not averse to complaining (loudly) of the city's endless inconveniences, yet they are the first to appreciate the historical and architectural marvels that surround them. Cynical, but hearty and filled with humanity, modern Romans propel themselves through the business of life with an enviable sense of style.

The crowds of pilgrims and the vast numbers of churches and convents exist side by side with fleshier and more earthbound distractions, the combination of which imbues many Romans with an overriding interest in pursuing the pleasures and distractions of the moment. This sense of theatricality can be seen in Roman driving habits; in animated conversations and gesticulations in restaurants and cafes; in the lavish displays of flowers, fountains, food, and architecture, the nation's trademark; and in the 27 centuries of building projects dedicated to the power and egos of long-dead potentates.

Despite the crowds, the pollution, the heat, and the virtual impossibility of efficiency, Romans for the most part take life with good cheer and *pazienza*. Translated as "patience," it seems to be the frequently uttered motto of modern Rome, and an appropriate philosophy for a city that has known everything from unparalleled glory to humiliation and despair. Romans know that since Rome wasn't built in a day, its charms should be savored slowly and with an appreciation for the cultures that contributed to this panoply.

1 Rome Past & Present

Many of the key events that shaped the rich and often gory tapestry of Italian history originated in Rome. Although parts of Italy (especially Sardinia and Sicily) were inhabited as early as the Bronze Age, the region around Rome was occupied relatively late. Some historians claim that the presence of active volcanoes in the region during the Bronze Age prevented prehistoric tribes from living here, but whatever the reason, Rome has unearthed far fewer prehistoric graves and implements than have neighboring Tuscany and Umbria.

THE ETRUSCANS　Among the early inhabitants of Italy, the most significant were the Etruscans—but who were they? No one knows, and the many inscriptions they left behind (mostly on graves) are of no help, since the Etruscan language has never been deciphered by modern scholars. It's thought they arrived on the eastern coast of Umbria several centuries before Rome was built, around 800 B.C. Their religious rites and architecture show an obvious contact with Mesopotamia; the Etruscans may have been refugees from Asia Minor who traveled westward about 1200 to 1000 B.C. Within 2 centuries, they had subjugated Tuscany and Campania and the Villanova tribes who lived there.

While the Etruscans built temples at Tarquinia and Caere (present-day Cerveteri), the few nervous Latin tribes who remained outside their sway gravitated to Rome, then little more than a sheepherding village. As its power grew, however, Rome increasingly profited from the strategically important Tiber crossing where the ancient Salt Way (Via Salaria) turned northeastward toward the central Apennines.

From their base at Rome, the Latins remained free of the Etruscans until about 600 B.C. But the Etruscan advance was inexorable, and though the tribes concentrated their forces at Rome for a last stand, they were swept away by the sophisticated Mesopotamian conquerors. The new overlords introduced gold tableware and jewelry, bronze urns and terra-cotta statuary, and the best of Greek and Asia Minor art and culture; they also made Rome the governmental

Dateline
- **Bronze Age** Tribes of Celts, Teutonics, and groups from the eastern Mediterranean inhabit the Italian peninsula.
- **1200 B.C.** The Etruscans migrate from the eastern Mediterranean (probably Mesopotamia) and occupy territory north and south of Rome.
- **800 B.C.** Sicily and southern Italy (especially Naples) flourish under Greek and Phoenician protection; independent of most outside domination, Rome evolves as an insignificant community of shepherds with loyalties divided among several Latin tribes.
- **753 B.C.** Rome's traditional founding date.
- **660 B.C.** Etruscans occupy Rome as the capital of their empire; the city grows rapidly and a major seaport (Ostia) opens at the mouth of the Tiber.
- **510–250 B.C.** The Latin tribes, still centered in Rome, maintain a prolonged revolt against the Etruscans; alpine Gauls attack the Etruscans from the north and Greeks living in Sicily destroy the Etruscan navy.
- **250 B.C.** The Romans and their allies finally purge the Etruscans from Italy; Rome flourishes as a republic and begins the accumulation of a vast empire.
- **250–50 B.C.** Rome obliterates its chief rival, Carthage, during two Punic Wars; Carthage's defeat allows unchecked Roman expansion into Spain, North Africa, Sardinia, and Corsica.

continues

- **44 B.C.** Julius Caesar is assassinated; his successor, Augustus, transforms Rome from a city of brick to a city of marble and solidifies Rome's status as a dictatorship.
- **40 B.C.** Rome and its armies control the entire Mediterranean world.
- **3rd century A.D.** Rome declines under a series of incompetent and corrupt emperors.
- **4th century A.D.** Rome is fragmented politically as administrative capitals are established in such cities as Milan and Trier, Germany.
- **395** The empire splits: Constantine establishes a "New Rome" at Constantinople (Istanbul); Goths invade Rome's provinces in northern Italy.
- **410–455** Rome is sacked by barbarians—Alaric the Goth, Attila the Hun, and Galseric the Vandal.
- **475** Rome falls, leaving only the primate of the Catholic church in control; the pope slowly adopts many of the responsibilities and the prestige once reserved for the Roman emperors.
- **731** Pope Gregory II renounces Rome's spiritual and political link to the authorities in Constantinople.
- **800** Charlemagne is crowned Holy Roman Emperor by Pope Leo III; Italy dissolves into a series of small warring kingdoms.
- **1065** The Holy Land falls to the Muslim Turks; the Crusades are launched.
- **1303–77** A papal schism occurs when a rival pope is established at Avignon.
- **1377** The "antipope" is removed from Avignon, and the Roman popes emerge as sole contenders to the legacy of St. Peter.

continues

seat of all Latium. Roma is an Etruscan name, and the kings of Rome had Etruscan names: Numa, Ancus, Tarquinius, and even Romulus. Under the combined influences of the Greeks and the Mesopotamian east, Rome grew enormously. A new port was opened at Ostia, near the mouth of the Tiber. Artists from Greece carved statues of Roman gods to resemble Greek divinities. From this enforced (and not always peaceable) mixture of Latin tribes and Etruscans grew the roots of what eventually became the Republic of Rome.

The Estruscans ruled until the Roman revolt around 510 B.C., and by 250 B.C., the Romans and their Campania allies had vanquished the Etruscans, wiping out their language and religion. However, many of the former rulers' manners and beliefs remained, assimilated into the culture. Even today, certain Etruscan customs and bloodlines are believed to exist in Italy, especially in Tuscany.

The best places to see the legacy left by these mysterious people are in Cerveteri and Tarquinia outside Rome. Especially interesting is the Etruscan necropolis, just 4 miles southeast of Tarquinia, where thousands of tombs have been discovered. See chapter 10 for details on all these sites. To learn more about the Etruscans, visit the Museo Nazionale di Villa Giulla in Rome (see chapter 6).

THE ROMAN REPUBLIC Gauls from the alpine regions invaded the northern Etruscan territory around 600 B.C., and the Latin tribes revolted in about 510 B.C., toppling the Etruscan-linked rulers from their power bases and establishing the southern boundary of Etruscan influence at the Tiber. Greeks from Sicily ended Etruscan sea power in 474 B.C. during the battle of Cumae off the Italian coastline just north of Naples. By 250 B.C., the Romans and their allies in Campagna had vanquished the Etruscans, wiping out their language and religion.

Tempered in the fires of military adversity, the stern Roman republic was characterized by belief in the gods, the necessity of learning from the past, strength of the family, education through books and public service, and, most important, obedience. The all-powerful Senate presided as Rome defeated rival powers one after the other in a steady stream of staggering military successes.

As the population grew, the Romans gave to their Latin allies and then to conquered peoples partial or complete Roman citizenship, always with the obligation of military service. Colonies of citizens were established on the borders of the growing empire and were populated with soldiers/farmers and their families. Later, as seen in the history of Britain and the European continent, colonies began to thrive as semi-autonomous units on their own, heavily fortified and linked to Rome by well-maintained military roads and a well-defined hierarchy of military command.

The final obstacle to the unrivaled supremacy of Rome was the defeat, during the 3rd century B.C., of the city-state of Carthage during the two Punic Wars. An ancient Phoenician trading post on the coast of Tunisia, Carthage had grown into one of the premier naval and agricultural powers of the Mediterranean with strongly fortified positions in Corsica, Sardinia, and Spain. Despite the impressive victories of the Carthaginian general Hannibal, Rome eventually eradicated Carthage in one of the most famous defeats in ancient history. Rome was able to immediately expand its power into North Africa, Sardinia, Corsica, and Iberia.

THE ROMAN EMPIRE By 49 B.C., Italy ruled all of the Mediterranean world either directly or indirectly, with all political, commercial, and cultural pathways leading directly to Rome. The wealth and glory to be found in Rome lured many there, but drained other Italian communities of human resources. As Rome transformed itself into an administrative headquarters, imports to the city from other parts of the empire hurt local farmers and landowners. The seeds for civil discord were sown early in the empire's existence, although, as Rome was embellished with temples, monuments, and the easy availability of slave labor from conquered territories, many of its social problems were overlooked in favor of expansion and glory.

No figure was more towering during the republic than Julius Caesar, the charismatic conqueror of Gaul—"the wife of every husband and the husband of every wife." After defeating the last resistance of the Pompeians in 45 B.C., he came to Rome and was made dictator and consul for 10 years. He was at that point almost a king. Conspirators led by Marcus Junius Brutus stabbed him to death in the Senate on March 15, 44 B.C. Beware the ides of March.

- **Mid-1400s** Originating in Florence, the Renaissance blossoms throughout Italy; Italian artists receive multiple commissions from the ecclesiastical communities of Rome.
- **1508** Ordered by the pope, Michelangelo begins work on the ceiling of the Vatican's Sistine Chapel.
- **1527** Rome is attacked and sacked by Charles V, who—to the pope's rage—is elected Holy Roman Emperor the following year.
- **1796–97** Napoléon's military conquests of Italy arouse Italian nationalism.
- **1861** Rome is declared the capital of the newly established Kingdom of Italy; the Papal States (but not the Vatican) are absorbed into the new nation.
- **1929** A concordat between the Vatican and the Italian government delineates the rights and responsibilities of both parties.
- **1935** Italian invasion of Abyssinia (Ethiopia).
- **1941** Italian invasion of Yugoslavia.
- **1943** General Patton lands in Sicily and soon controls the island.
- **1945** Mussolini killed by a mob in Milan.
- **1946** Establishment of Rome as the capital of the newly created Republic of Italy.
- **1960s** Rise of left-wing terrorist groups; flight of capital from Italy; continuing problems of the impoverished south cause an exodus from the countryside into such cities as Rome.
- **1980s** *Il Sorpasso* imbues Rome (and the rest of Italy) with dreams of an economic rebirth.
- **1994** Right-wing forces win in Italian national elections.
- **1996** Dini steps down as prime minister, as the

continues

president dissolves both houses of Parliament; in general elections, the center-left coalition known as the Olive Tree sweeps both the Senate and the Chamber of Deputies; Romano Prodi becomes prime minister.

- **1997–98** Prodi survives Neo-Communist challenge and continues to press for budget cuts in an effort to join Europe in 1999.
- **1999** Rome officially goes under the euro umbrella as it prepares for the millennium.
- **2000** Italy welcomes Jubilee visitors in wake of political discontent.

Marc Antony then assumed control by seizing Caesar's papers and wealth. Intent on expanding the Republic, Antony met with Cleopatra at Tarsus in 41 B.C. She seduced him, and he stayed in Egypt for a year. When Antony eventually returned to Rome, still smitten with Cleopatra, he made peace with Caesar's willed successor, Octavius, and, through the pacts of Brundisium, soon found himself married to Octavius's sister, Octavia. This marriage, however, didn't prevent him from openly marrying Cleopatra in 36 B.C. The furious Octavius gathered western legions and defeated Antony at the Battle of Actium on September 2, 31 B.C. Cleopatra fled to Egypt, followed by Antony, who committed suicide in disgrace a year later. Cleopatra, unable to seduce his successor and, thus, retain her rule of Egypt, followed suit with the help of an asp.

Born Gaius Octavius in 63 B.C., Augustus, the first Roman emperor, reigned from 27 B.C. to A.D. 14. His reign, called "the golden age of Rome," led to the Pax Romana, or 2 centuries of peace. He had been adopted by, and eventually became the heir of, his great-uncle Julius Caesar. In Rome you can still visit the remains of the Forum of Augustus, built before the birth of Christ, and the Domus Augustana, where the imperial family lived on the Palatine Hill.

On the eve of the birth of Jesus, Rome was a mighty empire whose generals had brought all of the Western world under the influence of Roman law, values, and civilization. Only in the eastern third of the Mediterranean did the existing cultures—notably the Greek—withstand the Roman incursions. Despite its occupation by Rome, Greece, more than any other culture, permeated Rome with new ideas, values, and concepts of art, architecture, religion, and philosophy.

The emperors, whose succession started with Augustus's principate after the death of Julius Caesar, brought Rome to new, almost giddy, heights. Augustus transformed the city from brick to marble, much the way Napoléon III transformed Paris many centuries later. But success led to corruption. The emperors wielded autocratic power, and the centuries witnessed a steady decay in the ideals and traditions on which the empire had been founded. The army became a fifth column of barbarian mercenaries, the tax collector became the scourge of the countryside, and for every good emperor (Augustus, Claudius, Trajan, Vespasian, and Hadrian, to name a few) there were three or four debased heads of state (Caligula, Nero, Domitian, Caracalla, and more).

The ideals of democratic responsibility in the heart of the empire had begun to break down. The populace began to object violently to a government that took little interest in commerce and seemed interested only in foreign politics. As taxes and levies increased, the poor emigrated in huge and idle numbers to Rome and the rich cities of the Po Valley. Entire generations of war captives, forced into the slave-driven economies of large Italian estates, were steeped in hatred and ignorance.

Christianity, a new and revolutionary religion, probably gained a foothold in Rome about 10 years after Jesus's crucifixion. Feared far more for its political implications than for its spiritual resuppositions, it was at first brutally suppressed before moving through increasingly tolerant stages of acceptability.

After Augustus died (by poison, perhaps), his widow, Livia—a crafty social climber who had divorced her first husband to marry Augustus—set up her son, Tiberius, as ruler through a series of intrigues and poisonings. A long series of murders ensued, and Tiberius, who ruled during Pontius Pilot's trial and crucifixion of Christ, was eventually murdered in an uprising of landowners. In fact, murder was so common that a short time later, Domitian (A.D. 81–96) became so obsessed with the possibility of assassination he had the walls of his palace covered in mica so he could see behind him at all times. (He was killed anyway.)

Excesses and scandal ruled the day: Caligula (a bit overfond of his sister Drusilla) appointed his horse a lifetime member of the Senate, lavished money on foolish projects, and proclaimed himself a god. Caligula's successor, his uncle Claudius, was deceived and publicly humiliated by one of his wives, the lascivious Messalina (he had her killed for her trouble); he was then poisoned by his final wife, his niece Agrippina, to secure the succession of Nero, her son by a previous marriage. Nero's thanks was later to murder not only his mother but also his wife, Claudius's daughter, and his rival, Claudius's son. The disgraceful Nero was removed as emperor while visiting Greece; he committed suicide with the cry, "What an artist I destroy."

By the 3rd century A.D., corruption was so prevalent there were 23 emperors in 73 years. How bad had things gotten? So bad that Caracalla, to secure control of the empire, had his brother Geta slashed to pieces while lying in his mother's arms.

As the decay progressed, the Roman citizen either lived on the increasingly swollen public dole and spent his days at gladiatorial games and imperial baths or was a disillusioned patrician at the mercy of emperors who might murder him for his property. The 3rd century saw so many emperors that it was common, as H. V. Morton tells us, to hear in the provinces of the election of an emperor together with a report of his assassination.

The 4th-century reforms of Diocletian held the empire together, but at the expense of its inhabitants, who were reduced to tax units. He reinforced imperial power while paradoxically weakening Roman dominance and prestige by dividing the empire into east and west halves and establishing administrative capitals at outposts like Milan and Trier, Germany. Diocletian instituted not only heavy taxes but also a socioeconomic system that made professions hereditary. This edict was so strictly enforced, the son of a silversmith could be tried as a criminal if he attempted to become a sculptor instead.

Constantine became emperor in A.D. 306, and in 330 he made Constantinople (or Byzantium) the new capital of the Empire, moving the administrative functions away from Rome altogether, an act that sounded a death knell for a city already threatened by the menace of barbarian attacks. The sole survivor of six rival emperors, Constantine recognized Christianity as the official religion of the Roman empire and built an entirely new, more easily defended capital on the banks of the Bosporus. Named in his honor (Constantinople, or Byzantium), it was later renamed Istanbul by the Ottoman Turks. When he moved to the new capital, Constantine and his heirs took with them the best of the artisans, politicians, and public figures of Rome. Rome, reduced to little more than a provincial capital controlling the threatened western half of the once-mighty empire, continued to founder and decay. As for the Christian church, although the popes of Rome were under the nominal auspices of an exarch from Constantinople, their power increased slowly and steadily as the power of the emperors declined.

Rome in Depth

THE EMPIRE FALLS The eastern and western sections of the Roman Empire split in 395, leaving Italy without the support it once received from east of the Adriatic. When the Goths moved toward Rome in the early 5th century, citizens in the provinces, who had grown to hate and fear the cruel bureaucracy set up by Diocletian and followed by succeeding emperors, welcomed the invaders. And then the pillage began.

Rome was first sacked by Alaric in August 410. The populace made no attempt to defend the city (other than trying vainly to buy off the Goth, a tactic that had worked 3 years before); most people simply fled into the hills or headed to their country estates if they were rich. The feeble Western emperor Honorius hid out in Ravenna the entire time.

More than 40 troubled years passed until the siege of Rome by Attila the Hun. Attila was dissuaded from attacking, thanks largely to a peace mission headed by Pope Leo I in 452. Yet, relief was short-lived: In 455, Gaiseric the Vandal carried out a 2-week sack that was unparalleled in its pure savagery. The empire of the West lasted for only another 20 years; finally the sacks and chaos ended it in 476, and Rome was left to the popes, under the nominal auspices of an exarch from Byzantium (Constantinople).

The last would-be Caesars to walk the streets of Rome were both barbarians: The first was Theodoric, who established an Ostrogoth kingdom at Ravenna from 493 to 526; and the second was Totila, who held the last chariot races in the Circus Maximus in 549. Totila was engaged in a running battle with Belisarius, the general of the Eastern emperor Justinian, who sought to regain Rome for the Eastern Empire. The city changed hands several times, recovering some of its ancient pride by bravely resisting Totila's forces but eventually being entirely depopulated by the continuing battles.

THE HOLY ROMAN EMPIRE So, a ravaged Rome entered the Middle Ages; its once-proud population scattered and unrecognizable in rustic exile. A modest population started life again in the swamps of the Campus Martius, while the seven hills, now without water since the aqueducts were cut, stood abandoned and crumbling.

After the fall of the Western Empire, the pope took on more and more imperial powers; yet, there was no political unity. Decades of rule by barbarians and then Goths were followed by takeovers in different parts of the country by various strong warriors, such as the Lombards. Italy was thus divided into several spheres of control. In 731, Pope Gregory II renounced Rome's dependence on Constantinople and, thus, ended the twilight era of the Greek exarch who had nominally ruled Rome.

Papal Rome turned toward Europe, where the papacy found a powerful ally in Charlemagne, a king of the barbarian Franks. In 800, he was crowned emperor by Pope Leo III. The capital he established at Aachen (Aix-la-Chapelle in French) lay deep within territory known to the Romans a half millennium ago as the heart of the barbarian world. Though Charlemagne pledged allegiance to the church and looked to Rome and its pope as the final arbiter in most religious and cultural affairs, he launched northwestern Europe on a course toward bitter political opposition to the meddling of the papacy in temporal affairs.

The successor to Charlemagne's empire was a political entity known as the Holy Roman Empire (962–1806). The new empire defined the end of the Dark Ages but ushered in a period of long bloody warfare. The Lombard leaders battled Franks. Magyars from Hungary invaded northeastern Lombardy and were in turn defeated by the increasingly powerful Venetians. Normans gained military control of Sicily in the 11th century, divided it from the rest of Italy, and altered forever the island's racial and ethnic makeup and its architecture. As Italy dissolved into a fragmented collection of city-states, the papacy fell under the power of Rome's feudal landowners. Eventually, even the process for choosing popes came into the hands of the increasingly Germanic Holy Roman emperors, though this power balance would very soon shift.

Rome during the Middle Ages was a quaint rural town. Narrow lanes with overhanging buildings filled many areas that had been planned as showcases of ancient imperial power, like the Campus Martius. Great basilicas were built and embellished with golden-hued mosaics. The forums, mercantile exchanges, temples, and theaters of the Imperial Era slowly disintegrated and collapsed. The decay of ancient Rome was assisted by periodic earthquakes, centuries of neglect, and, in particular, the growing need for building materials. Rome receded into a dusty provincialism. As the seat of the Roman Catholic church, the state was almost completely controlled by priests, who had an insatiable need for new churches and convents.

By the end of the 11th century, the popes shook off control of the Roman aristocracy, rid themselves of what they considered the excessive influence of the emperors at Aachen, and began an aggressive expansion of church influence and acquisitions. The deliberate organization of the church into a format modeled on the hierarchies of the ancient Roman Empire put it on a collision course with the empire and the other temporal leaders of Europe, resulting in an endless series of power struggles.

THE MIDDLE AGES   The papacy soon became essentially a feudal state, and the pope became a medieval (later Renaissance) prince engaged in many of the worldly activities that brought criticism on the church in later centuries. The fall of the Holy Land to the Turks in 1065 catapulted the papacy into the forefront of world politics, primarily because of the Crusades, most of which were judged to be military and economic disasters and many of which the popes directly caused or encouraged. During the 12th and 13th centuries, the bitter rivalries that rocked the secular and spiritual bastions of Europe took their toll on the stability of the Holy Roman Empire, which grew weaker as city-states buttressed by mercantile and trade-related prosperity grew stronger. Also, France emerged as a strong nation in its own right during this period. Each investiture of a new bishop to any influential post became a cause for endless jockeying for power among many political and ecclesiastical factions.

These conflicts achieved their most visible impasse in 1303 with the full-fledged removal of the papacy from Rome to the French city of Avignon. For more than 70 years, until 1377, viciously competing popes (one in Rome, another under the protection of the French kings in Avignon) made simultaneous claims to the legacy of St. Peter, underscoring as never before the degree to which the church was both a victim and a victimizer of European politics.

The seat of the papacy was eventually returned to Rome, where a series of popes proved every bit as fascinating as the Roman emperors they replaced. The great families—Barberini, Medici, Borgia—enhanced their status and fortunes impressively whenever one of their sons was elected pope.

In the mid–14th century, the Black Death ravaged Europe, killed a third of Italy's population. Despite such setbacks, northern Italian city-states grew wealthy from Crusade booty, trade with one another and with the Middle East, and banking. These wealthy principalities and pseudorepublics ruled by the merchant elite flexed their muscles in the absence of a strong central authority.

THE RENAISSANCE Rome's age of siege was not over. In 1527 Charles V spearheaded the worst sacking in the city's history. To the horror of Pope Clement VII (a Medici), the entire city was brutally pillaged by the man who was crowned Holy Roman Emperor the following year.

During the years of the Renaissance, Reformation, and the Counter-Reformation, Rome underwent major physical changes. The old centers of culture reverted to pastures and fields, and great churches and palaces were built with the stones of ancient Rome. This building boom, in fact, did far more damage to the temples of the caesars than did any barbarian or Teutonic sack. Rare marbles were stripped from the imperial baths and used as altar pieces or sent to lime kilns. So enthusiastic was the papal destruction of imperial Rome that it's a miracle anything is left.

This era is best remembered because of its art. The great ruling families, especially the Medicis in Florence, the Gonzagas in Mantua, and the Estes in Ferrara, not only reformed law and commerce but also sparked a renaissance in art. Out of this period arose such towering figures as Leonardo da Vinci and Michelangelo. Many visitors come to Italy to view what's left of the art and glory of that era, including Michelangelo's Sistine Chapel at the Vatican.

THE MOVE TOWARD A UNITED ITALY During the 17th, 18th, and 19th centuries the fortunes of Rome rose and fell with the general political and economic situation of the rest of Italy. Since the end of the 13th century, Italy had been divided into a series of regional states, each with mercenary soldiers, its own judicial system, and an interlocking series of alliances and enmities that had created a network of intensely competitive city-states. (Some of these families had attained formidable power under such *signori* as the Este family in Ferrara, the Medici in Florence, and the Sforza in Milan.) Rome, headquarters of the Papal States, maintained its independence and (usually) the integrity of its borders, although at least some of the city's religious power had been diluted as increasing numbers of Europeans converted to Protestantism.

Napoléon made a bid for power in Italy beginning in 1796, fueling his propaganda machines with what was considered a relatively easy victory. During the 1815 Congress of Vienna, which followed Napoléon's defeat, Italy was once again divided among many different factions: Austria was given Lombardy and Venetia, and the Papal States were returned to the popes. Some duchies were put back into the hands of their hereditary rulers; whereas, southern Italy and Sicily went to a newly imported dynasty related to the Bourbons. One historic move, which eventually assisted in the unification of Italy, was the assignment of the former republic of Genoa to Sardinia (which at the time was governed by the House of Savoy).

By now, political unrest had become a fact of Italian (and Roman) life, at least some of it encouraged by the rapid industrialization of the north and the almost total lack of industrialization in the south. Despite these barriers, in 1861 the Kingdom of Italy was proclaimed, and Victor Emmanuel II of the House of Savoy, king of Sardinia, became head of the new monarchy. In 1861 the designated capital of the newly united country, following a 2,000-year-old precedent, became Rome.

Garibaldi, the most respected of all Italian heroes, must be singled out for his efforts, which included taking Sicily, then returning to the mainland and marching north to meet Victor Emmanuel II at Teano, and finally declaring a unified Italy (with the important exception of Rome itself). It must have seemed especially sweet to a man whose efforts at unity had caused him to flee the country fearing for his life on four occasions. It's a tribute to the tenacity

It is not impossible to govern Italians. It is merely useless.

— Benito Mussolini

of this red-bearded hero that he never gave up, even in the early 1850s, when he was forced to wait out one of his exiles as a candlemaker on Staten Island in New York.

In a controversial move that engendered resentment many decades later, the borders of the Papal States were eradicated from the map as Rome was incorporated into the new nation of Italy. The Vatican, however, did not yield its territory to the new order despite guarantees of nonintervention proffered by the Italian government, and relations between the pope and the political leaders of Italy remained rocky until 1929.

WORLD WAR II & THE AXIS   On October 28, 1922, Benito Mussolini, who had started his Fascist Party in 1919, knew the time was ripe for change. He gathered 50,000 supporters for a march on Rome. Inflation was soaring and workers had just called a general strike, so King Victor Emmanuel II, rather than recognizing a state under siege, recognized Mussolini as the new government leader. In 1929, Il Duce defined the divisions between the Italian government and the Vatican by signing a concordat granting political and fiscal autonomy to Vatican City. It also made Roman Catholicism the official state religion—but that designation was removed in 1978 through a revision of the concordat.

During the Spanish Civil War (1936–39), Mussolini's support of Franco's Fascist party, which staged a coup against the democratically elected government of Spain, helped encourage the formation of the "Axis" alliance between Italy and Nazi Germany. Despite its outdated military equipment, Italy added to the general horror of the era by invading Abyssinia (Ethiopia) in 1935. In 1940, Italy invaded Greece through Albania and, in 1942, it sent thousands of Italian troops to assist Hitler in his disastrous campaign along the Russian front. In 1943, Allied forces, under the command of U.S. Gen. George Patton and British Gen. Bernard Montgomery, landed in Sicily and quickly secured the island as they prepared to move north toward Rome.

In the face of likely defeat and humiliation, Mussolini was overthrown by his own cabinet (Grand Council). The Allies made a separate deal with Victor Emmanuel III, who had collaborated with the Fascists during the previous 2 decades and now easily shifted allegiances. A politically divided Italy watched as battalions of fanatical German Nazis released Mussolini from his Italian jail cell to establish the short-lived Republic of Salò, headquartered on the edge of Lake Garda. Mussolini had hoped for a groundswell of popular opinion in favor of Italian Fascism, but events quickly proved this nothing more than a futile dream.

In April 1945, with almost half a million Italians rising in a mass demonstration against him and the German war machine, Mussolini was captured by Italian partisans as he fled to Switzerland. Along with his mistress, Claretta Petacci, and several others of his intimates, he was shot and strung upsidedown from the roof of a Milan gas station.

MODERN ROME   Disaffected with the monarchy and its identification with the fallen Fascist dictatorship, Italian voters in 1946 voted for the establishment of a republic. The major political party that emerged following World

War II was the Christian Democratic Party, a right-of-center group whose leader, Alcide De Gasperi (1881–1954), served as premier until 1953. The second-largest party was the Communist Party; however, by the mid-1970s it had abandoned its revolutionary program in favor of a democratic form of "Eurocommunism" (in 1991, the Communists even changed their name, to the Democratic Party of the Left).

Though after the war Italy was stripped of all its overseas colonies, it quickly succeeded, in part because of U.S. aid under the Marshall Plan (1948–52), in rebuilding its economy. By the 1960s, as a member of the European Community (founded in Rome in 1957), Italy had become one of the world's leading industrialized nations, prominent in the manufacture of automobiles and office equipment.

But the country continued to be plagued by economic inequities between the prosperous industrialized north and the economically depressed south. It suffered an unprecedented flight of capital (frequently aided by Swiss banks only too willing to accept discreet deposits from wealthy Italians) and an increase in bankruptcies, inflation (almost 20% during much of the 1970s), and unemployment.

During the late 1970s and early 1980s, Italy was rocked by the rise of terrorism, instigated both by neo-Fascists and by left-wing intellectuals from the Socialist-controlled universities of the north.

In the 1990s some 6,000 businesspeople and politicians were implicated in a billion-dollar government graft scandal. Such familiar figures as Bettino Craxi, former head of the Socialist party, and Giulio Andreotti, a seven-time prime minister, were accused of corruption.

Hoping for a renewal after all this exposure of greed, Italian voters in March 1994 turned to the right wing to head their government. In overwhelming numbers, voters elected a former cruise-ship singer turned media billionaire, Silvio Berlusconi, as their new leader. His Forza Italia (Go, Italy) party formed an alliance with the neo-fascist National Alliance and the secessionist Northern League to sweep to victory. These elections were termed "the most critical" for Italy in 4 decades. The new government was beset with an almost hopeless array of new problems, including destabilization caused by the Mafia and its underground economies and, when the Northern League defected from the coalition in December 1994, Berlusconi resigned.

Treasury Minister Lamberto Dini, a nonpolitical international banker, replaced him. Dini signed on merely as a transitional player in Italy's topsy-turvy political game. His austerity measures enacted to balance Italy's budget, including cuts in pensions and health care, were not popular among the mostly blue-collar Italian workers or the very influential labor unions. Pending a predicted defeat in a no-confidence vote, Dini also stepped down. His resignation in January 1996 left beleaguered Italians shouting *Basta!* (enough). This latest shuffling in Italy's political deck prompted President Oscar Scalfaro to dissolve both houses of the Italian Parliament.

Once again Italians were faced with forming a new government. Elections in April 1996 proved quite a shocker, not only for the defeated politicians but also for the victors. The center-left coalition known as the Olive Tree, led by Romano Prodi, swept both the Senate and the Chamber of Deputies. The Olive Tree, whose roots stem from the old Communist party, achieved victory by shifting toward the center and focusing its campaign on a strong platform protecting social benefits and supporting Italy's bid to become a solid member of the European Union. Prodi carried through on his commitment when he announced a stringent budget for 1997 in a bid to be among the first countries to enter the monetary union.

The year 1997 saw further upheavals as the Prodi government continued to push ahead with cuts to the country's generous social security system. In the autumn of 1997 Prodi was forced to submit his resignation when he lost critical support in Parliament from the Communist Refounding party, which balked at further pension and welfare cuts in the 1998 budget. The party eventually backed off with its demands, and Prodi was returned to office.

Italy and the United States faced tense relations in the spring of 1999 when a military jury cleared marine captain Richard J. Ashby of charges brought against him for flying his plane over a ski resort and severing gondola cables, plunging 20 people to their deaths in 1998. After a year of painful recriminations on both sides of the Atlantic and a bitter, 3-week-long trial, the not-guilty verdict came in with stunning finality.

As 1999 neared its end, Rome rushed to put the finishing touches on its many monuments, including churches and museums, and everybody was ready for the scaffolding to come down before the arrival of 2000. Italy spent all of 2000 welcoming Jubilee Year visitors from around the world, as its political cauldron bubbled. One particularly notable clash in 2000 pitted the church and social conservatives against more progressive young Italians, as the pope lashed out at the World Gay Pride rally held in the summer of 2000. His condemnation sparked much debate in the media, but the actual event went off without a hitch and, in fact, was labeled as rather tame when compared to more raucous Gay Pride rallies elsewhere around the globe.

In December of 1999, under Prime Minister Massimo D'Alema, Italy received its 57th new government since 1945. But it didn't last long. In April of 2000, former prime minister Giuliano Amato, a onetime Socialist, returned to power. The aim of Amato, as the designated leader of an unwieldy coalition of a dozen political parties ranging from former Communists to former Christian Democrats, is to govern until the legislature's term ends in the spring of 2001.

2 Architecture 101

The mysterious **Etruscans,** whose earliest origins probably lay somewhere in Mesopotamia, brought the first truly impressive architecture to mainland Italy. Little remains of their building, but historical writings by the Romans themselves record their powerful walls, bridges, and aqueducts, which were very similar to the Mycenaean architecture of Crete. As Rome asserted its own identity and overpowered its Etruscan masters, it borrowed heavily from their established themes.

In architecture, **ancient Rome** flourished magnificently, advancing in size and majesty far beyond the examples set by the Greeks. Part of this was because of the development of a primitive form of concrete, but even more important was the fine-tuning of the arch, which was used with a logic, rhythm, and ease never before seen. Monumental buildings were erected, each an embodiment of the strength, power, and careful organization of the empire itself. Examples include forums and baths scattered across the Mediterranean world (the greatest of which were Trajan's Forum and the Baths of Caracalla, both in Rome). Equally magnificent were the Colosseum and a building that later greatly influenced the Palladians during the Renaissance, Hadrian's Pantheon. These immense achievements were made possible by two major resources: almost

limitless funds pouring in from all regions of the empire and an unending supply of slaves captured during military campaigns.

The influence of Roman architecture was to have enormous impact on
building throughout most of the world, leading to a neoclassic revival centuries later in Britain and America. Although unromantic, it was the use of
concrete that had such a major influence on buildings to come. Concrete
seemingly lasts forever, as evidenced by the giant concrete dome of Rome's
Pantheon and the Baths of Caracalla, and makes vast buildings possible. Even in
Roman times this allowed *insulae* (apartment blocks) to climb to seven floors or
higher, something almost unheard of before. Even though Rome didn't invent
the arch or the aqueduct, or even concrete, Romans perfected these building
forms.

Following in the footprints of the Romans, **early Christians** copied Roman
architectural styles, although they lacked the rich marbles, slave labor, and
other materials that made Rome glorious. The earliest basilicas were hastily
constructed and poorly designed. Basilicas were entered at the west, with the
apse in the east (the direction of Palestine). None of the basilicas remaining
from this period is intact, as all were altered or changed entirely over the
centuries.

Because the Christian world was also ruled from the East, **Byzantine** architecture came into play. The roofing device of the Near East—covering a building with a dome—was adapted to the basic rectangular plan of the early
Christian basilica.

The art and architecture in the centuries that followed the collapse of Rome
became known as early medieval or **Romanesque.** In its many variations, it
flourished between A.D. 1000 and 1200.

Roman architecture was so innovative and powerful that it continued to
influence builders even beyond the Romanesque and during the **Gothic**
period. The best examples of domestic Gothic architecture in Italy, however,
are in Florence and Siena, not in Rome. Santa Maria Sopra Minerva (see chapter 6) is the only real exception.

The **Renaissance** flowered in Italy almost 2 centuries before it reached such
countries as England. In the early Renaissance, architecture in Rome was still
heavily influenced by classicism, although using building techniques perfected
during the Gothic period. Rome's greatest building achievement of the Renaissance is St. Peter's Basilica, the largest church ever constructed until the last
decade. Its sheer massiveness overwhelms (it's about five times the area of a
football field). Urbino-born Donato Bramante (1444–1514) was only the first
in a series of architects who created this monumental design. Regrettably, very
little is left of Bramante's concept—the decorative excess of the present building was not in his original vision. Even Michelangelo was an architect of
St. Peter's (from 1547 to 1564), designing and beginning construction of the
massive dome.

In the early 17th century and into the 18th century, the **baroque** (meaning
absurd or irregular) movement swept Europe, including Rome. This development was linked to the much-needed reforms and restructuring of the
Catholic church that followed the upheavals of the Protestant Reformation.
Many great Italian churches and *palazzi* were constructed during this period.

The great name from this period was **Giovanni Lorenzo Bernini**
(1598–1680), whose chief work is the piazza in front of St. Peter's. Completion of the basilica itself was the greatest architectural accomplishment of the
early baroque period. **Francesco Borromini** (1559–1667) was another great

architect of the age. His Church of Sant'Agnese in Rome reveals his mastery, with curved indentations on its facade.

As is obvious to any visitor to Rome, the 19th and 20th centuries did not see the grand architectural achievements of the Romanesque or Renaissance periods. The later baroque and flamboyant excesses of their more recent past were dismissed as "gay excesses" by 19th-century architects, and a revival of **neoclassicism** swept Europe in the late 1700s and lasted through the 18th century and well into the 19th. Italian architecture between 1780 and 1920 was lackluster. Rather than responding to Italy's former role as an innovator, architects simply copied classical monuments, perhaps adding a hint of Byzantine decoration. In the early 20th century Mussolini was more intent on producing pompous neoclassical buildings than in achieving breakthroughs in modern architectural design. Many of the buildings constructed in Rome during his dictatorship have been called fascist, uninspired architecture (visit the EUR district south of the center for an example).

If Italy produced any great modern architect in the 20th century, it was **Pier Luigi Nervi,** born in 1891 in Milan. He faced the same problems the Romans did: covering a vast enclosure with concrete vaulting. Nervi's innovative buildings are both poetic and practical; his daring styles and shapes are perhaps best represented by Rome's Palazzo dello Sport designed for the 1960 Olympics. He went on to build a smaller sports arena in Rome, the Palazzetto, which is still called "the world's most beautiful sports arena."

3 Art Through the Ages

There is an amazing richness of Italian art, though sadly neither enough room to display such artistic bounty nor enough resources to maintain the art and protect it from thieves. In fact, some world-class masterpieces that would be the focal point of many museums are tucked away in obscure rooms of rarely visited galleries. Others hide in dark church corners illuminated only by coin-operated lights.

How did it all begin?

As ancient Rome continued to develop its empire, its artisans began to turn out an exact, realistic **portrait sculpture** that became its hallmark. It differed distinctly from the more idealized forms of Greek sculpture. Rome was preoccupied with sculpted images—in fact, sculptors made bodies en masse and later fitted a particular head on the sculpture on the demand of a Roman citizen. Most Roman painting that survives is in the form of **murals in the fresco technique,** and most of these were uncovered when Pompeii and Herculaneum, on the Bay of Naples, were excavated. Rome's greatest artistic expression was in architecture, not in painting.

The aesthetic concepts of the Roman empire eventually evolved into **early Christian and Byzantine art.** More concerned with moral and spiritual values than with the physical beauty of the human form or the celebration of political grandeur, early Christian artists turned to the supernatural and spiritual world for their inspiration. Basilicas and churches were lavishly decorated with mosaics and colored marble, with paintings depicting the earthly suffering and heavenly rewards of martyrs and saints. Supported by monasteries or churches, art was almost wholly concerned with ecclesiastical subjects, frequently with the intention of educating the illiterate worshippers who studied it. Biblical parables were often carved in stone or painted into frescoes, useful teaching aids for a church eager to spread its messages.

Know Your Gods & Goddesses

Although modern visitors know Rome as the headquarters of Catholicism, the city also developed one of the world's most influential bodies of ancient mythology.

During the days when Rome was little more than a cluster of sheepherder's villages, a body of gods whose characters remained basically unchanged throughout the course of Roman history were worshipped. To this panoply, however, were added and assimilated the deities of other conquered territories (especially Greece) until the roster of Roman gods bristled with imports from around the Mediterranean. In its corrupted (later) version, the list grew impossibly unwieldy as more or less demented emperors forced their own deification and worship on the Roman masses. After the Christianizing of Europe, the original and ancient gods retained their astrological significance and have provided poetic fodder for endless literary and lyrical comparisons.

A brief understanding of each of the major gods' functions will add insights during your explorations of the city's museums and excavations.

Apollo was the representative of music, the sun, prophecy, healing, the arts, and philosophy. He was the brother of **Diana** (symbol of chastity and goddess of the hunt, the moon, wild animals, and later, of commerce) and the son of **Jupiter** (king of the gods and god of lightning), by a lesser female deity named Leto. **Cupid** was the god of falling in love.

Juno, the wife of Jupiter, was attributed with vague but awesome powers and a very human sense of outrage and jealousy. Her main job seemed to be wreaking vengeance against the hundreds of nymphs that Jupiter seduced and punishment of the thousands of children he supposedly fathered.

Mars, the dignified but bloodthirsty god of war, was reputed to be the father of **Romulus,** cofounder of Rome.

Early in the 1300s, Tuscan artists like Cimabue and Giotto blazed new trails and brought emotional realism into their work in what was later seen as a complete break from Byzantine gloom and rigidity, and an early harbinger of the Renaissance. However, artists in Rome continued to retain reminders of ancient Rome in their work.

The Italian **Renaissance** was born in Florence during the 15th century and almost immediately spread to Rome. Brunelleschi designed a dome for Florence's cathedral that has been hailed ever since as "a miracle of design." Keenly competitive with Florence, ecclesiastical planners in Rome hired Donato Bramante to work on a design for an amplified version of St. Peter's Basilica, the most significant and imposing building of the High Renaissance. Its interior required massive amounts of sculpture and decoration. To fill the void, artists from throughout Italy, including Michelangelo, flooded into Rome.

Perhaps it was in painting, however, that the Renaissance excelled. The artistic giant Raffaello (Raphael) Santi was commissioned to fresco the apartments of Pope Julius II in Rome. Simultaneously, Michelangelo painted the ceiling frescoes of the Sistine Chapel, an assignment that took 4 back-breaking years to complete. With infinite input from the patrons and artists in Rome, Italy remained Europe's artistic leader for nearly 200 years.

Mercury, symbol of such Geminis (twins) as Romulus and Remus, was one of the most diverse and morally ambiguous of the gods. He served as the guide to the dead as they approached the underworld, and as the patron of eloquence, travel, negotiation, diplomacy, good sense, prudence, and (to a very limited extent) thieving.

Neptune, god of the sea, was assigned almost no moral attributes but represents solely the watery domains of the earth.

Minerva was the goddess of wisdom, arts and crafts, and (occasionally) of war. A goddess whose allure was cerebral and whose discipline was severe, she wears a helmet and breastplate emblazoned with the head of **Medusa** (the snake-haired monster whose gaze could turn men into stone). During the Renaissance she became a symbol much associated, oddly enough, with the wisdom and righteousness of the Christian popes.

Venus, whose mythological power grew as the empire expanded, was the goddess of gardens and every conceivable variety of love. She was reportedly the mother of **Aeneas,** mythical ancestor of the Romans. Both creative and destructive, Venus's appeal and duality are as primeval as the earth itself.

Ceres, goddess of the earth and of the harvest, mourned for half of every year (during winter) when her daughter, **Proserpine,** abandoned her to live in the house of **Pluto,** god of death and the underworld.

Vulcan was the half-lame god of metallurgy, volcanoes, and furnaces, whose activities at his celestial forge crafted superweapons for an array of military heroes beloved by the ancient Romans.

Finally, **Bacchus,** the god of wine, undisciplined revelry, drunkenness, and absence of morality, gained importance in Rome as the city grew decadent and declined.

The transitional period between the Renaissance and the baroque came to be called **mannerism.** Although Venice's Tintoretto remains the most famous artist of this group, out of this period emerged such other (Rome-based) artists as Giulio Romano, Perin del Vaga, Rosso Fiorentino, and Parmigianino. Although little remains of their work (Rome was sacked and many artworks destroyed or carried away in 1527 during the siege of the city by Charles V), their restless and sometimes contorted style soon spread from Rome throughout the rest of Italy.

In the early 17th century and into the 18th century, the baroque age altered forever the architectural skyline of Rome (see "Architecture 101," earlier in this chapter). Simultaneously, great artists emerged, including Bernini, renowned both as a sculptor and painter; Carracci, who decorated the Roman palace of Cardinal Farnese; and Caravaggio, one of the baroque masters of earthy realism and dramatic tension.

Shortly thereafter the even more flamboyant **rococo** grew out of the baroque style. The baroque age also represented the high point of **trompe l'oeil** (illusionistic painting) whereby ceilings and walls were painted with disturbingly realistic landscapes that fool the eye with architecturally sophisticated perspectives and angles. Drop in on the second floor of Trastevere's

Villa Farnesina for an excellent example (see "Walking Tour 4: Trastevere," in chapter 7).

During the 17th, 18th, and 19th centuries the great light had gone out of art in Italy. Rome in particular, capitalizing on the vast ruins that lay scattered within its boundaries, became a magnet for the **neoclassical** craze sweeping through France, Britain, and Germany. Thousands of foreign and Italian artists descended on Rome to feed off its 2,000 years of artistic treasures. The era's return to the aesthetic ideals of ancient Greece and Rome helped fuel the growing sense of pan-Italian nationalism. By the 19th century the beacon of artistic creativity was picked up by France, whose artists ushered in a wide array of different artistic traditions (including Impressionism) whose tenets were for the most part ignored in Italy.

The 20th century witnessed the creative zeniths of several major Italian artists whose works once again captured the imagination of the world. De Chirico and Modigliani (the latter's greatest contribution lay in a new concept of portraiture) are two among many. Today the works of many of Italy's successful futurist and metaphysical painters can be seen in Rome's Galleria Nazionale d'Arte Moderna. Sadly, although many of the works contained therein are world-class art of international stature, they tend to be overlooked in a city whose artworks encompass two millennia of treasures.

4 Literature: The Classics & Beyond

The passion for empire building spilled over into the development of forms of Roman literature that affected every literary development in the Western world for 2,000 years.

The first true Latin poet was **Livius Andronicus** (ca. 284–204 B.C.), a Greek slave who translated Homer's *Odyssey* into Latin, but abandoned the poetic rhythms of ancient Greek in favor of Latin's Saturnian rhythm. **Quintus Ennius** (239–169 B.C.) was the father of Roman epic literature; his *Annales* were permeated with a sense of the divine mission of Rome to civilize the world. Quintus's bitter rival was **M. Porcius Cato the Censor** (234–149 B.C.), who passionately rejected Rome's dependence on Hellenistic models in favor of a distinctly Latin literary form.

Part of the common appeal of Latin literature lay in comedies performed in front of vast audiences. The Latin cadences and rhythms of **Plautus** (254–184 B.C.) were wholly original, and **C. Lucilius** (ca. 180–102 B.C.) is credited as the first satirist, developing a deliberately casual, sometimes lacerating method of revealing the shortcomings and foibles of individuals and groups of people (statesmen, poets, gourmands, etc.).

Latin prose and oratory reached their perfect form with the cadences of **Marcus Tullius Cicero** (106–43 B.C.). A successful and popular general and politician, he is credited with the development of the terms and principles of oratory, which are still used by debating societies everywhere. His speeches and letters are triumphs of diplomacy, and his public policies are credited with binding Rome together during some of its most wrenching civil wars.

Poetry also flourished. The works of **Catullus** (84–54 B.C.), primarily concerned with the immediacy and strength of his own emotions, presented romantic passion in startlingly vivid ways. Banned by some of the English Victorians, Catullus's works continue to shock anyone who bothers to translate them.

One of the Roman republic's most respected historians was **Livy,** whose saga of early Rome is more or less the accepted version. **Julius Caesar** himself (perhaps the most pivotal and biased eyewitness to the events he recorded) wrote accounts of his military exploits in Gaul and his transformation of the Roman republic into a dictatorship. Military and political genius combine with literary savvy in his *De Bello Gallica* (Gallic Wars) and *De Bello Civili* (Civil War).

Ancient Roman literature reached its most evocative peak during the Golden Age of Augustus (42 B.C.–A.D. 17). **Virgil's** (70–19 B.C.) *The Aeneid,* a 12-volume Roman creation myth linking Rome to the demolished city of Troy, has been judged equal to the epics of Homer.

Horace (Quintus Horatius Flaccus; 63–8 B.C.) became a master of satire, as well as the epic "Roman Odes," whose grandeur of style competes with Virgil. Frequently used as an educational text for princes and kings during the Renaissance 1,500 years later, Horace's works often reveal the anxiety he felt about the centralization of unlimited power in Rome after the end of the Republic. Many centuries later some of the themes of Horace were embraced during the Enlightenment of 17th-century Europe and were even used as ideological buttresses for the tenets that led to the French Revolution.

Ovid (43 B.C.–A.D. 17), master of the elegy, had an ability to write prose that reflected the traumas and priorities of his own life and emotional involvements. Avoiding references to politics (the growing power of the emperors was becoming increasingly repressive), the elegy grew into a superb form of lyric verse focused on such tenets as love, wit, beauty, pleasure, and amusement. Important works that are read thousands of years later for their charm and mastery of Latin include *Metamorphoses* and *The Art of Love.*

Between A.D. 17 and 170 Roman literature was stifled by a growing fear of such autocrats as Tiberius, Claudius, Nero, and Caligula. An exception is the work of the great Stoic writer **Lucius Annaeus Seneca** (4 B.C.?–A.D. 65), whose work commented directly and sometimes satirically on events of his time, advocating self-sufficiency, moderation, and emotional control.

For several hundred years after the collapse of the Roman empire very little was written of any enduring merit in Rome. The exceptions include Christian Latin-language writings from such apologists and theologians as **St. Jerome** (A.D. 340–420) and **St. Augustine** (354–430), whose works helped bridge the gap to the beginning of the Middle Ages.

From this time onward, literature in Rome parallels the development of Italian literature in general. Medieval Italian literature was represented by religious poetry, secular lyric poetry, and sonnets. Although associated with Florence, not Rome, **Dante Alighieri** (1265–1321) broke the monotony of a thousand-year literary silence with the difficult-to-translate *terza rima* of *The Divine Comedy.* Called the first masterpiece in Italian (to the detriment of Rome, the Tuscan dialect in which he wrote gradually became accepted as the purest form of Italian), it places Dante, rivaled only by medieval Italian-language poets Petrarch and Boccaccio, in firm control as the founder of both the Italian language and Italian literature.

Rome, however, continued to pulsate with its own distinctive dialect and preoccupations. The imbroglios of the city's power politics during the 1400s and 1500s, and the mores of its ruling aristocracy, were recorded in *The Courtier,* by **Baldassare Castiglione** (1478–1529), still read as a source of insight into customs, habits, and ambitions during the Renaissance.

From 1600 to around 1850, as the reins of international power and creativity shifted from Italy, literature took a second tier to such other art forms as music, opera, and architecture. The publication of **Alessandro Manzoni's** (1785–1873) romantic epic *I Promessi Sposi* (The Betrothed) in 1827 signaled the birth of the modern Italian novel.

During the 19th century, Rome's literary voice found its most provocative spokesperson in **Giuseppe Gioacchino Belli** (1792–1863), who wrote more than 2,000 satirical sonnets (*I Sonetti Romaneschi,* published 1886–96) in Roman dialect rather than academic Italian. A statue in his honor decorates Piazza Belli in Trastevere.

In modern times, **Alberto Moravia** has won an international following. Born in Rome of a well-to-do family, Moravia (the pseudonym of Alberto Pincherle) initiated the neorealist movement in the Italian novel, winning fame for *Two Women* and *The Empty Canvas.* His novels describe in painful detail the apparent emptiness of life in an era of mass conformity. In theater, **Pirandello** and **Goldoni** remain perennial favorites.

5 Recommended Books

GENERAL & HISTORY

Presenting a "warts and all" view of the Italian character, Luigi Barzini's *The Italians* (Macmillan, 1964) should almost be required reading for anyone contemplating a trip to Rome. It's lively, fun, and not at all academic.

Edward Gibbon's 1776 *The History of the Decline and Fall of the Roman Empire* is published in six volumes, but Penguin issues a manageable abridgement. This work has been hailed as one of the greatest histories ever written. No one has ever captured the saga of the glory that was Rome the way Gibbon did.

One of the best books on the long history of the papacy—detailing its excesses, triumphs, defeats, and most vivid characters—is Michael Walsh's *An Illustrated History of the Popes: Saint Peter to John Paul II* (St. Martin's Press, 1980). The story is so dramatic it could be turned into one of the longest running miniseries in the history of TV.

In the 20th century the most fascinating period in Italian history was the rise and fall of fascism, as detailed in countless works. One of the best biographies of Il Duce is Denis M. Smith's *Mussolini: A Biography* (Random House, 1983). Another subject that's always engrossing is the Mafia, which is detailed, godfathers and all, in Pino Arlacchi's *Mafia Business: The Mafia Ethic and the Spirit of Capitalism* (Routledge, Chapman & Hall, 1987).

William Murray's *The Last Italian: Portrait of a People* (Prentice Hall Press, 1991) is his second volume of essays on his favorite subject—Italy, its warm people, and astonishing civilization. The *New York Times* called it "a lover's keen, observant diary of his affair."

Once Upon a Time in Italy: The Vita Italiana of an American Journalist, by Jack Casserly (Roberts Rinehart, 1995), is the entertaining and affectionate memoir of a former bureau chief in Rome from 1957 to 1964. He captures the spirit of Italia sparita (bygone Italy) with such celebrity cameos as Maria Callas and the American expatriate singer Bricktop.

ART & ARCHITECTURE

From the Colosseum to Michelangelo, T. W. Potter provides one of the best accounts of the art and architecture of Rome in *Roman Italy* (University of California Press, 1987), which is also illustrated. Another good book on the same subject is *Roman Art and Architecture,* by Mortimer Wheeler (World of Art Series, Thames & Hudson, 1990).

The Sistine Chapel: A Glorious Restoration, by Michael Hirst et al. (Abrams, 1994), uses nearly 300 color photographs to illustrate the lengthy and painstaking restoration of Michelangelo's 16th-century frescoes in the Vatican.

FICTION & BIOGRAPHY

No one does it better than John Hersey's Pulitzer Prize–winning *A Bell for Adano* (Knopf, 1944), a frequently reprinted classic. It's a well-written and disturbing story of the American invasion of Italy.

One of the best known Italian writers published in England is Alberto Moravia, born in 1907. His neorealistic novels are immensely entertaining and are read around the world. Notable works include *Roman Tales* (Farrar, Straus, and Cudahy, 1957), *The Woman of Rome* (Penguin, 1957; also available in the Playboy paperback series), and *The Conformist* (Greenwood Press, 1975).

For the most wildly entertaining books on ancient Rome, detailing its most flamboyant personalities and excesses, read *I, Claudius* (Vintage, 1989) and *Claudius the God* (Vintage, 1989) both by Robert Graves. Borrowing from the histories of Tacitus and Suetonius, the series begins at the end of the Emperor Augustus's reign and ends with the death of Claudius in the first century A.D. In 1998 the Modern Library placed *I, Claudius* at number 14 on its list of the 100 finest English-language novels published this century.

Colleen McCullough's "Masters of Rome" series is rich, fascinating, and historically detailed, bringing to vivid life such greats as Gaius Marius (*The First Man in Rome,* Avon, 1991), Lucius Cornelius Sulla (*The Grass Crown,* Avon, 1992), and Julius Caesar (*Fortune's Favorites,* Avon, 1994, and *Casar's Women,* Avon, 1997.)

Irving Stone's *The Agony and the Ecstasy* (Doubleday, 1961), filmed with Charlton Heston playing Michelangelo, is the easiest to read and the most pop version of the life of this great artist. Heston still views it as his greatest role and still—at least on TV—tries to keep Michelangelo from coming out of the closet.

Many other writers have tried to capture the peculiar nature of Italy. Notable works include Italo Calvino's *The Baron in the Trees,* Umberto Eco's *The Name of the Rose,* E. M. Forster's *Where Angels Fear to Tread* and *A Room with a View,* Henry James's *The Aspern Papers,* Giuseppe di Lampedusa's *The Leopard,* Carlo Levi's *Christ Stopped at Eboli,* Thomas Mann's *Death in Venice,* Susan Sontag's *The Volcano Lover,* and Mark Helprin's underappreciated masterwork, *A Soldier of the Great War.*

Appendix B: Molto Italiano

1 Basic Vocabulary

ENGLISH-ITALIAN PHRASES

English	Italian	Pronunciation
Thank you	**Grazie**	*graht*-tzee-yey
You're welcome	**Prego**	*prey*-go
Please	**Per favore**	*pehr* fah-*vohr*-eh
Yes	**Si**	see
No	**No**	noh
Good morning or Good day	**Buongiorno**	bwohn-*djor*-noh
Good evening	**Buona sera**	*bwohn*-ah *say*-rah
Good night	**Buona notte**	*bwohn*-ah *noht*-tay
How are you?	**Come sta?**	*koh*-may *stah*
Very well	**Molto bene**	*mohl*-toh *behn*-ney
Goodbye	**Arrivederci**	ahr-ree-vah-*dehr*-chee
Excuse me (to get attention)	**Scusi**	*skoo*-zee
Excuse me (to get past someone)	**Permesso**	pehr-*mehs*-soh
Where is . . . ?	**Dovè . . . ?**	doh-*vey*
the station	**la stazione**	lah stat-tzee-*oh*-neh
a hotel	**un albergo**	oon ahl-*behr*-goh
a restaurant	**un ristorante**	oon reest-ohr-*ahnt*-eh
the bathroom	**il bagno**	eel *bahn*-nyoh
To the right	**A destra**	ah *dehy*-stra
To the left	**A sinistra**	ah see-*nees*-tra
Straight ahead	**Avanti (or sempre diritto)**	ahv-vahn-tee (*sehm*-pray dee-*reet*-toh)
How much is it?	**Quanto costa?**	*kwan*-toh *coh*-sta?
The check, please	**Il conto, per favore**	eel kon-toh *pehr* fah-*vohr*-eh
When?	**Quando?**	*kwan*-doh
Yesterday	**Ieri**	ee-*yehr*-ree
Today	**Oggi**	*oh*-jee
Tomorrow	**Domani**	doh-*mah*-nee
Breakfast	**Prima colazione**	*pree*-mah coh-laht-tzee-*ohn*-ay

English	Italian	Pronunciation
Lunch	**Pranzo**	*prahn*-zoh
Dinner	**Cena**	*chay*-nah
What time is it?	**Che ore sono?**	kay *or*-ay *soh*-noh
Monday	**Lunedì**	loo-nay-*dee*
Tuesday	**Martedì**	mart-ay-*dee*
Wednesday	**Mercoledì**	mehr-cohl-ay-*dee*
Thursday	**Giovedì**	joh-vay-*dee*
Friday	**Venerdì**	ven-nehr-*dee*
Saturday	**Sabato**	*sah*-bah-toh
Sunday	**Domenica**	doh-*mehn*-nee-kah

NUMBERS

1	**uno** (*oo*-noh)		30	**trenta** (*trayn*-tah)
2	**due** (*doo*-ay)		40	**quaranta** (kwah-*rahn*-tah)
3	**tre** (tray)		50	**cinquanta** (cheen-*kwan*-tah)
4	**quattro** (*kwah*-troh)		60	**sessanta** (sehs-*sahn*-tah)
5	**cinque** (*cheen*-kway)		70	**settanta** (seht-*tahn*-tah)
6	**sei** (say)		80	**ottanta** (oht-*tahn*-tah)
7	**sette** (*set*-tay)		90	**novanta** (noh-*vahnt*-tah)
8	**otto** (*oh*-toh)		100	**cento** (*chen*-toh)
9	**nove** (*noh*-vay)		1,000	**mille** (*mee*-lay)
10	**dieci** (dee-*ay*-chee)		5,000	**cinque milla**
11	**undici** (*oon*-dee-chee)			(*cheen*-kway *mee*-lah)
20	**venti** (*vehn*-tee)		10,000	**dieci milla**
21	**ventuno** (vehn-*toon*-oh)			(dee-*ay*-chee *mee*-lah)
22	**venti due** (*vehn*-tee *doo*-ay)			

Molto Italiano

2 A Glossary of Architectural Terms

Ambone   A pulpit, either serpentine or simple in form, erected in an Italian church.

Apse   The half-rounded extension behind the main altar of a church; Christian tradition dictates it be placed at the eastern end of an Italian church, the side closest to Jerusalem.

Atrium   A courtyard, open to the sky, in an ancient Roman house; the term also applies to the courtyard nearest the entranceway of an early Christian church.

Baldacchino (also ciborium)   A columned stone canopy, usually placed above the altar of a church; spelled in English, *baldachin* or *baldaquin*.

Baptistry   A separate building or a separate area in a church where the rite of baptism is held.

Basilica   Any rectangular public building, usually divided into three aisles by rows of columns; in ancient Rome, this architectural form was frequently used for places of public assembly and law courts; later, Roman Christians adapted the form for many of their early churches.

Caldarium   The steam room of a Roman bath.

Campanile   A bell tower, often detached, of a church.

Capital   The top of a column, often carved and usually categorized into one of three orders: Doric, Ionic, or Corinthian.

Castrum   A carefully planned Roman military camp, whose rectangular form, straight streets, and systems of fortified gates quickly became standardized throughout the Empire; modern cities that began as Roman camps and still more or less maintain their original forms include Chester (England), Barcelona (Spain), and such Italian cities as Lucca, Aosta, Como, Brescia, Florence, and Ancona.

Cavea The curved row of seats in a classical theater; the most prevalent shape was that of a semicircle.

Cella The sanctuary, or most sacred interior section, of a Roman pagan temple.

Chancel Section of a church containing the altar.

Cornice The decorative flange defining the uppermost part of a classical or neoclassical facade.

Cortile Courtyard or cloisters ringed with a gallery of arches or lintels set atop columns.

Crypt A church's main burial place, usually below the choir.

Cupola A dome.

Duomo Cathedral.

Forum The main square and principal gathering place of any Roman town, usually adorned with the city's most important temples and civic buildings.

Grotesques Carved and painted faces, deliberately ugly, used by everyone from the Etruscans to the architects of the Renaissance; they're especially amusing when set into fountains.

Hyypogeium Subterranean burial chambers, usually of pre-Christian origins.

Loggia Roofed balcony or gallery.

Lozenge An elongated four-sided figure that, along with stripes, was one of the distinctive signs of the architecture of Pisa.

Narthex The anteroom, or enclosed porch, of a Christian church.

Nave The largest and longest section of a church, usually devoted to sheltering and/or seating worshipers and often divided by aisles.

Palazzo A palace or other important building.

Piano Nobile The main floor of a palazzo (sometimes the second floor).

Pietra Dura Richly ornate assemblage of semiprecious stones mounted on a flat decorative surface, perfected during the 1600s in Florence.

Pieve A parish church.

Portico A porch, usually crafted from wood or stone.

Pulvin A four-sided stone serving as a substitute for the capital of a column, often decoratively carved, sometimes into biblical scenes.

Putti Plaster cherubs whose chubby forms often decorate the interiors of baroque chapels and churches.

Stucco Colored plaster composed of sand, powdered marble, water, and lime, either molded into statuary or applied in a thin concretelike layer to the exterior of a building.

Telamone Structural column carved into a standing male form; female versions are called *caryatids*.

Thermae Roman baths.

Transenna Stone (usually marble) screen separating the altar area from the rest of an early Christian church.

Travertine The stone from which ancient and Renaissance Rome was built, it's known for its hardness, light coloring, and tendency to be pitted or flecked with black.

Tympanum The half-rounded space above the portal of a church, whose semicircular space usually showcases a sculpture.

3 Italian Menu Terms

Abbacchio   Roast haunch or shoulder of lamb baked and served in a casserole and sometimes flavored with anchovies.

Agnolotti   A crescent-shaped pasta shell stuffed with a mix of chopped meat, spices, vegetables, and cheese; when prepared in rectangular versions, the same combination of ingredients is identified as **ravioli.**

Amaretti   Crunchy, sweet almond-flavored macaroons.

Anguilla alla veneziana   Eel cooked in a sauce made from tuna and lemon.

Antipasti   Succulent tidbits served at the beginning of a meal (before the pasta), whose ingredients might include slices of cured meats, seafood (especially shellfish), and cooked and seasoned vegetables.

Aragosta   Lobster.

Arrosto   Roasted meat.

Baccalà   Dried and salted codfish.

Bagna cauda   Hot and well-seasoned sauce, heavily flavored with anchovies, designed for dipping raw vegetables; literally translated as "hot bath."

Bistecca alla fiorentina   Florentine-style steaks, coated before grilling with olive oil, pepper, lemon juice, salt, and parsley.

Bocconcini   Veal layered with ham and cheese, then fried.

Bollito misto   Assorted boiled meats served on a single platter.

Braciola   Pork chop.

Bresaola   Air-dried, spiced beef.

Bruschetta   Toasted bread, heavily slathered with olive oil and garlic and often topped with tomatoes.

Bucatini   Coarsely textured hollow spaghetti.

Busecca alla Milanese   Tripe (beef stomach) flavored with herbs and vegetables.

Cacciucco ali livornese   Seafood stew.

Calzone   Pizza dough rolled with the chef's choice of sausage, tomatoes, cheese, and so on, then baked into a kind of savory turnover.

Cannelloni   Tubular dough stuffed with meat, cheese, or vegetables, then baked in a creamy white sauce.

Cappellacci alla ferrarese   Pasta stuffed with pumpkin.

Cappelletti   Small ravioli ("little hats") stuffed with meat or cheese.

Carciofi   Artichokes.

Carpaccio   Thin slices of raw cured beef, sometimes in a piquant sauce.

Cassatta alla siciliana   A richly caloric dessert combining layers of sponge cake, sweetened ricotta cheese, and candied fruit, bound together with chocolate butter cream icing.

Cervello al burro nero   Brains in black-butter sauce.

Cima alla genovese   Baked fillet of veal rolled into a tube-shaped package containing eggs, mushrooms, and sausage.

Coppa   Cured morsels of pork fillet encased in sausage skins, served in slices.

Costoletta alla milanese   Veal cutlet dredged in bread crumbs, fried, and sometimes flavored with cheese.

Cozze   Mussels.

Fagioli   White beans.

Fave   Fava beans.

Fegato alla veneziana   Thinly sliced calves' liver fried with salt, pepper, and onions.

Foccacia   Ideally, concocted from potato-based dough left to rise slowly for several hours, then garnished with tomato sauce, garlic, basil, salt, and pepper and drizzled with olive oil; similar to a deep-dish pizza most popular in the deep south, especially Bari.

Fontina   Rich cow's-milk cheese.

Frittata   Italian omelette.

Fritto misto   A deep-fried medley of whatever small fish, shellfish, and squid are available in the marketplace that day.

Fusilli   Spiral-shaped pasta.

Gelato (produzione propria)   Ice cream (homemade).

Gnocchi   Dumplings usually made from potatoes (*gnocchi alla patate*) or from semolina (*gnocchi alla romana*), often stuffed with combinations of cheese, spinach, vegetables, or whatever combinations strike the chef's fancy.

Gorgonzola   One of the most famous blue-veined cheeses of Europe—strong, creamy, and aromatic.

Granita   Flavored ice, usually with lemon or coffee.

Insalata di frutti di mare   Seafood salad (usually including shrimp and squid) garnished with pickles, lemon, olives, and spices.

Involtini   Thinly sliced beef, veal, or pork, rolled, stuffed, and fried.

Minestrone   A rich and savory vegetable soup usually sprinkled with grated parmigiano and studded with noodles.

Mortadella   Mild pork sausage, fashioned into large cylinders and served sliced; the original lunchmeat bologna (because its most famous center of production is Bologna).

Mozzarella   A nonfermented cheese, made from the fresh milk of a buffalo (or, if unavailable, from a cow), boiled and then kneaded into a rounded ball, served fresh.

Mozzarella con pomodori (also "caprese")   Fresh tomatoes with fresh mozzarella, basil, pepper, and olive oil.

Nervetti   A northern Italian antipasto made from chewy pieces of calves' foot or shin.

Osso bucco   Beef or veal knuckle slowly braised until the cartilage is tender, then served with a highly flavored sauce.

Pancetta   Herb-flavored pork belly, rolled into a cylinder and sliced—the Italian bacon.

Panettone   Sweet yellow-colored bread baked in the form of a brioche.

Panna   Heavy cream.

Pansotti   Pasta stuffed with greens, herbs, and cheeses, usually served with a walnut sauce.

Pappardelle alle lepre   Pasta with rabbit sauce.

Parmigiano   Parmesan, a hard and salty yellow cheese usually grated over pastas and soups but also eaten alone; also known as *granna*. The best is *parmigiano reggiano*.

Peperoni   Green, yellow, or red sweet peppers (not to be confused with pepperoni).

Pesci al cartoccio   Fish baked in a parchment envelope with onions, parsley, and herbs.

Pesto   A flavorful green sauce made from basil leaves, cheese, garlic, marjoram, and (if available) pine nuts.

Piccata al marsala   Thin escalope of veal braised in a pungent sauce flavored with marsala wine.

Piselli al prosciutto   Peas with strips of ham.

Pizza   Specific varieties include *capricciosa* (its ingredients can vary widely depending on the chef's culinary vision and the ingredients at hand), *margherita* (with tomato sauce, cheese, fresh basil, and memories of the first queen of Italy, Marguerite di Savoia, in whose honor it was first made by a Neapolitan chef), *napoletana* (with ham, capers, tomatoes, oregano, cheese, and the distinctive taste of anchovies), *quatro stagione* (translated as "four seasons" because of the array of fresh vegetables in it; it also contains ham and bacon), and *siciliana* (with black olives, capers, and cheese).

Pizzaiola   A process whereby something (usually a beefsteak) is covered in a tomato-and-oregano sauce.

Polenta   Thick porridge or mush made from cornmeal flour.

Polenta de uccelli   Assorted small birds roasted on a spit and served with polenta.

Polenta e coniglio   Rabbit stew served with polenta.

Polla alla cacciatore   Chicken with tomatoes and mushrooms cooked in wine.

Pollo all diavola   Highly spiced grilled chicken.

Ragù   Meat sauce.

Ricotta   A soft bland cheese made from cow's or sheep's milk.

Risotto   Italian rice.

Risotto alla milanese   Rice with saffron and wine.

Salsa verde   "Green sauce," made from capers, anchovies, lemon juice and/or vinegar, and parsley.

Saltimbocca   Veal scallop layered with prosciutto and sage; its name literally translates as "jump in your mouth," a reference to its tart and savory flavor.

Salvia   Sage.

Scaloppina alla Valdostana   Escalope of veal stuffed with cheese and ham.

Scaloppine   Thin slices of veal coated in flour and sautéed in butter.

Semifreddo   A frozen dessert; usually ice cream with sponge cake.

Seppia   Cuttlefish (a kind of squid); its black ink is used for flavoring in certain sauces for pasta and also in risotto dishes.

Sogliola   Sole.

Spaghetti   A long, round, thin pasta, variously served: *alla bolognese* (with ground meat, mushrooms, peppers, and so on), *alla carbonara* (with bacon, black pepper, and eggs), *al pomodoro* (with tomato sauce), *al sugo/ragù* (with meat sauce), and *alle vongole* (with clam sauce).

Spiedini   Pieces of meat grilled on a skewer over an open flame.

Strangolaprete   Small nuggets of pasta, usually served with sauce; the name is literally translated as "priest-choker."

Stufato   Beef braised in white wine with vegetables.

Tagliatelle   Flat egg noodles.

Tiramisu   Richly caloric dessert containing layers of triple-cream cheeses and rum-soaked sponge cake.

Tonno   Tuna.

Tortelli   Pasta dumplings stuffed with ricotta and greens.

Tortellini   Rings of dough stuffed with minced and seasoned meat and served either in soups or as a full-fledged pasta covered with sauce.

Trenette   Thin noodles served with pesto sauce and potatoes.

Trippe alla fiorentina   Beef tripe (stomach).

Vermicelli   Very thin spaghetti.

Molto Italiano

Vitello tonnato   Cold sliced veal covered with tuna-fish sauce.

Zabaglione/zabaione   Egg yolks whipped into the consistency of a custard, flavored with marsala, and served warm as a dessert.

Zampone   Pig's trotter stuffed with spicy seasoned port, boiled and sliced.

Zuccotto   A liqueur-soaked sponge cake, molded into a dome and layered with chocolate, nuts, and whipped cream.

Zuppa inglese   Sponge cake soaked in custard.

Malto Italiano

Index

See also Accommodations and Restaurant indexes, below.

270

General Index

FROMMER'S® COMPLETE TRAVEL GUIDES

Alaska
Amsterdam
Arizona
Atlanta
Australia
Austria
Bahamas
Barcelona, Madrid &
  Seville
Beijing
Belgium, Holland &
  Luxembourg
Bermuda
Boston
British Columbia & the
  Canadian Rockies
Budapest & the Best of
  Hungary
California
Canada
Cancún, Cozumel &
  the Yucatán
Cape Cod, Nantucket &
  Martha's Vineyard
Caribbean
Caribbean Cruises & Ports
  of Call
Caribbean Ports of Call
Carolinas & Georgia
Chicago
China
Colorado
Costa Rica
Denmark
Denver, Boulder & Colorado
  Springs
England
Europe

European Cruises & Ports
  of Call
Florida
France
Germany
Greece
Greek Islands
Hawaii
Hong Kong
Honolulu, Waikiki & Oahu
Ireland
Israel
Italy
Jamaica
Japan
Las Vegas
London
Los Angeles
Maryland & Delaware
Maui
Mexico
Montana & Wyoming
Montréal & Québec City
Munich & the Bavarian
  Alps
Nashville & Memphis
Nepal
New England
New Mexico
New Orleans
New York City
New Zealand
Nova Scotia, New Brunswick
  & Prince Edward Island
Oregon
Paris
Philadelphia & the
  Amish Country

Portugal
Prague & the Best of the
  Czech Republic
Provence & the Riviera
Puerto Rico
Rome
San Antonio & Austin
San Diego
San Francisco
Santa Fe, Taos & Albuquerque
Scandinavia
Scotland
Seattle & Portland
Shanghai
Singapore & Malaysia
South Africa
Southeast Asia
South Florida
South Pacific
Spain
Sweden
Switzerland
Thailand
Tokyo
Toronto
Tuscany & Umbria
USA
Utah
Vancouver & Victoria
Vermont, New Hampshire
  & Maine
Vienna & the Danube Valley
Virgin Islands
Virginia
Walt Disney World &
  Orlando
Washington, D.C.
Washington State

FROMMER'S® DOLLAR-A-DAY GUIDES

Australia from $50 a Day
California from $60 a Day
Caribbean from $70 a Day
England from $70 a Day
Europe from $70 a Day

Florida from $70 a Day
Hawaii from $70 a Day
Ireland from $60 a Day
Italy from $70 a Day
London from $85 a Day

New York from $80 a Day
Paris from $80 a Day
San Francisco from $60 a Day
Washington, D.C.,
  from $70 a Day

FROMMER'S® PORTABLE GUIDES

Acapulco, Ixtapa &
  Zihuatanejo
Alaska Cruises & Ports of Call
Bahamas
Baja & Los Cabos
Berlin
California Wine Country
Charleston & Savannah
Chicago
Dublin

Hawaii: The Big Island
Las Vegas
London
Los Angeles
Maine Coast
Maui
Miami
New Orleans
New York City
Paris

Puerto Vallarta, Manzanillo
  & Guadalajara
San Diego
San Francisco
Sydney
Tampa & St. Petersburg
Venice
Washington, D.C.